SHAPING TRADITION

. . .

Art and Diversity in the Essay

Sandra Fehl Tropp

Boston University

Harcourt Brace Jovanovich College Publishers

Fort Worth   Philadelphia   San Diego   New York   Orlando   Austin
San Antonio   Toronto   Montreal   London   Sydney   Tokyo

Publisher: Ted Buchholz
Acquisitions Editor: Michael Rosenberg
Developmental Editor: Stacy Schoolfield
Production Manager: Erin Gregg
Editorial, Design, and Production Services: Editorial Services of New England, Inc.
Cover Design: Jeanette Barber
Compositor: Publication Services, Inc.

Library of Congress Cataloging-in-Publication Data

Tropp, Sandra Fehl, 1944–
    Shaping tradition: art and diversity in the essay / Sandra Fehl Tropp.
      p.   cm.
    Includes index.
    ISBN 0-03-049518-0
    1. College readers. 2. English language—Rhetoric. 3. Essays.
I. Title.
PE1417.T76   1992
808.84—dc20   91-39199
                                        CIP

Address Editorial Correspondence To:
Harcourt Brace Jovanovich, Publishers
301 Commerce Street, Suite 3700
Fort Worth, TX 76102

Address Orders To:
Harcourt Brace Jovanovich, Publishers
6277 Sea Harbor Drive
Orlando, FL 32887
1-800-782-4479, or 1-800-433-0001 (in Florida)

Printed in the United States of America

1 2 3 4 016 9 8 7 6 5 4 3 2 1

Harcourt Brace Jovanovich
The Dryden Press
Saunders College Publishing

• • •

For my daughters, Elena and Rachel,
and their grandfathers, Samuel and Herman

· · ·

Preface

Like most texts, this one has taken shape in response to experiences in the classroom. A few years ago I began my freshman composition courses with three essays, two by Samuel Johnson and one by Lord Chesterfield. I found that when my students had succeeded in understanding, in accurately summarizing, and, finally, in comparing the ideas (and most did), they knew they had learned something of value. Their effort granted them insight into the power of language to connect the past to the present. They recognized that Johnson's punctuation does not conform to the rules of standard academic English today just as many regional dialects do not conform. But they also learned that all three of these forms of English, Johnson's, standard, and regional, encode rules that encourage elegance as well as individuality.

The insights my students gained by studying two writers from the eighteenth century prompted me to search for a collection of essays revealing the variety of styles that have emerged over the last four hundred years, a book that would allow students of writing to see how words reveal the connection between subject, style, and writer. But at that time, no such collection was in print. The idea that students could, should, or would want to learn from the essayists of the past was also not in fashion.

Meanwhile, I devised a two-semester Themes in Composition course centering on new developments in several areas, including science and literature. The segment on literature provided an overview of literary theory as well as a discussion of the canon wars. The following year I devised a regular freshman composition course based on readings from Bacon to Twain. That leap from the old to the new and back to the old showed me, as well as my students, the connections between the two and led, finally, to the development of this text.

Shaping Tradition reflects the importance of the ideas expressed by Samuel Johnson, Benjamin Franklin, and other humanists of the eighteenth century, especially their faith in human reason, in the freedom to express one's opinions, and in the benefits of a middle path between extremes. There are, as Leslie Epstein reminds us in "Civility and Its Discontents," "lasting truths" that are "to be handed down from one generation to another," but these truths must be selected, modified, added to, and reshaped for each succeeding generation, always and primarily to show the value we see in controversy, the importance of allowing the expression of diverse points of view, and the virtue inherent in change prompted by reason.

As teachers and students we need to use our capacity to think and write, not to separate us into different and competing constituencies but to learn to respect differences and cherish what unites us. Among these unifying qualities are the reliance on tradition, the appreciation of art, and the pleasure we take in diversity.

This text is directed to a diverse audience — to teachers and students who are investigating the art of the essay as a genre of literature and to those who are investigating the various ways of writing essays. The selections and apparatus in this text have been chosen with both groups in mind. The variety of selections over the past four hundred years presented in chronological order allows students to study the development of the essay as art; the multiple examples from various stylists allow students to study and apply the techniques of professionals.

The essays chosen vary in length and complexity to allow instructors to design courses suitable for beginning readers and writers as well as for those at intermediate and advanced levels. Freshmen may rely heavily on the biographies, footnotes, and glossary; graduate students may need only some of this material. This text can be used with a grammar handbook in composition courses or used alone for a study of the history of the essay. It is intentionally too big to be included in its entirety on any one syllabus. Like tradition itself, it offers a selection of possibilities that will be further narrowed by each instructor.

As in any text, the choices made reflect a theoretical approach toward both the material and its instructors and students. For example, while questions commonly found at the end of each essay in other composition readers direct students to points of interest, they also at some level imply that neither students nor teachers can be trusted to devise their own questions. Moreover, the regular appearance of such questions after each essay suggests that the main focus of all essays lies in the answers to a set of specific questions. Hence, in this text, I have chosen to supply this direction in the Instructor's Manual.

The Instructor's Manual contains suggestions for writing assignments in composition courses, ways to incorporate the biographies into assignments and classroom discussion, a sample syllabus, handouts, and fifteen suggested small groupings of the essays (supplementing the Thematic Contents) on such subjects as death, advice, teenagers, satire, smells, and the origin of *Homo sapiens*. For each essay in Part One the manual provides additional biographical and critical information about the essayist and a list of topics, rhetorical strategies, and connections to other essays in the book. In addition, for both parts of the text the manual provides a brief bibliography of recent criticism of each author's works to aid instructors in research and students in writing critical papers. For Part Two the manual contains suggestions for ways to approach the modern essays and ways to integrate them with those in Part One.

Because the theoretical approach of a text is important to all of its readers, the Introduction (page xxvii) is addressed to both instructors and students. The Introduction describes the elements of this text, including the chronological and thematic Contents, footnotes, glossary, and biographies. Each of these elements serves two purposes: to help instructors develop their own approaches to the material and to increase students' confidence in their ability to master it.

I am indebted to all those who helped with advice, information, and encouragement in the development of this text. I am particularly grateful to Sarah Gates Turell, who read the original proposal with care. I owe much to Ellen Grover Wickersham, who supplied me with translations of all of the Greek and much of the Latin. What is accurate can be credited to her; the rest, alas, to me. I am grateful also to Xavier Gonan and Susan K. Jackson for their help with Chesterfield's French. Thanks go to Sylvia Baldwin, Burton Cooper, Bonnie Costello, and Celia Millward for advice; to Rabbi Samuel Chiel and Mrs. Jeanette Chiel for a specific piece of information; and to many graduate students at Boston University, particularly Nina Allen, Andrew Harrington, Katie Kodat, Joellen Masters, Katheryn Murphy-Anderson, and Matthew Pelikan, for listening to me talk about the early stages of this work. Thanks must also go to my friends and neighbors whose confidence inspired me and to my students at Boston University whose work inspired the creation of this text.

Thanks go also to the staff of the New England Mobile Bookfair and to the staff of the following libraries: Babson College Library, Boston Public Library, Brandeis Library, Mugar Library at Boston University, Newton Public Library, Wellesley College Library, Wellesley Public Library, Pine Manor College, and the Harvard University libraries.

I also want to thank the reviewers of this text for offering thoughtful and sound advice: Lucien Agosta, California State University; Earl Dachslager, University of Houston; John Griffith, University of Washington; Martin Jacobi, Clemson University; Carol Johnson, Virginia Wesleyan College; I. Hashimoto, Whitman College; Kenneth Rainey, Memphis State University; Susan Seyfarth, Middle Tennesee State University; Dickie Spurgeon, Southern Illinois University at Edwardsville; Steven Strang, Wheaton University; Priscilla Tate, Texas Christian University.

I am especially indebted to my editors, Michael Rosenberg, who had faith in this project, and Stacy Schoolfield, who retained her sense of humor as she led me every step of the way.

My deepest appreciation is reserved for my husband, Martin Tropp, whose support, patience, editorial advice, and research assistance have made this book possible.

Contents

PART TWO
Twentieth-Century Essayists

Thematic Contents

WRITING, STYLE, AND THE ESSAY

PARENTS AND CHILDREN

ETHICS AND PHILOSOPHY

EDUCATION

Introduction

W hen Henry Louis Gates, Jr., now general editor of an anthology of African-American literature and head of African-American Studies at Harvard, wrote a detective spoof about the canon in the *New York Times Book Review* (March 25, 1990), his mission was to find those conspiring to keep some writers in and some writers out. Despite his comic stance, his point was serious: what we read does indeed shape us. It contributes not only to the information we know but also to the ways we have of obtaining that information. If specific groups of people are missing or misrepresented, our perceptions of these people will be affected. If complexity is not built into the works we read, we won't understand or appreciate complexity. Literary traditions shape our understanding and our expectations of the world, our sensitivity to language and to the values it expresses.

Knowing how much our literary tradition matters, Gates was seeking those who shape it. Although he failed to uncover a conspiracy, he was on the right track. The shapers of tradition—the writers, as well as their publishers, readers, and scholar-editors—are in a sort of collusion. Since no one can read or assign a text that has not been written or published, the writer and the marketplace are the final arbiters. Nevertheless, the four groups check and balance one another.

The Literary Canon

Any written tradition survives and multiplies in a range of forms between two extremes—between the vast, continually expanding possibility consisting of any-thing that has ever been written, published, and preserved in some library and the narrow list of selections on somebody's syllabus. How does a work move from one to the other? Although any work can theoretically appear on any syllabus, most teachers rely on what is currently available from publishers, that is, on a canon determined by the thousands of choices specific teachers make year after year. And teachers are most influenced by each other. Battles about what to include have a long history and are themselves traditional. Swift (in *The Battle of the Books*) and Chesterfield (in "On Prejudice") set the ancients (Homer and Virgil) against the moderns (Milton and Tasso). T.H. Huxley debated Matthew Arnold over the inclusion of science in the curriculum. F.R. Leavis issued *The Great Tradition*, decreeing Lawrence in and Joyce out. T.S. Eliot resurrected the metaphysical poets. Some of these dicta lasted more than a decade. Some did not. Nonetheless, publishers responded to the perceived need. Thus each member of each group—writers, publishers, readers, and scholars—is responsible for what we as a nation pass on to the next generation to read. Change is inevitable. Tradition shapes us while we shape it.

A Definition of the Essay

The essay has not always been considered a legitimate part of the literary tradition. It lacks the prestige of poetry, drama, and fiction. Part of the problem lies in its definition, slippery from the beginning. Its inventor, Montaigne, said (in "Of Democritus and Heraclitus") he could include anything in it, stopping anytime he pleased. Mixing fable and fact, history and personal experience, the essay was never limited to nonfiction, even before postmodernism. How can such a hodge-podge be defined?

In this book the essay is defined by its length and its voice. Although its length can vary considerably, one essay can be read at one sitting. Written in the first person, the essay is as much an expression of the author's voice as of the author's thoughts. In other words, while the information and opinions the author conveys may be important, they are no more important than the style the author creates to convey them.

Essays Excerpted from Books   Historically, the essay was published as a part of a collection. Any particular essay written by Montaigne, Bacon, and Browne, for instance, is an excerpt from a book. Only after the rise of the periodical essay in the eighteenth century were essays published as individual pieces. Even then, their longevity was assured primarily by reprinting them in book form. Moreover, while some essays by men such as Joseph Addison or Samuel Johnson were written in the form of fictitious letters, others by men such as Benjamin Franklin originally were actual letters, later published with other essays in book form. From the nineteenth and twentieth centuries I have included pieces that were originally speeches (by T.H. Huxley, Mark Twain, and Virginia Woolf) because they were later edited by their authors and printed as essays in books. I have also included excerpts from autobiographies written in the twentieth century (by Zora Neale Hurston, Richard Rodriguez, and Annie Dillard) because, like the chapters or sections from Thomas Browne's autobiographical *Religio Medici*, they are in fact self-contained essays published in book form.

The Essay as Art   Long or short, comic or dramatic, plain or baroque, centered on the self or the outside world, as casual as Montaigne claimed or highly structured, the essay is always arranged, deliberately patterned for effect. Thus it is art.

The Essay Canonized   As an art form the essay deserves to be respected, studied, and appreciated in its historical context. For a variety of reasons—its convenient length, our postmodern emphasis on the flux of fact into fiction, and the desire of the younger generation to topple the staid opinions of the past—the essay is experiencing a renaissance in the late twentieth century comparable to the rise of the periodical essay two centuries before.

The Essay and the Reading Public   Joseph Addison and Richard Steele developed the periodical essay as an instrument for the molding of English sensibility, outlining a middle path between the hard rock of Puritanism and the whirlpool of excess that had taken hold in the reign of Charles II. In essays such as "On Attributing Our Neighbours' Misfortunes to Judgments" and "Defence and Happiness of Married Life," for instance, Addison attempted to shape his readers' conceptions of God and their attitudes toward marriage. Benjamin Franklin also saw in the essay an opportunity to shape the values of his countrymen during a period of revolution. In both the aphorisms of Poor Richard and essays such as " 'What Are the Poor Young Women to Do?' The Speech of Polly Baker" or "Advice on the Choice of a Mistress," Franklin advocated productivity in business and marriage as the way to develop a new country.

Similarly, in the second half of the twentieth century, attitudes in western countries, particularly in America, are changing—people such as blacks, Jews, and those from non-western backgrounds, once considered at best oddities and at worst less than human, are more often respected. Part of the renewed popularity of the essay arises because it offers a convenient forum for a diversity of voices heretofore excluded from the western canon of literature. Writers such as Zora Neale Hurston, Cynthia Ozick, Richard Rodriguez, and Amy Tan, whose works would once have been ignored on the basis of their authors' gender, religion, or color of skin, are now published regularly.

Once again the essay, enriched by these voices, is proving a popular forum for shaping the attitudes and values of the reading public. Whether or not the celebration of diversity in our culture and the renewed respect for the essay are connected, it is true that, for the first time since the emphasis on English rhetoric in the eighteenth century, English departments across the country are establishing courses in the essay as an art form. It is also true that teachers and publishers are eager for new voices that articulate the experiences of a variety of Americans in multicultural contexts.

The Interplay of Past and Present   This collection shows how diverse modern essayists illuminate and fit within a tradition of essay writers in English, how writers like Stephen Jay Gould and Shelby Steele extend and modify the course of the essay as set by Francis Bacon and Thomas Browne. Their voices change our view of the past. In "Tradition and the Individual Talent" T.S. Eliot says "the past should be altered by the present as much as the present is directed by the past." He does not mean by this statement that the past should be censored to suit the preferences of the present. He does not mean, for instance, that Lamb's anti-Semiticism should be ignored or suppressed or that works of art should be revered only because those who wrote them were demeaned. What he later makes clear is more subtle and significant: our new knowledge acts as a telescope, bringing the past into focus so that we can see the writers of the past more objectively than they could see themselves. Contemporary essayists such as Cynthia Ozick and Stephen Jay Gould counteract Lamb's prejudice, either directly or indirectly, by the eloquence of their words. By helping to correct the errors of the past these new voices carry on the tradition of the essay in English.

The Chronological Organization of the Text

In this book the first Contents is arranged chronologically to reveal the continuity of influence from the first essayist, Michel de Montaigne, who wrote in French and was translated into English by John Florio, (the son of an Italian minister), to the last essayist, Amy Tan, an American of Chinese descent.

The Essayists: Part One   Part One opens with Michel de Montaigne, the father of a new genre of writing which he called the *essai*, the attempt, the testing or trying of one word against another. Next are Francis Bacon, Montaigne's British contemporary in the sixteenth century; then Sir Thomas Browne in the seventeenth century; Joseph Addison, the Fourth Earl of Chesterfield, Benjamin Franklin, and Samuel Johnson in the eighteenth century; Charles Lamb and William Hazlitt in the Romantic Period; and, finally T.H. Huxley and Mark Twain in the nineteenth century. All of these writers have been in the main lineage of the essay since its inception. They are exclusively male, white, and deceased.

The Essayists: Part Two   Part Two opens the essay in the twentieth century with Virginia Woolf, the first female essayist in English to be widely read both in her own time and in the present. She is followed by E.B. White, Zora Neale Hurston, George Orwell, James Baldwin, Cynthia Ozick, Edward Hoagland, Joan Didion, Stephen Jay Gould, Alice Walker, Richard Rodriguez, Annie Dillard, Michael Dorris, Shelby Steele, and Amy Tan.

The writers in Part Two constitute three groups—two who fit the parameters set in Part One (George Orwell and E.B. White), three who in the past would have been excluded for reasons of gender or race but are now so widely taught that they have entered the canon (Virginia Woolf, James Baldwin, and Zora Neale Hurston, who has only recently been rediscovered) and ten living writers (from Cynthia Ozick to Amy Tan). Works from many of these living writers appear frequently in collections of modern essayists. The last six, born during or after the Second World War, (Alice Walker, Richard Rodriguez, Annie Dillard, Michael Dorris, Shelby Steele, and Amy Tan), are not only currently writing, but writing at a time when their place in the tradition is by no means clear. They are represented by only one, two, or three essays, reflecting the sense that their best work may still be ahead of them, while what they have already published may not yet be extensive enough to establish a secure reputation. Thus fifteen essayists in this text represent the twentieth century compared to eleven from the four previous centuries.

Shaping the Canon   It is clear that in centuries to come only some, if any, of these names will remain on syllabi across the nation. Who from the past will continue to be read and who from the present will become traditional, like Browne's speculations about the song the sirens sang, is not beyond conjecture. The works here represent one range of possibilities—a collection of styles readers can appreciate and writers can adapt for themselves. The chronological arrangement shows that essays written for magazines and journals within the last few years are part of an ongoing enterprise, a shared tradition that extends from the sixteenth century to the present and is, like architecture, painting, and all the arts, ever changing, ever expanding, at once embracing the new and seeking a revision of the past. What works are passed on to future generations depends on the choices made by writers, publishers, editors, and readers. Thus as teachers, students, and, especially, as potential writers ourselves, we are the ones who will make those choices.

Traditions of Influence

Style   Because the essay is an art, its practitioners have studied each other; they shape each other's style. Francis Bacon adapted Montaigne's essay form to his own personality and interests, creating a detached, succinct style. Note, for example, the casual informality of this line from Montaigne: "The simplest and meerely-naturall smels are most pleasing unto me; which care ought to chiefly concern women." Bacon follows Montaigne in offering advice, but whereas Montaigne offers it slyly and centers his comments on himself, Bacon offers it bluntly and impersonally in a series of balanced don'ts: "As for the Passions and Studies of the Minde; Avoide Envie; Anxious Feares; Anger fretting inwards; Subtill and knottie Inquisitions."

   In the seventeenth century Sir Thomas Browne developed a baroque style, full of surprising modifying phrases and clauses: "I could lose an arme without a teare, and with few groans, mee thinkes, be quartered into pieces; yet can I weepe most seriously at a Play, and receive with a true passion, the counterfeit griefes of those knowne and professed impostures."

   Both styles, the plain one employed by Bacon and the baroque employed by Browne, were used by these men to express their interests in science, and both are represented by later essayists on science, the direct style by Benjamin Franklin, T.H. Huxley, and Stephen Jay Gould, and the baroque by Annie Dillard. Gould adopts the direct approach favored by Bacon but is less severe: "False lures and dangers often come in pairs in our legends and metaphors—consider the frying pan and the fire, or the devil and the deep blue sea." Dillard, on the other hand, like Browne, surprises with her modifying phrases and clauses: "She [a moth] burned for two hours without changing, without swaying or kneeling—only glowing within, like a building fire glimpsed through silhouetted walls, like a hollow saint, like a flame-faced virgin gone to God, while I read by her light, kindled, while Rimbaud in Paris burnt out his brain with a thousand poems, while night pooled wetly at my feet."

The great journalistic essayists of the eighteenth century—Joseph Addison, Benjamin Franklin, and Samuel Johnson—moralists as well as stylists, adapted the balance of Bacon and the variety of Montaigne. In their advocacy of faithful marriages and earnest virtue, they pose a sharp moral contrast to their contemporary Chesterfield, whose letters to his illegitimate son promote, in the balanced style of the period, the use of flattery and expedience to rise in society. Like their predecessors, modern journalistic essayists such as James Baldwin, Joan Didion, and Richard Rodriguez also engage in debates about current issues involving racism, sexism, and ethics, Baldwin employing the complex balance also heard in Johnson, Didion developing a more succinct, Baconian style that reflects, like the style of Rodriguez, the influence of George Orwell. Orwell himself combined the "plain style" of Hazlitt with the fervor and honesty of Johnson to create what will probably be seen as the most influential essays of the twentieth century.

In the Romantic Period, Charles Lamb molded his style on that of Browne, creating a warm, serene, archaic voice that harks back to the idioms of a former period, while William Hazlitt developed a direct, vigorous, self-assured voice stemming from Montaigne and Addison. Here is the archaic Lamb on love: "Methinks, it is better that I should have pined away seven of my goldenest years, when I was thrall to the fair hair and fairer eyes, of Alice W——n, than that so passionate a love adventure should be lost." (Alfred Lord Tennyson composed his more memorable rendition of this sentiment—" 'Tis better to have loved and lost/Than never to have loved at all"—in *In Memoriam* some years later.) Here in direct contrast to Lamb is the plain-speaking Hazlitt on women: "Women in general have no ideas, except personal ones. They are mere egotists. They have no passion for truth, nor any love of what is purely ideal." Both writers are strongly opinionated, and both have counterparts in the essayists of the twentieth century. E.B. White, for instance, maintains Lamb's warmth and gentle humor, yet adds to these the vigor of Hazlitt's direct, modern style.

Later in the nineteenth century Thomas Henry Huxley, famous for explaining Darwin's science to a general audience, wrote in a clear, elegant, and metaphoric style that continues to influence current scientific writers such as Stephen Jay Gould. In "The Coming of Age of the 'Origin of Species,' " for instance, Huxley develops an extended comparison between Darwin's book and the birth and growth of a child. Like Huxley, Gould regularly employs metaphors to make his points (as in the quotation from "Darwin's Middle Road" cited above), although his are usually not as extended as those of Huxley.

Mark Twain, another great essayist of the nineteenth century, also used metaphors to drive his direct, colloquial approach, concentrating the gently humorous and ironic styles of Addison and Franklin to a comic acidity. In "Different Classes of Female Orators," for instance, Addison suggests dissecting women's tongues in search of unusual "juices" or "fibres" which could account for women's volubility. Yet he ends his essay with the confession that he is "charmed" by women's speech and would not want to "discourage it." But Mark Twain in "The Lowest Animal" appends no such disavowal to his diatribe against every aspect of man, from his moral character, assassinated in the first part of the essay, to his physical being, destroyed in the last: "He [man] is but a basket of pestilent corruption provided for the support and entertainment of swarming armies of bacilli—armies commissioned to rot him and destroy him, and each army equipped with a special detail of the work. The process of waylaying him, persecuting him, rotting him, killing him, begins with his first breath, and there is no mercy, no pity, no truce, till he draws his last one."

Together Huxley and Twain open the door to the twentieth century. The impassioned eloquence of writers such as Zora Neale Hurston, James Baldwin, and Alice Walker combine the urgent intellectual commitment of Huxley with the sharp observation and colloquial style of Twain. Here, for instance, is Alice Walker writing about the history of Zora Neale Hurston's reputation: "And I do believe that now, in the seventies, we do not expect (though we may wish and pray) every black who speaks *always* to speak *correctly* (since this is impossible): and if we *do* expect it, we deserve all the silent leadership we are likely to get."

Acknowledgment and Reference   Because these essayists influence one another, they also refer to one another frequently. In Part One, for instance, Addison, Chesterfield, and Franklin cite Bacon; Lamb disagrees with Browne; and Hazlitt has something to say about nearly everyone. In Part Two Woolf writes about Hazlitt and mentions Montaigne, Addison, and Lamb; Orwell writes about Twain; White and Hoagland refer to Montaigne; Didion responds to Orwell; Ozick responds to Johnson and Woolf; Walker writes about Hurston; and Gould cites both Franklin and Huxley.

The newest voices included in the text, Alice Walker, Richard Rodriguez, Annie Dillard, Michael Dorris, Shelby Steele, and Amy Tan, are also influenced by essayists of the past. Walker and Rodriguez acknowledge in these selections and elsewhere their debt to major figures: Walker to Woolf and Hurston; Rodriguez to Montaigne and Orwell. Although the last four essayists do not refer to their predecessors directly, they too speak in voices shaped by tradition. What Mikhail Bakhtin has said about style in the novel (in "Discourse in the Novel") also applies to style in the essay: we can see "each work as a rejoinder in a given dialogue, whose style is determined by its interrelationship with other rejoinders in the same dialogue (in the totality of the conversation)." The topics covered and the shapes taken by the essay in the twentieth century have been developed in part through a continuing conversation with essayists of the past.

The Continuing Conversation

While the chronological organization reveals a continuity of style and reference, a thematic organization reveals a continuity of thought. In a panel discussion at Boston University in the fall of 1990, Cynthia Ozick said that as a child she wrote not only to convince her contemporaries, but to convince the writers of the past as well, as if the whole tradition were her audience. The essayists in this text participate in a continuing conversation covered in seven themes: Writing Style and the Essay, Women and Men, Parents and Children, Science and Health, Ethics and Philosophy, Education, and Prejudice. These themes reveal both the continuity and the diversity within the genre, showing that dissension is part of the tradition. Each grouping addresses a topic from a variety of stances that encourage readers to think and respond, to argue and compare, to reject some views and embrace others.

The first theme, Writing Style and the Essay, includes essays designed to help apprentice writers. While some of these essayists contradict each other, others do not follow their own admonitions. From this section writers learn that rules and advice help but can sometimes be ignored and that essay writing requires hard work. Montaigne and Hoagland explain what the essay is and how it works; Chesterfield and Johnson encourage careful word choice; Johnson urges the proper allotment of time; Twain recommends plenty of practice; Hazlitt assesses the efforts of his fellows; Orwell and Didion explain their motivations; and Walker shows the importance of a tradition. All convey an exemplary devotion to their art.

The essays under the theme of Women and Men trace relationships between the sexes from Montaigne and Bacon to Woolf and Tan. In Part One the writers are all male, since before Woolf women essayists were not included in the canon. Although there were popular women essayists in the past, such as Elizabeth Carter (who wrote two essays for Johnson's *Rambler*) as well as Alice Meynell and Mona Caird in the late 1800s, Part One deals only with those essayists permitted to join and thus help shape the tradition.

Excluded as writers, women were nonetheless popular subjects to extol, and, more often, to satirize, criticize, and analyze. Franklin and Johnson, like actors on the Shakespearian stage, even impersonate the voices of women to present their views, often with humor and surprising sensitivity. In Part Two the voices silenced in Part One make themselves heard, not as spokespeople for all women, but as individuals contributing to the ongoing discussion about how the two genders should and do interact.

The theme of Parents and Children includes essays which address the relationship from both viewpoints, offering conflicting advice and provocative descriptions of family life. Franklin and Addison encourage large families; a youthful Browne disagrees. Bacon recommends firm parental control over a child's studies, whereas Johnson, impersonating a sixteen-year-old girl, makes a case for self-determination. Woolf describes her father, Ozick describes her mother, and

Hurston describes both parents. Baldwin recounts the day his father died. White and Didion reflect on attempts to return as adults to the world of the past.

The essays included under the theme of Science and Health explore the search for health as well as the progress of science. Bacon makes suggestions about choosing a doctor, and Browne presents the physician's point of view. Orwell describes the dying poor, and White suffers during the fatal illness of his pig. Also in this section Orwell defines science, Gould describes its methods, Franklin parodies a scientific paper, and Twain satirizes one. Here too readers can follow a history of science from a respectful disagreement with ancient authorities in Browne to the setting up of pratical experiments in Franklin, from Addison's description of the comfortable chain of being to Huxley's explanation of the theory of natural selection. These changes in our perception of the world help readers to understand the nature of scientific theory, to see that what we now believe to be true may be revised in later generations. They learn that science and the arts both rely on experience and imagination, on the interplay between the details or data and the pattern or theory which interprets them.

The fifth theme, Ethics and Philosophy, includes essays on such subjects as death, fame, advice, happiness, and passion. These issues address a major question we all confront—What is the best way to live? Thus every essayist in the collection is included under this theme, for each responds to this question, either directly or indirectly; most of them stimulate responses in their readers as well. Addison questions the causes of misfortune in life; Didion discovers the meaning of self-respect; Hoagland modifies the golden rule; many essayists investigate the relationship of love-of-self to love-of-others.

The sixth theme, Education, comprises essays that offer advice about how and what to learn and present a variety of sometimes surprising opinions on the value of education and the subjects likely to prove of lasting worth. While Franklin and Johnson offer sound advice on how to read and how to approach difficult subjects, Gould points to social pressures as a source of problems in education. Rodriguez and Dorris recommend learning on the job, while Johnson, Lamb, White, and others mull over the traditional opposition between studies and experience, learning and doing, the intellectual and the practical man.

The stereotypes of the intellectual and practical man lead directly to the final theme, Prejudice. The essays included illustrate the variety of views expressed by British and American essayists toward those who differ from themselves. One group of essays in this section addresses the subject of prejudice from a theoretical perspective, examining the broad range of possibilities implicit in the term. Others treat specific groups such as blacks, native Americans, and Jews. Here readers will see that Charles Lamb can be sensitive to the rights and dignity of women yet intolerant of Jews and blacks. Here Alice Walker's personal testimony about her disfiguring eye stands in vivid contrast to Bacon's assertion that those with deformities are exceptionally "bold" and bent on revenge. Here Franklin extols the noble American Indian and Twain blasts that stereotype, replacing it with yet another. Thomas Browne's logical dismissal of the once popular belief that Jews emit a characteristic odor serves as an early example of the pervasive influence of prejudice in the western tradition and the power of reason to dispel it.

Biographies

Joseph Addison opens his first *Spectator* essay with these words: "I have observed, that a reader seldom peruses a book with pleasure, till he knows whether the writer of it be a black or a fair man, of a mild or choleric disposition, married or a bachelor, with other particulars of the like nature, that conduce very much to the right understanding of an author." He in fact devotes the first two issues to gratifying "this curiosity, which is so natural to a reader." Although Addison gives the self he describes as the Spectator a fictional biography, it shares characteristics of his own, since, in the essay, the two voices merge into one.

Only recently, some fifty years after New Criticism detached a work from its author and its time, are the lives of the authors again examined along with their literary creations. Postmodernists, however, cannot speak with Addison's conviction about the "right understanding" of an author nor about the significance of the life of a writer to her work. Now the examination produces heated argument over the connection, if any, between the two. Scholars argue about the effect of T.S. Eliot's anti-Semitism on his poetry and the deconstructionist Paul de Man's Nazi sympathies on his literary criticism. Each writer denied the relevance of the life to the work. Eliot, for instance, proposed an "Impersonal theory of poetry" wherein "Impressions and experiences which are important for the man may take no place in the poetry, and those which become important in the poetry may play quite a negligible part in the man." These serious literary and ethical questions must, in the end, be left to the judgment of individual readers. But such a judgment can be made only if the facts of the life are available.

The lives of the essayists in this collection are subject to scrutiny not only to help readers judge the works, but also, and perhaps primarily, to satisfy what Addison called our natural curiosity. The biographies assure us that the conveyers of tradition were and are individuals, people moved by the stresses and joys that strike us all. The information in each biography is keyed as much as possible to the seven themes the essayists address. For instance, since Bacon opens the discussion of marriage and children by asserting that men without children produce the most noble works, readers will want to know whether Bacon was married or had children, and in general, will want to compare the lives of the writers with the values they espouse. Readers will also see that opinions change as do the fortunes of life. The young Browne professed little interest in women or children, yet in later life married well and produced a large family. Of course, as Johnson made clear both in his life and his art, few live up to their own standards, though none should live without hope.

The biographies reveal the essayists to be a diverse lot: single, married, divorced, with children and without, heterosexual, homosexual, bisexual, bold and fearful, caring and cold, honest and deceitful, enthusiastic and disdainful, by turns embodying all kinds of emotions and behaviors. There is perhaps only one characteristic that connects them all—these writers are readers.

Discussions of Style   In the classic handbook *The Elements of Style*, E.B. White warns the beginner to approach style "warily, realizing that it is himself he is approaching, no other." Such words can terrorize new writers faced with the task of revision, for many believe that if the words they write are indeed reflections of the self, they must be sacred and immutable. If not, the self must change. Either way, the news is bad. Fortunately, despite the truth in White's warning, style is also a combination of discreet choices, each in itself unthreatening, each made possible by an awareness of the options open to the writer—options that can be selected only if they are perceived. Hence writers must be readers.

Appended to each biography is a brief assessment of the author's style. These comments direct readers to distinctive characteristics, to one or two of the specific choices each author makes. Readers should attend to the possibilities implicit in such words as "diction" and "syntax." "Diction" includes patterns of metaphor and sound, movement between formal and colloquial, abstract and concrete, emphatic verbs and emphatic nouns, words of one syllable and words of many. "Syntax" points to the order of subject and verb, the placement of detail, and the pattern of development. Sentences can be cumulative (loose), with the point presented first in an independent clause, followed by an accumulation of detail; periodic, putting off until the end the point to be made; or some combination of the two (mixed). Such choices also shape patterns within and among paragraphs.

Thus Johnson's propensity for latinate diction and ponderous, balanced sentences leads him to construct complex and carefully balanced essays as well. In "The Necessity of Literary Courage," for instance, he devotes an equal number of paragraphs to the ignorant and the learned. Most of his essays, in fact, are composed of equal halves which sometimes support the thesis initially presented and sometimes, as in "The usefulness of advice. . .," carefully undermine what is commonly thought to be true. Much of the pleasure in reading and rereading comes from discovering such patterns. The information on style suggests paths to explore.

The Sources for the Biographies   Information about the lives of the writers in Part One comes primarily from *A Dictionary of National Biography (DNB)*, edited by Virginia Woolf's father, Sir Leslie Stephen. I have supplemented the material I found there with information from Samuel Johnson's *Lives of the Poets* and from the work of more recent biographers, such as, in the case of Samuel Johnson, the great work of Walter Jackson Bate. Wherever I have relied on sources other than the *DNB*, I have referred to the authors by name (except in the case of Montaigne and Florio, whose biographical facts are readily available in many reference books).

I have relied heavily on recent biographers for the material on the authors in Part Two, again indicating each source by name. For the most recent authors, unascribed information comes from *Who's Who, Current Biography,* and *Contemporary Authors*. I have also relied on interviews published in newspapers and periodicals, again referring to each source by name. Some of the material on Cynthia Ozick and Stephen Jay Gould comes from personal telephone conversations. Finally, a large percentage of the information about these writers has been culled from their own essays, for essayists often write about themselves.

Orthography, Footnotes, and Glossary

Like all the ancillary material, the historically accurate spelling and punctuation in the text are designed to increase the readers' understanding of the writer in his time. The sense of chronology is enhanced by preserving the words as they were printed in each author's lifetime (as often as possible—Chesterfield's letters, for instance, were not published until after his death). Despite their daunting appearance, the early essays are not in fact a stumbling block after the initial reading or rereading. And the practical understanding of the history of the language is worth the expense of energy.

Like the biographies, the notes and glossary are provided to gratify the reader's curiosity. In the footnotes difficult or unusual words are defined, references identified, and dates supplied. The glossary contains similar information pertaining to people, places, or events that are mentioned more than once in the text. Persons or words included in the glossary are indicated by a degree sign (°) following the name or phrase. This mark appears every time the word appears, because at any time a reader's curiosity may suddenly be piqued.

Entering the Tradition   The tradition of the essay, from which this collection is derived, provides examples of clear, reasoned, evocative prose which readers can appreciate, imitate, and adapt. Whether or not a collection such as this is made available to a wide audience, the tradition itself will endure. Western culture, like all cultures, has always maintained an elite, well-educated group from which its leaders can be drawn. The great innovation of democracy is that the knowledge and thus the power invested in the elite can become the province of everyone.

Assuming that these works are too difficult or irrelevant for the majority isolates them from the privileges conferred by a shared literacy and ultimately silences their voices. If teachers underestimate their students' capacity for patience and attentiveness, students will underestimate themselves. Instead, let us join together as readers and writers to explore the art and diversity of the essay, assured in the knowledge that *we* are the shapers of tradition.

PART ONE

Sixteenth-Century to Nineteenth-Century Essayists

. . .

• • •

Michel de Montaigne

(1533–1592)

Michel de Montaigne was the third of five sons and three daughters born to Pierre Eyquem, a magistrate of Bordeaux whose family had been in the herring business and had bought the title and land of Montaigne in 1477. His mother, Antoinette de Louppes, was the daughter of Jewish refugees who, having been expelled from Spain in 1492, converted to Protestantism. Thus although Michel, his father, and most of the children were Catholic, his mother and a brother and sister were Protestant, and many of his family's friends were newly converted Jews. This early familiarity with religious diversity no doubt contributed to Montaigne's tolerance in an age of extreme religious persecution.

Montaigne's education, like his religious upbringing, was unusual: his father insisted that Michel hear and speak nothing but Latin until he was six years old. At that time he was sent to the Collège du Guyenne in Bordeaux and from there to study law. Montaigne then served as a magistrate until 1570 and as mayor of Bordeaux from 1581 to 1585, as his father had before him. While serving in the Bordeaux parliament he met a young lawyer, Étienne de la Boétie, who became his closest friend and whose death a few years later was a source of grief for the rest of Montaigne's life. At thirty-three, after a vigorous pursuit of the young ladies, Montaigne acquiesced to the wishes of his family by marrying Françoise de la Chassaigne, daughter of a Bordeaux magistrate. Two years later, when his beloved father died, Montaigne dropped the name Eyquem and took over the family property, living with his wife, his mother, and two of his sisters.

In 1571 Montaigne retired from the law to write, although even in his retirement he remained active in the affairs of his country, trying to reconcile the Protestant and Catholic rivals for the throne from 1574 to 1576. During this time his wife bore him six daughters; all but the second, Leonor, died in early infancy. The first edition of the *Essays,* including the first two books, was published in 1580; the third book, written after 1586, was published along with revisions of the first two in 1588. That year an eighteen-year-old girl of great intelligence met Montaigne in Paris and expressed her admiration for his essays. The two developed a strong friendship, and Marie de Gournay became his literary executor. In 1590 Leonor married François de la Tour and bore a daughter, Françoise, in 1591. Montaigne, survived by his mother, died in 1592, leaving his property to his daughter and his literary output to Marie de Gournay, who prepared a further edition of his *Essays* in 1595.

Montaigne's introspective, ambling essays probe the mind of an individual man, a man he thought to be typical and thus representative of all men. The loose design of his new form of writing, as described in "Of Democritus and Heraclitus," permits him to follow his meandering mind, shifting direction whenever his knowledge or interest in a subject falters or whenever another idea takes precedence. Having been granted such power, his voice is confident and casual, addressing with intimate ease both men and women—anyone, in fact, who can read his words. With a comic unflappability, Montaigne advises women against heavy perfume, recognizes the difficulty of their role in society, and encourages them in "Of Three Good Women" to love their husbands honestly in life and be prepared to join them in death. Like any conversationalist, he enjoys telling a story, peppering his essays with anecdotes from the ancients and the moderns, from plausible tales from the past as well as from his own imagined scenarios, such as the blinded men returning to their waiting mistresses in "How A Man Should Not Counterfeit To Be Sicke." Thus when he derides those who devise their own tales rather than rely on the exemplars of old ("Of Three Good Women"), he has merely, once again, changed his mind. Either way, as Montaigne and the reader both know, the success of the anecdote depends on the way it is told.

Montaigne's vivid diction, like "the close-smacking, sweetnesse-moving, love-alluring, and greedi-smirking kisses of youth," lingers long in the reader's memory. His sensuality, temperament, wit, integrity, and tolerance have engaged readers for centuries and have helped us to recognize that the exploration of the inner self, of thoughts and feelings, can be as significant and as rewarding as the exploration of the outer world.

John Florio (1553–1625), Montaigne's translator, was the son of a Protestant minister from Florence who had an Italian congregation in London. Educated at Oxford and under the patronage of men such as Leicester, Southhampton, and Pembroke, John Florio composed *First Fruits,* dialogues in English and Italian, in 1578, a book of Italian proverbs in 1591, and *World of Words,* an Italian English dictionary, in 1598. His most famous work, however, remains his translation of Montaigne, first published in 1603. The version offered here is from the 1613 edition, "Done Into English according to the last French Edition by John Florio Reader of Italian Tongue Unto the

Soveraigne Majestie of Anna,[1] Queen of England, Scotland, France, and Ireland, etc. and one of the Gentleman of Hir Royall Privie Chamber 1613."

The English that Florio wrote, although considered excellent in his day, might appall an uninformed English teacher in the twentieth century. His paragraphing is nearly nonexistent; he uses *it's* for the possessive *its,* never uses the apostrophe to indicate possession, substitutes *then* for *than,* and spells and capitalizes erratically. He misuses the semicolon, devises both run-on sentences and sentence fragments, and inserts commas with abandon. Montaigne's French was no better. Actually, in both cases, the orthography and punctuation were controlled by the printer, not the writer. In 1635, the French language was regularized when the French Academy, founded by Cardinal Richelieu,° set standards for the purity of the language, including its grammar, orthography, and rhetoric. The English language has never been regularized to the extent of the French, but the pressures of printers as well as the advice of seventeenth- and eighteenth-century grammars eventually resulted in a more consistent appearance of the printed English language than is found in the words of the first few essayists in this text. ✍

Of Democritus and Heraclitus

THE FIRST BOOKE, THE FIFTIETH CHAPTER

Judgement is an instrument for all subjects, and medleth every where, And therefore in the Essayes I make of it, there is no maner of occasion, I seeke not to employ therein. If it be a subject I understand not my selfe, therein I make triall of it, sounding afarre off the depth of the ford, and finding the same over deepe for my reach, I keepe my selfe on the shoare. And to acknowledge not to be able to wade through, is a part of it's effect, yea of such, whereof he vanteth[2] most. If I light upon a vaine and idle subject, I assay to trie, and endevour to see, whether I may find a good ground to worke upon, and matter to frame a body, and wherewith to build and underlay it. Sometimes I addresse my judgement and contrive it to a noble and out-worne subject, wherein is nothing found subsisting of it selfe, the high way to it, being so bare-trodden, that it cannot march, but in other steps. There he pleaseth himselfe in chusing the course he thinkes best, and a thousand paths sometimes he saith, this or that was best chosen. I take my first Argument of fortune: All are alike unto me: And I never purpose to handle them throughly: For, there is nothing wherein I can perceive the full perfection: Which they doe not that promise to shew it us. Of a hundred parts and visages that every thing hath, I take one, which sometimes I slightly runne over, and other times but

---

[1]Wife of James I.
[2]Boasts.

cursorily glance at. And yet other whilst I pinch it to the quicke. And give it a Stockado,[1] not the widest, but the deepest I can. And for the most part I love to seize upon them by some unwonted[2] lustre. I would adventure to treat and discourse of some matter to the depth; knew I my selfe lesse, or were I deceived in mine owne impuissance;[3] Scattering here one and there another word: Scant-lings[4] taken from their maine groundwork, disorderly dispersed, without any well-grounded designe and promise. I am not bound to make it good, nor without varying to keepe my selfe close-tied unto it; whensoever it shall please me to yeeld my selfe to doubt, to uncertaintie, and to my Mistris forme, which is ignorance. Each motion sheweth and discovereth what we are. The very same minde of Caesar,° we see in directing, marshalling, and setting the battel of Pharsalia,[5] is likewise seene to order, dispose, and contrive, idle, trifling and amorous devices. We judge of a horse, not only by seeing him ridden, and cunningly managed, but also by seeing him trot, or pace; yea, if we but looke upon him as he stands in the stable. Amongst the functions of the soule, some are but meane and base. He that seeth her no further, can never know her thorowly. And he that seeth her march her naturall and simple pace, doth peradventure observe her best. The winds of passions take her most in her highest pitch, seeing she entirely coucheth her selfe upon every matter, and wholy therein exerciseth her selfe: and handleth but one at once; not according to it, but according to herselfe. Things severall in them-selves have peradventure, weight, measure, and condition: But inwardly, in us, she cuts it out for them, as she understandeth the same herselfe. Death is fearefull and ugly unto Cicero;° wished for and desired of Cato°: and indifferent unto Socrates.° Health, well-fare, conscience, authoritie, riches, glorie, beautie, and their contraries are dispoyled at the entrance, and receive a new vesture at the soules hand. Yea, and what coulour she pleaseth; browne, bright, greene, sad, or any hew else: sharpe or sweete, deepe or superficiall, and what each of them pleaseth. For none of them did ever verifie their stiles, their rules, or formes in common; each one severally is a Queene in her owne estate. Therefore let us take no more excuses from externall qualities of things. To us it belongeth to give our selves accoumpt of it. Our good, and our evill hath no dependancy, but from our selves. Let us offer our vowes and offerings unto it; and not to fortune. She hath no power over our manners. Why shall I not judge of Alexander,° as I am sitting and drinking at Table, and talking in good company? Or if hee were playing at Chesse, what string of his wit doth not touch or harpe on this fond-childish, and time-consuming play?[6] I lothe and shun it, only because there is not sport enough in it, and that in his recreation, he is over serious with us, being ashamed I must

---

[1]Stockade built in water.

[2]Unusual.

[3]Weakness.

[4]Small bits.

[5]Name given to battle in 48 B.C. in which Caesar° skillfully defeated the forces of his great rival Pompey (106–48 B.C.) in the civil war begun when Caesar° crossed the Rubicon in 49 B.C.

[6]Alexander° applied all his intelligence to chess, which is merely a game and not worthy, Montaigne believes, of such effort.

apply that attention therunto, as might be imployed on some good subject. He was no more busied in levying his forces and preparing for his glorious passage into India; nor this other in disintangling and discovering of a passage, whence dependeth the well-fare and safety of mankind. See how much our mind troubleth this ridiculous amuzing,[1] if all her sinnewes bandy not.[2] How amply she giveth every one Law in that, to know and directly to judge of himselfe. I doe not more universally view and feele my selfe in any other posture. What passion doth not exercise us thereunto? Choller,[3] spight, hatred, impatience, and vehement ambition to overcome, in a matter wherein it were haply more excusable to be ambitious for to be vanquished. For, a rare pre-excellencie,[4] and beyond the common reach, in so frivolous a thing,[5] is much mis-seeming a man of honour. What I say of this example, may be spoken of all others. Every parcell, every occupation of a man, accuseth, and sheweth him equal unto another. Democritus° and Heraclitus° were two Philosophers, the first of which, finding and deeming humane condition to be vaine and ridiculous, did never walke abroad, but with a laughing, scorneful and mocking countenance: Whereas Heraclitus taking pitie and compassion of the very same condition of ours, was continually seene with a sad, mournfull, and heavie cheere, and with teares trickling downe his blubbered eyes.

——*Alter*
Ridebat quoties à limine moverat unum
Protulerátque pedem, flebat contrarius alter.

One from his doore, his foot no sooner past,
But straight he laught; the other wept as fast.

I like the first humor[6] best, not because it is more pleasing to laugh, than to weepe; but for it is more disdainfull, and doth more condemne us than the other. And methinkes we can never bee sufficiently despised, according to our merit. Bewailing and commiseration, are commixed with some estimation of the thing moaned and wailed. Things scorned and contemned, are thought to be of no worth. I cannot be perswaded, there can be so much ill lucke in us, as there is apparant vanitie, nor so much malice, as sottishnesse.[7] We are not so full of evill, as of voydnesse and inanitie. We, are not so miserable, as base and abject. Even so Diogenes,° who did nothing but trifle, toy, and dally with himselfe, in rumbling and rowling of his tub, and flurting at[8] Alexander,° accompting us but flies, and bladders puft with winde, was a more sharp, a more bitter, and a more stinging

---

[1] Amusement, that is, chess.
[2] Do not join in the fight.
[3] Choler.
[4] Of surpassing excellence.
[5] Chess.
[6] Disposition.
[7] Foolishness.
[8] Striking at.

judge, and by consequence, more just and fitting my humor, than Timon,[1] surnamed the hater of all mankinde. For looke what a man hateth, the same thing he takes to hart. Timon wisht all evill might light on us; He was passionate in desiring our ruine. He shunned and loathed our conversation, as dangerous and wicked, and of a depraved nature: Whereas the other so little regarded us, that wee could neither trouble nor alter him by our contagion; for-sooke our company, not for feare, but for disdaine of our commerce: He never thought us capable or sufficient to doe either good or evill. Of the same stampe was the answer of Statilius[2] to whom Brutus° spake to win him to take part, and adhere to the conspiracie against Caesar.° He allowed the enterprize to be very just, but disalowed of the men that should performe the same, as unworthy that any man should put himself in any adventure for them: Conformable to the discipline of Hegesias,[3] who said, 'That a wise man ought never to doe any thing, but for himselfe'; forasmuch as he alone is worthy to have any action performed for him: and to that of Theodorus,[4] who thought it an 'injustice, that a wise man should in any case hazard himselfe for the good and benefit of his countrie, or to indanger his wisdome for fooles.' Our owne condition is as ridiculous, as risible; as much to be laught at, as able to laugh. ✍

Of Smels and Odors

THE FIRST BOOKE, THE FIFTY-FIFTH CHAPTER

It is reported of some, namely of Alexander,° that their sweat, through some rare and extraordinary complexion, yeelded a sweet smelling savour; whereof Plutarke[5] and others seeke to finde out the cause. But the common sort of bodies are cleane contrarie, and the best qualitie they have, is to be cleare of any smell at all. The sweetnesse of the purest breaths hath nothing more perfect in them, than to bee without savour, that may offend us: as are those of healthy sound children. And therefore saith Plautus:[6]

---

[1]Greek philosopher (c. 320–230 B.C.).

[2]General of Augustus.°

[3]Greek philosopher (c. 340 B.C.) who believed happiness to be unattainable and whose lectures in Alexandria drove so many men to suicide that he was nicknamed "counselor of death." He was stopped from teaching by King Ptolemy.

[4]The Atheist of Cyrene (c. 317 B.C.), who believed that happiness should depend on the disposition of the mind.

[5]See Plutarch.°

[6]Titus Maccius (c. 254–184 B.C.), Roman comic playwright who wrote in a racy, idiomatic Latin, developing from Greek sources such stock comic figures as the bragging soldier, the parasite, and the clever slave. Of his twenty-one extant plays, including *Mostellaria, Miles gloriosus* is perhaps most famous.

Mulier tum bene, olet, ubi nihil olet.[1]

Then smel's a woman purely well,
When she of nothing else doth smell.

The most exquisit and sweetest savour of a woman, it is to smell of nothing;
and sweet, well-smelling, strange savours, may rightly be held suspicious in such
as use them; and a man may lawfully thinke, that who useth them, doth it to cover
some naturall defect: whence proceed these ancient Poeticall sayings. 'To smell
sweet, is to stinke.'

Rides nos Coracine nil olentes,
Malo quam bene olere, nil olere,

You laugh at us that we of nothing savour,
Rather smell so, than sweeter (by your favor).

And else where.

Posthume non bene olet, qui bene semper olet.

Good sir, he smels not ever sweet,
Who smels still sweeter than is meet.[2]

Yet love I greatly to be entertained with sweet smels, and hate exceedingly all
manner of sowre and ill savours, which I shall sooner smell, than any other.

——*Namque sagacius unus odoror,*
Polypus, an gravis hirsutis cubet hircus in alis,
Quam canis acer ubi lateat sus.

Sooner smell I, whether a cancred nose,
Or ranke gote-smel in hairie arme-pits lie,
Than sharpest hounds, where rowting bores repose.

The simplest and meerely-naturall smels are most pleasing unto me; which
care ought chiefly to concerne women. In the verie heart of Barbarie, the Scithian°
women, after they had washed themselves, did sprinkle, dawbe, and powder all
their bodies and faces over, with a certaine odoriferous drug, that groweth in their
Countrie: which dust and dawbing being taken away, when they come neere men,
or their husbands, they remaine verie cleane, and with a verie sweet savouring
perfume. What odor soever it be, it is strange to see, what hold it will take on me,
and how apt my skin is to receive it. He that complaineth against nature, that she
hath not created man with a fit instrument, to carrie sweet smels fast-tied to his
nose, is much to blame: for, they carrie themselves. As for me in particular, my
mostachoes, which are verie thicke, serve me for that purpose. Let me but
approach my gloves or my hand-kercher to them, their smell will sticke upon
them a whole day. They manifest the place I come from. The close-smacking,

---

[1]*Mostellaria* 1.3.
[2]Proper.

sweetnesse-moving, love-alluring, and greedi-smirking kisses of youth, were theretofore wont to sticke on them many houres after; yet am I little subject to those popular diseases, that are taken by conversation, and bred by the contagion of the ayre: And I have escaped those of my time, of which there hath beene many and severall kinds, both in the Townes about me, and in our Armie. We read of Socrates,° that during the time of many plagues and relapses of the pestilence, which so often infested the Citie of Athens, he never forsooke or went out of the Towne: yet was he the only man, that was never infected, or that felt any sicknesse. Physitians might (in mine opinion) draw more use and good from odours, than they doe. For, my selfe have often perceived, that according unto their strength and qualitie, they change and alter, and move my spirits, and worke strange effects in me: which makes me approve the common saying, that the invention of incense and perfumes in Churches, so ancient and so far-dispersed throughout all nations and religions, had an especiall regard to rejoyce, to comfort, to quicken, to rowze, and to purifie our senses, that so we might be the apter and readier unto contemplation. And the better to judge of it, I would I had my part of the skill, which some Cookes have, who can so curiously season and temper strange odors with the savour and rellish of their meats. As it was especially observed in the service of the King of Tunes,[1] who in our dayes landed at Naples, to meet and enter-parly[2] with the Emperour Charles the fifth.[3] His viands were so exquisitely farced,[4] and so sumptuously seasoned with sweet odoriferous drugs, and aromaticall spices, that it was found upon his booke of accompt, the dressing of one peacocke, and two fesants amounted to one hundred duckets;[5] which was their ordinarie manner of cooking his meats. And when they were carved up, not only the dining chambers, but all the roomes of his pallace, and the streets round about it were replenished with an exceeding odoriferous and aromaticall vapour, which continued a long time after. The principall care I take, wheresoever I am lodged, is to avoid, and be far from all manner of filthy, foggy, ill-savouring, and unwholsome aires. These goodly Cities of strangely-seated Venice, and huge-built Paris, by reason of the muddy, sharp, and offending savors, which they yeeld; the one by her fennie and marish situation,[6] the other by her durtie uncleannesse, and continuall mire, do greatly alter and diminish the favour which I beare them. ✿

---

[1]Tunis; in Montaigne's time, a popular center for trade with Europe.
[2]Confer.
[3]Holy Roman emperor from 1519 to 1556.
[4]Spiced.
[5]Gold coins.
[6]Marshy location.

How A Man Should Not Counterfeit To Be Sicke

THE SECOND BOOKE, THE TWENTY-FIFTH CHAPTER

There is an epigram in Martiall,[1] that may passe for a goode one (for there are all sortes in him) wherein he pleasantly relateth the storie of Caelius, who to avoide the courting of certaine great men in Rome, to give attendance at their rising, and to waite, assist, and follow them, fained to be troubled with the goute; and to make his excuse more likely, he caused his legges to be ointed and swathed, and lively counterfeted the behavior and countenance of a goutie man. In the end fortune did him the favour to make him goutie indeede.

> *Tantum cura potest et ars doloris,*
> *Desiit fingere Caelius podagram.*

> So much the care and cunning can of paine:
> Caelius (growne gowty) leaves the gowt to faine.

As farre as I remember, I have read a like History in some place of Appian,[2] of one who purposing to escape the proscriptions of the Triumvirat of Rome,[3] and to conceale himselfe from the knowledge of those who pursued him, kept himselfe close and disguised, adding this other invention to it, which was to counterfeit blindnes in one eye, who when he came somewhat to recover his liberty, and would have left off the plaister he had long time worne over his eyes, he found that under that mask he had altogether lost the sight of it. It may be the action of his sight was weakned, having so long continued without exercise and the usual vertue was wholly converted into the other eye: For, we may plainly perceive, that holding one eye shut, it convaieth some part of it's effect into his fellow; in such sort as it will swell and growe bigger. As also the idlenes, together with the warmth of the medicaments and swathing might very wel draw some goutie humor into the legge of Martials° goutie fellow. Reading in Froisart,[4] the vow which a gallant troupe of young English-men had made, to weare their left eyes hudwink't, untill such time as they should passe into France and there performe some notable exploite of armes upon us, I have often laughed with my self to think what they would have imagined, if as to the fore aleaged, it had hapned to them, and had all beene blind of the left eye, at what time they returned to look upon their mistresses, for whose sake they had made their vowe and undertaken such an enterprise. Mothers have great reason to chide their children when they counterfeit to be blind with one eye, crompt-backe, squint-eyed, or lame, and such other

---

[1] See Martial.°

[2] Greek-born writer (second century A.D.) of Roman history from the founding of the city to the ruler Trajan (98–117). Although he wrote in Greek, Appian was biased in favor of the Romans.

[3] See Caesar.°

[4] Jean Froissart (c.1337–1410?), French poet, priest, and courtier who extended the chronicle of western Europe begun by Jean le Bel, describing events from the early 1300s to 1400 in vivid and biased detail.

deformities of the body; for besides that the body thus tender may easily receive some ill custome, I know not how, it seemeth that fortune is glad to take us at our word; And I have heard diverse examples of some, who have falen sicke in very deede, because they had purposed to faine sicknes. I have at all times enured my selfe, whether I be on horsebacke or a foote to carry a good heavie wand or cudgell in my hand; yea I have endevoured to doe it handsomely, with an effected kinde of countenance to continue so. Many have threatned me, that fortune will one time or other turne this my wantonnes into necessitie. I presume upon this, that I should be the first of my race,[1] that ever was troubled with the gowt. But lett us somewhat amplifie this chapter, and patch it up with another piece concerning blindnes. Plinie[2] reports of one, who dreaming in his sleepe, that he was blind, awaking the next morning, was found to be starke blinde, having never had any precedent sicknes. The power of imagination may very well further such things, as eleswhere I have shewed; And Plinie[3] seemeth to bee of this opinion; but it is more likely, that the motions, which the body felt inwardly (whereof Physitians, may if they please, find out the cause) and which tooke away his sight, were the occasion of his dreame. Let us also adde another storie, concerning this purpose, which Seneca° reporteth in his *Epistles.* 'Thou knowest' (saith he writing to Lucilius) 'that Harpaste my wives foole, is left upon me as an hereditarie charge; for by mine owne nature, I am an enemie unto such monsters, and if I have a desire to laugh at a foole, I neede not seeke one farre; I laugh at my selfe. This foolish woman hath sodainly lost hir sight. I report a strange thing, but yet very true. She will not beleeve she is blind; and urgeth her keeper uncessantly to lead her, saying still, My house is very darke. What we laugh at in hir, I entreat thee to beleeve, that the same hapneth to each of us. No man knoweth himselfe to be covetous, or niggardly. Even the blind require a guide, but wee stray from our selves. I am not ambitious, say we, but no man can live otherwise at Rome: I am not sumptuous, but the Cittie requireth great charges. It is not my fault, if I be collerike;[4] If I have not yet set downe a sure course of my life the fault is in youth. Let us not seeke our evill out of us; it is within us, it is rooted in our entrailes. And only because we perceive not that we are sick, makes our recoverie to prove more difficult. If we beginne not betimes to cure our selves, when shall we provide for so many sores, for so many evils? Yet have we a most sweete and gentle medicine of Philosophy; for of others, no man feeles the pleasure of them, but after his recoverie, whereas she pleaseth, easeth, and cureth all a once.' Lo here what Seneca° saith, who hath somewhat diverted me from my purpose: But there is profit in the exchange. ✍

---

[1]Lineage.
[2]See Pliny the Elder.°
[3]See Pliny the Elder.°
[4]Choleric.

Of Three Good Women

THE SECOND BOOKE, THE THIRTY-FIFTH CHAPTER

They[1] are not to be had by dozens, as each one knowes, namely in rights and duties of mariage; For, it is a bargaine full of so many thornie circumstances, that it is hard the will of a woman should long keepe her selfe whole and perfect therein.[2] And although men have somewhat a better condition in the same, yet have they much to doe. The touchstone and perfect triall of a good mariage, respects the time that the societie continueth; whether it have constantly beene milde, loyall and commodious. In our age, they more commonly reserve to enstall their good offices, and set foorth the vehemence of their affections toward their lost husbands: And then seeke they at least to yeeld some testimonie of their good wil. O late testimonie and out of season, whereby they rather shew, they never love them but when they are dead. Our life is full of combustion and scolding, but our disease full of love and of curtesie. As fathers conceale affection toward their children; so they to maintaine an honest respect, cloake their love toward their husbands. This mystery answereth not my taste. They may long enough scratch and dishevell themselves; let me enquire of a chamber-maide or of a secretarie, how they were, how they did, and how they have lived together: I can never forget this good saying, *Iactantius moerent, quœ minus dolent.* 'They keepe a howling with most ostentation, who are lesse sorrowfull at heart.' Their lowring[3] and puling[4] is hatefull to the living, and vaine to the dead. Wee shall easily dispence with them to laugh at us when we are dead, upon condition they smile upon us while wee live. Is not this the way to revive a man with spite; that he who hath spitten in my face when I was living, shal come and claw my feet when I am dead? If there be any honour for a woman to weepe for hir husband, it belongs to hir that hath smiled upon him when she had him. Such as have wept when they lived, let them laugh when they are dead, as well outwardly as inwardly. Moreover regard not those blubbred eyes, nor that pitty moving voice; but view that demeanor, that colour and cheerefull good plight of those cheekes, under their great vailes; thence it is she speaks plaine French. There are few whose health doth not daily grow better and better; a quality that cannot lie. This ceremonious countenance looketh not so much backward, as forward: It is rather a purchase then a payment. In mine infancie an honest and most faire Ladie (who yet liveth, the widdowe of a Prince) had somewhat more of I wot not what in her attires, then the lawes of widdow-hood would well permit. To such as blamed hir for it: It is (said shee) because I intend no more new acquaintances, and have no mind at all to marry againe. Because I will not altogether dissent from our custome, I have heere made choise

---

[1]Good women.
[2]It is hard for her wholly and perfectly to fulfill the rights and duties.
[3]Bellowing.
[4]Whining.

of three women, who have also imployed the utmost endevor of their goodnes and affection, about their husbands deaths. Yet are they examples somewhat different and so urging[1] that they hardly draw life into consequence. Plinie the yonger,° had dwelling neere to a house of his in Italie, a neighbour wonderfuly tormented with certaine ulcers, which much troubled him in his secret parts. His wife perceiving him to droope and languish away, entreated him she might leasurely search and neerely view the quality of his disease, and she would more freely then any other tell him what he was to hope for: Which having obtained, and curiously considered the same, she found it impossible ever to be cured, and all he might expect was but to lead a long, dolorous, and languishing life; and therefore for his more safetie and soveraigne remedie, perswaded him to kill himselfe. And finding him somewhat nice[2] and backeward to effect so rude an enterprise: Thinke not my deare friend (quoth shee) but that the sorrowes and griefes, I see thee feele, touch me as neere and more, if more may be, as thy selfe, and that to be rid of them, I will applie the same remedie to my selfe, which I prescribe to thee. I will accompany thee in thy cure as I have done in thy sicknesse: remoove all feare, and assure thy selfe, we shall have pleasure in this passage, which shall deliver us from all torments, for we will happily goe together: That said, and having cheared up hir husbands courage, she determined they should both headlong throw themselves into the sea from out a window of their house, that overlooked the same: and to maintaine this loyall, vehement and never to be severed affection to the end, wherewith shee had during his life embraced him, she would also have him die in her armes; and fearing they might faile her, and through the fall, or feare or apprehension her hold-fast might be loosed, shee caused herselfe to be fast bound unto him by the middle: And thus for the ease of her husbands life she was contented to forgoe her owne. She was but of meane[3] place and low fortune: and amidde such condition of people, it is not so strange to see some parts of rare vertue and exemplar goodnesse.

> ——*extrema per illos*
> *Iustitia excedens terris vestigia fecit.*[4]

Justice departing from the earth did take
Of them her leave, through them last passage make.

The other two are noble and Rich; where examples of vertue are rarely lodged. Arria wife unto Cecinna Paetus, a man that had been Consul, was mother of another Arria, wife to Thrasea Paetus whose vertue was so highly renowned during the time of Nero;° and by meane of his sonne-in-law, grandmother to Fannia. For, the resemblance of these mens and womens names and fortunes hath

---

[1]Compelling.
[2]Reluctant.
[3]Inferior.
[4]Virgil° *Georgics* 2.473.

made diverse to mistake them. This first Arria, her husband Cecinna Paetus having beene taken prisoner by the Souldiers of Claudius the Emperour,° after the overthrow of Scribonianus, whose faction he had followed, entreated those who led him prisoner to Rome, to take her into their ship, where for the service of her husband shee should be of lesse charge and incommoditie to them, then a number of other persons, which they must necessarily have, and that she alone might supply and stead him in his chamber, in his kitchen and all other offices; which they utterly refused, and so hoised sailes, but shee leaping into a fishers boate, that she immediately hired, followed him aloofe from the further shore of Sclaviona. Being come to Rome, one day, in the Emperours presence, Iunia the widdow of Scribonianus, by reason of the neerenesse and society of their fortunes, familiarly accosted her, but she rudely, with these words, thrust her away: What (quoth shee) shall I speake to thee, or shall I listen what thou saiest? Thou, in whose lappe Scribonianus thy husband was slaine, and thou yet livest? and thou breathest? These words with divers other signes, made her kinsfolkes and friends perceive that she purposed to make herselfe away, as impatient to abide her husbands fortune. And Thrasea her son-in-law, taking hold of her speeches, beseeching her that she would not so unheedily spoile her selfe, he thus bespake her: What? If I were in Cecinnaes fortune or the like, would you have my wife your daughter to do so? What else? make you a question of it? (answered she) Yes marry would I, had she lived so long and in so good-agreeing sort with thee, as I have done with my husband. These and such like answers, encreased the care they had of her; and made them more heedfull to watch, and neerely to look unto her. One day, after she had uttered these words to her keepers; You may looke long enough to me, well may you make me die worse, but you shall never be able to keepe me from dying: and therewith furiously flinging her selfe out of a chaire (wherein she sate) with all the strength she had, she fiercely ranne her head against the next wall; with which blow having sore hurt her selfe, and falling into a dead swowne, after they had with much adoe brought her to her selfe againe: Did I not tell you (quoth she) that if you kept me from one easi death, I would choose another, how hard and difficult soever? The end of so admirable a vertue was this. Her husband Paetus wanting the courage to doe himselfe to death, unto which the Emperors cruelty reserved him; one day having first employed discourses and exhortations, befitting the counsell she gave him to make himselfe away, shee tooke a Dagger that her husband wore, and holding it outright in her hand, for the period of her exhortation: Doe thus Paetus (said she) and at that instant, stabbing her selfe mortally to the heart, and presently pulling the dagger out againe she reached the same unto her husband, and so yeelded up the ghost, uttering this noble, generous and immortall speech, *Paete non dolet,*[1] she had not the leasure to pronounce other than these three wordes, in substance materiall and worthy her selfe, "Holde Paetus, it hath done me no hurt."

---

[1]Montaigne translates in the following lines: *Paetus, it does not hurt.*

Custae suo gladium cum traderet Arria Paeto,
   Quem de visceribus traxerat ipsa suis;
Si qua fides, vulnus quod feci, non dolet, inquit,
   Sed quod tu facies, id mihi Paete dolet.[1]

Chast Arria when she gave her Paetus that sharpe sword,
   Which from her bowells she had drawne forth bleeding new,
The wound I gave and have, if you will trust my word,
   Griev's not, said she, but that which shall be made by you.

It is much more lively in his owne naturall, and of a richer Sense; for both her husbands wound and death, and her owne hurts, she was so farre from grieving to have beene the counselor and motive of them, that shee rejoyced to have performed so haughty[2] and couragious an act, onely for the behoofe of her deere husband, and at the last gaspe of her life, she only regarded him; and to remove all feare from him, to follow her in death, which Paetus beholding, he immediately wounded himselfe with the same dagger, ashamed (as I suppose) to have had need of so deare an instruction, and precious a teaching. Pompea Paulina, an high and noble-borne yong Romane Ladie, had wedded Seneca,° being very aged. Nero° (his faire disciple) having sent his Satellites or officers toward him, to denounce the decree of his death to him: which in those dayes was done after this manner. When the Roman Emperors had condemned any man of quality to death, they were wont to send their officers unto him, to chuse what death he pleased, and to take it within such and such a time, which according to the temper of their choller,[3] they prescribed unto him, sometimes shorter, and some times longer, giving him that time to dispose of his affaires, which also by reason of some short warning they divers times tooke from him: And if the condemned partie seemed in any sort to strive against their will, they would often send men of purpose to execute him, either cutting the veins of his armes and legs, or compelling him to take and swallow poison. But men of honor stayed not that enforcement, but to that effect used their own Phisitions or Surgeons. Seneca,° with a reposed and undanted countenance listned attentively to their charge, and presently demaunded for paper and inke to make his last wil and testament, which the Captaine refusing him, he turned towards his friends, and thus bespake them: Sith[4] (my loving friends) I cannot bequeath you any other thing in remembrance or acknowledgement of what I owe you, I leave you at least the richest and best portion I have, that is, the image of my maners and my life, which I beseech you to keepe in memory; which doing, you may acquire the glory and purchase the name of truly sincere and absolutely true friends. And therewithall sometimes appeasing the sharpenes of the sorow he saw them endure for his sake, with mild and gentle speeches, sometime raising his voice to chide them; Where are (said he) those memorable precepts of Philosophy? What is become of those provisions, which for so many yeares together we have laid up against the brunts

---

[1] Martial° *Epigrams* 1.15.1.
[2] Lofty.
[3] Choler.
[4] Since.

and accidents of Fortune? Was Neroes° innated[1] cruelty unknowne unto us? What might we expect or hope for at his hands, who had murdred his mother and massacred his Brother, but that he would also do his Tutor and Governor to death that hath fostred and brought him up? Having uttered these words to al the by-standers, he turned him to his wife, as she was ready to sinke downe, and with the burthen of her griefe to faint in heart and strength; he colled and embraced her about the necke, and heartily entreated her, for the love of him, somewhat more patiently to beare this accident; and that his houre was come, wherein he must shew no longer by discourse and disputation, but in earnest effect, declare the fruit he had reaped by his studie; and that undoubtedly he embraced death, not only without griefe but with exceeding joy. Wherefore my deere-deere heart, do not dishonor it by thy teares, lest thou seeme to love thy selfe more than my reputation. Asswage thy sorrowes, and comfort thy selfe in the knowledge thou hast had of me and of my actions; leading the rest of thy life by the honest occupations to which thou art addicted. To whom Paulina, having somwhat rouzed her drooping spirits, and by a thrice-noble affection awakened the magnanimitie of her high-setled courage, answered thus: No Seneca,° thinke not that in this necessitie I will leave you without my company.

I would not have you imagin that the vertuous examples of your life have not also taught me to die: And when shal I be able to do it or better, or more honestly, or more to mine own liking, then with your selfe? And be resolved I wil go with you and be partaker of your fortune. Seneca° taking so generous a resolve, and glorious a determination of his wife in good part, and to free himselfe from the feare he had to leave her after his death, to his enemies mercie and cruelty: Oh my deare Paulina, I had (quoth he) perswaded thee what I thought was convenient, to leade thy life more happily, and doost thou then rather choose the honour of a glorious death? Assuredly I will not envy thee: Be the constancie and resolution answerable to our common end, but be the beautie and glory greater on thy side. That said, the veines of both their armes were cut, to the end they might bleede to death; but because Senecaes° were somwhat shrunken up through age and abstinence, and his bloud could have no speedy course, he commaunded the veines of his thighes to be launced: And fearing lest the torments he felt, might in some sort entender his wifes heart; as also to deliver himselfe from the affliction, which greatly yearned him to see her in so pittious plight: after he had most lovingly taken leave of her, he besought her to be pleased she might be caried into the next chamber, which was accordingly performed. But all those incisions being unable to make him die, he willed Statius Anneus his Phisition to give him some poysoned potion, which wrought but small effect in him, for through the weaknesse and coldenesse of his members, it could not come unto his heart. And therefore they caused a warme bath to be prepared, wherein they layd him, then perceiving his end to approch, so long as he had breath, he continued his excellent discourses, concerning the subject of the estate wherein he found himselfe, which his Secretaries, so long as they could heare his voice, collected very diligently, whose last words continued long time after in high esteem and

---

[1]Inborn.

honor amongst the better sort of men, as Oracles; but they were afterward lost, and great pittie it is they never came unto our handes. But when he once beganne to feele the last pangs of death, taking some of the water, wherein he lay bathing, all bloody, he therewith washed his head, saying, I vow this water unto Jupiter the Deliverer. Nero° being advertised of all this, fearing lest Paulinaes death (who was one of the best alied[1] Ladies in Rome, and to whom he bare no particular grudge) might cause him some reproach, sent in all poste haste to have her incisions closed up againe, and if possibly it could be, to save her life; which hir servants by unwrithing her, performed, she being more then halfe dead and voyd of any sence. And that afterward, contrary to her intent, she lived, it was very honourable, and as befitted her vertue, shewing by the pale hew and wanne colour of her face, how much of her life she had wasted by her incisions. Loe heere my three true stories, which in my conceit are as pleasant and as tragicall, as any we devise at our pleasures, to please the vulgar sort withall: and I wonder, that those who invent so many fabulous tales, do not rather make choise of infinite excellent, and quaint stories, that are found in bookes, wherein they should have lesse trouble to write them, and might doubtlesse proove more pleasing to the hearer, and profitable to the Reader. And whosoever would undertake to frame a compleate and well joynted bodie of them, neede neither employe nor adde any thing of his owne unto it except the ligaments, as the soldring of another mettall, and by this meanes might compact sundry events of all kindes, disposing and diversifying them, according as the beauty and lustre of the worke should require: And very neere, as Ovid° hath sowen and contrived his *Metamorphosis,* with that strange number of diverse fables. In the last couple this is also worthy consideration, that Paulina offreth willingly to leave her life for her husbands sake, and that her husband had also other times quit death for the love of her. There is no great counterpoyze[2] in this exchange for us: but according to his Stoike[3] humour, I suppose he perswaded himselfe to have done as much for hir, prolonging his life for hir availe, as if he had died for hir. In one of his letters, he writeth to Lucilius, after he hath given him to understand how an ague having surprised him in Rome, contrary to his wives opinion, who would needs have stayed him, he sodainly tooke his Coach, to goe unto a house of his into the country; and how he told her that the ague he had was no bodily fever, but of the place: and followeth thus: 'At last she let me goe, earnestly recommending my health unto me. Now I who know, how her life lodgeth in mine, begin to provide for my self, that conse-quently I may provide for her: The priviledge my age hath bestowed on me, making me more constant, and more resolute in many things, I lose it; when ever I call to minde, that in this aged corps there harboureth a yoong woman, to whom I bring some profit. Since I cannot induce her to love me more couragiously, shee induceth me to love my selfe more carefully; for something must be lent to honest

---

[1]Connected.
[2]Balance.
[3]See Stoics.°

affections, and sometimes, although occasions urge us to the contrary, life must be revoked againe, yea with torment. The soule must be held fast with ones teeth, since the lawe to live an honest man, is not to live as long as they please, but so long as they ought. He who esteemeth not his wife or a friend so much, as that he will not lengthen his life for them, and wil obstinately die, that man is over-nice,[1] and too effeminate: The soule must commaund that unto her selfe, when the utilitie of our friends requireth it: we must sometimes lend our selves unto our friends, and when we would die for us, we ought for their sakes to interrupt our deseigne. It is a testimony of high courage to returne to life for the respect of others as diverse notable men have done: and to preserve age is a part of singular integritie (the chiefest commoditie whereof, is the carelesnesse of her continuance, and a more couragious and disdainefull use of life) if a man perceive such an office to be pleasing, acceptable and profitable to any well-affected friend. And who doeth it, receiveth thereby a gratefull meede and pleasing recompence: for what can bee sweeter, than to be so deare unto his wife, that in respect of her a man become more deere unto himselfe? So my Paulina, hath not onely charged me with her feare, but also with mine. It hath not beene sufficient for me to consider, how resolutely I might dye, but I have also considered how irresolutely she might endure it. I have enforced my selfe to live: And to live is sometime magnanimitie': Reade heere his owne wordes, as excellent as is his use.[2] *ø*

---

[1]Delicate.

[2]Custom, that is, as excellent as his words usually are.

* * *

Francis Bacon

(1561–1626)

Francis Bacon was born into a family favored by royalty; his father, Sir Nicholas, was Lord Keeper of the Great Seal. The last of eight children (six by his father's first wife), he attended Trinity College, Cambridge, with his older full-brother, Anthony. From there, Bacon went to Gray's Inn to study law and shortly thereafter to France for three years. After the death of his father, he returned to Gray's Inn and was admitted to the Bar in 1582 and to Parliament in 1584. But his objection to a bill supported by the Queen so impeded his advancement under Elizabeth that by 1598 he was arrested for debt.

After the Queen's death in 1603, Bacon began to rise in the government, becoming king's council for James I in 1604, solicitor-general in 1607, attorney-general in 1613, privy councillor in 1616, lord keeper in 1617, and finally lord chancellor in 1618. In 1606, at the age of forty-five, he married Alice Bartham. The couple had no children. Bacon was knighted when James I gained the throne, was made Baron Verulam in 1618, and became Viscount St. Albans in 1621. In that same year, convicted of accepting bribes, he fell from power and was forced to retire in disgrace. He died in March 1626 from bronchitis that developed after he had been gathering snow to test its effectiveness in preserving a chicken.

Bacon is remembered for his brilliant attempts to consolidate what was known and to compare it with what could be known. *The Advancement of Learning* (1605) and *Novum Organum* (1620) were to be parts of this grand scientific treatise. Because he advocated the formation of learned societies to promote scientific knowledge, he is credited with contributing to the founding of the Royal Society thirty-four years after his death.

The *Essays*, ten in number, were first published in 1597 and were dedicated to Anthony, who, during his twelve years in France, had met and befriended Montaigne. The essays were revised and expanded to thirty-eight in 1612 and finally to fifty-eight in 1625, establishing Bacon as the first

English essayist. He dedicated this edition, published simultaneously in English and Latin (Latin being the tongue Bacon thought most certain to endure), to the Duke of Buckingham: "For that, as it seemes, They come home, to mens Businesse, and Bosomes. I have enlarged them, both in Number, and Weight; So that they are indeed a New Worke."

Unlike Montaigne, Bacon wrote concise, assertive pieces nearly devoid of direct personal reference. Yet his personality is stamped on every page; in his balanced phrases and authoritative tone he distills his experience as an observer of man and nature, confident, as he states more than once in his essays, that the "care of Posterity, is most in them" who are childless men and thus free to serve the public. Unlike Montaigne, he has little use for tales, particularly if they disturb the imagination and distract us from reality. For Bacon, the great task of the writer is to pass on knowledge accumulated in all fields, philosophical and interpersonal as well as scientific, so that future generations might be better equipped to face the human condition. Much of this knowledge he conveys in aphoristic assertions of the golden mean or of a sensible alternation between extremes: "Use Fasting, and full Eating, but rather full Eating; Watching and Sleep, but rather Sleep; Sitting, and Exercise, but rather Exercise; and the like. So shall Nature be cherished, and yet taught Masteries." The pervasive parallelism of his sentences matches the pleasure he takes in mediating opposites. The content shapes the form. Thus the essay in English ranges in form from the internal, imaginative wanderings of Florio's Montaigne to the external, practical directives of Bacon. ✒

II. Of Death

Men feare Death, as Children feare to goe in the darke: And as that Natural Feare in Children, is increased with Tales, so is the other. Certainly, the Contemplation of Death, as the wages of sinne, and Passage to another world, is Holy, and Religious; But the Feare of it, as a Tribute due unto Nature, is weake. Yet in Religious Meditations, there is sometimes, Mixture of Vanitie, and of Superstition. You shal reade, in some of the Friars Books of Mortification, that a man should thinke with himselfe, what the Paine is, if he have but his Fingers end Pressed, or Tortured; And thereby imagine, what the Paines of Death are, when the whole Body, is corrupted and dissolved; when many times, Death passeth with lesse paine, then the Torture of a Limme: For the most vitall parts, are not the quickest of Sense. And by him, that spake onely as a Philosopher, and Naturall Man, it was well said; *Pompa Mortis magis terret, quam Mors ipsa.*[1] Groanes and Convulsions, and a discoloured Face, and Friends weeping, and Blackes,[2] and

---

[1] The parade of Death terrifies more than Death itself.
[2] Mourning clothes.

Obsequies, and the like, shew Death Terrible. It is worthy the observing, that there is no passion in the minde of man, so weake, but it Mates, and Masters, the Feare of Death; And therefore Death, is no such terrible Enemie, when a man hath so many Attendants, about him, that can winne the combat of him. Revenge triumphs over Death; Love slights it; Honour aspireth to it; Griefe flieth to it; Feare pre-occupateth it; Nay we reade, after Otho the Emperour[1] had slaine himselfe, Pitty (which is the tenderest of Affections) provoked many to die, out of meere compassion to their Soveraigne, and as the truest sort of Followers. Nay Seneca° addes Nicenesse[2] and Saciety;[3] *Cogita quam diu eadem feceris; Mori velle non tantum Fortis, aut Miser, sed etiam Fastidiosus potest.*[4] A man would die, though he were neither valiant, nor miserable, onely upon a wearinesse to doe the same thing, so oft over and over. It is no lesse worthy to observe, how little Alteration, in good Spirits, the Approaches of Death make; For they appeare, to be the same Men, till the last Instant, Augustus Caesar° died in a Complement; *Livia, Conjugii nostri memor, vive et vale,*[5] Tiberius[6] in dissimulation;[7] As Tacitus° saith of him; *Iam Tiberium Vires, et Corpus, non Dissimulatio, deserebant,*[8] Vespasian° in a jest; Sitting upon the Stoole, *Ut puto Deus fio,*[9] Galba[10] with a Sentence; *Feri, si ex re sit populi Romani,*[11] Tacitus°; Holding forth his Necke. Septimius Severus[12] in dispatch; *Adeste, si quid mihi restat agendum,*[13] And the like. Certainly, the Stoikes[14] bestowed too much cost upon Death, and by their great preparations, made it appeare more fearefull. Better saith he, *Qui Finem Vitae extremum inter*

---

[1]Marcus Salvius (A.D. 32–69), Roman emperor from January to April A.D. 69 and friend to Nero.°
  When Nero° took Otho's wife as his mistress, he gave a province to Otho. In 68 Otho revolted against Nero,° killed Galba, who had succeeded Nero,° and named himself emperor. But when Vetellius challenged his claim, Otho was defeated and committed suicide.

[2]Fastidiousness.

[3]Satiety or the condition of being fully satisfied.

[4]Think how long you have done the same things; not only the brave, or the wretched, but even the fastidious can wish to die.

[5]Livia, mindful of our marriage, live and be well.

[6]Tiberius Julius Caesar Augustus (42 B.C.–A.D. 37), second Roman emperor (A.D. 14–37). Known as a suspicious ruler, he ordered the death of Sejanus, his chief advisor, in A.D. 31, five years after Tiberius had retired to Capri to conduct the affairs of the Roman empire by letter.

[7]Deception.

[8]Now strength and body, but not dissimulation, were forsaking Tiberius.

[9]"I think that I am becoming a God." Vespasian° is making fun of the Roman custom of deifying great men when they die. The line comes from Suetonius.°

[10]Servius Sulpicius Galba (3 B.C.–A.D. 69), Roman emperor from 68 to 69, succeeded Nero° after his suicide but was defeated by Otho.

[11]Strike, if it be for the benefit of the Roman people.

[12]Lucius Septimius Severus (A.D. 146–211), Roman emperor (193–211) who brought peace after the murder of the previous emperor (Pertinax). He constructed new buildings in Rome and repaired Hadrian's° wall in Britain. He died in York while planning an invasion of Scotland.

[13]Come, if there is anything left for me to do.

[14]See Stoics.°

Munera ponat Naturae.[1] It is as Naturall to die, as to be borne; And to a little
Infant, perhaps, the one, is as painfull, as the other. He that dies in an earnest
Pursuit, is like one that is wounded in hot Bloud; who, for the time, scarce feeles
the Hurt; And therefore, a Minde fixt, and bent upon somewhat that is good, doth
avert the Dolors of Death; But above all, beleeve it, the sweetest Canticle[2] is, *Nunc
dimittis;*[3] when a Man hath obtained worthy Ends, and Expectations. Death hath
this also; That it openeth the Gate, to good Fame, and extinguisheth Envie.
—*Extinctus amabitur idem.*[4]

VII. *Of Parents and Children*

The joyes of Parents are Secret; And so are their Griefes, and Feares; They cannot
utter the one; Nor they will not utter the other. Children sweeten Labours; But
they make Misfortunes more bitter; They increase the Cares of Life; but they
mitigate the Remembrance of Death. The Perpetuity by Generation is common to
Beasts; But Memory, Merit, and Noble workes, are proper to Men; And surely a
Man shall see, the Noblest workes, and Foundations, have proceeded from
Childlesse Men; which have sought to expresse the Images of their Minds; where
those of their Bodies have failed; So the care of Posterity, is most in them, that
have no Posterity. They that are the first Raisers of their Houses,[5] are most
Indulgent towards their Children; Beholding them, as the Continuance, not only
of their kinde, but of their Worke; And so both Children, and Creatures.

    The difference in Affection, of Parents, towards their severall Children, is
many times unequall; And sometimes unworthy; Especially in the mother; As
Salomon[6] saith; A wise sonne rejoyceth the Father; but an ungracious sonne
shames the Mother.[7] A Man shall see, where there is a House full of Children, one
or two, of the Eldest, respected, and the Youngest made wantons; But in the
middest, some that are, as it were forgotten, who, many times, neverthelesse,
prove the best. The Illiberalitie of Parents, in allowance towards their Children, is
an harmefull Errour; Makes them base; Acquaints them with Shifts;[8] Makes them
sort with meane[9] Company; And makes them surfet[10] more, when they come to

---

[1]Who puts the final end of life among the gifts of Nature.
[2]Little song.
[3]"Now thou dost dismiss," spoken by Simeon after seeing the infant Jesus; Luke 2:29.
[4]"He will be loved just the same when dead" (Horace°).
[5]Those who first bring honor to their families.
[6]See Solomon.°
[7]Proverbs 10:1.
[8]Fraud.
[9]Poor.
[10]Indulge to excess.

Plenty; And therefore, the Proofe is best, when Men keepe their Authority towards their Children, but not their Purse. Men have a foolish manner (both Parents, and Schoole-masters, and Servants) in creating and breeding an Emulation between Brothers, during Childhood, which many times sorteth to Discord, when they are Men; And disturbeth Families. The Italians make little difference betweene Children, and Nephewes, or neere Kinsfolkes; But so they be of the Lumpe, they care not, though they passe not through their owne Body. And, to say Truth, in Nature, it is much a like matter; In so much, that we see a Nephew, sometimes, resembleth an Uncle, or a Kinsman, more then his owne Parent; As the Bloud happens. Let Parents choose betimes, the Vocations, and Courses, they meane their Children should take; For then they are most flexible; And let them not too much apply themselves, to the Disposition of their Children, as thinking they will take best to that, which they have most Minde to. It is true, that if the Affection or Aptnesse of the Children, be Extraordinary, then it is good, not to crosse it; But generally, the Precept is good; *Optimum elige, suave et facile illud faciet Consuetudo.*[1] Younger Brothers are commonly Fortunate, but seldome or never, where the Elder are disinherited.

VIII. *Of Marriage and Single Life*

He that hath Wife and Children, hath given Hostages to Fortune; For they are Impediments, to great Enterprises, either of Vertue, or Mischiefe. Certainly, the best workes, and of greatest Merit for the Publike, have proceeded from the unmarried, or Childlesse Men; which, both in Affection, and Meanes, have married and endowed the Publike. Yet it were great Reason, that those that have Children, should have greatest care of future times; unto which, they know, they must transmit, their dearest pledges.

Some there are, who though they lead a Single Life, yet their Thoughts doe end with themselves, and account future Times, Impertinences.[2] Nay, there are some other, that account Wife and Children, but as Bills of charges. Nay more, there are some foolish rich covetous Men, that take a pride in having no Children, because they may be thought, so much the richer. For perhaps, they have heard some talke; Such an one is a great rich Man; And another except to it; Yea, but he hath a great charge of Children: As if it were an Abatement to his Riches. But the most ordinary cause of a Single Life, is Liberty; especially, in certaine Selfe-pleasing, and humorous[3] Mindes, which are so sensible of every restraint, as they will goe neare, to thinke their Girdles, and Garters, to be Bonds and Shackles.

---

[1]Choose the best, custom will make it sweet and easy.
[2]Irrelevant folly.
[3]Capricious, fantastic.

Unmarried Men are best Friends; best Masters; best Servants; but not alwayes best Subjects; For they are light to runne away; And almost all Fugitives, are of that Condition. A Single Life doth well with Church men; For Charity will hardly water the Ground, where it must first fill a Poole. It is indifferent for judges and Magistrates; For if they be facile, and corrupt, you shall have a Servant, five times worse than a Wife. For Souldiers, I finde the Generalls commonly in their Hortatives,[1] put Men in minde of their Wives and Children. And I thinke the Despising of Marriage, amongst the Turkes, maketh the vulgar souldier more base. Certainly, Wife and Children, are a kinde of Discipline of Humanity; And single Men, though they be many times more Charitable, because their Meanes are lesse exhaust; yet, on the other side, they are more cruell, and hard hearted, (good to make severe Inquisitors) because their Tendernesse, is not so oft called upon.

Grave Natures, led by Custome, and therfore constant, are commonly loving Husbands; As was said of Ulysses; *Vetulam suam praetulit Immortalitati.*[2] Chast Women are often Proud, and froward, as Presuming upon the merit of their Chastity. It is one of the best Bonds, both of Chastity and Obedience, in the Wife, if She thinke her Husband Wise; which She will never doe, if She finde him jealous. Wives are young Mens Mistresses; Companions for middle Age; and old Mens Nurses. So as a Man may have a Quarrell[3] to marry, when he will. But yet, he was reputed one of the wise Men, that made Answer to the Question; When a Man should marry? A young Man not yet, an Elder Man not at all.[4] It is often seene, that bad Husbands, have very good Wives; whether it be, that it rayseth the Price of their Husbands Kindnesse, when it comes; Or that the Wives take a Pride, in their Patience. But this never failes, if the bad Husbands were of their owne choosing, against their Friends consent; For then, they will be sure, to make good their owne Folly.

XXX. *Of Regiment of Health*

There is a wisdome in this, beyond the Rules of Physicke:[5] A Mans owne Observation, what he findes Good of, and what he findes Hurt of, is the best Physicke to preserve Health.

---

[1] Exhortations.

[2] "He preferred his old wife to immortality"; that is, he chose to return to Penelope rather than stay with Calypso or Circe.

[3] Reason or argument.

[4] Bacon elsewhere attributes this saying to Thales, one of the Seven Sages.°

[5] Medical science; also medicine.

But it is a safer Conclusion to say; This agreeth not well with me, therefore I will not continue it; Then this; I finde no offence of this, therefore I may use it. For Strength of Nature in youth, passeth over many Excesses, which are owing a Man till his Age.

Discerne of the comming on of Yeares, and thinke not, to doe the same Things still; For Age will not be Defied. Beware of sudden Change in any great point of Diet, and if necessity inforce it, fit the rest to it. For it is a Secret, both in Nature, and State; That it is safer to change Many Things, then one. Examine thy Customes, of Diet, Sleepe, Exercise, Apparell, and the like; And trie in any Thing, thou shalt judge hurtfull, to discontinue it by little and little; But so, as if thou doest finde any Inconvenience by the Change, thou come backe to it againe; For it is hard to distinguish, that which is generally held good, and wholesome, from that, which is good particularly, and fit for thine owne Body. To be free minded, and cheerefully disposed, at Houres of Meat and of Sleep and of Exercise is one of the best Precepts of Long lasting. As for the Passions and Studies of the Minde; Avoid Envie; Anxious Feares; Anger fretting inwards; Subtill and knottie Inquisitions; Joyes, and Exhilarations in Excesse; Sadnesse not Communicated. Entertaine Hopes; Mirth rather then Joy; Varietie of Delights, rather then Surfet of them; Wonder, and Admiration, and therefore Novelties; Studies that fill the Minde with Splendide and Illustrious Objects, as Histories, Fables, and Contemplations of Nature. If you flie Physicke in Health altogether, it will be too strange for your Body, when you shall need it. If you make it too familiar, it will worke no Extraordinary Effect, when Sicknesse commeth. I commend rather, some Diet, for certaine Seasons, then frequent Use of Physicke, Except it be growen into a Custome. For those Diets alter the Body more, and trouble it lesse.

Despise no new Accident,[1] in your Body, but aske Opinion of it.[2] In Sicknesse, respect Health principally; And in Health, Action. For those that put their Bodies, to endure in Health, may in most Sicknesses, which are not very sharpe, be cured onely with Diet, and Tendering.

Celsus[3] could never have spoken it as a Physician, had he not been a Wise Man withall; when he giveth it, for one of the great precepts of Health and Lasting; That a Man doe vary, and enterchange Contraries; But with an Inclination to the more benigne Extreme: Use Fasting, and full Eating, but rather full Eating; Watching and Sleep, but rather Sleep; Sitting, and Exercise, but rather Exercise; and the like. So shall Nature be cherished, and yet taught Masteries.

Physicians are some of them so pleasing, and conformable to the Humor of the Patient,[4] as they presse not the true Cure of the Disease; And some other are so Regular, in proceeding according to Art, for the Disease, as they respect not

---

[1]Change or difference.

[2]That is, from a doctor.

[3]Aulus Cornelius, author of *De re medicina* (c. A.D. 30), a popular work in the Renaissance because of its eloquent Latin.

[4]Indulgent to the patient's wishes.

sufficiently the Condition of the Patient. Take one of a Middle Temper; Or if it may not be found in one Man, combine two of either sort; And forget not to call, as well the best acquainted with your Body, as the best reputed of for his Faculty.[1]

XXXII. Of Discourse

Some in their Discourse, desire rather Commendation of Wit, in being able to hold all Arguments, then of judgment, in discerning what is True: As if it were a Praise, to know what might be Said and not what should be Thought. Some have certaine Common Places, and Theames, wherein they are good, and want[2] Variety: Which kinde of Poverty is for the most part Tedious, and when it is once perceived, Ridiculous.

The Honourablest Part of Talke, is to give the Occasion; And againe to Moderate and passe to somewhat else; For then a Man leads the Daunce. It is good, in Discourse, and Speech of Conversation, to vary, and entermingle Speech, of the present Occasion with Arguments; Tales with Reasons, Asking of Questions, with telling of Opinions; and jest with Earnest: For it is a dull Thing to Tire, and, as we say now, to jade,[3] any Thing too farre.

As for jest, there be certaine Things, which ought to be priviledged from it; Namely Religion, Matters of State, Great Persons, Any Mans present Businesse of Importance, And any Case that deserveth Pitty. Yet there be some, that thinke their Wits have been asleepe; Except they dart out somewhat, that is Piquant, and to the Quicke:[4] That is a Vaine, which would be brideled; *Parce Puer stimulis, et fortius utere Loris.*[5] And generally, Men ought to finde the difference, between Saltnesse and Bitternesse. Certainly, he that hath a Satyricall vaine, as he maketh others afraid of his Wit, so he had need be afraid of others Memory. He that questioneth much, shall learne much, and content much; But especially, if he apply his Questions, to the Skill of the Persons, whom he asketh; For he shall give them occasion, to please themselves in Speaking,[6] and himselfe shall continually gather Knowledge. But let his Questions, not be troublesome; For that is fit for a Poser.[7] And let him be sure, to leave other Men their Turnes to speak. Nay, if there be any, that would raigne, and take up all the time, let him finde meanes to take them off, and to bring Others on; As Musicians use to doe, with those, that dance too long Galliards.

If you dissemble sometimes your knowledge, of that you are thought to know; you shall be thought another time, to know that, you know not. Speach of

---

[1]Ability.
[2]Lack.
[3]Exhaust.
[4]Some sharp sarcasm.
[5]"Spare the boy the whips, and use the reins more" (Ovid° *Metamorphoses*).
[6]Show off their knowledge.
[7]Apposer, one who asks difficult questions or interrogates the opposition.

a Mans Selfe ought to be seldome, and well chosen. I knew One, was wont to say, in Scorne; He must needs be a Wise Man, he speakes so much of Himselfe: And there is but one Case, wherein a Man may Commend Himselfe, with good Grace; And that is in commending Vertue in Another; Especially, if it be such a Vertue, whereunto Himselfe pretendeth.[1] Speech of Touch[2] towards Others, should be sparingly used; For Discourse ought to be as a Field, without comming home to any Man.[3] I knew two Noble-men, of the West Part of England; Whereof the one was given to Scoffe, but kept ever Royal Cheere in his House; The other, would aske of those, that had beene at the Others Table; Tell truely, was there never a Flout or drie Blow[4] given; To which the Guest would answer; Such and such a Thing passed; The Lord would say; I thought he would marre a good Dinner.

Discretion of Speech, is more then Eloquence; And to speak agreeably to him, with whom we deale, is more then to speake in good Words, or in good Order.

A good continued Speech, without a good Speech of Interlocution,[5] shews Slownesse; And a Good Reply, or Second Speech, without a good Setled[6] Speech, sheweth Shallownesse and Weaknesse. As we see in Beasts, that those that are Weakest in the Course, are yet Nimblest in the Turne; As it is betwixt the Grey-hound, and the Hare.

To use too many Circumstances,[7] ere one come to the Matter, is Wearisome; To use none at all, is Blunt.

XLIV. Of Deformity

Deformed Persons are commonly even with[8] Nature; For as Nature hath done ill by them; So doe they by Nature: Being for the most part, (as the Scripture saith)[9] void of Naturall Affection; And so they have their Revenge of Nature. Certainly there is a Consent between the Body and the Minde; And where Nature erreth in the One, she ventureth in the Other. *Ubi peccat in uno, periclitatur in altero.* But because, there is in Man, an Election[10] touching the Frame of his Minde, and a Necessity in the Frame of his Body, the Starres of Naturall Inclination, are sometimes obscured, by the Sun of Discipline, and Vertue. Therefore, it is good to consider of Deformity, not as a Signe, which is more Deceivable; But as a Cause, which seldome faileth of the Effect. Whosoever hath any Thing fixed in his

---

[1]To which he himself lays claim.
[2]With stings.
[3]General, without particular application, like a field rather than a road.
[4]A jeering speech or hostile witticism.
[5]Reply.
[6]First.
[7]To digress with material surrounding the point.
[8]Usually revenge themselves on.
[9]Romans 1:31.
[10]Choice.

Person, that doth enduce Contempt, hath also a perpetuall Spurre in himselfe, to rescue and deliver himselfe from Scorne: Therefore all Deformed Persons are extreme Bold. First, as in their own Defence, as being exposed to Scorn; But in Processe of Time, by a Generall Habit. Also it stirreth in them Industry, and especially of this kinde, to watch and observe the Weaknesse of Others, that they may have somewhat to repay. Againe, in their Superiours, it quencheth jealousie towards them, as Persons that they think they may at pleasure despise: And it layeth their Competitours and Emulatours asleepe; As never beleeving, they should be in possibility of advancement, till they see them in Possession. So that, upon the matter, in a great Wit, Deformity is an Advantage to Rising. Kings in Ancient Times, (And at this present in some Countries,) were wont to put Great Trust in eunuchs; Because they, that are Envious towards All, are more Obnoxious[1] and Officious[2] towards One. But yet their Trust towards them, hath rather beene as to good Spialls,[3] and good Whisperers; then good Magistrates, and Officers. And much like is the Reason of Deformed Persons. Still the Ground[4] is, they will, if they be of Spirit, seeke to free themselves from Scorne; Which must be, either by Vertue, or Malice: And therefore, let it not be Marvelled, if sometimes they prove Excellent Persons; As was Agesilaus,[5] Zanger the Sonne of Solyman,[6] Aesope,[7] Gasca President of Peru;[8] And Socrates° may goe likewise amongst them; with Others.

L. Of Studies

Studies serve for Delight, for Ornament, and for Ability. Their Chiefe Use for Delight, is in Privatenesse and Retiring; For Ornament, is in Discourse; And for Ability, is in the judgement and Disposition of Businesse. For Expert Men[9] can Execute, and perhaps Judge of particulars, one by one; But the generall Counsels, and the Plots, and Marshalling of Affaires, come best from those that are Learned.

To spend too much Time in Studies, is Sloth; To use them too much for Ornament, is Affectation; To make Judgement wholly by their Rules is the Humour[10] of a Scholler. They perfect Nature, and are perfected by Experience: For Naturall Abilities, are like Naturall Plants, that need Proyning by Study: And

---

[1] Submissive.

[2] Attentive.

[3] Ones who spy all.

[4] Rule.

[5] Agesilaus II (c. 444–360 B.C.), king of Sparta during its ruin by the Persians.

[6] Sulayman (1494–1566), Ottoman sultan.

[7] See Aesop.°

[8] (1485–1567) Spanish priest, lawyer, and administrator put in charge of restoring peace in Peru in 1547.

[9] Those with practical experience.

[10] Particular folly.

Studies themselves, doe give forth Directions too much at Large, except they be bounded in by experience.

Crafty Men Contemne Studies; Simple Men Admire them; and Wise Men Use them; For they teach not their owne Use; But that is a Wisdome without them, and above them, won by Observation.

Reade not to Contradict, and Confute; Nor to Beleeve and Take for granted; Nor to Finde Talke and Discourse; But to weigh and Consider.

Some Bookes are to be Tasted, Others to be Swallowed, and Some Few to be Chewed and Digested; That is, some Bookes are to be read onely in Parts; Others to be read but not Curiously;[1] And some Few to be read wholly, and with Diligence and Attention. Some Bookes also may be read by Deputy, and Extracts made of them by Others; But that would be, onely in the lesse important Arguments, and the Meaner Sort of Bookes; else distilled Bookes, are like Common distilled Waters, Flashy[2] Things.

Reading maketh a Full[3] Man; Conference[4] a Ready[5] Man; And Writing an Exact Man. And therefore, If a Man Write little, he had need have a Great memory; If he Conferre little, he had need have a Present Wit; And if he Reade litle, he had need have much Cunning, to seeme to know that, he doth not.

Histories make Men Wise; Poets Witty; The Mathematicks Subtill; Naturall Philosophy deepe; Morall Grave; Logick and Rhetorick Able to Contend. *Abeunt studia in Mores.*[6] Nay there is no Stond[7] or Impediment in the Wit, but may be wrought out by Fit Studies; Like as Diseases of the Body, may have Appropriate Exercises. Bowling is good for the Stone and Reines;[8] Shooting for the Lungs and Breast; Gentle Walking for the Stomacke; Riding for the Head; And the like. So if a Mans Wit be Wandring, let him Study the Mathematicks; For in Demonstrations, if his Wit be called away never so little, he must begin again; If his Wit be not Apt to distinguish or find differences, let him Study the Schoole-men; For they are *Cymini sectores.*[9]

If he be not Apt to beat over Matters,[10] and to call up one Thing, to Prove and Illustrate another, let him Study the Lawyers Cases; So every Defect of the Minde, may have a Speciall Receit.[11]

---

[1]With care.

[2]Overmoist, and thus insipid or tasteless.

[3]Well-informed.

[4]Discussions.

[5]Fluent.

[6]"Studies change character" (Ovid° *Heroides*). Bacon himself translated this line in *The Advancement of Learning* as "Studies have an influence and operation upon the manners of those that are conversant in them."

[7]Obstruction.

[8]Gall bladder and kidneys.

[9]Followers of a carver or divider of cumin, one of the smallest of seeds, that is, one who makes fine distinctions.

[10]Examine them carefully.

[11]Prescription.

. . .

Thomas Browne

(1605–1682)

Thomas Browne was born in London, the only son among four children of a textile dealer. His father died when Thomas was eight, and his mother remarried a sea captain, Sir Thomas Dutton, who later built a house on an estate in Ireland. Thomas Browne was educated first at Oxford (1623–1629) and then at Montpellier (France), Padua (Italy), and finally at Leiden (Holland), where he received his medical degree in 1633. When his stepfather died the next year from an injury received during a quarrel, his mother remained in Ireland and Browne went on to practice medicine in Yorkshire and possibly Oxfordshire.

In Yorkshire Browne wrote and privately distributed to a few friends his first work, *Religio Medici,* which was published in a pirated version in 1642 and again the next year in an authorized version. At age thirty-two (1637) Thomas Browne settled in the city of Norwich, where he spent the rest of his life as a doctor and writer. Four years later he married Dorothy Mileham, who bore him twelve children, four dying in infancy. Of the remaining eight only one son and three daughters survived their parents. In 1646 Browne published *Pseudodoxia Epidemica* and in 1658 *Hydriotaphia* and *The Garden of Cyrus*. At sixty-six, having remained a quiet loyalist during the period of Puritanism and civil war, he was knighted by Charles II. Browne died of a stomach ailment at seventy-seven and was buried in the Church of St. Peter in Norwich. When, in 1840, workers accidentally broke open his tomb, they found his bones intact and his auburn hair preserved. His skull was placed in a glass case in the hospital in Norwich.

Sir Thomas Browne was an erudite, scholarly man whose mind was incessantly ruminative, filled with curiosities, intrigued by mysteries like those in his most famous line in the fifth and final chapter of *Hydriotaphia or Urn Buriall:* "What song the Syrens sang, or what name Achilles assumed when he hid himself among women, though puzling Questions are not beyond all conjecture." While firmly believing in witches and angels,

Browne was dedicated to examining the opinions of the ancients and the moderns on scientific matters and to deducing through logic the truth or falsehood of their views. Along with Bacon, he is credited with acknowledging the primacy of experimental evidence over hearsay and ancient wisdom. And, although he did not himself contribute to the field of science, the books in his library show that he did read and make use of the best work in his field, including Harvey on the circulation of the blood and Leeuwenhoek on revelations from the microscope.

Browne combines qualities of both Montaigne and Bacon, sharing the introspection of the one and the scientific bent of the other. Yet he is unquestionably original. Although his protestations of modesty were questioned even by his first commentator, Sir Kenelm Digby, in 1643, few would question his faith or his determination to root out error in popular beliefs. His was a rare mind, weaving the practical and the mystical in a baroque fabric. In the short selections from *Religio Medici,* the reflective, imaginative side of Browne confronts mortality (it shames him) and the effects of prejudice: "by a word wee wound a thousand, and at one blow assassine the honour of a Nation." Yet he will not judge others; no one can, he says, "because no man knowes himselfe." In these essays Browne allows waywardness to prevail. Part 2, section 9, for instance, begins with a statement about marriage, moves to music, thence to comments about his patients and against infallibility, and ends with the prospect of immortality. In the selections from *Pseudodoxia Epidemica* his rational, practical side systematically dismisses both false "facts," such as the salamander's protection from fire, and false beliefs, prejudices against those who differ from the typical Englishman. In these essays, Browne follows a uniform pattern of argument; after treating the opposition with respect, he sets up his own assertion and proves it.

In "Of the Jews" Browne shows with relentless logic that Jews do not emit a characteristic odor. (The belief that the outsider stinks persists today: it was reported recently that many English fear that when the Channel Tunnel opens, garlic-laden French air will pollute the English countryside.) Moreover, Browne believed, and could prove through logic, that the skin color of blacks was not the result of the curse of Cain, as he does in "Of the Blackness of Negroes, continued." These two essays reveal Browne's love of arcane knowledge and his respect for ancient authorities, but they show most clearly his profound faith in reason and his determination to hold to it despite the ignorance and prejudice of those around him. Samuel Johnson's comments in his biography of Browne remain true whether Browne is following the vagaries of the internal mind or the intricacies of a logical pattern: "the spirit and vigour of his pursuit always gives delight; and the reader follows him, without reluctance, through his mazes, in themselves flowery and pleasing, and ending at the point originally in view." ✒

I am naturally bashful

RELIGIO MEDICI, PART 1, SECT. 40

I am naturally bashful, nor hath conversation, age, or travell, beene able to effront, or enharden me, yet I have one part of modesty which I have seldome discovered in another, that is (to speake truly) I am not so much afraid of death, as ashamed thereof; 'tis the very disgrace and ignominy of our natures, that in a moment can so disfigure us that our nearest friends, Wife, and Children, stand afraid and start at us. The Birds and Beasts of the field that before in a naturall feare obeyed us, forgetting all allegiance, begin to prey upon us. This very conceite hath in a tempest disposed and left me willing to be swallowed up in the abysse of waters; wherein I had perished unseene, unpityed, without wondring eyes, teares of pity, Lectures of morality, and none had said, *quantum mutatus ab illo!*[1] Not that I am ashamed of the Anatomy of my parts, or can accuse nature for playing the bungler in any part of me, or my owne vitious[2] life for contracting any shamefull disease upon me, whereby I might not call my selfe as wholesome a morsell for the wormes as any. ✐

Some upon the courage of a fruitfull issue

RELIGIO MEDICI, PART 1, SECT. 41[3]

Some upon the courage of a fruitfull issue, wherein, as in the truest Chronicle, they seem to outlive themselves, can with greater patience away with death. This conceit and counterfeit subsisting in our progenies seemes to mee a meere fallacy, unworthy the desires of a man, that can but conceive a thought of the next world; who, in a nobler ambition, should desire to live in his substance in Heaven rather than in his name and shadow in the earth. And therefore at my death I meane to take a totall adieu of the world, not caring for a Monument, History, or Epitaph, not so much as the bare memory of my name to be found any where but in the universall Register of God: I am not yet so Cynicall as to approve the Testament of *Diogenes*° *(Who willed his friend not to bury him, but to hang him up with a staffe in his hand to fright away the Crowes.);[4] nor doe I altogether allow that *Rodomontado*[5] of *Lucan;*°

——*coelo tegitur, qui non habet urnam.*

---

[1]"How changed he is from himself!" spoken by Aeneas° about Hector's shade in the *Aeneid* 2.274.

[2]Imperfect.

[3]Originally labeled Sect. 40 in a misprint.

[4]Parentheses plus asterisk indicate Browne's notes, which were originally located in the margins.

[5]Derived from Rodomant, a great boaster and Saracen° leader in Ariosto's *Orlando Furioso.*

He that unburied lies wants not his Herse,
For unto him a tombe's the Universe.

But commend in my calmer judgement those ingenuous intentions that
desire to sleepe by the urnes of their Fathers, and strive to goe the nearest way
unto corruption. I doe not envie the temper of Crowes and Dawes,[1] nor the
numerous weary dayes of our Fathers before the Flood. If there bee truth in
Astrology, I may outlive a Jubilee;[2] as yet I have seene one revolution of *Saturne*,[3]
nor hath my pulse beate thirty yeares, and yet excepting one, have seene the
Ashes, and left under ground, all the Kings of *Europe,* have beene contemporary
to three Emperours, four Grand Signiours,[4] and many Popes; mee thinkes I have
outlived my selfe, and begin to bee weary of the Sunne; I have shaked hands with
delight in my warme blood and Canicular dayes;[5] I perceive I doe Anticipate the
vices of age, the world to mee is but a dreame, or mockshow, and wee all therein
but Pantalones and Antickes[6] to my severer contemplations. 🙵

Now for that other Vertue of Charity

RELIGIO MEDICI, PART 2, SECT. 1

Now for that other Vertue of Charity, without which Faith is a meer notion, and
of no existence, I have ever endeavoured to nourish the mercifull disposition and
humane inclination I borrowed from my Parents, and regulate it to the written and
prescribed Lawes of Charity; and if I hold the true Anatomy of my selfe, I am
delineated and naturally framed to such a piece of vertue: for I am of a constitution
so generall, that it consorts and sympathizeth with all things; I have no antipathy,
or rather Idio-syncrasie, in dyet, humour,[7] ayre, any thing; I wonder not at the
French, for their dishes of frogges, snailes, and toadstooles, nor at the Jewes for
Locusts and Grasse-hoppers, but being amongst them, make them my common
viands; and I finde they agree with my stomach as well as theirs; I could digest a
Sallad gathered in a Church-yard, as well as in a Garden. I cannot start at the
presence of a Serpent, Scorpion, Lizard, or Salamander; at the sight of a Toad, or
Viper, I finde in me no desire to take up a stone to destroy them. I feele not in my
selfe those common antipathies that I can discover in others: Those nationall

---

[1]Birds known for their longevity.

[2]According to Leviticus 25:8–17, a period of rest, restitution, and remission occurring every fifty
years.

[3]Twenty-nine and a half years.

[4]Sultans of Turkey.

[5]Hot days around August 11 when the dog star rises, that is, during his hot youth.

[6]Fools and grotesques; Pantalone was a skinny, foolish old man in glasses, slippers, and panta-
loons in old Italian comedy.

[7]Temperament.

repugnances doe not touch me, nor doe I behold with prejudice the *French,* *Italian, Spaniard,* or *Dutch;* but where I find their actions in ballance with my Countreymens, I honour, love, and embrace them in the same degree; I was borne in the eighth Climate,[1] but seeme for to bee framed, and constellated unto all; I am no Plant that will not prosper out of a Garden. All places, all ayres make unto me one Country; I am in *England* every where, and under any meridian; I have beene shipwrackt,[2] yet am not enemy with sea or winds; I can study, play, or sleepe in a tempest. In briefe, I am averse from nothing, my conscience would give mee the lie if I should say I absolutely detest or hate any essence but the Devill, or so at least abhorre any thing but that wee might come to composition. If there be any among those common objects of hatred I doe contemne and laugh at, it is that great enemy of reason, vertue, and religion, the multitude, that numerous piece of monstrosity, which taken asunder seeme men, and the reasonable crea- tures of God; but confused together, make but one great beast, and a monstrosity more prodigious than Hydra;[3] it is no breach of Charity to call these fooles, it is the stile all holy Writers have afforded them, set downe by *Solomon*° in canonicall Scripture, and a point of our faith to beleeve so. Neither in the name of multitude doe I onely include the base and minor sort of people; there is a rabble even amongst the Gentry, a sort of Plebeian heads, whose fancy moves with the same wheele[4] as these; men in the same Levell with Mechanickes, though their fortunes doe somewhat guild their infirmities, and their purses compound for their follies. But as in casting account three or foure men together come short in account of one man placed by himself below them:[5] So neither are a troope of these Doradoes,[6] of that true esteeme and value, as many a forlorne person, whose condition doth place them below their feet. Let us speake like Politicians; there is a Nobility without Heraldry, a naturall dignity, whereby one man is ranked with another, another Filed before him, according to quality of his desert, and preheminence of his good parts. Though the corruption of these times, and the byas of present practise wheele another way, thus it was in the first and primitive Common- wealths, and is yet in the integrity and Cradle of well-order'd polities, till corrup- tion getteth ground, ruder desires labouring after that which wiser considerations contemn, every one having a liberty to amasse and heape up riches, and they a licence or faculty to doe or purchase any thing. ✒

---

[1]Strip of the earth's surface between two parallel latitudes. In Chaucer's time people referred to seven climates between the two poles, analogous to the seven planets. By 1800 thirty such climates had been posited.

[2]In 1630 when traveling between England and Ireland.

[3]In Greek mythology, a many-headed monster who grew two new heads when one was cut off. Hercules's second labor was to kill the hydra, which he did by cauterizing the necks after cutting off the heads.

[4]Of fortune.

[5]This accounting system seems to be based on an inverted pyramid shape in which the top and longest line is composed of 100 ones, the second line of 10 tens, and the third of 5 twenties.

[6]Wealthy men.

There is another offence unto Charity

RELIGIO MEDICI, PART 2, SECT. 4

There is another offence unto Charity, which no Author hath ever written of, and few take notice of, and that's the reproach, not of whole professions, mysteries, and conditions, but of whole nations, wherein by opprobrious Epithets wee miscall each other, and by an uncharitable Logicke from a disposition in a few conclude a habit in all.

> Le mutin Anglois, et le bravache Escossois;
> Le bougre Italien, et le fol Francois;
> Le poultron Romain, le larron de Gascongne,
> L'Espagnol superbe, et l'Aleman yvrongne.[1]

St. *Paul*, that cals the *Cretians* lyers,[2] doth it but indirectly and upon quotation of their owne Poet. It is as bloody a thought in one way as *Neroes*° was in another. For by a word wee wound a thousand, and at one blow assassine the honour of a Nation. It is as compleate a piece of madnesse to miscall and rave against the times, or thinke to recall men to reason, by a fit of passion: *Democritus*° that thought to laugh the times into goodnesse, seemes to mee as deeply Hypochondriack, as *Heraclitus*° that bewailed them; it moves not my spleen to behold the multitude in their proper humours, that is, in their fits of folly and madnesse, as well understanding that Wisedome is not prophan'd unto the World, and 'tis the priviledge of a few to be vertuous. They that endeavour to abolish vice destroy also vertue, for contraries, though they destroy one another, are yet the life of one another. Thus vertue (abolish vice) is an Idea; againe, the communitie of sinne doth not disparage goodnesse; for when vice gaines upon the major part, vertue, in whom it remaines, becomes more excellent, and being lost in some, multiplies its goodnesse in others which remaine untouched, and persists intire in the generall inundation. I can therefore behold vice without a Satyre,[3] content onely with an admonition, or instructive reprehension; for Noble natures, and such as are capable of goodnesse, are railed into vice, that might as easily bee admonished into vertue; and we should be all so farre the Orators of goodnesse, as to protect her from the power of vice and maintaine the cause of injured truth. No man can justly censure or condemne another, because indeed no man truely knowes another. This I perceive in my selfe, for I am in the darke to all the world, and my

---

[1] "The surly English, and the swaggering Scots; / The buggering Italian, and the insane French; / The upstart Roman, the thief of Gascony, / The proud Spaniard, and the drunken German." H. G. Ward first noted that Browne is here misquoting Sonnet 68 "Les Regrets" by Du Bellay (1524–1560) in which Du Bellay lists characteristics of nationalities that he hates. Ironically, in the last line of the poem, the poet directs his climactic hatred at pedantic learning, of which Browne might well have been accused.

[2] Titus 1:12.

[3] Satire, or without mockery.

nearest friends behold mee but in a cloud, those that know mee but superficially, thinke lesse of me than I doe of my selfe; those of my neere acquaintance thinke more; God, who truely knowes mee, knowes that I am nothing, for hee onely beholds me, and all the world, who lookes not on us through a derived ray,[1] or a trajection of a sensible species, but beholds the substance without the helpes of accidents, and the formes of things, as wee their operations. Further, no man can judge another, because no man knowes himselfe; for we censure others but as they disagree from that humour[2] which wee fancy laudable in our selves, and commend others but for that wherein they seeme to quadrate[3] and consent with us. So that in conclusion, all is but that we all condemne, selfe-love. 'Tis the generall complaint of these times, and perhaps of those past, that charity growes cold; which I perceive most verified in those which most doe manifest the fires and flames of zeale; for it is a vertue that best agrees with coldest natures, and such as are complexioned for humility: But how shall we expect charity towards others, when we are uncharitable to our selves? Charity begins at home, is the voyce of the world, yet is every man his owne greatest enemy, and as it were, his owne executioner. *Non occides,*[4] is the Commandement of God, yet scarse observed by any man; for I perceive every man is his owne *Atropos,*[5] and lends a hand to cut the thred of his owne dayes. *Cain* was not therefore the first murtherer, but *Adam,* who brought in death; whereof hee beheld the practise and example in his owne sonne *Abel,* and saw that verified in the experience of another, which faith could not perswade him in the Theory of himselfe. ✐

There is I thinke no man that apprehends his owne miseries lesse than my selfe

RELIGIO MEDICI, PART 2, SECT. 5

There is I thinke no man that apprehends his owne miseries lesse than my selfe, and no man that so neerely apprehends anothers. I could lose an arme without a teare, and with few groans, mee thinkes, be quartered into pieces; yet can I weepe most seriously at a Play, and receive with a true passion, the counterfeit griefes of those knowne and professed impostures. It is a barbarous part of inhumanity to adde unto any afficted parties misery, or endeavour to multiply in any man a passion, whose single nature is already above his patience; this was the greatest affliction of *Job,* and those oblique expostulations of his friends a deeper injury

---

[1]Indirectly and through the "accidents" of physical reality.
[2]Quality.
[3]To square and thus agree.
[4]Thou shalt not kill.
[5]The Greek goddess who cuts the thread of life; one of the Three Fates. The others are Clotho, who weaves the thread, and Lachesis, who measures it.

than the downe-right blowes of the Devill. It is not the teares of our owne eyes onely, but of our friends also, that doe exhaust the current of our sorrowes, which, falling into many streames, runne more peaceably, and is contented with a narrower channel. It is an act within the power of charity, to translate a passion out of one breast into another, and to divide a sorrow almost out of it selfe; for an affliction, like a dimension, may be so divided, as if not indivisible, at least to become insensible. Now with my friend I desire not to share or participate, but to engrosse his sorrowes, that by making them mine owne, I may more easily discusse them; for in mine owne reason, and within my selfe I can command that, which I cannot entreate without my selfe, and within the circle of another. I have often thought those Noble paires and examples of friendship not so truely Histories of what had beene, as fictions of what should be, but I now perceive nothing in them but possibilities, nor any thing in the Heroick examples of *Damon* and *Pythias,*[1] *Achilles* and *Patroclus,*[2] which mee thinkes upon some grounds I could not performe within the narrow compasse of my selfe. That a man should lay down his life for his friend, seemes strange to vulgar affections, and such as confine themselves within that worldly principle, Charity beginnes at home. For mine owne part I could never remember the relations that I held unto my selfe, nor the respect that I owe unto mine owne nature, in the cause of God, my Country, and my Friends. Next to these three, I doe embrace my selfe; I confesse I doe not observe that order that the Schooles ordaine our affections, to love our Parents, Wifes, Children, and then our friends, for excepting the injunctions of Religion, I doe not finde in my selfe such a necessary and indissoluble Sympathy to all those of my bloud. I hope I doe not breake the fifth Commandement, if I conceive I may love my friend before the nearest of my bloud, even those to whom I owe the principles of life; I never yet cast a true affection on a Woman,[3] but I have loved my Friend as I do vertue, my soule, my God. From hence me thinkes I doe conceive how God loves man, what happinesse there is in the love of God. Omitting all other, there are three most mysticall unions: Two natures in one person; three persons in one nature; one soule in two bodies. For though indeed they bee really divided, yet are they so united, as they seeme but one, and make rather a duality then two distinct soules. ✍

---

[1]When Pythias, condemned to death, asked his friend Damon to take his place while he went home to put his affairs in order, Damon agreed. Pythias returned as he had promised just in time for the execution. The ruler was so impressed with the friendship that he freed them both.

[2]In the *Iliad*, when Achilles refuses to fight because of Agamemnon's theft of Briseis, his loyal friend Patroclus wears the armor of Achilles, fights in his stead, and succumbs to Hector. The death of his friend finally moves Achilles to reenter the battle.

[3]He married six years later.

Not that I disallow of second marriage

RELIGIO MEDICI, PART 2, SECT. 9

I was never yet once, and commend their resolutions who never marry twice, not that I disallow of second marriage; as neither in all cases of Polygamy, which, considering some times and the unequall number of both sexes, may bee also necessary. The whole woman was made for man, but the twelfth part of man for woman: man is the whole world and the breath of God, woman the rib and crooked piece of man. I could be content that we might procreate like trees, without conjunction, or that there were any way to perpetuate the world without this triviall and vulgar way of coition; It is the foolishest act a wise man commits in all his life, nor is there any thing that will more deject his coold imagination, when hee shall consider what an odde and unworthy piece of folly hee hath committed; I speake not in prejudice, nor am averse from that sweet sexe, but naturally amorous of all that is beautifull; I can looke a whole day with delight upon a handsome picture, though it be but of an Horse. It is my temper, and I like it the better, to affect[1] all harmony, and sure there is musicke even in the beauty, and the silent note which *Cupid* strikes, farre sweeter than the sound of an instrument. For there is a musicke where-ever there is a harmony, order, or proportion, and thus farre we may maintain the musick of the spheares; for those well ordered motions, and regular paces, though they give no sound unto the eare, yet to the understanding they strike a note most full of harmony. Whatsoever is harmonically composed, delights in harmony; which makes me much distrust the symmetry of those heads[2] which declaime against all Church musicke. For my selfe, not only from my obedience, but my particular genius, I doe embrace it; for even that vulgar and Taverne Musicke, which makes one man merry, another mad, strikes in mee a deepe fit of devotion, and a profound contemplation of the first Composer, there is something in it of Divinity more than the eare discovers. It is an Hieroglyphicall and shadowed lesson of the whole world, and Creatures of God, such a melody to the eare, as the whole world well understood, would afford the understanding. In briefe, it is a sensible fit of that Harmony, which intellectually sounds in the eares of God. I will not say with *Plato,*° the Soule is an Harmony, but harmonicall, and hath its neerest sympathy unto musicke: thus some, whose temper of body agrees, and humours[3] the constitution of their soules, are borne Poets, though indeed all are naturally inclined unto Rhythme. This made *Tacitus,*° in the very first line of his Story, fall upon a verse *(Urbem Romam in principio Reges habuere.);*[4] and *Cicero,*° the worst of Poets, but declaym-

---

[1]To aspire to.
[2]Roundheads or Puritans.
[3]Complies with.
[4]That the city of Rome had kings in the beginning.

ing for a Poet *(Pro Archia Poeta),[1] falls in the very first sentence upon a perfect *Hexameter (In qua me non inficior mediocriter esse).[2] I feele not in me those sordid, and unchristian desires of my profession, doe not secretly implore and wish for Plagues, rejoyce at Famines, revolve Ephemerides,[3] and Almanacks, in expectation of malignant Aspects, fatal conjunctions, and Eclipses: I rejoyce not at unwholsome Springs, nor unseasonable Winters; my Prayer goes with the Husbandmans;[4] I desire every thing in its proper season, that neither men nor the times bee out of temper. Let mee bee sicke my selfe, if sometimes the malady of my patient be not a disease unto me; I desire rather to cure his infirmities than my owne necessities; where I do him no good me thinkes it is scarce honest gaine, though I confesse 'tis but the worthy salary of our well-intended endeavours: I am not onely ashamed, but heartily sorry, that besides death, there are diseases incurable, yet not for my own sake, or that they be beyond my art, but for the generall cause and sake of humanity whose common cause I apprehend as mine own: And to speak more generally, those three Noble professions[5] which al civil Common wealths doe honour, are raised upon the fall of Adam, and are not any way exempt from their infirmities; there are not onely diseases incurable in Physicke, but cases indissoluble in Lawes, Vices incorrigible in Divinity: if general Councells may erre, I doe not see why particular Courts should be infallible; their perfectest rules are raised upon the erroneous reasons of Man, and the Lawes of one, doe but condemn the rules of another; as Aristotle° oft-times the opinions of his predecessours, because, though agreeable to reason, yet were not consonant to his owne rules, and the Logicke of his proper principles. Againe, to speake nothing of the sinne against the Holy Ghost, whose cure not onely, but whose nature is unknowne; I can cure the gout or stone in some, sooner than Divinity, Pride or Avarice in others. I can cure vices by Physicke, when they remaine incurable by Divinity, and shall obey my pils, when they contemne their precepts. I boast nothing, but plainely say, we all labour against our owne cure, for death is the cure of all diseases. There is no Catholicon or universall remedy I know but this, which thogh nauseous to queasie stomachs, yet to prepared appetites is Nectar, and a pleasant potion of immortality. ✿

---

[1]Just as an ancient poet.
[2]In which I do not deny that I am mediocre.
[3]Study astronomical guides.
[4]Farmer's.
[5]Medicine, law, and religion.

Of the Salamander

PSEUDODOXIA EPIDEMICA, BOOK 3, CHAP. XIV

That a Salamander is able to live in flames, to endure and put out fire, is an assertion, not only of great antiquity, but confirmed by frequent, and not contemptible testimony. The *Egyptians* have drawn it into their Hieroglyphicks, *Aristotle*° seemeth to embrace it; more plainly *Nicander,*[1] Serenus Samimonicus,[2] *AElian*[3] and *Pliny,*°[4] who assigns the cause of this effect: An Animal (saith he) so cold that it extinguisheth the fire like Ice. All which notwithstanding, there is on the negative, Authority and Experience; *Sextius* a Physitian, as *Pliny*°[5] delivereth, denied this effect; *Dioscorides*° affirmed it a point of folly to believe it; *Galen*° that it endureth the fire but in continuance is consumed therein. For experimental conviction, Mathiolus[6] affirmeth, he saw a Salamander burnt in a very short time: and of the like assertion is *Amatus Lusitanus;*[7] and most plainly *Pierius,*[8] whose words in his Hieroglyphicks are these: *Whereas it is commonly said that a Salamander extinguisheth fire, we have found by experience, that it is so far from quenching hot coals, that it dieth immediately therein.* As far the contrary assertion of Aristotle,° it is but by hear say, as common opinion believeth, *Haec enim (ut aiunt) ignem ingrediens, eum extinguit;*[9] and therefore there was no absurdity in *Galen,*° when as a Septical medicine he commended the ashes of a Salamander *(A corruptive Medicine destroying the parts like Arsenike.); and *Magicians* in vain from the power of this Tradition, at the burning of Towns or Houses expect a relief from Salamanders.

The ground[10] of this opinion, might be some sensible resistance of fire observed in the Salamander: which being, as *Galen*° determineth, cold in the fourth, and moist in the third degree,[11] and having also a mucous humidity above

---

[1]Greek grammarian, physician, and poet (185–135 B.C.). Of his two extant poems, one describes poisonous animals and the wounds they can make and the other describes poisons and their antidotes.

[2]Murdered A.D. 212. Wealthy Roman intimate of the court whose works on mathematics, natural history, and medicine were esteemed in the Middle Ages.

[3]Claudius Aelianus (second century A.D.), a Roman who taught rhetoric and wrote in Greek. His works include *Historical Miscellanies, Peasant Letters,* and *On the Characteristics of Animals.*

[4]The Elder.

[5]The Elder.

[6](1500–1577) Physician and botanist from Sienna.

[7]Spanish Jewish physician and scientist (1511–1568) who was born in Portugal and wrote, in Latin, seven hundred medical case histories, including the treatment and results for each case.

[8]Piero Valerianus (1477–1558), an Italian who wrote on the hieroglyphics of Roman obelisks and on the changes in Roman life following the war of 1527.

[9]It certainly (as they say) upon entering the fire, extinguishes it.

[10]Basis.

[11]Stages of intensity in the four elemental qualities of bodies (heat and cold, dryness and moisture) in the Middle Ages; the four stages were sometimes refined into eight by Browne's time, with fire being hot in the eighth degree and dry in the fourth.

and under the skin, by vertue thereof it may a while endure the flame: which being consumed, it can resist no more. Such an humidity there is observed in Newtes, or Water-Lizards, especially if their skins be perforated or pricked. Thus will Frogs and Snails endure the Flame: thus will whites of Eggs, vitreous or glassie flegm extinguish a coal: thus are unguents made which protect a while from the fire: and thus beside the *Hirpini*[1] there are later stories of men that have passed untouch through the fire. And therefore some truth we allow in the tradition: truth according unto *Galen,*° that it may for a time resist a flame, or as *Scaliger*[2] avers, extinguish or put out a coal: for thus much will many humid bodies perform: but that it perseveres and lives in that destructive element, is a fallacious enlargement. Nor do we reasonably conclude, because for a time it endureth fire, it subdueth and extinguisheth the same, because by a cold and aluminous moisture, it is able a while to resist it: from a peculiarity of Nature it subsisteth and liveth in it.

It hath been much promoted by Stories of incombustible napkins and textures which endure the fire, whose materials are called by the name of Salamanders wool. Which many too literally apprehending,[3] conceive some investing part, or tegument[4] of the Salamander: wherein beside that they mistake the condition of this Animal (which is a kind of Lizard, a quadruped corticated[5] and depilous, that is, without wool, fur, or hair) they observe not the method and general rule of nature; whereby all Quadrupeds oviparous, as Lizards, Frogs, Tortois, Chamelions, Crocodiles, are without hair, and have no covering part or hairy investment at all. And if they conceive that from the skin of the Salamander, these incremable pieces are composed; beside the experiments made upon the living, that of *Brassavolus*[6] will step in, who in the search of this truth, did burn the skin of one dead.

Nor is this Salamanders wool desumed from any Animal, but a Mineral substance. Metaphorically so called from this received opinion. For beside *Germanicus*[7] his heart, and *Pyrrhus*[8] his great Toe, which would not burn with the rest of their bodies, there are in the number of Minerals some bodies incombustible; more remarkably that which the Ancients named *Asbeston,* and *Pancirollus*[9] treats

---

[1]Samnite people living in central Italy in the fourth century B.C.

[2]Julius Caesar (1484–1558), Italian scholar and physician in France who wrote on Cicero,° Virgil,° and Seneca° and also on medicine and botany.

[3]Understanding.

[4]Coating.

[5]Having a tough skin.

[6]Of Ferrara, sixteenth-century botanist and physician.

[7]Caesar (15 B.C.–A.D. 19), Roman general, adopted by Emperor Tiberius; he was poisoned by the governor of Syria.

[8]King of Epirus (c. 318–272 B.C.) who fought and defeated the Romans twice but suffered such losses that he declared, "One more such victory and I am lost." Later the Romans and the Spartans defeated him, and, when Pyrrhus escaped to Argos, he was killed by a mob.

[9]Guido (1523–1599), Italian jurist and scholar who wrote *De claris legum interpretibus,* a history of Roman and medieval law.

of in the Chapter of *Linum vivum*[1] *(Plutarch°. Suetonius°). Whereof by Art were weaved Napkins, Shirts, and Coats, inconsumable by fire; and wherein in ancient times to preserve their ashes pure, and without commixture, they burnt the bodies of Kings. A Napkin hereof *Pliny*°[2] reports that *Nero*° had, and the like saith *Paulus Venetus* the Emperour of *Tartary*[3] sent unto Pope Alexander; and also affirms that in some part of *Tartary* there were Mines of Iron whose filaments were weaved into incombustible cloth. Which rare Manufacture, although delivered for lost by *Pancirollus,* yet *Salmuth* his Commentator affirmeth, that one *Podocaterus* a Cyprian, had shewed the same at *Venice;* and his materials were from *Cyprus,* where indeed *Dioscorides*° placeth them; the same is also ocularly confirmed by *Vives* upon *Austin,* and *Maiolus* in his Colloquies. And thus in our days do men practise to make long-lasting Snasts[4] for Lamps out of Alumen plumosum;[5] and by the same we read in *Pausanius,*[6] that there always burnt a Lamp before the Image of *Minerva.*°

Of the Jews

PSEUDODOXIA EPIDEMICA, BOOK 4, CHAP. X

That the *Jews* stink naturally, that is, that in their race and nation there is an evil savour, is a received opinion we know not how to admit; although we concede many questionable points, and dispute not the verity of sundry opinions which are of affinity hereto. We will acknowledg that certain odours attend on animals, no less then certain colours; that pleasant smels are not confined unto vegetables, but found in divers animals, and some more richly then in plants. And though the Problem of *Aristotle*° enquire why no animal smels sweet beside the Parde?[7] yet later discoveries add divers sorts of *Monkeys,* the *Civet Cat* and *Gazela,* from which our Musk proceedeth. We confess that beside the smell of the species, there may be individual odours, and every Man may have a proper and peculiar savour; which although not perceptible unto Man, who hath this sense, but weak, yet sensible unto *Dogs,* who hereby can single out their masters in the dark. We will not deny that particular Men have sent forth a pleasant savour, as *Theophrastus*[8]

[1]Life thread.
[2]The Elder.
[3]Ancient land in central Asia.
[4]Wicks.
[5]Feathery alum.
[6]Traveler (c. A.D. 174) who wrote *Description of Greece*, which provides details about the places and legends of ancient Greece.
[7]Leopard.
[8]Greek philosopher (c. 372–287 B.C.) and successor to Aristotle° as head of the Peripatetics (so named because the followers of Aristotle walked under the arcades—*peripatos*—of the Lyceum

and *Plutarch*° report of *Alexander*° the great, and *Tzetzes*[1] and *Cardan*[2] do testifie of themselves. That some may also emit an unsavory odour, we have no reason to deny; for this may happen from the quality of what they have taken; the Faetor[3] whereof may discover it self by sweat and urine, as being unmasterable by the natural heat of Man, not to be dulcified by concoction beyond an unsavory condition: the like may come to pass from putrid humours,[4] as is often discoverible in putrid and malignant feavers. And sometime also in gross and humid bodies even in the latitude of sanity; the natural heat of the parts being insufficient for a perfect and thorough digestion, and the errors of one concoction not rectifiable by another. But that an unsavory odour is gentilitious[5] or national unto the *Jews*, if rightly understood, we cannot well concede; nor will the information of reason or sence induce it.

For first, Upon consult of reason, there will be found no easie assurance to fasten a material or temperamental propriety upon any nation; there being scarce any condition (but what depends upon clime) which is not exhausted or obscured from the commixture of introvenient[6] nations either by commerce or conquest; much more will it be difficult to make out this affection in the *Jews*; whose race however pretended to be pure, must needs have suffered inseparable commixtures with nations of all sorts; not only in regard of their proselytes, but their universal dispersion; some being posted from several parts of the earth, others quite lost, and swallowed up in those nations where they planted. For the tribes of *Ruben, Gad,* part of *Manasses* and *Napthali,* which were taken by *Assur,*[7] and the rest at the Sacking of *Samaria,* which were led away by *Salmanasser*[8] into Assyria, and after a year and half arrived at *Arsereth,* as is delivered in *Esdras;*[9] these I say never returned, and are by the *Jews* as vainly expected as their *Messias.* Of those of the tribe of *Judah* and *Benjamin,* which were led captive into *Babylon* by *Nebuchadnezzar,*[10] many returned under *Zorobabel;*[11] the rest remained, and

---

discussing philosophy). He is known for his work on plant physiology and his zoological studies, particularly on color adaptation in animals, and for his *Characters,* portraits of types of men in Greece in his period.

[1]Greek poet (twelfth century A.D.) who lived in Constantinople and wrote histories, stories, and commentaries on classical writers.

[2]Geronimo Cardano (1501–1576), Italian medical astrologer and mathematician who wrote on natural history, probability in games of chance, and systems for communicating with the blind and the deaf.

[3]Unpleasant odor.

[4]Vapors.

[5]Characteristic.

[6]Incoming.

[7]Chief god of Assyria.

[8]King of Assyria, died 1290.

[9]Books I and II of the Apocrypha.

[10]King of Babylonia (d. 562 B.C.) who crushed a revolt by Judea and put in place the puppet king Zedekiah.

[11]Zerubbabel, Prince of Judah, who led a group of exiles back to Jerusalem and encouraged the rebuilding of the temple. See the book of Ezra.

from thence long after upon invasion of the *Saracens,*° fled as far as *India;* where yet they are said to remain, but with little difference from the *Gentiles.*

The Tribes that returned to *Judea,* were afterward widely dispersed; for beside sixteen thousand which *Titus*[1] sent to *Rome* unto the triumph of his father *Vespasian,*° he sold no less then an hundred thousand for slaves. Not many years after *Adrian*[2] the Emperour, who ruined the whole Countrey, transplanted many thousands into *Spain,* from whence they dispersed into divers Countreys, as into *France* and *England,* but were banished after from both. From *Spain* they dispersed into *Africa, Italy, Constantinople,* and the Dominions of the *Turk,* where they remain as yet in very great numbers. And if (according to good relations) where they may freely speak it, they forbear not to boast that there are at present many thousand *Jews* in *Spain, France* and *England,* and some dispensed withall, even to the degree of Priesthood; it is a matter very considerable, and could they be smelled out, would much advantage, not only the Church of Christ, but also the coffers of Princes.

Now having thus lived in several Countries, and alwaies in subjection, they must needs have suffered many commixtures; and we are sure they are not exempted from the common contagion of Venery[3] contracted first from Christians. Nor are fornications unfrequent between them both; there commonly passing opinions of invitement,[4] that their Women desire copulation with them rather then their own Nation, and affect[5] Christian carnality above circumcised venery. It being therefore acknowledged, that some are lost, evident that others are mixed, and not assured that any are distinct, it will be hard to establish this quality upon the *Jews,* unless we also transfer the same unto those whose generations are mixed, whose genealogies are *Jewish,* and naturally derived from them.

Again, if we concede a National unsavouriness in any people, yet shall we find the *Jews* less subject hereto then any, and that in those regards which most powerfully concur to such effects, that is, their diet and generation.[6] As for their diet whether in obedience unto the precepts of reason, or the injunctions of parsimony, therein they are very temperate; seldom offending in ebriety or excess of drink, nor erring in gulosity[7] or superfluity of meats; whereby they prevent indigestion and crudities,[8] and consequently putrescence of humors.[9] They have in abomination all flesh maimed, or the inwards any way vitiated;[10] and therefore

---

[1]Titus Flavius Sabinus Vespasianus (A.D. 39–81), Roman emperor who captured Jerusalem in A.D. 70. Mt. Vesuvius erupted during his reign, burying Pompeii and Herculaneum.

[2]See Hadrian.°

[3]Pursuit of sexual gratification.

[4]About allurement.

[5]Aspire to.

[6]Procreation.

[7]Gluttony.

[8]Indigestible matter in the stomach.

[9]Vapors.

[10]Spoiled.

eat no meat but of their own killing. They observe not only fasts at certain times, but are restrained unto very few dishes at all times; so few, that whereas *St. Peters* sheet[1] will hardly cover our Tables, their Law doth scarce permit them to set forth a Lordly feast; nor any way to answer the luxury of our times, or those of our fore-fathers. For of flesh their Law restrains them many sorts, and such as compleat our feasts *(Quanta est gula, quae sibi totos ponit Apros![2] Animal propter convivia natum[3])*: That Animal, *Propter convivia natum,* they touch not,[4] nor any of its preparations, or parts so much in respect at *Roman* Tables, nor admit they unto their board, *Hares, Conies, Herons, Plovers* or *Swans.* Of *Fishes* they only taste of such as have both fins and scales; which are comparatively but few in number, such only, saith *Aristotle,°* whose Egg or spawn is arenaceous;[5] whereby are excluded all cetaceous[6] and cartilagious *Fishes;* many pectinal,[7] whose ribs are rectilineal;[8] many costal,[9] which have their ribs embowed; all spinal, or such as have no ribs, but only a back bone, or somewhat analogous thereto, as *Eels, Congers, Lampries;* all that are testaceous,[10] as *Oysters, Cocles, Wilks, Scollops, Muscles;* and likewise all crustaceous,[11] as *Crabs, Shrimps and Lobsters.* So that observing a spare and simple diet, whereby they prevent the generation of crudities; and fasting often whereby they might also digest them; they must be less inclinable unto this infirmity then any other Nation, whose proceedings are not so reasonable to avoid it.

As for their generations and conceptions (which are the purer from good diet,) they become more pure and perfect by the strict observation of their Law; upon the injunctions whereof, they severely observe the times of Purification, and avoid all copulation, either in the uncleanness of themselves, or impurity of their Women. A Rule, I fear, not so well observed by Christians; whereby not only conceptions are prevented, but if they proceed, so vitiated[12] and defiled, that durable inquinations[13] remain upon the birth. Which, when the conception meets with these impurities, must needs be very potent; since in the purest and most fair conceptions, learned Men derive the cause of *Pox* and *Meazels,* from principles of that nature *(The original or material causes of the Pox and Measles.);* that is, the monstrous impurities in the Mothers blood, and virulent tinctures contracted by the Infant, in the nutriment of the womb.

---

[1] In a vision Peter saw a huge sheet and numerous unkosher animals descend from heaven, at which time God told him they were all fit to eat; see Acts 10:11 and 11:5.
[2] How great is gluttony, which places whole wild boars for itself!
[3] Animal born for the sake of feasts.
[4] That is, the pig.
[5] Living in sand.
[6] Aquatic mammals.
[7] Shaped like a comb.
[8] Straight.
[9] Pertaining to the ribs.
[10] Having a shell.
[11] Having a hard shell.
[12] Spoiled.
[13] Corruptions.

Lastly, Experience will convict it; for this offensive odor is no way discoverable in their Synagogues where many are, and by reason of their number could not be concealed: nor is the same discernable in commerce or conversation with such as are cleanly in Apparel, and decent in their Houses. Surely the Viziars[1] and *Turkish Basha's*[2] are not of this opinion; who as Sir *Henry Blunt*[3] informeth, do generally keep a *Jew* of their private Counsel. And were this true, the *Jews* themselves do not strictly make out the intention of their Law, for in vain do they scruple to approach the dead, who livingly are cadaverous, or fear any outward pollution, whose temper pollutes themselves. And lastly, were this true, yet our opinion is not impartial; for unto converted *Jews* who are of the same seed, no Man imputeth this unsavoury odor; as though Aromatized by their conversion, they lost their scent with their Religion, and smelt no longer then they savoured of the *Jew*.

Now the ground[4] that begat or propagated this assertion, might be the distasteful aversness of the Christian from the *Jew*, upon the villany of that fact, which made them abominable and stink in the nostrils of all Men. Which real practise, and metaphorical expression, did after proceed into a literal construction; but was a fraudulent illation;[5] for such an evil savour their father *Jacob* acknowledged in himself *(Gen.34) when he said, his sons had made him stink in the land, that is, to be abominable unto the inhabitants thereof. Now how dangerous it is in sensible things to use metaphorical expressions unto the people, and what absurd conceits they will swallow in their literals, an impatient[6] example we have in our profession; who having called an eating *ulcer* by the name of a *Wolf*, common apprehension conceives a reality therein; and against our selves,[7] ocular affirmations are pretended[8] to confirm it.

The nastiness of that Nation, and sluttish course of life hath much promoted the opinion, occasioned by their servile condition at first, and inferiour ways of parsimony ever since; as is delivered by Mr. *Sandys:*[9] They are generally fat, saith he, and rank of the savours which attend upon sluttish corpulency. The *Epithetes* assigned them by ancient times, have also advanced the same; for *Ammianus Marcellinus*[10] describeth them in such language; and *Martial°* more ancient, in such a relative expression sets forth unsavoury *Bassa*.

---

[1]High officers in Muslim government.

[2]Pashas, high officers in the Ottoman Empire.

[3]British scholar (1602–1682) who studied law and then traveled extensively through not only France and Italy but also Poland, Bulgaria, Turkey, and Egypt, studying artifacts and customs wherever he went. He was knighted by Charles I.

[4]Basis.

[5]Deduction.

[6]Intolerable.

[7]Despite our refutations.

[8]Offered.

[9]The opening lines of this paragraph present the anti-Semitic views of a Mr. Sandys. Browne then demolishes them.

[10]Roman historian (c. 330–c. 400) who continued Tacitus's° history of the Roman Empire from the years A.D. 96 to 378, though only the years 353 to 378 are extant.

Quod jejunia Sabbatariorum.
Mallem, quam quod oles, olere Bassa. [1]

From whence notwithstanding we cannot infer an inward imperfection in the temper of that Nation; it being but an effect in the breath from outward observation, in their strict and tedious fasting; and was a common effect in the breaths of other Nations, became a Proverb among the *Greeks,* and the reason thereof begot a Problem in *Aristotle*° *(Νηστείας ὄζειν. *Jejunia olere*[2]).

Lastly, If all were true, and were this savour conceded, yet are the reasons alleadged for it no way satisfactory. *Hucherius,* and after him *Alsarius Crucius* *(de Sterilitate Cruc. Med. Epist.),* imputes this effect unto their abstinence from salt or salt meats; which how to make good in the present diet of the Jews, we know not; nor shall we conceive. It was observed of old, if we consider they seasoned every Sacrifice, and all oblations[3] whatsoever; whereof we cannot deny a great part was eaten by the Priests. And if the offering were of flesh, it was salted no less then thrice, that is, once in the common chamber of salt, at the foot-step of the Altar, and upon the top thereof as is at large delivered by *Maimonides.*° Nor if they refrained all salt, is the illation[4] very urgent;[5] for many there are, not noted for ill odours, which eat no salt at all; as all carnivorous Animals, most Children, many whole Nations, and probably our Fathers after the Creation; there being indeed in every thing we eat, a natural and concealed salt, which is separated by digestions, as doth appear in our tears, sweat and urines, although we refrain all salt, or what doth seem to contain it.

Another cause is urged by *Campegius,*[6] and much received by Christians; that this ill savour is a curse derived upon them by Christ, and stands, as a badge or brand of a generation that crucified their *Salvator.* But this is a conceit without all warrant; and an easie way to take off dispute in what point of obscurity soever. A method of many Writers, which much depreciates the esteem and value of miracles; that is, therewith to salve, not only real verities, but also non-existencies. Thus have elder times not only ascribed the immunity of *Ireland* from any venemous beast, unto the staff or rod of *Patrick;*° but the long tails of *Kent,* unto the malediction of *Austin.*[7]

Thus therefore, although we concede that many opinions are true which hold some conformity unto this, yet in assenting hereto, many difficulties must arise:

---

[1]This the fast of the Sabboth / I would rather smell like this than like you, Bassa.
[2]Greek and Latin, both meaning "to smell of fasting."
[3]Offerings.
[4]Deduction.
[5]Compelling.
[6]Probably Lorenzo Campeggio (1472–1539), Italian jurist and then cardinal of the Roman Catholic church, who was sent on delicate political missions, such as to England for the divorce of Catherine of Aragon and to Germany to pacify the Protestants.
[7]St. Augustine of Canterbury (d. 604). The first archbishop of Canterbury, Austin or Augustine was sent by Pope Gregory as a missionary to Kent. The "long tails of *Kent*" do not appear in Bede's history (see page 53, footnote 2).

it being a dangerous point to annex a constant property unto any Nation, and much more this unto the *Jew;* since this quality is not verifiable by observation; since the grounds are feeble that should establish it, and lastly, since if all were true, yet are the reasons alledged for it, of no sufficiency to maintain it. ✒

Of the Blackness of Negroes, continued

PSEUDODOXIA EPIDEMICA, BOOK 6, CHAP. XI

A second opinion there is, that this complexion was first a curse of God derived unto them from Cham,[1] upon whom it was inflicted for discovering the naked-nesse of Noah.[2] Which notwithstanding is sooner affirmed then proved, and carrieth with it sundry improbabilities. For first, if we derive the curse on Cham, or in generall upon his posterity, we shall denigrate a greater part of the earth then ever was so conceived; and not only paint the Aethiopians, and reputed sonnes of Cush, but the people also of Aegypt, Arabia, Assyria, and Chaldea; for by his race were these Countries also peopled. And if concordantly unto Berosus,[3] the fragment of Cato°[4] *de Originibus,* some things of Halicarnasseus, Macrobius,[5] and out of them of Leandro and Annius, we shall conceive of the travels of Camese or Cham; we may introduce a generation of Negroes as high as Italy; which part was never culpable of deformity,[6] but hath produced the magnified examples of beauty.

Secondly, The curse mentioned in Scripture was not denounced upon Cham, but Canaan his youngest son; and the reasons thereof are divers. The first, from the Jewish Tradition, whereby it is conceived, that Canaan made the discovery of the nakednesse of Noah, and notified it unto Cham. Secondly, to have cursed Cham had been to curse all his posterity, whereof but one was guilty of the fact. And lastly, he spared Cham, because he had blessed him before. Now if we confine this curse unto Canaan, and think the same fulfilled in his posterity; then doe we induce this complexion on the Sidonians,[7] then was the promised land a tract of Negroes; For from Canaan were descended the Canaanites, Jebusites, Amorites, Gergezites, and Hivites, which were possessed of that Land.

Thirdly, Although we should place the originall of this curse upon one of the sonnes of Cham, yet were it not known from which of them to derive it. For the

---

[1]One of Noah's three sons: (C)ham, Shem, and Japhet.
[2]See Genesis 9:20–27.
[3]Babylonian historian (third century B.C.) who wrote in Greek about Mesopotamian myths of creation. His work is quoted by Josephus.°
[4]The Elder.
[5]Latin writer and philosopher (fifth century A.D.) whose *Saturnalia,* about Virgil,° contains many quotations from other writers.
[6]Later in the essay Browne shows that color is not, in fact, a deformity.
[7]Who occupied what is now Lebanon.

particularity of their descents is imperfectly set down by accountants, nor is it distinctly determinable from whom thereof the Aethiopians are proceeded. For whereas these of Africa are generally esteemed to be the Issue of Chus, the elder sonne of Cham, it is not so easily made out. For the land of Chus, which the Septuagint[1] translates Aethiopia, makes no part of Africa; nor is it the habitation of Blackmores, but the Country of Arabia, especially the Happy, and Stony;[2] possessions and Colonies of all the sonnes of Chus, excepting Nimrod, and Havilah; possessed and planted wholly by the children of Chus, that is, by Sabtah and Raamah, Sabtacha, and the sonnes of Raamah, Dedan and Sheba, according unto whose names the Nations of those parts have received their denominations, as may be collected from Pliny°[3] and Ptolomy;[4] and as we are informed by credible Authors, they hold a fair Analogy in their names, even unto our daies. So the wife of Moses translated in Scripture an Aethiopian, and so confirmed by the fabulous relation of Josephus,° was none of the daughters of Africa, nor any Negroe of Aethiopia, but the daughter of Jethro, Prince and Priest of Madian; which was a part of Arabia the Stony, bordering upon the Red Sea. So the Queen of Sheba came not unto Solomon° out of Aethiopia, but from Arabia, and that part thereof which bore the name of the first planter, the sonne of Chus. So whether the Eunuch which Philip the Deacon baptised,[5] were servant unto Candace Queen of the African Aethiopia (although Damianus à Goes, Codignus, and the Aethiopick relations averre[6]) is yet by many, and with strong suspitions doubted. So that Army of a million, which Zerah King of Aethiopia is said to bring against Asa,[7] was drawn out of Arabia, and the plantations of Chus; not out of Aethiopia, and the remote habitations of the Moors. For it is said that Asa pursuing his victory, took from him the City Gerar; now Gerar was no city in or near Aethiopia, but a place between Cadesh and Zur, where Abraham formerly sojourned. Since therefore these African Aethiopians are not convinced by the common acception to be the sons of Chus, whether they be not the posterity of Phut, or Mizraim, or both, it is not assuredly determined. For Mizraim, he possessed Aegypt, and the East parts of Africa. From Lubym his son came the Lybians, and perhaps from them the Aethiopians: Phut possessed Mauritania, and the Western parts of Africa, and from these perhaps descended the Moors of the West, of Mandinga, Meleguette and Guinie. But from Canaan, upon whom the curse was pronounced, none of these had their

---

[1]From the Latin for "the Seventy," referring to the legendary seventy or seventy-two Jewish scholars who, in the third century B.C., translated the Old Testament from Hebrew into Greek.
[2]The ancients divided Arabia into three parts: Felix, Petraea, and Deserta (the Happy, the Stony, and the Desert).
[3]The Elder.
[4]Second-century geographer?
[5]See Acts 8:25–40.
[6]Affirm.
[7]King of Judah.

originall, for he was restrained unto Canaan and Syria; although in after Ages many Colonies dispersed, and some thereof upon the coasts of Africa, and prepossessions of his elder brothers.[1]

Fourthly, To take away all doubt or any probable divarication,[2] the curse is plainly specified in the Text, nor need we dispute it, like the mark of Cain; *Servus servorum erit fratribus suis.* Cursed be Canaan, a servant of servants shall he be unto his brethren;[3] which was after fulfilled in the conquest of Canaan, subdued by the Israelites, the posterity of Sem. Which Prophecy Abraham well understanding, took an oath of his servant not to take a wife for his son Isaac out of the daughters of the Canaanites; And the like was performed by Isaac in the behalf of his Son Jacob. As for Cham and his other sons, this curse attained them not; for Nimrod the son of Chus set up his kingdom in Babylon, and erected the first great Empire; Mizraim and his posterity grew mighty Monarchs in Egypt; and the Empire of the Aethiopians hath been as large, as either. Nor did the curse descend in generall upon the posterity of Canaan: for the Sidonians, Arkites, Hamathites, Sinites, Arvadites, and Zemarites seem exempted. But why there being eleven sonnes, five only were condemned, and six escaped the malediction, is a secret beyond discovery.

Lastly, Whereas men affirm this colour as a Curse, I cannot make out the propriety of that name, it neither seeming so to them, nor reasonably unto us; for they take so much content therein, that they esteem deformity by other colours,[4] describing the Devil, and terrible objects, White. And if we seriously consult the definitions of beauty, and exactly perpend[5] what wise men determine thereof, we shall not apprehend a curse, or any deformity therein. For first, some place the essence thereof in the proportion of parts; conceiving it to consist in a comely commensurability of the whole unto the parts, and the parts between themselves; which is the determination of the best and learned Writers. Now hereby the Moors are not excluded from beauty; there being in this description no consideration of colours, but an apt connexion and frame of parts and the whole. Others there be, and those most in number, which place it not only in proportion of parts, but also in grace of colour. But to make Colour essentiall unto Beauty, there will arise no slender difficulty; For Aristotle° in two definitions of pulchritude, and Galen° in one, have made no mention of colour. Neither will it agree unto the Beauty of Animals; wherein notwithstanding there is an approved pulchritude. Thus horses are handsome under any colour, and the symmetry of parts obscures the consideration of complexions. Thus in concolour[6] animals and such as are confined unto one colour, we measure not their Beauty thereby; for if a Crow or

---

[1]See Genesis 10 for these geneologies.

[2]Disagreement.

[3]See Genesis 9:25.

[4]That they see other colors as deformities.

[5]Weigh.

[6]One color.

Black-bird grow white, we generally account it more pretty; And even in monstrosity descend not to opinion of deformity. By this way likewise the Moores escape the curse of deformity; there concurring no stationary colour, and sometimes not any unto Beauty.

The Platonick contemplators reject both these descriptions founded upon parts and colours, or either; as M. Leo the Jew[1] hath excellently discoursed in his *Genealogy of Love:*[2] defining Beauty a formall grace, which delights and moves them to love which comprehend it. This grace say they, discoverable outwardly, is the resplendor and Raye of some interiour and invisible Beauty, and proceedeth from the forms of compositions amiable. Whose faculties if they can aptly contrive their matter, they beget in the subject an agreeable and pleasing beauty; if over-ruled thereby, they evidence not their perfections, but runne into deformity. For seeing that out of the same materials Thersites[3] and Paris,[4] Beauty and monstrosity, may be contrived; the forms and operative faculties introduce and determine their perfections. Which in naturall bodies receive exactnesse in every kinde, according to the first Idea of the Creator, and in contrived bodies the phancy of the Artificer. And by this consideration of Beauty, the Moores also are not excluded, but hold a common share therein with all mankinde.

Lastly, In whatsoever its Theory consisteth, or if in the generall, we allow the common conceit of symmetry and of colour, yet to descend unto singularities, or determine in what symmetry or colour it consisted, were a slippery designation. For Beauty is determined by opinion, and seems to have no essence that holds one notion with all; that seeming beauteous unto one, which hath no favour with another; and that unto every one, according as custome hath made it naturall, or sympathy and conformity of mindes shall make it seem agreeable. Thus flat noses seem comely unto the Moore, an Aquiline or hawked one unto the Persian, a large and prominent nose unto the Romane; but none of all these are acceptable in our opinion. Thus some think it most ornamentall to wear their Bracelets on their Wrests, others say it is better to have them about their Ancles; some think it most comely to wear their Rings and jewels in the Ear, others will have them about their Privities; a third will not think they are compleat except they hang them in their lips, cheeks or noses. Thus Homer° to set off Minerva° calleth her γλαυκῶπις, that is, gray or light-blew eyed: now this unto us seems farre lesse amiable then the black. Thus we that are of contrary complexions accuse the blacknesse of the Mores as ugly: But the Spouse in the *Canticles*[5] excuseth this conceit, in that

---

[1] Judah Abramel (c. 1465–1535).

[2] 1535.

[3] The ugliest Greek soldier in the *Iliad,* who was killed by Achilles for mocking him.

[4] In the *Iliad,* son of Priam and Hecuba, brother of Hector. For choosing Aphrodite as most beautiful of the three goddesses (the others were Hera and Athena) quarreling over the apple of discord, Paris was awarded Helen, whom he abducted from the Greek Menelaus, thereby starting the Trojan War.

[5] Song of Solomon.°

description of hers, *I am black, but comely.* And howsoever Cerberus,[1] and the furies of hell be described by the Poets under this complexion, yet in the beauty of our Saviour blacknesse is commended, when it is said, his locks are bushie and black as a Raven. So that to inferre this as a curse, or to reason it as a deformity, is no way reasonable; the two foundations of beauty, Symmetry and Complexion, receiving such various apprehensions; that no deviation will be expounded so high as a curse or undeniable deformity, without a manifest and confessed degree of monstrosity.

Lastly, It is a very injurious method unto Philosophy, and a perpetuall promotion of ignorance in points of obscurity not open unto easie considerations, to fall upon a present refuge unto Miracles; or recurre unto immediate contrivance from the insearchable hands of God. Thus in the conceit of the evil odor of the Jews, Christians without a farther research into the verity of the thing, or enquiry into the cause, draw up a judgement upon them from the passion of their Saviour. Thus in the wondrous effects of the clime of Ireland, and the freedom from all venemous creatures, the credulity of common conceit imputes this immunity unto the benediction of St. Patrick,° as Beda[2] and Gyraldus[3] have left recorded. Thus the Asse having a peculiar mark of a crosse made by a black list[4] down his back, and another athwart, or at right angles down his shoulders; common opinion ascribes this figure unto a peculiar signation;[5] since that beast had the honour to bear our Saviour on his back. Certainly this is a course more desperate then Antipathies, Sympathies or occult qualities;[6] wherein by a finall and satisfactive discernment of faith, we lay the last and particular effects upon the first and generall cause of all things; whereas in the other,[7] we doe but palliate[8] our determinations untill our advanced endeavours doe totally reject or partially salve their evasions. ✍

---

[1]In Greek mythology, the three-headed dog guarding the entrance to Hades.

[2]The Venerable Bede (673–735), British historian and Benedictine monk in the monasteries of Wearmouth and Jarrow who was the most learned man of his time. He wrote *Ecclesiastical History of the English Nation* in Latin, covering English history from 597 to 731, as well as many theological and scientific works.

[3]Giraldus Cambrensis (1146–1223), British historian connected to the English court who wrote histories of Ireland and Wales.

[4]Strip.

[5]Signing of the cross.

[6]Supposed magical affinities or repulsions.

[7]The occult explanations.

[8]Soften.

• • •

Joseph Addison

(1672–1719)

Joseph Addison was born in Wiltshire in 1672, the first of four children of a clergyman, Lancelot Addison, later the dean of Lichfield, and his first wife, Jane. When Addison was fourteen, he met Richard Steele at the Charterhouse school. There they began a lifelong friendship, both attending Oxford and much later collaborating in the publication of *The Tatler* and *The Spectator*. Unlike his lighthearted friend, Addison was shy around most people, able to expose his wit only to his closest friends. He was also a more serious scholar than Steele.

Addison completed his studies at Oxford, made a reputation for himself as a Latin poet, and was accepted as a don of Magdalen College in 1698. A year later, with money given him by Whigs, Addison left for a tour of the Continent to prepare for a career as a diplomat. When he returned in 1704, he published a poem in English on Marlborough's victory at Blenheim, reaffirmed his association with the Whigs, and renewed his friendship with Steele, helping with the revision of Steele's comedy *The Tender Husband*. In 1706 he was appointed under secretary of state and in 1708 became secretary to the lord lieutenant of Ireland, a post he held until the fall of the Whigs in 1710.

In 1709, his friend Steele began a periodical called *The Tatler*, published three times a week, to which Addison contributed a number of essays. Thus, when Addison lost his job, his new career as essayist was already well under way. In March of 1711 he established *The Spectator*, a daily (except Sundays) publication to replace *The Tatler*, which had come to an end that January. Steele had gotten Swift's permission to use his Sir Isaac Bickerstaff as the persona for the author of *The Tatler*, and Addison had invented a group of characters, including Sir Roger de Coverly, country gent, Andrew Freeport, merchant, and Will Honeycomb, man of fashion, as vehicles for his commentary on the morals and manners of his reading public. The readers of both publications consisted of members of the middle classes who required instruction in a middle course between the restrictions of the Puritans and the scandals of the elite. Such people gathered in the numerous chocolate and coffee houses to exchange gossip and display the wit and manners taught by these two essayists. Despite contributions from others in nearly fifty of the essays, both men felt the strain of putting out a daily paper, and on December 6, 1712, Steele wrote the last essay for *The Spectator*.

In 1713 Addison published his formal tragedy *Cato* and bought an estate in Warwickshire. After a short revival of *The Spectator* in 1714, Addison resumed his career in government as secretary to the regency and the Irish government. In 1716, at the age of forty-four, he married the dowager Countess of Warwick, whom he had pursued for some time after becoming a tutor to her son. According to friends, the marriage was not a comfortable one, for the Countess never forgot her social position, nor that of her new husband. A year later Addison reached his highest appointment as secretary of state, but like the long-sought-after marriage, his new position in government failed to gain him happiness.

In his biography of Addison, Samuel Johnson explains that Addison's inadequacies as a speaker forced him to claim ill health as the cause of an early retirement. In 1718 a political dispute ended his long friendship with Steele. In January of 1719, at forty-seven, he became the father of his only child, Charlotte, and six months later he died. Near the end, he called for his wife's son, the young man he had tutored, saying, "I have sent for you, that you may see how a Christian can die." Jonathan Swift described Addison's sister, Dorothy, as "sort of a wit, very like him." He added, " I am not fond of her." From Swift's comment one can conclude that Addison was not beloved by all.

Addison is generally considered a better stylist than Steele, but both are credited with the development of the periodical essay and with the shaping of the tastes and manners of the age. Writing on all topics except politics, Addison showed himself to be less introspective than Montaigne, less formal than Bacon, less scholarly than Browne, but an engaging individual with an alert mind, interested in philosophy, science, men and women, fashion and style, both in literature and in everyday life.

Like Montaigne, Addison is fond of anecdotes, ancient and imagined, "fables," as he calls them in "On Giving Advice." Through his various personae, he mingles fact and fiction to present his version of truth as surely as do such modern essayists as Edward Hoagland and Cynthia Ozick. Indeed, in his analysis of the role of the reader of such fables, Addison seems akin to the modern exponent of reader-response theory:

> In Writings of this Kind, the Reader comes in for half of the Performance; Every thing appears to him like a Discovery of his own; he is busied all the while in applying Characters and Circumstances, and is in this respect both a Reader and a Composer.

In his understanding of science, however, Addison is a confident man of his time: "It is much more probable that an hundred Million of Dice should be casually thrown an hundred Million of Times in the same Number, than that the Body of any single Animal should be produced by the fortuitous Concourse of Matter." Nonetheless, his subjects—the great variety of species, how humans came to be, the role of chance in nature—continue to provoke speculation and misunderstanding, as the essays of Stephen Jay Gould so well attest.

Whereas Addison's science may be outmoded, his prose is not. Both of the quotations above illustrate the truth of Samuel Johnson's judgment: "Whoever wishes to attain an English style, familiar but not coarse, and elegant but not ostentatious, must give his days and nights to the volumes of Addison." ✍

Reflections in Westminster Abbey

THE SPECTATOR, NO. 26

Friday, March 30, 1711

Pallidia mors aequo pulsat pede pauperum tabernas
Regumque turres, O beate Sexti.
Vitae summa brevis spem nos vetat inchoare longam:
Jam te premet nox, fabulaeque manes,
Et domus exilis Plutonia——[1]

HORACE°

When I am in a serious Humour, I very often walk by my self in Westminster Abbey; where the Gloominess of the Place, and the Use to which it is applied, with the Solemnity of the Building, and the Condition of the People who lye in it, are apt to fill the Mind with a kind of Melancholy, or rather Thoughtfulness, that is not disagreeable. I Yesterday pass'd a whole Afternoon in the Church-yard, the Cloysters, and the Church, amusing my self with the Tomb-stones and Inscriptions that I met with in those several Regions of the Dead. Most of them recorded nothing else of the buried Person, but that he was born upon one Day and died upon another: The whole History of his Life, being comprehended in those two Circumstances that are common to all Mankind. I could not but look upon these Registers of Existence, whether of Brass or Marble, as a kind of Satyr[2] upon the departed Persons; who had left no other Memorial of them, but that they were born and that they died. They put me in mind of several Persons mentioned in the Battles of Heroic Poems, who have sounding[3] Names given them, for no other

---

[1]Pale death beats on the apartments of the poor / And castles of princes alike, O happy Sestius. / Life's short span forces us to begin a long hope: / Soon night will be upon you, as will the storied shades of the underworld / And the ghostly house of Pluto.
[2]Satire.
[3]Sonorous.

Reason but that they may be killed, and are celebrated for nothing but being knocked on the Head.

Γλαῦκόν τε Μέδοντά τε Θερσίλοχόν τε.[1]

HOMER°

Glaucumque, Medontaque, Thersilochumque.[1]

VIRGIL°

The Life of these Men is finely described in Holy Writ, by the Path of an arrow which is immediately closed up and lost.

Upon my going into the Church, I entertain'd my self with the digging of a Grave; and saw in every Shovelfull of it that was thrown up, the Fragment of a Bone or Skull intermixt with a kind of fresh mouldering Earth that some time or other had a Place in the Composition of an humane Body. Upon this, I began to consider with my self what innumerable Multitudes of People lay confus'd together under the Pavement of that ancient Cathedral; how Men and Women, Friends and Enemies, Priests and Soldiers, Monks and Prebendaries,[2] were crumbled amongst one another, and blended together in the same common Mass; how Beauty, Strength, and Youth, with Old-age, Weakness, and Deformity, lay undistinguish'd in the same promiscuous Heap of Matter.

After having thus surveyed this great Magazine[3] of Mortality, as it were in the Lump; I examined it more particularly by the Accounts which I found on several of the Monuments which are raised in every Quarter of that ancient Fabrick. Some of them were covered with such extravagant Epitaphs, that, if it were possible for the dead Person to be acquainted with them, he would blush at the Praises which his Friends have bestow'd upon him. There are others so excessively modest, that they deliver the Character of the Person departed in Greek or Hebrew, and by that Means are not understood once in a Twelve-month. In the poetical Quarter, I found there were Poets who had no Monuments, and Monuments which had no Poets. I observed indeed that the present War[4] had filled the Church with many of these uninhabited Monuments, which had been erected to the Memory of Persons whose Bodies were perhaps buried in the Plains of Blenheim[5] or in the Bosom of the Ocean.

I could not but be very much delighted with several modern Epitaphs, which are written with great Elegance of Expression and Justness of Thought, and therefore do Honour to the Living as well as to the Dead. As a Foreigner is very apt to conceive an Idea of the Ignorance or Politeness of a Nation from the Turn of their publick Monuments and Inscriptions, they should be submitted to the

---

[1]Characters in the *Iliad:* "Glaukos, Medon, and Thersilochus," named in Greek and in Latin.
[2]Clergymen holding stipends from the cathedral.
[3]Storehouse.
[4]War of the Spanish Succession, 1701–1714.
[5]Village in Bavaria where John Churchill, First Duke of Marlborough, joined the Austrians in 1704 to put the Franco-Bavarian forces on the defensive.

Perusal of Men of Learning and Genius before they are put in Execution. Sir Cloudesly Shovel's Monument has very often given me great Offence: Instead of the brave rough English Admiral, which was the distinguishing Character of that plain gallant Man, he is represented on his Tomb by the Figure of a Beau, dress'd in a long Perriwig, and reposing himself upon Velvet Cushions under a Canopy, of State. The Inscription is answerable to the Monument; for instead of celebrating the many remark'able Actions he had performed in the Service of his Country, it acquaints us only with the Manner of his Death, in which it was impossible for him to reap any Honour.[1] The Dutch, whom we are apt to despise for want of Genius, shew an infinitely greater Taste of Antiquity and Politeness in their Buildings and Work's of this Nature, than what we meet with in those of our own Country. The Monuments of their Admirals, which have been erected at the publick Expence, represent them like themselves; and are adorn'd with rostral Crowns[2] and naval Ornaments, with beautiful Festoons of Sea-weed, Shells, and Coral.

But to return to our Subject. I have left the Repository of our English Kings for the Contemplation of another Day, when I shall find my Mind disposed for so serious an Amusement. I know that Entertainments of this Nature, are apt to raise dark and dismal Thoughts in timorous Minds and gloomy Imaginations; but for my own Part, though I am always serious, I do not know what it is to be melancholy; and can therefore take a View of Nature in her deep and solemn Scenes, with the same Pleasure as in her most gay and delightful ones. By this Means I can improve my self with those Objects, which others consider with Terrour. When I look upon the Tombs of the Great, every Emotion of Envy dies in me; when I read the Epitaphs of the Beautiful, every inordinate Desire goes out; when I meet with the Grief of Parents upon a Tomb-stone, my Heart melts with Compassion; when I see the Tomb of the Parents themselves, I consider the Vanity of grieving for those whom we must quick'ly follow. When I see Kings lying by those who deposed them, when I consider rival Wits plac'd Side by Side, or the holy Men that divided the World with their Contests and Disputes, I reflect with sorrow and Astonishment on the little Competitions, Factions, and Debates of Mankind. When I read the several Dates of the Tombs, of some that dy'd Yesterday, and some six hundred Years ago, I consider that great Day when we shall all of us be Contemporaries, and make our Appearance together. ✎

---

[1]Shovel was shipwrecked near the coast of England after returning from a successful battle. His still living body washed ashore and was found by a woman who was so taken with the emerald ring on his finger that she killed him and removed it. Years later, following a deathbed confession, the ring was returned to the family of the admiral.
[2]Golden crowns decorated with miniature images of the prows of ships, awarded to those who first got aboard enemy vessels.

Simonides's Satire on Women

THE SPECTATOR, NO. 209

Tuesday, October 30, 1711

Γυναικὸς οὐδὲ χρῆμ' ἀνὴρ ληίζεται
'Εσθλῆς ἄμεινον, οὐδὲ ῥίγιον κυκῆς.[1]

SIMONIDES

There are no Authors I am more pleased with than those who shew Human Nature in a variety of Views, and describe the several Ages of the World in their different Manners. A Reader cannot be more rationally entertained, than by comparing the Virtues and Vices of his own Times, with those which prevailed in the Times of his Fore-fathers; and drawing a Parallel in his Mind between his own private Character, and that of other Persons, whether of his own Age, or of the Ages that went before him. The Contemplation of Mankind under these changeable Colours is apt to shame us out of any particular Vice, or animate us to any particular Virtue, to make us pleased or displeased with our selves in the most proper Points, to clear our Minds of Prejudice and Prepossession, and to rectifie that Narrowness of Temper which inclines us to think amiss of those who differ from our selves.

If we look into the Manners of the most remote Ages of the World, we discover Human Nature in her Simplicity; and the more we come downward towards our own Times, may observe her hiding herself in Artifices and Refinements, Polished insensibly out of her Original Plainness, and at length entirely lost under Form and Ceremony, and (what we call) Good-breeding. Read the Accounts of Men and Women as they are given us by the most Ancient Writers, both Sacred and Prophane, and you would think, you were reading the History of another Species.

Among the Writers of Antiquity, there are none who instruct us more openly in the Manners of their respective Times in which they lived, than those who have employed themselves in Satyr,[2] under what Dress soever it may appear; as there are no other Authors, whose Province it is to enter so directly into the ways of Men, and set their Miscarriages in so strong a Light. Simonides,[3] a Poet famous in his Generation, is I think, Author of the oldest Satyr that is now extant; and, as some say, of the first that was ever written. This Poet flourished about four hundred Years after the Siege of Troy, and shews by his way of Writing, the Simplicity, or rather Coarseness of the Age in which he lived. I have taken notice, in my Hundred and sixty first Speculation, that the Rule of observing what the French call the *bienseance*,[4] in an Allusion, has been found out of latter Years; and

---

[1]A man does not acquire anything better than a good woman, or worse than a bad one.
[2]Satire.
[3]Semonides of Amorgos (c. 650 B.C.).
[4]Appropriate grace.

that the Ancients, provided there was a Likeness in their Similitudes,[1] did not much trouble themselves about the Decency of the Comparison. The Satyr or Iambicks of Simonides, with which I shall entertain my Readers in the present Paper, are a remarkable Instance of what I formerly advanced. The Subject of this Satyr is Woman. He describes the Sex in their several Characters, which he derives to them from a fanciful Supposition raised upon the Doctrine of Pre-existence. He tells us, that the Gods formed the Souls of Women out of those Seeds and Principles which compose several kinds of Animals and Elements, and that their Good or Bad Dispositions arise in them according as such and such Seeds and Principles predominate in their Constitutions. I have translated the Author very faithfully, and if not Word for Word (which our Language would not bear) at least, so as to comprehend every one of his Sentiments, without adding any thing of my own. I have already apologized for this Author's want[2] of Delicacy, and must further premise, that the following Satyr affects only some of the lower part of the Sex, and not those who have been refined by a Polite Education, which was not so common in the Age of this Poet.

"In the Beginning God made the Souls of Womankind out of different Materials and in a separate State from their Bodies.

The Souls of one kind of Women were formed out of those Ingredients which compose a Swine. A Woman of this Make is a Slutt in her House, and a Glutton at her Table. She is uncleanly in her Person, a Slattern in her Dress; and her Family is no better than a Dunghill.

"A Second sort of Female Soul was formed out of the same Materials that enter into the Composition of a Fox. Such an one is what we call a notable discerning Woman, who has an Insight into every thing, whether it be good or bad. In this Species of Females there are some Vertuous and some Vicious.

"A Third kind of Women were made up of Canine Particles. These are what we commonly call Scolds, who imitate the Animals out of which they were taken, that are always busy and barking, that snarl at every one who comes in their way, and live in perpetual Clamour.

"The Fourth kind of Women were made out of the Earth. These are your Sluggards, who pass away their Time in Indolence and Ignorance, hover over the Fire a whole Winter, and apply themselves with Alacrity to no kind of Business but Eating.

"The Fifth Species of Females were made out of the Sea. These are Women of variable uneven Tempers, sometimes all Storm and Tempest, sometimes all Calm and Sunshine. The Stranger who sees one of these in her Smiles and Smoothness would cry her up for a Miracle of good Humour; but on a sudden her Looks and her Words are changed, she is nothing but Fury and Outrage, noise and Hurricane.

"The Sixth Species were made up of the Ingredients which compose an Ass, or a Beast of Burden. These are naturally exceeding Slothful, but upon the Husbands exerting his Authority will live upon hard Fare, and do every thing to

---

[1] Metaphors or similes.
[2] Lack.

please him. They are however far from being averse to Venereal Pleasure, and seldom refuse a male companion.

"The Cat furnished Materials for a seventh Species of Women, who are of a melancholy, froward, unamiable nature, and so repugnant to the Offers of Love, that they fly in the Face of their Husband when he approaches them with Conjugal Endearments. This Species of Women are likewise subject to little Thefts, Cheats, and Pilferings.

"The Mare with a flowing Mane, which was never broke to any Servile Toil and Labour, composed an Eighth Species of Women. These are they who have little regard for their Husbands, who pass away their Time in Dressing, Bathing and Perfuming; who throw their Hair into the nicest Curls, and trick it up with the fairest Flowers and Garlands. A Woman of this Species is a very pretty thing for a Stranger to look upon, but very detrimental to her Owner, unless it be a king or Prince, who takes a Fancy to such a Toy.

"The ninth Species of Females were taken out of the Ape. These are such as are both ugly and ill-natured, who have nothing beautiful in themselves, and endeavour to detract from or ridicule every thing which appears so in others.

"The Tenth and Last Species of Women were made out of the Bee, and happy is the Man who gets such an one for his Wife. She is altogether faultless and unblameable. Her Family flourishes and improves by her good Management. She loves her Husband, and is beloved by him. She brings him a Race of beautiful and vertuous Children. She distinguishes her self among her Sex. She is surrounded with Graces. She never sits among the loose Tribe of Women, nor passes away her Time with them in wanton Discourses. She is full of Vertue and Prudence, and is the best Wife that Jupiter can bestow on Man."

I shall conclude these Iambicks with the Motto of this Paper, which is a Fragment of the same Author. "A Man cannot possess any thing that is better than a good Woman, nor any thing that is worse than a bad one."

As the Poet has shewn a great Penetration in this Diversity of Female Characters, he has avoided the Fault which Juvenal° and Monsieur Boileau° are guilty of, the former in his Sixth, and the other in his last Satyr, where they have endeavoured to expose the Sex in general, without doing justice to the valuable Part of it. Such levelling Satyrs are of no use to the World, and for this reason I have often wondered how the French Author above-mentioned, who was a Man of exquisite judgment, and a Lover of Virtue, could think Human Nature a proper Subject for Satyr in another of his celebrated Pieces, which is called "The Satyr upon Man." What Vice or Frailty can a Discourse correct, which censures the whole Species alike, and endeavours to shew by some Superficial Strokes of Wit, that Brutes are the more excellent Creatures of the two? A Satyr should expose nothing but what is corrigible, and make a due Discrimination between those who are, and those who are not, the proper Objects of it. ✍

Different Classes of Female Orators

THE SPECTATOR, NO. 247

Thursday, December 13, 1711

——Τῶν δ' ἀκάματος ῥέει αὐδὴ
'Εκ οτομάτων ἡδεῖα——[1]

HESIOD°

We are told by some Ancient Authors, that Socrates° was instructed in Eloquence by a Woman, whose Name, if I am not mistaken, was Aspasia.[2] I have indeed very often looked upon that Art as the most proper for the Female Sex and I think the Universities would do well to consider whether they should not fill their Rhetorick Chairs with She Professors.

It has been said in the Praise of some Men, that they could Talk whole Hours together upon any thing; but it must be owned to the Honour of the other Sex, that there are many among them who can Talk whole Hours together upon nothing. I have known a Woman branch out into a long extempore Dissertation upon the edging of a Petticoat, and chide her Servant for breaking a China Cup in all the Figures of Rhetorick.

Were Women admitted to plead in Courts of judicature, I am persuaded they would carry the Eloquence of the Bar to greater heights than it has yet arrived at. If any one doubts this, let him but be present at those Debates which frequently arise among the Ladies of the British Fishery.

The first kind therefore of Female Orators which I shall take notice of, are those who are employed in stirring up the Passions, a part of Rhetorick in which Socrates° his Wife[3] had perhaps made a greater Proficiency than his above-mentioned Teacher.

The second kind of Female Orators are those who deal in Invectives, and who are commonly known by the Name of the Censorious. The Imagination and Elocution of this Sett of Rhetoricians is wonderful. With what a fluency of Invention, and Copiousness of Expression, will they enlarge upon every little slip in the Behaviour of another! With how many different Circumstances, and with what variety of Phrases, will they tell over the same Story! I have known an old Lady make an unhappy Marriage the Subject of a Month's Conversation. She blamed the Bride in one place; pitied her in another; laught at her in a third; wonder'd at her in a fourth; was angry with her in a fifth; and in short, wore out a pair of Coach-horses in expressing her Concern for her. At length, after having

---

[1] Sweet talk flows untiringly out of mouths.
[2] Of Miletus (fl. c. 440 B.C.) lover of Pericles. He would have divorced his wife and married Aspasia had it not been for the law forbidding marriage to foreign women. Although Aspasia was a confidante of philosophers and statesmen, some doubt her connection with Socrates.°
[3] Xanthippe, said to be a shrew.

quite exhausted the Subject on this side, she made a Visit to the new married Pair, praised the Wife for the prudent Choice she had made, told her the unreasonable Reflections which some malicious People had cast upon her, and desired that they might be better acquainted. The Censure and Approbation of[1] this kind of Women are therefore only to be consider'd as Helps to Discourse.

A third kind of Female Orators may be comprehended under the Word Gossips. Mrs. Fiddle Faddle is perfectly accomplished in this sort of Eloquence; she launches out into Descriptions of Christenings, runs Divisions[2] upon a Head-dress, knows every Dish of Meat that is served up in her Neighbourhood, and entertains her Company a whole Afternoon together with the Wit of her little Boy, before he is able to speak.

The Coquet may be looked upon as a fourth kind of Female Orator. To give her self the larger Field for Discourse, she Hates and Loves in the same Breath, Talks to her Lap-Dog or Parrot, is uneasie in all kinds of Weather, and in every part of the Room: she has false Quarrels, and feign'd Obligations to all the Men of her Acquaintance; Sighs when she is not Sad, and Laughs when she is not Merry. The Coquet is in particular a great Mistress of that part of Oratory which is called Action, and indeed seems to speak for no other Purpose, but as it gives her an Opportunity of stirring a Limb, or varying a Feature, of glancing her Eyes, or playing with her Fan.

As for News-mongers, Politicians, Mimicks, Story-Tellers, with other Characters of that nature, which give Birth to Loquacity, they are as commonly found among the Men as the Women; for which Reason I shall pass them over in Silence.

I have been often puzzled to assign a Cause, why Women should have this Talent of a ready Utterance in so much greater Perfection than Men. I have sometimes fancied that they have not a Retentive Power, or the Faculty of suppressing their Thoughts, as Men have, but that they are necessitated to speak every thing they think; and if so, it would perhaps furnish a very strong Argument to the Cartesians,[3] for the supporting of their Doctrine, that the Soul always thinks. But as several are of Opinion that the Fair Sex are not altogether Strangers to the arts of Dissembling, and concealing their Thoughts, I have been forced to relinquish that Opinion, and have therefore endeavoured to seek after some better Reason. In order to it, a Friend of mine, who is an excellent Anatomist, has promised me by the first Opportunity to dissect a Woman's Tongue, and to examine whether there may not be in it certain Juices which render it so wonderfully voluble and flippant, or whether the Fibres of it may not be made up of a finer or more pliant Thread, or whether there are not in it some particular Muscles, which dart it up and down by such sudden Glances and Vibrations; or whether, in the last place, there may not be certain undiscovered Channels running from the Head and the Heart, to this little Instrument of Loquacity, and conveying into it a perpetual

---

[1]Used by.
[2]Creates variations.
[3]Followers of Descartes.°

Affluence of animal Spirits. Nor must I omit the Reason which Hudibras[1] has given, why those who can talk on Trifles, speak with the greatest Fluency; namely, that the Tongue is like a Race-Horse, which runs the faster the lesser Weight it carries.

Which of these Reasons so ever may be looked upon as the most probable, I think the Irishman's Thought was very natural, who after some Hours Conversation with a Female Orator told her, that he believed her Tongue was very glad when she was asleep, for that it had not a Moment's Rest all the while she was awake.

That excellent old Ballad of the Wanton Wife of Bath has the following remarkable Lines.

> I think, quoth Thomas, Womens Tongues of
> Aspen Leaves are made.[2]

And Ovid,° though in the description of a very Barbarous Circumstance, tells us, that when the Tongue of a beautiful Female was cut out, and thrown upon the Ground, it could not forbear muttering even in that posture.

> ——*Comprehensam forcipe linguam*
> *Abstulit ense fero. Radix micat ultima linguae.*
> *Ipsa jacet, terraeque tremens immurmurat atrae;*
> *Utque salire solet mutilatae cauda colubrae,*
> *Palpitat.*[3]
>
> OVID°

If a Tongue would be talking without a Mouth, what could it have done when it had all its Organs of Speech, and Accomplices of Sound about it! I might here mention the Story of the Pippin-Woman,[4] had not I some reason to look upon it as Fabulous.

I must confess I am so wonderfully charmed with the Musick of this little Instrument, that I would by no means discourage it. All that I aim at, by this Dissertation, is, to Cure it of several disagreeable Notes, and in particular of those little Jarrings and Dissonances which arise from Anger, Censoriousness, Gossiping and Coquettry. In short, I would have it always tuned by Good-Nature, Truth, Discretion, and Sincerity. ✐

---

[1]Main character in the anti-Puritan mock heroic poem of the same name by Samuel Butler (1612–1680).

[2]The aspen or willow tree is known as the quaking aspen because its flattened leaves quiver in the slightest breeze. The ballad is not in Chaucer.

[3]He cut off the tongue, / Seized with pincers the sharp bronze. The last root of the tongue glimmered. / The tongue itself lies on the black earth trembling and murmurs; / Just as the tail of a mutilated snake is accustomed to jump, / It throbs.

[4]According to Donald F. Bond, editor of the Oxford edition of *The Spectator*, an apple seller's head was said to have been severed when the Thames froze over in 1709.

On Attributing Our Neighbours' Misfortunes to Judgments

THE SPECTATOR, NO. 483

Saturday, September 13, 1712

Nec Deus intersit, nisi dignus vindice nodus
    Inciderit———[1]

    HORACE°

We cannot be guilty of a greater Act of Uncharitableness, than to interpret the Afflictions which befall our Neighbours, as Punishments and Judgments. It aggravates the Evil to him who suffers, when he looks upon himself as the Mark of Divine Vengeance, and abates the Compassion of those towards him, who regard him in so dreadful a Light. This Humour, of turning every Misfortune into a judgment, proceeds from wrong Notions of Religion, which, in its own Nature, produces Good-will towards Men, and puts the mildest Construction upon every Accident that befalls them. In this Case, therefore, it is not Religion that sowers a Man's Temper, but it is his Temper that sowers his Religion: People of gloomy unchearful Imaginations, or of envious malignant Tempers, whatever kind of Life they are engaged in, will discover their natural Tincture of Mind in all their Thoughts, Words, and Actions. As the finest Wines have often the Taste of the Soil, so even the most religious Thoughts often draw something, that is particular, from the Constitution of the Mind in which they arise. When Folly or Superstition strike in with this natural Depravity of Temper, it is not in the Power, even of Religion it self, to preserve the Character of the Person who is possessed with it, from appearing highly absurd and ridiculous.

An old Maiden Gentlewoman, whom I shall conceal under the Name of Nemesis,[2] is the greatest Discoverer of Judgments that I have met with. She can tell you what Sin it was that set such a Man's House on Fire, or blew down his Barns. Talk to her of an unfortunate young Lady that lost her Beauty by the Small Pox, she fetches a deep Sigh, and tells you, that when she had a fine Face she was always looking on it in her Glass. Tell her of a Piece of good Fortune that has befallen one of her Acquaintance, and she wishes it may prosper with her; but her Mother used one of her Neices very barbarously. Her usual Remarks turn upon People who had great Estates, but never enjoyed them, by reason of some Flaw in their own, or their Forefather's Behaviour. She can give you the Reason why such an one died Childless: Why such an one was cut off in the Flower of his Youth: Why such an one was Unhappy in her Marriage: Why one broke his Leg on such a particular Spot of Ground, and why another was killed with a Back-sword, rather

---

[1]And the god does not intervene, unless difficulty worthy of judgment / Occurs.
[2]The Greek goddess of vengeance or just retribution.

than with any other kind of Weapon. She has a Crime for every Misfortune that can befall any of her Acquaintance, and when she hears of a Robbery that has been made, or a Murder that has been committed, enlarges more on the Guilt of the suffering Person, than on that of the Thief, or the Assassin. In short, she is so good a Christian, that whatever happens to her-self is a Tryal, and whatever happens to her Neighbours, is a judgment.

The very Description of this Folly, in ordinary Life, is sufficient to expose it; but when it appears in a Pomp and Dignity of Stile, it is very apt to amuse and terrify the Mind of the Reader. Herodotus[1] and Plutarch° very often apply their judgments as impertinently as the old Woman I have before mentioned, though their manner of relating them makes the Folly it self appear venerable. Indeed, most Historians, as well Christian as Pagan, have fallen into this idle Superstition, and spoken of ill Successes, unforeseen Disasters, and terrible Events, as if they had been let into the Secrets of Providence, and made acquainted with that private Conduct by which the World is governed. One would think several of our own Historians in particular, had many Revelations of this Kind made to them. Our old English Monks seldom let any of their Kings depart in Peace, who had endeavoured to diminish the Power or Wealth of which the Ecclesiasticks were in those times possessed. William the Conqueror's° Race generally found their judgments in the New Forest, where their Father had pulled down Churches and Monasteries. In short, read one of the Chronicles, written by an Author of this Frame of Mind, and you would think you were reading an History of the Kings of Israel or Judah where the Historians were actually inspired, and where, by a particular Scheme of Providence, the Kings were distinguished by judgments or Blessings, according as they promoted Idolatry, or the Worship of the true God.

I cannot but look upon this manner of judging upon Misfortunes, not only to be very uncharitable, in regard to the Person whom they befall, but very presumptuous in regard to him who is supposed to inflict them. It is a strong Argument for a State of Retribution hereafter, that in this World virtuous Persons are very often unfortunate, and vicious Persons prosperous, which is wholly repugnant to the Nature of a Being, who appears infinitely wise and good in all his Works, unless we may suppose that such a promiscuous and undistinguishing Distribution of Good and Evil, which was necessary for carrying on the Designs of Providence in this Life, will be rectified and made amends for in another. We are not, therefore, to expect that Fire should fall from Heaven in the ordinary Course of Providence; nor when we see triumphant Guilt, or depressed Virtue in particular Persons, that Omnipotence will make bare its Holy Arm in the Defence of the one, or Punishment of the other. It is sufficient, that there is a Day set apart for the hearing and requiting of both, according to their respective Merits.

The Folly of ascribing Temporal judgments to any particular Crimes, may appear from several Considerations. I shall only mention two. First, that, generally speaking, there is no Calamity or Affliction, which is supposed to have

---

[1]Greek historian (484–425 B.C.) who wrote the first Western narrative history. His work includes information and stories about the ancient world as well as material on the Persian wars.

happened, as a judgment, to a vicious Man, which does not sometimes happen to Men of approved Religion and Virtue. When Diagoras, the Atheist,[1] was on board one of the Athenian Ships, there arose a very violent Tempest; upon which the Mariners told him, that it was a just judgment upon them for having taken so impious a Man on Board. Diagoras begged them to look upon the rest of the Ships, that were in the same Distress and asked them whether or no Diagoras was on board every Vessel in the Fleet. We are all involved in the same Calamities, and subject to the same Accidents; and when we see any one of the Species under any particular Oppression, we should look upon it as arising from the common Lot of Human Nature, rather than from the Guilt of the Person who suffers.

Another Consideration, that may check our Presumption in putting such a Construction upon a Misfortune is this, That it is impossible for us to know what are Calamities, and what are Blessings. How many Accidents have passed for Misfortunes, which have turned to the Welfare and Prosperity of the Persons in whose Lot they have fallen? How many Disappointments have, in their Consequences, saved a Man from Ruin? If we could look into the Effects of every thing, we might be allowed to pronounce boldly upon Blessings and judgments; but for a Man to give his Opinion of what he sees but in part, and in its Beginnings, is an unjustifiable Piece of Rashness and Folly. The Story of Biton and Cleobis, which was in great Reputation among the Heathens, for we see it quoted by all the Ancient Authors, both Greek and Latin, who have written upon the Immortality of the Soul, may teach us a Caution in this Matter. These two Brothers, being the Sons of a Lady who was Priestess to Juno, drew their Mother's Chariot to the Temple at the time of a great Solemnity, the Persons being absent who by their Office were to have drawn her Chariot on that Occasion. The Mother was so transported with this Instance of filial Duty, that she petitioned her Goddess to bestow upon them the greatest Gift that could be given to Men, upon which they were both cast into a deep Sleep, and the next Morning found dead in the Temple. This was such an Event, as would have been construed into a judgment, had it happened to the two Brothers after an Act of Disobedience, and would doubtless have been represented as such by any Ancient Historian, who had given us an Account of it. ✍

---

[1]Greek philosopher (fl. 416 B.C.) and follower of Democritus.° Diagoras rejected religion and Divine Providence when he saw a perjurer escape punishment.

Defence and Happiness of Married Life

THE SPECTATOR, NO. 500

Friday, October 3, 1712

——*huc natas adjice septem,*
Et totidem juvenes, et mox generosque nurusque.
Quaerite nunc, habeat quam nostra superbia causam.[1]

OVID° *Metamorphosis.*

Sir,[2] You who are so well acquainted with the story of Socrates,° must have read how, upon his making a Discourse concerning Love, he pressed his Point with so much Success that all the Batchelors in his Audience took a Resolution to Marry by the first Opportunity, and that all the married Men immediately took Horse and galloped home to their Wives. I am apt to think your Discourses, in which you have drawn so many agreeable Pictures of Marriage, have had a very good Effect this way in England. We are obliged to you at least, for having taken off that Senseless Ridicule, which for many Years the Witlins of the Town have turned upon their Fathers and Mothers. For my own part, I was born in Wedlock, and I don't care who knows it: For which Reason, among many others, I should look upon my self as a most Insufferable Coxcomb,[3] did I endeavour to maintain that Cuckoldom was inseparable from Marriage, or to make use of Husband and Wife as Terms of Reproach. Nay, Sir, I will go one Step further, and declare to you before the whole World, that I am a married Man, and at the same time I have so much Assurance as not to be ashamed of what I have done.

Among the several Pleasures that accompany this State of Life, and which you have described in your former Papers, there are two you have not taken Notice of, and which are seldom cast into the Account, by those who write on this Subject. You must have observed, in your Speculations on Human Nature, that nothing is more gratifying to the Mind of Man than Power or Dominion, and this I think my self amply possessed of, as I am the Father of a Family. I am perpetually taken up in giving out Orders, in prescribing Duties, in hearing Parties, in Administering justice, and in distributing Rewards and Punishments. To speak in the Language of the Centurion,[4] I say unto one, go and he goeth, and to another come and he cometh, and to my Servant do this and he doeth it. In short, Sir, I look, upon my Family as a Patriarchal Sovereignty, in which I am my self both King and Priest. All great Governments are nothing else but Clusters of these little private Royalties, and therefore I consider the Masters of Families as small Deputy-Governors

---

[1]To this add seven daughters, / And just as many sons, and soon the sons and daughters-in-law. / Ask now whether my pride has its cause.

[2]Addison here impersonates a married man.

[3]Fool.

[4]Commander of one hundred men in the Roman army.

presiding over the several little Parcels and Divisions of their Fellow Subjects. As I take great Pleasure in the Administration of my Government in particular, so I look upon my self not only as a more useful, but as a much greater and happier Man than any Batchelor in England of my own Rank and Condition.

There is another accidental Advantage in Marriage, which has likewise fallen to my Share, I mean the having a multitude of Children. These I cannot but regard as very great Blessings. When I see my little Troop before me, I rejoyce in the Additions which I have made to my Species, to my Country, and to my Religion, in having produced such a number of reasonable Creatures, Citizens, and Christians. I am pleased to see my self thus perpetuated, and as there is no Production comparable to that of an human Creature, I am more proud of having been the Occasion of ten such glorious Productions, than if I had built an hundred Pyramids at my own Expence, or published as many Volumes of the finest Wit and Learning. In what a beautiful Light has the Holy Scripture represented Abdon, one of the judges of Israel, who had forty Sons and thirty Grandsons, that rode on Threescore and Ten Ass-Colts, according to the Magnificence of the Eastern Countries? How must the Heart of the old Man rejoice, when he saw such a beautiful Procession of his own Descendents, such a numerous Cavalcade of his own raising? For my own part, I can sit in my Parlour with great Content, when I take a Review of half a dozen of my little Boys mounted upon Hobby-Horses, and of as many little Girls tutoring their Babies, each of them endeavouring to excell the rest, and to do something that may gain my Favour and Approbation. I cannot question but he who has blessed me with so many Children, will assist my Endeavours in providing for them. There is one thing I am able to give each of them, which is a virtuous Education. I think, it is Sir Francis Bacon's Observation, that in a numerous Family of Children the eldest is often spoiled by the Prospect of an Estate, and the youngest by being the Darling of the Parent; but that some one or other in the middle, who has not perhaps been regarded, has made his Way in the World, and over-topp'd the rest. It is my Business to implant in every one of my Children the same Seeds of Industry, and the same honest Principles. By this Means I think I have a fair Chance, that one or other of them may grow considerable in some or other way of Life, whether it be in the Army, or in the Fleet, in Trade, or any of the three learned Professions;[1] for you must know, Sir, that from long Experience and Observation, I am perswaded of what seems a Paradox to most of those with whom I converse, namely, that a Man who has many Children, and gives them a good Education, is more likely to raise a Family, than he who has but one, notwithstanding he leaves him his whole Estate. For this Reason I cannot forbear amusing my self with finding out a General, an Admiral, or an Alderman of London, a Divine, a Physician, or a Lawyer, among my little People who are now perhaps in Petticoats; and when I see the Motherly Airs of my little Daughters when they are playing with their Puppets,[2] I cannot but flatter my

---

[1]Law, medicine, and religion.
[2]Dolls.

self that their Husbands and Children will be happy, in the possession of such Wives and Mothers.

If you are a Father, you will not perhaps think, this Letter impertinent; but if you are a single Man, you will not know the Meaning of it, and probably throw it into the Fire; whatever you determine of it, you may assure your self that it comes from one who is Your most humble Servant and Well-wisher, Philogamus.[1] ✄

On Giving Advice

THE SPECTATOR, NO. 512

Friday, October 17, 1712

Lectorem delectando pariterque monendo.[2]

HORACE°

There is nothing which we receive with so much Reluctance as Advice. We look upon the Man who gives it us as offering an Affront to our Understanding, and treating us like Children or Idiots. We consider the Instruction as an implicit Censure, and the Zeal which any one shews for our Good on such an Occasion as a Piece of Presumption or Impertinence. The Truth of it is, the Person who pretends to advise, does, in that Particular, exercise a Superiority over us, and can have no other Reason for it, but that, in comparing us with himself, he thinks us defective either in our Conduct or our Understanding. For these Reasons, there is nothing so difficult as the Art of making Advice agreeable; and indeed all the Writers, both Ancient and Modern, have distinguished themselves among one another, according to the Perfection at which they have arrived in this Art. How many Devices have been made use of, to render this bitter Potion palatable? Some convey their Instructions to us in the best chosen Words, others in the most harmonious Numbers,[3] some in Points of Wit, and others in short Proverbs.

But among all the different Ways of giving Counsel, I think the finest, and that which pleases the most universally, is Fable, in whatsoever Shape it appears. If we consider this way of instructing or giving Advice, it excells all others, because it is the least shocking, and the least subject to those Exceptions which I have before mentioned.

This will appear to us, if we reflect, in the first place, that upon the reading of a Fable we are made to believe we advise our selves. We peruse the Author for the sake of the Story, and consider the Precepts rather as our own Conclusions, than his Instructions. The Moral insinuates it self imperceptibly, we are taught by

---

[1]Lover of marriage.
[2]To equally entertain and instruct the reader.
[3]Metrical rhythm.

Surprise, and become wiser and better unawares. In short, by this Method a Man is so far over-reached as to think he is directing himself, whilst he is following the Dictates of another, and consequently is not sensible of that which is the most unpleasing Circumstance in Advice.

In the next Place, if we look into Human Nature, we shall find that the Mind is never so much pleased, as when she exerts her self in any Action that gives her an Idea of her own Perfections and Abilities. This natural Pride and Ambition of the Soul is very much gratified in the reading of a Fable; for in Writings of this Kind, the Reader comes in for half of the Performance; Every thing appears to him like a Discovery of his own; he is busied all the while in applying Characters and Circumstances, and is in this respect both a Reader and a Composer. It is no wonder therefore that on such Occasions, when the Mind is thus pleased with it self, and amused with its own Discoveries, that it is highly delighted with the Writing which is the Occasion of it. For this Reason the Absalon and Achitophel[1] was one of the most popular Poems that ever appeared in English. The Poetry is indeed very fine, but had it been much finer it would not have so much pleased, without a Plan which gave the Reader an Opportunity of exerting his own Talents.

This oblique manner of giving Advice is so inoffensive, that if we look into ancient Histories, we find the Wise Men of old very often chose to give Counsel to their Kings in Fables. To omit many which will occur to every ones Memory, there is a pretty Instance of this Nature in a Turkish Tale, which I do not like the worse for that little Oriental Extravagance which is mixed with it.

We are told that the Sultan Mahmoud, by his perpetual Wars abroad, and his Tyranny at home had filled his Dominions with Ruin and Desolation and half-unpeopled the Persian Empire. The Visier[2] to this great Sultan, (whether an Humourist or an Enthusiast we are not informed) pretended to have learned of a certain Dervise[3] to understand the Language of Birds, so that there was not a Bird that could open his Mouth but the Visier knew what it was he said. As he was one Evening with the Emperor, in their Return from hunting, they saw a couple of Owls upon a Tree that grew near an old Wall out of an heap of Rubbish. I would fain know, says the Sultan, what those two Owls are saying to one another; listen to their Discourse, and give me an account of it. The Visier approached the Tree, pretending to be very attentive to the two Owls. Upon his Return to the Sultan, Sir, says he, I have heard part of their Conversation, but dare not tell you what it is. The Sultan would not be satisfied with such an Answer, but forced him to repeat Word for Word every thing the Owls had said. You must know then, said the Visier, that one of these Owls has a Son, and the other a Daughter, between whom they are now upon a Treaty of Marriage. The Father of the Son said to the Father of the Daughter, in my hearing, ''Brother, I consent to this Marriage, provided you will settle upon your Daughter fifty ruined Villages for her Portion.'' To which the

---

[1]Political satire by John Dryden° in which biblical characters stood for real people.
[2]Chief minister.
[3]Mohammedan friar who has taken vows of poverty and austerity.

Father of the Daughter replied, "Instead of fifty I will give her five hundred, if you please. God grant a long life to Sultan Mahmoud! whilst he reigns over us we shall never want ruined Villages."

The Story says, the Sultan was so touched with the Fable, that he rebuilt the Towns and Villages which had been destroyed, and from that time forward consulted the Good of his People.

To fill up my Paper, I shall add a most ridiculous Piece of natural Magick, which was taught by no less a Philosopher than Democritus,° namely, that if the Blood of certain Birds, which he mentioned, were mixed together, it would produce a Serpent of such a wonderful Virtue that whoever did eat it should be skill'd in the Language of Birds, and understand every thing they said to one another. Whether the Dervise above-mentioned might not have eaten such a Serpent, I shall leave to the Determinations of the Learned. *

Meditation on Animal Life

THE SPECTATOR, NO. 519

Saturday, October 25, 1712

Inde hominum pecudumque genus, vitaeque volantum,
  Et quae marmoreo fert monstra sub aequore pontus.[1]
    VIRGIL°

Though there is a great deal of Pleasure in contemplating the Material World, by which I mean that System of Bodies into which Nature has so curiously wrought the Mass of dead Matter, with the several Relations which those Bodies bear to one another; there is still, methinks, something more wonderful and surprizing in Contemplations on the World of Life, by which I mean all those Animals with which every Part of the Universe is furnished. The Material World is only the Shell of the Universe: The World of Life are its Inhabitants.

If we consider those Parts of the Material World which lie the nearest to us, and are therefore subject to our Observations and Enquiries, it is amazing to consider the Infinity of Animals with which it is stock'ed. Every part of Matter is peopled: Every green Leaf swarms with Inhabitants. There is scarce a single Humour[2] in the Body of a Man, or of any other Animal, in which our Glasses[3] do not discover Myriads of living Creatures. The Surface of Animals is also covered with other Animals, which are in the same manner the Basis of other Animals that

---

[1]"Hence the race of men and animals, and the lives of the flying / And the monsters that ocean brings forth below her smooth surface" (*Aeneid* 6. 728, 729).
[2]Fluid.
[3]Microscopes.

live upon it; nay, we find in the most solid Bodies, as in Marble it self, innumerable Cells and Cavities that are crouded with such imperceptible Inhabitants, as are too little for the naked Eye to discover. On the other Hand, if we look into the more bulky Parts of Nature, we see the Seas, Lakes and Rivers teeming with numberless Kinds of living Creatures: We find every Mountain and Marsh, Wilderness and Wood, plentifully stocked with Birds and Beasts, and every part of Matter affording proper Necessaries and Conveniencies for the Livelihood of Multitudes which inhabit it.

The Author of the Plurality of Worlds[1] draws a very good Argument from this Consideration, for the peopling of every Planet, as indeed it seems very probable from the Analogy of Reason, that if no part of Matter, which we are acquainted with, lies waste and useless, those great Bodies which are at such a Distance from us should not be desert and unpeopled, but rather that they should be furnished with Beings adapted to their respective Situations.

Existence is a Blessing to those Beings only which are endowed with Perception, and is, in a manner, thrown away upon dead Matter, any further than as it is subservient to Beings which are conscious of their Existence. Accordingly we find, from the Bodies which lie under our Observation, that Matter is only made as the Basis and Support of Animals, and that there is no more of the one, than what is necessary for the Existence of the other.

Infinite Goodness is of so communicative a Nature, that it seems to delight in the conferring of Existence upon every degree of Perceptive Being. As this is a Speculation, which I have often pursued with great Pleasure to my self, I shall enlarge farther upon it, by considering that part of the Scale of Beings, which comes within our Knowledge.

There are some living Creatures which are raised but just above dead Matter. To mention only that Species of Shellfish, which are formed in the Fashion of a Cone, that grow to the Surface of several Rocks, and immediately die upon their being severed from the Place where they grow. There are many other Creatures but one Remove from these, which have no other Sense besides that of Feeling and Taste. Others have still an additional one of Hearing; others of Smell, and others of Sight. It is wonderful to observe, by what a gradual Progress the World of Life advances through a prodigious Variety of Species, before a Creature is formed that is compleat in all its Senses, and even among these there is such a different degree of Perfection in the Sense, which one Animal enjoys beyond what appears in another, that though the Sense in different Animals be distinguished by the same common Denomination, it seems almost of a different Nature. If after this we look into the several inward Perfections of Cunning and Sagacity, or what we generally call Instinct, we find them rising after the same manner, imperceptibly one above

---

[1]Bernard le Bovier de Fontenelle (1657–1757), French writer of books on superstition and religion as well as *Entretiens sur la pluralité des mondes* (1686), a description of the Copernican (sun-centered) system.

another, and receiving additional Improvements, according to the Species in which they are implanted. This Progress in Nature is so very gradual, that the most perfect of an inferior Species comes very near to the most imperfect, of that which is immediately above it.

The exuberant and overflowing Goodness of the Supreme Being, whose Mercy extends to all his Works, is plainly seen, as I have before hinted, from his having made so very little Matter, at least what falls within our Knowledge, that does not Swarm with Life: Nor is his Goodness less seen in the Diversity, than in the Multitude of living Creatures. Had he only made one Species of Animals, none of the rest would have enjoyed the Happiness of Existence; he has, therefore, specified in his Creation every degree of Life, every Capacity of Being. The whole Chasm in Nature, from a Plant to a Man, is filled up with diverse Kinds of Creatures, rising one over another, by such a gentle and easie Ascent, that the little Transitions and Deviations from one Species to another, are almost insensible. This intermediate Space is so well husbanded and managed, that there is scarce a degree of Perception which does not appear in some one part of the World of Life. Is the Goodness, or Wisdom of the Divine Being, more manifested in this his Proceeding?

There is a Consequence, besides those I have already mentioned, which seems very naturally deducible from the foregoing Considerations. If the Scale of Being rises by such a regular Progress, so high as Man, we may by a Parity of Reason suppose that it still proceeds gradually through those Beings which are of a Superior Nature to him, since there is an infinitely greater Space and Room for different Degrees of Perfection, between the Supreme Being and Man, than between Man and the most despicable Insect. This Consequence of so great a Variety of Beings which are superior to us, from that Variety which is inferior to us, is made by Mr. Lock,[1] in a Passage which I shall here set down, after having premised, that notwithstanding there is such infinite room between Man and his Maker for the Creative Power to exert it self in, it is impossible that it should ever be filled up, since there will be still an infinite Gap or Distance between the highest created Being, and the Power which produced him.

"That there should be more Species of intelligent Creatures above us, than there are of sensible and material below us, is probable to me from hence; That in all the visible corporeal World, we see no Chasms, or no Gaps. All quite down from us, the descent is by easie steps, and a continued series of things, that in each remove, differ very little one from the other. There are Fishes that have Wings, and are not Strangers to the airy Regions, and there are some Birds, that are Inhabitants of the Water, whose Blood is cold as Fishes, and their Flesh so like in taste, that the scrupulous are allowed them on Fish-days. There are Animals so near of kin both to Birds and Beasts, that they are in the middle between both. Amphibious Animals link the Terrestrial and Aquatique together; Seals live at Land and at Sea, and Porpoises have the warm Blood and Entrails of a Hog, not to mention

---

[1]See Locke.°

what is confidently reported of Mermaids, or Sea-men. There are some Brutes, that seem to have as much knowledge and Reason, as some that are called Men; and the Animal and Vegetable kingdoms are so nearly joyn'd, that if you will take the lowest of one, and the highest of the other, there will scarce be perceived any great difference between them; and so on till we come to the lowest and the most inorganical parts of Matter, we shall find every where that the several Species are linked together, and differ but in almost insensible degrees. And when we consider the infinite Power and Wisdom of the Maker, we have reason to think, that it is suitable to the magnificent Harmony of the Universe, and the great Design and infinite Goodness of the Architect, that the Species of Creatures should also, by gentle degrees, Ascend upward from us toward his infinite Perfection, as we see they gradually descend from us downwards: which if it be probable, we have reason then to be persuaded, that there are far more Species of Creatures above us, than there are beneath; we being in degrees of perfection, much more remote from the infinite Being of God, than we are from the lowest state of Being, and that which approaches nearest to nothing. And yet of all those distinct Species, we have no clear distinct Ideas.''

In this System of Being, there is no Creature so wonderful in its Nature, and which so much deserves our particular Attention, as Man, who fills up the middle Space between the Animal and Intellectual Nature, the visible and invisible World, and is that Link in the Chain of Beings which has been often termed the *nexus utriusque mundi*.[1] So that he, who in one Respect is associated with Angels and Arch-Angels, may look upon a Being of infinite Perfection as his Father, and the highest Order of Spirits as his Brethren, may in another Respect say to Corruption, thou art my Father, and to the Worm, thou art my Mother and my Sister. ✍

Meditation on the Frame of the Human Body

THE SPECTATOR, NO. 543

Saturday, November 22, 1712

——*facies non omnibus una,*
Nec diversa tamen——[2]

    OVID°

Those who were skillful in Anatomy among the Ancients, concluded from the outward and inward Make of an Human Body, that it was the Work of a Being transcendently Wise and Powerful. As the World grew more enlightened in this Art, their Discoveries gave them fresh Opportunities of admiring the Conduct of

---

[1]The connecting of both of two worlds.

[2]Not one appearance for all, / Nor many either.

Providence in the Formation of an Human Body. Galen° was converted by his Dissections, and could not but own a Supreme Being upon a Survey of this his Handywork. There were, indeed, many Parts of which the old Anatomists did not know the certain Use, but as they saw that most of those which they examined were adapted with admirable Art to their several functions, they did not question but those, whose Uses they could not determine, were contrived with the same Wisdom for respective Ends and Purposes. Since the Circulation of the Blood has been found out and many other great Discoveries have been made by our Modern Anatomists, we see new Wonders in the Human Frame, and discern several important Uses for those Parts, which Uses the Ancients knew nothing of. In short, the Body of Man is such a Subject as stands the utmost Test of Examination. Though it appears formed with the nicest[1] Wisdom upon the most superficial Survey of it, it still mends upon the Search, and produces our Surprise and Amazement in Proportion as we pry into it. What I have here said of an Human Body, may be applied to the Body of every Animal which has been the Subject of Anatomical Observations.

The Body of an Animal is an Object adequate to our Senses. It is a particular System of Providence, that lies in a narrow Compass. The Eye is able to command it, and by successive Enquiries can search into all its Parts. Cou'd the Body of the whole Earth, or indeed the whole Universe, be thus submitted to the Examination of our Senses, were it not too big and disproportioned for our Enquiries, too unwieldy for the Management of the Eye and Hand, there is no Question but it would appear to us as curious and well-contrived a Frame as that of an Human Body. We should see the same Concatenation[2] and Subserviency, the same Necessity and Usefullness, the same Beauty and Harmony in all and every of its Parts, as what we discover in the Body of every single Animal.

The more extended our Reason is, and the more able to grapple with immense Objects, the greater still are those Discoveries which it makes of Wisdom and Providence in the Work of the Creation. A Sir Isaac Newton,° who stands up as the Miracle of the present Age, can look, through a whole Planetary System; consider it in its Weight, Number, and Measure; and draw from it as many Demonstrations of infinite Power and Wisdom, as a more confined Understanding is able to deduce from the System of an Human Body.

But to return to our Speculations on Anatomy, I shall here consider the Fabrick and Texture of the Bodies of Animals in one particular View, which, in my Opinion, shews the Hand of a thinking and all-wise Being in their Formation, with the Evidence of a thousand Demonstrations. I think we may lay this down as an incontested Principle, that Chance never acts in a perpetual Uniformity and Consistence with it self. If one should always fling the same Number with ten thousand Dice, or see every Throw just five times less, or five times more in Number, than the Throw which immediately preceded it, who would not imagine

---

[1]Finest.
[2]Linking.

there is some invisible Power which directs the Cast? This is the Proceeding which we find in the Operations of Nature. Every kind of Animal is diversifyed by different Magnitudes, each of which gives rise to a different Species. Let a Man trace the Dog or Lion Kind, and he will observe how many of the Works of Nature are published, if I may use the Expression, in a variety of Editions. If we look into the Reptile World, or into those different Kinds of Animals that fill the Element of Water, we meet with the same Repetitions among several Species, that differ very little from one another, but in Size and Bulk. You find the same Creature, that is drawn at large, copied out in several Proportions, and ending in Miniature. It would be tedious to produce Instances of this regular Conduct in Providence, as it would be superfluous to those who are versed in the Natural History of Animals. The magnificent Harmony of the Universe is such, that we may observe innumerable Divisions[1] running upon the same Ground. I might also extend this Speculation to the dead Parts of Nature, in which we may find Matter disposed into many similar Systems, as well in our Survey of Stars and Planets, as of Stones, Vegetables, and other sublunary Parts of the Creation. In a Word, Providence has shewn the Richness of its Goodness and Wisdom, not only in the Production of many Original Species, but in the multiplicity of Descants[2] which it has made on every Original Species in particular.

But to pursue this Thought still farther: Every living Creature, considered in it self, has many very complicated Parts that are exact Copies of some other Parts which it possesses, and which are complicated in the same manner. One Eye would have been sufficient for the Subsistence and Preservation of an Animal; but, in order to better his Condition, we see another placed with a Mathematical Exactness in the same most advantageous Situation, and in every Particular of the same Size and Texture. Is it possible for Chance to be thus delicate and uniform in her Operations? Should a Million of Dice turn up twice together the same Number, the Wonder would be nothing in Comparison with this. But when we see this Similitude and Resemblance in the Arm, the Hand, the Fingers; when we see one half of the Body entirely correspond with the other in all those minute Strokes, without which a Man might have very well subsisted; nay, when we often see a single Part repeated an hundred times in the same Body, notwithstanding it consists of the most intricate weaving of numberless Fibres, and these Parts differing still in Magnitude, as the Convenience of their particular Situation requires, sure a Man must have a strange Cast of Understanding, who does not discover the Finger of God in so wonderful a Work. These Duplicates in those Parts of the Body, without which a Man might have very well subsisted, tho' not so well as with them, are a plain Demonstration of an all-wise Contriver; as those more numerous Copyings, which are found among the Vessels of the same Body, are evident Demonstrations that they could not be the Work of Chance. This Argument receives additional Strength, if we apply it to every Animal and Insect,

---

[1]Variations.
[2]Themes.

within our Knowledge, as well as to those numberless living Creatures that are Objects too minute for an Human Eye; and if We consider how the several Species in this whole World of Life resemble one another in very many Particulars, so far as is convenient for their respective States of Existence. It is much more probable that an hundred Million of Dice should be casually thrown an hundred Million of Times in the same Number, than that the Body of any single Animal should be produced by the fortuitous Concourse of Matter. And that the like Chance should arise in innumerable Instances, requires a Degree of Credulity that is not under the direction of Common-Sense. We may carry this Consideration yet further, if we reflect on the two Sexes in every living Species, with their Resemblances to each other, and those particular Distinctions that were necessary for the keeping up of this great World of Life.

There are many more Demonstrations of a Supreme Being, and of his transcendent Wisdom, Power and Goodness in the Formation of the Body of a living Creature, for which I refer my Reader to other Writings, particularly to the Sixth Book of the Poem Entitled Creation[1] where the Anatomy of the human Body is described with great Perspicuity and Elegance. I have been particular on the Thought which runs through this Speculation, because I have not seen it enlarged upon by others. ✑

---

[1] Donald F. Bond, editor of the Oxford edition of the *Spectator*, identifies this as a poem by Sir Richard Blackmore published in 1712.

Philip Dormer Stanhope, Fourth Earl of Chesterfield

(1694–1773)

Philip Dormer Stanhope, the first of five sons, was educated at Trinity Hall, Cambridge, traveled to France, and held a seat in the House of Commons as a Whig from Cornwall before his appointment in 1715 as gentleman of the bedchamber to George, Prince of Wales. From this position he developed a close relationship with the king's son and a lifelong friendship with George's mistress, Henrietta Howard. When his father died in 1726, Chesterfield took his seat in the House of Lords, and, when the king died in 1727, the king's son, George II, retained Chesterfield and promoted him to lord of the bedchamber. However, when the king wanted to appoint Chesterfield privy councillor, Sir Robert Walpole, Chesterfield's longtime political enemy, vehemently opposed the appointment, suggesting the English Embassy at The Hague instead.

Chesterfield arrived at The Hague in 1728. In 1730 he became a knight of the garter and in 1731 was instrumental in the signing of the Second Treaty of Vienna. While in Holland, he met Mlle. du Bouchet and fathered an illegitimate son in 1732. Soon after, he returned to Parliament because of a persistent fever. Throughout this affair, he had kept up his correspondence with Henrietta Howard and thus remained in the king's favor. In 1733, at the age of thirty-nine, Chesterfield married the forty-year-old Countess of Walsingham, the daughter of King George I and his mistress, the Duchess of Kendall. Chesterfield took up residence next door to his wife in Grosvenor Square. Although their relationship was cordial, the marriage was merely a financial transaction; Chesterfield soon took on a new mistress, Fanny Shirley.

Meanwhile Lord Chesterfield pursued his political career as lord lieutenant of Ireland in 1744 and secretary of state in 1746, interrupting his work in Ireland to perform diplomatic missions to The Hague in 1745 and to recuperate from illness in 1746. In 1748 he resigned as secretary of state and returned to Parliament, undertaking such efforts as the reformation of the calendar in 1751 and the support of the bill for naturalization of the Jews, which passed in 1752 but was repealed the following year because of, in Chesterfield's words, "the groundless and senseless" intolerance of the populace. He retired from the House of Lords in 1755 and in the same year was elected to the Academy of Inscriptions in Paris. After a stint of gambling at White's Club, Chesterfield occupied himself with designing additional gardens and galleries for the house built for him in 1749.

For many years Chesterfield had been corresponding with his son, Philip Stanhope, encouraging him to develop the talents and skills necessary to take a proper place in society. When his son died in 1768 at the age of thirty-six, Chesterfield was shocked to discover that Philip had secretly married a woman of a lower class and had fathered two sons. Despite this severe blow, Chesterfield sent the two grandsons to school and began another correspondence, this time with his godson, a distant cousin and his presumptive heir, also called Philip Stanhope (b. 1757).

Although nearly deaf and increasingly ill, Chesterfield never lost the qualities for which he is now remembered—his wit and good manners. Near the end of his life he told a friend, "Trelawny and I have been dead these two years, but we do not choose to have it known." And, according to his doctor, his dying words were a request that a visitor be given a chair. After Chesterfield's death in 1773, his son's widow, Eugenia Stanhope, prepared two volumes of the letters to her husband, which were published in 1774 and garnered great popularity. The letters to the godson were published in 1880. On these letters, particularly those to his son, Chesterfield's literary and moral reputation rest.

Written in a balanced, witty, allusive style, the letters conjoin the parallelisms and imperatives of Bacon with the graceful assurance of Addison. Unlike Addison, however, Chesterfield values manners above morals. At his best, he combines political insight with biting wit, didactic zeal, and honest reflection. And, as one might expect of a man who values appearances, his writing is well seasoned with topical references, foreign languages, and famous people—proofs of his ease in the world of fashion. At his worst, however, Chesterfield's hectoring undermines the very graces he wishes so desperately to inculcate in his son: "I repeat it, and repeat it again, and shall never cease repeating it to you: air, manners, graces, style, elegance, and all those ornaments, must now be the only objects of your attention; it is now or never that you must acquire them."

In his revelation of his best and his worst to his son, Chesterfield shows himself to be poignantly human, intent on allowing freedom of religion yet totally convinced of the foolishness of women, attuned to what most displeases men in society yet unable to refrain from alienating his own son by those very means: "Men are much more unwilling to have their weaknesses and their imperfections known than their crimes; and if you hint to a man that you think him silly, ignorant, or even ill-bred, or awkward, he will hate you more and longer, than if you tell him plainly, that you think him a rogue." But however marred Chesterfield is, Samuel Johnson probably exaggerated when he said that the letters "teach the morals of a whore and the manners of a dancing master." ✍

The Art of Pleasing

London, October 16, O.S.° 1747.

Dear Boy:

The art of pleasing is a very necessary one to possess; but a very difficult one to acquire. It can hardly be reduced to rules; and your own good sense and observation will teach you more of it than I can. Do as you would be done by, is the surest method that I know of pleasing. Observe carefully what pleases you in others, and probably the same thing in you will please others. If you are pleased with the complaisance and attention of others to your humours,[1] your tastes, or your weaknesses, depend upon it the same complaisance and attention, on your part to theirs, will equally please them. Take the tone of the company that you are in, and do not pretend to give it; be serious, gay, or even trifling, as you find the present humour of the company; this is an attention due from every individual to the majority. Do not tell stories in company; there is nothing more tedious and disagreeable; if by chance you know a very short story, and exceedingly applicable to the present subject of conversation, tell it in as few words as possible; and even then, throw out that you do not love to tell stories; but that the shortness of it tempted you. Of all things, banish the egotism out of your conversation, and never think of entertaining people with your own personal concerns, or private affairs; though they are interesting to you, they are tedious and impertinent to everybody else; besides that, one cannot keep one's own private affairs too secret. Whatever you think your own excellencies may be, do not affectedly display them in company; nor labor, as many people do, to give that turn to the conversation, which may supply you with an opportunity of exhibiting them. If they are real, they will infallibly be discovered, without your pointing them out yourself, and with much more advantage. Never maintain an argument with heat and clamor, though you think or know yourself to be in the right: but give your opinion modestly and coolly, which is the only way to convince; and, if that does not do, try to change the conversation, by saying, with good humour, "We shall hardly convince one another, nor is it necessary that we should, so let us talk of something else."

---

[1]Moods.

Remember that there is a local propriety to be observed in all companies; and that what is extremely proper in one company, may be, and often is, highly improper in another.

The jokes, the *bon-mots*,[1] the little adventures, which may do very well in one company, will seem flat and tedious, when related in another. The particular characters, the habits, the cant[2] of one company, may give merit to a word, or a gesture, which would have none at all if divested of those accidental circumstances. Here people very commonly err; and fond of something that has entertained them in one company, and in certain circumstances, repeat it with emphasis in another, where it is either insipid, or, it may be, offensive, by being ill-timed or misplaced. Nay, they often do it with this silly preamble; "I will tell you an excellent thing"; or, "I will tell you the best thing in the world." This raises expectations, which, when absolutely disappointed, make the relater of this excellent thing look, very deservedly, like a fool.

If you would particularly gain the affection and friendship of particular people, whether men or women, endeavor to find out their predominant excellency, if they have one, and their prevailing weakness, which everybody has; and do justice to the one, and something more than justice to the other. Men have various objects in which they may excel, or at least would be thought to excel; and, though they love to hear justice done to them, where they know that they excel, yet they are most and best flattered upon those points where they wish to excel, and yet are doubtful whether they do or not. As, for example, Cardinal Richelieu,° who was undoubtedly the ablest statesman of his time, or perhaps of any other, had the idle vanity of being thought the best poet too; he envied the great Corneille° his reputation, and ordered a criticism to be written upon the "Cid." Those, therefore, who flattered skillfully, said little to him of his abilities in state affairs, or at least but *en passant*,[3] and as it might naturally occur. But the incense which they gave him, the smoke of which they knew would turn his head in their favor, was as a *bel esprit*[4] and a poet. Why? Because he was sure of one excellency, and distrustful as to the other.

You will easily discover every man's prevailing vanity, by observing his favorite topic of conversation; for every man talks most of what he has most a mind to be thought to excel in. Touch him but there, and you touch him to the quick. The late Sir Robert Walpole° (who was certainly an able man) was little open to flattery upon that head; for he was in no doubt himself about it; but his prevailing weakness was, to be thought to have a polite and happy turn to gallantry, of which he had undoubtedly less than any man living. It was his

---

[1]Clever remarks.
[2]Mindless platitudes.
[3]In passing.
[4]Sophisticated wit.

favorite and frequent subject of conversation, which proved, to those who had any penetration, that it was his prevailing weakness. And they applied to it with success.

Women have, in general, but one object, which is their beauty; upon which, scarce any flattery is too gross for them to swallow. Nature has hardly formed a woman ugly enough to be insensible to flattery upon her person; if her face is so shocking, that she must in some degree, be conscious of it, her figure and her air, she trusts, make ample amends for it. If her figure is deformed, her face, she thinks, counterbalances it. If they are both bad, she comforts herself that she has graces; a certain manner; a *je ne sais quoi*,[1] still more engaging than beauty. This truth is evident from the studied and elaborate dress of the ugliest women in the world. An undoubted, uncontested, conscious beauty, is of all women, the least sensible of flattery upon that head; she knows that it is her due, and is therefore obliged to nobody for giving it her. She must be flattered upon her understanding; which, though she may possibly not doubt of herself, yet she suspects that men may distrust.

Do not mistake me, and think that I mean to recommend to you abject and criminal flattery: no; flatter nobody's vices or crimes: on the contrary, abhor and discourage them. But there is no living in the world without a complaisant indulgence for people's weaknesses, and innocent, though ridiculous vanities. If a man has a mind to be thought wiser, and a woman handsomer than they really are, their error is a comfortable one to themselves, and an innocent one with regard to other people; and I would rather make them my friends, by indulging them in it, than my enemies, by endeavoring (and that to no purpose) to undeceive them.

There are little attentions, likewise, which are infinitely engaging, and which sensibly affect that degree of pride and self-love, which is inseparable from human nature; as they are unquestionable proofs of the regard and consideration which we have for the person to whom we pay them. As, for example, to observe the little habits, the likings, the antipathies, and the tastes of those whom we would gain; and then take care to provide them with the one, and to secure them from the other; giving them, genteelly, to understand, that you had observed that they liked such a dish, or such a room; for which reason you had prepared it: or, on the contrary, that having observed they had an aversion to such a dish, a dislike to such a person, etc., you had taken care to avoid presenting them. Such attention to such trifles flatters self-love much more than greater things, as it makes people think themselves almost the only objects of your thoughts and care.

These are some of the *arcana*[2] necessary for your initiation in the great society of the world. I wish I had known them better at your age; I have paid the price of three-and-fifty years for them, and shall not grudge it, if you reap the advantage. Adieu! ✐

---

[1] "I don't know what," that is, an inexpressible quality.

[2] Esoteric or secret knowledge.

A Keen Study of the Feminine

London, September 5, O.S.° 1748.

Dear Boy:

I have received yours, with the inclosed German letter to Mr. Gravenkop,[1] which he assures me is extremely well written, considering the little time that you have applied yourself to that language. As you have now got over the most difficult part, pray go on diligently, and make yourself absolutely master of the rest. Whoever does not entirely possess a language, will never appear to advantage, or even equal to himself, either in speaking or writing it. His ideas are fettered, and seem imperfect or confused, if he is not master of all the words and phrases necessary to express them. I therefore desire, that you will not fail writing a German letter once every fortnight to Mr. Gravenkop; which will make the writing of that language familiar to you; and moreover, when you shall have left Germany and be arrived at Turin, I shall require you to write even to me in German; that you may not forget with ease what you have with difficulty learned. I likewise desire, that while you are in Germany, you will take all opportunities of conversing in German, which is the only way of knowing that, or any other language, accurately. You will also desire your German master to teach you the proper titles and superscriptions to be used to people of all ranks; which is a point so material in Germany, that I have known many a letter returned unopened, because one title in twenty has been omitted in the direction.

St. Thomas's day[2] now draws near, when you are to leave Saxony and go to Berlin; and I take it for granted, that if anything is yet wanting to complete your knowledge of the state of that electorate, you will not fail to procure it before you go away. I do not mean, as you will easily believe, the number of churches, parishes, or towns; but I mean the constitution, the revenues, the troops, and the trade of that electorate. A few questions, sensibly asked, of sensible people, will produce you the necessary informations; which I desire you will enter in your little book.

Berlin will be entirely a new scene to you, and I look upon it, in a manner, as your first step into the great world; take care that step be not a false one, and that you do not stumble at the threshold. You will there be in more company than you have yet been; manners and attentions will therefore be more necessary. Pleasing in company is the only way of being pleased in it yourself. Sense and knowledge are the first and necessary foundations for pleasing in company; but they will by no means do alone, and they will never be perfectly welcome if they are not accompanied with manners and attentions. You will best acquire these by frequenting the companies of people of fashion; but then you must resolve to acquire them, in those companies, by proper care and observation; for I have known people, who, though they have frequented good company all their lifetime, have

---

[1]Danish gentleman who worked as a page for the Earl of Marchmont and later for Chesterfield.
[2]December 21.

done it in so inattentive and unobserving a manner, as to be never the better for it, and to remain as disagreeable, as awkward, and as vulgar, as if they had never seen any person of fashion. When you go into good company (by good company is meant the people of the first fashion of the place) observe carefully their turn, their manners, their address; and conform your own to them.

But this is not all neither; go deeper still; observe their characters, and pry, as far as you can, into both their hearts and their heads. Seek for their particular merit, their predominant passion, or their prevailing weakness; and you will then know what to bait your hook with to catch them. Man is a composition of so many, and such various ingredients, that it requires both time and care to analyze him: for though we have all the same ingredients in our general composition, as reason, will, passions, and appetites; yet the different proportions and combinations of them in each individual, produce that infinite variety of characters, which, in some particular or other, distinguishes every individual from another. Reason ought to direct the whole, but seldom does. And he who addresses himself singly to another man's reason, without endeavoring to engage his heart in his interest also, is no more likely to succeed, than a man who should apply only to a king's nominal minister, and neglect his favorite.

I will recommend to your attentive perusal, now that you are going into the world, two books, which will let you as much into the characters of men, as books can do. I mean, *Les Reflections Morales de la Rochefoucault*, and *Les Caractères de la Bruyère:*° but remember, at the same time, that I only recommend them to you as the best general maps to assist you in your journey, and not as marking out every particular turning and winding that you will meet with. There your own sagacity and observation must come to their aid.

La Rochefoucault,[1] is, I know, blamed, but I think without reason, for deriving all our actions from the source of self-love. For my own part, I see a great deal of truth, and no harm at all, in that opinion. It is certain that we seek our own happiness in everything we do; and it is as certain, that we can only find it in doing well, and in conforming all our actions to the rule of right reason, which is the great law of nature. It is only a mistaken self-love that is a blamable motive, when we take the immediate and indiscriminate gratification of a passion, or appetite, for real happiness. But am I blamable if I do a good action, upon account of the happiness which that honest consciousness will give me? Surely not. On the contrary, that pleasing consciousness is a proof of my virtue. The reflection which is the most censured in Monsieur de la Rochefoucault's book as a very ill-natured one, is this, *On trouve dans le malheur de son meilleur ami, quelque chose qui ne déplait pas.*[2] And why not? Why may I not feel a very tender and real concern for the misfortune of my friend, and yet at the same time feel a pleasing consciousness

---

[1]François, duc de La Rochefoucauld (1613-1680), French writer of nobility who opposed Richelieu° and later settled in Paris, where he wrote *Mémoirs* and *Réflexions ou sentences et maximes morales.*

[2]One finds in the misfortune of his best friend something that does not displease.

at having discharged my duty to him, by comforting and assisting him to the utmost of my power in that misfortune? Give me but virtuous actions, and I will not quibble and chicane[1] about the motives. And I will give anybody their choice of these two truths, which amount to the same thing: He who loves himself best is the honestest man; or, The honestest man loves himself best.

The characters of La Bruyère° are pictures from the life; most of them finely drawn, and highly colored. Furnish your mind with them first, and when you meet with their likeness, as you will every day, they will strike you the more. You will compare every feature with the original; and both will reciprocally help you to discover the beauties and the blemishes.

As women are a considerable, or at least a pretty numerous part of company; and as their suffrages[2] go a great way toward establishing a man's character in the fashionable part of the world (which is of great importance to the fortune and figure he proposes to make in it), it is necessary to please them. I will therefore, upon this subject, let you into certain *Arcana*[3] that will be very useful for you to know, but which you must, with the utmost care, conceal and never seem to know. Women, then, are only children of a larger growth;[4] they have an entertaining tattle, and sometimes wit; but for solid, reasoning good sense, I never knew in my life one that had it, or who reasoned or acted consequentially for four-and-twenty hours together. Some little passion or humour always breaks upon their best resolutions. Their beauty neglected or controverted, their age increased, or their supposed understandings depreciated, instantly kindles their little passions, and overturns any system of consequential conduct, that in their most reasonable moments they might have been capable of forming. A man of sense only trifles with them, plays with them, humours and flatters them, as he does with a sprightly forward child; but he neither consults them about, nor trusts them with serious matters; though he often makes them believe that he does both; which is the thing in the world that they are proud of; for they love mightily to be dabbling in business (which by the way they always spoil); and being justly distrustful that men in general look upon them in a trifling light, they almost adore that man who talks more seriously to them, and who seems to consult and trust them; I say, who seems; for weak men really do, but wise ones only seem to do it. No flattery is either too high or too low for them. They will greedily swallow the highest, and gratefully accept of the lowest; and you may safely flatter any woman from her understanding down to the exquisite taste of her fan. Women who are either indisputably beautiful, or indisputably ugly, are best flattered upon the score of their understandings; but those who are in a state of mediocrity, are best flattered upon their beauty, or at least their graces; for every woman who is not absolutely ugly thinks herself handsome; but not hearing often that she is so,

---

[1]Wrangle.
[2]Opinions.
[3]Esoteric or secret knowledge.
[4]See Dryden's° *All for Love* 4.1.43: "Men are but children of a larger growth."

is the more grateful and the more obliged to the few who tell her so; whereas a decided and conscious beauty looks upon every tribute paid to her beauty only as her due; but wants to shine, and to be considered on the side of her understanding; and a woman who is ugly enough to know that she is so, knows that she has nothing left for it but her understanding, which is consequently and probably (in more senses than one) her weak side.

But these are secrets which you must keep inviolably, if you would not, like Orpheus,[1] be torn to pieces by the whole sex; on the contrary, a man who thinks of living in the great world, must be gallant, polite, and attentive to please the women. They have, from the weakness of men, more or less influence in all courts; they absolutely stamp every man's character in the *beau monde*,[2] and make it either current, or cry it down, and stop it in payments.[3] It is, therefore, absolutely necessary to manage, please, and flatter them: and never to discover[4] the least marks of contempt, which is what they never forgive; but in this they are not singular, for it is the same with men; who will much sooner forgive an injustice than an insult. Every man is not ambitious, or courteous, or passionate; but every man has pride enough in his composition to feel and resent the least slight and contempt. Remember, therefore, most carefully to conceal your contempt, however just, wherever you would not make an implacable enemy. Men are much more unwilling to have their weaknesses and their imperfections known than their crimes; and if you hint to a man that you think him silly, ignorant, or even ill-bred, or awkward, he will hate you more and longer, than if you tell him plainly, that you think him a rogue. Never yield to that temptation, which to most young men is very strong, of exposing other people's weaknesses and infirmities, for the sake either of diverting the company, or showing your own superiority. You may get the laugh on your side by it for the present; but you will make enemies by it forever; and even those who laugh with you then, will, upon reflection, fear, and consequently hate you; besides that it is ill-natured, and a good heart desires rather to conceal than expose other people's weaknesses or misfortunes. If you have wit, use it to please, and not to hurt: you may shine, like the sun in the temperate zones, without scorching. Here it is wished for; under the Line[5] it is dreaded.

These are some of the hints which my long experience in the great world enables me to give you; and which, if you attend to them, may prove useful to you

---

[1]In Greek mythology, a musician who could tame the beasts with his lyre. He married Eurydice, who died after a bite from a snake. When Orpheus went to Hades to find her, he was promised her return if he did not look back as he brought her out. But he did look back, and she disappeared. Heartbroken, Orpheus wandered the Thracian countryside, a devotee of Dionysus. The women of Thrace tore him to pieces, either because of his lack of attention to them or because Dionysus was jealous of Orpheus's praise of Apollo° above other gods.

[2]World of fashion and high society.

[3]Label it untrustworthy.

[4]Reveal.

[5]The equator.

in your journey through it. I wish it may be a prosperous one; at least, I am sure that it must be your own fault if it is not.

Make my compliments to Mr. Harte,° who, I am very sorry to hear, is not well. I hope by this time he is recovered. Adieu! ✍

On Prejudices

London, February 7, O.S.° 1749.

Dear Boy:

You are now come to an age capable of reflection, and I hope you will do, what, however, few people at your age do, exert it for your own sake in the search of truth and sound knowledge. I will confess (for I am not unwilling to discover my secrets to you) that it is not many years since I have presumed to reflect for myself. Till sixteen or seventeen I had no reflection; and for many years after that, I made no use of what I had. I adopted the notions of the books I read, or the company I kept, without examining whether they were just or not; and I rather chose to run the risk of easy error, than to take the time and trouble of investigating truth. Thus, partly from laziness, partly from dissipation, and partly from the *mauvaise honte*[1] of rejecting fashionable notions, I was (as I have since found) hurried away by prejudices, instead of being guided by reason; and quietly cherished error, instead of seeking for truth. But since I have taken the trouble of reasoning for myself, and have had the courage to own that I do so, you cannot imagine how much my notions of things are altered, and in how different a light I now see them, from that in which I formerly viewed them, through the deceitful medium of prejudice or authority. Nay, I may possibly still retain many errors, which, from long habit, have perhaps grown into real opinions; for it is very difficult to distinguish habits, early acquired and long entertained, from the result of our reason and reflection.

My first prejudice (for I do not mention the prejudices of boys and women, such as hobgoblins, ghosts, dreams, spilling salt, etc.) was my classical enthusiasm, which I received from the books I read, and the masters who explained them to me. I was convinced there had been no common sense nor common honesty in the world for these last fifteen hundred years; but that they were totally extinguished with the ancient Greek and Roman governments. Homer° and Virgil° could have no faults, because they were ancient; Milton° and Tasso[2] could

---

[1]Terrible shame.

[2]Torquato (1544–1595), Italian poet of the Renaissance who wrote *Rinaldo*, a narrative, at eighteen and *Aminta*, a pastoral play, eleven years later. His masterpiece, *Jerusalem Delivered*, an epic about the First Crusade, is full of religious support for the Catholic Reformation and chivalric exploits of love and adventure.

have no merit, because they were modern. And I could almost have said, with regard to the ancients, what Cicero,° very absurdly and unbecomingly for a philosopher, says with regard to Plato,° *Cum quo errare malim quam cum aliis recte sentire.*[1] Whereas now, without any extraordinary effort of genius, I have discovered that nature was the same three thousand years ago as it is at present; that men were but men then as well as now; that modes and customs vary often, but that human nature is always the same. And I can no more suppose that men were better, braver, or wiser, fifteen hundred or three thousand years ago, than I can suppose that the animals or vegetables were better then than they are now. I dare assert too, in defiance of the favorers of the ancients, that Homer's° hero, Achilles,° was both a brute and a scoundrel, aud consequently an improper character for the hero of an epic poem; he had so little regard for his country, that he would not act in defense of it, because he had quarreled with Agamemnon° about a w—e;[2] and then afterward, animated by private resentment only, he went about killing people basely, I will call it, because he knew himself invulnerable; and yet, invulnerable as he was, he wore the strongest armor in the world; which I humbly apprehend to be a blunder; for a horse-shoe clapped to his vulnerable heel would have been sufficient. On the other hand, with submission to the favorers of the moderns, I assert with Mr. Dryden,° that the devil is in truth the hero of Milton's° poem; his plan, which he lays, pursues, and at last executes, being the subject of the poem. From all which considerations I impartially conclude that the ancients had their excellencies amid their defects, their virtues and their vices, just like the moderns; pedantry and affectation of learning decide clearly in favor of the former; vanity and ignorance, as peremptorily in favor of the latter.

Religious prejudices kept pace with my classical ones; and there was a time when I thought it impossible for the honestest man in the world to be saved out of the pale[3] of the Church of England, not considering that matters of opinion do not depend upon the will; and that it is as natural, and as allowable, that another man should differ in opinion from me, as that I should differ from him; and that if we are both sincere, we are both blameless; and should consequently have mutual indulgence for each other.

The next prejudices that I adopted were those of the *beau monde*,[4] in which as I was determined to shine, I took what are commonly called the genteel vices to be necessary. I had heard them reckoned so, and without further inquiry I believed it, or at least should have been ashamed to have denied it, for fear of exposing myself to the ridicule of those whom I considered as the models of fine gentlemen. But I am now neither ashamed nor afraid to assert that those genteel vices, as they are falsely called, are only so many blemishes in the character of even a man of the world and what is called a fine gentleman, and degrade him in the

---

[1] I would prefer to be wrong with him than to be correct with others.
[2] Whore.
[3] Outside the fence marking the boundary.
[4] World of fashion and high society.

opinions of those very people, to whom he hopes to recommend himself by them. Nay, this prejudice often extends so far, that I have known people pretend to vices they had not, instead of carefully concealing those they had.

Use and assert your own reason; reflect, examine, and analyze everything, in order to form a sound and mature judgment; let no ουτος εφα[1] impose upon your understanding, mislead your actions, or dictate your conversation. Be early what, if you are not, you will when too late wish you had been. Consult your reason betimes: I do not say that it will always prove an unerring guide; for human reason is not infallible; but it will prove the least erring guide that you can follow. Books and conversation may assist it; but adopt neither blindly and implicitly; try both by that best rule, which God has given to direct us,—reason. Of all the troubles, do not decline, as many people do, that of thinking. The herd of mankind can hardly be said to think; their notions are almost all adoptive;[2] and, in general, I believe it is better that it should be so, as such common prejudices contribute more to order and quiet than their own separate reasonings would do, unculti-vated and unimproved as they are. We have many of those useful prejudices in this country, which I should be very sorry to see removed. The good Protestant conviction, that the Pope is both Antichrist and the Whore of Babylon, is a more effectual preservative in this country against popery, than all the solid and unan-swerable arguments of Chillingworth.[3]

The idle story of the pretender's[4] having been introduced in a warming pan into the Queen's bed, though as destitute of all probability as of all foundation, has been much more prejudicial to the cause of Jacobitism than all that Mr. Locke° and others have written, to show the unreasonableness and absurdity of the doctrines of indefeasible hereditary right, and unlimited passive obedience. And that silly, sanguine notion, which is firmly entertained here, that one En-glishman can beat three Frenchmen, encourages, and has sometimes enabled, one Englishman in reality to beat two.

A Frenchman ventures his life with alacrity *pour l'honeur du Roi*;[5] were you to change the object, which he has been taught to have in view, and tell him that it was *pour le bien de la Patrie*,[6] he would very probably run away. Such gross local prejudices prevail with the herd of mankind, and do not impose upon cultivated,

---

[1] One of higher authority.

[2] Derivative.

[3] William (1602–1644), English theologian who, after converting to Roman Catholicism, left that faith and took orders in the Church of England, writing a book called *The Religion of Protestants: A Safe Way to Salvation,* which defended the individual's right to interpret the Bible. During the civil war, he was a chaplain in the king's army and died a prisoner.

[4] Belief in the right of the exiled branch of the Stuarts to the throne of England was called Jacobitism. After the Glorious Revolution of 1688, James II fled to France, from where, for more than fifty years, several "pretenders" attempted to regain the throne. The pretender Chesterfield refers to is Bonnie Prince Charlie (grandson of James II), who had only recently been defeated (1746), ending for good all hopes of the Stuarts.

[5] For the honor of the king.

[6] For the good of the country.

informed, and reflecting minds. But then there are notions equally false, though not so glaringly absurd, which are entertained by people of superior and improved understandings, merely for want of the necessary pains to investigate, the proper attention to examine, and the penetration requisite to determine the truth. Those are the prejudices which I would have you guard against by a manly exertion and attention of your reasoning faculty.

To mention one instance of a thousand that I could give you: It is a general prejudice, and has been propagated for these sixteen hundred years, that arts and sciences cannot flourish under an absolute government; and that genius must necessarily be cramped where freedom is restrained. This sounds plausible, but is false in fact. Mechanic arts, as agriculture, etc., will indeed be discouraged where the profits and property are, from the nature of the government, insecure. But why the despotism of a government should cramp the genius of a mathematician, an astronomer, a poet, or an orator, I confess I never could discover. It may indeed deprive the poet or the orator of the liberty of treating of certain subjects in the manner they would wish, but it leaves them subjects enough to exert genius upon, if they have it. Can an author with reason complain that he is cramped and shackled, if he is not at liberty to publish blasphemy, bawdry, or sedition? all which are equally prohibited in the freest governments, if they are wise and well-regulated ones. This is the present general complaint of the French authors; but indeed chiefly of the bad ones. No wonder, say they, that England produces so many great geniuses; people there may think as they please, and publish what they think. Very true, but what hinders them from thinking as they please?

If indeed they think in manner destructive of all religion, morality, or good manners, or to the disturbance of the state, an absolute government will certainly more effectually prohibit them from, or punish them for publishing such thoughts, than a free one could do. But how does that cramp the genius of an epic, dramatic, or lyric poet? or how does it corrupt the eloquence of an orator in the pulpit or at the bar? The number of good French authors, such as Corneille,° Racine,° Molière,° Boileau,° and La Fontaine,[1] who seemed to dispute it with the Augustan age, flourished under the despotism of Louis XIV; and the celebrated authors of the Augustan age did not shine till after the fetters were riveted upon the Roman people by that cruel and worthless Emperor.[2] The revival of letters was not owing, neither, to any free government, but to the encouragement and protection of Leo X.[3] and Francis I.,[4] the one as absolute a pope, and the other as despotic a prince, as ever reigned. Do not mistake, and imagine that while I am

---

[1]Jean de (1621–1695), French poet famous for his *Fables choisies, mises en vers*, a collection of twelve books of fables drawn from Aesop,° Horace,° and others, which he transforms with his wit and style, treating animals like men and painting a satiric portrait of the times.

[2]Caesar Augustus.°

[3]Pope from 1513 to 1521.

[4]King of France (1515–1547) who fought and lost four wars against Spain's Charles V in attempting to become the greatest power in Europe. He did, however, sign a concordat with Leo X, and he expanded his powers as monarch. In his reign the French Renaissance flourished.

only exposing a prejudice, I am speaking in favor of arbitrary power; which from my soul I abhor, and look upon as a gross and criminal violation of the natural rights of mankind. Adieu! ✐

The Importance of Style

London, November 24, O.S.° 1749.

Dear Boy:

Every rational being (I take it for granted) proposes to himself some object more important than mere respiration and obscure animal existence. He desires to distinguish himself among his fellow-creatures; and, *alicui negotio intentus, praeclari facinoris, aut artis bonae, faman quaerit.*[1] Caesar,° when embarking in a storm, said, that it was not necessary he should live; but that it was absolutely necessary he should get to the place to which he was going. And Pliny[2] leaves mankind this only alternative; either of doing what deserves to be written, or of writing what deserves to be read. As for those who do neither, *eorum vitam mortemque juxta aestumo; quoniam de utraque siletur.*[3] You have, I am convinced, one or both of these objects in view; but you must know and use the necessary means, or your pursuit will be vain and frivolous. In either case, *Sapere est principum et fons,*[4] but it is by no means all. That knowledge must be adorned, it must have lustre as well as weight, or it will be oftener taken for lead than for gold. Knowledge you have, and will have: I am easy upon that article. But my business, as your friend, is not to compliment you upon what you have, but to tell you with freedom what you want;[5] and I must tell you plainly, that I fear you want everything but knowledge.

I have written to you so often, of late, upon good-breeding, address, *les manieres liantes,*[6] the Graces, etc., that I shall confine this letter to another subject, pretty near akin to them, and which, I am sure, you are full as deficient in; I mean Style.

Style is the dress of thoughts; and let them be ever so just, if your style is homely, coarse, and vulgar, they will appear to as much disadvantage, and be as ill received as your person, though ever so well proportioned, would, if dressed in rags, dirt, and tatters. It is not every understanding that can judge of matter; but every ear can and does judge, more or less, of style: and were I either to speak or

---

[1]One intent on some business seeks fame in notorious crime or great art.

[2]The passage is actually from the preface to *Catalina* by the Roman historian Sallust (Caius Sallustius Crispus, 86 B.C.–c. 34 B.C.).

[3]I value each life equally with each death; since of both there is silence.

[4]To be wise is the beginning and the fountain.

[5]Lack.

[6]Sociable manners.

write to the public, I should prefer moderate matter, adorned with all the beauties and elegancies of style, to the strongest matter in the world, ill-worded and ill-delivered. Your business is negotiation abroad, and oratory in the House of Commons at home. What figure can you make, in either case, if your style be inelegant, I do not say bad? Imagine yourself writing an office-letter to a secretary of state, which letter is to be read by the whole Cabinet Council, and very possibly afterward laid before Parliament; any one barbarism, solecism, or vulgarism in it, would, in a very few days, circulate through the whole kingdom, to your disgrace and ridicule. For instance, I will suppose you had written the following letter from The Hague to the Secretary of State at London; and leave you to suppose the consequences of it: —

> My Lord: I HAD, last night, the honor of your Lordship's letter of the 24th; and SET ABOUT DOING the orders contained THEREIN; And IF SO BE that I can get that affair done by the next post, I will not fail FOR to give your Lordship an account of it by NEXT POST. I have told the French Minister, AS HOW THAT IF that affair be not soon concluded, your Lordship would think it ALL LONG OF HIM; and that he must have neglected FOR TO have wrote to his court about it. I must beg leave to put your Lordship in mind AS HOW, that I am now full three quarter in arrear; and if so BE that I do not very soon receive at least one-half year, I shall CUT A VERY BAD FIGURE; FOR THIS HERE place is very dear. I shall be VASTLY BEHOLDEN to your Lordship for THAT THERE mark of your favor; and so I REST or REMAIN, Your, etc.

You will tell me, possibly, that this is a *caricatura* of an illiberal and inelegant style: I will admit it; but assure you, at the same time, that a dispatch with less than half these faults would blow you up forever. It is by no means sufficient to be free from faults, in speaking and writing; but you must do both correctly and elegantly. In faults of this kind, it is not *ille optimus qui minimis arguetur*;[1] —but he is unpardonable who has any at all, because it is his own fault: he need only attend to, observe, and imitate the best authors.

It is a very true saying, that a man must be born a poet, but that he may make himself an orator; and the very first principal of an orator is to speak his own language, particularly, with the utmost purity and elegance. A man will be forgiven even great errors in a foreign language; but in his own, even the least slips are justly laid hold of and ridiculed.

A person of the House of Commons, speaking two years ago upon naval affairs, asserted, that we had then the finest navy UPON THE FACE OF THE YEARTH. This happy mixture of blunder and vulgarism, you may easily imagine, was matter of immediate ridicule; but I can assure you that it continues so still, and will be remembered as long as he lives and speaks. Another, speaking in defense of a gentleman, upon whom a censure was moved, happily said that he thought that gentleman was more LIABLE to be thanked and rewarded, than censured. You know, I presume, that LIABLE can never be used in a good sense.

---

[1]He is best who is accused least.

You have with you three or four of the best English authors, Dryden,° Atterbury,[1] and Swift;° read them with the utmost care, and with a particular view to their language, and they may possibly correct that CURIOUS INFELICITY OF DICTION, which you acquired at Westminster. Mr. Harte° excepted, I will admit that you have met with very few English abroad, who could improve your style; and with many, I dare say, who speak as ill as yourself, and, it may be, worse; you must, therefore, take the more pains, and consult your authors and Mr. Harte° the more. I need not tell you how attentive the Romans and Greeks, particularly the Athenians, were to this object. It is also a study among the Italians and the French; witness their respective academies and dictionaries for improving and fixing their languages. To our shame be it spoken, it is less attended to here than in any polite country; but that is no reason why you should not attend to it; on the contrary, it will distinguish you the more. Cicero° says, very truly, that it is glorious to excel other men in that very article, in which men excel brutes; SPEECH.

Constant experience has shown me, that great purity and elegance of style, with a graceful elocution, cover a multitude of faults, in either a speaker or a writer. For my own part, I confess (and I believe most people are of my mind) that if a speaker should ungracefully mutter or stammer out to me the sense of an angel, deformed by barbarism and solecisms,[2] or larded with vulgarisms, he should never speak to me a second time, if I could help it. Gain the heart, or you gain nothing; the eyes and the ears are the only roads to the heart. Merit and knowledge will not gain hearts, though they will secure them when gained. Pray, have that truth ever in your mind. Engage the eyes by your address, air, and motions; soothe the ears by the elegance and harmony of your diction; the heart will certainly follow; and the whole man, or woman, will as certainly follow the heart. I must repeat it to you, over and over again, that with all the knowledge which you may have at present, or hereafter acquire, and with all merit that ever man had, if you have not a graceful address, liberal and engaging manners, a prepossessing air, and a good degree of eloquence in speaking and writing, you will be nobody; but will have the daily mortification of seeing people, with not one-tenth part of your merit or knowledge, get the start of you, and disgrace you, both in company and in business.

You have read "Quintilian,"[3] the best book in the world to form an orator; pray read Cicero° Te Oratore, the best book in the world to finish one. Translate and re-translate from and to Latin, Greek, and English; make yourself a pure and elegant English style: it requires nothing but application. I do not find that God

---

[1]Francis (1662–1732), minor writer and bishop of Rochester who was arrested in 1722 and sent to the Tower on charges of treason as a Jacobite. He lost his case before the House of Lords, was stripped of his ecclesiastical office, and spent the rest of his life in Brussels and Paris.

[2]Grammatical errors or nonstandard usage.

[3]Marcus Fabius Quintilianus (A.D. 35–95), Roman rhetorician and public teacher, salaried by Vespasian,° famous for his good style, taste, and moderation. He wrote Institutio oratoria, a survey of rhetoric in twelve books.

has made you a poet; and I am very glad that he has not: therefore, for God's sake, make yourself an orator, which you may do. Though I still call you boy, I consider you no longer as such;[1] and when I reflect upon the prodigious quantity of manure that has been laid upon you, I expect that you should produce more at eighteen, than uncultivated soils do at eight-and-twenty.

Pray tell Mr. Harte° that I have received his letter of the 13th, N.S.° Mr. Smith was much in the right not to let you go, at this time of the year, by sea; in the summer you may navigate as much as you please; as, for example, from Leghorn to Genoa, etc. Adieu! ✒

Of Religion and Morality

London, January 8, O.S.° 1750.

Dear Boy:

I have seldom or never written to you upon the subject of religion and morality; your own reason, I am persuaded, has given you true notions of both; they speak best for themselves; but if they wanted assistance, you have Mr. Harte° at hand, both for precept and example; to your own reason, therefore, and to Mr. Harte,° shall I refer you for the reality of both, and confine myself in this letter to the decency, the utility, and the necessity of scrupulously preserving the appearances of both. When I say the appearances of religion, I do not mean that you should talk or act like a missionary or an enthusiast, nor that you should take up a controversial cudgel against whoever attacks the sect you are of; this would be both useless and unbecoming your age; but I mean that you should by no means seem to approve, encourage, or applaud, those libertine notions, which strike at religions equally, and which are the poor threadbare topics of half-wits and minute philosophers. Even those who are silly enough to laugh at their jokes, are still wise enough to distrust and detest their characters; for putting moral virtues at the highest, and religion at the lowest, religion must still be allowed to be a collateral security, at least, to virtue, and every prudent man will sooner trust to two securities than to one. Whenever, therefore, you happen to be in company with those pretended *Esprits forts*,[2] or with thoughtless libertines, who laugh at all religion to show their wit, or disclaim it, to complete their riot, let no word or look of yours intimate the least approbation; on the contrary, let a silent gravity express your dislike: but enter not into the subject and decline such unprofitable and indecent controversies. Depend upon this truth, that every man is the worse looked upon, and the less trusted for being thought to have no religion; in spite

---

[1]His son was then seventeen.
[2]Free thinkers.

of all the pompous and specious epithets he may assume, of *Esprit fort*, freethinker, or moral philosopher; and a wise atheist (if such a thing there is) would, for his own interest and character in this world, pretend to some religion.

Your moral character must be not only pure, but, like Caesar's° wife, unsuspected. The least speck or blemish upon it is fatal. Nothing degrades and vilifies more, for it excites; and unites detestation and contempt. There are, however, wretches in the world profligate enough to explode all notions of moral good and evil; to maintain that they are merely local, and depend entirely upon the customs and fashions of different countries; nay, there are still, if possible, more unaccountable wretches; I mean those who affect to preach and propagate such absurd and infamous notions without believing them themselves. These are the devil's hypocrites. Avoid, as much as possible, the company of such people; who reflect a degree of discredit and infamy upon all who converse with them. But as you may, sometimes, by accident, fall into such company, take great care that no complaisance, no good-humor, no warmth of festal mirth, ever make you seem even to acquiesce, much less to approve or applaud, such infamous doctrines. On the other hand, do not debate nor enter into serious argument upon a subject so much below it: but content yourself with telling these APOSTLES that you know they are not serious; that you have a much better opinion of them than they would have you have; and that, you are very sure, they would not practice the doctrine they preach. But put your private mark upon them, and shun them forever afterward.

There is nothing so delicate as your moral character, and nothing which it is your interest so much to preserve pure. Should you be suspected of injustice, malignity, perfidy, lying, etc., all the parts and knowledge in the world will never procure you esteem, friendship, or respect. A strange concurrence of circumstances has sometimes raised very bad men to high stations, but they have been raised like criminals to a pillory, where their persons and their crimes, by being more conspicuous, are only the more known, the more detested, and the more pelted and insulted. If, in any case whatsoever, affectation and ostentation are pardonable, it is in the case of morality; though even there, I would not advise you to a pharisaical[1] pomp of virtue. But I will recommend to you a most scrupulous tenderness for your moral character, and the utmost care not to say or do the least thing that may ever so slightly taint it. Show yourself, upon all occasions, the advocate, the friend, but not the bully of virtue. Colonel Chartres,[2] whom you have certainly heard of (who was, I believe, the most notorious blasted rascal in the world, and who had, by all sorts of crimes, amassed immense wealth), was so sensible of the disadvantage of a bad character, that I heard him once say, in his

---

[1]Resembling the Pharisees, that is, strict in form but not in spirit; hypocritical.

[2](1675-1731) A rake known for gambling, usury, and rape who supported Walpole° and was satirized in Pope's° *Imitations of Horace* as a cheater who could neither read nor write. It is said that at his funeral a mob tried to pull the body from the coffin and succeeded in throwing dead dogs into the grave.

impudent, profligate manner, that though he would not give one farthing for virtue, he would give ten thousand pounds for a character; because he should get a hundred thousand pounds by it; whereas, he was so blasted, that he had no longer an opportunity of cheating people. Is it possible, then, that an honest man can neglect what a wise rogue would purchase so dear?

There is one of the vices above mentioned, into which people of good education, and, in the main, of good principles, sometimes fall, from mistaken notions of skill, dexterity, and self-defense, I mean lying; though it is inseparably attended with more infamy and loss than any other. The prudence and necessity of often concealing the truth, insensibly seduces people to violate it. It is the only art of mean[1] capacities, and the only refuge of mean spirits. Whereas, concealing the truth upon proper occasions, is as prudent and as innocent, as telling a lie, upon any occasion, is infamous and foolish. I will state you a case in your own department. Suppose you are employed at a foreign court, and that the minister of that court is absurd or impertinent enough to ask you what your instructions are? Will you tell him a lie, which as soon as found out (and found out it certainly will be) must destroy your credit, blast your character, and render you useless there? No. Will you tell him the truth then, and betray your trust? As certainly, No. But you will answer with firmess, That you are surprised at such a question, that you are persuaded he does not expect an answer to it; but that, at all events, he certainly will not have one. Such an answer will give him confidence in you; he will conceive an opinion of your veracity, of which opinion you may afterward make very honest and fair advantages. But if, in negotiations, you are looked upon as a liar and a trickster, no confidence will be placed in you, nothing will be communicated to you, and you will be in the situation of a man who has been burned in the cheek; and who, from that mark, cannot afterward get an honest livelihood if he would, but must continue a thief.

Lord Bacon, very justly, makes a distinction between simulation[2] and dissimulation;[3] and allows the latter rather than the former; but still observes, that they are the weaker sort of politicians who have recourse to either. A man who has strength of mind and strength of parts, wants[4] neither of them.[5] *Certainly* (says he) *the ablest men that ever were, have all had an openness and frankness of dealing, and a name of certainty and veracity; but then, they were like horses well managed; for they could tell, passing well, when to stop or turn; and at such times, when they thought the case indeed required some dissimulation, if then they used it, it came to pass that the former opinion spread abroad of their good faith and clearness of dealing, made them almost invisible.*

---

[1]Poor or weak.

[2]Outright lying.

[3]Prudent dissembling to maintain secrecy; from Bacon's Essay No. 6.

[4]Needs.

[5]Chesterfield closely paraphrases Bacon's "strong wit and a strong heart" and "it is the weaker sort of politics that are the great dissemblers."

There are people who indulge themselves in a sort of lying, which they reckon innocent, and which in one sense is so; for it hurts nobody but themselves. This sort of lying is the spurious offspring of vanity, begotten upon folly: these people deal in the marvelous; they have seen some things that never existed; they have seen other things which they never really saw, though they did exist, only because they were thought worth seeing. Has anything remarkable been said or done in any place, or in any company? they immediately present and declare themselves eye or ear witnesses of it. They have done feats themselves, unattempted, or at least unperformed by others. They are always the heroes of their own fables; and think that they gain consideration, or at least present attention, by it. Whereas, in truth, all that they get is ridicule and contempt, not without a good degree of distrust; for one must naturally conclude, that he who will tell any lie from idle vanity, will not scruple telling a greater for interest. Had I really seen anything so very extraordinary as to be almost incredible I would keep it to myself, rather than by telling it give anybody room to doubt, for one minute, of my veracity. It is most certain, that the reputation of chastity is not so necessary for a woman, as that of veracity is for a man; and with reason; for it is possible for a woman to be virtuous, though not strictly chaste, but it is not possible for a man to be virtuous without strict veracity. The slips of the poor woman are sometimes mere bodily frailties; but a lie in a man is a vice of the mind and of the heart. For God's sake be scrupulously jealous of the purity of your moral character; keep it immaculate, unblemished, unsullied; and it will be unsuspected. Defamation and calumny never attack, where there is no weak place; they magnify, but they do not create.

There is a very great difference between the purity of character, which I so earnestly recommend to you, and the stoical gravity and austerity of character, which I do by no means recommend to you. At your age, I would no more wish you to be a Cato[1] than a Clodius.[2] Be, and be reckoned, a man of pleasure as well as a man of business. Enjoy this happy and giddy time of your life; shine in the pleasures, and in the company of people of your own age. This is all to be done, and indeed only can be done, without the least taint to the purity of your moral character; for those mistaken young fellows, who think to shine by an impious or immoral licentiousness, shine only from their stinking, like corrupted flesh, in the dark. Without this purity, you can have no dignity of character; and without dignity of character it is impossible to rise in the world. You must be respectable, if you will be respected. I have known people slattern away their character, without really polluting it; the consequence of which has been, that they have become innocently contemptible; their merit has been dimmed, their

---

[1] See Cato the Elder.°

[2] Publius Clodius Pulcher (d. 52 B.C.), Roman politician who caused a scandal by dressing as a woman and infiltrating the women's mysteries held in Julius Caesar's° house. Prosecuted by Cicero° for sacrilege, he was acquitted and later was made tribune by the First Triumvirate. Once in power, he exiled Cicero,° removed Cato the Younger° to Cyprus, and encouraged riots and gang wars until he was killed.

pretensions unregarded, and all their views defeated. Character must be kept bright, as well as clean. Content yourself with mediocrity in nothing. In purity of character and in politeness of manners labor to excel all, if you wish to equal many. Adieu! ✍

Portrait of Johnson

London, February 28, O.S.° 1751.

My Dear Friend:

This epigram in Martial°—

Non amo te, Sabidi, nec possum dicere quare;
  Hoc tantum possum dicere, non amo te[1]

has puzzled a great many people, who cannot conceive how it is possible not to love anybody, and yet not to know the reason why. I think I conceive Martial's° meaning very clearly, though the nature of epigram, which is to be short, would not allow him to explain it more fully; and I take it to be this: O Sabidis, you are a very worthy deserving man; you have a thousand good qualities, you have a great deal of learning; I esteem, I respect, but for the soul of me I cannot love you, though I cannot particularly say why. You are not *aimable*:[2] you have not those engaging manners, those pleasing attentions, those graces, and that address, which are absolutely necessary to please, though impossible to define. I cannot say it is this or that particular thing that hinders me from loving you; it is the whole together; and upon the whole you are not agreeable.

How often have I, in the course of my life, found myself in this situation, with regard to many of my acquaintance, whom I have honored and respected, without being able to love. I did not know why, because, when one is young, one does not take the trouble, nor allow one's self the time, to analyze one's sentiments and to trace them up to their source. But subsequent observation and reflection have taught me why. There is a man, whose moral character, deep learning, and superior parts, I acknowledge, admire, and respect; but whom it is so impossible for me to love, that I am almost in a fever whenever I am in his company. His figure (without being deformed) seems made to disgrace or ridicule the common struc-ture of the human body. His legs and arms are never in the position which, according to the situation of his body, they ought to be in, but constantly

---

[1] "I do not love thee, Sabidi, why I cannot say; / This only can I say, I do not love thee." These lines are better known in the nursery rhyme version of a translation by Thomas Brown (1663–1704), who was poking fun at the dean of Christ Church, Oxford: "I do not love thee, Dr. Fell. / The reason why I cannot tell. / But this I know and know full well, / I do not love thee, Dr. Fell."
[2] Amiable.

employed in committing acts of hostility upon the Graces. He throws anywhere, but down his throat, whatever he means to drink, and only mangles what he means to carve. Inattentive to all the regards of social life, he mistimes or misplaces everything. He disputes with heat and indiscriminately, mindless of the rank, character, and situation of those with whom he disputes; absolutely ignorant of the several gradations of familiarity or respect, he is exactly the same to his superiors, his equals, and his inferiors; and therefore, by a necessary consequence, absurd to two of the three. Is it possible to love such a man? No. The utmost I can do for him, is to consider him as a respectable Hottentot.[1]

I remember, that when I came from Cambridge, I had acquired, among the pedants of that illiberal seminary, a sauciness of literature, a turn to satire and contempt, and a strong tendency to argumentation and contradiction. But I had been but a very little while in the world, before I found that this would by no means do; and I immediately adopted the opposite character; I concealed what learning I had; I applauded often, without approving; and I yielded commonly without conviction. *Suaviter in modo*[2] was my law and my prophets; and if I pleased (between you and me) it was much more owing to that than to any superior knowledge or merit of my own. *A propos*, the word PLEASING puts one always in mind of Lady Hervey;[3] pray tell her, that I declare her responsible to me for your pleasing; that I consider her as a pleasing Falstaff,° who not only pleases, herself, but is the cause of pleasing in others; that I know she can make anything of anybody; and that, as your governess, if she does not make you please, it must be only because she will not, and not because she cannot. I hope you are *dubois dont on en fait*[4] and if so, she is so good a sculptor, that I am sure she can give you whatever form she pleases. A versatility of manners is as necessary in social, as a versatility of parts is in political life. One must often yield, in order to prevail; one must humble one's self, to be exalted; one must, like St. Paul, become all things to all men,[5] to gain some; and, by the way, men are taken by the same means,

---

[1]The identity of the "Hottentot" provoked great speculation. Although many, including Boswell, assumed this man to be Samuel Johnson, no evidence has been found to prove it. Johnson believed him to be the thin, awkward, and absentminded Lord George Lyttelton (1709–1773), declaring in his own defense that Chesterfield had never seen him eat. Chesterfield had promised Johnson financial support to help him compile his *Dictionary* but had never paid him. Then when the *Dictionary* was completed, Chesterfield apparently tried to take credit for supporting Johnson. Johnson wrote his famous letter (see page 158) in reply. Clearly, since that letter was written in 1755, this portrait could not have been written in retaliation. Nevertheless, it does fall within the period in which Johnson was working on his dictionary.

[2]Charmingly in moderation.

[3]Mary Lepell Hervey (1700–1768), a bold, attractive woman, maid of honor to the Princess of Wales, married to John Hervey in 1720, and widely admired by men like Pope,° Voltaire,° and Walpole.° In a letter dated October 22, 1750 Chesterfield notes that Lady Hervey "understands Latin" but "wisely conceals it."

[4]Of workable wood.

[5]1 Cor. 9:22.

mutatis mutandis[1] that women are gained—by gentleness, insinuation, and submission: and these lines of Mr. Dryden° will hold to a minister as well as to a mistress:.—

> *"The prostrate lover, when he lowest lies,*
> *But stoops to conquer, and but kneels to rise."*[2]

In the course of the world, the qualifications of the chameleon are often necessary; nay, they must be carried a little further, and exerted a little sooner; for you should, to a certain degree, take the hue of either the man or the woman that you want, and wish to be upon terms with. *A propos*, have you yet found out at Paris, any friendly and hospitable Madame de Lursay,[3] *qui veut bien se charger du soin de vous éduquer?*[4] And have you had any occasion of representing to her, *qu'elle faisoit donc des noeds?*[5] But I ask your pardon, Sir, for the abruptness of the question, and acknowledge that I am meddling with matters that are out of my department. However, in matters of less importance, I desire to be *de vos secrets le fidèle dépositaire.*[6] Trust me with the general turn and color of your amusements at Paris. Is it *le fracas du grand monde, comédies, bals, opéras, cour, etc.?*[7] Or is it *des petites sociétés, moins bruyantes, mais pas pour cela moins agréables?*[8] Where are you the most *établi?*[9] Where are you *le petit Stanhope? Voyez vous encore jour, à quelque arrangement honnête?*[10] Have you made many acquaintances among the young Frenchmen who ride at your Academy; and who are they? Send to me this sort of chit-chat in your letters, which, by the bye, I wish you would honor me with somewhat oftener. If you frequent any of the myriads of polite Englishmen who infest Paris, who are they? Have you finished with Abbé Nolèt,[11] and are you *au*

---

[1]"Having changed what must be changed"; that is, substituting the male for the female.
[2]From Dryden's° play *Amphytrion*, the last lines of Act 3: "Th'offending Lover, when he lowest lies, / Submits, to conquer; and but kneels, to rise." Goldsmith's° play *She Stoops to Conquer* was first produced in 1773.
[3]Character in *Égaremens du Coeur et de l'Esprit (Wanderings of the Heart and Mind)*, a popular novel by Claude Crebillon (1707–1777) about the memoirs of Mr. de Meilcour. Madame de Lursay, a friend of the narrator's mother, initiates the seventeen-year-old in the ways of love.
[4]Who wants to be entrusted with the care of educating you?
[5]"That she was making knots?" Chesterfield probably intends a three-way pun here. The word *noed* ("knot") means first a kind of handicraft like macrame that was popular at the time, but it also refers to the third act of the classical five-act play in which the plot is knotted or entangled, the last act being the "denouement" or untangling of the plot. Finally, here Chesterfield means to ask if such a lady were ensnaring, entangling, or catching his son in her seductive knots.
[6]The faithful repository of your secrets.
[7]The acclaim of high society, comedies, balls, operas, the court, etc.?
[8]Small social gatherings, less talked about, but not for that less pleasant?
[9]Established in society.
[10]Young Stanhope? Do you see another day, for some honorable or advantageous understanding?
[11]Jean-Antoine Nollet (1700–1770), preceptor in natural philosophy to the French royal family. He devised his own theory of electricity and wrote to Benjamin Franklin to dispute with the great American. Confident in the truth of his views, Franklin declined to respond.

fait[1] of all the properties and effects of air? Were I inclined to quibble, I would say, that the effects of *air*,[2] at least, are best to be learned of Marcel.[3] If you have quite done with l'Abbé Nolèt, ask my friend l'Abbé Sallier[4] to recommend to you some meagre philomath,[5] to teach you a little geometry and astronomy; not enough to absorb your attention and puzzle your intellects, but only enough not to be grossly ignorant of either. I have of late been a sort of *astronome malgré moi*,[6] by bringing in last Monday into the House of Lords a bill for reforming our present Calendar and taking the New Style.[7] Upon which occasion I was obliged to talk some astronomical jargon, of which I did not understand one word, but got it by heart, and spoke it by rote from a master. I wished that I had known a little more of it myself; and so much I would have you know. But the great and necessary knowledge of all is, to know yourself and others: this knowledge requires great attention and long experience; exert the former, and may you have the latter! Adieu!

P.S. I have this moment received your letters of the 27th February, and the 2d March, N.S.° The seal shall be done as soon as possible. I am glad that you are employed in Lord Albemarle's[8] *bureau*; it will teach you, at least, the mechanical part of that business, such as folding, entering, and docketing letters; for you must not imagine that you are let into the *fin fin*[9] of the correspondence, nor indeed is it fit that you should, at your age. However, use yourself to secrecy as to the letters you either read or write, that in time you may be trusted with SECRET, VERY SECRET, SEPARATE, APART, etc. I am sorry that this business interferes with your riding; I hope it is seldom; but I insist upon its not interfering with your dancing-master, who is at this time the most useful and necessary of all the masters you have or can have.

---

[1]Well aware.

[2]Appearance.

[3]The son's dancing master.

[4]Claude Sallier (1685–1761), French philologist who served in the king's library and wrote many essays for the Académie des Inscriptions.

[5]Lover of math.

[6]Astronomer in spite of myself.

[7]See N.S.°

[8]The second Earl of Albemarle, ambassador at Paris, died in 1754. In a letter dated 27 May 1752, Chesterfield tells his son that Albemarle lacked estate, fortune, birth, and political acumen. He made his way in the world by means of the graces only and was thus a perfect object lesson for Chesterfield's son.

[9]The most subtle and complete particulars.

Benjamin Franklin

(1706 –1790)

Benjamin Franklin was born in Boston, the eighth child of Josiah and Abiah and the fifteenth of Josiah's seventeen children. At age ten, Franklin left school to work in his father's soap and candle shop, but, finding the work not to his liking, he was apprenticed at twelve to his brother James, nine years his senior, to learn the printing trade. He learned quickly, despite conflicts between the two brothers, and, at sixteen, published his first essays under the name Silence Dogood. In his autobiography, Franklin attributed his literary success to his self- discipline and diligence in imitating Addison's essays from *The Spectator*:

> I took some of the papers, and making short hints of the sentiments in each sentence, laid them by a few days, and then, without looking at the book, tried to complete the papers again, by expressing each hinted sentiment at length, and as fully as it had been expressed before, in any suitable words that should occur to me. Then I compared my *Spectator* with the original, discovered some of my faults, and corrected them.

He increased his vocabulary by turning Addison's essays into verse and back again and improved his organization by jumbling Addison's ideas and later reordering them until he had not only corrected his faults but sometimes, he believed, exceeded even Addison in the variety and order of his prose.

Between 1723 and 1757 Franklin published *Poor Richard's Almanac*, established the first library in America, and formed a debating club that became the American Philosophical Society and an academy that became the University of Pennsylvania. At forty-two he claimed to have retired from his first career as printer and businessman to devote himself to study and scientific experiment. He had already urged the paving of the streets of Philadelphia and invented the Franklin stove, bifocal glasses, and the glass harmonica, when his work with electricity and his invention of the lightning rod won the acclaim of scientists in England and on the Continent.

Franklin's career as public servant began when he served as deputy postmaster (1753–1774) and delegate from Pennsylvania to the Albany Congress in 1754. In 1757 he left for England as emissary for the colonies, where he remained for all but two of the next seventeen years, finally returning in 1775 to be a delegate to the Continental Congress. In that year he was also appointed postmaster general and, a year later, became a member of the committee that drafted the Declaration of Independence. In 1776 he left for France to serve for nine years as diplomat and agent for the United States. At eighty-one he helped develop the compromise that led to the adoption of the Constitution in 1788 and lived to see his friend George Washington elected president of the United States.

Despite his reputation as a friend of the ladies in the salons of France and the racy, teasing tone he sometimes adopted in his letters to the many women, young and old, with whom he corresponded, there is no proof that, once married (1730), Franklin was unfaithful to his wife. Before he married Deborah Read, he had fathered a son, William, whom he publicly affirmed was illegitimate; he never revealed the name of the mother. No doubt William was one of the many "difficulties" that, Franklin states in his autobiography, he and Read had to overcome in agreeing to marry. Another was her earlier marriage to John Rogers, a scoundrel who had run off soon after the wedding. According to rumor, Rogers was a bigamist and dead; nonetheless, the Franklins were married in a civil, not a religious, ceremony.

Their marriage proved convenient for both, rescuing Read from the misery and shame of abandonment and pacifying Franklin's guilty conscience for having made promises to her that he had ignored while in England. Not a marriage based on passion, it was nonetheless a successful and enduring one, in which, in Franklin's words, they "throve together," devoted to the principles of frugality and hard work. Of necessity, they also throve apart, writing many letters to one another while Franklin was in England. Occasionally he asked his wife to join him, knowing full well that her fear of the crossing would keep her at home. She died two months before Franklin's return in 1775. According to one biographer, Ronald W. Clark, even William, not a favorite with her, believed at that point that she might have fared better had Franklin been able to return sooner.

The couple had two children of their own: another son, Francis, whose death at age four of smallpox led Franklin in his later years to urge that all children be vaccinated, and a daughter, Sarah, called Sally. Although William proved a disappointment, siding with the British during the War of Independence, and Sally was not an able pupil, Franklin found satisfaction in his grandchildren and in Mary Stevenson, often called Polly, the daughter of his landlady in England. Like Montaigne's Marie de Gourney, Polly became a second daughter to Franklin and was with him in Philadelphia when he died.

Franklin's honesty, clarity, and good humor pervade all he wrote, from the lines of Poor Richard to the many essays and letters he penned over the years. Although his tone is benign and self-confident like that of both Addison and Montaigne, Franklin's style is more direct than that of either man, and, because he was practical and self-taught, far less dependent on allusions to the ancients. Instead, Franklin derives his philosophy from his observation and analysis of the behavior of man and nature. Thus his focus parallels that of the earlier scientist, Bacon. Less abrupt than Bacon, however, he employs Browne's method of treating with respect the opposing point of view. In "Restoration of Life by Sun Rays," Franklin grants the possibility of a toad's survival while buried in sand, but he does not cite the sources for this hearsay as Browne would have done. Moreover, he concludes his opinion with evidence from an experiment he himself performed.

Combining the balance of Bacon with the amplitude of Addison, Franklin's style is a vigorous adaptation of the parallelism characteristic of eighteenth-century prose. In "The Handsome and Deformed Leg," for instance, Franklin sets up a circular paragraph composed of a single sentence that contrasts the optimist and the pessimist in a series of ten parallel phrases, moving from the general "conveniencies and inconveniencies" through specifics such as food, weather, government, and art, back to the general "good and bad qualities" of man. The most engaging quality of Franklin's style, however, is his wit, which is less biting and more pervasive than that of Chesterfield and adapted to all subjects—women (for whom he has far greater respect than any of his predecessors), philosophy, and even science. "On Perfumes," his parody of a scientific proposal, introduces what Addison calls a "want of Delicacy" and ends on a resounding pun that would no doubt have shocked the fastidious Chesterfield as much as it obviously tickled its author. ✍

Advice on the Choice of a Mistress

Philadelphia, June 25, 1745

My dear Friend:

I know of no medicine fit to diminish the violent natural inclinations you mention; and if I did, I think I should not communicate it to you. Marriage is the proper remedy. It is the most natural state of man, and therefore the state in which you are most likely to find solid happiness. Your reasons against entering into it at present appear to me not well founded. The circumstantial advantages you have in view by postponing it are not only uncertain, but they are small in comparison with that of the thing itself, the being married and settled. It is the man and woman united that make the complete human being. Separate, she wants his force of body and strength of reason; he, her fitness, sensibility, and acute discernment. Together they are more likely to succeed in the world. A single man has not nearly the value he would have in the state of union. He is an incomplete animal. He resembles the odd half of a pair of scissors. If you get a prudent, healthy wife, your industry in your profession, with her good economy, will be a fortune sufficient.

But if you will not take this counsel and persist in thinking a commerce with the sex inevitable, then I repeat my former advice, that in all your amours you should prefer old women to young ones.

You call this a paradox and demand my reasons. They are these:

1. Because they have more knowledge of the world, and their minds are better stored with observations, their conversation is more improving and more lastingly agreeable.

2. Because when women cease to be handsome they study to be good. To maintain their influence over men, they supply the diminution of beauty by an augmentation of utility. They learn to do a thousand services small and great, and are the most tender and useful of friends when you are sick. Thus they continue amiable. And hence there is hardly such a thing to be found as an old woman who is not a good woman.

3. Because there is no hazard of children, which irregularly produced may be attended with much inconvenience.

4. Because through more experience they are more prudent and discreet in conducting an intrigue to prevent suspicion. The commerce with them is therefore safer with regard to your reputation. And with regard to theirs, if the affair should happen to be known, considerate people might be rather inclined to excuse an old woman, who would kindly take care of a young man, form his manners by her good counsels, and prevent his ruining his health and fortune among mercenary prostitutes.

5. Because in every animal that walks upright the deficiency of the fluids that fill the muscles appears first in the highest part. The face first grows lank and wrinkled; then the neck; then the breast and arms; so that covering all above with a basket, and regarding only what is below the girdle, it is impossible of two women to tell an old one from a young one. As in the dark all cats are gray, the pleasure of corporal enjoyment with an old woman is at least equal, and frequently superior; every knack being, by practice, capable of improvement.

6. Because the sin is less. The debauching a virgin may be her ruin, and make her for life unhappy.

7. Because the compunction is less. The having made a young girl miserable may give you frequent bitter reflection; none of which can attend the making an old woman happy.

8th and lastly. They are so grateful!!

Thus much for my paradox. But still I advise you to marry directly; being sincerely

Your affectionate friend,
B. Franklin

"What Are the Poor Young Women to Do?"
The Speech of Polly Baker

1747

The speech of Miss Polly Baker before a Court of Judicature, at Connecticut near Boston in New England; where she was prosecuted the fifth time for having a bastard child: Which influenced the court to dispense with her punishment, and which induced one of her judges to marry her the next day—by whom she had fifteen children.

"May it please the honorable bench to indulge me in a few words: I am a poor, unhappy woman,[1] who have no money to fee lawyers to plead for me, being hard put to it to get a living. I shall not trouble your honors with long speeches; for I have not the presumption to expect that you may, by any means, be prevailed on to deviate in your sentence from the law, in my favor. All I humbly hope is that your honors would charitably move the governor's goodness on my behalf, that my fine may be remitted. This is the fifth time, gentlemen, that I have been dragged before your court on the same account; twice I have paid heavy fines, and twice have been brought to public punishment, for want[2] of money to pay those fines. This may have been agreeable to the laws, and I don't dispute it; but since laws are sometimes unreasonable in themselves, and therefore repealed; and others bear too hard on the subject in particular circumstances, and therefore there is left a power somewhere to dispense with the execution of them; I take the liberty to say that I think this law, by which I am punished, both unreasonable in itself, and particularly severe with regard to me, who have always lived an inoffensive life in the neighborhood where I was born, and defy my enemies (if I have any) to say I ever wronged any man, woman, or child. Abstracted from the law, I cannot conceive (may it please your honors) what the nature of my offense is. I have brought five fine children into the world, at the risk of my life; I have maintained them well by my own industry, without burdening the township, and would have done it better if it had not been for the heavy charges and fines I have paid. Can it be a crime (in the nature of things, I mean) to add to the king's subjects, in a new country, that really wants[3] people? I own it, I should think it rather a praiseworthy than a punishable action. I have debauched no other woman's husband, nor enticed any other youth; these things I never was charged with; nor has anyone the least cause of complaint against me, unless, perhaps, the ministers of justice, because I have had children without being married, by which they have missed a wedding fee. But can this be a fault of mine? I appeal to your honors. You are pleased to allow I don't want[4] sense; but I must be stupefied to the last degree, not to prefer the honorable state of wedlock to the condition I have

---

[1]Franklin here impersonates a woman.

[2]Lack.

[3]Needs.

[4]Lack.

lived in. I always was, and still am, willing to enter into it; and doubt not my behaving well in it, having all the industry, frugality, fertility, and skill in economy appertaining to a good wife's character. I defy anyone to say I ever refused an offer of the sort: on the contrary, I readily consented to the only proposal of marriage that ever was made me, which was when I was a virgin, but too easily confiding in the person's sincerity that made it, I unhappily lost my honor by trusting to his; for he got me with child, and then forsook me.

"That very person, you all know, he is now become a magistrate of this country; and I had hopes he would have appeared this day on the bench, and have endeavored to moderate the court in my favor; then I should have scorned to have mentioned it; but I must now complain of it, as unjust and unequal, that my betrayer and undoer, the first cause of all my faults and miscarriages (if they must be deemed such), should be advanced to honor and power in this government that punishes my misfortunes with stripes and infamy. I should be told, 'tis like, that were there no act of assembly in the case, the precepts of religion are violated by my transgressions. If mine is a religious offense, leave it to religious punishments. You have already excluded me from the comforts of your church communion. Is not that sufficient? You believe I have offended heaven, and must suffer eternal fire: Will not that be sufficient? What need is there then of your additional fines and whipping? I own I do not think as you do, for, if I thought what you call a sin was really such, I could not presumptuously commit it. But, how can it be believed that heaven is angry at my having children, when to the little done by me toward it, God has been pleased to add his divine skill and admirable workmanship in the formation of their bodies, and crowned the whole by furnishing them with rational and immortal souls?

"Forgive me, gentlemen, if I talk a little extravagantly on these matters; I am no divine, but if you, gentlemen, must be making laws, do not turn natural and useful actions into crimes by your prohibitions. But take into your wise consideration the great and growing number of bachelors in the country, many of whom, from the mean fear of the expenses of a family, have never sincerely and honorably courted a woman in their lives; and by their manner of living leave unproduced (which is little better than murder) hundreds of their posterity to the thousandth generation. Is not this a greater offense against the public good than mine? Compel them, then, by law, either to marriage, or to pay double the fine of fornication every year. What must poor young women do, whom customs and nature forbid to solicit the men, and who cannot force themselves upon husbands, when the laws take no care to provide them any, and yet severely punish them if they do their duty without them; the duty of the first and great command of nature and nature's God, *increase and multiply*; a duty, from the steady performance of which nothing has been able to deter me, but for its sake I have hazarded the loss of the public esteem, and have frequently endured public disgrace and punishment; and therefore ought, in my humble opinion, instead of a whipping, to have a statue erected to my memory." ✒

How to Get the Most Out of Reading

To Miss Mary Stevenson[1]   Craven Street London, May 17, 1760

I send my good girl the books I mentioned to her last night. I beg her to accept them as a small mark of my esteem and friendship. They are written in the familiar, easy manner, for which the French are so remarkable, and afford a good deal of philosophic and practical knowledge, unembarrassed with the dry mathematics used by more exact reasoners, but which is apt to discourage young beginners.

I would advise you to read with a pen in your hand, and enter in a little book short hints of what you find that is curious, or that may be useful; for this will be the best method of imprinting such particulars in your memory, where they will be ready, either for practice on some future occasion, if they are matters of utility, or at least to adorn and improve your conversation, if they are rather points of curiosity. And, as many of the terms of science are such as you cannot have met with in your common reading and may therefore be unacquainted with, I think it would be well for you to have a good dictionary at hand, to consult immediately when you meet with a word you do not comprehend the precise meaning of. This may at first seem troublesome and interrupting; but it is a trouble that will daily diminish, as you will daily find less and less occasion for your dictionary, as you become more acquainted with the terms; and in the meantime you will read with more satisfaction, because with more understanding.

When any point occurs, in which you would be glad to have further information than your book affords you, I beg you would not in the least apprehend that I should think it a trouble to receive and answer your questions. It will be a pleasure and no trouble. For though I may not be able, out of my own little stock of knowledge, to afford you what you require, I can easily direct you to the books where it may most readily be found. Adieu, and believe me ever, my dear friend, yours affectionately,

B. Franklin

Early Marriages Are Happy Ones

To John Alleyne   Craven Street, August 9, 1768

Dear Jack:

You desire, you say, my impartial thoughts on the subject of an early marriage, by way of answer to the numberless objections that have been made by numerous persons to your own. You may remember, when you consulted me on the occasion, that I thought youth, on both sides, to be no objection. Indeed, from the matches that have fallen under my observation, I am rather inclined to think

---

[1]She was about eighteen at the time.

that early ones stand the best chance for happiness. The tempers and habits of young people are not yet become so stiff and uncomplying as when more advanced in life; they form more easily to each other, and hence many occasions of disgust are removed. And if youth has less of that prudence that is necessary to manage a family, yet the parents and elder friends of young married persons are generally at hand to afford their advice, which amply supplies that defect; and by early marriage youth is sooner formed to regular and useful life; and possibly some of those accidents, or connections, that might have injured either the constitution, or the reputation, or both, are thereby happily prevented.

Particular circumstances of particular persons may, possibly, sometimes make it prudent to delay entering into that state; but in general, when nature has rendered our bodies fit for it, the presumption is in nature's favor, that she has not judged amiss in making us desire it. Late marriages are often attended, too, with this further inconvenience, that there is not the same chance that the parents shall live to see their offspring educated. "*Late children*," says the Spanish proverb, "*are early orphans*." A melancholy reflection to those whose case it may be!

With us in America, marriages are generally in the morning of life; our children are therefore educated and settled in the world by noon; and thus, our business being done, we have an afternoon and evening of cheerful leisure to ourselves; such as our friend at present enjoys. By these early marriages we are blest with more children; and from the mode among us, founded by nature, of every mother suckling and nursing her own child, more of them are raised. Thence the swift progress of population among us, unparalleled in Europe. In fine, I am glad you are married, and congratulate you most cordially upon it. You are now in the way of becoming a useful citizen; and you have escaped the unnatural state of celibacy for life,—the fate of many here, who never intended it, but who, having too long postponed the change of their condition, find at length that it is too late to think of it, and so live all their lives in a situation that greatly lessens a man's value. An odd volume of a set of books bears not the value of its proportion of the set, and what think you of the odd half of a pair of scissors? it can't well cut anything; it may possibly serve to scrape a trencher.[1]

Pray make my compliments and best wishes acceptable to your bride. I am old and heavy, or I should ere this have presented them in person. I shall make but small use of the old man's privilege, that of giving advice to younger friends. Treat your wife always with respect; it will procure respect to you, not from her only but from all that observe it. Never use a slighting expression to her, even in jest; for slights in jest, after frequent bandyings, are apt to end in angry earnest. Be studious in your profession, and you will be learned. Be industrious and frugal, and you will be rich. Be sober and temperate, and you will be healthy. Be in general virtuous, and you will be happy. At least, you will, by such conduct, stand the best chance for such consequences.

I pray God to bless you both; being ever your affectionate friend,

B. Franklin ✒

---

[1]A wooden plate.

Restoration of Life by Sun Rays

To Jaques Barbeu Dubourg[1]   London, 1773

Dear Sir:

Your observations on the causes of death, and the experiments which you propose for recalling to life those who appear to be killed by lightning, demonstrate equally your sagacity and your humanity. It appears that the doctrines of life and death in general are yet but little understood.

A toad buried in sand will live, it is said, till the sand becomes petrified; and then, being enclosed in the stone, it may still live for we know not how many ages. The facts which are cited in support of this opinion are too numerous, and too circumstantial, not to deserve a certain degree of credit. As we are accustomed to see all the animals with which we are acquainted eat and drink, it appears to us difficult to conceive how a toad can be supported in such a dungeon; but if we reflect that the necessity of nourishment which animals experience in their ordinary state proceeds from the continual waste of their substance by perspiration, it will appear less incredible that some animals in a torpid state, perspiring less because they use no exercise, should have less need of aliment; and that others, which are covered with scales or shells, which stop perspiration, such as land and sea turtles, serpents, and some species of fish, should be able to subsist a considerable time without any nourishment whatever. A plant, with its flowers, fades and dies immediately if exposed to the air without having its root immersed in a humid soil, for which it may draw a sufficient quantity of moisture to supply that which exhales from its substance and is carried off continually by the air. Perhaps, however, if it were buried in quicksilver, it might preserve for a considerable space of time its vegetable life, its smell, and color. If this be the case it might prove a commodious[2] method of transporting from distant countries those delicate plants which are unable to sustain the inclemency of the weather at sea and which require particular care and attention. I have seen an instance of common flies preserved in a manner somewhat similar. They had been drowned in Madeira wine, apparently about the time when it was bottled in Virginia, to be sent hither (to London). At the opening of one of the bottles, at the house of a friend where I then was, three drowned flies fell into the first glass that was filled. Having heard it remarked that drowned flies were capable of being revived by the rays of the sun, I proposed making the experiment upon these; they were therefore exposed to the sun upon a sieve, which had been employed to strain them out of the wine. In less than three hours, two of them began by degrees to recover life. They commenced by some convulsive motions of the thighs, and at length they

---

[1]French doctor and botanist (1709–1779), author of *Le Botanist français*. He helped Franklin secure the aid of France in the American Revolution and edited *Oeuvres de Franklin*, translated by L'Ecuy and published in 1773.

[2]Convenient.

raised themselves upon their legs, wiped their eyes with their fore feet, beat and brushed their wings with their hind feet, and soon after began to fly, finding themselves in Old England, without knowing how they came thither. The third continued lifeless till sunset, when, losing all hopes of him, he was thrown away.

I wish it were possible, from this instance, to invent a method of embalming drowned persons in such a manner that they may be recalled to life at any period, however distant; for having a very ardent desire to see and observe the state of America a hundred years hence, I should prefer to any ordinary death the being immersed in a cask of Madeira wine, with a few friends, till that time, to be then recalled to life by the solar warmth of my dear country! But since in all probability we live in an age too early and too near the infancy of science to hope to see such an art brought in our time to its perfection, I must for the present content myself with the treat, which you are so kind as to promise me, of the resurrection of a fowl or a turkey cock.

> I am, &c.,
> B. Franklin ✎

The Handsome and Deformed Leg

1780

There are two sorts of people in the world, who with equal degrees of health, and wealth, and the other comforts of life, become, the one happy, and the other miserable. This arises very much from the different views in which they consider things, persons, and events; and the effect of those different views upon their own minds.

In whatever situation men can be placed, they may find conveniencies and inconveniencies: in whatever company, they may find persons and conversation more or less pleasing; at whatever table, they may meet with meats and drinks of better and worse taste, dishes better and worse dressed; in whatever climate they will find good and bad weather; under whatever government, they may find good and bad laws, and good and bad administration of those laws; in whatever poem or work of genius they may see faults and beauties; in almost every face and every person, they may discover fine features and defects, good and bad qualities.

Under these circumstances, the two sorts of people above mentioned fix their attention,—those who are disposed to be happy, on the conveniencies of things, the pleasant parts of conversation, the well-dressed dishes, the goodness of the wines, the fine weather, etc., and enjoy all with cheerfulness. Those who are to be unhappy, think and speak only of the contraries. Hence they are continually discontented themselves, and by their remarks sour the pleasures of society, offend personally many people, and make themselves everywhere disagreeable.

If this turn of mind was founded in nature, such unhappy persons would be the more to be pitied. But as the disposition to criticize and to be disgusted, is perhaps taken up originally by imitation, and is unawares grown into a habit, which though at present strong may nevertheless be cured when those who have it are convinced of its bad effects on their felicity, I hope this little admonition may be of service to them, and put them on changing a habit, which, though in the exercise it is chiefly an act of imagination, yet has serious consequences in life, as it brings on real griefs and misfortunes. For as many are offended by, and nobody well loves this sort of people, no one shows them more than the most common civility and respect, and scarcely that; and this frequently puts them out of humor, and draws them into disputes and contentions. If they aim at obtaining some advantage in rank or fortune, nobody wishes them success, or will stir a step, or speak a word, to favor their pretensions. If they incur public censure or disgrace, no one will defend or excuse, and many join to aggravate their misconduct and render them completely odious.

If these people will not change this bad habit, and condescend to be pleased with what is pleasing, without fretting themselves and others about the contraries, it is good for others to avoid an acquaintance with them, which is always disagreeable, and sometimes very inconvenient, especially when one finds one's self entangled in their quarrels.

An old philosophical friend of mine was grown from experience very cautious in this particular, and carefully avoided any intimacy with such people. He had, like other philosophers, a thermometer to show him the heat of the weather, and a barometer to mark when it was likely to prove good or bad; but, there being no instrument invented to discover, at first sight, this unpleasing disposition in a person, he for that purpose made use of his legs; one of which was remarkably handsome, the other by some accident, crooked and deformed. If a stranger, at the first interview, regarded his ugly leg more than his handsome one, he doubted him. If he spoke of it, and took no notice of the handsome leg, that was sufficient to determine my philosopher to have no further acquaintance with him. Everybody has not this two-legged instrument; but everyone, with a little attention, may observe signs of that carping, fault-finding disposition, and take the same resolution of avoiding the acquaintance of those infected with it. I therefore advise those critical, querulous, discontented, unhappy people, that if they wish to be respected and beloved by others, and happy in themselves, they should *leave off looking at the ugly leg.* ✒

The Savages of North America

Savages we call them, because their manners differ from ours, which we think the perfection of civility; they think the same of theirs.

Perhaps, if we could examine the manners of different nations with impartiality, we should find no people so rude as to be without any rules of politeness, nor any so polite as not to have some remains of rudeness.

The Indian men, when young, are hunters and warriors; when old, council-lors; for all their government is by the council or advice of the sages; there is no force, there are no prisons, no officers to compel obedience, or inflict punish-ment. Hence, they generally study oratory, —the best speaker having the most influence. The Indian women till the ground, dress the food, nurse and bring up the children, and preserve and hand down to posterity the memory of public transactions. These employments of men and women are accounted natural and honorable. Having few artificial wants, they have abundance of leisure for im-provement by conversation.

Our laborious manner of life, compared with theirs, they esteem slavish and base; and the learning on which we value ourselves they regard as frivolous and useless. An instance of this occurred at the treaty of Lancaster, in Pennsylvania, anno 1749, between the government of Virginia and the Six Nations. After the principal business was settled, the commissioners from Virginia acquainted the Indians, by a speech, that there was at Williamsburg a college, with a fund, for educating Indian youth; and that, if the chiefs of the Six Nations would send down half a dozen of their sons to that college, the government would take care that they should be well provided for, and instructed in all the learning of the white people.

It is one of the Indian rules of politeness not to answer a public proposition the same day that it is made; they think it would be treating it as a light matter, and that they show it respect by taking time to consider it, as of a matter important. They therefore deferred their answer till the day following; when their speaker began by expressing their deep sense of the kindness of the Virginia government, in making them that offer; "for we know," says he, "that you highly esteem the kind of learning taught in those colleges, and that the maintenance of our young men, while with you, would be very expensive to you; we are convinced, therefore, that you mean to do us good by your proposal, and we thank you heartily. But you, who are wise, must know that different nations have different conceptions of things; and you will therefore not take it amiss if our ideas of this kind of education happen not to be the same with yours. We have had some experience of it; several of our young people were formerly brought up at the colleges of the northern provinces; they were instructed in all your sciences, but when they came back to us they were bad runners, ignorant of every means of living in the woods, unable to bear either cold or hunger, knew neither how to build a cabin, take a deer, or kill an enemy, spoke our language imperfectly, —were therefore neither fit for hunters, warriors, nor councillors; they were totally good for nothing. We are, however, not the less obliged by your kind offer, though we decline accepting it; and, to show our grateful sense of it, if the gentlemen of Virginia will send us a dozen of their sons, we will take great care of their education, instruct them in all we know, and make *men* of them."

Having frequent occasions to hold public councils, they have acquired great order and decency in conducting them. The old men sit in the foremost ranks, the warriors in the next, and the women and children in the hindmost. The business of the women is to take exact notice of what passes, imprint it in their memo-ries, —for they have no writing, —and communicate it to their children. They are the records of the council, and they preserve the tradition of the stipulations in treaties a hundred years back; which, when we compare with our writings, we always find exact. He that would speak rises. The rest observe a profound silence. When he has finished and sits down, they leave him five or six minutes to recollect, that, if he has omitted anything he intended to say, or has anything to add, he may rise again and deliver it. To interrupt another, even in common conversation, is reckoned highly indecent. How different this is from the conduct of a polite British House of Commons, where scarce a day passes without some confusion, that makes the speaker hoarse in calling *to order*; and how different from the mode of conversation in many polite companies of Europe, where, if you do not deliver your sentence with great rapidity, you are cut off in the middle of it by the impatient loquacity of those you converse with, and never suffered to finish it!

The politeness of these savages in conversation is indeed carried to excess, since it does not permit them to contradict or deny the truth of what is asserted in their presence. By this means they indeed avoid disputes; but then it becomes difficult to know their minds, or what impression you make upon them. The missionaries who have attempted to convert them to Christianity all complain of this as one of the great difficulties of their mission. The Indians hear with patience the truths of the gospel explained to them, and give their usual tokens of assent and approbation; you would think they were convinced. No such matter. It is mere civility.

A Swedish minister, having assembled the chiefs of the Susquehanna Indians, made a sermon to them, acquainting them with the principal historical facts on which our religion is founded; such as the fall of our first parents by eating an apple, the coming of Christ to repair the mischief, his miracles and suffering, &c. When he had finished, an Indian orator stood up to thank him. "What you have told us," says he, "is all very good. It is indeed bad to eat apples. It is better to make them all into cider. We are much obliged by your kindness in coming so far to tell us those things which you have heard from your mothers. In return, I will tell you some of those we have heard from ours.

"In the beginning, our fathers had only the flesh of animals to subsist on, and, if their hunting was unsuccessful, they were starving. Two of our young hunters, having killed a deer, made a fire in the woods to broil some parts of it. When they were about to satisfy their hunger they beheld a beautiful young woman descend from the clouds, and seat herself on that hill which you see yonder among the Blue Mountains. They said to each other, 'It is a spirit that perhaps has smelt our broiling venison, and wishes to eat of it; let us offer some to her.' They presented her with the tongue: she was pleased with the taste of it, and said, 'Your kindness shall be rewarded; come to this place after thirteen moons, and you shall find something that will be of great benefit in nourishing you and your children to the latest generations.' They did so, and, to their surprise, found plants they had never seen before, but which, from that ancient time, have been constantly cultivated among us, to our great advantage. Where her right hand had touched it they found maize, where her left hand had touched it they found kidney-beans, and where her backside had sat on it they found tobacco."

The good missionary, disgusted with this idle tale, said: "What I delivered to you were sacred truths; but what you tell me is mere fable, fiction and falsehood."

The Indian, offended, replied: "My brother, it seems your friends have not done you justice in your education; they have not well instructed you in the rules of common civility. You saw that we, who understand and practise those rules, believed all your stories; why do you refuse to believe ours?"

When any of them come into our towns, our people are apt to crowd round them, gaze upon them, and incommode them where they desire to be private; this they esteem great rudeness, and the effect of the want[1] of instruction in the rules of civility and good manners. "We have," say they, "as much curiosity as you, and when you come into our towns we wish for opportunities of looking at you; but for this purpose we hide ourselves behind bushes where you are to pass, and never intrude ourselves into your company."

Their manner of entering one another's villages has likewise its rules. It is reckoned uncivil, in travelling strangers, to enter a village abruptly, without giving notice of their approach. Therefore, as soon as they arrive within hearing, they stop and halloo, remaining there till invited to enter. Two old men usually come out to them, and lead them in. There is in every village a vacant dwelling, called the stranger's house. Here they are placed, while the old men go round from hut to hut, acquainting the inhabitants that strangers are arrived, who are probably hungry and weary; and every one sends them what he can spare of victuals, and skins to repose on. When the strangers are refreshed, pipes and tobacco are brought; and then, but not before, conversation begins, with inquiries who they are, whither bound, what news, &c., and it usually ends with offers of service, if the strangers have occasion for guides, or any necessaries for continuing their journey; and nothing is exacted for the entertainment.

The same hospitality, esteemed among them as a principal virtue, is practised by private persons; of which *Conrad Weiser*, our interpreter, gave me the following instance. He had been naturalized among the Six Nations, and spoke well the Mohawk language. In going through the Indian country, to carry a message from our governor to the council at Onondaga, he called at the habitation of Canassetego, an old acquaintance, who embraced him, spread furs for him to sit on, and placed before him some boiled beans and venison, and mixed some rum and water for his drink. When he was well refreshed, and had lit his pipe, Canassetego began to converse with him; asked how he had fared the many years since they had seen each other, whence he then came, what occasioned the journey, &c. Conrad answered all his questions, and, when the discourse began to flag, the Indian, to continue it, said: "Conrad, you have lived long among the white people, and know something of their customs; I have been sometimes at Albany, and have observed that once in seven days they shut up their shops, and assemble all in the great house; tell me what it is for. What do they do there?"

"They meet there," says Conrad, "to hear and learn *good things*."

---

[1]Lack.

"I do not doubt," says the Indian, "that they tell you so; they have told me the same; but I doubt the truth of what they say, and I will tell you my reasons. I went lately to Albany, to sell my skins, and buy blankets, knives, powder, rum, &c. You know I used generally to deal with Hans Hanson, but I was a little inclined this time to try some other merchants. However, I called first upon Hans, and asked him what he would give for beaver. He said he could not give any more than four shillings a pound; but, says he, I cannot talk on business now; this is the day when we meet together to learn *good things*, and I am going to meeting. So I thought to myself, since I cannot do any business to-day, I may as well go to the meeting too, and I went with him.

"There stood up a man in black, and began to talk to the people very angrily. I did not understand what he said; but, perceiving that he looked much at me and at Hanson I imagined he was angry at seeing me there. So I went out, sat down near the house, struck fire, and lit my pipe, waiting till the meeting should break up. I thought, too, that the man had mentioned something of beaver, and I suspected it might be the subject of their meeting. So, when they came out, I accosted my merchant. 'Well, Hans,' says I, 'I hope you have agreed to give more than four shillings a pound?' 'No,' says he, 'I cannot give so much; I cannot give more than three shillings and sixpence.' I then spoke to several other dealers; but they all sung the same song,—three and sixpence,—three and sixpence. This made it clear to me that my suspicion was right; and that, whatever they pretended of meeting to learn *good things*, the real purpose was to consult how to cheat Indians in the price of beaver. Consider but a little, Conrad, and you must be of my opinion. If they met so often to learn *good things*, they would certainly have learned some before this time. But they are still ignorant. You know our practice.

"If a white man, in travelling through our country, enters one of our cabins, we all treat him as I do you; we dry him if he is wet, we warm him if he is cold, and give him meat and drink that he may allay his thirst and hunger, and we spread soft furs for him to rest and sleep on: we demand nothing in return. But, if I go into a white man's house at Albany, and ask for victuals and drink, they say, 'Where is your money?' and, if I have none, they say, 'Get out, you Indian dog!' You see they have not yet learned those little *good things* that we need no meetings to be instructed in, because our mothers taught them to us, when we were children; and, therefore, it is impossible their meetings should be, as they say, for any such purpose, or have any such effect; they are only to contrive *the cheating of Indians in the price of beaver*." ✐

On Perfumes

A Letter to the Royal Academy of Brussels

Gentlemen:

I have perused your late mathematical prize question, proposed in lieu of one in natural philosophy for the ensuing year, viz: "*Une figure quelconque donnée, on demande d'y inscrire le plus grand nombre de fois possible une autre figure plus petite quelconque, qui est aussi donnée.*"[1]

I was glad to find by these following words, "*L'Académie a jugé que cette découverte, en étendant les bornes de nos connoissances, ne seroit pas sans utilité,*"[2] that you esteem *utility* an essential point in your inquiries, which has not always been the case with all academies; and I conclude therefore that you have given this question instead of a philosophical, or, as the learned express it, a *physical* one, because you could not at the time think of a physical one that promised greater *utility*.

Permit me then humbly to propose one of that sort for your consideration, and through you, if you approve it, for the serious inquiry of learned physicians, chemists, etc., of this enlightened age.

It is universally well known that, in digesting our common food, there is created or produced in the bowels of human creatures a great quantity of wind.

That the permitting this air to escape and mix with the atmosphere is usually offensive to the company, from the fetid smell that accompanies it.

That all well-bred people therefore, to avoid giving such offense, forcibly restrain the efforts of nature to discharge that wind.

That so retained contrary to nature, it not only gives frequently great present pain, but occasions future diseases such as habitual cholics,[3] ruptures, tympanies,[4] etc., often destructive of the constitution, and sometimes of life itself.

Were it not for the odiously offensive smell accompanying such escapes, polite people would probably be under no more restraint in discharging such wind in company than they are in spitting or in blowing their noses.

My prize question therefore should be: To discover some drug, wholesome and not disagreeable, to be mixed with our common food, or sauces, that shall render the natural discharges of wind from our bodies not only inoffensive, but agreeable as perfumes.

---

[1] "For whatever figure given, inscribe therein the greatest number of times possible another figure smaller than the first which is also given."

[2] "The Academy has ruled that this discovery, in extending the boundaries of our knowledge, will not be without use."

[3] Stomach pain.

[4] Swellings.

That this is not a chimerical project and altogether impossible, may appear from these considerations. That we already have some knowledge of means capable of *varying* that smell. He that dines on stale flesh, especially with much addition of onions, shall be able to afford a stink that no company can tolerate; while he that has lived for some time on vegetables only, shall have that breath so pure as to be insensible to the most delicate noses; and if he can manage so as to avoid the report,[1] he may anywhere give vent to his griefs, unnoticed. But as there are many to whom an entire vegetable diet would be inconvenient, and as a little quicklime thrown into a jakes[2] will correct the amazing quantity of fetid air arising from the vast mass of putrid matter contained in such places, and render it rather pleasing to the smell, who knows but that a little powder of lime (or some other thing equivalent), taken in our food, perhaps a glass of limewater drunk at dinner, may have the same effect on the air produced in and issuing from our bowels? This is worth the experiment. Certain it is also that we have the power of changing by slight means the smell of another discharge, that of our water. A few stems of asparagus eaten shall give our urine a disagreeable odor; and a pill of turpentine no bigger than a pea shall bestow on it the pleasing smell of violets. And why should it be thought more impossible in nature to find means of making perfume of our wind than of our water?

For the encouragement of this inquiry (from the immortal honor to be reasonably expected by the inventor), let it be considered of how small importance to mankind, or to how small a part of mankind have been useful those discoveries in science that have heretofore made philosophers famous. Are there twenty men in Europe this day the happier, or even the easier, for any knowledge they have picked out of Aristotle?° What comfort can the vortices of Descartes° give to a man who has whirlwinds in his bowels! The knowledge of Newton's° mutual *attraction* of the particles of matter, can it afford ease to him who is racked by their mutual *repulsion*, and the cruel distensions it occasions? The pleasure arising to a few philosophers, from seeing, a few times in their lives, the threads of light untwisted, and separated by the Newtonian° prism into seven colors, can it be compared with the ease and comfort every man living might feel seven times a day, by discharging freely the wind from his bowels? Especially if it be converted into a perfume; for the pleasures of one sense being little inferior to those of another, instead of pleasing the *sight*, he might delight the *smell* of those about him, and make numbers happy, which to a benevolent mind must afford infinite satisfaction. The generous soul, who now endeavors to find out whether the friends he entertains like best claret or Burgundy, champagne or Madeira, would then inquire also whether they chose musk or lily, rose or bergamot, and provide

---

[1]Sound.
[2]Latrine.

accordingly. And surely such a liberty of *ex-pressing one's scent-iments, and pleasing one another*, is of infinitely more importance to human happiness than that liberty of the *press*, or of *abusing one another*, which the English are so ready to fight and die for.

In short, this invention, if completed, would be, as *Bacon* expresses it, *bringing philosophy home to men's business and bosoms.*[1] And I cannot but conclude that in comparison therewith for *universal* and *continual utility*, the science of the philosophers abovementioned, even with the addition, gentlemen, of your "*figure quelconque*," and the figures inscribed in it, are, all together, scarcely worth a   Fart-hing. ✍

---

[1]From Bacon's dedication to the 1625 edition of his *Essays*.

Samuel Johnson

(1709 – 1784)

Samuel Johnson, the older of two sons of a struggling bookseller in Lichfield, began his life in distress, suffering from the sores of scrofula, deafness in one ear, near blindness in one eye, and a melancholy, inherited, he believed, from his father, which oppressed him all his life. At Lichfield Grammar School, where Addison had also studied, he learned much under the whip of the schoolmaster, and thus became convinced that punishment, unlike praise, reduces unpleasant rivalry. He also attended Stourbridge Grammar School in Worcestershire and entered Pembroke College, Oxford, as a commoner in 1728, using funds supplied by a small legacy to his mother. During his time at Oxford, plagued by poverty and a newly discovered religious intensity, he suffered a breakdown and sent a description of it in Latin to his godfather, Dr. Swynfen. In 1731 he returned home without a degree and without a career in mind.

Although the pride of his parents, Johnson was clearly unfit for the tedium of a bookseller, more interested in reading than in selling books. His father, now seventy-four, was so poor that he had to accept grants from a charitable trust and so ill that he could not always get up from bed. When his father asked him one day to go to a bookstall some distance away to try to sell some books, Samuel refused, and shortly after, in December of 1731, Michael Johnson died. Fifty years later, Samuel Johnson spent an hour in the crowded marketplace on the spot where the bookstall had been, head bare in unpleasant weather, subject to the ridicule of passersby, to atone at last for his youthful arrogance.

Uncertain of his future, Johnson spent the next few years in fitful indolence, working for a time at a school and, at a friend's insistence, completing a translation from the French of Father Lobo's *Voyage to Abyssinia*. In 1735 he married Elizabeth Jervis Porter, forty-five, the widow of his friend Harry, much to the dismay of her family, particularly her two sons,

Jervis Henry, seventeen, and Joseph, eleven. Only her daughter, Lucy, nine-teen, approved of Elizabeth's marriage to this poor, odd young man whom Lucy later described to Boswell as "lean and lank, so that his immense structure of bones was hideously striking to the eye, and the scars of scrophula were deeply visible. He also wore his hair,[1] which was straight and stiff, and separated behind; and he often had, seemingly, convulsive starts and odd gesticulations, which tended to excite at once surprize and ridi-cule." Nevertheless, Mrs. Porter told Lucy that he was "the most sensible man that I ever saw in my life."

Mrs. Porter brought with her enough money to give Johnson financial security, at least for a time, and the two opened a private school in Edial, where David Garrick was a pupil and where Johnson worked on his tragedy *Irene*. In that same year, 1736, Johnson's younger brother, Nathaniel, set up shop as a bookseller in Stourbridge, suffering, as his father had before him, from financial difficulties. Poverty had its effects on both brothers: while Samuel tortured himself with guilt over his indolence, Nathaniel apparently resorted to immoral behavior, possibly even forgery, to overcome his debts, and the following year he died mysteriously at the age of twenty-five.

When the school failed, Johnson went to London with Garrick to earn his living as a writer. He contributed anonymously to *Gentleman's Magazine* and published a variety of material, including *An Account of the Life of Mr. Richard Savage* in 1744, the Prologue for the opening of Garrick's Drury Lane Theatre and the *Plan of a Dictionary of the English Language* in 1747, and *The Vanity of Human Wishes*, his first signed work, in 1749. Meanwhile his marriage to Elizabeth deteriorated as she aged, took to drink, and isolated herself in her bed, unable even to attend Garrick's staging of *Irene*. Johnson spent most of the money he earned trying to provide his wife with the comforts she had been used to before their marriage had separated her from her family, friends, and former way of life. He was at this time at work on the *Dictionary*, which he published in 1755, and on the essays due twice weekly for *The Rambler*. Amid all this activity, Johnson continued to battle his melancholy and indolence; too often, he finished the last pages of these essays while the messenger from the printer waited, hand extended, at the door (see, for instance, No. 134). However hurriedly written, the *Rambler* essays particularly pleased his ailing wife; she died in March of 1752, two weeks after the last one was published.

In the years following his wife's death Johnson filled his house with people in need; he had at one time four permanent and quarreling guests: the blind and elderly Anna Williams, the impecunious and silent Dr. Levett, the widowed daughter of his godfather, Mrs. Desmoulins, and a Miss Car-michael, probably a prostitute Johnson had found lying ill on the streets of London. The household also included two elderly servants who depended

---

[1]Had no wig.

on Johnson, as well as Francis Barber, his Negro servant whom he had raised and educated, and, years later, Barber's wife and children. Others came and went. Often at the edge of poverty himself, Johnson was arrested for debt in 1759 and saved from prison by the loan of six guineas from Samuel Richardson. To supplement the meager funds earned by writing essays for *The Idler* between 1758 and 1760, he published *Rasselas*, claiming "No man but a blockhead ever wrote except for money."

In 1760 he met Benjamin Franklin, whose work on electricity he had admired. Johnson was himself a member of a society devoted to the practical use of scientific discoveries and later briefly experimented with chemicals in the Thrales'[1] backyard. He was not, however, a supporter of the colonies, because, among other reasons, he abhorred the slavery on the plantations. In fact, the meeting of the two men, as recorded in a letter from Franklin to his wife, took place at a gathering of the associates of Dr. Bray,[2] a philanthropical group devoted to the improvement of the status of Negroes. Neither man then suspected that the colonies would separate from Britain, though more than ten years later, while Franklin was a delegate to the Continental Congress, Johnson was writing *Taxation No Tyranny* in support of King George.

Finally, in 1762 Johnson was granted a royal pension that, along with his friendship with Boswell begun in 1763 and with the Thrales in 1765, led to a more comfortable existence for Johnson and his eccentric household. Largely because of Boswell's remarkable biography of Johnson, he is best known for his odd, slovenly appearance and his witty conversation. When Boswell began taking his notes on his subject, Johnson was at the height of his celebrity; in 1764 he established his famous Literary Club with Reynolds, Burke,° Goldsmith,° and others, and in 1765 he published his long-awaited edition of Shakespeare. In 1773, at age sixty-four, Johnson toured Scotland and the Hebrides with Boswell, publishing his description of the journey in 1775. That was also the year Oxford granted him a doctoral degree in civil law (he'd received an LL.D. from Dublin in 1765), and he was thereafter known as Dr. Johnson. His last major work, *The Lives of the Poets*, was completed in 1781. During the final years of his life, Johnson suffered from his recurrent melancholia as well as from a variety of diseases of the circulation and lungs, but he retained his mental acuity, his wit, and his religious resolve to the end of his days.

Twentieth-century biographers of Johnson, such as Walter Jackson Bate,[3] led critics beyond Boswell's vision of Johnson the conversationalist to a reexamination of Johnson's writing and a reappraisal of his style, including that of his *Rambler* essays, which in the nineteenth century were readily

---

[1] Close friends.

[2] See Maurice J. Quinlan, "Johnson's American Acquaintances" in *Johnson, Boswell, and Their Circle,* Oxford, 1965.

[3] Most of the facts in this biography are derived from Bate's *Samuel Johnson.*

dismissed as too ponderous to appeal. These essays are indeed full of the latinate diction Johnson defended as "useful" and "significant," though sometimes "superfluous," in his biography of Browne. But they are also, like Addison's, directed to the middle-class reading public, and intended, again like Addison's, to teach and delight his audience. They succeed in both. More formal than Addison's in tone, Johnson's voice recalls that of Bacon, for both men speak eloquently about great truths applicable to all men. But, where Bacon is concise, Johnson is expansive, drawing on his enormous learning but even more on his relentless self-examination to derive moral lessons for his reading public. Whether openly didactic or masquerading as a social type, Johnson shows an understanding and sympathy for the morally lax that he rarely allowed himself in private. It is this kindness, as well as the wit and cadence of his prose, that continues to delight his readers. ✍

Every Man Chiefly Happy or Miserable at Home. The Opinion of Servants.

THE RAMBLER, NO. 68

Saturday, November 10, 1750

Vivendum recte, cum propter plurima, tunc his
Praecipue causis, ut linguas mancipiorum
Contemnas; nam lingua mali pars pessima servi.

JUVENAL°

Let us live well: were it alone for this
The baneful tongues of servants to despise:
Slander, that worst of poisons, ever finds
An easy entrance to ignoble minds.

HERVEY

The younger Pliny° has very justly observed, that of actions that deserve our attention, the most splendid are not always the greatest. Fame, and wonder, and applause, are not excited but by external and adventitious circumstances, often distinct and separate from virtue and heroism. Eminence of station, greatness of effect, and all the favours of fortune, must concur to place excellence in publick view; but fortitude, diligence, and patience, divested of their show, glide unobserved through the crowd of life, and suffer and act, though with the same vigour and constancy, yet without pity and without praise.

This remark may be extended to all parts of life. Nothing is to be estimated by its effect upon common eyes and common ears. A thousand miseries make silent and invisible inroads on mankind, and the heart feels innumerable throbs, which never break into complaint. Perhaps, likewise, our pleasures are for the most part equally secret, and most are borne up by some private satisfaction, some internal consciousness, some latent hope, some peculiar prospect, which they never communicate, but reserve for solitary hours, and clandestine meditation.

The main of life is, indeed, composed of small incidents and petty occurrences; of wishes for objects not remote, and grief for disappointments of no fatal consequence; of insect vexations which sting us and fly away, impertinences which buzz awhile about us, and are heard no more; of meteorous pleasures which dance before us and are dissipated; of compliments which glide off the soul like other musick, and are forgotten by him that gave, and him that received them.

Such is the general heap out of which every man is to cull his own condition: for, as the chemists tell us, that all bodies are resolvable into the same elements, and that the boundless variety of things arises from the different proportions of very few ingredients; so a few pains and a few pleasures are all the materials of human life, and of these the proportions are partly allotted by Providence, and partly left to the arrangement of reason and of choice.

As these are well or ill disposed, man is for the most part happy or miserable. For very few are involved in great events, or have their thread of life entwisted with the chain of causes on which armies or nations are suspended; and even those who seem wholly busied in publick affairs, and elevated above low cares, or trivial pleasures, pass the chief part of their time in familiar and domestick scenes; from these they came into publick life, to these they are every hour recalled by passions not to be suppressed; in these they have the reward of their toils, and to these at last they retire.

The great end of prudence is to give cheerfulness to those hours, which splendour cannot gild, and acclamation cannot exhilarate; those soft intervals of unbended amusement, in which a man shrinks to his natural dimensions, and throws aside the ornaments or disguises, which he feels in privacy to be useless incumbrances, and to lose all effect when they became familiar. To be happy at home is the ultimate result of all ambition, the end to which every enterprise and labour tends, and of which every desire prompts the prosecution.

It is, indeed, at home that every man must be known by those who would make a just estimate either of his virtue or felicity; for smiles and embroidery are alike occasional, and the mind is often dressed for show in painted honour and fictitious benevolence.

Every man must have found some whose lives, in every house but their own, was a continual series of hypocrisy, and who concealed under fair appearances bad qualities, which, whenever they thought themselves out of the reach of censure, broke out from their restraint, like winds imprisoned in their caverns, and whom every one had reason to love, but they whose love a wise man is chiefly solicitous to procure. And there are others who, without any show of general goodness, and without the attractions by which popularity is conciliated, are received among their own families as bestowers of happiness, and reverenced as instructors, guardians, and benefactors.

The most authentick witnesses of any man's character are those who know him in his own family, and see him without any restraint or rule of conduct, but such as he voluntarily prescribes to him self. If a man carries virtue with him into his private apartments, and takes no advantage of unlimited power or probable secrecy; if we trace him through the round of his time, and find that his character, with those allowances which mortal frailty must always want, is uniform and regular, we have all the evidence of his sincerity that one man can have with regard to another: and, indeed, as hypocrisy cannot be its own reward, we may, without hesitation, determine that his heart is pure.

The highest panegyrick,[1] therefore, that private virtue can receive, is the praise of servants. For, however vanity or insolence may look down with contempt on the suffrage[2] of men undignified by wealth, and unenlightened by education, it very seldom happens that they commend or blame without justice. Vice and virtue are easily distinguished. Oppression, according to Harrington's aphorism,[3] will be felt by those that cannot see it; and, perhaps, it falls out very often that, in moral questions, the philosophers in the gown, and in the livery,[4] differ not so much in their sentiments, as in their language, and have equal power of discerning right, though they cannot point it out to others with equal address.[5]

There are very few faults to be committed in solitude, or without some agents, partners, confederates, or witnesses; and, therefore, the servant must commonly know the secrets of a master, who has any secrets to entrust; and failings, merely personal, are so frequently exposed by that security which pride and folly generally produce, and so inquisitively watched by that desire of reducing the inequalities of condition, which the lower orders of the world will always feel, that the testimony of a menial domestick can seldom be considered as defective for want[6] of knowledge. And though its impartiality may be sometimes suspected, it is at least as credible as that of equals, where rivalry instigates censure, or friendship dictates palliations.[7]

The danger of betraying our weakness to our servants, and the impossibility of concealing it from them, may be justly considered as one motive to a regular and irreproachable life. For no condition is more hateful or despicable, than his who has put him self in the power of his servant; in the power of him whom, perhaps, he has first corrupted by making him subservient to his vices, and whose fidelity he therefore cannot enforce by any precepts of honesty or reason. It is seldom known that authority thus acquired, is possessed without insolence, or that the master is not forced to confess by his tameness or forbearance, that he has enslaved himself by some foolish confidence. And his crime is equally punished, whatever part he takes of the choice to which he is reduced; and he is from that

---

[1]Compliment.

[2]Opinion.

[3]James Harrington (1611–1677), author of *Oceana* (1656), a theoretical model of a republic, as well as *Aphorisms Political* and *A System of Politics delineated in Short and Easy Aphorisms*.

[4]Costumes worn by scholars and servants.

[5]Aplomb and skills.

[6]Lack.

[7]Excuses.

fatal hour, in which he sacrifices his dignity to his passions, in perpetual dread of insolence or defamation; of a controller at home, or an accuser abroad. He is condemned to purchase, by continual bribes, that secrecy which bribes never secured, and which, after a long course of submission, promises, and anxieties, he will find violated in a fit of rage, or in a frolick of drunkenness.

To dread no eye, and to suspect no tongue, is the great prerogative of innocence; an exemption granted only to invariable virtue. But guilt has always its horrours and solicitudes; and to make it yet more shameful and detestable, it is doomed often to stand in awe of those, to whom nothing could give influence or weight, but their power of betraying. ✄

A Young Lady's Impatience of Control.

THE RAMBLER, NO. 84

Saturday, January 5, 1751

Cunarum fueras motor, CHARIDEME, *mearum,*
  Et pueri custos, assidusque comes.
Jam mihi nigrescunt tonsa sudaria barba,—
Sed tibi non crevi: te noster villicus horret:
  Te dispensator, te domus ipsa pavet.
Corripis, observas, quereris, suspiria ducis,
  Et vix a ferulis abstinet ira manum.

    MARTIAL°

You rock'd my cradle, were my guide,
In youth still tending at my side:
But now, dear sir, my beard is grown,
Still I'm a child to thee alone.
Our steward, butler, cook, and all,
You fright, nay e'en the very wall;
You pry, and frown, and growl, and chide,
And scarce will lay the rod aside.

    F. LEWIS

To The Rambler.[1]

Sir,

You seem in all your papers to be an enemy to tyranny, and to look with impartiality upon the world; I shall therefore lay my case before you, and hope by your decision to be set free from unreasonable restraints, and enabled to justify myself against the accusations which spite and peevishness produce against me.

---

[1]Johnson here impersonates a young girl.

At the age of five years I lost my mother, and my father, being not qualified to superintend the education of a girl, committed me to the care of his sister, who instructed me with the authority, and, not to deny her what she may justly claim, with the affection of a parent. She had not very elevated sentiments, or extensive views, but her principles were good, and her intentions pure; and, though some may practise more virtues, scarce any commit fewer faults.

Under this good lady I learned all the common rules of decent behaviour, and standing maxims of domestick prudence; and might have grown up by degrees to a country gentlewoman, without any thoughts of ranging beyond the neighborhood, had not Flavia[1] come down, last summer, to visit her relations in the next village. I was taken, of course, to compliment the stranger, and was, at the first sight, surprised at the unconcern with which she saw herself gazed at by the company whom she had never known before; at the carelessness with which she received compliments, and the readiness with which she returned them. I found she had something which I perceived myself to want,[2] and could not but wish to be like her, at once easy and officious,[3] attentive and unembarrassed. I went home, and for four days could think and talk of nothing but Miss Flavia; though my aunt told me, that she was a forward slut,[4] and thought herself wise before her time.

In a little time she repaid my visit, and raised in my heart a new confusion of love and admiration. I soon saw her again, and still found new charms in her air, conversation, and behaviour. You, who have perhaps seen the world, may have observed, that formality soon ceases between young persons. I know not how others are affected on such occasions, but I found myself irresistibly allured to friendship and intimacy, by the familiar complaisance and airy gaity of Flavia; so that in a few weeks I became her favourite, and all the time was passed with me, that she could gain from ceremony and visit.

As she came often to me, she necessarily spent some hours with my aunt, to whom she paid great respect by low courtesies, submissive compliance, and soft acquiescence; but as I became gradually more accustomed to her manners, I discovered that her civility was general; that there was a certain degree of deference shewn by her to circumstances and appearances; that many went away flattered by her humility, whom she despised in her heart; that the influence of far the greatest part of those with whom she conversed ceased with their presence; and that sometimes she did not remember the names of them, whom, without any intentional insincerity or false commendation, her habitual civility had sent away with very high thoughts of their own importance.

It was not long before I perceived that my aunt's opinion was not of much weight in Flavia's deliberations, and that she was looked upon by her as a woman of narrow sentiments, without knowledge of books, or observations on mankind.

---

[1]From the Latin name of the clan of Vespasian,° Titus, and Domitian, Roman emperors.
[2]Lack.
[3]Obliging.
[4]A bold, impudent girl.

I had hitherto considered my aunt as entitled, by her wisdom and experience, to the highest reverence; and could not forbear to wonder that any one so much younger should venture to suspect her of errour, or ignorance; but my surprise was without uneasiness, and being now accustomed to think *Flavia* always in the right, I readily learned from her to trust my own reason, and to believe it possible, that they who had lived longer might be mistaken.

Flavia had read much, and used so often to converse on subjects of learning, that she put all the men in the country to flight, except the old parson, who declared himself much delighted with her company, because she gave him opportunities to recollect the studies of his younger years, and, by some mention of ancient story, had made him rub the dust off his *Homer*,° which had lain unregarded in his closet. With *Homer*,° and a thousand other names familiar to *Flavia*, I had no acquaintance, but began, by comparing her accomplishments with my own, to repine at my education, and wish that I had not been so long confined to the company of those from whom nothing but housewifery was to be learned. I then set myself to peruse such books as *Flavia* recommended, and heard her opinion of their beauties and defects. I saw new worlds hourly bursting upon my mind, and was enraptured at the prospect of diversifying life with endless entertainment.

The old lady, finding that a large screen, which I had undertaken to adorn with turkey-work[1] against winter, made very slow advances, and that I had added in two months but three leaves to a flowered apron then in the frame, took the alarm, and with all the zeal of honest folly exclaimed against my new acquaintance, who had filled me with idle notions, and turned my head with books. But she had now lost her authority, for I began to find innumerable mistakes in her opinions, and improprieties in her language; and therefore thought myself no longer bound to pay much regard to one who knew little beyond her needle and her dairy, and who professed to think that nothing more is required of a woman than to see that the house is clean, and that the maids go to bed and rise at a certain hour.

She seemed however to look upon *Flavia* as seducing me, and to imagine that when her influence was withdrawn, I should return to my allegiance; she therefore contented herself with remote hints, and gentle admonitions, intermixed with sage histories of the miscarriages of wit, and disappointments of pride. But since she has found, that though *Flavia* is departed, I still persist in my new scheme, she has at length lost her patience, she snatches my book out of my hand, tears my paper if she finds me writing, burns *Flavia*'s letters before my face when she can seize them, and threatens to lock me up, and to complain to my father of my perverseness. If women, she says, would but know their duty and their interest, they would be careful to acquaint themselves with family affairs, and many a penny might be saved; for while the mistress of the house is scribbling and reading, servants are junketing,[2] and linen is wearing out. She then takes me

---

[1]Needlepoint done in imitation of Turkish tapestry.

[2]Off making merry.

round the rooms, shews me the worked hangings, and chairs of tent-stitch,[1] and asks whether all this was done with a pen and a book.

I cannot deny that I sometimes laugh and sometimes am sullen; but she has not delicacy enough to be much moved either with my mirth or my gloom, if she did not think the interest of the family endangered by this change of my manners. She had for some years marked out young Mr. *Surly*, an heir in the neighbour-hood, remarkable for his love of fighting-cocks, as an advantageous match; and was extremely pleased with the civilities which he used to pay me, till under *Flavia's* tuition I learned to talk of subjects which he could not understand. This, she says, is the consequence of female study: girls grow too wise to be advised, and too stubborn to be commanded; but she is resolved to try who shall govern, and will thwart my humour[2] till she breaks my spirit.

These menaces, Mr. *Rambler*, sometimes make me quite angry; for I have been sixteen these ten weeks, and think myself exempted from the dominion of a governess, who has no pretensions to more sense or knowledge than myself. I am resolved, since I am as tall and as wise as other women, to be no longer treated like a girl. Miss *Flavia* has often told me, that ladies of my age go to assemblies and routs,[3] without their mothers and their aunts; I shall therefore, from this time, leave asking advice, and refuse to give accounts. I wish you would state the time at which young ladies may judge for themselves, which I am sure you cannot but think ought to begin before sixteen; if you are inclined to delay it longer, I shall have very little regard to your opinion.

My aunt often tells me of the advantages of experience, and of the deference due to seniority; and both she and all the antiquated part of the world, talk of the unreserved obedience which they paid to the commands of their parents, and the undoubting confidence with which they listened to their precepts; of the terrors which they felt at a frown, and the humility with which they supplicated forgive-ness whenever they had offended. I cannot but fancy that this boast is too general to be true, and that the young and the old were always at variance. I have, however, told my aunt, that I will mend whatever she will prove to be wrong; but she replies that she has reasons of her own, and that she is sorry to live in an age when girls have the impudence to ask for proofs.

I beg once again, Mr. *Rambler*, to know whether I am not as wise as my aunt, and whether, when she presumes to check me as a baby, I may not pluck up a spirit and return her insolence? I shall not proceed to extremities without your advice, which is therefore impatiently expected by

MYRTILLA.[4]

P. S. Remember I am past sixteen. ✍

---

[1] Embroidery in which parallel stitches are arranged diagonally across the intersection of threads.
[2] Mood.
[3] Groups of disorderly people.
[4] From the Latin meaning "crowned with myrtle," as were the winners of ancient Olympic games.

The History of Hymenaeus's Courtship.

THE RAMBLER, NO. 113

Tuesday, April l6, 1751

———*Uxorem, Posthume ducis?*
Die qua Tisephone, quibus exagitare colubris?

JUVENAL°

A sober man like thee to change his life!
What fury would possess thee with a wife?

DRYDEN°

To The Rambler.[1]

Sir, I know not whether it is always a proof of innocence to treat censure with contempt. We owe so much reverence to the wisdom of mankind, as justly to wish, that our own opinion of our merit may be ratified by the concurrence of other suffrages;[2] and since guilt and infamy must have the same effect upon intelligences unable to pierce beyond external appearance, and influenced often rather by example than precept, we are obliged to refute a false charge, lest we should countenance the crime which we have never committed. To turn away from an accusation with supercilious silence, is equally in the power of him that is hardened by villany, and inspirited by innocence. The wall of brass which Horace° erects upon a clear conscience,[3] may be sometimes raised by impudence or power; and we should always wish to preserve the dignity of virtue by adorning her with graces which wickedness cannot assume.

For this reason I have determined no longer to endure, with either patient or sullen resignation, a reproach, which is, at least in my opinion, unjust; but will lay my case honestly before you, that you or your readers may at length decide it.

Whether you will be able to preserve your boasted impartiality, when you hear that I am considered as an adversary by half the female world, you may surely pardon me for doubting, notwithstanding the veneration to which you may imagine yourself entitled by your age, your learning, your abstraction, or your virtue. Beauty, Mr. Rambler, has often overpowered the resolutions of the firm, and the reasonings of the wise, roused the old to sensibility, and subdued the rigorous to softness.

I am one of those unhappy beings, who have been marked out as husbands for many different women, and deliberated a hundred times on the brink of matrimony. I have discussed all the nuptial preliminaries so often, that I can

---

[1]Johnson here impersonates a bachelor.
[2]Opinions.
[3]*Epistles* I.1.60–61.

repeat the forms in which jointures[1] are settled, pin-money[2] secured, and provisions for younger children ascertained;[3] but am at last doomed by general consent to everlasting solitude, and excluded by an irreversible decree from all hopes of connubial felicity. I am pointed out by every mother, as a man whose visits cannot be admitted without reproach; who raises hopes only to embitter disappointment, and makes offers only to seduce girls into a waste of that part of life, in which they might gain advantageous matches, and become mistresses and mothers.

I hope you will think, that some part of this penal severity may justly be remitted, when I inform you, that I never yet professed love to a woman without sincere intentions of marriage; that I have never continued an appearance of intimacy from the hour that my inclination changed, but to preserve her whom I was leaving from the shock of abruptness, or the ignominy of contempt; that I always endeavoured to give the ladies an opportunity of seeming to discard me; and that I never forsook a mistress for larger fortune, or brighter beauty, but because I discovered some irregularity in her conduct, or some depravity in her mind; not because I was charmed by another, but because I was offended by herself.

I was very early tired of that succession of amusements by which the thoughts of most young men are dissipated, and had not long glittered in the splendour of an ample patrimony[4] before I wished for the calm of domestick happiness. Youth is naturally delighted with sprightliness and ardour, and therefore I breathed out the sighs of my first affection at the feet of the gay, the sparkling, the vivacious Ferocula.[5] I fancied to myself a perpetual source of happiness in wit never exhausted, and spirit never depressed; looked with veneration on her readiness of expedients,[6] contempt of difficulty, assurance of address,[7] and promptitude of reply; considered her as exempt by some prerogative of nature from the weakness and timidity of female minds; and congratulated myself upon a companion superior to all common troubles and embarrassments. I was, indeed, somewhat disturbed by the unshaken perseverance with which she enforced her demands of an unreasonable settlement; yet I should have consented to pass my life in union with her, had not my curiosity led me to a crowd gathered in the street, where I found Ferocula, in the presence of hundreds, disputing for six-pence with a chairman.[8] I saw her in so little need of assistance, that it was no breach of the laws of chivalry to forbear interposition, and I spared myself the shame of owning her acquaintance. I forgot some point of ceremony at our next interview, and soon provoked her to forbid me her presence.

---

[1]The holding of property by both husband and wife and, in the event of the husband's death, the permission for the wife to use the property until her death.

[2]Annual allowance given to a woman for her personal expenses for clothing or whatever.

[3]The oldest inherits the title and estate.

[4]Estate inherited from one's father or ancestors.

[5]From the Latin for "overbearing" or "insolent."

[6]The ease with which she could come up with the means to her ends.

[7]Certainty of her poise in conversation.

[8]One who carries people in sedan-chairs.

My next attempt was upon a lady of great eminence for learning and philosophy. I had frequently observed the barrenness and uniformity of connubial conversation, and therefore thought highly of my own prudence and discernment, when I selected from a multitude of wealthy beauties, the deep-read, *Misothea*,[1] who declared herself the inexorable enemy of ignorant pertness, and puerile levity; and scarcely condescended to make tea, but for the linguist, the geometrician, the astronomer, or the poet. The queen of the Amazons[2] was only to be gained by the hero who could conquer her in single combat; and *Misothea's* heart was only to bless the scholar who could overpower her by disputation. Amidst the fondest transports of courtship she could call for a definition of terms, and treated every argument with contempt that could not be reduced to regular syllogism. You may easily imagine, that I wished this courtship at an end; but when I desired her to shorten my torments, and fix the day of my felicity, we were led into a long conversation, in which *Misothea* endeavoured to demonstrate the folly of attributing choice and self-direction to any human being. It was not difficult to discover the danger of committing myself for ever to the arms of one who might at any time mistake the dictates of passion, or the calls of appetite, for the decree of fate; or consider cuckoldom as necessary to the general system, as a link in the everlasting chain of successive causes. I therefore told her, that destiny had ordained us to part, and that nothing should have torn me from her but the talons of necessity.

I then solicited the regard of the calm, the prudent, the economical *Sophronia*,[3] a lady who considered wit as dangerous, and learning as superfluous, and thought that the woman who kept her house clean, and her accounts exact, took receipts for every payment, and could find them at a sudden call, inquired nicely[4] after the condition of the tenants, read the price of stocks once a-week, and purchased every thing at the best market, could want[5] no accomplishments necessary to the happiness of a wise man. She discoursed with great solemnity on the care and vigilance which the superintendence of a family demands; observed how many were ruined by confidence in servants; and told me, that she never expected honesty but from a strong chest, and that the best storekeeper was the mistress's eye. Many such oracles of generosity she uttered, and made every day new improvements in her schemes for the regulations of her servants, and the distribution of her time. I was convinced that, whatever I might suffer from *Sophronia*, I should escape poverty; and we therefore proceeded to adjust the settlements according to her own rule, fair and softly. But one morning her maid came to me in tears to intreat my interest for a reconciliation with her mistress, who had turned her out at night for breaking six teeth in a tortoise-shell comb; she

---

[1]From the Greek *misos* for "hatred" and *theos* for "god," meaning, perhaps, "hateful goddess."
[2]A warring tribe of women in Greek mythology; their men tended the domestic chores while the women fought. Each woman had to kill a man before she could marry.
[3]From the Greek for "skillful" or "clever."
[4]Precisely.
[5]Lack.

had attended her lady from a distant province, and having not lived long enough to save much money, was destitute among strangers, and, though of a good family, in danger of perishing in the streets, or of being compelled by hunger to prostitution. I made no scruple of promising to restore her; but upon my first application to *Sophronia*, was answered with an air which called for approbation,[1] that if she neglected her own affairs, I might suspect her of neglecting mine; that the comb stood her in three half crowns; that no servant should wrong her twice; and that indeed she took the first opportunity of parting with *Phillida*,[2] because, though she was honest, her constitution was bad, and she thought her very likely to fall sick. Of our conference I need not tell you the effect; it surely may be forgiven me, if on this occasion I forgot the decency of common forms.

From two more ladies I was disengaged by finding, that they entertained my rivals at the same time, and determined their choice by the liberality of our settlements. Another, I thought myself justified in forsaking, because she gave my attorney a bribe to favour her in the bargain; another because I could never soften her to tenderness, till she heard that most of my family had died young; and another, because, to increase her fortune by expectations, she represented her sister as languishing and consumptive.

I shall in another letter give the remaining part of my history of courtship. I presume that I should hitherto have injured the majesty of female virtue, had I not hoped to transfer my affection to higher merit.

I am, &c.
HYMENAEUS.[3] ✐

The Sequel of Hymenaeus's Courtship.

THE RAMBLER, NO. 115

Tuesday, April 23, 1751

Quaedam parva quidem, sed non tolerunda maritis.
JUVENAL°

Some faults, though small, intolerable grow.
DRYDEN°

Sir,

I sit down, in pursuance of my late engagement, to recount the remaining part of the adventures that befel me in my long quest of conjugal felicity, which,

---

[1]Expected approval.
[2]From the Greek for "friendship."
[3]From Hymen, the Greek god of marriage.

though I have not yet been so happy as to obtain it, I have at least endeavoured to deserve by unwearied diligence, without suffering from repeated disappointments any abatement of my hope, or repression of my activity.

You must have observed in the world a species of mortals who employ themselves in promoting matrimony, and without any visible motive of interest or vanity, without any discoverable impulse of malice or benevolence, without any reason, but that they want[1] objects of attention and topicks of conversation, are incessantly busy in procuring wives and husbands. They fill the ears of every single man and woman with some convenient match, and when they are informed of your age and fortune, offer a partner for life with the same readiness, and the same indifference, as a salesman, when he has taken measure by his eye, fits his customer with a coat.

It might be expected that they should soon be discouraged from this officious[2] interposition by resentment or contempt; and that every man should determine the choice on which so much of his happiness must depend, by his own judgment and observation: yet it happens, that as these proposals are generally made with a shew of kindness, they seldom provoke anger, but are at worst heard with patience, and forgotten. They influence weak minds to approbation; for many are sure to find in a new acquaintance, whatever qualities report has taught them to expect; and in more powerful and active understandings they excite curiosity, and sometimes, by a lucky chance, bring persons of similar tempers within the attraction of each other.

I was known to possess a fortune, and to want a wife; and therefore was frequently attended by these hymeneal solicitors, with whose importunity I was sometimes diverted, and sometimes perplexed; for they contended for me as vultures for a carcase; each employing all his eloquence, and all his artifices, to enforce and promote his own scheme, from the success of which he was to receive no other advantage than the pleasure of defeating others equally eager, and equally industrious.

An invitation to sup with one of those busy friends, made me, by a concerted chance, acquainted with *Camilla*,[3] by whom it was expected that I should be suddenly and irresistibly enslaved. The lady, whom the same kindness had brought without her own concurrence into the lists of love, seemed to think me at least worthy of the honour of captivity; and exerted the power, both of her eyes and wit, with so much art and spirit, that though I had been too often deceived by appearances to devote myself irrevocably at the first interview, yet I could not suppress some raptures of admiration, and flutters of desire. I was easily persuaded to make nearer approaches; but soon discovered, that an union with *Camilla* was not much to be wished. *Camilla* professed a boundless contempt for the folly, levity, ignorance, and impertinence of her own sex; and very frequently

---

[1]Lack.

[2]Obliging.

[3]A female warrior in the *Aeneid*.

expressed her wonder that men of learning or experience could submit to trifle away life with beings incapable of solid thought. In mixed companies, she always associated with the men, and declared her satisfaction when the ladies retired. If any short excursion into the country was proposed, she commonly insisted upon the exclusion of women from the party; because, where they were admitted, the time was wasted in frothy compliments, weak indulgences, and idle ceremonies. To shew the greatness of her mind, she avoided all compliance with the fashion; and to boast the profundity of her knowledge, mistook the various textures of silk, confounded tabbies with damasks,[1] and sent for ribands[2] by wrong names. She despised the commerce of stated visits, a farce of empty form without instruction; and congratulated herself, that she never learned to write message cards.[3] She often applauded the noble sentiment of *Plato,*° who rejoiced that he was born a man rather than a woman; proclaimed her approbation of *Swift's*° opinion, that women are only a higher species of monkeys; and confessed, that when she considered the behaviour, or heard the conversation, of her sex, she could not but forgive the Turks for suspecting them to want souls.

It was the joy and pride of *Camilla* to have provoked, by this insolence, all the rage of hatred, and all the persecutions of calumny; nor was she ever more elevated with her own superiority, than when she talked of female anger, and female cunning. Well, says she, has nature provided that such virulence should be disabled by folly, and such cruelty be restrained by impotence.

Camilla doubtless expected, that what she lost on one side, she should gain on the other; and imagined that every male heart would be open to a lady, who made such generous advances to the borders of virility. But man, ungrateful man, instead of springing forward to meet her, shrunk back at her approach. She was persecuted by the ladies as a deserter, and at best received by the men only as a fugitive. I, for my part, amused myself awhile with her fopperies,[4] but novelty soon gave way to detestation, for nothing out of the common order of nature can be long borne. I had no inclination to a wife who had the ruggedness of a man without his force, and the ignorance of a woman without her softness; nor could I think my quiet[5] and honour to be entrusted to such audacious virtue as was hourly courting danger, and soliciting assault.

My next mistress was *Nitella,*[6] a lady of gentle mien, and soft voice, always speaking to approve, and ready to receive direction from those with whom chance had brought her into company. In *Nitella* I promised myself an easy friend, with whom I might loiter away the day without disturbance or altercation. I therefore soon resolved to address her, but was discouraged from prosecuting my courtship, by observing, that her apartments were superstitiously regular; and that,

---

[1]Stiff striped silk taffetas (tabbies) as opposed to soft elaborately patterned silks (damasks).
[2]Ribbons.
[3]Invitations.
[4]Foolishness.
[5]Peace.
[6]From the Latin for "gleam."

unless she had notice of my visit, she was never to be seen. There is a kind of anxious cleanliness which I have always noted as the characteristick of a slattern; it is the superfluous scrupulosity of guilt, dreading discovery, and shunning suspicion: it is the violence of an effort against habit, which, being impelled by external motives, cannot stop at the middle point.

Nitella was always tricked out rather with nicety than elegance; and seldom could forbear to discover, by her uneasiness and constraint, that her attention was burdened, and her imagination engrossed: I therefore concluded, that being only occasionally and ambitiously dressed, she was not familiarized to her own ornaments. There are so many competitors for the fame of cleanliness, that it is not hard to gain information of those that fail, from those that desire to excel: I quickly found that *Nitella* passed her time between finery and dirt; and was always in a wrapper, nightcap, and slippers, when she was not decorated for immediate show.

I was then led by my evil destiny to *Charybdis*,[1] who never neglected an opportunity of seizing a new prey when it came within her reach. I thought myself quickly made happy by permission to attend her to publick places; and pleased my own vanity with imagining the envy which I should raise in a thousand hearts, by appearing as the acknowledged favourite of *Charybdis*. She soon after hinted her intention to take a ramble for a fortnight, into a part of the kingdom which she had never seen. I solicited the happiness of accompanying her, which, after a short reluctance, was indulged me. She had no other curiosity on her journey, than after all possible means of expense; and was every moment taking occasion to mention some delicacy, which I knew it my duty upon such notices to procure.

After our return, being now more familiar, she told me, whenever we met, of some new diversion; at night she had notice of a charming company that would breakfast in the gardens; and in the morning had been informed of some new song in the opera, some new dress at the playhouse, or some performer at a concert whom she longed to hear. Her intelligence was such, that there never was a show, to which she did not summon me on the second day; and as she hated a crowd, and could not go alone, I was obliged to attend at some intermediate hour, and pay the price of a whole company. When we passed the streets, she was often charmed with some trinket in the toy-shops; and from moderate desires of seals and snuff-boxes,[2] rose, by degrees, to gold and diamonds. I now began to find the smile of *Charybdis* too costly for a private purse, and added one more to six and forty lovers, whose fortune and patience her rapacity had exhausted.

Imperia[3] then took possession of my affections; but kept them only for a short time. She had newly inherited a large fortune, and having spent the early part of her life in the perusal of romances, brought with her into the gay world all the pride of *Cleopatra*; expected nothing less than vows, altars, and sacrifices; and

---

[1] In Greek mythology, the whirlpool opposite the cave of Scylla, the sea monster.

[2] Seals: engraved stamps used to make impressions in wax for use on letters; snuff-boxes: small decorated boxes for carrying powdered tobacco which the user inhaled through the nose.

[3] From the Latin for "the right to command."

thought her charms dishonoured, and her power infringed, by the softest opposition to her sentiments, or the smallest transgression of her commands. Time might indeed cure this species of pride in a mind not naturally undiscerning, and vitiated[1] only by false representations; but the operations of time are slow; and I therefore left her to grow wise at leisure, or to continue in errour at her own expense.

Thus I have hitherto, in spite of myself, passed my life in frozen celibacy. My friends, indeed, often tell me, that I flatter my imagination with higher hopes than human nature can gratify; that I dress up an ideal charmer in all the radiance of perfection, and then enter the world to look for the same excellence in corporeal beauty. But surely, Mr. Rambler, it is not madness to hope for some terrestrial lady unstained by the spots which I have been describing; at least I am resolved to pursue my search; for I am so far from thinking meanly of marriage, that I believe it able to afford the highest happiness decreed to our present state; and if, after all these miscarriages, I find a woman that fills up my expectation, you shall hear once more from

> Yours, &c.
> HYMENAEUS. ✍

Tranquilla's Account of Her Lovers, Opposed to Hymenaeus.

THE RAMBLER, NO. 119

Tuesday, May 7, 1751

Iliacos intra muros peccatur, et extra.

HORACE

Faults lay on either side the Trojan tow'rs.

ELPHINSTON

To The Rambler[2]

Sir,

As, notwithstanding all that wit, or malice, or pride, or prudence will be able to suggest, men and women must at last pass their lives together, I have never therefore thought those writers friends to human happiness, who endeavour to excite in either sex a general contempt or suspicion of the other. To persuade

---

[1]Spoiled.
[2]Johnson here impersonates a woman of "antiquated virginity."

them who are entering the world, and looking abroad for a suitable associate, that all are equally vitious,[1] or equally ridiculous; that they who trust are certainly betrayed, and they who esteem are always disappointed; is not to awaken judgment, but to inflame temerity.[2] Without hope there can be no caution. Those who are convinced, that no reason for preference can be found, will never harass their thoughts with doubt and deliberation; they will resolve, since they are doomed to misery, that no needless anxiety shall disturb their quiet; they will plunge at hazard into the crowd, and snatch the first hand that shall be held toward them.

That the world is over-run with vice, cannot be denied; but vice, however predominant, has not yet gained an unlimited dominion. Simple and unmingled good is not in our power, but we may generally escape a greater evil by suffering a less; and therefore, those who undertake to initiate the young and ignorant in the knowledge of life, should be careful to inculcate the possibility of virtue and happiness, and to encourage endeavours by prospects of success.

You, perhaps, do not suspect, that these are the sentiments of one who has been subject for many years to all the hardships of antiquated virginity; has been long accustomed to the coldness of neglect, and the petulance of insult; has been mortified in full assemblies by inquiries after forgotten fashions, games long disused, and wits and beauties of ancient renown; has been invited, with malicious importunity, to the second wedding of many acquaintances; has been ridiculed by two generations of coquets in whispers intended to be heard; and been long considered by the airy and gay, as too venerable for familiarity, and too wise for pleasure. It is indeed natural for injury to provoke anger, and by continual repetition to produce an habitual asperity;[3] yet I have hitherto struggled with so much vigilance against my pride and my resentment, that I have preserved my temper uncorrupted. I have not yet made it any part of my employment to collect sentences against marriage; nor am inclined to lessen the number of the few friends whom time has left me, by obstructing that happiness which I cannot partake, and venting my vexation in censures of the forwardness and indiscretion of girls, or the inconstancy, tastelessness, and perfidy of men.

It is, indeed, not very difficult to bear that condition to which we are not condemned by necessity, but induced by observation and choice; and therefore I, perhaps, have never yet felt all the malignity with which a reproach, edged with the appellation of old maid, swells some of those hearts in which it is infixed. I was not condemned in my youth to solitude, either by indigence or deformity, nor passed the earlier part of life without the flattery of courtship, and the joys of triumph. I have danced the round of gaiety amidst the murmurs of envy, and gratulations of applause; been attended from pleasure to pleasure by the great, the sprightly, and the vain; and seen my regard solicited by the obsequiousness of gallantry, the gaiety of wit, and the timidity of love. If, therefore, I am yet a stranger

---

[1]Corrupt.
[2]Recklessness.
[3]Irritability.

to nuptial happiness, I suffer only the consequences of my own resolves, and can look back upon the succession of lovers, whose addresses I have rejected, without grief, and without malice.

When my name first began to be inscribed upon glasses, I was honoured with the amorous professions of the gay *Venustulus*,[1] a gentleman, who, being the only son of a wealthy family, had been educated in all the wantonness of expense, and softness of effeminacy. He was beautiful in his person, and easy in his address, and, therefore, soon gained upon my eye at an age when the sight is very little overruled by the understanding. He had not any power in himself of gladdening or amusing; but supplied his want[2] of conversation by treats and diversions; and his chief art of courtship was to fill the mind of his mistress with parties, rambles, musick, and shows. We were often engaged in short excursions to gardens and seats, and I was for a while pleased with the care which *Venustulus* discovered in securing me from any appearance of danger, or possibility of mischance. He never failed to recommend caution to his coachman, or to promise the waterman a reward if he landed us safe; and always contrived to return by day-light for fear of robbers. This extraordinary solicitude was represented for a time as the effect of his tenderness for me; but fear is too strong for continued hypocrisy. I soon discovered, that *Venustulus* had the cowardice as well as elegance of a female. His imagination was perpetually clouded with terrours, and he could scarcely refrain from screams and outcries at any accidental surprise. He durst not enter a room if a rat was heard behind the wainscot, nor cross a field where the cattle were frisking in the sunshine; the least breeze that waved upon the river was a storm, and every clamour in the street was a cry of fire. I have seen him lose his colour when my squirrel had broke his chain; and was forced to throw water in his face on the sudden entrance of a black cat. Compassion once obliged me to drive away with my fan, a beetle that kept him in distress, and chide off a dog that yelped at his heels, to which he would gladly have given up me to facilitate his own escape. Women naturally expect defence and protection from a lover or a husband, and therefore you will not think me culpable in refusing a wretch, who would have burdened life with unnecessary fears, and flown to me for that succor which it was his duty to have given.

My next lover was *Fungoso*,[3] the son of a stockjobber,[4] whose visits my friends, by the importunity of persuasion, prevailed upon me to allow. *Fungoso* was no very suitable companion; for having been bred in a counting-house,[5] he spoke a language unintelligible in any other place. He had no desire of any reputation but that of an acute prognosticator of the changes in the funds; nor had any means of raising merriment, but by telling how somebody was over-reached

---

[1] From the Latin for "charming."
[2] Lack.
[3] From the Latin for "busy."
[4] Member of the stock exchange who deals in stocks on his own account.
[5] Office of finance.

in a bargain by his father. He was, however, a youth of great sobriety and prudence, and frequently informed us how carefully he would improve my fortune. I was not in haste to conclude the match, but was so much awed by my parents, that I durst not dismiss him, and might perhaps have been doomed for ever to the grossness of pedlary, and the jargon of usury, had not a fraud been discovered in the settlement, which set me free from the persecution of grovelling pride, and pecuniary impudence.

I was afterwards six months without any particular notice, but at last became the idol of the glittering *Flosculus*,[1] who prescribed the mode of embroidery to all the fops[2] of his time, and varied at pleasure the cock of every hat, and the sleeve of every coat that appeared in fashionable assemblies. *Flosculus* made some impression upon my heart by a compliment which few ladies can hear without emotion; he commended my skill in dress, my judgment in suiting colours, and my art in disposing ornaments. But *Flosculus* was too much engaged by his own elegance, to be sufficiently attentive to the duties of a lover, or to please with varied praise an ear made delicate by riot of adulation. He expected to be repaid part of his tribute, and staid away three days, because I neglected to take notice of a new coat. I quickly found, that *Flosculus* was rather a rival than an admirer; and that we should probably live in a perpetual struggle of emulous finery, and spend our lives in stratagems to be first in the fashion.

I had soon after the honour at a feast of attracting the eyes of *Dentatus*,[3] one of those human beings whose only happiness is to dine. *Dentatus* regaled me with foreign varieties, told me of measures that he had laid for procuring the best cook in France, and entertained me with bills of fare, prescribed the arrangement of dishes, and taught me two sauces invented by himself. At length, such is the uncertainty of human happiness, I declared my opinion too hastily upon a pie made under his own direction; after which he grew so cold and negligent, that he was easily dismissed.

Many other lovers, or pretended lovers, I have had the honour to lead a while in triumph. But two of them I drove from me, by discovering that they had no taste or knowledge in musick; three I dismissed, because they were drunkards; two, because they paid their addresses at the same time to other ladies; and six, because they attempted to influence my choice by bribing my maid. Two more I discarded at the second visit for obscene allusions; and five for drollery on religion. In the latter part of my reign, I sentenced two to perpetual exile, for offering me settlements, by which the children of a former marriage would have been injured; four, for representing falsely the value of their estates; three for concealing their debts; and one, for raising the rent of a decrepit tenant.

I have now sent you a narrative, which the ladies may oppose to the tale of *Hymenaeus*. I mean not to depreciate the sex which has produced poets and

---

[1]From the Latin for "little flower" or "pride."
[2]Fools.
[3]From the Latin for "having teeth."

philosophers, heroes and martyrs; but will not suffer the rising generation of beauties to be dejected by partial satire; or to imagine that those who censured them have not likewise their follies, and their vices. I do not yet believe happiness unattainable in marriage, though I have never yet been able to find a man, with whom I could prudently venture an inseparable union. It is necessary to expose faults, that their deformity may be seen; but the reproach ought not to be extended beyond the crime, nor either sex to be contemned, because some women, or men, are indelicate or dishonest.

I am, &c.
TRANQUILLA [1] 🖋

Idleness an Anxious and Miserable State.

THE RAMBLER, NO. 134

Saturday, June 29, 1751

Quis scit an adjiciant hodiernae crastina summae
Tempora Dii superi?

HORACE°

Who knows if heav'n, with ever-bounteous pow'r,
Shall add tomorrow to the present hour?

FRANCIS

I sat yesterday morning employed in deliberating on which, among the various subjects that occurred to my imagination, I should bestow the paper of today. After a short effort of meditation by which nothing was determined, I grew every moment more irresolute, my ideas wandered from the first intention, and I rather wished to think, than thought upon any settled subject; till at last I was awakened from this dream of study by a summons from the press; the time was now come for which I had been thus negligently purposing to provide, and, however dubious or sluggish, I was now necessitated to write.

Though to a writer whose design is so comprehensive and miscellaneous, that he may accommodate himself with a topick from every scene of life, or view of nature, it is no great aggravation of his task to be obliged to a sudden composition; yet I could not forbear to reproach myself for having so long neglected what was unavoidably to be done, and of which every moment's idleness increased the difficulty. There was however, some pleasure in reflecting that I, who had only trifled till diligence was necessary, might still congratulate myself upon my superiority to multitudes, who have trifled till diligence is vain; who can by no

---

[1]From the Latin for "calm."

degree of activity or resolution recover the opportunities which have slipped away; and who are condemned by their own carelessness to hopeless calamity and barren sorrow.

The folly of allowing ourselves to delay what we know cannot be finally escaped, is one of the general weaknesses, which, in spite of the instruction of moralists, and the remonstrances of reason, prevail to a greater or less degree in every mind; even they who most steadily withstand it, find it, if not the most violent, the most pertinacious[1] of their passions, always renewing its attacks, and though often vanquished, never destroyed.

It is indeed natural to have particular regard to the time present, and to be most solicitous for that which is by its nearness enabled to make the strongest impressions. When therefore any sharp pain is to be suffered, or any formidable danger to be incurred, we can scarcely exempt ourselves wholly from the seducements of imagination; we readily believe that another day will bring some support or advantage which we now want;[2] and are easily persuaded, that the moment of necessity which we desire never to arrive, is at a great distance from us.

Thus life is languished away in the gloom of anxiety, and consumed in collecting resolutions which the next morning dissipates; in forming purposes which we scarcely hope to keep, and reconciling ourselves to our own cowardice by excuses, which, while we admit them, we know to be absurd. Our firmness is by the continual contemplation of misery, hourly impaired; every submission to our fear enlarges its dominion; we not only waste that time in which the evil we dread might have been suffered and surmounted, but even where procrastination produces no absolute increase of our difficulties, make them less superable[3] to ourselves by habitual terrours. When evils cannot be avoided, it is wise to contract the interval of expectation; to meet the mischiefs which will overtake us if we fly; and suffer only their real malignity, without the conflicts of doubt, and anguish of anticipation.

To act is far easier than to suffer; yet we every day see the progress of life retarded by the *vis inertiae*,[4] the mere repugnance to motion, and find multitudes repining at the want[5] of that which nothing but idleness hinders them from enjoying. The case of *Tantalus*, in the region of poetick punishment, was somewhat to be pitied, because the fruits that hung about him retired from his hand; but what tenderness can be claimed by those who, though perhaps they suffer the pains of *Tantalus*, will never lift their hands for their own relief?

There is nothing more common among this torpid generation than murmurs and complaints; murmurs at uneasiness which only vacancy and suspicion expose them to feel, and complaints of distresses which it is in their own power to remove. Laziness is commonly associated with timidity. Either fear originally

---

[1] Stubbornly persistent.
[2] Lack.
[3] Able to be overcome.
[4] Force of inertia.
[5] Lack.

prohibits endeavours by infusing despair of success; or the frequent failure of irresolute struggles, and the constant desire of avoiding labour, impress by degrees false terrours on the mind. But fear, whether natural or acquired, when once it has full possession of the fancy, never fails to employ it upon visions of calamity, such as, if they are not dissipated by useful employment, will soon overcast it with horrours, and embitter life not only with those miseries by which all earthly beings are really more or less tormented, but with those which do not yet exist, and which can only be discerned by the perspicacity[1] of cowardice.

Among all who sacrifice future advantage to present inclination, scarcely any gain so little as those that suffer themselves to freeze in idleness. Others are corrupted by some enjoyment of more or less power to gratify the passions; but to neglect our duties, merely to avoid the labour of performing them, a labour which is always punctually rewarded, is surely to sink under weak temptations. Idleness never can secure tranquillity; the call of reason and of conscience will pierce the closest[2] pavilion of the sluggard, and though it may not have force to drive him from his down,[3] will be loud enough to hinder him from sleep. Those moments which he cannot resolve to make useful, by devoting them to the great business of his being, will still be usurped by powers that will not leave them to his disposal; remorse and vexation will seize upon them, and forbid him to enjoy what he is so desirous to appropriate.

There are other causes of inactivity incident to more active faculties and more acute discernment. He to whom many objects of pursuit arise at the same time, will frequently hesitate between different desires, till a rival has precluded him, or change his course as new attractions prevail, and harass himself without advancing. He who sees different ways to the same end, will, unless he watches carefully over his own conduct, lay out too much of his attention upon the comparison of probabilities, and the adjustment of expedients, and pause in the choice of his road till some accident intercepts his journey. He whose penetration extends to remote consequences, and who, whenever he applies his attention to any design, discovers new prospects of advantage, and possibilities of improvement, will not easily be persuaded that his project is ripe for execution; but will superadd one contrivance to another, endeavour to unite various purposes in one operation, multiply complications, and refine niceties, till he is entangled in his own scheme, and bewildered in the perplexity of various intentions. He that resolves to unite all the beauties of situation in a new purchase,[4] must waste his life in roving to no purpose from province to province. He that hopes in the same house

---

[1] Clear-sightedness.

[2] Most tightly closed.

[3] Johnson may be punning on *down*, which may refer to a down pillow as well as the depressed spirits of the sluggard.

[4] All the best characteristics of a plot of land in one place; Johnson may be punning here on the word *purchase*, meaning something bought and a position attained, both physically and metaphorically.

to obtain every convenience, may draw plans and study *Palladio*,[1] but will never lay a stone. He will attempt a treatise on some important subject, and amass materials, consult authors, and study all the dependant and collateral parts of learning, but never conclude himself qualified to write. He that has abilities to conceive perfection, will not easily be content without it; and since perfection cannot be reached, will lose the opportunity of doing well in the vain hope of unattainable excellence.

The certainty that life cannot be long, and the probability that it will be much shorter than nature allows, ought to awaken every man to the active prosecution of whatever he is desirous to perform. It is true, that no diligence can ascertain success; death may intercept the swiftest career; but he who is cut off in the execution of an honest undertaking, has at least the honour of falling in his rank, and has fought the battle though he missed the victory. ✄

The Necessity of Literary Courage.

THE RAMBLER, NO. 137

Tuesday, July 9, 1751

Dum vitant stulti vitia, in contraria currunt.

HORACE°

——whilst fools one vice condemn,
They run into the opposite extreme.

CREECH

That wonder is the effect of ignorance, has been often observed. The awful stillness of attention, with which the mind is overspread at the first view of an unexpected effect, ceases when we have leisure to disentangle complications and investigate causes. Wonder is a pause of reason, a sudden cessation of the mental progress, which lasts only while the understanding is fixed upon some single idea, and is at an end when it recovers force enough to divide the object into its parts, or mark the intermediate gradations from the first agent to the last consequence.

It may be remarked with equal truth, that ignorance is often the effect of wonder. It is common for those who have never accustomed themselves to the labour of inquiry, nor invigorated their confidence by conquests over difficulty, to sleep in the gloomy quiescence[2] of astonishment, without any effort to animate

---

[1]Andrea (1508–1580), Italian architect of the Renaissance who wrote *The Four Books of Architecture* and designed town palaces and villas in Vicenza. The arch and column design is now called the Palladian motif.
[2]Inactivity.

inquiry, or dispel obscurity. What they cannot immediately conceive, they consider as too high to be reached, or too extensive to be comprehended; they therefore content themselves with the gaze of folly, forbear to attempt what they have no hopes of performing, and resign the pleasure of rational contemplation to more pertinacious study,[1] or more active faculties.[2]

Among the productions of mechanick art, many are of a form so different from that of their first materials, and many consist of parts so numerous and so nicely adapted to each other, that it is not possible to view them without amazement. But when we enter the shops of artificers, observe the various tools by which every operation is facilitated, and trace the progress of a manufacture through the different hands, that, in succession to each other, contribute to its perfection, we soon discover that every single man has an easy task, and that the extremes, however remote, of natural rudeness and artificial elegance, are joined by a regular concatenation[3] of effects, of which every one is introduced by that which precedes it, and equally introduces that which is to follow.

The same is the state of intellectual and manual performances. Long calculations or complex diagrams affright the timorous and unexperienced from a second view; but if we have skill sufficient to analyze them into simple principles, it will be discovered that our fear was groundless. *Divide and conquer*, is a principle equally just in science[4] as in policy.[5] Complication is a species of confederacy,[6] which, while it continues united, bids defiance to the most active and vigorous intellect; but of which every member is separately weak, and which may therefore be quickly subdued, if it can once be broken.

The chief art of learning, as *Locke*° has observed, is to attempt but little at a time. The widest excursions of the mind are made by short flights frequently repeated; the most lofty fabricks of science are formed by the continued accumulation of single propositions.

It often happens, whatever be the cause, that impatience of labour,[7] or dread of miscarriage,[8] seizes those who are most distinguished for quickness of apprehension;[9] and that they who might with greatest reason promise themselves victory, are least willing to hazard the encounter. This diffidence,[10] where the attention is not laid asleep by laziness, or dissipated by pleasures, can arise only from confused and general views, such as negligence snatches in haste, or from

---

[1] Those more persistent in their studies.

[2] Alert minds.

[3] Chain.

[4] Knowledge acquired by study.

[5] Political science.

[6] A thing is complicated because it is made up of many interconnected parts.

[7] Desire for immediate results.

[8] Fear of failure.

[9] Understanding.

[10] Shyness or hesitation.

the disappointment of the first hopes formed by arrogance without reflection. To expect that the intricacies of science will be pierced by a careless glance, or the eminences of fame ascended without labour, is to expect a particular privilege, a power denied to the rest of mankind; but to suppose that the maze is inscrutable to diligence, or the heights inaccessible to perseverance, is to submit tamely to the tyranny of fancy, and enchain the mind in voluntary shackles.

It is the proper ambition of the heroes in literature to enlarge the boundaries of knowledge by discovering and conquering new regions of the intellectual world. To the success of such undertakings perhaps some degree of fortuitous happiness[1] is necessary, which no man can promise or procure to himself; and therefore doubt and irresolution may be forgiven in him that ventures into the unexplored abysses of truth, and attempts to find his way through the fluctuations of uncertainty, and the conflicts of contradiction. But when nothing more is required, than to pursue a path already beaten, and to trample obstacles which others have demolished, why should any man so much distrust his own intellect as to imagine himself unequal to the attempt?

It were to be wished that they who devote their lives to study would at once believe nothing too great for their attainment, and consider nothing as too little for their regard; that they would extend their notice alike to science[2] and to life, and unite some knowledge of the present world to their acquaintance with past ages and remote events.

Nothing has so much exposed men of learning to contempt and ridicule, as their ignorance of things which are known to all but themselves. Those who have been taught to consider the institutions of the schools, as giving the last perfection to human abilities, are surprised to see men wrinkled with study, yet wanting[3] to be instructed in the minute circumstances of propriety, or the necessary forms of daily transaction; and quickly shake off their reverence for modes of education, which they find to produce no ability above the rest of mankind.

Books, says Bacon, *can never teach the use of books*. The student must learn by commerce[4] with mankind to reduce his speculations to practice, and accommodate his knowledge to the purposes of life.

It is too common for those who have been bred to scholastick professions, and passed much of their time in academies where nothing but learning confers honours, to disregard every other qualification, and to imagine that they shall find mankind ready to pay homage to their knowledge, and to crowd about them for instruction. They therefore step out from their cells into the open world with all the confidence of authority and dignity of importance; they look round about them at once with ignorance and scorn on a race of beings to whom they are

---

[1]Luck.
[2]Book learning.
[3]Needing.
[4]Interaction.

equally unknown and equally contemptible, but whose manners they must imitate, and with whose opinions they must comply, if they desire to pass their time happily among them.

To lessen that disdain with which scholars are inclined to look on the common business of the world, and the unwillingness with which they condescend to learn what is not to be found in any system of philosophy, it may be necessary to consider that though admiration is excited by abstruse researches and remote discoveries, yet pleasure is not given, nor affection conciliated,[1] but by softer accomplishments, and qualities more easily communicable to those about us. He that can only converse upon questions, about which only a small part of mankind has knowledge sufficient to make them curious, must lose his days in unsocial silence, and live in the crowd of life without a companion. He that can only be useful on great occasions, may die without exerting his abilities, and stand a helpless spectator of a thousand vexations which fret away happiness, and which nothing is required to remove but a little dexterity of conduct and readiness of expedients.[2]

No degree of knowledge attainable by man is able to set him above the want[3] of hourly assistance, or to extinguish the desire of fond endearments, and tender officiousness;[4] and therefore, no one should think it unnecessary to learn those arts by which friendship may be gained. Kindness is preserved by a constant reciprocation of benefits or interchange of pleasures; but such benefits only can be bestowed, as others are capable to receive, and such pleasures only imparted, as others are qualified to enjoy.

By this descent from the pinnacles of art no honour will be lost; for the condescensions of learning[5] are always overpaid by gratitude. An elevated genius employed in little things, appears, to use the simile of *Longinus,°* like the sun in his evening declination: he remits[6] his splendour but retains his magnitude, and pleases more though he dazzles less. ✍

Genius and Learning in the Arts and Sciences.

THE RAMBLER, NO. 154

Saturday, September 7, 1751

——*Tibi res antiquae laudis et artis*
Aggredior, sanctos ausus recludere fontes.

VIRGIL°

---

[1]Gained.
[2]Availability of appropriate means to desired ends.
[3]Need.
[4]Eagerness to help others.
[5]Descent from the ivory tower of the learned.
[6]Gives up.

For thee my tuneful accents will I raise,
And treat of arts disclos'd in ancient days;
Once more unlock for thee the sacred spring.
        DRYDEN°

The direction of *Aristotle*° to those that study politicks, is first to examine and understand what has been written by the ancients upon government; then to cast their eyes round upon the world, and consider by what causes the prosperity of communities is visibly influenced, and why some are worse, and others better administered.

The same method must be pursued by him who hopes to become eminent in any other part of knowledge. The first task is to search books, the next to contemplate nature. He must first possess himself of the intellectual treasures which the diligence of former ages has accumulated, and then endeavour to increase them by his own collections.

The mental disease of the present generation, is impatience of study, contempt of the great masters of ancient wisdom, and a disposition to rely wholly upon unassisted genius and natural sagacity. The wits of these happy days have discovered a way to fame, which the dull caution of our laborious ancestors durst never attempt; they cut the knots of sophistry[1] which it was formerly the business of years to untie, solve difficulties by sudden irradiations of intelligence, and comprehend long processes of argument by immediate intuition.

Men who have flattered themselves into this opinion of their own abilities, look down on all who waste their lives over books, as a race of inferior beings, condemned by nature to perpetual pupilage, and fruitlessly endeavouring to remedy their barrenness by incessant cultivation, or succour[2] their feebleness by subsidiary strength. They presume that none would be more industrious than they, if they were not more sensible of deficiencies; and readily conclude, that he who places no confidence in his own powers, owes his modesty only to his weakness.

It is however certain, that no estimate is more in danger of erroneous calculations than those by which a man computes the force of his own genius. It generally happens at our entrance into the world, that, by the natural attraction of similitude, we associate with men like ourselves, young, sprightly, and ignorant, and rate our accomplishments by comparison with theirs; when we have once obtained an acknowledged superiority over our acquaintances, imagination and desire easily extend it over the rest of mankind, and if no accident forces us into new emulations, we grow old, and die in admiration of ourselves.

Vanity, thus confirmed in her dominion, readily listens to the voice of idleness, and sooths the slumber of life with continual dreams of excellence and greatness. A man, elated by confidence in his natural vigour of fancy and sagacity

---

[1]Faulty reasoning.
[2]Relieve.

of conjecture,[1] soon concludes that he already possesses whatever toil and inquiry can confer. He then listens with eagerness to the wild objections which folly has raised against the common means of improvement; talks of the dark chaos of indigested knowledge; describes the mischievous effects of heterogeneous sciences fermenting in the mind; relates the blunders of lettered ignorance; expatiates on the heroick merit of those who deviate from prescription, or shake off authority; and gives vent to the inflations of his heart by declaring that he owes nothing to pedants and universities.

All these pretensions, however confident, are very often vain. The laurels which superficial acuteness gains in triumphs over ignorance unsupported by vivacity, are observed by *Locke*° to be lost, whenever real learning and rational diligence appear against her; the sallies of gaiety are soon repressed by calm confidence; and the artifices of subtilty are readily detected by those, who, having carefully studied the question, are not easily confounded or surprised.

But, though the contemner[2] of books had neither been deceived by others nor himself, and was really born with a genius surpassing the ordinary abilities of mankind; yet surely such gifts of Providence may be more properly urged as incitements to labour, than encouragements to negligence. He that neglects the culture of ground naturally fertile, is more shamefully culpable, than he whose field would scarcely recompense his husbandry.[3]

Cicero° remarks, that not to know what has been transacted in former times, is to continue always a child. If no use is made of the labours of past ages, the world must remain always in the infancy of knowledge. The discoveries of every man must terminate in his own advantage, and the studies of every age be employed on questions which the past generation had discussed and determined. We may with as little reproach borrow science[4] as manufactures from our ancestors; and it is as rational to live in caves till our own hands have erected a palace, as to reject all knowledge of architecture which our understandings will not supply.

To the strongest and quickest mind it is far easier to learn than to invent. The principles of arithmetick and geometry may be comprehended by a close attention in a few days; yet who can flatter himself that the study of a long life would have enabled him to discover them, when he sees them yet unknown to so many nations, whom he cannot suppose less liberally endowed with natural reason, than the *Grecians* or *Egyptians*?

Every science was thus far advanced towards perfection, by the emulous[5] diligence of contemporary students, and the gradual discoveries of one age improving on another. Sometimes unexpected flashes of instruction were struck out by the fortuitous collision of happy incidents, or an involuntary concurrence

---

[1]His own strong imagination and the wisdom of his guesses.
[2]Despiser.
[3]Hardly repay the work put into it.
[4]Knowledge.
[5]Imitative.

of ideas, in which the philosopher to whom they happened had no other merit than that of knowing their value, and transmitting, unclouded, to posterity, that light which had been kindled by causes out of his power. The happiness of these casual illuminations no man can promise to himself, because no endeavours can procure them; and therefore whatever be our abilities or application, we must submit to learn from others what perhaps would have lain hid for ever from human penetration, had not some remote inquiry brought it to view; as treasures are thrown up by the ploughman and the digger in the rude[1] exercise of their common occupations.

The man whose genius qualifies him for great undertakings, must at least be content to learn from books the present state of human knowledge; that he may not ascribe to himself the invention of arts generally known; weary his attention with experiments of which the event has been long registered; and waste, in attempts which have already succeeded or miscarried, that time which might have been spent with usefulness and honour upon new undertakings.

But, though the study of books is necessary, it is not sufficient to constitute literary eminence. He that wishes to be counted among the benefactors of posterity, must add by his own toil to the acquisitions of his ancestors, and secure his memory from neglect by some valuable improvement. This can only be effected by looking out upon the wastes of the intellectual world, and extending the power of learning over regions yet undisciplined and barbarous; or by surveying more exactly our ancient dominions, and driving ignorance from the fortresses and retreats where she skulks undetected and undisturbed. Every science[2] has its difficulties, which yet call for solution before we attempt new systems of knowledge; as every country has its forests and marshes, which it would be wise to cultivate and drain, before distant colonies are projected as a necessary discharge of the exuberance of inhabitants.

No man ever yet became great by imitation. Whatever hopes for the veneration of mankind must have invention in the design or the execution; either the effect must itself be new, or the means by which it is produced. Either truths hitherto unknown must be discovered, or those which are already known enforced by stronger evidence, facilitated by clearer method, or elucidated by brighter illustrations.

Fame cannot spread wide or endure long that is not rooted in nature, and manured by art. That which hopes to resist the blast of malignity, and stand firm against the attacks of time, must contain in itself some original principle of growth. The reputation which arises from the detail or transportation of borrowed sentiments, may spread for awhile, like ivy on the rind of antiquity, but will be torn away by accident or contempt, and suffered to rot unheeded on the ground. ✍

---

[1] Humble.
[2] Area of knowledge.

The Usefulness of Advice. The Danger of Habits. The Necessity of Reviewing Life.

THE RAMBLER, NO. 155

Tuesday, September 1, 1751

——*Steriles transmissimus annos,*
Haec avi mihi prima dies, haec limina vitae.

STATIUS°

——Our barren years are past;
Be this of life the first, of sloth the last.

ELPHINSTON

No weakness of the human mind has more frequently incurred animadversion,[1] than the negligence with which men overlook their own faults, however flagrant, and the easiness with which they pardon them, however frequently repeated.

It seems generally believed, that as the eye cannot see itself, the mind has no faculties by which it can contemplate its own state, and that therefore we have not means of becoming acquainted with our real characters; an opinion which, like innumerable other postulates, an inquirer finds himself inclined to admit upon very little evidence, because it affords a ready solution of many difficulties. It will explain why the greatest abilities frequently fail to promote the happiness of those who possess them; why those who can distinguish with the utmost nicety[2] the boundaries of vice and virtue, suffer them to be confounded[3] in their own conduct; why the active and vigilant resign their affairs implicitly to the management of others; and why the cautious and fearful make hourly approaches towards ruin, without one sigh of solicitude or struggle for escape.

When a position teems thus with commodious consequences,[4] who can without regret confess it to be false? Yet it is certain that declaimers have indulged a disposition to describe the dominion of the passions as extended beyond the limits that nature assigned. Self-love is often rather arrogant than blind; it does not hide our faults from ourselves, but persuades us that they escape the notice of others, and disposes us to resent censures lest we should confess them to be just. We are secretly conscious of defects and vices, which we hope to conceal from the publick eye, and please ourselves with innumerable impostures, by which, in reality, nobody is deceived.

In proof of the dimness of our internal sight, or the general inability of man to determine rightly concerning his own character, it is common to urge the success of the most absurd and incredible flattery, and the resentment always raised by advice, however soft, benevolent, and reasonable. But flattery, if its

---

[1]Hostile criticism.
[2]Precision.
[3]Mixed and confused.
[4]So many convenient explanations.

operation be nearly[1] examined, will be found to owe its acceptance, not to ignorance, but knowledge of our failures, and to delight us rather as it consoles our wants[2] than displays our possessions. He that shall solicit the favour of his patron by praising him for qualities which he can find in himself, will be defeated by the more daring panegyrist[3] who enriches him with adscititious[4] excellence. Just praise is only a debt, but flattery is a present. The acknowledgment of those virtues on which conscience congratulates us, is a tribute that we can at any time exact with confidence; but the celebration of those which we only feign, or desire without any vigorous endeavours to attain them, is received as a confession of sovereignty over regions never conquered, as a favourable decision of disputable claims, and is more welcome as it is more gratuitous.[5]

Advice is offensive, not because it lays us open to unexpected regret, or convicts us of any fault which had escaped our notice, but because it shews us that we are known to others as well as to our selves; and the officious monitor[6] is persecuted with hatred, not because his accusation is false, but because he assumes that superiority which we are not willing to grant him, and has dared to detect what we desired to conceal.

For this reason advice is commonly ineffectual. If those who follow the call of their desires, without inquiry whither they are going, had deviated ignorantly from the paths of wisdom, and were rushing upon dangers unforeseen, they would readily listen to information that recalls them from their errours, and catch the first alarm by which destruction or infamy is denounced. Few that wander in the wrong way mistake it for the right, they only find it more smooth and flowery, and indulge their own choice rather than approve it: therefore few are persuaded to quit it by admonition or reproof, since it impresses no new conviction, nor confers any powers of action or resistance. He that is gravely informed how soon profusion[7] will annihilate his fortune, hears with little advantage what he knew before, and catches at the next occasion of expense, because advice has no force to suppress his vanity. He that is told how certainly intemperance will hurry him to the grave, runs with his usual speed to a new course of luxury, because his reason is not invigorated, nor his appetite weakened.

The mischief of flattery is, not that it persuades any man that he is what he is not, but that it suppresses the influence of honest ambition, by raising an opinion that honour may be gained without the toil of merit; and the benefit of advice arises commonly not from any new light imparted to the mind, but from the discovery which it affords of the publick suffrages.[8] He that could withstand conscience is frighted at infamy, and shame prevails when reason was defeated.

---

[1]Closely.
[2]Makes us feel better about what we lack.
[3]Offerer of elaborate praise.
[4]Extra; not inherent.
[5]Undeserved.
[6]Dutiful inspector.
[7]Excessive spending.
[8]Opinions.

As we all know our own faults, and know them commonly with many aggravations which human perspicacity[1] cannot discover, there is, perhaps, no man, however hardened by impudence or dissipated by levity, sheltered by hypocrisy or blasted by disgrace, who does not intend some time to review his conduct, and to regulate the remainder of his life by the laws of virtue. New temptations indeed attack him, new invitations are offered by pleasure and interest, and the hour of reformation is always delayed; every delay gives vice another opportunity of fortifying itself by habit; and the change of manners, though sincerely intended and rationally planned, is referred to the time when some craving passion shall be fully gratified, or some powerful allurement cease its importunity.[2]

Thus procrastination is accumulated on procrastination, and one impediment succeeds another, till age shatters our resolution, or death intercepts the project of amendment. Such is often the end of salutary purposes, after they have long delighted the imagination, and appeased that disquiet which every mind feels from known misconduct, when the attention is not diverted by business or by pleasure.

Nothing surely can be more unworthy of a reasonable nature, than to continue in a state so opposite to real happiness, as that all the peace of solitude, and felicity of meditation, must arise from resolutions of forsaking it. Yet the world will often afford examples of men, who pass months and years in a continual war with their own convictions, and are daily dragged by habit, or betrayed by passion, into practices which they closed and opened their eyes with purposes to avoid; purposes which, though settled on conviction, the first impulse of momentary desire easily overthrows.

The influence of custom is indeed such, that to conquer it will require the utmost efforts of fortitude and virtue; nor can I think any man more worthy of veneration and renown, than those who have burst the shackles of habitual vice. This victory, however, has different degrees of glory as of difficulty; it is more heroick as the objects of guilty gratification are more familiar,[3] and the recurrence of solicitation more frequent. He that, from experience of the folly of ambition, resigns his offices, may set himself free at once from temptation to squander his life in courts, because he cannot regain his former station. He who is enslaved by an amorous passion, may quit his tyrant in disgust, and absence will, without the help of reason, overcome by degrees the desire of returning. But those appetites to which every place affords their proper object, and which require no preparatory measures or gradual advances, are more tenaciously adhesive; the wish is so near the enjoyment, that compliance often precedes consideration, and, before the powers of reason can be summoned, the time for employing them is past.

Indolence is therefore one of the vices from which those whom it once infects are seldom reformed. Every other species of luxury operates upon some appetite

---

[1]Clear-sightedness.
[2]Insistent appeal.
[3]Close at hand.

that is quickly satiated, and requires some concurrence of art or accident which every place will not supply; but the desire of ease acts equally at all hours, and the longer it is indulged is the more increased. To do nothing is in every man's power; we can never want[1] an opportunity of omitting duties. The lapse to indolence is soft and imperceptible, because it is only a mere cessation of activity; but the return to diligence is difficult, because it implies a change from rest to motion, from privation to reality:

> ——*Facilis descensus averni:*
> *Noctes atque dies patet atri janua ditis;*
> *Sed revocare gradum, superasque evadere ad auras,*
> *Hoc opus, hic labor est.*
>
> VIRGIL°

> ——The gates of hell are open night and day;
> Smooth the descent, and easy is the way;
> But to return, and view the cheerful skies,
> In this the task and mighty labour lies.
>
> DRYDEN°

Of this vice, as of all others, every man who indulges it is conscious: we all know our own state, if we could be induced to consider it, and it might perhaps be useful to the conquest of all these ensnarers of the mind, if, at certain stated days, life was reviewed. Many things necessary are omitted, because we vainly imagine that they may be always performed; and what cannot be done without pain will for ever be delayed, if the time of doing it be left unsettled. No corruption is great but by long negligence, which can scarcely prevail in a mind regularly and frequently awakened by periodical remorse. He that thus breaks his life into parts, will find in himself a desire to distinguish every stage of his existence by some improvement, and delight himself with the approach of the day of recollection, as of the time which is to begin a new series of virtue and felicity. ✍

Poetry Debased by Mean Expressions.
An Example from Shakespeare.

THE RAMBLER, NO. 168

Saturday, October 26, 1751

> ——*Decipit*
> *Frons prima multos; rara mens intelligit,*
> *Quod interiore condidit cura angulo.*
>
> PHAEDRUS

---

[1]Lack.

The tinsel glitter, and the specious mien,[1]
Delude the most; few pry behind the scene.

It has been observed by *Boileau*,° that a "mean or common thought expressed in pompous diction, generally pleases more than a new or noble sentiment delivered in low and vulgar language; because the number is greater of those whom custom has enabled to judge of words, than whom study has qualified to examine things."

This solution might satisfy, if such only were offended with meanness of expression as are unable to distinguish propriety of thought, and to separate propositions or images from the vehicles by which they are conveyed to the understanding. But this kind of disgust is by no means confined to the ignorant or superficial; it operates uniformly and universally upon readers of all classes; every man, however profound or abstracted, perceives himself irresistibly alienated by low terms; they who profess the most zealous adherence to truth are forced to admit that she owes part of her charms to her ornaments; and loses much of her power over the soul, when she appears disgraced by a dress uncouth or ill-adjusted.

We are all offended by low terms, but are not disgusted alike by the same compositions, because we do not all agree to censure the same terms as low. No word is naturally or intrinsically meaner than another; our opinion therefore of words, as of other things arbitrarily and capriciously established, depends wholly upon accident and custom. The cottager thinks those apartments splendid and spacious, which an inhabitant of palaces will despise for their inelegance; and to him who has passed most of his hours with the delicate and polite, many expressions will seem sordid, which another, equally acute, may hear without offence; but a mean term never fails to displease him to whom it appears mean, as poverty is certainly and invariably despised, though he who is poor in the eyes of some, may, by others, be envied for his wealth.

Words become low by the occasions to which they are applied, or the general character of them who use them; and the disgust which they produce, arises from the revival of those images with which they are commonly united. Thus if, in the most solemn discourse, a phrase happens to occur which has been successfully employed in some ludicrous narrative, the gravest auditor finds it difficult to refrain from laughter, when they who are not prepossessed by the same accidental association, are utterly unable to guess the reason of his merriment. Words which convey ideas of dignity in one age, are banished from elegant writing or conversation in another, because they are in time debased by vulgar mouths, and can be no longer heard without the involuntary recollection of unpleasing images.

When *Macbeth*[2] is confirming himself in the horrid purpose of stabbing his king, he breaks out amidst his emotions into a wish natural to a murderer:

---

[1]False bearing.
[2]Actually Lady Macbeth; see 1.5.48–52.

————Come, thick night!
And pall thee in the dunnest smoke of hell,
That my keen knife see not the wound it makes;
Nor heav'n peep through the blanket of the dark,
To cry, hold! hold!

In this passage is exerted all the force of poetry; that force which calls new powers into being, which embodies sentiment, and animates matter: yet, perhaps, scarce any man now peruses it without some disturbance of his attention from the counteraction of the words to the ideas. What can be more dreadful than to implore the presence of night, invested not in common obscurity, but in the smoke of hell? Yet the efficacy of this invocation is destroyed by the insertion of an epithet now seldom heard but in the stable, and *dun*[1] night may come or go without any other notice than contempt.

If we start into raptures when some hero of the *Iliad* tells us that δόρυ μαίνεται, his lance rages with eagerness to destroy; if we are alarmed at the terrour of the soldiers commanded by *Caesar°* to hew down the sacred grove, who dreaded, says *Lucan,°* lest the axe aimed at the oak should fly back upon the striker:

————*Si robora sacra ferirent,*
In sua credebant redituras membra secures,

None dares with impious steel the grove to rend,
Lest on himself the destin'd stroke descend;

we cannot surely but sympathise with the horrours of a wretch about to murder his master, his friend, his benefactor, who suspects that the weapon will refuse its office, and start back from the breast which he is preparing to violate. Yet this sentiment is weakened by the name of an instrument used by butchers and cooks in the meanest employments: we do not immediately conceive that any crime of importance is to be committed with a *knife*; or who does not, at last, from the long habit of connecting a knife with sordid offices, feel aversion rather than terrour?

Macbeth proceeds to wish, in the madness of guilt, that the inspection of heaven may be intercepted, and that he may, in the involutions of infernal darkness, escape the eye of Providence. This is the utmost extravagance of determined wickedness; yet this is so debased by two unfortunate words, that while I endeavour to impress on my reader the energy of the sentiment, I can scarce check my risibility, when the expression forces itself upon my mind; for who, without some relaxation of his gravity, can hear of the avengers of guilt *peeping through a blanket*?

These imperfections of diction are less obvious to the reader, as he is less acquainted with common usages; they are therefore wholly imperceptible to a foreigner, who learns our language from books, and will strike a solitary academick less forcibly than a modish lady.

---

[1]Connected with the greyish brown color of a horse and a proverb about a horse called Dun who is stuck in the mire.

Among the numerous requisites that must concur to complete an author, few are of more importance than an early entrance into the living world. The seeds of knowledge may be planted in solitude, but must be cultivated in publick. Argumentation may be taught in colleges, and theories formed in retirement; but the artifice of embellishment, and the powers of attraction, can be gained only by general converse.

An acquaintance with prevailing customs and fashionable elegance is necessary likewise for other purposes. The injury that grand imagery suffers from unsuitable language, personal merit may fear from rudeness and indelicacy. When the success of *Aeneas°* depended on the favour of the queen upon whose coasts he was driven, his celestial protectress thought him not sufficiently secured against rejection by his piety or bravery, but decorated him for the interview with preternatural beauty. Whoever desires, for his writings or himself, what none can reasonably contemn, the favour of mankind, must add grace to strength, and make his thoughts agreeable as well as useful. Many complain of neglect who never tried to attract regard. It cannot be expected that the patrons of science or virtue should be solicitous to discover excellencies, which they who possess them shade and disguise. Few have abilities so much needed by the rest of the world as to be caressed on their own terms; and he that will not condescend to recommend himself by external embellishments, must submit to the fate of just sentiment meanly expressed, and be ridiculed and forgotten before he is understood. ✍

To the Right Honorable Earl of Chesterfield

February 7, 1755

My Lord

I have been lately informed by the proprietor of *The World* that two papers in which my *Dictionary* is recommended to the public were written by your Lordship. To be so distinguished is an honor which, being very little accustomed to favors from the great, I know not well how to receive, or in what terms to acknowledge.

When upon some slight encouragement I first visited your Lordship I was overpowered like the rest of mankind by the enchantment of your address, and could not forbear to wish that I might boast myself *le vainqueur du vainqueur de la terre*,[1] that I might obtain that regard for which I saw the world contending, but found my attendance so little encouraged that neither pride nor modesty would suffer me to continue it. When I had once addressed your Lordship in public, I had exhausted all the art of pleasing which a retired and uncourtly scholar can

---

[1] The conqueror of the conqueror of the world.

possess. I had done all that I could, and no man is well pleased to have his all neglected, be it ever so little.

Seven years, my lord, have now past since I waited in your outward rooms or was repulsed from your door, during which time I have been pushing on my work through difficulties of which it is useless to complain, and have brought it at last to the verge of publication without one act of assistance, one word of encouragement, or one smile of favor. Such treatment I did not expect, for I never had a Patron before.

The shepherd in Virgil° grew at last acquainted with Love, and found him a native of the rocks.[1] Is not a Patron, my lord, one who looks with unconcern on a man struggling for life in the water and when he has reached ground encumbers him with help? The notice which you have been pleased to take of my labors, had it been early, had been kind; but it has been delayed till I am indifferent and cannot enjoy it, till I am solitary and cannot impart it,[2] till I am known and do not want[3] it.

I hope it is no very cynical asperity[4] not to confess obligation where no benefit has been received, or to be unwilling that the public should consider me as owing that to a patron, which Providence has enabled me to do for myself.

Having carried on my work thus far with so little obligation to any favorer of learning I shall not be disappointed though I should conclude it, if less be possible, with less, for I have been long wakened from that dream of hope, in which I once boasted myself with so much exultation, my Lord your Lordship's most humble, most obedient servant,

SAM JOHNSON ✒

---

[1] *Eclogue* No. 8.
[2] Probably an allusion to his wife's death in 1752.
[3] Need.
[4] Sharpness of temper.

• • •

Charles Lamb

(1775 –1834)

Like Samuel Johnson, Charles Lamb was born into the working class, his father having come to London as the scrivener to Samuel Salt, senior member of the Inner Temple, which was one of the four legal societies in England known as the Inns of Court. Salt provided lodging in chambers of the Temple to John Lamb and his wife Elizabeth Field, and here they raised their family, Elizabeth bearing seven children, three of whom survived infancy. The oldest child was John, born in 1763, the second was Mary, born a year later, and the third was Charles, nine years younger than his sister.

Charles spent his first seven years in the Temple, where his mother worked as housekeeper for Salt, who undertook the early education of his servants' sons. Later, through Samuel Salt's influence, Charles was educated at Christ's Hospital, a school that had been established for needy children during the Reformation. When he left in 1789, he joined his brother, John, as clerk in the South Sea House and in 1792, at seventeen, took a position as clerk in the accounting office of the East India House, where he remained until his retirement. The year 1792 marks not only the start of his working career but also, with the death of his grandmother, the end of his frequent idyllic vacations in Hertfordshire. His loquacious maternal grandmother, Mary Field, had served as housekeeper at Blakesware (in Hertfordshire), an otherwise empty house owned by a wealthy family from the next county. Here Charles developed his unrequited affection for Ann Simmons, a young woman living with her mother in a cottage in nearby Blenheims. Ann later married a Mr. Bartram, who maintained a commercial address in Leicester Square.

By this time, Lamb's mother had become an invalid in the care of her sister Hetty and her daughter Mary. In 1796 Mary, in a fit of insanity, chased a serving girl about, wounded their father, and fatally stabbed their mother before Charles could wrest away the knife. Mary was taken to the asylum. After the death of Aunt Hetty the next year and of their father in 1799, Mary was released in the custody of Charles, who cared for her the rest of his life.

Although her fits of insanity periodically forced Charles to send her back to the asylum, Mary was generally an intelligent and pleasant companion.

Before leaving school, Lamb had met Coleridge,° two years his senior, and had developed through him a friendship with Wordsworth,° Hazlitt, and many other poets and writers of the period. Such men met often at the Lamb household. Gradually the Wednesday night literary gatherings became a regular occurrence. Despite his stutter, his underlying melancholy, and his occasional overindulgence in drink, Lamb became famous for his generous hospitality and his amusing wit.

During these early years together, to earn needed extra money and to entertain themselves as well, Mary and Charles wrote and published in 1807 *Tales from Shakespeare,* a book for children. In 1808 Charles published *Specimens of English Dramatic Poets Who Lived About the Time of Shakespeare,* which contributed to the revival of Elizabethan drama. Aside from some minor love sonnets and unsuccessful plays, however, his major works were written after 1820, when Lamb contributed twenty-five essays, about one a month, to the *London Magazine,* edited by John Scott.

In 1821, Lamb's brother, John, died. Charles and Mary went abroad in 1822 but returned when Mary had another attack. In 1823 his collected essays were published as *Essays of Elia,* the pseudonym taken from an Italian clerk at the South Sea House, where Lamb had briefly worked with his brother. A year later, he and Mary adopted an orphan, Emma Isola, whose father had taught Wordsworth, and brought her to live with them. Following Lamb's severe illness in 1825, the India House granted him a pension of three-quarters of his salary. He continued to write intermittently for various periodicals, and in 1833 he published the last of the *Essays of Elia.* Also in that year Emma, who had become a teacher, married one of the Lambs' friends, the publisher Edward Moxon. Near the end of his life Charles enjoyed long walks with Mary, though Coleridge's death in 1834 increased his loneliness; in December he fell, injuring his face, and died of eurysipelas, an infection under the skin.

Lamb's style, deliberately old-fashioned and whimsical, cultivates the voice of a bemused observer of city life and recalls, in its distinctively personal tone, the voices of Montaigne and Browne. Mildly and amusingly self-deprecating, he also directs what he believes to be gentle satire at the foibles of those around him. According to Lamb, the trouble with the schoolmaster, for instance, is "that he wants to be teaching *you.* One of these professors, upon my complaining that these little sketches of mine were anything but methodical, and that I was unable to make them otherwise, kindly offered to instruct me in the method by which young gentlemen in *his* seminary were taught to compose English themes." Such ruminations on the manners of men and women delighted the readers of his day.

Now, however, it is clear that what Lamb took to be harmless and humorous satire is often, in fact, insidious prejudice that moves from what is merely offensive in his characterization of the Scots to what is intolerable in his attitudes toward Jews and blacks. Unfortunately, "Imperfect Sympathies" probably expresses the majority opinion of the time. Yet the times do not exonerate him; Browne, his admired model, was not only able to resist such malignity of spirit but was motivated to use logic to dispel its concomitant superstitions. Even Chesterfield, preferring appearance to all, was more keenly attuned to the humanity of others than was Lamb. Lamb's tone in this and all his essays shows him to be confident that what amuses him will also amuse others. At their best, his essays are disarmingly honest and gently comic. Occasionally they are cloying and affected. At their worst they reveal the smug satisfaction of blatant prejudice.

Although he knew and loved Browne's prose, Lamb lacked Browne's natural charity. And, although he shared with Johnson his preference for London over nature, Lamb lacked Johnson's zeal and his moral stature. Unlike Addison, who also writes with warmth and gentle humor, Lamb rarely intends to instruct. Nonetheless, Lamb's influence over the essay has been considerable: E. B. White, for instance, adopts Lamb's bemused tone and comic self-deprecation; Edward Hoagland adopts his focus on the self as the center of the essay. This focus on the self as central originates, of course, in the essays of Montaigne. Lamb's unique contribution to the tradition of the essay thus resides in his own personality, in his "intellectual frame," as he calls it in "The Old and the New Schoolmaster." In all his writing Lamb heeds the advice he gives in that essay: "Your way of thinking, the mould in which your thoughts are cast, must be your own." ✐

New Year's Eve

Every man hath two birthdays: two days at least, in every year, which set him upon revolving the lapse[1] of time, as it affects his mortal duration. The one is that which in an especial manner he termeth his. In the gradual desuetude[2] of old observances, this custom of solemnizing our proper birthday hath nearly passed away, or is left to children, who reflect nothing at all about the matter, nor understand anything in it beyond cake and orange. But the birth of a New Year is of an interest too wide to be pretermitted[3] by king or cobbler. No one ever regarded the First of January with indifference. It is that from which all date their time, and count upon what is left. It is the nativity of our common Adam.

---

[1]Turning over in his mind the passing.
[2]Disuse.
[3]Neglected.

Of all sound of all bells — (bells, the music nighest bordering upon heaven) — most solemn and touching is the peal which rings out the Old Year. I never hear it without a gathering-up of my mind to a concentration of all the images that have been diffused over the past twelvemonth; all I have done or suffered, performed or neglected, in that regretted time. I begin to know its worth, as when a person dies. It takes a personal colour; nor was it a poetical flight in a contemporary, when he exclaimed —

"I saw the skirts of the departing Year." [1]

It is no more than what in sober sadness every one of us seems to be conscious of, in that awful leave-taking. I am sure I felt it, and all felt it with me, last night; [2] though some of my companions affected rather to manifest an exhilaration at the birth of the coming year, than any very tender regrets for the decease of its predecessor. But I am none of those who —

"Welcome the coming, speed the parting guest." [3]

I am naturally, beforehand, shy of novelties; new books, new faces, new years, — from some mental twist which makes it difficult in me to face the prospective. I have almost ceased to hope; and am sanguine [4] only in the prospects of other (former years). I plunge into foregone visions and conclusions. I encounter pell-mell with past disappointments. I am armour-proof against old discouragements. I forgive or overcome in fancy, old adversaries. I play over again *for love*, as the gamesters phrase it, games for which I once paid so dear. I would scarce now have any of those untoward accidents and events of my life reversed. I would no more alter them than the incidents of some well-contrived novel. Methinks, it is better that I should have pined away seven of my goldenest years, when I was thrall to the fair hair and fairer eyes, of Alice W——n, [5] than that so passionate a love adventure should be lost. It was better that our family should have missed that legacy, which old Dorrell [6] cheated us of, than that I should have at this moment two thousand pounds *in banco*, and be without the idea of that specious [7] old rogue.

In a degree beneath manhood, it is my infirmity to look back upon those early days. Do I advance a paradox when I say, that, skipping over the intervention of forty years, a man may have leave to love *himself* without the imputation of self-love?

---

[1] From Coleridge's° "Ode to the Departing Year," 1797.

[2] New Year's Eve, 1820.

[3] From Pope's° *Second Satire of Horace°* 2.160.

[4] Cheerful or optimistic.

[5] Ann Simmons; see biography.

[6] Probably an actual adversary.

[7] Deceptive.

If I know aught of myself, no one whose mind is introspective—and mine is painfully so—can have a less respect for his present identity than I have for the man Elia.[1] I know him to be light, and vain, and humoursome;[2] a notorious ***; addicted to ***; averse from counsel, neither taking it, nor offering it;—***[3] besides; a stammering buffoon; what you will; lay it on, and spare not; I subscribe to it all, and much more, than thou canst be willing to lay at his door:—but for the child Elia—that "other me," there, in the background—I must take leave to cherish the remembrance of that young master—with as little reference, I protest, to this stupid changeling of five-and-forty, as if it had been a child of some other house, and not of my parents. I can cry over its patient small-pox at five, and rougher medicaments. I can lay its poor fevered head upon the sick pillow at Christ's, and wake with it in surprise at the gentle posture of maternal tenderness hanging over it, that unknown had watched its sleep. I know how it shrank from any the least colour of falsehood.—God help thee, Elia, how art thou changed!—Thou art sophisticated.—I know how honest, how courageous (for a weakling) it was—how religious, how imaginative, how hopeful! From what have I not fallen, if the child I remember was indeed myself,—and not some dissembling guardian, presenting a false identity, to give the rule to my unpractised steps, and regulate the tone of my moral being!

That I am fond of indulging, beyond a hope of sympathy, in such retrospection, may be the symptom of some sickly idiosyncrasy. Or is it owing to another cause: simply, that being without wife or family, I have not learned to project myself enough out of myself; and having no offspring of my own to dally with, I turn back upon memory, and adopt my own early idea, as my heir and favourite? If these speculations seem fantastical to thee, reader—(a busy man, perchance), if I tread out of the way of thy sympathy, and am singularly conceited only, I retire, impenetrable to ridicule, under the phantom cloud of Elia.

The elders, with whom I was brought up, were of a character not likely to let slip the sacred observance of any old institution; and the ringing out of the Old Year was kept by them with circumstances of peculiar ceremony.—In those days the sound of those midnight chimes, though it seemed to raise hilarity in all around me, never failed to bring a train of pensive imagery into my fancy. Yet I then scarce conceived what it meant, or thought of it as a reckoning that concerned me. Not childhood alone, but the young man till thirty, never feels practically that he is mortal. He knows it indeed, and, if need were, he could preach a homily on the fragility of life; but he brings it not home to himself, any more than in a hot June we can appropriate to our imagination the freezing days of December. But now, shall I confess a truth?—I feel these audits but too powerfully. I begin to count the probabilities of my duration, and to grudge at the

---

[1]Lamb's pseudonym as an essay writer; see biography.
[2]Capricious and peevish.
[3]Asterisks indicate words Lamb pretends to have censored.

expenditure of moments and shortest periods, like miser's farthings. In proportion as the years both lessen and shorten, I set more count upon their periods, and would fain lay my ineffectual finger upon the spoke of the great wheel.[1] I am not content to pass away "like a weaver's shuttle."[2] Those metaphors solace me not, nor sweeten the unpalatable draught of mortality. I care not to be carried with the tide, that smoothly bears human life to eternity; and reluct at the inevitable course of destiny. I am in love with this green earth; the face of town and country; the unspeakable rural solitudes, and the sweet security of streets. I would set up my tabernacle here. I am content to stand still at the age to which I am arrived; I, and my friends: to be no younger, no richer, no handsomer. I do not want to be weaned by age; or drop, like mellow fruit, as they say, into the grave.— Any alteration, on this earth of mine, in diet or in lodging, puzzles and discomposes me. My household-gods[3] plant a terrible fixed foot, and are not rooted up without blood. They do not willingly seek Lavinian shores.[4] A new state of being staggers me.

Sun, and sky, and breeze, and solitary walks, and summer holidays, and the greenness of fields, and the delicious juices of meats and fishes, and society, and the cheerful glass, and candlelight, and fireside conversations, and innocent vanities, and jests, and *irony itself*—do these things go out with life?

Can a ghost laugh, or shake his gaunt sides, when you are pleasant with him?

And you, my midnight darlings, my Folios; must I part with the intense delight of having you (huge armfuls) in my embraces? Must knowledge come to me, if it come at all, by some awkward experiment of intuition, and no longer by this familiar process of reading?

Shall I enjoy friendships there, wanting[5] the smiling indications which point me to them here,—the recognisable face—the "sweet assurance of a look"?[6]

In winter this intolerable disinclination to dying—to give it its mildest name—does more especially haunt and beset me. In a genial August noon, beneath a sweltering sky, death is almost problematic. At those times do such poor snakes as myself enjoy an immortality. Then we expand and burgeon. Then we are as strong again, as valiant again, as wise again, and a great deal taller. The blast that nips and shrinks me, puts me in thoughts of death. All things allied to the insubstantial, wait upon that master feeling; cold, numbness, dreams, perplexity; moonlight itself, with its shadowy and spectral appearances,— that cold ghost of the sun, or Phoebus' sickly sister,[7] like that innutritious

---

[1]Of fortune.

[2]Job 7:6.

[3]Lares and penates, two kinds of Roman household gods carried whenever the Romans moved, came to signify the continuity of the family.

[4]Lavinius is the town in Latium (Italy) founded by Aeneas° after the Trojan War.

[5]Lacking.

[6]E. V. Lucas, an early editor of Lamb's work, attributes this quotation to Sidney.°

[7]Phoebus is Apollo, Greek god of the sun, and his sister, Artemis, is the moon.

one denounced in the Canticles:[1] —I am none of her minions—I hold with the Persian.[2]

Whatsoever thwarts, or puts me out of my way, brings death unto my mind. All partial evils, like humours,[3] run into that capital plague-sore.—I have heard some profess an indifference to life. Such hail the end of their existence as a port of refuge; and speak of the grave as of some soft arms, in which they may slumber as on a pillow. Some have wooed death—but out upon thee, I say, thou foul, ugly phantom! I detest, abhor, execrate, and (with Friar John)[4] give thee to six score thousand devils, as in no instance to be excused or tolerated, but shunned as an universal viper; to be branded, proscribed, and spoken evil of! In no way can I be brought to digest thee, thou thin, melancholy *Privation*, or more frightful and confounding *Positive!*[5]

Those antidotes, prescribed against the fear of thee, are altogether frigid and insulting, like thyself. For what satisfaction hath a man, that he shall "lie down with kings and emperors in death," who in his lifetime never greatly coveted the society of such bed-fellows?—or, forsooth, that "so shall the fairest face appear"?—why, to comfort me, must Alice W——n be a goblin? More than all, I conceive disgust at those impertinent and misbecoming familiarities, inscribed upon your ordinary tombstones. Every dead man must take upon himself to be lecturing me with his odious truism, that "Such as he now is I must shortly be." Not so shortly, friend, perhaps, as thou imaginest. In the meantime I am alive. I move about. I am worth twenty of thee. Know thy betters! Thy New Years' days are past. I survive, a jolly candidate for 1821. Another cup of wine—and while that turncoat bell, that just now mournfully chanted the obsequies of 1820 departed, with changed notes lustily rings in a successor, let us attune to its peal the song made on a like occasion, by hearty, cheerful Mr. Cotton.[6]

> *The New Year*
> HARK, the cock crows, and yon bright star
> Tells us, the day himself's not far;
> And see where, breaking from the night,
> He gilds the western hills with light.
> With him old Janus[7] doth appear,

---

[1]Song of Solomon° 8:8.

[2]According to E. V. Lucas, a worshiper of the sun.

[3]Morbid fluids.

[4]E. V. Lucas identifies him as a character from Rabelais° who sent his slain enemies "to all the devils in hell!"

[5]That which truly exists; a reality.

[6]Charles Cotton (1630–1687), minor poet of the Restoration who translated Montaigne's *Essays* and wrote *Poems on Several Occasions*, lyrics admired by Coleridge,° Wordsworth,° and Lamb.

[7]Roman God of beginnings, gates, and doorways, whose two bearded faces look in opposite directions. Because his festival was celebrated on the first day of the year, the first month, January, is named in his honor.

Peeping into the future year,
With such a look as seems to say
The prospect is not good that way.
Thus do we rise ill sights to see,
And 'gainst ourselves to prophesy;
When the prophetic fear of things
A more tormenting mischief brings,
More full of soul-tormenting gall
Than direst mischiefs can befall.
But stay! but stay! methinks my sight,
Better informed by clearer light,
Discerns sereneness in that brow
That all contracted seemed but now.
His revers'd face may show distaste,
And frown upon the ills are past;
But that which this way looks is clear,
And smiles upon the New-born Year.
He looks too from a place so high,
The year lies open to his eye;
And all the moments open are
To the exact discoverer.
Yet more and more he smiles upon
The happy revolution.
Why should we then suspect or fear
The influences of a year,
So smiles upon us the first morn,
And speaks us good so soon as born?
Plague on't! the last was ill enough,
This cannot but make better proof;
Or, at the worst, as we brush'd through
The last, why so we may this too;
And then the next in reason shou'd
Be superexcellently good:
For the worst ills (we daily see)
Have no more perpetuity
Than the best fortunes that do fall;
Which also bring us wherewithal
Longer their being to support,
Than those do of the other sort:
And who has one good year in three,
And yet repines at destiny,
Appears ungrateful in the case,
And merits not the good he has.
Then let us welcome the New Guest
With lusty brimmers of the best:
Mirth always should Good Fortune meet,
And renders e'en Disaster sweet:

And though the Princess[1] turn her back
Let us but line ourselves with sack,
We better shall by far hold out,
Till the next year she face about.

How say you, reader—do not these verses smack of the rough magnanimity of the old English vein? Do they not fortify like a cordial; enlarging the heart, and productive of sweet blood, and generous spirits, in the concoction? Where be those puling[2] fears of death, just now expressed or affected?—Passed like a cloud—absorbed in the purging sunlight of clear poetry—clean washed away by a wave of genuine Helicon,[3] your only Spa for these hypochondries. And now another cup of the generous! and a merry New Year, and many of them to you all, my masters! ✐

Imperfect Sympathies

> I am of a constitution so general, that it consorts and sympathiseth with all things; I have no antipathy, or rather idiosyncrasy in anything. Those natural repugnancies do not touch me, nor do I behold with prejudice the French, Italian, Spaniard, or Dutch.
>
> *Religio Medici.*[4]

That the author of the Religio Medici mounted upon the airy stilts of abstraction, conversant about notional[5] and conjectural essences; in whose categories of Being the possible took the upper hand of the actual; should have overlooked the impertinent individualities of such poor concretions as mankind, is not much to be admired. It is rather to be wondered at, that in the genus of animals he should have condescended to distinguish that species at all. For myself—earth-bound and fettered to the scene of my activities,— "Standing on earth, not rapt above the sky,"[6] I confess that I do feel the differences of mankind, national or individual, to an unhealthy excess. I can look with no indifferent eye upon things or persons. Whatever is, is to me a matter of taste or distaste; or when once it becomes indifferent, it begins to be disrelishing. I am, in plainer words, a bundle of prejudices—made up of likings and dislikings—the veriest thrall to sympathies, apathies, antipathies. In a certain sense, I hope it may be said of me that I am a lover of my species. I can feel for all indifferently, but I cannot feel towards all equally. The more purely-English word that expresses sympathy, will better

---

[1]Fortune.
[2]Whining.
[3]The mountain in Boetia sacred to the muses; Lamb here seems to treat it as a body of water with waves.
[4]Lamb juxtaposes two sentences from part 2, section 1.
[5]Speculative.
[6]*Paradise Lost* 7.23, where "pole" replaces Lamb's "sky."

explain my meaning. I can be a friend to a worthy man, who upon another account cannot be my mate or *fellow*. I cannot *like* all people alike. [I would be understood as confining myself to the subject of imperfect sympathies.[1] To nations or classes of men there can be no direct antipathy. There may be individuals born and constellated so opposite to another individual nature, that the same sphere cannot hold them. I have met with my moral antipodes, and can believe the story of two persons meeting (who never saw one another before in their lives) and instantly fighting.

> ——We by proof find there should be
> "Twixt man and man such an antipathy,
> That though he can show no just reason why
> For any former wrong or injury,
> Can neither find a blemish in his fame,
> Nor aught in face or feature justly blame,
> Can challenge or accuse him of no evil,
> Yet notwithstanding hates him as a devil.

The lines are from old Heywood's° "Hierarchie of Angels," and he subjoins a curious story in confirmation, of a Spaniard who attempted to assassinate a king Ferdinand of Spain, and being put to the rack could give no other reason for the deed but an inveterate antipathy which he had taken to the first sight of the king.

> ——The cause which to that act compell'd him
> Was, he ne'er loved him since he first beheld him.]

I have been trying all my life to like Scotchmen, and am obliged to desist from the experiment in despair. They cannot like me—and in truth, I never knew one of that nation who attempted to do it. There is something more plain and ingenuous in their mode of proceeding. We know one another at first sight. There is an order of imperfect intellects (under which mine must be content to rank) which in its constitution is essentially anti-Caledonian.[2] The owners[3] of the sort of faculties I allude to, have minds rather suggestive than comprehensive. They have no pretences to much clearness or precision in their ideas, or in their manner of expressing them. Their intellectual wardrobe (to confess fairly) has few whole pieces in it. They are content with fragments and scattered pieces of Truth. She presents no full front to them—a feature or side-face at the most. Hints and glimpses, germs and crude essays[4] at a system, is the utmost they pretend to.[5] They beat up a little game[6] peradventure—and leave it to knottier heads, more robust constitutions, to run it down. The light that lights them is not steady and

---

[1]All material shown here in brackets appeared as footnotes in the original text.
[2]Caledonia was the Roman name for Scotland.
[3]Lamb, for instance.
[4]Attempts.
[5]Aim for.
[6]Lamb is using the hunt as a metaphor here.

polar, but mutable and shifting: waxing, and again waning. Their conversation is accordingly. They will throw out a random word in or out of season, and be content to let it pass for what it is worth. They cannot speak always as if they were upon their oath—but must be understood, speaking or writing, with some abatement.[1] They seldom wait to mature a proposition, but e'en bring it to market in the green ear. They delight to impart their defective discoveries as they arise, without waiting for their full development. They are no systematizers, and would but err more by attempting it. Their minds, as I said before, are suggestive merely. The brain of a true Caledonian (if I am not mistaken) is constituted upon quite a different plan. His Minerva° is born in panoply.[2] You are never admitted to see his ideas in their growth—if, indeed, they do grow, and are not rather put together upon principles of clock-work. You never catch his mind in an undress. He never hints or suggests anything, but unlades[3] his stock of ideas in perfect order and completeness. He brings his total wealth into company, and gravely unpacks it. His riches are always about him. He never stoops to catch a glittering something in your presence to share it with you, before he quite knows whether it be true touch[4] or not. You cannot cry *halves* to anything that he finds. He does not find, but bring. You never witness his first apprehension of a thing. His understanding is always at its meridian[5]—you never see the first dawn, the early streaks.—He has no falterings of self-suspicion. Surmises, guesses, misgivings, half-intuitions, semi-consciousnesses, partial illuminations, dim instincts, embryo conceptions, have no place in his brain or vocabulary. The twilight of dubiety never falls upon him. Is he orthodox—he has no doubts. Is he an infidel—he has none either. Between the affirmative and the negative there is no border-land with him. You cannot hover with him upon the confines of truth, or wander in the maze of a probable argument. He always keeps the path. You cannot make excursions with him—for he sets you right. His taste never fluctuates. His morality never abates. He cannot compromise, or understand middle actions. There can be but a right and a wrong. His conversation is as a book. His affirmations have the sanctity of an oath. You must speak upon the square with him. He stops a metaphor like a suspected person in an enemy's country. "A healthy book!"—said one of his countrymen to me, who had ventured to give that appellation to John Buncle,[6]—"Did I catch rightly what you said? I have heard of a man in health, and of a healthy state of body, but I do not see how that epithet can be properly applied

---

[1]Moderation.

[2]In the complete arms and armor of a warrior; Minerva (Athena) was born fully mature from the head of Jupiter (Zeus).

[3]Unpacks.

[4]Tested for its quality, as a precious stone is by being rubbed on a touchstone such as black quartz or jasper.

[5]Zenith.

[6]Title character in *The Life of John Buncle, Esq.* by Thomas Amory, published in two parts in 1756 and 1766; Hazlitt called Amory "the English Rabelais.°"

to a book." Above all, you must beware of indirect expressions before a Caledonian. Clap an extinguisher upon your irony, if you are unhappily blest with a vein of it. Remember you are upon your oath. I have a print of a graceful female after Leonardo da Vinci,° which I was showing off to Mr. **** After he had examined it minutely, I ventured to ask him how he liked MY BEAUTY (a foolish name it goes by among my friends)—when he very gravely assured me, that "he had considerable respect for my character and talents" (so he was pleased to say), "but had not given himself much thought about the degree of my personal pretensions." The misconception staggered me, but did not seem much to disconcert him.—Persons of this nation are particularly fond of affirming a truth —which nobody doubts. They do not so properly affirm, as annunciate it. They do indeed appear to have such a love of truth (as if, like virtue, it were valuable for itself) that all truth becomes equally valuable, whether the proposition that contains it be new or old, disputed, or such as is impossible to become a subject of disputation. I was present not long since at a party of North Britons, where a son of Burns° was expected; and happened to drop a silly expression (in my South British way), that I wished it were the father instead of the son—when four of them started up at once to inform me, that "that was impossible, because he was dead." An impracticable wish, it seems, was more than they could conceive. Swift° has hit off this part of their character, namely their love of truth, in his biting way, but with an illiberality that necessarily confines the passage to the margin. [There are some people who think they sufficiently acquit themselves, and entertain their company, with relating facts of no consequence, not at all out of the road of such common incidents as happen every day; and this I have observed more frequently among the Scots than any other nation, who are very careful not to omit the minutest circumstances of time or place; which kind of discourse, if it were not a little relieved by the uncouth terms and phrases, as well as accent and gesture, peculiar to that country, would be hardly tolerable.—*Hints toward an Essay on Conversation*.] The tediousness of these people is certainly provoking. I wonder if they ever tire one another!—In my early life I had a passionate fondness for the poetry of Burns.° I have sometimes foolishly hoped to ingratiate myself with his countrymen by expressing it. But I have always found that a true Scot resents your admiration of his compatriot even more than he would your contempt of him. The latter he imputes to your "imperfect acquaintance with many of the words which he uses"; and the same objection makes it a presumption in you to suppose that you can admire him.—Thomson[1] they seem to have forgotten. Smollett° they have neither forgotten nor forgiven for his delineation of Rory[2]

---

[1]James (1700–1748), Scottish poet, friend of Pope,° forerunner of romanticism, who wrote *The Seasons*, a descriptive poem of four parts.

[2]Title character in *Roderick Random*, Smollett's° autobiographical first novel about a young Scotsman trained in surgery who comes to London and, overcome by poverty, sails as surgeon's mate on a ship to the West Indies.

and his companion, upon their first introduction to our metropolis.—Speak of Smollett° as a great genius, and they will retort upon you Hume's° History compared with *his* Continuation of it. What if the historian had continued Humphrey Clinker?[1]

I have, in the abstract, no disrespect for Jews. They are a piece of stubborn antiquity, compared with which Stonehenge is in its nonage.[2] They date beyond the pyramids. But I should not care to be in habits of familiar intercourse with any of that nation. I confess that I have not the nerves to enter their synagogues. Old prejudices cling about me. I cannot shake off the story of Hugh of Lincoln.[3] Centuries of injury, contempt, and hate, on the one side,—of cloaked revenge, dissimulation, and hate, on the other, between our and their fathers, must and ought to affect the blood of the children. I cannot believe it can run clear and kindly yet; or that a few fine words, such as candour, liberality, the light of a nineteenth century, can close up the breaches of so deadly a disunion. A Hebrew is nowhere congenial to me. He is least distasteful on 'Change[4]—for the mercantile spirit levels all distinctions, as all are beauties in the dark. I boldly confess that I do not relish the approximation[5] of Jew and Christian, which has become so fashionable. The reciprocal endearments have, to me, something hypocritical and unnatural in them. I do not like to see the Church and Synagogue kissing and congeeing[6] in awkward postures of an affected civility. If *they* are converted, why do they not come over to us altogether? Why keep up a form of separation, when the life of it is fled? If they can sit with us at table, why do they keck[7] at our cookery? I do not understand these half convertites. Jews christianizing—Christians judaizing—puzzle me. I like fish or flesh. A moderate Jew is a more confounding piece of anomaly than a wet Quaker.[8] The spirit of the synagogue is essentially *separative*. B—— would have been more in keeping if he had abided by the faith of his forefathers. There is a fine scorn in his face, which nature meant to be of— Christians. The Hebrew spirit is strong in him, in spite of his proselytism. He cannot conquer the Shibboleth.[9] How it breaks out, when he sings, "The Children of Israel passed through the Red Sea!" The auditors, for the moment, are as Egyptians to him, and he rides over our necks in triumph. There is no mistaking

---

[1]Smollett's° epistolary novel about a coach tour through Britain.
[2]Youth.
[3]Little Christian boy in "The Prioress's Tale" from Chaucer's *Canterbury Tales* whose throat is slit by Jews. Such anti-Semitic accusations were common in the Middle Ages.
[4]Stock exchange.
[5]The advance toward a union.
[6]Bowing formally.
[7]Make the sound of vomiting.
[8]One who drinks alcohol.
[9]Password that distinguishes one group from another; from the Hebrew for "ear of corn"—see Judges 12:6.

him. B—— has a strong expression of sense in his countenance, and it is confirmed by his singing. The foundation of his vocal excellence is sense. He sings with understanding, as Kemble[1] delivered dialogue. He would sing the Commandments, and give an appropriate character to each prohibition. His nation, in general, have not over-sensible countenances. How should they?—but you seldom see a silly expression among them.—Gain, and the pursuit of gain, sharpen a man's visage. I never heard of an idiot being born among them.—Some admire the Jewish female-physiognomy. I admire it—but with trembling. Jael[2] had those full dark inscrutable eyes.

In the Negro countenance you will often meet with strong traits of benignity. I have felt yearnings of tenderness towards some of these faces—or rather masks—that have looked out kindly upon one in casual encounters in the streets and highways. I love what Fuller[3] beautifully calls—these "images of God cut in ebony." But I should not like to associate with them, to share my meals and my good nights with them—because they are black.

I love Quaker ways, and Quaker worship. I venerate the Quaker principles. It does me good for the rest of the day when I meet any of their people in my path. When I am ruffled or disturbed by any occurrence, the sight, or quiet voice of a Quaker, acts upon me as a ventilator, lightening the air, and taking of a load from the bosom. But I cannot like the Quakers (as Desdemona would say) "to live with them."[4] I am all over sophisticated—with humours,[5] fancies, craving hourly sympathy. I must have books, pictures, theatres, chit-chat, scandal, jokes, ambiguities, and a thousand whimwhams, which their simpler taste can do without. I should starve at their primitive banquet. My appetites are too high for the salads which (according to Evelyn[6]) Eve dressed for the angel; my gusto too excited "To sit a guest with Daniel at his pulse."[7]

The indirect answers which Quakers are often found to return to a question put to them may be explained, I think, without the vulgar assumption, that they are more given to evasion and equivocating than other people. They naturally look to their words more carefully, and are more cautious of committing themselves.

---

[1]J. P. (1757–1823), formal tragic actor who played Hamlet and Coriolanus. Kemble became manager of the Drury Lane Theatre in 1789 and manager of Covent Garden in 1803, reopening it when it was destroyed by fire in 1808. The actress Sarah Siddons was his sister.

[2]See Judges 4–5, where Jael, one of the enslaved people of Israel, became a heroine by appearing to provide safety for the enemy Sisera and then murdering him while he slept.

[3]Thomas (1608–1661), a popular Cavalier preacher and writer who wrote *The Holy and Profane States*, a miscellany of essays and character types, *Good Thoughts in Bad Times*, and *The History of the Worthies of England*. Lamb published an edition of Fuller's writings in 1811.

[4]*Othello* 1.3.249.

[5]Whims.

[6]John (1620–1706), English diarist who developed extensive gardens at his residence at Sayes Court, Deptford, and wrote *Acetaria: A Discourse of Sallets,* to which Lamb here refers.

[7]Porridge made from seeds like lentils (*Paradise Regained* 2.278).

upon their veracity. A Quaker is by law exempted from taking an oath. The custom of resorting to an oath in extreme cases, sanctified as it is by all religious antiquity, is apt (it must be confessed) to introduce into the laxer sort of minds the notion of two kinds of truth—the one applicable to the solemn affairs of justice, and the other to the common proceedings of daily intercourse. As truth bound upon the conscience by an oath can be but truth, so in the common affirmations of the shop and the marketplace a latitude is expected and conceded upon questions wanting this solemn covenant. Something less than truth satisfies. It is common to hear a person say, "You do not expect me to speak as if I were upon my oath." Hence a great deal of incorrectness and inadvertency, short of falsehood, creeps into ordinary conversation; and a kind of secondary or laic-truth is tolerated, where clergy-truth—oath-truth, by the nature of the circumstances, is not required. A Quaker knows none of this distinction. His simple affirmation being received upon the most sacred occasions, without any further test, stamps a value upon the words which he is to use upon the most indifferent topics of life. He looks to them, naturally, with more severity. You can have of him no more than his word. He knows, if he is caught tripping in a casual expression, he forfeits, for himself at least, his claim to the invidious exemption. He knows that his syllables are weighed—and how far a consciousness of this particular watchfulness, exerted against a person, has a tendency to produce indirect answers, and a diverting of the question by honest means, might be illustrated, and the practice justified by a more sacred example than is proper to be adduced[1] upon this occasion. The admirable presence of mind, which is notorious in Quakers upon all contingencies, might be traced to this imposed self-watchfulness—if it did not seem rather an humble and secular scion[2] of that old stock of religious constancy, which never bent or faltered, in the Primitive Friends, or gave way to the winds of persecution, to the violence of judge or accuser, under trials and racking examinations. "You will never be the wiser, if I sit here answering your questions till midnight," said one of those upright Justicers to Penn,[3] who had been putting law-cases with a puzzling subtlety. "Thereafter as the answers may be," retorted the Quaker. The astonishing composure of this people is sometimes ludicrously displayed in lighter instances.—I was travelling in a stage-coach with three male Quakers, buttoned up in the straitest nonconformity of their sect. We stopped to bait[4] at Andover, where a meal, partly tea apparatus, partly supper was set before us. My friends confined themselves to the tea-table. I in my way took supper. When the landlady brought in the bill, the eldest of my companions discovered that she had charged for both meals. This was resisted. Mine hostess was very clamorous and positive. Some mild arguments were used on the part of the Quakers, for which

---

[1]Cited.

[2]Descendant.

[3]William (1644–1718), English Quaker, once imprisoned in the Tower of London for his religious views, who established in 1682 the colony of religious toleration that became the state of Pennsylvania.

[4]Feed horses and passengers.

the heated mind of the good lady seemed by no means a fit recipient. The guard They have a peculiar character to keep up on this head. They stand in a manner came in with his usual peremptory notice. The Quakers pulled out their money and formally tendered it—so much for tea—I, in humble imitation, tendering mine—for the supper which I had taken. She would not relax in her demand. So they all three quietly put up their silver,[1] as did myself, and marched out of the room, the eldest and gravest going first, with myself closing up the rear, who thought I could not do better than follow the example of such grave and warrantable[2] personages. We got in. The steps went up. The coach drove off. The murmurs of mine hostess, not very indistinctly or ambiguously pronounced, became after a time inaudible—and now my conscience, which the whimsical scene had for a while suspended, beginning to give some twitches, I waited, in the hope that some justification would be offered by these serious persons for the seeming injustice of their conduct. To my great surprise not a syllable was dropped on the subject. They sat as mute as at a meeting. At length the eldest of them broke silence, by inquiring of his next neighbour, "Hast thee heard how indigos go at the India House?"[3] and the question operated as a soporific on my moral feeling as far as Exeter. ✍

The Old and the New Schoolmaster

My reading has been lamentably desultory[4] and immethodical. Odd, out of the way, old English plays, and treatises, have supplied me with most of my notions, and ways of feeling. In everything that relates to *science*, I am a whole Encyclopaedia behind the rest of the world. I should have scarcely cut a figure among the franklins, or country gentlemen, in King John's[5] days. I know less geography than a schoolboy of six weeks' standing. To me a map of old Ortelius is as authentic as Arrowsmith.[6] I do not know whereabout Africa merges into Asia; whether Ethiopia lie in one or other of those great divisions; nor can form the remotest

---

[1]Put away their money.

[2]Authoritative.

[3]The price of blue-dyed cloth from India at the office of the East India Company in London.

[4]Haphazard.

[5](1167–1216) Son of Henry II and Eleanor of Aquitaine. He rebelled against his brother Richard's° rule. Richard forgave him, and John became king upon his brother's death. In June 1215 he signed the Magna Carta.

[6]Abraham Ortelius (1527–1598) was a Flemish geographer who published the first modern atlas, *Theatrum Orbis Terrarum*, in 1570. Aaron Arrowsmith (1750–1823) was an English geographer who founded a mapmaking business that was later continued by his sons and nephew. Their maps were the best of the time.

conjecture of the position of New South Wales, or Van Diemen's Land.[1] Yet do I hold a correspondence with a very dear friend in the first-named of these two Terrae Incognitae. I have no astronomy. I do not know where to look for the Bear, or Charles's Wain;[2] the place of any star; or the name of any of them at sight. I guess at Venus only by her brightness—and if the sun on some portentous morn were to make his first appearance in the West, I verily believe, that, while all the world were gasping in apprehension about me, I alone should stand unterrified, from sheer incuriosity and want[3] of observation. Of history and chronology I possess some vague points, such as one cannot help picking up in the course of miscellaneous study; but I never deliberately sat down to a chronicle, even of my own country. I have most dim apprehensions of the four great monarchies;[4] and sometimes the Assyrian, sometimes the Persian, floats as *first* in my fancy. I make the widest conjectures concerning Egypt, and her shepherd kings. My friend M., with great painstaking, got me to think I understood the first proposition in Euclid,[5] but gave me over in despair at the second. I am entirely unacquainted with the modern languages; and, like a better man than myself, have "small Latin and less Greek."[6] I am a stranger to the shapes and texture of the commonest trees, herbs, flowers—not from the circumstance of my being town-born—for I should have brought the same inobservant spirit into the world with me, had I first seen it "on Devon's leafy shores,"[7] —and am no less at a loss among purely town objects, tools, engines, mechanic processes. —Not that I affect ignorance— but my head has not many mansions, nor spacious; and I have been obliged to fill it with such cabinet[8] curiosities as it can hold without aching. I sometimes wonder how I have passed my probation with so little discredit in the world, as I have done, upon so meagre a stock. But the fact is, a man may do very well with a very little knowledge, and scarce be found out, in mixed company; everybody is so much more ready to produce his own, than to call for a display of your acquisitions. But in a *tête-à-tête* there is no shuffling. The truth will out. There is nothing which I dread so much, as the being left alone for a quarter of an hour with a sensible, well-informed man, that does not know me. I lately got into a dilemma of this sort. —

---

[1]Tasmania, island off Australia.

[2]Wagon, that is, the Big Dipper.

[3]Lack.

[4]Assyrian, Persian, Roman, Greek.

[5]Greek mathematician (fl. 300 B.C.) who taught at Alexandria and wrote *Elements*, a treatise of thirteen books on plane and solid geometry, the theory of numbers, and problems in arithmetic.

[6]Said of Shakespeare by the poet and dramatist Ben Jonson (1572–1637) in "To the Memory of Shakespeare."

[7]From Wordsworth's° *Excursion* 3.518.

[8]A room arranged to display art or museum pieces.

In one of my daily jaunts between Bishopsgate and Shacklewell, the coach stopped to take up a staid-looking gentleman, about the wrong side of thirty, who was giving his parting directions (while the steps were adjusting), in a tone of mild authority, to a tall youth, who seemed to be neither his cleric, his son, nor his servant, but something partaking of all three. The youth was dismissed, and we drove on. As we were the sole passengers, he naturally enough addressed his conversation to me; and we discussed the merits of the fare; the civility and punctuality of the driver; the circumstance of an opposition coach having been lately set up, with the probabilities of its success—to all which I was enabled to return pretty satisfactory answers, having been drilled into this kind of etiquette by some years' daily practice of riding to and fro in the stage aforesaid—when he suddenly alarmed me by a startling question, whether I had seen the show of prize cattle that morning in Smithfield? Now, as I had not seen it, and do not greatly care for such sort of exhibitions, I was obliged to return a cold negative. He seemed a little mortified, as well as astonished, at my declaration, as (it appeared) he was just come fresh from the sight, and doubtless had hoped to compare notes on the subject. However, he assured me that I had lost a fine treat, as it far exceeded the show of last year. We were now approaching Norton Folgate, when the sight of some shop-goods *ticketed*[1] freshened him up into a dissertation upon the cheapness of cottons this spring. I was now a little in heart, as the nature of my morning avocations had brought me into some sort of familiarity with the raw material; and I was surprised to find how eloquent I was becoming on the state of the India market; when, presently, he dashed my incipient vanity to the earth at once, by inquiring whether I had ever made any calculation as to the value of the rental of all the retail shops in London. Had he asked of me what song the Sirens sang, or what name Achilles assumed when he hid himself among women, I might, with Sir Thomas Browne, have hazarded a "wide solution." [Urn Burial] My companion saw my embarrassment, and, the almshouses beyond Shoreditch just coming in view, with great goodnature and dexterity shifted his conversation to the subject of public charities; which led to the comparative merits of provision for the poor in past and present times, with observations on the old monastic institutions, and charitable orders; but, finding me rather dimly impressed with some glimmering notions from old poetic associations, than strongly fortified with any speculations reducible to calculation on the subject, he gave the matter up; and, the country beginning to open more and more upon us, as we approached the turnpike at Kingsland (the destined termination of his journey), he put a home thrust upon me, in the most unfortunate position he could have chosen, by advancing some queries relative to the North Pole Expedition.[2] While

---

[1]Priced.

[2]When this essay first appeared in *London Magazine* in 1821, John Franklin and other British naval officers were exploring the polar region (1819–1823).

I was muttering out something about the Panorama[1] of those strange regions (which I had actually seen), by way of parrying the question, the coach stopping relieved me from any further apprehensions. My companion getting out, left me in the comfortable possession of my ignorance; and I heard him, as he went off, putting questions to an outside passenger, who had alighted with him, regarding an epidemic disorder that had been rife about Dalston, and which my friend assured him had gone through five or six schools in that neighbourhood. The truth now flashed upon me, that my companion was a schoolmaster; and that the youth, whom he had parted from at our first acquaintance, must have been one of the bigger boys, or the usher.[2]—He was evidently a kind-hearted man, who did not seem so much desirous of provoking discussion by the questions which he put, as of obtaining information at any rate. It did not appear that he took any interest, either, in such kind of inquiries, for their own sake; but that he was in some way bound to seek for knowledge. A greenish-coloured coat, which he had on, forbade me to surmise that he was a clergyman. The adventure gave birth to some reflections on the difference between persons of his profession in past and present times.

Rest to the souls of those fine old Pedagogues; the breed, long since extinct, of the Lilys,[3] and the Linacres:[4] who believing that all learning was contained in the languages which they taught, and despising every other acquirement as superficial and useless, came to their task as to a sport! Passing from infancy to age, they dreamed away all their days as in a grammar-school. Revolving in a perpetual cycle of declensions, conjugations, syntaxes, and prosodies; renewing constantly the occupations which had charmed their studious childhood; rehearsing continually the part of the past; life must have slipped from them at last like one day. They were always in their first garden, reaping harvests of their golden time, among their *Flori-* and their *Spici-legia;*[5] in Arcadia[6] still, but kings; the ferule[7] of their sway not much harsher, but of like dignity with that mild

---

[1]Invented by R. Barker c. 1789, it was a picture or landscape unrolled and passed in front of the spectator as a continuous scene.

[2]Schoolmaster's assistant.

[3]William (c. 1468–1523), Oxford humanist, first headmaster of St. Paul's School in the center of London, who collaborated with the English humanist Desiderius Erasmus (1466–1536) and John Colet (1467–1519) on the famous Latin grammar.

[4]Thomas (1460–1524), English physician and humanist who wrote a Latin grammar and taught Desiderius Erasmus and Sir Thomas More (1478–1535), the famous Roman Catholic martyr and author of *Utopia*. Linacres translated works by Aristotle° and Galen° into Latin and founded the Royal College of Physicians.

[5]Latin for "flowers" and "ears of grain," meaning the anthologies and gleanings from the Latin that they selected for their students to translate.

[6]Mountains of Greece where ancient peoples were said to have lived in simple, rustic bliss.

[7]The metal ring attached to a cane to prevent it from splitting; often used to mean the cane itself.

sceptre attributed to king Basilius; the Greek and Latin, their stately Pamela and their Philoclea; with the occasional duncery of some untoward Tyro, serving for a refreshing interlude of a Mopsa, or a clown Damoetas![1]

With what a savour doth the Preface to Colet's,[2] or (as it is sometimes called) Paul's Accidence, set forth! "To exhort every man to the learning of grammar, that intendeth to attain the understanding of the tongues, wherein is contained a great treasury of wisdom and knowledge, it would seem but vain and lost labour; for so much as it is known, that nothing can surely be ended, whose beginning is either feeble or faulty; and no building be perfect, whereas the foundation and ground-work is ready to fall, and unable to uphold the burden of the frame." How well doth this stately preamble (comparable to those which Milton° commendeth[3] as "having been the usage to prefix to some solemn law, then first promulgated by Solon[4] or Lycurgus"[5]) correspond with and illustrate that pious zeal for confor-mity, expressed in a succeeding clause, which would fence about grammar-rules with the severity of faith-articles! —"as for the diversity of grammars, it is well profitably taken away by the King's Majesties wisdom, who foreseeing the incon-venience, and favourably providing the remedie, caused one kind of grammar by sundry learned men to be diligently drawn, and so to be set out, only everywhere to be taught for the use of learners, and for the hurt in changing of schoolmaist-ers." What a *gusto* in that which follows: "wherein it is profitable that he (the pupil) can orderly decline his noun and his verb." *His* noun!

The fine dream is fading away fast; and the least concern of a teacher in the present day is to inculcate grammar-rules.

The modern schoolmaster is expected to know a little of everything, because his pupil is required not to be entirely ignorant of anything. He must be super-ficially, if I may so say, omniscient. He is to know something of pneumatics;[6] of chemistry; of whatever is curious or proper to excite the attention of the youthful mind; an insight into mechanics is desirable, with a touch of statistics; the quality of soils, etc., botany, the constitution of his country, *cum multis aliis.*[7] You may get a notion of some part of his expected duties by consulting the famous Tractate on Education, addressed to Mr. Hartlib.[8]

---

[1]King Basilius, Pamela, Philoclea, Mopsa, and Damoetas are all characters in Sidney's° *Arcadia.* Tyro: beginner.

[2]The famous Latin Grammar, called "Paul's Accidence" and later the "Eton Grammar."

[3]In *Tractate on Education*; see footnote 8 below.

[4](c. 639–559 B.C.) One of the Seven Sages,° reformer of Athens who opened the assembly to all free men, established the Council of Four Hundred to represent the landed class, and developed a humane code of law to replace the law of Draco.

[5]Seventh century B.C.; founder of the Spartan constitution, described in detail by Plutarch,° though much of the information is said to be legendary.

[6]Branch of physics dealing with the properties of air and gasses.

[7]With many others.

[8]By Milton,° published in 1644.

All these things—these, or the desire of them—he is expected to instil, not by set lessons from professors, which he may charge in the bill, but at school intervals, as he walks the streets, or saunters through green fields (those natural instructors), with his pupils. The least part of what is expected from him is to be done in school-hours. He must insinuate knowledge at the *mollia tempora fandi*.[1] He must seize every occasion—the season of the year—the time of the day—a passing cloud—a rainbow—a wagon of hay—a regiment of soldiers going by—to inculcate something useful. He can receive no pleasure from a casual glimpse of Nature, but must catch at it as an object of instruction. He must interpret beauty into the picturesque. He cannot relish a beggar-man, or a gipsy, for thinking of the suitable improvement. Nothing comes to him, not spoiled by the sophisticating medium of moral uses. The Universe—that Great Book, as it has been called—is to him, indeed, to all intents and purposes, a book out of which he is doomed to read tedious homilies to distasting schoolboys.—Vacations themselves are none to him, he is only rather worse off than before; for commonly he has some intrusive upper-boy fastened upon him at such times; some cadet of a great family; some neglected lump of nobility, or gentry; that he must drag after him to the play, to the Panorama, to Mr. Bartley's Orrery,[2] to the Panopticon,[3] or into the country, to a friend's house, or his favourite watering-place. Wherever he goes, this uneasy shadow attends him. A boy is at his board, and in his path, and in all his movements. He is boy-rid, sick of perpetual boy.

Boys are capital fellows in their own way, among their mates; but they are unwholesome companions for grown people. The restraint is felt no less on the one side than on the other.—Even a child, that "plaything for an hour,"[4] tires *always*. The noises of children, playing their own fancies—as I now hearken to them, by fits, sporting on the green before my window, while I am engaged in these grave speculations at my neat suburban retreat at Shacklewell—by distance made more sweet—inexpressibly take from the labour of my task. It is like writing to music. They seem to modulate my periods. They ought at least to do so—for in the voice of that tender age there is a kind of poetry, far unlike the harsh prose-accents of man's conversation.—I should but spoil their sport, and diminish my own sympathy for them, by mingling in their pastime.

I would not be domesticated all my days with a person of very superior capacity to my own—not, if I know myself at all, from any considerations of jealousy or self-comparison, for the occasional communion with such minds has constituted the fortune and felicity of my life—but the habit of too constant

---

[1] *Aeneid* 4.293–294: misquoted from *mollissima fandi tempora,* "the best time for telling."

[2] A machine invented by George Graham about 1700 that presents the motions of the planets around the sun by means of clockwork. It was named after Charles Boyle, the Earl of Orrery, for whom it was invented. According to E. V. Lucas, a comedian named George Bartley (1782–1858) was lecturing on astronomy and poetry at the time Lamb was writing this essay.

[3] A showroom for novelties.

[4] Quotation from Charles and Mary Lamb's *Poetry for Children*.

intercourse with spirits above you, instead of raising you, keeps you down. Too frequent doses of original thinking from others restrain what lesser portion of that faculty you may possess of your own. You get entangled in another man's mind, even as you lose yourself in another man's grounds.[1] You are walking with a tall varlet,[2] whose strides out-pace yours to lassitude. The constant operation of such potent agency would reduce me, I am convinced, to imbecility. You may derive thoughts from others; your way of thinking, the mould in which your thoughts are cast, must be your own. Intellect may be imparted, but not each man's intellectual frame. —

As little as I should wish to be always thus dragged upward, as little (or rather still less) is it desirable to be stunted downwards by your associates. The trumpet does not more stun you by its loudness, than a whisper teases you by its provoking inaudibility.

Why are we never quite at our ease in the presence of a schoolmaster? — because we are conscious that he is not quite at his ease in ours. He is awkward, and out of place in the society of his equals. He comes like Gulliver from among his little people,[3] and he cannot fit the stature of his understanding to yours. He cannot meet you on the square. He wants a point given him, like an indifferent whist-player.[4] He is so used to teaching, that he wants to be teaching *you*. One of these professors, upon my complaining that these little sketches of mine were anything but methodical, and that I was unable to make them otherwise, kindly offered to instruct me in the method by which young gentlemen in *his* seminary were taught to compose English themes. — The jests of a schoolmaster are coarse, or thin. They do not *tell* out of school. He is under the restraint of a formal and didactive hypocrisy in company, as a clergyman is under a moral one. He can no more let his intellect loose in society than the other can his inclinations. He is forlorn among his coevals; his juniors cannot be his friends.

"I take blame to myself," said a sensible man of this profession, writing to a friend respecting a youth who had quitted his school abruptly, "that your nephew was not more attached to me. But persons in my situation are more to be pitied than can well be imagined. We are surrounded by young, and, consequently, ardently affectionate hearts, but *we* can never hope to share an atom of their affections. The relation of master and scholar forbids this. *How pleasing this must be to you, how I envy your feelings!* my friends will sometimes say to me, when they see young men whom I have educated, return after some years' absence from school, their eyes shining with pleasure, while they shake hands with their old

---

[1] Property.

[2] Rascal.

[3] Swift's° hero from *Gulliver's Travels* who meets, among many groups, peoples both smaller (Lilliputians) and larger (Brobdinagians) than he.

[4] The parent game of bridge, whist is a card game in which two pairs of players vie for thirteen tricks.

master, bringing a present of game to me, or a toy to my wife, and thanking me in the warmest terms for my care of their education. A holiday is begged for the boys; the house is a scene of happiness; I, only, am sad at heart.—This fine-spirited and warm-hearted youth, who fancies he repays his master with gratitude for the care of his boyish years—this young man—in the eight long years I watched over him with a parent's anxiety, never could repay me with one look of genuine feeling. He was proud, when I praised; he was submissive, when I reproved him; but he did never *love* me—and what he now mistakes for gratitude and kindness for me, is but the pleasant sensation which all persons feel at revisiting the scenes of their boyish hopes and fears; and the seeing on equal terms the man they were accustomed to look up to with reverence." "My wife, too," this interesting correspondent goes on to say, "my once darling Anna, is the wife of a school-master.—When I married her—knowing that the wife of a schoolmaster ought to be a busy notable creature, and fearing that my gentle Anna would ill supply the loss of my dear bustling mother, just then dead, who never sat still, was in every part of the house in a moment, and whom I was obliged sometimes to threaten to fasten down in a chair, to save her from fatiguing herself to death—I expressed my fears that I was bringing her into a way of life unsuitable to her; and she, who loved me tenderly, promised for my sake to exert herself to perform the duties of her new situation. She promised, and she has kept her word. What wonders will not woman's love perform?—My house is managed with a propriety and decorum unknown in other schools; my boys are well fed, look healthy, and have every proper accommodation; and all this performed with a careful economy, that never descends to meanness. But I have lost my gentle *helpless* Anna! When we sit down to enjoy an hour of repose after the fatigue of the day, I am compelled to listen to what have been her useful (and they are really useful) employments through the day, and what she proposes for her tomorrow's task. Her heart and her features are changed by the duties of her situation. To the boys, she never appears other than the *master's wife*, and she looks up to me as the *boys' master*; to whom all show of love and affection would be highly improper, and unbecoming the dignity of her situation and mine. Yet *this* my gratitude forbids me to hint to her. For my sake she submitted to be this altered creature, and can I reproach her for it?"—For the communication of this letter I am indebted to my cousin Bridget.[1] ✍

Modern Gallantry

In comparing modern with ancient manners, we are pleased to compliment ourselves upon the point of gallantry; a certain obsequiousness,[2] or deferential respect, which we are supposed to pay to females, as females.

---

[1] His sister Mary.
[2] Compliance.

I shall believe that this principle actuates our conduct, when I can forget, that in the nineteenth century of the era from which we date our civility, we are but just beginning to leave off the very frequent practice of whipping females in public, in common with the coarsest male offenders.

I shall believe it to be influential, when I can shut my eyes to the fact that in England women are still occasionally—hanged.

I shall believe in it, when actresses are no longer subject to be hissed off a stage by gentlemen.

I shall believe in it, when Dorimant[1] hands a fishwife across the kennel;[2] or assists the apple-woman to pick up her wandering fruit, which some unlucky dray[3] has just dissipated.

I shall believe in it, when the Dorimants in humbler life, who would be thought in their way notable adepts in this refinement, shall act upon it in places where they are not known, or think themselves not observed—when I shall see the traveller for some rich tradesman part with his admired box-coat,[4] to spread it over the defenceless shoulders of the poor woman, who is passing to her parish on the roof of the same stage-coach with him, drenched in the rain—when I shall no longer see a woman standing up in the pit of a London theatre, till she is sick and faint with the exertion with men about her seated at their ease, and jeering at her distress; till one, that seems to have more manners or conscience than the rest, significantly declares "she should be welcome to his seat, if she were a little younger and handsomer." Place this dapper warehouseman, or that rider, in a circle of their own female acquaintance, and you shall confess you have not seen a politer-bred man in Lothbury.[5]

Lastly, I shall begin to believe that there is some such principle influencing our conduct, when more than one-half of the drudgery and coarse servitude of the world shall cease to be performed by women.

Until that day comes I shall never believe this boasted point to be anything more than a conventional fiction; a pageant got up between the sexes, in a certain rank, and at a certain time of life, in which both find their account equally.

I shall be even disposed to rank it among the salutary[6] fictions of life, when in polite circles I shall see the same attentions paid to age as to youth, to homely features as to handsome, to coarse complexions as to clear—to the woman, as she is a woman, not as she is a beauty, a fortune, or a title.

I shall believe it to be something more than a name, when a well-dressed gentleman in a well-dressed company can advert to the topic of *female old age*

---

[1]A rake; from the main character in *The Man of Mode*, a Restoration comedy by Sir George Etherege (1635–1691).

[2]Gutter.

[3]Cart.

[4]Heavy overcoat worn by those riding outside the coach.

[5]Street in London where the Bank of England and other such banks are located.

[6]Beneficial.

without exciting, and intending to excite, a sneer:—when the phrases "anti-quated virginity,"[1] and such a one has "overstood her market," pronounced in good company, shall raise immediate offence in man, or woman, that shall hear them spoken.

Joseph Paice, of Bread-street-hill, merchant, and one of the Directors of the South Sea company—the same to whom Edwards, the Shakspeare commentator,[2] has addressed a fine sonnet—was the only pattern of consistent gallantry I have met with. He took me under his shelter at an early age, and bestowed some pains upon me. I owe to his precepts and example whatever there is of the man of business (and that is not much) in my composition. It was not his fault that I did not profit more. Though bred a Presbyterian, and brought up a merchant, he was the finest gentleman of his time. He had not one system of attention to females in the drawingroom, and another in the shop, or at the stall. I do not mean that he made no distinction. But he never lost sight of sex, or overlooked it in the casualties of a disadvantageous situation. I have seen him stand bareheaded—smile if you please—to a poor servant-girl, while she has been inquiring of him the way to some street—in such a posture of unforced civility, as neither to embarrass her in the acceptance, nor himself in the offer, of it. He was no dangler, in the common acceptation of the word, after women; but he reverenced and upheld, in every form in which it came before him, womanhood. I have seen him—nay, smile not—tenderly escorting a marketwoman, whom he had encountered in a shower, exalting his umbrella over her poor basket of fruit, that it might receive no damage, with as much carefulness as if she had been a Countess. To the reverend form of Female Eld[3] he would yield the wall[4] (though it were to an ancient beggar-woman) with more ceremony than we can afford to show our grandams. He was the Preux Chevalier[5] of Age; the Sir Calidore, or Sir Tristan,[6] to those who have no Calidores or Tristans to defend them. The roses, that had long faded thence, still bloomed for him in those withered and yellow cheeks.

He was never married, but in his youth he paid his addresses to the beautiful Susan Winstanley—old Winstanley's daughter of Clapton—who dying in the early days of their courtship, confirmed in him the resolution of perpetual bachelorship. It was during their short courtship, he told me, that he had been one day treating his mistress with a profusion of civil speeches—the common

---

[1]See Johnson's *Rambler* No. 119.

[2]Thomas Edwards (1699–1757), barrister and critic.

[3]Old woman.

[4]Give up the inner side of the sidewalk or pavement, where one is less likely to be splashed by the traffic.

[5]Valiant Knight.

[6]Sir Calidore, who represents courtesy, is the hero of the sixth book of Spenser's *Fairie Queen*. Sir Tristan is the hero of the medieval legend of Tristan and Isolde retold by Malory and others.

gallantries—to which kind of thing she had hitherto manifested no repugnance—but in this instance with no effect. He could not obtain from her a decent acknowledgment in return. She rather seemed to resent his compliments. He could not set it down to caprice, for the lady had always shown herself above that littleness. When he ventured on the following day, finding her a little better humoured, to expostulate with her on her coldness of yesterday, she confessed, with her usual frankness, that she had no sort of dislike to his attentions; that she could even endure some high-flown compliments; that a young woman placed in her situation had a right to expect all sorts of civil things said to her; that she hoped she could digest a dose of adulation, short of insincerity, with as little injury to her humility as most young women; but that—a little before he had commenced his compliments—she had overheard him by accident, in rather rough language, rating[1] a young woman, who had not brought home his cravats[2] quite to the appointed time, and she thought to herself, "As I am Miss Susan Winstanley, and a young lady—a reputed beauty, and known to be a fortune—I can have my choice of the finest speeches from the mouth of this very fine gentleman who is courting me—but if I had been poor Mary Such-a-one (*naming the milliner*[3]),—and had failed of bringing home the cravats to the appointed hour—though perhaps I had sat up half the night to forward them—what sort of compliments should I have received then?—And my woman's pride came to my assistance; and I thought, that if it were only to do *me* honour, a female, like myself, might have received handsomer usage; and I was determined not to accept any fine speeches to the compromise of that sex, the belonging to which was after all my strongest claim and title to them."

I think the lady discovered both generosity, and a just way of thinking, in this rebuke which she gave her lover; and I have sometimes imagined, that the uncommon strain of courtesy, which through life regulated the actions and behaviour of my friend towards all of womankind indiscriminately, owed its happy origin to this seasonable lesson from the lips of his lamented mistress. I wish the whole female world would entertain the same notion of these things that Miss Winstanley showed. Then we should see something of the spirit of consistent gallantry; and no longer witness the anomaly of the same man—a pattern of true politeness to a wife—of cold contempt, or rudeness, to a sister—the idolater of his female mistress—the disparager and despiser of his no less female aunt, or unfortunate—still female—maiden cousin. Just so much respect as a woman derogates[4] from her own sex, in whatever condition placed—her hand-maid, or dependent—she deserves to have diminished from herself on that score; and

---

[1]Scolding with anger.
[2]Men's linen or silk handkerchiefs passed twice around the neck outside the shirt collar.
[3]Seller of clothing, originally material manufactured in Milan.
[4]Detracts.

probably will feel the diminution, when youth, and beauty, and advantages, not inseparable from sex, shall lose of their attraction. What a woman should demand of a man in courtship, or after it, is first—respect for her as she is a woman;—and next to that—to be respected by him above all other women. But let her stand upon her female character as upon a foundation; and let the attentions, incident to individual preference, be so many pretty additaments[1] and ornaments—as many, and as fanciful, as you please—to that main structure. Let her first lesson be—with sweet Susan Winstanley—to *reverence her sex.* ✒

A Bachelor's Complaint of the Behaviour of Married People

As a single man, I have spent a good deal of my time in noting down the infirmities of Married People, to console myself for those superior pleasures, which they tell me I have lost by remaining as I am.

I cannot say that the quarrels of men and their wives ever made any great impression upon me, or had much tendency to strengthen me in those antisocial resolutions which I took up long ago upon more substantial considerations. What oftenest offends me at the houses of married persons where I visit, is an error of quite a different description;—it is that they are too loving.

Not too loving neither: that does not explain my meaning. Besides, why should that offend me? The very act of separating themselves from the rest of the world, to have the fuller enjoyment of each other's society, implies that they prefer one another to all the world.

But what I complain of is, that they carry this preference so undisguisedly, they perk it up in the faces of us single people so shamelessly, you cannot be in their company a moment without being made to feel, by some indirect hint or open avowal, that *you* are not the object of this preference. Now there are some things which give no offence, while implied or taken for granted merely; but expressed, there is much offence in them. If a man were to accost the first homely-featured or plain-dressed young woman of his acquaintance, and tell her bluntly, that she was not handsome or rich enough for him, and he could not marry her, he would deserve to be kicked for his ill-manners; yet no less is implied in the fact, that having access and opportunity of putting the question to her, he has never yet thought fit to do it. The young woman understands this as clearly as if it were put into words; but no reasonable young woman would think of making this the ground of a quarrel. Just as little right have a married couple to tell me by speeches, and looks that are scarce less plain than speeches, that I am not the

---

[1]Additions.

happy man,—the lady's choice. It is enough that I know I am not: I do not want this perpetual reminding.

The display of superior knowledge or riches may be made sufficiently mortifying, but these admit of a palliative.[1] The knowledge which is brought out to insult me, may accidentally improve me; and in the rich man's houses and pictures,—his parks and gardens, I have a temporary usufruct[2] at least. But the display of married happiness has none of these palliatives: it is throughout pure, unrecompensed, unqualified insult.

Marriage by its best title is a monopoly, and not of the least invidious sort. It is the cunning of most possessors of any exclusive privilege to keep their advantage as much out of sight as possible, that their less favoured neighbours, seeing little of the benefit, may the less be disposed to question the right. But these married monopolists thrust the most obnoxious part of their patent[3] into our faces.

Nothing is to me more distasteful than that entire complacency and satisfaction which beam in the countenances of a new-married couple,—in that of the lady particularly: it tells you, that her lot is disposed of in this world: that *you* can have no hopes of her. It is true, I have none: nor wishes either, perhaps: but this is one of those truths which ought, as I said before, to be taken for granted, not expressed.

The excessive airs which those people give themselves, founded on the ignorance of us unmarried people, would be more offensive if they were less irrational. We will allow them to understand the mysteries belonging to their own craft better than we, who have not had the happiness to be made free of the company: but their arrogance is not content within these limits. If a single person presume to offer his opinion in their presence, though upon the most indifferent subject, he is immediately silenced as an incompetent person. Nay, a young married lady of my acquaintance, who, the best of the jest was, had not changed her condition above a fortnight before, in a question on which I had the misfortune to differ from her, respecting the properest mode of breeding oysters for the London market, had the assurance to ask with a sneer, how such an old Bachelor as I could pretend to know anything about such matters!

But what I have spoken of hitherto is nothing to the airs which these creatures give themselves when they come, as they generally do, to have children. When I consider how little of a rarity children are,—that every street and blind alley swarms with them,—that the poorest people commonly have them in most abundance,—that there are few marriages that are not blest with at least one of these bargains,—how often they turn out ill, and defeat the fond hopes of their parents, taking to vicious courses, which end in poverty, disgrace, the gallows, etc.—I cannot for my life tell what cause for pride there can possibly be in having

---

[1] A reduction of pain or intensity.

[2] Enjoyment.

[3] Contract.

them. If they were young phoenixes,[1] indeed, that were born but one in a year, there might be a pretext. But when they are so common——

I do not advert to[2] the insolent merit which they assume with their husbands on these occasions. Let *them* look to that. But why *we*, who are not their natural-born subjects, should be expected to bring our spices, myrrh, and incense,—our tribute and homage of admiration,—I do not see.

"Like as the arrows in the hand of the giant, even so are the young children"; so says the excellent office in our Prayer-book appointed for the churching of women. "Happy is the man that hath his quiver full of them." So say I; but then don't let him discharge his quiver upon us that are weaponless;—let them be arrows, but not to gall and stick us. I have generally observed that these arrows are double-headed: they have two forks, to be sure to hit with one or the other. As for instance, where you come into a house which is full of children, if you happen to take no notice of them (you are thinking of something else, perhaps, and turn a deaf ear to their innocent caresses), you are set down as untractable, morose, a hater of children. On the other hand, if you find them more than usually engaging,—if you are taken with their pretty manners, and set about in earnest to romp and play with them,—some pretext or other is sure to be found for sending them out of the room; they are too noisy or boisterous, or Mr.—— does not like children. With one or other of these forks the arrow is sure to hit you.

I could forgive their jealousy, and dispense with toying with their brats, if it gives them any pain; but I think it unreasonable to be called upon to *love* them, where I see no occasion,—to love a whole family, perhaps eight, nine, or ten, indiscriminately,—to love all the pretty dears, because children are so engaging!

I know there is a proverb, "Love me, love my dog": that is not always so very practicable, particularly if the dog be set upon you to tease you or snap at you in sport. But a dog, or a lesser thing—any inanimate substance, as a keepsake, a watch or a ring, a tree, or the place where we last parted when my friend went away upon a long absence, I can make shift to love, because I love him, and anything that reminds me of him; provided it be in its nature indifferent, and apt to receive whatever hue fancy can give it. But children have a real character, and an essential being of themselves: they are amiable or unamiable *per se*; I must love or hate them as I see cause for either in their qualities. A child's nature is too serious a thing to admit of its being regarded as a mere appendage to another being, and to be loved or hated accordingly; they stand with me upon their own stock, as much as men and women do. Oh! but you will say, sure it is an attractive age,—there is something in the tender years of infancy that of itself charms us? That is the very reason why I am more nice[3] about them. I know that a sweet child is the sweetest thing in nature, not even excepting the delicate creatures which bear them; but the prettier the kind of a thing is, the more desirable it is that it should be pretty of its kind. One daisy

---

[1] Mythical birds that rise up from their own ashes every five hundred years.
[2] Pay attention to.
[3] Discriminating.

differs not much from another in glory; but a violet should look and smell the daintiest.—I was always rather squeamish in my women and children.

But this is not the worst: one must be admitted into their familiarity at least, before they can complain of inattention. It implies visits, and some kind of intercourse. But if the husband be a man with whom you have lived on a friendly footing before marriage—if you did not come in on the wife's side—if you did not sneak into the house in her train, but were an old friend in fast habits of intimacy before their courtship was so much as thought on,—look about you—your tenure is precarious—before a twelvemonth shall roll over your head, you shall find your old friend gradually grow cool and altered towards you, and at last seek opportunities of breaking with you. I have scarce a married friend of my acquaintance, upon whose firm faith I can rely, whose friendship did not commence *after the period of his marriage*. With some limitations, they can endure that; but that the good man should have dared to enter into a solemn league of friendship in which they were not consulted, though it happened before they knew him,—before they that are now man and wife ever met,—this is intolerable to them. Every long friendship, every old authentic intimacy must be brought into their office to be new stamped with their currency, as a sovereign prince calls in the good old money that was coined in some reign before he was born or thought of, to be new marked and minted with the stamp of his authority, before he will let it pass current in the world. You may guess what luck generally befalls such a rusty piece of metal as I am in these *new mintings*.

Innumerable are the ways which they take to insult and worm you out of their husband's confidence. Laughing at all you say with a kind of wonder, as if you were a queer kind of fellow that said good things, *but an oddity*, is one of the ways;—they have a particular kind of stare for the purpose;—till at last the husband, who used to defer to your judgment, and would pass over some excrescences[1] of understanding and manner for the sake of a general vein of observation (not quite vulgar) which he perceived in you, begins to suspect whether you are not altogether a humorist,[2]—a fellow well enough to have consorted with in his bachelor days, but not quite so proper to be introduced to ladies. This may be called the staring way; and is that which has oftenest been put in practice against me.

Then there is the exaggerating way, or the way of irony; that is, where they find you an object of especial regard with their husband, who is not so easily to be shaken from the lasting attachment founded on esteem which he has conceived towards you; by never qualified exaggerations to cry up all that you say or do, till the good man, who understands well enough that it is all done in compliment to him, grows weary of the debt of gratitude which is due to so much candour, and by relaxing a little on his part, and taking down a peg or two in his enthusiasm, sinks at length to the kindly level of moderate esteem—that "decent

---

[1]Exuberant outbursts.
[2]One subject to whims.

affection and complacent kindness'' towards you, where she herself can join in sympathy with him without much stretch and violence to her sincerity.

Another way (for the ways they have to accomplish so desirable a purpose are infinite) is, with a kind of innocent simplicity, continually to mistake what it was which first made their husband fond of you. If an esteem for something excellent in your moral character was that which riveted the chain which she is to break, upon any imaginary discovery of a want[1] of poignancy in your conversation, she will cry, "I thought, my dear, you described your friend, Mr.——, as a great wit?" If, on the other hand, it was for some supposed charm in your conversation that he first grew to like you, and was content for this to overlook some trifling irregularities in your moral deportment, upon the first notice of any of these she as readily exclaims, "This, my dear, is your good Mr.——!" One good lady whom I took the liberty of expostulating with for not showing me quite so much respect as I thought due to her husband's old friend, had the candour to confess to me that she had often heard Mr.—— speak of me before marriage, and that she had conceived a great desire to be acquainted with me, but that the sight of me had very much disappointed her expectations; for, from her husband's representations of me, she had formed a notion that she was to see a fine, tall, officer-like looking man (I use her very words), the very reverse of which proved to be the truth. This was candid; and I had the civility not to ask her in return, how she came to pitch upon[2] a standard of personal accomplishments for her husband's friends which differed so much from his own; for my friend's dimensions as near as possible approximate to mine; he standing five feet five in his shoes, in which I have the advantage of him by about half an inch; and he no more than myself exhibiting any indications of a martial character in his air[3] or countenance.

These are some of the mortifications which I have encountered in the absurd attempt to visit at their houses. To enumerate them all would be a vain endeavour; I shall therefore just glance at the very common impropriety of which married ladies are guilty,—of treating us as if we were their husbands, and *vice versa*. I mean, when they use us with familiarity, and their husbands with ceremony. *Testacea*,[4] for instance, kept me the other night two or three hours beyond my usual time of supping, while she was fretting because Mr.—— did not come home, till the oysters were all spoiled, rather than she would be guilty of the impoliteness of touching one in his absence. This was reversing the point of good manners: for ceremony is an invention to take of the uneasy feeling which we derive from knowing ourselves to be less the object of love and esteem with a fellow-creature than some other person is. It endeavours to make up, by superior attentions in little points, for that invidious preference which it is forced to deny in the greater. Had *Testacea* kept the oysters back for me, and withstood her

---

[1]Lack.
[2]Settle on.
[3]Bearing.
[4]From the Latin for "shellfish."

husband's importunities to go to supper, she would have acted according to the strict rules of propriety. I know no ceremony that ladies are bound to observe to their husbands, beyond the point of a modest behaviour and decorum: therefore I must protest against the vicarious gluttony of *Cerasia*,[1] who at her own table sent away a dish of Morellas,[2] which I was applying to with great good-will, to her husband at the other end of the table, and recommended a plate of less extraordinary gooseberries to my unwedded palate in their stead. Neither can I excuse the wanton affront of——

But I am weary of stringing up all my married acquaintance by Roman denominations. Let them amend and change their manners, or I promise to record the full-length English of their names, to the terror of all such desperate offenders in future. ✄

---

[1]From the Latin for "cherry."
[2]Dark red, sour cherries.

• • •

William Hazlitt

(1778–1830)

William Hazlitt was born in 1778 at Maidstone in Kent, the youngest of the three children, two boys and a girl, of William and Grace Hazlitt. His father was a Unitarian minister so devoted to liberty that he transported his family to America in 1783 and remained there for three years, living for a time in Philadelphia and founding the first Unitarian church in Boston. Still devoted to freedom of conscience, the father returned with his family to England in 1787 when he was called to lead a congregation at Wem in Shropshire.

Educated at home, Hazlitt at thirteen wrote his first published piece, a letter to a newspaper defending Joseph Priestley's right to celebrate Bastille Day and protesting against the mob that had attacked the scientist's house in Birmingham. Two years later, Hazlitt enrolled in a Unitarian college in Hackney to study theology, but by the time he met Coleridge° in 1798 he had given up that calling and was uncertain about his future. Coleridge° had been invited to visit Hazlitt's father after preaching in nearby Shrewsbury, where he was to be offered a permanent position as minister. But after their visit Coleridge° was given a stipend to devote himself to poetry, and Hazlitt, entranced by his conversations with the great poet, was invited to Nether Stowey to meet Wordsworth° and to continue discussing philosophy and literature, the two fields in which Hazlitt was reading with great pleasure.

Despite this literary stimulation, Hazlitt remained uncertain of his career. His brother, John, eleven years older, had become a fairly successful miniature portrait painter, and so, following John's lead, Hazlitt studied art and went to Paris in 1802 to copy portraits in the Louvre. Although he displayed a modest talent (his painting of Charles Lamb hangs in the National Portrait Gallery), Hazlitt found painting unsatisfactory. Still unsettled, he wrote several political and philosophical essays, but he did not discover his career until he fell in love and married Sarah Stoddart, a friend of the Lambs, in 1808. After this, financial realities impelled him to write.

Hazlitt first published an English grammar. After the death in infancy of his first son and the birth of his second, William, in 1811, the family moved to London, where Hazlitt supported them by delivering ten lectures on modern philosophy at the Russell Institute and by writing reviews of plays and reports of Parliament for the *Morning Chronicle*. Finally, in 1814, at the age of thirty-six, Hazlitt began writing the essays on English literature that gained him a lasting reputation. By 1820, when he joined the staff of the *London Magazine*, he had written and published a book on Thomas Holcroft, *The Characters of Shakespeare's Plays*, a collection of his essays from various periodicals titled *The Round Table*, a collection of his theatrical pieces in *A View of the English Stage*, and three collections of lectures: *The English Poets*, *The English Comic Writers*, and *The Dramatic Literature of the Age of Elizabeth*. Two years later, he published *Table Talk*, two volumes of original essays.

During this period of prolific writing, Hazlitt was plagued by marital troubles and by his own temperament and political fervor. His wife, an intelligent woman, was apparently a slovenly housekeeper and, worse, not as impressed with her husband's talents as he would have wished. She was probably unimpressed by his essay "Education of Women," written in 1815. By 1819 the two were living apart. At the same time Hazlitt's politics led him to quarrel with many of his friends over what he saw as their loss of faith in the causes of liberty and the French Revolution. All who knew him agreed that he was among the most volatile and miserable of men, quick to anger, difficult, proud, fiercely protective of his ideas. He managed to quarrel even with his close friend Lamb over a review copy of Wordsworth's° *Excursion*. In "My First Acquaintance with Poets" (1823), Hazlitt describes himself somewhat differently: "reading books, looking at pictures, going to plays, hearing, thinking, writing on what pleased me best. I have wanted only one thing to make me happy; but wanting that, have wanted everything!" That one thing was his landlord's daughter, Sarah Walker, who flirted with Hazlitt, inspired him to travel to Scotland to divorce his wife, and later jilted him for someone else. *Liber Amoris* (1823) documents this disappointment with love. Undaunted, Hazlitt married a Mrs. Bridgewater in 1824, and the two went off to tour Europe, Hazlitt mailing descriptions of France and Italy to the *Morning Chronicle*. Within the next three years the marriage dissolved, but the essays were collected and published in 1826 as *Notes of a Journey Through France and Italy*.

During the last four years of his life, as his health declined, Hazlitt published two of his best works, *Spirit of the Age* and *Plain Speaker*, and his worst, *Life of Napoleon*, a work uniformly disliked by his friends and his enemies. Despite his ill temper, Hazlitt's last words were said to be "Well, I've had a happy life." In "My First Acquaintance with Poets," Hazlitt makes an observation that underlines the disparity between his outward disposition and his own assessment of his life: "So if we look back to past generations (as far as the eye can reach) we see the same hopes, fears, wishes, followed by the same disappointments, throbbing in the human heart; and so we may see them (if we look forward) rising up forever, and disappearing, like vaporish bubbles, in the human breast!'' However much his daily life was marred by resentments, bitterness, and disappointment, it was also enlivened by the senses, the emotions, and the opinions that led to those miseries.

Hazlitt's essays, full of opinionated judgments, contradictory reflections, and astute observations, explore the variety and vigor of the mind. His vocal range is greater than that of most of his predecessors, such as Bacon, Addison, Franklin, and Johnson, and his focus is less subjective than that of the first great master of vocal range, Montaigne. Moreover, despite the massive number of allusions in his prose, his style matches that which he advocated in "On Familiar Style"—"plain words" used in "popular modes of construction." His criticism of the prose style of Johnson is particularly apt: "His subjects are familiar, but the author is always upon stilts. He has neither ease nor simplicity . . ." One need only compare this witty metaphor with some of the analytical lines from "On Prejudice" and with the emotional outpouring on the pleasures of living in "On the Feeling of Immortality in Youth" to appreciate the variety of tones Hazlitt can command. In his originality, range of voice, breadth of subject, and choice of diction, Hazlitt is representative of his time and place—Romantic England. ✒

Education of Women

The Examiner.   February 12, 1815.

We do not think a classical education proper for women. It may pervert their minds, but it cannot elevate them. It has been asked, Why a woman should not learn the dead languages as well as the modern ones? For this plain reason, that the one are still spoken, and have immediate associations connected with them, and the other not. A woman may have a lover who is a Frenchman, or an Italian, or a Spaniard; and it is well to be provided against every contingency in that way. But what possible interest can she feel in those old-fashioned persons, the Greeks and Romans, or in what was done two thousand years ago? A modern widow would doubtless prefer Signor Tramezzani to Aeneas,° and Mr. Conway would be a formidable rival to Paris.°[1] No young lady in our days, in conceiving an idea of Apollo,° can go a step beyond the image of her favourite poet: nor do we wonder

---

[1]In *A View of the English Stage* Hazlitt accuses the popular Italian tenor Signor Tramezzani of overacting, especially in love scenes, and so vehemently denigrates the talents of actor William Conway in his role as Romeo that Hazlitt was later moved to defend his criticisms as directed at the acting, not the man himself.

that our old friend, the Prince Regent,[1] passes for a perfect Adonis[2] in the circles of beauty and fashion. Women in general have no ideas, except personal ones. They are mere egotists. They have no passion for truth, nor any love of what is purely ideal. They hate to think, and they hate every one who seems to think of any thing but themselves. Everything is to them a perfect nonentity which does not touch their senses, their vanity, or their interest. Their poetry, their criticism, their politics, their morality, and their divinity, are downright affectation. That line in Milton° is very striking—

'He for God only, she for God in him.'[3]

Such is the order of nature and providence; and we should be sorry to see any fantastic improvements on it. Women are what they were meant to be; and we wish for no alteration in their bodies or their minds. They are the creatures of the circumstances in which they are placed, of sense, of sympathy and habit. They are exquisitely susceptible of the passive impressions of things: but to form an idea of pure understanding or imagination, to feel an interest in the true and the good beyond themselves, requires an effort of which they are incapable. They want[4] principle, except that which consists in an adherence to established custom; and this is the reason of the severe laws which have been set up as a barrier against every infringement of decorum and propriety in women. It has been observed by an ingenious writer of the present day, that women want[5] imagination. This requires explanation. They have less of that imagination which depends on intensity of passion, on the accumulation of ideas and feelings round one object, on bringing all nature and all art to bear on a particular purpose, on continuity and comprehension of mind; but for the same reason, they have more fancy, that is greater flexibility of mind, and can more readily vary and separate their ideas at pleasure. The reason of that greater presence of mind which has been remarked in women is, that they are less in the habit of speculating on what is best to be done, and the first suggestion is decisive. The writer of this article confesses that he never met with any woman who could reason, and with but one reasonable woman.[6] There is no instance of a woman having been a great mathematician or metaphysician or poet or painter: but they can dance and sing and act and write novels and fall in love, which last quality alone makes more than angels of them. Women are no judges of the characters of men, except as men. They have no real respect for men, or they never respect them for those qualities, for which they are respected by men. They in fact regard all such qualities as interfering with their own pretensions, and creating a jurisdiction different from their own. Women

---

[1]George, Prince of Wales, regent for George III, who had been declared insane.

[2]In Greek mythology, an especially handsome young man loved by two goddesses.

[3]*Paradise Lost* 4.299.

[4]Lack.

[5]Lack.

[6]Critics identify Mary Lamb here, in her periods of sanity, of course.

naturally wish to have their favourites all to themselves, and flatter their weaknesses to make them more dependent on their own good opinion, which, they think, is all that they want. We have, indeed, seen instances of men, equally respectable and amiable, equally admired by the women and esteemed by the men, but who have been ruined by an excess of virtues and accomplishments. ✍

On the Periodical Essayists[1]

"The proper study of mankind is man."[2]

I now come to speak of that sort of writing which has been so successfully cultivated in this country by our periodical Essayists, and which consists in applying the talents and resources of the mind to all that mixed mass of human affairs, which, though not included under the head of any regular art, science, or profession, falls under the cognisance of the writer, and "comes home to the business and bosoms of men."[3] *Quicquid agunt homines nostri farrago libelli,*[4] is the general motto of this department of literature. It does not treat of minerals or fossils, of the virtues of plants, or the influence of planets; it does not meddle with forms of belief or systems of philosophy, nor launch into the world of spiritual existences; but it makes familiar with the world of men and women, records their actions, assigns their motives, exhibits their whims, characterises their pursuits in all their singular and endless variety, ridicules their absurdities, exposes their inconsistencies, "holds the mirror up to nature, and shews the very age and body of the time its form and pressure;"[5] takes minutes of our dress, air, looks, words, thoughts, and actions; shews us what we are, and what we are not; plays the whole game of human life over before us, and by making us enlightened spectators of its many-coloured scenes, enables us (if possible) to become tolerably reasonable agents in the one in which we have to perform a part. "The act and practic part of life is thus made the mistress of our theorique."[6] It is the best and most natural course of study. It is in morals and manners what the experimental is in natural philosophy, as opposed to the dogmatical method. It does not deal in sweeping clauses of proscription and anathema,[7] but in nice[8] distinction and liberal constructions. It makes up its general accounts from details, its few theories from many facts. It does not try to prove all black or all white as it wishes, but lays on the intermediate colours, (and

---

[1] This essay was first published as part of *Lectures on the English Comic Writers* in 1819.
[2] From Pope's *Essay on Man* 2.2.
[3] From Bacon's dedication to the 1625 edition of his *Essays*.
[4] "Whatever things men do form the mixed subject of our book" (Juvenal° *Satires* 1.85). This quotation is the motto of the early issues of the *Tatler*.
[5] A loose rendition of parts of *Hamlet* 3.2.24–26.
[6] A variation on *Henry V* 1.1.51–52.
[7] Prohibition and denunciation.
[8] Precise.

most of them not unpleasing ones,) as it finds them blended with "the web of our life, which is of a mingled yarn, good and ill together."[1] It inquires what human life is and has been, to shew what it ought to be. It follows it into courts and camps, into town and country, into rustic sports or learned disputations, into the various shades of prejudice or ignorance, of refinement or barbarism, into its private haunts or public pageants, into its weaknesses and littlenesses, its professions and its practices—before it pretends to distinguish right from wrong, or one thing from another. How, indeed, should it do so otherwise?

> "Quid sit pulchrum, quid turpe, quid utile, quid non,
> Plenius et melius Chrysippo et Crantore dicit."[2]

The writers I speak of are, if not moral philosophers, moral historians, and that's better: or if they are both, they found the one character upon the other; their premises precede their conclusions; and we put faith in their testimony, for we know that it is true.

Montaigne was the first person who in his *Essays* led the way to this kind of writing among the moderns. The great merit of Montaigne then was, that he may be said to have been the first who had the courage to say as an author what he felt as a man. And as courage is generally the effect of conscious strength, he was probably led to do so by the richness, truth, and force of his own observations on books and men. He was, in the truest sense, a man of original mind, that is, he had the power of looking at things for himself, or as they really were, instead of blindly trusting to, and fondly repeating what others told him that they were. He got rid of the go-cart of prejudice and affectation, with the learned lumber[3] that follows at their heels, because he could do without them. In taking up his pen he did not set up for a philosopher, wit, orator, or moralist, but he became all these by merely daring to tell us whatever passed through his mind, in its naked simplicity and force, that he thought any ways worth communicating. He did not, in the abstract character of an author, undertake to say all that could be said upon a subject, but what in his capacity as an inquirer after truth he happened to know about it. He was neither a pedant nor a bigot. He neither supposed that he was bound to know all things, nor that all things were bound to conform to what he had fancied or would have them to be. In treating of men and manners, he spoke of them as he found them, not according to preconceived notions and abstract dogmas; and he began by teaching us what he himself was. In criticising books he did not compare them with rules and systems, but told us what he saw to like or dislike in them. He did not take his standard of excellence "according to an exact scale" of Aristotle,° or fall out with a work that was good for any thing, because "not one

---

[1]*All's Well That Ends Well* 4.3.71–72.

[2]"Crantor [c. 300 B.C., Greek philosopher], he speaks more completely and better to Chrysippus [290–210 B.C., Stoic° philosopher] about whatever would be beautiful, whatever ugly, whatever useful, whatever not [useful]."

[3]Useless odds and ends.

of the angles at the four corners was a right one."[1] He was, in a word, the first author who was not a book-maker, and who wrote not to make converts of others to established creeds and prejudices, but to satisfy his own mind of the truth of things. In this respect we know not which to be most charmed with, the author or the man. There is an inexpressible frankness and sincerity, as well as power, in what he writes. There is no attempt at imposition or concealment, no juggling tricks or solemn mouthing, no laboured attempts at proving himself always in the right, and every body else in the wrong; he says what is uppermost, lays open what floats at the top or the bottom of his mind, and deserves Pope's° character of him, where he professes to

> ——pour out all as plain
> As downright Shippen, or as old Montaigne.[2]

[Why Pope° should say in reference to him, "Or *more wise* Charron,[3] " is not easy to determine.][4] He does not converse with us like a pedagogue with his pupil, whom he wishes to make as great a blockhead as himself, but like a philosopher and friend who has passed through life with thought and observation, and is willing to enable others to pass through it with pleasure and profit. A writer of this stamp, I confess, appears to me as much superior to a common bookworm, as a library of real books is superior to a mere book-case, painted and lettered on the outside with the names of celebrated works. As he was the first to attempt this new way of writing, so the same strong natural impulse which prompted the undertaking, carried him to the end of his career. The same force and honesty of mind which urged him to throw off the shackles of custom and prejudice, would enable him to complete his triumph over them. He has left little for his successors to achieve in the way of just and original speculation on human life. Nearly all the thinking of the two last centuries of that kind which the French denominate *morale observatrice,*[5] is to be found in Montaigne's *Essays*: there is the germ, at least, and generally much more. He sowed the seed and cleared away the rubbish, even where others have reaped the fruit, or cultivated and decorated the soil to a greater degree of nicety[6] and perfection. There is no one to whom the old Latin adage is more applicable than to Montaigne, "*Pereant isti qui ante nos nostra dixerunt.*" (Confound the fellows who have said our good things before us). There has been no new impulse given to thought since his time. Among the specimens of criticisms on authors which he has left us, are those on Virgil,° Ovid,° and Boccaccio,° in the account of books which he thinks worth reading, or (which is the same thing) which he finds he can read in his old age, and which may be reckoned among the few criticisms which are worth reading at any age.[7]

---

[1]From Sterne's° *Tristram Shandy*, book 3, chapter 12.
[2]*Imitations of Horace,*° Satire 1.
[3]Skeptical French Roman Catholic theologian (1541–1603) and friend of Montaigne.
[4]All material shown here in brackets appeared as footnotes in the original text.
[5]Moral observations.
[6]Precision.
[7]A lengthy quotation from Montaigne, appearing here as a footnote, has been deleted.

Montaigne's *Essays* were translated into English by Charles Cotton,[1] who was one of the wits and poets of the age of Charles II;[2] and Lord Halifax, one of the noble critics of that day, declared it to be "the book in the world he was the best pleased with." This mode of familiar Essay-writing, free from the trammels of the schools, and the airs of professed authorship, was successfully imitated, about the same time, by Cowley[3] and Sir William Temple,[4] in their miscellaneous *Essays*, which are very agreeable and learned talking upon paper. Lord Shaftesbury[5] on the contrary, who aimed at the same easy, *dégagé*[6] mode of communicating his thoughts to the world, has quite spoiled his matter, which is sometimes valuable, by his manner, in which he carries a certain flaunting, flowery, figurative, flirting style of amicable condescension to the reader, to an excess more tantalising than the most starched and ridiculous formality of the age of James I.[7] There is nothing so tormenting as the affectation of ease and freedom from affectation.

The ice being thus thawed, and the barrier that kept authors at a distance from common-sense and feeling broken through, the transition was not difficult from Montaigne and his imitators, to our Periodical Essayists. These last applied the same unrestrained expression of their thoughts to the more immediate and passing scenes of life, to temporary and local matters; and in order to discharge the invidious office of *Censor Morum*[8] more freely, and with less responsibility, assumed some fictitious and humorous disguise, which, however, in a great degree corresponded to their own peculiar habits and character. By thus concealing their own name and person under the title of the *Tatler, Spectator,* etc. they were enabled to inform us more fully of what was passing in the world, while the dramatic contrast and ironical point of view to which the whole is subjected added a greater liveliness and *piquancy* to the descriptions. The philosopher and wit here commences newsmonger, makes himself master of "the perfect spy o' th' time",[9] and from his various walks and turns through life, brings home little curious specimens of the humours,[10] opinions, and manners of his contemporaries, as the botanist brings home different plants and weeds, or the mineralogist different shells and fossils, to illustrate their several theories, and be useful to mankind.

The first of these papers that was attempted in this country was set up by Steele in the beginning of the last century; and of all our Periodical Essayists, the *Tatler* (for that was the name he assumed) has always appeared to me the most amusing and agreeable. Montaigne, whom I have proposed to consider as the father of this kind of personal authorship among the moderns, in which the reader

---

[1](1630–1687) He dedicated the translation to Halifax.

[2]Reigned from 1660 to 1685.

[3]Abraham (1618–1667), poet and, in his forties, a writer of eleven *Essays in Prose and Verse*.

[4](1628–1699) Diplomat and writer of political prose and essays.

[5]Anthony Ashley Cooper (1671–1713), third Earl of Shaftsbury and writer of *Characteristicks*.

[6]Offhand.

[7]Reigned from 1603 to 1625.

[8]Judge of Custom.

[9]*Macbeth* 3.1.130.

[10]Whims.

is admitted behind the curtain, and sits down with the writer in his gown and slippers, was a most magnanimous and undisguised egotist; but Isaac Bickerstaff, Esq.[1] was the more disinterested gossip of the two. The French author is contented to describe the peculiarities of his own mind and constitution, which he does with a copious and unsparing hand. The English journalist good-naturedly lets you into the secret both of his own affairs and those of others. A young lady, on the other side Temple Bar,[2] cannot be seen at her glass for half a day together, but Mr. Bickerstaff takes due notice of it; and he has the first intelligence of the symptoms of the *belle passion*[3] appearing in any young gentleman at the West-end of the town. The departures and arrivals of widows with handsome jointures,[4] either to bury their grief in the country, or to procure a second husband in town, are punctually recorded in his pages. He is well acquainted with the celebrated beauties of the preceding age at the court of Charles II;[5] and the old gentleman (as he feigns himself) often grows romantic in recounting "the disastrous strokes which his youth suffered"[6] from the glances of their bright eyes, and their unaccountable caprices. In particular, he dwells with a secret satisfaction on the recollection of one of his mistresses, who left him for a richer rival, and whose constant reproach to her husband, on occasion of any quarrel between them, was "I, that might have married the famous Mr. Bickerstaff, to be treated in this manner!"[7] The club at the Trumpet consists of a set of persons almost as well worth knowing as himself. The cavalcade of the justice of the peace, the knight of the shire, the country squire, and the young gentleman, his nephew, who came to wait on him at his chambers, in such form and ceremony, seem not to have settled the order of their precedence to this hour;[8] and I should hope that the upholsterer and his companions, who used to sun themselves in the Green Park, and who broke their rest and fortunes to maintain the balance of power in Europe, stand as fair a chance for immortality as some modern politicians. Mr. Bickerstaff himself is a gentleman and a scholar, a humourist, and a man of the world; with a great deal of nice easy naivete about him. If he walks out and is caught in a shower of rain, he makes amends for this unlucky accident by a criticism on the shower in Virgil,° and concludes with a burlesque copy of verses on a city-shower. He entertains us, when he dates from his own apartment, with a quotation from Plutarch,° or a moral reflection; from the Grecian coffee-house with politics; and from Will's, or the Temple, with the poets and players, the beaux and men of wit

---

[1]See biography for Addison.

[2]Once the gate at Fleet Street and Strand that marked the western limit of London. The grand arch for carriages, with two walkways on either side, was built by Wren in the 1670s but was removed in 1877 to ease congestion.

[3]Love.

[4]Estates settled on women at the deaths of their husbands.

[5]Ruled from 1660 to 1685.

[6]Variation on *Othello* 1.3.157–158.

[7]*Tatler* No. 107.

[8]*Tatler* No. 125.

and pleasure about town.[1] In reading the pages of the *Tatler,* we seem as if suddenly carried back to the age of Queen Anne,[2] of toupees and full-bottomed periwigs. The whole appearance of our dress and manners undergoes a delightful metamorphosis. The beaux and the belles are of a quite different species from what they are at present; we distinguish the dappers, the smarts, and the pretty fellows, as they pass by Mr. Lilly's shop-windows in the Strand;[3] we are introduced to Betterton and Mrs. Oldfield behind the scenes; are made familiar with the persons and performances of Will Estcourt or Tom Durfey; we listen to a dispute at a tavern, on the merits of the Duke of Marlborough, or Marshal Turenne; or are present at the first rehearsal of a play by Vanbrugh,[4] or the reading of a new poem by Mr. Pope.° The privilege of thus virtually transporting ourselves to past times, is even greater than that of visiting distant places in reality. London, a hundred years ago, would be much better worth seeing than Paris at the present moment.

It will be said, that all this is to be found, in the same or a greater degree, in the *Spectator.* For myself, I do not think so; or at least, there is in the last work a much greater proportion of commonplace matter. I have, on this account, always preferred the *Tatler* to the *Spectator.* Whether it is owing to my having been earlier or better acquainted with the one than the other, my pleasure in reading these two admirable works is not in proportion to their comparative reputation. The *Tatler* contains only half the number of volumes, and, I will venture to say, nearly an equal quantity of sterling wit and sense. "The first sprightly runnings"[5] are there: it has more of the original spirit, more of the freshness and stamp of nature. The indications of character and strokes of humour are more true and frequent; the reflections that suggest themselves arise more from the occasion, and are less spun out into regular dissertations. They are more like the remarks which occur in sensible conversation, and less like a lecture. Something is left to the understanding of the reader. Steele seems to have gone into his closet chiefly to set down what he observed outdoors. Addison seems to have spent most of his time in his study, and to have spun out and wire-drawn[6] the hints, which he borrowed

---

[1] In the first issue of the *Tatler* (Tuesday, April 12, 1709), Steele describes the coffeehouses from which his news is gathered: "All Accounts of GALLANTRY, PLEASURE, and ENTERTAINMENT, shall be under the Article of WHITE'S CHOCOLATE HOUSE; POETRY, under that of WILL'S COFFEE-HOUSE; LEARNING under the Title of GRAECIAN; FOREIGN and DOMESTICK NEWS, you will have from ST. JAMES'S COFFEE-HOUSE and what else I have to offer on any other Subject, shall be dated from my own APARTMENT."

[2] Reigned from 1702 to 1714.

[3] Charles Lillie sold perfume as well as the *Tatler* and the *Spectator* and is mentioned in these periodicals.

[4] Betterton, Oldfield, and Estcourt were actors; Durfey wrote plays and songs; the Duke of Marlborough (1650–1722) was a great English commander and Marshal Turenne (1611–1675) a great French commander; Sir John Vanbrugh (1664–1726) translated plays from the French and wrote *The Relapse* and *The Provok'd Wife.*

[5] From *Aureng-Zebe* 4.1, Dryden's° last heroic play in rhyme.

[6] Stretched out.

from Steele, or took from nature, to the utmost. I am far from wishing to deprecate Addison's talents, but I am anxius to do justice to Steele, who was, I think, upon the whole, a less artificial and more original writer. The humorous descriptions of Steele resemble loose sketches, or fragments of a comedy; those of Addison are rather comments or ingenious paraphrases on the genuine text. The characters of the club not only in the *Tatler,* but in the *Spectator,* were drawn by Steele. That of Sir Roger de Coverly is among the number. Addison has, however, gained himself immortal honour by his manner of filling up this last character. Who is there that can forget, or be insensible to, the inimitable nameless graces and varied traits of nature and of old English character in it—to his unpretending virtues and aimiable weaknesses—to his modesty, generosity, hospitality, and eccentric whims—to the respect of his neighbours, and the affection of his domestics—to his wayward, hopeless, secret passion for his fair enemy, the widow, in which there is more of real romance and true delicacy, than in a thousand tales of knight-errantry—(we perceive the hectic flush of his cheek, the faltering of his tongue in speaking of her bewitching airs and "the whiteness of her hand")[1] —to the havoc he makes among the game in his neighborhood—to his speech from the bench, to shew the Spectator what is thought of him in the country—to his unwillingness to be put up as a sign-post, and his having his own likeness turned into the Saracen's° head—to his gentle reproof of the baggage of a gypsy that tells him "he has a widow in his line of life"—to his doubts as to the existence of witchcraft, and protection of reputed witches—to his account of the family pictures, and his choice of a chaplain—to his falling asleep at church and his reproof of John Williams, as soon as he recovered from his nap, for talking in sermon-time. The characters of Will. Wimble, and Will. Honeycomb[2] are not a whit behind their friend, Sir Roger, in delicacy and felicity. The delightful simplicity and good-humoured officiousness[3] in the one, are set off by the graceful affectation and courtly pretension in the other. How long since I first became acquainted with these two characters in the *Spectator!* What old-fashioned friends they seem, and yet I am not tired of them, like so many other friends, nor they of me! How airy these abstractions of the poet's pen stream over the dawn of our acquaintance with human life! how they glance their fairest colours on the prospect before us! how pure they remain in it to the last, like the rainbow in the evening-cloud, which the rude hand of time and experience can neither soil nor dissipate! What a pity that we cannot find the reality, and yet if we did, the dream would be over. I once thought I knew a Will. Wimble, and a Will. Honeycomb, but they turned out but indifferently; the originals in the *Spectator* still read, word for word, the same that they always did. We have only to turn the page, and find them where we left them!—many of the most exquisite pieces in the *Tatler,* it is to be observed, are Addison's, as the Court of Honour, the Personification of

---

[1]*Spectator* No. 113.
[2]Wimble was a younger son of Sir Roger de Coverly. Honeycomb was a man of fashion.
[3]Helpfulness.

Musical Instruments, with almost all those papers that form regular sets or series. I do not know whether the picture of the family of an old college acquaintance, in the *Tatler,* where the children run to let Mr. Bickerstaff in at the door, and where the one that loses the race that way, turns back to tell the father that he is come; with the nice gradation of incredulity in the little boy, who is got into *Guy of Warwick,*[1] and the *Seven Champions,*[2] and who shakes his head at the improbability of AEsop's *Fables,* is Steele's or Addison's, though I believe it belongs to the former.[3] The account of the two sisters, one of whom held up her head higher than ordinary, from having on a pair of flowered garters, and that of the married lady who complained to the *Tatler* of the neglect of her husband, with her answers to some *home* questions that were put to her, are unquestionably Steele's.—If the *Tatler* is not inferior to the *Spectator* as a record of manners and character, it is superior to it in the interest of many of the stories. Several of the incidents related there by Steele have never been surpassed in the heart-rending pathos of private distress. I might refer to those of the lover and his mistress, when the theatre, in which they were, caught fire; of the bridegroom, who by accident kills his bride on the day of their marriage; the story of Mr. Eustace and his wife; and the fine dream about his own mistress when a youth. What has given its superior reputation to the *Spectator,* is the greater gravity of its pretensions, its moral dissertations and critical reasonings, by which I confess myself less edified than by other things, which are thought more lightly of. Systems and opinions change, but nature is always true. It is the moral and didactic tone of the *Spectator* which makes us apt to think of Addison (according to Mandeville's sarcasm) as "a parson in a tie-wig."[4] Many of his moral Essays are, however, exquisitely beautiful and quite happy. Such are the reflections on cheerfulness, those in Westminster Abbey, on the Royal Exchange, and particularly some very affecting ones on the death of a young lady in the fourth volume. These, it must be allowed, are the perfection of elegant sermonising. His critical Essays are not so good. I prefer Steele's occasional selection of beautiful poetical passages, without any affectation of analysing their beauties, to Addison's finer-spun theories. The best criticism in the *Spectator,* that on the Cartoons of Raphael,° of which Mr. Fuseli[5] has availed himself with great spirit in his *Lectures,* is by Steele. [The antithetical style and verbal paradoxes which Burke° was so fond of, in which the epithet is a seeming contradiction to the substantive, such as 'proud submission and dignified obedience,' are, I think, first to be found in the *Tatler.*] I owed this acknowledgment to a writer who has so often put me in good humour with myself, and

---

[1] English romance c. 1300.

[2] Unremarkable prose fiction (1596) by Richard Johnson.

[3] *Tatler* No. 95 was indeed written by Steele.

[4] Bernard Mandeville (1670?–1733), satiric author of *Grumbling Hive* (1705) and *Fable of the Bees* (1714).

[5] Henry (1741–1825), Anglo-Swiss painter born in Zurich who studied in London, worked in Italy, and returned to England, where he displayed his romantic and grotesque works, such as *Nightmare.*

every thing about me, when few things else could, and when the tomes of casuistry and ecclesiastical history, with which the little duodecimo[1] volumes of the *Tatler* were overwhelmed and surrounded, in the only library to which I had access when a boy, had tried their tranquillising effects upon me in vain. I had not long ago in my hands, by favour of a friend, an original copy of the quarto[2] edition of the *Tatler*, with a list of the subscribers. It is curious to see some names there which we should hardly think of (that of Sir Isaac Newton° is among them,) and also to observe the degree of interest excited by those of the different persons, which is not determined according to the rules of the Herald's College.[3] One literary name lasts as long as a whole race of heroes and their descendants! The *Guardian*, which followed the *Spectator*, was, as may be supposed, inferior to it.

The dramatic and conversational turn which forms the distinguishing feature and greatest charm of the *Spectator* and *Tatler*, is quite lost in the *Rambler* by Dr. Johnson. There is no reflected light thrown on human life from an assumed character, nor any direct one from a display of the author's own. The *Tatler* and *Spectator* are, as it were, made up of notes and memorandums of the events and incidents of the day, with finished studies after nature, and characters fresh from the life, which the writer moralises upon, and turns to account as they come before him: the *Rambler* is a collection of moral Essays, or scholastic theses, written on set subjects, and of which the individual characters and incidents are merely artificial illustrations, brought in to give a pretended relief to the dryness of didactic discussion. The *Rambler* is a splendid and imposing common-place-book of general topics, and rhetorical declamation on the conduct and business of human life. In this sense, there is hardly a reflection that has been suggested on such subjects which is not to be found in this celebrated work, and there is, perhaps, hardly a reflection to be found in it which had not been already suggested and developed by some other author, or in the common course of conversation. The mass of intellectual wealth here heaped together is immense, but it is rather the result of gradual accumulation, the produce of the general intellect, labouring in the mine of knowledge and reflection, than dug out of the quarry, and dragged into the light by the industry and sagacity of a single mind. I am not here saying that Dr. Johnson was a man without originality, compared with the ordinary run of men's minds, but he was not a man of original thought or genius, in the sense in which Montaigne or Lord Bacon was. He opened no new vein of precious ore, nor did he light upon any single pebbles of uncommon size and unrivalled lustre. We seldom meet with anything to "give us pause";[4] he does not set us thinking for the first time. His reflections present themselves like reminiscences; do not disturb the ordinary march of our thoughts; arrest our attention by the stateliness of their appearance, and the costliness of their garb, but pass on

---

[1] A book composed of pages formed by folding the printer's sheet into twelve leaves.
[2] A book composed of pages formed by folding a printer's sheet into four leaves.
[3] Organization chartered in 1483 to trace ancestry and assign coats of arms; its rules are those that define the design of the shield on the coat of arms.
[4] *Hamlet* 3.1.68.

and mingle with the throng of our impressions. After closing the volumes of the *Rambler*, there is nothing that we remember as a new truth gained to the mind, nothing indelibly stamped upon the memory; nor is there any passage that we wish to turn to as embodying any known principle or observation, with such force and beauty that justice can only be done to the idea in the author's own words. Such, for instance, are many of the passages to be found in Burke,° which shine by their own light, belong to no class, have neither equal nor counterpart, and of which we say that no one but the author could have written them! There is neither the same boldness of design, nor mastery of execution in Johnson. In the one, the spark of genius seems to have met with its congenial matter: the shaft is sped; the forked lightning dresses up the face of nature in ghastly smiles, and the loud thunder rolls far away from the ruin that is made. Dr. Johnson's style, on the contrary, resembles rather the rumbling of mimic thunder at one of our theatres; and the light he throws upon a subject is like the dazzling effect of phosphorus, or an *ignis fatuus*[1] of words. There is a wide difference, however, between perfect originality and perfect common-place: neither ideas nor expressions are trite or vulgar because they are not quite new. They are valuable, and ought to be repeated, if they have not become quite common; and Johnson's style both of reasoning and imagery holds the middle rank between startling novelty and vapid common-place. Johnson has as much originality of thinking as Addison; but then he wants[2] his familiarity of illustration, knowledge of character, and delightful humour. —What most distinguishes Dr. Johnson from other writers is the pomp and uniformity of his style. All his periods are cast in the same mould, are of the same size and shape, and consequently have little fitness to the variety of things he professes to treat of. His subjects are familiar, but the author is always upon stilts. He has neither ease nor simplicity, and his efforts at playfulness, in part, remind one of the lines in Milton:° —

> "——The elephant
> To make them sport wreath'd his proboscis lithe."[3]

His Letters from Correspondents, in particular, are more pompous and unwieldy than what he writes in his own person. This want[4] of relaxation and variety of manner has, I think, after the first effects of novelty and surprise were over, been prejudicial to the matter. It takes from the general power, not only to please, but to instruct. The monotony of style produces an apparent monotony of ideas. What is really striking and valuable, is lost in the vain ostentation and circumlocution of the expression; for when we find the same pains and pomp of diction bestowed upon the most trifling as upon the most important parts of a sentence or discourse, we grow tired of distinguishing between pretension and reality, and are

---

[1] Foolish fire.
[2] Lacks.
[3] Variation on *Paradise Lost* 4.345–347.
[4] Lack.

disposed to confound the tinsel and bombast of the phraseology with want of weight in the thoughts. Thus, from the imposing and oracular nature of the style, people are tempted at first to imagine that our author's speculations are all wisdom and profundity: till having found out their mistake in some instances, they suppose that there is nothing but common-place in them, concealed under verbiage and pedantry; and in both they are wrong. The fault of Dr. Johnson's style is, that it reduces all things to the same artificial and unmeaning level. It destroys all shades of difference, the association between words and things. It is a perpetual paradox and innovation. He condescends to the familiar till we are ashamed of our ʿinterest in it: he expands the little till it looks big. "If he were to write a fable of little fishes," as Goldsmith° said of him, "he would make them speak like great whales."[1] We can no more distinguish the most familiar objects in his descriptions of them, than we can a well-known face under a huge painted mask. The structure of his sentences, which was his own invention, and which has been generally imitated since his time, is a species of rhyming in prose, where one clause answers to another in measure and quantity, like the tagging of syllables at the end of a verse; the close of the period follows as mechanically as the oscillation of a pendulum, the sense is balanced with the sound; each sentence, revolving round its centre of gravity, is contained with itself like a couplet, and each paragraph forms itself into a stanza. Dr. Johnson is also a complete balance-master in the topics of morality. He never encourages hope, but he counteracts it by fear; he never elicits a truth, but he suggests some objection in answer to it. He seizes and alternately quits the clue of reason, lest it should involve him in the labyrinths of endless error: he wants[2] confidence in himself and his fellows. He dares not trust himself with the immediate impressions of things, for fear of compromising his dignity; or follow them into their consequences, for fear of committing his prejudices. His timidity is the result, not of ignorance, but of morbid apprehension.[3] "He runs the great circle, and is still at home." No advance is made by his writings in any sentiment, or mode of reasoning. Out of the pale[4] of established authority and received dogmas, all is sceptical, loose, and desultory: he seems in imagination to strengthen the dominion of prejudice, as he weakens and dissipates that of reason; and round the rock of faith and power, on the edge of which he slumbers blindfold and uneasy, the waves and billows of uncertain and dangerous opinion roar and heave for evermore. His *Rasselas* is the most melancholy and debilitating moral speculation that ever was put forth. Doubtful of the faculties of his mind, as of his organs of vision, Johnson trusted only to his feelings and his fears. He cultivated a belief in witches as an out-guard[5] to the evidences of religion; and abused Milton,° and patronised Lauder, in spite

---

[1] In Boswell's *Life of Johnson.*
[2] Lacks.
[3] Fear.
[4] Fence marking a boundary.
[5] A outpost or guard sent some distance from the main army.

of his aversion to his countrymen, as a step to secure the existing establishment in church and state.[1] This was neither right feeling nor sound logic.

The most triumphant record of the talents and character of Johnson is to be found in Boswell's Life of him. The man was superior to the author. When he threw aside his pen, which he regarded as an incumbrance, he became not only learned and thoughtful, but acute, witty, humorous, natural, honest; hearty and determined, "the king of good fellows and wale[2] of old men."[3] There are as many smart repartees, profound remarks, and keen invectives to be found in Boswell's "inventory of all he said," as are recorded of any celebrated man. The life and dramatic play of his conversation forms a contrast to his written works. His natural powers and undisguised opinions were called out in convivial intercourse. In public he practised with the foils on:[4] in private, he unsheathed the sword of controversy, and it was "the Ebro's[5] temper." The eagerness of opposition roused him from his natural sluggishness and acquired timidity; he returned blow for blow; and whether the trial were of argument or wit, none of his rivals could boast much of the encounter. Burke° seems to have been the only person who had a chance with him; and it is the unpardonable sin of Boswell's work, that he has purposely omitted their combats of strength and skill. Goldsmith° asked, "Does he wind into a subject like a serpent, as Burke° does?" And when exhausted with sickness, he himself said, "If that fellow Burke° were here now, he would kill me." It is to be observed, that Johnson's colloquial style was as blunt, direct, and downright, as his style of studied composition was involved and circuitous. As when Topham Beauclerc and Langton knocked him up at his chambers, at three in the morning, and he came to the door with the poker in his hand, but seeing them, exclaimed, "What, is it you, my lads? then I'll have a frisk with you!" and he afterwards reproaches Langton, who was a literary milksop, for leaving them to go to an engagement "with some *un-idead*[6] girls." What words to come from the mouth of the great moralist and lexicographer! His good deeds were as many as his good sayings. His domestic habits, his tenderness to servants, and readiness to oblige his friends; the quantity of strong tea that he drank to keep down sad thoughts; his many labours reluctantly begun, and irresolutely laid aside; his honest acknowledgment of his own, and indulgence to the weaknesses of others; his throwing himself back in the post-chaise with Boswell, and saying

---

[1]In his biography of Johnson (London: Hogarth Press, 1984, 253–254), Walter Jackson Bate explains that Lauder, a deceitful Scottish scholar, claimed that Milton° had plagiarized from "modern" Latin poems to write *Paradise Lost*. Johnson wrote a preface to Lauder's supposed proof (drawn in fact from a Latin translation of Milton's° epic), unaware of the fraud and interested only in seeing what he thought might be the underlying materials for the poem. As soon as the fraud came to light, Johnson apologized in writing and insisted that Lauder publicly confess his crime. Hazlitt's accusations here have no basis in fact.

[2]Choice.

[3]Burns.°

[4]With a sword with a guard for the hand and a blunt point to prevent injury.

[5]The Ebro is a long, wild river in Spain.

[6]In Boswell for the year 1753 the phrase is "un-idea'd girls," that is, girls lacking ideas.

"Now I think I am a good-humoured fellow," though nobody thought him so, and yet he was; his quitting the society of Garrick and his actresses, and his reason for it; his dining with Wilkes, and his kindness to Goldsmith;° his sitting with the young ladies on his knee at the Mitre,[1] to give them good advice, in which situation, if not explained, he might be taken for Falstaff;° and last and noblest, his carrying the unfortunate victim of disease and dissipation on his back up through Fleet Street, (an act which realises the parable of the good Samaritan) — all these, and innumerable others, endear him to the reader, and must be remembered to his lasting honour. He had faults, but they lie buried with him. He had his prejudices and his intolerant feelings; but he suffered enough in the conflict of his own mind with them. For if no man can be happy in the free exercise of his reason, no wise man can be happy without it. His were not time-serving, heartless, hypocritical prejudices; but deep, inwoven, not to be rooted out but with life and hope, which he found from old habit necessary to his own peace of mind, and thought so to the peace of mankind. I do not hate, but love him for them. They were between himself and his conscience, and should be left to that higher tribunal, "where they in trembling hope repose, the bosom of his Father and his God."[2] In a word, he has left behind him few wiser or better men.

The herd of his imitators shewed what he was by their disproportionate effects. The Periodical Essayists, that succeeded the *Rambler,* are, and deserve to be, little read at present. The *Adventurer,* by Hawksworth, is completely trite and vapid, aping all the faults of Johnson's style, without any thing to atone for them. The sentences are often absolutely unmeaning; and one half of each might regularly be left blank. The *World,* and *Connoisseur,* which followed, are a little better; and in the last of these there is one good idea, that of a man in indifferent health, who judges of every one's title to respect from their possession of this blessing, and bows to a sturdy beggar with sound limbs and a florid complexion, while he turns his back upon a lord who is a valetudinarian.[3]

Goldsmith's° *Citizen of the World,* like all his works, bears the stamp of the author's mind. It does not "go about to cozen reputation without the stamp of merit." He is more observing, more original, more natural and picturesque than Johnson. His work is written on the model of the *Persian Letters;*[4] and contrives to give an abstracted and somewhat perplexing view of things, by opposing foreign prepossessions[5] to our own, and thus stripping objects of their customary disguises. Whether truth is elicited in this collision of contrary absurdities, I do not know; but I confess the process is too ambiguous and full of intricacy to be very amusing to my plain understanding. For light summer reading, it is like walking in a garden full of traps and pitfalls. It necessarily gives rise to paradoxes,

---

[1]Tavern on Fleet Street.

[2]The last two lines from Gray's° "Elegy Written in a Country Churchyard."

[3]Chronic invalid.

[4]*Letters from a Persian in England to his Friend at Isaphan* (1735) by Lord George Lyttelton (1709–1773), minor poet and essayist, friend of men like Pope° and Smollett.° See also page 100, footnote 1.

[5]Preconceptions.

and there are some very bold ones in the *Essays,* which would subject an author less established to no very agreeable sort of *censura literaria.*[1] Thus the Chinese philosopher exclaims very unadvisedly, "The bonzes[2] and priests of all religions keep up superstition and imposture: all reformations begin with the laity." Goldsmith,° however, was staunch in his practical creed, and might bolt[3] speculative extravagances with impunity. There is a striking difference in this respect between him and Addison, who, if he attacked authority, took care to have common sense on his side, and never hazarded anything offensive to the feelings of others, or on the strength of his own discretional opinion. There is another inconvenience in this assumption of an exotic character and tone of sentiment, that it produces an inconsistency between the knowledge which the individual has time to acquire, and which the author is bound to communicate. Thus the Chinese has not been in England three days before he is acquainted with the characters of the three countries which compose this kingdom, and describes them to his friend at Canton, by extracts from the newspapers of each metropolis. The nationality of Scotchmen is thus ridiculed: — "Edinburgh. We are positive when we say, that Sanders Macgregor, lately executed for horse-stealing, is not a native of Scotland, but born at Carrickfergus."[4] Now this is very good; but how should our Chinese philosopher find it out by instinct? Beau Tibbs, a prominent character in this little work, is the best comic sketch since the time of Addison; unrivalled in his finery, his vanity, and his poverty.

I have only to mention the names of the *Lounger* and the *Mirror,*[5] which are ranked by the author's admirers with Sterne° for sentiment, and with Addison for humour. I shall not enter into that: but I know that the story of La Roche is not like the story of Le Fevre,[6] nor one hundredth part so good. Do I say this from prejudice to the author? No: for I have read his novels. Of the *Man of the World* I cannot think so favourably as some others; nor shall I here dwell on the picturesque and romantic beauties of Julia de Roubigne, the early favourite of the author of *Rosamond Gray;*[7] but of the *Man of Feeling* I would speak with grateful recollections: nor is it possible to forget the sensitive, irresolute, interesting Harley;[8] and that lone figure of Miss Walton[9] in it, that floats in the horizon, dim and ethereal, the day-dream of her lover's youthful fancy—better, far better than all the realities of life! ✍

---

[1] Literary judgment.
[2] Buddhist monks in China and Japan who teach social concern and salvation for all.
[3] Examine by sifting.
[4] A borough in Northern Ireland.
[5] Periodicals written mostly by Henry Mackenzie (1745–1831), who also wrote the "Story of La Roche" (in the *Mirror*) and the novels *Man of the World, Julia de Roubigne,* and *Man of Feeling.*
[6] From *Tristram Shandy.*
[7] Charles Lamb.
[8] Sentimental hero of Mackenzie's *Man of Feeling.*
[9] Rich, upper-class woman whom Harley loves.

On the Feeling of Immortality in Youth

"Life is a pure flame, and we live by an invisible sun within us."

SIR THOMAS BROWNE [1]

No young man believes he shall ever die. It was a saying of my brother's, and a fine one. There is a feeling of Eternity in youth, which makes us amends for every thing. To be young is to be as one of the Immortal Gods. One half of time indeed is flown—the other half remains in store for us with all its countless treasures; for there is no line drawn, and we see no limit to our hopes and wishes. We make the coming age our own.

"The vast, the unbounded prospect lies before us."[2]

Death, old age, are words without a meaning, that pass by us like the idle air which we regard not. Others may have undergone, or may still be liable to them—we "bear a charmed life,"[3] which laughs to scorn all such sickly fancies. As in setting out on a delightful journey, we strain our eager gaze forward— "Bidding the lovely scenes at distance hail,"[4]—and see no end to the landscape, new objects presenting themselves as we advance; so, in the commencement of life, we set no bounds to our inclinations, nor to the unrestricted opportunities of gratifying them. We have as yet found no obstacle, no disposition to flag; and it seems that we can go on so for ever. We look round in a new world, full of life and ceaseless progress; and feel in ourselves all the vigor and spirit to keep pace with it, and do not forsee from any present signs how we shall be left behind in the race, decline into old age, and drop into the grave. It is the simplicity and as it were abstractedness of our feelings in youth, that (so to speak) identifies us with nature and (our experience being weak and our passions strong) makes us fancy ourselves immortal like it. Our short-lived connection with being, we fondly flatter ourselves, is an indissoluble and lasting union. As infants smile and sleep we are rocked in the cradle of our desires, and hushed into fancied security by the roar of the universe around us—we quaff the cup of life with eager thirst without draining it, and joy and hope seem ever mantling[5] to the brim—objects press around us, filling the mind with their magnitude and with the throng of desires that wait upon them, so that there is no room for the thoughts of death. We are too much dazzled by the gorgeousness and novelty of the bright waking dream about us to discern the dim shadow lingering for us in the distance. Nor would the hold that life has taken of us permit us to detach our thoughts that way, even

---

[1]*Hydrotaphia* 4. This epigraph appears in the second and longer version of this essay published in *Literary Remains*; the essay given here is the first printed version, appearing unsigned in the *Monthly Magazine* in March of 1827.

[2]See Addison's *Cato* 5.1: "The wide, the unbounded prospect, lies before me."

[3]*Macbeth* 5.7.41.

[4]P. P. Howe, editor of Hazlitt's complete works, has located this quotation in Collins's ode "The Passions," line 32.

[5]Frothing.

if we could. We are too much absorbed in present objects and pursuits. While the spirit of youth remains unimpaired, ere the "wine of life is drunk,"[1] we are like people intoxicated or in a fever, who are hurried away by the violence of their own sensations: it is only as present objects begin to pall upon the sense, as we have been disappointed in our favourite pursuits, cut off from our closest ties, that we by degrees become weaned from the world, that passion loosens its hold upon futurity, and that we begin to contemplate "as in a glass, darkly,"[2] the possibility of parting with it for good. Till then, the example of others has no effect upon us. Casualties we avoid: the slow approaches of age we play at *hide and seek* with. Like the foolish fat scullion, in Sterne,° who hears that Master Bobby[3] is dead, our only reflection is "So am not I!" The idea of death, instead of staggering our confidence, only seems to strengthen and enhance our sense of the possession and our enjoyment of life. Others may fall around us like leaves, or be mowed down by the scythe of Time like grass: these are but metaphors to the unreflecting buoyant ears and overweening presumption of youth. It is not till we see the flowers of Love, Hope, and Joy, withering around us, that we give up the flattering delusions that before led us on, and that the emptiness and dreariness of the prospect before us reconciles us hypothetically to the silence of the grave.

Life is indeed a strange gift, and its privileges are most mysterious. No wonder when it is first granted to us that our gratitude, our admiration, and our delight should prevent us from reflecting on our own nothingness, or from thinking it will ever be recalled. Our first and strongest impressions are borrowed from the mighty scene that is open to us, and we unconsciously transfer its durability as well as its splendour to ourselves. So newly found, we cannot think of parting with it yet, or at least put off that consideration *sine die*.[4] Like a rustic at a fair, we are full of amazement and rapture, and have no thought of going home, or that it will soon be night. We know our existence only by ourselves, and confound our knowledge with the objects of it. We and Nature are therefore one. Otherwise, the illusion, "the feast of reason and the flow of soul,"[5] to which we were invited, is a mockery and a cruel insult. We do not go from a play till the last act is ended, and the lights are about to be extinguished. But the fairy face of Nature still shines on; shall we be called away, before the curtain falls, or ere we have scarce had a glimpse of what is going on? Like children, our step-mother Nature holds us up to see the raree-show[6] of the universe; and then, as if life were a burthen to her to support, lets us fall down again. Yet what brave sublunary things does not this pageant present like a ball or *fete* of the universe!

To see the golden sun, the azure sky, the out-stretched ocean; to walk upon the green earth, and be lord of a thousand creatures; to look down yawning precipices or over distant sunny vales; to see the world spread out under one's feet

---

[1]*Macbeth* 2.3.96—"The wine of life is drawn."

[2]1 Cor. 13:12.

[3]In *Tristram Shandy*.

[4]"Without a day"; indefinitely.

[5]Pope,° *Imitations of Horace*,° 1.128.

[6]A show contained or carried about in a box.

on a map; to bring the stars near; to view the smallest insects in a microscope; to read history, and consider the revolutions of empire and the succession of generations, to hear of the glory of Tyre,[1] of Sidon,[2] of Babylon[3] and of Susa,[4] and to say all these were before me and are now nothing; to say I exist in such a point of time, and in such a point of space; to be a spectator and a part of its ever-moving scene; to witness the change of season, of spring and autumn, of winter and summer; to feel hot and cold, pleasure and pain, beauty and deformity, right and wrong; to be sensible to the accidents of nature; to consider the mighty world of eye and ear; to listen to the stockdove's[5] notes amid the forest deep; to journey over moor and mountain; to hear the midnight sainted choir; to visit lighted halls, or the cathedral's gloom, or sit in crowded theatres and see life itself mocked; to study the works of art and refine the sense of beauty to agony; to worship fame, and to dream of immortality, to look upon the Vatican and to read Shakspear; to gather up the wisdom of the ancients, and to pry into the future; to listen to the trump of war, the shout of victory; to question history as to the movements of the human heart; to seek for truth; to plead the cause of humanity; to overlook the world as if time and nature poured their treasures at our feet — to be and to do all this, and then in a moment to be nothing — to have it all snatched from us as by a juggler's trick, or a phantasmagoria! There is something in this transition from all to nothing that shocks us and damps the enthusiasm of youth new flushed with hope and pleasure, and we cast the comfortless thought as far from us as we can. In the first enjoyment of the estate of life we discard the fear of debts and duns,[6] and never think of the final payment of our great debt to Nature. Art we know is long; life we flatter ourselves, should be so too. We see no end of the difficulties and delays we have to encounter: perfection is slow of attainment, and we must have time to accomplish it in. The fame of the great names we look up to is immortal: and shall we who contemplated imbibe a portion of ethereal fire, the *divinae particula aurae,*[7] which nothing can extinguish? A wrinkle in Rembrandt° or in Nature takes whole days to resolve itself into its component parts, its softenings and its sharpnesses; we refine upon our perfections, and unfold intricacies of nature. What a prospect for the future! What a task have we not begun! And shall we be arrested in the middle of it? We do not count our time thus employed lost, or our pains thrown away; we do not flag or grow tired, but

---

[1]Ancient Phoenician city (now in Lebanon) that flourished under numerous rulers as a port and later as an industrial center for textiles and purple dye from about 1400 B.C. until it was destroyed by Muslims in 1291 A.D.

[2]Also an ancient Phoenician city and trade center, known for dyes and glass.

[3]Ancient city of Mesopotamia, site of the Hanging Gardens (one of the Seven Wonders of the Ancient World), famed in the days of Nebuchadnezzar (c. 540 B.C.) for walls, palace, and gates.

[4]Ancient city of Elam (now Iran), whose inhabitants conquered Babylon and carried off the code of Hammurabi and numerous art objects.

[5]Common gray European bird, smaller than a pigeon, living in hollow tree trunks.

[6]Creditors or agents employed to collect debts.

[7]A portion of the divine breath.

gain new vigour at our endless task. Shall Time, then, grudge us to finish what we have begun, and have formed a compact with Nature to do? Why not fill up the blank that is left us in this manner? I have looked for hours at a Rembrandt,° without being conscious of the flight of time, but with ever new wonder and delight, have thought that not only my own but another existence I could pass in the same manner. This rarefied, refined existence seemed to have no end, nor stint, nor principle of decay in it. The print would remain long after I who looked on it had become the prey of worms. The thing seems in itself out of all reason: health, strength, appetite are opposed to the idea of death, and we are not ready to credit it till we have found our illusions vanished, and our hopes grown cold. Objects in youth, from novelty, &c., are stamped upon the brain with such force and integrity that one thinks nothing can remove or obliterate them. They are riveted there, and appear to us as an element of our nature. It must be a mere violence that destroys them, not a natural decay. In the very strength of this persuasion we seem to enjoy an age by anticipation. We melt down years into a single moment of intense sympathy, and by anticipating the fruits defy the ravages of time. If, then, a single moment of our lives is worth years, shall we set any limits to its total value and extent? Again, does it not happen that so secure do we think ourselves of an indefinite period of existence, that at times, when left to ourselves, and impatient of novelty, we feel annoyed at what seems to us the slow and creeping progress of time, and argue that if it always moves at this tedious snail's pace it will never come to an end? How ready we are to sacrifice any space of time which separates us from a favourite object, little thinking that before long we shall find it move too fast.

For my part, I started in life with the French Revolution, and I have lived, alas! to see the end of it. But I did not foresee this result. My sun rose with the first dawn of liberty, and I did not think how soon both must set. The new impulse to ardour given to men's minds imparted a congenial warmth and glow to mine; we were strong to run a race together, and I little dreamed that long before mine was set, the sun of liberty would turn to blood, or set once more in the night of despotism. Since then, I confess, I have no longer felt myself young, for with that my hopes fell.

I have since turned my thoughts to gathering up some of the fragments of my early recollections, and putting them into a form to which I might occasionally revert. The future was barred to my progress, and I turned for consolation and encouragement to the past. It is thus, that when we find our personal and substantial identity vanishing from us, we strive to gain a reflected and vicarious one in our thoughts: we do not like to perish wholly, and wish to bequeath our names at least to posterity. As long as we can make our cherished thoughts and nearest interests live in the minds of others, we do not appear to have retired altogether from the stage. We still occupy the breasts of others, and exert an influence and power over them, and it is only our bodies that are reduced to dust and powder. Our favourite speculations still find encouragement, and we make as great a figure in the eye of the world, or perhaps a greater, than in our life-time. The demands of our self-love are thus satisfied, and these are the most imperious and unremitting. Besides, if by our intellectual superiority we survive ourselves in this world, by our virtues and faith we may attain an interest in another, and a higher state of being, and may thus be recipients at the same time of men and of angels.

"Even from the tomb the voice of Nature cries,
Even in our ashes live their wonted fires."[1]

As we grow old, our sense of the value of time becomes vivid. Nothing else, indeed, seems of any consequence. We can never cease wondering that that which has ever been should cease to be. We find many things remain the same: why then should there be change in us. This adds a convulsive grasp of whatever is, a sense of a fallacious hollowness in all we see. Instead of the full, pulpy feeling of youth tasting existence and every object in it, all is flat and vapid,—a whited sepulchre, fair without but full of ravening[2] and all uncleanness within.[3] The world is a witch that puts us off with false shows and appearances. The simplicity of youth, the confiding expectation, the boundless raptures are gone: we only think of getting out of it as well as we can, and without any great mischance or annoyance. The flush of illusion, even the complacent retrospect of past joys and hopes, is over: if we can slip out of life without indignity, can escape with little bodily infirmity, and frame our minds to the calm and respectable composure of *still-life*[4] before we return to physical nothingness, it is as much as we can expect. We do not die wholly at our deaths: we have mouldered away gradually long before. Faculty after faculty, attachment after attachment disappear: we are torn from ourselves while living, year after year sees us no longer the same, and death only consigns the last fragment of what we were to the grave. That we should wear out by slow stages, and dwindle at last into nothing, is not wonderful, when even in our prime our strongest impressions leave little trace but for the moment, and we are the creatures of petty circumstance. How little effect is made on us in our best days by the books we have read, the scenes we have witnessed, the sensations we have gone through! Think only of the feelings we experience in reading a fine romance (one of Sir Walter's,[5] for instance); what beauty, what sublimity, what interest, what heart-rending emotions! You would suppose the feelings you then experienced would last for ever, or subdue the mind to their own harmony and tone: while we are reading, it seems as if nothing could ever put us out of our way, or trouble us:—the first splash of mud that we get on entering the street, the first twopence that we are cheated of, the whole feeling vanishes clean out of our minds, and we become the prey of petty and annoying circumstances. The mind soars to the lofty: it is at home in the grovelling, the disagreeable, and the little. And yet we wonder that age should be feeble and querulous—that the freshness of youth should fade away. Both worlds would hardly satisfy the extravagance of our desires and of our presumption. ✐

---

[1]Gray's° "Elegy Written in a Country Churchyard," 91–92.
[2]Plunder.
[3]See Mathew 23:27.
[4]A picture of inanimate objects such as fruits and flowers.
[5]Sir Walter Scott.°

On Prejudice[1]

It is a mistake to suppose that all prejudices are false, though it is not an easy matter to distinguish between true and false prejudice. Prejudice is properly an opinion or feeling, not for which there is no reason, but of which we cannot render a satisfactory account on the spot. It is not always possible to assign a "reason for the faith that is in us,"[2] not even if we take time and summon up all our strength; but it does not therefore follow that our faith is hollow and unfounded. A false impression may be defined to be an effect without a cause, or without any adequate one; but the effect may remain and be true, though the cause is concealed or forgotten. The grounds of our opinions and tastes may be deep, and be scattered over a large surface; they may be various, remote and complicated, but the result will be sound and true, if they have existed at all, though we may not be able to analyse them into classes, or to recall the particular time, place, and circumstances of each individual case or branch of the evidence. The materials of thought and feeling, the body of facts and experience, are infinite, are constantly going on around us, and acting to produce an impression of good or evil, of assent or dissent to certain inferences; but to require that we should be prepared to retain the whole of this mass of experience in our memory, to resolve it into its component parts, and be able to quote chapter and verse for every conclusion we unavoidably draw from it, or else to discard the whole together as unworthy the attention of a rational being, is to betray an utter ignorance both of the limits and the several uses of the human capacity. The *feeling* of the truth of anything, or the soundness of the judgment formed upon it from repeated, actual impressions, is one thing: the power of vindicating and enforcing it, by distinctly appealing to or explaining those impressions, is another. The most fluent talkers or most plausible reasoners are not always the justest thinkers. To deny that we can, in a certain sense, know and be justified in believing anything of which we cannot give the complete demonstration, or the exact *why* and *how,* would only be to deny that the clown, the mechanic (and not even the greatest philosopher), can know the commonest thing; for in this new and dogmatical process of reasoning, the greatest philosopher can trace nothing *above,* nor proceed a single step without taking something for granted;[3] [Berkeley,[4] in his *Minute Philosopher,* attacks Dr. Halley, who had objected to faith and mysteries in religion, on this score; and contends that the mathematician, no less than the theologian, is obliged to presume on certain *postulates,* or to resort, before he could establish a single theorem, to a formal definition of those undefinable and hypothetical existances, points, lines, and surfaces; and, according to the ingenious and learned Bishop of

---

[1]This essay first appeared in the *Monthly Magazine* in 1830.
[2]1 Peter 3:15: "a reason of the hope that is in you."
[3]Hazlitt appends the following bracketed material as a footnote here.
[4]George (1685–1753) Anglo-Irish bishop and philosopher who believed that the external world is dependent upon perception and that God instills our sense of an otherwise nonexistent world.

Cloyne, *solids* would fare no better than *superficials* in this war of words and captious contradiction.] and it is well if he does not take more things for granted than the most vulgar and illiterate, and what he knows a great deal less about. A common mechanic can tell how to work an engine better than the mathematician who invented it. A peasant is able to foretell rain from the appearance of the clouds, because (time out of mind) he has seen that appearance followed by that consequence; and shall a pedant catechise him out of a conviction which he has found true in innumerable instances, because he does not understand the composition of the elements, or cannot put his notions into a logical shape? There may also be some collateral circumstance (as the time of day), as well as the appearance of the clouds, which he may forget to state in accounting for his prediction; though, as it has been a part of his familiar experience, it has naturally guided him in forming it, whether he was aware of it or not. This comes under the head of the well known principle of the *association of ideas;* by which certain impressions, from frequent recurrence, coalesce and act in unison truly and mechanically— that is, without our being conscious of anything but the general and settled result. On this principle it has been well said, that "there is nothing so true as habit"; but it is also blind: we feel and can produce a given effect from numberless repetitions of the same cause; but we neither inquire into the cause, nor advert[1] to the mode. In learning any art or exercise, we are obliged to take lessons, to watch others, to proceed step by step, to attend to the details and means employed; but when we are masters of it, we take all this for granted, and do it without labour and without thought, by a kind of habitual instinct—that is, by the trains of our ideas and volitions having been directed uniformly, and at last flowing of themselves into the proper channel.

We never do anything well till we cease to think about the manner of doing it. This is the reason why it is so difficult for any but natives to speak a language correctly or idiomatically. They do not succeed in this from knowledge or reflection, but from inveterate custom, which is a cord that cannot be loosed. In fact, in all that we do feel or think there is a leaven of *prejudice* (more or less extensive) viz., something implied of which we do not know or have forgotten the grounds.

If I am required to prove the possibility, or demonstrate the mode of whatever I do before I attempt it, I can neither speak, walk, nor see; nor have the use of my hands, senses, or common understanding. I do not know what muscles I use in walking, nor what organs I employ in speech: those who do cannot speak or walk better on that account nor can they tell how these organs and muscles themselves act. Can I not discover that one object is near, and another at a distance from the eye alone or from continual impressions of sense and custom concurring to make the distinction, without going through a course of perspective and optics?—or am I not to be allowed an opinion on the subject, or to act upon it, without being accused of being a very *prejudiced* and obstinate person? An artist knows that, to imitate an object in the horizon, he must use less colour; and the naturalist knows

---

[1]Call attention.

that this effect is produced by the intervention of a greater quantity of air: but a country fellow, who knows nothing of either circumstance, must not only be ignorant but a blockhead, if he could be persuaded that a hill ten miles off was close before him, only because he could not state the grounds of his opinion scientifically. Not only must we (if restricted to reason and philosophy) distrust the notices of sense, but we must also dismiss all that mass of knowledge and perception which falls under the head of *common sense* and *natural feeling,* which is made up of the strong and urgent, but undefined impressions of things upon us, and lies between the two extremes of absolute proof and the grossest ignorance. Many of these pass for instinctive principles and *innate ideas;* but there is nothing in them "more than natural."[1]

Without the aid of prejudice and custom, I should not be able to find my way across the room; nor know how to conduct myself in any circumstances, nor what to feel in any relation of life. Reason may play the critic, and correct certain errors afterwards; but if we were to wait for its formal and absolute decisions in the shifting and multifarious combinations of human affairs, the world would stand still. Even men of science, after they have gone over the proofs a number of times, abridge the process, and *jump at a conclusion:* is it therefore false, because they have always found it to be true? Science after a certain time becomes presumption; and learning reposes in ignorance. It has been observed, that women have more *tact* and insight into character than men, that they find out a pedant, a pretender, a blockhead, sooner. The explanation is, that they trust more to the first impressions and natural indications of things, without troubling themselves with a learned theory of them; whereas men, affecting greater gravity, and thinking themselves bound to justify their opinions, are afraid to form any judgment at all, without the formality of proofs and definitions, and blunt the edge of their understandings, lest they should commit some mistake. They stay for facts, till it is too late to pronounce on the characters. Women are naturally physiognomists,[2] and men phrenologists.[3] The first judge by sensations; the last by rules. Prejudice is so far then an involuntary and stubborn *association of ideas,* of which we cannot assign the distinct grounds and origin; and the answer to the question, "How do we know whether the prejudice is true or false?" depends chiefly on that other, whether the first connection between our ideas has been real or imaginary. This again resolves into the inquiry—Whether the subject in dispute falls under the province of our own experience, feeling, and observation, or is referable to the head of authority, tradition, and fanciful conjecture? Our practical conclusions are in this respect generally right; our speculative opinions are just as likely to be wrong. What we derive from our personal acquaintance with things (however narrow in its scope or imperfectly digested), is, for the most part, built on a solid foundation—that of Nature; it is in trusting to others (who give themselves out for

---

[1]P. P. Howe glosses these words with a reference to *Hamlet* 2.2.385.
[2]Those who judge character from facial features.
[3]Those who judge character from the shape of the skull and the bumps on it.

guides and doctors) that we are *all abroad,* and at the mercy of quackery, impudence, and imposture. Any impression, however absurd, or however we may have imbibed it, by being repeated and indulged in, becomes an article of implicit and incorrigible belief. The point to consider is, how we have first taken it up, whether from ourselves or the arbitrary dictation of others. "Thus shall we try the doctrines, whether they be of nature or of man."[1]

So far then from the charge lying against vulgar and illiterate prejudice as the bane of truth and common sense, the argument turns the other way; for the greatest, the most solemn, and mischievous absurdities that mankind have been the dupes of, they have imbibed from the dogmatism and vanity or hypocrisy of the self-styled wise and learned, who have imposed profitable fictions upon them for self-evident truths, and contrived to enlarge their power with their pretensions to knowledge. Every boor sees that the sun shines above his head; that "the moon is made of green cheese," is a fable that has been taught him. Defoe° says, that there were a hundred thousand stout country-fellows in his time ready to fight to the death against popery, without knowing whether popery was a man or a horse. This, then, was a prejudice that they did not fill up of their own heads. All the great points that men have founded a claim to superiority, wisdom, and illumination upon, that they have embroiled the world with, and made matters of the last importance, are what one age and country differ diametrically with each other about, have been successively and justly exploded, and have been the levers of opinion and the grounds of contention, precisely because, as their expounders and believers are equally in the dark about them, they rest wholly on the fluctuations of will and passion, and as they can neither be proved nor disproved, admit of the fiercest opposition or the most bigoted faith. In what "comes home to the business and bosoms of men,"[2] there is less of this uncertainty and presumption; and there, in the little world of our own knowledge and experience, we can hardly do better than attend to the "still, small voice"[3] of our own hearts and feelings, instead of being browbeat by the effrontery, or puzzled by the sneers and cavils of pedants and sophists, of whatever school or description.

If I take a prejudice against a person from his face, I shall very probably be in the right; if I take a prejudice against a person from hearsay, I shall quite as probably be in the wrong. We have a prejudice in favour of certain books, but it is hardly without knowledge, if we have read them with delight over and over again. Fame itself is a prejudice, though a fine one. Natural affection is a prejudice: for though we have cause to love our nearest connections better than others, we have no reason to think them better than others. The error here is, when that which is properly a dictate of the heart passes out of its sphere, and becomes an overweening decision of the understanding. So in like manner of the love of country; and there is a prejudice in favour of virtue, genius, liberty, which (though

---

[1]P. P. Howe cites 1 John 4:1 here, but the connection is tenuous.
[2]Dedication to the 1625 edition of Bacon's *Essays.*
[3]1 Kings 19:12 .

it were possible) it would be a pity to destroy. The passions, such as avarice, ambition, love, &c., are prejudices, that is amply exaggerated views of certain objects, made up of habit and imagination beyond their real value; but if we ask what is the real value of any object, independently of its connection with the power of habit, or its affording natural scope for the imagination, we shall perhaps be puzzled for an answer. To reduce things to the scale of abstract reason would be to annihilate our interest in them, instead of raising our affections to a higher standard; and by striving to make man rational, we should leave him merely brutish.

Animals are without prejudice: they are not led away by authority or custom, but it is because they are gross, and incapable of being taught. It is, however, a mistake to imagine that only the vulgar and ignorant, who can give no account of their opinions, are the slaves of bigotry and prejudice; the noisiest declaimers, the most subtle casuists, and most irrefragable[1] doctors, are as far removed from the character of true philosophers, while they strain and pervert all their powers to prove some unintelligible dogma, instilled into their minds by early education, interest, or self-importance; and if we say the peasant or artisan is a Mahometan because he is born in Turkey, or a papist because he is born in Italy, the mufti at Constantinople or the cardinal at Rome is so, for no better reason, in the midst of all his pride and learning. Mr. Hobbes° used to say, that if he had read as much as others, he should have been as ignorant as they.

After all, most of our opinions are a mixture of reason and prejudice, experience and authority. We can only judge for ourselves in what concerns ourselves, and in things about us: and even there we must trust continually to established opinion and current report; in higher and more abstruse points we must pin our faith still more on others. If we believe only what we know at first hand, without trusting to authority at all, we shall disbelieve a great many things that really exist; and the suspicious coxcomb[2] is as void of judgment as the credulous fool. My habitual conviction of the existence of such a place as Rome is not strengthened by my having seen it; it might be almost said to be obscured and weakened, as the reality falls short of the imagination. I walk along the streets without fearing that the houses will fall on my head, though I have not examined their foundation; and I believe firmly in the Newtonian° system, though I have never read the *Principia*. In the former case, I argue that if the houses were inclined to fall they would not wait for me; and in the latter I acquiesce in what all who have studied the subject, and are capable of understanding it, agree in, having no reason to suspect the contrary. That *the earth turns round* is agreeable to my understanding, though it shocks my sense, which is however too weak to grapple with so vast a question. ✐

---

[1]Indisputable.
[2]Fool.

Thomas Henry Huxley

(1825–1895)

T. H. Huxley, the seventh and youngest surviving child of eight, was the son of an assistant master at a school in Ealing, a suburb of London. At the age of eight he entered his father's school, but left two years later when his family moved to Coventry. From then on he educated himself, making use, like Hazlitt, of his father's library to read whatever pleased him at the time: at twelve he read James Hutton's° *Theory of the Earth* and at fifteen taught himself Italian and German. Influenced by his two sisters' husbands, both physicians, Huxley went to London in 1841 as an apprentice to one of his brothers-in-law and, after graduating from London University at seventeen, won a scholarship to Charing Cross Hospital. In 1845 he earned his medical degree and began to merge his medical education with his interest in structural anatomy; during this time he discovered a layer of cells in the root sheath of hair.

Like Charles Darwin, Huxley was profoundly affected by his experiences at sea: fifteen years after Darwin set sail on the *Beagle*, Huxley sailed as assistant surgeon and naturalist aboard the *Rattlesnake*, commissioned by the navy to survey the waters between Australia and the Great Barrier Reef. During his four years on the *Rattlesnake*, Huxley studied the structure of coral, hydrazoa, sea anemones, and other examples of invertebrate marine life, sent back papers on his discoveries, and, at Sydney, during the ship's regular port of call, met and wooed Miss Henrietta Heathhorn, daughter of an Australian merchant.

When Huxley returned in 1850 he had established his reputation as a scientist and was elected the next year as a Fellow of the Royal Society. Nonetheless, as a member of the navy, he could not be paid to pursue his scientific research, and he lacked sufficient funds to marry Henrietta. Frustrated in his career and his private life, Huxley applied unsuccessfully for positions at various colleges, until in 1854 he was able to resign from the navy and take over a course of lectures at the Royal School of Mines for a friend who had accepted a professorship in Edinburgh.

In 1855, securely employed at the Mines school, he married Henrietta and began his teaching career, having already published over thirty scientific papers. In the early years of their marriage, the Huxleys were happy but anxious about health: on her arrival in London Henrietta had been told by a doctor that she had only a few months to live, and Huxley repeatedly suffered from digestive problems which he attributed to hypochondria. Nonetheless, each was kept busy, Henrietta with their growing family (Noel born in 1856, Jessie in 1858, Marion in 1859, and Leonard in 1860, followed by Rachel, Henrietta, and Henry) and Huxley with his publications, his lectures, and his increasing commitment to the scientific education of the working classes.

By the time Huxley undertook a review of *Origin of Species* in the London *Times* in 1859, he was already a controversial speaker, having questioned Richard Owen's[1] ideas about archetypical structures in his lecture "On the Theory of the Vertebrate Skull" before the Royal Society in 1858. For the rest of his life, Huxley was surrounded by the controversies stemming from his defense of Darwin's work and his promotion of the free expression of truths discovered through verifiable experiment. In 1860 he defended Darwin against Bishop Wilberforce at the British Association for the Advancement of Science at Oxford. In 1870 he was elected to the first London School Board, where he promoted both the teaching of science and the reading of the Bible (for moral instruction) at the elementary level. In 1871 he was elected secretary of the Royal Society. In 1880 he engaged in a controversy with Matthew Arnold° over the replacement at the college level of the study of classics with the study of science. Although his disagreement with Arnold° has been called a conflict between science and the humanities, it was not. Huxley was adamant in his belief that the study of literature, history, philosophy, and languages is as important as the study of science, but he argued that students, particularly those destined for careers in medicine or science, should study modern languages and modern literature rather than the languages and literature of the ancients.

In 1885, now president of the Royal Society, Huxley debated with Gladstone° over biblical interpretation; in 1889 he was embroiled in another controversy, this time over agnosticism, a term which he himself had coined to express doubt in the absence of logical evidence about theological issues. Darwin also professed to be an agnostic, both men having encountered some of their doubt at the deaths of their children, Darwin's ten-year-old daughter in 1851 and Huxley's four-year-old son Noel in 1860. Despite his agnosticism, Huxley retained the fervor of his dissenting background: "We live

---

[1](1804–1892) British zoologist and anatomist, superintendent for twenty-seven years of the natural history department of the British Museum. He opposed Darwin's theory of evolution.

in a world which is full of misery and ignorance, and the plain duty of each and all of us is to try to make the little corner he can influence somewhat less miserable and somewhat less ignorant than it was before he entered it." Huxley thought that this goal was to be achieved through "two beliefs": that "the order of nature" can be examined and understood "to an extent which is practically unlimited" and that "our volition counts for something as a condition of the course of events."

Failing health forced Huxley to move from London to Eastbourne in 1890, and in 1895 he died of a kidney ailment; his wife Henrietta outlived him by nineteen years. He had spent the last five years of his life writing, delivering lectures, and collecting his lectures and essays, nine volumes in all, for publication. His essays attest to his faith in doubt, in the necessity for the verification of every scientific assertion, and in the perfectibility of scientific knowledge. What we believe today may be shown to be faulty in generations to come, he believed, but reliance on the scientific method will bring us ever closer to truth. Directly contradicting Hazlitt's limitations on the essay, that it "not treat of minerals or fossils, of the virtues of plants, or the influence of planets," Huxley's essays fit the tradition established by Browne and Franklin.

Like Franklin before him, Huxley admired Addison's style and consciously tinkered with language as he prepared his collected essays. But his writing is more metaphorical than either Addison's or Franklin's and more exhortative—a result, no doubt, of his years of teaching and lecturing. "The Coming of Age of the *Origin of Species*," for instance, begins with an extended metaphor, uplifts in its praises of Darwin's book, yet follows the pattern of the scientific argument, aligning evidence first to counter and then to convince the opponent. Speaking of the first part of that essay, Huxley says, "It may remove dissent, but it does not compell assent." The second section of his essay does. Like that of Bacon, Franklin, and Hazlitt, Huxley's voice is clear and direct, speaking without condescension or pretension to all who would participate in the common concerns of humanity. ✍

The Coming of Age of the "Origin of Species"[1]

Many of you will be familiar with the aspect[2] of this small green-covered book. It is a copy of the first edition of the "Origin of Species," and bears the date of its production—the 1st of October 1859. Only a few months, therefore, are needed to complete the full tale of twenty-one years since its birthday.

---

[1]Huxley published this lecture, originally delivered in 1880, in 1896 as part of his collection of essays on Darwin entitled *Darwiniana*. All material shown here in brackets appeared as footnotes in the original text.

[2]Appearance.

Those whose memories carry them back to this time will remember that the infant was remarkably lively, and that a great number of excellent persons mistook its manifestations of a vigorous individuality for mere naughtiness; in fact there was a very pretty turmoil about its cradle. My recollections of the period are particularly vivid, for, having conceived a tender affection for a child of what appeared to me to be such remarkable promise, I acted for some time in the capacity of a sort of under-nurse, and thus came in for my share of the storms which threatened the very life of the young creature. For some years it was undoubtedly warm work; but considering how exceedingly unpleasant the apparition of the new-comer must have been to those who did not fall in love with him at first sight, I think it is to the credit of our age that the war was not fiercer, and that the more bitter and unscrupulous forms of opposition died away as soon as they did.

I speak of this period as of something past and gone, possessing merely an historical, I had almost said an antiquarian interest. For, during the second decade of the existence of the "Origin of Species," opposition, though by no means dead, assumed a different aspect. On the part of all those who had any reason to respect themselves, it assumed a thoroughly respectful character. By this time, the dullest began to perceive that the child was not likely to perish of any congenital weakness or infantile disorder, but was growing into a stalwart personage, upon whom mere goody scoldings and threatenings with the birch-rod were quite thrown away.

In fact, those who have watched the progress of science within the last ten years will bear me out to the full, when I assert that there is no field of biological inquiry in which the influence of "Origin of Species" is not traceable; the foremost men of science in every country are either avowed champions of its leading doctrines, or at any rate abstain from opposing them; a host of young and ardent investigators seek for and find inspiration and guidance in Mr. Darwin's great work; and the general doctrine of evolution, to one side of which it gives expression, obtains, in the phenomena of biology, a firm base of operations whence it may conduct its conquest of the whole realm of Nature.

History warns us, however, that it is the customary fate of new truths to begin as heresies and to end as superstitions; and, as matters now stand, it is hardly rash to anticipate that, in another twenty years, the new generation, educated under the influences of the present day, will be in danger of accepting the main doctrines of the "Origin of Species," with as little reflection, and it may be with as little justification, as so many of our contemporaries, twenty years ago, rejected them.

Against any such consummation[1] let us all devoutly pray; for the scientific spirit is of more value than its products, and irrationally held truths may be more harmful than reasoned errors. Now the essence of the scientific spirit is criticism. It tells us that whenever a doctrine claims our assent we should reply, Take it if you can compel it. The struggle for existence holds as much in the intellectual as

---

[1]End.

in the physical world. A theory is a species of thinking, and its right to exist is coextensive with its power of resisting extinction by its rivals.

From this point of view it appears to me that it would be but a poor way of celebrating the Coming of Age of the "Origin of Species," were I merely to dwell upon the facts, undoubted and remarkable as they are, of its far-reaching influence and of the great following of ardent disciples who are occupied in spreading and developing its doctrines. Mere insanities and inanities have before now swollen to portentous size in the course of twenty years. Let us rather ask this prodigious change in opinion to justify itself: let us inquire whether anything has happened since 1859, which will explain, on rational grounds, why so many are worshipping that which they burned, and burning that which they worshipped. It is only in this way that we shall acquire the means of judging whether the movement we have witnessed is a mere eddy of fashion, or truly one with the irreversible current of intellectual progress, and, like it, safe from retrogressive reaction.

Every belief is the product of two factors: the first is the state of the mind to which the evidence in favour of that belief is presented; and the second is the logical cogency of the evidence itself. In both these respects, the history of biological science during the last twenty years appears to me to afford an ample explanation of the change which has taken place; and a brief consideration of the salient events of that history will enable us to understand why, if the "Origin of Species" appeared now, it would meet with a very different reception from that which greeted it in 1859.

One-and-twenty years ago, in spite of the work commenced by Hutton° and continued with rare skill and patience by Lyell,° the dominant view of the past history of the earth was catastrophic. Great and sudden physical revolutions, wholesale creations and extinctions of living beings, were the ordinary machinery of the geological epic brought into fashion by the misapplied genius of Cuvier.° It was gravely maintained and taught that the end of every geological epoch was signalised by a cataclysm, by which every living being on the globe was swept away, to be replaced by a brand-new creation when the world returned to quiescence. A scheme of nature which appeared to be modelled on the likeness of a succession of rubbers of whist,[1] at the end of each of which the players upset the table and called for a new pack, did not seem to shock anybody.

I may be wrong, but I doubt if, at the present time, there is a single responsible representative of these opinions left. The progress of scientific geology has elevated the fundamental principle of uniformitarianism, that the explanation of the past is to be sought in the study of the present, into the position of an axiom; and the wild speculations of the catastrophists, to which we all listened with respect a quarter of a century ago, would hardly find a single patient hearer at the present day. No physical geologist now dreams of seeking outside the range of

---

[1]The parent game of bridge, whist is a card game in which two pairs of players vie for thirteen tricks. Rubbers consist of three or five games from which a clear winner can emerge.

known natural causes, for the explanation of anything that happened millions of years ago, any more than he would be guilty of the like absurdity in regard to current events.

The effect of this change of opinion upon biological speculation is obvious. For, if there have been no periodical general physical catastrophes, what brought about the assumed general extinctions and re-creations of life which are the corresponding biological catastrophes? And, if no such interruptions of the ordinary course of nature have taken place in the organic, any more than in the inorganic, world, what alternative is there to the admission of evolution?

The doctrine of evolution in biology is the necessary result of the logical application of the principles of uniformitarianism to the phenomena of life. Darwin is the natural successor of Hutton° and Lyell,° and the "Origin of Species" the logical sequence of the "Principles of Geology."

The fundamental doctrine of the "Origin of Species," as of all forms of the theory of evolution applied to biology, is "that the innumerable species, genera, and families of organic beings with which the world is peopled have all descended, each within its own class or group, from common parents, and have all been modified in the course of descent." [*Origin of Species*, ed. 1, p. 457.]

And, in view of the facts of geology, it follows that all living animals and plants "are the lineal descendants of those which lived long before the Silurian epoch." [*Origin of Species*, p. 458.]

It is an obvious consequence of this theory of descent with modification, as it is sometimes called, that all plants and animals, however different they may now be, must, at one time or other, have been connected by direct or indirect intermediate gradations, and that the appearance of isolation presented by various groups of organic beings must be unreal.

No part of Mr. Darwin's work ran more directly counter to the prepossessions[1] of naturalists twenty years ago than this. And such prepossessions were very excusable, for there was undoubtedly a great deal to be said, at that time, in favour of the fixity of species and of the existence of great breaks, which there was no obvious or probable means of filling up, between various groups of organic beings.

For various reasons, scientific and unscientific, much had been made of the hiatus between man and the rest of the higher mammalia, and it is no wonder that issue was first joined on this part of the controversy. I have no wish to revive past and happily forgotten controversies; but I must state the simple fact that the distinctions in the cerebral and other characters, which were so hotly affirmed to separate man from all other animals in 1860, have all been demonstrated to be nonexistent, and that the contrary doctrine is now universally accepted and taught.

But there were other cases in which the wide structural gaps asserted to exist between one group of animals and another were by no means fictitious; and,

---

[1]Preconceptions.

when such structural breaks were real Mr. Darwin could account for them only by supposing that the intermediate forms which once existed had become extinct. In a remarkable passage he says—

"We may thus account even for the distinctness of whole classes from each other—for instance of birds from all other vertebrate animals—by the belief that many animal forms of life have been utterly lost, through which the early progenitors of birds were formerly connected with the early progenitors of the other vertebrate classes." [*Origin of Species*, p. 431.]

Adverse criticism made merry over such suggestions as these. Of course it was easy to get out of the difficulty by supposing extinction; but where was the slightest evidence that such intermediate forms between birds and reptiles as the hypothesis required ever existed? And then probably followed a tirade upon this terrible forsaking of the paths of "Baconian induction."

But the progress of knowledge has justified Mr. Darwin to an extent which could hardly have been anticipated. In 1862, the specimen of *Archaeopteryx*, which, until the last two or three years, has remained unique, was discovered; and it is an animal which, in its feathers and the greater part of its organisation, is a veritable bird, while, in other parts, it is as distinctly reptilian.

In 1868, I had the honour of bringing under your notice, in this theatre, the results of investigations made, up to that time, into the anatomical characters of certain ancient reptiles, which showed the nature of the modifications in virtue of which the type of the quadrupedal reptile passed into that of a bipedal bird; and abundant confirmatory evidence of the justice of the conclusions which I then laid before you has since come to light.

In 1875, the discovery of the toothed birds of the cretaceous formation in North America by Professor Marsh[1] completed the series of transitional forms between birds and reptiles, and removed Mr. Darwin's proposition that "many animal forms of life have been utterly lost, through which the early progenitors of birds were formerly connected with the early progenitors of the other vertebrate classes," from the region of hypothesis to that of demonstrable fact.

In 1859, there appeared to be a very sharp and clear hiatus between vertebrated and invertebrated animals, not only in their structure, but, what was more important, in their development. I do not think that we even yet know the precise links of connection between the two; but the investigations of Kowalewsky[2] and others upon the development of *Amphioxus*[3] and of the *Tunicata*[4] prove, beyond a doubt, that the differences which were supposed to constitute a barrier between

---

[1]Othniel Charles Marsh (1831–1899) established the field of vertebrate paleontology in the United States and was president of the National Academy of Sciences from 1830 to 1895. The discoveries Huxley refers to occurred during Marsh's four expeditions to South Dakota, Nebraska, and Wyoming.

[2]Aleksandr Onufriyevich Kovalevsky (1840–1901), Russian founder of comparative embryology who demonstrated a common pattern of development in multicellular animals.

[3]Primitive chordate, sharp at both ends.

[4]Chordate marine animals with roundish bodies and tough outer coverings.

the two are non-existent. There is no longer any difficulty in understanding how the vertebrate type may have arisen from the invertebrate though the full proof of the manner in which the transition was actually effected may still be lacking.

Again, in 1859 there appeared to be a no less sharp separation between the two great groups of flowering and flowerless plants. It is only subsequently that the series of remarkable investigations inaugurated by Hofmeister[1] has brought to light the extraordinary and altogether unexpected modifications of the reproductive apparatus in the *Lycopodiaceae*,[2] the *Rhizocarpeae*,[3] and the *Gymnospermeae*,[4] by which the ferns and the mosses are gradually connected with the Phanerogamic[5] division of the vegetable world.

So, again, it is only since 1859 that we have acquired that wealth of knowledge of the lowest forms of life which demonstrates the futility of any attempt to separate the lowest plants from the lowest animals, and shows that the two kingdoms of living nature have a common borderland which belongs to both, or to neither.

Thus it will be observed that the whole tendency of biological investigation, since 1859, has been in the direction of removing the difficulties which the apparent breaks in the series created at that time; and the recognition of gradation is the first step towards the acceptance of evolution.

As another great factor in bringing about the change of opinion which has taken place among naturalists, I count the astonishing progress which has been made in the study of embryology. Twenty years ago, not only were we devoid of any accurate knowledge of the mode of development of many groups of animals and plants, but the methods of investigation were rude and imperfect. At the present time, there is no important group of organic beings the development of which has not been carefully studied; and the modern methods of hardening and section-making enable the embryologist to determine the nature of the process, in each case, with a degree of minuteness and accuracy which is truly astonishing to those whose memories carry them back to the beginnings of modern histology.[6] And the results of these embryological investigations are in complete harmony with the requirements of the doctrine of evolution. The first beginnings of all the higher forms of animal life are similar, and however diverse their adult conditions, they start from a common foundation. Moreover, the process of development of the animal or the plant from the primary egg, or germ, is a true process of evolution—a progress from almost formless to more or less highly organised matter, in virtue of the properties inherent in that matter.

To those who are familiar with the process of development, all *a priori* objections to the doctrine of biological evolution appear childish. Any one who

---

[1]Wilhelm (1824–1877), German botanist.

[2]Club mosses.

[3]Ferns.

[4]Conifers.

[5]Pertaining to plants with flowers and true seeds.

[6]Study of the anatomy of microscopic plant and animal tissue.

has watched the gradual formation of a complicated animal from the protoplasmic mass, which constitutes the essential element of a frog's or a hen's egg, has had under his eyes sufficient evidence that a similar evolution of the whole animal world from the like foundation is, at any rate, possible.

Yet another product of investigation has largely contributed to the removal of the objections to the doctrine of evolution current in 1859. It is the proof afforded by successive discoveries that Mr. Darwin did not over-estimate the imperfection of the geological record. No more striking illustration of this is needed than a comparison of our knowledge of the mammalian fauna of the Tertiary epoch[1] in 1859 with its present condition. M. Gaudry's[2] researches on the fossils of Pikermi were published in 1868, those of Messrs. Leidy, Marsh, and Cope,[3] on the fossils of the Western Territories of America, have appeared almost wholly since 1870, those of M. Filhol[4] on the phosphorites of Quercy in 1878. The general effect of these investigations has been to introduce to us a multitude of extinct animals, the existence of which was previously hardly suspected; just as if zoologists were to become acquainted with a country, hitherto unknown, as rich in novel forms of life as Brazil or South Africa once were to Europeans. Indeed, the fossil fauna of the Western Territories of America bid fair to exceed in interest and importance all other known Tertiary deposits put together; and yet, with the exception of the case of the American tertiaries, these investigations have extended over very limited areas; and, at Pikermi, were confined to an extremely small space.

Such appear to me to be the chief events in the history of the progress of knowledge during the last twenty years, which account for the changed feeling with which the doctrine of evolution is at present regarded by those who have followed the advance of biological science, in respect of those problems which bear indirectly upon that doctrine.

But all this remains mere secondary evidence. It may remove dissent, but it does not compel assent. Primary and direct evidence in favour of evolution can be furnished only by palaeontology. The geological record, so soon as it approaches completeness, must, when properly questioned, yield either an affirmative or a negative answer: if evolution has taken place, there will its mark be left; if it has not taken place, there will lie its refutation.

---

[1]First period of the Cenozoic era characterized by the appearance of modern flora as well as of apes and other large mammals.

[2]Albert Jean Gaudry (1827–1908), French paleontologist who conducted expeditions in the Mediterranean in 1853 and again at Attica and Pikermi (Greece) from 1855 to 1860.

[3]American paleontologist Edward Drinker Cope (1840–1897) was Marsh's bitter rival. Each charged the other with unethical conduct, but Marsh outmaneuvered Cope in funding and publication, forcing his competitor to go on lecture tours to raise money. Cope sold his fossils to the American Museum of Natural History in 1894.

[4]Antoine-Pierre-Henri Filhol (1844–1902), French geologist and paleontologist, member of the French Academies of Science and Medicine, who spent time on islands in the Pacific, visited America, and published extensively on marine and vertebrate fossils.

What was the state of matters in 1859? Let us hear Mr. Darwin, who may be trusted always to state the case against himself as strongly as possible.

"On this doctrine of the extermination of an infinitude of connecting links between the living and extinct inhabitants of the world, and at each successive period between the extinct and still older species, why is not every geological formation charged with such links? Why does not every collection of fossil remains afford plain evidence of the gradation and mutation of the forms of life? We meet with no such evidence, and this is the most obvious and plausible of the many objections which may be urged against my theory." [*Origin of Species*, ed. 1, p. 463.]

Nothing could have been more useful to the opposition than this characteristically candid avowal, twisted as it immediately was into an admission that the writer's views were contradicted by the facts of palaeontology. But, in fact, Mr. Darwin made no such admission. What he says in effect is, not that palaeontological evidence is against him, but that it is not distinctly in his favour; and, without attempting to attenuate the fact, he accounts for it by the scantiness and the imperfection of that evidence.

What is the state of the case now, when, as we have seen, the amount of our knowledge respecting the mammalia of the Tertiary epoch is increased fifty-fold, and in some directions even approaches completeness?

Simply this, that, if the doctrine of evolution had not existed, palaeontologists must have invented it,[1] so irresistibly is it forced upon the mind by the study of the remains of the Tertiary mammalia which have been brought to light since 1859.

Among the fossils of Pikermi, Gaudry found the successive stages by which the ancient civets passed into the more modern hyaenas; through the Tertiary deposits of Western America, Marsh tracked the successive forms by which the ancient stock of the horse has passed into its present form; and innumerable less complete indications of the mode of evolution of other groups of the higher mammalia have been obtained. In the remarkable memoir on the phosphorites of Quercy, to which I have referred, M. Filhol describes no fewer than seventeen varieties of the genus *Cynodictis*, which fill up all the interval between the viverine animals[2] and the bear-like dog *Amphicyon*; nor do I know any solid ground of objection to the supposition that, in this *Cynodictis-Amphicyon* group, we have the stock whence all the Viveridae, Felidae, Hyaenidae, Canidae, and perhaps the Procyonidae and Ursidae, of the present fauna have been evolved. On the contrary, there is a great deal to be said in favour.

In the course of summing up his results, M. Filhol observes: —

"During the epoch of the phosphorites, great changes took place in animal forms, and almost the same types as those which now exist became defined from one another.

---

[1] A play on Voltaire's° famous line: "If God did not exist, it would be necessary to invent Him."
[2] Carniverous mammals like the civet and mongoose.

"Under the influence of natural conditions of which we have no exact knowledge, though traces of them are discoverable, species have been modified in a thousand ways: races have arisen which, becoming fixed, have thus produced a corresponding number of secondary species."

In 1859, language of which this is an unintentional paraphrase, occurring in the "Origin of Species," was scouted as wild speculation; at present, it is a sober statement of the conclusions to which an acute and critically-minded investigator is led by large and patient study of the facts of palaeontology. I venture to repeat what I have said before, that so far as the animal world is concerned, evolution is no longer a speculation, but a statement of historical fact. It takes its place alongside of those accepted truths which must be reckoned with by philosophers of all schools.

Thus when, on the first day of October next, the "Origin of Species" comes of age, the promise of its youth will be amply fulfilled; and we shall be prepared to congratulate the venerated author of the book, not only that the greatness of his achievement and its enduring influence upon the progress of knowledge have won him a place beside our Harvey;° but, still more, that, like Harvey,° he has lived long enough to outlast detraction and opposition, and to see the stone that the builders rejected become the head-stone of the corner.[1] ✎

Charles Darwin

[*Nature*, April 27th, 1882][2]

Very few, even among those who have taken the keenest interest in the progress of the revolution in natural knowledge set afoot by the publication of the "Origin of Species," and who have watched, not without astonishment, the rapid and complete change which has been effected both inside and outside the boundaries of the scientific world in the attitude of men's minds towards the doctrines which are expounded in that great work, can have been prepared for the extraordinary manifestation of affectionate regard for the man, and of profound reverence for the philosopher, which followed the announcement, on Thursday last, of the death of Mr. Darwin.

Not only in these islands, where so many have felt the fascination of personal contact with an intellect which had no superior, and with a character which was even nobler than the intellect: but, in all parts of the civilised world, it would seem that those whose business it is to feel the pulse of nations and to know what interests the masses of mankind, were well aware that thousands of their readers would think the world the poorer for Darwin's death, and would dwell with eager

---

[1]See Psalms 118:22; Mt. 21:42; Acts 4:11; Pet. 2:7.

[2]Reprinted in *Darwiniana*. All material shown here in brackets appeared as footnotes in the original text.

interest upon every incident of his history. In France, in Germany, in Austro-Hungary, in Italy, in the United States, writers of all shades of opinion, for once unanimous, have paid a willing tribute to the worth of our great countryman, ignored in life by the official representatives of the kingdom, but laid in death among his peers in Westminster Abbey by the will of the intelligence of the nation.

It is not for us to allude to the sacred sorrows of the bereaved home at Down; but it is no secret that, outside that domestic group, there are many to whom Mr. Darwin's death is a wholly irreparable loss. And this not merely because of his wonderfully genial, simple, and generous nature; his cheerful and animated conversation, and the infinite variety and accuracy of his information; but because the more one knew of him, the more he seemed the incorporated ideal of a man of science. Acute as were his reasoning powers, vast as was his knowledge, marvellous as was his tenacious industry, under physical difficulties which would have converted nine men out of ten into aimless invalids;[1] it was not these qualities, great as they were, which impressed those who were admitted to his intimacy with involuntary veneration, but a certain intense and almost passionate honesty by which all his thoughts and actions were irradiated,[2] as by a central fire.

It was this rarest and greatest of endowments which kept his vivid imagination and great speculative powers within due bounds; which compelled him to undertake the prodigious labours of original investigation and of reading, upon which his published works are based; which made him accept criticisms and suggestions from anybody and everybody, not only without impatience, but with expressions of gratitude sometimes almost comically in excess of their value; which led him to allow neither himself nor others to be deceived by phrases, and to spare neither time nor pains in order to obtain clear and distinct ideas upon every topic with which he occupied himself.

One could not converse with Darwin without being reminded of Socrates.° There was the same desire to find some one wiser than himself; the same belief in the sovereignty of reason; the same ready humour; the same sympathetic interest in all the ways and works of men. But instead of turning away from the problems of Nature as hopelessly insoluble, our modern philosopher devoted his whole life to attacking them in the spirit of Heraclitus° and of Democritus,° with results which are the substance of which their speculations were anticipatory shadows.

The due appreciation, or even enumeration, of these results is neither practicable nor desirable at this moment. There is a time for all things—a time for glorying in our ever-extending conquests over the realm of Nature, and a time for mourning over the heroes who have led us to victory.

None have fought better, and none have been more fortunate, than Charles Darwin. He found a great truth trodden underfoot, reviled by bigots, and ridiculed by all the world; he lived long enough to see it, chiefly by his own efforts,

---

[1]See "Darwin's Illness" in *Pluto's Republic* by Peter Medawar (1984) for an analysis of Darwin's mysterious ailment, thought by many to be psychosomatic but more likely contracted in Argentina when Darwin was bitten by the "great black bug of the Pampas."
[2]Illuminated.

irrefragably[1] established in science, inseparably incorporated with the common thoughts of men, and only hated and feared by those who would revile, but dare not. What shall a man desire more than this? Once more the image of Socrates° rises unbidden, and the noble peroration[2] of the "Apology" rings in our ears as if it were Charles Darwin's farewell: —

"The hour of departure has arrived, and we go our ways—I to die and you to live. Which is the better, God only knows." ✍

Autobiography[3]

'My Dear Mr. Engel, —

'You really are the most pertinaciously persuasive of men. When you first wrote to me, I said I would have nothing whatever to do with anything you might please to say about me, that I had a profound objection to write about myself, and that I could not see what business the public had with my private life. I think I even expressed to you my complete sympathy with Dr. Johnson's desire to take Boswell's life when he heard of the latter's occupation with his biography.

'Undeterred by all this, you put before me the alternative of issuing something that may be all wrong, unless I furnish you with something authoritative; I do not say all right, because autobiographies are essentially works of fiction, whatever biographies may be. So I yield, and send you what follows, in the hope that those who find it to be mere egotistical gossip will blame you and not me.

'I am

'Yours faithfully,
'T.H. Huxley.'

I was born about eight o'clock in the morning on the 4th of May, 1825, at Ealing, which was, at that time, as quiet a little country village as could be found within half a dozen miles of Hyde Park Corner. Now it is a suburb of London with, I believe, 30,000 inhabitants. I am not aware that any portents preceded my arrival in this world; but, in my childhood, I remember hearing a traditional account of the manner in which I lost the chance of an endowment of great practical value. The windows of my mother's room were open, in consequence of the unusual warmth of the weather. For the same reason, probably, a neighbouring beehive had swarmed, and the new colony, pitching on the window-sill, was making its way into the room when the horrified nurse shut down the sash. If that well-meaning woman had only abstained from her ill-timed interference, the swarm might have settled on my lips, and I should have been endowed with that mellifluous[4] eloquence which, in this country, leads far more surely than worth,

---

[1] Incontrovertibly.
[2] The end of a work or speech.
[3] February 1889.
[4] Honeyed, that is, flowing with honey.

capacity, or honest work, to the highest places in Church and State. But the opportunity was lost and I have been obliged to content myself through life with saying what I mean in the plainest of plain language; than which, I suppose, there is no habit more ruinous to a man's prospects of advancement. Why I was christened Thomas Henry I do not know; but it is a curious chance that my parents should have fixed for my usual denomination upon the name of that particular Apostle with whom I have always felt most sympathy.[1] Physically and mentally I am the son of my mother so completely—even down to peculiar movements of the hands, which made their appearance in me as I reached the age she had when I noticed them—that I can hardly find any trace of my father in myself except an inborn faculty for drawing, which unfortunately, in my case, has never been cultivated; a hot temper; and that amount of tenacity of purpose, which unfriendly observers sometimes call obstinacy.

My mother was a slender brunette, of an emotional and energetic temperament, and possessed of the most piercing black eyes I ever saw in a woman's head. With no more education than other women of the middle classes in her day, she had an excellent mental capacity. Her most distinguishing characteristic, however, was rapidity of thought. If one ventured to suggest that she had not taken much time to arrive at any conclusion, she would say, 'I cannot help it, things flash across me.' That peculiarity has been passed on to me in full strength; it has often stood me in good stead; it has sometimes played me sad tricks, and it has always been a danger. But after all, if my time were to come over again, there is nothing I would less willingly part with than my inheritance of mother wit.

I have next to nothing to say about my childhood. In later years, my mother, looking at me almost reproachfully, would sometimes say, 'Ah! you were such a pretty boy!' whence I had no difficulty in concluding that I had not fulfilled my early promise in the matter of looks. In fact, I have a distinct recollection of certain curls, of which I was vain, and of a conviction that I closely resembled that handsome courtly gentleman, Sir Herbert Oakley, who was vicar of our parish, and who was as a god to us country folk, because he was occasionally visited by the then Prince George of Cambridge.[2] I remember turning my pinafore wrong side forwards, in order to represent a surplice,[3] and preaching to my mother's maids in the kitchen, as nearly as possible in Sir Herbert's manner, one Sunday morning when the rest of the family were at church. That is the earliest indication I can call to mind of the strong clerical affinities which my friend Mr. Herbert Spencer[4] has always ascribed to me, though I fancy they have for the most part remained in a latent state.

---

[1] Doubting Thomas; see John 20:24–29.
[2] (1762–1830) Later became George IV.
[3] White gown worn over a black robe cassock by some members of the clergy.
[4] (1820–1903) English philosopher and author of *Synthetic Philosophy,* which applies principles of evolution to all areas of life.

My regular school training was of the briefest, perhaps fortunately, for though my way of life has made me acquainted with all sorts and conditions of men, from the highest to the lowest, I deliberately affirm that the society I fell into at school was the worst I have ever known. We boys were average lads, with much the same inherent capacity for good and evil as any others; but the people who were set over us cared about as much for our intellectual and moral welfare as if they were baby farmers. We were left to the operation of the struggle for existence among ourselves, and bullying was the least of the ill practices current among us. Almost the only cheerful reminiscence in connection with the place, which arises in my mind, is that of a battle I had with one of my classmates, who had bullied me until I could stand it no longer. I was a very slight lad, but there was a wild-cat element in me which, when roused, made up for lack of weight, and I licked my adversary effectually. However, one of my first experiences of the extremely rough-and-ready nature of justice, as exhibited by the course of things in general, arose out of the fact that I, the victor, had a black eye, while he, the vanquished, had none; so that I got into disgrace, and he did not. We made it up, and thereafter I was unmolested. One of the greatest shocks I ever received in my life was to be told, a dozen years afterwards, by the groom who brought me my horse, in a stable-yard in Sydney, that he was my quondam[1] antagonist. He had a long story of family misfortune to account for his position; but at that time it was necessary to deal very cautiously with mysterious strangers in New South Wales, and on inquiry I found that the unfortunate young man had not only been 'sent out'[2] but had undergone more than one colonial conviction.

As I grew older, my great desire was to be a mechanical engineer, but the Fates were against this; and, while very young, I commenced the study of Medicine under a medical brother-in-law. But, though the Institute of Mechanical Engineers would certainly not own me, I am not sure that I have not, all along, been a sort of mechanical engineer *in partibus infidelium*.[3] I am now occasionally horrified to think how very little I ever knew or cared about Medicine as the art of healing. The only part of my professional course which really and deeply interested me was Physiology, which is the mechanical engineering of living machines; and, notwithstanding that natural science has been my proper business, I am afraid there is very little of the genuine naturalist in me. I never collected anything, and species work was always a burden to me; what I cared for was the architectural and engineering part of the business, the working out of the wonderful unity of plan in the thousands and thousands of diverse living constructions, and the modifications of similar apparatuses to serve diverse ends. The extraordinary attraction I felt towards the study of the intricacies of living structure nearly proved fatal to me at the outset. I was a mere boy—I think between thirteen and fourteen years of age—when I was taken by some older student friends of mine to

---

[1] Former.

[2] In 1788 the first penal colony was established in what was to become Sydney, and by 1820 the whole continent had been claimed by Britain.

[3] In some respect disloyal.

the first post-mortem examination I ever attended. All my life I have been most unfortunately sensitive to the disagreeables which attend anatomical pursuits; but on this occasion, my curiosity overpowered all other feelings, and I spent two or three hours in gratifying it. I did not cut myself and none of the ordinary symptoms of dissection poison supervened, but poisoned I was somehow, and I remember sinking into a strange state of apathy. By way of a last chance I was sent to the care of some good, kind people, friends of my father's, who lived in a farmhouse in the heart of Warwickshire. I remember staggering from my bed to the window on the bright spring morning after my arrival, and throwing open the casement. Life seemed to come back on the wings of the breeze; and, to this day, the faint odour of wood-smoke, like that which floated across the farmyard in the early morning, is as good to me as the 'sweet south upon a bed of violets.'[1] I soon recovered; but for years I suffered from occasional paroxysms of internal pain, and from that time my constant friend, hypochondriacal dyspepsia, commenced his half century of co-tenancy of my fleshly tabernacle.

Looking back on my 'Lehrjahre,'[2] I am sorry to say that I do not think that any account of my doings as a student would tend to edification. In fact, I should distinctly warn ingenuous[3] youth to avoid imitating my example. I worked extremely hard when it pleased me, and when it did not (which was a very frequent case) I was extremely idle (unless making caricatures of one's pastors and masters is to be called a branch of industry), or else wasted my energies in wrong directions. I read everything I could lay hands upon, including novels, and took up all sorts of pursuits, to drop them again quite as speedily. No doubt it was very largely my own fault, but the only instruction from which I ever obtained the proper effect of education was that which I received from Mr. Wharton Jones, who was the Lecturer on Physiology at the Charing Cross School of Medicine. The extent and precision of his knowledge impressed me greatly, and the severe exactness of his method of lecturing was quite to my taste. I do not know that I have ever felt so much respect for anybody before or since. I worked hard to obtain his approbation, and he was extremely kind and helpful to the youngster who, I am afraid, took up more of his time than he had any right to do. It was he who suggested the publication of my first scientific paper[4]—a very little one—in the Medical Gazette of 1845, and most kindly corrected the literary faults which abounded in it, short as it was; for at that time, and for many years afterwards, I detested the trouble of writing, and would take no pains over it.

It was in the early spring of 1846 that, having finished my obligatory medical studies, and passed the first M.D. examination at the London University (though I was still too young to qualify at the College of Surgeons), I was talking to a fellow-student — the present eminent physician, Sir Joseph Fayrer — and wondering what I should do to meet the imperative necessity for earning my own bread,

---

[1]See *Twelfth Night*, 1.1.5.
[2]Apprenticeship.
[3]Innocent or unsophisticated.
[4]On the human hair sheath.

when my friend suggested that I should write to Sir William Burnett, at that time Director-General for the Medical Service of the Navy, for an appointment. I thought this rather a strong thing to do as Sir William was personally unknown to me, but my cheery friend would not listen to my scruples, so I went to my lodgings and wrote the best letter I could devise. A few days afterwards I received the usual official circular of acknowledgment, but at the bottom there was written an instruction to call at Somerset House on such a day. I thought that looked like business, so, at the appointed time, I called and sent in my card, while I waited in Sir William's ante-room. He was a tall, shrewd-looking old gentleman, with a broad Scotch accent—and I think I see him now as he entered with my card in his hand. The first thing he did was to return it, with the frugal reminder that I should probably find it useful on some other occasion. The second was to ask whether I was an Irishman. I suppose the air of modesty about my appeal must have struck him. I satisfied the Director-General that I was English to the backbone and he made some inquiries as to my student career, finally desiring me to hold myself ready for examination. Having passed this, I was in Her Majesty's Service, and entered on the books of Nelson's old ship Victory[1] for duty at Haslar Hospital, about a couple of months after I made my application.

My official chief at Haslar was a very remarkable person—the late Sir John Richardson, an excellent naturalist, and far-famed as an indomitable Arctic traveller. He was a silent, reserved man outside the circle of his family and intimates; and, having a full share of youthful vanity, I was extremely disgusted to find that 'Old John,' as we irreverent youngsters called him, took not the slightest notice of my worshipful self either the first time I attended him, as it was my duty to do, or for some weeks afterwards. I am afraid to think of the lengths to which my tongue might have run on the subject of the churlishness of the chief who was in truth one of the kindest-hearted and most considerate of men. But one day, as I was crossing the Hospital square, Sir John stopped me, and heaped coals of fire on my head by telling me that he had tried to get me one of the resident appointments, much coveted by the assistant-surgeons, but that the Admiralty had put in another man. 'However,' said he, 'I mean to keep you here till I can get you something you will like,' and turned upon his heel without waiting for the thanks I stammered out. That explained how it was I had not been packed off to the West Coast of Africa, like some of my juniors, and why, eventually, I remained altogether seven months at Haslar.

After a long interval, during which 'Old John' ignored my existence almost as completely as before, he stopped me again as we met in a casual way, and describing the service on which the Rattlesnake was likely to be employed, said that Captain Owen Stanley, who was to command the ship, had asked him to recommend an assistant-surgeon who knew something of science; would I like that? Of course I jumped at the offer. 'Very well, I give you leave; go to London at once and see Captain Stanley.' I went, saw my future commander, who was very

---

[1]Horatio Nelson (1758–1805), English admiral who died on board the Victory at Trafalgar. See Tennyson's "Ode to the Duke of Wellington," stanza 6.

civil to me and promised to ask that I should be appointed to his ship, as in due time I was. It is a singular thing that, during the few months of my stay at Haslar, I had among my messmates two future Directors-General of the Medical Service of the Navy (Sir Alexander Armstrong and Sir John Watt-Reid), with the present President of the College of Physicians and my kindest of doctors, Sir Andrew Clark. Life on board Her Majesty's ships in those days was a very different affair from what it is now; and ours was exceptionally rough as we were often many months without receiving letters or seeing any civilised people but ourselves. In exchange, we had the interest of being about the last voyagers, I suppose, to whom it could be possible to meet with people who knew nothing of fire-arms—as we did on the South Coast of New Guinea—and of making acquaintance with a variety of interesting savage and semi-civilised people. But, apart from experience of this kind, and the opportunities offered for scientific work, to me, personally, the cruise was extremely valuable. It was good for me to live under sharp discipline; to be down on the realities of existence by living on bare necessaries; to find out how extremely well worth living life seemed to be, when one woke up from a night's rest on a soft plank, with the sky for canopy and cocoa and weevilly biscuit the sole prospect for breakfast; and more especially to learn to work for the sake of what I got for myself out of it, even if it all went to the bottom and I along with it. My brother officers were as good fellows as sailors ought to be and generally are; but, naturally, they neither knew nor cared anything about my pursuits, nor understood why I should be so zealous in pursuit of the objects which my friends the Middies[1] christened 'Buffons,' after the title conspicuous on a volume of the *Suites à Buffon,*[2] which stood on my shelf in the chart room.

During the four years of our absence, I sent home communication after communication to the 'Linnean Society,'[3] with the same result as that obtained by Noah when he sent the raven out of his ark. Tired at last of hearing nothing about them, I determined to do or die, and, in 1849, I drew up a more elaborate paper[4] and forwarded it to the Royal Society. This was my dove, if I had only known it. But owing to the movements of the ship, I heard nothing of that either, until my return to England in the latter end of the year 1850, when I found that it was printed and published, and that a huge packet of separate copies awaited me. When I hear some of my young friends complain of want of sympathy and encouragement, I am inclined to think that my naval life was not the least valuable part of my education.

Three years after my return were occupied by a battle between my scientific friends on the one hand, and the Admiralty on the other, as to whether the latter

[1]Sailors, from "midshipmen," noncommissioned officers ranking below sublieutenant in the Royal British Navy.
[2]"Followers of Buffon" (French naturalist Georges-Louis Leclerc, Comte de Buffon, 1707–1788).
[3]Scientific society founded in 1788 and named after Carolus Linnaeus (1707–1778), the Swedish botanist who created the system for classifying plants and animals.
[4]On the anatomy of the family of Medusae.

ought, or ought not, to act up to the spirit of a pledge they had given to encourage officers who had done scientific work, by contributing to the expense of publishing mine. At last, the Admiralty, getting tired, I suppose, cut short the discussion by ordering me to join a ship. Which thing I declined to do, and as Rastignac, in the *Père Goriot*,[1] says to Paris, I said to London, *à nous deux*.[2] I desired to obtain a Professorship of either Physiology or Comparative Anatomy; and as vacancies occurred, I applied, but in vain. My friend, Professor Tyndall, and I were candidates at the same time, he for the Chair of Physics and I for that of Natural History, in the University of Toronto, which fortunately, as it turned out, would not look at either of us. I say fortunately, not from any lack of respect for Toronto, but because I soon made up my mind that London was the place for me, and hence I have steadily declined the inducements to leave it which have at various times been offered. At last, in 1854, on the translation of my warm friend, Edward Forbes, to Edinburgh, Sir Henry De la Beche, the Director General of the Geological Survey, offered me the post Forbes vacated of Paleontologist and Lecturer on Natural History. I refused the former point blank, and accepted the latter provisionally, telling Sir Henry that I did not care for fossils, and that I should give up Natural History as soon as I could get a physiological post. But I held the office for thirty-one years, and a large part of my work has been paleontological.

At that time I disliked public speaking, and had a firm conviction that I should break down every time I opened my mouth. I believe I had every fault a speaker could have (except talking at random or indulging in rhetoric) when I spoke to the first important audience I ever addressed, on a Friday evening, at the Royal Institution, in 1852. Yet I must confess to having been guilty, *malgré moi*,[3] of as much public speaking as most of my contemporaries, and for the last ten years it ceased to be so much of a bugbear to me. I used to pity myself for having to go through this training; but I am now more disposed to compassionate the unfortunate audiences, especially my ever friendly hearers at the Royal Institution, who were the subjects of my oratorical experiments.

The last thing that it would be proper for me to do would be to speak of the work of my life, or to say at the end of the day, whether I think I have earned my wages or not. Men are said to be partial judges of themselves—young men may be, I doubt if old men are. Life seems terribly foreshortened as they look back; and the mountain they set themselves to climb in youth turns out to be a mere spur of immeasurably higher ranges, when, with failing breath, they reach the top. But if I may speak of the objects I have had more or less definitely in view since I began the ascent of my hillock, they are briefly these: to promote the increase of natural knowledge and to forward the application of scientific methods of investigation to all the problems of life to the best of my ability, in the conviction—which has grown with my growth and strengthened with my strength—that there is no

---

[1] Novel by Honoré Balzac; Rastignac is a law student determined to rise in Parisian society.
[2] "Between us two," meaning that Rastignac pits himself against the social world of Paris.
[3] In spite of myself.

alleviation for the sufferings of mankind except veracity of thought and of action, and the resolute facing of the world as it is, when the garment of make-believe, by which pious hands have hidden its uglier features, is stripped off.

It is with this intent that I have subordinated any reasonable or unreasonable ambition for scientific fame, which I may have permitted myself to entertain, to other ends; to the popularisation of science; to the development and organisation of scientific education; to the endless series of battles and skirmishes over evolution; and to untiring opposition to that ecclesiastical spirit, that clericalism, which in England, as everywhere else, and to whatever denomination it may belong, is the deadly enemy of science.

In striving for the attainment of these objects, I have been but one among many, and I shall be well content to be remembered, or even not remembered, as such. Circumstances, among which I am proud to reckon the devoted kindness of many friends, have led to my occupation of various prominent positions, among which the Presidency of the Royal Society is the highest. It would be mock modesty on my part, with these and other scientific honours which have been bestowed upon me, to pretend that I have not succeeded in the career which I have followed, rather because I was driven into it, than of my own free will; but I am afraid I should not count even these things as marks of success, if I could not hope that I had somewhat helped that movement of opinion which has been called the New Reformation.[1] ✍

---

[1] That is, evolution by means of natural selection.

• • •

Mark Twain

(1835–1910)

Samuel Langhorne Clemens was born in Florida, Missouri, where the family had moved at the suggestion of his maternal uncle, John Quarles, who owned a successful farm and hoped that his sister's family could also prosper there. Sam was the fifth of six children of John Marshall Clemens, a sober lawyer and shopkeeper perpetually in search of better fortune, and his wife, Jane Lampton Clemens, a cheerful, plucky woman who loved stories. When Sam was four, John Clemens moved the family to Hannibal, Missouri, but Sam returned to his uncle's farm in Florida every summer until he was twelve.

Pleasure, piety, and peril shaped Twain's early life. On the farm in Florida he ate well, played hard with his many cousins, and listened to the stories and songs of the slaves his uncle owned. In Hannibal, he swam, fished, skated, spelunked, and watched the riverboats on the Mississippi. For piety, he was sent to three grammar schools, each devoted to the development of good manners and morals, and to Methodist and later Presbyterian Sunday schools and church services, which, with his mother's help, created in Twain a tender and stinging conscience. For peril, Sam had only to look about him. His nine-year-old sister Margaret died of fever when he was not quite four, and his ten-year-old brother Ben sickened and died within a week when Sam was eight. Before he was twelve Sam had seen slaves chained and beaten on their way south and had witnessed three murders. In his chaotic autobiography, written near the end of his life, Twain says that he drew on his memories from these early years to write *The Adventures of Tom Sawyer* and *The Adventures of Huckleberry Finn*.

In 1847, after a series of financial disasters forced him to sell all he could to pay his debts, John Clemens died of pneumonia, leaving his wife and children (Orion, twenty-one; Pamela, nineteen; Sam, twelve; and Henry, ten) with a house and little else. A year later Sam quit school and, like Ben Franklin, went to work as a printer, first for the *Missouri Courier* and then at sixteen for his brother Orion, who had started a paper in 1850. Also like Ben Franklin, Sam found it hard to work for his older brother; when he was eighteen he left Hannibal and for the next four years worked as a printer in St. Louis, New York, Philadelphia, Keokuk (Iowa), and Cincinnati, learning the printing business and developing an ear for regional idiosyncrasies.

In 1857 Sam took a steamboat to New Orleans. He had planned to go to South America but instead became apprenticed to Horace Bixby, senior pilot on a Mississippi steamboat. He earned his license in two years, saw his brother Henry, then about twenty, die from injuries suffered in a steamboat explosion, and piloted over twenty-one ships before the Civil War ended all steamboat traffic in 1861.

After a two-week stint in the Confederate Army, Twain set off in a stagecoach with his remaining brother, Orion, for Carson City, Nevada. For the next five years, Twain wrote articles, essays, and comic pieces for various newspapers, particularly the *Virginia City Territorial Enterprise*, where the name Mark Twain[1] first appeared in 1863, and for three papers in San Francisco. In 1865 he wrote a story based on a tale he'd heard in a mining camp, "Jim Smiley and His Jumping Frog," which was printed in New York and then picked up by papers around the country. Suddenly Mark Twain was a famous name. The next year, Twain sailed to the Sandwich Islands (now Hawaii) as a correspondent for the *Sacramento Union*, and by 1866 he was lecturing on his travels. In 1867 he published his first book, *The Celebrated Jumping Frog of Calaveras County, and Other Sketches*, and arrived in New York to lecture and to sail on the *Quaker City* to the Holy Land as correspondent for the San Francisco *Alta Californian*.

This voyage, like Huxley's aboard the *Rattlesnake*, proved pivotal for Twain, both personally and professionally. Among his fellow passengers was Charles Langdon, the eighteen-year-old son of a coal merchant in Elmira, New York, who one day showed Twain a picture of his sister Olivia. From that day on, Twain told his friend and biographer Albert Bigelow Paine, he was in love. He met Olivia shortly after the voyage ended and became engaged to her in 1869. Meanwhile Twain collected the letters he'd sent to the paper in San Francisco and devised from them his second publication, *Innocents Abroad*, which confirmed his national reputation as an American humorist.

With a loan from Olivia's father, Twain bought a partnership in the *Buffalo Express,* and in 1870 he and Olivia were married. Despite the death from diphtheria of their two-year-old son Langdon and the delicate health of his wife, the family was a happy one, Olivia bearing three daughters, Susy in 1872, Clara in 1874, and Jean in 1880. Twain continued to lecture in both America and England and to publish, drawing on his travels and later on his early life for his materials. *Roughing It*, based on the stagecoach trip with Orion, came out in 1872, *The Adventures of Tom Sawyer* in 1876, *A Tramp*

---

[1]A river call denoting a depth of two fathoms.

Abroad in 1880, *The Prince and the Pauper* in 1882, and *Life on the Mississippi* in 1883. From 1876 to 1883 he worked on his masterpiece, *The Adventures of Huckleberry Finn*, which was published in 1885.

During these years the family prospered, moved to a twenty-eight-room house in Hartford, Connecticut, employed six servants, and entertained guests with warmth and splendor. But this happiness did not last. In 1890, at age ten, their daughter Jean was diagnosed as epileptic. In the early 1890s Twain took his family to Europe for a prolonged visit, but by 1894 he was bankrupt, plunged into debt because of investments in the Paige typesetting machine. Like his father before him, Twain was determined to pay off all his debts, which he did in 1895–1896 by performing a grueling lecture trip around the world to raise the necessary funds. While he and his wife were away, Susy, the daughter most like Twain, died of meningitis. By 1898 Twain had paid off the last of his debts, and by 1903, having published prodigiously and recouped his fortunes, he was able to travel with his wife to Italy in hopes of improving her failing health. She died the following year.

Throughout his changing fortunes, Twain continued in his private life and in his writing to deflate pretension and pomposity with humor and honesty. In the 1930s Van Wyck Brooks and others attributed the increasingly sardonic and bitter tone of Twain's later works, such as *The Man That Corrupted Hadleyburg and Other Stories and Essays* (1900) and *What Is Man?* (published privately in 1906), to a release of feelings he had suppressed to please his conventional wife. However, research has turned up no evidence to support this view. His bitterness has also been attributed to a mechanistic philosophy adopted as a result of private misfortunes. Yet Twain's last years, like his first ones, were marked by pleasures as well as by pangs of conscience and sensitivity to the perils of life. He was pleased by the popular acclaim he received on his return to America in 1900 and by his honorary degrees from Yale (1901), the University of Missouri (1902), and Oxford (1907). He continued to enjoy good food, good company, and travel, visiting Bermuda and England in 1907 and Bermuda again in 1909. That year his daughter Clara married a concert pianist, and his daughter Jean, who had suffered periodic attacks from epilepsy, died. After Jean's death, he returned to Bermuda but came home again in April 1910, suffering from bronchitis and ready to fulfill the prediction he had made to Albert Bigelow Paine: "I came in with Halley's comet in 1835. It is coming again next year, and I expect to go out with it." He did.

The essays of Mark Twain share with those of his fellow countryman Ben Franklin a disarming directness. Both writers take pleasure in surprising the reader; both enjoy a joke. Both exploit the levels of language, the humor gained from the juxtaposition of an erudite term with a bit of slang. In their comic essays on science, Franklin and Twain rely on this technique, the one to parody the scientific treatise, the other to satirize it. Although Twain is a master of satire, he is not always as right as he believes himself to be; his satire of science, for instance, although always funny, does not always hit the mark. His essay on the American Indian, like Franklin's, is based on personal experience, but is nonetheless inflammatory. And his essay on man, "The Lowest Animal," would have inflamed even the mild-mannered Addison on two counts, the first for inverting the Great Chain of Being, and the second for defying his definition of proper satire (proffered in "Simonides' Satire on Women").

But when Twain's targets are the conventions of his day, as in "Corn-Pone Opinions" or "Elinor Glyn and the Passions," he is at his best. In "Corn-Pone Opinions" he notes the effects of convention on prose style: "Our prose standard, three quarters of a century ago, was ornate and diffuse; some authority or other changed it in the direction of compactness and simplicity, and conformity followed, without argument." In fact, of course, Twain himself was one of those responsible for introducing a new fashion for American dialects, particularly in novels, and for colloquial diction in essays. In his essay on science, Twain substitutes an adjective for an adverb as he plays the part of the stereotypical lowbrow besting the stereotypical intellectual:[1] "Bones do not keep good in coffins. There is no sure way but to cord them up in caves." The word *cord*, alliterating with *coffins* and *caves*, underlines the sophistication of his wit, but cannot, in the end, compensate for Twain's lack of expertise in the field. The common-sense assumption that coffins are the best receptacle for preserving bones is not true in this case. The stereotypical intellectual who lacks common sense is correct. Thus, although the humor remains intact, the satire fails. Nonetheless the juxtaposition of the ungrammatical with the alliterative, the comic with the barb, is typical of the enormously successful format he developed for his lectures, a mixture of wit and seriousness, humor and satire, aimed always at the pretensions of humanity. ✍

Female Suffrage

Editors Missouri Democrat:[2]

I have read the long list of lady petitioners in favor of female suffrage, and as a husband[3] and a father I want to protest against the whole business. It will never do to allow women to vote. It will never do to allow them to hold office. You know, and I know, that if they were granted these privileges there would be no more peace on earth. They would swamp the country with debt. They like to hold office

---

[1] These are the types Samuel Johnson took great care to describe and instruct in "The Necessity of Literary Courage." (See page 145.)

[2] First published in 1867.

[3] Twain married three years after this essay was published.

too well. They like to be Mrs. President Smith of the Dorcas society,[1] or Mrs. Secretary Jones of the Hindoo aid association, or Mrs. Treasurer of something or other. They are fond of the distinction of the thing, you know; they revel in the sweet jingle of the title. They are always setting up sanctified confederations of all kinds, and then running for president of them. They are even so fond of office that they are willing to serve without pay. But you allow them to vote and to go to the Legislature once, and then see how it will be. They will go to work and start a thousand more societies, and cram them full of salaried offices. You will see a state of things then that will stir your feelings to the bottom of your pockets. The first fee bill would exasperate you some. Instead of the usual schedule for judges, State printer, Supreme court clerks, &c., the list would read something like this:

OFFICES AND SALARIES.

President Dorcas society..$4,000
Subordinate Officers of same, each...................................2,000
President Ladies' Union prayer meeting 3,000
President Pawnee Educational society 4,000
President Of Ladies' society for Dissemination
    of Belles Lettres among the Shoshones.........................5,000
State Crinoline Directress..10,000
State Superintendent of waterfalls...................................10,000
State Hair Oil inspectress 10,000
State Milliner[2] 50,000

You know what a state of anarchy and social chaos that fee bill would create. Every woman in the commonwealth of Missouri would let go everything and run for State Milliner. And instead of ventilating each other's political antecedents, as men do, they would go straight after each other's private moral character. (I know them—they are all like my wife.) Before the canvass was three days old it would be an established proposition that every woman in the State was "no better than she ought to be."[3] Only think how it would lacerate me to have an opposition candidate say that about my wife. That is the idea, you know—having other people say these hard things. Now, I know that my wife isn't any better than she ought to be, poor devil—in fact, in matters of orthodox doctrine, she is particularly shaky—but still I would not like these things aired in a political contest. I don't really suppose that that woman will stand any more show hereafter than—however, she may improve—she may even become a beacon light for the saving of others—but if she does, she will burn rather dim, and she will flicker a good deal, too. But, as I was saying, a female political canvass would be an outrageous thing.

----

[1]A benevolent religious organization for women named after Dorcas (in Greek; Tabitha in Aramaic), a woman who made clothes for the poor; see Acts 9:36–43.
[2]Hatmaker.
[3]A famous phrase, probably from Burns's° "A Dedication to Gavin Hamilton": "He's just—nae better than he should be."

Think of the torch-light processions that would distress our eyes. Think of the curious legends on the transparencies:[1] "Robbins forever! Vote for Sallie Robbins, the only virtuous candidate in the field!"

And this: "Chastity, modesty, patriotism! Let the great people stand by Maria Sanders, the champion of morality and progress, and the only candidate with a stainless reputation!"

And this: "Vote for Judy McGinniss, the incorruptible! Nine children—one at the breast!"

In that day a man shall say to his servant, "What is the matter with the baby?" And the servant shall reply, "It has been sick for hours." "And where is its mother?" "She is out electioneering for Sallie Robbins." And such conversations as these shall transpire between ladies and servants applying for situations. "Can you cook?" "Yes." "Wash?" "Yes." "Do general housework?" "Yes." "All right; who is your choice for State Milliner?" "Judy McGinniss." "Well, you can tramp." And women shall talk politics instead of discussing the fashions; and they shall neglect the duties of the household to go out and take a drink with candidates; and men shall nurse the baby while their wives travel to the polls to vote. And also in that day the man who hath beautiful whiskers shall beat the homely man of wisdom for Governor, and the youth who waltzes with exquisite grace shall be Chief of Police, in preference to the man of practiced sagacity and determined energy.

Every man, I take it, has a selfish end in view when he pours out eloquence in behalf of the public good in the newspapers, and such is the case with me. I do not want the privileges of women extended, because my wife already holds office in nineteen different infernal female associations and I have to do all her clerking.[2] If you give the women full sweep with the men in political affairs, she will proceed to run for every confounded office under the new dispensation. That will finish me. It is bound to finish me. She would not have time to do anything at all then, and the one solitary thing I have shirked up to the present time would fall on me and my family would go to destruction; for I am *not* qualified for a wet nurse.

Mark Twain 🖉

About Smells[3]

In a recent issue of the "Independent," the Rev. T. De Witt Talmage, of Brooklyn, has the following utterance on the subject of "Smells":

I have a good Christian friend who, if he sat in the front pew in church, and a working man should enter the door at the other end, would smell him instantly. My friend is not to blame for the sensitiveness of his nose, any more than you

---

[1] Photographic slides in which the images are made visible by a light shining through from behind.
[2] Record keeping.
[3] First published in 1870.

would flog a pointer for being keener on the scent than a stupid watch-dog. The fact is, if you had all the churches free, by reason of the mixing up of the common people with the uncommon, you would keep one-half of Christendom sick at their stomach. If you are going to kill the church thus with bad smells, I will have nothing to do with this work of evangelization.

We have reason to believe that there will be laboring men in heaven; and also a number of negroes, and Esquimaux, and Terra del Fuegans,[1] and Arabs, and a few Indians, and possibly even some Spaniards and Portuguese. All things are possible with God. We shall have all these sorts of people in heaven; but, alas! in getting them we shall lose the society of Dr. Talmage. Which is to say, we shall lose the company of one who could give more real "tone" to celestial society than any other contribution Brooklyn could furnish. And what would eternal happiness be without the Doctor? Blissful, unquestionably—we know that well enough—but would it be distingué,[2] would it be recherché[3] without him? St. Matthew[4] without stockings or sandals; St. Jerome[5] bareheaded, and with a coarse brown blanket robe dragging the ground; St. Sebastian[6] with scarcely any raiment at all—these we should see, and should enjoy seeing them;[7] but would we not miss a spike-tailed coat and kids,[8] and turn away regretfully, and say to parties from the Orient: "These are well enough, but you ought to see Talmage of Brooklyn." I fear me that in the better world we shall not even have Dr. Talmage's "good Christian friend." For if he were sitting under the glory of the Throne, and the keeper of the keys admitted a Benjamin Franklin or other laboring man, that "friend," with his fine natural powers infinitely augmented by emancipation from hampering flesh, would detect him with a single sniff, and immediately take his hat and ask to be excused.

To all outward seeming, the Rev. T. De Witt Talmage is of the same material as that used in the construction of his early predecessors in the ministry; and yet one feels that there must be a difference somewhere between him and the Saviour's first disciples. It may be because here, in the nineteenth century, Dr. T. has had advantages which Paul and Peter and the others could not and did not have. There was a lack of polish about them, and a looseness of etiquette, and a want[9] of exclusiveness, which one cannot help noticing. They healed the very beggars, and held intercourse with people of a villainous odor every day. If the subject of these remarks had been chosen among the original Twelve Apostles, he

---

[1]These people were believed at the time to be the most primitive people on earth; they lived on the extreme southeastern tip of South America.
[2]Distinguished.
[3]Exquisite.
[4]One of the twelve Apostles of Christ and the author of the first Gospel.
[5](A.D. 340–420) Translated the Bible from Hebrew into Latin (the *Vulgate*).
[6]Third-century Roman martyr executed by a squad of archers.
[7]All three descriptions are derived from popular paintings of these figures.
[8]Gloves of kidskin, soft leather made from the skin of a young goat.
[9]Lack.

would not have associated with the rest, because he could not have stood the fishy smell of some of his comrades who came from around the Sea of Galilee. He would have resigned his commission with some such remark as he makes in the extract quoted above: "Master, if thou art going to kill the church thus with bad smells, I will have nothing to do with this work of evangelization." He is a disciple, and makes that remark to the Master; the only difference is, that he makes it in the nineteenth instead of the first century.

Is there a choir in Mr. T.'s church? And does it occur that they have no better manners than to sing that hymn which is so suggestive of laborers and mechanics:

> "Son of the Carpenter! receive
>   This humble work of mine?"

Now, can it be possible that in a handful of centuries the Christian character has fallen away from an imposing heroism that scorned even the stake, the cross, and the axe, to a poor little effeminacy that withers and wilts under an unsavory smell? We are not prepared to believe so, the reverend Doctor and his friend to the contrary notwithstanding. ✎

A General Reply[1]

When I was sixteen or seventeen years old, a splendid idea burst upon me—a bran-new one, which had never occurred to anybody before. I would write some "pieces" and take them down to the editor of the "Republican," and ask him to give me his plain, unvarnished opinion of their value! Now, as old and threadbare as the idea was, it was fresh and beautiful to me, and it went flaming and crashing through my system like the genuine lightning and thunder of originality. I wrote the pieces. I wrote them with that placid confidence and that happy facility which only want[2] of practice and absence of literary experience can give. There was not one sentence in them that cost half an hour's weighing and shaping and trimming and fixing. Indeed, it is possible that there was not one sentence whose mere wording cost even one-sixth of that time. If I remember rightly, there was not one single erasure or interlineation[3] in all that chaste manuscript. [I have since lost that large belief in my powers, and likewise that marvellous perfection of execution.] I started down to the "Republican" office with my pocket full of manuscripts, my brain full of dreams, and a grand future opening out before me. I knew perfectly well that the editor would be ravished with my pieces. But presently—

---

[1]First published in 1870.
[2]Lack.
[3]Insertion between the lines.

However, the particulars are of no consequence. I was only about to say that a shadowy sort of doubt just then intruded upon my exaltation. Another came, and another. Pretty soon a whole procession of them. And at last, when I stood before the "Republican" office and looked up at its tall, unsympathetic front, it seemed hardly *me* that could have "chinned" its towers ten minutes before, and was now so shrunk up and pitiful that if I dared to step on the gratings I should probably go through.

At about that crisis the editor, the very man I had come to consult, came down stairs, and halted a moment to pull at his wristbands and settle his coat to its place, and he happened to notice that I was eyeing him wistfully. He asked me what I wanted. I answered, "NOTHING!" with a boy's own meekness and shame; and, dropping my eyes, crept humbly round till I was fairly in the alley, and then drew a big grateful breath of relief, and picked up my heels and ran!

I was satisfied. I wanted no more. It was my first attempt to get a "plain unvarnished opinion" out of a literary man concerning my compositions, and it has lasted me until now. And in these latter days, whenever I receive a bundle of MS. through the mail, with a request that I will pass judgment upon its merits, I feel like saying to the author, "If you had only taken your piece to some grim and stately newspaper office, where you did not know anybody, you would not have so fine an opinion of your production as it is easy to see you have now."

Every man who becomes editor of a newspaper or magazine straightway begins to receive MSS. from literary aspirants, together with requests that he will deliver judgment upon the same. And after complying in eight or ten instances, he finally takes refuge in a general sermon upon the subject, which he inserts in his publication, and always afterward refers such correspondents to that sermon for answer. I have at last reached this station in my literary career. I now cease to reply privately to my applicants for advice, and proceed to construct my public sermon.

As all letters of the sort I am speaking of contain the very same matter, differently worded, I offer as a fair average specimen the last one I have received:

Oct. 3.

MARK TWAIN, Esq:

DEAR SIR: I am a youth, just out of school and ready to start in life. I have looked around, but don't see anything that suits exactly. Is a literary life easy and profitable, or is it the hard times it is generally put up for? It *must* be easier than a good many if not most of the occupations, and I feel drawn to launch out on it, make or break, sink or swim, survive or perish. Now, what are the conditions of success in literature? You need not be afraid to paint the thing just as it is. I can't do any worse than fail. Every thing else offers the same. When I thought of the law—yes, and five or six other professions—I found the same thing was the case every time, viz: *all full—overrun—every profession so crammed that success is rendered impossible—too many hands and not enough work.* But I must try *something*, and so I turn at last to literature. Something tells me that that is the true bent of my genius, if I have any. I enclose some of my pieces. Will you read them over and give me your candid and unbiassed opinion of them? And now I hate to trouble you, but you have been a young man yourself, and what I want is for you to get me a newspaper job of writing to do. You know many newspaper people, and I am entirely unknown. And will you make the best terms you can for me? though I do not expect what might be called high wages at first, of course. Will you candidly say what such articles as these I enclose are worth? I have plenty of them. If you should sell these and let me know, I can send you more, as good and may be better than these. An early reply, etc.

Yours truly, etc.

I will answer you in good faith. Whether my remarks shall have great value or not, or my suggestions be worth following, are problems which I take great pleasure in leaving entirely to you for solution. To begin: There are several questions in your letter which only a man's life experience can eventually answer for him—not another man's words. I will simply skip those.

1. Literature, like the ministry, medicine, the law, and *all other* occupations, is cramped and hindered for want[1] of men to do the work, not want of work to do. When people tell you the reverse, they speak that which is not true. If you desire to test this, you need only hunt up a first-class editor, reporter, business manager, foreman of a shop, mechanic, or artist in any branch of industry, and *try to hire him*. You will find that he is already hired. He is sober, industrious, capable, and reliable, and is always in demand. He cannot get a day's holiday except by courtesy of his employer, or his city, or the great general public. But if you need idlers, shirkers, half-instructed, unambitious, and comfort-seeking editors, reporters, lawyers, doctors, and mechanics, apply anywhere. There are millions of them to be had at the dropping of a handkerchief.

2. No; I must not and will not venture any opinion whatever as to the literary merit of your productions. The public is the only critic whose judgment is worth anything at all. Do not take my poor word for this, but reflect a moment and take your own. For instance, if Sylvanus Cobb or T. S. Arthur had submitted their maiden MSS. to you, you would have said, with tears in your eyes, "Now please don't write any more!" But you see yourself how popular they are. And if it had been left to you, you would have said the "Marble Faun"[2] was tiresome, and that even "Paradise Lost" lacked cheerfulness; but you know they sell. Many wiser and better men than you pooh-poohed Shakespeare, even as late as two centuries ago; but still that old party has outlived those people. No, I will not sit in judgment upon your literature. If I honestly and conscientiously praised it, I might thus help to inflict a lingering and pitiless bore upon the public; if I honestly and conscientiously condemned it, I might thus rob the world of an undeveloped and unsuspected Dickens° or Shakespeare.

3. I shrink from hunting up literary labor for you to do and receive pay for. Whenever your literary productions have proved for themselves that they have a real value, you will never have to go around hunting for remunerative literary work to do. You will require more hands than you have now, and more brains than you

---

[1]Lack.
[2]Novel by Nathaniel Hawthorne° published in 1860.

probably ever will have, to do even half the work that will be offered you. Now, in order to arrive at the proof of value hereinbefore spoken of, one needs only to adopt a very simple and certainly very sure process; and that is, *to write without pay until somebody offers pay*. If nobody offers pay within three years, the candidate may look upon this circumstance with the most implicit confidence as the sign that sawing wood is what he was intended for. If he has any wisdom at all, then, he will retire with dignity and assume his heaven-appointed vocation.

In the above remarks I have only offered a course of action which Mr. Dickens° and most other successful literary men had to follow; but it is a course which will find no sympathy with my client, perhaps. The young literary aspirant is a very, very curious creature. He knows that if he wished to become a tinner, the master smith would require him to prove the possession of a good character, and would require him to promise to stay in the shop three years—possibly four—and would make him sweep out and bring water and build fires all the first year, and let him learn to black stoves in the intervals; and for these good honest services would pay him two suits of cheap clothes and his board; and next year he would begin to receive instructions in the trade, and a dollar a week would be added to his emoluments;[1] and two dollars would be added the third year, and three the fourth; and *then*, if he had become a first-rate tinner, he would get about fifteen or twenty, or may be thirty dollars a week, with never a possibility of getting seventy-five while he lived. If he wanted to become a mechanic of any other kind, he would have to undergo this same tedious, ill-paid apprenticeship. If he wanted to become a lawyer or a doctor, he would have fifty times worse; for he would get nothing at all during his long apprenticeship, and in addition would have to pay a large sum for tuition, and have the privilege of boarding and clothing himself. The literary aspirant knows all this, and yet he has the hardihood to present himself for reception into the literary guild and ask to share its high honors and emoluments, without a single twelvemonth's apprenticeship to show in excuse for his presumption! He would smile pleasantly if he were asked to make even so simple a thing as a ten-cent tin dipper without previous instruction in the art; but, all green and ignorant, wordy, pompously-assertive, ungrammatical, and with a vague, distorted knowledge of men and the world acquired in a back country village, he will serenely take up so dangerous a weapon as a pen, and attack the most formidable subject that finance, commerce, war, or politics can furnish him withal. It would be laughable if it were not so sad and so pitiable. The poor fellow would not intrude upon the tin-shop without an apprenticeship, but is willing to seize and wield with unpractised hand an instrument which is able to overthrow dynasties, change religions, and decree the weal or woe of nations.

If my correspondent will write free of charge for the newspapers of his neighborhood, it will be one of the strangest things that ever happened if he does not get all the employment he can attend to on those terms. And as soon as ever his writings are worth money, plenty of people will hasten to offer it.

---

[1]Payment.

And by way of serious and well-meant encouragement, I wish to urge upon him once more the truth that acceptable writers for the Press are so scarce that book and periodical publishers are seeking them constantly, and with a vigilance that never grows heedless for a moment.

The Noble Red Man[1]

In books he is tall and tawny, muscular, straight, and of kingly presence; he has a beaked nose and an eagle eye.

His hair is glossy, and as black as the raven's wing; out of its massed richness springs a sheaf of brilliant feathers; in his ears and nose are silver ornaments; on his arms and wrists and ankles are broad silver bands and bracelets; his buckskin hunting suit is gallantly fringed, and the belt and the moccasins wonderfully flowered with colored beads; and when, rainbowed with his war-paint, he stands at full height, with his crimson blanket wrapped about him, his quiver at his back, his bow and tomahawk projecting upward from his folded arms, and his eagle eye gazing at specks against the far horizon which even the paleface's field-glass could scarcely reach, he is a being to fall down and worship.

His language is intensely figurative. He never speaks of the moon, but always of "the eye of the night"; nor of the wind *as* the wind, but as "the whisper of the Great Spirit"; and so forth and so on. His power of condensation is marvellous. In some publications he seldom says anything but "Waugh!" and this, with a page of explanation by the author, reveals a whole world of thought and wisdom that before lay concealed in that one little word.

He is noble. He is true and loyal; not even imminent death can shake his peerless faithfulness. His heart is a well-spring of truth, and of generous impulses, and of knightly magnanimity. With him, gratitude is religion; do him a kindness, and at the end of a lifetime he has not forgotten it. Eat of his bread, or offer him yours, and the bond of hospitality is sealed—a bond which is forever inviolable with him.

He loves the dark-eyed daughter of the forest, the dusky maiden of faultless form and rich attire, the pride of the tribe, the all-beautiful. He talks to her in a low voice, at twilight, of his deeds on the war-path and in the chase, and of the grand achievements of his ancestors; and she listens with downcast eyes, "while a richer hue mantles her dusky cheek."

Such is the Noble Red Man in print. But out on the plains and in the mountains, not being on dress parade, not being gotten up to see company, he is under no obligation to be other than his natural self, and therefore:

---

[1]First published in 1870.

He is little, and scrawny, and black, and dirty; and, judged by even the most charitable of our canons[1] of human excellence, is thoroughly pitiful and contemptible. There is nothing in his eye or his nose that is attractive, and if there is anything in his hair that—however, that is a feature which will not bear too close examination. He wears no feathers in his hair, and no ornament or covering on his head. His dull-black, frowsy[2] locks hang straight down to his neck behind, and in front they hang just to his eyes, like a curtain, being cut straight across the forehead, from side to side, and never parted on top. He has no pendants in his ears, and as for his—however, let us not waste time on unimportant particulars, but hurry along. He wears no bracelets on his arms or ankles; his hunting suit is gallantly fringed, but not intentionally; when he does not wear his disgusting rabbit-skin robe, his hunting suit consists wholly of the half of a horse blanket brought over in the Pinta or the Mayflower, and frayed out and fringed by inveterate use. He is not rich enough to possess a belt; he never owned a moccasin or wore a shoe in his life; and truly he is nothing but a poor, filthy, naked scurvy vagabond, whom to exterminate were a charity to the Creator's worthier insects and reptiles which he oppresses. Still, when contact with the white man has given to the Noble Son of the Forest certain cloudy impressions of civilization, and aspirations after a nobler life, he presently appears in public with one boot on and one shoe—shirtless, and wearing ripped and patched and buttonless pants which he holds up with his left hand—his execrable rabbit-skin robe flowing from his shoulders—an old hoop-skirt on, outside of it—a necklace of battered sardine-boxes and oyster-cans reposing on his bare breast—a venerable flintlock musket in his right hand—a weather-beaten stove-pipe hat on, canted "gallusly"[3] to starboard,[4] and the lid off and hanging by a thread or two; and when he thus appears, and waits patiently around a saloon till he gets a chance to strike a "swell"[5] attitude before a looking-glass, he is a good, fair, desirable subject for extermination if ever there was one. [This is not a fancy picture; I have seen it many a time in Nevada, just as it is here limned.—M. T.]

There is nothing figurative, or moonshiny, or sentimental about his language. It is very simple and unostentatious, and consists of plain, straightforward lies. His "wisdom" conferred upon an idiot would leave that idiot helpless indeed.

He is ignoble—base and treacherous, and hateful in every way. Not even imminent death can startle him into a spasm of virtue. The ruling trait of all savages is a greedy and consuming selfishness, and in our Noble Red Man it is found in its amplest development. His heart is a cesspool of falsehood, of treachery, and of low and devilish instincts. With him, gratitude is an unknown emotion; and when one does him a kindness, it is safest to keep the face toward

---

[1]Standards.
[2]Unkempt.
[3]From galluses or suspenders.
[4]Hanging to the right.
[5]Elegant.

him, lest the reward be an arrow in the back. To accept of a favor from him is to assume a debt which you can never repay to his satisfaction, though you bankrupt yourself trying. To give him a dinner when he is starving, is to precipitate the whole hungry tribe upon your hospitality, for he will go straight and fetch them, men, women, children, and dogs, and these they will huddle patiently around your door, or flatten their noses against your window, day after day, gazing beseechingly upon every mouthful you take, and unconsciously swallowing when you swallow! The scum of the earth!

And the Noble Son of the Plains becomes a mighty hunter in the due and proper season. That season is the summer, and the prey that a number of the tribes hunt is crickets and grasshoppers! The warriors, old men, women, and children, spread themselves abroad in the plain and drive the hopping creatures before them into a ring of fire. I could describe the feast that then follows, without missing a detail, if I thought the reader would stand it.

All history and honest observation will show that the Red Man is a skulking coward and a windy braggart, who strikes without warning—usually from an ambush or under cover of night, and nearly always bringing a force of about five or six to one against his enemy; kills helpless women and little children, and massacres the men in their beds; and then brags about it as long as he lives, and his son and his grandson and great-grandson after him glorify it among the "heroic deeds of their ancestors." A regiment of Fenians[1] will fill the whole world with the noise of it when they are getting ready to invade Canada; but when the Red Man declares war, the first intimation his friend the white man whom he supped with at twilight has of it, is when the war-whoop rings in his ears and the tomahawk sinks into his brain. In June, seven Indians went to a small station on the Plains where three white men lived, and asked for food; it was given them, and also tobacco. They stayed two hours, eating and smoking and talking, waiting with Indian patience for their customary odds of seven to one to offer, and as soon as it came they seized the opportunity; that is, when two of the men went out, they killed the other the instant he turned his back to do some solicited favor; then they caught his comrades separately, and killed one, but the other escaped.

The Noble Red Man seldom goes prating loving foolishness to a splendidly caparisoned[2] blushing maid at twilight. No; he trades a crippled horse, or a damaged musket, or a dog, a gallon of grasshoppers, and an inefficient old mother for her, and makes her work like an abject slave all the rest of her life to compensate him for the outlay. He never works himself. She builds the habitation, when they use one (it consists in hanging half a dozen rags over the weather side of a sage-brush bush to roost under); gathers and brings home the fuel; takes care of the raw-boned pony when they possess such grandeur; she walks and

---

[1]Members of a secret organization in America and Ireland in the midnineteenth century whose goal was the overthrow of British rule in Ireland.
[2]Ornamented.

carries her nursing cubs while he rides. She wears no clothing save the fragrant rabbit-skin robe which her greatgrandmother before her wore, and all the "blushing" she does can be removed with soap and a towel, provided it is only four or five weeks old and not caked.

Such is the genuine Noble Aborigine. I did not get him from books, but from personal observation.

By Dr. Keim's excellent book it appears that from June, 1868, to October, 1869 the Indians *massacred nearly 200 white persons and ravished over forty women captured in peaceful outlying settlements along the border, or belonging to emigrant trains traversing the settled routes of travel. Children were burned alive in the presence of their parents. Wives were ravished before their husbands' eyes. Husbands were mutilated, tortured, and scalped, and their wives compelled to look on*. These facts and figures are official, and they exhibit the misunderstood Son of the Forest in his true character—as a creature devoid of brave or generous qualities, but cruel, treacherous, and brutal. During the Pi-Ute war the Indians often dug the sinews out of the backs of white men before they were dead. (The sinews are used for bow-strings.) But their favorite mutilations cannot be put into print. Yet it is this same Noble Red Man who is always greeted with a wail of humanitarian sympathy from the Atlantic seaboard whenever he gets into trouble; the maids and matrons throw up their hands in horror at the bloody vengeance wreaked upon him, and the newspapers clamor for a court of inquiry to examine into the conduct of the inhuman officer who inflicted the little pleasantry upon the "poor abused Indian." (They always look at the matter from the abused-Indian point of view, never from that of the bereaved white widow and orphan.) But it is a great and unspeakable comfort to know that, let them be as prompt about it as they may, the inquiry has always got to come *after* the good officer has administered his little admonition. ✐

A Brace of Brief Lectures on Science[1]
I. Paleontology

What a noble science is paleontology! And what really startling sagacity its votaries[2] exhibit!

Immediately after the Nathan murder, twenty practiced detectives went and viewed the dead body; examined the marks on the throat and on the head; followed the bloody tracks; looked at the bloody clothes, the broken safe, and the curious, unusual, mysterious "dog."[3] They took note of the stolen diamond studs

---

[1]First published in 1871, the same year that Darwin published *The Descent of Man*.
[2]Ardent enthusiasts.
[3]Philanthropist Benjamin Nathan (1813–1870), one of the wealthiest men in New York City, was found murdered in his bedroom, covered with blood from repeated beatings with a carpenter's

and set a watch on the pawnbrokers, and they set watches upon all the known thieves and housebreakers, and upon their fast women. They had the detectives of all the wide world to help them watch and work, and the telegraph to facilitate communication. They had the testimony of fifty witnesses in point[1] and conveniently at hand for reference, a knowledge of everything that transpired about the Nathan mansion during the entire eventful night with the exception of the single hour during which the murder was committed. Thus we perceive that the mystery was narrowed down to a very small compass, and the clues and helps were abundant and excellent. Yet what is the result? Nothing. The "dog" has told no tales, the bloody tracks have led no whither, the murderer has not been found. Why, it is not even known whether there was one murderer, or twenty—or whether men or women did the deed—or how entrance was gained to the house or how exit was accomplished!

The reader perceives how illiterate detectives can blunder along, with whole volumes of clues to guide them, and yet achieve nothing. Now let me show him what "science" can do. Let me show what might have been done if New York had been intelligent enough to employ one deep paleontologist in the work instead of a dozen detectives.—Let me demonstrate that with no other clue than one small splinter off that "iron dog," or a gill[2] of the water the bloody shirt was washed in, any cultivated paleontologist would have walked right off and fetched you that murderer with as unerring certainty as he would take a fragment of an unknown bone and build you the animal it used to belong to, and tell you which end his tail was on and what he preferred for dinner.[3]

In this lesson I will treat only of one subject of paleontological "research"— PRIMEVAL MAN. Geology has revealed the fact that the crust of the earth is composed of five layers or strata. We exist on the surface of the fifth. Geology teaches, with scientific accuracy, that each of these layers was from ten thousand to two million years forming or cooling. [A disagreement as to a few hundred thousand years is a matter of little consequence to science.] The layer immediately under our layer, is the fourth or "quaternary"; under that is the third, or tertiary, etc. Each of these layers had its peculiar animal and vegetable life, and when each layer's mission was done, it and its animals and vegetables ceased from their labors and were forever buried under the new layer, with its new-shaped and new fangled animals and vegetables. So far, so good. Now the geologists Thompson, Johnson, Jones and Ferguson state that our own layer has been ten thousand years forming. The geologists Herkimer, Hildebrand, Boggs and Walker all claim that

---

"dog" or mechanical grip. Although a bloody handprint had been left on the wall, the murder has never been solved because fingerprint detection was not introduced until thirty years later.

[1]In proper order.

[2]Four fluid ounces.

[3]In *Discours preliminaire*, 1812, Georges Cuvier° had indeed claimed that an expert could reconstruct the complete animal from a single bone. For a history of the rebuttal of this claim, see "Everlasting Legends" by Stephen Jay Gould in *Natural History,* June 1990.

our layer has been four hundred thousand years forming. Other geologists just as reliable, maintain that our layer has been from one to two million years forming. Thus we have a concise and satisfactory idea of how long our layer has been growing and accumulating.

That is sufficient geology for our present purpose. The paleontologists Hooker, Baker, Slocum and Hughes claim that Primeval Man existed during the quaternary period—consequently he existed as much as ten thousand, and possibly two million, years ago. The paleontologists Howard, Perkins, de Warren and Von Hawkins[1] assert that Primeval Man existed as far back as the *tertiary* period—and consequently he walked the earth at a time so remote that if you strung ciphers after a unit till there were enough to answer for a necklace for a mastodon you could not adequately represent the billions of centuries ago it happened. Now, you perceive, we begin to cramp this part of our subject into a corner where we can grasp it, as it were, and contemplate it intelligently. Let us—"for a flier," as the learned Von Humboldt[2] phrases it—consider that this Primeval Man transpired eight or nine hundred thousand years ago, and not day before yesterday, like the Nathan murder.—What do we know of him, and how do we find it out? Listen, while I reduce the "revelations" of paleontology to a few paragraphs:

1. Primeval Man existed in the quaternary period—because his bones are found in caves along with bones of now extinct animals *of* that period—such as the "cave-hyena," the mammoth, etc.

2. The incredible antiquity of the Primeval Man's bones is further proven by their extreme "fragility."—No bones under a million years old "could be so fragile." [I quote strictly from the scientific authorities.] The reason royal skeletons in Westminster crumble to dust when exposed, although only a trifling eight hundred years old, is because they are shut up in leaden coffins, I suppose. Bones do not keep good in coffins. There is no sure way but to cord them up in caves. Paleontology reveals that they will then last you a million years without any inconvenience.

3. The Primeval Man possessed weapons—because along with his bones are found rude chips and flakes of flint that the paleontologist knows very well were regarded as knives by the Primeval Man; and also flints of a rude oval shape that in his pretty simplicity he regarded as "hatchets." These things have been found in vast quantities with his bones.

4. The Primeval Man "WORE CLOTHES—because, along with his bones have been found skeletons of the reindeer, "*with marks still visible about the base of the horns, such as are made in our day when we cut there to loosen the hide in order to skin*

---

[1]Since only one of the names in these lists appears in standard lists of scientists of the time (Thompson on page 255 could be Zadock Thompson [1796–1856], American geographer who wrote on the history of Canada and Vermont), it is likely that the names are fictitious.

[2]Friedrich Wilhelm Heinrich Alexander Von Humboldt (1769–1859), German scientist, South American explorer, astronomer, and world traveler who made maps and popularized scientific information.

the animal." Could this paleontologist find the Nathan murderer? —Undoubtedly he could. The ignorant need not say that possibly the Primeval Man wore no
clothes, but wanted the hide for a tent, or for bow-strings, or lassos, or beds, or
to trade off for glass beads and whisky. The paleontologist knows what he wanted
with the hide.

5. The Primeval Man had not only inventive powers and gropings toward
civilization, as evidenced by his contriving and manufacturing flint hatchets and
knives and wearing clothes, but he also had marked and unmistakable "art"
inspirations—because, along with his bones have been found figures scratched
on bone, vaguely suggestive of possible fishes; and a boar's tooth rudely carved
into the shape of a bird's head, and "with a hole in it *to enable him to hang it around
his neck.*" [I quote from authority.] I ask, could this person discover the Nathan
murderer?

6. The Primeval Man "eat his wild game roasted"—because, "along with his
bones are found the bones of wild animals which seem to have been scorched"
some millions of years ago.

7. The Primeval Man was "passionately fond of marrow" [I still quote from
the scientific authorities,]—because, along with his bones have been found
animal bones *broken lengthwise*, "which shows that they had been thus broken *to
extract the marrow*, of which our primitive forefathers were *inordinately fond*," says
the "Paleontological Investigations." Could *this* man read the secrets of an iron
dog and a bloody shirt, or could he not?

8. The Primeval Man was—a—cannibal!—because, in Italy, and also in Scotland, along with his bones have found children's bones which had "first been
carefully cleansed and emptied to satisfy the inordinate taste for marrow, and then
gnawed."(!) This is horrible, but true. Let not the ignorant say that a dog might have
done this gnawing, for paleontology has looked into that and decided that—

9. The Primeval Man had no dog—because "*there is no trace of dogs having
been domesticated then.*" Which settles that point.

10. The Primeval hyena gnawed bones, however—because paleontology
proves that "the marks on some bones found in France were not made by dog,
human, cat or mastodon teeth, but by the teeth of a hyena." And paleontology is
aware that the hyena gnawed the bones "*after the Primeval Man*" was done with
them—which was clever, but paleontology keeps the reasons for knowing this a
scientific secret.

11. Primeval Man had graveyards—"because, along with great quantities of
the roasted and gnawed bones of primeval animals, have been found quantities of
human bones and flint weapons." And it is a precious privilege to live in an epoch
of paleontologists, for the uneducated investigator would not be able to tell a
primeval graveyard from a primeval restaurant.

12. The Primeval Man always had a banquet and a good time after a funeral—
because, down the hill a little way from his graveyard (there is only one on record,)
"*a bed of ashes was unearthed.*" Von Rosenstein and some others say the banquet
occurred *before* the funeral, but most paleontologists agree that it was nearly a
week after the obsequies.

13. Primeval Man "made his flint knives and hatchets with a stone hammer"—and an English paleontologist has "proved" this, and overwhelmed all cavilers[1] with confusion, and won thunders of applause and incalculable gratitude from his fellow-scientists by actually *making* a flint hatchet *with a stone hammer*. The fact that these weapons are so independent in form that if a man chipped a piece of flint with his eyes shut the result would infallibly be a primeval flint knife or flint hatchet, one or the other, in spite of him, has got nothing to do with the matter. If cavilers say that the fact that we *could* carve our bread with an axe is no sign that we *do* carve it with an axe, I simply say that such an argument begs the question, inasmuch as it applies to the present time, whereas the science of paleontology only treats of matters of remote antiquity.

Now I come to the most marvellous "revelation" of all—the most unexpected, the most surprising, the most gratifying. It is this. Paleontology has discovered that—

14. THE PRIMEVAL MAN BELIEVED IN IMMORTALITY!" —because, "else why did he bury those huge quantities of flint hatchets and other weapons with his dead, just as all savages do who desire to provide the loved and lost with means of amusement and subsistence in the happy hunting grounds of eternity?" Aha! What saith the caviler now? Poor purblind[2] croaker, in this grand and awful evidence of the Primeval Man's belief in the immortality of his soul, *you* would find only evidence that the primeval cemetery, the primeval restaurant and the primeval arsenal were purposely compacted into the same premises to save rent. Idiot!

The lesson is ended. Do you see, now, how simple and easy "science" makes a thing? Do you see how—

Some animal bones, split, scratched and scorched; located in quaternary ground;

Some full sized human bones with them—and very "fragile";

Some small bones, marrowless and scratched;

Some flints of several uncertain shapes;

Some rude scratchings and carvings, done possibly by design;

Some deer horns, scratched at their bases;

An ash-pile;

The absence of dog-tracks;—

Do you see how these clues and "evidences" are all the materials the science of paleontology needs in order to give to the world the wonder of a—

Primeval Man;

And not only that but tell what was the particular period he lived in;

What weapons he carried;

What kind of clothes he wore;

---

[1]Carpers.
[2]Dull.

What his art predilections and capacities were;

What he made his weapons with;

What his funeral customs were;

What part of a bear or a child he preferred for breakfast;

What animal got the remains of his feasts, and what animal didn't;

And finally, what the foundation and cornerstone of the religion of the lost and lamented old antediluvian commander-in-chief of all the fossils, was!

What a crying pity it is that the Nathan murder was not committed two million years ago—for I *do* so want to know all about it. [Some of my own paleontological deductions differing in some respects from those of other paleontological authorities, I reserve them for expression in another chapter on "Science," which will appear next month.]

II. Paleontology Concluded—Primeval Man

My brother Paleontologists have "proved" by the finding of weapons (for use in the happy hunting grounds,) side by side with the Primeval Man's bones, that the Primeval Man was a believer in immortality. And I think they have done more than this. I think that in "proving" that he always broke the bones of animals "lengthwise" to get at the marrow, they have come near proving the Primeval Man an ass. For why should he break bones lengthwise to get at the marrow when anybody except a scientist knows that it is a deal easier to break a bone crosswise than lengthwise, and still more convenient to smash your stone down on it and let it break any way it pleases; and we all know that the marrow will taste just the same, no matter what plan of fracture you pursue. And yet nothing would suit this primeval "galoot"[1] but the lengthwise style—it does *not* look reasonable. And I must call notice to the fact that neither the Primeval Man's elk-horn instruments, nor his flint knife, nor yet the awe-inspiring quoit[2] which *he* thought was a flint "hatchet," could split a slippery, crooked, uneasy and vexatious bone lengthwise with facility—and I have always noticed that your Primeval Man looks to convenience *first*. That is his way, if I know whereof I speak—and if I do not, what am I a paleontologist for?

2. Somehow I cannot feel satisfied that those bears (whose bones are found mingled with those of the Primeval Man), were not the real parties that ate that marrow—and also the animals that used to own it. And without nibbling at heresy any further, I may as well come out and suggest that perhaps they ate the Primeval Man himself. Here is a pile of bones of primeval man and beast all mixed together, with no more damning evidence that the man ate the bears than that the bears ate the man—yet paleontology holds a coroner's inquest here in the fifth

---

[1]Stupid fellow.

[2]Flat ring.

geologic period on an "unpleasantness" which transpired in the quaternary, and calmly lays it on the MAN, and then adds to it what purports to be evidence of CANNIBALISM. I ask the candid reader, Does not this look like taking advantage of a gentleman who has been dead two million years, and whose surviving friends and relatives—. But the subject is too painful. Are we to have another Byron-scandal case?[1] Here are savage ways and atrocious appetites attributed to the dead and helpless Primeval Man—have we any assurance that the same hand will not fling mud at the Primeval Man's mother, next?

3. Again. Is there anything really so surprising about the absence of the marrow from bones a few hundred thousand years old as to make it worth while to sit up nights trying to figure out how it came to be absent? Now *is* there, considering that there are so many good chances that Age, Worms and Decay got the marrow?

4. If the student should ask why paleontologists call the Primeval Man a cannibal, I should answer that it was because they find toothmarks on primeval children's bones which they "*recognize as the marks of human teeth.*" If the student should ask why paleontologists assert that primeval hyenas gnawed the bones of roasted animals after the Primeval Man had finished his meal, I should answer that they find teeth-marks upon said bones which they "*recognize as hyena teeth-marks.*" If the student should ask me how the paleontologist tells the difference between hyena and human teeth-marks on a *bone*, and particularly a bone which has been rotting in a cave since the everlasting hills were builded, I should answer that I don't know.

A man could leave a sort of a tooth-mark (till decay set in,) in any fleshy substance that might remain sticking to a bone, but that he could make a tooth-mark on the bone itself I am obliged to question. Let the earnest student try to bite the handle of his tooth-brush and see if he can leave an autograph that will defy the ages. Aha! where are you *now*!

5. The frivolous are apt to take notice of a certain paleontological custom, which, not understanding, they take to be proper prey for their wit. I refer to the common paleontological custom of "proving" the vast age of primeval bones by their "*extreme fragility*," and then accounting for their wonderful preservation by the fact that they were "*petrified and fossilized* by deposits of calcareous salts." If cavilers had brains enough to comprehend this, they would not cavil so much about it.

6. In the celebrated paleontological "cave of Aurignac"[2] were found bones of primeval men, woolly elephants, huge bears and elks and wolves of a singular pattern, and also bones of the august mastodon. What do my fellow paleontologists call that place? A "primeval *graveyard*." Why? Why graveyard? Reader, I have

---

[1]Twain is perhaps referring to Byron,° the English poet whose wife separated from him because of his incestuous relationship with his half-sister.

[2]In the south of France; it became famous in 1860 when sculptures, artifacts, and drawings from the Stone Age were discovered there.

looked carefully into this matter and discovered the significant fact that they never found a single tomb-stone. Nor any sign of a grave. Then *why* call it a graveyard? Does a tangled mess of bones of men and beasts necessarily constitute a grave-yard? I would not disturb any man's faith in the primeval cemetery, though, merely to hear myself talk. I have opened the subject for a nobler purpose—to give the paleontological student's faith a new direction and a worthier one. I have investigated the evidences and now feel tolerably satisfied that the contents of the cave of Aurignac are not the remains of a primeval graveyard, but of a primeval menagerie. I ask the intelligent reader if it is likely that such rare creatures as a woolly elephant, a mastodon, and those huge and peculiar bears, wolves, etc., would simply *happen* together, along with a man or two, in a comfortable, roomy cave, with a small, low door, just suited to the admission of single files of country people, to say nothing of children and servants at half price? I simply ask the candid reader that question and let him sweat—as the historian Josephus° used to say. If I should be asked for further suggestions in support of my hypothesis, I should hazard the thought that the treasurer of the menagerie was guilty of a hideous general massacre, while the proprietor and the beasts were asleep, and that his object was robbery. It is admitted by nearly one-sixth of all the paleon-tologists (observe the unusual unanimity) that the first part of the quaternary period must have been an uncommonly good season for public exhibitions—and in this one fact alone you have almost a confirmation of the criminal motive attributed to the treasurer. If I am asked for final and incontrovertible proof of my position, I point to the significant fact that *the bones of the treasurer have never been found*, and THE CASH BOX IS GONE. It is enough to make one's hair stand on end.

I desire nothing more than my dues. If I have thrown any light on the mystery of the cave of Aurignac, I desire that it shall be acknowledged—if I have not, I desire that it may be as though I had never spoken.

7. As concerns the proud paleontological trophy, the "flint hatchet" and its companion the "flint knife," I am compelled again to differ with the other scientists. I cannot think that the so-called "flint knife" is a knife at all. I cannot disabuse my mind of the impression that it is a file. No knife ever had such a scandalous blade as that. If asked by scholars of the established faith what the Primeval Man could want with a file, I should, with customary paleontological diplomacy, ask what he could want with such a *knife*? Because he *might* file something with that thing, but I will hang if he could ever *cut* anything with it.

8. And as for the oval shaped flint which stands for the lauded primeval "hatchet," I cannot rid myself of the idea that it was only a paper-weight. If incensed brother-paleontologists storm at me and say the Primeval Man had no paper, I shall say calmly, "As long as it was nobody's business but his own, couldn't he carry his paper-weight around till he got some?"

But there is nothing intractable about me. If gentlemen wish to compromise and call it a petrified hoecake,[1] or anything in *reason*, I am agreeable; for the

---

[1]Thin cornmeal cake, originally baked on the blade of a hoe.

Primeval Man had to have food, and might have had hoecakes, but he didn't have to have a flint "hatchet" like this thing, which he could not even cut his butter with without mashing it.

If any one should find fault with any arguments used by me in the course of the above chapter, and say that I jump to a conclusion over so much ground that the feat is in a manner ungraceful; and if he should say further, that in establishing one paleontological position of mine I generally demolish another, I would answer that these things are inseparable from scientific investigation. We all do it—all scientists. No one can regret it more than we do ourselves, but there really seems to be no remedy for it. First we had to recede from our assertion that a certain fossil was a primeval man, because afterward when we had found multitudes of saurians[1] and had grown glib and facile in descanting[2] upon them, we found that that other creature was of the same species. What could we do? It was too big a job to turn a thousand saurians into primeval men, and so we turned the solitary primeval man into a saurian. It was the cheapest way.[3] And so it has always been with us. Every time we get a chance to assert something, we have to take back something. When we announced and established the great discovery of the "Glacial Period," how we did have to cart the dead animals around! Because, do not you see, the indiscriminate sort of distribution of fossil species which we had accommodated to the characteristic action of a general flood would not answer for a nicely discriminating "glacial period" which *ought* to transport only walruses, white bears, and other frigid creatures, from the North Pole down into Africa and not meddle with any other kind of animals. Well, we had only got the several species of fossil animals located to "back up" the "glacial period" when here comes some idiot down from Behring's Strait with a fossil elephant a hundred thousand years old! Of course we had to go to work and account for *him.* You see how it is. Science is as sorry as you are that this year's science is no more like last year's science than last year's was like the science of twenty years gone by. But science cannot help it. Science is full of change. Science is progressive and eternal. The scientists of twenty years ago laughed at the ignorant men who had groped in the intellectual darkness of twenty years before.

We derive pleasure from laughing at *them.* We have accounted for that elephant, at last, on the hypothesis that when he was alive Alaska was in the tropics. Twenty or thirty years from now the new crop of paleontologists will be just as likely as not to find an elephant and a petrified iceberg roosting in the same quaternary cave together up there in Alaska, and if they do, down *we* go, with our tropical theory, that is all. ✐

---

[1]Reptiles.

[2]Commenting at length.

[3]Twain is referring here to the principle called Occam's razor, after William of Occam or Ockham (c. 1285–c. 1349), a scholastic philosopher who said, "What can be done with fewer is done in vain with more." This principle acts as a razor, shaving off unnecessarily elaborate explanations.

On Training Children[1]

Editor Christian Union:

I have just finished reading the admirably told tale entitled "What Ought He to have Done?" in your No. 24, and I wish to take a chance at that question myself before I cool off. What a happy literary gift that mother has!—and yet, with all her brains, she manifestly thinks there is a difficult conundrum concealed in that question of hers. It makes a body's blood boil to read her story!

I am a fortunate person, who has been for thirteen years accustomed, daily and hourly, to the charming companionship of thoroughly well-behaved, well-trained, well-governed children. Never mind about taking my word; ask Mrs. Harriet Beecher Stowe,°[2] or Charles Dudley Warner[3] or any other near neighbor of mine,[4] if this is not the exact and unexaggerated truth. Very well, then, I am quite competent to answer that question of "What ought he to have done?" and I will proceed to do it by stating what he would have done, and what would have followed, if "John Senior" had been me, and his wife had been my wife, and the cub our mutual property. To wit:

When John Junior "entered the library, marched audaciously up to the desk, snatched an open letter from under his father's busy fingers, threw it upon the floor," and struck the ill-mannered attitude described in the succeeding paragraph, his mother would have been a good deal surprised, and also grieved: surprised that her patient training of her child to never insult any one—even a parent—should so suddenly and strangely have fallen to ruin; and grieved that she must witness the shameful thing.

At this point John Senior—meaning me—would not have said, either "judicially" or otherwise, "Junior is a naughty boy." No; he would have known more than this John Senior knew—for he would have known enough to keep still. He wouldn't have aggravated a case which was already bad enough, by making any such stupid remark—stupid, unhelpful, undignified. He would have known and felt that there was one present who was quite able to deal with the case, in any stage it might assume, without any assistance from him. Yes, and there is another thing which he would have known, and does at this present writing know: that in an emergency of the sort which we are considering, he is always likely to be as thorough going and ludicrous an ass as this John Senior proved himself to be in the little tale.

No—he would have kept still. Then the mother would have led the little boy to a private place, and taken him on her lap, and reasoned with him, and loved

---

[1] First published in 1885.

[2] Mother of six children.

[3] (1829–1900) Essayist and publisher of the *Hartford Courant* who collaborated with Twain on the novel *The Gilded Age* (1873).

[4] In Nook Farm, Connecticut.

him out of his wrong mood, and shown him that he had mistreated one of the best and most loving friends he had in the world; and in no very long time the child would be convinced, and be sorry, and would run with eager sincerity and ask the father's pardon. And that would be the end of the matter.

But, granting that it did not turn out in just this way, but that the child grew stubborn, and stood out against reasoning and affection. In that case, a whipping would be promised. That would have a prompt effect upon the child's state of mind; for it would know, with its mature two years' experience, that no promise of any kind was ever made to a child in our house and not rigidly kept. So this child would quiet down at this point, become repentant, loving, reasonable; in a word, its own charming self again; and would go and apologize to the father, receive his caresses, and bound away to its play, light-hearted and happy again, although well aware that at the proper time it was going to get that whipping, sure.

The "proper time" referred to is any time after both mother and child have got the sting of the original difficulty clear out of their minds and hearts, and are prepared to give and take a whipping on purely business principles—disciplinary principles—and with hearts wholly free from temper. For whippings are not given in our house for revenge; they are not given for spite, nor ever in anger; they are given partly for punishment, but mainly by way of impressive reminder, and protector against a repetition of the offense. The interval between the promise of a whipping and its infliction is usually an hour or two. By that time both parties are calm, and the one is judicial, the other receptive. The child never goes from the scene of punishment until it has been loved back into happy-heartedness and a joyful spirit. The spanking is never a cruel one, but it is always an honest one. It hurts. If it hurts the child, imagine how it must hurt the mother. Her spirit is serene, tranquil. She has not the support which is afforded by anger. Every blow she strikes the child bruises her own heart. The mother of my children adores them—there is no milder term for it; and they worship her; they even worship anything which the touch of her hand has made sacred. They know her for the best and truest friend they have ever had, or ever shall have; they know her for one who never did them a wrong, and cannot do them a wrong; who never told them a lie, nor the shadow of one; who never deceived them by even an ambiguous gesture; who never gave them an unreasonable command, nor ever contented herself with anything short of a perfect obedience; who has always treated them as politely and considerately as she would the best and oldest in the land, and has always required of them gentle speech and courteous conduct toward all, of whatsoever degree, with whom they chanced to come in contact; they know her for one whose promise, whether of reward or punishment, is gold, and always worth its face, to the uttermost farthing. In a word, they know her, and I know her, for the best and dearest mother that lives—and by a long, long way the wisest.

You perceive that I have never got *down* to where the mother in the tale really asks her question. For the reason that I cannot realize the situation. The spectacle of that treacherously-reared boy, and that wordy, namby-pamby father, and that weak, namby-pamby mother, is enough to make one ashamed of his species. And if I could cry, I would cry for the fate of that poor little boy—a fate which has cruelly placed him in the hands and at the mercy of a pair of grown up children, to have his disposition ruined, to come up ungoverned, and be a nuisance to himself and everybody about him, in the process, instead of being the solacer of care, the disseminator of happiness, the glory and honor and joy of the house, the welcomest face in all the world to them that gave him being—as he ought to be, was sent to be, and would be, but for the hard fortune that flung him into the clutches of these paltering incapables.

In all my life I have never made a single reference to my wife in print before, as far as I can remember, except once in the dedication of a book; and, so, after these fifteen years of silence, perhaps I may unseal my lips this one time without impropriety or indelicacy. I will institute one other novelty. I will send this manuscript to the press without her knowledge, and without asking her to edit it. This will save it from getting edited into the stove.

Mark Twain ✍

The Lowest Animal[1]

In August, 1572, similar things were occurring in Paris and elsewhere in France. In this case it was Christian against Christian. The Roman Catholics, by previous concert, sprang a surprise upon the unprepared and unsuspecting Protestants, and butchered them by thousands—both sexes and all ages. This was the memorable St. Bartholomew's Day. At Rome the Pope and the Church gave public thanks to God when the happy news came.

During several centuries hundreds of heretics were burned at the stake every year because their religious opinions were not satisfactory to the Roman Church.

In all ages the savages of all lands have made the slaughtering of their neighboring brothers and the enslaving of their women and children the common business of their lives.

Hypocrisy, envy, malice, cruelty, vengefulness, seduction, rape, robbery, swindling, arson, bigamy, adultery, and the oppression and humiliation of the poor and the helpless in all ways have been and still are more or less common among both the civilized and uncivilized peoples of the earth.

For many centuries "the common brotherhood of man" has been urged—on Sundays—and "patriotism" on Sundays and weekdays both. Yet patriotism *contemplates the opposite of a common brotherhood.*

Woman's equality with man has never been conceded by any people, ancient or modern, civilized or savage.

---

[1]Written in 1897. Bernard DeVoto, the editor of *Letters from the Earth,* from which this essay is taken, explains that the essay was to have been accompanied by newspaper clippings dealing with religious persecutions in Crete, presumably in connection with the uprising against the Turks in 1897.

I have been studying the traits and dispositions of the "lower animals" (so-called), and contrasting them with the traits and dispositions of man. I find the result humiliating to me. For it obliges me to renounce my allegiance to the Darwinian theory of the Ascent of Man from the Lower Animals; since it now seems plain to me that that theory ought to be vacated in favor of a new and truer one, this new and truer one to be named the Descent of Man from the Higher Animals.

In proceeding toward this unpleasant conclusion I have not guessed or speculated or conjectured, but have used what is commonly called the scientific method. That is to say, I have subjected every postulate that presented itself to the crucial test of actual experiment, and have adopted it or rejected it according to the result. Thus I verified and established each step of my course in its turn before advancing to the next. These experiments were made in the London Zoological Gardens, and covered many months of painstaking and fatiguing work.

Before particularizing any of the experiments, I wish to state one or two things which seem to more properly belong in this place than further along. This in the interest of clearness. The massed experiments established to my satisfaction certain generalizations, to wit:

1. That the human race is of one distinct species. It exhibits slight variations—in color, stature, mental caliber, and so on—due to climate, environment, and so forth but it is a species by itself, and not to be confounded with any other.

2. That the quadrupeds are a distinct family, also. This family exhibits variations—in color, size, food preferences and so on; but it is a family by itself.

3. That the other families—the birds, the fishes, the insects, the reptiles, etc:—are more or less distinct, also. They are in the procession. They are links in the chain which stretches down from the higher animals to man at the bottom.

Some of my experiments were quite curious. In the course of my reading I had come across a case where, many years ago, some hunters on our Great Plains organized a buffalo hunt for the entertainment of an English earl—that, and to provide some fresh meat for his larder. They had charming sport. They killed seventy-two of those great animals; and ate part of one of them and left the seventy-one to rot. In order to determine the difference between an anaconda and an earl—if any—I caused seven young calves to be turned into the anaconda's cage. The grateful reptile immediately crushed one of them and swallowed it, then lay back satisfied. It showed no further interest in the calves, and no disposition to harm them. I tried this experiment with other anacondas; always with the same result. The fact stood proven that the difference between an earl and an anaconda is that the earl is cruel and the anaconda isn't; and that the earl wantonly destroys what he has no use for, but the anaconda doesn't. This seemed to suggest that the anaconda was not descended from the earl. It also seemed to suggest that the earl was descended from the anaconda, and had lost a good deal in the transition.

I was aware that many men who have accumulated more millions of money than they can ever use have shown a rabid hunger for more, and have not scrupled to cheat the ignorant and the helpless out of their poor servings in order to partially appease that appetite. I furnished a hundred different kinds of wild and tame animals the opportunity to accumulate vast stores of food, but none of them would do it. The squirrels and bees and certain birds made accumulations, but stopped when they had gathered a winter's supply, and could not be persuaded to add to it either honestly or by chicane.[1] In order to bolster up a tottering reputation the ant pretended to store up supplies, but I was not deceived. I know the ant. These experiments convinced me that there is this difference between man and the higher animals: he is avaricious and miserly, they are not.

In the course of my experiments I convinced myself that among the animals man is the only one that harbors insults and injuries, broods over them, waits till a chance offers, then takes revenge. The passion of revenge is unknown to the higher animals.

Roosters keep harems, but it is by consent of their concubines; therefore no wrong is done. Men keep harems, but it is by brute force, privileged by atrocious laws which the other sex were allowed no hand in making. In this matter man occupies a far lower place than the rooster.

Cats are loose in their morals, but not consciously so. Man, in his descent from the cat, has brought the cat's looseness with him but has left the unconsciousness behind—the saving grace which excuses the cat. The cat is innocent, man is not.

Indecency, vulgarity, obscenity—these are strictly confined to man; he invented them. Among the higher animals there is no trace of them. They hide nothing; they are not ashamed. Man, with his soiled mind, covers himself. He will not even enter a drawing room with his breast and back naked, so alive are he and his mates to indecent suggestion. Man is "The Animal that Laughs:" But so does the monkey, as Mr. Darwin pointed out;[2] and so does the Australian bird that is called the laughing jackass. No—Man is the Animal that Blushes. He is the only one that does it—or has occasion to.

At the head of this article we see how "three monks were burnt to death" a few days ago, and a prior[3] "put to death with atrocious cruelty." Do we inquire into the details? No; or we should find out that the prior was subjected to unprintable mutilations. Man—when he is a North American Indian—gouges out his prisoner's eyes; when he is King John,° with a nephew to render untroublesome, he uses a red-hot iron; when he is a religious zealot dealing with heretics in the Middle Ages, he skins his captive alive and scatters salt on his back; in the first Richard's° time he shuts up a multitude of Jew families in a tower and sets fire to it; in Columbus's time he captures a family of Spanish Jews and—but that is not printable; in our day in England a man is fined ten shillings for beating his mother nearly to death with a chair, and another man is fined forty shillings for having four pheasant eggs in his possession without being able to satisfactorily

[1]Trickery.
[2]In *The Expression of the Emotions in Man and Animals*, 1872.
[3]An administrating monk ranking just below the abbot of an abbey.

explain how he got them. Of all the animals, man is the only one that is cruel. He is the only one that inflicts pain for the pleasure of doing it. It is a trait that is not known to the higher animals. The cat plays with the frightened mouse; but she has this excuse, that she does not know that the mouse is suffering. The cat is moderate—unhumanly moderate: she only scares the mouse, she does not hurt it; she doesn't dig out its eyes, or tear off its skin, or drive splinters under its nails—man-fashion; when she is done playing with it she makes a sudden meal of it and puts it out of its trouble. Man is the Cruel Animal. He is alone in that distinction.

The higher animals engage in individual fights, but never in organized masses. Man is the only animal that deals in that atrocity of atrocities, War. He is the only one that gathers his brethren about him and goes forth in cold blood and with calm pulse to exterminate his kind. He is the only animal that for sordid wages will march out, as the Hessians[1] did in our Revolution, and as the boyish Prince Napoleon[2] did in the Zulu war,[3] and help to slaughter strangers of his own species who have done him no harm and with whom he has no quarrel.

Man is the only animal that robs his helpless fellow of his country—takes possession of it and drives him out of it or destroys him. Man has done this in all the ages. There is not an acre of ground on the globe that is in possession of its rightful owner, or that has not been taken away from owner after owner, cycle after cycle, by force and bloodshed.

Man is the only Slave. And he is the only animal who enslaves. He has always been a slave in one form or another, and has always held other slaves in bondage under him in one way or another. In our day he is always some man's slave for wages, and does that man's work; and this slave has other slaves under him for minor wages, and they do *his* work. The higher animals are the only ones who exclusively do their own work and provide their own living.

Man is the only Patriot. He sets himself apart in his own country, under his own flag, and sneers at the other nations, and keeps multitudinous uniformed assassins on hand at heavy expense to grab slices of other people's countries, and keep *them* from grabbing slices of *his*. And in the intervals between campaigns he washes the blood off his hands and works for "the universal brotherhood of man"—with his mouth.

Man is the Religious Animal. He is the only Religious Animal. He is the only animal that has the True Religion—several of them. He is the only animal that loves his neighbor as himself, and cuts his throat if his theology isn't straight. He has made a graveyard of the globe in trying his honest best to smooth his brother's path to happiness and heaven. He was at it in the time of the Caesars, he was at it in Mahomet's time, he was at it in the time of the Inquisition, he was at it in

---

[1]West German mercenaries in the British army during the Revolution.
[2]Louis Napoleon Bonaparte (1808–1873), son of the king of Holland and later Napoleon III, emperor of France from 1852 to 1870.
[3]1838.

France a couple of centuries, he was at it in England in Mary's day,[1] he has been at it ever since he first saw the light, he is at it today in Crete—as per the telegrams quoted above—he will be at it somewhere else tomorrow. The higher animals have no religion. And we are told that they are going to be left out, in the Hereafter. I wonder why? It seems questionable taste.

Man is the Reasoning Animal. Such is the claim. I think it is open to dispute. Indeed, my experiments have proven to me that he is the Unreasoning Animal. Note his history, as sketched above. It seems plain to me that whatever he is he is *not* a reasoning animal. His record is the fantastic record of a maniac. I consider that the strongest count against his intelligence is the fact that with that record back of him he blandly sets himself up as the head animal of the lot: whereas by his own standards he is the bottom one.

In truth, man is incurably foolish. Simple things which the other animals easily learn, he is incapable of learning. Among my experiments was this. In an hour I taught a cat and a dog to be friends. I put them in a cage. In another hour I taught them to be friends with a rabbit. In the course of two days I was able to add a fox, a goose, a squirrel and some doves. Finally a monkey. They lived together in peace; even affectionately.

Next, in another cage I confined an Irish Catholic from Tipperary, and as soon as he seemed tame I added a Scotch Presbyterian from Aberdeen. Next a Turk from Constantinople; a Greek Christian from Crete; an Armenian; a Methodist from the wilds of Arkansas; a Buddhist from China; a Brahman from Benares. Finally, a Salvation Army Colonel from Wapping. Then I stayed away two whole days. When I came back to note results, the cage of Higher Animals was all right, but in the other there was but a chaos of gory odds and ends of turbans and fezzes and plaids and bones and flesh—not a specimen left alive. These Reasoning Animals had disagreed on a theological detail and carried the matter to a Higher Court.

One is obliged to concede that in true loftiness of character, Man cannot claim to approach even the meanest of the Higher Animals. It is plain that he is constitutionally incapable of approaching that altitude; that he is constitutionally afflicted with a Defect which must make such approach forever impossible, for it is manifest that this defect is permanent in him, indestructible, ineradicable.

I find this Defect to be *the Moral Sense.* He is the only animal that has it. It is the secret of his degradation. It is the quality *which enables him to do wrong.* It has no other office. It is incapable of performing any other function. It could never have been intended to perform any other. Without it, man could do no wrong. He would rise at once to the level of the Higher Animals.

---

[1]Mary Tudor (1516–1558), daughter of Henry VIII and Katherine of Aragon, and queen of England from 1553 to 1558. She was brought up a Roman Catholic like her mother. In 1554 she married Philip of Spain and reinstated Catholicism as the religion of Great Britain; from then on religious persecutions, including the burning of three hundred people at the stake, caused her to be called "Bloody Mary," although she was personally of a mild disposition.

Since the Moral Sense has but the one office, the one capacity—to enable man to do wrong—it is plainly without value to him. It is as valueless to him as is disease. In fact, it manifestly is a disease. *Rabies* is bad, but it is not so bad as this disease. Rabies enables a man to do a thing which he could not do when in a healthy state: kill his neighbor with a poisonous bite. No one is the better man for having rabies. The Moral Sense enables a man to do wrong. It enables him to do wrong in a thousand ways. Rabies is an innocent disease, compared to the Moral Sense. No one, then, can be the better man for having the Moral Sense. What, now, do we find the Primal Curse to have been? Plainly what it was in the beginning: the infliction upon man of the Moral Sense; the ability to distinguish good from evil; and with it, necessarily, the ability to *do* evil; for there can be no evil act without the presence of consciousness of it in the doer of it.

And so I find that we have descended and degenerated, from some far ancestor—some microscopic atom wandering at its pleasure between the mighty horizons of a drop of water perchance—insect by insect, animal by animal, reptile by reptile, down the long highway of smirchless innocence, till we have reached the bottom stage of development—namable as the Human Being. Below us— nothing. Nothing but the Frenchman.

There is only one possible stage below the Moral Sense; that is the Immoral Sense. The Frenchman has it. Man is but little lower than the angels. This definitely locates him. He is between the angels and the French.

Man seems to be a rickety poor sort of a thing, any way you take him; a kind of British Museum of infirmities and inferiorities. He is always undergoing re- pairs. A machine that was as unreliable as he is would have no market. On top of his specialty—the Moral Sense—are piled a multitude of minor infirmities; such a multitude, indeed, that one may broadly call them countless. The higher animals get their teeth without pain or inconvenience. Man gets his through months and months of cruel torture; and at a time of life when he is but ill able to bear it. As soon as he has got them they must all be pulled out again, for they were of no value in the first place, not worth the loss of a night's rest. The second set will answer for a while, by being reinforced occasionally with rubber or plugged up with gold; but he will never get a set which can really be depended on till a dentist makes him one. This set will be called "false" teeth—as if he had ever worn any other kind.

In a wild state—a natural state—the Higher Animals have a few diseases; diseases of little consequence; the main one is old age. But man starts in as a child and lives on diseases till the end, as a regular diet. He has mumps, measles, whooping cough, croup, tonsilitis, diphtheria, scarlet fever, almost as a matter of course. Afterward, as he goes along, his life continues to be threatened at every turn: by colds, coughs, asthma, bronchitis, itch, cholera, cancer, consumption, yellow fever, bilious fever, typhus fevers, hay fever, ague, chilblains, piles,[1] in-

---

[1]Ague: recurrent chills and fever; chilblains: inflammation on hands, feet, or ears caused by exposure to cold; piles: hemorrhoids.

flammation of the entrails, indigestion, toothache, earache, deafness, dumbness, blindness, influenza, chicken pox, cowpox, smallpox, liver complaint, constipation, bloody flux,[1] warts, pimples, boils, carbuncles,[2] abscesses, bunions, corns, tumors, fistulas,[3] pneumonia, softening of the brain, melancholia and fifteen other kinds of insanity; dysentery, jaundice, diseases of the heart, the bones, the skin, the scalp, the spleen, the kidneys, the nerves, the brain, the blood; scrofula, paralysis, leprosy, neuralgia, palsy, fits, headache, thirteen kinds of rheumatism, forty-six of gout, and a formidable supply of gross and unprintable disorders of one sort and another. Also—but why continue the list? The mere names of the agents appointed to keep this shackly machine out of repair would hide him from sight if printed on his body in the smallest type known to the founder's art. He is but a basket of pestilent corruption provided for the support and entertainment of swarming armies of bacilli—armies commissioned to rot him and destroy him, and each army equipped with a special detail of the work. The process of waylaying him, persecuting him, rotting him, killing him, begins with his first breath, and there is no mercy, no pity, no truce till he draws his last one.

Look at the workmanship of him, in certain of its particulars. What are his tonsils for? They perform no useful function; they have no value. They have no business there. They are but a trap. They have but the one office, the one industry: to provide tonsilitis and quinsy[4] and such things for the possessor of them. And what is the vermiform[5] appendix for? It has no value; it cannot perform any useful service. It is but an ambuscaded[6] enemy whose sole interest in life is to lie in wait for stray grapeseeds and employ them to breed strangulated hernia. And what are the male's mammals[7] for? For business, they are out of the question; as an ornament, they are a mistake. What is his beard for? It performs no useful function; it is a nuisance and a discomfort; all nations hate it; all nations persecute it with the razor. And because it is a nuisance and a discomfort, Nature never allows the supply of it to fall short, in any man's case, between puberty and the grave. You never see a man bald-headed on his chin. But his hair! It is a graceful ornament, it is a comfort, it is the best of all protections against certain perilous ailments, man prizes it above emeralds and rubies. And because of these things Nature puts it on, half the time, so that it won't stay. Man's sight, smell, hearing, sense of locality—how inferior they are. The condor sees a corpse at five miles; man has no telescope that can do it. The bloodhound follows a scent that is two days old. The robin hears the earthworm burrowing his course under the ground. The cat, deported in a closed basket, finds its way home again through twenty miles of country which it has never seen.

---

[1] Diarrhea.
[2] Large boils with several openings.
[3] Abnormal openings from an abscess to skin.
[4] Inflammation of the tonsils, often leading to abscess.
[5] Wormlike.
[6] Ambushed.
[7] Nipples.

Certain functions lodged in the other sex perform in a lamentably inferior way as compared with the performance of the same functions in the Higher Animals. In the human being, menstruation, gestation and parturition are terms which stand for horrors. In the Higher Animals these things are hardly even inconveniences.

For style, look at the Bengal tiger—that ideal of grace, beauty, physical perfection, majesty. And then look at Man—that poor thing. He is the Animal of the Wig, the Trepanned Skull,[1] the Ear Trumpet, the Glass Eye, the Pasteboard Nose, the Porcelain Teeth, the Silver Windpipe, the Wooden Leg—a creature that is mended and patched all over, from top to bottom. If he can't get renewals of his bric-a-brac in the next world, what will he look like?

He has just one stupendous superiority. In his intellect he is supreme. The Higher Animals cannot touch him there. It is curious, it is noteworthy, that no heaven has ever been offered him wherein his one sole superiority was provided with a chance to enjoy itself. Even when he himself has imagined a heaven, he has never made provision in it for intellectual joys. It is a striking omission. It seems a tacit confession that heavens are provided for the Higher Animals alone. This is matter for thought; and for serious thought. And it is full of a grim suggestion: that we are not as important, perhaps, as we had all along supposed we were. ✒

Corn-Pone Opinions[2]

Fifty years ago, when I was a boy of fifteen and helping to inhabit a Missourian village on the banks of the Mississippi, I had a friend whose society was very dear to me because I was forbidden by my mother to partake of it. He was a gay and impudent and satirical and delightful young black man—a slave—who daily preached sermons from the top of his master's woodpile, with me for sole audience. He imitated the pulpit style of the several clergymen of the village, and did it well, and with fine passion and energy. To me he was a wonder. I believed he was the greatest orator in the United States and would some day be heard from. But it did not happen; in the distibution of rewards he was overlooked. It is the way, in this world.

He interrupted his preaching, now and then, to saw a stick of wood; but the sawing was a pretense—he did it with his mouth; exactly imitating the sound the bucksaw makes in shrieking its way through the wood. But it served its purpose; it kept his master from coming out to see how the work was getting along. I

---

[1]One with surgical holes bored into it.
[2]First published in 1901.

listened to the sermons from the open window of a lumber room at the back of the house. One of his texts was this:

"You tell me whar a man gits his corn pone, en I'll tell you what his 'pinions is."

I can never forget it. It was deeply impressed upon me. By my mother. Not upon my memory, but elsewhere. She had slipped in upon me while I was absorbed and not watching. The black philosopher's idea was that a man is not independent, and cannot afford views which might interfere with his bread and butter. If he would prosper, he must train with the majority; in matters of large moment, like politics and religion, he must think and feel with the bulk of his neighbors, or suffer damage in his social standing and in his business prosperities. He must restrict himself to corn-pone opinions—at least on the surface. He must get his opinions from other people; he must reason out none for himself; he must have no first-hand views.

I think Jerry was right, in the main, but I think he did not go far enough.

1. It was his idea that a man conforms to the majority view of his locality by calculation and intention.

This happens, but I think it is not the rule.

2. It was his idea that there is such a thing as a first-hand opinion; an original opinion; an opinion which is coldly reasoned out in a man's head, by a searching analysis of the facts involved, with the heart unconsulted, and the jury room closed against outside influences. It may be that such an opinion has been born somewhere, at some time or other, but I suppose it got away before they could catch it and stuff it and put it in the museum.

I am persuaded that a coldly-thought-out and independent verdict upon a fashion in clothes, or manners, or literature, or politics, or religion, or any other matter that is projected into the field of our notice and interest, is a most rare thing—if it has indeed ever existed.

A new thing in costume appears—the flaring hoopskirt, for example—and the passersby are shocked, and the irreverent laugh. Six months later everybody is reconciled; the fashion has established itself; it is admired, now, and no one laughs. Public opinion resented it before, public opinion accepts it now, and is happy in it. Why? Was the resentment reasoned out? Was the acceptance reasoned out? No. The instinct that moves to conformity did the work. It is our nature to conform; it is a force which not many can successfully resist. What is its seat? The inborn requirement of self-approval. We all have to bow to that; there are no exceptions. Even the woman who refuses from first to last to wear the hoopskirt comes under that law and is its slave; she could not wear the skirt and have her own approval; and that she *must* have, she cannot help herself. But as a rule our self-approval has its source in but one place and not elsewhere—the approval of other people. A person of vast consequences can introduce any kind of novelty in dress and the general world will presently adopt it—moved to do it, in the first place, by the natural instinct to passively yield to that vague something recognized as authority, and in the second place by the human instinct to train with the multitude and have its approval. An empress introduced the hoopskirt, and we know the result. A nobody introduced the bloomer, and we know the result. If Eve should come again, in her ripe renown, and reintroduce her quaint styles—well, we know what would happen. And we should be cruelly embarrassed, along at first.

The hoopskirt runs its course and disappears. Nobody reasons about it. One woman abandons the fashion; her neighbor notices this and follows her lead; this influences the next woman; and so on and so on, and presently the skirt has vanished out of the world, no one knows how nor why, nor cares, for that matter. It will come again, by and by and in due course will go again.

Twenty-five years ago, in England, six or eight wine glasses stood grouped by each person's plate at a dinner party, and they were used, not left idle and empty; to-day there are but three or four in the group, and the average guest sparingly uses about two of them. We have not adopted this new fashion yet, but we shall do it presently. We shall not think it out; we shall merely conform, and let it go at that. We get our notions and habits and opinions from outside influences; we do not have to study them out.

Our table manners, and company manners, and street manners change from time to time, but the changes are not reasoned out; we merely notice and conform. We are creatures of outside influences; as a rule we do not think, we only imitate. We cannot invent standards that will stick; what we mistake for standards are only fashions, and perishable. We may continue to admire them, but we drop the use of them. We notice this in literature. Shakespeare is a standard, and fifty years ago we used to write tragedies which we couldn't tell from—from somebody else's; but we don't do it any more, now. Our prose standard, three quarters of a century ago, was ornate and diffuse; some authority or other changed it in the direction of compactness and simplicity, and conformity followed, without argument. The historical novel starts up suddenly, and sweeps the land. Everybody writes one, and the nation is glad. We had historical novels before, but nobody read them, and the rest of us conformed—without reasoning it out. We are conforming in the other way, now, because it is another case of everybody.

The outside influences are always pouring in upon us, and we are always obeying their orders and accepting their verdicts. The Smiths like the new play; the Joneses go to see it, and they copy the Smith verdict. Morals, religions, politics, get their following from surrounding influences and atmospheres, almost entirely; not from study, not from thinking. A man must and will have his own approval first of all, in each and every moment and circumstance of his life—even if he must repent of a self-approved act the moment after its commission, in order to get his self-approval *again*: but, speaking in general terms, a man's self-approval in the large concerns of life has its source in the approval of the peoples about him, and not in a searching personal examination of the matter. Mohammedans are Mohammedans because they are born and reared among that sect, not because they have thought it out and can furnish sound reasons for being

Mohammedans; we know why Catholics are Catholics; why Presbyterians are Presbyterians; why Baptists are Baptists; why Mormons are Mormons; why thieves are thieves; why monarchists are monarchists; why Republicans are Republicans and Democrats, Democrats. We know it is a matter of association and sympathy, not reasoning and examination; that hardly a man in the world has an opinion upon morals, politics, or religion which he got otherwise than through his associations and sympathies. Broadly speaking, there are none but corn-pone opinions. And broadly speaking, corn-pone stands for self-approval. Self-approval is acquired mainly from the approval of other people. The result is conformity. Sometimes conformity has a sordid business interest—the bread-and-butter interest—but not in most cases, I think. I think that in the majority of cases it is unconscious and not calculated; that it is born of the human being's natural yearning to stand well with his fellows and have their inspiring approval and praise—a yearning which is commonly so strong and so insistent that it cannot be effectually resisted, and must have its way.

A political emergency brings out the corn-pone opinion in fine force in its two chief varieties—the pocketbook variety, which has its origin in self-interest, and the bigger variety, the sentimental variety—the one which can't bear to be outside the pale;[1] can't bear to be in disfavor; can't endure the averted face and the cold shoulder; wants to stand well with his friends, wants to be smiled upon, wants to be welcome, wants to hear the precious words, "*He's* on the right track!" Uttered, perhaps by an ass, but still an ass of high degree, an ass whose approval is gold and diamonds to a smaller ass, and confers glory and honor and happiness, and membership in the herd. For these gauds many a man will dump his life-long principles into the street, and his conscience along with them. We have seen it happen. In some millions of instances.

Men think they think upon great political questions, and they do; but they think with their party, not independently; they read its literature, but not that of the other side; they arrive at convictions, but they are drawn from a partial view of the matter in hand and are of no particular value. They swarm with their party, they feel with their party, they are happy in their party's approval; and where the party leads they will follow, whether for right and honor, or through blood and dirt and a mush of mutilated morals.

In our late canvass half of the nation passionately believed that in silver lay salvation, the other half as passionately believed that that way lay destruction.[2] Do you believe that a tenth part of the people, on either side, had any rational excuse for having an opinion about the matter at all? I studied that mighty question to the bottom—and came out empty. Half of our people passionately believe in high tariff, the other half believe otherwise. Does this mean study and examination, or

---

[1]The fence marking a boundary.
[2]William Jennings Bryan had electrified the 1896 Democratic convention with his famous Cross of Gold speech; with the election of the Republican president William McKinley, the nation went on the gold standard in 1900.

only feeling? The latter, I think. I have deeply studied that question, too—and didn't arrive. We all do no end of feeling, and we mistake it for thinking. And out of it we get an aggregation which we consider a Boon. Its name is Public Opinion. It is held in reverence. It settles everything. Some think it the Voice of God. Pr'aps.

I suppose that in more cases than we should like to admit, we have two sets of opinions: one private, the other public; one secret and sincere, the other corn-pone, and more or less tainted. ✎

Elinor Glyn and the Passions[1]

Two or three weeks ago Elinor Glyn[2] called on me one afternoon and we had a long talk, of a distinctly unusual character, in the library. It may be that by the time this chapter reaches print she may be less well known to the world than she is now, therefore I will insert a word or two of information about her. She is English. She is an author. The newspapers say she is visiting America with the idea of finding just the right kind of a hero for the principal character in a romance which she is proposing to write. She has come to us upon the stormwind of a vast and sudden notoriety.

The source of this notoriety is a novel of hers called *Three Weeks*. In this novel the hero is a fine and gifted and cultivated young English gentleman of good family, who imagines he has fallen in love with the ungifted, uninspired, commonplace daughter of the rector. He goes to the Continent on an outing, and there he happens upon a brilliant and beautiful young lady of exceedingly foreign extraction, with a deep mystery hanging over her. It transpires later that she is the childless wife of a king or kinglet, a coarse and unsympathetic animal whom she does not love.

She and the young Englishman fall in love with each other at sight. The hero's feeling for the rector's daughter was pale, not to say colorless, and it is promptly consumed and extinguished in the furnace fires of his passion for the mysterious stranger—passion is the right word, passsion is what the pair of strangers feel for

---

[1] First published on January 13, 1908.

[2] (1864–1943) British author of *Three Weeks, One Day, Sequel to Three Weeks, The Point of View,* and her autobiography *Romantic Adventure*, in which she presents her view of her interview with Twain: "He told me that he liked *Three Weeks* very much, and understood its meaning, and I found that he did, indeed, know it well, for he discussed every point, and made a profound analysis of the whole book. He also made many interesting comments of his own concerning human instincts and their control. I said I would write an approximation of all he said, and send it to him to read. I did, and he wrote me a most witty reply, in which he said my summary had only the value of a 'cromo-lithograph' [a picture printed in colors from stone], because if I had really set down what he had said it would have Satan roasting a Sunday School! He also added that I was grossly misunderstood, but that he had no intention of defending me, since he was not on earth 'to do good'—at least not intentionally! He was always exquisitely whimsical, the dear old man" (*Romantic Adventure*, 1937).

each other, what they recognize as real love, the only real love, the only love worthy to be called by that great name—whereas the feeling which the young man had for the rector's daughter is perceived to have been only a passing partiality.

The queenlet and the Englishman flit away privately to the mountains and take up sumptuous quarters in a remote and lonely house there—and then business begins. They recognize that they were highly and holily created for each other and that their passion is a sacred thing, that it is their master by divine right, and that its commands must be obeyed. They get to obeying them at once and they keep on obeying them and obeying them, to the reader's intense delight and disapproval, and the process of obeying them is described, several times, almost exhaustively, but not quite—some little rag of it being left to the reader's imagination, just at the end of each infraction, the place where his imagination is to take up and do the finish being indicated by stars.

The unstated argument of the book is that the laws of Nature are paramount and properly take precedence of the interfering and impertinent restrictions obtruded upon man's life by man's statutes.

Mme. Glyn called, as I have said, and she was a picture! Slender, young, faultlessly formed and incontestably beautiful—a blonde with blue eyes, the incomparable English complexion, and crowned with a glory of red hair of a very peculiar, most rare, and quite ravishing tint. She was clad in the choicest stuffs and in the most perfect taste. There she is, just a beautiful girl; yet she has a daughter fourteen years old. She isn't winning; she has no charm but the charm of beauty, and youth, and grace, and intelligence and vivacity; she *acts* charm, and does it well, exceedingly well in fact, and it does not convince, it doesn't stir the pulse, it doesn't go to the heart, it leaves the heart serene and unemotional. Her English hero would have prodigiously admired her; he would have loved to sit and look at her and hear her talk, but he would have been able to get away from that lonely house with his purity in good repair, if he wanted to.

I talked with her with daring frankness, frequently calling a spade a spade instead of coldly symbolizing it as a snow shovel; and on her side she was equally frank. It was one of the damnedest conversations I have ever had with a beautiful stranger of her sex, if I do say it myself that shouldn't. She wanted my opinion of her book and I furnished it. I said its literary workmanship was excellent, and that I quite agreed with her view that in the matter of the sexual relation man's statutory regulations of it were a distinct interference with a higher law, the law of Nature. I went further and said I couldn't call to mind a written law of any kind that had been promulgated in any age of the world in any statute book or any Bible for the regulation of man's conduct in *any* particular, from assassination all the way up to Sabbath-breaking, that wasn't a violation of the law of Nature, which I regarded as the highest of laws, the most peremptory and absolute of all laws—Nature's laws being in my belief plainly and simply the laws of God, since He instituted them, He and no other, and the said laws, by authority of this divine origin taking precedence of all the statutes of man. I said that her pair of indelicate lovers were obeying the law of their make and disposition; that therefore they were obeying the clearly enunciated law of God, and in His eyes must manifestly be blameless.

Of course what she wanted of me was support and defense—I knew that but I said I couldn't furnish it. I said we were the servants of convention; that we could not subsist, either in a savage or a civilized state, without conventions; that we must accept them and stand by them, even when we disapproved of them; that while the laws of Nature, that is to say the laws of God, plainly made every human being a law unto himself, we must steadfastly refuse to obey those laws, and we must as steadfastly stand by the conventions which ignore them, since the statutes furnish us peace, fairly good government, and stability, and therefore are better for us than the laws of God, which would soon plunge us into confusion and disorder and anarchy, if we should adopt them. I said her book was an assault upon certain old and well-established and wise conventions, and that it would not find many friends, and indeed would not deserve many.

She said I was very brave, the bravest person she had ever met (gross flattery which could have beguiled me when I was very very young), and she implored me to publish these views of mine, but I said, "No, such a thing is unthinkable." I said that if I, or any other wise, intelligent, and experienced person, should suddenly throw down the walls that protect and conceal his real opinion on almost any subject under the sun, it would at once be perceived that he had lost his intelligence and his wisdom and ought to be sent to the asylum. I said I had been revealing to her my private sentiments, *not* my public ones; that I, like all other human beings, expose to the world only my trimmed and perfumed and carefully barbered public opinions and conceal carefully, cautiously, wisely, my private ones.

I explained that what I meant by that phrase "public opinions" was *published* opinions, opinions spread broadcast[1] in print. I said I was in the common habit, in private conversation with friends, of revealing every private opinion I possessed relating to religion, politics, and men, but that I should never dream of *printing* one of them, because they are individually and collectively at war with almost everybody's public opinion, while at the same time they are in happy agreement with almost everybody's private opinion. As an instance, I asked her if she had encountered an intelligent person who privately believed in the Immaculate Conception[2]—which of course she hadn't; and I also asked her if she had ever seen an intelligent person who was daring enough to publicly deny his belief in that fable and print the denial. Of course she hadn't encountered any such person.

I said I had a large cargo of the most interesting and important private opinions about every great matter under the sun, but that they were not for print. I reminded her that we all break over the rule two or three times in our lives and fire a disagreeable and unpopular private opinion of ours into print, but we never do it when we can help it, we never do it except when the desire to do it is too

---

[1]Over a wide area.

[2]The doctrine that Mary was conceived without sin, often confused, as Twain has done here, with the Virgin Birth of Christ.

strong for us and overrides and conquers our cold, calm, wise judgement. She mentioned several instances in which I had come out publicly in defense of unpopular causes, and she intimated that what I had been saying about myself was not perhaps in strict accordance with the facts; but I said they were merely illustrations of what I had just been saying, that when I publicly attacked the American missionaries in China and some other iniquitous persons and causes, I did not do it for any reason but just the one, that the inclination to do it was stronger than my diplomatic instincts, and I had to obey and take the consequences. But I said I was not moved to defend her book in public; that it was not a case where inclination was overpowering and unconquerable, and that therefore I could keep diplomatically still and should do it.

The lady was young enough, and inexperienced enough, to imagine that whenever a person has an unpleasant opinion in stock which could be of educational benefit to Tom, Dick, and Harry, it is his *duty* to come out in print with it and become its champion. I was not able to convince her that we never do *any* duty for the duty's sake but only for the mere personal satisfaction we get out of doing that duty. The fact is, she was brought up just like the rest of the world, with the ingrained and stupid superstition that there is such a thing as *duty for duty's sake*, and so I was obliged to let her abide in her darkness. She believed that when a man held a private unpleasant opinion of an educational sort, which would get him hanged if he published it, he ought to publish it anyway and was a coward if he didn't. Take it all round, it was a very pleasant conversation, and glaringly unprintable, particularly those considerable parts of it which I haven't had the courage to more than vaguely hint at in this account of our talk.

Some days afterward I met her again for a moment, and she gave me the startling information that she had written down every word I had said, just as I had said it, without any softening and purifying modifications, and that it was "just splendid, just wonderful." She said she had sent it to her husband, in England. Privately I didn't think that was a very good idea, and yet I believed it would interest him. She begged me to let her publish it and said it would do infinite good in the world, but I said it would damn me before my time and I didn't wish to be useful to the world on such expensive conditions. ✒

PART TWO
Twentieth-Century
Essayists

. . .

· · ·

Virginia Woolf

(1882–1941)

L ike the first male essayists, the first female essayist to gain a wide reading
public was born into the comfortable middle class. Virginia Stephen was
the daughter of Leslie Stephen, a prominent British philosopher, and his
second wife, Julia Prinsep, widow of Herbert Duckworth. Her mother had
seven children, George (1868-1934), Stella (1869–1897), and Gerald
(1870–1937) from her first marriage, and Vanessa (1879–1961), Thoby
(1880–1906), Virginia, and Adrian (1883–1948) from her second. Also
living at the house where Virginia was born was her insane half-sister Laura
(1870–1945), the only child of Leslie Stephen's first marriage to a daughter
of William Thackeray.°

The household was ideal for the development of the intellect. The year
Virginia was born her father, already editor of the *Cornhill Magazine*, became
editor of *A Dictionary of National Biography*. Many famous Victorians, such as
Thomas Hardy,° Henry James,° and George Meredith,° visited the Stephens
regularly, both at their London home and at their summer house, St. Ives, in
Cornwall. While the boys were sent to preparatory school, the girls were
taught Greek, Latin, mathematics, drawing, dancing, and music at home. All
were allowed to browse at will in Leslie Stephen's marvelous library.

It was a heady world for the development of both emotions and perceptions. The four younger children, all quite close in age, formed a special
group of their own, Virginia excelling in words and her sister in the visual
arts. Both sisters admired their brother Thoby, the leader of most of their
adventures. At St. Ives they climbed rocks, picnicked, collected butterflies
and moths, went wading and boating, bowled and played cricket. Back in
London, when Virginia was nine, the children started a weekly family newspaper, the *Hyde Park Gate News*, full of comic character sketches and imitations of the literary styles the children had come to know through their own
reading and through their father's regular sessions of reading aloud.

But Virginia's early life was also scarred, like Twain's, by suffering and loss. She was subjected to incestuous sexual advances, at age six from Gerald and later from George, who indulged in improper fondling off and on for more than five years. These episodes, along with her recognition of the special education accorded her brothers, awakened in her a distaste for male domination and aggression and no doubt contributed significantly to her emotional fragility. Between the ages of thirteen and twenty-four she suffered the loss of four close family members. The death in 1895 of her mother, when Virginia was thirteen, precipitated her first emotional breakdown. Stella took charge of the children after their mother's death, but two years later, just after her marriage, Stella also died, of peritonitis.

During the next few years Virginia practiced her writing, imitating novelists, and according to her nephew and biographer Quentin Bell,[1] composing a history of women and an imitation of Sir Thomas Browne called *Religio Laici*; neither work remains. Meanwhile her brother Thoby entered Trinity College, and in 1900 her father completed his editorship of the sixty-three volumes of *A Dictionary of National Biography*. The following year her sister Vanessa entered art school and Virginia took private lessons in Greek and learned to bind books. In 1902 she developed her first intense friendship with a woman, Violet Dickinson, her younger brother Adrian entered Trinity College, and her father became ill with cancer. When her father died in 1904, Virginia suffered her second major breakdown.

Following their father's death, the Stephen siblings moved to 46 Gordon Square, Bloomsbury, where Thoby's friends from Cambridge, particularly the biographer Lytton Strachey and the art critic Clive Bell, began meeting for Thursday evening discussions of literature, art, love, and religion. Here too, encouraged by Violet Dickinson, Virginia began writing reviews for publication in the *Guardian* and a memoir of her father for his biographer, F. W. Maitland. For three years, she taught literature and writing at Morley College, an institute for working men and women. In the early fall of 1906 Virginia, Violet, Vanessa, Thoby, and Adrian left Bloomsbury for a tour of Greece. But first Vanessa and then Thoby became ill. In November, the trip concluded, both were in bed with fever. On November 20 Thoby died of typhoid fever; two days later Vanessa announced her decision to marry Clive Bell.

By 1907 Vanessa had married, and Virginia and Adrian had moved to 29 Fitzroy Square. Despite her fragile emotional health, Virginia began working on a novel. Over the next few years she and Adrian shocked their more conventional friends and the members of the Duckworth side of the family by including nonfamily members in their household, now located in Brunswick Square: the economist John Maynard Keynes, the artist Duncan Grant, and, when he returned from Ceylon, the Jewish socialist and political activist Leonard Woolf. These men and others, such as the art critic Roger Fry and occasionally the novelist E. M. Forster,° became part of what is

---

[1]*Virginia Woolf: A Biography* (1974). The facts in this biography come from Bell's book.

called the Bloomsbury Group, whose members were brilliant, creative, and radical in their ideas and in their personal relationships. In 1911 Virginia suffered a mild breakdown and consulted a psychologist. She felt at this time that she ought to marry. Although she had considered marrying several men, particularly her old friend Lytton Strachey, she did not feel she could love any of them. Finally, in 1912, after much thought, she married Leonard Woolf, a man who lacked the financial resources of many of the Bloomsbury Group but who loved her faithfully and provided the stability she required during her creative years as novelist and critic.

In 1913, after completing her first novel, *The Voyage Out*, Virginia broke down and attempted suicide. For the next two years, her health was uncertain; just after her novel was published in 1915, she suffered a terrible relapse. By 1917, however, she had recovered and was writing regularly for the *Times Literary Supplement*. That July she and Leonard each published a short story on their own printing press set up in the dining room and named, after their house in Richmond, the Hogarth Press. The press proved to be of value in several ways. The physical work of reading manuscripts, setting type, and binding and stacking books provided a relief from emotional preoccupations. Moreover, the press provided a necessary addition to their income and served as a means of introducing some of the best literature of the period, including works by Katherine Mansfield, T. S. Eliot,° and Virginia Woolf herself. Their one major mistake was to reject Joyce's° *Ulysses*.

In 1919 the Woolfs bought Monks House, a cottage in Rodmell on the river Ouse in Sussex, as a retreat from the sometimes stressful social life of Hogarth House in Richmond. In these two houses, between bouts of mania and depression, Virginia Woolf wrote her best novels and essays, *Jacob's Room* (1922), *Mrs. Dalloway* (1925), *The Common Reader* (1925), *To the Lighthouse* (1927), *Orlando* (1928), *A Room of One's Own* (1929), *The Waves* (1931), *The Common Reader: Second Series* (1932), *The Years* (1937), and *Three Guineas* (1938).

By 1941 Virginia Woolf had completed the biography of her friend Roger Fry and had written a draft of an eighth novel, *Between the Acts*, when she felt another period of insanity descending on her. On the morning of March 28, after writing three letters, one to her sister Vanessa and two to Leonard, she drowned herself in the river Ouse. In the note addressed to Leonard that she left on the mantle she explained that she no longer wanted to burden him with her illness. This note, which Quentin Bell reproduces in his biography, also reveals the gratitude she felt for Leonard's constant solicitude and support. "If anybody could have saved me it would have been you," she wrote. Despite the several close relationships Virginia had developed over the years with women like Violet Dickinson, Katherine Mansfield, Lady Ottoline Morrell, and especially Vita Sackville-West, her relationship with her husband had given her "the greatest possible happiness."

In her novels, Virginia Woolf turned away from the description of external reality so well depicted by the Victorians; instead, like the painters of the modern period, she concentrated on the personal impressions of her characters, on life as it feels when lived. Although many of her essays, like those of Addison, Johnson, Hazlitt, and Twain, were written for periodicals, and others, like those of Hazlitt, Huxley, and Twain, were originally lectures, they too convey her interest in the impress of thought and feeling, this time on the critic. In her essay "Women and Fiction," Woolf says that fiction "is the easiest thing for a woman to write." Although her diaries and letters show how difficult writing fiction actually was for her, she nevertheless believed it to be easier for women than poetry, easier even than writing essays, which she calls, somewhat ironically, one of "the sophisticated arts."

Certainly writing essays does not require the emotional or even the physical endurance needed to write novels. But an essay writer does require confidence and breadth of knowledge, qualities hard to come by in either sex, but particularly scarce in women, then and even now. Yet Virginia Woolf had the courage to write clearly and directly about her impressions of books and life. She conveys her sense of the rapture of thought and feeling through precise, declarative sentences: "The same energy which inspired the rooks, the ploughmen, the horses, and even, it seemed, the lean bare-backed downs, sent the moth fluttering from side to side of his square of the window-pane." This sentence from "The Death of the Moth," for instance, is packed with the detail and the allusive precision of poetry. The energy of life inspires, breathes life into, not only the living creatures outside her window but also the fields themselves, which, with their bare backs, are like horses. Yet their pattern, one field adjacent to another, from the eye of a rook, at least, is a square, like the square of the window-pane that encompasses the moth. Because of her precise description of the reality outside the window and because of the authority of her voice, Virginia Woolf's vision of the doomed embodiment of life in a square of the world becomes ours as well. ✒

Women and Fiction[1]

The title of this article can be read in two ways; it may allude to women and the fiction that they write, or to women and the fiction that is written about them. The ambiguity is intentional, for in dealing with women as writers, as much elasticity as possible is desirable; it is necessary to leave oneself room to deal with other things besides their work, so much has that work been influenced by conditions that have nothing whatever to do with art.

The most superficial inquiry into women's writing instantly raises a host of questions. Why, we ask at once, was there no continuous writing done by women before the eighteenth century? Why did they then write almost as habitually as

---

[1]First published in the *Forum* in 1929.

men, and in the course of that writing produce, one after another, some of the classics of English fiction? And why did their art then, and why to some extent does their art still, take the form of fiction?

A little thought will show us that we are asking questions to which we shall get, as answer, only further fiction. The answer lies at present locked in old diaries, stuffed away in old drawers, half obliterated in the memories of the aged. It is to be found in the lives of the obscure—in those almost unlit corridors of history where the figures of generations of women are so dimly, so fitfully perceived. For very little is known about women. The history of England is the history of the male line, not of the female. Of our fathers we know always some fact, some distinction. They were soldiers or they were sailors; they filled that office or they made that law. But of our mothers, our grandmothers, our great-grandmothers, what remains? Nothing but a tradition. One was beautiful; one was red-haired; one was kissed by a Queen. We know nothing of them except their names and the dates of their marriages and the number of children they bore.

Thus, if we wish to know why at any particular time women did this or that, why they wrote nothing, why on the other hand they wrote masterpieces, it is extremely difficult to tell. Anyone who should seek among those old papers, who should turn history wrong side out and so construct a faithful picture of the daily life of the ordinary woman in Shakespeare's time, in Milton's° time, in Johnson's time, would not only write a book of astonishing interest, but would furnish the critic with a weapon which he now lacks. The extraordinary woman depends on the ordinary woman. It is only when we know what were the conditions of the average woman's life—the number of her children, whether she had money of her own, if she had a room to herself, whether she had help in bringing up her family, if she had servants, whether part of the housework was her task—it is only when we can measure the way of life and the experience of life made possible to the ordinary woman that we can account for the success or failure of the extraordinary woman as a writer.

Strange spaces of silence seem to separate one period of activity from another. There was Sappho° and a little group of women all writing poetry on a Greek island six hundred years before the birth of Christ. They fall silent. Then about the year 1000 we find a certain court lady, the Lady Murasaki, writing a very long and beautiful novel in Japan.[1] But in England in the sixteenth century, when the dramatists and poets were most active, the women were dumb. Elizabethan literature is exclusively masculine. Then, at the end of the eighteenth century and in the beginning of the nineteenth, we find women again writing—this time in England—with extraordinary frequency and success.

Law and custom were of course largely responsible for these strange intermissions of silence and speech. When a woman was liable, as she was in the fifteenth century, to be beaten and flung about the room if she did not marry

---

[1]Her novel, *Genji-Monigatari, Tale of Genji,* about a prince and his descendants, describes a complex Japanese society.

the man of her parents' choice, the spiritual atmosphere was not favourable to the production of works of art. When she was married without her own consent to a man who thereupon became her lord and master, 'so far at least as law and custom could make him,' as she was in the time of the Stuarts,[1] it is likely she had little time for writing, and less encouragement. The immense effect of environment and suggestion upon the mind, we in our psychoanalytical age are beginning to realize. Again, with memoirs and letters to help us, we are beginning to understand how abnormal is the effort needed to produce a work of art, and what shelter and what support the mind of the artist requires. Of those facts the lives and letters of men like Keats° and Carlyle° and Flaubert° assure us.

Thus it is clear that the extraordinary outburst of fiction in the beginning of the nineteenth century in England was heralded by innumerable slight changes in law and customs and manners. And women of the nineteenth century had some leisure; they had some education. It was no longer the exception for women of the middle and upper classes to choose their own husbands. And it is significant that of the four great women novelists—Jane Austen,° Emily Brontë,° Charlotte Brontë,° and George Eliot°—not one had a child, and two were unmarried.

Yet, though it is clear that the ban upon writing had been removed, there was still, it would seem, considerable pressure upon women to write novels. No four women can have been more unlike in genius and character than these four. Jane Austen° can have had nothing in common with George Eliot;° George Eliot° was the direct opposite of Emily Brontë.° Yet all were trained for the same profession; all, when they wrote, wrote novels.

Fiction was, as fiction still is, the easiest thing for a woman to write. Nor is it difficult to find the reason. A novel is the least concentrated form of art. A novel can be taken up or put down more easily than a play or a poem. George Eliot° left her work to nurse her father. Charlotte Brontë° put down her pen to pick the eyes out of the potatoes. And living as she did in the common sitting-room, surrounded by people, a woman was trained to use her mind in observation and upon the analysis of character. She was trained to be a novelist and not to be a poet.

Even in the nineteenth century, a woman lived almost solely in her home and her emotions. And those nineteenth-century novels, remarkable as they were, were profoundly influenced by the fact that the women who wrote them were excluded by their sex from certain kinds of experience. That experience has a great influence upon fiction is indisputable. The best part of Conrad's° novels, for instance, would be destroyed if it had been impossible for him to be a sailor. Take away all that Tolstoy° knew of war as a soldier, of life and society as a rich young man whose education admitted him to all sorts of experience, and *War and Peace* would be incredibly impoverished.

Yet *Pride and Prejudice*, *Wuthering Heights*, *Villette*, and *Middlemarch* were written by women from whom was forcibly withheld all experience save that which could be met with in a middle-class drawing-room. No first-hand experience of war

---

[1]From James I to Queen Anne (1603–1714), except for the period of the Commonwealth and Protectorate (1649–1659).

or seafaring or politics or business was possible for them. Even their emotional life was strictly regulated by law and custom. When George Eliot° ventured to live with Mr. Lewes without being his wife, public opinion was scandalized. Under its pressure she withdrew into a suburban seclusion which, inevitably, had the worst possible effects upon her work. She wrote that unless people asked of their own accord to come and see her, she never invited them. At the same time, on the other side of Europe, Tolstoy° was living a free life as a soldier, with men and women of all classes, for which nobody censured him and from which his novels drew much of their astonishing breadth and vigour.

But the novels of women were not affected only by the necessarily narrow range of the writer's experience. They showed, at least in the nineteenth century, another characteristic which may be traced to the writer's sex. In *Middlemarch* and in *Jane Eyre* we are conscious not merely of the writer's character, as we are conscious of the character of Charles Dickens,° but we are conscious of a woman's presence—of someone resenting the treatment of her sex and pleading for its rights. This brings into women's writing an element which is entirely absent from a man's, unless, indeed, he happens to be a working man, a negro, or one who for some other reason is conscious of disability. It introduces a distortion and is frequently the cause of weakness. The desire to plead some personal cause or to make a character the mouthpiece of some personal discontent or grievance always has a distressing effect, as if the spot at which the reader's attention is directed were suddenly twofold instead of single.

The genius of Jane Austen° and Emily Brontë° is never more convincing than in their power to ignore such claims and solicitations and to hold on their way unperturbed by scorn or censure. But it needed a very serene or a very powerful mind to resist the temptation to anger. The ridicule, the censure, the assurance of inferiority in one form or another which were lavished upon women who practised an art, provoked such reactions naturally enough. One sees the effect in Charlotte Brontë's° indignation, in George Eliot's° resignation. Again and again one finds it in the work of the lesser women writers—in their choice of a subject, in their unnatural self-assertiveness, in their unnatural docility. Moreover, insincerity leaks in almost unconsciously. They adopt a view in deference to authority. The vision becomes too masculine or it becomes too feminine; it loses its perfect integrity and, with that, its most essential quality as a work of art.

The great change that has crept into women's writing is, it would seem, a change of attitude. The woman writer is no longer bitter. She is no longer angry. She is no longer pleading and protesting as she writes. We are approaching, if we have not yet reached, the time when her writing will have little or no foreign influence to disturb it. She will be able to concentrate upon her vision without distraction from outside. The aloofness that was once within the reach of genius and originality is only now coming within the reach of ordinary women. Therefore the average novel by a woman is far more genuine and far more interesting today than it was a hundred or even fifty years ago.

But it is still true that before a woman can write exactly as she wishes to write, she has many difficulties to face. To begin with, there is the technical difficulty—

so simple, apparently; in reality, so baffling—that the very form of the sentence does not fit her. It is a sentence made by men; it is too loose, too heavy, too pompous for a woman's use. Yet in a novel, which covers so wide a stretch of ground, an ordinary and usual type of sentence has to be found to carry the reader on easily and naturally from one end of the book to the other. And this a woman must make for herself, altering and adapting the current sentence until she writes one that takes the natural shape of her thought without crushing or distorting it.

But that, after all, is only a means to an end, and the end is still to be reached only when a woman has the courage to surmount opposition and the determination to be true to herself. For a novel, after all, is a statement about a thousand different objects—human, natural, divine; it is an attempt to relate them to each other. In every novel of merit these different elements are held in place by the force of the writer's vision. But they have another order also, which is the order imposed upon them by convention. And as men are the arbiters of that convention, as they have established an order of values in life, so too, since fiction is largely based on life, these values prevail there also to a very great extent.

It is probable, however, that both in life and in art the values of a woman are not the values of a man. Thus, when a woman comes to write a novel, she will find that she is perpetually wishing to alter the established values—to make serious what appears insignificant to a man, and trivial what is to him important. And for that, of course, she will be criticized; for the critic of the opposite sex will be genuinely puzzled and surprised by an attempt to alter the current scale of values, and will see in it not merely a difference of view, but a view that is weak, or trivial, or sentimental, because it differs from his own.

But here, too, women are coming to be more independent of opinion. They are beginning to respect their own sense of values. And for this reason the subject matter of their novels begins to show certain changes. They are less interested, it would seem, in themselves; on the other hand, they are more interested in other women. In the early nineteenth century, women's novels were largely autobiographical. One of the motives that led them to write was the desire to expose their own suffering, to plead their own cause. Now that this desire is no longer so urgent, women are beginning to explore their own sex, to write of women as women have never been written of before; for of course, until very lately, women in literature were the creation of men.

Here again there are difficulties to overcome, for, if one may generalize, not only do women submit less readily to observation than men, but their lives are far less tested and examined by the ordinary processes of life. Often nothing tangible remains of a woman's day. The food that has been cooked is eaten; the children that have been nursed have gone out into the world. Where does the accent fall? What is the salient point for the novelist to seize upon? It is difficult to say. Her life has an anonymous character which is baffling and puzzling in the extreme. For the first time, this dark country is beginning to be explored in fiction; and at the same moment a woman has also to record the changes in women's minds and habits which the opening of the professions has introduced. She has to observe how their lives are ceasing to run underground; she has to discover what new colours and shadows are showing in them now that they are exposed to the outer world.

If, then, one should try to sum up the character of women's fiction at the present moment, one would say that it is courageous; it is sincere; it keeps closely to what women feel. It is not bitter. It does not insist upon its femininity. But at the same time, a woman's book is not written as a man would write it. These qualities are much commoner than they were, and they give even to second- and third-rate work the value of truth and the interest of sincerity.

But in addition to these good qualities, there are two that call for a word more of discussion. The change which has turned the English woman from a nonde-script influence, fluctuating and vague, to a voter, a wage-earner, a responsible citizen, has given her both in her life and in her art a turn toward the impersonal. Her relations now are not only emotional; they are intellectual, they are political. The old system which condemned her to squint askance at things through the eyes or through the interests of husband or brother, has given place to the direct and practical interests of one who must act for herself, and not merely influence the acts of others. Hence her attention is being directed away from the personal centre which engaged it exclusively in the past to the impersonal, and her novels naturally become more critical of society, and less analytical of individual lives.

We may expect that the office of gadfly to the state, which has been so far a male prerogative, will now be discharged by women also. Their novels will deal with social evils and remedies. Their men and women will not be observed wholly in relation to each other emotionally, but as they cohere and clash in groups and classes and races. That is one change of some importance. But there is another more interesting to those who prefer the butterfly to the gadfly— that is to say, the artist to the reformer. The greater impersonality of women's lives will encourage the poetic spirit, and it is in poetry that women's fiction is still weakest. It will lead them to be less absorbed in facts and no longer content to record with astonishing acuteness the minute details which fall under their own observation. They will look beyond the personal and political relationships to the wider questions which the poet tries to solve—of our destiny and the meaning of life.

The basis of the poetic attitude is of course largely founded upon material things. It depends upon leisure, and a little money, and the chance which money and leisure give to observe impersonally and dispassionately. With money and leisure at their service, women will naturally occupy themselves more than has hitherto been possible with the craft of letters. They will make a fuller and a more subtle use of the instrument of writing. Their technique will become bolder and richer.

In the past, the virtue of women's writing often lay in its divine spontaneity, like that of the blackbird's song or the thrush's. It was untaught; it was from the heart. But it was also, and much more often, chattering and garrulous—mere talk spilt over paper and left to dry in pools and blots. In future, granted time and books and a little space in the house for herself, literature will become for women, as for men, an art to be studied. Women's gift will be trained and strengthened.

The novel will cease to be the dumping-ground for the personal emotions. It will become, more than at present, a work of art like any other, and its resources and its limitations will be explored.

From this it is a short step to the practice of the sophisticated arts, hitherto so little practised by women—to the writing of essays and criticism, of history and biography. And that, too, if we are considering the novel, will be of advantage; for besides improving the quality of the novel itself, it will draw off the aliens who have been attracted to fiction by its accessibility while their hearts lay elsewhere. Thus will the novel be rid of those excrescences of history and fact which, in our time, have made it so shapeless.

So, if we may prophesy, women in time to come will write fewer novels, but better novels; and not novels only, but poetry and criticism and history. But in this, to be sure, one is looking ahead to that golden, that perhaps fabulous, age when women will have what has so long been denied them—leisure, and money, and a room to themselves. ✍

Professions for Women[1]

When your secretary invited me to come here, she told me that your Society[2] is concerned with the employment of women and she suggested that I might tell you something about my own professional experiences. It is true I am a woman; it is true I am employed; but what professional experiences have I had? It is difficult to say. My profession is literature; and in that profession there are fewer experiences for women than in any other, with the exception of the stage—fewer, I mean, that are peculiar to women. For the road was cut many years ago—by Fanny Burney,[3] by Aphra Behn,[4] by Harriet Martineau,[5] by Jane Austen,° by George Eliot°—many famous women, and many more unknown and forgotten, have been before me, making the path smooth, and regulating my steps. Thus, when I came to write, there were very few material obstacles in my way. Writing was a reputable and harmless occupation. The family peace was not broken by the scratching of a pen. No demand was made upon the family purse. For ten and

---

[1]First published in *The Death of the Moth* (1942) but written in 1931.

[2]The Women's Service League.

[3]Madame D'Arblay (1752–1840), English novelist who was well read but lacked a formal education; she was a member of Samuel Johnson's circle. Her novels include *Evelina* (1778), *Cecilia* (1782), *Camilla* (1796), and *The Wanderer* (1814).

[4]Known as the first English woman to write professionally, Behn (1640–1689) was an English spy in the Dutch wars and an inmate in debtors' prison before she wrote a successful play, *The Rover*, and her famous novel *Oroonoko* (1688), a philosophical love story.

[5]English author and journalist (1802–1876), deaf from childhood, who wrote on a variety of subjects, including religion, the economy, the abolition of slavery, and philosophy. She also wrote a novel, *Deerbrook* (1839), and *Letters on Mesmerism* (1845).

sixpence one can buy paper enough to write all the plays of Shakespeare—if one has a mind that way. Pianos and models, Paris, Vienna and Berlin, masters and mistresses, are not needed by a writer. The cheapness of writing paper is, of course, the reason why women have succeeded as writers before they have succeeded in the other professions.

But to tell you my story—it is a simple one. You have only got to figure to yourselves a girl in a bedroom with a pen in her hand. She had only to move that pen from left to right—from ten o'clock to one. Then it occurred to her to do what is simple and cheap enough after all—to slip a few of those pages into an envelope, fix a penny stamp in the corner, and drop the envelope into the red box at the corner. It was thus that I became a journalist; and my effort was rewarded on the first day of the following month—a very glorious day it was for me—by a letter from an editor containing a cheque for one pound ten shillings and six-pence. But to show you how little I deserve to be called a professional woman, how little I know of the struggles and difficulties of such lives, I have to admit that instead of spending that sum upon bread and butter, rent, shoes and stockings, or butcher's bills, I went out and bought a cat—a beautiful cat, a Persian cat, which very soon involved me in bitter disputes with my neighbours.

What could be easier than to write articles and to buy Persian cats with the profits? But wait a moment. Articles have to be about something. Mine, I seem to remember, was about a novel by a famous man. And while I was writing this review, I discovered that if I were going to review books I should need to do battle with a certain phantom. And the phantom was a woman, and when I came to know her better I called her after the heroine of a famous poem, The Angel in the House.[1] It was she who used to come between me and my paper when I was writing reviews. It was she who bothered me and wasted my time and so tormented me that at last I killed her. You who come of a younger and happier generation may not have heard of her—you may not know what I mean by the Angel in the House. I will describe her as shortly as I can. She was intensely sympathetic. She was immensely charming. She was utterly unselfish. She excelled in the difficult arts of family life. She sacrificed herself daily. If there was chicken, she took the leg; if there was a draught she sat in it—in short she was so constituted that she never had a mind or a wish of her own, but preferred to sympathize always with the minds and wishes of others. Above all—I need not say it—she was pure. Her purity was supposed to be her chief beauty—her blushes, her great grace. In those days— the last of Queen Victoria—every house had its Angel. And when I came to write I encountered her with the very first words. The shadow of her wings fell on my page; I heard the rustling of her skirts in the room. Directly, that is to say, I took my pen in hand to review that novel by a famous man, she slipped behind me and whispered: "My dear, you are a young woman. You are writing about a book that has been written by a man. Be sympathetic; be tender; flatter; deceive; use all the arts and wiles of our sex. Never let anybody

---

[1]See Patmore.°

guess that you have a mind of your own. Above all, be pure." And she made as if to guide my pen. I now record the one act for which I take some credit to myself, though the credit rightly belongs to some excellent ancestors of mine who left me a certain sum of money—shall we say five hundred pounds a year?—so that it was not necessary for me to depend solely on charm for my living. I turned upon her and caught her by the throat. I did my best to kill her. My excuse, if I were to be had up in a court of law, would be that I acted in self-defence. Had I not killed her she would have killed me. She would have plucked the heart out of my writing. For, as I found, directly I put pen to paper, you cannot review even a novel without having a mind of your own, without expressing what you think to be the truth about human relations, morality, sex. And all these questions, according to the Angel in the House, cannot be dealt with freely and openly by women; they must charm, they must conciliate, they must—to put it bluntly—tell lies if they are to succeed. Thus, whenever I felt the shadow of her wing or the radiance of her halo upon my page, I took up the inkpot and flung it at her. She died hard. Her fictitious nature was of great assistance to her. It is far harder to kill a phantom than a reality. She was always creeping back when I thought I had despatched her. Though I flatter myself that I killed her in the end, the struggle was severe; it took much time that had better have been spent upon learning Greek grammar; or in roaming the world in search of adventures. But it was a real experience; it was an experience that was bound to befall all women writers at that time. Killing the Angel in the House was part of the occupation of a woman writer.

But to continue my story. The Angel was dead; what then remained? You may say that what remained was a simple and common object—a young woman in a bedroom with an inkpot. In other words, now that she had rid herself of false-hood, that young woman had only to be herself. Ah, but what is "herself"? I mean, what is a woman? I assure you, I do not know. I do not believe that you know. I do not believe that anybody can know until she has expressed herself in all the arts and professions open to human skill. That indeed is one of the reasons why I have come here—out of respect for you, who are in process of showing us by your experiments what a woman is, who are in process of providing us, by your failures and successes, with that extremely important piece of information.

But to continue the story of my professional experiences. I made one pound ten and six by my first review; and I bought a Persian cat with the proceeds. Then I grew ambitious. A Persian cat is all very well, I said; but a Persian cat is not enough. I must have a motor car. And it was thus that I became a novelist—for it is a very strange thing that people will give you a motor car if you will tell them a story. It is a still stranger thing that there is nothing so delightful in the world as telling stories. It is far pleasanter than writing reviews of famous novels. And yet, if I am to obey your secretary and tell you my professional experiences as a novelist, I must tell you about a very strange experience that befell me as a novelist. And to understand it you must try first to imagine a novelist's state of mind. I hope I am not giving away professional secrets if I say that a novelist's chief desire is to be as unconscious as possible. He has to induce in himself a state of perpetual lethargy. He wants life to proceed with the utmost quiet and regularity. He wants to see the same faces, to read the same books, to do the same things day after day, month after month, while he is writing, so that nothing may break the illusion in which he is living—so that nothing may disturb or disquiet the mysterious nosings about, feelings round, darts, dashes and sudden discoveries of that very shy and illusive spirit, the imagination. I suspect that this state is the same both for men and women. Be that as it may, I want you to imagine me writing a novel in a state of trance. I want you to figure to yourselves a girl sitting with a pen in her hand, which for minutes, and indeed for hours, she never dips into the inkpot. The image that comes to my mind when I think of this girl is the image of a fisherman lying sunk in dreams on the verge of a deep lake with a rod held out over the water. She was letting her imagination sweep unchecked round every rock and cranny of the world that lies submerged in the depths of our unconscious being. Now came the experience, the experience that I believe to be far commoner with women writers than with men. The line raced through the girl's fingers. Her imagination had rushed away. It had sought the pools, the depths, the dark places where the largest fish slumber. And then there was a smash. There was an explosion. There was foam and confusion. The imagination had dashed itself against something hard. The girl was roused from her dream. She was indeed in a state of the most acute and difficult distress. To speak without figure she had thought of something, something about the body, about the passions which it was unfitting for her as a woman to say. Men, her reason told her, would be shocked. The consciousness of what men will say of a woman who speaks the truth about her passions had roused her from her artist's state of unconsciousness. She could write no more. The trance was over. Her imagination could work no longer. This I believe to be a very common experience with women writers—they are impeded by the extreme conventionality of the other sex. For though men sensibly allow themselves great freedom in these respects, I doubt that they realize or can control the extreme severity with which they condemn such freedom in women.

These then were two very genuine experiences of my own. These were two of the adventures of my professional life. The first—killing the Angel in the House—I think I solved. She died. But the second, telling the truth about my own experiences as a body, I do not think I solved. I doubt that any woman has solved it yet. The obstacles against her are still immensely powerful—and yet they are very difficult to define. Outwardly, what is simpler than to write books? Outwardly, what obstacles are there for a woman rather than for a man? Inwardly, I think, the case is very different; she has still many ghosts to fight, many prejudices to overcome. Indeed it will be a long time still, I think, before a woman can sit down to write a book without finding a phantom to be slain, a rock to be dashed against. And if this is so in literature, the freest of all professions for women, how is it in the new professions which you are now for the first time entering?

Those are the questions that I should like, had I time, to ask you. And indeed, if I have laid stress upon these professional experiences of mine, it is because I believe that they are, though in different forms, yours also. Even when the path is nominally open—when there is nothing to prevent a woman from being a doctor, a lawyer, a civil servant—there are many phantoms and obstacles, as I believe, looming in her way. To discuss and define them is I think of great value and importance; for thus only can the labour be shared, the difficulties be solved. But besides this, it is necessary also to discuss the ends and the aims for which we are fighting, for which we are doing battle with these formidable obstacles. Those aims cannot be taken for granted; they must be perpetually questioned and examined. The whole position, as I see it—here in this hall surrounded by women practising for the first time in history I know not how many different professions—is one of extraordinary interest and importance. You have won rooms of your own in the house hitherto exclusively owned by men. You are able, though not without great labour and effort, to pay the rent. You are earning your five hundred pounds a year. But this freedom is only a beginning; the room is your own, but it is still bare. It has to be furnished; it has to be decorated; it has to be shared. How are you going to furnish it, how are you going to decorate it? With whom are you going to share it, and upon what terms? These, I think, are questions of the utmost importance and interest. For the first time in history you are able to ask them; for the first time you are able to decide for yourselves what the answers should be. Willingly would I stay and discuss those questions and answers—but not tonight. My time is up; and I must cease. ✒

Leslie Stephen[1]

By the time that his children were growing up, the great days of my father's life were over. His feats on the river and on the mountains had been won before they were born. Relics of them were to be found lying about the house—the silver cup on the study mantelpiece; the rusty alpenstocks that leaned against the bookcase in the corner; and to the end of his days he would speak of great climbers and explorers with a peculiar mixture of admiration and envy. But his own years of activity were over, and my father had to content himself with pottering about the Swiss valleys or taking a stroll across the Cornish moors.

That to potter and to stroll meant more on his lips than on other people's is becoming obvious now that some of his friends have given their own version of those expeditions. He would start off after breakfast alone, or with one companion. Shortly after dinner he would return. If the walk had been successful, he would have out his great map and commemorate a new short cut in red ink. And he was quite capable, it appears, of striding all day across the moors without speaking more than a word or two to his companion. By that time, too, he had written the *History of English Thought in the Eighteenth Century*, which is said by some to be his masterpiece; and the *Science of Ethics*—the book which interested him most; and *The Playground of Europe*, in which is to be found "The Sunset on Mont Blanc"—in his opinion the best thing he ever wrote. He still wrote daily and methodically, though never for long at a time.

---

[1]First published in *The Captain's Death Bed* (1950) but written in 1932.

In London he wrote in the large room with three long windows at the top of the house. He wrote lying almost recumbent in a low rocking chair which he tipped to and fro as he wrote, like a cradle, and as he wrote he smoked a short clay pipe, and he scattered books round him in a circle. The thud of a book dropped on the floor could be heard in the room beneath. And often as he mounted the stairs to his study with his firm, regular tread he would burst, not into song, for he was entirely unmusical, but into a strange rhythmical chant, for verse of all kinds, both "utter trash," as he called it, and the most sublime words of Milton° and Wordsworth,° stuck in his memory, and the act of walking or climbing seemed to inspire him to recite whichever it was that came uppermost or suited his mood.

But it was his dexterity with his fingers that delighted his children before they could potter along the lanes at his heels or read his books. He would twist a sheet of paper beneath a pair of scissors and out would drop an elephant, a stag, or a monkey, with trunks, horns, and tails delicately and exactly formed. Or, taking a pencil, he would draw beast after beast—an art that he practiced almost unconsciously as he read, so that the flyleaves of his books swarm with owls and donkeys as if to illustrate the "Oh, you ass!" or "Conceited dunce" that he was wont to scribble impatiently in the margin. Such brief comments, in which one may find the germ of the more temperate statements of his essays, recall some of the characteristics of his talk. He could be very silent, as his friends have testified. But his remarks, made suddenly in a low voice between the puffs of his pipe, were extremely effective. Sometimes with one word—but his one word was accompanied by a gesture of the hand—he would dispose of the tissue of exaggerations which his own sobriety seemed to provoke. "There are 40,000,000 unmarried women in London alone!" Lady Ritchie once informed him. "Oh, Annie, Annie!" my father exclaimed in tones of horrified but affectionate rebuke. But Lady Ritchie, as if she enjoyed being rebuked, would pile it up even higher next time she came.

The stories he told to amuse his children of adventures in the Alps—but accidents only happened, he would explain, if you were so foolish as to disobey your guides—or of those long walks, after one of which, from Cambridge to London on a hot day, "I drank, I am sorry to say, rather more than was good for me," were told very briefly, but with a curious power to impress the scene. The things that he did not say were always there in the background. So, too, though he seldom told anecdotes, and his memory for facts was bad, when he described a person—and he had known many people, both famous and obscure—he would convey exactly what he thought of him in two or three words. And what he thought might be the opposite of what other people thought. He had a way of upsetting established reputations and disregarding conventional values that could be disconcerting, and sometimes perhaps wounding, though no one was more respectful of any feeling that seemed to him genuine. But when, suddenly opening his bright blue eyes and rousing himself from what had seemed complete abstraction, he gave his opinion, it was difficult to disregard it. It was a habit, especially when deafness made him unaware that this opinion could be heard, that had its inconveniences.

"I am the most easily bored of men," he wrote, truthfully as usual; and when, as was inevitable in a large family, some visitor threatened to stay not merely for tea but also for dinner, my father would express his anguish at first by twisting and untwisting a certain lock of hair. Then he would burst out, half to himself, half to the powers above, but quite audibly, "Why can't he go? Why can't he go?" Yet such is the charm of simplicity—and did he not say, also truthfully, that "bores are the salt of the earth"?—that the bores seldom went, or, if they did, forgave him and came again.

Too much, perhaps, has been said of his silence, too much stress has been laid upon his reserve. He loved clear thinking; he hated sentimentality and gush; but this by no means meant that he was cold and unemotional, perpetually critical and condemnatory in daily life. On the contrary, it was his power of feeling strongly and of expressing his feeling with vigor that made him sometimes so alarming as a companion. A lady, for instance, complained of the wet summer that was spoiling her tour in Cornwall. But to my father, though he never called himself a democrat, the rain meant that the corn was being laid; some poor man was being ruined; and the energy with which he expressed his sympathy—not with the lady—left her discomfited. He had something of the same respect for farmers and fishermen that he had for climbers and explorers. So, too, he talked little of patriotism, but during the South African War[1]—and all wars were hateful to him—he lay awake thinking that he heard the guns on the battlefield. Again, neither his reason nor his cold common sense helped to convince him that a child could be late for dinner without having been maimed or killed in an accident. And not all his mathematics together with a bank balance which he insisted must be ample in the extreme could persuade him, when it came to signing a check, that the whole family was not "shooting Niagara to ruin," as he put it. The pictures that he would draw of old age and the bankruptcy court, of ruined men of letters who have to support large families in small houses at Wimbledon (he owned a very small house at Wimbledon), might have convinced those who complain of his understatements that hyperbole was well within his reach had he chosen.

Yet the unreasonable mood was superficial, as the rapidity with which it vanished would prove. The checkbook was shut; Wimbledon and the workhouse were forgotten. Some thought of a humorous kind made him chuckle. Taking his hat and his stick, calling for his dog and his daughter, he would stride off into Kensington Gardens, where he had walked as a little boy, where his brother Fitzjames and he had made beautiful bows to young Queen Victoria and she had swept them a curtsy; and so, round the Serpentine, to Hyde Park Corner, where he had once saluted the great Duke[2] himself; and so home. He was not then in the least "alarming"; he was very simple, very confiding; and his silence, though one might last unbroken from the Round Pond to the Marble Arch, was curiously full

---

[1]Also known as the Boer War (1899–1902), fought between the Dutch and British settlers of South Africa. The British won but only after much cruelty on both sides, which left a legacy of bitterness.

[2]The Duke of Wellington (1769–1852), who defeated Napoleon at Waterloo in 1815.

of meaning, as if he were thinking half aloud, about poetry and philosophy and people he had known.

He himself was the most abstemious of men. He smoked a pipe perpetually, but never a cigar. He wore his clothes until they were too shabby to be tolerable; and he held old-fashioned and rather puritanical views as to the vice of luxury and the sin of idleness. The relations between parents and children today have a freedom that would have been impossible with my father. He expected a certain standard of behavior, even of ceremony, in family life. Yet if freedom means the right to think one's own thoughts and to follow one's own pursuits, then no one respected and indeed insisted upon freedom more completely than he did. His sons, with the exception of the Army and Navy, should follow whatever professions they chose; his daughters, though he cared little enough for the higher education of women, should have the same liberty. If at one moment he rebuked a daughter sharply for smoking a cigarette — smoking was not in his opinion a nice habit in the other sex — she had only to ask him if she might become a painter, and he assured her that so long as she took her work seriously he would give her all the help he could. He had no special love for painting; but he kept his word. Freedom of that sort was worth thousands of cigarettes.

It was the same with the perhaps more difficult problem of literature. Even today there may be parents who would doubt the wisdom of allowing a girl of fifteen the free run of a large and quite unexpurgated library. But my father allowed it. There were certain facts — very briefly, very shyly he referred to them. Yet "Read what you like," he said, and all his books, "mangy and worthless," as he called them, but certainly they were many and various, were to be had without asking. To read what one liked because one liked it, never to pretend to admire what one did not — that was his only lesson in the art of reading. To write in the fewest possible words, as clearly as possible, exactly what one meant — that was his only lesson in the art of writing. All the rest must be learned for oneself. Yet a child must have been childish in the extreme not to feel that such was the teaching of a man of great learning and wide experience, though he would never impose his own views or parade his own knowledge. For, as his tailor remarked when he saw my father walk past his shop up Bond Street, "There goes a gentleman that wears good clothes without knowing it."

In those last years, grown solitary and very deaf, he would sometimes call himself a failure as a writer; he had been "jack of all trades, and master of none." But whether he failed or succeeded as a writer, it is permissible to believe that he left a distinct impression of himself on the minds of his friends. Meredith° saw him as "Phoebus Apollo° turned fasting friar" in his earlier days; Thomas Hardy,° years later, looked at the "spare and desolate figure" of the Schreckhorn and thought of

——him,
Who scaled its horn with ventured life and limb,
Drawn on on by vague imaginings, maybe,
Of semblance to his personality
In its quaint glooms, keen lights, and rugged trim.

But the praise he would have valued most, for though he was an agnostic nobody believed more profoundly in the worth of human relationships, was Meredith's° tribute after his death: "He was the one man to my knowledge worthy to have married your mother." And Lowell,[1] when he called him "L.S., the most lovable of men," has best described the quality that makes him, after all these years, unforgettable. *

William Hazlitt[2]

Had one met Hazlitt no doubt one would have liked him on his own principle that "We can scarcely hate any one we know." But Hazlitt has been dead now a hundred years, and it is perhaps a question how far we can know him well enough to overcome those feelings of dislike, both personal and intellectual, which his writings still so sharply arouse. For Hazlitt—it is one of his prime merits—was not one of those non-committal writers who shuffle off in a mist and die of their own insignificance. His essays are emphatically himself. He has no reticence and he has no shame. He tells us exactly what he thinks, and he tells us—the confidence is less seductive—exactly what he feels. As of all men he had the most intense consciousness of his own existence, since never a day passed without inflicting on him some pang of hate or of jealousy, some thrill of anger or of pleasure, we cannot read him for long without coming in contact with a very singular character—ill conditioned yet high minded; mean yet noble; intensely egotistical yet inspired by the most genuine passion for the rights and liberties of mankind.

Soon, so thin is the veil of the essay as Hazlitt wore it, his very look comes before us. We see him as Coleridge° saw him, "browhanging, shoe-contemplative, strange." He comes shuffling into the room, he looks nobody straight in the face, he shakes hands with the fin of a fish; occasionally he darts a malignant glance from his corner. "His manners are 99 in a 100 singularly repulsive," Coleridge° said. Yet now and again his face lit up with intellectual beauty, and his manner became radiant with sympathy and understanding. Soon, too, as we read on, we become familiar with the whole gamut of his grudges and his grievances. He lived, one gathers, mostly at inns. No woman's form graced his board. He had quarrelled with all his old friends, save perhaps with Lamb. Yet his only fault had been that he had stuck to his principles and "not become a government tool." He was the object of malignant persecution—Blackwood's reviewers[3] called him "pimply Hazlitt," though his cheek was pale as alabaster. These lies, however, got into print, and then he was afraid to visit his friends because the footman had read

---

[1]James Russell (1819–1891), American poet, critic, editor, and ambassador to London from 1877 to 1885; he was also Virginia Woolf's godfather.
[2]First published in *The Common Reader: Second Series*, 1932.
[3]Reviewers for the magazine *Blackwood's*, first published in Edinburgh in 1817.

the newspaper and the housemaid tittered behind his back. He had—no one could deny it—one of the finest minds, and he wrote indisputably the best prose style of his time. But what did that avail with women? Fine ladies have no respect for scholars, nor chambermaids either—so the growl and plaint of his grievances keeps breaking through, disturbing us, irritating us; and yet there is something so independent, subtle, fine, and enthusiastic about him—when he can forget himself he is so rapt in ardent speculation about other things—that dislike crumbles and turns to something much warmer and more complex. Hazlitt was right:

> It is the mask only that we dread and hate; the man may have something human about him! The notions in short which we entertain of people at a distance, or from partial representation, or from guess-work, are simple, uncompounded ideas, which answer to nothing in reality; those which we derive from experience are mixed modes, the only true and, in general, the most favourable ones.

Certainly no one could read Hazlitt and maintain a simple and uncompounded idea of him. From the first he was a twy-minded man—one of those divided natures which are inclined almost equally to two quite opposite careers. It is significant that his first impulse was not to essay-writing but to painting and philosophy. There was something in the remote and silent art of the painter that offered a refuge to his tormented spirit. He noted enviously how happy the old age of painters was—"their minds keep alive to the last"; he turned longingly to the calling that takes one out of doors, among fields and woods, that deals with bright pigments, and has solid brush and canvas for its tools and not merely black ink and white paper. Yet at the same time he was bitten by an abstract curiosity that would not let him rest in the contemplation of concrete beauty. When he was a boy of fourteen he heard his father, the good Unitarian minister, dispute with an old lady of the congregation as they were coming out of Meeting as to the limits of religious toleration, and, he said, "it was this circumstance that decided the fate of my future life." It set him off "forming in my head . . . the following system of political rights and general jurisprudence." He wished "to be satisfied of the reason of things." The two ideals were ever after to clash. To be a thinker and to express in the plainest and most accurate of terms "the reason of things," and to be a painter gloating over blues and crimsons, breathing fresh air and living sensually in the emotions—these were two different, perhaps incompatible ideals, yet like all Hazlitt's emotions both were tough and each strove for mastery. He yielded now to one, now to the other. He spent months in Paris copying pictures at the Louvre. He came home and toiled laboriously at the portrait of an old woman in a bonnet day after day, seeking by industry and pains to discover the secret of Rembrandt's° genius; but he lacked some quality—perhaps it was invention—and in the end cut the canvas to ribbons in a rage or turned it against the wall in despair. At the same time he was writing the *Essay on the Principles of Human Action* which he preferred to all his other works. For there he wrote plainly and truthfully, without glitter or garishness, without any wish to please or to make money, but solely to gratify the urgency of his own desire for truth. Naturally, "the book dropped still-born from the press." Then, too, his political hopes, his belief that the age of freedom had come and that the tyranny of kingship was over, proved vain. His friends deserted to the Government, and he was left to uphold the doctrines of liberty, fraternity, and revolution in that perpetual minority which requires so much self-approval to support it.

Thus he was a man of divided tastes and of thwarted ambition; a man whose happiness, even in early life, lay behind. His mind had set early and bore for ever the stamp of first impressions. In his happiest moods he looked not forwards but backwards—to the garden where he had played as a child, to the blue hills of Shropshire and to all those landscapes which he had seen when hope was still his, and peace brooded upon him and he looked up from his painting or his book and saw the fields and woods as if they were the outward expression of his own inner quietude. It is to the books that he read then that he returns—to Rousseau° and to Burke° and to the *Letters of Junius*.[1] The impression that they made upon his youthful imagination was never effaced and scarcely overlaid; for after youth was over he ceased to read for pleasure, and youth and the pure and intense pleasures of youth were soon left behind.

Naturally, given his susceptibility to the charms of the other sex, he married; and naturally, given his consciousness of his own "misshapen form made to be mocked," he married unhappily. Miss Sarah Stoddart pleased him when he met her at the Lambs by the common sense with which she found the kettle and boiled it when Mary absent-mindedly delayed. But of domestic talents she had none. Her little income was insufficient to meet the burden of married life, and Hazlitt soon found that instead of spending eight years in writing eight pages he must turn journalist and write articles upon politics and plays and pictures and books of the right length, at the right moment. Soon the mantelpiece of the old house at York Street where Milton° had lived was scribbled over with ideas for essays. As the habit proves, the house was not a tidy house, nor did geniality and comfort excuse the lack of order. The Hazlitts were to be found eating breakfast at two in the afternoon, without a fire in the grate or a curtain to the window. A valiant walker and a clear-sighted woman, Mrs. Hazlitt had no delusions about her husband. He was not faithful to her, and she faced the fact with admirable common sense. But "he said that I had always despised him and his abilities," she noted in her diary, and that was carrying common sense too far. The prosaic marriage came lamely to an end. Free at last from the encumbrance of home and husband, Sarah Hazlitt pulled on her boots and set off on a walking tour through Scotland, while Hazlitt, incapable of attachment or comfort, wandered from inn to inn, suffered tortures of humiliation and disillusionment, but, as he drank cup after cup of very strong tea and made love to the innkeeper's daughter, he wrote those essays that are of course among the very best that we have.

---

[1] A collection of political letters written over a period of three years beginning in 1768 and addressed to the editor of the *Public Advertiser* by an unknown writer who opposed the government of George III and supported freedom of the press and the British constitution.

That they are not quite the best—that they do not haunt the mind and remain entire in the memory as the essays of Montaigne or Lamb haunt the mind—is also true. He seldom reaches the perfection of these great writers or their unity. Perhaps it is the nature of these short pieces that they need unity and a mind at harmony with itself. A little jar there makes the whole composition tremble. The essays of Montaigne, Lamb, even Addison, have the reticence which springs from composure, for with all their familiarity they never tell us what they wish to keep hidden. But with Hazlitt it is different. There is always something divided and discordant even in his finest essays, as if two minds were at work who never succeed save for a few moments in making a match of it. In the first place there is the mind of the inquiring boy who wishes to be satisfied of the reason of things—the mind of the thinker. It is the thinker for the most part who is allowed the choice of the subject. He chooses some abstract idea, like Envy, or Egotism, or Reason and Imagination. He treats it with energy and independence. He explores its ramifications and scales its narrow paths as if it were a mountain road and the ascent both difficult and inspiring. Compared with this athletic progress, Lamb's seems the flight of a butterfly cruising capriciously among the flowers and perching for a second incongruously here upon a barn, there upon a wheelbarrow. But every sentence in Hazlitt carries us forward. He has his end in view and, unless some accident intervenes, he strides towards it in that "pure conversational prose style" which, as he points out, is so much more difficult to practise than fine writing.

There can be no question that Hazlitt the thinker is an admirable companion. He is strong and fearless; he knows his mind and he speaks his mind forcibly yet brilliantly too, for the readers of newspapers are a dull-eyed race who must be dazzled in order to make them see. But besides Hazlitt the thinker there is Hazlitt the artist. There is the sensuous and emotional man, with his feeling for colour and touch, with his passion for prize-fighting and Sarah Walker, with his sensibility to all those emotions which disturb the reason and make it often seem futile enough to spend one's time slicing things up finer and finer with the intellect when the body of the world is so firm and so warm and demands so imperatively to be pressed to the heart. To know the reason of things is a poor substitute for being able to feel them. And Hazlitt felt with the intensity of a poet. The most abstract of his essays will suddenly glow red-hot or white-hot if something reminds him of his past. He will drop his fine analytic pen and paint a phrase or two with a full brush brilliantly and beautifully if some landscape stirs his imagination or some book brings back the hour when he first read it. The famous passages about reading *Love for Love*[1] and drinking coffee from a silver pot, and reading *La Nouvelle Héloïse*[2] and eating a cold chicken are known to all, and yet how oddly they often break into the context, how violently we are switched from reason to rhapsody—how embarrassingly our austere thinker falls upon our

---

[1] 1695; play by William Congreve.°
[2] 1761; novel by Jean Jacques Rousseau.°

shoulders and demands our sympathy! It is this disparity and the sense of two forces in conflict that trouble the serenity and cause the inconclusiveness of some of Hazlitt's finest essays. They set out to give us a proof and they end by giving us a picture. We are about to plant our feet upon the solid rock of Q.E.D.,[1] and behold the rock turns to quagmire and we are knee-deep in mud and water and flowers. "Faces pale as the primrose with hyacinthine locks" are in our eyes; the woods of Tuderly breathe their mystic voices in our ears. Then suddenly we are recalled, and the thinker, austere, muscular, and sardonic, leads us on to analyse, to dissect, and to condemn.

Thus if we compare Hazlitt with the other great masters in his line it is easy to see where his limitations lie. His range is narrow and his sympathies few if intense. He does not open the doors wide upon all experience like Montaigne, rejecting nothing, tolerating everything, and watching the play of the soul with irony and detachment. On the contrary, his mind shut hard with egotistic tenacity upon his first impressions and froze them to unalterable convictions. Nor was it for him to make play, like Lamb, with the figures of his friends, creating them afresh in fantastic flights of imagination and reverie. His characters are seen with the same quick sidelong glance full of shrewdness and suspicion which he darted upon people in the flesh. He does not use the essayist's licence to circle and meander. He is tethered by his egotism and by his convictions to one time and one place and one being. We never forget that this is England in the early days of the nineteenth century; indeed, we feel ourselves in the Southampton Buildings[2] or in the inn parlour that looks over the downs and on to the high road at Winterslow[3] He has an extraordinary power of making us contemporary with himself. But as we read on through the many volumes which he filled with so much energy and yet with so little love of his task, the comparison with the other essayists drops from us. These are not essays, it seems, independent and self-sufficient, but fragments broken off from some larger book—some searching inquiry into the reason for human actions or into the nature of human institutions. It is only accident that has cut them short, and only deference to the public taste that has decked them out with gaudy images and bright colours. The phrase which occurs in one form or another so frequently and indicates the structure which if he were free he would follow—"I will here try to go more at large into the subject and then give such instances and illustrations of it as occur to me"— could by no possibility occur in the *Essays of Elia* or *Sir Roger de Coverley*.[4] He loves to grope among the curious depths of human psychology and to track down the reason of things. He excels in hunting out the obscure causes that lie behind some common saying or sensation, and the drawers of his mind are well stocked with illustrations and arguments. We can believe him when he says that for twenty

---

[1] *Quod erat demonstrandum*, Latin for "which was to be demonstrated."
[2] Possibly Nos. 18–23 Bloomsbury Square, London, which occupy the space of the Southampton House, built in 1657 for the fourth earl and demolished in 1850.
[3] The small town near Salisbury in Wiltshire where Hazlitt once lived.
[4] By Lamb and Addison, respectively.

years he had thought hard and suffered acutely. He is speaking of what he knows from experience when he exclaims, "How many ideas and trains of sentiment, long and deep and intense, often pass through the mind in only one day's thinking or reading!" Convictions are his life-blood; ideas have formed in him like stalactites, drop by drop, year by year. He has sharpened them in a thousand solitary walks; he has tested them in argument after argument, sitting in his corner, sardonically observant, over a late supper at the Southampton Inn. But he has not changed them. His mind is his own and it is made up.

Thus however threadbare the abstraction—*Hot and Cold*, or *Envy*, or *The Conduct of Life*, or *The Picturesque and the Ideal*—he has something solid to write about. He never lets his brain slacken or trusts to his great gift of picturesque phrasing to float him over a stretch of shallow thought. Even when it is plain from the savagery and contempt with which he attacks his task that he is out of the mood and only keeps his mind to the grindstone by strong tea and sheer force of will we still find him mordant and searching and acute. There is a stir and trouble, a vivacity and conflict in his essays as if the very contrariety of his gifts kept him on the stretch. He is always hating, loving, thinking, and suffering. He could never come to terms with authority or doff his own idiosyncrasy in deference to opinion. Thus chafed and goaded the level of his essays is extraordinarily high. Often dry, garish in their bright imagery, monotonous in the undeviating energy of their rhythm—for Hazlitt believed too implicitly in his own saying, "mediocrity, insipidity, want of character, is the great fault," to be an easy writer to read for long at a stretch—there is scarcely an essay without its stress of thought, its thrust of insight, its moment of penetration. His pages are full of fine sayings and unexpected turns and independence and originality. "All that is worth remembering of life is the poetry of it." "If the truth were known, the most disagreeable people are the most amiable." "You will hear more good things on the outside of a stagecoach from London to Oxford, than if you were to pass a twelve-month with the undergraduates or heads of colleges of that famous University." We are constantly plucked at by sayings that we would like to put by to examine later.

But besides the volumes of Hazlitt's essays there are the volumes of Hazlitt's criticism. In one way or another, either as lecturer or reviewer, Hazlitt strode through the greater part of English literature and delivered his opinion of the majority of famous books. His criticism has the rapidity and the daring, if it has also the looseness and the roughness, which arise from the circumstances in which it was written. He must cover a great deal of ground, make his points clear to an audience not of readers but of listeners, and has time only to point to the tallest towers and the brightest pinnacles in the landscape. But even in his most perfunctory criticism of books we feel that faculty for seizing on the important and indicating the main outline which learned critics often lose and timid critics never acquire. He is one of those rare critics who have thought so much that they can dispense with reading. It matters very little that Hazlitt had read only one poem by Donne;° that he found Shakespeare's sonnets unintelligible; that he never read a book through after he was thirty; that he came indeed to dislike reading altogether. What he had read he had read with fervour. And since in his view it was the duty of a critic to "reflect the colours, the light and shade, the soul and body of a work," appetite, gusto, enjoyment were far more important than analytic subtlety or prolonged and extensive study. To communicate his own fervour was his aim. Thus he first cuts out with vigorous and direct strokes the figure of one author and contrasts it with another, and next builds up with the freest use of imagery and colour the brilliant ghost that the book has left glimmering in his mind. The poem is re-created in glowing phrases—"A rich distilled perfume emanates from it like the breath of genuis; a golden cloud envelops it; a honeyed paste of poetic diction encrusts it, like the candied coat of the auricula."[1] But since the analyst in Hazlitt is never far from the surface, this painter's imagery is kept in check by a nervous sense of the hard and lasting in literature, of what a book means and where it should be placed, which models his enthusiasm and gives it angle and outline. He singles out the peculiar quality of his author and stamps it vigorously. There is the "deep, internal, sustained sentiment" of Chaucer; "Crabbe[2] is the only poet who has attempted and succeeded in the *still life* of tragedy." There is nothing flabby, weak, or merely ornamental in his criticism of Scott°—sense and enthusiasm run hand in hand. And if such criticism is the reverse of final, if it is initiatory and inspiring rather than conclusive and complete, there is something to be said for the critic who starts the reader on a journey and fires him with a phrase to shoot off on adventures of his own. If one needs an incentive to read Burke,° what is better than "Burke's style was forked and playful like the lightning, crested like the serpent"? Or again, should one be trembling on the brink of a dusty folio, the following passage is enough to plunge one in midstream:

> It is delightful to repose on the wisdom of the ancients; to have some great name at hand, besides one's own initials always staring one in the face; to travel out of one's self into the Chaldee, Hebrew, and Egyptian characters; to have the palm-trees waving mystically in the margin of the page, and the camels moving slowly on in the distance of three thousand years. In that dry desert of learning, we gather strength and patience, and a strange and insatiable thirst of knowledge. The ruined monuments of antiquity are also there, and the fragments of buried cities (under which the adder lurks) and cool springs, and green sunny spots, and the whirlwind and the lion's roar, and the shadow of angelic wings.

Needless to say that is not criticism. It is sitting in an armchair and gazing into the fire, and building up image after image of what one has seen in a book. It is loving and taking the liberties of a lover. It is being Hazlitt.

But it is likely Hazlitt will survive not in his lectures, nor in his travels, nor in his *Life of Napoleon*, nor in his *Conversations of Northcote*, full as they are of energy and integrity, of broken and fitful splendour and shadowed with the shape of some vast unwritten book that looms on the horizon. He will live in a volume of essays in which is distilled all those powers that are dissipated and distracted elsewhere, where the parts of his complex and tortured spirit come together in a

---

[1]A species of primrose, from the Latin for "little ear."

[2]George (1754–1832), English poet and physician, friend of Burke's.° Crabbe wrote *The Village*, a grim depiction of rustic life, in response to Goldsmith's° idealized *Deserted Village*.

truce of amity and concord. Perhaps a fine day was needed, or a game of fives[1] or a long walk in the country, to bring about this consummation. The body has a large share in everything that Hazlitt writes. Then a mood of intense and spontaneous reverie came over him; he soared into what Patmore° called "a calm so pure and serene that one did not like to interrupt it." His brain worked smoothly and swiftly and without consciousness of its own operations; the pages dropped without an erasure from his pen. Then his mind ranged in a rhapsody of well-being over books and love, over the past and its beauty, the present and its comfort, and the future that would bring a partridge hot from the oven or a dish of sausages sizzling in the pan.

> I look out of my window and see that a shower has just fallen: the fields look green after it, and a rosy cloud hangs over the brow of the hill; a lily expands its petals in the moisture, dressed in its lovely green and white; a shepherd-boy has just brought some pieces of turf with daisies and grass for his young mistress to make a bed for her skylark, not doomed to dip his wings in the dappled dawn—my cloudy thoughts draw off, the storm of angry politics has blown over—Mr. Blackwood,[2] I am yours—Mr. Croker,[3] my service to you—Mr. T. Moore,[4] I am alive and well.

There is then no division, no discord, no bitterness. The different faculties work in harmony and unit. Sentence follows sentence with the healthy ring and chime of a blacksmith's hammer on the anvil; the words glow and the sparks fly; gently they fade and the essay is over. And as his writing had such passages of inspired description, so, too, his life had its seasons of intense enjoyment. When he lay dying a hundred years ago in a lodging in Soho his voice rang out with the old pugnacity and conviction: "Well, I have had a happy life." One has only to read him to believe it. ✒

The Death of the Moth[5]

Moths that fly by day are not properly to be called moths; they do not excite that pleasant sense of dark autumn nights and ivy-blossom which the commonest yellow-underwing asleep in the shadow of the curtain never fails to rouse in us. They are hybrid creatures, neither gay like butterflies nor sombre like their own species. Nevertheless the present specimen, with his narrow hay-coloured wings, fringed with a tassel of the same colour, seemed to be content with life. It was a

---

[1]A game for two or four people played by using the hand to hit a hard ball against the front wall of a three-sided court.

[2]William (1776–1834), founder and publisher of *Blackwood's Magazine*.

[3]John Wilson (1780–1857), secretary to the Admiralty (1810–1830), British Tory politician who attacked Keats's° *Endymion* in the *Quarterly Review* in 1818.

[4]Thomas (1779–1852), popular Irish poet and lawyer who wrote *Irish Melodies*, a group of lyrics set to music by John Stevenson, as well as a biography of his friend Byron.°

[5]First published in *The Death of the Moth* in 1942.

pleasant morning, mid-September, mild, benignant, yet with a keener breath than that of the summer months. The plough was already scoring the field opposite the window, and where the share had been, the earth was pressed flat and gleamed with moisture. Such vigour came rolling in from the fields and the down beyond that it was difficult to keep the eyes strictly turned upon the book. The rooks too were keeping one of their annual festivities; soaring round the tree tops until it looked as if a vast net with thousands of black knots in it had been cast up into the air; which, after a few moments sank slowly down upon the trees until every twig seemed to have a knot at the end of it. Then, suddenly, the net would be thrown into the air again in a wider circle this time, with the utmost clamour and vociferation, as though to be thrown into the air and settle slowly down upon the tree tops were a tremendously exciting experience.

The same energy which inspired the rooks, the ploughmen, the horses, and even, it seemed, the lean bare-backed downs, sent the moth fluttering from side to side of his square of the window-pane. One could not help watching him. One was, indeed, conscious of a queer feeling of pity for him. The possibilities of pleasure seemed that morning so enormous and so various that to have only a moth's part in life, and a day moth's at that, appeared a hard fate, and his zest in enjoying his meagre opportunities to the full, pathetic. He flew vigorously to one corner of his compartment, and, after waiting there a second, flew across to the other. What remained for him but to fly to a third corner and then to a fourth? That was all he could do, in spite of the size of the downs, the width of the sky, the far-off smoke of houses, and the romantic voice, now and then, of a steamer out at sea. What he could do he did. Watching him, it seemed as if a fibre, very thin but pure, of the enormous energy of the world had been thrust into his frail and diminutive body. As often as he crossed the pane, I could fancy that a thread of vital light became visible. He was little or nothing but life.

Yet, because he was so small, and so simple a form of the energy that was rolling in at the open window and driving its way through so many narrow and intricate corridors in my own brain and in those of other human beings, there was something marvellous as well as pathetic about him. It was as if someone had taken a tiny bead of pure life and decking it as lightly as possible with down and feathers, had set it dancing and zigzagging to show us the true nature of life. Thus displayed one could not get over the strangeness of it. One is apt to forget all about life, seeing it humped and bossed and garnished and cumbered so that it has to move with the greatest circumspection and dignity. Again, the thought of all that life might have been had he been born in any other shape caused one to view his simple activities with a kind of pity.

After a time, tired by his dancing apparently, he settled on the window ledge in the sun, and, the queer spectacle being at an end, I forgot about him. Then, looking up, my eye was caught by him. He was trying to resume his dancing, but seemed either so stiff or so awkward that he could only flutter to the bottom of the window-pane; and when he tried to fly across it he failed. Being intent on other matters I watched these futile attempts for a time without thinking, unconsciously waiting for him to resume his flight, as one waits for a machine, that has stopped momentarily, to start again without considering the reason of its failure. After perhaps a seventh attempt he slipped from the wooden ledge and fell, fluttering his wings, on to his back on the window sill. The helplessness of his attitude roused me. It flashed upon me that he was in difficulties; he could no longer raise himself; his legs struggled vainly. But, as I stretched out a pencil, meaning to help him to right himself, it came over me that the failure and awkwardness were the approach of death. I laid the pencil down again.

The legs agitated themselves once more. I looked as if for the enemy against which he struggled. I looked out of doors. What had happened there? Presumably it was midday, and work in the fields had stopped. Stillness and quiet had replaced the previous animation. The birds had taken themselves off to feed in the brooks. The horses stood still. Yet the power was there all the same, massed outside indifferent, impersonal, not attending to anything in particular. Somehow it was opposed to the little hay-coloured moth. It was useless to try to do anything. One could only watch the extraordinary efforts made by those tiny legs against an oncoming doom which could, had it chosen, have submerged an entire city, not merely a city, but masses of human beings; nothing, I knew had any chance against death. Nevertheless after a pause of exhaustion the legs fluttered again. It was superb this last protest, and so frantic that he succeeded at last in righting himself. One's sympathies, of course, were all on the side of life. Also, when there was nobody to care or to know, this gigantic effort on the part of an insignificant little moth, against a power of such magnitude, to retain what no one else valued or desired to keep, moved one strangely. Again, somehow, one saw life, a pure bead. I lifted the pencil again, useless though I knew it to be. But even as I did so, the unmistakable tokens of death showed themselves. The body relaxed, and instantly grew stiff. The struggle was over. The insignificant little creature now knew death. As I looked at the dead moth, this minute wayside triumph of so great a force over so mean an antagonist filled me with wonder. Just as life had been strange a few minutes before, so death was now as strange. The moth having righted himself now lay most decently and uncomplainingly composed. O yes, he seemed to say, death is stronger than I am. ✿

Old Mrs. Grey[1]

There are moments even in England, now, when even the busiest, most contented suddenly let fall what they hold—it may be the week's washing. Sheets and pyjamas crumble and dissolve in their hands, because, though they do not state this in so many words, it seems silly to take the washing round to Mrs. Peel when out there over the fields over the hills, there is no washing; no pinning of clothes

---

[1]First published in *The Death of the Moth* in 1942.

to lines; mangling[1] and ironing; no work at all, but boundless rest. Stainless and boundless rest; space unlimited; untrodden grass; wild birds flying; hills whose smooth uprise continue that wild flight.

Of all this however only seven foot by four could be seen from Mrs. Grey's corner. That was the size of her front door which stood wide open, though there was a fire burning in the grate. The fire looked like a small spot of dusty light feebly trying to escape from the embarrassing pressure of the pouring sunshine.

Mrs. Grey sat on a hard chair in the corner looking—but at what? Apparently at nothing. She did not change the focus of her eyes when visitors came in. Her eyes had ceased to focus themselves; it may be that they had lost the power. They were aged eyes, blue, unspectacled. They could see, but without looking. She had never used her eyes on anything minute and difficult; merely upon faces, and dishes and fields. And now at the age of ninety-two they saw nothing but a zigzag of pain wriggling across the door, pain that twisted her legs as it wriggled; jerked her body to and fro like a marionette. Her body was wrapped round the pain as a damp sheet is folded over a wire. The wire was spasmodically jerked by a cruel invisible hand. She flung out a foot, a hand. Then it stopped. She sat still for a moment.

In that pause she saw herself in the past at ten, at twenty, at twenty-five. She was running in and out of a cottage with eleven brothers and sisters. The line jerked. She was thrown forward in her chair.

"All dead. All dead," she mumbled. "My brothers and sisters. And my husband gone. My daughter too. But I go on. Every morning I pray God to let me pass."

The morning spread seven foot by four green and sunny. Like a fling of grain the birds settled on the land. She was jerked again by another tweak of the tormenting hand.

"I'm an ignorant old woman. I can't read or write, and every morning when I crawls down stairs, I say I wish it were night; and every night, when I crawls up to bed, I say, I wish it were day. I'm only an ignorant old woman. But I prays to God: O let me pass. I'm an ignorant old woman—I can't read or write."

So when the colour went out of the doorway, she could not see the other page which is then lit up; or hear the voices that have argued, sung, talked for hundreds of years.

The jerked limbs were still again.

"The doctor comes every week. The parish doctor now. Since my daughter went, we can't afford Dr. Nicholls. But he's a good man. He says he wonders I don't go. He says my heart's nothing but wind and water. Yet I don't seem able to die."

So we—humanity—insist that the body shall still cling to the wire. We put out the eyes and the ears; but we pinion it there, with a bottle of medicine, a cup of tea, a dying fire, like a rook on a barn door; but a rook that still lives, even with a nail through it. ✎

---

[1]Wringing out of clothes.

E. B. White

(1899–1985)

Elwyn Brooks White was born in Mt. Vernon, New York, the last child of Samuel Tilly White, vice president and secretary of the Waters Piano Company, and his wife, Jesse Hart White. At the time of his birth, July 11, 1899, the household consisted of a maid, a cook, his parents, and five siblings: Marion, eighteen; Clara, fifteen; Albert, eleven; Stanley, eight; and Lillian, five. Elwyn's position in the family was particularly advantageous because, having attained a comfortable income, his father was finally able to spend time with his family and to provide his youngest child with such luxuries as the first bicycle on the block and later a canoe of his own to use during summer vacations on Great Pond, North Belgrade, Maine. From his brother Stanley, Elwyn learned how to paddle a canoe, cut with a jackknife, and read both books and nature. From Lillian he learned to laugh at the old-fashioned ways of their parents and to develop some social graces. But by the time Elwyn was twelve all his brothers and sisters had left home.

Like Mark Twain, E. B. White drew on his childhood for the materials in his fiction, *Stuart Little* (1945), *Charlotte's Web* (1952), and *Trumpet of the Swan* (1970), but White's experiences, unlike Twain's, included few of life's perils. All his siblings prospered, the older girls marrying at eighteen and twenty and producing numerous healthy children, the boys going off to Cornell, and finally Lillian leaving for boarding school and later for Vassar. White spent these lonely years skiing and playing hockey in the winter, biking, roller-skating, climbing trees, swimming, and boating in the summer. He sported with his dogs, Mac and Beppo, and made trips into New York City to visit the circus and the zoo. He watched eggs hatch, observed the activities of salamanders, caterpillars, snakes, frogs, pigeons, geese, turkeys, ducks, rabbits, and horses, and once, when he was sick, he kept a pet mouse.

Despite this apparently idyllic environment, White was a fearful child and became subject to attacks of panic and hypochondria in his teenage years, a condition that plagued him all his life. Some of his fear probably derived from his persistent hay fever and from the effects of elderly, solicitous parents and a circumscribed social life consisting primarily of Sunday visits to the homes of his married sisters. Although disasters never happened to him or his family, he knew that they could, that they had happened to neighbors and other people he read about in the newspaper. And he saw death regularly in the world of nature. His biographer, Scott Elledge,[1] argues that writing became for White a way of escaping and controlling his loneliness and fears.

He began writing early, winning a prize for a poem about a mouse from the *Women's Home Companion* in 1909 and two prizes for pieces about nature from *St. Nicholas Magazine* when he was eleven and fourteen. In high school he was assistant editor of the literary magazine, and he kept a journal of poems, both comic and serious, as well as reflections about the war, his desire for independence, and his uncertainty about the future. (His concerns about the war led him to register for the draft in September of his sophomore year of college at Cornell University—two months before the armistice.)

At Cornell he kept up his journal and his poetry, was a reporter for and later editor-in-chief of the student newspaper, the *Cornell Daily Sun*, and joined two literary groups. But his interests lay more in journalism and the practical requirements of what he called a "material world" than in the pursuit of literary criticism. (Although exempted from Freshman Composition, he got a D in his second semester in English.)

After graduation, White worked for a while in Manhattan as a reporter and writer of press releases until, in March of 1922, restless and uncertain, he set off in his Model T Ford for parts west. He and a friend, Howard Cushman, drove through Ohio, Kentucky, Indiana, Illinois, Wisconsin, North Dakota, and Montana, washing dishes, playing the piano, picking fruit, and sandpapering floors to pay their way. They reached Seattle in September; White stayed on for nine months, working as a reporter and writer of light verse for the *Seattle Times*. In June of 1923 he spent most of his money on a ticket to Skagway, Alaska, aboard the SS *Buford*, bound for Siberia and back again. At Skagway, the ship's captain gave him a job as saloon boy so that he could remain aboard through the return trip. After the boat docked, he took a train home to New York, still discouraged, still uncertain of his future.

Though unaware of the pattern himself, E. B. White was enacting the typical apprenticeship of the essayist, followed by men like Hazlitt and Twain before him. Like them, he eventually made use of his travels in his writing, publishing "Farewell My Lovely" in 1936 (based on a suggestion from Richard L. Strout), about the Model T, and "The Years of Wonder" in 1961, about the trip to Alaska. Back in Manhattan, White worked for an advertising agency while keeping up his journal and publishing a few poems

---

[1]*E.B. White* (1984). The facts in this biography come from Elledge's book.

in the *New York World*. Meanwhile, Harold Ross began publishing a new weekly magazine, *The New Yorker*; E. B. White bought the first issue the day it appeared, February 19, 1925. By 1927, *The New Yorker* was an established enterprise and E. B. White one of its main contributors; he wrote witty responses to comic headlines and mistakes that he compiled from newspapers across the country, as well as "Notes and Comments," essays, and light verse. That year also he met and fell in love with Katherine Sergeant Angell, seven years older than he and the literary editor of *The New Yorker*. After a long and complicated courtship, they married in November of 1929. Katherine had been increasingly unhappy in her marriage to Ernest Angell, a lawyer, but she had two children: Nancy, who was twelve when her mother remarried, and Roger, who was nine. In the end, custody was given to their father. The marriage was a success, marred only by Katherine's illnesses and White's attacks of panic and hypochondria. In December 1930 their son, Joel, was born.

With both partners working, the family prospered despite the Depression. By 1933 they were able to buy a waterfront farm in Maine, where White could indulge his three favorite passions—sailing, writing, and farming. That purchase set up an enduring conflict for White between the weekly deadlines of *The New Yorker* in the city and his longing for unlimited time to write in the country. Moreover, he felt confined by Ross's requirement that he use the editorial "we" in his unsigned essays in "Notes and Comments." Finally, in 1938, he agreed to write a signed monthly column for *Harper's Magazine* and moved the family to the farm. Katherine continued to work for *The New Yorker*, reading manuscripts in Maine, but she missed the staff and the activity of the city. Nonetheless, both were productive; by 1944, when the two edited *A Subtreasury of American Humor*, White had published twelve books, including *Is Sex Necessary?* with Thurber (1929) and *One Man's Meat* (1942), a collection of the essays from *Harper's*. While writing for *Harper's*, White developed the themes and the introspective tone, both wry and poetic, that have made him famous.

In 1943 the Whites moved back to New York City to help Ross with *The New Yorker*. White had become interested in the war effort and hoped to communicate his ideas about internationalism and a world government through his pieces in *The New Yorker*. One result was a book of his political writing, *The Wild Flag*, published in 1946. During the next eleven years, frequently troubled by Katherine's illnesses and White's depression and hypochondria, the couple traveled back and forth from city to country but kept their primary residence in New York. In addition to his regular contributions to *The New Yorker*, White wrote *Charlotte's Web* and, in 1954, published *Second Tree from the Corner*, a collection of his essays from *The New Yorker*.

In 1957, when Katherine gave up her full-time work at *The New Yorker*, the Whites moved permanently to Maine. While Katherine worked part-time, White revised Strunk's "little book," *The Elements of Style* (1959). By this time the family had a combined total of nine grandchildren and a handsome income from White's best-selling children's books. In 1961 poor health forced Katherine to retire from her editorial work; though increasingly ill, she continued to help her husband and work on her garden until her death in 1977.

From his farmhouse, enlarged over the years to eleven rooms on forty acres of land, White continued to write his *New Yorker* essays, collected in *The Points of My Compass* (1962), *An E. B. White Reader* (1966), *Essays of E. B. White* (1977), *Poems and Sketches* (1981), and a reissue of *One Man's Meat* with an introduction (1982). Although he received honorary degrees from the University of Maine, Dartmouth, Yale, Bowdoin, Harvard, and Colby, his highest recognition was a Pulitzer citation in 1978 for excellence in writing. White spent his last years enjoying visits with his family, writing letters to friends, doing his farm chores, sailing, and watching the sea.

White's prose style, informal, often intimate and humorous, recalls the style of Montaigne. His introspection, his intense love of life, and his preoccupation with time also recall the prose of William Hazlitt and Charles Lamb. Less literary than Hazlitt, White nonetheless practices the plain style, creating affecting metaphors from the social and physical world around him, from the fashions of wartime Paris and the painted pinecones of Florida. Like Lamb, he depends for his success on the strength of his admittedly solipsistic narrative voice. And, like Lamb, he reveals prejudices. But, unlike Lamb, White uses his writing to draw attention to injustice and to prod his own conscience. He also uses it to transform his persistent bouts of hypochondria into wry comedy, balancing the disarray of his emotions with the ordered cycles of nature to create poignant reminders of the brevity and the joy of life.

This sentence from "The Ring of Time," in which White describes a circus rider's handling of the broken strap of her bathing suit, shows the wealth he can reveal in the simplest of actions: "She just rolled the strap into a neat ball and stowed it inside her bodice while the horse rocked and rolled beneath her in dutiful innocence." The sexually suggestive situation, the disposal of the broken strap belonging to an attractive young girl, is comically deflected first by the verb *stowed*, suggestive of camp gear, then by the old-fashioned term *bodice* for the area of storage, and finally by the words *dutiful innocence*, wittily ascribed to the horse. All the while the horse is rocking and rolling "beneath her." With the words *rocked and rolled*, *just*, and *neat*, White adapts the colloquial language of his subject, a fifties teenager, a practice generally not recommended by Strunk and White. Yet it is precisely these words that convey the matter-of-fact control the girl exerts over this potentially embarrassing situation. As White reflects on this scene, he considers the youth of the performer, the brevity of time, and the polished enchantment of art, investing her simple act with profound meaning and a wide range of emotions. ✐

Memoirs of a Master[1]

There were always servants in my father's house, and now there are servants in mine. This morning, from a vantage point in the upstairs hall of my house in the city, I counted five. We have a cook, a chambermaid-and-waitress, a nurse, a laundress, and a furnace man. There are times when amity and peace brood over the home, when the servants remain with us and I begin to have a bowing acquaintance with some of them. There are other periods when the arrivals and departures are frequent and dramatic, and the house takes on the momentous character of the North Beach Airport.

Whenever a new servant is due to arrive, my wife and I always prepare the room for her with our own hands—with a sort of loving suspicion, as you might make a nest for a litter of lion cubs. I have just this minute come from the top floor, where we are fixing up a room for an incoming cook. Her name is said to be Gloria. It sounds implausible; but to me, an old master, nothing is impossible, not even a cook named Gloria. Nothing is even remotely unlikely. I await Gloria with head held high. The encounter with Gloria's bedroom suite, however, has exhausted me; and as I sit here on my study couch, I feel a great wave of fatigue engulf me—the peculiar weariness that afflicts a man who has always had everything done for him. I call it *Meisterschmerz*.[2] I realize that I am not getting any younger and that the day may come when I shall no longer have the physical stamina to be waited on hand and foot by a corps of well-trained domestics.

When bachelors enjoy a reverie, I understand that all the girls of their past float before their eyes in rings of smoke from their pipe. My benedictine[3] smoke dreams are full, not of past loves but of former servants. I dream of Alma, Estelle, Mrs. Farrell, Sylvia, Susan, Anna (who chose a brief interlude with us to have gallstones), Gaston and Eugénie, Elaine the beautiful, Zelda, Otto and Mildred, Mrs. Farnsworth, Joan, Claire. I like to sit here now and dream about them, count them over, like beads in a rosary, and think of all the bright, fierce times I have had with them, sharing their sorrows and their joys, their sickness and their health, taking their phone calls, filling in for them on their days out, driving them to distant churches in remote country districts. They have had some magnificent sicknesses, these old friends of mine, vivid bits of malaise, and truly distinguished indispositions. Every name calls up some bright recollection of bygone days.

Sylvia, for example. Sylvia to me means Christmas, and Christmas in turn means pneumonia. Someone in my family is always sick at Christmas, and when it isn't I, it is quite apt to be a servant. The year we had Sylvia, it was she. Sylvia

---

[1]Published in *The New Yorker*, December 1939.

[2]German for "master pain"; pun on *Mittelschmertz*, the pain of ovulation women sometimes feel at midcycle.

[3]From St. Benedict (c. 480–c. 543), founder of a monastery in Monte Cassino, Italy, and author of *The Rule of St. Benedict*, which established the principles of Western monasticism. It is also the name of a liqueur originally made by the monks.

had been looking a bit stringy for several days before the twenty-fifth, and we could feel something coming on. We nursed her along and refused to let her do any work, but her fever began on the twenty-fourth, with the early-afternoon carol singing, and rose steadily with the dusk. At last her conversation faded out and she just mumbled something and went to bed. I wasn't feeling any too fit myself, so at six o'clock my wife took first Sylvia's temperature and then mine. Sylvia had me by four and two-tenths degrees, and it was decided that *she* would be the one to go to the hospital. Our doctor verified this and mentioned pneumonia. I simply picked up the phone and said those magic words which I had read so many times on the cover of the directory: "I want an ambulance."

To my astonishment, an ambulance soon appeared in the street below. Police arrived with it, and the living room soon smelled pleasantly of balsam wreaths and Irishmen. The children, of course, adored having police on Christmas Eve—it gave a gala touch to the holiday—but the whole business presented special problems to us parents because all the gifts were hidden in Sylvia's room, and we had the devil's own time keeping the youngsters from running in and out with the cops.

None of us could think of Sylvia's last name, not even Sylvia; but I gave "Cassidy" to the ambulance doctor, and he bundled her downstairs to the waiting car, and away she went through the merry streets, myself following along afoot (with my low-grade fever) like one of the Magi, to attend to the admittance problem—which is part of the servant problem. I shall never forget the hospital's reception of Sylvia. To begin with, the place was jammed—the holiday rush—and the pneumonia ward was full to bursting. Sylvia was rolled into a downstairs corridor and parked there for about half an hour, while sisters of mercy flitted about conjuring up an extra bed. Finally it was arranged, and I accompanied Sylvia up to the ward to tuck her in and wish her a last Merry Christmas, although the poor girl was barely conscious by this time of what was going on. It was after nine o'clock, and the corridor was lit only by a small red night light. Just as our little procession groped its way into the ward, with its dim forms of sickness and the smell of calamity, we were welcomed by a woman's delirious scream.

"Sylvia!" the voice cried, in unworldly pain. "Seeelvyah!" And then a short, rapid "Sylvia, Sylvia, Sylvia," ending with a mournful wolf note, "Seeeeeeelvyah!"

It was the cry of a female who must have had a Sylvia in her family, or in her past, or both. But it was too much for my Sylvia. I think she imagined herself crossed over into purgatory. "Dear God!" I heard her mumble. "Dear God, get me out of here!" Feeling definitely pneumonic myself, and damn sorry for Sylvia and for the world in general, I trudged shakily home and spent the rest of the holy night putting together a child's fire truck, which had arrived from a department store that must have known of our domestic quandary, for they sent the thing in knockdown form—a mass of wheels, axles, bolts, screws, nuts, bars, and cotter pins.

Well, that was all a long while ago. Sylvia pulled through all right, but took a place in the country, where the air would be better for her. I thought, in those days, that I knew what sickness was; but I tell you now that nobody knows what sickness is till he's had an upstairs maid with gallstones. Anna had been with us only six days when her seizure came. In fact, I had never actually seen Anna—her paths and mine never crossed—and I knew her only by hearsay and by the sound of her typewriter tap-tapping on the floor above me. She was an elderly sort, my wife said, with eyes set too near together, like Franklin D. Roosevelt's. I inquired about the presence of the typewriter and my wife explained that Anna had taken up typing, hoping to improve herself. I couldn't very well object, because I had been up to the same trick myself for some years.

Anna, it turned out, was more than a typist—she was a Christian Scientist as well, and waited grimly through three hours of torture before letting out the yell that began our acquaintanceship. The yell came at four o'clock in the morning, and my wife and I sprang out of bed and instinctively rushed up one flight to see what was the matter.

"Mister," groaned Anna, recognizing me instantly as a friend, "please get me some morphine—it's my gallbladder!"

"Call the doctor!" said my wife. "And," she added peremptorily, "you better get dressed, you may have to go somewhere and you might as well be ready."

As I pattered downstairs, I remember trying to decide between my blue unfinished worsted (whose pockets contained everything necessary for a gallstone operation, such as money, fountain pen, and keys) and my brown tweed, which seemed a more workaday proposition but needed servicing. I knew the day would come and go before I slept again, and I figured I might as well be dressed correctly.

When the doctor arrived, I was fully attired in the blue and ready for anything. He seemed suspicious of Anna's familiarity with morphine, but admitted that her gallbladder might be on the blink and said we'd better get in touch with her relatives. Now, the relatives of domestics are an even more mysterious band of people than domestics themselves. I knew from experience that sometimes they didn't even have names. I also knew that they never had telephones, although they sometimes lived in the same building with a telephone. However, we grilled Anna on the subject of relatives, after the doctor had relieved her, and eventually, by an elaborate bit of telephoning through third parties, we dug up a beauty—a niece, Anna said she was. We asked her to come as soon as possible. She turned out to be one of the most beautiful women I have ever seen in my life. She arrived about nine that morning, with a fourteen-month-old child in rather bad repair. I let her in, and she immediately handed the baby to me. "Would you mind?" she said. "I have a terrible hangover and can hardly stand up. Isn't it a shame about Bumpo?"

"About who?" I asked.

"Bumpo," she said. "That's what we call my Aunt Anna."

"Oh, I didn't know," I replied. "Yes, it's a dreadful thing, with much pain. I'm sorry *you* don't feel good, either," I added courteously.

"I'll be all right as soon as I get a drink," she said. "I was on a bender last night after the show. I have a walk-on part in the 'Scandals,' you know. Have you seen it?"

"No, but I will," I replied.

Together we marched upstairs. The baby was heavy and soggy, a rather spiritless child. With him in my lap, I made a quick phone call to the office and told them that it didn't look as though I'd be in till afternoon.

I sometimes think that that morning, as I stood around pacifying the grand-nephew of a stricken domestic named Bumpo, my career as a master reached a minor pinnacle, achieved something like nobility. It didn't last, though. Anna had been gone hardly an hour when my wife and I found ourselves engaged in the cheap, vulgar trick of reading the diary which she had left behind her. We discovered it on her bureau. Our intentions were honorable enough at first—we were simply thumbing through it hoping to come across her niece's address, which in the confusion she had neglected to leave us. Gradually, however, we became absorbed; Anna's story began to grip us and sweep us along. Written in ink, in a fine, close hand, the diary covered a period of about two years and chronicled her goings and comings in two previous places. For the most part it was a rather dreary recital of a cheerless life. "The madam out this afternoon." "Getting colder." "Robert Taylor was at the Strand yesterday but didn't get to go." We waded, fascinated, through page after page of this commonplace stuff, and suddenly, as though we had been hit across the eyes with a board, we came upon the following terse item: "Phoned Milwaukee police today."

That was all there was to it. Nothing led up to it. Nothing led away from it. It stood there all alone, a tiny purple chapter in a gray little book. We still don't know what it was all about, and we still dream about it sometimes.

Anna had her stones out in good shape and soon grew fit again. We volun-teered to pay for the operation, but she refused financial help. Although we held the situation open for her, she never came back to us—which rather disappointed me, as I wanted to get to know her well enough to call her Bumpo. She is probably even now tapping away at her portable machine somewhere—a one-act play, perhaps, or a friendly note to the Department of Justice.

The presence in my house of a group of persons with whom I have merely a contractual relationship is a constant source of wonder to me. Left to my own devices, I believe I would never employ a domestic but would do my own work, which would take me about twenty minutes a day. However, all matters pertain-ing to the operation of the home are settled agreeably and competently for me by my wife, who dearly loves complexity and whose instinctive solution of any dilemma like marriage is to get about four or five other people embroiled in it. Although the picturesque and lurid role of householder saps my strength and keeps me impoverished, I must admit it gives life a sort of carnival aspect, almost as though there were an elephant swaying in the dining room. And then, once in a lifetime, some thoroughly indispensable and noble person walks casually into one's home, like Antoinette Ferraro, who proceeds to become a member of the family, blood or no blood. Antoinette has been fooling around our house for thirteen or fourteen years, and we would as lief part with her as with our own children. There is no danger of any separation, however. I am perfectly sure that when I draw my last breath, Antoinette will still be somewhere about the premises, performing some grotesquely irrelevant act, like ironing a dog's blanket.

Her name is really Antonietta, and I suspect that I had better not go on with these memoirs without taking her up in some detail, as she is the core of our domestic apple. Without her we should perish; and *with* her (such is the pressure of her outside obligations) we very nearly do. The other night, as my wife and I were sitting by Antoinette's side in the crowded auditorium of a trade school, watching her legitimate son Pietro graduate with honors in my blue serge suit, I had a chance to study the beatific face of this remarkable woman and brood about my good fortune in having encountered her in this world. She was born, I believe, in northern Italy, and speaks an impartial blend of Italian, French, and English. The only form of an English verb which appeals to her, however, is the present participle. In fact, she speaks almost entirely in participles, joining them by French conjunctions, to which she is loyal. If you ask if she'd be good enough to boil you an egg, her reply is simply, "*Oui*, I'm boiling." Once, on New Year's, she got a little tight on some mulled wine of her own concoction, and when we inquired of her next day if she had reached the Sixth Avenue "El" safely the night before, she blinked her long lashes shyly and said, "Oh, *oui*. Hah! I'm so running! Oh, my!"

Although she ostensibly works full time for us, and gets paid for it, this is merely a mutual conceit on our parts, for she has a full, absorbing life of her own—an apartment full of birds and plants, a son on whom she pours the steady stream of her affection, two boarders for whom she prepares two meals a day, and a thoroughbred Cairn bitch, which (like Antoinette herself) is forever being taken advantage of by an inferior male. The last time this animal had puppies, Antoinette brought one over, tenderly, for us to see. It was something of a monster, with chow characteristics and a set of inflamed bowels. When we offered our condolences on the continuance of the bitch's bitter destiny, Antoinette sighed. "*Ah, oui*," she said, dreamily. "Wazz that night on the roof."

I marvel that we go on paying Antoinette anything. It takes her two hours and a half to dust one side of a wooden candlestick, and even then she forgets to put it back on the mantelpiece and our Boston terrier carries it to the cellar and worries it in the coalbin. All we gain from the arrangement is Antoinette's rich account of the little adventure, including a perfect imitation of the dog. "He so hoppy," she will explain, "holding in mouth, like beeg cigar, *mais*[1] never dropping. Oh, he barking, he jumping. . . ."

It doesn't sound reasonable, I know, that we should pay anyone to sit around our house and imitate a dog, but we do, nevertheless. One morning she showed up, ready for work, accompanied by a sick bird in a gilded cage, her bitch (again pregnant), and her own family wash, which she always seems to do on our time. "Antoinette," said my wife, exasperated, "I honestly don't see how you expect to do anything for *us* today." Antoinette fluttered her wonderful lashes. "Is all right," she announced, "I'm doing." She never leaves any opening for you at the end of a sentence.

---

[1] French for "but."

She is a magnificent cook, easily the best we ever encountered, but, because our hours interfere with the proper functioning of her own domestic establishment, she has given up cooking for us and prepares food now only for our dog, kneading raw meat and carrots with kindly red hands and adding a few drops of "colliver oily" as cautiously and precisely as a gourmet fussing over a salad dressing. There have been times when I have looked into the dog's dish with unfeigned envy, for the instant Antoinette's hand touches food, it becomes mysteriously delectable. When I think of her risotto,[1] the tears come to my eyes.

I suppose our affection for Antoinette is temperamental: she likes the same things we do, has the same standards, reacts the same in any situation. She drinks moderately and likes to see other people drink and have a good time; consequently, when you ask her to bring you some ice, she does it with gusto and a twinkle in the eye. We usually manage to sneak her a glass of wine at night, when the other, more straitlaced members of the staff aren't looking. She smokes our brand of cigarettes, and is a chain smoker. She is fond of dogs, and indeed is the only domestic of my acquaintance whose first concern, when a dog is sick on the rug, is for the dog. I can't help liking that in her, even though I often have to clean the rug myself while she is comforting the animal. If you give her an old flannel shirt to launder, she lavishes all her love and skill upon it, and it comes back to you the same size as when it went to the tub. And then, Antoinette has that great Latin quality: she is a realist. Life is life, and it's the way it is. We had a manservant one time—a middle-aged Belgian who went hog wild one morning about ten o'clock, kicked pots and pans all over the pantry, and wound up by taking off all his clothes and running naked up and down the laundry, hoping by this sudden noisy revel to engage Antoinette's fancy. Neither my wife nor I was home, and when we apologized later to Antoinette for this unexpected bit of goatishness, she chuckled reminiscently. "La, that old fellow," she snickered. "Is nothing."

This same old fellow who was nothing was my first experience with a manservant. His name was Gaston, and his career with us was brief but colorful. He was one half of a "couple," and nobody has had any experience of a domestic nature till he has employed a couple. I was against the idea, but my wife assured me that a couple would be more economical because then the man could tend the furnace. Unimpressed by this flimsy bit of logic, I went to a nursemaid then in our employ and asked her if she had ever worked in the same house with a couple. "Oh, sure, I like it," she replied. "It's fun to come down in the morning and see which one has the bruises."

I really held out for quite a while against a couple.

"But why?" asked my wife doggedly. "What earthly reason is against it?"

"Well," I said, "I'm not going to have any man pussyfooting around this house, bowing and scraping."

"What's wrong with a man?"

---

[1] Italian dish of rice cooked in stock and seasonings and served with vegetables and grated cheese or chopped meat or seafood.

"Well, I don't know," I cried, "it's just sort of immoral, that's all."

"Immoral! What kind of crazy reason is that? It's no more immoral than having *you* around."

"You know what manservants do sometimes, don't you?" I asked.

"What do they do?"

"They steam open your letters. I saw one do it in the movies one time."

"Oh, my God," said my wife, and the talk ended. Gaston and Eugénie arrived the following Monday, in a cab.

They were, as I have said, Belgians. It seemed to me then, and still seems, an inspired bit of deviltry on my wife's part to engage a couple neither of whom could speak or understand English. I myself neither speak nor understand any other language. I can usually grasp Antoinette's meanings, because she puts in a liberal dash of English participles and nouns. Gaston and Eugénie spoke a mixture of French and Flemish, which gave even my bilingual wife a little trouble. In fact, until Gaston and I worked out a system of arm signals and small guttural cries, there was practically no communication between any of us in the home.

"He'll soon learn English," my wife assured me. And indeed the old fellow did make a stab at it. One evening, after a formal dinner party at which Gaston had officiated, we men stepped out into the garden for a smoke while the ladies withdrew, genteelly, to the living room upstairs. I was half through a cigarette when Gaston appeared in the garden, his bald streak shining in the moon, his gray curls festooned like tiny vines around his big, rascally ears. With his index finger pointing upward, he placed his heels neatly together, bowed, and said, "*Pardon, M'sieu. Café*[1] oops."

"How's that, Gaston?" I said sheepishly, while my fascinated guests watched. "*Café* what?"

"*Café* oops, *M'sieu*. Oopstair."

"*Ah, oui. Ah, oui,*[2] Gaston," I replied glibly, and led the gentlemen aloft to their coffee.

In the long roster of persons who have been attached at one period or another to our house, Gaston and Eugénie were far from being the most successful, but they were in many ways the most distinguished. The head of the employment agency where my wife found them had been most enthusiastic—they were the "perfect servants" and had been trained in the household of a Washington diplomat, an ambassador, I believe. I think my wife was just a shade impressed by this. Anyway, she failed to foresee the unhealthy effect it would have on Gaston to go straight from serving an ambassador to serving a screwball like me. I always felt rather sorry for the old boy, with his courtly manner and his bucktoothed little wife, who grinned and said yes even when she didn't understand what you said, which was always. The very first meeting between Gaston and myself was unpropitious and drab. I had a rotten cold on the Monday when he arrived, and spent the morning wrapped in an old button-up-the-front sweater in my third-floor

---

[1] French for "Excuse me, Sir. Coffee."

[2] French for "Oh yes."

study among some diseased house plants and empty picture frames. My wife left early in the morning, to be gone all day, and had given instructions to the breathless new couple to prepare for me, the unseen master, a lunch, explaining that I was unwell, in the chambers above, but would descend to the dining room for the noon meal.

"*M'sieu est* grippy," she said, in her best Flemish.

"*Oui, Madame*," Gaston had replied respectfully.

At one o'clock, I heard stealthy footsteps outside the door, then a rap. "Yes?" I said. The door opened, and there he was—a faded, gray little man, beautifully if unsuitably attired in tails. There was something tragic about the appearance, in my dismal doorway on a Monday noon, of a Belgian husband in evening dress. Against the peeling plaster walls, he looked wrong, and I knew then and there that our adventure with a couple was ill-starred. His skin was a cigarette-ash gray, and his bow tie was not much less dingy. Having been instructed by my wife never to address me in French or Flemish, and being incapable of announcing lunch in any other tongue, he simply raised one arm in a long, eloquent sweep toward the stairs and the smell of meat balls, and departed.

Lunch turned out to be a considerably gayer occasion than I reckoned on. I was joined at table by my small son, Bertrand, and our Boston terrier, Palsy. The latter, far from being depressed by the sight of a tailcoat at noontide, was exhilarated. He took up a wing-back position near the woodbox and executed a brilliant series of line bucks through Gaston's skinny legs. Ordinarily, Bertrand would have welcomed a free-for-all of this sort with howls of encouragement, but to my amazement the little boy sat spellbound and quiet, his steady gaze never wavering from Gaston's contorted features, his grave demeanor in strange contrast to Palsy's clowning. There was something genuinely compelling in Gaston's hauteur, and throughout the meal Bertie spoke only in whispers. I kept blowing my nose and scolding Palsy, but there wasn't much use in it. Finally I said to Gaston, "I am sorry, Gaston, that the little dog attacks you foolishly. Soon he will get to know you."

"*M'sieu?*" queried Gaston, trembling with incomprehension.

"The little dog," I said, pointing. "I fear he is a great trouble to you."

Gaston considered this speech carefully, searching for meanings. Then his features composed into a hideous smile. Picking up a meat ball between thumb and forefinger, he bent stiffly from the waist and handed it to Palsy, dreaming, I do not doubt, of his life in Washington, among decent people.

When we fired Gaston and Eugénie for Gaston's vile interlude in the laundry, he put on quite a scene, at first refusing flatly to accept the dismissal. I stood by while my wife alternately discharged him in French and translated his protests to me in English. We were, he said (and his great, melodious voice dipped deep into the lower register and then swooped up again like some dark bird), making the supreme mistake of our lives, dispensing with the services of himself and his so talented wife. We countered. Liquor, we said, had unquestionably debased him. Eugénie, hearing the word "liquor," nodded violently in agreement: liquor had made Gaston gross, but we should not concern ourselves with such harmless derelictions. Gaston grew more and more surly. A discharge was out of the question, and he was willing to lay the whole unfortunate affair to our inexperience as master and mistress of a household. "He says we're inexperienced, darling," said my wife.

This, for some reason, made me mad, for I remembered Anna's gallstones and a thousand and one other nights.[1] "By God, nobody's going to stand there and call me inexperienced!" I shouted. "You get out of here, you lecherous old scarecrow."

Half an hour later they were gone, but not before Gaston had got in the last word. He appeared on the second-floor landing with his trunk, set it down, and turned to salute us.

"*S'il faut partir, il faut partir. Pfui!*"[2] And with a quick little push, he launched the trunk into the air and watched it go roaring down to the floor below, chipping off pieces of stair as it went. Thus departed the perfect servant.

My wife is not easily discouraged, and Gaston and Eugénie were followed closely by another wedded pair, Otto and Mildred. They were young Germans, but they spoke English clearly enough — it just came natural to them. Otto was the *Turnverein*[3] type, big, blue-eyed, vain, and strong; well-being oozed from every pore. I always felt that he should wear shorts and a small rucksack when waiting on table. He loved moving heavy objects, because it showed off his strength, and he frequently went down cellar and threw boxes and crates around for no particular reason. When my Aunt Helen, who is a fairly fleshy old lady, returned to our house to convalesce after she'd had her appendix out, the problem came of getting her upstairs. "Dot's nudding," said Otto, appraising her quickly. And before any of us could stop him, he gathered Aunt Helen in his arms, scar tissue and all, and bounded up two flights of stairs with her. "So!" he said, plopping her down on the bed.

Otto loved to be in the same room with me. When he discovered I was a writing man, he determined to be of the greatest possible assistance to me, and was always busting into my study, clad in a zipper campus jacket and bearing a greasy clipping from the *Daily Mirror*. "Here's a tchoke for you," he would announce, handing me some unattractive oddity in the news, such as a cat mothering a baby robin. I had to give up trying to work at home during the time he was with us. I used to go to the reading room of the Public Library and sit with other escapists at long oak desks.

There is something about our household which invariably makes it seem like a comedown to servants after other houses they have been in. Gaston and Eugénie

---

[1]Allusion to the thousand and one tales in *The Arabian Nights* narrated by the fictional Scheherazade.
[2]French for "If it is necessary to leave, it is necessary to leave. Phooey!"
[3]German for "gymnastic club."

were gravely disappointed that our home wasn't an embassy. Otto was crushed when he found out I didn't own two Duesenbergs.[1] The man he worked for just before he came to us had two Duesenbergs, and Otto kept throwing them in my face. Even had I allowed Otto to drive my old Hudson sedan, which I never did, I'm sure it wouldn't have filled the void in his life. I think it was the humdrum of our home that drove him into aviation as a sideline. He managed to combine the two vocations charmingly—waiting on table here and spending his Thursday and Sunday afternoons off at an airfield in Flushing, taking flying lessons.

I asked him if it wasn't pretty expensive. "Na," he replied. "Ten dollars an hour, dot's all." His goggles, which he showed me one day, cost $27.50.

He progressed rapidly in the air. When he got so he could solo, he used to fly across the river and circle above our house, banking sharply at the prescribed altitude and showing off as much as he could without violating the Bureau of Air Commerce regulations. It was a perfect outlet for his Aryan spirits, but it was just one more straw for my tired old back. I got damned sick of hearing the drone of my employee's plane over my rooftop, and I never got quite used to having my Friday-morning coffee poured by a man lately down from the skies. I felt earth-bound, insignificant, and stuffy; and I began to compensate for this, unconsciously, in my attitude toward Otto.

"Well," I would say sourly, "I see you didn't break your neck yesterday."

Otto would laugh—a loud, bold laugh. "Na, I'm too schmart."

He *was* too smart, too. He left our household not as the result of any aerial mishap but because he couldn't get on with Bertrand's nurse, Katie, a pretty little Irish girl who called him Tarzan behind his back and was no more impressed by his gorgeous torso than I was.

I guess Otto's most notable quality was his readiness to answer all questions, at table. We first noticed this in him the day Aunt Helen went to the hospital for her appendectomy, which was very soon after Otto's arrival.

"I wish I knew how much the operation is going to cost," I remarked to my wife at dinner.

"Fifty dollars," replied Otto, coming up on my left with a dish of broccoli.

I was delighted at this sign of alertness in him and soon discovered that his store of information covered every subject. If a guest, for example, filled in a dull pause at dinner by remarking that she had found a terribly nice little flower shop but she couldn't remember whether it was on Fifty-first Street or Fifty-second Street, Otto would pipe up, "Fifty-first." If you speculated as to what theater a certain show was playing in, Otto would announce, "Broadhurst."

I never knew him to be right about anything, but he was an enormous comfort just the same. There are lots of times when you like to get a quick answer, even though it means nothing.

Another thing I rather enjoyed about Otto was his identification with the world of crime. Otto hadn't been with us three days when a jeweler's wife was murdered in a small suburban apartment building by a lover in a state of pique.

---

[1] Now defunct German luxury automobile.

"It's funny how dot feller got in her hallway," said Otto, taking a quick glance over my shoulder at the newspaper.

"What's so funny about it?" I replied. "He got in by pushing somebody else's bell and walking in when they clicked."

"Dot's what *you* think," said Otto. "But dot building ain't dot way. You godda be let in."

"How do you know so much about it?"

"I worked there."

It soon became clear that Otto had worked not only at the scene of that crime but at the scene of all crimes. While police wallowed in the darkness of an unsolved mystery, Otto and I walked in the light of exact knowledge. I consulted him whenever I was in doubt about any point, and always got a direct, clear answer.

Smoke dreams! How charmingly these dear people drift before me as I sit here with my pipe and my memories! I think back to the soft spring evening, ten years ago, when I was in the dining room lingering over coffee. The door opened and a young peasant woman entered, carrying a dustpan full of horse manure. It was some which she had discovered in front of the house, following the fitful passage through our street of a Borden's delivery wagon. The young woman, surprised to find me still in the dining room, blushed prettily, then carried her treasure out into the back garden and spread it tenderly on the exhausted little plot of soil which supported our privet bush.

The smoke curls in wreaths around my head. I see the thin, competent form of Mrs. Farrell, whom Antoinette always called Farola and who in turn called me Dearie. I think of Minnie, the Bahai, whose piety allowed her to partake of food only before sunrise and after sundown, and whose abstinence so weakened her that she used to run the eggbeater in the kitchen to drown out the noise of her lamentation. And of Mrs. Farnsworth, the aged eccentric, whom, in the course of a five-hundred-mile motor journey, I regaled with a dollar-and-a-quarter chicken dinner only to see her sweep the entire contents of her plate off into her purse, to take to the little dog that was the delight of her life.

I count them over, one by one. Today, however, I feel a great lethargy creep over me. Sometimes I wish I could relive all those strange and golden times; but there are other moments, when the radio is particularly loud in Francine's room and the *Meisterschmertz* is strong upon me, when I know that all I want is peace. ✒

Education[1]

I have an increasing admiration for the teacher in the country school where we have a third-grade scholar in attendance. She not only undertakes to instruct her charges in all the subjects of the first three grades, but she manages to function quietly and effectively as a guardian of their health, their clothes, their habits, their mothers, and their snowball engagements. She has been doing this sort of Augean[2] task for twenty years, and is both kind and wise. She cooks for the children on the stove that heats the room, and she can cool their passions or warm their soup with equal competence. She conceives their costumes, cleans up their messes, and shares their confidences. My boy already regards his teacher as his great friend, and I think tells her a great deal more than he tells us.

The shift from city school to country school was something we worried about quietly all last summer. I have always rather favored public school over private school, if only because in public school you meet a greater variety of children. This bias of mine, I suspect, is partly an attempt to justify my own past (I never knew anything but public schools) and partly an involuntary defense against getting kicked in the shins by a young ceramist on his way to the kiln. My wife was unacquainted with public schools, never having been exposed (in her early life) to anything more public than the washroom of Miss Winsor's. Regardless of our backgrounds, we both knew that the change in schools was something that concerned not us but the scholar himself. We hoped it would work out all right. In New York our son went to a medium-priced private institution with semi-progressive ideas of education, and modern plumbing. He learned fast, kept well, and we were satisfied. It was an electric, colorful, regimented existence with moments of pleasurable pause and giddy incident. The day the Christmas angel fainted and had to be carried out by one of the Wise Men was educational in the highest sense of the term. Our scholar gave imitations of it around the house for weeks afterward, and I doubt if it ever goes completely out of his mind.

His days were rich in formal experience. Wearing overalls and an old sweater (the accepted uniform of the private seminary), he sallied forth at morn accompanied by a nurse or a parent and walked (or was pulled) two blocks to a corner where the school bus made a flag stop. This flashy vehicle was as punctual as death: seeing us waiting at the cold curb, it would sweep to a halt, open its mouth, suck the boy in, and spring away with an angry growl. It was a good deal like a train picking up a bag of mail. At school the scholar was worked on for six or seven hours by half a dozen teachers and a nurse, and was revived on orange juice in midmorning. In a cinder court he played games supervised by an athletic instructor, and in a cafeteria he ate lunch worked out by a dietitian. He soon learned

---

[1]First published in March 1939.

[2]Reference in Greek mythology to the Augean Stables, left untouched for thirty years, which Hercules had to clean as one of the twelve labors imposed on him for killing his wife and children in a fit of madness induced by Hera.

to read with gratifying facility and discernment and to make Indian weapons of a semi-deadly nature. Whenever one of his classmates fell low of a fever the news was put on the wires and there were breathless phone calls to physicians, discussing periods of incubation and allied magic.

In the country all one can say is that the situation is different, and somehow more casual. Dressed in corduroys, sweatshirt, and short rubber boots, and carrying a tin dinner-pail, our scholar departs at crack of dawn for the village school, two and a half miles down the road, next to the cemetery. When the road is open and the car will start, he makes the journey by motor, courtesy of his old man. When the snow is deep or the motor is dead or both, he makes it on the hoof. In the afternoons he walks or hitches all or part of the way home in fair weather, gets transported in foul. The schoolhouse is a two-room frame building, bungalow type, shingles stained a burnt brown with weather-resistant stain. It has a chemical toilet in the basement and two teachers above stairs. One takes the first three grades, the other the fourth, fifth, and sixth. They have little or no time for individual instruction, and no time at all for the esoteric. They teach what they know themselves, just as fast and as hard as they can manage. The pupils sit still at their desks in class, and do their milling around outdoors during recess.

There is no supervised play. They play cops and robbers (only they call it "Jail") and throw things at one another—snowballs in winter, rose hips in fall. It seems to satisfy them. They also construct darts, pinwheels, and "pick-up sticks" (jackstraws), and the school itself does a brisk trade in penny candy, which is for sale right in the classroom and which contains "surprises." The most highly prized surprise is a fake cigarette, made of cardboard, fiendishly lifelike.

The memory of how apprehensive we were at the beginning is still strong. The boy was nervous about the change too. The tension, on that first fair morning in September when we drove him to school, almost blew the windows out of the sedan. And when later we picked him up on the road, wandering along with his little blue lunch-pail, and got his laconic report "All right" in answer to our inquiry about how the day had gone, our relief was vast. Now, after almost a year of it, the only difference we can discover in the two school experiences is that in the country he sleeps better at night—and *that* probably is more the air than the education. When grilled on the subject of school-in-country vs. school-in-city, he replied that the chief difference is that the day seems to go so much quicker in the country. "Just like lightning," he reported.

It is just a year ago as I write this that I made my spring visit to Peter Henderson in Cortlandt Street, home of Convolvulus Major[1] and the early pea. I bought nineteen dollars' worth of seeds, flower and vegetable. It took the clerk almost an hour, opening and shutting the white drawers, to fish them out; together we studied the list, checked it for errors. Carrying the bundle home in the subway, I was struck with how heavy the seeds were—they weighed as much as a time bomb.

---

[1]Genus of trailing and twining plants such as the morning glory.

A negro came into the seed store while I was there. He was in clericals[1] and seemed to be quite a fellow. "Give a penny to de Lawd!" he cried, addressing no one in particular. "Give a penny to de Lawd, who makes all dese wonderful seeds to jeminate!" He was a slick one and got a pretty good haul. I put all my money, however, into direct cultivation—the seeds themselves. They did well enough, and we are still eating them out of jars.

Now we're in New York again, for a visit, not just to consult with Peter Henderson but to get back into the good graces of the dentist and to catch up with the theater. I suppose there is no reason for not going to the dentist in the country, but teeth are like sunken reefs: you feel better about them if they are gone over by someone who possesses what the pilot book calls "local knowledge," someone who's been over them before. Also, dentistry is more impressive in town—what the rural man calls cleaning the teeth is called "prophylaxis"[2] in New York.

Quite apart from teeth and dramaturgy and seed buying, it is necessary to come up to the town after a long spell in the country, for a period of privacy and rest. I don't get enough sleep in the country, as the days are too short for my enterprises, with the result that I rise early, go to bed late, and in general prolong the waking hours. And of course there is no privacy in rural surroundings, where a man can't even blow his nose without exciting the community. I thought at first I was going to mind this limelight terribly, this being stared at: the men working on the road, looking up, watching, the men in front of the store, in dooryards, old men coming in through the dusk with an armful of stovewood, stopping in their tracks to watch the car go by, women tending the hens, everywhere the fixed eye. I discovered, however, that the situation was instantly relieved as soon as I acquired the knack of staring back. You've got to stare back. Besides, after you've lived in the country a while you learn that keeping track of the comings and goings of one's friends and neighbors is a very sensible thing indeed, and that it cannot be set down to idle curiosity. Not a car or team passes my door now but I look up, check its speed and direction, identify the driver if possible, and guess the errand. This isn't mere gossip hunting, it is a valuable personal intelligence service. I used to waste hours of time hunting up people who, if I'd used my eyes and ears, I should have known were some place else. It's like war: you've got to have a map with pins. The location of the mail truck, the progress of the snow plow, the whereabouts of the expressman and the fish peddler—such information becomes vastly important. I find that keeping abreast of my neighbors' affairs has increased, not diminished, my human sympathies (if any); and when I get up in the morning and spy one man heading south on foot with a dog and shotgun, and another heading north with a sick child in a blue coupé, the pattern of the day becomes clear and I can conduct my own affairs more wisely and usefully than if I lacked that knowledge. Of course one's horizon tends to close in: in New York I rise and scan Europe in the *Times*; in the country I get up and look at the

---

[1]The clothing of a clergyman.
[2]Preventative treatment for disease.

thermometer—a thoroughly self-contained point of view which, if it could infect everybody everywhere, would I am sure be the most salutary thing that could now happen to the world. My isolation is shortlived, however. An hour later I stop by the store to buy a package of soap chips and I hear the radio telling me the temperature in Providence, Rhode Island. Immediately the shell of my comfortable little world is rudely shattered and I shudder in sympathetic response to Rhode Island's raw mercurial destiny.

There was a time when only God could make a tree, but now John D. Rockefeller, Jr.[1] can do it too. Our visit to New York happens to coincide with the arrival of the great elms along Fifth Avenue, those lovely seventy-foot trees which are springing full grown from the pavement in front of Radio City. I attended the first of the eight miracles and felt like a character in the Old Testament. Nelson Rockefeller[2] was there wearing rubbers (although it was a dry night) and carrying a brief case. The last time I had seen him was at a groundbreaking, when Radio City was still a blueprint. He looked unchanged by the years (I hastily wondered if I did too) but was less camera-shy and more poised, now that the buildings were there, throwing their majestic weight in support of the whole visionary idea. The elm itself, at first horizontal on a truck, lay as though dead, but soon managed, with the help of a winch, to sit bolt upright and look around. Mr. Rockefeller leapt easily to the bole of earth, and the photographers lay down on their backs on the sidewalk for the angle shot which was to distinguish their art. It was the first time I had ever seen a man lie down on Fifth Avenue, although I once saw a fellow down in a fit.

A woman, passing, seeing that somebody was up to the prank of setting out a tree in the shopping district, remarked that she thought it was a mighty silly thing, a tree. "What do they want a tree for?" she said. "It will just be in the way."

I think elm-birth is the prettiest fairy tale in the city's wonderbook, for the big trees are delivered at night, when earth hangs down away from the light and fowls are stirring on their roosts. In all the long swing of time there has never been a fortnight such as this—these midnights when late strolling citizens come suddenly on a giant elm, arriving furtively in the marketplace and sliding into position for early risers to discover on their way to work. ✐

---

[1](1874–1960) Son of the philanthropic oil-refining magnate. He took over from his father in 1911 and gave money to build the Riverside Baptist Church in New York City, restore colonial Williamsburg, Virginia, create Rockefeller Center, and fund many other philanthropical undertakings.

[2](1908–1979) Son of John D. Rockefeller, Jr. Nelson Rockefeller, a Republican, was governor of New York from 1959 to 1973 and vice president of the United States from 1974 to 1977.

Freedom[1]

I have often noticed on my trips up to the city that people have recut their clothes to follow the fashion. On my last trip, however, it seemed to me that people had remodeled their ideas too—taken in their convictions a little at the waist, shortened the sleeves of their resolve, and fitted themselves out in a new intellectual ensemble copied from a smart design out of the very latest page of history. It seemed to me they had strung along with Paris[2] a little too long.

I confess to a disturbed stomach. I feel sick when I find anyone adjusting his mind to the new tyranny which is succeeding abroad. Because of its fundamental strictures, fascism does not seem to me to admit of any compromise or any rationalization, and I resent the patronizing air of persons who find in my plain belief in freedom a sign of immaturity. If it is boyish to believe that a human being should live free, then I'll gladly arrest my development and let the rest of the world grow up.

I shall report some of the strange remarks I heard in New York. One man told me that he thought perhaps the Nazi ideal was a sounder ideal than our constitutional system "because have you ever noticed what fine alert young faces the young German soldiers have in the newsreel?" He added: "Our American youngsters spend all their time at the movies—they're a mess." That was his summation of the case, his interpretation of the new Europe. Such a remark leaves me pale and shaken. If it represents the peak of our intelligence, then the steady march of despotism will not receive any considerable setback at our shores.

Another man informed me that our democratic notion of popular government was decadent and not worth bothering about—"because England is really rotten and the industrial towns there are a disgrace." That was the only reason he gave for the hopelessness of democracy; and he seemed mightily pleased with himself, as though he were more familiar than most with the anatomy of decadence, and had detected subtler aspects of the situation than were discernible to the rest of us.

Another man assured me that anyone who took *any* kind of government seriously was a gullible fool. You could be sure, he said, that there is nothing but corruption "because of the way Clemenceau acted at Versailles."[3] He said it didn't make any difference really about this war. It was just another war. Having relieved himself of this majestic bit of reasoning, he subsided.

---

[1]First published in July 1940.

[2]In July 1940, Marshal Henri Petain set up the Vichy government after the Franco-German armistice of June; the Allies never recognized this fascist government.

[3]Georges Clemenceau (1841–1929), twice premier of France (1906–1909 and 1917–1920) and leader of the French delegation at the Paris Peace Conference, opposed the Versailles Treaty because he thought it endangered the security of France against the Germans; he was nonetheless defeated in the next election for appearing lenient to the Germans.

Another individual, discovering signs of zeal creeping into my blood, berated me for having lost my detachment, my pure skeptical point of view. He announced that he wasn't going to be swept away by all this nonsense, but would prefer to remain in the role of innocent bystander, which he said was the duty of any intelligent person. (I noticed, however, that he phoned later to qualify his remark, as though he had lost some of his innocence in the cab on the way home.)

Those are just a few samples of the sort of talk that seemed to be going round—talk which was full of defeatism and disillusion and sometimes of a too studied innocence. Men are not merely annihilating themselves at a great rate these days, but they are telling one another enormous lies, grandiose fibs. Such remarks as I heard are fearfully disturbing in their cumulative effect. They are more destructive than dive bombers and mine fields, for they challenge not merely one's immediate position but one's main defenses. They seemed to me to issue either from persons who could never have really come to grips with freedom, so as to understand her, or from renegades. Where I expected to find indignation, I found paralysis, or a sort of dim acquiescence, as in a child who is dully swallowing a distasteful pill. I was advised of the growing anti-Jewish sentiment by a man who seemed to be watching the phenomenon of intolerance not through tears of shame but with a clear intellectual gaze, as through a well-ground lens.

The least a man can do at such a time is to declare himself and tell where he stands. I believe in freedom with the same burning delight, the same faith, the same intense abandon which attended its birth on this continent more than a century and a half ago. I am writing my declaration rapidly, much as though I were shaving to catch a train. Events abroad give a man a feeling of being pressed for time. Actually I do not believe I am pressed for time, and I apologize to the reader for a false impression that may be created. I just want to tell, before I get slowed down, that I am in love with freedom and that it is an affair of long standing and that it is a fine state to be in, and that I am deeply suspicious of people who are beginning to adjust to fascism and dictators merely because they are succeeding in war. From such adaptable natures a smell rises. I pinch my nose.

For as long as I can remember I have had a sense of living somewhat freely in a natural world. I don't mean I enjoyed freedom of action, but my existence seemed to have the quality of free-ness. I traveled with secret papers pertaining to a divine conspiracy. Intuitively I've always been aware of the vitally important pact which a man has with himself, to be all things to himself, and to be identified with all things, to stand self-reliant, taking advantage of his haphazard connection with a planet, riding his luck, and following his bent with the tenacity of a hound. My first and greatest love affair was with this thing we call freedom, this lady of infinite allure, this dangerous and beautiful and sublime being who restores and supplies us all.

It began with the haunting intimation (which I presume every child receives) of his mystical inner life; of God in man; of nature publishing herself through the "I." This elusive sensation is moving and memorable. It comes early in life: a boy, we'll say, sitting on the front steps on a summer night, thinking of nothing in particular, suddenly hearing as with a new perception and as though for the first time the pulsing sound of crickets, overwhelmed with the novel sense of identi-fication with the natural company of insects and grass and night, conscious of a faint answering cry to the universal perplexing question: "What is 'I'?" Or a little girl, returning from the grave of a pet bird leaning with her elbows on the windowsill, inhaling the unfamiliar draught of death, suddenly seeing herself as part of the complete story. Or to an older youth, encountering for the first time a great teacher who by some chance word or mood awakens something and the youth beginning to breathe as an individual and conscious of strength in his vitals. I think the sensation must develop in many men as a feeling of identity with God—an eruption of the spirit caused by allergies and the sense of divine existence as distinct from mere animal existence. This is the beginning of the affair with freedom.

But a man's free condition is of two parts: the instinctive freeness he expe-riences as an animal dweller on a planet, and the practical liberties he enjoys as a privileged member of human society. The latter is, of the two, more generally understood, more widely admired, more violently challenged and discussed. It is the practical and apparent side of freedom. The United States, almost alone today, offers the liberties and the privileges and the tools of freedom. In this land the citizens are still invited to write their plays and books, to paint their pictures, to meet for discussion, to dissent as well as to agree, to mount soapboxes in the public square, to enjoy education in all subjects without censorship, to hold court and judge one another, to compose music, to talk politics with their neighbors without wondering whether the secret police are listening, to exchange ideas as well as goods, to kid the government when it needs kidding, and to read real news of real events instead of phony news manufactured by a paid agent of the state. This is a fact and should give every person pause.

To be free, in a planetary sense, is to feel that you belong to earth. To be free, in a social sense, is to feel at home in a democratic framework. In Adolf Hitler, although he is a freely flowering individual, we do not detect either type of sensibility. From reading his book I gather that his feeling for earth is not a sense of communion but a driving urge to prevail. His feeling for men is not that they co-exist, but that they are capable of being arranged and standardized by a superior intellect—that their existence suggests not a fulfillment of their person-alities but a submersion of their personalities in the common racial destiny. His very great absorption in the destiny of the German people somehow loses some of its effect when you discover, from his writings, in what vast contempt he holds *all* people. "I learned," he wrote, ". . . to gain an insight into the unbelievably primitive opinions and arguments of the people." To him the ordinary man is a primitive, capable only of being used and led. He speaks continually of people as sheep, halfwits, and impudent fools—the same people from whom he asks the utmost in loyalty, and to whom he promises the ultimate in prizes.

Here in America, where our society is based on belief in the individual, not contempt for him, the free principle of life has a chance of surviving. I believe that it must and will survive. To understand freedom is an accomplishment which all men may acquire who set their minds in that direction; and to love freedom is a tendency which many Americans are born with. To live in the same room with freedom, or in the same hemisphere, is still a profoundly shaking experience for me.

One of the earliest truths (and to him most valuable) that the author of *Mein Kampf*[1] discovered was that it is not the written word, but the spoken word, which in heated moments moves great masses of people to noble or ignoble action. The written word, unlike the spoken word, is something which every person examines privately and judges calmly by his own intellectual standards, not by what the man standing next to him thinks. "I know," wrote Hitler, "that one is able to win people far more by the spoken than by the written word. . . ." Later he adds contemptuously: "For let it be said to all knights of the pen and to all the political dandies, especially of today: the greatest changes in this world have never yet been brought about by a goose quill! No, the pen has always been reserved to motivate these changes theoretically."

Luckily I am not out to change the world—that's being done for me, and at a great clip. But I know that the free spirit of man is persistent in nature; it recurs, and has never successfully been wiped out, by fire or flood. I set down the above remarks merely (in the words of Mr. Hitler) to motivate that spirit, theoretically. Being myself a knight of the goose quill, I am under no misapprehension about "winning people"; but I am inordinately proud these days of the quill, for it has shown itself, historically, to be the hypodermic which inoculates men and keeps the germ of freedom always in circulation, so that there are individuals in every time in every land who are the carriers, the Typhoid Mary's,[2] capable of infecting others by mere contact and example. These persons are feared by every tyrant— who shows his fear by burning the books and destroying the individuals. A writer goes about his task today with the extra satisfaction which comes from knowing that he will be the first to have his head lopped off—even before the political dandies. In my own case this is a double satisfaction, for if freedom were denied me by force of earthly circumstance, I am the same as dead and would infinitely prefer to go into fascism without my head than with it, having no use for it any more and not wishing to be saddled with so heavy an encumbrance. ✒

Sanitation[3]

The good world will be impossible to achieve until parents quit teaching their children about materialism. Children are naturally active and somewhat materialistic, but they are not incurably purposeful. Their activity has a fanciful quality, and partakes of the solid gaiety of Negroes, and is harmless although often destructive to property.

---

[1]German for "*My Struggle*" (1933).

[2]Immune herself, Mary Mallon (1870–1938), a cook in the New York City area, carried the typhoid bacillus to fifty-one people and caused at least three deaths.

[3]First published in *The New Yorker* in September 1940.

We teach our child many things I don't believe in, and almost nothing I do believe in. We teach punctuality, but I do not honestly think there is any considerable good in punctuality, particularly if the enforcement of it disturbs the peace. My father taught me, by example, that the greatest defeat in life was to miss a train. Only after many years did I learn that an escaping train carries away with it nothing vital to my health. Railroad trains are such magnificent objects we commonly mistake them for Destiny.

We teach cleanliness, sanitation, hygiene; but I am suspicious of these practices. A child who believes that every scratch needs to be painted with iodine has lost a certain grip on life which he may never regain, and has acquired a frailty of spirit which may unfit him for living. The sterile bandage is the flag of modern society, but I notice more and more of them are needed all the time, so terrible are the wars.

We teach our child manners, but the only good manners are those which take shape somewhat instinctively, from a feeling of kinship with, or admiration for, other people who are behaving in a gentle fashion. Manners are a game which adults play among themselves and with children to make life easier for themselves, but frequently they do not make life easier but harder. Often a meal hour is given over to the business of enforcing certain standards on a child, who becomes petulant and refractory, as do the parents, and the good goes out of the food and the occasion. It is impossible for a mature person to take manners seriously if he observes how easily they shape themselves to fit the circumstances. Ten or fifteen years ago it was customary in a restaurant to rise when someone approached your table. But when the Pullman-type booth[1] was invented men discovered they couldn't rise out of their seat without barking their belly on the edge of the table—so they abandoned the rule and kept their seat. This is most revealing. If a man were truly bent on showing respect for ladies he would do so even if it meant upsetting every table in the room.

I teach my child to look at life in a thoroughly materialistic fashion. If he escapes and becomes the sort of person I hope he will become, it will be because he sees through the hokum that I hand out. He already shows signs of it.

I guess there are two reasons for my not interpreting life more honestly for my son. First, it is too hard. (It's almost a full-time job to interpret life honestly.) Second, if you tell a child about the hollowness of some of the conventions he will be back in ten minutes using his information against you.

When three coasting schooners, one right after another, tacked into our cove and dropped anchor I knew there must be something wrong. In these days one schooner is news, three in a bunch are almost unheard of. It soon was apparent that the vessels were dude-carriers. Their decks, instead of being loaded with pulp wood, held that most precious freight—men and women on excursion. I rowed out into the cove to see the sights and was invited aboard one of the vessels by an

---

[1] Restaurant booths that resembled the narrow individual accommodations for sleeping in a railway carriage.

enthusiastic old sea dog who, after three full days of life afloat, was bursting with information of a feverishly nautical character. He kept tying knots in things, and rushed me all over the little ship, above and below, showing off its rude appointments and instructing me in the proper handling of a coasting schooner in fair weather and foul, including the management of a sail which he called the "jib flapsail." The schooners' yawl boats were busy taking passengers ashore for a lobster dinner on the beach, and our usually quiet cove, whose only regular night visitors are myself and a great blue heron, was soon gay with the vagrant screams and cries of persons temporarily removed from their normal environment.

I was told that the schooners were all owned by the same man—he has five or six of them and is buying others as fast as he can find them. Dude business is good. Not much has to be done to the ships—some bunks built into the hold, a toilet installed, a new sail or two, and some paint. They are old boats, most of them, but plenty good enough for summertime cruising, and are competently sailed by Maine captains, who accept the arrival of vacationers on their foredeck with the same stoical reserve with which they accept fog on a flood tide at evening.

The invasion of western ranches and eastern schooners by paying guests who are neither cowboys nor sailors is an American phenomenon which we have grown used to. Some of the ranches have even moved east, to be nearer their cash customers. It's hard to say why the spectacle is saddening to the spirit, but there is no denying the way I feel when I see a coaster that has lost her legitimate deckload and acquired a new crew of part-time gypsies. There is nothing wrong about it—anybody who is having a good time can't be wrong—yet the eternal quest for the romantic past which lives in the minds of men and causes them to strike attitudes of hardihood in clothes that don't quite fit them is so obviously a quest for the unattainable. And it ends so abruptly in reality. A dude, at best, is merely an inexperienced actor in the revival of an old melodrama.

One change which has come about since the World War is the change in people's feelings about dachshunds. I remember that in the last war if a man owned a dachshund he was suspected of being pro-German. The growth in popularity of the standard breeds has brought about a spirit of tolerance, almost a spirit of understanding. My neighbors here in the country don't seem to attach any dark significance to our dachshunds, Fred and Minnie. In this war if you own a dachshund people don't think you are pro-Nazi; they just think you are eccentric.

If there was a shadow of a doubt about my Americanism, on account of the dachshunds, it was completely dispelled in the town hall the other night when I won a wire-haired fox terrier puppy on a twenty-five-cent lottery ticket. Everyone knows that a man's allegiance belongs to the country where the jackpot is.

In a news broadcast the other morning, I heard a minor item which has stuck in my mind. The reporter said that the Nazis were "re-Germanizing" the land of Alsace, eliminating all French influence. He mentioned some rules which had been made to this end: Alsation men named Henri would have to write their name Henrich, and all inscriptions on tombstones would have to be in German. It seemed to me that the German ideal of purity had suddenly met its match, when it sought to "re-Germanize" not only the quick Alsatians but also the old bones in the cemeteries. To say that a man shall remember his dead in German is like saying that he shall perspire in German, or taste his spit in German. I doubt that the memory of the dead is capable of revision at the caprice of a conqueror.

Conquest in the disciplined German manner seems curiously lacking in the lustiness which is traditionally associated with victory in war. In earlier, more robust times, the victorious soldiery roared through town, drinking the bars dry and ravishing the girls. Today the new conquest seems to be mechanical, inhibited, orderly, and grim. A man back from ambulance service with the French army tells me that the German soldiers he saw in occupied France were well behaved: they all had excellent cameras and went round taking pictures of everything in sight.

In Alsace, they not only snap pictures, they diligently revise the legends on gravestones.

I was spreading some poison in the barn the other day for mine enemies the rats, when I came upon an unopened copy of the *Boston American*, dated Sunday, October 31, 1909. It was a special "Achievement Number" and contained 128 pages—at that time the largest newspaper that had ever been published in New England. Probably there haven't been many bigger ones since, either. It contained fifteen sections, each one of them something of a journalistic nosegay.

By inquiring around I discovered that the paper was one which had been in possession of my wife's father. She remembers that, as a little girl, the *Boston American* was never allowed in her house; and apparently her father, true to his principles, had declined to open the Achievement Number which had been sent to him and which, we discovered, contained his picture along with the pictures of some other Boston industrialists of the 1900's. He didn't throw the paper away, but just set it aside, and it has moved about from garret to storage warehouse to barn for thirty years, while its achievements dimmed and its pages yellowed.

It made pretty good reading. In thirty years the greatest change has really been in our feeling about achievement itself. The *Boston American* of 1909 exuded a supreme sense of calm and pride in America. That is no longer a typical newspaper reaction. Even on that October Sunday in the proud and prosperous Boston of 1909, the news of the day failed somehow to corroborate the dream of achievement. Holdup men had victimized two ladies of Quincy. In South Braintree a young husband, after shooting his wife, had hurried to the cellar and slashed his throat. In Melrose a young boy ran stark mad through the streets, driven out of his mind by a thwarted desire to play on the Melrose High School team. And there was immorality in Scollay Square.[1] The leading story on Page One was the most sobering and contradictory of all—it was the account of the Harvard-Army game. Harvard had managed to win the game for the Achievement Number, but in doing so had broken the neck of Army's left tackle, E. A. Byrne, and the player had died on the field. ✐

---

[1]Once the red light district of Boston, the area is now Government Center.

On a Florida Key[1]

I am writing this in a beach cottage on a Florida key. It is raining to beat the cars. The rollers from a westerly storm are creaming along the shore, making a steady boiling noise instead of the usual intermittent slap. The Chamber of Commerce has drawn the friendly blind against this ugliness and is busy getting out some advance notices of the style parade which is to be held next Wednesday at the pavilion. The paper says cooler tomorrow.

The walls of my room are of matched boarding, applied horizontally and painted green. On the floor is a straw mat. Under the mat is a layer of sand that has been tracked into the cottage and has sifted through the straw. I have thought some of taking the mat up and sweeping the sand into a pile and removing it, but have decided against it. This is the way keys form, apparently, and I have no particular reason to interfere. On a small wooden base in one corner of the room is a gas heater, supplied from a tank on the premises. This device can raise the temperature of the room with great rapidity by converting the oxygen of the air into heat. In deciding whether to light the heater or leave it alone, one has only to choose whether he wants to congeal in a well-ventilated room or suffocate in comfort. After a little practice, a nice balance can be established—enough oxygen left to sustain life, yet enough heat generated to prevent death from exposure.

On the west wall hangs an Indian rug, and to one edge of the rug is pinned a button which carries the legend: Junior Programs Joop Club. Built into the north wall is a cabinet made of pecky cypress. On the top shelf are three large pine cones, two of them painted emerald-green, the third painted brick-red. Also a gilded candlestick in the shape of a Roman chariot. Another shelf holds some shells which, at the expenditure of considerable effort on somebody's part, have been made to look like birds. On the bottom shelf is a tiny toy collie, made of rabbit fur, with a tongue of red flannel.

In the kitchenette just beyond where I sit is a gas stove and a small electric refrigerator of an ancient vintage. The ice trays show deep claw marks, where people have tried to pry them free, using can openers and knives and screwdrivers and petulance. When the refrigerator snaps on it makes a noise which can be heard all through the cottage and the lights everywhere go dim for a second and then return to their normal brilliancy. This refrigerator contains the milk, the butter, and the eggs for tomorrow's breakfast. More milk will arrive in the morning, but I will save it for use on the morrow, so that every day I shall use the milk of the previous day, never taking advantage of the opportunity to enjoy perfectly fresh milk. This is a situation which could be avoided if I had the guts to throw away a whole bottle of milk, but nobody has that much courage in the world today. It is a sin to throw away milk and we know it.

The water that flows from the faucets in the kitchen sink and in the bathroom contains sulphur and is not good to drink. It leaves deep-brown stains around the

---

[1] First published in February 1941.

drains. Applied to the face with a shaving brush, it feels as though fine sandpaper were being drawn across your jowls. It is so hard and sulphurous that ordinary soap will not yield to it, and the breakfast dishes have to be washed with a washing powder known as Dreft.

On the porch of the cottage, each in a special stand, are two carboys of spring water—for drinking, making coffee, and brushing teeth. There is a deposit of two dollars on bottle and stand, and the water itself costs fifty cents. Two rival companies furnish water to the community, and I happened to get mixed up with both of them. Every couple of days a man from one or the other of the companies shows up and hangs around for a while, whining about the presence on my porch of the rival's carboy. I have made an attempt to dismiss one company and retain the other, but to accomplish it would require a dominant personality and I haven't one. I have been surprised to see how long it takes a man to drink up ten gallons of water. I should have thought I could have done it in half the time it has taken me.

This morning I read in the paper of an old Negro, one hundred-and-one years old, and he was boasting of the quantity of whiskey he had drunk in his life. He said he had once worked in a distillery and they used to give him half a gallon of whiskey a day to take home, which kept him going all right during the week, but on weekends, he said, he would have to buy a gallon extra, to tide him over till Monday.

In the kitchen cabinet is a bag of oranges for morning juice. Each orange is stamped "Color Added." The dyeing of an orange, to make it orange, is man's most impudent gesture to date. It is really an appalling piece of effrontery, carrying the clear implication that Nature doesn't know what she is up to. I think an orange, dyed orange, is as repulsive as a pine cone painted green. I think it is about as ugly a thing as I have ever seen, and it seems hard to believe that here, within ten miles, probably, of the trees that bore the fruit, I can't buy an orange that somebody hasn't smeared with paint. But I doubt that there are many who feel that way about it, because fraudulence has become a national virtue and is well thought of in many circles. In the last twenty-four hours, I see by this morning's paper, 136 cars of oranges have been shipped. There are probably millions of children today who have never seen a natural orange—only an artificially colored one. If they should see a natural orange they might think something had gone wrong with it.

There are two moving picture theaters in the town to which my key is attached by a bridge. In one of them colored people are allowed in the balcony. In the other, colored people are not allowed at all. I saw a patriotic newsreel there the other day which ended with a picture of the American flag blowing in the breeze, and the words: one nation indivisible, with liberty and justice for all. Everyone clapped, but I decided I could not clap for liberty and justice (for all) while I was in a theater from which Negroes had been barred. And I felt there were too many people in the world who think liberty and justice for all means liberty and justice for themselves and their friends. I sat there wondering what would happen to me if I were to jump up and say in a loud voice: "If you folks like liberty and justice so much, why do you keep Negroes from this theater?" I am sure it would have surprised everybody very much and it is the kind of thing I dream about doing but never do. If I had done it I suppose the management would have taken me by the arm and marched me out of the theater, on the grounds that it is disturbing the peace to speak up for liberty just as the feature is coming on. When a man is in the South he must do as the Southerners do; but although I am willing to call my wife "sugar" I am not willing to call a colored person a nigger.

Northerners are quitely likely to feel that Southerners are bigoted on the race question, and Southerners almost invariably figure that Northerners are without any practical experience and therefore their opinions aren't worth much. The Jim Crow° philosophy of color is unsatisfying to a Northerner, but is regarded as sensible and expedient to residents of towns where the Negro population is as large as or larger than the white. Whether one makes a practical answer or an idealistic answer to a question depends partly on whether one is talking in terms of one year, or ten years, or a hundred years. It is, in other words, conceivable that the Negroes of a hundred years from now will enjoy a greater degree of liberty if the present restrictions on today's Negroes are not relaxed too fast. But that doesn't get today's Negroes in to see Hedy Lamarr.

I have to laugh when I think about the sheer inconsistency of the Southern attitude about color: the Negro barred from the movie house because of color, the orange with "color added" for its ultimate triumph. Some of the cities in this part of the State have fête days to commemorate the past and advertise the future, and in my mind I have been designing a float that I would like to enter in the parades. It would contain a beautiful Negro woman riding with the other bathing beauties and stamped with the magic words, Color Added.

In the cottage next door is a lady who is an ardent isolationist and who keeps running in and out with pamphlets, books, and marked-up newspapers, hoping to convince me that America should mind its own business. She tracks sand in, as well as ideas, and I have to sweep up after her two or three times a day.

Floridians are complaining this year that business is below par. They tell you that the boom in industry causes this unwholesome situation. When tycoons are busy in the North they have no time for sunning themselves, or even for sitting in a semitropical cottage in the rain. Miami is appropriating a few extra thousand dollars for its advertising campaign, hoping to lure executives away from the defense program for a few golden moments.

Although I am no archeologist, I love Florida as much for the remains of her unfinished cities as for the bright cabanas on her beaches. I love to prowl the dead sidewalks that run off into the live jungle, under the broiling sun of noon, where the cabbage palms throw their spiny shade across the stillborn streets and the creepers bind old curbstones in a fierce sensual embrace and the mocking birds dwell in song upon the remembered grandeur of real estate's purple hour. A boulevard which has been reclaimed by Nature is an exciting avenue; it breathes a strange prophetic perfume, as of some century still to come, when the birds will remember, and the spiders, and the little quick lizards that toast themselves on the smooth hard surfaces that once held the impossible dreams of men. Here along these bristling walks is a decayed symmetry in a living forest—straight lines softened by a kindly and haphazard Nature, pavements nourishing life with the beginnings of topsoil, the cracks in the walks possessed by root structures, the brilliant blossoms of the domesticated vine run wild, and overhead the turkey buzzard in the clear sky, on quiet wings, awaiting new mammalian death among the hibiscus, the yucca, the Spanish bayonet, and the palm. I remember the wonderful days and the tall dream of rainbow's end; the offices with the wall charts, the pins in the charts, the orchestras playing gently to prepare the soul of the wanderer for the mysteries of subdivision,[1] the free bus service to the rainbow's beginning, the luncheon served on the little tables under the trees, the warm sweet air so full of the deadly contagion, the dotted line, the signature, and the premonitory qualms and the shadow of the buzzard in the wild wide Florida sky.

I love these rudimentary cities that were conceived in haste and greed and never rose to suffer the scarifying effects of human habitation, cities of not quite forgotten hopes, untouched by neon and by filth. And I love the beaches too, out beyond the cottage colony, where they are wild and free still, visited by the sandpipers that retreat before each wave, like children, and by an occasional hip-sprung farmwife hunting shells, or sometimes by a veteran digging for *Donax variabilis*[2] to take back to his hungry mate in the trailer camp.

The sound of the sea is the most time-effacing sound there is. The centuries reroll in a cloud and the earth becomes green again when you listen, with eyes shut, to the sea—a young green time when the water and the land were just getting acquainted and had known each other for only a few billion years and the mollusks were just beginning to dip and creep in the shallows; and now man the invertebrate, under his ribbed umbrella, anoints himself with oil and pulls on his Polaroid glasses to stop the glare and stretches out his long brown body at ease upon a towel on the warm sand and listens.

The sea answers all questions, and always in the same way; for when you read in the papers the interminable discussions and the bickering and the prognostications and the turmoil, the disagreements and the fateful decisions and agreements and the plans and the programs and the threats and the counter threats, then you close your eyes and the sea dispatches one more big roller in the unbroken line since the beginning of the world and it combs and breaks and returns foaming and saying: "So soon?" ✒

---

[1]Development.
[2]Fake Latin for "various gifts," that is, found coins.

Once More to the Lake[1]

One summer, along about 1904, my father rented a camp on a lake in Maine and took us all there for the month of August. We all got ringworm from some kittens and had to rub Pond's Extract on our arms and legs night and morning, and my father rolled over in a canoe with all his clothes on; but outside of that the vacation was a success and from then on none of us ever thought there was any place in the world like that lake in Maine. We returned summer after summer— always on August 1 for one month. I have since become a salt-water man, but sometimes in summer there are days when the restlessness of the tides and the fearful cold of the sea water and the incessant wind that blows across the afternoon and into the evening make me wish for the placidity of a lake in the woods. A few weeks ago this feeling got so strong I bought myself a couple of bass hooks and a spinner and returned to the lake where we used to go, for a week's fishing and to revisit old haunts.

I took along my son, who had never had any fresh water up his nose and who had seen lily pads only from train windows. On the journey over to the lake I began to wonder what it would be like. I wondered how time would have marred this unique, this holy spot—the coves and streams, the hills that the sun set behind, the camps and the paths behind the camps. I was sure that the tarred road would have found it out, and I wondered in what other ways it would be desolated. It is strange how much you can remember about places like that once you allow your mind to return into the grooves that lead back. You remember one thing, and that suddenly reminds you of another thing. I guess I remembered clearest of all the early mornings, when the lake was cool and motionless, remembered how the bedroom smelled of the lumber it was made of and of the wet woods whose scent entered through the screen. The partitions in the camp were thin and did not extend clear to the top of the rooms, and as I was always the first up I would dress softly so as not to wake the others, and sneak out into the sweet outdoors and start out in the canoe, keeping close along the shore in the long shadows of the pines. I remembered being very careful never to rub my paddle against the gunwale for fear of disturbing the stillness of the cathedral.

The lake had never been what you would call a wild lake. There were cottages sprinkled around the shores, and it was in farming country although the shores of the lake were quite heavily wooded. Some of the cottages were owned by nearby farmers, and you would live at the shore and eat your meals at the farmhouse. That's what our family did. But although it wasn't wild, it was a fairly large and undisturbed lake and there were places in it that, to a child at least, seemed infinitely remote and primeval.

I was right about the tar: it led to within half a mile of the shore. But when I got back there, with my boy, and we settled into a camp near a farmhouse and

---

[1]First published in August 1941.

into the kind of summertime I had known, I could tell that it was going to be pretty much the same as it had been before—I knew it, lying in bed the first morning, smelling the bedroom and hearing the boy sneak quietly out and go off along the shore in a boat. I began to sustain the illusion that he was I, and therefore, by simple transposition, that I was my father. This sensation persisted, kept cropping up all the time we were there. It was not an entirely new feeling, but in this setting it grew much stronger. I seemed to be living a dual existence. I would be in the middle of some simple act, I would be picking up a bait box or laying down a table fork, or I would be saying something, and suddenly it would be not I but my father who was saying the words or making the gesture. It gave me a creepy sensation.

We went fishing the first morning. I felt the same damp moss covering the worms in the bait can, and saw the dragonfly alight on the tip of my rod as it hovered a few inches from the surface of the water. It was the arrival of this fly that convinced me beyond any doubt that everything was as it always had been, that the years were a mirage and that there had been no years. The small waves were the same, chucking the rowboat under the chin as we fished at anchor, and the boat was the same boat, the same color green and the ribs broken in the same places, and under the floorboards the same fresh-water leavings and débris—the dead helgramite,[1] the wisps of moss, the rusty discarded fishhook, the dried blood from yesterday's catch. We stared silently at the tips of our rods, at the dragonflies that came and went. I lowered the tip of mine into the water, tentatively, pensively dislodging the fly, which darted two feet away, poised, darted two feet back, and came to rest again a little farther up the rod. There had been no years between the ducking of this dragonfly and the other one—the one that was part of memory. I looked at the boy, who was silently watching his fly, and it was my hands that held his rod, my eyes watching. I felt dizzy and didn't know which rod I was at the end of.

We caught two bass, hauling them in briskly as though they were mackerel, pulling them over the side of the boat in a businesslike manner without any landing net, and stunning them with a blow on the back of the head. When we got back for a swim before lunch, the lake was exactly where we had left it, the same number of inches from the dock, and there was only the merest suggestion of a breeze. This seemed an utterly enchanted sea, this lake you could leave to its own devices for a few hours and come back to, and find that it had not stirred, this constant and trustworthy body of water. In the shallows, the dark, water-soaked sticks and twigs, smooth and old, were undulating in clusters on the bottom against the clean ribbed sand, and the track of the mussel was plain. A school of minnows swam by, each minnow with its small individual shadow, doubling the attendance, so clear and sharp in the sunlight. Some of the other campers were in swimming, along the shore, one of them with a cake of soap, and the water felt thin and clear and unsubstantial. Over the years there had been this person with the cake of soap, this cultist, and here he was. There had been no years.

---

[1]Large brown insect (dobson fly) larva used as bait for bass.

Up to the farmhouse to dinner through the teeming, dusty field, the road under our sneakers was only a two-track road. The middle track was missing, the one with the marks of the hooves and the splotches of dried, flaky manure. There had always been three tracks to choose from in choosing which track to walk in; now the choice was narrowed down to two. For a moment I missed terribly the middle alternative. But the way led past the tennis court, and something about the way it lay there in the sun reassured me; the tape had loosened along the backline, the alleys were green with plantains and other weeds, and the net (installed in June and removed in September) sagged in the dry noon, and the whole place steamed with midday heat and hunger and emptiness. There was a choice of pie for dessert, and one was blueberry and one was apple, and the waitresses were the same country girls, there having been no passage of time, only the illusion of it as in a dropped curtain—the waitresses were still fifteen; their hair had been washed, that was the only difference—they had been to the movies and seen the pretty girls with the clean hair.

Summertime, oh summertime, pattern of life indelible, the fadeproof lake, the woods unshatterable, the pasture with the sweetfern and the juniper forever and ever, summer without end; this was the background, and the life along the shore was the design, the cottagers with their innocent and tranquil design, their tiny docks with the flagpole and the American flag floating against the white clouds in the blue sky, the little paths over the roots of the trees leading from camp to camp and the paths leading back to the outhouses and the can of lime for sprinkling, and at the souvenir counters at the store the miniature birch-bark canoes and the postcards that showed things looking a little better than they looked. This was the American family at play, escaping from the city heat, wondering whether the newcomers in the camp at the head of the cove were "common" or "nice," wondering whether it was true that the people who drove up for Sunday dinner at the farmhouse were turned away because there wasn't enough chicken.

It seemed to me, as I kept remembering all this, that those times and those summers had been infinitely precious and worth saving. There had been jollity and peace and goodness. The arriving (at the beginning of August) had been so big a business in itself, at the railway station the farm wagon drawn up, the first smell of the pine-laden air, the first glimpse of the smiling farmer, and the great importance of the trunks and your father's enormous authority in such matters, and the feel of the wagon under you for the long ten-mile haul, and at the top of the last long hill catching the first view of the lake after eleven months of not seeing this cherished body of water. The shouts and cries of the other campers when they saw you, and the trunks to be unpacked, to give up their rich burden. (Arriving was less exciting nowadays, when you sneaked up in your car and parked it under a tree near the camp and took out the bags and in five minutes it was all over, no fuss, no loud wonderful fuss about trunks.)

Peace and goodness and jollity. The only thing that was wrong now, really, was the sound of the place, an unfamiliar nervous sound of the outboard motors. This was the note that jarred, the one thing that would sometimes break the illusion and set the years moving. In those other summertimes all motors were inboard; and when they were at a little distance, the noise they made was a sedative, an ingredient of summer sleep. They were one-cylinder and two-cylinder engines, and some were make-and-break and some were jump-spark, but they all made a sleepy sound across the lake. The one-lungers throbbed and fluttered, and the twin-cylinder ones purred and purred, and that was a quiet sound, too. But now the campers all had outboards. In the daytime, in the hot mornings, these motors made a petulant, irritable sound; at night, in the still evening when the afterglow lit the water, they whined about one's ears like mosquitoes. My boy loved our rented outboard, and his great desire was to achieve single-handed mastery over it, and authority, and he soon learned the trick of choking it a little (but not too much), and the adjustment of the needle valve. Watching him I would remember the things you could do with the old one-cylinder engine with the heavy flywheel, how you could have it eating out of your hand if you got really close to it spiritually. Motorboats in those days didn't have clutches, and you would make a landing by shutting off the motor at the proper time and coasting in with a dead rudder. But there was a way of reversing them, if you learned the trick, by cutting the switch and putting it on again exactly on the final dying revolution of the flywheel, so that it would kick back against compression and begin reversing. Approaching a dock in a strong following breeze, it was difficult to slow up sufficiently by the ordinary coasting method, and if a boy felt he had complete mastery over his motor, he was tempted to keep it running beyond its time and then reverse it a few feet from the dock. It took a cool nerve, because if you threw the switch a twentieth of a second too soon you would catch the flywheel when it still had speed enough to go up past center, and the boat would leap ahead, charging bull-fashion at the dock.

We had a good week at the camp. The bass were biting well and the sun shone endlessly, day after day. We would be tired at night and lie down in the accumulated heat of the little bedrooms after the long hot day and the breeze would stir almost imperceptibly outside and the smell of the swamp drift in through the rusty screens. Sleep would come easily and in the morning the red squirrel would be on the roof, tapping out his gay routine. I kept remembering everything, lying in bed in the mornings—the small steamboat that had a long rounded stern like the lip of a Ubangi,[1] and how quietly she ran on the moonlight sails, when the older boys played their mandolins and the girls sang and we ate doughnuts dipped in sugar, and how sweet the music was on the water in the shining night, and what it had felt like to think about girls then. After breakfast we would go up to the store and the things were in the same place—the minnows in a bottle, the plugs and spinners disarranged and pawed over by the youngsters from the boys' camp, the Fig Newtons and the Beeman's gum. Outside, the road was tarred and cars stood in front of the store. Inside, all was just as it had always been, except there was more Coca-Cola and not so much Moxie and root beer and birch beer

---

[1]Member of a group of people living in the Central African Republic. The women were known for using disks to extend their lips.

and sarsaparilla. We would walk out with a bottle of pop apiece and sometimes the pop would backfire up our noses and hurt. We explored the streams, quietly, where the turtles slid off the sunny logs and dug their way into the soft bottom; and we lay on the town wharf and fed worms to the tame bass. Everywhere we went I had trouble making out which was I, the one walking at my side, the one walking in my pants.

One afternoon while we were there at that lake a thunderstorm came up. It was like the revival of an old melodrama that I had seen long ago with childish awe. The second-act climax of the drama of the electrical disturbance over a lake in America had not changed in any important respect. This was the big scene, still the big scene. The whole thing was so familiar, the first feeling of oppression and heat and a general air around camp of not wanting to go very far away. In midafternoon (it was all the same) a curious darkening of the sky, and a lull in everything that had made life tick; and then the way the boats suddenly swung the other way at their moorings with the coming of a breeze out of the new quarter, and the premonitory rumble. Then the kettle drum, then the snare, then the bass drum and cymbals, then crackling light against the dark, and the gods grinning and licking their chops in the hills. Afterward the calm, the rain steadily rustling in the calm lake, the return of light and hope and spirits, and the campers running out in joy and relief to go swimming in the rain, their bright cries perpetuating the deathless joke about how they were getting simply drenched, and the children screaming with delight at the new sensation of bathing in the rain, and the joke about getting drenched linking the generations in a strong indestructible chain. And the comedian who waded in carrying an umbrella.

When the others went swimming, my son said he was going in, too. He pulled his dripping trunks from the line where they had hung all through the shower and wrung them out. Languidly, and with no thought of going in, I watched him, his hard little body, skinny and bare, saw him wince slightly as he pulled up around his vitals the small, soggy, icy garment. As he buckled the swollen belt, suddenly my groin felt the chill of death. ✍

Book Learning[1]

Farmers are interested in science, in modern methods, and in theory, but they are not easily thrown off balance and they maintain a healthy suspicion of book learning and of the shenanigans of biologists, chemists, geneticists, and other late-rising students of farm practice and management. They are, I think, impressed by education, but they have seen too many examples of the helplessness and the impracticality of educated persons to be either envious or easily budged from their position.

---

[1]First published in *The New Yorker* in 1942.

I was looking at a neighbor's hens with him one time when he said something which expressed the feeling farmers have about colleges and books. He was complaining about the shape of the henhouse, but he wanted me to understand that it was all his own fault it had turned out badly. "I got the plan for it out of a book, fool-fashion," he said. And he gazed around at his surroundings in gentle disgust, with a half-humorous, half-disappointed look, as one might look back at any sort of youthful folly.

Scientific agriculture, however sound in principle, often seems strangely unrelated to, and unaware of, the vital, gruelling job of making a living by farming. Farmers sense this quality in it as they study their bulletins, just as a poor man senses in a rich man an incomprehension of his own problems. The farmer of today knows, for example, that manure loses some of its value when exposed to the weather; but he also knows how soon the sun goes down on all of us, and if there is a window handy at the cow's stern he pitches the dressing out into the yard and kisses the nitrogen good-by. There is usually not time in one man's lifetime to do different. The farmer knows that early-cut hay is better feed than hay which has been left standing through the hot dry days of late July. He hasn't worked out the vitamin losses, but he knows just by looking at the grass that some of the good has gone out of it. But he knows also that to make hay he needs settled weather—better weather than you usually get in June.

I've always tried to cut my hay reasonably early, but this year I wasn't able to get a team until the middle of July. It turned out to be just as well. June was a miserable month of rains and fog mulls. The people who stuck to their theories and cut their hay in spite of the weather, took a beating. A few extremists, fearful of losing a single vitamin, mowed in June, choosing a day when the sun came out for a few minutes. Their hay lay in the wet fields and rotted day after day, while Rommel[1] took Tobruk and careened eastward toward Alexandria.

The weather was unprecedented—weeks of damp and rain and fog. Everybody talked about it. One day during that spell I was holding forth to a practical farmer on the subject of hay. Full of book learning, I was explaining (rather too glibly) the advantages of cutting hay in June. I described in detail the vitamin loss incurred by letting hay stand in the field after it has matured, and how much greater the feed value was per unit weight in early-cut hay, even though the quantity might be slightly less. The farmer was a quiet man, with big hands for curling round a scythe handle. He listened attentively. My words swirled around his head like summer flies. Finally, when I had exhausted my little store of learning and paused for a moment, he ventured a reply.

"The time to cut hay," he said firmly, "is in hayin' time." ✒

---

[1]Erwin (1891–1944), German field marshal who commanded a division in the attack on France in 1940, led the Afrika Korps into Libya, where he was nicknamed "the desert fox" in 1941, and nearly took Alexandria, but who was overrun by the British at Alamein in 1942. He died when forced to take poison for his part in the plot on Hitler's life in July 1944.

Death of a Pig[1]

I spent several days and nights in mid-September with an ailing pig and I feel driven to account for this stretch of time, more particularly since the pig died at last, and I lived, and things might easily have gone the other way round and none left to do the accounting. Even now, so close to the event, I cannot recall the hours sharply and am not ready to say whether death came on the third night or the fourth night. This uncertainty afflicts me with a sense of personal deterioration; if I were in decent health I would know how many nights I had sat up with a pig.

The scheme of buying a spring pig in blossomtime, feeding it through summer and fall, and butchering it when the solid cold weather arrives, is a familiar scheme to me and follows an antique pattern. It is a tragedy enacted on most farms with perfect fidelity to the original script. The murder, being premeditated, is in the first degree but is quick and skillful, and the smoked bacon and ham provide a ceremonial ending whose fitness is seldom questioned.

Once in a while something slips—one of the actors goes up in his lines and the whole performance stumbles and halts. My pig simply failed to show up for a meal. The alarm spread rapidly. The classic outline of the tragedy was lost. I found myself cast suddenly in the role of pig's friend and physician—a farcical character with an enema bag for a prop. I had a presentiment, the very first afternoon, that the play would never regain its balance and that my sympathies were now wholly with the pig. This was slapstick—the sort of dramatic treatment that instantly appealed to my old dachshund, Fred, who joined the vigil, held the bag, and, when all was over, presided at the interment. When we slid the body into the grave, we both were shaken to the core. The loss we felt was not the loss of ham but the loss of pig. He had evidently become precious to me, not that he represented a distant nourishment in a hungry time, but that he had suffered in a suffering world. But I'm running ahead of my story and shall have to go back.

My pigpen is at the bottom of an old orchard below the house. The pigs I have raised have lived in a faded building that once was an icehouse. There is a pleasant yard to move about in, shaded by an apple tree that overhangs the low rail fence. A pig couldn't ask for anything better—or none has, at any rate. The sawdust in the icehouse makes a comfortable bottom in which to root, and a warm bed. This sawdust, however, came under suspicion when the pig took sick. One of my neighbors said he thought the pig would have done better on new ground—the same principle that applies in planting potatoes. He said there might be something unhealthy about that sawdust, that he never thought well of sawdust.

It was about four o'clock in the afternoon when I first noticed that there was something wrong with the pig. He failed to appear at the trough for his supper, and when a pig (or a child) refuses supper a chill wave of fear runs through any household, or icehousehold. After examining my pig, who was stretched out in

[1]First published in 1947.

the sawdust inside the building, I went to the phone and cranked it four times. Mr. Dameron answered. "What's good for a sick pig?" I asked. (There is never any identification needed on a country phone; the person on the other end knows who is talking by the sound of the voice and by the character of the question.)

"I don't know, I never had a sick pig," said Mr. Dameron, "but I can find out quick enough. You hang up and I'll call Henry."

Mr. Dameron was back on the line again in five minutes. "Henry says roll him over on his back and give him two ounces of castor oil or sweet oil, and if that doesn't do the trick give him an injection of soapy water. He says he's almost sure the pig's plugged up, and even if he's wrong, it can't do any harm."

I thanked Mr. Dameron. I didn't go right down to the pig, though. I sank into a chair and sat still for a few minutes to think about my troubles, and then I got up and went to the barn, catching up on some odds and ends that needed tending to. Unconsciously I held off, for an hour, the deed by which I would officially recognize the collapse of the performance of raising a pig; I wanted no interruption in the regularity of feeding, the steadiness of growth, the even succession of days. I wanted no interruption, wanted no oil, no deviation. I just wanted to keep on raising a pig, full meal after full meal, spring into summer into fall. I didn't even know whether there were two ounces of castor oil on the place.

Shortly after five o'clock I remembered that we had been invited out to dinner that night and realized that if I were to dose a pig there was no time to lose. The dinner date seemed a familiar conflict: I move in a desultory society and often a week or two will roll by without my going to anybody's house to dinner or anyone's coming to mine, but when an occasion does arise, and I am summoned, something usually turns up (an hour or two in advance) to make all human intercourse seem vastly inappropriate. I have come to believe that there is in hostesses a special power of divination, and that they deliberately arrange dinners to coincide with pig failure or some other sort of failure. At any rate, it was after five o'clock and I knew I could put off no longer the evil hour.

When my son and I arrived at the pigyard, armed with a small bottle of castor oil and a length of clothesline, the pig had emerged from his house and was standing in the middle of his yard, listlessly. He gave us a slim greeting. I could see that he felt uncomfortable and uncertain. I had brought the clothesline thinking I'd have to tie him (the pig weighed more than a hundred pounds) but we never used it. My son reached down, grabbed both front legs, upset him quickly, and when he opened his mouth to scream I turned the oil into his throat—a pink, corrugated area I had never seen before. I had just time to read the label while the neck of the bottle was in his mouth. It said Puretest. The screams, slightly muffled by oil, were pitched in the hysterically high range of pigsound, as though torture were being carried out, but they didn't last long: it was all over rather suddenly, and, his legs released, the pig righted himself.

In the upset position the corners of his mouth had been turned down, giving him a frowning expression. Back on his feet again, he regained the set smile that a pig wears even in sickness. He stood his ground, sucking slightly at the residue of oil; a few drops leaked out of his lips while his wicked eyes, shaded by their coy little lashes, turned on me in disgust and hatred. I scratched him gently with oily fingers and he remained quiet, as though trying to recall the satisfaction of being scratched when in health, and seeming to rehearse in his mind the indignity to which he had just been subjected. I noticed, as I stood there, four or five small dark spots on his back near the tail end, reddish brown in color, each about the size of a housefly. I could not make out what they were. They did not look troublesome but at the same time they did not look like mere surface bruises or chafe marks. Rather they seemed blemishes of internal origin. His stiff white bristles almost completely hid them and I had to part the bristles with my fingers to get a good look.

Several hours later, a few minutes before midnight, having dined well and at someone else's expense, I returned to the pighouse with a flashlight. The patient was asleep. Kneeling, I felt his ears (as you might put your hand on the forehead of a child) and they seemed cool, and then with the light made a careful examination of the yard and the house for a sign that the oil had worked. I found none and went to bed.

We had been having an unseasonable spell of weather—hot, close days, with the fog shutting in every night, scaling for a few hours in midday, then creeping back again at dark, drifting in first over the trees on the point, then suddenly blowing across the fields, blotting out the world and taking possession of houses, men, and animals. Everyone kept hoping for a break, but the break failed to come. Next day was another hot one. I visited the pig before breakfast and tried to tempt him with a little milk in his trough. He just stared at it, while I made a sucking sound through my teeth to remind him of past pleasures of the feast. With very small, timid pigs, weanlings, this ruse is often quite successful and will encourage them to eat; but with a large, sick pig the ruse is senseless and the sound I made must have made him feel, if anything, more miserable. He not only did not crave food, he felt a positive revulsion to it. I found a place under the apple tree where he had vomited in the night.

At this point, although a depression settled over me, I didn't suppose that I was going to lose my pig. From the lustiness of a healthy pig a man derives a feeling of personal lustiness; the stuff that goes into the trough and is received with such enthusiasm is an earnest of some later feast of his own, and when this suddenly comes to an end and the food lies stale and untouched, souring in the sun, the pig's imbalance becomes the man's, vicariously, and life seems insecure, displaced, transitory.

As my own spirits declined, along with the pig's, the spirits of my vile old dachshund rose. The frequency of our trips down the footpath through the orchard to the pigyard delighted him, although he suffers greatly from arthritis, moves with difficulty, and would be bedridden if he could find anyone willing to serve him meals on a tray.

He never missed a chance to visit the pig with me, and he made many professional calls on his own. You could see him down there at all hours, his white face parting the grass along the fence as he wobbled and stumbled about, his stethoscope dangling—a happy quack, writing his villainous prescriptions and grinning his corrosive grin. When the enema bag appeared, and the bucket of warm suds, his happiness was complete, and he managed to squeeze his enormous body between the two lowest rails of the yard and then assumed full charge of the irrigation. Once, when I lowered the bag to check the flow, he reached in and hurridly drank a few mouthfuls of the suds to test their potency. I have noticed that Fred will feverishly consume any substance that is associated with trouble—the bitter flavor is to his liking. When the bag was above reach, he concentrated on the pig and was everywhere at once, a tower of strength and inconvenience. The pig, curiously enough, stood rather quietly through this colonic carnival, and the enema, though ineffective, was not as difficult as I had anticipated.

I discovered, though, that once having given a pig an enema there is no turning back, no chance of resuming one of life's more stereotyped roles. The pig's lot and mine were inextricably bound now, as though the rubber tube were the silver cord. From then until the time of his death I held the pig steadily in the bowl of my mind; the task of trying to deliver him from his misery became a strong obsession. His suffering soon became the embodiment of all earthly wretchedness. Along toward the end of the afternoon, defeated in physicking, I phoned the veterinary twenty miles away and placed the case formally in his hands. He was full of questions, and when I casually mentioned the dark spots on the pig's back, his voice changed its tone.

"I don't want to scare you," he said, "but when there are spots, erysipelas[1] has to be considered."

Together we considered erysipelas, with frequent interruptions from the telephone operator, who wasn't sure the connection had been established.

"If a pig has erysipelas can he give it to a person?" I asked.

"Yes, he can," replied the vet.

"Have they answered?" asked the operator.

"Yes, they have," I said. Then I addressed the vet again. "You better come over here and examine this pig right away."

"I can't come myself," said the vet, "but McFarland can come this evening if that's all right. Mac knows more about pigs than I do anyway. You needn't worry too much about the spots. To indicate erysipelas they would have to be deep hemorrhagic infarcts."[2]

"Deep hemorrhagic what?" I asked.

"Infarcts," said the vet.

"Have they answered?" asked the operator.

"Well," I said, "I don't know what you'd call these spots, except they're about the size of a housefly. If the pig has erysipelas I guess I have it, too, by this time, because we've been very close lately."

"McFarland will be over," said the vet.

---

[1] Acute streptococcal infection under the skin (the cause of Lamb's death).
[2] Areas of dead tissue caused by loss of local blood supply.

I hung up. My throat felt dry and I went to the cupboard and got a bottle of whiskey. Deep hemorrhagic infarcts—the phrase began fastening its hooks in my head. I had assumed that there could be nothing much wrong with a pig during the months it was being groomed for murder; my confidence in the essential health and endurance of pigs had been strong and deep, particularly in the health of pigs that belonged to me and that were part of my proud scheme. The awakening had been violent and I minded it all the more because I knew that what could be true of my pig could be true also of the rest of my tidy world. I tried to put this distasteful idea from me, but it kept recurring. I took a short drink of the whiskey and then, although I wanted to go down to the yard and look for fresh signs, I was scared to. I was certain I had erysipelas.

It was long after dark and the supper dishes had been put away when a car drove in and McFarland got out. He had a girl with him. I could just make her out in the darkness—she seemed young and pretty. "This is Miss Owen," he said. "We've been having a picnic supper on the shore, that's why I'm late."

McFarland stood in the driveway and stripped off his jacket, then his shirt. His stocky arms and capable hands showed up in my flashlight's gleam as I helped him find his coverall and get zipped up. The rear seat of his car contained an astonishing amount of paraphernalia, which he soon overhauled, selecting a chain, a syringe, a bottle of oil, a rubber tube, and some other things I couldn't identify. Miss Owen said she'd go along with us and see the pig. I led the way down the warm slope of the orchard, my light picking out the path for them, and we all three climbed the fence, entered the pighouse, and squatted by the pig while McFarland took a rectal reading. My flashlight picked up the glitter of an engagement ring on the girl's hand.

"No elevation," said McFarland, twisting the thermometer in the light. "You needn't worry about erysipelas." He ran his hand slowly over the pig's stomach and at one point the pig cried out in pain.

"Poor piggledy-wiggledy!" said Miss Owen.

The treatment I had been giving the pig for two days was then repeated, somewhat more expertly, by the doctor, Miss Owen and I handing him things as he needed them—holding the chain that he had looped around the pig's upper jaw, holding the syringe, holding the bottle stopper, the end of the tube, all of us working in darkness and in comfort, working with the instinctive teamwork induced by emergency conditions, the pig unprotesting, the house shadowy, protecting, intimate. I went to bed tired but with a feeling of relief that I had turned over part of the responsibility of the case to a licensed doctor. I was beginning to think, though, that the pig was not going to live.

He died twenty-four hours later, or it might have been forty-eight—there is a blur in time here, and I may have lost or picked up a day in the telling and the pig one in the dying. At intervals during the last day I took cool fresh water down to him and at such times as he found the strength to get to his feet he would stand with head in the pail and snuffle his snout around. He drank a few sips but no more; yet it seemed to comfort him to dip his nose in water and bobble it about, sucking in and blowing out through his teeth. Much of the time, now, he lay indoors half buried in sawdust. Once, near the last, while I was attending him I saw him try to make a bed for himself but he lacked the strength, and when he set his snout into the dust he was unable to plow even the little furrow he needed to lie down in.

He came out of the house to die. When I went down, before going to bed, he lay stretched in the yard a few feet from the door. I knelt, saw that he was dead, and left him there: his face had a mild look, expressive neither of deep peace nor of deep suffering, although I think he had suffered a good deal. I went back up to the house and to bed, and cried internally—deep hemorrhagic intears. I didn't wake till nearly eight the next morning, and when I looked out the open window the grave was already being dug, down beyond the dump under a wild apple. I could hear the spade strike against the small rocks that blocked the way. Never send to know for whom the grave is dug, I said to myself, it's dug for thee.[1] Fred, I well knew, was supervising the work of digging, so I ate breakfast slowly.

It was a Saturday morning. The thicket in which I found the gravediggers at work was dark and warm, the sky overcast. Here, among alders and young hackmatacks, at the foot of the apple tree, Lennie had dug a beautiful hole, five feet long, three feet wide, three feet deep. He was standing in it, removing the last spadefuls of earth while Fred patrolled the brink in simple but impressive circles, disturbing the loose earth of the mound so that it trickled back in. There had been no rain for weeks and the soil, even three feet down, was dry and powdery. As I stood and stared, an enormous earthworm which had been partially exposed by the spade at the bottom dug itself deeper and made a slow withdrawal, seeking even remoter moistures at even lonelier depths. And just as Lennie stepped out and rested his spade against the tree and lit a cigarette, a small green apple separated itself from a branch overhead and fell into the hole. Everything about this last scene seemed overwritten—the dismal sky, the shabby woods, the imminence of rain, the worm (legendary bedfellow of the dead), the apple (conventional garnish of a pig).

But even so, there was a directness and dispatch about animal burial, I thought, that made it a more decent affair than human burial: there was no stopover in the undertaker's foul parlor, no wreath nor spray; and when we hitched a line to the pig's hind legs and dragged him swiftly from his yard, throwing our weight into the harness and leaving a wake of crushed grass and smoothed rubble over the dump, ours was a businesslike procession, with Fred, the dishonorable pallbearer, staggering along in the rear, his perverse bereavement showing in every seam in his face; and the post mortem performed handily and swiftly right at the edge of the grave, so that the inwards that had caused the pig's death preceded him into the ground and he lay at last resting squarely on the cause of his own undoing.

---

[1]Allusion to Donne's *Devotions upon Emergent Occasions*, "Meditation" XVII: "And therefore never send to know for whom the bell tolls; it tolls for thee."

I threw in the first shovelful, and then we worked rapidly and without talk, until the job was complete. I picked up the rope, made it fast to Fred's collar (he is a notorious ghoul), and we all three filed back up the path to the house, Fred bringing up the rear and holding back every inch of the way, feigning unusual stiffness. I noticed that although he weighed far less than the pig, he was harder to drag, being possessed of the vital spark.

The news of the death of my pig travelled fast and far, and I received many expressions of sympathy from friends and neighbors, for no one took the event lightly and the premature expiration of a pig is, I soon discovered, a departure which the community marks solemnly on its calendar, a sorrow in which it feels fully involved. I have written this account in penitence and in grief, as a man who failed to raise his pig, and to explain my deviation from the classic course of so many raised pigs. The grave in the woods is unmarked, but Fred can direct the mourner to it unerringly and with immense good will, and I know he and I shall often revisit it, singly and together, in seasons of reflection and despair, on flagless memorial days of our own choosing. ✍

The Future of Reading[1]

In schools and colleges, in these audio-visual days, doubt has been raised as to the future of reading—whether the printed word is on its last legs. One college president has remarked that in fifty years "only five per cent of the people will be reading." For this, of course, one must be prepared. But how prepare? To us it would seem that even if only one person out of a hundred and fifty million should continue as a *reader*, he would be the one worth saving, the nucleus around which to found a university. We think this not impossible person, this Last Reader, might very well stand in the same relation to the community as the queen bee to the colony of bees, and that the others would quite properly dedicate themselves wholly to his welfare, serving special food and building special accommodations. From his nuptial, or intellectual, flight would come the new race of men, linked perfectly with the long past by the unbroken chain of the intellect, to carry on the community. But it is more likely that our modern hive of bees, substituting a coaxial cable[2] for spinal fluid, will try to perpetuate the race through audio-visual devices, which ask no discipline of the mind and which are already giving the room the languor of an opium parlor.

Reading is the work of the alert mind, is demanding, and under ideal conditions produces finally a sort of ecstasy. As in the sexual experience, there are never more than two persons present in the act of reading—the writer, who is the

---

[1]First published in 1954.

[2]High-frequency cable used for telephones and televisions in which a core wire is enclosed in a metal conducting tube.

impregnator, and the reader, who is the respondent. This gives the experience of reading a sublimity and power unequalled by any other form of communication. It would be just as well, we think, if educators clung to this great phenomenon and did not get sidetracked, for although books and reading may at times have played too large a part in the educational process, that is not what is happening today. Indeed, there is very little true reading, and not nearly as much writing as one would suppose from the towering piles of pulpwood in the dooryards of our paper mills. Readers and writers are scarce, as are publishers and reporters. The reports we get nowadays are those of men who have not gone to the scene of the accident, which is always farther inside one's own head than it is convenient to penetrate without galoshes. ✍

The Ring of Time[1]

After the lions had returned to their cages, creeping angrily through the chutes, a little bunch of us drifted away and into an open doorway nearby, where we stood for a while in semidarkness, watching a big brown circus horse go harumphing around the practice ring. His trainer was a woman of about forty, and the two of them, horse and woman, seemed caught up in one of those desultory[2] treadmills of afternoon from which there is no apparent escape. The day was hot, and we kibitzers were grateful to be briefly out of the sun's glare. The long rein, or tape, by which the woman guided her charge counterclockwise in his dull career formed the radius of their private circle, of which she was the revolving center; and she, too, stepped a tiny circumference of her own, in order to accommodate the horse and allow him his maximum scope. She had on a short-skirted costume and a conical straw hat. Her legs were bare and she wore high heels, which probed deep into the loose tanbark[3] and kept her ankles in a state of constant turmoil. The great size and meekness of the horse, the repetitious exercise, the heat of the afternoon, all exerted a hypnotic charm that invited boredom; we spectators were experiencing a languor—we neither expected relief nor felt entitled to any. We had paid a dollar to get into the grounds, to be sure, but we had got our dollar's worth a few minutes before, when the lion trainer's whiplash had got caught around a toe of one of the lions. What more did we want for a dollar?

Behind me I heard someone say, "Excuse me, please," in a low voice. She was halfway into the building when I turned and saw her—a girl of sixteen or seventeen, politely threading her way through us onlookers who blocked the entrance. As she emerged in front of us, I saw that she was barefoot, her dirty little feet fighting the uneven ground. In most respects she was like any of two or three

---

[1]Written on March 22, 1956.
[2]Aimless.
[3]Shredded bark from which the tannin has been removed, used to cover circus areas and other surfaces.

dozen showgirls you encounter if you wander about the winter quarters of Mr. John Ringling North's circus, in Sarasota—cleverly proportioned, deeply browned by the sun, dusty, eager, and almost naked. But her grave face and the naturalness of her manner gave her a sort of quick distinction and brought a new note into the gloomy octagonal building where we had all cast our lot for a few moments. As soon as she had squeezed through the crowd, she spoke a word or two to the older woman, whom I took to be her mother, stepped to the ring, and waited while the horse coasted to a stop in front of her. She gave the animal a couple of affectionate swipes on his enormous neck and then swung herself aboard. The horse immediately resumed his rocking canter, the woman goading him on, chanting something that sounded like "Hop! Hop!"

In attempting to recapture this mild spectacle, I am merely acting as recording secretary for one of the oldest of societies—the society of those who, at one time or another, have surrendered, without even a show of resistance, to the bedazzlement of a circus rider. As a writing man, or secretary, I have always felt charged with the safekeeping of all unexpected items of worldly or unworldly enchantment, as though I might be held personally responsible if even a small one were to be lost. But it is not easy to communicate anything of this nature. The circus comes as close to being the world in microcosm as anything I know; in a way, it puts all the rest of show business in the shade. Its magic is universal and complex. Out of its wild disorder comes order; from its rank smell rises the good aroma of courage and daring; out of its preliminary shabbiness comes the final splendor. And buried in the familiar boasts of its advance agents lies the modesty of most of its people. For me the circus is at its best before it has been put together. It is at its best at certain moments when it comes to a point, as through a burning glass, in the activity and destiny of a single performer out of so many. One ring is always bigger than three. One rider, one aerialist, is always greater than six. In short, a man has to catch the circus unawares to experience its full impact and share its gaudy dream.

The ten-minute ride the girl took achieved—as far as I was concerned, who wasn't looking for it, and quite unbeknownst to her, who wasn't even striving for it—the thing that is sought by performers everywhere, on whatever stage, whether struggling in the tidal currents of Shakespeare or bucking the difficult motion of a horse. I somehow got the idea she was just cadging a ride, improving a shining ten minutes in the diligent way all serious artists seize free moments to hone the blade of their talent and keep themselves in trim. Her brief tour included only elementary postures and tricks, perhaps because they were all she was capable of, perhaps because her warmup at this hour was unscheduled and the ring was not rigged for a real practice session. She swung herself off and on the horse several times, gripping his mane. She did a few knee-stands—or whatever they are called—dropping to her knees and quickly bouncing back up on her feet again. Most of the time she simply rode in a standing position, well aft on the beast, her hands hanging easily at her sides, her head erect, her straw-colored ponytail lightly brushing her shoulders, the blood of exertion showing faintly through the tan of her skin. Twice she managed a one-foot stance—a sort of ballet pose, with arms outstretched. At one point the neck strap of her bathing suit broke and she went twice around the ring in the classic attitude of a woman making minor repairs to a garment. The fact that she was standing on the back of a moving horse while doing this invested the matter with a clownish significance that perfectly fitted the spirit of the circus—jocund, yet charming. She just rolled the strap into a neat ball and stowed it inside her bodice while the horse rocked and rolled beneath her in dutiful innocence. The bathing suit proved as self-reliant as its owner and stood up well enough without benefit of strap.

The richness of the scene was in its plainness, its natural condition—of horse, of ring, of girl, even to the girl's bare feet that gripped the bare back of her proud and ridiculous mount. The enchantment grew not out of anything that happened or was performed but out of something that seemed to go round and around and around with the girl, attending her, a steady gleam in the shape of a circle—a ring of ambition, of happiness, of youth. (And the positive pleasures of equilibrium under difficulties.) In a week or two, all would be changed, all (or almost all) lost; the girl would wear makeup, the horse would wear gold, the ring would be painted, the bark would be clean for the feet of the horse, the girl's feet would be clean for the slippers that she'd wear. All, all would be lost.

As I watched with the others, our jaws adroop, our eyes alight, I became painfully conscious of the element of time. Everything in the hideous old building seemed to take the shape of a circle, conforming to the course of the horse. The rider's gaze, as she peered straight ahead, seemed to be circular, as though bent by force of circumstance; then time itself began running in circles, and so the beginning was where the end was, and the two were the same, and one thing ran into the next and time went round and around and got nowhere. The girl wasn't so young that she did not know the delicious satisfaction of having a perfectly behaved body and the fun of using it to do a trick most people can't do, but she was too young to know that time does not really move in a circle at all. I thought: "She will never be as beautiful as this again"—a thought that made me acutely unhappy—and in a flash my mind (which is too much of a busybody to suit me) had projected her twenty-five years ahead, and she was now in the center of the ring, on foot, wearing a conical hat and high-heeled shoes, the image of the older woman, holding the long rein, caught in the treadmill of an afternoon long in the future. "She is at that enviable moment in life [I thought] when she believes she can go once around the ring, make one complete circuit, and at the end be exactly the same age as at the start." Everything in her movements, her expression, told you that for her the ring of time was perfectly formed, changeless, predictable, without beginning or end, like the ring in which she was traveling at this moment with the horse that wallowed under her. And then I slipped back into my trance, and time was circular again—time, pausing quietly with the rest of us, so as not to disturb the balance of a performer.

Her ride ended as casually as it had begun. The older woman stopped the horse, and the girl slid to the ground. As she walked toward us to leave, there was a quick, small burst of applause. She smiled broadly, in surprise and pleasure; then her face suddenly regained its gravity and she disappeared through the door.

It has been ambitious and plucky of me to attempt to describe what is indescribable, and I have failed, as I knew I would. But I have discharged my duty to my society; and besides, a writer, like an acrobat, must occasionally try a stunt that is too much for him. At any rate, it is worth reporting that long before the circus comes to town, its most notable performances have already been given. Under the bright lights of the finished show, a performer need only reflect the electric candle power that is directed upon him; but in the dark and dirty old training rings and in the makeshift cages, whatever light is generated, whatever excitement, whatever beauty, must come from original sources—from internal fires of professional hunger and delight, from the exuberance and gravity of youth. It is the difference between planetary light and the combustion of stars.

The South is the land of the sustained sibilant. Everywhere, for the appreciative visitor, the letter "s" insinuates itself in the scene: in the sound of the sea and sand, in the singing shell, in the heat of sun and sky, in the sultriness of the gentle hours, in the siesta, in the stir of birds and insects. In contrast to the softness of its music, the South is also cruel and hard and prickly. A little striped lizard, flattened along the sharp green bayonet of a yucca, wears in its tiny face and watchful eye the pure look of death and violence. And all over the place, hidden at the bottom of their small sandy craters, the ant lions[1] lie in wait for the ant that will stumble into their trap. (There are three kinds of lions in this region: the lions of the circus, the ant lions, and the Lions of the Tampa Lions Club,[2] who roared their approval of segregation at a meeting the other day—all except one, a Lion named Monty Gurwit, who declined to roar and thereby got his picture in the paper.)

The day starts on a note of despair: the sorrowing dove, alone on its telephone wire, mourns the loss of night, weeps at the bright perils of the unfolding day. But soon the mockingbird wakes and begins an early rehearsal, setting the dove down by force of character, running through a few slick imitations, and trying a couple of original numbers into the bargain. The redbird takes it from there. Despair gives way to good humor. The Southern dawn is a pale affair, usually, quite different from our northern daybreak. It is a triumph of gradualism; night turns to day imperceptibly, softly, with no theatrics. It is subtle and undisturbing. As the first light seeps through the blinds I lie in bed half awake, despairing with the dove, sounding the A for the brothers Alsop.[3] All seems lost, all seems sorrowful. Then a mullet jumps in the bayou outside the bedroom window. It falls back into the water with a smart smack. I have asked several people why the mullet incessantly jump and I have received a variety of answers. Some say the mullet jump to shake off a parasite that annoys them. Some say they jump for the love of jumping—as

---

[1] Also called doodlebugs, they are insect larvae that dig holes to trap ants and other insects for food.
[2] International Association of Lions Clubs, founded in 1917 and composed of business and professional men committed to citizenship, patriotism, and the improvement of the community.
[3] Joseph Wright Alsop, Jr. (1910–   ), and Stewart Johonnot Oliver Alsop (1914–1974) were journalists who covered Washington politics and wrote a column together from 1946 to 1958 called "Matter of Fact."

the girl on the horse seemed to ride for the love of riding (although she, too, like all artists, may have been shaking off some parasite that fastens itself to the creative spirit and can be got rid of only by fifty turns around a ring while standing on a horse).

In Florida at this time of year, the sun does not take command of the day until a couple of hours after it has appeared in the east. It seems to carry no authority at first. The sun and the lizard keep the same schedule; they bide their time until the morning has advanced a good long way before they come fully forth and strike. The cold lizard waits astride his warming leaf for the perfect moment; the cold sun waits in his nest of clouds for the crucial time.

On many days, the dampness of the air pervades all life, all living. Matches refuse to strike. The towel, hung to dry, grows wetter by the hour. The newspaper, with its headlines about integration, wilts in your hand and falls limply into the coffee and the egg. Envelopes seal themselves. Postage stamps mate with one another as shamelessly as grasshoppers. But most of the time the days are models of beauty and wonder and comfort, with the kind sea stroking the back of the warm sand. At evening there are great flights of birds over the sea, where the light lingers; the gulls, the pelicans, the terns, the herons stay aloft for half an hour after land birds have gone to roost. They hold their ancient formations, wheel and fish over the Pass, enjoying the last of day like children playing outdoors after suppertime.

To a beachcomber from the North, which is my present status, the race problem has no pertinence, no immediacy. Here in Florida I am a guest in two houses—the house of the sun, the house of the State of Florida. As a guest, I mind my manners and do not criticize the customs of my hosts. It gives me a queer feeling, though, to be at the center of the greatest social crisis of my time and see hardly a sign of it. Yet the very absence of signs seems to increase one's awareness. Colored people do not come to the public beach to bathe, because they would not be made welcome there; and they don't fritter away their time visiting the circus, because they have other things to do. A few of them turn up at the ballpark, where they occupy a separate but equal section of the left-field bleachers and watch Negro players on the visiting Braves team using the same bases as the white players, instead of separate (but equal) bases. I have had only two small encounters with "color." A colored woman named Viola, who had been a friend of my wife's sister years ago, showed up one day with some laundry of ours that she had consented to do for us, and with the bundle she brought a bunch of nasturtiums, as a sort of natural accompaniment to the delivery of clean clothes. The flowers seemed a very acceptable thing and I was touched by them. We asked Viola about her daughter, and she said she was at Kentucky State College, studying voice.

The other encounter was when I was explaining to our cook, who is from Finland, the mysteries of bus travel in the American Southland. I showed her the bus stop, armed her with a timetable, and then, as a matter of duty, mentioned the customs of the Romans. "When you get on the bus," I said, "I think you'd better sit in one of the front seats—the seats in back are for colored people." A look of great weariness came into her face, as it does when we use too many dishes, and she replied, "Oh, I know—isn't it silly!"

Her remark, coming as it did all the way from Finland and landing on this sandbar with a plunk, impressed me. The Supreme Court said nothing about silliness, but I suspect it may play more of a role than one might suppose. People are, if anything, more touchy about being thought silly than they are about being thought unjust. I note that one of the arguments in the recent manifesto of Southern Congressmen in support of the doctrine of "separate but equal" was that it had been founded on "common sense." The sense that is common to one generation is uncommon to the next. Probably the first slave ship, with Negroes lying in chains on its decks, seemed commonsensical to the owners who operated it and to the planters who patronized it. But such a vessel would not be in the realm of common sense today. The only sense that is common, in the long run, is the sense of change—and we all instinctively avoid it, and object to the passage of time, and would rather have none of it.

The Supreme Court decision[1] is like the Southern sun, laggard in its early stages, biding its time. It has been the law in Florida for two years now, and the years have been like the hours of the morning before the sun has gathered its strength. I think the decision is as incontrovertible and warming as the sun, and, like the sun, will eventually take charge.

But there is certainly a great temptation in Florida to duck the passage of time. Lying in warm comfort by the sea, you receive gratefully the gift of the sun, the gift of the South. This is true seduction. The day is a circle—morning, afternoon, and night. After a few days I was clearly enjoying the same delusion as the girl on the horse—that I could ride clear around the ring of day, guarded by wind and sun and sea and sand, and be not a moment older.

P.S. (April 1962).   When I first laid eyes on Fiddler Bayou, it was wild land, populated chiefly by the little crabs that gave it its name, visited by wading birds and by an occasional fisherman. Today, houses ring the bayou, and part of the mangrove shore has been bulkheaded with a concrete wall. Green lawns stretch from patio to water's edge, and sprinklers make rainbows in the light. But despite man's encroachment, Nature manages to hold her own and assert her authority: high tides and high winds in the gulf sometimes send the sea crashing across the sand barrier, depositing its wrack on lawns and ringing everyone's front door bell. The birds and the crabs accommodate themselves quite readily to the changes that have taken place; every day brings herons to hunt around among the roots of the mangroves, and I have discovered that I can approach to within about eight feet of a Little Blue Heron simply by entering the water and swimming slowly toward him. Apparently he has decided that when I'm in the water, I am without guile—possibly even desirable, like a fish.

The Ringling circus has quit Sarasota and gone elsewhere for its hibernation. A few circus families still own homes in the town, and every spring the students

---

[1] The order to desegregate the public schools in *Brown vs. Board of Education of Topeka Kansas* (1954).

at the high school put on a circus, to let off steam, work off physical requirements, and provide a promotional spectacle for Sarasota. At the drugstore you can buy a postcard showing the bed John Ringling slept in. Time has not stood still for anybody but the dead, and even the dead must be able to hear the acceleration of little sports cars and know that things have changed.

From the all-wise *New York Times*, which has the animal kingdom ever in mind, I have learned that one of the creatures most acutely aware of the passing of time is the fiddler crab himself. Tiny spots on his body enlarge during daytime hours, giving him the same color as the mudbank he explores and thus protecting him from his enemies. At night the spots shrink, his color fades, and he is almost invisible in the light of the moon. These changes are synchronized with the tides, so that each day they occur at a different hour. A scientist who experimented with the crabs to learn more about the phenomenon discovered that even when they are removed from their natural environment and held in confinement, the rhythm of their bodily change continues uninterrupted, and they mark the passage of time in their laboratory prison, faithful to the tides in their fashion. ✍

Afternoon of an American Boy[1]

When I was in my teens, I lived in Mount Vernon, in the same block with J. Parnell Thomas, who grew up to become chairman of the House Committee on Un-American Activities.° I lived on the corner of Summit and East Sidney at No. 101 Summit Avenue, and Parnell lived four or five doors north of us on the same side of the avenue, in the house the Diefendorfs used to live in.

Parnell was not a playmate of mine, as he was a few years older, but I used to greet him as he walked by our house on his way to and from the depot. He was a good-looking young man, rather quiet and shy. Seeing him, I would call "Hello, Parnell!" and he would smile and say "Hello, Elwyn!" and walk on. Once I remember dashing out of our yard on roller skates and executing a rink turn in front of Parnell, to show off, and he said, "Well! Quite an artist, aren't you?" I remember the words. I was delighted at praise from an older man and sped away along the flagstone sidewalk, dodging the cracks I knew so well.

The thing that made Parnell a special man in my eyes in those days was not his handsome appearance and friendly manner but his sister. Her name was Eileen. She was my age and was a quiet, nice-looking girl. She never came over to my yard to play, and I never went over there, and, considering that we lived so near each other, we were remarkably uncommunicative; nevertheless, she was the girl I singled out, at one point, to be of special interest to me. Being of special interest to me involved practically nothing on a girl's part—it simply meant that she was

---

[1]First published in 1977.

under constant surveillance. On my own part, it meant that I suffered an astonishing disintegration when I walked by her house, from embarrassment, fright, and the knowledge that I was in enchanted territory.

In the matter of girls, I was different from most boys of my age. I admired girls a lot, but they terrified me. I did not feel that I possessed the peculiar gifts or accomplishments that girls liked in their male companions—the ability to dance, to play football, to cut up a bit in public, to smoke, and to make small talk. I couldn't do any of these things successfully, and seldom tried. Instead, I stuck with the accomplishments I was sure of: I rode my bicycle sitting backward on the handle bars, I made up poems, I played selections from *Aïda*[1] on the piano. In winter, I tended goal in the hockey games on the frozen pond in the dell. None of these tricks counted much with girls. In the four years I was in the Mount Vernon High School, I never went to a school dance and I never took a girl to a drugstore for a soda or to the Westchester Playhouse or to Proctor's. I wanted to do these things but did not have the nerve. What I finally did manage to do, however, and what is the subject of this memoir, was far brassier, far gaudier. As an exhibit of teen-age courage and ineptitude, it never fails to amaze me in retrospect. I am not even sure it wasn't un-American.

My bashfulness and backwardness annoyed my older sister very much, and at about the period of which I am writing she began making strong efforts to stir me up. She was convinced that I was in a rut, socially, and she found me a drag in her own social life, which was brisk. She kept trying to throw me with girls, but I always bounced. And whenever she saw a chance she would start the phonograph and grab me, and we would go charging around the parlor in the toils of the one-step, she gripping me as in a death struggle, and I hurling her finally away from me through greater strength. I was a skinny kid but my muscles were hard, and it would have taken an unusually powerful woman to have held me long in the attitude of the dance.

One day, through a set of circumstances I have forgotten, my sister managed to work me into an afternoon engagement she had with some others in New York. To me, at that time, New York was a wonderland largely unexplored. I had been to the Hippodrome[2] a couple of times with my father, and to the Hudson-Fulton Celebration,[3] and to a few matinées; but New York, except as a setting for extravaganzas, was unknown. My sister had heard tales of tea-dancing at the Plaza Hotel. She and a girl friend of hers and another fellow and myself went there to give it a try. The expedition struck me as a slick piece of arrangement on her part.

---

[1]Italian opera by Giuseppe Verdi (1813–1901).

[2]Built in 1905 by Frederick Thompson and Elmer S. Dundy, the Hippodrome, 51 Forty-third Street, was the location of numerous shows involving diving girls, chorus girls, prizefighters, opera companies, and elephants.

[3]From September 25 to October 11, 1909, New York City celebrated the three-hundredth anniversary of Henry Hudson's discovery of the Hudson River and the one-hundredth anniversary of the first steam navigation of the river in Robert Fulton's *Clermont*.

I was the junior member of the group and had been roped in, I imagine, to give symmetry to the occasion. Or perhaps Mother had forbidden my sister to go at all unless another member of the family was along. Whether I was there for symmetry or for decency I can't really remember, but I was there.

The spectacle was a revelation to me. However repulsive the idea of dancing was, I was filled with amazement at the setup. Here were tables where a fellow could sit so close to the dance floor that he was practically on it. And you could order cinnamon toast and from the safety of your chair observe girls and men in close embrace, swinging along, the music playing while you ate the toast, and the dancers so near to you that they almost brushed the things off your table as they jogged by. I was impressed. Dancing or no dancing, this was certainly high life, and I knew I was witnessing a scene miles and miles ahead of anything that took place in Mount Vernon. I had never seen anything like it, and a ferment must have begun working in me that afternoon.

Incredible as it seems to me now, I formed the idea of asking Parnell's sister Eileen to accompany me to a tea dance at the Plaza. The plan shaped up in my mind as an expedition of unparalleled worldliness, calculated to stun even the most blasé girl. The fact that I didn't know how to dance must have been a powerful deterrent, but not powerful enough to stop me. As I look back on the affair, it's hard to credit my own memory, and I sometimes wonder if, in fact, the whole business isn't some dream that has gradually gained the status of actuality. A boy with any sense, wishing to become better acquainted with a girl who was "of special interest," would have cut out for himself a more modest assignment to start with—a soda date or a movie date—something within reasonable limits. Not me. I apparently became obsessed with the notion of taking Eileen to the Plaza and not to any darned old drugstore. I had learned the location of the Plaza, and just knowing how to get to it gave me a feeling of confidence. I had learned about cinnamon toast, so I felt able to cope with the waiter when he came along. And I banked heavily on the general splendor of the surroundings and the extreme sophistication of the function to carry the day, I guess.

I was three days getting up nerve to make the phone call. Meantime, I worked out everything in the greatest detail. I heeled myself with a safe amount of money. I looked up trains. I overhauled my clothes and assembled an outfit I believed would meet the test. Then, one night at six o'clock, when Mother and Father went downstairs to dinner, I lingered upstairs and entered the big closet off my bedroom where the wall phone was. There I stood for several minutes, trembling, my hand on the receiver, which hung upside down on the hook. (In our family, the receiver always hung upside down, with the big end up.)

I had rehearsed my first line and my second line. I planned to say, "Hello, can I please speak to Eileen?" Then, when she came to the phone, I planned to say, "Hello Eileen, this is Elwyn White." From there on, I figured I could ad-lib it.

At last, I picked up the receiver and gave the number. As I had suspected, Eileen's mother answered.

"Can I please speak to Eileen?" I asked, in a low, troubled voice.

"Just a minute," said her mother. Then, on second thought, she asked, "Who is it, please?"

"It's Elwyn," I said.

She left the phone, and after quite a while Eileen's voice said, "Hello, Elwyn." This threw my second line out of whack, but I stuck to it doggedly.

"Hello, Eileen, this is Elwyn White," I said.

In no time at all I laid the proposition before her. She seemed dazed and asked me to wait a minute. I assume she went into a huddle with her mother. Finally, she said yes, she would like to go tea-dancing with me at the Plaza, and I said fine, I would call for her at quarter past three on Thursday afternoon, or whatever afternoon it was—I've forgotten.

I do not know now, and of course did not know then, just how great was the mental and physical torture Eileen went through that day, but the incident stacks up as a sort of unintentional un-American activity, for which I was solely responsible. It all went off as scheduled: the stately walk to the depot; the solemn train ride, during which we sat staring shyly into the seat in front of us; the difficult walk from Grand Central across Forty-second to Fifth, with pedestrians clipping us and cutting in between us; the bus ride to Fifty-ninth Street; then the Plaza itself, and the cinnamon toast, and the music, and the excitement. The thundering quality of the occasion must have delivered a mental shock to me, deadening my recollection, for I have only the dimmest memory of leading Eileen onto the dance floor to execute two or three unspeakable rounds, in which I vainly tried to adapt my violent sister-and-brother wrestling act into something graceful and appropriate. It must have been awful. And at six o'clock, emerging, I gave no thought to any further entertainment, such as dinner in town. I simply herded Eileen back all the long, dreary way to Mount Vernon and deposited her, a few minutes after seven, on an empty stomach, at her home. Even if I had attempted to dine her, I don't believe it would have been possible; the emotional strain of the afternoon had caused me to perspire uninterruptedly, and any restaurant would have been justified in rejecting me solely on the ground that I was too moist.

Over the intervening years, I've often felt guilty about my afternoon at the Plaza, and many years ago, during Parnell's investigation of writers, my feeling sometimes took the form of a guilt sequence in which I imagined myself on the stand, in the committee room, being questioned. It went something like this:

PARNELL: Have you ever written for the screen, Mr. White?

ME: No, sir.

PARNELL: Have you ever been, or are you now, a member of the Screen Writers' Guild?

ME: No, sir.

PARNELL: Have you ever been, or are you now, a member of the Communist Party?

ME: No, sir.

Then, in this imaginary guilt sequence of mine, Parnell digs deep and comes up with the big question, calculated to throw me.

PARNELL: Do you recall an afternoon, along about the middle of the second decade of this century, when you took my sister to the Plaza Hotel for tea under the grossly misleading and false pretext that you knew how to dance?

And as my reply comes weakly, "Yes, sir," I hear the murmur run through the committee room and see reporters bending over their notebooks, scribbling hard. In my dream, I am again seated with Eileen at the edge of the dance floor, frightened, stunned, and happy—in my ears the intoxicating drumbeat of the dance, in my throat the dry, bittersweet taste of cinnamon.

I don't know about the guilt, really. I guess a good many girls might say that an excursion such as the one I conducted Eileen on belongs in the un-American category. But there must be millions of aging males, now slipping into their anecdotage, who recall their Willie Baxter period[1] with affection, and who remember some similar journey into ineptitude, in that precious, brief moment in life before love's pages, through constant reference, had become dog-eared, and before its narrative, through sheer competence, had lost the first, wild sense of derring-do. ✒

Foreword[2]

The essayist is a self-liberated man, sustained by the childish belief that everything he thinks about, everything that happens to him, is of general interest. He is a fellow who thoroughly enjoys his work, just as people who take bird walks enjoy theirs. Each new excursion of the essayist, each new "attempt," differs from the last and takes him into new country. This delights him. Only a person who is congenitally self-centered has the effrontery and the stamina to write essays.

There are as many kinds of essays as there are human attitudes or poses, as many essay flavors as there are Howard Johnson ice creams. The essayist arises in the morning and, if he has work to do, selects his garb from an unusually extensive wardrobe: he can pull on any sort of shirt, be any sort of person, according to his mood or his subject matter—philosopher, scold, jester, raconteur, confidant, pundit, devil's advocate, enthusiast. I like the essay, have always liked it, and even as a child was at work, attempting to inflict my young thoughts and experiences on others by putting them on paper. I early broke into print in the pages of *St. Nicholas*. I tend still to fall back on the essay form (or lack of form)

---

[1]From the hero of *Seventeen* (1916), a novel of adolescence by Booth Tarkington (1869–1946); the novel was made into a hit play that ran in 1918 and again in 1926.

[2]First published in *Essays of E. B. White* (1977).

when an idea strikes me, but I am not fooled about the place of the essay in twentieth-century American letters—it stands a short distance down the line. The essayist, unlike the novelist, the poet, and the playwright, must be content in his self-imposed role of second-class citizen. A writer who has his sights trained on the Nobel Prize or other earthly triumphs had best write a novel, a poem, or a play, and leave the essayist to ramble about, content with living a free life and enjoying the satisfactions of a somewhat undisciplined existence. (Dr. Johnson called the essay "an irregular, undigested piece"; this happy practitioner has no wish to quarrel with the good doctor's characterization.)

There is one thing the essayist cannot do, though—he cannot indulge himself in deceit or in concealment, for he will be found out in no time. Desmond MacCarthy, in his introductory remarks to the 1928 E. P. Dutton & Company edition of Montaigne, observes that Montaigne "had the gift of natural candour. . . ." It is the basic ingredient. And even the essayist's escape from discipline is only a partial escape: the essay, although a relaxed form, imposes its own disciplines, raises its own problems, and these disciplines and problems soon become apparent and (we all hope) act as a deterrent to anyone wielding a pen merely because he entertains random thoughts or is in a happy or wandering mood.

I think some people find the essay the last resort of the egoist, a much too self-conscious and self-serving form for their taste; they feel that it is presumptuous of a writer to assume that his little excursions or his small observations will interest the reader. There is some justice in their complaint. I have always been aware that I am by nature self-absorbed and egoistical; to write of myself to the extent I have done indicates a too great attention to my own life, not enough to the lives of others. I have worn many shirts, and not all of them have been a good fit. But when I am discouraged or downcast I need only fling open the door of my closet, and there, hidden behind everything else, hangs the mantle of Michel de Montaigne, smelling slightly of camphor.[1]

The essays in this collection cover a long expanse of time, a wide variety of subjects. I have chosen the ones that have amused me in the rereading, along with a few that seemed to have the odor of durability clinging to them. Some, like "Here Is New York," have been seriously affected by the passage of time and now stand as period pieces. I wrote about New York in the summer of 1948, during a hot spell. The city I described has disappeared, and another city has emerged in its place—one that I'm not familiar with. But I remember the former one, with longing and with love. David McCord,[2] in his book *About Boston* tells of a journalist from abroad visiting this country and seeing New York for the first time. He reported that it was "inspiring but temporary in appearance." I know what he

---

[1] A volatile compound used as an insect repellant.
[2] Born 1897; writer, curator, poet for children, author of *Every Time I Climb a Tree* (1967) and many other books.

means. The last time I visited New York, it seemed to have suffered a personality change, as though it had a brain tumor as yet undetected.

Two of the Florida pieces have likewise experienced a sea change. My remarks about the conditions of the black race in the South have happily been nullified, and the pieces are merely prophetic, not definitive.

To assemble these essays I have rifled my other books and have added a number of pieces that are appearing for the first time between covers. Except for extracting three chapters, I have let "One Man's Meat" alone, since it is a sustained report of about five years of country living—a report I prefer not to tamper with. The arrangement of the book is by subject matter or by mood or by place, not by chronology. Some of the pieces in the book carry a dateline, some do not. Chronology enters into the scheme, but neither the book nor its sections are perfectly chronological. Sometimes the reader will find me in the city when he thinks I am in the country, and the other way round. This may cause a mild confusion; it is unavoidable and easily explained. I spent a large part of the first half of my life as a city dweller, a large part of the second half as a countryman. In between, there were periods when nobody, including myself, quite knew (or cared) where I was: I thrashed back and forth between Maine and New York for reasons that seemed compelling at the time. Money entered into it, affection for *The New Yorker* magazine entered in. And affection for the city.

I have finally come to rest. ✐

· · ·

Zora Neale Hurston

(1901–1960)

Zora Neale Hurston was born[1] in Eatonville, Florida, the sixth of eight children of Lucy Ann Potts and John Hurston, a Baptist preacher, carpenter, and three-term mayor of the all-black town. In her autobiography, *Dust Tracks on a Road* (1942), Hurston describes herself as an exceptionally strong, confident, and imaginative child, unafraid of snakes, who believed that the moon followed only her. She was also curious. On her errands to Joe Clarke's store, "the heart and spring of the town," she overheard men talking about women in language not intended for children's ears, and she lingered to hear their "lying" sessions, when they outdid each other swapping folk tales about God, the Devil, and animals that talked. She read voraciously—fairy tales, Greek and Roman myths, stories of the Norse, books such as *The Swiss Family Robinson*, and, of course, the Bible. Immersed in this wealth of material, Hurston began making up her own tall tales; her mother approved, but her maternal grandmother called her a liar; her father had always complained that she "had too much spirit."

When she was still quite young, Hurston saw visions of twelve unhappy scenes that she was convinced she must endure before achieving happiness. Overwhelmed by "a cosmic loneliness," she sensed the end of her childhood, and shortly thereafter, when she was nine, her mother died, the family dispersed, and Hurston was sent off to school in Jacksonville. Although her early childhood had indeed ended, several of its aspects—isolation from the racism outside Eatonville, a wealth of local folk tales, the poetry of her father's Baptist services, and her mother's challenge to "jump at de sun"—had given her a pride in herself and her race that remained undiminished all her life.

Lack of funds soon forced Hurston to leave the Jacksonville school, but she despised her new stepmother and her father's house no longer seemed

---

[1]Most critics give Hurston's date of birth as 1901, though all agree that the date is uncertain; biographical evidence suggests a date closer to 1895.

like home. Hurston and her younger siblings were sent on to various relatives who expected children to work rather than read. For the next ten years, she worked sporadically as a maid, receptionist, dishwasher, and, finally, in 1915, as a wardrobe girl with a traveling Gilbert and Sullivan repertory company, all the time hoping to save enough money to return to school. After the Gilbert and Sullivan tour, she enrolled in night school in Maryland, working days as a waitress, and graduated from high school in 1918. That summer she worked in Washington as a manicurist before entering Howard University, where she studied with Alain Locke, philosophy professor and editor of *Stylus*, the literary magazine where, in 1921, Hurston published her first story, "John Redding Goes to Sea."

In 1925 Hurston left Howard for New York City, finances again keeping her from finishing school. But by then she had published several short stories based on life in Eatonville ("Drenched in Light" in 1924, "Spunk" and "Magnolia Flower" in 1925), and, with the backing of Locke and other intellectuals of the Harlem Renaissance,° Hurston was soon in the center of that society, entertaining friends with her flamboyance and her tales from Eatonville. When she won second place at an awards dinner for her short story "Spunk," a contest judge, novelist Fanny Hurst, hired Hurston as secretary and later as traveling companion. At the same dinner, one of the founders of Barnard College, also impressed with Hurston's talent, offered her a scholarship to Barnard beginning in the fall of 1925.

At Barnard, Hurston studied anthropology under Dr. Franz Boas and shifted her interests from that of creative artist to that of recorder and collector of folk tales and black culture. Her new enthusiasm led her to measure heads on the streets of Harlem to supply evidence for Boas's refutation of nineteenth-century assertions about racial differences in brain size. In 1927, just before her graduation from Barnard, she was given a fellowship to study folklore in the South. While in Florida, Hurston married Herbert Sheen, a man she had met at Howard in 1920. He had worked his way through school as a waiter and pianist and had then moved to Chicago to enter medical school. Unfortunately, both the fieldwork and the marriage proved unsuccessful. Alienated by her Barnard education, Hurston's informants refused to cooperate, and commitment to separate careers, one in Chicago and the other in New York and the South, eroded the marriage. Hurston drove back from her fieldwork with the poet Langston Hughes.° Four years later Hurston and Sheen divorced.

Hurston arrived in New York, to report to Boas on her fieldwork on folklore, miserable and nearly empty-handed. The one article she did manage to produce was found, years later (by William Stewart in 1972), to have been plagiarized. Her biographer, Robert Hemenway,[1] argues that plagiarism "may be an unconscious attempt at academic suicide." He

---

[1]*Zora Neale Hurston,* University of Illinois Press, 1980. The facts in this biography come from Hurston's autobiography and Hemenway's book.

explains that Hurston was torn between her love of art and her respect for science, for neither alone could convey the power and integrity of black folk culture to a nation dominated by racial prejudice. As an artist she felt she lacked credibility, yet as an anthropologist she was forced to suppress her imagination and to publish in scholarly journals read only by those knowledgeable in the field. Moreover, she was afraid of failure as a scientist. She knew that if discovered the plagiarism would destroy her career, but the discovery would also have solved her dilemma. As it was, she was left to solve the dilemma herself.

By December of 1927 Hurston had found another sponsor for her fieldwork, Mrs. Charlotte Osgood Mason, rich, white, and the patron of Langston Hughes° and other black artists. In return for her funding Mason required absolute loyalty and a contract that gave her ownership of all collected material and control over all publishing of this material. In fact, Mason refused to let Hurston publish anything; she was to collect only. Mason's strict control and her preference for science over art eventually led first Hughes° and then Hurston to reject her money. But without this money Hurston would not have been able to regain her confidence as an anthropologist. On this second venture Hurston was quite successful. Masquerading as a runaway from a bootlegging husband, she lived for a time with the workers of the Everglades Cypress Lumber Company and later worked as an apprentice hoo-doo doctor in New Orleans. In 1929 she went to the Bahamas to collect Afro-Caribbean folklore, songs, and hoo-doo material. Although Mason funded Hurston's fieldwork for three years, the money was barely enough to keep Hurston in gas and shoes, and she longed to publish some of her findings, particularly the songs and dances, in the form of drama, which Mason absolutely forbade. While she was writing up her notes, she was also, behind Mason's back, conspiring with Hughes° on a play to be called "Mule Bone." Never produced in her lifetime,[1] the play caused the breakup of Hurston's friendship with Hughes° (they argued over who had written what and over the addition of a third party to the project), but it also pointed up Hurston's own struggles between what she saw as sterile reporting and imaginative art. Worse, when Mason was finally ready to allow Hurston to publish her findings, no one was willing to publish her material without extensive revisions. Mason now wanted a return for her investment. Using some of the material from her notes, Hurston created a musical show, *The Great Day*, which was an artistic success but not a financial one. It was largely underwritten, again, by Mason. This production marked the end of Hurston's financial dependence on Mason. Finally, when Hurston returned to Eatonville in 1932, she was able to write the manuscript that became *Mules and Men*, a combination of the folk material she had collected and a first-person narrative that was neither fiction nor pure research.

---

[1]It was recently produced in New York City to mixed reviews.

For the next ten years, Hurston supported herself through odd jobs and her writing, both fiction and nonfiction. She was drama instructor at Bethune Cookman College in Daytona in 1933 and producer of another *Great Day* in Chicago in 1934. When the publisher Lippincott read her short story "The Gilded Six-Bits" (1933) and asked if she had a novel to submit, Hurston said yes and quickly produced her first novel, *Jonah's Gourd Vine* (1934). After that, her publisher was willing, finally, to publish *Mules and Men* (1935) as well. Hurston worked for the Federal Theatre Project in New York, went to the West Indies on a Guggenheim Fellowship in 1936, and wrote *Their Eyes Were Watching God* in Haiti in 1937, infusing the story with the passion she had felt for a young man, a member of the cast of *The Great Day*, whom after much soul-searching she had forsaken, again because of her career. Unlike that novel, her next book, *Tell My Horse* (1938), based on her collections of material in the West Indies, did not sell well, and Hurston joined the writers' project in Florida in 1938. In 1939 she published her third novel, *Moses, Man of the Mountain*, married Albert Price III, whom she divorced four years later, and took a job as manager of a drama program at the North Carolina College for Negroes at Durham. In 1941 she was in New York and in 1942 was living in California with a wealthy friend. There Hurston wrote her autobiography, *Dust Tracks on a Road* (1942), and consulted at Paramount Studios. The autobiography was so successful that she was asked to write numerous articles for magazines during the forties. But she was still living hand to mouth, even in 1944 after she had received an award from Howard University. In the midforties she worked for the Republicans in political campaigns in New York, and in 1948 she published *Seraph on the Sewanee*, a novel about white people in the South.

Hurston's writing during the forties has perplexed and annoyed many of her admirers, who see this work, particularly the autobiography and the last novel, as rejections of the goals she had pursued in the twenties and thirties. The manuscript for the autobiography shows that her publisher had cut out Hurston's criticism of the United States's racist policies, but even so, her writing seems to be patriotic in time of war and shaped to please a white audience. Hurston became even more conservative after she was arrested and falsely accused of child molestation in 1948. Although she proved that she had been out of the country at the time of the supposed incidents and although the case against her was dropped, a black newspaper picked up the story in lurid headlines and Hurston was deeply hurt.

Depressed but not beaten, Hurston returned to Florida, wrote articles for magazines, and lived for a while in a houseboat. During the fifties she shocked many blacks by her anticommunism, her support for Republicans, and particularly by her rejection of the 1954 Supreme Court decision forbidding separate but equal public education. But it was Hurston's pride in the all-black community of Eatonville that had led her to this position. She spent much of her last years researching and reading the works of Flavius

Josephus° in order to write a novel about Herod the Great, which, like Hazlitt's book on Napoleon, found merit in the eyes of the author only. It was rejected in 1955. Nonetheless, Hurston continued to believe in her book and supported herself while rewriting by working as a maid, librarian, reporter, and part-time teacher. She had suffered much of her life from periodic stomach ailments, including appendicitis, gall bladder attacks, and gastroenteritis picked up on her trips to the Bahamas and the West Indies. In later years she had become obese and finally suffered a stroke. In 1959, when she could no longer care for herself, she entered the Saint Lucie County welfare home, where she died a year later. She was buried in the segregated cemetery of Fort Pierce, Florida.

Hurston's prose style is informal and metaphoric. She makes use of the conventions of speech familiar to her in her childhood and puts words together to create alliterative poetic images: "There is something about poverty that smells like death. Dead dreams dropping off the heart like leaves in a dry season and rotting around the feet; impulses smothered too long in the fetid air of underground caves. The soul lives in a sickly air. People can be slave-ships in shoes." At other times her words amuse with their outrageous audacity; when Lippincott accepted her first novel, she wrote about the thrill she felt: "You know the feeling when you found your first pubic hair. Greater than that." Both quotations come from her autobiography and show that, like Twain, Hurston was adept at juxtaposing levels of diction. Unlike Twain, she remained an optimist. Viewing pity with disdain, she insisted that the internal life of black men and women is as important as the external barriers against them. She railed against those barriers, but she also wrote with pride about black people living in America. ✎

How It Feels to Be Colored Me[1]

I am colored but I offer nothing in the way of extenuating circumstances except the fact that I am the only Negro in the United States whose grandfather on the mother's side was *not* an Indian chief.

I remember the very day that I became colored. Up to my thirteenth year I lived in the little Negro town of Eatonville, Florida. It is exclusively a colored town. The only white people I knew passed through the town going to or coming from Orlando. The native whites rode dusty horses, the Northern tourists chugged down the sandy village road in automobiles. The town knew the Southerners and never stopped cane chewing when they passed. But the Northerners were something else again. They were peered at cautiously from behind curtains

---

[1] First published in *World Tomorrow*, May 1928, this essay had been submitted before Hurston signed her contract with Mrs. Mason.

by the timid. The more venturesome would come out on the porch to watch them go past and got just as much pleasure out of the tourists as the tourists got out of the village.

The front porch might seem a daring place for the rest of the town, but it was a gallery seat for me. My favorite place was atop the gate-post. Proscenium[1] box for a born first-nighter. Not only did I enjoy the show, but I didn't mind the actors knowing that I liked it. I usually spoke to them in passing. I'd wave at them and when they returned my salute, I would say something like this: "Howdy-do-well-I-thank-you-where-you-goin'?" Usually the automobile or the horse paused at this, and after a queer exchange of compliments, I would probably "go a piece of the way" with them, as we say in farthest Florida. If one of my family happened to come to the front in time to see me, of course negotiations would be rudely broken off. But even so, it is clear that I was the first "welcome-to-our-state" Floridian, and I hope the Miami Chamber of Commerce will please take notice.

During this period, white people differed from colored to me only in that they rode through town and never lived there. They liked to hear me "speak pieces" and sing and wanted to see me dance the parse-me-la,[2] and gave me generously of their small silver for doing these things, which seemed strange to me for I wanted to do them so much that I needed bribing to stop. Only they didn't know it. The colored people gave no dimes. They deplored any joyful tendencies in me, but I was their Zora nevertheless. I belonged to them, to the nearby hotels, to the county—everybody's Zora.

But changes came in the family when I was thirteen, and I was sent to school in Jacksonville.[3] I left Eatonville, the town of the oleanders,[4] as Zora. When I disembarked from the river-boat at Jacksonville, she was no more. It seemed that I had suffered a sea change. I was not Zora of Orange County any more, I was now a little colored girl. I found it out in certain ways. In my heart as well as in the mirror, I became a fast[5] brown—warranted not to rub or run.

But I am not tragically colored. There is no great sorrow dammed up in my soul, nor lurking behind my eyes. I do not mind at all. I do not belong to the sobbing school of Negrohood who hold that nature somehow has given them a lowdown dirty deal and whose feelings are all hurt about it. Even in the helter-skelter skirmish that is my life, I have seen that the world is to the strong regardless of a little pigmentation more or less. No, I do not weep at the world—I am too busy sharpening my oyster knife.

Someone is always at my elbow reminding me that I am the granddaughter of slaves. It fails to register depression with me. Slavery is sixty years in the past. The operation was successful and the patient is doing well, thank you. The terrible

---

[1]Area between the curtain and the orchestra in a theater.
[2]From "La Pas Ma La" (1895), a tune for dancing.
[3]In her autobiography, she says she was nine when she went to Jacksonville.
[4]Poisonous evergreen shrubs with fragrant pink, white, or red flowers.
[5]Permanent.

struggle that made me an American out of a potential slave said "On the line!" The Reconstruction said "Get set!"; and the generation before said "Go!" I am off to a flying start and I must not halt in the stretch to look behind and weep. Slavery is the price I paid for civilization, and the choice was not with me. It is a bully adventure and worth all that I have paid through my ancestors for it. No one on earth ever had a greater chance for glory. The world to be won and nothing to be lost. It is thrilling to think—to know that for any act of mine, I shall get twice as much praise or twice as much blame. It is quite exciting to hold the center of the national stage, with the spectators not knowing whether to laugh or weep.

The position of my white neighbor is much more difficult. No brown specter pulls up a chair beside me when I sit down to eat. No dark ghost thrusts its leg against mine in bed. The game of keeping what one has is never so exciting as the game of getting.

I do not always feel colored. Even now I often achieve the unconscious Zora of Eatonville before the Hegira.[1] I feel most colored when I am thrown against a sharp white background.

For instance at Barnard. "Beside the waters of the Hudson" I feel my race. Among the thousand white persons, I am a dark rock surged upon, and over-swept, but through it all, I remain myself. When covered by the waters, I am; and the ebb but reveals me again.

Sometimes it is the other way around. A white person is set down in our midst, but the contrast is just as sharp for me. For instance, when I sit in the drafty basement that is The New World Cabaret with a white person, my color comes. We enter chatting about any little nothing that we have in common and are seated by the jazz waiters. In the abrupt way that jazz orchestras have, this one plunges into a number. It loses no time in circumlocutions, but gets right down to business. It constricts the thorax and splits the heart with its tempo and narcotic harmonies. This orchestra grows rambunctious, rears on its hind legs and attacks the tonal veil with primitive fury, rending it, clawing it until it breaks through to the jungle beyond. I follow those heathen—follow them exultingly. I dance wildly inside myself; I yell within, I whoop; I shake my assegai[2] above my head, I hurl it true to the mark *yeeeooww*! I am in the jungle and living in the jungle way. My face is painted red and yellow and my body is painted blue. My pulse is throbbing like a war drum. I want to slaughter something—give pain, give death to what, I do not know. But the piece ends. The men of the orchestra wipe their lips and rest their fingers. I creep back slowly to the veneer we call civilization with the last tone and find the white friend sitting motionless in his seat, smoking calmly.

"Good music they have here," he remarks, drumming the table with his fingertips.

---

[1]A flight from danger, from the flight to Medina in A.D. 622 of the monotheistic Muhammad from the polytheistic inhabitants of Mecca marking the beginning of the Muslim era; the abbreviation A.H. is used to indicate the period before the hegira.

[2]A javelin made from the tree of that name in southern Africa.

Music. The great blobs of purple and red emotion have not touched him. He has only heard what I felt. He is far away and I see him but dimly across the ocean and the continent that have fallen between us. He is so pale with his whiteness then and I am *so* colored.

At certain times I have no race, I am *me*. When I set my hat at a certain angle and saunter down Seventh Avenue, Harlem City, feeling as snooty as the lions in front of the Forty-Second Street Library, for instance. So far as my feelings are concerned, Peggy Hopkins Joyce[1] on the Boule Mich[2] with her gorgeous raiment, stately carriage, knees knocking together in a most aristocratic manner, has nothing on me. The cosmic Zora emerges. I belong to no race nor time. I am the eternal feminine with its string of beads.

I have no separate feeling about being an American citizen and colored. I am merely a fragment of the Great Soul that surges within the boundaries. My country, right or wrong.

Sometimes, I feel discriminated against, but it does not make me angry. It merely astonishes me. How *can* any deny themselves the pleasure of my company? It's beyond me.

But in the main, I feel like a brown bag of miscellany propped against a wall. Against a wall in company with other bags, white, red and yellow. Pour out the contents, and there is discovered a jumble of small things priceless and worthless. A first-water[3] diamond, an empty spool, bits of broken glass, lengths of string, a key to a door long since crumbled away, a rusty knife-blade, old shoes saved for a road that never was and never will be, a nail bent under the weight of things too heavy for any nail, a dried flower or two still a little fragrant. In your hand is the brown bag. On the ground before you is the jumble it held—so much like the jumble in the bags, could they be emptied, that all might be dumped in a single heap and the bags refilled without altering the content of any greatly. A bit of colored glass more or less would not matter. Perhaps that is how the Great Stuffer of Bags filled them in the first place—who knows? ✍

---

[1]Born Peggy Upton in Norfolk, Virginia, she ran away from home at fifteen, married the first of her six rich husbands the next day (she met him on the train), and went on to become the most famous gold digger of the 1920s. In Paris on a honeymoon with her third husband, Stanley Joyce, she ran off with Henri Letellier, the "richest man in Paris." By collecting precious stones and cash as well as husbands, she died wealthy in 1957, a legend from a lost time.

[2]The Boulevard St. Michel in Paris.

[3]Highest degree of quality in gems or pearls.

My Birthplace[1]

Like the dead-seeming, cold rocks, I have memories within that come out of the material that went to make me. Time and place have had their say.

So you will have to know something about the time and place where I came from, in order that you may interpret the incidents and directions of my life.

I was born in a Negro town. I do not mean by that the black back-side of an average town. Eatonville, Florida, is, and was at the time of my birth, a pure Negro town—charter, mayor, council, town marshal and all. It was not the first Negro community in America, but it was the first to be incorporated, the first attempt at organized self-government on the part of Negroes in America.

Eatonville is what you might call hitting a straight lick with a crooked stick. The town was not in the original plan. It is a by-product of something else.

It all started with three white men on a ship off the coast of Brazil. They had been officers in the Union Army. When the bitter war had ended in victory for their side, they had set out for South America. Perhaps the post-war distress made their native homes depressing. Perhaps it was just that they were young, and it was hard for them to return to the monotony of everyday being after the excitement of military life, and they, like numerous other young men, set out to find new frontiers.

But they never landed in Brazil. Talking together on the ship, these three decided to return to the United States and try their fortunes in the unsettled country of South Florida. No doubt the same thing which had moved them to go to Brazil caused them to choose South Florida.

This had been dark and bloody country since the mid-1700's. Spanish, French, English, Indian, and American blood had been bountifully shed.

The last great struggle was between the resentful Indians and the white planters of Georgia, Alabama, and South Carolina. The strong and powerful Cherokees, aided by the conglomerate Seminoles, raided the plantations and carried off Negro slaves into Spanish-held Florida. Ostensibly they were carried off to be slaves to the Indians, but in reality the Negro men were used to swell the ranks of the Indian fighters against the white plantation owners. During lulls in the long struggle, treaties were signed, but invariably broken. The sore point of returning escaped Negroes could not be settled satisfactorily to either side. Who was an Indian and who was a Negro? The whites contended all who had Negro blood. The Indians contended all who spoke their language belonged to the tribe. Since it was an easy matter to teach a slave to speak enough of the language to pass in a short time, the question could never be settled. So the wars went on.

---

[1] Chapter 1 of *Dust Tracks on a Road* (1942).

The names of Oglethorpe,[1] Clinch[2] and Andrew Jackson[3] are well known on the white side of the struggle. For the Indians, Miccanopy,[4] Billy Bow-legs[5] and Osceola.[6] The noble Osceola was only a sub-chief, but he came to be recognized by both sides as the ablest of them all. Had he not been captured by treachery, the struggle would have lasted much longer than it did. With an offer of friendship, and a new rifle (some say a beautiful sword) he was lured to the fort seven miles outside of St. Augustine, and captured. He was confined in sombre Fort Marion that still stands in the city, escaped, was recaptured, and died miserably in the prison of a fort in Beaufort, South Carolina. Without his leadership, the Indian cause collapsed. The Cherokees and most of the Seminoles, with their Negro adherents, were moved west. The beaten Indians were moved to what is now Oklahoma. It was far from the then settlements of the whites. And then too, there seemed to be nothing there that white people wanted, so it was a good place for Indians. The wilds of Florida heard no more clash of battle among men.

The sensuous world whirled on in the arms of ether for a generation or so. Time made and marred some men. So into this original hush came the three frontier-seekers who had been so intrigued by its prospects that they had turned back after actually arriving at the coast of Brazil without landing. These young men were no poor, refuge-seeking, wayfarers. They were educated men of family and wealth.

The shores of Lake Maitland were beautiful, probably one reason they decided to settle there, on the northern end where one of the old forts—built against the Indians, had stood. It had been commanded by Colonel Maitland, so the lake and the community took their names in memory of him. It was Mosquito County then and the name was just. It is Orange County now for equally good reason. The

---

[1] James Edward Oglethorpe (1696–1785), English general, founder of the colony of Georgia for debtors. He forbade slavery in the colony and defeated the Spanish in 1742, ensuring the stability of Georgia, before he returned to England. He was a member of the House of Commons for thirty-two years and a friend of Samuel Johnson.

[2] Duncan Lamont Clinch (1787–1849), general in the Seminole War in Florida in 1835. The year after he won the Battle of Ouithlacooche (December 31, 1835), he resigned from the army and was elected to Congress as a Whig; he served until 1845. Fort Clinch in Florida, named after him, was seized by Confederates in the Civil War.

[3] (1767–1845); seventh president of the United States (1829–1837) and military hero in the War of 1812. He fought the Seminoles near the Florida border in 1818, achieving wide popularity among farmers and the middle class.

[4] Seminole Indian chief who, with a force of five hundred, joined Chief Osceola in the Seminole War of 1835 and helped kill General Thompson, causing the Battle of Ouithlacoochee.

[5] Corruption of "Bowleck," name of the Seminole Indian chief who in 1812, during the Seminole Wars, joined King Paine, another Seminole chief and head of a band of Negroes and Indians, to attack settlements in northern Florida. On 11 September 1812 they defeated a small force under Captain Williams. Their band increased, and they attacked General Neuman; Paine was killed, Bowleck wounded, and the band defeated.

[6] A leader of the Seminole Indians (c. 1800–1838) who fought their removal farther west and was captured in St. Augustine, where he had agreed to meet General Jessup, supposedly under a truce.

men persuaded other friends in the north to join them, and the town of Maitland began to be in a great rush.

Negroes were found to do the clearing. There was the continuous roar of the crashing of ancient giants of the lush woods, of axes, saws and hammers. And there on the shores of Lake Maitland rose stately houses, surrounded by beautiful grounds. Other settlers flocked in from upper New York State, Minnesota and Michigan, and Maitland became a center of wealth and fashion. In less than ten years, the Plant System, later absorbed into the Atlantic Coast Line Railroad, had been persuaded to extend a line south through Maitland, and the private coaches of millionaires and other dignitaries from North and South became a common sight on the siding.[1] Even a president of the United States visited his friends at Maitland.

These wealthy homes, glittering carriages behind blooded[2] horses and occupied by well-dressed folk, presented a curious spectacle in the swampy forests so dense that they are dark at high noon. The terrain swarmed with the deadly diamond-back rattlesnake, and huge, decades-old bull alligators bellowed their challenges from the uninhabited shores of lakes. It was necessary to carry a lantern when one walked out at night, to avoid stumbling over these immense reptiles in the streets of Maitland.

Roads were made by the simple expedient of driving buggies and wagons back and forth over the foot trail, which ran for seven miles between Maitland and Orlando. The terrain was as flat as a table and totally devoid of rocks. All the roadmakers had to do was to curve around the numerous big pine trees and oaks. It seems it was too much trouble to cut them down. Therefore, the road looked as if it had been laid out by a playful snake. Now and then somebody would chop down a troublesome tree. Way late, the number of tree stumps along the route began to be annoying. Buggy wheels bumped and jolted over them and took away the pleasure of driving. So a man was hired to improve the road. His instructions were to round off the tops of all stumps so that the wheels, if and when they struck stumps, would slide off gently instead of jolting the teeth out of riders as before. This was done, and the spanking rigs of the bloods whisked along with more assurance.

Now, the Negro population of Maitland settled simultaneously with the white. They had been needed, and found profitable employment. The best of relations existed between employer and employee. While the white estates flourished on the three-mile length of Lake Maitland, the Negroes set up their hastily built shacks around St. John's Hole, a lake as round as a dollar, and less than a half-mile wide. It is now a beauty spot in the heart of Maitland, hard by United States Highway Number 17. They call it Lake Lily.

The Negro women could be seen every day but Sunday squatting around St. John's Hole on their haunches, primitive style, washing clothes and fishing, while

---

[1]A short line of track connected to the main line to provide storage space.

[2]Thoroughbred.

their men went forth and made their support in cutting new ground, building, and planting orange groves. Things were moving so swiftly that there was plenty to do, with good pay. Other Negroes in Georgia and West Florida heard of the boom in South Florida from Crescent City to Cocoa and they came. No more back-bending over rows of cotton; no more fear of the fury of the Reconstruction. Good pay, sympathetic white folks and cheap land, soft to the touch of a plow. Relatives and friends were sent for.

Two years after the three adventurers entered the primeval forests of Mosquito County, Maitland had grown big enough, and simmered down enough, to consider a formal city government.

Now, these founders were, to a man, people who had risked their lives and fortunes that Negroes might be free. Those who had fought in the ranks had thrown their weight behind the cause of Emancipation. So when it was decided to hold an election, the Eatons, Lawrences, Vanderpools, Hurds, Halls, the Hills, Yateses and Galloways, and all the rest including Bishop Whipple, head of the Minnesota diocese, never for a moment considered excluding the Negroes from participation. The whites nominated a candidate, and the Negroes, under the aggressive lead of Joe Clarke, a muscular, dynamic Georgia Negro, put up Tony Taylor as their standard-bearer.

I do not know whether it was the numerical superiority of the Negroes, or whether some of the whites, out of deep feeling, threw their votes to the Negro side. At any rate, Tony Taylor became the first mayor of Maitland with Joe Clarke winning out as town marshal. This was a wholly unexpected turn, but nobody voiced any open objections. The Negro mayor and marshal and the white city council took office peacefully and served their year without incident.

But during that year, a yeast was working. Joe Clarke had asked himself, why not a Negro town? Few of the Negroes were interested. It was too vaulting for their comprehension. A pure Negro town! If nothing but their own kind was in it, who was going to run it? With no white folks to command them, how would they know what to do? Joe Clarke had plenty of confidence in himself to do the job, but few others could conceive of it.

But one day by chance or purpose, Joe Clarke was telling of his ambitions to Captain Eaton, who thought it a workable plan. He talked it over with Captain Lawrence and others. By the end of the year, all arrangements had been made. Lawrence and Eaton bought a tract of land a mile west of Maitland for a town site. The backing of the whites helped Joe Clarke to convince the other Negroes, and things were settled.

Captain Lawrence at his own expense erected a well-built church on the new site, and Captain Eaton built a hall for general assembly and presented it to the new settlement. A little later, the wife of Bishop Whipple had the first church rolled across the street and built a larger church on the same spot, and the first building was to become a library, stocked with books donated by the white community.

So on August 18, 1886, the Negro town, called Eatonville, after Captain Eaton, received its charter of incorporation from the state capital, Tallahassee, and made history by becoming the first of its kind in America, and perhaps in the world. So, in a raw, bustling frontier, the experiment of self-government for Negroes was tried. White Maitland and Negro Eatonville have lived side by side for fifty-six years without a single instance of enmity. The spirit of the founders has reached beyond the grave.

The whole lake country of Florida sprouted with life—mostly Northerners, and prosperity was everywhere. It was in the late eighties that the stars fell, and many of the original settlers date their coming "just before, or just after the stars fell."[1] ✍

My Folks[2]

Into this burly, boiling, hard-hitting, rugged-individualistic setting walked one day a tall, heavy-muscled mulatto who resolved to put down roots.

John Hurston, in his late twenties, had left Macon County, Alabama, because the ordeal of share-cropping on a southern Alabama cotton plantation was crushing to his ambition. There was no rise to the thing.

He had been born near Notasulga, Alabama, in an outlying district of landless Negroes, and whites not too much better off. It was "over the creek," which was just like saying on the wrong side of the railroad tracks. John Hurston had learned to read and write somehow between cotton-choppings and cotton-picking, and it might have satisfied him in a way. But somehow he took to going to Macedonia Baptist Church on the right side of the creek. He went one time, and met up with dark-brown Lucy Ann Potts, of the land-owning Richard Potts, which might have given him the going habit.

He was nearly twenty years old then, and she was fourteen. My mother used to claim with a smile that she saw him looking and looking at her up there in the choir and wondered what he was looking at her for. She wasn't studying about *him*. However, when the service was over and he kept standing around, never far from her, she asked somebody, "Who is dat bee-stung yaller nigger?"

"Oh, dat's one of dem niggers from over de creek, one of dem Hurstons—call him John I believe."

That was supposed to settle that. Over-the-creek niggers lived from one white man's plantation to the other. Regular hand-to-mouth folks. Didn't own pots to pee in, nor beds to push 'em under. Didn't have no more pride than to let themselves be hired by poor-white trash. No more to 'em than the stuffings out of a zero. The inference was that Lucy Ann Potts had asked about nothing and had been told.

Mama thought no more about him, she said. Of course, she couldn't help noticing that his gray-green eyes and light skin stood out sharply from the

---

[1] 1833? In Faulkner's *Go Down Moses* (1942), in the section titled "The Bear," the ledger records June 1833 as "yr stars fell." The phrase refers to a meteor shower.

[2] Chapter 2 of *Dust Tracks on a Road* (1942).

black-skinned, black-eyed crowd he was in. Then, too, he had a build on him that made you look. A stud-looking buck like that would have brought a big price in slavery time. Then, if he had not kept on hanging around where she couldn't help from seeing him, she would never have remembered that she had seen him two or three times before around the cotton-gin in Notasulga, and once in a store. She had wondered then who he was, handling bales of cotton like suitcases.

After that Sunday, he got right worrisome. Slipping her notes between the leaves of hymn-books and things like that. It got so bad that a few months later she made up her mind to marry him just to get rid of him. So she did, in spite of the most violent opposition of her family. She put on the little silk dress which she had made with her own hands, out of goods bought from egg-money she had saved. Her ninety pounds of fortitude set out on her wedding night alone, since none of the family except her brother Jim could bear the sight of her great come-down in the world. She who was considered the prettiest and the smartest black girl was throwing herself away and disgracing the Pottses by marrying an over-the-creek nigger, and a bastard at that. Folks said he was a certain white man's son. But here she was, setting out to walk two miles at night by herself, to keep her pledge to him at the church. Her father, more tolerant than her mother, decided that his daughter was not going alone, nor was she going to walk to her wedding. So he hitched up the buggy and went with her. Nobody much was there. Her brother Jim slipped in just before she stood on the floor.

So she said her words and took her stand for life, and went off to a cabin on a plantation with him. She never forgot how the late moon shone that night as his two hundred pounds of bone and muscle shoved open the door and lifted her in his arms over the doorsill.

That cabin on a white man's plantation had to be all for the present. She had been pointedly made to know that the Potts plantation was nothing to her any more. Her father soon softened and was satisfied to an extent, but her mother, never. To her dying day her daughter's husband was never John Hurston to her. He was always "dat yaller bastard." Four years after my mother's marriage, and during her third pregnancy, she got to thinking of the five acres of cling-stone peaches on her father's place, and the yearning was so strong that she walked three miles to get a few. She was holding the corners of her apron with one hand and picking peaches with the other when her mother spied her, and ordered her off the place.

It was after his marriage that my father began to want things. Plantation life began to irk and bind him. His over-the-creek existence was finished. What else was there for a man like him? He left his wife and three children behind and went out to seek and see.

Months later he pitched into the hurly-burly of South Florida. So he heard about folks building a town all out of colored people. It seemed like a good place to go. Later on, he was to be elected Mayor of Eatonville for three terms, and to write the local laws. The village of Eatonville is still governed by the laws formulated by my father. The town clerk still consults a copy of the original printing which seems to be the only one in existence now. I have tried every way I know how to get this copy for my library, but so far it has not been possible. I had it once, but the town clerk came and took it back.

When my mother joined Papa a year after he had settled in Eatonville, she brought some quilts, her featherbed and bedstead. That was all they had in the house that night. Two burlap bags were stuffed with Spanish moss for the two older children to sleep on. The youngest child was taken into the bed with them.

So these two began their new life. Both of them swore that things were going to better, and it came to pass as they said. They bought land, built a roomy house, planted their acres and reaped. Children kept coming—more mouths to feed and more feet for shoes. But neither of them seemed to have minded that. In fact, my father not only boasted among other men about "his house full of young'uns" but he boasted that he had never allowed his wife to go out and hit a lick of work for anybody a day in her life. Of weaknesses, he had his share, and I know that my mother was very unhappy at times, but neither of them ever made any move to call the thing off. In fact, on two occasions, I heard my father threaten to kill my mother if she ever started towards the gate to leave him. He was outraged and angry one day when she said lightly that if he did not want to do for her and his children, there was another man over the fence waiting for his job. That expression is a folksaying and Papa had heard it used hundreds of times by other women, but he was outraged at hearing it from Mama. She definitely understood, before he got through carrying on, that the saying was not for her lips.

On another occasion Papa got the idea of escorting the wife of one of his best friends, and having the friend escort Mama. But Mama seemed to enjoy it more than Papa thought she ought to—though she had opposed the idea when it was suggested—and it ended up with Papa leaving his friend's wife at the reception and following Mama and his friend home, and marching her into the house with the muzzle of his Winchester rifle in her back. The friend's wife, left alone at the hall, gave both her husband and Papa a good cussing out the next day. Mama dared not laugh, even at that, for fear of stirring Papa up more. It was a month or so before the two families thawed out again. Even after that, the subject could never be mentioned before Papa or the friend's wife, though both of them had been red-hot for the experiment.

My mother rode herd on one woman with a horsewhip about Papa, and "spoke out" another one. This, instead of making Papa angry, seemed to please him ever so much. The woman who got "spoken out" threatened to whip my mother. Mother was very small and the other woman was husky. But when Papa heard of the threats against Mama, he notified the outside woman that if she could not whip him too, she had better not bring the mess up. The woman left the county without ever breaking another breath with Papa. Nobody around there knew what became of her.

So, looking back, I take it that Papa and Mama, in spite of his meanderings, were really in love. Maybe he was just born before his time.

We lived on a big piece of ground with two big chinaberry trees shading the front gate and Cape jasmine bushes with hundreds of blooms on either side of the walks. I loved the fleshy, white, fragrant blooms as a child but did not make too much of them. They were too common in my neighborhood. When I got to New York and found out that the people called them gardenias, and that the flowers cost a dollar each, I was impressed. The home folks laughed when I went back down there and told them. Some of the folks did not want to believe me. A dollar for a Cape jasmine bloom! Folks up north there must be crazy.

There were plenty of orange, grapefruit, tangerine, guavas and other fruits in our yard. We had a five-acre garden with things to eat growing in it, and so we were never hungry. We had chicken on the table often; home-cured meat, and all the eggs we wanted. It was a common thing for us smaller children to fill the iron tea-kettle full of eggs and boil them, and lay around in the yard and eat them until we were full. Any left-over boiled eggs could always be used for missiles. There was plenty of fish in the lakes around the town, and so we had all that we wanted. But beef stew was something rare. We were all very happy whenever Papa went to Orlando and brought back something delicious like stew-beef. Chicken and fish were too common with us. In the same way, we treasured an apple. We had oranges, tangerines and grapefruit to use as hand-grenades on the neighbors' children. But apples were something rare. They came from way up north.

Our house had eight rooms, and we called it a two-story house; but later on I learned it was really one story and a jump. The big boys all slept up there, and it was a good place to hide and shirk from sweeping off the front porch or raking up the back yard.

Downstairs in the dining-room there was an old "safe," a punched design in its tin doors. Glasses of guava jelly, quart jars of pear, peach and other kinds of preserves. The left-over cooked foods were on the lower shelves.

There were eight children in the family, and our house was noisy from the time school turned out until bedtime. After supper we gathered in Mama's room, and everybody had to get their lessons for the next day. Mama carried us all past long division in arithmetic, and parsing sentences in grammar, by diagrams on the blackboard. That was as far as she had gone. Then the younger ones were turned over to my oldest brother, Bob, and Mama sat and saw to it that we paid attention. You had to keep on going over things until you did know. How I hated the multiplication tables—especially the sevens!

We had a big barn, and a stretch of ground well covered with Bermuda grass. So on moonlight nights, two-thirds of the village children from seven to eighteen would be playing hide and whoop, chick-mah-chick, hide and seek, and other boisterous games in our yard. Once or twice a year we might get permission to go and play at some other house. But that was most unusual. Mama contended that we had plenty of space to play in; plenty of things to play with; and, furthermore, plenty of us to keep each other's company. If she had her way, she meant to raise her children to stay at home. She said that there was no need for us to live like no-count Negroes and poor-white trash—too poor to sit in the house—had to come outdoors for any pleasure, or hang around somebody else's house. Any of her children who had any tendencies like that must have got it from the Hurston side. It certainly did not come from the Pottses. Things like that gave me my first glimmering of the universal female gospel that all good traits and leanings come from the mother's side.

Mama exhorted her children at every opportunity to "jump at de sun." We might not land on the sun, but at least we would get off the ground. Papa did not feel so hopeful. Let well enough alone. It did not do for Negroes to have too much spirit. He was always threatening to break mine or kill me in the attempt. My mother was always standing between us. She conceded that I was impudent and given to talking back, but she didn't want to "squinch my spirit" too much for fear that I would turn out to be a mealy-mouthed rag doll by the time I got grown. Papa always flew hot when Mama said that. I do not know whether he feared for my future, with the tendency I had to stand and give battle, or that he felt a personal reference in Mama's observation. He predicted dire things for me. The white folks were not going to stand for it. I was going to be hung before I got grown. Somebody was going to blow me down for my sassy tongue. Mama was going to suck sorrow for not beating my temper out of me before it was too late. Posses with ropes and guns were going to drag me out sooner or later on account of that stiff neck I toted. I was going to tote a hungry belly by reason of my forward ways. My older sister was meek and mild. She would always get along. Why couldn't I be like her? Mama would keep right on with whatever she was doing and remark, "Zora is my young'un, and Sarah is yours. I'll be bound mine will come out more than conquer. You leave her alone. I'll tend to her when I figger she needs it." She meant by that that Sarah had a disposition like Papa's, while mine was like hers.

Behind Mama's rocking-chair was a good place to be in times like that. Papa was not going to hit Mama. He was two hundred pounds of bone and muscle and Mama weighed somewhere in the nineties. When people teased him about Mama being the boss, he would say he could break her of her headstrong ways if he wanted to, but she was so little that he couldn't find any place to hit her. My Uncle Jim, Mama's brother, used to always take exception to that. He maintained that if a woman had anything big enough to sit on, she had something big enough to hit on. That was his firm conviction, and he meant to hold on to it as long as the bottom end of his backbone pointed towards the ground—don't care who the woman was or what she looked like, or where she came from. Men like Papa who held to any other notion were just beating around the bush, dodging the issue, and otherwise looking like a fool at a funeral.

Papa used to shake his head at this and say, "What's de use of me taking my fist to a poor weakly thing like a woman? Anyhow, you got to submit yourself to 'em, so there ain't no use in beating on 'em and then have to go back and beg 'em pardon."

But perhaps the real reason that Papa did not take Uncle Jim's advice too seriously was because he saw how it worked out in Uncle Jim's own house. He could tackle Aunt Caroline, all right, but he had his hands full to really beat her. A knockdown didn't convince her that the fight was over at all. She would get up and come right on in, and she was nobody's weakling. It was generally conceded that he might get the edge on her in physical combat if he took a hammer or a trace-chain[1] to her, but in other ways she always won. She would watch his various philandering episodes just so long, and then she would go into action. One time she saw all, and said nothing. But one Saturday afternoon, she watched him rush in with a new shoe-box which he thought that she did not see him take out to the barn and hide until he was ready to go out. Just as the sun went down, he went out, got his box, cut across the orange grove and went on down to the store.

He stopped long enough there to buy a quart of peanuts, two stalks of sugarcane, and then tripped on off to the little house in the woods where lived a certain transient light of love. Aunt Caroline kept right on ironing until he had gotten as far as the store. Then she slipped on her shoes, went out in the yard and got the axe, slung it across her shoulder and went walking very slowly behind him.

The men on the store porch had given Uncle Jim a laughing sendoff. They all knew where he was going and why. The shoes had been bought right there at the store. Now here came "dat Cal'line" with her axe on her shoulder. No chance to warn Uncle Jim at all. Nobody expected murder, but they knew that plenty of trouble was on the way. So they just sat and waited. Cal'line had done so many side-splitting things to Jim's lights of love—all without a single comment from her—that they were on pins to see what happened next.

About an hour later, when it was almost black dark, they saw a furtive figure in white dodging from tree to tree until it hopped over Clark's strawberry-patch fence and headed towards Uncle Jim's house until it disappeared.

"Looked mightily like a man in long drawers and nothing else," Walter Thomas observed. Everybody agreed that it did, but who and what could it be?

By the time the town lamp which stood in front of the store was lighted, Aunt Caroline emerged from the blackness that hid the woods and passed the store. The axe was still over her shoulder, but now it was draped with Uncle Jim's pants, shirt and coat. A new pair of women's oxfords were dangling from the handle by their strings. Two stalks of sugarcane were over her other shoulder. All she said was, "Good-evening, gentlemen," and kept right on walking towards home.

The porch rocked with laughter. They had the answer to everything. Later on when they asked Uncle Jim how Cal'line managed to get into the lady's house, he smiled sourly and said, "Dat axe was her key." When they kept on teasing him, he said, "Oh, dat old stubborn woman I married, you can't teach her nothing. I can't teach her no city ways at all."

On another occasion, she caused another lady who couldn't give the community anything but love, baby, to fall off of the high, steep church steps on her head. Aunt Cal'line might have done that just to satisfy her curiosity, since it was said that the lady felt that anything more than a petticoat under her dresses would be an encumbrance. Maybe Aunt Caroline just wanted to verify the rumor. The way the lady tumbled, it left no doubt in the matter. She was really a free soul. Evidently Aunt Caroline was put out about it, because she had to expectorate at that very moment, and it just happened to land where the lady was bare. Aunt

---

[1]Strap connecting a draft animal to the vehicle it pulls.

Caroline evidently tried to correct her error in spitting on her rival, for she took her foot and tried to grind it in. She never said a word as usual, so the lady must have misunderstood Aunt Caroline's curiosity. She left town in a hurry—a speedy hurry—and never was seen in those parts again.

So Papa did not take Uncle Jim's philosophy about handling the lady people too seriously. Every time Mama cornered him about some of his doings, he used to threaten to wring a chair over her head. She never even took enough notice of the threat to answer. She just went right on asking questions about his doings and then answering them herself until Papa slammed out of the house looking like he had been whipped all over with peach hickories. But I had better not let out a giggle at such times, or it would be just too bad.

Our house was a place where people came. Visiting preachers, Sunday school and B.Y.P.U.[1] workers, and just friends. There was fried chicken for visitors, and other such hospitality as the house afforded.

Papa's bedroom was the guest-room. Store-bought towels would be taken out of the old round-topped trunk in Mama's room and draped on the washstand. The pitcher and bowl were scrubbed out before fresh water from the pump was put in for the use of the guest. Sweet soap was company soap. We knew that. Otherwise, Octagon laundry soap was used to keep us clean. Bleached-out meal sacks served the family for bath towels ordinarily, so that the store-bought towels could be nice and clean for visitors.

Company got the preference in toilet paper, too. Old newspapers were put out in the privy house for family use. But when the company came, something better was offered them. Fair to middling guests got sheets out of the old Sears, Roebuck catalogue. But Mama would sort over her old dress patterns when really fine company came, and the privy house was well scrubbed, lime thrown in, and the soft tissue paper pattern stuck on a nail inside the place for the comfort and pleasure of our guests. ✎

The "Pet" Negro System[2]

Brothers and sisters, I take my text this morning from the Book of Dixie.[3] I take my text and I take my time.

Now it says here, "And every white man shall be allowed to pet himself a Negro. Yea, he shall take a black man unto himself to pet and to cherish, and this same Negro shall be perfect in his sight. Nor shall hatred among the races of men, nor conditions of strife in the walled cities, cause his pride and pleasure in his own Negro to wane."

---

[1]Baptist Young People's Union.

[2]First published in *American Mercury*, May 1943.

[3]The southern states of the Confederacy during the Civil War, possibly from a ten-dollar bill with *Dix* printed on both sides that was issued in New Orleans before the war.

Now, beloved Brothers and Sisters, I see you have all woke up and you can't wait till the service is over to ask me how come? So I will read you further from the sacred word which says here:

"Thus spake the Prophet of Dixie when slavery was yet a young thing, for he saw the yearning in the hearts of men. And the dwellers in the bleak North, they who pass old-made phrases through their mouths, shall cry out and say, 'What are these strange utterances? Is it not written that the hand of every white man in the South is raised against his black brother? Do not the sons of Japheth[1] drive the Hammites before them like beasts? Do they not lodge them in shacks and hovels and force them to share the crops? Is not the condition of black men in the South most horrible? Then how doth this scribe named Hurston speak of pet Negroes? Perchance she hath drunk of new wine, and it has stung her like an adder?'"

Now, my belov-ed, before you explode in fury you might look to see if you know your facts or if you merely know your phrases. It happens that there are more angles to this race-adjustment business than are ever pointed out to the public, white, black or in-between. Well-meaning outsiders make plans that look perfect from where they sit, possibly in some New York office. But these plans get wrecked on hidden snags. John Brown[2] at Harpers Ferry is a notable instance. The simple race-agin-race pattern of those articles and speeches on the subject is not that simple at all. The actual conditions do not jibe with the fulminations of the so-called spokesmen of the white South, nor with the rhetoric of the champions of the Negro cause either.

II.[3]   Big men like Bilbo,° Heflin[4] and Tillman[5] bellow threats which they know they couldn't carry out even in their own districts. The orators at both extremes may glint and glitter in generalities, but the South lives and thinks in individuals. The North has no interest in the particular Negro, but talks of justice for the whole. The South has no interest, and pretends none, in the mass of Negroes but is very much concerned about the individual. So that brings us to the pet Negro, because to me at least it symbolizes the web of feelings and mutual dependencies spun by generations and generations of living together and natural adjustment. It isn't half as pretty as the ideal adjustment of theorizers, but it's a lot more real and durable, and a lot of black folk, I'm afraid, find it mighty cozy.

The pet Negro, belov-ed, is someone whom a particular white person or persons wants to have and to do all the things forbidden to other Negroes. It can

---

[1]Third son of Noah; Ham, the first son, cursed for seeing his father naked, was said to be the father of the Ethiopians; see Genesis 9:20–27, in which Canaan, son of Ham, is condemned to slavery under Japheth. See also Browne, "The Color of Negroes, Continued."

[2]American abolitionist (1800–1859) who on October 16, 1859 captured the arsenal at Harpers Ferry but lost to Col. Robert E. Lee. He was hanged December 2.

[3]There is no I. in the original.

[4]James Thomas, U.S. senator (1920–1930) from Alabama known for his crusades in favor of white supremacy and against Catholics.

[5]Benjamin Ryan, U.S. senator (1895–1918) from South Carolina who favored force to keep blacks from voting.

be Aunt Sue, Uncle Stump, or the black man at the head of some Negro organization. Let us call him John Harper. John Harper is the pet of Colonel Cary and his lady, and Colonel Cary swings a lot of weight in his community.

The Colonel will tell you that he opposes higher education for Negroes. It makes them mean and cunning. Bad stuff for Negroes. He is against having lovely, simple blacks turned into rascals by too much schooling. But there are exceptions. Take John, for instance. Worked hard, saved up his money and went up there to Howard University and got his degree in education. Smart as a whip! Seeing that John had such a fine head, of course he helped John out when necessary. Not that he would do such a thing for the average darky, no sir! He is no nigger lover. Strictly unconstructed Southerner, willing to battle for white supremacy! But his John is different.

So naturally when John finished college and came home, Colonel Cary knew he was the very man to be principal of the Negro high school, and John got the post even though someone else had to be eased out. And making a fine job of it. Decent, self-respecting fellow. Built himself a nice home and bought himself a nice car. John's wife is county nurse; the Colonel spoke to a few people about it and she got the job. John's children are smart and have good manners. If all the Negroes were like them he wouldn't mind what advancement they made. But the rest of them, of course, lie like the cross-ties from New York to Key West. They steal things and get drunk. Too bad, but Negroes are like that.

Now there are some prominent white folk who don't see eye to eye with Colonel Cary about this John Harper. They each have a Negro in mind who is far superior to John. They listen to eulogies about John only because they wish to be listened to about their own pets. They pull strings for the Colonel's favorites knowing that they will get the same thing done for theirs.

Now, how can the Colonel make his attitude towards John Harper jibe with his general attitude towards Negroes? Easy enough. He got his general attitude by tradition, and he has no quarrel with it. But he found John truthful and honest, clean, reliable and a faithful friend. He *likes* John and so considers him as white inside as anyone else. The treatment made and provided for Negroes generally is suspended, restrained and done away with. He knows that John is able to learn what white people of similar opportunities learn. Colonel Cary's affection and respect for John, however, in no way extend to black folk in general.

When you understand that, you can see why it is so difficult to change certain things in the South. His particular Negroes are not suffering from the strictures, and the rest are no concern of the Colonel's. Let their own white friends do for them. If they are worth the powder and lead it would take to kill them, they have white friends; if not, then they belong in the "stray nigger" class and nobody gives a damn about them. If John should happen to get arrested for anything except assault and murder upon the person of a white man, or rape, the Colonel is going to stand by him and get him out. It would be a hard-up Negro who would work for a man who couldn't get his black friends out of jail.

And mind you, the Negroes have their pet whites, so to speak. It works both ways. Class-consciousness of Negroes is an angle to be reckoned with in the

South. They love to be associated with "the quality" and consequently are ashamed to admit that they are working for "strainers." It is amusing to see a Negro servant chasing the madam or the boss back on his or her pedestal when they behave in an unbecoming manner. Thereby he is to a certain extent preserving his own prestige, derived from association with that family.

If ever it came to the kind of violent showdown the orators hint at, you could count on all the Colonel Carys tipping off and protecting their John Harpers; and you could count on all the John Harpers and Aunt Sues to exempt their special white folk. And that means that pretty nearly everybody on both sides would be exempt, except the "pore white trash" and the "stray niggers," and not all of them.

III.   An outsider driving through a street of well-off Negro homes, seeing the great number of high-priced cars, will wonder why he has never heard of this side of Negro life in the South. He has heard about the shacks and the sharecroppers. He has had them before him in literature and editorials and crusading journals. But the other side isn't talked about by the champions of white supremacy, because it makes their stand, and their stated reasons for keeping the Negro down, look a bit foolish. The Negro crusaders and their white adherents can't talk about it because it is obviously bad strategy. The worst aspects must be kept before the public to force action.

It has been so generally accepted that all Negroes in the South are living under horrible conditions that many friends of the Negro up North actually take offense if you don't tell them a tale of horror and suffering. They stroll up to you, cocktail glass in hand, and say, "I am a friend of the Negro, you know, and feel awful about the terrible conditions down there." That's your cue to launch into atrocities amidst murmurs of sympathy. If, on the other hand, just to find out if they really have done some research down there, you ask "What conditions do you refer to?" you get an injured, and sometimes a malicious, look. Why ask foolish questions? Why drag in the many Negroes of opulence and education? Yet these comfortable, contented Negroes are as real as the sharecroppers.

There is, in normal times, a regular stream of high-powered cars driven by Negroes headed North each summer for a few weeks' vacation. These people go, have their fling, and hurry back home. Doctors, teachers, lawyers, businessmen, they are living and working in the South because that is where they want to be. And why not? Economically, they are at ease and more. The professional men do not suffer from the competition of their white colleagues to anything like they do up North. Personal vanity, too, is served. The South makes a sharp distinction between the upper-class and lower-class Negro. Businessmen cater to him. His word is *good* downtown. There is some Mr. Big in the background who is interested in him and will back his fall. All the plums that a Negro can get are dropped in his mouth. He wants no part of the cold, impersonal North. He notes that there is segregation and discrimination up there, too, with none of the human touches of the South.

As I have said, belov-ed, these Negroes who are petted by white friends think just as much of their friends across the line. There is a personal attachment that will ride over practically anything that is liable to happen to either. They have their fingers crossed, too, when they say they don't like white people. "White people" does not mean their particular friends, any more than niggers means John Harper to the Colonel. This is important. For anyone, or any group, counting on a solid black South, or a solid white South in opposition to each other will run into a hornet's nest if he discounts these personal relations. Both sides admit the general principle of opposition, but when it comes to putting it into practice, behold what happens. There is a quibbling, a stalling, a backing and filling that nullifies all the purple oratory.

So well is this underground hookup established, that it is not possible to keep a secret from either side. Nearly everybody spills the beans to his favorite on the other side of the color line—in strictest confidence, of course. That's how the "petting system" works in the South.

Is it a good thing or a bad thing? Who am I to pass judgment? I am not defending the system, belov-ed, but trying to explain it. The lowdown fact is that it weaves a kind of basic fabric that tends to stabilize relations and give something to work from in adjustments. It works to prevent hasty explosions. There are some people in every community who can always talk things over. It may be the proof that this race situation in America is not entirely hopeless and may even be worked out eventually.

There are dangers in the system. Too much depends on the integrity of the Negro so trusted. It cannot be denied that this trust has been abused at times. What was meant for the whole community has been turned to personal profit by the pet. Negroes have long groaned because of this frequent division of general factors into the channels of private benefits. Why do we not go to Mr. Big and expose the Negro in question? Sometimes it is because we do not like to let white people know that we have folks of that ilk. Sometimes we make a bad face and console ourselves, "At least one Negro has gotten himself a sinecure[1] not usually dealt out to us." We curse him for a yellow-bellied sea-buzzard, a ground-mole and a woods-pussy, call him a white-folkses nigger, an Uncle Tom, and a handkerchief-head and let it go at that. In all fairness, it must be said that these terms are often flung around out of jealousy: somebody else would like the very cinch[2] that the accused has grabbed himself.

But when everything is discounted, it still remains true that white people North and South have promoted Negroes—usually in the capacity of "representing the Negro"—with little thought of the ability of the person promoted but in line with the "pet system." In the South it can be pointed to scornfully as a residue of feudalism; in the North no one says what it is. And that, too, is part of the illogical, indefensible but somehow useful "pet system."

---

[1] A paid position requiring little work, from the Latin for "without care."
[2] Certainty.

IV.   The most powerful reason why Negroes do not do more about false "representation" by pets is that they know from experience that the thing is too deep-rooted to be budged. The appointer has his reasons, personal or political. He can always point to the beneficiary and say, "Look, Negroes, you have been taken care of. Didn't I give a member of your group a big job?" White officials assume that the Negro element is satisfied and they do not know what to make of it when later they find that so large a body of Negroes charge indifference and double-dealing. The white friend of the Negroes mumbles about ingratitude and decides that you simply can't understand Negroes . . . just like children.

A case in point is Dr. James E. Sheppard,[1] President of the North Carolina State College for Negroes. He has a degree in pharmacy, and no other. For years he ran a one-horse religious school of his own at Durham, North Carolina. But he has always been in politics and has some good friends in power at Raleigh. So the funds for the State College for Negroes were turned over to him, and his little church school became the Negro college so far as that State is concerned. A fine set of new buildings has been erected. With a host of Negro men highly trained as educators within the State, not to mention others who could be brought in, a pharmacist heads up higher education for Negroes in North Carolina. North Carolina can't grasp why Negroes aren't perfectly happy and grateful.

In every community there is some Negro strong man or woman whose word is going to go. In Jacksonville, Florida, for instance, there is Eartha White.[2] You better see Eartha if you want anything from the white powers-that-be. She happens to be tremendously interested in helping the unfortunates of her city and she does get many things for them from the whites.

I have white friends with whom I would, and do, stand when they have need of me, race counting for nothing at all. Just friendship. All the well-known Negroes could honestly make the same statement. I mean that they all have strong attachments across the line whether they intended them in the beginning or not. Carl Van Vechten° and Henry Allen Moe[3] could ask little of me that would be refused. Walter White,[4] the best known race champion of our time, is hand and glove with Supreme Court Justice Black, a native of Alabama and an ex-Klansman. So you see how this friendship business makes a sorry mess of all the rules made and provided. James Weldon Johnson,[5] the crusader for Negro rights, was bogged

---

[1]According to Hurston's biographer Hemenway, Shepherd was an excellent educator who hired Hurston as director of drama in 1939. But Hurston, for whatever reasons, failed to produce even one play and left, embittered, in 1940.

[2](1876–1974) A black businesswoman and community leader in Jacksonville, Florida, known as the Angel of Mercy; her many activities supporting racial equality included the founding of an orphanage for black children, a nursing home, and the Clara White Mission to feed and house the poor.

[3]Director of the Guggenheim Foundation who granted Hurston a fellowship in 1935 and 1937; Hurston wrote a number of letters to Moe.

[4]Secretary of the National Association for the Advancement of Colored People (NAACP) from 1931 to his death in 1955.

[5](1871–1938) One of the founders of the NAACP, he was also the first black lawyer in Florida, an American consul, a professor at Fiske, and the author of several books.

to his neck in white friends whom he loved and who loved him. Dr. William E. Burkhardt Du Bois,° the bitterest opponent of the white race that America has ever known, loved Joel Spingarn[1] and was certainly loved in turn by him. The thing doesn't make sense. It just makes beauty.

Friendship, however it comes about, is a beautiful thing. The Negro who loves a white friend is shy in admitting it because he dreads the epithet "white folks' nigger!" The white man is wary of showing too much warmth for his black friends for fear of being called "nigger-lover," so he explains his attachment by extolling the extraordinary merits of his black friend to gain tolerance for it.

This is the inside picture of things, as I see it. Whether you like it or not, is no concern of mine. But it is an important thing to know if you have any plans for racial manipulations in Dixie. You cannot batter in doors down there, and you can save time and trouble, and I do mean trouble, by hunting up the community keys.

In a way, it is a great and heartening tribute to human nature. It will be bound by nothing. The South frankly acknowledged them long ago in its laws against marriage between blacks and whites. If the Southern lawmakers were so sure that racial antipathy would take care of racial purity, there would have been no need for the laws.

"And no man shall seek to deprive a man of his Pet Negro. It shall be unwritten-lawful for any to seek to prevent him in his pleasure thereof. Thus spoke the Prophet of Dixie." *Selah.*[2] 🖉

My Most Humiliating Jim Crow Experience[3]

My most humiliating Jim Crow° experience came in New York instead of the South as one would have expected. It was in 1931 when Mrs. R. Osgood Mason was financing my researches in anthropology. I returned to New York from the Bahama Islands ill with some disturbances of the digestive tract.

Godmother (Mrs. Mason liked for me to call her Godmother) became concerned about my condition and suggested a certain white specialist at her expense. His office was in Brooklyn.

Mr. Paul Chapin[4] called up and made the appointment for me. The doctor told the wealthy and prominent Paul Chapin that I would get the best of care.

---

[1] (1875–1939) A professor at Columbia, an expert in comparative literature, and an officer of the NAACP. In 1913 he funded the Spingarn medal, awarded every year to an outstanding Negro.

[2] Hebrew for "to lift up," appearing intermittently at the end of verses in the Psalms. It is thought to be a signal to singers or musicians, but the intent of the signal is unknown.

[3] First published in 1944.

[4] Perhaps James Paul Chapin (1889–1964), ornithologist for the American Museum in New York City who did his fieldwork in the Belgian Congo and wrote papers on his work in 1932, 1938, 1953, and 1954.

So two days later I journeyed to Brooklyn to submit myself to the care of the great specialist.

His reception room was more than swanky, with a magnificent hammered copper door and other decor on the same plane as the door.

But his receptionist was obviously embarrassed when I showed up. I mentioned the appointment and got inside the door. She went into the private office and stayed a few minutes, then the doctor appeared in the door all in white, looking very important, and also very unhappy from behind his rotund stomach.

He did not approach me at all, but told one of his nurses to take me into a private examination room.

The room was private all right, but I would not rate it highly as an examination room. Under any other circumstances, I would have sworn it was a closet where the soiled towels and uniforms were tossed until called for by the laundry. But I will say this for it, there was a chair in there wedged in between the wall and the pile of soiled linen.

The nurse took me in there, closed the door quickly and disappeared. The doctor came in immediately and began in a desultory manner to ask me about symptoms. It was evident he meant to get me off the premises as quickly as possible. Being the sort of objective person I am, I did not get up and sweep out angrily as I was first disposed to do. I stayed to see just what would happen, and further to torture him more. He went through some motions, stuck a tube down my throat to extract some bile from my gall bladder, wrote a prescription and asked for twenty dollars as a fee.

I got up, set my hat at a reckless angle and walked out, telling him that I would send him a check, which I never did. I went away feeling the pathos of Anglo-Saxon civilization.

And I still mean pathos, for I know that anything with such a false foundation cannot last. Whom the gods would destroy, they first made mad.[1] ✐

Crazy for This Democracy[2]

They tell me this democracy form of government is a wonderful thing. It has freedom, equality, justice, in short, everything! Since 1937 nobody has talked about anything else.

The late Franklin D. Roosevelt sort of re-decorated it, and called these United States the boastful name of "The Arsenal of Democracy."

The radio, the newspapers, and the columnists inside the newspapers, have said how lovely it was.

---

[1]From Euripedes:° "Whom God wishes to destroy he first made mad." The quotation exists in many forms.

[2]First published in *Negro Digest* in December 1945.

And this talk and praise-giving has got me in the notion to try some of the stuff. All I want to do is to get hold of a sample of the thing, and I declare, I sure will try it. I don't know for myself, but I have been told that it is really wonderful.

Like the late Will Rogers,[1] all I know is what I see by the papers. It seems like now, I do not know geography as well as I ought to, or I would not get the wrong idea about so many things. I heard so much about "global" "world-freedom" and things like that, that I must have gotten mixed up about oceans.

I thought that when they said Atlantic Charter,[2] that meant me and everybody in Africa and Asia and everywhere. But it seems like the Atlantic is an ocean that does not touch anywhere but North America and Europe.

Just the other day, seeing how things were going in Asia, I went out and bought myself an atlas and found out how narrow this Atlantic ocean was. No wonder those Four Freedoms[3] couldn't get no further than they did! Why, that poor little ocean can't even wash up some things right here in America, let alone places like India, Burma, Indo-China, and the Netherlands East Indies. We need two more whole oceans for that.

Maybe, I need to go out and buy me a dictionary, too. Or perhaps a spelling-book would help me out a lot. Or it could be that I just mistook the words. Maybe I mistook a British pronunciation for a plain American word. Did F.D.R., aristocrat from Groton and Harvard, using the British language say "arse-and-all" of Democracy when I thought he said plain arsenal? Maybe he did, and I have been mistaken all this time. From what is going on, I think that is what he must have said.

That must be what he said, for from what is happening over on that other, unmentioned ocean, we look like the Ass-and-All of Democracy. Our weapons, money, and the blood of millions of our men have been used to carry the English, French and Dutch and lead them back on the millions of unwilling Asiatics. The Ass-and-all-he-has has been very useful.

The Indo-Chinese are fighting the French now in Indo-China to keep the freedom that they have enjoyed for five or six years now. The Indonesians are trying to stay free from the Dutch, and the Burmese and Malayans from the British.

But American soldiers and sailors are fighting along with the French, Dutch and English to rivet these chains back on their former slaves. How can we so

---

[1]American humorist (1879–1935) who was a cowboy in Oklahoma before he traveled around the world. When he returned to the United States, he performed as a rope twirler and joke teller in vaudeville, joined the Ziegfeld Follies, and wrote several books and a syndicated newspaper column. The "cowboy philosopher," an avid fan of the airplane, died in a plane crash in Alaska.

[2]Peace charter devised by Winston Churchill, Prime Minister of Great Britain, and Franklin Delano Roosevelt, President of the United States, on August 14, 1941, four months before the United States entered the war. The charter opposed changes in territory made against the wishes of those affected and supported the restoration of self-government, the easing of trade restrictions, and world cooperation in the achievement of economic and social security and freedom.

[3]Described in Roosevelt's annual message to Congress on January 6, 1941, which outlined the war aims. They are "freedom of speech and expression," "freedom of every person to worship God in his own way," "freedom from want," and "freedom from fear."

admire the fire and determination of Toussaint Louverture[1] to resist the orders of Napoleon to "Rip the gold braids off those Haitian slaves and put them back to work" after four years of freedom, and be indifferent to these Asiatics for the same feelings under the same circumstances?

Have we not noted that not one word has been uttered about the freedom of the Africans? On the contrary, there have been mutterings in undertones about being fair and giving different nations sources of raw materials there? The Ass-and-All of Democracy has shouldered the load of subjugating the dark world completely.

The only Asiatic power[2] able to offer any effective resistance has been double-teened[3] by the combined powers of the Occident and rendered incapable of offering or encouraging resistance, and likewise removed as an example to the dark people of the world.

The inference is, that God has restated the superiority of the West. God always does like that when a thousand white people surround one dark one. Dark people are always "bad" when they do not admit the Divine Plan like that. A certain Javanese man who sticks up for Indonesian Independence is very low-down by the papers, and suspected of being a Japanese puppet. Wanting the Dutch to go back to Holland and go to work for themselves! The very idea! A very, very bad man, that Javanese.

As for me, I am just as sceptical as this contrary Javanese. I accept this idea of Democracy. I am all for trying it out. It must be a good thing if everybody praises it like that. If our government has been willing to go to war and to sacrifice billions of dollars and millions of men for the idea, I think that I ought to give the thing a trial.

The only thing that keeps me from pitching headlong into the thing is the presence of numerous Jim Crow° laws on the statute books of the nation. I am crazy about the idea of this Democracy. I want to see how it feels. Therefore, I am all for the repeal of every Jim Crow° law in the nation here and now. Not in another generation or so. The Hurstons have already been waiting eighty years for that. I want it here and now.

And why not? A lot of people in these United States have been saying all this time that things ought to be equal. Numerous instances of inequality have been pointed out, and fought over in the courts and in the newspapers. That seems like a waste of time to me.

The patient has the small-pox. Segregation and things like that are the bumps and blisters on the skin, and not the disease, but evidence and symptoms of the sickness. The doctors around the bedside of the patient are desperately picking bumps. Some assume that the opening of one blister will cure the case. Some strangely assert that a change of climate is all that is needed to kill the virus in the blood!

---

[1]François Dominique Toussaint L'Ouverture (c. 1744–1803); Haitian revolutionary, freed slave, and martyr who helped the French expel the British and Spanish in 1798 but was seized by the French in 1802. He died in prison.

[2]Possibly Japan, the only strong Asiatic military power, crushed by the Allies and the bomb.

[3]From double-teamed: to cover an offensive player with two defensive players simultaneously.

But why this sentimental over-simplification in diagnosis? Do the doctors not know anything about the widespread occurrence of this disease? It is NOT peculiar to the South. Canada, once the refuge of escaping slaves, has now its denomination of second-class citizens, and they are the Japanese and other non-Caucasians. The war cannot explain it, because enemy Germans are not put in that second class.

Jim Crow° is the rule in South Africa, and is even more extensive than in America. More rigid and grinding. No East Indian may ride first-class in the trains of British-held India. Jim Crow° is common in all colonial Africa, Asia and the Netherlands East Indies. There, too, a Javanese male is punished for flirting back at a white female. So why this stupid assumption that "moving North" will do away with social smallpox? Events in northern cities do not bear out this juvenile contention.

So why the waste of good time and energy, and further delay the recovery of the patient by picking him over bump by bump and blister to blister? Why not the shot of serum that will kill the thing in the blood? The bumps are symptoms. The symptoms cannot disappear until the cause is cured.

These Jim Crow° laws have been put on the books for a purpose, and that purpose is psychological. It has two edges to the thing. By physical evidence, back seats in trains, back-doors of houses, exclusion from certain places and activities, to promote in the mind of the smallest white child the conviction of First by Birth, eternal and irrevocable like the place assigned to the Levites by Moses over the other tribes of the Hebrews. Talent, capabilities, nothing has anything to do with the case. Just FIRST BY BIRTH.

No one of darker skin can ever be considered an equal. Seeing the daily humiliations of the darker people confirms the child in its superiority, so that it comes to feel it the arrangement of God. By the same means, the smallest dark child is to be convinced of its inferiority, so that it is to be convinced that competition is out of the question, and against all nature and God.

All physical and emotional things flow from this premise. It perpetuates itself. The unnatural exaltation of one ego, and the equally unnatural grinding down of the other. The business of some whites to help pick a bump or so is even part of the pattern. Not a human right, but a concession from the throne has been made. Otherwise why do they not take the attitude of Robert Ingersoll[1] that all of it is wrong? Why the necessity for the little concession? Why not go for the underskin injection? Is it a bargaining with a detail to save the whole intact? It is something to think about.

As for me, I am committed to the hypodermic and the serum. I see no point in the picking of a bump. Others can erupt too easily. That same one can burst out again. Witness the easy scrapping of FEPC.[2] No, I give my hand, my heart and my head to the total struggle. I am for complete repeal of All Jim Crow° Laws in the

---

[1]Famous lecturer and lawyer (1833–1899) who fought for the Union in the Civil War and became known as "the great agnostic" for his speeches questioning Christianity.
[2]The Fair Employment Practices Code, created by the Committee on Fair Employment Practices, established in 1941 to eliminate discrimination in hiring.

United States once and for all, and right now. For the benefit of this nation and as a precedent to the world.

I have been made to believe in this democracy thing, and I am all for tasting this democracy out. The flavor must be good. If the Occident is so intent in keeping the taste out of darker mouths that it spends all those billions and expends all those millions of lives, colored ones too, to keep it among themselves, then it must be something good. I crave to sample this gorgeous thing. So I cannot say anything different from repeal of all Jim Crow° laws! Not in some future generation, but repeal *now* and forever!! ✐

What White Publishers Won't Print[1]

I have been amazed by the Anglo-Saxon's lack of curiosity about the internal lives and emotions of the Negroes, and for that matter, any non-Anglo-Saxon peoples within our borders, above the class of unskilled labor.

This lack of interest is much more important than it seems at first glance. It is even more important at this time than it was in the past. The internal affairs of the nation have bearings on the international stress and strain, and this gap in the national literature now has tremendous weight in world affairs. National coherence and solidarity is implicit in a thorough understanding of the various groups within a nation, and this lack of knowledge about the internal emotions and behavior of the minorities cannot fail to bar out understanding. Man, like all the other animals, fears and is repelled by that which he does not understand, and mere difference is apt to connote something malign.

The fact that there is no demand for incisive and full-dress stories around Negroes above the servant class is indicative of something of vast importance to this nation. This blank is NOT filled by the fiction built around upper-class Negroes exploiting the race problem. Rather, it tends to point it up. A college-bred Negro still is not a person like other folks, but an interesting problem, more or less. It calls to mind a story of slavery time. In this story, a master with more intellectual curiosity than usual, set out to see how much he could teach a particularly bright slave of his. When he had gotten him up to higher mathematics and to be a fluent reader of Latin, he called in a neighbor to show off his brilliant slave, and to argue that Negroes had brains just like the slave-owners had, and given the same opportunities, would turn out the same.

The visiting master of slaves looked and listened, tried to trap the literate slave in Algebra and Latin, and failing to do so in both, turned to his neighbor and said:

"Yes, he certainly knows his higher mathematics, and he can read Latin better than many white men I know, but I cannot bring myself to believe that he understands a thing that he is doing. It is all an aping of our culture. All on the outside. You are crazy if you think that it has changed him inside in the least. Turn

---

[1]First published in *Negro Digest* in April 1950.

him loose, and he will revert at once to the jungle. He is still a savage, and no amount of translating Virgil° and Ovid° is going to change him. In fact, all you have done is to turn a useful savage into a dangerous beast."

That was in slavery time, yes, and we have come a long, long way since then, but the troubling thing is that there are still too many who refuse to believe in the ingestion and digestion of western culture as yet. Hence the lack of literature about the higher emotions and love life of upper-class Negroes and the minorities in general.

Publishers and producers are cool to the idea. Now, do not leap to the conclusion that editors and producers constitute a special class of unbelievers. That is far from true. Publishing houses and theatrical promoters are in business to make money. They will sponsor anything that they believe will sell. They shy away from romantic stories about Negroes and Jews because they feel that they know the public indifference to such works, unless the story or play involves racial tension. It can then be offered as a study in Sociology, with the romantic side subdued. They know the scepticism in general about the complicated emotions in the minorities. The average American just cannot conceive of it, and would be apt to reject the notion, and publishers and producers take the stand that they are not in business to educate, but to make money. Sympathetic as they might be, they cannot afford to be crusaders.

In proof of this, you can note various publishers and producers edging forward a little, and ready to go even further when the trial balloons show that the public is ready for it. This public lack of interest is the nut of the matter.

The question naturally arises as to the why of this indifference, not to say scepticism, to the internal life of educated minorities.

The answer lies in what we may call THE AMERICAN MUSEUM OF UNNATURAL HISTORY. This is an intangible built on folk belief. It is assumed that all non-Anglo-Saxons are uncomplicated stereotypes. Everybody knows all about them. They are lay figures mounted in the museum where all may take them in at a glance. They are made of bent wires without insides at all. So how could anybody write a book about the nonexistent?

The American Indian is a contraption of copper wires in an eternal war-bonnet, with no equipment for laughter, expressionless face and that says "How" when spoken to. His only activity is treachery leading us to massacres. Who is so dumb as not to know all about Indians, even if they have never seen one, nor talked with anyone who ever knew one?

The American Negro exhibit is a group of two. Both of these mechanical toys are built so that their feet eternally shuffle, and their eyes pop and roll. Shuffling feet and those popping, rolling eyes denote the Negro and no characterization is genuine without this monotony. One is seated on a stump picking away on his banjo and singing and laughing. The other is a most amoral character before a share-cropper's shack mumbling about injustice. Doing this makes him out to be a Negro "intellectual." It is as simple as all that.

The whole museum is dedicated to the convenient "typical." In there is the "typical" Oriental, Jew, Yankee, Westerner, Southerner, Latin, and even out-of-favor Nordics like the German. The Englishman "I say old chappie," and the gesticulating Frenchman. The least observant American can know all at a glance. However, the public willingly accepts the untypical in Nordics, but feels cheated if the untypical is portrayed in others. The author of *Scarlet Sister Mary*[1] complained to me that her neighbors objected to her book on the grounds that she had the characters thinking, "and everybody know that Nigras don't think."

But for the national welfare, it is urgent to realize that the minorities do think, and think about something other than the race problem. That they are very human and internally, according to natural endowment, are just like everybody else. So long as this is not conceived, there must remain that feeling of unsurmountable difference, and difference to the average man means something bad. If people were made right, they would be just like him.

The trouble with the purely problem arguments is that they leave too much unknown. Argue all you will or may about injustice, but as long as the majority cannot conceive of a Negro or a Jew feeling and reacting inside just as they do, the majority will keep right on believing that people who do not feel like them cannot possibly feel as they do, and conform to the established pattern. It is well known that there must be a body of waived matter, let us say, things accepted and taken for granted by all in a community before there can be that commonality of feeling. The usual phrase is having things in common. Until this is thoroughly established in respect to Negroes in America, as well as of other minorities, it will remain impossible for the majority to conceive of a Negro experiencing a deep and abiding love and not just the passion of sex. That a great mass of Negroes can be stirred by the pageants of Spring and Fall; the extravaganza of summer, and the majesty of winter. That they can and do experience discovery of the numerous subtle faces as a foundation for a great and selfless love, and the diverse nuances that go to destroy that love as with others. As it is now, this capacity, this evidence of high and complicated emotions, is ruled out. Hence the lack of interest in a romance uncomplicated by the race struggle has so little appeal.

This insistence on defeat in a story where upperclass Negroes are portrayed, perhaps says something from the subconscious of the majority. Involved in western culture, the hero or the heroine, or both, must appear frustrated and go down to defeat, somehow. Our literature reeks with it. Is it the same as saying, "You can translate Virgil,° and fumble with the differential calculus, but can you really comprehend it? Can you cope with our subtleties?"

That brings us to the folklore of "reversion to type." This curious doctrine has such wide acceptance that it is tragic. One has only to examine the huge literature on it to be convinced. No matter how high we may *seem* to climb, put us under strain and we revert to type, that is, to the bush. Under a superficial layer of western culture, the jungle drums throb in our veins.

---

[1]1928, a book by Julia Mood (1880–1961), who also published *Black April* (1927) and *Roll, Jordan, Roll* (1933). Her collected short stories were published in 1970.

This ridiculous notion makes it possible for that majority who accept it to conceive of even a man like the suave and scholarly Dr. Charles S. Johnson[1] to hide a black cat's bone on his person, and indulge in a midnight voodoo ceremony, complete with leopard skin and drums if threatened with the loss of the presidency of Fisk University, or the love of his wife. "Under the skin . . . better to deal with them in business, etc., but otherwise keep them at a safe distance and under control. I tell you, Carl Van Vechten,° think as you like, but they are just not like us."

The extent and extravagance of this notion reaches the ultimate in nonsense in the widespread belief that the Chinese have bizarre genitals, because of that eye-fold that makes their eyes seem to slant. In spite of the fact that no biology has ever mentioned any such difference in reproductive organs makes no matter. Millions of people believe it. "Did you know that a Chinese has . . ." Consequently, their quiet contemplative manner is interpreted as a sign of slyness and a treacherous inclination.

But the opening wedge for better understanding has been thrust into the crack. Though many Negroes denounced Carl Van Vechten's° *Nigger Heaven* because of the title, and without ever reading it, the book, written in the deepest sincerity, revealed Negroes of wealth and culture to the white public. It created curiosity even when it aroused scepticism. It made folks want to know. Worth Tuttle Hedden's *The Other Room*[2] has definitely widened the opening. Neither of these well-written works take a romance of upper-class Negro life as the central theme, but the atmosphere and the background is there. These works should be followed up by some incisive and intimate stories from the inside.

The realistic story around a Negro insurance official, dentist, general practitioner, undertaker and the like would be most revealing. Thinly disguised fiction around the well known Negro names is not the answer, either. The "exceptional" as well as the Ol' Man Rivers has been exploited all out of context already. Everybody is already resigned to the "exceptional" Negro, and willing to be entertained by the "quaint." To grasp the penetration of western civilization in a minority, it is necessary to know how the average behaves and lives. Books that deal with people like in Sinclair Lewis' *Main Street*[3] is the necessary metier. For

---

[1](1893–1956) Social scientist at Fisk University and author of many books still reprinted, including *The Negro in American Civilization* (1930), *The Negro College Graduate* (1938), *Growing Up in the Black Belt: Negro Youth in the Rural South* (1941), and *Patterns of Negro Segregation* (1943).

[2]Hurston here seems to have confused Hedden with Lyman Abbott (1835–1922) who wrote *The Other Room* (1915). Abbott succeeded Henry Ward Beecher as pastor of the Plymouth Congregational Church in Brooklyn.

[3]Sinclair Lewis (1885–1951) was an American novelist whose satires of middle-class life and hypocrisy helped Americans reassess their views of conformity and success. Most influential among his works were *Main Street* (1920), about small towns in America, followed by *Babbitt* (1922) about businessmen, *Arrowsmith* (1925) about doctors, and *Elmer Gantry* (1927) about religion.

various reasons, the average, struggling, non-morbid Negro is the best-kept secret in America. His revelation to the public is the thing needed to do away with that feeling of difference which inspires fear and which ever expresses itself in dislike.

It is inevitable that this knowledge will destroy many illusions and romantic traditions which America probably likes to have around. But then, we have no record of anybody sinking into a lingering death on finding out that there was no Santa Claus. The old world will take it in its stride. The realization that Negroes are no better nor no worse, and at times just as boring as everybody else, will hardly kill off the population of the nation.

Outside of racial attitudes, there is still another reason why this literature should exist. Literature and other arts are supposed to hold up the mirror to nature. With only the fractional "exceptional" and the "quaint" portrayed, a true picture of Negro life in America cannot be. A great principle of national art has been violated.

These are the things that publishers and producers, as the accredited representatives of the American people, have not as yet taken into consideration sufficiently. Let there be light! ✐

George Orwell

(1903–1950)

Eric Arthur Blair was born in Motihari, Bengal. His father, Richard Walmesley Blair, forty-six, was an opium agent in the Indian Civil Service; his mother, Ida Mabel Limouzin Blair, twenty-eight, had lived outside of England most of her life, first in Burma, where her father had sold teak, and later in India with her husband. The Blairs were thus members of what Orwell called the "lower-upper-middle class," their position secured by imperialism and maintained by proper education. When Eric was nearly two, his mother brought him and his seven-year-old sister Marjorie to England to live in Henley, Oxfordshire, where, in 1908, his younger sister Avril was born. Because Marjorie was five years older and Avril five years younger than he, Orwell lived a somewhat lonely childhood. Moreover, aside from occasional brief leaves, his father did not live with the family until he retired from the Indian Civil Service in 1912, too late to develop a close relationship with his son.

The year before his father returned, Eric had been sent, at age eight, to a private boarding school, St. Cyprian's, in Sussex. For the next five years, as he describes the experience in "Such, Such Were the Joys . . . ," he inhabited a cruel world where the rules were impossible to obey and where the rich were treated with respect and the poor with ridicule. Moreover, the school encouraged a conformity that Orwell felt himself unable to achieve. Although he knew he was supposed to love God and his father, he felt he could not. According to the standards of St. Cyprian's, he saw himself as "damned." He relates, "I had no money, I was weak, I was ugly, I was unpopular, I had a chronic cough, I was cowardly, I smelt." Yet it was his scholarship to this school that maintained his social status and kept him from becoming in his own eyes, and in the eyes of all he knew, a total failure.

Despite his misery, the schooling achieved its goal: in 1917, after a term at Wellington College, Eric entered Eton, again on scholarship, to complete his indoctrination in the values of the British upper middle class. His position as both an outsider and an insider, a believer who cannot believe, served Orwell all his life and provided him with the courage and perhaps the compulsion to tell the truth or say nothing at all. His writings show that loyalty to abstract virtues such as honor, duty, courage, and patriotism (as opposed to nationalism) persisted side by side with prejudices against birth control advocates and the "smells" of the poor, even when he had become the passionate champion of socialism and the working class.

After Eton, where he ranked in the bottom third among the scholarship boys, Eric followed in his father's footsteps, taking a post not in India but in Burma, as an assistant administrator of police. He worked there for five years, again both an insider and an outsider: "I was stuck between my hatred of the empire I served and my rage against the evil-spirited little beasts who tried to make my job impossible." When he returned to England on leave in 1927, he informed his family that he'd decided to resign to pursue a career as a writer.

For the next five years, like Hazlitt, Twain, White, and others, Eric Blair foundered in a pattern typical of the developing writer practicing his craft. While living with his parents in Southwold, Suffolk, a community popular with retired servants of the empire in India, he began his forays into the underside of British life, walking the roads in dirty, torn clothes and staying at run-down lodging houses, but reappearing among his friends periodically to discuss his ideas and take long walks in the country. His behavior mystified his friends, some attributing it to guilt caused by serving the empire, some to his need for material to write about. Blair acknowledged both motives; he also knew that his parents were disappointed in his behavior. In the spring of 1928, he left for a working-class area in Paris (near his mother's sister Nellie) to write. Although some of his essays were accepted by *Le Monde* and *Le Progrès civique*, the two novels and numerous short stories he composed were rejected and no longer survive. In 1929 he caught pneumonia and spent time in the Hôpital Cochin, which he describes in detail in his essay "How the Poor Die." After working as a dishwasher and a kitchen helper, Blair returned to England and began writing *Down and Out in Paris and London* and articles for *Adelphi*, a leftist literary journal. By 1933 he had taught school in London, suffered another bout of pneumonia, lived at home, worked at a bookstore in Hampstead, and written three novels: *Burmese Days*, about the unpleasant behavior of both the rulers and the ruled, and *A Clergyman's Daughter* and *Keep the Aspidistra Flying*, both about the struggling middle class to which he clearly belonged.

In 1933 Blair finally found a publisher, leftist Victor Gollancz, for *Down and Out in Paris and London*, which was published under the pseudonym that gradually became Blair's public self. Later, rejecting *Burmese Days* (first published in America) for fear of political repercussions, Gollancz accepted Orwell's two middle-class novels under the name Eric Blair. This dual perspective, a part of Orwell since his days at St. Cyprian's, was perpetuated, his older friends knowing him as Blair and his newer friends as Orwell. Taken from the river Orwell in his parents' community of Southwold, his pseudonym, like the man it represents, retains a muted connection with the lower upper middle class.

By 1935 Gollancz had agreed to publish *Burmese Days* and Orwell had met his future wife, Eileen O'Shaughnessy, a graduate of Oxford with a degree in English who was studying psychology at University College, London. In his relationship with women, as in most other aspects of his life, Orwell "had a power of facing unpleasant facts." According to several women he courted in those days, he clearly wanted a woman who would admire him, listen to him, and recognize that his writing would always come first in their lives. And in 1935 his prospects for earning money seemed dim. Knowing all this, Eileen O'Shaughnessy still married George Orwell in June of 1936 in Wallington, Hertfordshire, a small village where Orwell had bought a country store with the advance he had been paid by Victor Gollancz and the Left Book Club to study the lives of the poor and unemployed miners in northern England. While Orwell wrote *The Road to Wigan Pier* and tended his garden and his goats and chickens, Eileen tended the store.

In 1937 the book was published, with an introductory disclaimer by Gollancz provoked by Orwell's irritating prejudice against feminists, vegetarians, and other "cranks" that Orwell believed gave socialists a bad name. As soon as he had finished writing the book, Orwell had gone to Spain to fight for the Republicans in the Spanish Civil War. He enlisted in the POUM (*Partido Obrero de Unificacion Marxista*, or Workers' Party of Marxist Unification) in Barcelona, where the workers were in fact running the city and class distinctions seemed to have disappeared. In February, when his wife arrived to be near him and to work as a secretary for the Independent Labour Party, Orwell was serving as a corporal in the front lines. The democracy he experienced at the front made a socialist of him, but he never lost his ability to see the "unpleasant facts." In Spain the facts that the leftists in Britain shunned infuriated Orwell: Stalin and the Communists, Orwell saw, were not interested in the POUM and the workers' revolution but in suppressing them as traitors: the Communists were as totalitarian as the Fascists. In May, during the fighting, Orwell was shot through the neck by a sniper and nearly died. In June he and his wife left for France and then Wallington, where Orwell wrote *Homage to Catalonia*, which Gollancz refused to publish because it contradicted the established leftist view of the Communist Party. (Like *Animal Farm* and *Nineteen Eighty-Four*, *Homage to Catalonia* was published by Secker & Warburg.)

For the last twelve years of his life Orwell was committed to a political ideal, the kind of democratic classless socialism he had seen at the front in the Spanish Civil War. He was also increasingly ill with tuberculosis. When he was first diagnosed as having the disease in March of 1938, he was sent to a sanatorium in Kent and later, through financial support from another writer, to Morocco with Eileen for rest. There he wrote *Coming Up for Air*, the last novel by Eric Blair. Rejected by the army as physically unfit, Orwell spent the war years in London as a sergeant in the Home Guard, a producer for the BBC, literary editor and writer of a weekly column for the *Tribune*, and frequent contributor to such journals as *Horizon* and *Partisan Review*. He published a collection of essays, *Inside the Whale*, in 1940 and a book urging revolution, *The Lion and the Unicorn*, in 1941. Meanwhile Eileen worked for the Censorship Department and later for the Ministry of Food, but she quit her job in 1944, while Orwell was finishing *Animal Farm*, because Orwell wanted very much to have a child. They adopted a baby, Richard Horatio Blair, in June.

Eight months later Orwell left for France as a reporter for the *Observer*, leaving Eileen behind with the baby. She had been feeling ill and was scheduled for what Orwell had called a minor operation but was in fact a hysterectomy for a cancerous tumor.[1] When he was in Cologne, he learned that his wife had died under the anesthetic. He had lost a true companion who had shared his struggles—economic, political, physical, and literary. Nonetheless, he was devoted to Richard and determined to raise him, alone if necessary.

In September of 1945 Orwell rented a cottage for himself and Richard on the island of Jura off the coast of Scotland. He liked it so well that he later rented a farmhouse, where, after the death of his older sister Margaret, his younger sister Avril came to live with him. During the winter of 1946 he returned to London and began *Nineteen Eighty-Four*. He proposed to more than one woman, again offering the "unpleasant truth" of his situation, but no one accepted, and Orwell went back to Jura in April of 1947, increasingly ill but committed to his son and his novel. Some of his friends believed that the move to Jura was suicidal, but others were convinced that the island appealed to some central need for beauty and peace. Orwell spent his time there writing, working on his garden, fishing, caring for his animals, and doing unremarkable carpentry. He and his son were clearly happy, though Orwell was torn between his fear of infecting Richard and his fear of the emotional distance that a greater physical distance between them could produce. By 1949 Orwell was placed in a sanatorium, and *Nineteen Eighty-Four* was published that June.

In October, from his hospital bed, Orwell married Sonia Brownell, a literary editor at *Horizon* who, according to Stephen Wadhams (*Remembering Orwell*, Penguin, 1984), had been one of those who had rejected Orwell's earlier proposals. After the wedding, he was looking forward to a trip to Switzerland and to writing a short book, but he never left his bed. He died on January 26, 1950.

Perhaps the best modern practitioner of Hazlitt's "familiar style," Orwell creates a voice on the page we hear and immediately recognize. In this sentence, for example, from "Why I Write," we hear his forthright, assertive

---

[1]See *The Orwell Mystique* by Daphne Patai, 1984, p. 286. Other facts in this biography come from *The Crystal Spirit* by George Woodcock, 1966, and *The World of George Orwell*, edited by Miriam Gross, 1971.

tone: "These magazines [school publications] were the most pitiful burlesque stuff that you could imagine, and I took far less trouble with them than I now would with the cheapest journalism." In one stroke he manages to deflate school magazines, his own careless youth, and the kind of journalism that he admits he writes, at least occasionally. His reference to his audience as "you," a casual, conversational, seemingly artless ploy, successfully draws the reader into a collaboration with Orwell in which writer and audience share an elite artistic judgment without rejecting, because of words like *stuff* and *cheapest*, a solid affiliation with the particular material they are impugning.

Like Lamb, Orwell has prejudices, but like Samuel Johnson, he is honest and passionate in his pursuit of morality, and unlike either Lamb or Browne or those writers who engage in abstract analyses of prejudice, he focuses on the unpleasant complexities that prejudice engenders. Indeed, his reputation rests on his ability to describe these complexities, such as the irony of being important enough to be hated when shooting an elephant or the collaborative shame in the "impulse . . . to snigger" after a hanging. Even in book reviews, Orwell manages to find a moral crux: Mark Twain, he says, did not write the books he should have written "because of that flaw in his own nature, his inability to despise success." He sees in Twain's art only the recording of "social history," because Orwell's rigid standards require a writer to limit his income to "reasonable proportions," whatever those may be. Thus Orwell tells the truth as he sees it even when that "truth" reveals Orwell's own lack of logic or awareness or even sometimes, as in the notoriously poorly organized "Politics and the English Language," good style. Always, however, his truth makes us think about our own. ✿

A Hanging[1]

It was in Burma, a sodden morning of the rains. A sickly light, like yellow tinfoil, was slanting over the high walls into the jail yard. We were waiting outside the condemned cells, a row of sheds fronted with double bars, like small animal cages. Each cell measured about ten feet by ten and was quite bare within except for a plank bed and a pot of drinking water. In some of them brown silent men were squatting at the inner bars, with their blankets draped round them. These were the condemned men, due to be hanged within the next week or two.

One prisoner had been brought out of his cell. He was a Hindu, a puny wisp of a man, with a shaven head and vague liquid eyes. He had a thick, sprouting moustache, absurdly too big for his body, rather like the moustache of a comic man on the films.[2] Six tall Indian warders were guarding him and getting him ready for

---

[1]First published in *Adelphi* in 1931, under the name Eric A. Blair.
[2]An allusion to Charlie Chaplin (1889–1977) in his guise as the tramp in such films as *The Kid* (1920), *The Gold Rush* (1924), and *City Lights* (1931).

the gallows. Two of them stood by with rifles and fixed bayonets, while the others handcuffed him, passed a chain through his handcuffs and fixed it to their belts, and lashed his arms tight to his sides. They crowded very close about him, with their hands always on him in a careful, caressing grip, as though all the while feeling him to make sure he was there. It was like men handling a fish which is still alive and may jump back into the water. But he stood quite unresisting, yielding his arms limply to the ropes, as though he hardly noticed what was happening.

Eight o'clock struck and a bugle call, desolately thin in the wet air, floated from the distant barracks. The superintendent of the jail, who was standing apart from the rest of us, moodily prodding the gravel with his stick, raised his head at the sound. He was an army doctor, with a grey toothbrush moustache and a gruff voice. "For God's sake hurry up, Francis," he said irritably. "The man ought to have been dead by this time. Aren't you ready yet?"

Francis, the head jailer, a fat Dravidian[1] in a white drill suit and gold spectacles, waved his black hand. "Yes sir, yes sir," he bubbled. "All iss satis-factorily prepared. The hangman iss waiting. We shall proceed."

"Well, quick march, then. The prisoners can't get their breakfast till this job's over."

We set out for the gallows. Two warders marched on either side of the prisoner, with their rifles at the slope; two others marched close against him, gripping him by arm and shoulder, as though at once pushing and supporting him. The rest of us, magistrates and the like, followed behind. Suddenly, when we had gone ten yards, the procession stopped short without any order or warning. A dreadful thing had happened—a dog, come goodness knows whence, had appeared in the yard. It came bounding among us with a loud volley of barks, and leapt round us wagging its whole body, wild with glee at finding so many human beings together. It was a large woolly dog, half Airedale, half pariah.[2] For a moment it pranced round us, and then, before anyone could stop it, it had made a dash for the prisoner, and jumping up tried to lick his face. Everyone stood aghast, too taken aback even to grab at the dog.

"Who let that bloody brute in here?" said the superintendent angrily. "Catch it, someone!"

A warder, detached from the escort, charged clumsily after the dog, but it danced and gambolled just out of his reach, taking everything as part of the game. A young Eurasian jailer picked up a handful of gravel and tried to stone the dog away, but it dodged the stones and came after us again. Its yaps echoed from the jail walls. The prisoner, in the grasp of the two warders, looked on incuriously, as though this was another formality of the hanging. It was several minutes before someone managed to catch the dog. Then we put my handkerchief through its collar and moved off once more, with the dog still straining and whimpering.

It was about forty yards to the gallows. I watched the bare brown back of the prisoner marching in front of me. He walked clumsily with his bound arms, but

---

[1]A native of southern India.

[2]From the Hindi for "outsider"; pye-dog or stray dog in Asia.

quite steadily, with that bobbing gait of the Indian who never straightens his knees. At each step his muscles slid neatly into place, the lock of hair on his scalp danced up and down, his feet printed themselves on the wet gravel. And once, in spite of the men who gripped him by each shoulder, he stepped slightly aside to avoid a puddle on the path.

It is curious, but till that moment I had never realised what it means to destroy a healthy, conscious man. When I saw the prisoner step aside to avoid the puddle, I saw the mystery, the unspeakable wrongness, of cutting a life short when it is in full tide. This man was not dying, he was alive just as we were alive. All the organs of his body were working—bowels digesting food, skin renewing itself, nails growing, tissues forming—all toiling away in solemn foolery. His nails would still be growing when he stood on the drop, when he was falling through the air with a tenth of a second to live. His eyes saw the yellow gravel and the grey walls, and his brain still remembered, foresaw, reasoned—reasoned even about puddles. He and we were a party of men walking together, seeing, hearing, feeling, understanding the same world; and in two minutes, with a sudden snap, one of us would be gone—one mind less, one world less.

The gallows stood in a small yard, separate from the main grounds of the prison, and overgrown with tall prickly weeds. It was a brick erection like three sides of a shed, with planking on top, and above that two beams and a crossbar with the rope dangling. The hangman, a grey-haired convict in the white uniform of the prison, was waiting beside his machine. He greeted us with a servile crouch as we entered. At a word from Francis the two warders, gripping the prisoner more closely than ever, half led, half pushed him to the gallows and helped him clumsily up the ladder. Then the hangman climbed up and fixed the rope round the prisoner's neck.

We stood waiting, five yards away. The warders had formed in a rough circle round the gallows. And then, when the noose was fixed, the prisoner began crying out on his god. It was a high, reiterated cry of "Ram! Ram! Ram! Ram!",[1] not urgent and fearful like a prayer or a cry for help, but steady, rhythmical, almost like the tolling of a bell. The dog answered the sound with a whine. The hangman, still standing on the gallows, produced a small cotton bag like a flour bag and drew it down over the prisoner's face. But the sound, muffled by the cloth, still persisted, over and over again: "Ram! Ram! Ram! Ram! Ram!"

The hangman climbed down and stood ready, holding the lever. Minutes seemed to pass. The steady, muffled crying from the prisoner went on and on, "Ram! Ram! Ram!" never faltering for an instant. The superintendent, his head on his chest, was slowly poking the ground with his stick; perhaps he was counting the cries, allowing the prisoner a fixed number—fifty, perhaps, or a hundred. Everyone had changed colour. The Indians had gone grey like bad coffee, and one or two of the bayonets were wavering. We looked at the lashed, hooded man on

[1]From *Rama*, a term for the three incarnations of Vishnu—Balarama, Parashurama, and Ramachandra; from the Sanskrit for "black."

the drop, and listened to his cries—each cry another second of life; the same thought was in all our minds: oh, kill him quickly, get it over, stop that abominable noise!

Suddenly the superintendent made up his mind. Throwing up his head he made a swift motion with his stick. "Chalo!" he shouted almost fiercely.

There was a clanking noise, and then dead silence. The prisoner had vanished, and the rope was twisting on itself. I let go of the dog, and it galloped immediately to the back of the gallows; but when it got there it stopped short, barked, and then retreated into a corner of the yard, where it stood among the weeds, looking timorously out at us. We went round the gallows to inspect the prisoner's body. He was dangling with his toes pointed straight downwards, very slowly revolving, as dead as a stone.

The superintendent reached out with his stick and poked the bare body; it oscillated, slightly. "*He's* all right," said the superintendent. He backed out from under the gallows, and blew out a deep breath. The moody look had gone out of his face quite suddenly. He glanced at his wrist-watch. "Eight minutes past eight. Well, that's all for this morning, thank God."

The warders unfixed bayonets and marched away. The dog, sobered and conscious of having misbehaved itself, slipped after them. We walked out of the gallows yard, past the condemned cells with their waiting prisoners, into the big central yard of the prison. The convicts, under the command of warders armed with lathis,[1] were already receiving their breakfast. They squatted in long rows, each man holding a tin pannikin,[2] while two warders with buckets marched round ladling out rice; it seemed quite a homely, jolly scene, after the hanging. An enormous relief had come upon us now that the job was done. One felt an impulse to sing, to break into a run, to snigger. All at once everyone began chattering gaily.

The Eurasian boy walking beside me nodded towards the way we had come, with a knowing smile: "Do you know, sir, our friend (he meant the dead man), when he heard his appeal had been dismissed, he pissed on the floor of his cell. From fright.—Kindly take one of my cigarettes, sir. Do you not admire my new silver case, sir? From the boxwallah,[3] two rupees eight annas. Classy European style."

Several people laughed—at what, nobody seemed certain.

Francis was walking by the superintendent, talking garrulously: "Well sir, all hass passed off with the utmost satisfactoriness. It wass all finished—flick! like that. It iss not always so—oah, no! I have known cases where the doctor wass obliged to go beneath the gallows and pull the prisoner's legs to ensure decease. Most disagreeable!"

"Wriggling about, eh? That's bad," said the superintendent.

---

[1] Heavy bamboo sticks bound with iron.
[2] Small container for drinks.
[3] Native itinerant peddler.

"Ach, sir, it iss worse when they become refractory! One man, I recall, clung to the bars of hiss cage when we went to take him out. You will scarcely credit, sir, that it took six warders to dislodge him, three pulling at each leg. We reasoned with him. 'My dear fellow,' we said, 'think of all the pain and trouble you are causing to us!' But no, he would not listen! Ach, he wass very troublesome!''

I found that I was laughing quite loudly. Everyone was laughing. Even the superintendent grinned in a tolerant way. "You'd better all come out and have a drink'' he said quite genially. "I've got a bottle of whiskey in the car. We could do with it.''

We went through the big double gates of the prison, into the road. "Pulling at his legs!'' exclaimed a Burmese magistrate suddenly, and burst into a loud chuckling. We all began laughing again. At that moment Francis's anecdote seemed extraordinarily funny. We all had a drink together, native and European alike, quite amicably. The dead man was a hundred yards away. ✄

Shooting an Elephant[1]

In Moulmein, in Lower Burma, I was hated by large numbers of people—the only time in my life that I have been important enough for this to happen to me. I was sub-divisional police officer of the town, and in an aimless, petty kind of way anti-European feeling was very bitter. No one had the guts to raise a riot, but if a European woman went through the bazaars alone somebody would probably spit betel juice over her dress. As a police officer I was an obvious target and was baited whenever it seemed safe to do so. When a nimble Burman tripped me up on the football field and the referee (another Burman) looked the other way, the crowd yelled with hideous laughter. This happened more than once. In the end the sneering yellow faces of young men that met me everywhere, the insults hooted after me when I was at a safe distance, got badly on my nerves. The young Buddhist priests were the worst of all. There were several thousands of them in the town and none of them seemed to have anything to do except stand on street corners and jeer at Europeans.

All this was perplexing and upsetting. For at that time I had already made up my mind that imperialism was an evil thing and the sooner I chucked up my job and got out of it the better. Theoretically—and secretly, of course—I was all for the Burmese and all against their oppressors, the British. As for the job I was doing, I hated it more bitterly than I can perhaps make clear. In a job like that you see the dirty work of Empire at close quarters. The wretched prisoners huddling in the stinking cages of the locks-ups, the grey, cowed faces of the long-term convicts, the scarred buttocks of the men who had been flogged with bamboos— all these oppressed me with an intolerable sense of guilt. But I could get nothing

---

[1]First published in *New Writing* in 1936.

into perspective. I was young and ill-educated and I had had to think out my problems in the utter silence that is imposed on every Englishman in the East. I did not even know that the British Empire is dying, still less did I know that it is a great deal better than the younger empires that are going to supplant it. All I knew was that I was stuck between my hatred of the empire I served and my rage against the evil-spirited little beasts who tried to make my job impossible. With one part of my mind I thought of the British Raj[1] as an unbreakable tyranny, as something clamped down, *in saecula saeculorum*,[2] upon the will of prostrate peoples; with another part I thought that the greatest joy in the world would be to drive a bayonet into a Buddhist priest's guts. Feelings like these are the normal by-products of imperialism; ask any Anglo-Indian official, if you can catch him off duty.

One day something happened which in a roundabout way was enlightening. It was a tiny incident in itself, but it gave me a better glimpse than I had had before of the real nature of imperialism—the real motives for which despotic governments act. Early one morning the sub-inspector at a police station the other end of the town rang me up on the phone and said that an elephant was ravaging the bazaar. Would I please come and do something about it? I did not know what I could do, but I wanted to see what was happening and I got on to a pony and started out. I took my rifle, an old .44 Winchester and much too small to kill an elephant, but I thought the noise might be useful *in terrorem*.[3] Various Burmans stopped me on the way and told me about the elephant's doings. It was not, of course, a wild elephant, but a tame one which had gone "must."[4] It had been chained up as tame elephants always are when their attack of "must" is due, but on the previous night it had broken its chain and escaped. Its mahout,[5] the only person who could manage it when it was in that state, had set out in pursuit, but he had taken the wrong direction and was now twelve hours' journey away, and in the morning the elephant had suddenly reappeared in the town. The Burmese population had no weapons and were quite helpless against it. It had already destroyed somebody's bamboo hut, killed a cow and raided some fruit-stalls and devoured the stock; also it had met the municipal rubbish van, and, when the driver jumped out and took to his heels, had turned the van over and inflicted violence upon it.

The Burmese sub-inspector and some Indian constables were waiting for me in the quarter where the elephant had been seen. It was a very poor quarter, a labyrinth of squalid bamboo huts, thatched with palm-leaf, winding all over a steep hillside. I remember that it was a cloudy stuffy morning at the beginning of

---

[1]British Rule, from the Hindi for "reign."
[2]"Generation after generation."
[3]To frighten.
[4]A period of wild sexual excitement in male camels and elephants.
[5]Elephant keeper.

the rains. We began questioning the people as to where the elephant had gone, and, as usual, failed to get any definite information. That is invariably the case in the East; a story always sounds clear enough at a distance, but the nearer you get to the scene of events the vaguer it becomes. Some of the people said that the elephant had gone in one direction, some said that he had gone in another, some professed not even to have heard of any elephant. I had almost made up my mind that the whole story was a pack of lies, when we heard yells a little distance away. There was a loud, scandalised cry of "Go away, child! Go away this instant!" and an old woman with a switch in her hand came round the corner of a hut, violently shooing away a crowd of naked children. Some more women followed, clicking their tongues and exclaiming; evidently there was something there that the children ought not to have seen. I rounded the hut and saw a man's dead body sprawling in the mud. He was an Indian, a black Dravidian coolie,[1] almost naked, and he could not have been dead many minutes. The people said that the elephant had come suddenly upon him round the corner of the hut, caught him with its trunk, put its foot on his back and ground him into the earth. This was the rainy season and the ground was soft, and his face had scored a trench a foot deep and a couple of yards long. He was lying on his belly with arms crucified and head sharply twisted to one side. His face was coated with mud, the eyes wide open, the teeth bared and grinning with an expression of unendurable agony. (Never tell me, by the way, that the dead look peaceful. Most of the corpses I have seen looked devilish.) The friction of the great beast's foot had stripped the skin from his back as neatly as one skins a rabbit. As soon as I saw the dead man I sent an orderly to a friend's house nearby to borrow an elephant rifle. I had already sent back the pony, not wanting it to go mad with fright and throw me if it smelled the elephant.

The orderly came back in a few minutes with a rifle and five cartridges, and meanwhile some Burmans had arrived and told us that the elephant was in the paddy fields below, only a few hundred yards away. As I started forward practically the whole population of the quarter flocked out of their houses and followed me. They had seen the rifle and were all shouting excitedly that I was going to shoot the elephant. They had not shown much interest in the elephant when he was merely ravaging their homes, but it was different now that he was going to be shot. It was a bit of fun to them, as it would be to an English crowd; besides, they wanted the meat. It made me vaguely uneasy. I had no intention of shooting the elephant—I had merely sent for the rifle to defend myself if necessary—and it is always unnerving to have a crowd following you. I marched down the hill, looking and feeling a fool, with the rifle over my shoulder and an ever-growing army of people jostling at my heels. At the bottom, when you got away from the huts, there was a metalled road and beyond that a miry waste of paddy fields a thousand yards across, not yet ploughed but soggy from the first rains and dotted with coarse

---

[1]Name given by Europeans to southern Indian laborers.

grass. The elephant was standing eighty yards from the road, his left side towards us. He took not the slightest notice of the crowd's approach. He was tearing up bunches of grass, beating them against his knees to clean them and stuffing them into his mouth.

I had halted on the road. As soon as I saw the elephant I knew with perfect certainty that I ought not to shoot him. It is a serious matter to shoot a working elephant—it is comparable to destroying a huge and costly piece of machinery— and obviously one ought not to do it if it can possibly be avoided. And at that distance, peacefully eating, the elephant looked no more dangerous than a cow. I thought then and I think now that his attack of "must" was already passing off; in which case he would merely wander harmlessly about until the mahout came back and caught him. Moreover, I did not in the least want to shoot him. I decided that I would watch him for a little while to make sure that he did not turn savage again, and then go home.

But at that moment I glanced round at the crowd that had followed me. It was an immense crowd, two thousand at the least and growing every minute. It blocked the road for a long distance on either side. I looked at the sea of yellow faces above the garish clothes—faces all happy and excited over this bit of fun, all certain that the elephant was going to be shot. They were watching me as they would watch a conjuror about to perform a trick. They did not like me, but with the magical rifle in my hands I was momentarily worth watching. And suddenly I realised that I should have to shoot the elephant after all. The people expected it of me and I had got to do it; I could feel their two thousand wills pressing me forward, irresistibly. And it was at this moment, as I stood there with the rifle in my hands, that I first grasped the hollowness, the futility of the white man's dominion in the East. Here was I, the white man with his gun, standing in front of the unarmed native crowd—seemingly the leading actor of the piece; but in reality I was only an absurd puppet pushed to and fro by the will of those yellow faces behind. I perceived in this moment that when the white man turns tyrant it is his own freedom that he destroys. He becomes a sort of hollow, posing dummy, the conventionalised figure of a sahib.[1] For it is the condition of his rule that he shall spend his life in trying to impress the "natives" and so in every crisis he has got to do what the "natives" expect of him. He wears a mask, and his face grows to fit it. I had got to shoot the elephant. I had committed myself to doing it when I sent for the rifle. A sahib has got to act like a sahib; he has got to appear resolute, to know his own mind and do definite things. To come all that way, rifle in hand, with two thousand people marching at my heels, and then to trail feebly away, having done nothing—no, that was impossible. The crowd would laugh at me. And my whole life, every white man's life in the East, was one long struggle not to be laughed at.

---

[1] From the Hindi for "master."

But I did not want to shoot the elephant. I watched him beating his bunch of grass against his knees, with that preoccupied grandmotherly air that elephants have. It seemed to me that it would be murder to shoot him. At that age I was not squeamish about killing animals, but I had never shot an elephant and never wanted to. (Somehow it always seems worse to kill a *large* animal.) Besides, there was the beast's owner to be considered. Alive, the elephant was worth at least a hundred pounds; dead, he would only be worth the value of his tusks—five pounds, possibly. But I had got to act quickly. I turned to some experienced-looking Burmans who had been there when we arrived, and asked them how the elephant had been behaving. They all said the same thing: he took no notice of you if you left him alone, but he might charge if you went too close to him.

It was perfectly clear to me what I ought to do. I ought to walk up to within, say, twenty-five yards of the elephant and test his behaviour. If he charged I could shoot, if he took no notice of me it would be safe to leave him until the mahout came back. But also I knew that I was going to do no such thing. I was a poor shot with a rifle and the ground was soft mud into which one would sink at every step. If the elephant charged and I missed him, I should have about as much chance as a toad under a steam-roller. But even then I was not thinking particularly of my own skin, only the watchful yellow faces behind. For at that moment, with the crowd watching me, I was not afraid in the ordinary sense, as I would have been if I had been alone. A white man mustn't be frightened in front of "natives"; and so, in general, he isn't frightened. The sole thought in my mind was that if anything went wrong those two thousand Burmans would see me pursued, caught, trampled on and reduced to a grinning corpse like that Indian up the hill. And if that happened it was quite probable that some of them would laugh. That would never do. There was only one alternative. I shoved the cartridges into the magazine and lay down on the road to get a better aim.

The crowd grew very still, and a deep, low, happy sigh, as of people who see the theatre curtain go up at last, breathed from innumerable throats. They were going to have their bit of fun after all. The rifle was a beautiful German thing with cross-hair sights. I did not then know that in shooting an elephant one should shoot to cut an imaginary bar running from ear-hole to ear-hole. I ought therefore, as the elephant was sideways on, to have aimed straight at his ear-hole; actually I aimed several inches in front of this, thinking the brain would be further forward.

When I pulled the trigger I did not hear the bang or feel the kick—one never does when a shot goes home—but I heard the devilish roar of glee that went up from the crowd. In that instant, in too short a time, one would have thought, even for the bullet to get there, a mysterious terrible change had come over the elephant. He neither stirred nor fell, but every line of his body had altered. He looked suddenly stricken, shrunken, immensely old, as though the frightful impact of the bullet had paralysed him without knocking him down. At last, after what seemed a long time—it might have been five seconds, I dare say—he sagged flabbily to his knees. His mouth slobbered. An enormous senility seemed to have settled upon him. One could have imagined him thousands of years old. I fired again into the same spot. At the second shot he did not collapse but climbed with desperate slowness to his feet and stood weakly upright, with legs sagging and head drooping. I fired a third time. That was the shot that did for him. You could see the agony of it jolt his whole body and knock the last remnant of strength from his legs. But in falling he seemed for a moment to rise, for as his hind legs collapsed beneath him he seemed to tower upwards like a huge rock toppling, his trunk reaching skyward like a tree. He trumpeted, for the first and only time. And then down he came, his belly towards me, with a crash that seemed to shake the ground even where I lay.

I got up. The Burmans were already racing past me across the mud. It was obvious that the elephant would never rise again, but he was not dead. He was breathing very rhythmically with long rattling gasps, his great mound of a side painfully rising and falling. His mouth was wide open—I could see far down into caverns of pale pink throat. I waited a long time for him to die, but his breathing did not weaken. Finally I fired my two remaining shots into the spot where I thought his heart must be. The thick blood welled out of him like red velvet, but still he did not die. His body did not even jerk when the shots hit him, the tortured breathing continued without a pause. He was dying, very slowly and in great agony, but in some world remote from me where not even a bullet could damage him further. I felt that I had got to put an end to that dreadful noise. It seemed dreadful to see the great beast lying there, powerless to move and yet powerless to die, and not even to be able to finish him. I sent back for my small rifle and poured shot after shot into his heart and down his throat. They seemed to make no impression. The tortured gasps continued as steadily as the ticking of a clock.

In the end I could not stand it any longer and went away. I heard later that it took him half an hour to die. Burmans were arriving with dahs and baskets even before I left, and I was told they had stripped his body almost to the bones by the afternoon.

Afterwards, of course, there were endless discussions about the shooting of the elephant. The owner was furious, but he was only an Indian and could do nothing. Besides, legally I had done the right thing, for a mad elephant has to be killed, like a mad dog, if its owner fails to control it. Among the Europeans opinion was divided. The older men said I was right, the younger men said it was a damn shame to shoot an elephant for killing a coolie, because an elephant was worth more than any damn Coringhee[1] coolie. And afterwards I was very glad that the coolie had been killed; it put me legally in the right and gave me sufficient pretext for shooting the elephant. I often wondered whether any of the others grasped that I had done it solely to avoid looking a fool. *

---

[1]Possibly someone from Coorg, the anglicized form of "Hodagu," a section of India whose capital is Mercara; it came under British rule in 1834.

Marrakech[1]

As the corpse went past the flies left the restaurant table in a cloud and rushed after it, but they came back a few minutes later.

The little crowd of mourners—all men and boys, no women—threaded their way across the market-place between the piles of pomegranates and the taxis and the camels, wailing a short chant over and over again. What really appeals to the flies is that the corpses here are never put into coffins, they are merely wrapped in a piece of rag and carried on a rough wooden bier on the shoulders of four friends. When the friends get to the burying-ground they hack an oblong hole a foot or two deep, dump the body in it and fling over it a little of the dried-up, lumpy earth, which is like broken brick. No gravestone, no name, no identifying mark of any kind. The burying-ground is merely a huge waste of hummocky[2] earth, like a derelict building-lot. After a month or two no one can even be certain where his own relatives are buried.

When you walk through a town like this—two hundred thousand inhabitants, of whom at least twenty thousand own literally nothing except the rags they stand up in—when you see how the people live, and still more how easily they die, it is always difficult to believe that you are walking among human beings. All colonial empires are in reality founded upon that fact. The people have brown faces—besides, there are so many of them! Are they really the same flesh as yourself? Do they even have names? Or are they merely a kind of undifferentiated brown stuff, about as individual as bees or coral insects? They rise out of the earth, they sweat and starve for a few years, and then they sink back into the nameless mounds of the graveyard and nobody notices that they are gone. And even the graves themselves soon fade back into the soil. Sometimes, out for a walk, as you break your way through the prickly pear, you notice that it is rather bumpy underfoot, and only a certain regularity in the bumps tells you that you are walking over skeletons.

I was feeding one of the gazelles in the public gardens.

Gazelles are almost the only animals that look good to eat when they are still alive, in fact, one can hardly look at their hindquarters without thinking of mint sauce. The gazelle I was feeding seemed to know that this thought was in my mind, for though it took the piece of bread I was holding out it obviously did not like me. It nibbled rapidly at the bread, then lowered its head and tried to butt me, then took another nibble and then butted again. Probably its idea was that if it could drive me away the bread would somehow remain hanging in mid-air.

---

[1]First published in *New Writing* in 1939.
[2]Bumpy, full of ridges.

An Arab navvy[1] working on the path nearby lowered his heavy hoe and sidled towards us. He looked from the gazelle to the bread and from the bread to the gazelle, with a sort of quiet amazement, as though he had never seen anything quite like this before. Finally he said shyly in French:

"I could eat some of that bread."

I tore off a piece and he stowed it gratefully in some secret place under his rags. The man is an employee of the Municipality.

When you go through the Jewish quarters you gather some idea of what the medieval ghettoes were probably like. Under their Moorish rulers the Jews were only allowed to own land in certain restricted areas, and after centuries of this kind of treatment they have ceased to bother about overcrowding. Many of the streets are a good deal less than six feet wide, the houses are completely window-less, and sore-eyed children cluster everywhere in unbelievable numbers, like clouds of flies. Down the centre of the street there is generally running a little river of urine.

In the bazaar huge families of Jews, all dressed in the long black robe and little black skull-cap, are working in dark fly-infested booths that look like caves. A carpenter sits cross-legged at a prehistoric lathe, turning chair-legs at lightning speed. He works the lathe with a bow in his right hand and guides the chisel with his left foot, and thanks to a lifetime of sitting in this position his left leg is warped out of shape. At his side his grandson, aged six, is already starting on the simpler parts of the job.

I was just passing the coppersmiths' booths when somebody noticed that I was lighting a cigarette. Instantly, from the dark holes all round, there was a frenzied rush of Jews, many of them old grandfathers with flowing grey beards, all clamouring for a cigarette. Even a blind man somewhere at the back of one of the booths heard a rumour of cigarettes and came crawling out, groping in the air with his hand. In about a minute I had used up the whole packet. None of these people, I suppose, works less than twelve hours a day, and every one of them looks on a cigarette as a more or less impossible luxury.

As the Jews live in self-contained communities they follow the same trades as the Arabs, except for agriculture. Fruit-sellers, potters, silversmiths, blacksmiths, butchers, leather-workers, tailors, water-carriers, beggars, porters—whichever way you look you see nothing but Jews. As a matter of fact there are thirteen thousand of them, all living in the space of a few acres. A good job Hitler isn't here. Perhaps he is on his way, however. You hear the usual dark rumours about the Jews, not only from the Arabs but from the poorer Europeans.

"Yes, *mon vieux*,[2] they took my job away from me and gave it to a Jew. The Jews! They're the real rulers of this country, you know. They've got all the money. They control the banks, finance—everything."

---

[1]British slang for a "laborer."
[2]French for "my old fellow."

"But," I said, "isn't it a fact that the average Jew is a labourer working for about a penny an hour?"

"Ah, that's only for show! They're all moneylenders really. They're cunning, the Jews."

In just the same way, a couple of hundred years ago, poor old women used to be burned for witchcraft when they could not even work enough magic to get themselves a square meal.

All people who work with their hands are partly invisible, and the more important the work they do, the less visible they are. Still, a white skin is always fairly conspicuous. In northern Europe, when you see a labourer ploughing a field, you probably give him a second glance. In a hot country, anywhere south of Gibraltar or east of Suez, the chances are that you don't even see him. I have noticed this again and again. In a tropical landscape one's eye takes in everything except the human beings. It takes in the dried-up soil, the prickly pear, the palm-tree and the distant mountain, but it always misses the peasant hoeing at his patch. He is the same colour as the earth, and a great deal less interesting to look at.

It is only because of this that the starved countries of Asia and Africa are accepted as tourist resorts. No one would think of running cheap trips to the Distressed Areas. But where the human beings have brown skins their poverty is simply not noticed. What does Morocco mean to a Frenchman? An orange-grove or a job in government service. Or to an Englishman? Camels, castles, palm-trees, Foreign Legionnaires, brass trays and bandits. One could probably live here for years without noticing that for nine-tenths of the people the reality of life is an endless, back-breaking struggle to wring a little food out of an eroded soil.

Most of Morocco is so desolate that no wild animal bigger than a hare can live on it. Huge areas which were once covered with forest have turned into a treeless waste where the soil is exactly like broken-up brick. Nevertheless, a good deal of it is cultivated, with frightful labour. Everything is done by hand. Long lines of women, bent double like inverted capital Ls, work their way slowly across the fields, tearing up the prickly weeds with their hands, and the peasant gathering lucerne[1] or fodder pulls it up stalk by stalk instead of reaping it, thus saving an inch or two on each stalk. The plough is a wretched wooden thing, so frail that one can easily carry it on one's shoulder, and fitted underneath with a rough iron spike which stirs the soil to a depth of about four inches. This is as much as the strength of the animals is equal to. It is usual to plough with a cow and a donkey yoked together. Two donkeys would not be quite strong enough, but on the other hand two cows would cost a little more to feed. The peasants possess no harrows, they merely plough the soil several times over in different directions, finally leaving it in rough furrows, after which the whole field has to be shaped with hoes into small oblong patches, to conserve water. Except for a day or two after the rare

---

[1]British term for alfalfa.

rainstorms there is never enough water. Along the edges of the fields channels are hacked out to a depth of thirty or forty feet to get at the tiny trickles which run through the subsoil.

Every afternoon a file of very old women passes down the road outside my house, each carrying a load of firewood. All of them are mummified with age and the sun, and all of them are tiny. It seems to be generally the case in primitive communities that the women, when they get beyond a certain age, shrink to the size of children. One day a poor old creature who could not have been more than four feet tall crept past me under a vast load of wood. I stopped her and put a five-sou piece (a little more than a farthing) into her hand. She answered with a shrill wail, almost a scream, which was partly gratitude but mainly surprise. I suppose that from her point of view, by taking any notice of her, I seemed almost to be violating a law of nature. She accepted her status as an old woman, that is to say as a beast of burden. When a family is travelling it is quite usual to see a father and a grown-up son riding ahead on donkeys, and an old woman following on foot, carrying the baggage.

But what is strange about these people is their invisibility. For several weeks, always at about the same time of day, the file of old women had hobbled past the house with their firewood, and though they had registered themselves on my eyeballs I cannot truly say that I had seen them. Firewood was passing—that was how I saw it. It was only that one day I happened to be walking behind them, and the curious up-and-down motion of a load of wood drew my attention to the human being underneath it. Then for the first time I noticed the poor old earth-coloured bodies, bodies reduced to bones and leathery skin, bent double under the crushing weight. Yet I suppose I had not been five minutes on Moroccan soil before I noticed the overloading of the donkeys and was infuriated by it. There is no question that the donkeys are damnably treated. The Moroccan donkey is hardly bigger than a St Bernard dog, it carries a load which in the British army would be considered too much for a fifteen-hands mule, and very often its pack-saddle is not taken off its back for weeks together. But what is peculiarly pitiful is that it is the most willing creature on earth, it follows its master like a dog and does not need either bridle or halter. After a dozen years of devoted work it suddenly drops dead, whereupon its master tips it into the ditch and the village dogs have torn its guts out before it is cold.

This kind of thing makes one's blood boil, whereas—on the whole—the plight of the human beings does not. I am not commenting, merely pointing to a fact. People with brown skins are next door to invisible. Anyone can be sorry for the donkey with its galled back, but it is generally owing to some kind of accident if one even notices the old woman under her load of sticks.

As the storks flew northward the Negroes were marching southward—a long, dusty column, infantry, screw-gun batteries and then more infantry, four or five thousand men in all, winding up the road with a clumping of boots and a clatter of iron wheels.

They were Senegalese, the blackest Negroes in Africa, so black that some-times it is difficult to see whereabouts on their necks the hair begins. Their splendid bodies were hidden in reach-me-down khaki uniforms, their feet squashed into boots that looked like blocks of wood, and every tin hat seemed to be a couple of sizes too small. It was very hot and the men had marched a long way. They slumped under the weight of their packs and the curiously sensitive black faces were glistening with sweat.

As they went past a tall, very young Negro turned and caught my eye. But the look he gave me was not in the least the kind of look you might expect. Not hostile, not contemptuous, not sullen, not even inquisitive. It was the shy, wide-eyed Negro look, which actually is a look of profound respect. I saw how it was. This wretched boy, who is a French citizen and has therefore been dragged from the forest to scrub floors and catch syphilis in garrison towns, actually has feelings of reverence before a white skin. He has been taught that the white race are his masters, and he still believes it.

But there is one thought which every white man (and in this connection it doesn't matter twopence if he calls himself a Socialist) thinks when he sees a black army marching past. "How much longer can we go on kidding these people? How long before they turn their guns in the other direction?"

It was curious, really. Every white man there has this thought stowed some-where or other in his mind. I had it, so had the other onlookers, so had the officers on their sweating chargers and the white NCOs[1] marching in the ranks. It was a kind of secret which we all knew and were too clever to tell; only the Negroes didn't know it. And really it was almost like watching a flock of cattle to see the long column, a mile or two miles of armed men, flowing peacefully up the road, while the great white birds drifted over them in the opposite direction, glittering like scraps of paper. ✍

Mark Twain — The Licensed Jester[2]

Mark Twain has crashed the lofty gates of the Everyman Library, but only with *Tom Sawyer* and *Huckleberry Finn*, already fairly well known under the guise of "children's books" (which they are not). His best and most characteristic books, *Roughing It*, *The Innocents at Home*, and even *Life on the Mississippi*, are little remembered in this country, though no doubt in America the patriotism which is everywhere mixed up with literary judgement keeps them alive.

---

[1]Noncommissioned officers.
[2]First published in the *Tribune* in November 1943.

Although Mark Twain produced a surprising variety of books, ranging from a namby-pamby "life" of Joan of Arc[1] to a pamphlet so obscene[2] that it has never been publicly printed, all that is best in his work centres about the Mississippi river and the wild mining towns of the West. Born in 1835 (he came of a Southern family, a family just rich enough to own one or perhaps two slaves), he had had his youth and early manhood in the golden age of America, the period when the great plains were opened up, when wealth and opportunity seemed limitless, and human beings felt free, indeed *were* free, as they had never been before and may not be again for centuries. *Life on the Mississippi* and the two other books that I have mentioned are a ragbag of anecdotes, scenic descriptions and social history both serious and burlesque, but they have a central theme which could perhaps be put into these words: "This is how human beings behave when they are not frightened of the sack." In writing these books Mark Twain is not consciously writing a hymn to liberty. Primarily he is interested in "character", in the fantastic, almost lunatic variations which human nature is capable of when economic pressure and tradition are both removed from it. The raftsmen, Mississippi pilots, miners and bandits whom he describes are probably not much exaggerated, but they are as different from modern men, and from one another, as the gargoyles of a medieval cathedral. They could develop their strange and sometimes sinister individuality because of the lack of any outside pressure. The State hardly existed, the churches were weak and spoke with many voices, and land was to be had for the taking. If you disliked your job you simply hit the boss in the eye and moved further west; and moreover, money was so plentiful that the smallest coin in circulation was worth a shilling. The American pioneers were not supermen, and they were not especially courageous. Whole towns of hardy gold miners let themselves be terrorised by bandits whom they lacked the public spirit to put down. They were not even free from class distinctions. The desperado who stalked through the streets of the mining settlement, with a Derringer pistol in his waistcoat pocket and twenty corpses to his credit, was dressed in a frock coat and shiny top-hat, described himself firmly as a "gentleman" and was meticulous about table manners. But at least it was not the case that a man's destiny was settled from his birth. The "log cabin to White House" myth was true while the free land lasted. In a way, it was for this that the Paris mob had stormed the Bastille, and when one reads Mark Twain, Bret Harte[3] and Whitman° it is hard to feel that their effort was wasted.

---

[1] *The Personal Recollections of Joan of Arc* (1896).

[2] A twenty-eight-page collection of blasphemous and scatalogical observations titled "1601: Conversation as it was by the Social Fireside in the time of the Tudors," written first as a letter in 1876, then privately printed and circulated. The participants in the conversation included Queen Elizabeth, Shakespeare, Francis Bacon, and Sir Walter Raleigh. Twain said he put in "grossnesses not to be found outside of Rabelais,° perhaps."

[3] American humorist (1836–1902) known for his short stories, particularly "The Luck of Roaring Camp," and for the local color of the West.

However, Mark Twain aimed at being something more than a chronicler of the Mississippi and the Gold Rush. In his own day he was famous all over the world as a humorist and comic lecturer. In New York, London, Berlin, Vienna, Melbourne and Calcutta vast audiences rocked with laughter over jokes which have now, almost without exception, ceased to be funny. (It is worth noticing that Mark Twain's lectures were only a success with Anglo-Saxon and German audiences. The relatively grown-up Latin races—whose own humour, he complained, always centred round sex and politics—never cared for them.) But in addition, Mark Twain had some pretentions to being a social critic, even a species of philosopher. He had in him an iconoclastic, even revolutionary vein which he obviously wanted to follow up and yet somehow never did follow up. He might have been a destroyer of humbugs and a prophet of democracy more valuable than Whitman,° because healthier and more humorous. Instead he became that dubious thing a "public figure", flattered by passport officials and entertained by royalty, and his career reflects the deterioration in American life that set in after the civil war.

Mark Twain has sometimes been compared with his contemporary, Anatole France.[1] This comparison is not so pointless as it may sound. Both men were the spiritual children of Voltaire,° both had an ironical, sceptical view of life, and a native pessimism overlaid by gaiety; both knew that the existing social order is a swindle and its cherished beliefs mostly delusions. Both were bigoted atheists and convinced (in Mark Twain's case this was Darwin's doing) of the unbearable cruelty of the universe. But there the resemblance ends. Not only is the Frenchman enormously more learned, more civilised, more alive aesthetically, but he is also more courageous. He does attack the things he disbelieves in; he does not, like Mark Twain, always take refuge behind the amiable mask of the "public figure" and the licensed jester. He is ready to risk the anger of the Church and to take the unpopular side in a controversy—in the Dreyfus° case, for example. Mark Twain, except perhaps in one short essay "What is Man?", never attacks established beliefs in a way that is likely to get him into trouble. Nor could he ever wean himself from the notion, which is perhaps especially an American notion, that success and virtue are the same thing.

In *Life on the Mississippi* there is a queer little illustration of the central weakness of Mark Twain's character. In the earlier part of this mainly autobiographical book the dates have been altered. Mark Twain describes his adventures as a Mississippi pilot as though he had been a boy of about seventeen at the time, whereas in fact he was a young man of nearly thirty. There is a reason for this. The same part of the book describes his exploits in the civil war, which were distinctly

---

[1]Jacques Anatole Thibault (1844–1924), popular novelist. Financially secure through the aid of his mistress of twenty-seven years, Mme de Caillavet, he wrote *L'Ile des pingouins* (*Penguin Island*), *Le Crime de Sylvestre Bonnard*, *Le Livre de mon ami* (*My Friend's Book*), *Les Deux ont soif* (*The Gods Are Athirst*), and a life of Joan of Arc, among other works.

inglorious. Moreover, Mark Twain started by fighting, if he can be said to have fought, on the Southern side, and then changed his allegiance before the war was over. This kind of behaviour is more excusable in a boy than in a man, whence the adjustment of the dates. It is also clear enough, however, that he changed sides because he saw that the North was going to win; and this tendency to side with the stronger whenever possible, to believe that might *must* be right, is apparent throughout his career. In *Roughing It* there is an interesting account of a bandit named Slade, who, among countless other outrages, had committed 28 murders. It is perfectly clear that Mark Twain admires this disgusting scoundrel. Slade was successful; therefore he was admirable. This outlook, no less common today, is summed up in the significant American expression "to *make good*".

In the money-grubbing period that followed the civil war it was hard for anyone of Mark Twain's temperament to refuse to be a success. The old, simple, stump-whittling, tobacco-chewing democracy which Abraham Lincoln typified was perishing: it was now the age of cheap immigrant labour and the growth of Big Business. Mark Twain mildly satirised his contemporaries in *The Gilded Age*, but he also gave himself up to the prevailing fever, and made and lost vast sums of money. He even for a period of years deserted writing for business; and he squandered his time on buffooneries, not merely lecture tours and public banquets, but, for instance, the writing of a book like *A Connecticut Yankee in King Arthur's Court*, which is a deliberate flattery of all that is worst and most vulgar in American life. The man who might have been a kind of rustic Voltaire° became the world's leading after-dinner speaker, charming alike for his anecdotes and his power to make businessmen feel themselves public benefactors.

It is usual to blame Mark Twain's wife for his failure to write the books he ought to have written, and it is evident that she did tyrannise over him pretty thoroughly. Each morning, Mark Twain would show her what he had written the day before, and Mrs Clemens (Mark Twain's real name was Samuel Clemens) would go over it with the blue pencil, cutting out everything that she thought unsuitable. She seems to have been a drastic blue-penciller even by nineteenth-century standards. There is an account in W.D. Howells's book *My Mark Twain*[1] of the fuss that occurred over a terrible expletive that had crept into *Huckleberry Finn*. Mark Twain appealed to Howells, who admitted that it was "just what Huck would have said," but agreed with Mrs Clemens that the word could not possibly be printed. The word was "hell". Nevertheless, no writer is really the intellectual slave of his wife. Mrs Clemens could not have stopped Mark Twain writing any book he really wanted to write. She may have made his surrender to society easier, but the surrender happened because of that flaw in his own nature, his inability to despise success.

Several of Mark Twain's books are bound to survive, because they contain invaluable social history. His life covered the great period of American expansion. When he was a child it was a normal day's outing to go with a picnic lunch and

---

[1]1910.

watch the hanging of an Abolitionist, and when he died the aeroplane was ceasing to be a novelty. This period in America produced relatively little literature, and but for Mark Twain our picture of a Mississippi paddle-steamer, or a stage-coach crossing the plains, would be much dimmer than it is. But most people who have studied his work have come away with a feeling that he might have done something more. He gives all the while a strange impression of being about to say something and then funking it, so that *Life on the Mississippi* and the rest of them seem to be haunted by the ghost of a greater and much more coherent book. Significantly, he starts his autobiography by remarking that a man's inner life is indescribable. We do not know what he would have said—it is just possible that the unprocurable pamphlet, *1601*,[1] would supply a clue but we may guess that it would have wrecked his reputation and reduced his income to reasonable proportions. ✍

As I Please (July 7, 1944)[2]

When the Caliph Omar[3] destroyed the libraries of Alexandria he is supposed to have kept the public baths warm for eighteen days with burning manuscripts, and great numbers of tragedies by Euripides° and others are said to have perished, quite irrecoverably. I remember that when I read about this as a boy it simply filled me with enthusiastic approval. It was so many less words to look up in the dictionary—that was how I saw it. For, though I am only forty-one, I am old enough to have been educated at a time when Latin and Greek were only escapable with great difficulty, while "English" was hardly regarded as a school subject at all.

Classical education is going down the drain at last, but even now there must be far more adults who have been flogged through the entire extant works of Aeschylus,° Sophocles,° Euripides,° Aristophanes,° Vergil,[4] Horace° and various other Latin and Greek authors than have read the English masterpieces of the eighteenth century. People pay lip service to Fielding° and the rest of them, of course, but they don't read them, as you can discover by making a few enquiries among your friends. How many people have ever read *Tom Jones*, for instance? Not so many have even read the later books of *Gulliver's Travels*.[5] *Robinson Crusoe*[6] has a sort of popularity in nursery versions, but the book as a whole is so little known

[1]See note 2, page 420; it was published as early as 1933 by the Golden Hind Press, New York.
[2]"As I Please" was the title of Orwell's weekly column in the *Tribune* published between December 1943 and February 1945. This essay appeared in the *Tribune*, July 7, 1944.
[3](c. 581–644) A convert to Islam in 618, he was an advisor to Muhammad and invaded Syria, Egypt, and Persia. In 642 he took over the city of Alexandria, already in decline since the days of Caesar,° and died two years later at the hand of a foreign slave.
[4]See Virgil.°
[5]See Swift.°
[6]See Defoe.°

that few people are even aware that the second part (the journey through Tartary) exists. Smollett,° I imagine, is the least read of all. The central plot of Shaw's° play, *Pygmalion*, is lifted out of *Peregrine Pickle*,[1] and I believe that no one has ever pointed this out in print, which suggests that few people can have read the book. But what is strangest of all is that Smollett,° so far as I know, has never been boosted by the Scottish Nationalists, who are so careful to claim Byron° for their own. Yet Smollett,° besides being one of the best novelists the English-speaking races have produced, *was* a Scotsman, and proclaimed it openly at a time when being so was anything but helpful to one's career.

> Life in the civilised world.
> (The family are at tea.)
> Zoom-zoom-zoom!
> "Is there an alert on?"
> "No, it's all clear."
> "I thought there was an alert on."
> Zoom-zoom-zoom!
> "There's another of those things coming!"
> "It's all right, it's miles away."
> Zoom-zoom-ZOOM!
> "Look out, here it comes! Under the table, quick!"
> Zoom-zoom-zoom!
> "It's all right, it's getting fainter."
> Zoom-zoom-ZOOM!
> "It's coming back!"
> "They seem to kind of circle round and come back again. They've got something on their tails that makes them do it. Like a torpedo."
> ZOOM-ZOOM-ZOOM!
> "Christ! It's bang overhead!"
> Dead silence.
> "Now get *right* underneath. Keep your head well down. What a mercy baby isn't here!"
> "Look at the cat! He's frightened too."
> "Of course animals *know*. They can feel the vibrations."
> BOOM!
> "It's all right, I told you it was miles away."
> (Tea continues.)

I see that Lord Winterton, writing in the *Evening Standard*, speaks of the "remarkable reticence (by no means entirely imposed by rule or regulation) which Parliament and press alike have displayed in this war to avoid endangering national security" and adds that it has "earned the admiration of the civilised world".

---

[1] By Smollett.°

It is not only in war-time that the British press observes this voluntary reticence. One of the most extraordinary things about England is that there is almost no official censorship, and yet nothing that is actually offensive to the governing class gets into print, at least in any place where large numbers of people are likely to read it. If it is "not done" to mention something or other, it just doesn't get mentioned. The position is summed up in the lines by (I think) Hilaire Belloc:°

> You cannot hope to bribe or twist
> Thank God! the English journalist:
> But seeing what the man will do
> Unbribed, there is no reason to.

No bribes, no threats, no penalties—just a nod and a wink and the thing is done. A well-known example was the business of the Abdication.[1] Weeks before the scandal officially broke, tens or hundreds of thousands of people had heard all about Mrs Simpson, and yet not a word got into the press, not even into the *Daily Worker*, although the American and European papers were having the time of their lives with the story. Yet I believe there was no definite official ban: just an official "request" and a general agreement that to break the news prematurely "would not do". And I can think of other instances of good news stories failing to see the light although there would have been no penalty for printing them.

Nowadays this kind of veiled censorship even extends to books. The MOI[2] does not, of course, dictate a party line or issue an *index expurgatorious*.[3] It merely "advises". Publishers take manuscripts to the MOI, and the MOI "suggests" that this or that is undesirable, or premature, or "would serve no clear purpose". And though there is no definite prohibition, no clear statement that this or that must not be printed, official policy is never flouted. Circus dogs jump when the trainer cracks his whip, but the really well-trained dog is the one that turns his somersault when there is no whip. And that is the state we have reached in this country, thanks to three hundred years of living together without a civil war.

Here is a little problem sometimes used as an intelligence test.

A man walked four miles due south from his house and shot a bear. He then walked two miles due west, then walked another four miles due north and was back at his home again. What was the colour of the bear?[4]

The interesting point is that—so far as my own observations go—men usually see the answer to this problem and women do not. ✍

---

[1] King Edward VIII abdicated in 1936 to marry Mrs. Wallace Warfield Simpson, an American divorcée.
[2] Ministry of Information.
[3] Latin for "index of censored works."
[4] White, because the hunter is at the North Pole.

As I Please (August 11, 1944)[1]

A few days ago a West African wrote to inform us that a certain London dance hall had recently erected a "colour bar," presumably in order to please the American soldiers who formed an important part of its clientele. Telephone conversations with the management of the dance hall brought us the answers: (a) that the "colour bar" had been cancelled, and (b) that it had never been imposed in the first place; but I think one can take it that our informant's charge had some kind of basis. There have been other similar incidents recently. For instance, during last week a case in a magistrate's court brought out the fact that a West Indian Negro working in this country had been refused admission to a place of entertainment when he was wearing Home Guard[2] uniform. And there have been many instances of Indians, Negroes and others being turned away from hotels on the ground that "we don't take coloured people".

It is immensely important to be vigilant against this kind of thing, and to make as much public fuss as possible whenever it happens. For this is one of those matters in which making a fuss can achieve something. There is no kind of legal disability against coloured people in this country, and, what is more, there is very little popular colour feeling. (This is not due to any inherent virtue in the British people, as our behaviour in India shows. It is due to the fact that in Britain itself there is no colour problem.)

The trouble always arises in the same way. A hotel, restaurant or what not is frequented by people who have money to spend who object to mixing with Indians or Negroes. They tell the proprietor that unless he imposes a colour bar they will go elsewhere. They may be a very small minority, and the proprietor may not be in agreement with them, but it is difficult for him to lose good customers; so he imposes the colour bar. This kind of thing cannot happen when public opinion is on the alert and disagreeable publicity is given to any establishment where coloured people are insulted. Anyone who knows of a provable instance of colour discrimination ought always to expose it. Otherwise the tiny percentage of colour-snobs who exist among us can make endless mischief, and the British people are given a bad name which, as a whole, they do not deserve.

In the nineteen-twenties, when American tourists were as much a part of the scenery of Paris as tobacco kiosks and tin urinals, the beginnings of a colour bar began to appear even in France. The Americans spent money like water, and restaurant proprietors and the like could not afford to disregard them. One evening, at a dance in a very well-known café, some Americans objected to the presence of a Negro who was there with an Egyptian woman. After making some feeble protests, the proprietor gave in, and the Negro was turned out.

Next morning there was a terrible hullabaloo and the café proprietor was hauled up before a Minister of the Government and threatened with prosecution.

---

[1]Published in the *Tribune* August 11, 1944.
[2]Volunteers trained to defend Great Britain in case of German invasion during World War II.

It had turned out that the offended Negro was the Ambassador of Haiti. People of that kind can usually get satisfaction, but most of us do not have the good fortune to be ambassadors, and the ordinary Indian, Negro or Chinese can only be protected against petty insult if other ordinary people are willing to exert themselves on his behalf. ✍

Antisemitism in Britain[1]

There are about 400,000 known Jews in Britain, and in addition some thousands or, at most, scores of thousands of Jewish refugees who have entered the country from 1934 onwards. The Jewish population is almost entirely concentrated in half a dozen big towns and is mostly employed in the food, clothing and furniture trades. A few of the big monopolies, such as the ICI,[2] one or two leading newspapers and at least one big chain of department stores are Jewish-owned or partly Jewish-owned, but it would be very far from the truth to say that British business life is dominated by Jews. The Jews seem, on the contrary, to have failed to keep up with the modern tendency towards big amalgamations and to have remained fixed in those trades which are necessarily carried out on a small scale and by old-fashioned methods.

I start off with these background facts, which are already known to any well-informed person, in order to emphasise that there is no real Jewish "problem" in England. The Jews are not numerous or powerful enough, and it is only in what are loosely called "intellectual circles" that they have any noticeable influence. Yet it is generally admitted that antisemitism is on the increase, that it has been greatly exacerbated by the war, and that humane and enlightened people are not immune to it. It does not take violent forms (English people are almost invariably gentle and law-abiding), but it is ill-natured enough, and in favourable circumstances it could have political results. Here are some samples of antisemitic remarks that have been made to me during the past year or two:

Middle-aged office employee: "I generally come to work by bus. It takes longer, but I don't care about using the Underground from Golders Green[3] nowadays. There's too many of the Chosen Race travelling on that line."

Tobacconist (woman): "No, I've got no matches for you. I should try the lady down the street. *She's* always got matches. One of the Chosen Race, you see."

Young intellectual, Communist or near-Communist: "No, I do *not* like Jews. I've never made any secret of that. I can't stick them. Mind you, I'm not antisemitic, of course."

Middle-class woman: "Well, no one could call me antisemitic, but I do think the

---

[1]First published in *Contemporary Jewish Record* in April 1945.
[2]Imperial Chemical Industries, a huge British chemical firm.
[3]Largely Jewish suburb of London, originally named for the goldsmiths who worked there.

way these Jews behave is too absolutely stinking. The way they push their way to the head of queues, and so on. They're so abominably selfish. I think they're responsible for a lot of what happens to them."

Milk roundsman: "A Jew don't do no work, not the same as what an Englishman does. 'E's too clever. We work with this 'ere" (flexes his biceps). "They work with that there" (taps his forehead).

Chartered accountant, intelligent, left-wing in an undirected way: "These bloody Yids are all pro-German. They'd change sides tomorrow if the Nazis got here. I see a lot of them in my business. They admire Hitler at the bottom of their hearts. They'll always suck up to anyone who kicks them."

Intelligent woman, on being offered a book dealing with antisemitism and German atrocities: "Don't show it me, *please* don't show it to me. It'll only make me hate the Jews more than ever."

I could fill pages with similar remarks, but these will do to go on with. Two facts emerge from them. One—which is very important and which I must return to in a moment—is that above a certain intellectual level people are ashamed of being antisemitic and are careful to draw a distinction between "antisemitism" and "disliking Jews". The other is that antisemitism is an irrational thing. The Jews are accused of specific offenses (for instance, bad behaviour in food queues) which the person speaking feels strongly about, but it is obvious that these accusations merely rationalise some deep-rooted prejudice. To attempt to counter them with facts and statistics is useless, and may sometimes be worse than useless. As the last of the above-quoted remarks shows, people can remain antisemitic, or at least anti-Jewish, while being fully aware that their outlook is indefensible. If you dislike somebody, you dislike him and there is an end of it: your feelings are not made any better by a recital of his virtues.

It so happens that the war has encouraged the growth of antisemitism and even, in the eyes of many ordinary people, given some justification for it. To begin with, the Jews are one people of whom it can be said with complete certainty that they will benefit by an Allied victory. Consequently the theory that "this is a Jewish war" has a certain plausibility, all the more so because the Jewish war effort seldom gets its fair share of recognition. The British Empire is a huge heterogeneous organisation held together largely by mutual consent, and it is often necessary to flatter the less reliable elements at the expense of the more loyal ones. To publicise the exploits of Jewish soldiers, or even to admit the existence of a considerable Jewish army in the Middle East, rouses hostility in South Africa, the Arab countries and elsewhere: it is easier to ignore the whole subject and allow the man in the street to go on thinking that Jews are exceptionally clever at dodging military service. Then again, Jews are to be found in exactly those trades which are bound to incur unpopularity with the civilian public in war-time. Jews are mostly concerned with selling food, clothes, furniture and tobacco—exactly the commodities of which there is a chronic shortage, with consequent overcharging, black-marketing and favouritism. And again, the common charge that Jews behave in an exceptionally cowardly way during air raids was given a certain amount of colour by the big raids of 1940. As it happened, the Jewish quarter of Whitechapel was one of the first areas to be heavily blitzed, with the natural result that swarms of Jewish refugees distributed themselves all over London. If one judged merely from these war-time phenomena, it would be easy to imagine that antisemitism is a quasi-rational thing, founded on mistaken premises. And naturally the antisemite thinks of himself as a reasonable being. Whenever I have touched on this subject in a newspaper article, I have always had a considerable "come-back", and invariably some of the letters are from well-balanced, middling people—doctors, for example—with no apparent economic grievance. These people always say (as Hitler says in *Mein Kampf*)[1] that they started out with no anti-Jewish prejudice but were driven into their present position by mere observation of the facts. Yet one of the marks of antisemitism is an ability to believe stories that could not possibly be true. One could see a good example of this in the strange accident that occurred in London in 1942, when a crowd, frightened by a bomb-burst nearby, fled into the mouth of an Underground station, with the result that something over a hundred people were crushed to death. The very same day it was repeated all over London that "the Jews were responsible". Clearly, if people will believe this kind of thing, one will not get much further by arguing with them. The only useful approach is to discover *why* they can swallow absurdities on one particular subject while remaining sane on others.

But now let me come back to that point I mentioned earlier—that there is widespread awareness of the prevalence of antisemitic feeling, and unwillingness to admit sharing it. Among educated people, antisemitism is held to be an unforgivable sin and in a quite different category from other kinds of racial prejudice. People will go to remarkable lengths to demonstrate that they are *not* antisemitic. Thus, in 1943 an intercession service on behalf of the Polish Jews was held in a synagogue in St John's Wood.[2] The local authorities declared themselves anxious to participate in it, and the service was attended by the mayor of the borough in his robes and chain, by representatives of all the churches, and by detachments of RAF,[3] Home Guards, nurses, Boy Scouts and what not. On the surface it was a touching demonstration of solidarity with the suffering Jews. But it was essentially a *conscious* effort to behave decently by people whose subjective feelings must in many cases have been very different. That quarter of London is partly Jewish, antisemitism is rife there, and, as I well knew, some of the men sitting round me in the synagogue were tinged by it. Indeed, the commander of my own platoon of Home Guards, who had been especially keen beforehand that we should "make a good show" at the intercession service, was an ex-member of

---

[1] German for "*My Struggle*" (1933).
[2] A relatively fancy section of London.
[3] Royal Air Force.

Mosley's Blackshirts.[1] While this division of feeling exists, tolerance of mass violence against Jews, or, what is more important, antisemitic legislation, are not possible in England. It is not at present possible, indeed, that antisemitism should *become respectable*. But this is less of an advantage than it might appear.

One effect of the persecutions in Germany has been to prevent antisemitism from being seriously studied. In England a brief inadequate survey was made by Mass Observation[2] a year or two ago, but if there has been any other investigation of the subject, then its findings have been kept strictly secret. At the same time there has been conscious suppression, by all thoughtful people, of anything likely to wound Jewish susceptibilities. After 1934 the "Jew joke" disappeared as though by magic from postcards, periodicals and the music-hall stage, and to put an unsympathetic Jewish character into a novel or short story came to be regarded as antisemitism. On the Palestine issue, too, it was *de rigueur*[3] among enlightened people to accept the Jewish case as proved and avoid examining the claims of the Arabs—a decision which might be correct on its own merits, but which was adopted primarily because the Jews were in trouble and it was felt that one must not criticise them. Thanks to Hitler, therefore, you had a situation in which the press was in effect censored in favour of the Jews while in private antisemitism was on the up-grade, even, to some extent, among sensitive and intelligent people. This was particularly noticeable in 1940 at the time of the internment of the refugees. Naturally, every thinking person felt that it was his duty to protest against the wholesale locking-up of unfortunate foreigners who for the most part were only in England because they were opponents of Hitler. Privately, however, one heard very different sentiments expressed. A minority of the refugees behaved in an exceedingly tactless way, and the feeling against them necessarily had an antisemitic undercurrent, since they were largely Jews. A very eminent figure in the Labour Party—I won't name him, but he is one of the most respected people in England—said to me quite violently: "We never asked these people to come to this country. If they choose to come here, let them take the consequences." Yet this man would as a matter of course have associated himself with any kind of petition or manifesto against the internment of aliens. This feeling that antisemitism is something sinful and disgraceful, something that a civilised person does not suffer from, is unfavourable to a scientific approach, and indeed many people will admit that they are frightened of probing too deeply into the subject. They are

---

[1]Sir Oswald Mosley (1896–1980), British anti-Semite who founded the British Union of Fascists in 1932 in imitation of Mussolini's Blackshirts. Through his second wife, Diana Guinness (sister to Jessica and Nancy Mitford), he became a friend of Hitler (guest of honor at their wedding in 1936). Mosley and his wife were interned from 1940 to 1943. As late as 1959 he was still in politics, running unsuccessfully for Parliament.

[2]In the thirties in England Charles Madge, a poet, began a movement to collect statistics about all aspects of life on a massive scale. On the day of George VI's coronation, May 12, 1936, observers all over England collected every scrap of information they could about everything.

[3]French for "proper" or "socially obligatory."

frightened, that is to say, of discovering not only that antisemitism is spreading, but that they themselves are infected by it.

To see this in perspective one must look back a few decades, to the days when Hitler was an out-of-work house-painter whom nobody had heard of. One would then find that though antisemitism is sufficiently in evidence now, it is probably *less* prevalent in England than it was thirty years ago. It is true that antisemitism as a fully thought-out racial or religious doctrine has never flourished in England. There has never been much feeling against intermarriage, or against Jews taking a prominent part in public life. Nevertheless, thirty years ago it was accepted more or less as a law of nature that a Jew was a figure of fun and—though superior in intelligence—slightly deficient in "character". In theory a Jew suffered from no legal disabilities, but in effect he was debarred from certain professions. He would probably not have been accepted as an officer in the navy, for instance, nor in what is called a "smart" regiment in the army. A Jewish boy at a public school almost invariably had a bad time. He could, of course, live down his Jewishness if he was exceptionally charming or athletic, but it was an initial disability comparable to a stammer or a birthmark. Wealthy Jews tended to disguise themselves under aristocratic English or Scottish names, and to the average person it seemed quite natural that they should do this, just as it seems natural for a criminal to change his identity if possible. About twenty years ago, in Rangoon, I was getting into a taxi with a friend when a small ragged boy of fair complexion rushed up to us and began a complicated story about having arrived from Colombo on a ship and wanting money to get back. His manner and appearance were difficult to "place", and I said to him:

"You speak very good English. What nationality are you?"

He answered eagerly in his chi-chi accent: "I am a *Joo*, sir!"

And I remember turning to my companion and saying, only partly in joke, "He admits it openly." All the Jews I had known till then were people who were ashamed of being Jews, or at any rate preferred not to talk about their ancestry, and if forced to do so tended to use the word "Hebrew".

The working-class attitude was no better. The Jew who grew up in Whitechapel took it for granted that he would be assaulted, or at least hooted at, if he ventured into one of the Christian slums nearby, and the "Jew joke" of the music halls and the comic papers was almost consistently ill-natured.[1] There was

---

[1] It is interesting to compare the "Jew joke" with that other stand-by of the music halls, the "Scotch joke", which superficially it resembles. Occasionally a story is told (e.g. the Jew and the Scotsman who went into a pub together and both died of thirst) which puts both races on an equality, but in general the Jew is credited *merely* with cunning and avarice while the Scotsman is credited with physical hardihood as well. This is seen, for example, in the story of the Jew and the Scotsman who go together to a meeting which has been advertised as free. Unexpectedly there is a collection, and to avoid this the Jew faints and the Scotsman carries him out. Here the Scotsman performs the athletic feat of carrying the other. It would seem vaguely wrong if it were the other way about. [Orwell's footnote.]

also literary Jew-baiting, which in the hands of Belloc,° Chesterton° and their followers reached an almost continental level of scurrility. Non-Catholic writers were sometimes guilty of the same thing in a milder form. There has been a perceptible antisemitic strain in English literature from Chaucer onwards, and without even getting up from this table to consult a book I can think of passages which *if written now* would be stigmatised as antisemitism, in the works of Shakespeare, Smollett,° Thackeray,° Bernard Shaw,° H.G. Wells,° T.S. Elliot,° Aldous Huxley° and various others. Offhand, the only English writers I can think of who, before the days of Hitler, made a definite effort to stick up for Jews are Dickens° and Charles Reade.° And however little the average intellectual may have agreed with the opinions of Belloc° and Chesterton,° he did not acutely disapprove of them. Chesterton's° endless tirades against Jews, which he thrust into stories and essays upon the flimsiest pretexts, never got him into trouble — indeed Chesterton° was one of the most generally respected figures in English literary life. Anyone who wrote in that strain *now* would bring down a storm of abuse upon himself, or more probably would find it impossible to get his writings published.

If, as I suggest, prejudice against Jews has always been pretty widespread in England, there is no reason to think that Hitler has genuinely diminished it. He has merely caused a sharp division between the politically conscious person who realises that this is not a time to throw stones at the Jews, and the unconscious person whose native antisemitism is increased by the nervous strain of the war. One can assume, therefore, that many people who would perish rather than admit to antisemitic feelings are secretly prone to them. I have already indicated that I believe antisemitism to be essentially a neurosis, but of course it has its rationalisations, which are sincerely believed in and are partly true. The rationalisation put forward by the common man is that the Jew is an exploiter. The partial justification for this is that the Jew, in England, is generally a small businessman — that is to say a person whose depredations are more obvious and intelligible than those of, say, a bank or an insurance company. Higher up the intellectual scale, antisemitism is rationalised by saying that the Jew is a person who spreads disaffection and weakens national morale. Again there is some superficial justification for this. During the past twenty-five years the activities of what are called "intellectuals" have been largely mischievous. I do not think it an exaggeration to say that if the "intellectuals" had done their work a little more thoroughly, Britain would have surrendered in 1940. But the disaffected intelligentsia inevitably included a large number of Jews. With some plausibility it can be said that the Jews are the enemies of our native culture and our national morale. Carefully examined, the claim is seen to be nonsense, but there are always a few prominent individuals who can be cited in support of it. During the past few years there has been what amounts to a counter-attack against the rather shallow Leftism which was fashionable in the previous decade and which was exemplified by such organisations as the Left Book Club. This counter-attack (see for instance such books as Arnold Lunn's *The Good Gorilla*[1] or Evelyn Waugh's° *Put Out More Flags*) has an antisemitic strain, and it would probably be more marked if the subject were not so obviously dangerous. It so happens that for some decades past Britain has had no nationalist intelligentsia worth bothering about. But British nationalism, i.e. nationalism of an intellectual kind, may revive, and probably will revive if Britain comes out of the present war greatly weakened. The young intellectuals of 1950 may be as naively patriotic as those of 1914. In that case the kind of antisemitism which flourished among the anti-Dreyfusards[2] in France, and which Chesterton° and Belloc° tried to import into this country, might get a foothold.

I have no hard-and-fast theory about the origins of antisemitism. The two current explanations, that it is due to economic causes, or on the other hand, that it is a legacy from the Middle Ages, seem to me unsatisfactory, though I admit that if one combines them they can be made to cover the facts. All I would say with confidence is that antisemitism is part of the larger problem of nationalism, which has not yet been seriously examined, and that the Jew is evidently a scapegoat, though *for what* he is a scapegoat we do not yet know. In this essay I have relied almost entirely on my own limited experience, and perhaps every one of my conclusions would be negatived by other observers. The fact is that there are almost no dates on this subject. But for what they are worth I will summarise my opinions. Boiled down, they amount to this:

There is more antisemitism in England than we care to admit, and the war has accentuated it, but it is not certain that it is on the increase if one thinks in terms of decades rather than years.

It does not at present lead to open persecution, but it has the effect of making people callous to the sufferings of Jews in other countries.

It is at bottom quite irrational and will not yield to argument.

The persecutions in Germany have caused much concealment of antisemitic feeling and thus obscured the whole picture.

The subject needs serious investigation.

Only the last point is worth expanding. To study any subject scientifically one needs a detached attitude, which is obviously harder when one's own interests or emotions are involved. Plenty of people who are quite capable of being objective about sea urchins, say, or the square root of 2, become schizophrenic if they have to think about the sources of their own income. What vitiates nearly all that is written about antisemitism is the assumption in the writer's mind that *he himself* is immune to it. "Since I know that antisemitism is irrational," he argues, "it

---

[1]Lunn (1888–1974) was an outdoorsman, mountaineer, and skier who invented the slalom and is known as the father of downhill ski racing. He fought in the Spanish Civil War and wrote about his disillusionment with the Republican cause in *Spanish Rehearsal* (1937).
[2]See Dreyfus.°

follows that I do not share it." He thus fails to start his investigation in the one place where he could get hold of some reliable evidence—that is, in his own mind.

It seems to me a safe assumption that the disease loosely called nationalism is now almost universal. Antisemitism is only one manifestation of nationalism, and not everyone will have the disease in that particular form. A Jew, for example, would not be antisemitic: but then many Zionist Jews seem to me to be merely antisemites turned upside-down, just as many Indians and Negroes display the normal colour prejudices in an inverted form. The point is that something, some psychological vitamin, is lacking in modern civilisation, and as a result we are all more or less subject to this lunacy of believing that whole races or nations are mysteriously good or mysteriously evil. I defy any modern intellectual to look closely and honestly into his own mind without coming upon nationalistic loyalties and hatreds of one kind or another. It is the fact that he can feel the emotional tug of such things, and yet see them dispassionately for what they are, that gives him his status as an intellectual. It will be seen, therefore, that the starting point for any investigation of antisemitism should not be "Why does this obviously irrational belief appeal to other people?" but "Why does antisemitism appeal to *me*? What is there about it that I feel to be true?" If one asks this question one at least discovers one's own rationalisations, and it may be possible to find out what lies beneath them. Antisemitism should be investigated—and I will not say by antisemites, but at any rate by people who know that they are not immune to that kind of emotion. When Hitler has disappeared a real enquiry into this subject will be possible, and it would probably be best to start not by debunking antisemitism, but by marshalling all the justifications for it that can be found, in one's own mind or anybody else's. In that way one might get some clues that would lead to its psychological roots. But that antisemitism will be definitively *cured*, without curing the larger disease of nationalism, I do not believe. ✍

What Is Science?[1]

In last week's *Tribune*, there was an interesting letter from Mr J. Stewart Cook, in which he suggested that the best way of avoiding the danger of a "scientific hierarchy" would be to see to it that every member of the general public was, as far as possible, scientifically educated. At the same time, scientists should be brought out of their isolation and encouraged to take a greater part in politics and administration.

As a general statement, I think most of us would agree with this, but I notice that, as usual, Mr Cook does not define science, and merely implies in passing

---

[1]First published in the *Tribune* in 1945.

that it means certain exact sciences whose experiments can be made under laboratory conditions. Thus, adult education tends "to neglect scientific studies in favour of literary, economic and social subjects", economics and sociology not being regarded as branches of science, apparently. This point is of great importance. For the word science is at present used in at least two meanings, and the whole question of scientific education is obscured by the current tendency to dodge from one meaning to the other.

Science is generally taken as meaning either (a) the exact sciences, such as chemistry, physics, etc, or (b) a method of thought which obtains verifiable results by reasoning logically from observed fact.

If you ask any scientist, or indeed almost any educated person, "What is science?" you are likely to get an answer approximating to (b). In everyday life, however, both in speaking and in writing, when people say "science" they mean (a). Science means something that happens in a laboratory: the very word calls up a picture of graphs, test-tubes, balances, Bunsen burners, microscopes. A biologist, an astronomer, perhaps a psychologist or a mathematician, is described as a "man of science": no one would think of applying this term to a statesman, a poet, a journalist or even a philosopher. And those who tell us that the young must be scientifically educated mean, almost invariably, that they should be taught more about radioactivity, or the stars, or the physiology of their own bodies, rather than that they should be taught to think more exactly.

This confusion of meaning, which is partly deliberate, has in it a great danger. Implied in the demand for more scientific education is the claim that if one has been scientifically trained one's approach to *all* subjects will be more intelligent than if one had had no such training. A scientist's political opinions, it is assumed, his opinions on sociological questions, on morals, on philosophy, perhaps even on the arts, will be more valuable than those of a layman. The world, in other words, would be a better place if the scientists were in control of it. But a "scientist", as we have just seen, means in practice a specialist in one of the exact sciences. It follows that a chemist or a physicist, as such, is politically more intelligent than a poet or a lawyer, as such. And, in fact, there are already millions of people who do believe this.

But is it really true that a "scientist", in this narrower sense, is any likelier than other people to approach non-scientific problems in an objective way? There is not much reason for thinking so. Take one simple test—the ability to withstand nationalism. It is often loosely said that "Science is international", but in practice the scientific workers of all countries line up behind their own governments with fewer scruples than are felt by the writers and the artists. The German scientific community, as a whole, made no resistance to Hitler. Hitler may have ruined the long-term prospects of German science, but there were still plenty of gifted men to do the necessary research on such things as synthetic oil, jet planes, rocket projectiles and the atomic bomb. Without them the German war machine could never have been built up.

On the other hand, what happened to German literature when the Nazis came to power? I believe no exhaustive lists have been published, but I imagine that the number of German scientists—Jews apart—who voluntarily exiled themselves or were persecuted by the regime was much smaller than the number of writers and journalists. More sinister than this, a number of German scientists swallowed the monstrosity of "racial science". You can find some of the statements to which they set their names in Professor Brady's *The Spirit and Structure of German Fascism*.

But, in slightly different forms, it is the same picture everywhere. In England, a large proportion of our leading scientists accept the structure of capitalist society, as can be seen from the comparative freedom with which they are given knighthoods, baronetcies and even peerages. Since Tennyson,° no English writer worth reading—one might, perhaps, make an exception of Sir Max Beerbohm[1]—has been given a title. And those English scientists who do not simply accept the *status quo* are frequently Communists, which means that, however intellectually scrupulous they may be in their own line of work, they are ready to be uncritical and even dishonest on certain subjects. The fact is that a mere training in one or more of the exact sciences, even combined with very high gifts, is no guarantee of a humane or sceptical outlook. The physicists of half a dozen great nations, all feverishly and secretly working away at the atomic bomb, are a demonstration of this.

But does all this mean that the general public should *not* be more scientifically educated? On the contrary! All it means is that scientific education for the masses will do little good, and probably a lot of harm, if it simply boils down to more physics, more chemistry, more biology, etc to the detriment of literature and history. Its probable effect on the average human being would be to narrow the range of his thoughts and make him more than ever contemptuous of such knowledge as he did not possess: and his political reactions would probably be somewhat less intelligent than those of an illiterate peasant who retained a few historical memories and a fairly sound aesthetic sense.

Clearly, scientific education ought to mean the implanting of a rational, sceptical, experimental habit of mind. It ought to mean acquiring a *method*—a method that can be used on any problem that one meets—and not simply piling up a lot of facts. Put it in those words, and the apologist of scientific education will usually agree. Press him further, ask him to particularise, and somehow it always turns out that scientific education means more attention to the exact sciences, in others words—more *facts*. The idea that science means a way of looking at the world, and not simply a body of knowledge, is in practice strongly resisted. I think sheer professional jealousy is part of the reason for this. For if science is simply a method or an attitude, so that anyone whose thought-processes are sufficiently rational can in some sense be described as a scientist—what then becomes of the

---

[1]English essayist, caricaturist, and parodist (1872–1956) who succeeded Shaw° as the drama critic for the *Saturday Review* and wrote *Zuleika Dobson* (1911), among many other works.

enormous prestige now employed by the chemist, the physicist, etc and his claim to be somehow wiser than the rest of us?

A hundred years ago, Charles Kingsley° described science as "making nasty smells in a laboratory". A year or two ago a young industrial chemist informed me, smugly, that he "could not see what was the use of poetry". So the pendulum swings to and fro, but it does not seem to me that one attitude is any better than the other. At the moment, science is on the up-grade, and so we hear, quite rightly, the claim that the masses should be scientifically educated: we do not hear, as we ought, the counter-claim that the scientists themselves would benefit by a little education. Just before writing this, I saw in an American magazine the statement that a number of British and American physicists refused from the start to do research on the atomic bomb, well knowing what use would be made of it. Here you have a group of sane men in the middle of a world of lunatics. And though no names were published, I think it would be a safe guess that all of them were people with some kind of general cultural background, some acquaintance with history or literature or the arts—in short, people whose interests were not, in the current sense of the word, purely scientific. ✍

Why I Write[1]

From a very early age, perhaps the age of five or six, I knew that when I grew up I should be a writer. Between the ages of about seventeen and twenty-four I tried to abandoned this idea, but I did so with the consciousness that I was outraging my true nature and that sooner or later I should have to settle down and write books.

I was the middle child of three, but there was a gap of five years on either side, and I barely saw my father before I was eight. For this and other reasons I was somewhat lonely, and I soon developed disagreeable mannerisms which made me unpopular throughout my schooldays. I had the lonely child's habit of making up stories and holding conversations with imaginary persons, and I think from the very start my literary ambitions were mixed up with the feeling of being isolated and undervalued. I knew that I had a facility with words and a power of facing unpleasant facts, and I felt that this created a sort of private world in which I could get my own back for my failure in everyday life. Nevertheless the volume of serious—i.e. seriously intended—writing which I produced all through my childhood and boyhood would not amount to half a dozen pages. I wrote my first poem at the age of four or five, my mother taking it down to dictation. I cannot remember anything about it except that it was about a tiger and the tiger had "chair-like teeth"—a good enough phrase, but I fancy the poem was a plagiarism

---

[1]First published in *Gangrel* in 1946.

of Blake's[1] "Tiger, Tiger". At eleven, when the war of 1914–18 broke out, I wrote a patriotic poem which was printed in the local newspaper, as was another, two years later, on the death of Kitchener.[2] From time to time, when I was a bit older, I wrote bad and usually unfinished "nature poems" in the Georgian[3] style. I also, about twice, attempted a short story which was a ghastly failure. That was the total of the would-be serious work that I actually set down on paper during all those years.

However, throughout this time I did in a sense engage in literary activities. To begin with there was the made-to-order stuff which I produced quickly, easily and without much pleasure to myself. Apart from school work, I wrote *vers d'occasion*,[4] semi-comic poems which I could turn out at what now seems to me astonishing speed—at fourteen I wrote a whole rhyming play, in imitation of Aristophanes,° in about a week—and helped to edit school magazines, both printed and in manuscript. These magazines were the most pitiful burlesque stuff that you could imagine, and I took far less trouble with them than I now would with the cheapest journalism. But side by side with all this, for fifteen years or more, I was carrying out a literary exercise of a quite different kind: this was the making up of a continuous "story" about myself, a sort of diary existing only in the mind. I believe this is a common habit of children and adolescents. As a very small child I used to imagine that I was, say, Robin Hood, and picture myself as the hero of thrilling adventures, but quite soon my "story" ceased to be narcissistic in a crude way and became more and more a mere description of what I was doing and the things I saw. For minutes at a time this kind of thing would be running through my head: "He pushed the door open and entered the room. A yellow beam of sunlight, filtering through the muslin curtains, slanted on to the table, where a matchbox, half open, lay beside the inkpot. With his right hand in his pocket he moved across to the window. Down in the street a tortoiseshell cat was chasing a dead leaf," etc etc. This habit continued till I was about twenty-five, right through my non-literary years. Although I had to search, and did search, for the right words, I seemed to be making this descriptive effort almost against my will, under a kind of compulsion from outside. The "story" must, I suppose, have reflected the styles of the various writers I admired at different ages, but so far as I remember it always had the same meticulous descriptive quality.

When I was about sixteen I suddenly discovered the joy of mere words, i.e. the sounds and associations of words. The lines from *Paradise Lost*,

> So hee with difficulty and labour hard
> Moved on: with difficulty and labour hee,

---

[1]Great English poet and engraver (1757–1827) whose *Songs of Innocence* (1789) and *Songs of Experience* (1794), where "Tiger, Tiger" appears, greatly influenced English Romanticism.
[2]Horatio Herbert (1850–1916), first earl of Kartoum and of Droone, British war hero and statesman who fought in the Boer War, led the British troops in India, and was made secretary of war at the onset of World War I. Criticized for the shortages at the front, he set off on a mission to strengthen the Russian contribution to the war, but his ship sank when it hit a German mine.
[3]Pastoral, decorative verse popular during the reign of King George V (1910–1936).
[4]Poems written for specific occasions.

which do not now seem to me so very wonderful, sent shivers down my backbone; and the spelling "hee" for "he" was an added pleasure. As for the need to describe things, I knew all about it already. So it is clear what kind of books I wanted to write, in so far as I could be said to want to write books at that time. I wanted to write enormous naturalistic novels with unhappy endings, full of detailed descriptions and arresting similes, and also full of purple passages in which words were used partly for the sake of their sound. And in fact my first completed novel, *Burmese Days*, which I wrote when I was thirty but projected much earlier, is rather that kind of book.

I give all this background information because I do not think one can assess a writer's motives without knowing something of his early development. His subject matter will be determined by the age he lives in—at least this is true in tumultuous, revolutionary ages like our own—but before he ever begins to write he will have acquired an emotional attitude from which he will never completely escape. It is his job, no doubt, to discipline his temperament and avoid getting stuck at some immature stage, or in some perverse mood: but if he escapes from his early influences altogether, he will have killed his impulse to write. Putting aside the need to earn a living, I think there are four great motives for writing, at any rate for writing prose. They exist in different degrees in every writer, and in any one writer the proportions will vary from time to time, according to the atmosphere in which he is living. They are:

1. Sheer egoism. Desire to seem clever, to be talked about, to be remembered after death, to get your own back on grown-ups who snubbed you in childhood, etc etc. It is humbug to pretend that this is not a motive, and a strong one. Writers share this characteristic with scientists, artists, politicians, lawyers, soldiers, successful businessmen—in short, with the whole top crust of humanity. The great mass of human beings are not acutely selfish. After the age of about thirty they abandon individual ambition—in many cases, indeed, they almost abandon the sense of being individuals at all—and live chiefly for others, or are simply smothered under drudgery. But there is also the minority of gifted, wilful people who are determined to live their own lives to the end, and writers belong in this class. Serious writers, I should say, are on the whole more vain and self-centered than journalists, though less interested in money.

2. Aesthetic enthusiasm. Perception of beauty in the external world, or, on the other hand, in words and their right arrangement. Pleasure in the impact of one sound on another, in the firmness of good prose or the rhythm of a good story. Desire to share an experience which one feels is valuable and ought not to be missed. The aesthetic motive is very feeble in a lot of writers, but even a pamphleteer or a writer of textbooks will have pet words and phrases which appeal to him for non-utilitarian reasons; or he may feel strongly about typography, width of margins, etc. Above the level of a railway guide, no book is quite free from aesthetic considerations.

3. Historical impulse. Desire to see things are they are, to find out true facts and store them up for the use of posterity.

4. Political purpose—using the word "political" in the widest possible sense. Desire to push the world in a certain direction, to alter other people's idea of the kind of society that they should strive after. Once again, no book is genuinely free from political bias. The opinion that art should have nothing to do with politics is itself a political attitude.

It can be seen how these various impulses must war against one another, and how they must fluctuate from person to person and from time to time. By nature—taking your "nature" to be the state you have attained when you are first adult—I am a person in whom the first three motives would outweigh the fourth. In a peaceful age I might have written ornate or merely descriptive books, and might have remained almost unaware of my political loyalties. As it is I have been forced into becoming a sort of pamphleteer. First I spent five years in an unsuitable profession (the Indian Imperial Police, in Burma), and then I underwent poverty and the sense of failure. This increased my natural hatred of authority and made me for the first time fully aware of the existence of the working classes, and the job in Burma had given me some understanding of the nature of imperialism: but these experiences were not enough to give me an accurate political orientation. Then came Hitler, the Spanish civil war, etc. By the end of 1935 I had still failed to reach a firm decision. I remember a little poem that I wrote at that date,[1] expressing my dilemma:

A happy vicar I might have been
Two hundred years ago,
To preach upon eternal doom
And watch my walnuts grow;

But born, alas, in an evil time,
I missed that pleasant haven,
For the hair has grown on my upper lip
And the clergy are all clean-shaven.

And later still the times were good,
We were so easy to please,
We rocked our troubled thoughts to sleep
On the bosoms of the trees.

All ignorant we dared to own
The joys we now dissemble;
The greenfinch on the apple bough
Could make my enemies tremble.

But girls' bellies and apricots,
Roach in a shaded stream,
Horses, ducks in flight at dawn,
All these are a dream.

[1] Published in *Adelphi*, December 1936, this poem, with its nursery rhyme rhythms and antibourgeois sentiments, is similar to many written in that period by W. H. Auden, Stephen Spender, C. Day Lewis, Louis MacNeice, and others.

It is forbidden to dream again;
We maim our joys or hide them;
Horses are made of chromium steel
And little fat men shall ride them.

I am the worm who never turned,
The eunuch without a harem;
Between the priest and the commissar[1]
I walk like Eugene Aram;[2]

And the commissar is telling my fortune
While the radio plays,
But the priest has promised an Austin Seven,[3]
For Duggie always pays.

I dreamed I dwelt in marble halls,[4]
And woke to find it true;
I wasn't born for an age like this;
Was Smith? Was Jones? Were you?

The Spanish war and other events in 1936–37 turned the scale and thereafter I knew where I stood. Every line of serious work that I have written since 1936 has been written, directly or indirectly, *against* totalitarianism and *for* democratic Socialism, as I understand it. It seems to me nonsense, in a period like our own, to think that one can avoid writing of such subjects. Everyone writes of them in one guise or another. It is simply a question of which side one takes and what approach one follows. And the more one is conscious of one's political bias, the more chance one has of acting politically without sacrificing one's aesthetic and intellectual integrity.

What I have most wanted to do throughout the past ten years is to make political writing into an art. My starting point is always a feeling of partisanship, a sense of injustice. When I sit down to write a book, I do not say to myself, "I am going to produce a work of art." I write it because there is some lie that I want to expose, some fact to which I want to draw attention, and my initial concern is to get a hearing. But I could not do the work of writing a book, or even a long magazine article, if it were not also an aesthetic experience. Anyone who cares to examine my work will see that even when it is downright propaganda it contains much that a full-time politician would consider irrelevant. I am not able, and I do not want, completely to abandon the world-view that I acquired in childhood. So

---

[1]Enforcer of party loyalty in the Communist Party.

[2](1704–1759) English linguist convicted and hanged as the murderer of his friend Daniel Clark, fourteen years after the crime. His story is told in Thomas Hood's ballad "The Dream of Eugene Aram" and in Bulwer-Lytton's novel *Eugene Aram*.

[3]Designed by Sir Herbert Austin in 1922, the seven-horsepower car was popular and cheap, often a family's first car, but at the same time it projected a certain glitz because of its marvelous performance in Class I motor races.

[4]Opening line of famous song by Thomas Moore, based on two lines from *The Bohemian Girl* by Alfred Bunn (1796–1860).

long as I remain alive and well I shall continue to feel strongly about prose style, to love the surface of the earth, and to take pleasure in solid objects and scraps of useless information. It is no use trying to suppress that side of myself. The job is to reconcile my ingrained likes and dislikes with the essentially public, non-individual activities that this age forces on all of us.

It is not easy. It raises problems of construction and of language, and it raises in a new way the problem of truthfulness. Let me give just one example of the cruder kind of difficulty that arises. My book about the Spanish civil war, *Homage to Catalonia*, is, of course, a frankly political book, but in the main it is written with a certain detachment and regard for form. I did try very hard in it to tell the whole truth without violating my literary instincts. But among other things it contains a long chapter, full of newspaper quotations and the like, defending the Trotskyists[1] who were accused of plotting with Franco.[2] Clearly such a chapter, which after a year or two would lose its interest for any ordinary reader, must ruin the book. A critic whom I respect read me a lecture about it. "Why did you put in all that stuff?" he said. "You've turned what might have been a good book into journalism." What he said was true, but I could not have done otherwise. I happened to know, what very few people in England had been allowed to know, that innocent men were being falsely accused. If I had not been angry about that I should never have written the book.

In one form or another this problem comes up again. The problem of language is subtler and would take too long to discuss. I will only say that of late years I have tried to write less picturesquely and more exactly. In any case I find that by the time you have perfected any style of writing, you have always out-grown it. *Animal Farm* was the first book in which I tried, with full consciousness of what I was doing, to fuse political purpose and artistic purpose into one whole. I have not written a novel for seven years, but I hope to write another fairly soon. It is bound to be a failure, every book is a failure, but I know with some clarity what kind of book I want to write.

Looking back through the last page or two, I see that I have made it appear as though my motives in writing were wholly public-spirited. I don't want to leave that as the final impression. All writers are vain, selfish and lazy, and at the very bottom of their motives there lies a mystery. Writing a book is a horrible, exhausting struggle, like a long bout of some painful illness. One would never undertake such a thing if one were not driven on by some demon whom one can neither resist nor understand. For all one knows that demon is simply the same instinct that makes a baby squall for attention. And yet it is also true that one can write nothing readable unless one constantly struggles to efface one's own personality. Good prose is like a window pane. I cannot say with certainty which of

---

[1] Followers of Leon Trotsky (1879–1940), leader of the Bolshevik Revolution who was ousted from the Communist Party by Stalin in 1929 and assassinated in Mexico.
[2] Francisco (1892–1975), Fascist dictator of Spain who defeated the Republicans in the Spanish Civil War and ruled the country until his death.

my motives are the strongest, but I know which of them deserve to be followed. And looking back through my work, I see that it is invariably where I lacked a *political* purpose that I wrote lifeless books and was betrayed into purple passages, sentences without meaning, decorative adjectives and humbug generally. ✍

As I Please (January 24, 1947)[1]

Recently I was listening to a conversation between two small businessmen in a Scottish hotel. One of them, an alert-looking, well-dressed man of about forty-five, was something to do with the Federation of Master Builders. The other, a good deal older, with white hair and a broad Scottish accent, was some kind of wholesale tradesman. He said grace before his meals, a thing I had not seen anyone do for many a year. They belonged, I should say, in the £2,000-a-year and the £1,000-a-year income groups respectively.

We were sitting round a rather inadequate peat fire, and the conversation started off with the coal shortage. There was no coal, it appeared, because the British miners refused to dig it out, but on the other hand it was important not to let Poles work in the pits because this would lead to unemployment. There was severe unemployment in Scotland already. The older man then remarked with quiet satisfaction that he was very glad—"varra glad indeed"—that Labour had won the General Election. Any government that had to clean up after the war was in for a bad time, and as a result of five years of rationing, housing shortage, unofficial strikes and so forth, the general public would see through the promises of the Socialists and vote Conservative next time.

They began talking about the housing problem, and almost immediately they were back to the congenial subject of the Poles. The younger man had just sold his flat in Edinburgh at a good profit and was trying to buy a house. He was willing to pay £2,700. The other was trying to sell his house for £1,500 and buy a smaller one. But it seemed that it was impossible to buy houses or flats nowadays. The Poles were buying them all up, and "where they get the money from is a mystery". The Poles were also invading the medical profession. They even had their own medical school in Edinburgh or Glasgow (I forget which) and were turning out doctors in great numbers while "our lads" found it impossible to buy practices. Didn't everyone know that Britain had more doctors than it could use? Let the Poles go back to their own country. There were too many people in this country already. What was needed was emigration.

The younger man remarked that he belonged to several business and civic associations, and that on all of them he made a point of putting forward resolutions that the Poles should be sent back to their own country. The older one added that the Poles were "very degraded in their morals." They were responsible for

---

[1]Published in the *Tribune*, January 24, 1947.

444 • George Orwell

much of the immorality that was prevalent nowadays. "Their ways are not our ways," he concluded piously. It was not mentioned that the Poles pushed their way to the head of queues, wore bright-coloured clothes and displayed cowardice during air raids, but if I had put forward a suggestion to this effect I am sure it would have been accepted.

One cannot of course, do very much about this kind of thing. It is the contemporary equivalent of antisemitism. By 1947, people of the kind I am describing would have caught up with the fact that antisemitism is discreditable, and so the scapegoat is sought elsewhere. But the race hatred and mass delusions which are part of the pattern of our time might be somewhat less bad in their effects if they were not reinforced by ignorance. If in the years before the war, for instance, the facts about the persecution of Jews in Germany had been better known, the subjective popular feeling against Jews would probably not have been less, but the actual treatment of Jewish refugees might have been better. The refusal to allow refugees in significant numbers into this country would have been branded as disgraceful. The average man would still have felt a grudge against the refugees, but in practice more lives would have been saved.

So also with the Poles. The thing that most depressed me in the above-mentioned conversation was the recurrent phrase, "let them go back to their own country". If I had said to those two businessmen, "Most of these people have no country to go back to," they would have gaped. Not one of the relevant facts would have been known to them. They would never have heard of the various things that have happened to Poland since 1939, any more than they would have known that the over-population of Britain is a fallacy or that local unemployment can coexist with a general shortage of labour. I think it is a mistake to give such people the excuse of ignorance. You can't actually change their feelings, but you can make them understand what they are saying when they demand that home-less refugees shall be driven from our shores, and the knowledge may make them a little less actively malignant.

The other week, in the *Spectator*, Mr Harold Nicolson[1] was consoling himself as best he could for having reached the age of sixty. As he perceived, the only positive satisfaction in growing older is that after a certain point you can begin boasting of having seen things that no one will ever have the chance to see again. It set me wondering what boasts I could make myself, at forty-four, or nearly. Mr Nicolson had seen the Czar, surrounded by his bodyguard of enormous Cossacks, blessing the Neva.[2] I never saw that, but I did see Marie Lloyd,[3] almost a legendary figure,

---

[1]Sir Harold Nicolson (1886–1968), biographer, diplomat, historian; the *Spectator* was and still is an independent conservative British journal of opinion.
[2]River in Russia.
[3](1870–1922) one of the most popular English music hall entertainers of all time, with an act noted for risqué humor and songs such as *My Old Man Said Follow the Van*.

and I saw Little Tich[1]—who, I think, did not die till about 1928, but who must have retired at about the same time as Marie Lloyd—and I have seen a whole string of crowned heads and other celebrities from Edward VII onwards. But on only two occasions did I feel, at the time, that I was seeing something significant, and on one of these occasions it was the circumstances and not the person concerned that made me feel this.

One of these celebrities was Pétain.[2] It was at Foch's[3] funeral in 1929. Pétain's personal prestige in France was very great. He was honoured as the defender of Verdun,[4] and the phrase "They shall not pass" was popularly supposed to have been coined by him. He was given a place to himself in the procession, with a gap of several yards in front of and behind him. As he stalked past—a tall, lean, very erect figure, though he must have been seventy years old or thereabouts, with great sweeping white moustaches like the wings of a gull—a whisper of *Voilà Pétain!* went rippling through the vast crowd. His appearance impressed me so much that I dimly felt, in spite of his considerable age, that he might still have some kind of distinguished future ahead of him.

The other celebrity was Queen Mary.[5] One day I was walking past Windsor Castle when a sort of electric shock seemed to go through the street. People were taking their hats off, soldiers springing to attention. And then, clattering over the cobbles, there came a huge, plum-coloured open carriage drawn by four horses with postilions.[6] I believe it was the first and last time in my life that I have seen a postilion. On the rear seat, with his back to the carriage, another groom sat stiffly upright, with his arms folded. The groom who sat at the back used to be called the tiger. I hardly noticed the Queen, my eyes were fixed on that strange, archaic figure at the back, immobile as a waxwork, with his white breeches that looked as though he had been poured into them, and the cockade[7] on his tophat. Even at that date (1920 or thereabouts) it gave me a wonderful feeling of looking backwards through a window into the nineteenth century. ✒

---

[1]A colleague of Marie Lloyd's who performed in the 1890s, he was known for his spoken absurd and satiric monologues, such as "One of the Deathless Army," about the horror of war.

[2](1856–1951) French military hero of World War I but head of the Vichy government in World War II.

[3]Ferdinand (1851–1929), marshal who commanded the unified armies of France, Great Britain, and America in World War I.

[4]The longest and bloodiest battle of World War I, fought from February to July of 1916. Over half a million soldiers were killed.

[5]Wife of George V, king from 1910 to 1936.

[6]Riders who guide the horses.

[7]A knot of ribbon.

How the Poor Die[1]

In the year 1929 I spent several weeks in the Hôpital X,[2] in the fifteenth *arrondissement* of Paris. The clerks put me through the usual third-degree at the reception desk, and indeed I was kept answering questions for some twenty minutes before they would let me in. If you have ever had to fill up forms in a Latin country you will know the kind of questions I mean. For some days past I had been unequal to translating Réaumur[3] into Fahrenheit, but I know that my temperature was round about 103, and by the end of the interview I had some difficulty in standing on my feet. At my back a resigned little knot of patients, carrying bundles done up in coloured handkerchiefs, waited their turn to be questioned.

After the questioning came the bath—a compulsory routine for all newcomers, apparently, just as in prison or the workhouse. My clothes were taken away from me, and after I had sat shivering for some minutes in five inches of warm water I was given a linen nightshirt and a short blue flannel dressing-gown—no slippers, they had none big enough for me, they said—and led out into the open air. This was a night in February and I was suffering from pneumonia. The ward we were going to was 200 yards away and it seemed that to get to it you had to cross the hospital grounds. Someone stumbled in front of me with a lantern. The gravel path was frosty underfoot, and the wind whipped the nightshirt round my bare calves. When we got into the ward I was aware of a strange feeling of familiarity whose origin I did not succeed in pinning down till later in the night. It was a long, rather low, ill-lit room, full of murmuring voices and with three rows of beds surprisingly close together. There was a foul smell, faecal and yet sweetish. As I lay down I saw on a bed nearly opposite me a small, round-shouldered, sandy-haired man sitting half naked while a doctor and a student performed some strange operation on him. First the doctor produced from his black bag a dozen small glasses like wine glasses, then the student burned a match inside each glass to exhaust the air, then the glass was popped on to the man's back or chest and the vacuum drew up a huge yellow blister. Only after some moments did I realise what they were doing to him. It was something called cupping, a treatment which you can read about in old medical text-books but which till then I had vaguely thought of as one of those things they do to horses.

The cold air outside had probably lowered my temperature, and I watched this barbarous remedy with detachment and even a certain amount of amusement. The next moment, however, the doctor and the student came across to my bed, hoisted me upright and without a word began applying the same set of

---

[1]First published in *Now* in 1946.

[2]Hôpital Cochin.

[3]René (1683–1757), French scientist, inventor of the alcohol thermometer and the temperature scale named after him, in which the freezing point of water is 0 and the boiling point is 80 degrees.

glasses, which had not been sterilised in any way. A few feeble protests that I uttered got no more response than if I had been an animal. I was very much impressed by the impersonal way in which the two men started on me. I had never been in the public ward of a hospital before, and it was my first experience of doctors who handle you without speaking to you, or, in a human sense, taking any notice of you. They only put on six glasses in my case, but after doing so they scarified the blisters and applied the glasses again. Each glass now drew out about a dessert-spoonful of dark-coloured blood. As I lay down again, humiliated, disgusted and frightened by the thing that had been done to me, I reflected that now at least they would leave me alone. But no, not a bit of it. There was another treatment coming, the mustard poultice, seemingly a matter of routine like the hot bath. Two slatternly nurses had already got the poultice ready, and they lashed it round my chest as tight as a strait jacket while some men who were wandering about the ward in shirt and trousers began to collect round my bed with half-sympathetic grins. I learned later that watching a patient have a mustard poultice was a favourite pastime in the ward. These things are normally applied for a quarter of an hour and certainly they are funny enough if you don't happen to be the person inside. For the first five minutes the pain is severe, but you believe you can bear it. During the second five minutes this belief evaporates, but the poultice is buckled at the back and you can't get it off. This is the period the onlookers most enjoy. During the last five minutes, I noted a sort of numbness supervenes. After the poultice had been removed a waterproof pillow packed with ice was thrust beneath my head and I was left alone. I did not sleep and to the best of my knowledge this was the only night of my life—I mean the only night spent in bed—in which I have not slept at all, not even a minute.

During my first hour in the Hôpital X, I had had a whole series of different and contradictory treatments, but this was misleading, for in general you got very little treatment at all, either good or bad, unless you were ill in some interesting and instructive way. At five in the morning the nurses came round, woke the patients and took their temperatures, but did not wash them. If you were well enough you washed yourself, otherwise you depended on the kindness of some walking patient. It was generally patients, too, who carried the bed-bottles and the grim bed-pan, nicknamed *la casserole*. At eight breakfast arrived, called army-fashion *la soupe*. It was soup, too, a thin vegetable soup with slimy hunks of bread floating about in it. Later in the day the tall, solemn, black-bearded doctor made his rounds, with an *interne* and a troop of students following at his heels, but there were about sixty of us in the ward and it was evident that he had other wards to attend to as well. There were many beds past which he walked day after day, sometimes followed by imploring cries. On the other hand if you had some disease with which the students wanted to familiarise themselves you got plenty of attention of a kind. I myself, with an exceptionally fine specimen of a bronchial rattle, sometimes had as many as a dozen students queueing up to listen to my chest. It was a very queer feeling—queer, I mean, because of their intense interest in learning their job, together with a seeming lack of any perception that the patients were human beings. It is strange to relate, but sometimes as some young student stepped forward to take his turn at manipulating you he would be actually tremulous with excitement, like a boy who has at last got his hands on some expensive piece of machinery. And then ear after ear—ears of young men, of girls, of Negroes—pressed against your back, relays of fingers solemnly but clumsily tapping, and not from any one of them did you get a word of conversation or a look direct in your face. As a non-paying patient, in the uniform nightshirt, you were primarily *a specimen*, a thing I did not resent but could never quite get used to.

After some days I grew well enough to sit up and study the surrounding patients. The stuffy room, with its narrow beds so close together that you could easily touch your neighbour's hand, had every sort of disease in it except, I suppose, acutely infectious cases. My right-hand neighbour was a little red-haired cobbler with one leg shorter than the other, who used to announce the death of any other patient (this happened a number of times, and my neighbour was always the first to hear of it) by whistling to me, exclaiming "*Numéro 43!*" (or whatever it was) and flinging his arms above his head. This man had not much wrong with him, but in most of the other beds within my angle of vision some squalid tragedy or some plain horror was being enacted. In the bed that was foot to foot with mine there lay, until he died (I didn't see him die—they moved him to another bed), a little weazened man who was suffering from I do not know what disease, but something that made his whole body so intensely sensitive that any movement from side to side, sometimes even the weight of the bed-clothes, would make him shout out with pain. His worst suffering was when he urinated, which he did with the greatest difficulty. A nurse would bring him the bed-bottle and then for a long time stand beside his bed, whistling, as grooms are said to do with horses, until at last with an agonised shriek of "*Je pisse!*" he would get started. In the bed next to him the sandy-haired man whom I had seen being cupped used to cough up blood-streaked mucus at all hours. My left-hand neighbour was a tall, flaccid-looking young man who used periodically to have a tube inserted into his back and astonishing quantities of frothy liquid drawn off from some part of his body. In the bed beyond that a veteran of the war of 1870 was dying, a handsome old man with a white imperial,[1] round whose bed, at all hours when visiting was allowed, four elderly female relatives dressed all in black sat exactly like crows, obviously scheming for some pitiful legacy. In the bed opposite me in the further row was an old bald-headed man with drooping moustaches and greatly swollen face and body, who was suffering from some disease that made him urinate almost incessantly. A huge glass receptable stood always beside his bed. One day his wife and daughter came to visit him. At the sight of them the old man's bloated face lit up with a smile of surprising sweetness, and as his daughter, a pretty girl of about twenty, approached the bed I saw that his hand was slowly working its way from under the bed-clothes. I seemed to see in advance the gesture that was

---

[1] A pointed beard growing from the lower lip and chin.

coming—the girl kneeling beside the bed, the old man's hand laid on her head in his dying blessing. But no, he merely handed her the bed-bottle, which she promptly took from him and emptied into the receptacle.

About a dozen beds away from me was *numéro 57*—I think that was his number—a cirrhosis of the liver case. Everyone in the ward knew him by sight because he was sometimes the subject of a medical lecture. On two afternoons a week the tall, grave doctor would lecture in the ward to a party of students, and on more than one occasion old *numéro 57* was wheeled on a sort of trolley into the middle of the ward, where the doctor would roll back his nightshirt, dilate with his fingers a huge flabby protuberance on the man's belly—the diseased liver, I suppose—and explain solemnly that this was a disease attributable to alcoholism, commoner in the wine-drinking countries. As usual he neither spoke to his patient nor gave him a smile, a nod or any kind of recognition. While he talked, very grave and upright, he would hold the wasted body beneath his two hands, sometimes giving it a gentle roll to and fro, in just the attitude of a woman handling a rolling-pin. Not that *numéro 57* minded this kind of thing. Obviously he was an old hospital inmate, a regular exhibit at lectures, his liver long since marked down for a bottle in some pathological museum. Utterly uninterested in what was said about him, he would lie with his colourless eyes gazing at nothing, while the doctor showed him off like a piece of antique china. He was a man of about sixty, astonishingly shrunken. His face, pale as vellum, had shrunken away till it seemed no bigger than a doll's.

One morning my cobbler neighbour woke me by plucking at my pillow before the nurses arrived. "*Numéro 57!*"—he flung his arms above his head. There was a light in the ward, enough to see by. I could see old *numéro 57* lying crumpled up on his side, his face sticking out over the side of the bed, and towards me. He had died some time during the night, nobody knew when. When the nurses came they received the news of his death indifferently and went about their work. After a long time, an hour or more, two other nurses marched in abreast like soldiers, with a great clumping of sabots,[1] and knotted the corpse up in the sheets, but it was not removed till some time later. Meanwhile, in the better light, I had had time for a good look at *numéro 57*. Indeed I lay on my side to look at him. Curiously enough he was the first dead European I had seen. I had seen dead men before, but always Asiatics and usually people who had died violent deaths. *Numéro 57*'s eyes were still open, his mouth also open, his small face contorted into an expression of agony. What most impressed me however was the whiteness of his face. It had been pale before, but now it was little darker than the sheets. As I gazed at the tiny, screwed-up face it struck me that this disgusting piece of refuse, waiting to be carted away and dumped on a slab in the dissecting room, was an example of "natural" death, one of the things you pray for in the Litany. There you are, then, I thought, that's what is waiting for you, twenty, thirty, forty years hence: that is how the lucky ones die, the ones who live to be old. One wants

---

[1]Wooden-soled shoes.

to live, of course, indeed one only stays alive by virtue of the fear of death, but I think now, as I thought then, that it's better to die violently and not too old. People talk about the horrors of war, but what weapon has man invented that even approaches in cruelty some of the commoner diseases? "Natural" death, almost by definition, means something slow, smelly and painful. Even at that, it makes a difference if you can achieve it in your own home and not in a public institution. This poor old wretch who had just flickered out like a candle-end was not even important enough to have anyone watching by his deathbed. He was merely a number, then a "subject" for the students' scalpels. And the sordid publicity of dying in such a place! In the Hôpital X the beds were very close together and there were no screens. Fancy, for instance, dying like the little man whose bed was for a while foot to foot with mine, the one who cried out when the bed-clothes touched him! I dare say *Je pisse!* were his last recorded words. Perhaps the dying don't bother about such things—that at least would be the standard answer: nevertheless dying people are often more or less normal in their minds till within a day or so of the end.

In the public wards of a hospital you see horrors that you don't seem to meet with among people who manage to die in their own homes, as though certain diseases only attacked people at the lower income levels. But it is a fact that you would not in any English hospitals see some of the things I saw in the Hôpital X. This business of people just dying like animals, for instance, with nobody standing by, nobody interested, the death not even noticed till the morning—this happened more than once. You certainly would not see that in England, and still less would you see a corpse left exposed to the view of the other patients. I remember that once in a cottage hospital in England a man died while we were at tea, and though there were only six of us in the ward the nurses managed things so adroitly that the man was dead and his body removed without our even hearing about it till tea was over. A thing we perhaps underrate in England is the advantage we enjoy in having large numbers of well-trained and rigidly-disciplined nurses. No doubt English nurses are dumb enough, they may tell fortunes with tea-leaves, wear Union Jack badges and keep photographs of the Queen on their mantle-pieces, but at least they don't let you lie unwashed and constipated on an unmade bed, out of sheer laziness. The nurses at the Hôpital X still had a tinge of Mrs Gamp[1] about them, and later, in the military hospitals of Republican Spain, I was to see nurses almost too ignorant to take a temperature. You wouldn't, either, see in England such dirt as existed in the Hôpital X. Later on, when I was well enough to wash myself in the bathroom, I found that there was kept there a huge packing-case into which the scraps of food and dirty dressings from the ward were flung, and the wainscottings were infested by crickets.

---

[1]Disreputable and tippling nurse from Dickens's° *Martin Chuzzlewit*. Famous for her bulky umbrella (the type became known as a "gamp"), Mrs. Gamp was known for citing the imaginary Mrs. Harris, who always agreed with her. Unsavory and uncertified maternity nurses also came to be called "gamps."

When I had got back my clothes and grown strong on my legs I fled from the Hôpital X, before my time was up and without waiting for a medical discharge. It was not the only hospital I have fled from, but its gloom and bareness, its sickly smell and, above all, something in its mental atmosphere stand out in my memory as exceptional. I had been taken there because it was the hospital belonging to my *arrondissement*, and I did not learn till after I was in it that it bore a bad reputation. A year or two later the celebrated swindler, Madame Hanaud, who was ill while on remand, was taken to the Hôpital X, and after a few days of it she managed to elude her guards, took a taxi and drove back to the prison, explaining that she was more comfortable there. I have no doubt that the Hôpital X was quite untypical of French hospitals even at that date. But the patients, nearly all of them working men, were surprisingly resigned. Some of them seemed to find the conditions almost comfortable, for at least two were destitute malingerers who found this a good way of getting through the winter. The nurses connived because the malingerers made themselves useful by doing odd jobs. But the attitude of the majority was: of course this is a lousy place, but what else do you expect? It did not seem strange to them that you should be woken at five and then wait three hours before starting the day on watery soup, or that people should die with no one at their bedside, or even that your chance of getting medical attention should depend on catching the doctor's eye as he went past. According to their traditions that was what hospitals were like. If you are seriously ill, and if you are too poor to be treated in your own home, then you must go into hospital, and once there you must put up with harshness and discomfort, just as you would in the army. But on top of this I was interested to find a lingering belief in the old stories that have now almost faded from memory in England—stories, for instance, about doctors cutting you open out of sheer curiosity or thinking it funny to start operating before you were properly "under". There were dark tales about a little operating room said to be situated just beyond the bathroom. Dreadful screams were said to issue from this room. I saw nothing to confirm these stories and no doubt they were all nonsense, though I did see two students kill a sixteen-year-old boy, or nearly kill him (he appeared to be dying when I left the hospital, but he may have recovered later) by a mischievous experiment which they probably could not have tried on a paying patient. Well within living memory it used to be believed in London that in some of the big hospitals patients were killed off to get dissection subjects. I didn't hear this tale repeated at the Hôpital X, but I should think some of the men there would have found it credible. For it was a hospital in which not the methods, perhaps, but something of the atmosphere of the nineteenth century had managed to survive, and therein lay its peculiar interest.

During the past fifty years or so there has been a great change in the relationship between doctor and patient. If you look at almost any literature before the later part of the nineteenth century, you find that a hospital is popularly regarded as much the same thing as a prison, and an old-fashioned, dungeon-like prison at that. A hospital is a place of filth, torture and death, a sort of antechamber to the tomb. No one who was not more or less destitute would have thought of going into such a place for treatment. And especially in the early part of the last century, when medical science had grown bolder than before without being any more successful, the whole business of doctoring was looked on with horror and dread by ordinary people. Surgery, in particular, was believed to be no more than a peculiarly gruesome form of sadism, and dissection, possibly only with the aid of body-snatchers, was even confused with necromancy. From the nineteenth century you could collect a large horror-literature connected with doctors and hospitals. Think of poor old George III,[1] in his dotage, shrieking for mercy as he sees his surgeons approaching to "bleed him till he faints"! Think of the conversations of Bob Sawyer and Benjamin Allen,[2] which no doubt are hardly parodies, or the field hospitals in La Débâcle[3] and War and Peace,[4] or that shocking description of an amputation in Melville's° Whitejacket! Even the names given to doctors in nineteenth-century English fiction, Slasher, Carver, Sawyer, Fillgrave and so on, and the generic nickname "sawbones", are about as grim as they are comic. The anti-surgery tradition is perhaps best expressed in Tennyson's° poem, "The Children's Hospital",[5] which is essentially a pre-chloroform document though it seems to have been written as late as 1880. Moreover, the outlook which Tennyson° records in this poem had a lot to be said for it. When you consider what an operation without anaesthetics must have been like, what it notoriously was like, it is difficult not to suspect the motives of people who would undertake such things. For these bloody horrors which the students so eagerly looked forward to ("A magnificent sight if Slasher does it!") were admittedly more or less useless: the patient who did not die of shock usually died of gangrene, a result which was taken for granted. Even now doctors can be found whose motives are questionable. Anyone who has had much illness, or who has listened to medical students talking, will know what I mean. But anaesthetics were a turningpoint, and disinfectants were another. Nowhere in the world, probably, would you now see the kind of scene described by Axel Munthe[6] in The Story of San Michele, when the sinister surgeon in top-hat and frock-coat, his starched shirtfront spattered with blood and pus, carves up patient after patient with the same knife and flings the severed limbs into a pile beside the table. Moreover, national health insurance

---

[1]Died in 1820.

[2]Crass members of the medical profession in Dickins's° novel The Pickwick Papers.

[3]By Zola.°

[4]By Tolstoy.°

[5]"In the Children's Hospital" is a poem of eight stanzas narrated by a devoted nurse who pits the old, kindly doctor against the new surgeon, a "coarse," red-haired man who is convinced of the benefits of bone setting over prayer, claiming "the good Lord Jesus has had his day." Emmie, a "meek" orphan, fond of flowers, overhears the doctor's plan to operate the next day and his fear that she'll not survive. When Emmie asks Annie, the child in the next cot, what to do, Annie tells her to cry to Jesus. During the long night, the nurse hears thunder, the sound of a lamb bleating, and imagines the "dreadful knife," but in the morning, when the surgeon arrives, the doctors and nurse find that "the Lord of the children had heard her [Emmie], and Emmie has past [sic] away."

[6]A physician (1857–1949) who wrote two books of biographical reminiscences, Memories and Vagaries (1930) and The Story of San Michele (1929).

has partly done away with the idea that a working-class patient is a pauper who deserves little consideration. Well into this century it was usual for "free" patients at the big hospitals to have their teeth extracted with no anaesthetic. They didn't pay, so why should they have an anaesthetic—that was the attitude. That too has changed.

And yet every institution will always bear upon it some lingering memory of its past. A barrack-room is still haunted by the ghost of Kipling,° and it is difficult to enter a workhouse without being reminded of *Oliver Twist*.[1] Hospitals began as a kind of casual ward for lepers and the like to die in, and they continued as places where medical students learned their art on the bodies of the poor. You can still catch a faint suggestion of their history in their characteristically gloomy architecture. I would be far from complaining about the treatment I have received in any English hospital, but I do know that it is a sound instinct that warns people to keep out of hospitals if possible, and especially out of the public wards. Whatever the legal position may be, it is unquestionable that you have far less control over your own treatment, far less certainty that frivolous experiments will not be tried on you, when it is a case of "accept the discipline or get out". And it is a great thing to die in your own bed, though it is better still to die in your boots. However great the kindness and the efficiency, in every hospital death there will be some cruel, squalid detail, something perhaps too small to be told but leaving terribly painful memories behind, arising out of the haste, the crowding, the impersonality of a place where every day people are dying among strangers.

The dread of hospitals probably still survives among the very poor and in all of us it has only recently disappeared. It is a dark patch not far beneath the surface of our minds. I have said earlier that, when I entered the ward at the Hôpital X, I was conscious of a strange feeling of familiarity. What the scene reminded me of, of course, was the reeking, pain-filled hospitals of the nineteenth century, which I had never seen but of which I had a traditional knowledge. And something, perhaps the black-clad doctor with his frowsy black bag, or perhaps only the sickly smell, played the queer trick of unearthing from my memory that poem of Tennyson's,° "The Children's Hospital," which I had not thought of for twenty years. It happened that as a child I had had it read aloud to me by a sick-nurse whose own working life might have stretched back to the time when Tennyson° wrote the poem. The horrors and sufferings of the old-style hospitals were a vivid memory to her. We had shuddered over the poem together, and then seemingly I had forgotten it. Even its name would probably have recalled nothing to me. But the first glimpse of the ill-lit, murmurous room, with the beds so close together, suddenly roused the train of thought to which it belonged, and in the night that followed I found myself remembering the whole story and atmosphere of the poem, with many of its lines complete. ✍

---

[1]See Dickens.°

James Baldwin

(1924–1987)

W hen James Arthur Baldwin was born in Harlem Hospital in August of 1924, the surname on his birth certificate was that of his mother, Emma Berdis Jones, for she never revealed the name of his father. The man who became Baldwin's father, gave him his name, and shaped his reality was David Baldwin, a preacher from New Orleans. He arrived in Harlem with his aging mother, a former slave, and a son, Samuel, age twelve, to marry Emma Jones when James was three. David Baldwin was a man of strong beliefs— hatred of whites, commitment to religion, and rejection of street life, theater, and movies. James knew that his father favored Samuel despite the older boy's fierce rebellion against his strict upbringing. Even after Samuel left home, James felt rejected by David Baldwin. Yet it was this same home that also supplied James with a sense of his own worth and helped him to withstand the degradations of prejudice. Through his mother's love and her reliance on James to help her with the growing family—three more boys and five girls—James developed a sense of responsibility and an understanding of the meaning of family, of the need for discipline and affection, and of the saving grace of love.

While his mother cleaned the houses of white people, James tended children, read Charles Dickens,° Harriet Beecher Stowe,° and Horatio Alger, ran errands, worked odd jobs, and attended school. Reading led to writing. By the time he was graduated from Public School 24 at age eleven he had already written a history of Harlem based on library research and had won a prize for a short story he'd sent to a church newspaper. At Frederick Douglass Junior High School he continued to write, contributing stories and editorials to the school magazine. When he was fourteen, entrapped by his hatred of his stepfather as well as his fear of succumbing to the lure of the racketeers and the drug addicts of the street, Baldwin underwent an anguished religious conversion at the hands of the Pentecostals. Soon he became an immensely popular preacher, succeeding to his great satisfaction in his stepfather's own profession. At this time, he entered De Witt Clinton High School and again took up writing, editing the *Magpie*, the school's literary magazine.

Three years after his conversion, James Baldwin gave up preaching, drawn away not only by his love of the literary life and the movies and plays forbidden by the church but also by his sexual experiences, with girls but also and especially with his first male lover. After high school, Baldwin left home, got a job laying railroad track for the army in New Jersey, and began writing what became, eleven years later, his first novel, *Go Tell It on the Mountain*. The following year, 1943, he was fired from his job, David Baldwin was dying, and James returned home. According to his friend and biographer, W. J. Weatherby, after his stepfather's funeral James found and lost job after job. Although his brothers were now old enough to work and contribute to the household finances, Baldwin knew that the family depended on him; he believed his best hope of supporting them was through his writing. Suffering from insomnia, he read Milton,° Shakespeare, Chaucer, and the black writer Richard Wright,° searching for techniques that would help him tell his own story about his life in Harlem. He realized finally that to become a writer he had to write the truth as he saw it and to do that he had to accept his homosexuality and he had to leave his home.

Baldwin then moved to the gay community of Greenwich Village, where he seemed to be the only black. Now twenty, he arranged through a friend to meet Wright,° who at thirty-six provided for Baldwin the role model he needed. In 1945, with Wright's° help, Baldwin was awarded the Eugene Saxton Fellowship, a grant of five hundred dollars from Harper's with the possibility of publishing the work with Harper's when it was finished. But Harper's turned him down. The next year Richard Wright° moved to France. Dejected and humiliated over his failure to publish his novel, Baldwin turned to drink. But the pride that had kept him from asking Wright° for more help also spurred him to try again. In bars and through connections made during a brief flirtation with socialism, he met editors and writers and eventually landed work writing a book review for the *Nation* and later steady work as a reviewer for the *New Leader*. For *Commentary* he wrote his first essay, "The Harlem Ghetto," which took him six months of rewriting because the topics, especially the anti-Semitism in Harlem, were painful for him to face and work out.

Although "The Harlem Ghetto" was widely admired, Baldwin was nearly broke when it was finally published in February of 1948. Comparing himself, Weatherby says, to Orwell in *Down and Out in Paris and London*, Baldwin joined with a photographer to write a book on storefront churches that remained unpublished but that earned him the Rosenwald Fellowship, money he hoped to use to write a different novel, about Greenwich Village and the gay community. When he was told of the suicide of a good friend who at twenty-four had jumped off the George Washington Bridge, Baldwin felt more and more hopeless and anxious. Finally he decided to spend all but forty dollars of the money from his fellowship on the airfare to Paris. He left his mother and brothers and sisters behind, believing that only by leaving America could he be free to write about it.

In Paris, friends met Baldwin at the airport and took him to Les Deux Magots, where Richard Wright° introduced him to the editor of a new magazine called *Zero* and recommended a cheap hotel. Baldwin soon became part of a group of American writers who were linked through Wright° and others to Sartre and the French intelligentsia. But his funds were running out, forcing him to borrow both money and clothes. In 1949 *Zero* published his essay "Everybody's Protest Novel," in which Baldwin compares *Uncle Tom's Cabin* with Wright's° *Native Son*, concluding that, though opposite, "Bigger[1] is Uncle Tom's descendant" because neither figure conveys the full humanity of an individual black man. Each character accepts the burden of a stultifying stereotype; each claims "that it is his categorization alone which is real and which cannot be transcended." These words caused a permanent rift between the two writers; when Wright° died in 1960 Baldwin called him "the man I fought so hard and who meant so much to me."

Baldwin lived in France and later in Switzerland for the next eight years, returning briefly to America in 1952 and 1956. In Europe he read Henry James,° developed a close friendship with a young Swiss named Lucien, and found the quiet and the determination to write about his life in Europe as well as about life in Harlem and in Greenwich Village. Essays such as "Stranger in the Village" and "Equal in Paris" were later collected in *Notes of a Native Son* (1955). His novels about Harlem and Greenwich Village, *Go Tell It on the Mountain* and *Giovanni's Room*, were published in 1953 and 1956. He also wrote a play, *The Amen Corner*, which was performed at Howard University in 1954–1955. By this time he had become famous, his books had brought him large royalties, and his self-confidence had increased.

Baldwin returned to New York in 1957 and soon after flew south. In Georgia he met Martin Luther King° in a hotel room, followed him to Alabama to hear him preach, and came away committed to the civil rights movement, despite the artist's traditional shunning of politics. Throughout the sixties, Baldwin drove himself to speak, protest, and witness for the movement. He spent all the money he earned traveling between the South and New York City, helping his family and friends, throwing and attending parties, drinking, and, miraculously, writing. Involved with the theatrical community in New York, he hoped to see a play develop from his novel about the homosexual world of Greenwich Village.

In these days Baldwin moved among celebrities from various fields— Harry Belafonte, Roy Innis of the Congress of Racial Equality (CORE),

---

[1]Protagonist of *Native Son*.

Norman Mailer,° Marlon Brando, Lorraine Hansberry, William Styron, Eli Kazan, and Sidney Poitier. Although *Giovanni's Room* was never produced as a play, Baldwin did publish a second collection of essays, *Nobody Knows My Name*, in 1961, including in it "Fifth Avenue, Uptown," a look at Harlem twelve years after his first essay was published, and "Alas, Poor Richard," his essay on the death of Richard Wright.° In 1962 he published a third novel, *Another Country*, met with Malcolm X,° and traveled to Africa. In 1963 he published *The Fire Next Time*, a long essay describing the rage and inhumanity produced by racism. By 1970 he had published two plays, *Blues for Mister Charlie* (1964) and *The Amen Corner* (1965), each of which had been produced in New York City, as well as a collaboration with photographer Richard Avedon, *Nothing Personal* (1964); a collection of short stories, *Going to Meet the Man* (1965); and another novel, *Tell Me How Long the Train's Been Gone* (1968).

According to his biographer, Baldwin believed that the death of Martin Luther King° in 1968 marked the death of the civil rights movement. Exhausted, Baldwin returned to Paris, but fame and misery drove him to Istanbul, London, and Italy before he collapsed and was hospitalized. Friends brought him to St. Paul-de-Venice, near Nice, where he settled permanently, making periodic visits to the United States.

In the 1970s, finding it increasingly difficult to write, Baldwin published a number of minor works, including transcripts of conversations, several extended essays, a children's book, and two more novels (*If Beale Street Could Talk*, 1974, and *Just Above My Head*, 1979). The reviews of these works were not favorable. Although he was often ill, depressed, and restless, he continued to produce short essays, such as "If Black English Isn't a Language, Then Tell Me, What Is?" (1979) for *The New York Times* and "Dark Days" (1980) for *Esquire*.

In 1983 and 1984, as a professor for Five Colleges, Inc. (University of Massachusetts, Hampshire College, Mount Holyoke, Smith, and Amherst), Baldwin taught at the University of Massachusetts at Amherst in the W. E. B. Du Bois° Department of African Studies, lecturing on the controversial subjects he had always met head on. One time, according to Weatherby, he lectured on blacks and Jews, reiterating his view that to many blacks Jews are simply "white Christians" and accepting with no comment the blatantly anti-Semitic responses his black students contributed during the question period. Transient emotional attachments as well as drinking, smoking, and working too hard had left him vulnerable to exhaustion and depression. On his way to a writing class he was teaching at Hampshire College, he suffered a heart attack.

In the following year, 1985, despite the publication of three books, Baldwin's reputation hit its lowest point. *Evidence of Things Not Seen*, a book about a series of child murders in Atlanta, received uniformly negative reviews; his book of poems, *Jimmy's Blues: Selected Poems*, was ignored; and the collection of fifty-one essays, none new, in one large volume entitled *The Price of the Ticket: Collected Non-Fiction 1948–85* showed, the critics said, that over the years his writing had traded power for bombast. In 1987 he was diagnosed as having cancer of the esophagus; his brother David kept the news from him as long as he could, allowing James to rest comfortably in his home outside Nice. When James Baldwin died in early December, his body was flown home to Harlem, where his funeral was attended by his mother, his brothers and sisters, his friends, his admirers, the famous and the unknown, homosexuals and heterosexuals, blacks and whites—a mixture of the humanity about which Baldwin had written and in whom, despite all odds, he had continued to place his trust.

In "Autobiographical Notes" Baldwin says that his writing was influenced by "the King James Bible, the rhetoric of the store-front church, something ironic and violent and perpetually understated in Negro speech—and something of Dickens'° love for bravura." His style also reflects the ironic, the understated, and some of Orwell's unflinching honesty, an honesty that Baldwin worked hard to discover for himself and to reveal to others in his first published essay, an honesty that survived the increasingly bitter and disappointing struggle for the acceptance of all men and women on the basis of their merits, not their religion or their skin color or their sexual preferences. His earlier essays project a hope for the future by means of metaphor, as if it were indeed possible to explain the state of the people of Harlem to the white world surrounding it: the people of Harlem wait as if for "winter: it is coming and it will be hard; there is nothing anyone can do about it." Harlem itself is "like the insistent, maddening, claustrophobic pounding in the skull that comes from trying to breathe in a very small room with all the windows shut." The sense of claustrophobia intensifies with each added detail, moving from the pounding inside of the head to the windows that are shut. There is no escape. Twelve years later, in "Fifth Avenue, Uptown," Baldwin sees in Harlem "the churches, block upon block of churches, niched in the walls like cannon in the walls of a fortress." What he had first perceived as an inner pain had by then become a fortress prepared for battle. Yet even then, Baldwin knew that the enemy and the self are one: "In the face of one's victim, one sees oneself. Walk through the streets of Harlem and see what we, this nation, have become." The mirror becomes a recurring image in Baldwin's writing, until he forgoes metaphor altogether, insisting to the end "We are a part of each other . . . But none of us can do anything about it." ✍

The Harlem Ghetto[1]

Harlem, physically at least, has changed very little in my parents' lifetime or in mine. Now as then the buildings are old and in desperate need of repair, the streets are crowded and dirty, there are too many human beings per square block. Rents are 10 to 58 percent higher than anywhere else in the city; food, expensive everywhere, is more expensive here and of an inferior quality; and now that the war is over and money is dwindling, clothes are carefully shopped for and seldom bought. Negroes, traditionally the last to be hired and the first to be fired, are finding jobs harder to get, and, while prices are rising implacably, wages are going down. All over Harlem now there is felt the same bitter expectancy with which, in my childhood, we awaited winter: it is coming and it will be hard; there is nothing anyone can do about it.

All of Harlem is pervaded by a sense of congestion, rather like the insistent, maddening, claustrophobic pounding in the skull that comes from trying to breathe in a very small room with all the windows shut. Yet the white man walking through Harlem is not at all likely to find it sinister or more wretched than any other slum.

Harlem wears to the casual observer a casual face; no one remarks that—considering the history of black men and women and the legends that have sprung up about them, to say nothing of the ever-present policemen, wary on the street corners—the face is, indeed, somewhat excessively casual and may not be as open or as careless as it seems. If an outbreak of more than usual violence occurs, as in 1935 or in 1943,[2] it is met with sorrow and surprise and rage; the social hostility of the rest of the city feeds on this as proof that they were right all along, and the hostility increases; speeches are made, committees are set up, investigations ensue. Steps are taken to right the wrong, without, however, expanding or demolishing the ghetto. The idea is to make it less of a social liability, a process about as helpful as make-up to a leper. Thus, we have the Boys' Club on West 134th Street, the playground at West 131st and Fifth Avenue; and, since Negroes will not be allowed to live in Stuyvesant Town,° Metropolitan Life is thoughtfully erecting a housing project called Riverton in the center of Harlem; however, it is not likely that any but the professional class of Negroes—and not all of them—will be able to pay the rent.

Most of these projects have been stimulated by perpetually embattled Negro leaders and by the Negro press. Concerning Negro leaders, the best that one can say is that they are in an impossible position and that the handful motivated by genuine concern maintain this position with heartbreaking dignity. It is unlikely

---

[1]First published in *Commentary*, February 1948.
[2]In March 1935, blacks in Harlem rioted after a rumor of a killing by a storeowner; the violence was directed against property, not people: two hundred stores were damaged. The Harlem riot of 1943 was also directed at property owned by white outsiders; casualties were largely blacks injured or killed by police and the National Guard.

that anyone acquainted with Harlem seriously assumes that the presence of one playground more or less has any profound effect upon the psychology of the citizens there. And yet it is better to have the playground; it is better than nothing; and it will, at least, make life somewhat easier for parents who will then know that their children are not in as much danger of being run down in the streets. Similarly, even though the American cult of literacy has chiefly operated only to provide a market for the *Reader's Digest* and the *Daily News*, literacy is still better than illiteracy; so Negro leaders must demand more and better schools for Negroes, though any Negro who takes this schooling at face value will find himself virtually incapacitated for life in this democracy. Possibly the most salutary effect of all this activity is that it assures the Negro that he is not altogether forgotten: people *are* working in his behalf, however hopeless or misguided they may be; and as long as the water is troubled it cannot become stagnant.

The terrible thing about being a Negro leader lies in the term itself. I do not mean merely the somewhat condescending differentiation the term implies, but the nicely refined torture a man can experience from having been created and defeated by the same circumstances. That is, Negro leaders have been created by the American scene, which thereafter works against them at every point; and the best that they can hope for is ultimately to work themselves out of their jobs, to nag contemporary American leaders and the members of their own group until a bad situation becomes so complicated and so bad that it cannot be endured any longer. It is like needling a blister until it bursts. On the other hand, one cannot help observing that some Negro leaders and politicians are far more concerned with their careers than with the welfare of Negroes, and their dramatic and publicized battles are battles with the wind. Again, this phenomenon cannot be changed without a change in the American scene. In a land where, it is said, any citizen can grow up and become president, Negroes can be pardoned for desiring to enter Congress.

The Negro press, which supports any man, provided he is sufficiently dark and well-known—with the exception of certain Negro novelists accused of drawing portraits unflattering to the race—has for years received vastly confusing criticism based on the fact that it is helplessly and always exactly what it calls itself, that is, a press devoted entirely to happenings in or about the Negro world. This preoccupation can probably be forgiven in view of the great indifference and frequent hostility of the American white press. The Negro press has been accused of not helping matters much—as indeed, it has not, nor do I see how it could have. And it has been accused of being sensational, which it is; but this is a criticism difficult to take seriously in a country so devoted to the sensational as ours.

The best-selling Negro newspaper, I believe, is the *Amsterdam Star-News*, which is also the worst, being gleefully devoted to murders, rapes, raids on love-nests, interracial wars, any item—however meaningless—concerning prominent Negroes, and whatever racial gains can be reported for the week—all in just about that order. Apparently, this policy works well; it sells papers—which is, after all, the aim; in my childhood we never missed an edition. The day the paper came out we could hear, far down the street, the news vendor screaming the latest scandal and people rushing to read about it.

The *Amsterdam* has been rivaled, in recent years, by the *People's Voice*, a journal, modeled on *PM*[1] and referred to as *PV*. *PV* is not so wildly sensational a paper as the *Amsterdam*, though its coverage is much the same (the news coverage of the Negro press is naturally pretty limited). *PV*'s politics are less murky, to the left of center (the *Amsterdam* is Republican, a political affiliation that has led it into some strange doubletalk), and its tone, since its inception, has been ever more hopelessly militant, full of warnings, appeals, and open letters to the government—which, to no one's surprise, are not answered—and the same rather pathetic preoccupation with prominent Negroes and what they are doing. Columns signed by Lena Horne[2] and Paul Robeson[3] appeared in *PV* until several weeks ago, when both severed their connections with the paper. Miss Horne's column made her sound like an embittered Eleanor Roosevelt,[4] and the only column of Robeson's I have read was concerned with the current witch hunt in Hollywood, discussing the kind of movies under attack and Hollywood's traditional treatment of Negroes. It is personally painful to me to realize that so gifted and forceful a man as Robeson should have been tricked by his own bitterness and by a total inability to understand the nature of political power in general, or Communist aims in particular, into missing the point of his own critique, which is worth a great deal of thought: that there are a great many ways of being un-American, some of them nearly as old as the country itself, and that the House Un-American Activities° Committee might find concepts and attitudes even more damaging to American life in a picture like *Gone With the Wind*[5] than in the possibly equally romantic but far less successful *Watch on the Rhine*.[6]

The only other newspapers in the field with any significant sale in Harlem are the Pittsburgh *Courier*, which has the reputation of being the best of the lot, and the *Afro-American*, which resembles the New York *Journal-American* in layout and type and seems to make a consistent if unsuccessful effort to be at once readable,

---

[1]A New York daily tabloid newspaper that had no advertising and was published from 1940 to 1948. Liberal in opinion and typographically modern, it was founded by Marshall Field and edited by Ralph Ingersoll.

[2]Singer and actress (1917–) known for her beauty as well as her voice. She started out at sixteen as a chorus dancer in Harlem.

[3]Singer and actor (1898–1976), son of an escaped slave and graduate of Rutgers and then Columbia Law School, who starred in O'Neil's *Emperor Jones* (1925), *Showboat* (1928), and *Othello* (1943–1945). After supporting some communist causes, he won the International Stalin Peace Prize in 1952, moved to England in 1958, and returned to the United States in 1963.

[4](1884–1962) Humanitarian, civil and consumer rights activist, First Lady from 1933 to 1945, diplomat during World War II, and delegate to the United Nations (1945–1953, 1961). She wrote a syndicated daily news column called "My Day" beginning in 1933.

[5]1939 epic film celebrating the South, based on the Pulitzer Prize–winning novel by Margaret Mitchell (1900–1949).

[6]1943 movie (based on the play by Lillian Hellman) starring Paul Lucas and Bette Davis; Lucas won an Oscar for his role as a patriot.

intelligent, and fiery. The *Courier* is a high-class paper, reaching its peak in the handling of its society news and in the columns of George S. Schuyler, whose Olympian serenity infuriates me, but who, as a matter of fact, reflects with great accuracy the state of mind and the ambitions of the professional, well-to-do Negro who has managed to find a place to stand. Mr. Schuyler, who is remembered still for a satirical novel I have not read, called *Black No More*, is aided enormously in this position by a genteel white wife and a child-prodigy daughter—who is seriously regarded in some circles as proof of the incomprehensible contention that the mating of white and black is more likely to produce genius than any other combination. (The *Afro-American* recently ran a series of articles on this subject, "The Education of a Genius," by Mrs. Amarintha Work, who recorded in detail the development of her mulatto son, Craig.)

Ebony and *Our World* are two big magazines in the field, *Ebony* looking and sounding very much like *Life*, and *Our World* being the black man's *Look*. *Our World* is a very strange, disorganized magazine indeed, sounding sometimes like a college newspaper and sometimes like a call to arms, but principally, like its more skillful brothers, devoted to the proposition that anything a white man can do a Negro can probably do better. *Ebony* digs feature articles out of such things as the "real" Lena Horne and Negro FBI agents, and it travels into the far corners of the earth for any news, however trivial, concerning any Negro or group of Negroes who are in any way unusual and/or newsworthy. The tone of both *Ebony* and *Our World* is affirmative; they cater to the "better class of Negro." *Ebony's* November 1947 issue carried an editorial entitled "Time To Count Our Blessings," which began by accusing Chester Himes[1] (author of the novel *Lonely Crusade*) of having a color psychosis, and went on to explain that there are Negro racists also who are just as blind and dangerous as Bilbo,° which is incontestably true, and that, compared to the millions of starving Europeans, Negroes are sitting pretty—which comparison, I hazard, cannot possibly mean anything to any Negro who has not seen Europe. The editorial concluded that Negroes had come a long way and that "as patriotic Americans" it was time "we" stopped singing the blues and realized just how bright the future was. These cheering sentiments were flanked—or underscored, if you will—by a photograph on the opposite page of an aging Negro farm woman carrying home a bumper crop of onions. It apparently escaped the editors of *Ebony* that the very existence of their magazine, and its table of contents for any month, gave the lie to this effort to make the best of a bad bargain.

The true *raison d'être*[2] of the Negro press can be found in the letters-to-the-editor sections, where the truth about life among the rejected can be seen in print. It is the terrible dilemma of the Negro press that, having no other model, it models

---

[1]Chester Bomar Himes (1909–1984) began writing while serving a seven-year sentence in the Ohio State Penitentiary. *Lonely Crusade* (1947), about blacks working in a defense plant, deals with racism, anti-Semitism, and union organizers. His other novels are *If He Hollars Let Him Go* (1945) and *Cast the First Stone* (1952).

[2]French for "reason for existing" or "purpose."

itself on the white press, attempting to emulate the same effortless, sophisticated tone—a tone its subject matter renders utterly unconvincing. It is simply impossible not to sing the blues, audibly or not, when the lives lived by Negroes are so inescapably harsh and stunted. It is not the Negro press that is at fault: whatever contradictions, inanities, and political infantilism can be charged to it can be charged equally to the American press at large. It is a black man's newspaper straining for recognition and a foothold in the white man's world. Matters are not helped in the least by the fact that the white man's world, intellectually, morally, and spiritually, has the meaningless ring of a hollow drum and the odor of slow death. Within the body of the Negro press all the wars and falsehoods, all the decay and dislocation and struggle of our society are seen in relief.

The Negro press, like the Negro, becomes the scapegoat for our ills. There is no difference, after all, between the *Amsterdam*'s handling of a murder on Lenox Avenue and the *Daily News*' coverage of a murder on Beekman Place,[1] nor is there any difference between the chauvinism of the two papers, except that the *News* is smug and the *Amsterdam* is desperate. Negroes live violent lives, unavoidably; a Negro press without violence is therefore not possible; and, further, in every act of violence, particularly violence against white men, Negroes feel a certain thrill of identification, a wish to have done it themselves, a feeling that old scores are being settled at last. It is no accident that Joe Louis[2] is the most idolized man in Harlem. He has succeeded on a level that white America indicates is the only level for which it has any respect. We (Americans in general, that is) like to point to Negroes and to most of their activities with a kind of tolerant scorn; but it is ourselves we are watching, ourselves we are damning, or—condescendingly— bending to save.

I have written at perhaps excessive length about the Negro press, principally because its many critics have always seemed to me to make the irrational demand that the nation's most oppressed minority behave itself at all times with a skill and foresight no one ever expected of the late Joseph Patterson[3] or ever expected of Hearst;[4] and I have tried to give some idea of its tone because it seems to me that it is here that the innate desperation is betrayed. As for the question of Negro advertising, which has caused so much comment, it seems to me quite logical that any minority identified by the color of its skin and the texture of its hair would eventually grow self-conscious about these attributes and avoid advertising

---

[1]Located next to Sutton Place. The two, Beekman and Sutton, encompass the area from Forty-eighth Street on the south to Fifty-ninth Street on the north and from First Avenue east to the East River. The large brownstones here were once the homes of the wealthy but were later left to the poor who worked in the slaughterhouses and coal yards. Gradually, after the 1920s, the area was again reclaimed by the rich.
[2]Prizefighter (1914–1981), holder of the heavyweight boxing title from 1937 to 1949.
[3](1879–1946) Son of the editor-in-chief of the *Chicago Tribune*, he founded in 1919 the first successful tabloid in the country, the New York City *Daily News*.
[4]William Randolph (1863–1951), who created a publishing empire including twenty-eight newspapers as well as popular magazines such as *Good Housekeeping* and *Harper's Bazaar*.

lotions that made the hair kinkier and soaps that darkened the skin. The American ideal, after all, is that everyone should be as much alike as possible.

It is axiomatic that the Negro is religious, which is to say that he stands in fear of the God our ancestors gave us and before whom we all tremble yet. There are probably more churches in Harlem than in any other ghetto in this city and they are going full blast every night and some of them are filled with praying people every day. This, supposedly, exemplifies the Negro's essential simplicity and good-will; but it is actually a fairly desperate emotional business.

These churches range from the august and publicized Abyssinian Baptist Church on West 138th Street to resolutely unclassifiable lofts, basements, store-fronts, and even private dwellings. Nightly, Holyroller ministers, spiritualists, self-appointed prophets and Messiahs gather their flocks together for worship and for strength through joy. And this is not, as *Cabin in the Sky*[1] would have us believe, merely a childlike emotional release. Their faith may be described as childlike, but the end it serves is often sinister. It may, indeed, "keep them happy"—a phrase carrying the inescapable inference that the way of life imposed on Negroes makes them quite actively unhappy—but also, and much more significantly, religion operates here as a complete and exquisite fantasy revenge: white people own the earth and commit all manner of abomination and injustice on it; the bad will be punished and the good rewarded, for God is not sleeping, the judgment is not far off. It does not require a spectacular degree of perception to realize that bitterness is here neither dead nor sleeping, and that the white man, believing what he wishes to believe, has misread the symbols. Quite often the Negro preacher descends to levels less abstract and leaves no doubt as to what is on his mind: the pressure of life in Harlem, the conduct of the Italian-Ethiopian war,° racial injustice during the recent war, and the terrible possibility of yet another very soon. All these topics provide excellent springboards for sermons thinly coated with spirituality but designed mainly to illustrate the injustice of the white American and anticipate his certain and long overdue punishment.

Here, too, can be seen one aspect of the Negro's ambivalent relation to the Jew. To begin with, though the traditional Christian accusation that the Jews killed Christ is neither questioned nor doubted, the term "Jew" actually operates in this initial context to include all infidels of white skin who have failed to accept the Savior. No real distinction is made: the preacher begins by accusing the Jews of having refused the light and proceeds from there to a catalog of their subsequent sins and the sufferings visited on them by a wrathful God. Though the notion of the suffering is based on the image of the wandering, exiled Jew, the context changes imperceptibly, to become a fairly obvious reminder of the trials of the Negro, while the sins recounted are the sins of the American republic.

At this point, the Negro identifies himself almost wholly with the Jew. The more devout Negro considers that he *is* a Jew, in bondage to a hard taskmaster and

---

[1]An MGM movie (1943) directed by Vincente Minnelli; it was a musical fantasy with an all-Negro cast starring Lena Horne, Ethel Waters, Duke Ellington, and Louis Armstrong.

waiting for a Moses to lead him out of Egypt. The hymns, the texts, and the most favored legends of the devout Negro are all Old Testament and therefore Jewish in origin: the flight from Egypt, the Hebrew children in the fiery furnace, the terrible jubilee songs of deliverance: *Lord, wasn't that hard trials, great tribulations, I'm bound to leave this land!* The covenant God made in the beginning with Abraham and which was to extend to his children and to his children's children forever is a covenant made with these latter-day exiles also: as Israel was chosen, so are they. The birth and death of Jesus, which adds a non-Judaic element, also implements this identification. It is the covenant made with Abraham again, renewed, signed with his blood. ("Before Abraham was, I am.")[1] Here the figure of Jesus operates as the intercessor, the bridge from earth to heaven; it was Jesus who made it possible, who made salvation free to all, "to the Jew first and afterwards the Gentile." The images of the suffering Christ and the suffering Jew are wedded with the image of the suffering slave, and they are one: the people that walked in darkness have seen a great light.

But if the Negro has bought his salvation with pain and the New Testament is used to prove, as it were, the validity of the transformation, it is the Old Testament which is clung to and most frequently preached from, which provides the emotional fire and anatomizes the path of bondage; and which promises vengeance and assures the chosen of their place in Zion. The favorite text of my father, among the most earnest of ministers, was not "Father, forgive them, for they know not what they do," but "How can I sing the Lord's song in a strange land?"

This same identification, which Negroes, since slavery, have accepted with their mother's milk, serves, in contemporary actuality, to implement an involved and specific bitterness. Jews in Harlem are small tradesmen, rent collectors, real estate agents, and pawnbrokers; they operate in accordance with the American business tradition of exploiting Negroes, and they are therefore identified with oppression and are hated for it. I remember meeting no Negro in the years of my growing up, in my family or out of it, who would really ever trust a Jew, and few who did not, indeed, exhibit for them the blackest contempt. On the other hand, this did not prevent their working for Jews, being utterly civil and pleasant to them, and, in most cases, contriving to delude their employers into believing that, far from harboring any dislike for Jews, they would rather work for a Jew than for anyone else. It is part of the price the Negro pays for his position in this society that, as Richard Wright° points out, he is almost always acting. A Negro learns to gauge precisely what reaction the alien person facing him desires, and he produces it with disarming artlessness. The friends I had, growing up and going to work, grew more bitter every day; and, conversely, they learned to hide this bitterness and to fit into the pattern Gentile and Jew alike had fixed for them.

The tension between Negroes and Jews contains an element not characteristic of Negro-Gentile tension, an element which accounts in some measure for the Negro's tendency to castigate the Jew verbally more often than the Gentile,

---

[1]See John 8:58.

and which might lead one to the conclusion that, of all white people on the face of the earth, it is the Jew whom the Negro hates most. When the Negro hates the Jew *as a Jew* he does so partly because the nation does and in much the same painful fashion that he hates himself. It is an aspect of his humiliation whittled down to a manageable size and then transferred; it is the best form the Negro has for tabulating vocally his long record of grievances against his native land.

At the same time, there is a subterranean assumption that the Jew should "know better," that he has suffered enough himself to know what suffering means. An understanding is expected of the Jew such as none but the most naïve and visionary Negro has ever expected of the American Gentile. The Jew, by the nature of his own precarious position, has failed to vindicate this faith. Jews, like Negroes, must use every possible weapon in order to be accepted, and must try to cover their vulnerability by a frenzied adoption of the customs of the country; and the nation's treatment of Negroes is unquestionably a custom. The Jew has been taught—and, too often, accepts—the legend of Negro inferiority; and the Negro, on the other hand, has found nothing in his experience with Jews to counteract the legend of Semitic greed. Here the American white Gentile has two legends serving him at once: he has divided these minorities and he rules.

It seems unlikely that within this complicated structure any real and systematic cooperation can be achieved between Negroes and Jews. (This is in terms of the over-all social problem and is not meant to imply that individual friendships are impossible or that they are valueless when they occur.) The structure of the American commonwealth has trapped both these minorities into attitudes of perpetual hostility. They do not dare trust each other—the Jew because he feels he must climb higher on the American social ladder and has, so far as he is concerned, nothing to gain from identification with any minority even more unloved than he; while the Negro is in the even less tenable position of not really daring to trust anyone.

This applies, with qualifications and yet with almost no exceptions, even to those Negroes called progressive and "unusual." Negroes of the professional class (as distinct from professional Negroes) compete actively with the Jew in daily contact; and they wear anti-Semitism as a defiant proof of their citizenship; their positions are too shaky to allow them any real ease or any faith in anyone. They do not trust whites or each other or themselves; and, particularly and vocally, they do not trust Jews. During my brief days as a Socialist I spent more than one meeting arguing against anti-Semitism with a Negro college student, who was trying to get into civil service and was supporting herself meanwhile as a domestic. She was by no means a stupid girl, nor even a particularly narrow-minded one: she was all in favor of the millenium,[1] even to working with Jews to

---

[1]The Second Coming of Christ; a period of joy, peace, and justice; from the Latin for "a span of a thousand years."

achieve it; but she was not prepared ever to accept a Jew as a friend. It did no good to point out, as I did, that the exploitation of which she accused the Jews was American, not Jewish, that in fact, behind the Jewish face stood the American reality. And *my* Jewish friends in high school were not like that, I said, they had no intention of exploiting *me*, we did not hate each other. (I remember, as I spoke, of being aware of doubt crawling like fog in the back of my mind.) This might all be very well, she told me, we were children now, with no need to earn a living. Wait until later, when your friends go into business and you try to get a job. You'll see!

It is this bitterness—felt alike by the inarticulate, hungry population of Harlem, by the wealthy on Sugar Hill,[1] and by the brilliant exceptions ensconced in universities—which has defeated and promises to continue to defeat all efforts at interracial understanding. I am not one of the people who believe that oppression imbues a people with wisdom or insight or sweet charity, though the survival of the Negro in this country would simply not have been possible if this bitterness had been all he felt. In America, though, life seems to move faster than anywhere else on the globe and each generation is promised more than it will get: which creates, in each generation, a furious, bewildered rage, the rage of people who cannot find solid ground beneath their feet. Just as a mountain of sociological investigations, committee reports, and plans for recreational centers have failed to change the face of Harlem or prevent Negro boys and girls from growing up and facing, individually and alone, the unendurable frustration of being always, everywhere, inferior—until finally the cancer attacks the mind and warps it—so there seems no hope for better Negro-Jewish relations without a change in the American pattern.

Both the Negro and the Jew are helpless; the pressure of living is too immediate and incessant to allow time for understanding. I can conceive of no Negro native to this country who has not, by the age of puberty, been irreparably scarred by the conditions of his life. All over Harlem, Negro boys and girls are growing into stunted maturity, trying desperately to find a place to stand; and the wonder is not that so many are ruined but that so many survive. The Negro's outlets are desperately constricted. In his dilemma he turns first upon himself and then upon whatever most represents to him his own emasculation. Here the Jew is caught in the American crossfire. The Negro, facing a Jew, hates, at bottom, not his Jewishness but the color of his skin. It is not the Jewish tradition by which he has been betrayed but the tradition of his native land. But just as a society must have a scapegoat, so hatred must have a symbol. Georgia has the Negro and Harlem has the Jew. ✍

---

[1] Handsome, residential section of tall apartment buildings and private houses in uptown Harlem, populated by the black bourgeoisie.

Notes of a Native Son[1]

One

On the twenty-ninth of July, in 1943, my father died. On the same day, a few hours later, his last child was born. Over a month before this, while all our energies were concentrated in waiting for these events, there had been, in Detroit, one of the bloodiest race riots of the century. A few hours after my father's funeral, while he lay in state in the undertaker's chapel, a race riot broke out in Harlem.[2] On the morning of the third of August, we drove my father to the graveyard through a wilderness of smashed plate glass.

The day of my father's funeral had also been my nineteenth birthday. As we drove him to the graveyard, the spoils of injustice, anarchy, discontent, and hatred were all around us. It seemed to me that God himself had devised, to mark my father's end, the most sustained and brutally dissonant of codas. And it seemed to me, too, that the violence which rose all about us as my father left the world had been devised as a corrective for the pride of his eldest son. I had declined to believe in that apocalypse which had been central to my father's vision; very well, life seemed to be saying, here is something that will certainly pass for an apocalypse until the real thing comes along. I had inclined to be contemptuous of my father for the conditions of his life, for the conditions of our lives. When his life had ended I began to wonder about that life and also, in a new way, to be apprehensive about my own.

I had not known my father very well. We had got on badly, partly because we shared, in our different fashions, the vice of stubborn pride. When he was dead I realized that I had hardly ever spoken to him. When he had been dead a long time I began to wish I had. It seems to be typical of life in America, where opportunities, real and fancied, are thicker than anywhere else on the globe, that the second generation has no time to talk to the first. No one, including my father, seems to have known exactly how old he was, but his mother had been born during slavery. He was of the first generation of free men. He, along with thousands of other Negroes, came North after 1919 and I was part of that generation which had never seen the landscape of what Negroes sometimes call the Old Country.

He had been born in New Orleans and had been a quite young man there during the time that Louis Armstrong,[3] a boy, was running errands for the dives and honky-tonks of what was always presented to me as one of the most wicked of cities—to this day, whenever I think of New Orleans, I also helplessly think of Sodom and Gomorrah.[4] My father never mentioned Louis Armstrong, except to forbid us to play his records; but there was a picture of him on our wall for a long

---

[1]First published in *Harper's Magazine*, November 1955.

[2]See footnote 2, p. 459.

[3]Jazz musician (1900–1971) nicknamed Satchmo. Born in New Orleans, he first became famous as a trumpeter and singer in 1922 as part of the King Oliver Band in Chicago.

[4]According to Genesis 19:24, these ancient Palestinian cities were so wicked that God destroyed them by fire and brimstone.

time. One of my father's strong-willed female relatives had placed it there and forbade my father to take it down. He never did, but he eventually maneuvered her out of the house and when, some years later, she was in trouble and near death, he refused to do anything to help her.

He was, I think, very handsome. I gather this from photographs and from my own memories of him, dressed in his Sunday best and on his way to preach a sermon somewhere, when I was little. Handsome, proud, and ingrown, "like a toenail," somebody said. But he looked to me, as I grew older, like pictures I had seen of African tribal chieftains: he really should have been naked, with warpaint on and barbaric mementos, standing among spears. He could be chilling in the pulpit and indescribably cruel in his personal life and he was certainly the most bitter man I have ever met; yet it must be said that there was something else in him, buried in him, which lent him his tremendous power and, even, a rather crushing charm. It had something to do with his blackness, I think—he was very black—with his blackness and his beauty, and with the fact that he knew that he was black but did not know that he was beautiful. He claimed to be proud of his blackness but it had also been the cause of much humiliation and it had fixed bleak boundaries to his life. He was not a young man when we were growing up and he had already suffered many kinds of ruin; in his outrageously demanding and protective way he loved his children, who were black like him and menaced, like him; and all these things sometimes showed in his face when he tried, never to my knowledge with any success, to establish contact with any of us. When he took one of his children on his knee to play, the child always became fretful and began to cry; when he tried to help one of us with our homework the absolutely unabating tension which emanated from him caused our minds and our tongues to become paralyzed, so that he, scarcely knowing why, flew into a rage and the child, not knowing why, was punished. If it ever entered his head to bring a surprise home for his children, it was, almost unfailingly, the wrong surprise and even the big watermelons he often brought home on his back in the summertime led to the most appalling scenes. I do not remember, in all those years, that one of his children was ever glad to see him come home. From what I was able to gather of his early life, it seemed that this inability to establish contact with other people had always marked him and had been one of the things which had driven him out of New Orleans. There was something in him, therefore, groping and tentative, which was never expressed and which was buried with him. One saw it most clearly when he was facing new people and hoping to impress them. But he never did, not for long. We went from church to smaller and more improbable church, he found himself in less and less demand as a minister, and by the time he died none of his friends had come to see him for a long time. He had lived and died in an intolerable bitterness of spirit and it frightened me, as we drove him to the graveyard through those unquiet, ruined streets, to see how powerful and overflowing this bitterness could be and to realize that this bitterness now was mine.

When he died I had been away from home for a little over a year. In that year I had had time to become aware of the meaning of all my father's bitter warnings, had discovered the secret of his proudly pursed lips and rigid carriage: I had discovered the weight of white people in the world. I saw that this had been for my ancestors and now would be for me an awful thing to live with and that the bitterness which had helped to kill my father could also kill me.

He had been ill a long time—in the mind, as we now realized, reliving instances of his fantastic intransigence in the new light of his affliction and endeavoring to feel a sorrow for him which never, quite, came true. We had not known that he was being eaten up by paranoia, and the discovery that his cruelty, to our bodies and our minds, had been one of the symptoms of his illness was not, then, enough to enable us to forgive him. The younger children felt, quite simply, relief that he would not be coming home anymore. My mother's observation that it was he, after all, who had kept them alive all these years meant nothing because the problems of keeping children alive are not real for children. The older children felt, with my father gone, that they could invite their friends to the house without fear that their friends would be insulted or, as had sometimes happened with me, being told that their friends were in league with the devil and intended to rob our family of everything we owned. (I didn't fail to wonder, and it made me hate him, what on earth we owned that anybody else would want.)

His illness was beyond all hope of healing before anyone realized that he was ill. He had always been so strange and had lived, like a prophet, in such unimaginably close communion with the Lord that his long silences which were punctuated by moans and hallelujahs and snatches of old songs while he sat at the living-room window never seemed odd to us. It was not until he refused to eat because, he said, his family was trying to poison him that my mother was forced to accept as a fact what had, until then, been only an unwilling suspicion. When he was committed, it was discovered that he had tuberculosis and, as it turned out, the disease of his mind allowed the disease of his body to destroy him. For the doctors could not force him to eat, either, and, though he was fed intravenously, it was clear from the beginning that there was no hope for him.

In my mind's eye I could see him, sitting at the window, locked up in his terrors; hating and fearing every living soul including his children who had betrayed him, too, by reaching toward the world which had despised him. There were nine of us. I began to wonder what it could have felt like for such a man to have had nine children whom he could barely feed. He used to make little jokes about our poverty, which never, of course, seemed very funny to us; they could not have seemed very funny to him, either, or else our all too feeble response to them would never have caused such rages. He spent great energy and achieved, to our chagrin, no small amount of success in keeping us away from the people who surrounded us, people who had all-night rent parties to which we listened when we should have been sleeping, people who cursed and drank and flashed razor blades on Lenox Avenue. He could not understand why, if they had so much energy to spare, they could not use it to make their lives better. He treated almost everybody on our block with a most uncharitable asperity and neither they, nor, of course, their children were slow to reciprocate.

The only white people who came to our house were welfare workers and bill collectors. It was almost always my mother who dealt with them, for my father's temper, which was at the mercy of his pride, was never to be trusted. It was clear that he felt their very presence in his home to be a violation: this was conveyed by his carriage, almost ludicrously stiff, and by his voice, harsh and vindictively polite. When I was around nine or ten I wrote a play which was directed by a young, white schoolteacher, a woman, who then took an interest in me, and gave me books to read and, in order to corroborate my theatrical bent, decided to take me to see what she somewhat tactlessly referred to as "real" plays. Theater-going was forbidden in our house, but, with the really cruel intuitiveness of a child, I suspected that the color of this woman's skin would carry the day for me. When, at school, she suggested taking me to the theater, I did not, as I might have done if she had been a Negro, find a way of discouraging her, but agreed that she should pick me up at my house one evening. I then, very cleverly, left all the rest to my mother, who suggested to my father, as I knew she would, that it would not be very nice to let such a kind woman make the trip for nothing. Also, since it was a schoolteacher, I imagine that my mother countered the idea of sin with the idea of "education," which word, even with my father, carried a kind of bitter weight.

Before the teacher came my father took me aside to ask *why* she was coming, what *interest* she could possibly have in our house, in a boy like me. I said I didn't know but I, too, suggested that it had something to do with education. And I understood that my father was waiting for me to say something—I didn't quite know what; perhaps that I wanted his protection against this teacher and her "education." I said none of these things and the teacher came and we went out. It was clear, during the brief interview in our living room, that my father was agreeing very much against his will and that he would have refused permission if he had dared. The fact that he did not dare caused me to despise him: I had no way of knowing that he was facing in that living room a wholly unprecedented and frightening situation.

Later, when my father had been laid off from his job, this woman became very important to us. She was really a very sweet and generous woman and went to a great deal of trouble to be of help to us, particularly during one awful winter. My mother called her by the highest name she knew: she said she was a "christian." My father could scarcely disagree but during the four or five years of our relatively close association he never trusted her and was always trying to surprise in her open, Midwestern face the genuine, cunningly hidden, and hideous motivation. In later years, particularly when it began to be clear that this "education" of mine was going to lead me to perdition, he became more explicit and warned me that my white friends in high school were not really my friends and that I would see, when I was older, how white people would do anything to keep a Negro down. Some of them could be nice, he admitted, but none of them were to be trusted and most of them were not even nice. The best thing was to have as little to do with them as possible. I did not feel this way and I was certain, in my innocence, that I never would.

But the year which preceded my father's death had made a great change in my life. I had been living in New Jersey, working in defense plants, working and living among southerners, white and black. I knew about the South, of course, and about how southerners treated Negroes and how they expected them to behave, but it had never entered my mind that anyone would look at me and expect *me* to behave that way. I learned in New Jersey that to be a Negro meant, precisely, that one was never looked at but was simply at the mercy of the reflexes the color of one's skin caused in other people. I acted in New Jersey as I had always acted, that is as though I thought a great deal of myself—I had to *act* that way—with results that were, simply, unbelievable. I had scarcely arrived before I had earned the enmity, which was extraordinarily ingenious, of all my superiors and nearly all my co-workers. In the beginning, to make matters worse, I simply did not know what was happening. I did not know what I had done, and I shortly began to wonder what *anyone* could possibly do, to bring about such unanimous, active, and unbearably vocal hostility. I knew about jim crow° but I had never experienced it. I went to the same self-service restaurant three times and stood with all the Princeton boys before the counter, waiting for a hamburger and coffee; it was always an extraordinarily long time before anything was set before me; but it was not until the fourth visit that I learned that, in fact, nothing had ever been set before me: I had simply picked something up. Negroes were not served there, I was told, and they had been waiting for me to realize that I was the only Negro present. Once I was told this, I determined to go there all the time. But now they were ready for me and, though some dreadful scenes were subsequently enacted in that restaurant, I never ate there again.

It was the same story all over New Jersey, in bars, bowling alleys, diners, places to live. I was always being forced to leave, silently, or with mutual imprecations. I very shortly became notorious and children giggled behind me when I passed and their elders whispered or shouted—they really believed that I was mad. And it did begin to work on my mind, of course; I began to be afraid to go anywhere and to compensate for this I went places to which I really should not have gone and where, God knows, I had no desire to be. My reputation in town naturally enhanced my reputation at work and my working day became one long series of acrobatics designed to keep me out of trouble. I cannot say that these acrobatics succeeded. It began to seem that the machinery of the organization I worked for was turning over, day and night, with but one aim: to eject me. I was fired once, and contrived, with the aid of a friend from New York, to get back on the payroll; was fired again, and bounced back again. It took a while to fire me for the third time, but the third time took. There were no loopholes anywhere. There was not even any way of getting back inside the gates.

That year in New Jersey lives in my mind as though it were the year during which, having an unsuspected predilection for it, I first contracted some dread, chronic disease, the unfailing symptom of which is a kind of blind fever, a pounding in the skull and fire in the bowels. Once this disease is contracted, one can never be really carefree again, for the fever, without an instant's warning, can recur at any moment. It can wreck more important things than race relations. There is not a Negro alive who does not have this rage in his blood—one has the choice, merely, of living with it consciously or surrendering to it. As for me, this fever has recurred in me, and does, and will until the day I die.

My last night in New Jersey, a white friend from New York took me to the nearest big town, Trenton, to go to the movies and have a few drinks. As it turned out, he also saved me from, at the very least, a violent whipping. Almost every detail of that night stands out very clearly in my memory. I even remember the name of the movie we saw because its title impressed me as being so patly ironical. It was a movie about the German occupation of France, starring Maureen O'Hara and Charles Laughton and called *This Land Is Mine*. I remember the name of the diner we walked into when the movie ended: it was the "American Diner." When we walked in the counterman asked what we wanted and I remember answering with the casual sharpness which had become my habit: "We want a hamburger and a cup of coffee, what do you think we want?" I do not know why, after a year of such rebuffs, I so completely failed to anticipate his answer, which was, of course, "we don't serve Negroes here." This reply failed to discompose me, at least for the moment. I made some sardonic comment about the name of the diner and we walked out into the streets.

This was the time of what was called the "brownout," when the lights in all American cities were very dim. When we reentered the streets something happened to me which had the force of an optical illusion, or a nightmare. The streets were very crowded and I was facing north. People were moving in every direction but it seemed to me, in that instant, that all of the people I could see, and many more than that, were moving toward me, against me, and that everyone was white. I remember how their faces gleamed. And I felt, like a physical sensation, a *click* at the nape of my neck as though some interior string connecting my head to my body had been cut. I began to walk. I heard my friend call after me, but I ignored him. Heaven only knows what was going on in his mind, but he had the good sense not to touch me—I don't know what would have happened if he had—and to keep me in sight. I don't know what was going on in my mind, either; I certainly had no conscious plan. I wanted to do something to crush these white faces, which were crushing me. I walked for perhaps a block or two until I came to an enormous, glittering, and fashionable restaurant in which I knew not even the intercession of the Virgin would cause me to be served. I pushed through the doors and took the first vacant seat I saw, at a table for two, and waited.

I do not know how long I waited and I rather wonder, until today, what I could possibly have looked like. Whatever I looked like, I frightened the waitress who shortly appeared, and the moment she appeared all of my fury flowed toward her. I hated her for her white face, and for her great, astounded, frightened eyes. I felt that if she found a black man so frightening I would make her fright worthwhile.

She did not ask me what I wanted, but repeated, as though she had learned it somewhere, "We don't serve Negroes here." She did not say it with the blunt, derisive hostility to which I had grown so accustomed, but, rather, with a note of apology in her voice, and fear. This made me colder and more murderous than ever. I felt I had to do something with my hands. I wanted her to come close enough for me to get her neck between my hands.

So I pretended not to have understood her, hoping to draw her closer. And she did step a very short step closer, with her pencil poised incongruously over her pad, and repeated the formula: ". . . don't serve Negroes here."

Somehow, with the repetition of that phrase, which was already ringing in my head like a thousand bells of a nightmare, I realized that she would never come any closer and that I would have to strike from a distance. There was nothing on the table but an ordinary watermug half full of water, and I picked this up and hurled it with all my strength at her. She ducked and it missed her and shattered against the mirror behind the bar. And, with that sound, my frozen blood abruptly thawed, I returned from wherever I had been, I *saw*, for the first time, the restaurant, the people with their mouths open, already, as it seemed to me, rising as one man, and I realized what I had done, and where I was, and I was frightened. I rose and began running for the door. A round, potbellied man grabbed me by the nape of the neck just as I reached the doors and began to beat me about the face. I kicked him and got loose and ran into the streets. My friend whispered, *"Run!"* and I ran.

My friend stayed outside the restaurant long enough to misdirect my pursuers and the police, who arrived, he told me, at once. I do not know what I said to him when he came to my room that night. I could not have said much. I felt, in the oddest, most awful way, that I had somehow betrayed him. I lived it over and over and over again, the way one relives an automobile accident after it has happened and one finds oneself alone and safe. I could not get over two facts, both equally difficult for the imagination to grasp, and one was that I could have been murdered. But the other was that I had been ready to commit murder. I saw nothing very clearly but I did see this: that my life, my *real* life, was in danger, and not from anything other people might do but from the hatred I carried in my own heart.

Two

I had returned home around the second week in June—in great haste because it seemed that my father's death and my mother's confinement were both but a matter of hours. In the case of my mother, it soon became clear that she had simply made a miscalculation. This had always been her tendency and I don't believe that a single one of us arrived in the world, or has since arrived anywhere else, on time. But none of us dawdled so intolerably about the business of being born as did my baby sister. We sometimes amused ourselves, during those endless, stifling weeks, by picturing the baby sitting within in the safe, warm dark, bitterly regretting the necessity of becoming a part of our chaos and stubbornly putting it off as long as possible. I understood her perfectly and congratulated her on showing such good sense so soon. Death, however, sat as purposefully at my father's bedside as life stirred within my mother's womb and it was harder to understand why he so lingered in that long shadow. It seemed that he had bent, and for a long time, too, all of his energies toward dying. Now death was ready for him but my father held back.

All of Harlem, indeed, seemed to be infected by waiting. I had never before known it to be so violently still. Racial tensions throughout this country were exacerbated during the early years of the war, partly because the labor market brought together hundreds of thousands of ill-prepared people and partly because Negro soldiers, regardless of where they were born, received their military training in the south. What happened in defense plants and army camps had repercussions, naturally, in every Negro ghetto. The situation in Harlem had grown bad enough for clergymen, policemen, educators, politicians, and social workers to assert in one breath that there was no "crime wave" and to offer, in the very next breath, suggestions as to how to combat it. These suggestions always seemed to involve playgrounds, despite the fact that racial skirmishes were occurring in the playgrounds, too. Playground or not, crime wave or not, the Harlem police force had been augmented in March, and the unrest grew— perhaps, in fact, partly as a result of the ghetto's instinctive hatred of policemen. Perhaps the most revealing news item, out of the steady parade of reports of muggings, stabbings, shootings, assaults, gang wars, and accusations of police brutality, is the item concerning six Negro girls who set upon a white girl in the subway because, as they all too accurately put it, she was stepping on their toes. Indeed she was, all over the nation.

I had never before been so aware of policemen, on foot, on horseback, on corners, everywhere, always two by two. Nor had I ever been so aware of small knots of people. They were on stoops and on corners and in doorways, and what was striking about them, I think, was that they did not seem to be talking. Never, when I passed these groups, did the usual sound of a curse or a laugh ring out and neither did there seem to be any hum of gossip. There was certainly, on the other hand, occurring between them communication extraordinarily intense. Another thing that was striking was the unexpected diversity of the people who made up these groups. Usually, for example, one would see a group of sharpies standing on the street corner, jiving the passing chicks; or a group of older men, usually, for some reason, in the vicinity of a barber shop, discussing baseball scores, or the numbers, or making rather chilling observations about women they had known. Women, in a general way, tended to be seen less often together—unless they were church women, or very young girls, or prostitutes met together for an unprofessional instant. But that summer I saw the strangest combinations: large, respectable, churchly matrons standing on the stoops or the corners with their hair tied up, together with a girl in sleazy satin whose face bore the marks of gin and the razor, or heavy-set, abrupt, no-nonsense older men, in company with the most disreputable and fanatical "race" men, or these same "race" men with the sharpies, or these sharpies with the churchly women. Seventh Day Adventists and Methodists and Spiritualists seemed to be hobnobbing with Holyrollers and they were all, alike, entangled with the most flagrant disbelievers; something heavy in their stance seemed to indicate that they had all, incredibly, seen a common vision, and on each face there seemed to be the same strange, bitter shadow.

The churchly women and the matter-of-fact, no-nonsense men had children in the Army. The sleazy girls they talked to had lovers there, the sharpies and the "race" men had friends and brothers there. It would have demanded an unquestioning patriotism, happily as uncommon in this country as it is undesirable, for these people not to have been disturbed by the bitter letters they received, by the newspaper stories they read, not to have been enraged by the posters, then to be found all over New York, which described the Japanese as "yellow-bellied Japs." It was only the "race" men, to be sure, who spoke ceaselessly of being revenged— how this vengeance was to be exacted was not clear—for the indignities and dangers suffered by Negro boys in uniform; but everybody felt a directionless, hopeless bitterness, as well as that panic which can scarcely be suppressed when one knows that a human being one loves is beyond one's reach, and in danger. This helplessness and this gnawing uneasiness does something, at length, to even the toughest mind. Perhaps the best way to sum all this up is to say that the people I knew felt, mainly, a peculiar kind of relief when they knew that their boys were being shipped out of the south, to do battle overseas. It was, perhaps, like feeling that the most dangerous part of a dangerous journey had been passed and that now, even if death should come, it would come with honor and without the complicity of their countrymen. Such a death would be, in short, a fact with which one could hope to live.

It was on the twenty-eighth of July, which I believe was a Wednesday, that I visited my father for the first time during his illness and for the last time in his life. The moment I saw him I knew why I had put off this visit so long. I had told my mother that I did not want to see him because I hated him. But this was not true. It was only that I *had* hated him and I wanted to hold on to this hatred. I did not want to look on him as a ruin: it was not a ruin I had hated. I imagine that one of the reasons people cling to their hates so stubbornly is because they sense, once hate is gone, that they will be forced to deal with pain.

We traveled out to him, his older sister and myself, to what seemed to be the very end of a very Long Island. It was hot and dusty and we wrangled, my aunt and I, all the way out, over the fact that I had recently begun to smoke and, as she said, to give myself airs. But I knew that she wrangled with me because she could not bear to face the fact of her brother's dying. Neither could I endure the reality of her despair, her unstated bafflement as to what had happened to her brother's life, and her own. So we wrangled and I smoked and from time to time she fell into a heavy reverie. Covertly, I watched her face, which was the face of an old woman; it had fallen in, the eyes were sunken and lightless; soon she would be dying, too.

In my childhood—it had not been so long ago—I had thought her beautiful. She had been quick-witted and quick-moving and very generous with all the children and each of her visits had been an event. At one time one of my brothers and myself had thought of running away to live with her. Now she could no longer produce out of her handbag some unexpected and yet familiar delight. She made me feel pity and revulsion and fear. It was awful to realize that she no longer caused me to feel affection. The closer we came to the hospital the more querulous she became and at the same time, naturally, grew more dependent on me. Between pity and guilt and fear I began to feel that there was another me trapped in my skull like a jack-in-the-box who might escape my control at any moment and fill the air with screaming.

She began to cry the moment we entered the room and she saw him lying there, all shriveled and still, like a little black monkey. The great, gleaming apparatus which fed him and would have compelled him to be still even if he had been able to move brought to mind, not beneficence, but torture; the tubes entering his arm made me think of pictures I had seen when a child, of Gulliver,[1] tied down by the pygmies on that island. My aunt wept and wept, there was a whistling sound in my father's throat; nothing was said; he could not speak. I wanted to take his hand, to say something. But I do not know what I could have said, even if he could have heard me. He was not really in that room with us, he had at last really embarked on his journey; and though my aunt told me that he said he was going to meet Jesus, I did not hear anything except that whistling in his throat. The doctor came back and we left, into that unbearable train again, and home. In the morning came the telegram saying that he was dead. Then the house was suddenly full of relatives, friends, hysteria, and confusion and I quickly left my mother and the children to the care of those impressive women, who, in Negro communities at least, automatically appear at times of bereavement armed with lotions, proverbs, and patience, and an ability to cook. I went downtown. By the time I returned, later the same day, my mother had been carried to the hospital and the baby had been born.

Three

For my father's funeral I had nothing black to wear and this posed a nagging problem all day long. It was one of those problems, simple, or impossible of solution, to which the mind insanely clings in order to avoid the mind's real trouble. I spent most of that day at the downtown apartment of a girl I knew, celebrating my birthday with whisky and wondering what to wear that night. When planning a birthday celebration one naturally does not expect that it will be up against competition from a funeral and this girl had anticipated taking me out that night, for a big dinner and a night club afterwards. Sometime during the course of that long day we decided that we would go out anyway, when my father's funeral service was over. I imagine I decided it, since, as the funeral hour approached, it became clearer and clearer to me that I would not know what to do with myself when it was over. The girl, stifling her very lively concern as to the possible effects of the whisky on one of my father's chief mourners, concentrated on being conciliatory and practically helpful. She found a black shirt for me somewhere and ironed it and, dressed in the darkest pants and jacket I owned, and slightly drunk, I made my way to my father's funeral.

The chapel was full, but not packed, and very quiet. There were, mainly, my father's relatives, and his children, and here and there I saw faces I had not seen

---

[1] See Swift.°

since childhood, the faces of my father's one-time friends. They were very dark and solemn now, seeming somehow to suggest that they had known all along that something like this would happen. Chief among the mourners was my aunt, who had quarreled with my father all his life; by which I do not mean to suggest that her mourning was insincere or that she had not loved him. I suppose that she was one of the few people in the world who had, and their incessant quarreling proved precisely the strength of the tie that bound them. The only other person in the world, as far as I knew, whose relationship to my father rivaled my aunt's in depth was my mother, who was not there.

It seemed to me, of course, that it was a very long funeral. But it was, if anything, a rather shorter funeral than most, nor, since there were no overwhelming, uncontrollable expressions of grief, could it be called—if I dare to use the word—successful. The minister who preached my father's funeral sermon was one of the few my father had still been seeing as he neared his end. He presented to us in his sermon a man whom none of us had ever seen—a man thoughtful, patient, and forbearing, a Christian inspiration to all who knew him, and a model for his children. And no doubt the children, in their disturbed and guilty state, were almost ready to believe this; he had been remote enough to be anything and, anyway, the shock of the incontrovertible, that it was really our father lying up there in that casket, prepared the mind for anything. His sister moaned and this grief-stricken moaning was taken as corroboration. The other faces held a dark, noncommittal thoughtfulness. This was not the man they had known, but they had scarcely expected to be confronted with *him*; this was, in a sense deeper than questions of fact, the man they had not known, and the man they had not known may have been the real one. The real man, whoever he had been, had suffered and now he was dead; this was all that was sure and all that mattered now. Every man in the chapel hoped that when his hour came he, too, would be eulogized, which is to say forgiven, and that all of his lapses, greeds, errors, and strayings from the truth would be invested with coherence and looked upon with charity. This was perhaps the last thing human beings could give each other and it was what they demanded, after all, of the Lord. Only the Lord saw the midnight tears, only He was present when one of His children, moaning and wringing hands, paced up and down the room. When one slapped one's child in anger the recoil in the heart reverberated through heaven and became part of the pain of the universe. And when the children were hungry and sullen and distrustful and one watched them, daily, growing wilder, and further away, and running headlong into danger, it was the Lord who knew what the charged heart endured as the strap was laid to the backside; the Lord alone who knew what one *would* have said if one had had, like the Lord, the gift of the living word. It was the Lord who knew of the impossibility every parent in that room faced: how to prepare the child for the day when the child would be despised and how to *create* in the child—by what means?—a stronger antidote to this poison than one had found for oneself. The avenues, side streets, bars, billiard halls, hospitals, police stations, and even the playgrounds of Harlem—not to mention the houses of correction, the jails, and the morgue— testified to the potency of the poison while remaining silent as to the efficacy of whatever antidote, irresistibly raising the question of whether or not such an antidote existed; raising, which was worse, the question of whether or not an antidote was desirable; perhaps poison should be fought with poison. With these several schisms in the mind and with more terrors in the heart than could be named, it was better not to judge the man who had gone down under an impossible burden. It was better to remember: *Thou knowest this man's fall; but thou knowest not his wrassling.*

While the preacher talked and I watched the children—years of changing their diapers, scrubbing them, slapping them, taking them to school, and scolding them had had the perhaps inevitable result of making me love them, though I am not sure I knew this then—my mind was busily breaking out with a rash of disconnected impressions. Snatches of popular songs, indecent jokes, bits of books I had read, movie sequences, faces, voices, political issues—I thought I was going mad; all these impressions suspended, as it were, in the solution of the faint nausea produced in me by the heat and liquor. For a moment I had the impression that my alcoholic breath, inefficiently disguised with chewing gum, filled the entire chapel. Then someone began singing one of my father's favorite songs and, abruptly, I was with him, sitting on his knee, in the hot, enormous, crowded church which was the first church we attended. It was the Abyssinian Baptist Church on 138th Street. We had not gone there long. With this image, a host of others came. I had forgotten, in the rage of my growing up, how proud my father had been of me when I was little. Apparently, I had had a voice and my father had liked to show me off before the members of the church. I had forgotten what he had looked like when he was pleased but now I remembered that he had always been grinning with pleasure when my solos ended. I even remembered certain expressions on his face when he teased my mother—had he loved her? I would never know. And when had it all begun to change? For now it seemed that he had not always been cruel. I remembered being taken for a haircut and scraping my knee on the footrest of the barber's chair and I remembered my father's face as he soothed my crying and applied the stinging iodine. Then I remembered our fights, fights which had been of the worst possible kind because my technique had been silence.

I remembered the one time in all our life together when we had really spoken to each other.

It was on a Sunday and it must have been shortly before I left home. We were walking, just the two of us, in our usual silence, to or from church. I was in high school and had been doing a lot of writing and I was, at about this time, the editor of the high school magazine. But I had also been a Young Minister and had been preaching from the pulpit. Lately, I had been taking fewer engagements and preached as rarely as possible. It was said in the church, quite truthfully, that I was "cooling off."

My father asked me abruptly, "You'd rather write than preach, wouldn't you?"

I was astonished at his question—because it was a real question. I answered, "Yes."

That was all we said. It was awful to remember that that was all we had *ever* said.

The casket now was opened and the mourners were being led up the aisle to look for the last time on the deceased. The assumption was that the family was too overcome with grief to be allowed to make this journey alone and I watched while my aunt was led to the casket and, muffled in black, and shaking, led back to her seat. I disapproved of forcing the children to look on their dead father, considering that the shock of his death, or, more truthfully, the shock of death as a reality, was already a little more than a child could bear, but my judgment in this matter had been overruled and there they were, bewildered and frightened and very small, being led, one by one, to the casket. But there is also something very gallant about children at such moments. It has something to do with their silence and gravity and with the fact that one cannot help them. Their legs, somehow, seem *exposed*, so that it is at once incredible and terribly clear that their legs are all they have to hold them up.

I had not wanted to go to the casket myself and I certainly had not wished to be led there, but there was no way of avoiding either of these forms. One of the deacons led me up and I looked on my father's face. I cannot say that it looked like him at all. His blackness had been equivocated by powder and there was no suggestion in that casket of what his power had or could have been. He was simply an old man dead, and it was hard to believe that he had ever given anyone either joy or pain. Yet, his life filled that room. Further up the avenue his wife was holding his newborn child. Life and death so close together, and love and hatred, and right and wrong, said something to me which I did not want to hear concerning man, concerning the life of man.

After the funeral, while I was downtown desperately celebrating my birthday, a Negro soldier, in the lobby of the Hotel Braddock, got into a fight with a white policeman over a Negro girl. Negro girls, white policemen, in or out of uniform, and Negro males—in or out of uniform—were part of the furniture of the lobby of the Hotel Braddock and this was certainly not the first time such an incident had occurred. It was destined, however, to receive an unprecedented publicity, for the fight between the policeman and the soldier ended with the shooting of the soldier. Rumor, flowing immediately to the streets outside, stated that the soldier had been shot in the back, an instantaneous and revealing invention, and that the soldier had died protecting a Negro woman. The facts were somewhat different— for example, the soldier had not been shot in the back, and was not dead, and the girl seems to have been as dubious a symbol of womanhood as her white counterpart in Georgia usually is, but no one was interested in the facts. They preferred the invention because this invention expressed and corroborated their hates and fears so perfectly. It is just as well to remember that people are always doing this. Perhaps many of those legends, including Christianity, to which the world clings began their conquest of the world with just some such concerted surrender to distortion. The effect, in Harlem, of this particular legend was like the effect of a lit match in a tin of gasoline. The mob gathered before the doors of the Hotel Braddock simply began to swell and to spread in every direction, and Harlem exploded.

The mob did not cross the ghetto lines. It would have been easy, for example, to have gone over Morningside Park on the west side or to have crossed the Grand Central railroad tracks at 125th Street on the east side, to wreak havoc in white neighborhoods. The mob seems to have been mainly interested in something more potent and real than the white face, that is, in white power, and the principal damage done during the riot of the summer of 1943 was to white business establishments in Harlem. It might have been a far bloodier story, of course, if, at the hour the riot began, these establishments had still been open. From the Hotel Braddock the mob fanned out, east and west along 125th Street, and for the entire length of Lenox, Seventh, and Eighth avenues. Along each of these avenues, and along each major side street—116th, 125th, 135th, and so on—bars, stores, pawnshops, restaurants, even little luncheonettes had been smashed open and entered and looted—looted, it might be added, with more haste than efficiency. The shelves really looked as though a bomb had struck them. Cans of beans and soup and dog food, along with toilet paper, corn flakes, sardines and milk tumbled every which way, and abandoned cash registers and cases of beer leaned crazily out of the splintered windows and were strewn along the avenues. Sheets, blankets, and clothing of every description formed a kind of path, as though people had dropped them while running. I truly had not realized that Harlem *had* so many stores until I saw them all smashed open; the first time the word *wealth* ever entered my mind in relation to Harlem was when I saw it scattered in the streets. But one's first, incongruous impression of plenty was countered immediately by an impression of waste. None of this was doing anybody any good. It would have been better to have left the plate glass as it had been and the goods lying in the stores.

It would have been better, but it would also have been intolerable, for Harlem had needed something to smash. To smash something is the ghetto's chronic need. Most of the time it is the members of the ghetto who smash each other, and themselves. But as long as the ghetto walls are standing there will always come a moment when these outlets do not work. That summer, for example, it was not enough to get into a fight on Lenox Avenue, or curse out one's cronies in the barber shops. If ever, indeed, the violence which fills Harlem's churches, pool halls, and bars erupts outward in a more direct fashion, Harlem and its citizens are likely to vanish in an apocalyptic flood. That this is not likely to happen is due to a great many reasons, most hidden and powerful among them the Negro's real relation to the white American. This relation prohibits, simply, anything as uncomplicated and satisfactory as pure hatred. In order really to hate white people, one has to blot so much out of the mind—and the heart—that this hatred itself becomes an exhausting and self-destructive pose. But this does not mean, on the other hand, that love comes easily: the white world is too powerful, too complacent, too ready with gratuitous humiliation, and, above all, too ignorant and too innocent for that. One is absolutely forced to make perpetual qualifications and one's own reactions are always canceling each other out. It is this, really, which has driven so many people mad, both white and black. One is always in the position of having to decide between amputation and gangrene. Amputation is swift but time may prove that the amputation was not necessary—or one may delay the amputation too long. Gangrene is slow, but it is impossible to be sure that one is reading one's symptoms right. The idea of going through life as a cripple is more than one can bear, and equally unbearable is the risk of swelling up slowly, in agony, with poison. And the trouble, finally, is that the risks are real even if the choices do not exist.

"But as for me and my house," my father had said, "we will serve the Lord." I wondered, as we drove him to his resting place, what this line had meant for him. I had heard him preach it many times. I had preached it once myself, proudly giving it an interpretation different from my father's. Now the whole thing came back to me, as though my father and I were on our way to Sunday school and I were memorizing the golden text: *And if it seem evil unto you to serve the Lord, choose you this day whom you will serve; whether the gods which your fathers served that were on the other side of the flood, or the gods of the Amorites, in whose land ye dwell: but as for me and my house, we will serve the lord.*[1] I suspected in these familiar lines a meaning which had never been there for me before. All of my father's texts and songs, which I had decided were meaningless, were arranged before me at his death like empty bottles, waiting to hold the meaning which life would give them for me. This was his legacy: nothing is ever escaped. That bleakly memorable morning I hated the unbelievable streets and the Negroes and whites who had, equally, made them that way. But I knew that it was folly, as my father would have said, this bitterness was folly. It was necessary to hold on to the things that mattered. The dead man mattered, the new life mattered; blackness and whiteness did not matter; to believe that they did was to acquiesce in one's own destruction. Hatred, which could destroy so much, never failed to destroy the man who hated and this was an immutable law.

It began to seem that one would have to hold in the mind forever two ideas which seemed to be in opposition. The first idea was acceptance, the acceptance, totally without rancor, of life as it is, and men as they are: in the light of this idea, it goes without saying that injustice is a commonplace. But this did not mean that one could be complacent, for the second idea was of equal power: that one must never, in one's own life, accept these injustices as commonplace but must fight them with all one's strength. This fight begins, however, in the heart and it now had been laid to my charge to keep my own heart free of hatred and despair. This intimation made my heart heavy and, now that my father was irrecoverable, I wished that he had been beside me so that I could have searched his face for the answers which only the future would give me now. ✒

---

[1]See Joshua 24:15.

Fifth Avenue, Uptown[1]
A Letter from Harlem

There is a housing project standing now where the house in which we grew up once stood, and one of those stunted city trees is snarling where our doorway used to be. This is on the rehabilitated side of the avenue. The other side of the avenue—for progress takes time—has not been rehabilitated yet and it looks exactly as it looked in the days when we sat with our noses pressed against the windowpane, longing to be allowed to go "across the street." The grocery store which gave us credit is still there, and there can be no doubt that it is still giving credit. The people in the project certainly need it—far more, indeed, than they ever needed the project. The last time I passed by, the Jewish proprietor was still standing among his shelves, looking sadder and heavier but scarcely any older. Farther down the block stands the shoe-repair store in which our shoes were repaired until reparation became impossible and in which, then, we bought all our "new" ones. The Negro proprietor is still in the window, head down, working at the leather.

These two, I imagine, could tell a long tale if they would (perhaps they would be glad to if they could), having watched so many, for so long, struggling in the fishhooks, the barbed wire, of this avenue.

The avenue is elsewhere the renowned and elegant Fifth. The area I am describing, which, in today's gang parlance, would be called "the turf," is bounded by Lenox Avenue on the west, the Harlem River on the east, 135th Street on the north, and 130th Street on the south. We never lived beyond these boundaries; this is where we grew up. Walking along 145th Street, for example, familiar as it is, and similar, does not have the same impact because I do not know any of the people on the block. But when I turn east on 131st Street and Lenox Avenue, there is first a soda-pop joint, then a shoeshine "parlor," then a grocery store, then a dry cleaners', then the houses. All along the street there are people who watched me grow up, people who grew up with me, people I watched grow up along with my brothers and sisters; and, sometimes in my arms, sometimes underfoot, sometimes at my shoulder—or on it—their children, a riot, a forest of children, who include my nieces and nephews.

When we reach the end of this long block, we find ourselves on wide, filthy, hostile Fifth Avenue, facing that project which hangs over the avenue like a monument to the folly, and the cowardice, of good intentions. All along the block, for anyone who knows it, are immense human gaps, like craters. These gaps are not created merely by those who have moved away, inevitably into some other ghetto; or by those who have risen, almost always into a greater capacity for self-loathing and self-delusion; or yet by those who, by whatever means—the

---

[1]First published in *Esquire*, July 1960.

Second World War, the Korean war, a policeman's gun or billy,[1] a gang war, a brawl, madness, an overdose of heroin, or, simply, unnatural exhaustion—are dead. I am talking about those who are left, and I am talking principally about the young. What are they doing? Well, some, a minority, are fanatical churchgoers, members of the more extreme of the Holy Roller sects. Many, many more are "moslems," by affiliation or sympathy, that is to say that they are united by nothing more—and nothing less—than a hatred of the white world and all its works. They are present, for example, at every Buy Black street-corner meeting— meetings in which the speaker urges his hearers to cease trading with white men and establish a separate economy. Neither the speaker nor his hearers can possibly do this, of course, since Negroes do not own General Motors or RCA or the A & P, nor, indeed, do they own more than a wholly insufficient fraction of anything else in Harlem (those who *do* own anything are more interested in their profits than in their fellows). But these meetings nevertheless keep alive in the participators a certain pride of bitterness without which, however futile this bitterness may be, they could scarcely remain alive at all. Many have given up. They stay home and watch the TV screen, living on the earnings of their parents, cousins, brothers, or uncles, and only leave the house to go to the movies or to the nearest bar. "How're you making it?" one may ask, running into them along the block, or in the bar. "Oh, I'm TV-ing it"; with the saddest, sweetest, most shamefaced of smiles, and from a great distance. This distance one is compelled to respect; anyone who has traveled so far will not easily be dragged again into the world. There are further retreats, of course, than the TV screen or the bar. There are those who are simply sitting on their stoops, "stoned," animated for a moment only, and hideously, by the approach of someone who may lend them the money for a "fix." Or by the approach of someone from whom they can purchase it, one of the shrewd ones, on the way to prison or just coming out.

And the others, who have avoided all of these deaths, get up in the morning and go downtown to meet "the man." They work in the white man's world all day and come home in the evening to this fetid block. They struggle to instill in their children some private sense of honor or dignity which will help the child to survive. This means, of course, that they must struggle, stolidly, incessantly, to keep this sense alive in themselves, in spite of the insults, the indifference, and the cruelty they are certain to encounter in their working day. They patiently browbeat the landlord into fixing the heat, the plaster, the plumbing; this demands prodigious patience; nor is patience usually enough. In trying to make their hovels habitable, they are perpetually throwing good money after bad. Such frustration, so long endured, is driving many strong, admirable men and women whose only crime is color to the very gates of paranoia.

One remembers them from another time—playing handball in the playground, going to church, wondering if they were going to be promoted at school.

---

[1] Club.

One remembers them going off to war—gladly, to escape this block. One remembers their return. Perhaps one remembers their wedding day. And one sees where the girl is now—vainly looking for salvation from some other embittered, trussed,[1] and struggling boy—and sees the all-but-abandoned children in the streets.

Now I am perfectly aware that there are other slums in which white men are fighting for their lives, and mainly losing. I know that blood is also flowing through those streets and that the human damage there is incalculable. People are continually pointing out to me the wretchedness of white people in order to console me for the wretchedness of blacks. But an itemized account of the American failure does not console me and it should not console anyone else. That hundreds of thousands of white people are living, in effect, no better than the "niggers" is not a fact to be regarded with complacency. The social and moral bankruptcy suggested by this fact is one of the bitterest, most terrifying kind.

The people, however, who believe that this democratic anguish has some consoling value are always pointing out that So-and-So, white, and So-and-So, black, rose from the slums into the big time. The existence—the public existence—of, say, Frank Sinatra[2] and Sammy Davis, Jr.,[3] proves to them that America is still the land of opportunity and that inequalities vanish before the determined will. It proves nothing of the sort. The determined will is rare—at the moment, in this country, it is unspeakably rare—and the inequalities suffered by the many are in no way justified by the rise of a few. A few have always risen—in every country, every era, and in the teeth of regimes which can by no stretch of the imagination be thought of as free. Not all of these people, it is worth remembering, left the world better than they found it. The determined will is rare, but it is not invariably benevolent. Furthermore, the American equation of success with the big times reveals an awful disrespect for human life and human achievement. This equation has placed our cities among the most dangerous in the world and has placed our youth among the most empty and most bewildered. The situation of our youth is not mysterious. Children have never been very good at listening to their elders, but they have never failed to imitate them. They must, they have no other models. That is exactly what our children are doing. They are imitating our immorality, our disrespect for the pain of others.

All other slum dwellers, when the bank account permits it, can move out of the slum and vanish altogether from the eye of persecution. No Negro in this country has ever made that much money and it will be a long time before any Negro does. The Negroes in Harlem, who have no money, spend what they have on such gimcracks as they are sold. These include "wider" TV screens, more "faithful" hi-fi sets, more "powerful" cars, all of which, of course, are obsolete

---

[1] Bound or confined.

[2] Popular white singer and actor (1915–) born in Hoboken, New Jersey, who sang with the Harry James and Tommy Dorsey bands in the late thirties and early forties.

[3] Black entertainer, actor, and singer (1925–1990) who first became popular in movies such as *Mr. Wonderful* (1956) and *Porgy and Bess* (1959).

long before they are paid for. Anyone who has ever struggled with poverty knows how extremely expensive it is to be poor; and if one is a member of a captive population, economically speaking, one's feet have simply been placed on the treadmill forever. One is victimized, economically, in a thousand ways—rent, for example, or car insurance. Go shopping one day in Harlem—for anything—and compare Harlem prices and quality with those downtown.

The people who have managed to get off this block have only got as far as a more respectable ghetto. This respectable ghetto does not even have the advantages of the disreputable one—friends, neighbors, a familiar church, and friendly tradesmen; and it is not, moreover, in the nature of any ghetto to remain respectable long. Every Sunday, people who have left the block take the lonely ride back, dragging their increasingly discontented children with them. They spend the day talking, not always with words, about the trouble they've seen and the trouble— one must watch their eyes as they watch their children—they are only too likely to see. For children do not like ghettos. It takes them nearly no time to discover exactly why they are there.

The projects in Harlem are hated. They are hated almost as much as policemen, and this is saying a great deal. And they are hated for the same reason: both reveal, unbearably, the real attitude of the white world, no matter how many liberal speeches are made, no matter how many lofty editorials are written, no matter how many civil-rights commissions are set up.

The projects are hideous, of course, there being a law, apparently respected throughout the world, that popular housing shall be as cheerless as a prison. They are lumped all over Harlem, colorless, bleak, high, and revolting. The wide windows look out on Harlem's invincible and indescribable squalor: the Park Avenue railroad tracks, around which, about forty years ago, the present dark community began; the unrehabilitated houses, bowed down, it would seem, under the great weight of frustration and bitterness they contain; the dark, the ominous schoolhouses from which the child may emerge maimed, blinded, hooked, or enraged for life; and the churches, churches, block upon block of churches, niched in the walls like cannon in the walls of a fortress. Even if the administration of the projects were not so insanely humiliating (for example: one must report raises in salary to the management, which will then eat up the profit by raising one's rent; the management has the right to know who is staying in your apartment; the management can ask you to leave, at their discretion), the projects would still be hated because they are an insult to the meanest intelligence.

Harlem got its first private project, Riverton[1]—which is now, naturally, a slum—about twelve years ago because at that time Negroes were not allowed to

---

[1]The inhabitants of Riverton were much embittered by this description; they have, apparently, forgotten how their project came into being; and have repeatedly informed me that I cannot possibly be referring to Riverton, but to another housing project which is directly across the street. It is quite clear, I think, that I have no interest in accusing any individuals or families of the depredations herein described: but neither can I deny the evidence of my own eyes. Nor do

live in Stuyvesant Town.° Harlem watched Riverton go up, therefore, in the most violent bitterness of spirit, and hated it long before the builders arrived. They began hating it at about the time people began moving out of their condemned houses to make room for this additional proof of how thoroughly the white world despised them. And they had scarcely moved in, naturally, before they began smashing windows, defacing walls, urinating in the elevators, and fornicating in the playgrounds. Liberals, both white and black, were appalled at the spectacle. I was appalled by the liberal innocence—or cynicism, which comes out in practice as much the same thing. Other people were delighted to be able to point to proof positive that nothing could be done to better the lot of the colored people. They were, and are, right in one respect: that nothing can be done as long as they are treated like colored people. The people in Harlem know they are living there because white people do not think they are good enough to live anywhere else. No amount of "improvement" can sweeten this fact. Whatever money is now being earmarked to improve this, or any other ghetto, might as well be burnt. A ghetto can be improved in one way only: out of existence.

Similarly, the only way to police a ghetto is to be oppressive. None of the Police Commissioner's men, even with the best will in the world, have any way of understanding the lives led by the people they swagger about in twos and threes controlling. Their very presence is an insult, and it would be, even if they spent their entire day feeding gumdrops to children. They represent the force of the white world, and that world's real intentions are, simply, for that world's criminal profit and ease, to keep the black man corraled up here, in his place. The badge, the gun in the holster, and the swinging club make vivid what will happen should his rebellion become overt. Rare, indeed, is the Harlem citizen, from the most circumspect church member to the most shiftless adolescent, who does not have a long tale to tell of police incompetence, injustice, or brutality. I myself have witnessed and endured it more than once. The businessmen and racketeers also have a story. And so do the prostitutes. (And this is not, perhaps, the place to discuss Harlem's very complex attitude toward black policemen, nor the reasons, according to Harlem, that they are nearly all downtown.)

It is hard, on the other hand, to blame the policeman, blank, good-natured, thoughtless, and insuperably innocent, for being such a perfect representative of the people he serves. He, too, believes in good intentions and is astounded and offended when they are not taken for the deed. He has never, himself, done anything for which to be hated—which of us has?—and yet he is facing, daily and nightly, people who would gladly see him dead, and he knows it. There is no way for him not to know it: there are few things under heaven more unnerving than the silent, accumulating contempt and hatred of a people. He moves through Harlem,

---

° I blame anyone in Harlem for making the best of a dreadful bargain. But anyone who lives in Harlem and imagines that he has *not* struck this bargain, or that what he takes to be his status (in whose eyes?) protects him against the common pain, demoralization, and danger, is simply self-deluded. [Baldwin's note.]

therefore, like an occupying soldier in a bitterly hostile country; which is precisely what, and where, he is, and is the reason he walks in twos and threes. And he is not the only one who knows why he is always in company: the people who are watching him know why, too. Any street meeting, sacred or secular, which he and his colleagues uneasily cover has as its explicit or implicit burden the cruelty and injustice of the white domination. And these days, of course, in terms increasingly vivid and jubilant, it speaks of the end of that domination. The white policeman standing on a Harlem street corner finds himself at the very center of the revolution now occurring in the world. He is not prepared for it—naturally, nobody is—and, what is possibly much more to the point, he is exposed, as few white people are, to the anguish of the black people around him. Even if he is gifted with the merest mustard grain[1] of imagination, something must seep in. He cannot avoid observing that some of the children, in spite of their color, remind him of children he has known and loved, perhaps even of his own children. He knows that he certainly does not want *his* children living this way. He can retreat from his uneasiness in only one direction: into a callousness which very shortly becomes second nature. He becomes more callous, the population becomes more hostile, the situation grows more tense, and the police force is increased. One day, to everyone's astonishment, someone drops a match in the powder keg and everything blows up. Before the dust has settled or the blood congealed, editorials, speeches, and civil-rights commissions are loud in the land, demanding to know what happened. What happened is that Negroes want to be treated like men.

Negroes want to be treated like men: a perfectly straightforward statement containing only seven words. People who have mastered Kant,° Hegel,° Shakespeare, Marx,° Freud,° and the Bible find this statement utterly impenetrable. The idea seems to threaten profound, barely conscious assumptions. A kind of panic paralyzes their features, as though they found themselves trapped on the edge of a steep place. I once tried to describe to a very well-known American intellectual the conditions among Negroes in the South. My recital disturbed him and made him indignant; and he asked me in perfect innocence, "Why don't all the Negroes in the South move North?" I tried to explain what *has* happened, unfailingly, whenever a significant body of Negroes move North. They do not escape Jim Crow:° they merely encounter another, not-less-deadly variety. They do not move to Chicago, they move to the South Side; they do not move to New York, they move to Harlem. The pressure within the ghetto causes the ghetto walls to expand, and this expansion is always violent. White people hold the line as long as they can, and in as many ways as they can, from verbal intimidation to physical violence. But inevitably the border which has divided the ghetto from the rest of the world falls into the hands of the ghetto. The white people fall back bitterly before the black horde; the landlords make a tidy profit by raising the rent, chopping up the rooms, and all but dispensing with the upkeep; and what has once been a neighborhood turns into a "turf." This is precisely what happened

---

[1]See Matthew 17:20.

when Puerto Ricans[1] arrived in their thousands—and the bitterness thus caused is, as I write, being fought out all up and down those streets.

Northerners indulge in an extremely dangerous luxury. They seem to feel that because they fought on the right side during the Civil War, and won, they have earned the right merely to deplore what is going on in the South, without taking any responsibility for it; and that they can ignore what is happening in northern cities because what is happening in Little Rock[2] or Birmingham[3] is worse. Well, in the first place, it is not possible for anyone who has not endured both to know which is "worse." I know Negroes who prefer the South and white southerners, because "At least there, you haven't got to play any guessing games!" The guessing games referred to have driven more than one Negro to the narcotics ward, the madhouse, or the river. I know another Negro, a man very dear to me, who says, with conviction and with truth, "The spirit of the South is the spirit of America." He was born in the North and did his military training in the South. He did not, as far as I can gather, find the South "worse"; he found it, if anything, all too familiar. In the second place, though, even if Birmingham *is* worse, no doubt Johannesburg, South Africa, beats it by several miles, and Buchenwald[4] was one of the worst things that ever happened in the entire history of the world. The world has never lacked for horrifying examples; but I do not believe that these examples are meant to be used as justification for our own crimes. This perpetual justification empties the heart of all human feeling. The emptier our hearts become, the greater will be our crimes. Thirdly, the South is not merely an embarrassingly backward region, but a part of this country, and what happens there concerns every one of us.

As far as the color problem is concerned, there is but one great difference between the southern white and the northerner: the southerner remembers, historically and in his own psyche, a kind of Eden in which he loved black people and they loved him. Historically, the flaming sword[5] laid across this Eden is the Civil War. Personally, it is the southerner's sexual coming of age, when, without any warning, unbreakable taboos are set up between himself and his past. Everything, thereafter, is permitted him except the love he remembers and has never ceased to need. The resulting, indescribable torment affects every southern mind and is the basis of the southern hysteria.

None of this is true for the northerner. Negroes represent nothing to him personally, except, perhaps, the dangers of carnality. He never sees Negroes. Southerners see them all the time. Northerners never think about them whereas southerners are never really thinking of anything else. Negroes are, therefore, ignored in the North and are under surveillance in the South, and suffer hideously

---

[1]East Harlem, also known as Spanish Harlem, developed after World War II.

[2]State capitol of Arkansas where in 1957 President Eisenhower sent federal troops to enforce the 1954 Supreme Court ruling against segregation in public schools.

[3]Largest city in Alabama; where the Birmingham bus boycott took place.

[4]Nazi extermination camp near Weimar, Germany.

[5]See Genesis 3:22.

in both places. Neither the southerner nor the northerner is able to look on the Negro simply as a man. It seems to be indispensable to the national self-esteem that the Negro be considered either as a kind of ward (in which case we are told how many Negroes, comparatively, bought Cadillacs last year and how few, comparatively, were lynched), or as a victim (in which case we are promised that he will never vote in our assemblies or go to school with our kids). They are two sides of the same coin and the South will not change—*cannot* change—until the North changes. The country will not change until it reexamines itself and discovers what it really means by freedom. In the meantime, generations keep being born, bitterness is increased by incompetence, pride, and folly, and the world shrinks around us.

It is a terrible, an inexorable, law that one cannot deny the humanity of another without diminishing one's own: in the face of one's victim, one sees oneself. Walk through the streets of Harlem and see what we, this nation, have become. ✍

If Black English Isn't a Language,
Then Tell Me, What Is?[1]

The argument concerning the use, or the status, or the reality, of black English is rooted in American history and has absolutely nothing to do with the question the argument supposes itself to be posing. The argument has nothing to do with language itself but with the role of language. Language, incontestably, reveals the speaker. Language, also, far more dubiously, is meant to define the other—and, in this case, the other is refusing to be defined by a language that has never been able to recognize him.

People evolve a language in order to describe and thus control their circumstances or in order not to be submerged by a situation that they cannot articulate. (And if they cannot articulate it, they are submerged.) A Frenchman living in Paris speaks a subtly and crucially different language from that of the man living in Marseilles; neither sounds very much like a man living in Quebec; and they would all have great difficulty in apprehending what the man from Guadeloupe, or Martinique, is saying, to say nothing of the man from Senegal—although the "common" language of all these areas is French. But each has paid, and is paying, a different price for this "common" language, in which, as it turns out, they are not saying, and cannot be saying, the same things: They each have very different realities to articulate, or control.

What joins all languages, and all men, is the necessity to confront life, in order, not inconceivably, to outwit death: The price for this is the acceptance, and

---

[1] First published in *The New York Times*, July 29, 1979.

achievement, of one's temporal identity. So that, for example, though it is not taught in the schools (and this has the potential of becoming a political issue) the south of France still clings to its ancient and musical Provençal,[1] which resists being described as a "dialect." And much of the tension in the Basque countries,[2] and in Wales, is due to the Basque and Welsh determination not to allow their languages to be destroyed. This determination also feeds the flames in Ireland for among the many indignities the Irish have been forced to undergo at English hands is the English contempt for their language.

It goes without saying, then, that language is also a political instrument, means, and proof of power. It is the most vivid and crucial key to identity: It reveals the private identity, and connects one with, or divorces one from, the larger, public, or community identity. There have been, and are, times and places, when to speak a certain language could be dangerous, even fatal. Or, one may speak the same language, but in such a way that one's antecedents are revealed, or (one hopes) hidden. This is true in France, and is absolutely true in England: The range (and reign) of accents on that damp little island make England coherent for the English and totally incomprehensible for everyone else. To open your mouth in England is (if I may use black English) to "put your business in the street." You have confessed your parents, your youth, your school, your salary, your self-esteem, and, alas, your future.

Now, I do not know what white Americans would sound like if there had never been any black people in the United States, but they would not sound the way they sound. *Jazz*, for example, is a very specific sexual term, as in *jazz me, baby*, but white people purified it into the Jazz Age. *Sock it to me*, which means, roughly, the same thing, has been adopted by Nathaniel Hawthorne's° descendants with no qualms or hesitations at all, along with *let it all hang out* and *right on! Beat to his socks*, which was once the black's most total and despairing image of poverty, was transformed into a thing called the Beat Generation, which phenomenon was, largely, composed of *uptight*, middle-class white people, imitating poverty, trying to *get down*, to get *with it*, doing their *thing*, doing their despairing best to be *funky*, which we, the blacks, never dreamed of doing—we were funky, baby, like *funk* was going out of style.

Now, no one can eat his cake, and have it, too, and it is late in the day to attempt to penalize black people for having created a language that permits the nation its only glimpse of reality, a language without which the nation would be even more *whipped* than it is.

I say that the present skirmish is rooted in American history, and it is. Black English is the creation of the black diaspora.° Blacks came to the United States chained to each other, but from different tribes. Neither could speak the other's language. If two black people, at that bitter hour of the world's history, had been

---

[1] Literary language of the medieval troubadours of this area of France.
[2] Northern Spain and southwest France (the western Pyrenees), where Basque, a language of eight dialects, is spoken.

able to speak to each other, the institution of chattel[1] slavery could never have lasted as long as it did. Subsequently, the slave was given, under the eye, and the gun, of his master, Congo Square, and the Bible—or, in other words, and under those conditions, the slave began the formation of the black church, and it is within this unprecedented tabernacle that black English began to be formed. This was not, merely, as in the European example, the adoption of a foreign tongue, but an alchemy that transformed ancient elements into a new language: *A language comes into existence by means of brutal necessity, and the rules of the language are dictated by what the language must convey.*

There was a moment, in time, and in this place, when my brother, or my mother, or my father, or my sister, had to convey to me, for example, the danger in which I was standing from the white man standing just behind me, and to convey this with a speed and in a language, that the white man could not possibly understand, and that, indeed, he cannot understand, until today. He cannot afford to understand it. This understanding would reveal to him too much about himself and smash that mirror before which he has been frozen for so long.

Now, if this passion, this skill, this (to quote Toni Morrison°) "sheer intelligence," this incredible music, the mighty achievement of having brought a people utterly unknown to, or despised by "history"—to have brought this people to their present, troubled, troubling, and unassailable and unanswerable place—if this absolutely unprecedented journey does not indicate that black English is a language, I am curious to know what definition of languages is to be trusted.

A people at the center of the western world, and in the midst of so hostile a population, has not endured and transcended by means of what is patronizingly called a "dialect." We, the blacks, are in trouble, certainly, but we are not inarticulate because we are not compelled to defend a morality that we know to be a lie.

The brutal truth is that the bulk of the white people in America never had any interest in educating black people, except as this could serve white purposes. It is not the black child's language that is despised. It is his experience. A child cannot be taught by anyone who despises him, and a child cannot afford to be fooled. A child cannot be taught by anyone whose demand, essentially, is that the child repudiate his experience, and all that gives him sustenance, and enter a limbo in which he will no longer be black, and in which he knows that he can never become white. Black people have lost too many black children that way.

And, after all, finally, in a country with standards so untrustworthy, a country that makes heroes of so many criminal mediocrities, a country unable to face why so many of the nonwhite are in prison, or on the needle, or standing, futureless, in the streets—it may very well be that both the child, and his elder, have concluded that they have nothing whatever to learn from the people of a country that has managed to learn so little. ✐

---

[1]Movable property.

Dark Days[1]

I hit the streets when I was seven. It was the middle of the Depression and I learned how to sing out of hard experience. To be black was to confront, and to be forced to alter, a condition forged by history. To be white was to be forced to digest a delusion called white supremacy. Indeed, without confronting the history that has either given white people an identity or divested them of it, it is hardly possible for anyone who thinks of himself as white to know what a black person is talking about at all. Or to know what education is.

Not one of us—black or white—knows how to walk when we get here. Not one of us knows how to open a window, unlock a door. Not one of us can master a staircase. We are absolutely ignorant of the almost certain results of falling out of a five-story window. None of us comes here knowing enough not to play with fire. Nor can one of us drive a tank, fly a jet, hurl a bomb, or plant a tree.

We must be taught all that. We have to learn all that. The irreducible price of learning is realizing that you do not know. One may go further and point out—as any scientist, or artist, will tell you—that the more you learn, the less you know; but that means that you have begun to accept, and are even able to rejoice in, the relentless conundrum of your life.

"What happens," black poet Langston Hughes° asks, "to a dream deferred?" What happens, one may now ask, when a reality finds itself on a collision course with a fantasy? For the white people of this country have become, for the most part, sleepwalkers, and their somnambulation is reflected in the caliber of U.S. politics and politicians. And it helps explain why the blacks, who walked all those dusty miles and endured all that slaughter to get the vote, are now not voting.

Education occurs in a context and has a very definite purpose. The context is mainly unspoken, and the purpose very often unspeakable. But education can never be aimless, and it cannot occur in a vacuum.

I went to school in Harlem, quite a long time ago, during a time of great public and private strain and misery. Yet I was somewhat luckier than the Harlem children are today. I was going to school in the thirties, after the stock market crash. My family lived on Park Avenue, just above the uptown railroad tracks. The poverty of my childhood differed from poverty today in that the TV set was not sitting in front of our faces, forcing us to make unbearable comparisons between the room we were sitting in and the rooms we were watching, neither were we endlessly being told what to wear and drink and buy. We knew that we were poor, but then, everybody around us was poor.

The stock market crash had very little impact on our house. We had made no investments, and we wouldn't have known a stockbroker if one had patted us on the head. The market was part of the folly that always seemed to be overtaking white people, and it was always leading them to the same end. They wept briny

---

[1]First published in *Esquire*, October 1980.

tears, they put pistols to their heads or jumped out of windows. "That's just like white folks," was my father's contemptuous judgment, and we took our cue from him and felt no pity whatever. "You reap what you sow," Daddy said, grimly, carrying himself and his lunch box off to the factory, while we carried *our* lunch boxes off to school and, soon, into the streets, where my brother and I shined shoes and sold shopping bags. Mama went downtown or to the Bronx to clean white ladies' apartments.

Yet there *is* a moment from that time that I remember today and will probably always remember—a photograph from the center section of the *Daily News*. We were starving, people all over the country were starving. Yet here were several photographs of farmers, somewhere in America, slaughtering hogs and pouring milk onto the ground in order to force prices up (or keep them up), in order to protect their profits. I was much too young to know what to make of this beyond the obvious. People were being forced to starve, and being driven to death for the sake of money.

One might say that my recollection of this photograph marks a crucial moment in my education but one must also say that my education must have begun long before that moment, and dictated my reaction to the photograph. My education began, as does everyone's, with the people who towered over me, who were responsible for me, who were forming me. There were the people who loved me, in their fashion—whom I loved, in mine. These were people whom I had no choice but to imitate and, in time, to outwit. One realizes later that there is no one to outwit but oneself.

When I say that I was luckier than the children are today, I am deliberately making a very dangerous statement, a statement that I am willing, even anxious, to be called on. A black boy born in New York's Harlem in 1924 was born of southerners who had but lately been driven from the land, and therefore was born into a southern community. And this was incontestably a community in which every parent was responsible for every child. Any grown-up, seeing me doing something he thought was wrong, could (and did) beat my behind and then carry me home to my Mama and Daddy and tell them why he beat my behind. Mama and Daddy would thank him and then beat my behind again.

I learned respect for my elders. And I mean respect. I do not mean fear. In spite of his howling, a child can tell when the hand that strikes him means to help him or to harm him. A child can tell when he is loved. One sees this sense of confidence emerge, slowly, in the conduct of the child—the first fruits of his education.

Every human being born begins to be *civilized* the moment he or she is born. Since we all arrive here absolutely helpless, with no way of getting a decent meal or of moving from one place to another without human help (and human help exacts a human price), there is no way around that. But this is civilization with a small *c*. Civilization with a large *C* is something else again. So is education with a small *e* different from Education with a large *E*. In the lowercase, education refers to the relations that actually obtain among human beings. In the uppercase, it refers to power. Or, to put it another way, my father, mother, brothers, sisters, lovers, friends, sons, daughters civilize me in quite another way than the state intends. And the education I can receive from an afternoon with *Picasso*,° or from taking one of my nieces or nephews to the movies, is not at all what the state has in mind when it speaks of Education.

For I still remember, lucky though I was, that reality altered when I started school. My mother asked me about one of my teachers; was she white or colored? My answer, which was based entirely on a child's observation, was that my teacher was "a little bit colored and a little bit white." My mother laughed. So did the teacher. I have no idea how she might react today. In fact, my answer had been far more brutally accurate than I could have had any way of knowing. But I wasn't penalized or humiliated for my unwitting apprehension of the Faulknerian° torment.

Harlem was not an all-black community during the time I was growing up. It was only during the Second World War that Harlem began to become entirely black. This transformation had something to do, in part, with the relations between black and white soldiers called together under one banner. These relations were so strained and volatile that, however equal the soldiers might be deemed, it was thought best to keep them separate when off the base. And Harlem, officially or not, was effectively off limits for white soldiers.

Harlem's transformation relates to the military in another way. The Second World War ended the Depression by throwing America into a war economy. We are in a war economy still, and we are only slightly embarrassed by the difficulty of officially declaring a Third World War. But where there's a will, I hate to suggest, there's often a way.

When I was growing up there were Finns, Jews, Poles, West Indians, and various other exotics scattered all over Harlem. We could all be found eating as much as we could hold in Father Divine's restaurants[1] for fifteen cents. I fought every campaign of the Italian-Ethiopian War° with the oldest son of the Italian fruit and vegetable vendor who lived next door to us. I lost. Inevitably. He knew who had the tanks.

The new prosperity caused many people to pack their bags and go. Some blacks got as far as Queens, Jamaica, or the Bronx. One might say that a certain rupture began during this time. We began to lose each other. The whites who left moved directly into the American mainstream, as we like to say, without the complexity

---

[1]George Baker (1880?–1965) opened a church in Brooklyn, proclaimed himself God, and established a nondenominational, interracial cult that demanded complete celibacy. In 1930 he took the name Father Divine and soon became enormously wealthy, one of the largest landlords in Harlem. Among many other enterprises, he ran restaurants and gave lavish free banquets to gain followers. After a series of scandals in the late 1930s, his influence waned; he moved to "exile" in Philadelphia, where he died.

of the smallest regret and without a backward look. The blacks moved into limbo. The doors opened for white people and (especially) for their children. The schools, the unions, industry, and the arts were not opened for blacks. Not then, and not now.

This means—and meant—that the black family had moved onto yet another sector of a vast and endless battlefield. The people I am speaking of came mainly from the South. They had been driven north by the sheer impossibility of remaining in the South. They came with nothing. And the good Lord knows it was a hard journey. Their children had never seen the South: their challenges came from the hard pavements of a hostile city, and their parents had no arms with which to protect them from its devastation.

When I went to work as a civilian for the Army in 1942, I earned about three times as much in a week as my father ever had. This was not without its effect on my father. His authority was being eroded, he was being cheated of the reality of his role. And I, of course, had absolutely no way of understanding the ferocious complexity of his reaction. I did not understand the depth and power and reality of his pain.

The blacks who moved out of Harlem were not received with open arms by their countrymen. They were mocked and despised and their children were in greater danger than ever. No friendly neighbor was likely to correct the child. The child would either rise up into a seeming responsibility and respectability, one step ahead of paranoia, or drop down to the needle and the prison. And since there is not a single institution in this country that is not a racist institution—beginning with the churches, and by no means ignoring the unions—blacks were unable to seize the tools with which they could forge a genuine autonomy.

The new prosperity also brought in the blight of housing projects to keep the nigger in his place. Whites, thinking "If you can't beat them, stone them," dumped drugs into the ghetto, and what had once been a community began to fragment. The space between people grew wider. The question of identity became a paralyzing one. Being "accepted" could cause even greater anguish, and was a more deadly danger, than being spat on as a nigger.

I was luckier in school than the children are today. My situation, however grim, was relatively coherent. I was not yet lost. Though most of my teachers were white, many were black. And some of the white teachers were very definitely on the Left. They opposed Franco's Spain and Mussolini's Italy and Hitler's Third Reich.[1] For these extreme opinions, several were placed in blacklists and drummed out of the academic community—to the everlasting shame of that community.

The black teachers, paradoxically, were another matter. They were laconic about politics but single-minded about the future of black students. Many of them were survivors of the Harlem Renaissance° and wanted us black students to know that we could do, become, anything. We were not, in any way whatever, to be

---

[1]All three were Fascist regimes.

limited by the Republic's estimation of black people. *They* had refused to be defined that way, and they had, after all, paid some dues.

I did not, then, obviously really know who some of these people were. Gertrude E. Ayers, for example, my principal at P.S. 24, was the first black principal in the history of New York City schools. I did not know, then, what this meant. Dr. Kenneth Clark[1] informed me in the early sixties that Ayers was the only one until 1963. And there was the never-to-be-forgotten Mr. Porter, my black math teacher, who soon gave up any attempt to teach me math. I had been born, apparently, with some kind of deformity that resulted in a total inability to count. From arithmetic to geometry, I never passed a single test. Porter took his failure very well and compensated for it by helping me run the school magazine. He assigned me a story about Harlem for this magazine, a story that he insisted demanded serious research. Porter took me downtown to the main branch of the public library at Forty-second Street and waited for me while I began my research. He was very proud of the story I eventually turned in. But I was so terrified that afternoon that I vomited all over his shoes in the subway.

The teachers I am talking about accepted my limits. I could begin to accept them without shame. I could trust them when they suggested the possibilities open to me. I understood why they changed the list of colleges they had hoped to send me to, since I was clearly never going to become either an athlete or a businessman.

I was an exceedingly shy, withdrawn, and uneasy student. Yet my teachers somehow made me believe that I could learn. And when I could scarcely see for myself any future at all, my teachers told me that the future was mine. The question of color was but another detail, somewhere between being six feet tall and being six feet under. In the long meantime, everything was up to me.

Every child's sense of himself is terrifyingly fragile. He is really at the mercy of his elders, and when he finds himself totally at the mercy of his peers, who know as little about themselves as he, it is because his peers' elders have abandoned them. I am talking, then, about morale, that sense of self *with which the child must be invested.* No child can do it alone.

But children, I submit, cannot be fooled. They can only be betrayed by adults, not fooled—for adults, unlike children, are fooled very easily, and only because they wish to be. Children—innocence being both real and monstrous—intimidate, harass, blackmail, terrify, and sometimes even kill one another. But no child can fool another child the way one adult can fool another. It would be impossible, for example, for children to bring off the spectacle—the scandal—of the Republican or Democratic conventions. They do not have enough to hide—or, if you like, to flaunt.

---

[1](1914–) Black psychologist, educator, and director of Metropolitan Applied Research Center; author of *Desegregation: An Appraisal of the Evidence* (1953), *Prejudice and Your Child* (1955), and *Dark Ghetto* (1965).

I remember being totally unable to recite the Pledge of Allegiance until I was seven years old. Why? At seven years old I was certainly not a card-carrying Communist, and no one had told me not to recite "with liberty and justice for all." In fact, my father thought that I should recite it for safety's sake. But I knew that he believed it no more than I, and that *his* recital of the pledge had done nothing to contribute to his safety, to say nothing of the tormented safety of his children.

How did I know that? How does any child know that? I knew it from watching my father's face, my father's hours, days, and nights. I knew it from scrubbing the floors of the tenements in which we lived, knew it from the eviction notices, knew it from the bitter winters when the landlord gave us no heat, knew it from my mother's face when a new child was born, knew it by contrasting the kitchens in which my mother was employed with *our* kitchen, knew it from the kind of desperate miasma in which you grow up realizing that you have been born to be despised. Forever.

It remains impossible to describe the Byzantine[1] labyrinth black people find themselves in when they attempt to save their children. A high school diploma, which had almost no meaning in my day, nevertheless suggested that you had been to school. But today it operates merely as a credential for jobs—for the most part nonexistent—that demand virtually nothing in the way of education. And the attendance certificate merely states that you have been through school without having managed to learn anything.

The educational system of this country is, in short, designed to destroy the black child. It does not matter whether it destroys him by stoning him in the ghetto or by driving him mad in the isolation of Harvard. And whoever has survived this crucible is a witness to the power of the Republic's educational system.

It is an absolute wonder and an overwhelming witness to the power of the human spirit that any black person in this country has managed to become, in any way whatever, educated. The miracle is that some have stepped out of the rags of the Republic's definitions to assume the great burden and glory of their humanity and of their responsibility for one another. It is an extraordinary achievement to be trapped in the dungeon of color and to dare to shake down its walls and to step out of it, leaving the jailhouse keeper in the rubble.

But for the black man with the attaché case, or for the black boy on the needle, it has always been the intention of the Republic to promulgate and guarantee his dependence on this Republic. For although one cannot really be educated to believe a lie, one can be forced to surrender to it.

And there is, after all, no reason *not* to be dependent on one's country or, at least, to maintain a viable and fruitful relationship with it. But this is not possible if you see your country and your country does not see you. It is not possible if the entire effort of your countrymen is an attempt to destroy your sense of reality.

---

[1]Complicated, labyrinthian, from the intricate art and architecture of Byzantium in the fifth century A.D.

This is an election year. I am standing in the streets of Harlem, Newark, or Watts,[1] and I have been asked a question.

Now, what am I to say concerning the presidential candidates, season after ignoble season? Carter[2] has learned to sing "Let my people go," speaking of the hostages[3] in Iran, while taking no responsibility at all for the political prisoners all over his home state of Georgia. He is prepared for massive retaliation against the Ayatollah Khomeini but, after Miami,[4] can only assure the city's blacks that violence is not the answer. This despite the fact that in the event of "massive retaliation," blacks will assuredly be sent to fight in Iran—and for what? Despite the news of the acquittal of the four Miami policemen who beat the black man McDuffie to death. That news made page twenty-four of *The New York Times*. The uprising resulting from the acquittal made page one.

The ghetto man, woman, or child who may already wonder why curbing inflation means starving him out of existence (or into the Army) may also wonder why violence is right for Carter, or for any other white man, but wrong for the black man. The ghetto people I am talking to, or about, are not at all stupid, and if I lie to them, how can I teach them?

Dark days. Recently I was back in the South, more than a quarter of a century after the Supreme Court[5] decision that outlawed segregation in the Republic's schools, a decision to be implemented with "all deliberate speed." My friends with whom I had worked and walked in those dark days are no longer in their teens, or even their thirties. Their children are now as old as their parents were then, and, obviously, some of my comrades are now roughly as old as I, and I am facing sixty. Dark days, for we know how much there is to be done and how unlikely it is that we will have another sixty years. We know, for that matter, how utterly improbable it is—indeed, miraculous—that we can still have a drink, or a pork chop, or a laugh together.

I walked into an Alabama courtroom, in Birmingham, where my old friend the Reverend Fred Shuttlesworth was sitting. I had not seen him in more than twenty years; his church was bombed[6] shortly after I last saw him. Now, something like twenty-two years later, the man accused of bombing the church was on trial. The Reverend Shuttlesworth was very cool, much cooler than I, given that the trial had been delayed twenty-two years. How slowly the mills of justice grind if one is black. What in the world can possibly happen in the mind and heart of a black student, observing, who must stumble out of this courtroom and back to Yale?

---

[1]Areas in New York, New Jersey, and Los Angeles with large, impoverished black populations.
[2]James Earl, Jr. (1924–), thirty-ninth president of the United States (1977–1981).
[3]Released on January 20, 1981, a few minutes after Ronald Reagan was sworn in as president.
[4]May 1980: 16 died, 371 were injured, and millions of dollars of property was damaged.
[5]1954.
[6]On September 15, 1963, the Sixteenth Street Baptist Church in Birmingham was bombed; four black children were killed and fourteen were injured.

It was a desegregated(!) courtroom, and it was certainly a mock trial. The only reason the defendant, J. B. Stoner, was not legally, openly acquitted was that the jury—mostly women, and one exceedingly visible black man dressed in a canary-colored suit (I had the feeling that no one ever addressed a word to him)—could not quite endorse Stoner's conviction (among his many others about blacks) that being born a Jew should be made a crime "punishable by death—legally." (He hastened to add, "I'm against illegal violence.") Forced to admit—by the reading of newspaper quotes—that he had crowed, upon hearing of the assassination of Martin Luther King, Jr.,° "Well, he's a good nigger *now*," Stoner said, "Hell, that ain't got nothing to do with violence. The man was already dead."

He was not acquitted, but he received the minimum sentence—ten years—and is free on bail.

If I put this travesty back to back with the case of—for example—The Wilmington Ten,[1] I will begin to suggest to my students the meaning of *education*.

On the first day of class last winter at Bowling Green State University, where I was a visiting writer-in-residence, one of my white students, in a racially mixed class, asked me, "Why does the white hate the nigger?"

I was caught off guard. I simply had not had the courage to open the subject right away. I underestimated the children, and I am afraid that most of the middle-aged do. The subject, I confess, frightened me, and it would never have occurred to me to throw it at them so nakedly. No doubt, since I am not totally abject, I would have found a way to discuss what we refer to as interracial tension. What my students made me realize (and I consider myself eternally in their debt) was that the notion of interracial tension hides a multitude of delusions and is, in sum, a cowardly academic formulation. In the ensuing discussion the children, very soon, did not need me at all, except as a vaguely benign adult presence. They began talking to one another, and they were not talking about race. They were talking of their desire to know one another, their need to know one another; each was trying to enter into the experience of the other. The exchanges were sharp and remarkably candid, but never fogged by an unadmitted fear or hostility. They were trying to become whole. They were trying to put themselves and their country together. They would be facing hard choices when they left this academy. And why was it a condition of American life that they would then be forced to be strangers?

The reality, the depth, and the persistence of the delusion of white supremacy in this country causes any real concept of education to be as remote, and as much to be feared, as change or freedom itself. What black men here have always known

---

[1]Nine blacks and one white were sentenced to terms of twenty-three to twenty-four years in prison for fire-bombing property and for conspiracy to assault during riots in Wilmington, North Carolina, in 1971.

is now beginning to be clear all over the world. Whatever it is that white Americans want, it is not freedom—neither for themselves nor for others.

"It's you who'll have the blues," Langston Hughes° said, "not me. Just wait and see." ✒

Here Be Dragons[1]

To be androgynous, *Webster's* informs us, is to have both male and female characteristics. This means that there is a man in every woman and a woman in every man. Sometimes this is recognized only when the chips are, brutally, down—when there is no longer any way to avoid this recognition. But love between a man and a woman, or love between any two human beings, would not be possible did we not have available to us the spiritual resources of both sexes.

To be androgynous does not imply both male and female sexual equipment, which is the state, uncommon, of the hermaphrodite. However, the existence of the hermaphrodite reveals, in intimidating exaggeration, the truth concerning every human being—which is why the hermaphrodite is called a freak. The human being does not, in general, enjoy being intimidated by what he/she finds in the mirror.

The hermaphrodite, therefore, may make his/her living in side shows or brothels, whereas the merely androgynous are running banks or filling stations or maternity wards, churches, armies or countries.

The last time you had a drink, whether you were alone or with another, you were having a drink with an androgynous human being; and this is true for the last time you broke bread or, as I have tried to suggest, the last time you made love.

There seems to be a vast amount of confusion in the western world concerning these matters, but love and sexual activity are not synonymous: Only by becoming inhuman can the human being pretend that they are. The mare is not obliged to love the stallion, nor is the bull required to love the cow. They are doing what comes naturally.

But this by no means sums up the state or the possibilities of the human being in whom the awakening of desire fuels imagination and in whom imagination fuels desire. In other words, it is not possible for the human being to be as simple as a stallion or a mare, because the human imagination is perpetually required to examine, control, and redefine reality, of which we must assume ourselves to be the center and the key. Nature and revelation are perpetually challenging each other; this relentless tension is one of the keys to human history and to what is known as the human condition.

---

[1]First published as "Freaks and the American Ideal of Manhood" in *Playboy*, January 1985.

Now, I can speak only of the western world and must rely on my own experience, but the simple truth of this universal duality, this perpetual possibility of communion and completion, seems so alarming that I have watched it lead to addiction, despair, death, and madness. Nowhere have I seen this panic more vividly than in my country and in my generation.

The American idea of sexuality appears to be rooted in the American idea of masculinity. Idea may not be the precise word, for the idea of one's sexuality can only with great violence be divorced or distanced from the idea of the self. Yet something resembling this rupture has certainly occurred (and is occurring) in American life, and violence has been the American daily bread since we have heard of America. This violence, furthermore, is not merely literal and actual but appears to be admired and lusted after, and the key to the American imagination.

All countries or groups make of their trials a legend or, as in the case of Europe, a dubious romance called "history." But no other country has ever made so successful and glamorous a romance out of genocide and slavery; therefore, perhaps the word I am searching for is not idea but ideal.

The American *ideal*, then, of sexuality appears to be rooted in the American ideal of masculinity. This ideal has created cowboys and Indians, good guys and bad guys, punks and studs, tough guys and softies, butch and faggot, black and white. It is an ideal so paralytically infantile that it is virtually forbidden—as an unpatriotic act—that the American boy evolve into the complexity of manhood.

The exigencies[1] created by the triumph of the Industrial Revolution—or, in other terms, the rise of Europe to global dominance—had, among many mighty effects, that of commercializing the roles of men and women. Men became the propagators, or perpetrators, of property, and women became the means by which that property was protected and handed down. One may say that this was nothing more than the ancient and universal division of labor—women nurtured the tribe, men battled for it—but the concept of property had undergone a change. This change was vast and deep and sinister.

For the first time in human history, a man was reduced not merely to a thing but to a thing the value of which was determined, absolutely, by that thing's commercial value. That this pragmatic principle dictated the slaughter of the native American, the enslavement of the black and the monumental rape of Africa—to say nothing of creating the wealth of the Western world—no one, I suppose, will now attempt to deny.

But this principle also raped and starved Ireland, for example, as well as Latin America, and it controlled the pens of the men who signed the Declaration of Independence—a document more clearly commercial than moral. This is how, and why, the American Constitution was able to define the slave as three-fifths of a man, from which legal and commercial definition it legally followed that a black man "had no rights a white man was bound to respect."

---

[1]Urgent requirements.

Ancient maps of the world—when the the world was flat—inform us, concerning that void where America was waiting to be discovered, HERE BE DRAGONS. Dragons may not have been here then, but they are certainly here now, breathing fire, belching smoke; or, to be less literary and biblical about it, attempting to intimidate the mores, morals, and morality of this particular and peculiar time and place. Nor, since this country is the issue of the entire globe and is also the most powerful nation currently to be found on it, are we speaking only of this time and place. And it can be said that the monumental struggles being waged in our time and not only in this place resemble, in awesome ways, the ancient struggle between those who insisted that the world was flat and those who apprehended that it was round.

Of course, I cannot possibly imagine what it can be like to have both male and female sexual equipment. That's a load of family jewels to be hauling about, and it seems to me that it must make choice incessant or impossible—or, in terms unavailable to me, unnecessary. Yet, not to be frivolous concerning what I know I cannot—or, more probably, dare not—imagine, I hazard that the physically androgynous state must create an all-but-intolerable loneliness, since we all exist, afer all, and crucially, in the eye of the beholder. We all react to and, to whatever extent, become what that eye sees. This judgment begins in the eyes of one's parents (the crucial, the definitive, the all-but-everlasting judgment), and so we move, in the vast and claustrophobic gallery of Others, on up or down the line, to the eye of one's enemy or one's friend or one's lover.

It is virtually impossible to trust one's human value without the collaboration or corroboration of that eye—which is to say that no one can live without it. One can, of course, instruct that eye as to what to see, but this effort, which is nothing less than ruthless intimidation, is wounding and exhausting: While it can keep humiliation at bay, it confirms the fact that humiliation is the central danger of one's life. And since one cannot risk love without risking humiliation, love becomes impossible.

I hit the streets when I was about six or seven, like most black kids of my generation, running errands, doing odd jobs. This was in the black world—my turf—which means that I felt protected. I think that I really was, though poverty is poverty and we were, if I may say so, among the truly needy, in spite of the tins of corned beef we got from home relief every week, along with prunes. (Catsup[1] had not yet become a vegetable; indeed, I don't think we had ever heard of it.) My mother fried corned beef, she boiled it, she baked it, she put potatoes in it, she put rice in it, she disguised it in corn bread, she boiled it in soup(!), she wrapped it in cloth, she beat it with a hammer, she banged it against the wall, she threw it onto the ceiling. Finally, she gave up, for nothing could make us eat it anymore,

---

[1]Reference to a suggestion, never implemented, during the Reagan administration (1980–1988), that catsup be defined as a vegetable in order to meet a dietary requirement that school lunches contain two vegetables.

and the tins reproachfully piled up on the shelf above the bathtub—along with the prunes, which we also couldn't eat anymore. While I won't speak for my brothers and sisters, I can't bear corned-beef hash or prunes even today.

Poverty. I remember one afternoon when someone dropped a dime in front of the subway station at 125th Street and Lenox Avenue and I and a man of about forty both scrambled for it. The man won, giving me a cheerful goodbye as he sauntered down the subway steps. I was bitterly disappointed, a dime being a dime, but I laughed, too.

The truly needy. Once, my father gave me a dime—the last dime in the house, though I didn't know that—to go to the store for kerosene for the stove, and I fell on the icy streets and dropped the dime and lost it. My father beat me with an iron cord from the kitchen to the back room and back again, until I lay, half-conscious, on my belly on the floor.

Yet—strange though it is to realize this, looking back—I never felt threatened in those years, when I was growing up in Harlem, my home town. I think this may be because it was familiar; the white people who lived there then were as poor as we, and there was no TV setting our teeth on edge with exhortations to buy what we could never hope to afford.

On the other hand, I was certainly unbelievably unhappy and pathologically shy, but that, I felt, was nobody's fault but mine. My father kept me in short pants longer than he should have, and I had been told, and I believed, that I was ugly. This meant that the idea of myself as a sexual possibility, or target, as a creature capable of desire, had never entered my mind. And it entered my mind, finally, by means of the rent made in my short boy-scout pants by a man who lured me into a hallway, saying that he wanted to send me to the store. That was the very last time I agreed to run an errand for any stranger.

Yet I was, in peculiar truth, a very lucky boy. Shortly after I turned sixteen, a Harlem racketeer, a man of about thirty-eight, fell in love with me, and I will be grateful to that man until the day I die. I showed him all my poetry, because I had no one else in Harlem to show it to, and even now, I sometimes wonder what on earth his friends could have been thinking, confronted with stingy-brimmed, mustachioed, razor-toting Poppa and skinny, popeyed Me when he walked me (rarely) into various shady joints, I drinking ginger ale, he drinking brandy. I think I was supposed to be his nephew, some nonsense like that, though he was Spanish and Irish, with curly black hair. But I knew that he was showing me off and wanted his friends to be happy for him—which, indeed, if the way they treated me can be taken as a barometer, they were. They seemed to feel that this was his business—that he would be in trouble if it became *their* business.

And though I loved him, too—in my way, a boy's way—I was mightily tormented, for I was still a child evangelist, which everybody knew, Lord. My soul looks back and wonders.

For what this really means is that all of the American categories of male and female, straight or not, black or white, were shattered, thank heaven, very early in my life. Not without anguish, certainly; but once you have discerned the meaning of a label, it may seem to define you for others, but it does not have the power to define you to yourself.

This prepared me for my life downtown, where I quickly discovered that my existence was the punch line of a dirty joke.

The condition that is now called gay was then called queer. The operative word was *faggot* and, later, pussy, but those epithets really had nothing to do with the question of sexual preference: You were being told simply that you had no balls.

I certainly had no desire to harm anyone, nor did I understand how anyone could look at me and suppose me physically capable of *causing* any harm. But boys and men chased me, saying I was a danger to their sisters. I was thrown out of cafeterias and rooming houses because I was "bad" for the neighborhood.

The cops watched all this with a smile, never making the faintest motion to protect me or to disperse my attackers; in fact, I was even more afraid of the cops than I was of the populace.

By the time I was nineteen, I was working in the Garment Center. I was getting on very badly at home and delayed going home after work as long as possible. At the end of the workday, I would wander east, to the Forty-second Street Library. Sometimes, I would sit in Bryant Park—but I discovered that I could not sit there long. I fled, to the movies, and so discovered Forty-second Street. Today that street is exactly what it was when I was an adolescent: It has simply become more blatant.

There were no X-rated movies then, but there were, so to speak, X-rated audiences. For example, I went in complete innocence to the Apollo, on Forty-second Street, because foreign films were shown there—*The Lower Depths, Childhood of Maxim Gorky, La Bête Humaine*—and I walked out as untouched (by human hands) as I had been when I walked in. There were the stores, mainly on Sixth Avenue, that sold "girlie" magazines. These magazines were usually to be found at the back of the store, and I don't so much remember them as I remember the silent men who stood there. They stood, it seemed, for hours, with the magazines in their hands and a kind of miasma in their eyes. There were all kinds of men, mostly young and, in those days, almost exclusively white. Also, for what it's worth, they were heterosexual, since the images they studied, at crotch level, were those of women.

Actually, I guess I hit Forty-second Street twice and have very nearly blotted the first time out. I was not at the mercy of the street the first time, for, though I may have dreaded *going* home, I hadn't *left* home yet. Then, I spent a lot of time in the library, and I stole odds and ends out of Woolworth's—with no compunction at all, due to the way they treated us in Harlem. When I went to the movies, I imagine that a combination of innocence and terror prevented me from too clearly apprehending the action taking place in the darkness of the Apollo— though I understood it well enough to remain standing a great deal of the time. This cunning stratagem failed when, one afternoon, the young boy I was standing behind put his hand behind him and grabbed my cock at the very same moment that a young boy came up behind me and put his cock against my hand: Ignobly enough, I fled, though I doubt that I was missed. The men in the men's room frightened me, so I moved in and out as quickly as possible, and I also dimly felt, I remember, that I didn't want to "fool around" and so risk hurting the feelings of my uptown friend.

But if I was paralyzed by guilt and terror, I cannot be judged or judge myself too harshly, for I remember the faces of the men. These men, so far from being or resembling faggots, looked and sounded like the vigilantes who banded together on weekends to beat faggots up. (And I was around long enough, suffered enough, and learned enough to be forced to realize that this was very often true. I might not have learned this if I had been a white boy; but sometimes a white man will tell a black boy anything, everything, weeping briny tears. He knows that the black boy can never betray him, for no one will believe his testimony.)

These men looked like cops, football players, soldiers, sailors, Marines or bank presidents, admen, boxers, construction workers; they had wives, mistresses, and children. I sometimes saw them in other settings—in, as it were, the daytime. Sometimes they spoke to me, sometimes not, for anguish has many days and styles. But I had first seen them in the men's room, sometimes on their knees, peering up into the stalls, or standing at the urinal stroking themselves, staring at another man, stroking, and with this miasma in their eyes. Sometimes, eventually, inevitably, I would find myself in bed with one of these men, a despairing and dreadful conjunction, since their need was as relentless as quicksand and as impersonal, and sexual rumor concerning blacks had preceded me. As for sexual roles, these were created by the imagination and limited only by one's stamina.

At bottom, what I had learned was that the male desire for a male roams everywhere, avid, desperate, unimaginably lonely, culminating often in drugs, piety, madness or death. It was also dreadfully like watching myself at the end of a long, slow-moving line: Soon I would be next. All of this was very frightening. It was lonely and impersonal and demeaning. I could not believe—after all, I was only nineteen—that I could have been driven to the lonesome place where these men and I met each other so soon, to stay.

The American idea of masculinity: There are few things under heaven more difficult to understand or, when I was younger, to forgive.

During the Second World War (the first one having failed to make the world safe for democracy)[1] and some time after the Civil War (which had failed, unaccountably, to liberate the slave), life for niggers was fairly rough in Greenwich Village. There were only about three of us, if I remember correctly, when I first hit those streets, and I was the youngest, the most visible, and the most vulnerable.

---

[1]The claim made at the start of World War I.

On every street corner, I was called a faggot. This meant that I was despised, and, however horrible this is, it is clear. What was *not* clear at that time of my life was what motivated the men and boys who mocked and chased me; for, if they found me when they were alone, they spoke to me very differently—frightening me, I must say, into a stunned and speechless paralysis. For when they were alone, they spoke very gently and wanted me to take them home and make love. (They could not take *me* home; they lived with their families.) The bafflement and the pain this caused in me remain beyond description. I was far too terrified to be able to accept their propositions, which could only result, it seemed to me, in making myself a candidate for gang rape. At the same time, I was moved by their loneliness, their halting, nearly speechless need. But I did not understand it.

One evening, for example, I was standing at the bottom of the steps to the Waverly Place subway station, saying goodbye to some friends who were about to take the subway. A gang of boys stood at the top of the steps and cried, in high, feminine voices, "Is this where the fags meet?"

Well. This meant that I certainly could not go back upstairs but would have to take the subway with my friends and get off at another station and maneuver my way home. But one of the gang saw me and, without missing a beat or saying a word to his friends, called my name and came down the steps, throwing one arm around me and asking where I'd been. He had let me know, some time before, that he wanted me to take him home—but I was surprised that he could be so open before his friends, who for their part seemed to find nothing astonishing in this encounter and disappeared, probably in search of other faggots.

The boys who are left of that time and place are all my age or older. But many of them are dead, and I remember how some of them died—some in the streets, some in the Army, some on the needle, some in jail. Many years later, we managed, without ever becoming friends—it was too late for that—to be friendly with one another. One of these men and I had a very brief, intense affair shortly before he died. He was on drugs and knew that he could not live long. "What a waste," he said, and he was right.

One of them said, "My God, Jimmy, you were moving so fast in those years, you never stopped to talk to me."

I said, "That's right, baby; I didn't stop because I didn't want you to think that I was trying to seduce you."

"Man," he said, indescribably, "why didn't you?"

But the queer—not yet gay—world was an even more intimidating area of this hall of mirrors. I knew that I was in the hall and present at this company—but the mirrors threw back only brief and distorted fragments of myself.

In the first place, as I have said, there were very few black people in the Village in those years, and of that handful, I was decidedly the most improbable. Perhaps, as they say in the theater, I was a hard type to cast; yet I was eager, vulnerable, and lonely. I was terribly shy, but boys *are* shy. I am saying that I don't think I felt absolutely, irredeemably grotesque—nothing that a friendly wave of the wand couldn't alter—but I was miserable. I moved through that world very quickly; I have described it as "my season in hell," for I was never able to make my peace with it.

It wasn't only that I didn't wish to seem or sound like a woman, for it was this detail that most harshly first struck my eye and ear. I am sure that I was afraid that I already seemed and sounded too much like a woman. In my childhood, at least until my adolescence, my playmates had called me a sissy. It seemed to me that many of the people I met were making fun of women, and I didn't see why. *I* certainly needed all the friends I could get, male *or* female, and women had nothing to do with whatever my trouble might prove to be.

At the same time, I had already been sexually involved with a couple of white women in the Village. There were virtually no black women there when I hit those streets, and none who needed or could have afforded to risk herself with an odd, raggedy-assed black boy who clearly had no future. (The first black girl I met who dug me I fell in love with, lived with and almost married. But I met her, though I was only twenty-two, many light-years too late.)

The white girls I had known or been involved with—different categories—had paralyzed me, because I simply did not know what, apart from my sex, they wanted. Sometimes it was great, sometimes it was just moaning and groaning, but, ultimately, I found myself at the mercy of a double fear. The fear of the world was bearable until it entered the bedroom. But it sometimes entered the bedroom by means of the motives of the girl, who intended to civilize you into becoming an appendage or who had found a black boy to sleep with because she wanted to humiliate her parents. Not an easy scene to play, in any case, since it can bring out the worst in both parties, and more than one white girl had already made me know that her color was more powerful than my dick.

Which had nothing to do with how I found myself in the gay world. I would have found myself there anyway, but perhaps the very last thing this black boy needed were clouds of imitation white women and speculations concerning the size of his organ: speculations sometimes accompanied by an attempt at the laying on of hands. "*Ooo!* Look at him! He's cute—he doesn't like you to touch him there!"

In short, I was black in that world, and I was used that way, and by people who truly meant me no harm.

And they could *not* have meant me any harm, because they did not see me. There were exceptions, of course, for I also met some beautiful people. Yet even today, it seems to me (possibly because I am black) very dangerous to model one's opposition to the arbitrary definition, the imposed ordeal, merely on the example supplied by one's oppressor.

The object of one's hatred is never, alas, conveniently outside but is seated in one's lap, stirring in one's bowels and dictating the beat of one's heart. And if one does not know this, one risks becoming an imitation—and, therefore, a continuation—of principles one imagines oneself to despise.

I, in any case, had endured far too much debasement willingly to debase myself. I had absolutely no fantasies about making love to the last cop or hoodlum who had beaten the shit out of me. I did not find it amusing, in any way whatever, to act out the role of the darky.

So I moved on out of there.

In fact, I found a friend—more accurately, a friend found *me*—an Italian, about five years older than I, who helped my morale greatly in those years. I was told that he had threatened to kill anyone who touched me. I don't know about that, but people stopped beating me up. Our relationship never seemed to worry him or his friends or his women.

My situation in the Village stabilized itself to the extent that I began working as a waiter in a black West Indian restaurant, The Calypso, on MacDougal Street. This led, by no means incidentally, to the desegregation of the San Remo, an Italian bar and restaurant on the corner of MacDougal and Bleecker. Every time I entered the San Remo, they threw me out. I had to pass it all the time on my way to and from work, which is, no doubt, why the insult rankled.

I had won the Saxton Fellowship, which was administered by Harper & Brothers, and I knew Frank S. MacGregor, the president of Harper's. One night, when he asked me where we should have dinner, I suggested, spontaneously, the San Remo.

We entered, and they seated us and we were served. I went back to MacGregor's house for a drink and then went straight back to the San Remo, sitting on a bar stool in the window. The San Remo thus began to attract a varied clientele, indeed—so much so that Allen Ginsberg[1] and company arrived there the year I left New York for Paris.

As for the people who ran and worked at the San Remo, they never bothered me again. Indeed, the Italian community never bothered me again—or rarely and, as it were, by accident. But the Village was full of white tourists, and one night, when a mob gathered before the San Remo, demanding that I come out, the owners closed the joint and turned the lights out and we sat in the back room, in the dark, for a couple of hours, until they judged it safe to drive me home.

This was a strange, great and bewildering time in my life. Once I was in the San Remo, for example, I was *in*, and anybody who messed with me was *out*—that was all there was to it, and it happened more than once. And no one seemed to remember a time when I had not been there.

I could not quite get it together, but it seemed to me that I was no longer black for them and they had ceased to be white for me, for they sometimes introduced me to their families with every appearance of affection and pride and exhibited not the remotest interest in whatever my sexual proclivities chanced to be.

---

[1]American poet (1926–) and follower of Whitman,° one of the founders of the Beat Generation, best known for *Howl* (1956). Other books include *Kadish and Other Poems* (1961) and *The Fall of America* (1973).

They had fought me very hard to prevent this moment, but perhaps we were all much relieved to have got beyond the obscenity of color.

Matters were equally bewildering, though in a different way, at The Calypso. All kinds of people came into our joint—I am now referring to white people—and one of their most vivid aspects, for me, was the cruelty of their alienation. They appeared to have no antecedents nor any real connections.

"Do you really *like* your mother?" someone asked me, seeming to be astounded, totally disbelieving the possibility.

I was astounded by the question. Certainly, my mother and I did not agree about everything, and I knew that she was very worried about the dangers of the life I lived, but that was normal, since I was a boy and she was a woman. Of course she was worried about me: She was my *mother*. But she knew I wasn't crazy and that I would certainly never do anything, deliberately, to hurt her. Or my tribe, my brothers and sisters, who were probably worried about me, too.

My family was a part of my life. I could not imagine life without them, might never have been able to reconcile myself to life without them. And certainly one of the reasons I was breaking my ass in the Village had to do with my need to try to move us out of our dangerous situation. I was perfectly aware of the odds—my father had made that very clear—but he had also given me my assignment. "Do you really *like* your mother?" did not cause me to wonder about my mother or myself but about the person asking the question.

And perhaps because of such questions, I was not even remotely tempted by the possibilities of psychiatry or psychoanalysis. For one thing, there were too many schools—Freud,° Horney,[1] Jung,° Reich° (to suggest merely the tip of that iceberg)—and, for another, it seemed to me that anyone who thought seriously that I had any desire to be "adjusted" to this society had to be ill; too ill, certainly, as time was to prove, to be trusted.

I sensed, then—without being able to articulate it—that this dependence on a formula for safety, for that is what it was, signaled a desperate moral abdication. People went to the shrink in order to find justification for the empty lives they led and the meaningless work they did. Many turned, helplessly, hopefully, to Wilhelm Reich° and perished in orgone[2] boxes.

I seem to have strayed a long way from our subject, but our subject is social and historical—and continuous. The people who leaped into orgone boxes in search of the perfect orgasm were later to turn to acid. The people so dependent on psychiatric formulas were unable to give their children any sense of right or

---

[1]Karen Horney (1885–1952), psychoanalyst born and educated in Germany who came to the United States in 1932. One of the founders of the Association for the Advancement of Psychoanalysis and the American Institute for Psychoanalysis, she wrote numerous books, such as *The Neurotic Personality of Our Time, Self-Analysis,* and *Feminine Psychology.*
[2]See Reich.°

wrong—indeed, this sense was in themselves so fragile that during the McCarthy[1] era, more than one shrink made a lot of money by convincing his patients, or clients, that their psychic health demanded that they inform on their friends. (Some of these people, after their surrender, attempted to absolve themselves in the civil rights movement.)

What happened to the children, therefore, is not even remotely astonishing. The flower children—who became the Weather Underground,[2] the Symbionese Liberation Army,[3] the Manson Family[4]—are creatures from this howling inner space.

I am not certain, therefore, that the present sexual revolution is either sexual or a revolution. It strikes me as a reaction to the spiritual famine of American life. The present androgynous "craze"—to underestimate it—strikes me as an attempt to be honest concerning one's nature, and it is instructive, I think, to note that there is virtually no emphasis on overt sexual activity. There is nothing more boring, anyway, than sexual activity as an end in itself, and a great many people who came out of the closet should reconsider.

Such figures as Boy George[5] do not disturb me nearly so much as do those relentlessly hetero(sexual?) keepers of the keys and seals, those who know what the world needs in the way of order and who are ready and willing to supply that order.

This rage for order can result in chaos, and in this country, chaos connects with color. During the height of my involvement in the civil rights movement, for example, I was subjected to hate mail of a terrifying precision. Volumes concerning what my sisters, to say nothing of my mother, were capable of doing; to say nothing of my brothers; to say nothing of the monumental size of *my* organ and what I did with it. Someone described, in utterly riveting detail, a scene he swore he had witnessed (I *think* it was a *he*—such mail is rarely signed) on the steps of houses in Baltimore of niggers fucking their dogs.

At the same time, I was also on the mailing list of one of the more elegant of the KKK[6] societies, and I still have some of that mail in my files. Someone, of course, eventually realized that the organization should not be sending that mail to this particular citizen, and it stopped coming—but not before I had time to be

---

[1]See Un-American Activities,° Committee on.

[2]Also called Weathermen, it was an underground organization of violent revolutionaries in the late 1960s. The name *weathermen* comes from a line in a Bob Dylan song, "Subterranean Homesick Blues": "You don't need a weatherman to know which way the wind is blowing."

[3]A small band of revolutionaries who kidnapped the heiress Patty Hearst in February 1974.

[4]A group of people under the influence of drugs and a charismatic ex-convict named Charles Manson. In August 1969, he ordered some of his disciples to kill rich white people, hoping that blacks would be blamed and a race war would begin. The murder of six people, including the actress Sharon Tate and a couple named LaBianca, followed. Manson and five members of his family were convicted and sent to prison the next year.

[5]Androgynous British rock star.

[6]Ku Klux Klan, a secret anti-black, anti-Jewish, and anti-Catholic organization founded in Georgia in 1915 and named after a similar society established after the Civil War to maintain the segregation of blacks from whites.

struck by the similarity of tone between the hate mail and the mail of the society, and not before the society had informed me, by means of a parody of an Audubon Society[1] postcard, what it felt and expected me to feel concerning a certain "Red-breasted" Martin Luther King, Jr.°

The Michael Jackson[2] cacophony is fascinating in that it is not about Jackson at all. I hope he has the good sense to know it and the good fortune to snatch his life out of the jaws of a carnivorous success. He will not swiftly be forgiven for having turned so many tables, for he damn sure grabbed the brass ring, and the man who broke the bank at Monte Carlo[3] has nothing on Michael. All that noise is about America, as the dishonest custodian of black life and wealth; the blacks, especially males, in America; and the burning, buried American guilt; and sex and sexual roles and sexual panic; money, success and despair—to all of which may now be added the bitter need to find a head on which to place the crown of Miss America.[4]

Freaks are called freaks and are treated as they are treated—in the main, abominably—because they are human beings who cause to echo, deep within us, our most profound terrors and desires.

Most of us, however, do not appear to be freaks—though we are rarely what we appear to be. We are, for the most part, visibly male or female, our social roles defined by our sexual equipment.

But we are all androgynous, not only because we are all born of a woman impregnated by the seed of a man but because each of us, helplessly and forever, contains the other—male in female, female in male, white in black and black in white. We are a part of each other. Many of my countrymen appear to find this fact exceedingly inconvenient and even unfair, and so, very often, do I. But none of us can do anything about it. ✎

---

[1]National Group devoted to the preservation of wildlife and the environment and named after John James Audubon (1785–1851), American naturalist and painter.
[2]Androgynous American rock star.
[3]Idiom for a millionaire, from a song of that title by Fred Gilbert (1850–1903).
[4]Allusion to Vanessa Williams, the first black Miss America, who lost her crown when *Penthouse* magazine published nude photographs of her.

Cynthia Ozick

(1928–)

Cynthia Ozick was born in New York City in April 1928, six years after the birth of her brother Julius. Her parents, William and Celia Regelson Ozick, later moved to Pelham Bay, the Bronx, where they owned a pharmacy. Both parents had emigrated from the province of Minsk, in northwestern Russia, her mother arriving in New York City in June of 1906 at the age of nine-and-a-half and her father in 1913 at the age of twenty-one. Both parents brought with them their language, Yiddish, and a love of family and study. Her father was also fluent in Russian, Hebrew, German, and Latin.

Ozick's father's parents had remained in Moscow, he a perpetual student of the Talmud and she an educated woman and industrious mother of seven who ran a dry goods store. Her mother's parents, on the other hand, had settled in America with their large family (eight children). This side of the family, then, directly affected the pattern of Cynthia Ozick's life. Although her maternal grandfather died before Ozick was born, he left the family a lasting legacy of artistic and intellectual passion. A carver of chairs by profession, he was also a great reader who often rose early and lost himself in the latest Hebrew literary magazines until night had fallen and it was too late to work. His son, Abraham Regelson (Ozick's uncle), became a well-known Hebrew poet; many of her cousins on her mother's side are artists as well. Ozick attributes her passion for her art to this side of her family. Her maternal grandmother, who died when Ozick was eleven, also continues to be a major influence in Ozick's life. In his biography Joseph Lowin writes that her grandmother introduced Ozick to feminism when she took her five-year-old granddaughter to study Hebrew and was told by the rabbi "a girl doesn't have to study." Ozick's grandmother took her right back the next day.

As a child Cynthia Ozick was subject to "brutally difficult" prejudice. Lowin records her memories of being called "Christ-killer" and of being pelted with stones as she passed two neighborhood churches. In "A Drugstore in Winter" Ozick remembers the prejudice she encountered in grammar school when she refused to sing Christmas carols. Also in public school Ozick felt lonely and ugly and stupid in math. But at home, in her own world, the power of books upheld her imagination and inspired her to become a writer.

This desire to write fired Ozick's ambition from grammar school on, inspiring her transformation from the duckling of PS 71 to the cygnet of Hunter College High School for girls where, she recalls in "The Question of Our Speech: The Return to Aural Culture," she learned the Latin of Virgil° and delivered the commencement speech to the class of 1946. In "Washington Square, 1946," Ozick describes her arrival at New York University, the day before the semester was actually to begin, seventeen-and-a-half years old, in her "mind's cradle," imbued with the miraculous excitement of names and words not yet deciphered. Before her graduation with a B.A. *cum laude*, in English, Ozick also began to understand the outer world, "hammer-struck with the shock of Europe's skull, the bled planet of death camp and war."

In 1950, at twenty-two, as she describes in ironic self-mockery in "The Lesson of the Master," Ozick dedicated her life to art, to writing novels: "I was a worshiper of literature, literature was my single altar." She had just finished her M.A. in English at Ohio State University, having written a thesis entitled "Parable in the Later Novels of Henry James.°" Years later, after reading Leon Edel's immense biography of James,° she explains, again in satiric tones, that she discovered she had been betrayed by her youth and innocence into misreading the words of an old man—"The great voices of Art never mean *only* art; they also mean Life, they always mean Life."

For the next fourteen years, Ozick wrote "steadily and obsessively"— poems, stories, essays, and a long, finally abandoned novel called *Mercy, Pity, Peace, and Love*. She has written that her marriage to lawyer Bernard Hallote in 1952 provided a kind of "grant from a very private, very poor, foundation." In 1953 Ozick read Leo Baeck's essay "Romantic Religion" and then *History of the Jews* by Heinrich Graetz. Thus began her intensified study of Judaism, leading gradually but inescapably to her recognition that to be a writer is to raise metaphysical questions.

Despite her devotion to reading and writing, Ozick says in her essay "Cyril Connolly and the Groans of Success," she began to feel herself a failure. She had not gained economic independence through her writing; she had hardly been published at all. Although she had read voraciously, written with equal fervor, and lusted after publication, by the time she was thirty-six she had in print only "a handful of poems, a couple of short stories, a single essay, and all in quirky little magazines." After *Mercy, Pity, Peace, and Love*, she'd written another novel in a matter of weeks, put it aside, and embarked in 1957 on a third novel which she finished in 1963.

In 1964 Ozick took a job as instructor at New York University, a step representing the end of her life as a "recluse." In September 1965 she gave birth to a daughter, Rachel. Finally, in 1966 with the publication of the third novel, *Trust*, Cynthia Ozick left behind forever the apprenticeship of her "despairing middle thirties." She has been a remarkably prolific and honored writer ever since.

Ozick's first highly praised short story, "The Pagan Rabbi," appeared in 1966 in *Hudson Review*. Since then her short stories, essays, and poems have appeared in such journals as *Commentary*, *New Criterion*, *Partisan Review*, *Esquire*, *The New York Times Book Review*, *The New York Review of Books*, and *The New Yorker*. In 1968 she was a Fellow of the National Endowment for the Arts, which helped her to produce her first collection of short stories (*The Pagan Rabbi and Other Stories*), issued by Knopf in 1971 and nominated for the National Book Award in 1972. In 1973 she won the American Academy and Institute of Arts and Letters Award for Literature. Her work appeared in *Best American Short Stories* five times between 1970 and 1984, and she won first prize in the *O. Henry Prize Stories* in 1975, 1981, and 1984. In 1976 Knopf published *Bloodshed and Three Novellas*. In 1981 Ozick was Distinguished Artist-in-Residence at the City University of New York, where she taught a seminar in creative writing. The following year Knopf published *Levitation: Five Fictions*. Also that year she won a Guggenheim Fellowship, was a nominee for the National Book Critics Circle Award (also in 1983 and 1990), and was the recipient of the American Academy and Institute of Arts and Letters Strauss Living Award from 1982 to 1987. Since 1984 she has received eleven honorary degrees.

Art & Ardor: Essays and a novel, *Cannibal Galaxy*, appeared in 1983. In 1984 Ozick won the Distinguished Service in Jewish Letters Award from the Jewish Theological Seminary, the Distinguished Alumnus Award from New York University, and nomination for the PEN-Faulkner Award (also in 1988). In 1985 she was Phi Beta Kappa Orator at Harvard University. The next year she received the Michael Rea Award for the Short Story. Another novel, *The Messiah of Stockholm*, came out in 1987, and in 1989 she published *Metaphor & Memory: Essays*; a work of fiction, *The Shawl*; and a "Critic at Large" essay, "T. S. Eliot at 101," in *The New Yorker* dated November 20, 1989. Her novella, "Puttermesser Paired," appeared in *The New Yorker* dated October 8, 1990, and another essay, "Alfred Chester's Wig," is forthcoming. A collection of her poems will be published by the Logan Elm Press (a division of Ohio State University Press) in 1992. She has been awarded the Bryn Mawr College Lucy Martin Donnelly Fellowship for 1991–1992 and is currently writing a play based on *The Shawl*. She is also at work on essays and a novel.

Cynthia Ozick has over the years lectured in the United States, Canada, Israel, Italy, Denmark, Sweden, and France, and in December of 1989 chaired a conference titled "The Middle East: Uncovering the Myths," held at Hunter College in New York. Her time is a precarious battlefield where two selves meet, the one proclaiming that art means life and the other defiantly resisting: "As for life, I don't like it. I notice no 'interplay of life and art.' Life is that which—pressingly, persistently, unfailingly, imperially—interrupts."

Ozick's essays reveal her love of carefully crafted language: "nothing matters to me so much as a comely and muscular sentence." Her wide-ranging diction moves from a "transcendent vocabulary" to comic barbs. In the last paragraphs of "The Seam of the Snail," Ozick contrasts her mother's profusion, a "horn of plenty," with her own precision, bound by the "tiny twin horns of the snail," to reach an apotheosis of words: "out of this thinnest thread, this ink-wet line of words, must rise a visionary fog, a mist, a smoke, forging cities, histories, sorrows, quagmires, entanglements, lives of sinners, even the life of my furnace-hearted mother." Her comic complaint in "Crocodiled Moats in the Kingdom of Letters" that the divisiveness she perceives in the humanities is an expression of "sour grapes" connecting New York and California shows that she is not above a pun. Her lists—the variety of sciences in "Crocodiled Moats" or the names of her teachers, "Miss Evangeline Trolander, Mrs. Olive Birch Davis, and Mrs. Ruby S. Papp (pronounced *pop*)" in "The Question of Our Speech"—reveal a pleasure in sounds martialled for humor as well as for sense.

Yet the overall impression left by Ozick's essays is of a mind passionately committed to intellectual rigor and truth. Nearly as allusive as Hazlitt, Ozick boldly delineates the ignorance of youth, her own as well as that of her students, engages with energy in literary battles, and reaffirms the importance of the Muse in the postmodern world, professing the essay a form of fiction—to keep it honest. ✍

Previsions of the Demise of the Dancing Dog[1]

Young women, . . . you are, in my opinion, disgracefully ignorant. You have never made a discovery of any importance. You have never shaken an empire or led an army into battle. The plays of Shakespeare are not by you, and you have never introduced a barbarous race to the blessings of civilization. What is your excuse?

VIRGINIA WOOLF, *A Room of One's Own*

No comradely socialist legislation on women's behalf could accomplish a millionth of what a bit more muscle tissue, gratuitously offered by nature, might do. . . .

ELIZABETH HARDWICK,° *A View of One's Own*

[1] First published in *Women in Sexist Society*, Basic Books, 1971.

Several years ago I devoted a year to Examining the Minds of the Young. It was a curious experience, like going into theater after theater in a single night, and catching bits of first acts only. How will the heroine's character develop? Will the hero turn out to be captain of his fate[1] or only of some minor industry? I never arrived at the second act, and undoubtedly I will never be witness to the denouement. But what I saw of all those beginnings was extraordinary: they were all so similar. All the characters were exactly the same age, and most had equal limitations of imagination and aspiration. Is "the individual," I wondered, a sacred certainty, and the human mind infinitely diversified, as we are always being told? Examine for yourself the Minds of the Young and it is possible you will begin to think the opposite. Democratic theory is depressingly correct in declaring all men equal. Just as every human hand is limited at birth by its five fingers, so is every human mind stamped from a single, equally obvious, pattern. "I have never in all my various travels seen but two sorts of people, and those very like one another; I mean men and women, who always have been, and ever will be, the same," wrote Lady Mary Wortley Montagu[2] in the middle of the eighteenth century. Human nature is one.

The vantage point from which I came to these not unusual conclusions was not from reading the great philosophers, or even from reading Lady Mary—it was from a job. I was hired by a large urban university to teach English to freshmen: three classes of nearly a hundred young men and young women, all seventeen, some city-born, some suburban, some well-off, some only scraping by, of every ethnic group and of every majority religion but Hindu. Almost all were equipped with B high-school averages; almost all were more illiterate than not; almost all possessed similar prejudices expressed in identical platitudes. Almost all were tall, healthy, strong-toothed, obedient, and ignorant beyond their years. They had, of course, very few ideas—at seventeen this can hardly be called a failing; but the ideas they had were plainly derived not from speculation but from indoctrination. They had identical minuscule vocabularies, made identical errors of grammar and punctuation, and were identically illogical. They were identically uneducated, and the minds of the uneducated young women were identical with the minds of the uneducated young men.

Now this last observation was the least surprising of all. Though unacquainted with the darkest underbrush of the human mind (and here it must be emphatically averred that deep scrutiny, at indecently short intervals, of one hundred freshman themes is the quickest and most scarifying method of achieving intimacy with the human mind in its rawest state), I had never doubted that the human mind was a democratic whole, that it was androgynous, epicene,

---

[1]A play on well-known lines from "Invictus" by the Victorian poet William Ernest Henley (1849–1903): "I am the master of my fate: / I am the captain of my soul."

[2](1689–1762) Best known for her four volumes of letters published from 1763 to 1767 describing English society and her life as the wife of the ambassador to Turkey, she is also the author of poems popular in her lifetime.

asexual, call it what you will; it had always seemed axiomatic to me that the minds of men and women were indistinguishable.

My students confirmed this axiom to the last degree. You could not tell the young men's papers from the young women's papers. They thought alike (badly), they wrote alike (gracelessly), and they believed alike (docilely). And what they all believed was this: that the minds of men and women are spectacularly unlike.

They believed that men write like men, and women like women; that men think like men, and women like women; that men believe like men, and women like women. And they were all identical in this belief.

But I have said, after all, that they were alike in illiteracy, undereducation, ignorance, and prejudice.

Still, to teach at a university is not simply to teach; the teacher is a teacher among students, but he is also a teacher among teachers. He has colleagues, and to have colleagues is to have high exchanges, fruitful discourses, enlightening quarrels. Colleagues, unlike students, are not merely literate but breathtakingly literary; not merely educated but bent under the weight of multitudinous higher degrees; not merely informed but dazzlingly knowledgeable; not merely unprejudiced but brilliantly questing. And my colleagues believed exactly what my students believed.

My colleagues were, let it be noted, members of the Department of English in the prestige college of an important university. I was, let it be revealed, the only woman instructor in that department. Some years before, the college had been all male. Then the coeds were invited in, and now and then in their wake a woman was admitted, often reluctantly, to the faculty. Before my own admittance, I had been living the isolated life of a writer—my occupation for some years had consisted in reading great quantities and in writing embarrassingly tiny quantities. I was, I suppose, not in that condition generally known as "being in touch with the world." I was in touch with novels, poetry, essays, enlarging meditations; but of "the world," as it turned out, I apparently knew little.

I came to the university in search of the world. I had just finished an enormous novel, the writing of which had taken many more years than any novel ought to take, and after so long a retreat my lust for the world was prodigious. I wanted Experience, I wanted to sleep under bridges—but finding that all the bridges had thickly trafficked cloverleaves under them, I came instead to the university. I came innocently. I had believed, through all those dark and hope-sickened years of writing, that it was myself ("myself"—whatever that means for each of us) who was doing the writing. In the university, among my colleagues, I discovered two essential points: (1) that it was a "woman" who had done the writing—not a mind—and that I was a "woman writer"; and (2) that I was now not a teacher, but a "woman teacher."

I was suspect from the beginning—more so among my colleagues than among my students. My students, after all, were accustomed to the idea of a "woman teacher," having recently been taught by several in high school. But my colleagues were long out of high school, and they distrusted me. I learned that I had no genuinely valid opinions, since every view I might hold was colored by my sex. If I said I didn't like Hemingway,° I could have no *critical* justification, no *literary* reason; it was only because, being a woman, I obviously could not be sympathetic toward Hemingway's° "masculine" subject matter—the hunting, the fishing, the bullfighting, which no woman could adequately digest. It goes without saying that among my colleagues there were other Hemingway° dissenters; but their reasons for disliking Hemingway,° unlike mine, were not taken to be simply ovarian.

In fact, both my students and my colleagues were equal adherents of the Ovarian Theory of Literature, or, rather, its complement, the Testicular Theory. A recent camp follower (I cannot call him a pioneer) of this explicit theory is, of course, Norman Mailer,° who has attributed his own gift, and the literary gift in general, solely and directly to the possession of a specific pair of organs. One writes with these organs, Mailer° has said in *Advertisements for Myself*; and I have always wondered with what shade of ink he manages to do it.

I recall my first encounter with the Ovarian Theory. My students had been assigned the reading of *Wise Blood*, the novel by Flannery O'Connor.° Somewhere in the discussion I referred to the author as "she." The class stirred in astonishment; they had not imagined that "Flannery" could connote a woman, and this somehow put a different cast upon the narrative and their response to it. Now among my students there was a fine young woman, intelligent and experimental rather than conforming, one of my rare literates, herself an anomaly because she was enrolled in the overwhelmingly male College of Engineering. I knew that her mind usually sought beyond the commonplace—she wrote with the askew glance of the really inquisitive. Up went her hand. "But I could *tell* she was a woman," she insisted. "Her sentences are a woman's sentences." I asked her what she meant and how she could tell. "Because they are sentimental," she said, "they're not concrete like a man's." I pointed out whole paragraphs, pages even, of unsentimental, so-called tough prose. "But she *sounds* like a woman—she has to sound that way because she is," said the future engineer, while I speculated whether her bridges and buildings would loom plainly as woman's work. Moreover, it rapidly developed that the whole class now declared that it too, even while ignorant of the author's sex, had nevertheless intuited all along that this was a woman's prose; it had to be, since Flannery was a she.

My second encounter with the idea of literature-as-physiology was odder yet. This time my interlocutor was a wonderfully gentle, deeply intellectual young fellow teacher; he was going to *prove* what my freshmen had merely maintained. "But of course style is influenced by physical make-up," he began in his judicious graduate-assistant way. Here was his incontrovertible evidence: "Take Keats,° right? Keats° fighting tuberculosis at the end of his life. You don't suppose Keats's° poetry was totally unaffected by his having had tuberculosis?" And he smiled with the flourish of a young man who has made an unanswerable point. "Ah, but *you* don't suppose," I put it to him cheerfully enough, "that being a woman is a *disease*?"

But comparing literary women with having a debilitating disease is the least of it. My colleague, after all, was a kindly sort, and stuck to human matters; he did not mention dogs. On the other hand, almost everyone remembers Dr. Johnson's remark upon hearing a woman preacher—she reminded him, he said, of a dog dancing on its hind legs; one marvels not at how well it is done, but that it is done at all. That was two centuries ago; wise Lady Mary was Johnson's contemporary. Two centuries, and the world of letters has not been altered by a syllable, unless you regard the switch from dogs to disease as a rudimentary advance. Perhaps it is. We have advanced so far that the dullest as well as the best of freshmen can scarcely be distinguished from Dr. Johnson, except by a bark.

And our own Dr. Johnson—I leave you to guess his name—hoping to insult a rival writer, announces that the rival "reminds me of nothing so much as a woman writer."

Consider, in this vein, the habits of reviewers. I think I can say in good conscience that I have never—repeat, *never*—read a review of a novel or, especially, of a collection of poetry by a woman that did not include somewhere in its columns a gratuitous allusion to the writer's sex and its supposed effects. The Ovarian Theory of Literature is the property of all society, not merely of freshmen and poor Ph.D. lackeys: you will find it in all the best periodicals, even the most highbrow. For example: a few years ago a critic in *The New York Review of Books* considered five novels, three of which were by women. And so his review begins: "Women novelists, we have learned to assume, like to keep their focus narrow." And from this touchstone—with no ground other than the "we have learned to assume"—falls his praise and his censure. The touchstone, of course, is properly qualified, as such touchstones always are, by reverent asides concerning the breadth of George Eliot° and the grasp of Jane Austen.° Ah, indispensable George and Jane! They have come into the world, one concludes, only to serve as exceptions to the strictures of reviewers; and they *are* exceptions. Genius always is; it is how genius is defined. But if the exception is to be dragged into every routine review of novelists and poets who are women, then the rule must drop equally on all. Let every new poet, male and female, be reviewed in the shadow of Emily Dickinson° and Coleridge.° Let every unknown novelist, male and female, be reviewed in the blaze of *Anna Karenina* and *Wuthering Heights*.[1] If this seems like nonsense, then reviewers must take merit as their point of concentration, not stale expectation, and not the glibbest of literary canards.[2]

Still, the canards are, in their way, small fun, being as flexible and fragile as other toys. A collection of canards is bound to be a gaggle of contradictions. When, for instance, my bright engineering student identified Flannery O'Connor° as "sentimental," she was squarely in one-half of a diluvial, though bifurcated, tradition. Within this tradition there are two hoary views of woman. One: she is sentimental, imprecise, irrational, overemotional, impatient, unperseveringly flighty, whimsical, impulsive, unreliable, unmechanical, not given to

---

[1] See Tolstoy° and Emily Brontë.°
[2] False or misleading information, from the French for "duck."

practicality, perilously vague, and so on. In this view she is always contrasted with man, who is, on the other hand, unsentimental, exact, rational, controlled, patient, hard-headed, mechanically gifted, a meeter of payrolls, firm of purpose, wary of impulse, anything but a dreamer. Description One accounts for why throughout her history she has been a leader neither of empires nor of trades nor of armies. But it is also declared that, her nature having failed her in the practical world, she cannot succeed in the world of invention either: she is unequipped, for example, for poetry, in that (here is Description Two) she is above all pragmatic, sensible and unsentimental, unvisionary, unadventurous, empirical, conservative, down-to-earth, unspontaneous, perseveringly patient and thus good at the minutiae of mechanical and manipulative tasks, and essentially unimaginative. In short, she will wander too much or she will wander not at all. She is either too emotional or not emotional enough. She is either too spontaneous or not spontaneous enough. She is either too sensitive (that is why she cannot be president of General Motors) or she is not sensitive enough (that is why she will never write *King Lear*°).

But none of this is to imply that woman is damned, and damned from every direction. Not at all. The fact is that woman qua woman is more often celebrated. If she cannot hear the muse, says Robert Graves,° what does it matter? She *is* the muse. *Man Does, Woman Is* is the title of Graves's° most recent collection of poetry. If we are expected to conclude from this that woman is an It rather than a Thou (to use Martin Buber's[1] categories), why deplore it? The Parthenon too is beautiful, passive, inspiring. Who would long to *build* it, if one can *be* it?

And even this is unfair, since it is simultaneously true that woman is frequently praised as the more "creative" sex. She does not need to make poems, it is argued; she has no drive to make poems, because she is privileged to make babies. A pregnancy is as fulfilling as, say, Yeats's° *Sailing to Byzantium*. Here is an interesting idea worth examination. To begin with, we would have to know what it cost Yeats°—I am speaking physically—to wring out a poem of genius. Perhaps we cannot know this. The writing of great and visionary literature is not a common experience and is not readily explorable. A. E. Housman[2]—a lesser poet than Yeats,° to be sure, though as pure a one—said of the genesis of a poem that it affected his flesh: that if a wisp of a line came to him while he was in the middle of shaving, for instance, he would sense the bristles standing on end. Most poets, if they speak of it at all, report extreme exhaustion accompanied by supreme exaltation. Yeats° himself spoke of the poet living amid whirlwinds. Virginia Woolf, a writer of a kind of prose very near poetry in tone and aspiration, was

---

[1]Austrian theologian (1878–1965) who interpreted Jewish mysticism and influenced Christians through *I and Thou* (1923), a book about his understanding of the dialogue between God and man.

[2]British pastoral poet (1859–1936) known for such poems as "Into My Heart an Air That Kills," "To an Athlete Dying Young," and "Loveliest of Trees."

racked in the heat of composition by seizures of profoundly tormenting head-aches. Isaac Babel[1] called himself a "galley slave." Conrad° was in a frenzy for weeks on end—"I turn in this vicious circle and the work itself becomes like the work in a treadmill—a thing without joy—a punishing task. . . . I am at it day after day, and I want all day, every minute of a day, to produce a beggarly tale of words or perhaps to produce nothing at all. . . . One's will becomes a slave of hallucinations, responds only to shadowy impulses, waits on imagination alone." Dostoyevsky° said plainly: "*I worked and was tortured.*" Flaubert° wrote, "You don't know what it is to stay a whole day with your head in your hands trying to squeeze your unfortunate brain so as to find a word." Tolstoy° told a friend, "One ought only to write when one leaves a piece of flesh in the ink-pot each time one dips one's pen." For Isak Dinesen,[2] the "great and difficult task" was pursued "without faith and without hope." And George Eliot° said of the writing of *Romola*—it occupied two years—that she began it young, and finished it old.

That is what "creativity" is. Is a pregnancy like that? The fact is, given health (and one must never assume the abnormal, since being a woman is really *not* like having a disease), the condition of pregnancy is—in the consciousness—very nearly like the condition of nonpregnancy. It is insulting to a poet to compare his titanic and agonized strivings with the so-called "creativity" of childbearing, where—consciously—nothing happens. One does not will the development of the fetus; one can be as dull or as active, or as bored or as intense, as one pleases—anything else is mere self-absorption and daydream: the process itself is as involuntary and as unaware as the beating of one's own heart. Of course, it is a miracle that one's heart goes on beating, that the fetus goes on growing—but it is not a human miracle, it is Nature's miracle. If we want to talk about Nature, very well—but now we are talking about literature. To produce a new human being out of a pair of cells is a marvel, but it is not *our* marvel. Once we, male and female, have joined two disparate cells by our human wills, the rest is done for us, not by us. The woman's body is a vessel, thereafter, for a parasite. For the presence of the zygote she is thereafter no more responsible than she is for the presence of her heart and lungs. To call a child a poem may be a pretty metaphor, but it is a slur on the labor of art. Literature cannot be equated with physiology, and woman through her reproductive system alone is no more a creative artist than was Joyce° by virtue of his kidneys alone, or James° by virtue of his teeth (which, by the way, were troublesome). A poem emerges from a mind, and mind is, so far as our present knowledge takes us, an unknowable abstraction. Perhaps it is a compli-ment to a woman of no gifts to say of her in compensation, "Ah, well, but she has made a child." But that is a cheap and slippery mythology, and a misleading one.

---

[1]Russian Jewish writer (1894–1941) who was arrested in 1938 and sent by Stalin to a concen-tration camp, where he died. He wrote two collections of short stories, *Odessa Tales* and *Red Cavalry*, as well as two plays and a novel.

[2]Pseudonym of Baroness Karen Blixen (1885–1962), Danish author who wrote in English and lived in British East Africa. She is best known for her novel *Out of Africa* and her supernatural tales.

It induces the false value of self-inflation in mediocre women. It is scarcely our duty to compliment the mediocre for their mediocrity when we are hardly employed enough in celebrating the gifted for their gifts, wrung out by the toil of desire and imagination. It takes something away from Yeats° to compare a mediocre child—and most children, like most parents, *are* mediocre—with *Sailing to Byzantium*. But it is just as irrelevant to compare a brilliant child with a brilliant poem. Biology is *there*: it does not need our praise, and if we choose to praise it, it is blasphemous to think we are praising not God but ourselves.[1]

All this is, one would think, almost stupefyingly obvious. It is embarrassing, it is humiliating, to be so obvious about the quality either of literature or of woman. She, at any rate, is not a muse, nor is she on the strength of her womb alone an artist. She is—how stupidly obvious—a person. She can be an artist if she was born talented. She can be a muse if she inspires a poet, but she too (if she was born talented) can find her own muse in another person. Madame de Sévigné's[2] muse was her daughter, and what male muse it was who inspired Emily Brontë's° Heathcliff, history continues to conjecture. The muse—*pace* Robert Graves°—has no settled sex or form, and can appear in the shape of a tree (*Howards End*)[3] or a city (the Paris of *The Ambassadors*)[4] or even—think of Proust°—a cookie.

Yet in our culture, in our country, much is not obvious. With respect to woman and with respect to literature (I refer you again to the reviewers), ours is among the most backward areas on earth. It is true that woman has had the vote for fifty years and has begun to enter most professions, though often without an invitation. We are far past the grievances Virginia Woolf grappled with in *A Room of One's Own* and *Three Guineas*—books still sneered at as "feminist."[5] In 1929, when Virginia Woolf visited Oxford (or was it Cambridge? she is too sly to say which), she was chased off a lawn forbidden to the feet of women. By then, of

---

[1]Sometimes the analogy is made not between poetry and childbearing proper, but between poetry and an idealized domesticity. Here is the versifier Phyllis McGinley writing in an advertisement for and in *The New York Times*: "I know a remarkable woman who is a true artist, domestic version. She creates an atmosphere in which her children and her husband can move with delight and peace, pouring out all the passion which Emily Dickinson° might have spent on perfecting a stanza or—to update the comparison—as Joan Sutherland does on interpreting an aria. Her masterpiece consists of her family, her house, her community duties." But would the gifted McGinley be willing to reverse the metaphor, and compare her witty verses with mopping under the bed? Or match Emily Dickinson's° "I Heard a Fly Buzz When I Died" with a good nourishing family breakfast, or a morning on the telephone for the PTA? Or liken rendering an aria to sitting down to an editorial in the *Times*? [Ozick's note.]

[2]Marie de Rabutin-Chantal, marquise de (1626–1696), French writer of elegant, witty letters to her daughter and others, first published in 1725.

[3]See E. M. Forster.°

[4]See Henry James.°

[5]The change since this was written is especially striking. These essays are now both the subject and the support of dozens of women's studies courses in many universities. Woolf the feminist has outstripped Woolf the woman of letters. An irony, since—for Virginia Woolf herself—the former was espoused in order to facilitate the latter. [Ozick's note.]

course, our colleges were already full of coeds, though not so full as now. And yet the question of justification remains. Only a few months ago, in my own college, a startling debate was held—"Should a Woman Receive a College Education?" The audience was immense, but the debaters were only three: an instructor in anthropology (female), a professor of history (male), and a fiercely bearded professor of psychology (ostentatiously male). According to the unironic conventions of chivalry, the anthropologist spoke first. She spoke of opportunities and of problems. She spoke of living wholly and well. She did not ignore the necessities and difficulties of housekeeping and childrearing; she spoke of the relations of parents, children, and work-in-the-world; she talked extensively about nursery schools. She took as her premise not merely that woman ought to be fully educated, but that her education should be fully used in society. She was reasoned and reasonable; she had a point of view. Perhaps it was a controversial point of view, perhaps not—her listeners never had the chance of a serious evaluation. Her point of view was never assailed or refuted. It was overlooked. She spoke—against mysterious whispered cackles in the audience—and sat. Then up rose the laughing psychologist, and cracked jokes through his beard. Then up rose the laughing historian, and cracked jokes through his field—I especially remember one about the despotism of Catherine the Great.[1] "That's what happens when a woman gets emancipated." Laughter from all sides. Were the historian and the psychologist laughing at the absurdity of the topic the callow students' committee had selected for debate? An absurd topic—it deserves to be laughed out of court, and surely that is exactly what is happening, since here in the audience are all these coeds, censuring and contradicting by their very presence the outrageous question. Yet look again: the coeds are laughing too. Everyone is laughing the laughter of mockery. They are not laughing at the absurdly callow topic. They are laughing at the buffoonery of the historian and the psychologist, who are themselves laughing at the subject of the topic: the whole huge room, packed to the very doors and beyond with mocking boys and girls, is laughing at the futility of an educated woman. *She* is the absurdity.

The idea of an educated woman is not yet taken seriously in American universities. She is not chased off the campus, she is even welcomed there—but she is not taken seriously as a student, and she will not be welcomed if she hopes to return as a serious lifelong scholar. Nor will she be welcomed afterward in the "world." A law firm may hire her, but it will hide her in its rear research offices, away from the eyes of clients. The lower schools will receive her, as they always have, since she is their bulwark; their bulwark, but not their principal, who is a man. We have seen her crawling like Griselda[2] through the long ordeal of medicine: she is almost always bound to be a pediatrician, since it is in her nature to "work with children."

---

[1]Catherine II (1729–1796), czarina of Russia from 1762 until her death.
[2]Patient heroine found in Boccaccio° and Chaucer who submits to trials imposed by her husband to test her loyalty to him.

I will not forget the appalling laughter of the two mocking debaters. But it was not so appalling as the laughter of the young men and the young women in the audience. In the laughter of the historian and the psychologist I heard the fussy cry—a cry of violated venerable decorum, no doubt—of the beadle who chased Virginia Woolf off the grass in 1929. But what of that youthful mockery? Their laughter was hideous; it showed something ugly and self-shaming about the nature of our society and the nature of our education—and by "our education" I do not mean the colleges, I mean the kindergartens, I mean the living rooms at home, I mean the fathers and the mothers, the men and the women.

In this country the women, by and large, are at home. Let us consider that first. Most of the women are at home. Why are they at home? Well, plainly because they belong there. They are there to rear the children, and if they have a whole lot of children (in our country they have an amazing number of children, without regard to the diet of algae they are imposing on their children's children), there will usually be a helpless baby. The mother is at home to take care of the helpless baby. That is right and reasonable. Everyone agrees—Nature agrees, the father agrees, Society agrees. Society agrees? That is very interesting. That too is an idea worth examination. It is very useful for society to have the mother at home. It keeps her out of the way. If, say, she stopped at only two children (but if she stopped at only two she would be in danger of reducing the birth rate, which now rivals India's), those two might be half-grown, and safely shut up in a school building most of the day, by the time she is thirty-five. And if she were thirty-five—a young, healthy, able, educated thirty-five—with no helpless baby to keep her at home, and most of the day free, what would she do? Society shudders at the possibility: she might want to get a job. But that would never do. Why, if you counted up all the young, healthy, able, educated, free women of thirty-five, it might come to nearly half the population! And, as things stand now, there are not even enough jobs for the other half of the population, the truly breadwinning half. And what about all those three-quarters-grown persons we call adolescents? Society shudders at them too: the economy is an inn with no room for adolescents and women. But if it will not allow adolescents and women to share in its work (how can it? so much of the work is done by machines), society must at least provide something else to keep the adolescents and women occupied, if only artificially. So, out of the largesse of its infinitely adaptable lap, it gives women knitting and adolescents transistor radios to dance to. (And for the adolescents of even mediocre capacities—here there is not so much discrimination by sex—it comes up with colleges, and fraudulent debates, and more dancing.) Society provides a complete—and in essence custodial—culture for each group it is forced to keep out of the way. It is a culture of busywork and make-believe and distraction. Society is very clever and always has been. Once upon a time, before machines, women and adolescents *were* needed and used to the last degree in the economy. Women were not educated because an unautomated house requires a work horse to maintain it, and a woman who cannot read or write is somehow better at hauling water in from the pump than one who can. (Why this should be, only the experience of society can explain.) But now society—so long as we fail to renovate it—can furnish work for only a quarter of the population, and so the rest must be lured into thinking it is performing a job when it is really not doing anything beyond breathing.

That is why there are in our society separate minority cultures for adolescents and for women. Each has its own set of opinions, prejudices, tastes, values, and—do not underestimate this last—magazines. You and I are here concerned only with the culture of women. Society, remember, is above men and women; it acts *in* men and women. So you must not make the mistake of thinking that the culture of women is the conspiracy of men. Not in the least. That is an old-fashioned, bluestocking view of the matter, and it is erroneous. The culture of women is believed in by both men and women, and it is the conspiracy of neither, because it is the creature neither of men alone, nor of women alone, but of society itself—that autonomous, cunning, insensitive sibling of history.

The culture of women consists of many, many things—products as well as attitudes, but attitudes mostly. The attitudes generate the products, and the products utilize the attitudes. The most overriding attitude is summed up in a cult word: "Home." (Notice that builders do not sell houses, they sell homes—a case of attitude and product coalescing.) But what does "Home" mean? It means curtains, rugs, furniture, a boiler in the cellar, magazines with dress patterns and recipes and articles full of adulterated Freud,° a dog, a box of cereal bones for the dog, a kitchen floor that conscience insists must be periodically waxed, and so forth: but mostly, of course, it means "Children." And "Children" are not regarded as incomplete or new persons, as unformed destinies, as embryo participants in the society; above all, they are not regarded simply as *children*: they are a make-believe entity in themselves, a symbol of need and achievement, just as the dog biscuits (not real bones) are a make-believe entity in themselves (does the dog think they are real?). "Children" as a concept have, in their present incarnation, a definite function, which is to bolster the whole airy system of make-believe. "Children" are there to justify "Home"; and "Home" is there to justify a third phantom entity—the heroine of the fairy tale, also an invention and an abstraction, the "Homemaker."

In this sense, neither "Home" nor "Children" nor "Homemaker" has any reality at all. All are dissemblances, fables, daydreams. All are abstractions designed to give the prestige of sham significance to a fairy tale. Nothing here is in the least related to living persons or to life itself. "Home" and "Children" and "Homemaker" are fabrications in the same sense that a bank is a fabrication: we pretend we are passing something called money, but meanwhile a bookkeeper (that is, a computer) is simply balancing the columns in an account book, more on this side of the line, less on that side. If we should all insist on exchanging metal again, the bank fabrication would dissolve. And when the "Children" grow up a little, refuse to be players in the game of gauze, and insist at last on being real persons, does "Home" dissolve, does "Homemaker" dissolve? Only partially. Because now society steps in and sweeps up the remains under the heading of "Womanhood." The children go away, the dog dies, the house wears out, but

"Womanhood" is eternal. Its possessor, the creature in whom "Womanhood" is immanent (divinely, as it were), has her magazines to prove her reality—her reality, mind you, as a concept called "Woman," endowed with another concept called "Womanhood"; she has the benevolent chorus of society to prove it, she has the bearded psychologist and the professor of history to prove it, she has the laughing girls and boys to prove it.

They "prove" it, perhaps—the Ptolemaic system[1] was also in error, and its proofs were magnificent—but they do not justify *her*. No fabrication can be justified. Only a person can be justified. A person is justified by the quality of her life; but a daydream is not a life, no matter how many propose to declare it so.

This is our "problem"—the problem of a majority's giving its credence and its loyalty to a daydream. And it is a bigger problem than any other we know of in this country, for the plain and terrifying reason that we have not even considered it to be a problem. Whenever the cliché-question is put, "What is the number one problem in America today?", the cliché-answer comes: "Civil rights—the Black Revolution." Scarcely. The solution to that problem is there—we have only to catch up to it, with all our might. If the debate at my college had dealt with civil rights it would have been serious, passionate, and argumentative. We had a Vietnam teach-in: *it* was serious and passionate and argumentative. But until now no one has been serious and passionate, and certainly no one has been argumentative, concerning attitudes about woman. Once a problem has been articulated, the answer is implicit; the answer is already fated. But this problem was never articulated; there was no answer, because no one ever asked the question. It was a question that had not yet found its incarnation. Its substance was, on every level, the stuff of primitive buffoonery.

Virginia Woolf is the artist-pioneer, the Margaret-Sanger°-as-bard, so to speak, of this social question. Among artists she has no successor. Not until art has seized and possessed and assimilated this question will it begin to interest the scientist-humanists.

But what are the components of the question? Perhaps they can once again crudely be set out, though they are so old and so tiresome, though we have no poet to speak them forth once and for all, though we handle them with the weariness of overuse. Here they are: no great female architects, painters, playwrights, sailors, bridge-builders, jurists, captains, composers, etc., etc. Everyone knows that list; everyone can recite it at length, now and then hesitating to allow for a Saint Joan[2] or an empress or an influential courtesan or a salon wit. But the list of omissions is long, as long almost as history, or, to use a more telling simile, as long almost as the history of the Jews.

---

[1] Theory that the earth remains motionless at the center of the universe while all other celestial bodies move in concentric circles around it, creating "the music of the spheres." This theory was believed valid until the sixteenth century, when Copernicus developed his heliocentric theory.

[2] Joan of Arc (1412?–1431), French national heroine who led the troops that defeated the English at Orléans and Patay in 1429. She was burned as a heretic in 1431 and canonized in 1920.

And here I think of a curious analogy. Say what you will about the gifted Jews, they have never, up until times so recent that they scarcely begin to count, been plastic artists. Where is the Jewish Michelangelo,° the Jewish Rembrandt,° the Jewish Rodin?° He has never come into being. Why? Have oppression and persecution erased the possibility of his existence? Hardly. Oppression and persecution often tend to reinforce gifts; to proscribe is more effective than to prescribe. Where then *is* the Jewish Michelangelo?° Is it possible that a whole people cannot produce a single painter? And not merely a single painter of note, but a single painter at all? Well, there have been artists among the Jews—artisans, we should more likely call them, decorators of trivial ceremonial objects, a wine cup here, a scroll cover there. Talented a bit, but nothing great. They never tried their hand at wood or stone or paint. "Thou shalt have no graven images"—the Second Commandment—prevented them. And it is not until a very, very little while ago, under the influence of a movement called "Emancipation" or "Enlightenment," that we begin to see creeping in a Chagall,° a Modigliani,° an Epstein,° who have ceased to believe that art insults the Unity of God. It will be a long, long time before the Jews have their Michelangelo.° Before a "David" can happen, a thousand naked Apollos° must be hewn. (And Apollo° *did* insult the Unity of God.) There must be a readied ground, a preparation—in short, a relevant living culture to frame the event.

The same, I think, with our problem. Gifts and brains are not transmitted, like hemophilia, from the immune sex to the susceptible sex. Genius is the property of both sexes and all nations alike. That is the humanist view. The Jews have had no artists not because they have no genius for art, but because their image of themselves as a culture inhibited the exercise of the latent gift. And all those nonexistent female Newtons° and Bachs° and Leonardos° and Shakespeares (all? surely they would be very few indeed, so rare is genius of that degree)—they have had no more chance of leaping from the prison of their societal fates than any Greek slave, or a nomad's child in Yemen today. The emancipation of women is spectacularly new. Emancipation does not instantly result in achievement. Enlightenment must follow. And the enlightenment has, for women, and especially by women, not yet occurred.

It has not yet occurred even at the most expressive point of all—in the universities. It is the function of a liberal university not to give right answers, but to ask right questions. And the ultimate humanist question, as we have seen, has not yet been expressed (my students had never in all their lives heard it put); the components of the unrealized question, as we have seen, are the experiences and needs and omissions and premises of a culture. A culture can have a seemingly unchanging premise, and then suddenly it will change; hence, among the Jews, Chagall° and Modigliani° and Epstein;° hence, in literature, the early epistolary artists—Madame de Sévigné and Lady Mary—and then, close on their heels, the genius novelists, Jane and George. Literature was the first to begin it, since literature could be pursued privately and at home. But here let us listen to Elizabeth Hardwick:° "Who is to say that *Remembrance of Things Past* is 'better' than the marvelous *Emma*? *War and Peace* better than *Middlemarch*? *Moby-Dick*[1] superior to *La Princesse de Clèves*?[2] But everybody says so! It is only the whimsical, the cantankerous, the eccentric . . . who would say that any literary work by a woman, marvelous as these may be, is on a level with the very greatest accomplishments of men."[3] I am not sure it is whimsical, cantankerous, or eccentric not to feel the need to make such distinctions, but even if the distinctions *are* justified—perhaps they are, I cannot tell—who is to say that *Emma* and *Middlemarch* and *La Princess de Clèves* are not simply forerunners? In England Lady Mary preceded Jane. In France Madame de Sévigné preceded George Sand.[4] Cultivation precedes fruition. Perhaps we cannot have our great women architects, painters, playwrights, sailors, bridge-builders, jurists, captains, composers, and so forth, until we have run-of-the-mill women in these roles, until all that is a commonplace—until, in short, women enter into the central stream of mankind's activities, until woman-as-person becomes as flat and unremarked a tradition as man-as-person. Reproduction, trick it out as you will in this or that myth, is still only reproduction, a natural and necessary biological function, and biology, however fancied up with tribal significance and mystical implication, is not enough. Unless you are on the extreme verge of death, it is never enough just to keep on breathing.

Even woman's differing muscular capacity—much is made of this, unsurprisingly—is, in the age of the comprehensive machine, an obstacle to almost no pursuit. It would be difficult to insist that a woman on board the sort of ship Conrad° describes in that remarkable novella "Youth" would be as efficient as most male members of the crew; but muscle is no longer an issue anywhere. Evolution has now become, in Julian Huxley's[5] words, a "psycho-social process"—that is, man is now able consciously to contribute to his own development. He lives, Huxley writes, "not only in relation with the physico-chemical and biological environment provided by nature, but with the psycho-social environment of material and mental habitats which he has himself created," and those habitats include the muscle-augmenting machine and its incalculable influences. Might a woman have written "Youth"? Who would dare to say yes? In Conrad's° day—in the scope of technology a very short time ago—almost no woman and very few men could have the stamina to wrest out Conrad's° strenuous

---

[1]See Proust,° Austen,° Tolstoy,° G. Eliot,° and Melville.°

[2]1678; a novel by the comtesse de La Fayette, considered a precursor of modern psychological fiction. The princess struggles to stay loyal to her husband, who dies in bitterness when she confesses her love for another.

[3] *A View of One's Own.* [Ozick's note.]

[4]Pseudonym of Amandine Aurore Lucie Dupin, baronne Dudevant (1804–1876), French novelist who divorced the baron in 1836 and left with her two children to live in Paris. There she wrote over eighty popular novels and had affairs with Sandeau, Musset, Chopin, and others. Her best-known works are *La Mare au diable* (*The Haunted Pool*), *Les Maîtres sonneurs* (*The Master Bell-Ringers*) and *La Petite Fadette* (*Fanchon the Cricket*).

[5]British biologist (1887–1975), brother of Aldous, grandson of T. H., professor of zoology at King's College, London, and secretary of the Zoological Society of London.

sea experience. Yet the machine widens experience for everyone and equalizes the physical endurance of men and women. A long journey is no longer a matter of muscle, but of jet schedules. Presumably it will become harder and harder to maintain that novelists who are women are condemned to a narrower focus than men because their lives are perforce narrower. The cult of Experience is, more and more, accessible to anyone who wishes to be lured by it: though it might well be argued that novels and poems grow out of something other than raw physical experience. "It is not suggested," Elizabeth Hardwick° continues, "that muscles write books, but there is a certain sense in which, talent and experience being equal, they may be considered a bit of an advantage. In the end, it is in the matter of experience that women's disadvantage is catastrophic. It is very difficult to know how this may be extraordinarily altered." Huxley's self-propelled evolutionary view is more optimistic, though perhaps both views, Hardwick's° and Huxley's, are at bottom equally irrelevant to the making of literature, which is, after all, as unknown a quantity as mind itself.

The question is, then, I believe, a question touching at least peripherally on art. Not merely literary art, but all the human arts, including those we call science. And I have ventured that the question must be formulated as a humanistic issue, not a sectarian one, not a divisive one. Art must belong to all human beings, not alone to a traditionally privileged segment; every endeavor, every passion must be available to the susceptible adult, without the intervention of myth or canard. Woman will cease solely to be man's muse—an It (as she is, curiously, for writers as disparate as Graves° and Mailer,° or as she was for Freud°)—and will acquire muses of her own when she herself ceases to be bemused with gaudy daydreams and romances—with lies reinforcing lies—about her own nature. She limits—she self-limits—her aspirations and her expectations. She joins the general mockery at her possibilities. I have heard her laughing at herself as though she were a dancing dog. You have seen her regard her life as a disease to be constantly tended and pacified. She does not yet really believe that she is herself accessible to poetry or science: she wills these into her sons, but not into her daughters. She surrounds herself with the devices and manipulations of an identity that is not an identity. Without protest she permits the intractable momentum of society to keep her from its worthiness and larger adventures, from its expressive labor. She lives among us like a docile captive; a consuming object; an accomplice; an It. She has even been successfully persuaded to work for and at her own imprisonment. No one can deny that imprisonment offers advantages, especially to the morally lazy. There have been slaves who have rejoiced in their slavery (think of the Children of Israel yearning day and night for the fleshpots of Egypt), and female infantilism is a kind of pleasurable slavishness. Dependency, the absence of decisions and responsibility, the avoidance of risk, the shutting-out of the gigantic toil of art—all these are the comforts of the condoning contented subject, and when these are combined, as they are in this country, with excessive leisure, it would almost seem that woman has a vested interest in her excluded role. If one were to bow to the tempting idea that her role has come about through a conspiracy (as it could not have, since custom is no plot), it would appear as though it were a conspiracy of sluggish women, and never of excluding men. The fervor and energies of the women who are not lazy, those rare activist personalities who feel the call of a Cause, are thrown pragmatically into the defense of that easy and comfortable role; the barricades of the pleasant prison are manned—no, wom-aned—by the inmates themselves, to prevent the rebels from breaking out.

But the rebels are few.

That is because among us for a long time no one rebelled, no one protested, no one wanted to renovate or liberate, no one asked any fundamental question. We have had, alas, and still have, the doubtful habit of reverence. Above all, we respect things as they are. If we want to step on the moon, it is not to explore an unknown surface or to divine a new era, but to bolster ourselves at home, among the old home rivals; there is more preening than science in that venture, less boldness than bravado. We are so placid that the smallest tremor of objection to anything at all is taken as a full-scale revolution. Should any soul speak up in favor of the obvious, it is taken as a symptom of the influence of the left, the right, the pink, the black, the dangerous. An idea for its own sake—especially an obvious idea—has no respectability.

Among my students—let us come back to *them*, since they are our societal prototypes—all this was depressingly plain. That is why they could not write intelligibly—no one had ever mentioned the relevance of writing to thinking, and thinking had never been encouraged or induced in them. By "thinking" I mean, of course, not the simple ability to make equations come out right, but the devotion to speculation on that frail but obsessive distraction known as the human condition. My students—male and female—did not need to speculate on what goals are proper to the full life; male and female, they already knew their goals. And their goals were identical. They all wanted to settle down into a perpetual and phantom coziness. They were all at heart sentimentalists—and sentimentalists, Yeats° said, are persons "who believe in money, in position, in a marriage bell, and whose understanding of happiness is to be so busy whether at work or play, that all is forgotten but the momentary aim." Accordingly, they had all determined, long ago, to pursue the steady domestic life, the enclosed life, the restricted life—the life, in brief, of the daydream, into which the obvious must not be permitted to thrust its scary beams.

By the "obvious" I mean, once again, the gifts and teachings and life-illuminations of art. The methods of art are variegated, flexible, abstruse, and often enough mysterious. But the burden of art is obvious: here is the world, here are human beings, here is childhood, here is struggle, here is hate, here is old age, here is death. None of these is a fantasy, a romance, or a sentiment, none is an imagining; all are obvious. A culture that does not allow itself to look clearly at the obvious through the universal accessibility of art is a culture of tragic delusion, hardly living; it will make room for a system of fantasy Offices on the one hand, and a system of fantasy Homes on the other, but it will forget that the earth lies beneath all. It will turn out role-playing stereotypes (the hideousness of the phrase is appropriate to the concept) instead of human beings. It will shut the children away from half the population. It will shut aspiration away from half the population. It will glut its colleges with young people enduringly maimed by illusions learned early and kept late. It will sup on make-believe. But a humanist society—you and I do not live in one—is one in which a voice is heard: "Come," it says, "here is a world requiring architects, painters, playwrights, sailors, bridge-builders, jurists, captains, composers, discoverers, and a thousand things besides, all real and all obvious. Partake," it says; "live."

Is it a man's voice or a woman's voice? Students, colleagues, listen again; it is two voices. "How obvious," you will one day reply, and if you laugh, it will be at the quaint folly of obsolete custom, which once failed to harness the obvious; it will not be at a dancing dog. ✍

A Drugstore in Winter[1]

This is about reading; a drugstore in winter; the gold leaf on the dome of the Boston State House; also loss, panic, and dread.

First, the gold leaf. (This part is a little like a turn-of-the-century pulp tale, though only a little. The ending is a surprise, but there is no plot.) Thirty years ago I burrowed in the Boston Public Library one whole afternoon, to find out—not out of curiosity—how the State House got its gold roof. The answer, like the answer to most Bostonian questions, was Paul Revere. So I put Paul Revere's gold dome into an "article," and took it (though I was just as scared by recklessness then as I am now) to the Boston Globe, on Washington Street. The Features Editor had a bare severe head, a closed parenthesis mouth, and silver Dickensian° spectacles. He made me wait, standing, at the side of his desk while he read; there was no bone in me that did not rattle. Then he opened a drawer and handed me fifteen dollars. Ah, joy of Homer,° joy of Milton!° Grub Street[2] bliss!

The very next Sunday, Paul Revere's gold dome saw print. Appetite for more led me to a top-floor chamber in Filene's department store: Window Dressing. But no one was in the least bit dressed—it was a dumbstruck nudist colony up there, a mob of naked frozen enigmatic manikins, tall enameled skinny ladies with bald breasts and skulls, and legs and wrists and necks that horribly unscrewed. Paul Revere's dome paled beside this gold mine! A sight—mute numb Walpurgisnacht[3]—easily worth another fifteen dollars. I had a Master's degree (thesis topic: "Parable in the Later Novels of Henry James"°) and a job as an advertising copywriter (9 a.m. to 6 p.m. six days a week, forty dollars per week; if you were male and had no degree at all, sixty dollars). Filene's Sale Days—Crib Bolsters! Lulla-Buys! Jonnie-Mops! Maternity Skirts with Expanding Invisible

---

[1]First published in The New York Times Book Review, January 21, 1982.
[2]Street in London, now called Milton Street, where poor journalists and literary hacks once lived.
[3]Nightmare world of the witches' Sabbath, said to occur on the night before May Day in Germany; from St. Walburga, whose feast day is May 1.

Trick Waist! And a company show; gold watches to mark the retirement of elderly Irish salesladies; for me the chance to write song lyrics (to the tune of "On Top of Old Smoky") honoring our Store. But "Mute Numb Walpurgisnacht in Secret Downtown Chamber" never reached the *Globe*. Melancholy and meaning business, the Advertising Director forbade it. Grub Street was bad form, and I had to promise never again to sink to another article. Thus ended my life in journalism.

Next: reading, and certain drugstore winter dusks. These come together. It is an aeon before Filene's, years and years before the Later Novels of Henry James.° I am scrunched on my knees at a round glass table near a plate glass door on which is inscribed, in gold leaf Paul Revere never put there, letters that must be read backward: PARK VIEW PHARMACY There is an evening smell of late coffee from the fountain, and all the librarians are lined up in a row on the tall stools, sipping and chattering. They have just stepped in from the cold of the Traveling Library, and so have I. The Traveling Library is a big green truck that stops, once every two weeks, on the corner of Continental Avenue, just a little way in from Westchester Avenue, not far from a house that keeps a pig. Other houses fly pigeons from their roofs, other yards have chickens, and down on Mayflower there is even a goat. This is Pelham Bay, the Bronx, in the middle of the Depression, all cattails and weeds, such a lovely place and tender hour! Even though my mother takes me on the subway far, far downtown to buy my winter coat in the frenzy of Klein's on Fourteenth Street, and even though I can recognize the heavy power of a quarter, I don't know it's the Depression. On the trolley on the way to Westchester Square I see the children who live in the boxcar strangely set down in an empty lot some distance from Spy Oak (where a Revolutionary traitor was hanged—served him right for siding with redcoats); the lucky boxcar children dangle their stick-legs from their train-house maw and wave; how I envy them! I envy the orphans of the Gould Foundation,[1] who have their own private swings and seesaws. Sometimes I imagine I am an orphan, and my father is an imposter pretending to be my father.

My father writes in his prescription book: *#59330 Dr. O'Flaherty Pow .60/ #59331 Dr. Mulligan Gtt .65/ #59332 Dr. Thron Tab .90.* Ninety cents! A terrifically expensive medicine; someone is really sick. When I deliver a prescription around the corner or down the block, I am offered a nickel tip. I always refuse, out of conscience; I am, after all, the Park View Pharmacy's own daughter, and it wouldn't be seemly. My father grinds and mixes powders, weighs them out in tiny snowy heaps on an apothecary scale, folds them into delicate translucent papers or meticulously drops them into gelatin capsules.

In the big front window of the Park View Pharmacy there is a startling display—goldfish bowls, balanced one on the other in amazing pyramids. A German lady enters, one of my father's cronies—his cronies are both women and men. My quiet father's eyes are water-color blue, he wears his small skeptical

---

[1]Edwin Gould Foundation for Children, established in 1923 "to promote the welfare of children" through grants and scholarships to institutions primarily in New York City.

quiet smile and receives the neighborhood's life-secrets. My father is discreet and inscrutable. The German lady pokes a punchboard with a pin, pushes up a bit of rolled paper, and cries out—she has just won a goldfish bowl, with two swimming goldfish in it! Mr. Jaffe, the salesman from McKesson & Robbins, arrives, trailing two mists: winter steaminess and the animal fog of his cigar,[1] which melts into the coffee smell, the tarpaper smell, the eerie honeyed tangled drugstore smell. Mr. Jaffe and my mother and father are intimates by now, but because it is the 1930s, so long ago, and the old manners still survive, they address one another gravely as Mr. Jaffe, Mrs. Ozick, Mr. Ozick. My mother calls my father Mr. O, even at home, as in a Victorian novel. In the street my father tips his hat to ladies. In the winter his hat is a regular fedora; in the summer it is a straw boater with a black ribbon and a jot of blue feather.

What am I doing at this round glass table, both listening and not listening to my mother and father tell Mr. Jaffe about their struggle with "Tessie," the lion-eyed landlady who has just raised, threefold, in the middle of that Depression I have never heard of, the Park View Pharmacy's devouring rent? My mother, not yet forty, wears bandages on her ankles, covering oozing varicose veins; back and forth she strides, dashes, runs, climbing cellar stairs or ladders; she unpacks cartons, she toils behind drug counters and fountain counters. Like my father, she is on her feet until one in the morning, the Park View's closing hour. My mother and father are in trouble, and I don't know it. I am too happy. I feel the secret center of eternity, nothing will ever alter, no one will ever die. Through the window, past the lit goldfish, the gray oval sky deepens over our neighborhood wood, where all the dirt paths lead down to seagull-specked water. I am familiar with every frog-haunted monument: Pelham Bay Park is thronged with WPA[2] art—statuary, fountains, immense rococo staircases cascading down a hillside, Bacchus°-faced stelae[3]—stone Roman glories afterward mysteriously razed by an avenging Robert Moses.[4] One year—how distant it seems now, as if even the climate is past returning—the bay froze so hard that whole families, mine among them, crossed back and forth to City Island, strangers saluting and calling out in the ecstasy of the bright trudge over such a sudden wilderness of ice.

In the Park View Pharmacy, in the winter dusk, the heart in my body is revolving like the goldfish fleet-finned in their clear bowls. The librarians are still warming up over their coffee. They do not recognize me, though only half an hour ago I was scrabbling in the mud around the two heavy boxes from the Traveling Library—oafish crates tossed with a thump to the ground. One box contains magazines—*Boy's Life, The American Girl, Popular Mechanix*. But the other, the

---

[1]Mr. Matthew Bruccoli, another Bronx drugstore child, has written to say that he remembers with certainty that Mr. Jaffe did not smoke. In my memory the cigar is somehow there, so I leave it. [Ozick's note.]

[2]Work Projects Administration agency established in 1935 by President Roosevelt (then called Works Progress Administration) to employ people and so improve the economy.

[3]Upright, inscribed stones or slabs; from the Greek for "pillar."

[4](1888–1981) New York City park commissioner from 1934 to 1960.

other! The other transforms me. It is tumbled with storybooks, with clandestine intimations and transfigurations. In school I am a luckless goosegirl, friendless and forlorn. In P.S. 71 I carry, weighty as a cloak, the ineradicable knowledge of my scandal—I am cross-eyed, dumb, an imbecile at arithmetic; in P.S. 71 I am publicly shamed in Assembly because I am caught not singing Christmas carols; in P.S. 71 I am repeatedly accused of deicide. But in the Park View Pharmacy, in the winter dusk, branches blackening in the park across the road, I am driving in rapture through the Violet Fairy Book and the Yellow Fairy Book, insubstantial chariots snatched from the box in the mud. I have never been *inside* the Traveling Library; only grownups are allowed. The boxes are for the children. No more than two books may be borrowed, so I have picked the fattest ones, to last. All the same, the Violet and the Yellow are melting away. Their pages dwindle. I sit at the round glass table, dreaming, dreaming. Mr. Jaffe is murmuring advice. He tells a joke about Wrong-Way Corrigan.[1] The librarians are buttoning up their coats. A princess, captive of an ogre, receives a letter from her swain and hides it in her bosom. I can visualize her bosom exactly—she clutches it against her chest. It is a tall and shapely vase, with a hand-painted flower on it, like the vase on the secondhand piano at home.

I am incognito. No one knows who I truly am. The teachers in P.S. 71 don't know. Rabbi Meskin, my *cheder* teacher,[2] doesn't know. Tessie the lion-eyed landlady doesn't know. Even Hymie the fountain clerk can't know—though he understands other things better than anyone: how to tighten roller skates with a skatekey, for instance, and how to ride a horse. On Friday afternoons, when the new issue is out, Hymie and my brother fight hard over who gets to see *Life* magazine first. My brother is older than I am, and doesn't like me; he builds radios in his bedroom, he is already W2LOM, and operates his transmitter (*da-di-da-dit, da-da-di-da*) so penetratingly on Sunday mornings that Mrs. Eva Brady, across the way, complains. Mrs. Eva Brady has a subscription to *The Writer*; I fill a closet with her old copies. How to Find a Plot. Narrative and Character, the Writer's Tools. Because my brother has his ham license, I say, "I have a license too." "What kind of license?" my brother asks, falling into the trap. "Poetic license," I reply; my brother hates me, but anyhow his birthday presents are transporting: one year *Alice in Wonderland*, *Pinocchio* the next, then *Tom Sawyer*. I go after Mark Twain, and find *Joan of Arc* and my first satire, *Christian Science*. My mother surprises me with *Pollyanna*, the admiration of her Lower East Side childhood, along with *The Lady of the Lake*. Mrs. Eva Brady's daughter Jeannie has outgrown her Nancy Drews and Judy Boltons, so on rainy afternoons I cross the street and borrow them, trying not to march away with too many—the child of

---

[1]Douglas Corrigan allegedly took off from New York in July 1938, heading for Los Angeles; he landed in Ireland twenty-seven hours later, supposedly unable to see the Atlantic Ocean because of fog. In fact, denied an application to fly to Ireland, he may have fabricated the famous tale of his 180° error.

[2]Religion teacher.

immigrants, I worry that the Bradys, true and virtuous Americans, will judge me greedy or careless. I wrap the Nancy Drews in paper covers to protect them. Old Mrs. Brady, Jeannie's grandmother, invites me back for more. I am so timid I can hardly speak a word, but I love her dark parlor; I love its black bookcases. Old Mrs. Brady sees me off, embracing books under an umbrella; perhaps she divines who I truly am. My brother doesn't care. My father doesn't notice. I think my mother knows. My mother reads the *Saturday Evening Post* and the *Woman's Home Companion*; sometimes the *Ladies Home Journal*, but never *Good Housekeeping*. I read all my mother's magazines. My father reads *Drug Topics* and *Der Tog*, the Yiddish daily. In Louie Davidowitz's house (waiting our turn for the rabbi's lesson, he teaches me chess in *cheder*) there is a piece of furniture I am in awe of: a shining circular table that is also a revolving bookshelf holding a complete set of Charles Dickens.° I borrow *Oliver Twist*. My cousins turn up with *Gulliver's Travels*, *Just So Stories*, *Don Quixote*,[1] Oscar Wilde's° *Fairy Tales*, uncannily different from the usual kind. Blindfolded, I reach into a Thanksgiving grabbag and pull out *Mrs. Leicester's School*, Mary Lamb's desolate stories of rejected children.[2] Books spill out of rumor, exchange, miracle. In the Park View Pharmacy's lending library I discover, among the nurse romances, a browning, brittle miracle: *Jane Eyre*.[3] Uncle Morris comes to visit (*his* drugstore is on the other side of the Bronx) and leaves behind, just like that, a three-volume Shakespeare. Peggy and Betty Provan, Scottish sisters around the corner, lend me their *Swiss Family Robinson*.[4] Norma Foti, a whole year older, transmits a rumor about Louisa May Alcott;° afterward I read *Little Women* a thousand times. Ten thousand! I am no longer incognito, not even to myself. I am Jo in her "vortex"; not Jo exactly, but some Jo-of-the-future. I am under an enchantment: who I truly am must be deferred, waited for and waited for. My father, silently filling capsules, is grieving over his mother in Moscow. I write letters in Yiddish to my Moscow grandmother, whom I will never know. I will never know my Russian aunts, uncles, cousins. In Moscow there is suffering, deprivation, poverty. My mother, threadbare, goes without a new winter coat so that packages can be sent to Moscow. Her fiery justice-eyes are semaphores I cannot decipher.

Some day, when I am free of P.S. 71, I will write stories; meanwhile, in winter dusk, in the Park View, in the secret bliss of the Violet Fairy Book, I both see and do not see how these grains of life will stay forever, papa and mama will live forever, Hymie will always turn my skatekey.

Hymie, after Italy, after the Battle of the Bulge, comes back from the war with a present: *From Here to Eternity*.[5] Then he dies, young. Mama reads *Pride and*

---

[1] See Swift,° Kipling,° and Cervantes.°

[2] See biography of Charles Lamb.

[3] See Charlotte Brontë.°

[4] Popular children's book by Swiss author Johann Wyss (1743–1818), translated into English in 1818.

[5] Novel (1951) by James Jones (1931–1977), American novelist whose works also include *Some Came Running* (1958), *The Thin Red Line* (1962) and *WW II* (1975).

Prejudice[1] and every single word of Willa Cather.° Papa reads in Yiddish, all of Sholem Aleichem[2] and Peretz.[3] He reads Malamud's[4] *The Assistant* when I ask him to.

Papa and mama, in Staten Island, are under the ground. Some other family sits transfixed in the sun parlor where I read *Jane Eyre* and *Little Women* and, long afterward, *Middlemarch*.[5] The Park View Pharmacy is dismantled, turned into a Hallmark card shop. It doesn't matter! I close my eyes, or else only stare, and everything is in its place again, and everyone.

A writer is dreamed and transfigured into being by spells, wishes, goldfish, silhouettes of trees, boxes of fairy tales dropped in the mud, uncles' and cousins' books, tablets and capsules and powders, papa's Moscow ache, his drugstore jacket with his special fountain pen in the pocket, his beautiful Hebrew paragraphs, his Talmudist's rationalism, his Russian-Gymnasium Latin and German, mama's furnace-heart, her masses of memoirs, her paintings of autumn walks down to the sunny water, her braveries, her reveries, her old, old school hurts.

A writer is buffeted into being by school hurts—Orwell, Forster,° Mann!°— but after a while other ambushes begin: sorrows, deaths, disappointments, subtle diseases, delays, guilts, the spite of the private haters of the poetry side of life, the snubs of the glamorous, the bitterness of those for whom resentment is a daily gruel, and so on and so on; and then one day you find yourself leaning here, writing at that selfsame round glass table salvaged from the Park View Pharmacy—writing this, an impossibility, a summary of how you came to be where you are now, and where, God knows, is that? Your hair is whitening, you are a well of tears, what you meant to do (beauty and justice) you have not done, papa and mama are under the earth, you live in panic and dread, the future shrinks and darkens, stories are only vapor, your inmost craving is for nothing but an old scarred pen, and what, God knows, is that? ✎

The Seam of the Snail[6]

In my Depression childhood, whenever I had a new dress, my cousin Sarah would get suspicious. The nicer the dress was, and especially the more expensive it looked, the more suspicious she would get. Finally she would lift the hem and

---

[1]See Austen.°

[2]Pseudonym for Solomon Rabinowitz (1859–1916), novelist and short story writer influential in establishing Yiddish as a literary language and best known for his humorous tales of Chelm. The best-known anthology is *The World of Shalom Aleichem* (1943).

[3]Isaac Loeb (1852–1915), novelist, poet, and dramatist, born in Poland, who wrote in Hebrew and Yiddish about the ghetto life of European Jews.

[4]Bernard (1914–1986), American writer of short stories (collected in *The Magic Barrel*) and novels, including *The Fixer* and *The Natural*.

[5]See George Eliot.°

[6]First published as "Excellence" in *MS.*, January 1985.

check the seams. This was to see if the dress had been bought or if my mother had sewed it. Sarah could always tell. My mother's sewing had elegant outsides, but there was something catch-as-catch-can about the insides. Sarah's sewing, by contrast, was as impeccably finished inside as out; not one stray thread dangled.

My uncle Jake built meticulous grandfather clocks out of rosewood; he was a perfectionist, and sent to England for the clockworks. My mother built service-able radiator covers and a serviceable cabinet, with hinged doors, for the pantry. She built a pair of bookcases for the living room. Once, after I was grown and in a house of my own, she fixed the sewer pipe. She painted ceilings, and also landscapes; she reupholstered chairs. One summer she planted a whole yard of tall corn. She thought herself capable of doing anything, and did everything she imagined. But nothing was perfect. There was always some clear flaw, never visible head-on. You had to look underneath, where the seams were. The corn thrived, though not in rows. The stalks elbowed one another like gossips in a dense little village.

"Miss Brrrroooobaker," my mother used to mock, rolling her Russian r's, whenever I crossed a t she had left uncrossed, or corrected a word she had misspelled, or became impatient with a v that had tangled itself up with a w in her speech. ("Vvventriloquist," I would say. "Vvventriloquist," she would obediently repeat. And the next time it would come out "wiolinist.") Miss Brubaker was my high school English teacher, and my mother invoked her name as an emblem of raging finical obsession. "Miss Brrrroooobaker," my mother's voice hoots at me down the years, as I go on casting and recasting sentences in a tiny handwriting on monomaniacally uniform paper. The loops of my mother's handwriting—it was the Palmer Method[1]—were as big as soup bowls, spilling generous splashy ebullience. She could pull off, at five minutes' notice, a satisfying dinner for ten concocted out of nothing more than originality and panache. But the napkin would be folded a little off center, and the spoon might be on the wrong side of the knife. She was an optimist who ignored trifles; for her, God was not in the details but in the intent. And all these culinary and agricultural efflorescences were extracurricular, accomplished in the crevices and niches of a fourteen-hour business day. When she scribbled out her family memoirs, in heaps of dog-eared notebooks, or on the backs of old bills, or on the margins of last year's calendar, I would resist typing them; in the speed of the chase she often omitted words like "the," "and," "will." The same flashing and bountiful hand fashioned and fired ceramic pots, and painted brilliant autumn views and vases of imaginary flowers and ferns, and decorated ordinary Woolworth platters with lavish enameled gardens. But bits of the painted petals would chip away.

Lavish: my mother was as lavish as nature. She woke early and saturated the hours with work and inventiveness, and read late into the night. She was all profusion, abundance, fabrication. Angry at her children, she would run after us whirling the cord of the electric iron, like a lasso or a whip; but she never caught

---

[1]Introduced in 1888, it taught penmanship using model letter forms (that adorned every ele-mentary classroom) and free-flowing forearm exercises to practice loops and circles.

us. When, in seventh grade, I was afraid of failing the Music Appreciation final exam because I could not tell the difference between "To a Wild Rose" and "Barcarole,"[1] she got the idea of sending me to school with a gauze sling rigged up on my writing arm, and an explanatory note that was purest fiction. But the sling kept slipping off. My mother gave advice like mad—she boiled over with so much passion for the predicaments of strangers that they turned into permanent cronies. She told intimate stories about people I had never heard of.

Despite the gargantuan Palmer loops (or possibly because of them), I have always known that my mother's was a life of—intricately abashing word!— excellence: insofar as excellence means ripe generosity. She burgeoned, she proliferated; she was endlessly leafy and flowering. She wore red hats, and called herself a gypsy. In her girlhood she marched with the suffragettes and for Margaret Sanger° and called herself a Red.[2] She made me laugh, she was so varied: like a tree on which lemons, pomegranates, and prickly pears absurdly all hang together. She had the comedy of prodigality.

My own way is a thousand times more confined. I am a pinched perfectionist, the ultimate fruition of Miss Brubaker; I attend to crabbed minutiae and am self-trammeled through taking pains. I am a kind of human snail, locked in and condemned by my own nature. The ancients believed that the moist track left by the snail as it crept was the snail's own essence, depleting its body little by little; the farther the snail toiled, the smaller it became, until it finally rubbed itself out. That is how perfectionists are. Say to us Excellence, and we will show you how we use up our substance and wear ourselves away, while making scarcely any progress at all. The fact that I am an exacting perfectionist in a narrow strait only, and nowhere else, is hardly to the point, since nothing matters to me so much as a comely and muscular sentence. It is my narrow strait, this snail's road; the track of the sentence I am writing now; and when I have eked out the wet substance, ink or blood, that is its mark, I will begin the next sentence. Only in treading out sentences am I perfectionist; but then there is nothing else I know how to do, or take much interest in. I miter every pair of abutting sentences as scrupulously as Uncle Jake fitted one strip of rosewood against another. My mother's worldly and bountiful hand has escaped me. The sentence I am writing is my cabin and my shell, compact, self-sufficient. It is the burnished horizon—a merciless planet where flawlessness is the single standard, where even the inmost seams, however hidden from a laxer eye, must meet perfection. Here "excellence" is not strewn casually from a tipped cornucopia, here disorder does not account for charm, here trifles rule like tyrants.

I measure my life in sentences pressed out, line by line, like the lustrous ooze on the underside of the snail, the snail's secret open seam, its wound, leaking attar.[3] My mother was too mettlesome to feel the force of a comma. She scorned

---

[1]"To a Wild Rose" (1986): music by Edward MacDowell (1861–1908); "Barcarolle": by J. Offenbach, from *The Tales of Hoffman* (1881), with lyrics by Jules Paul Barbier (1822–1901).

[2]A communist.

[3]A fragrant oil extracted from the petals of flowers.

minutiae. She measured her life according to what poured from the horn of plenty, which was her own seamless, ample, cascading, elastic, susceptible, inexact heart. My narrower heart rides between the tiny twin horns of the snail, dwindling as it goes.

And out of this thinnest thread, this ink-wet line of words, must rise a visionary fog, a mist, a smoke, forging cities, histories, sorrows, quagmires, entanglements, lives of sinners, even the life of my furnace-hearted mother: so much wilderness, waywardness, plenitude on the head of the precise and impeccable snail, between the horns. (Ah, if this could be!) ✍

Crocodiled Moats in the Kingdom of Letters[1]

> For constantly I felt I was moving among two groups—comparable in intelligence, identical in race, not grossly different in social origin, earning about the same incomes, who had almost ceased to communicate at all, who in intellectual, moral and psychological climate had so little in common that . . . one might have crossed an ocean.
>
> C.P. SNOW, *The Two Cultures and the Scientific Revolution*

Disraeli° in his novel *Sybil* spoke of "two nations," the rich and the poor. After the progress of more than a century, the phrase (and the reality) remains regrettably apt. But in the less than three decades since C. P. Snow[2] proposed his "two cultures" thesis—the gap of incomprehension between the scientific and literary elites—the conditions of what we still like to call culture have altered so drastically that Snow's arguments are mostly dissolved into pointlessness. His compatriot and foremost needler, the Cambridge critic F. R. Leavis,[3] had in any case set out to flog Snow's hypothesis from the start. Snow, he said, "rides on an advancing swell of cliché," "doesn't know what literature is," and hasn't "had the advantage of an intellectual discipline of any kind." And besides—here Leavis emitted his final boom—"there is only one culture."

---

[1]First published as "Science and Letters—God's Work and Ours" in *The New York Times Book Review*, September 27, 1987.

[2]Charles Percy, Baron of Leicester (1905–1980), English writer and physicist who held various offices in government and wrote eleven novels entitled collectively *Strangers and Brothers*. *The Two Cultures* (1959) caused as much heated discussion among academics as the publication of *Cultural Literacy* (1987) by E. D. Hirsch and *The Closing of the American Mind* (1987) by Allan Bloom has caused in more recent times.

[3]Frank Raymond (1895–1978), British critic and teacher, editor of the literary quarterly *Scrutiny* from its founding in 1932 until its demise in 1953. His pronouncements on literature in the quarterly and in such works as *New Bearings in English Poetry* (1932) and especially *The Great Tradition* (1948), in which Leavis created his own literary canon (D. H. Lawrence, for instance, was in, whereas James Joyce° was out), caused considerable controversy in academia.

In the long run both were destined to be mistaken—Leavis perhaps more than Snow. In 1959, when Snow published *The Two Cultures*, we had already had well over a hundred years to get used to the idea of science as a multi-divergent venture—dozens and dozens of disciplines, each one nearly a separate nation with its own governance, psychology, entelechy.[1] It might have been possible to posit, say, a unitary medical culture in the days when barbers were surgeons; but in recent generations we don't expect our dentist to repair a broken kneecap, or our orthopedist to practice cardiology. And nowadays we are learning that an ophthalmologist with an understanding of the cornea is likely to be a bit shaky on the subject of the retina. Engineers are light-years from astrophysicists. Topology is distinct from topography, paleobotany from paleogeology. In reiterating that scientific culture is specialist culture—who doesn't know this?—one risks riding an advancing swell of cliché. Yet science, multiplying, fragmented, in hot pursuit of split ends, is in a way a species of polytheism, or, rather, animism: every grain of matter, every path of conceptualization, has its own ruling spirit, its differentiated lawgiver and traffic director. Investigative diversity and particularizing empiricism have been characteristic of science since—well, since alchemy turned into physical chemistry (and lately into superconductivity); since the teakettle inspired the locomotive; since Icarus° took off his wax wings to become Pan Am; since Archimedes° stepped out of his tub into Einstein's° sea.

Snow was in command of all this, of course—he was pleased to identify himself as an exceptional scientist who wrote novels—and still he chose to make a monolith out of splinters. Why did he do it? In order to have one unanimity confront another. While it may have been a polemical contrivance to present a diversiform scientific culture as unitary, it was patently not wrong, thirty years ago, to speak of literary culture as a single force or presence. That was what was meant by the peaceable word "humanities." And it was what Leavis meant, too, when he growled back at Snow that one culture was all there was worth having. "Don't mistake me," Leavis pressed, "I am not preaching that we should defy, or try to reverse, the accelerating movement of external civilization (the phrase sufficiently explains itself, I hope) that is determined by advancing technology. . . . What I *am* saying is that such a concern is not enough—disastrously not enough." Not enough, he argued, for "a human future . . . in full intelligent possession of its full humanity." For Leavis, technology was the mere outer rind of culture, and the job of literature (the hot core at the heart of culture) was not to oppose science but to humanize it. Only in Snow's wretchedly deprived mind did literature stand apart from science; Snow hardly understood what literature was *for*. And no wonder: Snow's ideas about literary intellectuals came, Leavis sneered, from "the reviewing in the Sunday papers."

It has never been easy to fashion a uniform image of science—which is why we tend to say "the sciences." But until not very long ago one could take it for

---

[1] In Aristotle,° the condition of full actualization as opposed to potential; selfhood.

granted (despite the headlong decline of serious high art) that there was, on the humanities side, a concordant language of sensibility, an embracing impulse toward integration, above all the conviction of human connectedness—even if that conviction occasionally partook of a certain crepuscular[1] nostalgia we might better have done without. Snow pictured literature and science as two angry armies. Leavis announced that there was only one army, with literature as its commander in chief. Yet it was plain that both Leavis and Snow, for all their antagonisms, saw the kingdom of letters as an intact and enduring power.

This feeling for literary culture as a glowing wholeness—it *was* a feeling, a stirring, a flush of idealism—is now altogether dissipated. The fragrant term that encapsuled it—belles-lettres—is nearly archaic and surely effete: it smacks of leather tooling for the moneyed, of posturing. But it was once useful enough. "Belles-lettres" stood for a binding thread of observation and civilizing emotion. It signified not so much that letters are beautiful as that the house of letters is encompassingly humane and undivisive, no matter how severally its windows are shaped, or who looks out or in. Poets, scholars, journalists, librarians, novelists, playwrights, art critics, philosophers, writers for children, historians, political theorists, and all the rest, may have inhabited different rooms, differently furnished, but it was indisputably one house with a single roof and plenty of connecting doors and passageways. And sometimes—so elastic and compressive was the humanist principle—poet, scholar, essayist, philosopher, etc., all lived side by side in the same head. Seamlessness (even if only an illusion) never implied locked and separate cells.

And now? Look around. Now "letters" suggests a thousand enemy camps, "genres" like fortresses, professions isolated by crocodiled moats. The living tissue of intuition and inference that nurtured the commonalty of the humanities is ruptured by an abrupt invasion of specialists. In emulation of the sciences? But we don't often hear of astronomers despising molecular biologists; in science, it may be natural for knowledge to run, like quicksilver, into crannies.

In the ex-community of letters, factions are in fashion, and the business of factions is to despise. Matthew Arnold's° mild and venerable dictum, an open-ended, open-armed definition of literature that clearly intends a nobility of inclusiveness—"the best that is known and thought in the world"—earns latter-day assaults and jeers. What can all that mean now but "canon," and what can a received canon mean but reactionary, racist, sexist, elitist closure? Politics presses against disinterestedness; what claims to be intrinsic is counted as no more than foregone conclusion. All categories are suspect, no category is allowed to display its wares without the charge of vested interest or ideological immanence. What Arnold° called the play of mind is asked to show its credentials and prove its legitimacy. "Our organs of criticism," Arnold complained in 1864 (a period as

---

[1]Hazy, from the Latin for "twilight."

uninnocent as our own), "are organs of men and parties having practical ends to serve, and with them those practical ends are the first thing and the play of mind the second."

And so it is with us. The culture of the humanities has split and split and split again, always for reasons of partisan ascendancy and scorn. Once it was not unusual for writers—Dreiser,[1] Stephen Crane,[2] Cather,° Hemingway!°—to turn to journalism for a taste of the workings of the world. Today novelists and journalists are alien breeds reared apart, as if imagination properly belonged only to the one and never to the other; as if society and instinct were designed for estrangement. The two crafts are contradictory even in method: journalists are urged to tell secrets in the top line; novelists insinuate suspensefully, and wait for the last line to spill the real beans. Dickens,° saturated in journalism, excelled at shorthand; was a court reporter; edited topical magazines.

In the literary academy, Jacques Derrida[3] has the authority that Duns Scotus[4] had for medieval scholastics—and it is authority, not literature, that mainly engages faculties. In the guise of maverick or rebel, professors kowtow to dogma. English departments have set off after theory, and use culture as an instrument to illustrate doctrinal principles, whether Marxist or "French Freud."[5] The play of mind gives way to signing up and lining up. College teachers were never cut off from the heat of poets dead or alive as they are now; only think of the icy distances separating syllables by, say Marianne Moore,[6] A. R. Ammons,[7] May Swenson,[8] or Amy Clampitt[9] from the papers read at last winter's Modern Language

---

[1]Theodore (1871–1945), American novelist who worked on newspapers in the Midwest and wrote for magazines in New York City before publishing such novels as *Sister Carrie* (1900) and *An American Tragedy* (1925).

[2]American short story writer and novelist (1871–1900) who worked as a free-lance writer in New York City before composing *The Red Badge of Courage* (1895). Later he served as a foreign correspondent in Cuba and Greece before publishing such collections of short stories as *The Open Boat and Other Tales* (1898) and *The Monster and Other Stories* (1899).

[3]French philosopher and literary critic (1930–), a founder of the deconstructionist movement. His works include *Grammatology* (1967), *Margins of Philosophy* (1972), and *Positions* (1972).

[4]Called the Subtle Doctor, Scotus (1266–1308) was born in Scotland and educated at Oxford, Paris, and Cologne. He founded a school of scholasticism that posits the "thisness" or essence of a thing as coming from God's will. His philosophy, explained in *On the First Principle*, remains influential in the Roman Catholic church today.

[5]A reference to Jacques Lacan (1901–1981), French psychoanalyst and founder of École freudienne de Paris. His writings were collected in *Écrits* (1966).

[6]American poet (1887–1972) who lived in New York City and worked as a librarian and as editor of *Dial* (1925–1929). Her poems are collected in *Poems, Observations, What Are Years?, Collected Poems, O to Be a Dragon,* and *Complete Poems.*

[7]American poet (1926–), author of *Tape for the Turn of the Year* (1965), one long poem written on adding machine roll, *The Snow Poems* (1977), and *A Coast of Trees* (1981). He won the National Book Award in 1973 for *Collected Poems.*

[8]American poet (1919–1989) born in Utah, whose works include *Another Animal* (1954), *More Poems to Solve* (1971), *New and Selected Things Taking Place* (1978), and a play, *The Floor* (1966).

[9]Iowa-born poet (1920–) whose works include *Multitudes and Multitudes* (1974), *The Kingfisher*

Association meeting—viz., "Written Discourse as Dialogic Interaction," "Abduction, Transference, and the Reading Stage," "The Politics of Feminism and the Discourse of Feminist Literary Criticism."

And more: poets trivialize novelists, novelists trivialize poets. Both trivialize critics. Critics trivialize reviewers. Reviewers retort that they *are* critics. Short-story writers assert transfigurations unavailable to novelists. Novelists declare the incomparable glories of the long pull. Novelizing aestheticians, admitting to literature no claims of moral intent, ban novelizing moralists. The moralists condemn the aestheticians as precious, barren, solipsist.[1] Few essayists essay fiction. Few novelists hazard essays. Dense-language writers vilify minimalists. Writers of plain prose ridicule complex sentences. Professors look down on commercial publishers. Fiction writers dread university presses. The so-called provinces envy and despise the provinciality of New York. New York sees sour grapes in California and everywhere else. The so-called mainstream judges which writers are acceptably universal and which are to be exiled as "parochial." The so-called parochial, stung or cowardly or both, fear all particularity and attempt impersonation of the acceptable "Star" writers—recall the 1986 International PEN Congress[2] in New York—treat lesser-knowns as invisible, negligible. The lesser-knowns, crushed, disparage the stars.

And even the public library, once the unchallenged repository of the best that is known and thought, begins to split itself off, abandons its mandate, and rents out Polaroid cameras and videotapes, like some semi-philanthropic Crazy Eddie.[3] My own local library, appearing to jettison the basic arguments of the age, flaunts shelf after shelf prominently marked Decorating, Consumer Power, How To, Cookery, Hooray for Hollywood, Accent on You, What Makes Us Laugh, and many more such chitchat categories. But there are no placards for Literature, History, Biography; and Snow and Leavis, whom I needed to moon over in order to get started on this essay, were neither one to be had. (I found them finally in the next town, in a much smaller if more traditionally bookish library.)

Though it goes against the grain of respected current belief to say so, literature is really *about* something. It is about us. That may be why we are drawn to think of the kingdom of letters as a unity, at least in potential. Science, teeming and multiform, is about how the earth and the heavens and the microbes and the insects and our mammalian bodies are constructed, but literature is about the meaning of the finished construction. Or, to set afloat a more transcendent vocabulary: science is about God's work; literature is about our work. If our work

---

(1983), and *What the Light Was Like* (1987). Her poems often contain erudite allusions and elaborate footnotes.

[1]Self-centered.

[2]A world association of poets, playwrights, editors, essayists, and novelists (hence the name PEN) founded in 1921 "to promote and maintain friendship and intellectual cooperation" among writers of all countries. It holds conferences and publishes a journal, the *PEN Bulletin*.

[3]The name of a now-defunct discount electronics chain as well as its "insane" TV pitchman, played by Jerry Carroll.

lies untended (and what is our work but aspiration?), if literary culture falls into a heap of adversarial splinters—into competing contemptuous clamorers for turf and mental dominance—then what will be left to tell us that we are one human presence?

To forward that strenuous telling, Matthew Arnold° (himself now among the jettisoned) advised every reader and critic to "try and possess one great literature, at least, besides his own; and the more unlike his own, the better." Not to split off from but to add on to the kingdom of letters: so as to uncover its human face.

An idea that—in a time of ten thousand self-segregating literary technologies—may be unwanted, if not obsolete. ✍

Forewarning[1]

Here is a late learning: a fiction writer who also writes essays is looking for trouble. While stories and novels under the eye of a good reader are permitted to bask in the light of the free imagination, essays are held to a sterner standard. No good reader of fiction will suppose that a character's ideas and emotions are consistently, necessarily, inevitably, the writer's ideas and emotions; but most good readers of essays unfailingly trust the veracity of non-narrative prose. A story is known to reflect in its "attitudes" the concrete particularities of its invention; every story is its own idiosyncratic occasion, and each occasion governs tone, point of view, conclusion. A story, in brief, is regarded as an ad hoc contrivance, and if it is called as witness, it is in the court of the conditional, the subjective, the provisional, even the lyrical.

An essay, by contrast, is almost always hauled before the most sobersided court of all, presided over by judges who will scrutinize the evidence for true belief: absolute and permanent congruence of the writer and what is on the page. An essay is rarely seen to be a bewitched contraption in the way of a story. An essayist is generally assumed to be a reliable witness, sermonizer, lecturer, polemicist, persuader, historian, advocate: a committed intelligence, a single-minded truth-speaker.

But when a writer writes both stories and essays, something else can happen: the essays will too often be forced into a tailoring job for which they were never intended. The essays, like chalk marks, are used to take the measure of the stories. The essays become the stories' interpreters: their clues, or cues, or concordances, as if the premises of the essays were incontrovertibly the premises of the stories as well. As if the stories were "illustrations" of the essays; as if the essays expressed the ideational (or even at times the ideological) matrix of the stories.

All these notions are, I am afraid, plain foolishness. They imagine that there is a commanding difference between essays and stories, and that the difference is

---

[1]Foreword to *Metaphor & Memory* (1989).

pure: essays are "honest" and stories are made up. The reality is otherwise: all good stories are honest and most good essays are not. Stories, when they succeed *as* stories, tend to be honest even when they concern themselves with fraudulence, or especially then (Tolstoy's° *The Death of Ivan Ilych* comes instantly to mind); stories are moods—illuminations—that last in their original form. A new story will hardly contradict a prior one: each has worked for, and argued, its own embodiment, its own consummation. Stories are understood to represent desire, or conviction, at its most mercurial. Originality, in fiction, *means* mercurial. Nobody wants all the stories a writer produces to resemble one another, to conform to a predictable line. The truth of one story is not implicated in the truth of the next.

But essays are expected to take a "position," to show a consistency of temperament, a stability of viewpoint. Essays are expected to make the writer's case. Sometimes, of course, they do; I feel fairly sure the book reviews in this volume incorporate judgments that time and temper will not seriously alter. Yet most essays, like stories, are not designed to stand still in this way. A story is a hypothesis, a tryout of human nature under the impingement of certain given materials; so is an essay. After which, the mind moves on. Nearly every essay, like every story, is an experiment, not a credo.

Or, to put it more stringently: an essay, like a story or a novel, is a fiction. A fiction, by definition, is that which is made up in response to an excited imagination. What is fictitious about the essay is that it is pretending not to be made up—so that reading an essay may be more dangerous than reading a story. This very foreword, for instance, may count as a little essay: ought it to be trusted? (Remember the Cretan captured by Greeks. Questioned, he replied: "All Cretans are liars." Was this a truthful confession, or only another sample of a Cretan lying? After all, even Tolstoy,° whom we think of as the quintessential novelist, was a kind of Cretan. First he wrote *Anna Karenina*; then he wrote "What Is Art?"—condemning the writing of novels. Which Tolstoy° should we believe?)

The point is not that essays are untrustworthy. Obviously, an essay will fail if it is not intellectually coherent, if it does not strike you as authentic (ideas must be earned, not merely learned), if it is not felt to be reliably truth-telling. An essay must show all these indispensable signs of consonance and conscience—but only for the duration of its reading, or a bit longer. If its "authenticity" is compelled to last much beyond that, the reader will be tying the writer down by small stakes and long strings, like Gulliver;[1] and no essayist (except maybe a Gibbon[2] or a Montaigne—certainly no contemporary essayist) is as big as that. In other words,

---

[1]See Swift.°

[2]Edward (1737–1794), English historian and member of Samuel Johnson's literary group who wrote *The History of the Decline and Fall of the Roman Empire* in six volumes (1776–1788) as well as six drafts of his autobiography, *Memoirs of His Life and Writings*, later published as *Autobiographies* (1896), and numerous miscellaneous pieces.

if a writer of stories is also a writer of essays, the essays ought not to be seized as a rod to beat the writer's stories with; or as a frame into which to squeeze the writer's stories; or, collectively, as a "philosophy" into which to pen the writer's outlook.

Does all this mean that virtually no essay can have an enduring probity? Well, if a story can be empowered with constancy and incorruptibility, so can an essay; but only in the same way, contingent on its immanent logic or marrow-song. No story, and no essay, has the practical capacity to act itself out in the world; or ought to. All the same, if it seems that I am denying plausible truth-telling to the essays in this book, or that I don't want them to represent me, it isn't so: each, little or long, was pressed out in a mania of (ad hoc, occasional, circumstantial) conviction: the juncture—as in any fiction—of predicament and nerve. The essays herein do represent me: didn't I tackle them, shouldn't I "take responsibility" for them, whatever unease (or even alienation) they may cause me afterward? What I *am* repudiating, though, is the inference that a handful of essays is equal to a *Weltanschauung*,[1] that an essay is generally anything more than simply another fiction—a short story told in the form of an argument, or a history, or even (once in a very great while) an illumination. But never a tenet. ✐

---

[1]Comprehensive worldview or philosophy.

Edward Hoagland

(1932–)

Born in New York City on December 21, 1932, Edward Hoagland can trace his family on his father's side to farmers who settled in America before the Revolution. His paternal grandfather was an obstetrician in Kansas; his father earned a scholarship to Yale and became a financial attorney for an oil company. The Morleys, his mother's side of the family, were businessmen, arriving in America somewhat later than the Hoaglands and making their money in saddles, hardware, department store merchandise, and banking.

Like E. B. White, Hoagland grew up in financial security and loved animals and the outdoors. During the Depression the family remained in the city, where they were able to employ a maid and send their son to "an English-type school called St. Bernard's and to birthday parties at the St. Regis Hotel." By the time Hoagland was ready for the Country Day School, the family had moved to a wealthy community in Fairfield County, Connecticut, to a house with maids, "a series of Negro and old Polish ladies," and "twenty rooms, artesian water, a shady lawn, a little orchard and many majestic maples and spruce." Hoagland prowled the woods and brooks on his neighbor's estate, kept dogs and chickens and alligators, and learned about falconry from the local veterinarian.

Also like White, Hoagland suffered as a child, primarily from a stutter that developed at the age of six but also from an allergy to fur and later from excess nerves. As an adolescent he rebelled against his upbringing. In "Home Is Two Places" he attributes some of his fury toward his parents to "a bunch of nerves," but he also recognizes that his Connecticut community, wealthy and prejudiced, probably produced most of this anger. In "On Not Being a Jew" Hoagland records the cruelty of the townspeople who dug a huge ditch around the house of a Jewish family "to keep their children penned in" and who voted in an open town meeting to reject the offer of an estate for a new public high school, choosing instead to build it in a swamp near a highway because most of their children attended private school. He also records here his own taunting of two Jewish store owners as well as his enforced golf lessons at the country club and his education at Deerfield Academy and Harvard College. His rebellion led him to spend summers fighting forest fires, traveling with the circus, tending retired MGM lions in California, sleeping in flophouses, "seeing," as he says in "Home Is Two Places," "what was foreign and maybe wretched, having experiences which were not strictly necessary in my case, and *caring*, however uselessly."

In "The Threshold and the Jolt of Pain" Hoagland describes his stutter as "vocal handcuffs" that made him "a desperate, devoted writer at twenty." By 1954, when he graduated from Harvard, Hoagland had had his first novel accepted for publication (*Cat Man*, 1956) and had hitchhiked through forty-three states. The next year, suffering from both asthma and his stutter, he convinced the doctor at his physical for the draft that he was fine, because he knew that either guilt or doubt would plague him if he became 4-F. In the army, which he calls one of "the core experiences," he gained weight, temporarily lost his stutter, mingled with those less privileged than he, and worked on his second novel.

After the army, in 1957, Hoagland returned to New York City, living at times on the Upper West Side, the Lower East Side, and in Greenwich Village, writing and learning, as he describes in "The Threshhold and the Jolt of Pain" and "The Lapping, Itchy Edge of Love," about women and love. In 1960 he married his first wife, Amy, an idealistic mathematician, and published two short stories as well as his second novel, *The Circle Home*, which received only three reviews and thus caused him "stomach trouble and neck and back cramps." He and Amy lived in Sicily, Spain, and the poorer sections of New York, both caught up in the powerful emotions of their twenties. He blames their troubles primarily on his refusal to have a child. Too late, after the divorce, Hoagland says, he realized that he loved her deeply; he cried in anguish and finally left for Europe and a "wild-oats bachelorhood."

During the sixties Hoagland taught at the New School for Social Research (1963–1964), Rutgers University (1966), Sarah Lawrence College (1967, 1971), and City College of the City University of New York (1967–1968). He published his third novel, *The Peacock's Tail*, in 1965, after receiving a Longfellow Foundation Award in 1961 and an American Academy of Arts and Letters Traveling Fellow Award and a Guggenheim Award in 1964. By the time of his second marriage, to Marion Magid in 1968, Hoagland had finished his first nonfiction book, *Notes from the Century Before: A Journal from British Columbia* (1969), and was ready to commit himself to wife, child (Molly), and the writing of essays, activities he has thoroughly enjoyed ever since. One of his earliest pieces, "The Draft Card Gesture," published in *Commentary* in 1968, describes his experiences in the march on Washington in 1963, the less joyous march to the United Nations in

1967, and his ambivalence about tearing up his draft card as a thirty-five-year-old veteran and mailing it to President Johnson to protest what he saw as an atrocious war.

In the late sixties and early seventies Hoagland produced several short stories but focused almost exclusively on his essays, regularly contributing to *Commentary*, the *Village Voice*, *Harper's*, and the *Atlantic*. By 1971 he had published his first collection of essays, *The Courage of Turtles*, won the O. Henry Award, declared himself an optimist, and purchased a second home—a house of eight rooms and forty acres in Vermont. The following year he was given awards for literature by Brandeis University and the New York State Council on the Arts. By 1980 Hoagland had taught at the University of Iowa (1978) and Columbia University (1980) and had published three more collections of essays, *Walking the Dead Diamond River* (1973), *Red Wolves and Black Bears* (1976), and *African Calliope: A Journey to the Sudan* (1979). Geoffrey Wolff edited *The Hoagland Reader* in 1979; a fourth collection of essays, *The Tugman's Passage*, appeared in 1982; and another novel, *Seven Rivers West*, appeared in 1987. Hoagland won a National Magazine Award for *Harper's* in 1989 for his essay on suicide, "An Urge for an End." He now lives in Vermont, where he teaches writing part-time at Bennington College, and continues to write and publish his essays in *Esquire* and elsewhere.

The effect of Hoagland's essays is as startling as Montaigne's must have been on his first audience and for the same reason: their shocking personal honesty. The two are alike also in the diversity of their subjects, from smells to morality in Montaigne, from turtles to horror in Hoagland. Hoagland's style is also reminiscent of Lamb's in its conversational tone and in its casual and candid handling of issues others would be afraid to tackle, such as the stereotypes he raises in "City Rat" and in "On Not Being a Jew." Whereas Lamb apparently feels no guilt and recognizes no wrongdoing in his comments about blacks, Jews, and Scots, Hoagland is acutely aware of his prejudices and of the complex issues involved in disliking a person as an individual, regardless of the stereotypes attributed to the group.

Whether writing of himself or someone else, the country or the city, Hoagland's direct, colloquial style often disguises, at least on the first reading, his artfulness. With exuberance and passion, he moves apparently at random in and around his topic, interweaving observation and commentary, all the while deftly designing a supporting scaffold. "City Rat," for instance, is built on Hoagland's jogging tour of the city, past and present, contrasting his youthful stride and his loping middle-aged swerve. Much of his meaning is conveyed in verbs (*slipping, shooting, banging, rubbernecking, grinning, breathing*) and comparisons (city people are rats, badgers, cougars, hedgehogs, coyotes). Verbs and comparisons underpin "The Courage of Turtles" as well: "Turtles cough, burp, whistle, grunt and hiss," as well as wander, hunch, lunge, creep, and thump, and they are compared to nearly every animal in the zoo.

Hoagland also uses sentence structure to create patterns. To express a journey from youth to adulthood in the second paragraph of "The Courage of Turtles," he uses a series of progressively longer and more intricate sets of dependent and independent clauses to articulate his circumscribed rambles as a ten-year-old and his increasingly extensive forays as a twelve-year-old and older youth, culminating in a detailed survey of his ever-widening domain. Through such rhetorical patterns of verb, sentence length, and metaphor, Hoagland, like Ozick, celebrates the fictive side of the essay, shaping his experience to fit the contrapuntal nature of his mind. ✐

The Courage of Turtles[1]

Turtles are a kind of bird with the governor turned low. With the same attitude of removal, they cock a glance at what is going on, as if they need only to fly away. Until recently they were also a case of virtue rewarded, at least in the town where I grew up, because, being humble creatures, there were plenty of them. Even when we still had a few bobcats in the woods the local snapping turtles,[2] growing up to forty pounds, were the largest carnivores. You would see them through the amber water, as big as greeny wash basins at the bottom of the pond, until they faded into the inscrutable mud as if they hadn't existed at all.

When I was ten I went to Dr. Green's Pond, a two-acre pond across the road. When I was twelve I walked a mile or so to Taggart's Pond, which was lusher, had big water snakes and a waterfall; and shortly after that I was bicycling way up to the adventuresome vastness of Mud Pond, a lake-sized body of water in the reservoir system of a Connecticut city, possessed of cat-backed little islands and empty shacks and a forest of pines and hardwoods along the shore. Otters, foxes and mink left their prints on the bank; there were pike and perch. As I got older, the estates and forgotten back lots in town were parceled out and sold for nice prices, yet, though the woods had shrunk, it seemed that fewer people walked in the woods. The new residents didn't know how to find them. Eventually, exploring, they did find them, and it required some ingenuity and doubling around on my part to go for eight miles without meeting someone. I was grown by now, I lived in New York, and that's what I wanted on the occasional weekends when I came out.

Since Mud Pond contained drinking water I had felt confident nothing untoward would happen there. For a long while the developers stayed away, until the drought of the mid-1960s. This event, squeezing the edges in, convinced the local water company that the pond really wasn't a necessity as a catch basin,

---

[1]First published in the *Village Voice*, December 12, 1968.

[2]Of the family Chelydridae, they are large, aggressive predators with powerful jaws capable of severing an unwary swimmer's toe.

however; so they bulldozed a hole in the earthen dam, bulldozed the banks to fill in the bottom, and landscaped the flow of water that remained to wind like an English brook and provide a domestic view for the houses which were planned. Most of the painted turtles[1] of Mud Pond, who had been inaccessible as they sunned on their rocks, wound up in boxes in boys' closets within a matter of days. Their footsteps in the dry leaves gave them away as they wandered forlornly. The snappers and the little musk turtles,[2] neither of whom leave the water except once a year to lay their eggs, dug into the drying mud for another siege of hot weather, which they were accustomed to doing whenever the pond got low. But this time it was low for good; the mud baked over them and slowly entombed them. As for the ducks, I couldn't stroll in the woods and not feel guilty, because they were crouched beside every stagnant pothole, or were slinking between the bushes with their heads tucked into their shoulders so that I wouldn't see them. If they decided I had, they beat their way up through the screen of trees, striking their wings dangerously, and wheeled about with that headlong, magnificent velocity to locate another poor puddle.

I used to catch possums and black snakes as well as turtles, and I kept dogs and goats. Some summers I worked in a menagerie with the big personalities of the animal kingdom, like elephants and rhinoceroses. I was twenty before these enthusiasms began to wane, and it was then that I picked turtles as the particular animal I wanted to keep in touch with. I was allergic to fur, for one thing, and turtles need minimal care and not much in the way of quarters. They're personable beasts. They see the same colors we do and they seem to see just as well, as one discovers in trying to sneak up on them. In the laboratory they unravel the twists of a maze with the hot-blooded rapidity of a mammal. Though they can't run as fast as a rat, they improve on their errors just as quickly, pausing at each crossroads to look left and right. And they rock rhythmically in place, as we often do, although they are hatched from eggs, not the womb. (A common explanation psychologists give for our pleasure in rocking quietly is that it recapitulates our mother's heartbeat in utero.)

Snakes, by contrast, are dryly silent and priapic.[3] They are smooth movers, legalistic, unblinking, and they afford the humor which the humorless do. But they make challenging captives; sometimes they won't eat for months on a point of order—if the light isn't right, for instance. Alligators are sticklers too. They're like war-horses, or German shepherds, and with their bar-shaped, vertical pupils adding emphasis, they have the idée fixe[4] of eating, eating, even when they choose to refuse all food and stubbornly die. They delight in tossing a salamander up towards the sky and grabbing him in their long mouths as he comes down. They're so eager that they get the jitters, and they're too much of a proposition for

---

[1]One of the four species of the genus *Chrysemys*, noted for their colorful shells.

[2]Species of the genus *Sternotherus*, capable of producing a yellowish foul-smelling fluid when threatened.

[3]Phallic, from the Greek and later Roman god Priapus, guardian of procreation, gardens, and vineyards.

[4]French for "obsession."

a casual aquarium like mine. Frogs are depressingly defenseless: that moist, extensive back, with the bones almost sticking through. Hold a frog and you're holding its skeleton. Frogs' tasty legs are the staff of life to many animals—herons, raccoons, ribbon snakes—though they themselves are hard to feed. It's not an enviable role to be the staff of life, and after frogs you descend down the evolutionary ladder a big step to fish.

Turtles cough, burp, whistle, grunt and hiss, and produce social judgments. They put their heads together amicably enough, but then one drives the other back with the suddenness of two dogs who have been conversing in tones too low for an onlooker to hear. They pee in fear when they're first caught, but exercise both pluck and optimism in trying to escape, walking for hundreds of yards within the confines of their pen, carrying the weight of that cumbersome box on legs which are cruelly positioned for walking. They don't feel that the contest is unfair; they keep plugging, rolling like sailorly souls—a bobbing, infirm gait, a brave, sea-legged momentum—stopping occasionally to study the lay of the land. For me, anyway, they manage to contain the rest of the animal world. They can stretch out their necks like a giraffe, or loom underwater like an apocryphal[1] hippo. They browse on lettuce thrown on the water like a cow moose which is partly submerged. They have a penguin's alertness, combined with a build like a Brontosaurus when they rise up on tiptoe. Then they hunch and ponderously lunge like a grizzly going forward.

Baby turtles in a turtle bowl are a puzzle in geometrics. They're as decorative as pansy petals, but they are also self-directed building blocks, propping themselves on one another in different arrangements, before upending the tower. The timid individuals turn fearless, or vice versa. If one gets a bit arrogant he will push the others off the rock and afterwards climb down into the water and cling to the back of one of those he has bullied, tickling him with his hind feet until he bucks like a bronco. On the other hand, when this same milder-mannered fellow isn't exerting himself, he will stare right into the face of the sun for hours. What could be more lionlike? And he's at home in or out of the water and does lots of metaphysical tilting. He sinks and rises, with an infinity of levels to choose from; or, elongating himself, he climbs out on the land again to perambulate, sits boxed in his box, and finally slides back in the water, submerging into dreams.

I have five of these babies in a kidney-shaped bowl. The hatchling, who is a painted turtle, is not as large as the top joint of my thumb. He eats chicken gladly. Other foods he will attempt to eat but not with sufficient perseverance to succeed because he's so little. The yellow-bellied terrapin[2] is probably a yearling, and he eats salad voraciously, but no meat, fish or fowl. The Cumberland terrapin[3] won't touch salad or chicken but eats fish and all of the meats except for bacon. The little

---

[1]False or counterfeit, from the fourteen books of the Apocrypha included in the Vulgate but not accepted by Protestants. Roman Catholics accept eleven of them.

[2]*Trachemys scripta scripta*, a species of turtle distinguished by a thick, uneven shell.

[3]*Trachemys scripta elegans*, also known as the red-eared slider, the most common pet turtle.

snapper, with a black crenelated[1] shell, feasts on any kind of meat, but rejects greens and fish. The fifth of the turtles is African. I acquired him only recently and don't know him well. A mottled brown, he unnerves the green turtles, dragging their food off to his lairs. He doesn't seem to want to be green—he bites the algae off his shell, hanging meanwhile at daring, steep, head-first angles.

The snapper was a Ferdinand[2] until I provided him with deeper water. Now he snaps at my pencil with his downturned and fearsome mouth, his swollen face like a napalm victim's. The Cumberland has an elliptical red mark on the side of his green-and-yellow head. He is benign by nature and ought to be as elegant as his scientific name (*Pseudemys scripta elegans*)[3] except he has contracted a disease of the air bladder which has permanently inflated it; he floats high in the water at an undignified slant and can't go under. There may have been internal bleeding, too, because his carapace[4] is stained along its ridge. Unfortunately, like flowers, baby turtles often die. Their mouths fill up with a white fungus and their lungs with pneumonia. Their organs clog up from the rust in the water, or diet troubles, and, like a dying man's, their eyes and heads become too prominent. Toward the end, the edge of the shell becomes flabby as felt and folds around them like a shroud.

While they live they're like puppies. Although they're vivacious, they would be a bore to be with all the time, so I also have an adult wood turtle[5] about six inches long. Her shell is the equal of any seashell for sculpturing, even a Cellini shell;[6] it's like an old, dusty, richly engraved medallion dug out of a hillside. Her legs are salmon-orange bordered with black and protected by canted,[7] heroic scales. Her plastron—the bottom shell—is splotched like a margay cat's[8] coat, with black ocelli[9] on a yellow background. It is convex to make room for the female organs inside, whereas a male's would be concave to help him fit tightly on top of her. Altogether, she exhibits every camouflage color on her limbs and shells. She has a turtleneck neck, a tail like an elephant's, wise old pachydermous hind legs and the face of a turkey—except that when I carry her she gazes at the passing ground with a hawk's eyes and mouth. Her feet fit to the fingers of my hand, one to each one, and she rides looking down. She can walk on the floor in perfect silence,

---

[1]Having square indentations.

[2]Hero of *Ferdinand the Bull* (1936), the classic story by Munro Leaf about the bull who wanted to "just sit and sniff the flowers."

[3]Hoagland is in error here: *Pseudemys* designates red-bellied turtles and river cooters, but there is no turtle by this name; the proper Latin name for the Cumberland terrapin or red slider is *Trachemys scripta elegans*.

[4]Fused plates of the shell.

[5]From the genus *Rhinoclemmys*, and including nine species similar to box turtles but found in Central and South America.

[6]Benvenuto Cellini (1500–1571) was an Italian sculptor and goldsmith who wrote a fascinating autobiography and was famous for his jewels and ornaments as well as his bronze and marble statues.

[7]Slanted.

[8]A small, long-tailed wildcat with spots.

[9]Spots that look like eyes.

but usually she lets her shell knock portentously, like a footstep, so that she resembles some grand, concise, slow-moving id.[1] But if an earthworm is presented, she jerks swiftly ahead, poises above it and strikes like a mongoose, consuming it with wild vigor. Yet she will climb on my lap to eat bread or boiled eggs.

If put into a creek, she swims like a cutter, nosing forward to intercept a strange turtle and smell him. She drifts with the current to go downstream, maneuvering behind a rock when she wants to take stock, or sinking to the nether levels, while bubbles float up. Getting out, choosing her path, she will proceed a distance and dig into a pile of humus, thrusting herself to the coolest layer at the bottom. The hole closes over her until it's as small as a mouse's hole. She's not as aquatic as a musk turtle, not quite as terrestrial as the box turtles[2] in the same woods, but because of her versatility she's marvelous, she's everywhere. And though she breathes the way we breathe, with scarcely perceptible movements of her chest, sometimes instead she pumps her throat ruminatively, like a pipe smoker sucking and puffing. She waits and blinks, pumping her throat, turning her head, then sets off like a loping tiger in slow motion, hurdling the jungly lumber, the pea vine and twigs. She estimates angles so well that when she rides over the rocks, sliding down a drop-off with her rugged front legs extended, she has the grace of a rodeo mare.

But she's well off to be with me rather than at Mud Pond. The other turtles have fled—those that aren't baked into the bottom. Creeping up the brooks to sad, constricted marshes, burdened as they are with that box on their backs, they're walking into a setup where all their enemies move thirty times faster than they. It's like the nightmare most of us have whimpered through, where we are weighted down disastrously while trying to flee; fleeing our home ground, we try to run.

I've seen turtles in still worse straits. On Broadway, in New York, there is a penny arcade which used to sell baby terrapins that were scrawled with bon mots in enamel paint, such as KISS ME BABY. The manager turned out to be a wholesaler as well, and once I asked him whether he had any larger turtles to sell. He took me upstairs to a loft room devoted to the turtle business. There were desks for the paper work and a series of racks that held shallow tin bins atop one another, each with several hundred babies crawling around in it. He was a smudgy-complexioned, serious fellow and he did have a few adult terrapins, but I was going to school and wasn't actually planning to buy; I'd only wanted to see them. They were aquatic turtles, but here they went without water, presumably for weeks, lurching about in those dry bins like handicapped citizens, living on gumption. An easel where the artist worked stood in the middle of the floor. She had a palette and a clip attachment for fastening the babies in place. She wore a smock and a beret, and was homely, short and eccentric-looking, with funny black hair, like some of the ladies who show their paintings in Washington Square in May. She had a cold, she was smoking, and her hand wasn't very steady,

---

[1]That part of the psyche that is instinctive and demands the satisfaction of primitive desires.
[2]Many species of the genus *Terrapine*, with domed shells; almost totally land dwelling.

although she worked quickly enough. The smile that she produced for me would have looked giddy if she had been happier, or drunk. Of course the turtles' doom was sealed when she painted them, because their bodies inside would continue to grow but their shells would not. Gradually, invisibly, they would be crushed. Around us their bellies—two thousand belly shells—rubbed on the bins with a mournful, momentous hiss.

Somehow there were so many of them I didn't rescue one. Years later, however, I was walking on First Avenue when I noticed a basket of living turtles in front of a fish store. They were as dry as a heap of old bones in the sun; nevertheless, they were creeping over one another gimpily, doing their best to escape. I looked and was touched to discover that they appeared to be wood turtles, my favorites, so I bought one. In my apartment I looked closer and realized that in fact this was a diamondback terrapin,[1] which was bad news. Diamondbacks are tidewater turtles from brackish estuaries, and I had no sea water to keep him in. He spent his days thumping interminably against the baseboards, pushing for an opening through the wall. He drank thirstily but would not eat and had none of the hearty, accepting qualities of wood turtles. He was morose, paler in color, sleeker and more Oriental in the carved ridges and rings that formed his shell. Though I felt sorry for him, finally I found his unrelenting presence exasperating. I carried him, struggling in a paper bag, across town to the Morton Street Pier on the Hudson. It was August but gray and windy. He was very surprised when I tossed him in; for the first time in our association, I think, he was afraid. He looked afraid as he bobbed about on top of the water, looking up at me from ten feet below. Though we were both accustomed to his resistance and rigidity, seeing him still pitiful, I recognized that I must have done the wrong thing. At least the river was salty, but it was also bottomless; the waves were too rough for him, and the tide was coming in, bumping him against the pilings underneath the pier. Too late, I realized that he wouldn't be able to swim to a peaceful inlet in New Jersey, even if he could figure out which way to swim. But since, short of diving in after him, there was nothing I could do, I walked away. ✍

The Problem of the Golden Rule[2]

Like a good many New Yorkers, I've often wondered whether I was going to be mugged. I've lived in a number of neighborhoods, and being a night walker, have many times changed my course or speeded my stride, eyeing a formidable-looking figure as he approached. But it's never happened, and I imagine that if it finally does there may actually be a kind of relief, even a species of exhilaration, as I pick

---

[1]*Malaclemys* terrapin, brought to the verge of extinction early this century because of its popularity as a gourmet dish.

[2]First published in *Commentary*, August 1969.

myself up—assuming that I am not badly hurt—because a danger anticipated for a long time may come to seem worse than the reality. People who come home and encounter a robber in their apartment who flees are likely to be less shaken up than the householder is who simply steps into a shambles of ransacked bureaus and upended beds: they've seen the fellow; they know he's human. A friend of mine wrestled a burglar for several minutes around the floor of his living room, both of them using the trips and hip throws that they remembered from their teens, until by the time my friend won and phoned the police they were old acquaintances.

I know, too, that to describe the few incidents of violence I've met with in the past makes them sound more grisly than they were in fact. In the army, my platoon was put in the charge of a peculiar sergeant who, mostly for reasons of his own, had us do squat jumps one noontime until we could no longer walk or stand up. Then he strolled among us kicking us to make sure that we weren't faking. It was a hot drill field strewn with packs and stacked rifles and other movie props, and yet the experience was not nearly as bad as one would anticipate if he were told at breakfast what to expect that day. We just followed orders until we couldn't get up and then we lay where we were on the ground until the sergeant was satisfied that we had done what was humanly possible. Even in a true atrocity situation that's all that is ever done: what is humanly possible. Afterwards one becomes unresponsive and fatalistic; terror is no longer a factor.

Next day the sergeant wanted to have it both ways, so he set us into formation and told us what he was going to make us do, and thereupon went off to the latrine to give us a chance to stand at attention and think and stew. Another sergeant promptly walked up and dismissed us, however. We hobbled away in every direction as fast as possible, while the two sergeants met to discuss the issue in the barracks door. They met person-to-person, and we had been punished person-to-person, and the facelessness of the mugger whom one anticipates meeting on Little West 12th Street was never a part of it. This, like our doing whatever was humanly possible, made the experience supportable.

I visualize Armageddon[1] not as a steel-muzzled affair of push-button silos under the earth but as a rusty freighter, flying the Liberian flag, perhaps, which sails inconspicuously up the Hudson past my apartment and goes off. Beyond that I don't see any details—though, as a non sequitur, I expect the tunnels and bridges would fill up with hikers leaving the city before it was too late. A woman I know says she sees Armageddon as getting under the bed. What we do with the insupportable is to turn it to terms we can file and forget. Unfortunately we are able to deal almost as handily with the nuclear bombs that have already gone off as we are with the ones that haven't. If as individual fighting men we had razed Hiroshima, then the horror of its destruction would persist as a legend to our great-

---

[1]The final battle between good and evil that signals the end of the world according to Revelation 16:16, from the Hebrew for "Megiddo," a mountainous area where great battles occur in the Old Testament.

grandchildren because it would have been witnessed and done on the spot—also because of the somber old notion that residing in every man is a spark of divinity, whether the man is an enemy or a friend. This putative spark is central to most religious belief; and right at the root of Western ethics is what is called, under one of its names, the Golden Rule. But spark or no spark, since in practice we cannot react to others with unabashed fellow-feeling, we usually reduce the Golden Rule to a sort of silver rule, doing to them just about what we think they would do to us if they had the opportunity. And this works—has been working—though the new impersonalized technology is challenging its workability, along with another behemoth[1] among changes, which is that today there are too many people. Where there are too many people, we get tired of following even the silver rule, tired of paying that much attention, of noticing whom we are with and who is who. For the agnostic as well, basing his reverence for life on its variety and on a Jeffersonian fascination with the glimmerings of talent in every man, the glut is discouraging. Although we don't ridicule these old ideas, the sentiments that people have for one another in a traffic jam are becoming our sentiments more and more. A groan goes up in any suburb when it's announced that a new complex of housing for two thousand souls is going to be built on Lone Tree Hill. And the vast sigh of impatience which greeted Pope Paul's traditionalist statement of faith in the sanctity of the seed germs of life points to the tone to come. *Life for the living*, people will say: body-counts in war and baby-counts in peace. We grant each union man his $10,500 a year, and then the hell with him. He, for his part, doesn't care if our garbage cans fester with rats when the union goes after $10,900.

Never have people dealt so briskly with strangers as now. Many of us have ceased to see strangers at all; our eyes simply don't register them except as verticals on the sidewalk, and when we must parley with them we find out quickly what they are asking from us, do it—maybe—and that's that. When I was a child I remember how my astonishment evolved as I realized that people often would not do the smallest thing to convenience another person or make him feel easier for the moment. Of course I'd known that *kids* wouldn't, but I had thought that was because they were kids. It was my first comprehension of the deadness of life. Everyone has discovered at some particular point life's deadness, but the galloping sense of deadness which alarms so many people lately, and especially the young, goes way beyond such individual discoveries to dimensions and contexts that have brought revolution to the U.S. Even in the arts the ancient austerities have been deemed insufficient, and we have actors who jump into the audience and do their acting there. When acting seems to fail, they improvise, and finally improvisation isn't enough either, and instead of having an actor play the drug addict, the addict himself must appear onstage and play himself—like the toothpaste tube blown up and hanging on the museum wall: "Look, if nothing else, I'm real." This is the era when students are so busy trying to teach their teachers that

---

[1] A huge animal described in Job 40:15–24.

they are hard to teach, and when the chip on the shoulder of the man in the street is his "personality"—personality is quarrelsomeness. The revolution, in any case, is overdue, but maybe our best hope is that we remain at least idiosyncratic creatures, absorbed close to home. Dog owners, when they walk their dogs, show nearly as exact an interest in their pets' defecations as they would in their own. The same communing silence steals over their faces, the look of musing solemnity, that usually only the bathroom mirror gets a glimpse of.

The worst public tragedy I've witnessed was in Boston, when from a distance I saw a brick wall fall on a company of firemen. Some, with a great shout, got away, but even the leap that they made while the rest crumpled is blurred as a memory compared to the images of two old men whom I knew very slightly at the time. Mr. Kate wrote cookbooks in the winter and hired out as a cook on a private yacht during the warm months. His other love, besides cooking, was opera, and he lived in a room shaped like a shoebox that cost him eight dollars a week. He served himself candlelit meals on a folding table and concocted all of his recipes on a hotplate set in the sink. By contrast, Mr. Hurth, although a somewhat less cultivated man, was an alumnus of Brown University and lived in a large ground-floor room in the same house. He had ruined himself in a scandal in St. Louis, where he had been a businessman, but that was all I learned. What he'd done next was to come to Boston and throw himself on the old-fashioned, private or "Christian" charity, as it used to be called, of a roommate from college, though thirty years had passed. He was a pleasant subdued man ordinarily, swinging from sweet to vaguely hangdog, but he was a drinker, and so this benefactor no longer asked him to Newton Centre[1] for Thanksgiving because he was likely to break the furniture. When he did, he'd leave his glasses behind by mistake so that he'd have to go back out again for a whole second festival of apologies. Through charitable intercession, Mr. Hurth was on the payroll of the John Hancock Insurance Company, being listed on the books as a claims investigator, though actually (charity compounding charity) his single duty was to work for the United Fund once a year on a loan basis. The campaign was a brief one, but he was a bitter, floundering functionary, faced with his fate if his drinking should snap off his last sticks of presence and respectability.

As I say, next to the memory of two nodding acquaintances the death of some distant firemen is small potatoes. I was reminded of that catastrophe the other night for the first time in years while watching a fire on Third Avenue. Here in the bigger city one is witness to such a cataract of appalling happenings that they pass remembering. I saw a man who had just been burned out of his apartment turned away from a hotel in the neighborhood because he had a little blacking on him, although the shock and fear stood in his eyes. "Sure, there was a fire there, all right," the manager told me with a laugh. "I never take them in, those victims. They're dirty and they're scared to death. They're not worth the nuisance."

---

[1]Comfortable suburb of Boston.

He was a modern, casual villain, however, impartial, just the kind who is not memorable. I came upon a much less gratuitous drama a few days afterwards. A child of two or three had been stuck inside one of those all-glass phone booths with a spring door which cannot be opened except by a grown person because of where the handle is placed. The world was passing—this was on the open street—but he was feeling his way around the glass in gathering panic, trying to find an escape route, reaching up and reaching down. Every few seconds he let out a thin, fluting scream so pure in pitch that it was hardly human; it was *pre*-human. You could see him thinking, learning, recording discoveries. He reached for the phone, but that was too high up; he thumped each pane of glass, searching for the door, and pounded on the metal frame, and screamed to find whether screaming would work. He was boxed into his terror, and you could see him grow older by leaps and bounds. I'm just this month a new father, so I was as transfixed as if he were my child. His governess or baby-sitter, baby-walker, or whatever she was, a short shadowy woman such as you might see managing a subway change booth, was standing right next to the glass, apparently feasting her eyes. Whether it was supposed to be a "punishment" or merely a pleasure fest, the child was too frightened by now to notice her.

Maybe our cruelty will save us. At least the cruel do pay attention, and the woman would probably have let him out before the crowd got around to hearing him. She had moved to the door, looking down at him intently as he pushed on the glass. I was seething, partly because I found that some of the woman's sexual excitement had communicated itself to me, which was intolerable, and partly because my cowardice in not interfering was equally outrageous. We've all become reluctant to stop and stick our noses in—a man is run over by a Breakstone cream-cheese truck and we pass quickly by. But cowardice was what it was in this particular event, since even under happy circumstances I stutter and it requires an enormous gearing up of nerve for me to step into a public fracas on the street. I strangle; I can't speak at all and must either use my hands on the stranger or gag and quaver, unable to put two words together. The seams of human nature frighten me in this regard, and the whole confrontation ethic of the sixties, much as I have entered into it on occasion, gives me nightmare visions because I have no conventional means of battling. I see myself as unable to protest in words to the person whose behavior has angered me and so using my hands on him; then just as unable to explain myself to the crowd that gathers, but only shuddering and stuttering; and then in court again enforcedly silent, dependent on the empathy or telepathic capacities of the people who are there to convey my side of the controversy.

Weaving like a nauseous moose, I was working my way toward her, when the woman, with a glance at me, pushed the door of the booth open, reached inside, and pulled the boy to her and walked away. In effect, I was let off, because only an exceptional well-doer would have tracked the woman down from that point on and questioned her about her psyche.

However, there are times one isn't let off, when one's very humanity hangs at issue and perhaps my specific problems with my stutter are an epitome of what each of us meets. Once in northern New England when I was snowshoeing, a hunter started shooting at me, really only to scare me, pinging with his .22 in my immediate vicinity. I was on an open hillside which I'd already realized was too slippery to climb, but as long as I kept scrabbling there in silence on the ice, like an animal in trouble, he was going to keep on pinging. Because a stutterer's every impulse is to stutter softly, unobtrusively, it's twice as hard to shout one's way through a stutter as to wedge through in quiet tones; but from the sheer imperatives of survival I shouted, "I CAN SEE YOU!" I shouted it several times again, although I couldn't see him; he was in the woods. I was insisting and reiterating that I was a human being: if I could get that message across to him he would stop shooting at me. It was even worse than my conception of a courtroom trial because this was one of those rare emergencies when we can't trust to all our faculties to operate together for us—the movements of our hands, our youth or age, our manner and expression—some compensating for the inadequacies of the others. I had to go to bat with my speaking abilities and nothing else. So I shouted to him that I could see him, by which I meant I was a man, and he stopped shooting.

More recently, I was on a tiny Danish island off the coast of Sweden, wandering around some seventeenth-century fortifications and the walled town, now a huddled fishing village. I had sat on the sea wall to watch the cloud action but was distracted by the spectacle below me of a boy mistreating a wild duck. Oddly enough, many times an incident where a person, rather than an animal, is being mauled and manhandled is easier to shrug off. The fact that he's a person complicates the case. As an onlooker you can see, for example, that he has gotten himself drunk and let his guard down, lost his dignity, talked out of turn. But the duck, with its wings clipped, presumably, was only trying to run away. The boy would catch it, pummel it and grip it tightly, trundling it about. Finally I got off my bench and went over and told him falteringly to cut that out. Many Danes speak English, but he was twelve or so and he may not have understood me. Like a mirror of myself, he stared at me without trying to say a word. Then he squeezed the duck again hard in both hands. My bugaboo about trying to explain myself to strangers rose in me, along with my indignation. Instead of looking for a local fellow to translate and take over, I lifted the duck from his arms, and with the sense of right and doom that I have dreaded in foreseeing a confrontation on the street, carried it down the stairs of the sea wall and released it on the beach. The boy ran for help; the duck paddled into the waves; I climbed to the promenade and started walking as deliberately as I could toward the small boat which had brought me to the island.

Uncannily soon, before I'd gone a dozen yards, practically the whole male populace was on the scene. "Hey! Turn around!" they yelled. I took another couple of steps away and then did so. They told me very plainly in English that they were going to throw me over the sea wall. They said the duck had been rescued by the boys of the island—their sons—after it had swum through an oil slick and almost drowned. Now, because of what I'd done, it really *was* about to drown, and when it went under, they would toss me over. This was not spoken in joking tones, and I could see the duck getting heavier in the water; its feathers, though as tidy to the eye as a healthy duck's feathers, had no buoyancy. Meanwhile, I'd fallen into something like what a prizefighter would call a clinch by refusing to acknowledge by any sign that I understood what was being said to me. It is a psychological necessity that when you punish somebody he understand the reason why. Even if he doesn't accept the guilty finding, you must explain to him why you are punishing him or you can't do it. So while they could scarcely contain their frustration, my face displayed bewilderment; I kept pretending to grope to understand. I was doing this instinctively, of course, and as their first impetus to violence passed, I found myself acting out with vehemence how I had seen the boy mistreat the duck. The men, who wanted at the least to take a poke at me, watched doubtfully, but there was a Coast Guardsman, an off-islander, who seemed to be arguing in Danish on my behalf. Another man went down to where the duck was swimming and reached out; the duck perceiving itself to be sinking, had moved cautiously closer to shore. And when the duck was saved I was saved; I only had the island's boys waiting for me in the embrasures[1] of the wall.

Yet this quite comic misadventure, when every dread came real—I couldn't say a single word to save my life—was just as numbing as those ninety-five squat jumps at Fort Dix—only later was it terrifying. And in a way it makes up for the memories I have as a teenager of watching flocks of bats murdered with brooms and frogs tormented—moments when I didn't interfere, but giggled ruefully to keep my popularity and stifle my outcries.

Sociology progresses; the infant mortality rate among Negroes goes down. Nevertheless we know that if the announcement were made that there was going to be a public hanging in Central Park, Sheep Meadow would be crowded with spectators, like Tyburn mall.[2] Sometimes at night my standing lamp shades itself into an observant phantom figure which takes a position next to my bed. It doesn't threaten me directly, and I stretch out to clutch its throat with careful anger. My final grab bumps the lamp over. This electric phantom is a holdover from my vivid night demons when I was eight or ten. I never saw them outright, thank the Lord, but for years I fell asleep facing the wall to avoid beholding my destruction. I'd "whisper," as I called it, when I went to bed, telling myself an installment of a round-robin story, and when the installment was over I'd wait for the demons, until I fell asleep. Later, just as invariably, I faced the outer room so I could see them come and have warning to fight. Such archaisms in our minds are not an unmixed evil, however, because they link us to humanity and to our history as human beings. My wife says every man she's been familiar with would smell his socks at night before he went to bed: just a whiff—each sock, not only one. I do this too, although the smell has been of no instrinsic interest to me for twenty years. The smell of each sock checks precisely with the other one and smells as vital as pigs do. Maybe it reassures us that we're among the living still. We need to know. In the fifties I also liked the smell of air pollution. I didn't think of it as

---

[1]Slanted openings in a wall.
[2]Until 1783 the site of public executions in London.

air pollution then—nobody did—but as the smell of industry and the highways I hitchhiked on, the big-shouldered America I loved.

In 1943 George Orwell said the problem of the times was the decay in the belief in personal immortality. Several French novelists had turned existentialist and several English novelists Catholic (possibly the same reaction), while he himself, like many of the more likable writers, had adopted a hardy humanist's masculine skepticism. Twenty-odd years later, the problem appears only to have grown more piercing, though it is not put into the same terms. You can't have as many people walking around as there are now and still simply see them as chips off the divine lodestone.[1] Nor is the future *1984*: that's too succinct. At first the new nuclear bullying, the new technocracy, made mere survival more the point, because we wanted to be sure of surviving here on earth before we worried about heaven. Lately, instead the talk has been about overpopulation, and city people have started venturing to the outback, buying acreage with all the premonitory fervor of Noah sawing logs. Everyone wants space to breathe; the character of city life has drastically deteriorated, and there's no questioning the statistics, just as there used to be no questioning the odds that eventually a nuclear war was going to penetrate our precautions through that old fontanel[2] of existence: human mix-up.

When we say that enough is enough, that we have enough people on hand now for any good purpose, we mean that the divine spark has become something of a conflagration, besides an embarrassment of riches. We're trying to make a start at sorting the riches, buying Edwardian clothes but also Volkswagens, and settling down to the process of zoning the little land there is. As we also begin to cogitate on how the quality of life can be improved, we may be in for a religious revival, too. It's a natural beginning, and faddism will probably swing that way, and after all, we *are* extraordinary—we're so extraordinary we're everywhere. Next to the new mysticisms, old-fashioned, run-of-the-mill religion is not so hard to swallow. The difficulty will be how we regard individual people, a question which involves not only whether we think we're immortal but whether we think they are. The crowded impatience of suburb-city living doesn't often evoke intimations of other people's immortality,[3] and neither do the hodge-podge leveling procedures of a modern democracy. So much of the vigor of the Victorian church, for instance, grew out of the contrast between its members and the raw, destitute brown masses who covered the rest of the globe. Among an elite, self-congratulatory minority even the greatest of attributes—immortality—seemed plausible.

But maybe I'm being overly sour. We have wiped tigers off the earth and yet our children hear as much about the symbolism of tigers as children did in the old days. And next to the subway station I use there is a newsdealer who was blinded

---

[1]Magnetic stone (magnetite) once used in compasses; the words also refer to the Hellenic Gnostic philosophy of the second century A.D. whose adherents believed, among other things, that man consists of flesh, soul, and spirit, the divine spark.

[2]Soft spot at the top of the newborn baby's head.

[3]See Wordsworth.°

in Orwell's war, the Spanish War, in the mountains behind Motril.[1] He wears the aura of a revolutionary volunteer. He dresses bulkily, as if for weather at the front, and rigs canvas around his hut as neatly as a soldier's tent. Not one of your meek blind men, he's on his feet most of the day, especially in tough weather, pacing, marching, standing tall. He's gray and grim, hard and spare, and doubtless lives surrounded by the companions that he had in the Sierra Nevada. But he's too bluff and energetic to be a museum piece. If you help him cross the street you get the rough edge of his tongue. He searches for the lamppost with his cane like a tennis player swinging backhand, and if he loses his bearings and bumps against something, he jerks abruptly back like a cavalier insulted, looking gaunt and fierce. I pity him, but I take note of him; he counts himself among the living. I buy a paper and go home to my newborn baby, who is as intense and focused (to my eye) as a flight of angels dancing on a pinhead.[2]

I don't believe in a god you can pray to, but I do find I believe in God—I do more than I don't. I believe in glee and in the exuberance I feel with friends and animals and in the fields, and in other emotions besides that. Anyway, as we know, it really isn't necessary to see sparks of a grand divinity in someone else to feel the old immediacy that he is kin; we can evolve a more sophisticated Golden Rule than that. We will be trying to refine and revivify the qualities of life, and the chief stumbling block is that we must somehow reduce the density of people in our own comings and goings without doing it as we do now, which is by simply not seeing them, by registering them as shadows to dodge by on the street. Without degenerating into callousness, we must develop our ability to switch on and off—sometimes analogous to what we do already with body temperature in a harsh world. Generally we'd button up if we were out walking, but when the Breakstone cream-cheese truck ran over an old man, this would be a time when our ancient instinct for cherishing a stranger would spring to being.

I live in a high-rise apartment and keep a pair of field glasses next to the window to use whenever somebody emerges on one of the rooftops nearby. There are ten or fifteen regulars—old people hanging wash, high school kids who have come up into the open to talk where they can be alone. All of them are neighbors to me now, though on the street I probably would turn away from them—even the bathing beauties would not be beauties there. Admittedly I am a bit of a voyeur, as who isn't, but the population density on the rooftops seems about right. In fact, I roused myself not long ago to drive some robbers off a roof across the street by gesticulating sternly. They waved back as they went down the stairs like people who've escaped a fall. ✐

---

[1]Town on the southern Spanish coast near Granada.

[2]A reference to the famous theological controversy attributed to medieval times concerning the number of angels that could fit on the head of a pin.

City Rat[1]

Delightedly, I used to cross Park Avenue wearing an undershirt on my way to digs far to the south and east. I could remember waiting, as a boy of eight, on almost the same street corner for the St. Bernard's school bus in a proper tweed blazer, striped tie and shiny shoes, and so this gulf between costumes seemed sweet. Sweaty, bare-shouldered, strolling the summer streets, I felt my class or creed unidentifiable, which very much pleased me. Physically I was in my prime, I liked to jog, and, long and loose like a runner, though still smooth-faced, I felt as if I were a thousand miles and a whole world away from that small boy. I'd sit around on door stoops after a walk of eighty blocks or so, up from the Battery or down from Yankee Stadium, and watch the world go by. If I'd been an out-of-towner, awed by the city, these walks would have been ideal for adjusting. Wherever I ran out of steam, I'd sit, keeping an eye peeled, and try to pretend that this was now my territory and I must figure it out quickly. It should be remembered that fifteen years ago violence in New York City was fairly well contained within a framework of teenage gangs attacking other gangs, not wayfarers; Negro bitterness bore down mainly on other Negroes, and though sometimes the Mafia in Brooklyn dumped a body on Avenue D, the Lower East Side itself and other such areas were quite peaceful.

I was in the theater district once, sitting on a stoop, enjoying the stream of life, when a brisk, well-preserved man with custom-fitted pants, a cane and good coloring halted in front of me. "Young man," he said abruptly, "are you trying to break into the theater?" Aware that it was a funny question, he raised his eyebrows while he waited, as if I'd been the one who'd asked. I was holding my knees and looking up at him. He tapped my feet with the point of his cane as though he were buying me and I was supposed to stand.

I was too nervous to answer. Superciliously he stared at me. "You'd better come along. There are a great many young men trying to get into the theater. I'm in the theater." He tapped me again. I still didn't trust myself to speak, and he glanced at my Army boots, laughed and said, "Are you a paratrooper? Come now, last chance, young man. Fame and fortune. There are a great many of you and one of me. What's going to set you apart?"

My embarrassed silence made him uncomfortable, as well as the possibility that somebody might recognize him standing there in this peculiar conversation. As he left, he called back, "Good luck, little friend, whoever you are." But I grinned more confidently at him as he got farther off, because a couple of months before I'd had my picture in *Time* as a blazing new author; perhaps he never had. That was the second fillip[2] to wandering in my undershirt along Fifth or Park Avenue: the fact that on other days I'd be wearing a snaky gray flannel suit,

---

[1]First published in *Audience*, March–April 1972.

[2]A slight goad or incentive.

slipping through the crowds in the skyscraper district, and shooting up high in a building for a swank lunch. I wasn't really masquerading as a carpenter; on the contrary, I'd made no choices yet—I was enjoying being free.

Banging around on a motor scooter down the length of Manhattan by way of the waterfront, I'd unwind in the evening after writing all day. New York was compartmentalized; Harlem was in Harlem, and on Delancey[1] Street there were live ducks for sale, and in a shop with big windows, shoemakers cutting soles for shoes. I looked at coming attractions under the various movie marquees and watched the traffic on the stairs to a second-floor whorehouse (sailors coming down and a cop going up). Since I was both bashful and lonely, I would leave notes on the bulletin boards of some of the coffeehouses—"Typist wanted"— then wait by the telephone. The girls were under no illusions about what I was up to when they called, except that they usually did want some work out of the arrangement as well, and, unfairly enough, that's what I was reluctant to give. I kept my manuscripts in the refrigerator as a precaution against fire and was a nut about safeguarding them. Inevitably, then, the sort of girl who'd phone me blind and invite me over for a screw on the strength of a note I'd left in a coffeehouse was not a girl I'd trust my typing to.

One girl had a beachboy crouching naked on the floor painting her bathtub red when I arrived; the rest of the apartment was a deep black. Another, on Houston Street,[1] immediately embraced me with her head swathed in bandages from the blows that her husband had bestowed the night before. Pulling the bookcases over, he'd strewn the books around, broken all the china and announced he was leaving. Nothing had been picked up since. The baby, only a year old, cried desperately in the playpen, and though his mother naturally hoped I would be able to step right into the father's role and comfort him, I wasn't that skillful. A window was broken, so it was cold. She took me to the bedroom, moaning, "Hit me! Hit me!" When things there didn't work out she led me downstairs to a kind of commune, introduced me around and announced to the members that I was impotent.

Still, I was busy, once sleeping with three different women in as many days, and covering the city better than most news reporters, it seemed to me, recognizing innumerable street nooks and faces which epitomized New York for me. Perhaps the air was rather sooty, but it didn't cause headaches or give people bleeding throats. Now I sometimes spit blood in the morning and feel raw sulfur in my gullet from breathing the air; in midtown or around Canal Street I breathe through my teeth like a survivalist who specializes in outlasting Black Lung. This morning when I went out to buy milk for breakfast I saw a clump of police cars and a yellow car which had slid out of the traffic and come to rest against the curb, empty except for a gray-looking dead man in his thirties slumped sideways against the wheel. I stood rubbernecking next to the delicatessen owner. One night last year I'd stood in a crowd and watched most of the building that houses his store

---

[1]Delancey and Houston are streets in the old Jewish section of Manhattan.

burn to a shell, all of us—he wasn't there—as silent and spellbound as if we were witnessing public copulation. Though he is not a friendly man, I like his Greek bluntness and at the time I'd felt guilty to be watching as a mere spectacle what was a catastrophe for him. But here he was, rubbernecking at this fellow's death just like me, only less solemnly; he chuckled, shaking his head. I kept a straight face and felt a pang, but while I crossed the street with the groceries and rode up in the elevator the incident entirely slipped my mind; I didn't even mention it when I got home.

Such imperviousness is a result of changes in the city as well as in me. If I have lost my bloom, so has the city, more drastically. Among the beggars who approach me, almost weekly I see a mugger who is clearly screwing up his nerve to do more than just *ask* for money. I have the New Yorker's quick-hunch posture for broken-field maneuvering, and he swerves away. A minute later, with pounding feet, there he goes, clutching a purse, with a young woman in forlorn pursuit. Recently, riding in a bus, I saw a policeman with his gun drawn and his free hand stretched out tiptoe hastily after a suspect through a crowd and make the nab as the bus pulled away. It's not any single event, it's the cumulative number of them—shouted arguments, funerals, playground contretemps, drivers leaning on their horns, adults in tears, bums falling down and hitting their heads, young men in triumph over a business deal—that one sees in the course of a midday walk which veneers one with callousness.

We each work out a system of living in the city. With music, for instance. I put trumpet voluntaries on the phonograph in the morning, organ fugues after supper, and whale songs or wolf howls in the silence at night. I go to a Village bar which is like a club, with the same faces in it day after day, although as a hangout it does acquire a tannic-acid[1] taste if you go too often because most of the people are divorced or on that road. The newspapermen see it as belonging to them; hungry poets and movie novelists view it as a literary saloon; the seamen, photographers, carpenters, folk singers, young real-estate impresarios, political lawyers, old union organizers and Lincoln Brigade[2] veterans all individually believe it's theirs.

I'm tired of Washington Square, Tompkins Square Park, Abingdon Square, even Central Park (I lived next to it for several years and found it to be ground as overused as the banks of the Ganges are). And the last time my wife and I picnicked in Van Cortlandt Park, which is more countrified, we needed to cut at top speed through the woods to escape two men who were stalking us. Space is important to me, and each of these public resting spots has its own character and defines a particular period for me. In the early sixties I was in Washington Square, watching, among other things, the early stirrings of Negro belligerence, still indirect. It seemed to take the form of their ballplaying, sometimes one man alone, throwing a rubber ball as high as he could and catching it on the second or

---

[1] Derived from bark, fruit, and teas and used in the process of tanning hides and clarifying wine and beer.

[2] Americans who fought as volunteers in the Spanish Civil War.

third bounce. They were lanky, like men just out of the Army or prison, and when they played catch they loped all over the park, taking possession everywhere. Already they had secret handshakes and contemptuous expressions, and this gobbling up the whole park with their legs and lofting a rubber ball into the stratosphere bespoke the blocked energy, the screened anger that would soon explode. The explosion is past; new developments are brewing in these parks, but I am fatigued with watching.

The Chinese laundryman we go to is mean of heart and keeps his children home from school to iron for him while he loafs. The two girls next to us are sleeping with the super, and sit in triumph while their apartment is painted, as a consequence. Perhaps he sleeps well, but I'm almost sleepless from fighting with my wife. And there are explosions going off nightly down in the street. I have no idea what they are; years ago I would have thought just firecrackers. New York is a city of the old and young, and looking out the window, I sometimes see old people fall. One man has cancer of the mouth. When he feels well he sits outside the barber shop or in the park, not looking up, withdrawn into his memories, but seeming tranquil there; certainly nobody enjoys the sunshine more. But the next day when you walk past he is sitting quietly hemorrhaging into his handkerchief, looking at it fearfully, then boosting himself off the bench to go back to the nursing home.

In the apartment on the other side of us are two young men who entertain a lot, and one day somebody leaned out their window with a rifle equipped with a spotting scope, searching the courtyard and the street. I assumed it was a toy, but in any case I simply pulled down the blinds; one can't react to everything. We'd had a stink in the corridor the week before that gradually grew stronger. It was a really hideous smell, subterraneanly terrifying, and we and some of the neighbors began to wonder whether somebody might not have died. It was pervasive, hard to isolate, and we were all city procrastinators—with so many emergencies, so many lonely people, why get involved? At least, however, where our consciences had failed, our noses got the better of us and we called the cops. It turned out to be a decomposing chicken which someone had defrosted before a trip and forgotten about. A month or so later the same putrid smell invaded our floor all over again. Holding our noses, we complained left and right, trying to ignore it. Even so, again the police had to be called. This time they found a young woman dead of an overdose of heroin, with her headband wrapped around her arm as a tourniquet and her cat still alive, having managed to subsist on her body fluids.

Year round, I keep my air conditioner on, its steady hum submerging the street sounds. But one of the neighbors upstairs, finding this noise, too, unnerving, has lent me a white-sound machine, an instrument which, like a sort of aural sun lamp, manufactures a sense of neutrality and well-being. Right now neutrality seems to be the first condition of peace; these devices have become commonplace. People are seeking to disengage, get out of town, or at least stay indoors and regale themselves with surfy sounds. The question everybody is asking is, Where does one live? New York is the action scene; one won't feel the kinesis of the 1970s in a Sicilian fishing village, and very few people are really quite ready to write all that off. Maybe the best of both worlds is to be a New Yorker outside New York. Anyway, I'm at my best as a traveler, and looking back when I am elderly, I may be fondest of some of my memories of hauling a suitcase along, grinning, questioning strangers, breathing the smoke of their wood fires, supported, although I was far from home, by the knowledge of where I'd come from. Arriving in Alaska, straight from New York, one feels tough as a badger, quick as a wolf. We New Yorkers see more death and violence than most soldiers do, grow a thick chitin[1] on our backs, grimace like a rat and learn to do a disappearing act. Long ago we outgrew the need to be blow-hards about our masculinity; we leave that to the Alaskans and Texans, who have more time for it. We think and talk faster, we've seen and know more, and when my friends in Vermont (who are much wiser folk than Alaskans) kid me every fall because I clear out before the first heavy snow, I smile and don't tell them that they no longer know what being tough is.

Setting out from home for the landmark of the Empire State Building, I arrive underneath it as a countryman might reach a nearby bluff, and push on to the lions at the public library, and St. Patrick's, and the fountain in front of the Plaza. Or in fifteen minutes I can take my two-year-old daughter to the Museum of Natural History, where, after waving good-by to the subway train, she strides inside, taking possession of the stuffed gorillas, antelopes, spiny anteaters, modeled Indian villages and birds and fish—the pre-twentieth-century world cooked down to some of its essentials. Six or seven puppet shows and several children's plays are being presented in the city this afternoon, and there are ships to watch, four full-scale zoos, and until recently goats, monkeys, chickens and ten horses were quartered on an eccentric half-acre a few blocks from our building. Just the city's lighted skyscrapers and bridges alone will be with my daughter forever if her first memories are like mine—she lies on her back looking upward out the window when we ride uptown in a taxi at night, with the lights opals and moons.

But is it worth the blood in the throat? Even when we go out on a pier to watch the big ships, what comes blowing in is smudgy smoke instead of a clean whiff of the sea. For me it's as disquieting as if we had to drink right out of the Hudson; our lungs must be as calloused as the soles of our feet. Is it worth seeing a dead man before breakfast and forgetting him by the time one sits down to one's orange juice? Sometimes when I'm changing records at night I hear shrieks from the street, sounds that the phonograph ordinarily drowns out. My old boyhood dreams of playing counterspy have declined in real life to washing perfume off my face once in a blue moon when, meeting an old girlfriend in a bar, I get smooched, but I still have a trotting bounce to my walk, like a middle-aged coyote who lopes along avoiding the cougars and hedgehogs, though still feeling quite capable of snapping up rabbits and fawns. Lightness and strength in the legs is important to

---

[1]Substance composing the outer crust on insects and crustaceans.

me; like the closed face, it's almost a must for the city. There's not a week when I don't think of leaving for good, living in a *house*, living in the West, perhaps, or a smaller town. I will never lose my New Yorker's grimace, New Yorker's squint and New Yorker's speed, but can't I live with them somewhere else? ✿

A Run of Bad Luck[1]

Bad ions[2] in the air, bad stars, or bad luck: call it what you will—a run of bad luck, in fact. I was driving down the Thruway in Vermont to consult a doctor in New York, and hit a deer. Didn't see the deer till the impact, sharing its surprise. Deer, unlike domestic animals, are afraid of cars and leap as you pass, either into you or away. It lay in the deep grass, heaving like a creature stranded on the beach.

Sure enough, as befitted the omen, in New York City the doctor's news was bad. Then within a day or two, Pier 50, a huge ramshackle structure across the street from where I live, caught fire and burned hectically for seven hours, although surrounded by fireboats, as only an abandoned pier can. The neighborhood was layered in smoke for a couple of days—for me, acrid testimony to what the doctor had said. There were also a few of the usual New York hang-up phone calls, and then, as if to push me into a sump[3] of depression, somebody—a vandal aroused by the fire, or someone who thought I had parked in his parking space—poured sugar into the gas tank of my car, not enough to destroy the engine but enough so that I returned to Vermont in relief.

In the meantime, my mother, in another city, had gone into the hospital for surgery, and one evening that week my daughter and I were out walking along a wooded road (I was carrying her on my shoulders), when a car passing another car bore down on us at high speed, its roar not easy to distinguish from that of the slower one; I barely heard it in time. This, in the context of the other incidents, particularly shook me because it seemed to bear a hint of malevolence; I felt very small. Then, within days, my next-door neighbor there, an old man as close as a relative to us, died of a stroke. Another good friend and country mentor went into the hospital after a heart attack. News came from New York as well that a friend in the city had killed herself. I marshaled a motley assortment of tranquilizers and sleeping pills left over from the past—divorce, career crisis, other bad occasions. I had that feeling of luck running out, that I must be *very careful*, although, on the contrary, I was becoming deadened, not alert. At such a time, the opposite of invulnerable, one must take care to move in a gingerly fashion and not get so rattled that an accident happens. I had considered myself a sort of a Sunday's child much of my life, but suddenly intimations of death and calamity were all about.

---

[1]First published in *Newsweek*, July 30, 1973.
[2]Electrically charged atoms.
[3]Cesspool.

I remembered talking to a woman who had survived a snowslide by swimming along on the surface while whooshing downhill for a hundred yards—as people caught in an undertow or even in quicksand save themselves by flattening out and floating if they can. Just so, I should ride the current until it turned. The best advice I have heard on bearing pain is to fix one's mind upon the idea that the pain is in one place—the other side of the room—and that you are in another; then, where you are, play cards or whatever. Cooking, fooling with my daughter, I realized more distinctly than at any time in years that although in fact my life was not at stake right now, I believed in some form of reincarnation or immortality— this a conviction, not a wish. I pray in airplanes during takeoff, but it is with a sense of praying *pro forma*,[1] as if the location of my belief weren't really there, but were more generalized, in a bigger God. There are ideas central to society which we seldom question in order that society will hold together—as, for instance, the notion basic to medical care that everybody has a contribution to make, or "a right to life." But there are other conceptions, such as the idea of God, which we disparage and scarcely consider, until later, smiling sheepishly in our mind's eye as if we had disputed the fact that the moon moves in the sky, we admit to having been wrong, and to having known all along that we were wrong.

Once, highborn ladies would flee to a convent if some unnerving sequence of events overtook them, not necessarily taking orders, but resting, collecting their wits. And when they strolled in the cloister around a bubbling fountain, the walkway itself possessed a soothing, perpetual quality, with each right-angle turn leading straight to another. Walking for many hours, they looked at the lindenwood saints, the robust faces—at the Virgin's implacable verve, or else at a dolor[2] portrayed with an equally saving exaggeration. Coincidentally, I went to New York's own Cloisters, and because the reality of each bad event had been dulled by the others, it was for me one of those queer times when people recognize how much they can adjust to—how quickly, for example, they could settle into the routine of life in a prison camp.

Of course I had my daughter to entertain, and in the country I walked in the woods, watching the aspens quake (said by legend to occur because Christ's cross was of aspen). I have an old army siren, hand-cranked, that I climbed with up on the mountain at twilight, to persuade a family of coyotes nearby to answer. I was relieved that the random incidents seemed to have ended. I thought of two friends in the city who had recently suffered crises—heart attacks at forty. One fellow, as the pain surged through him, found himself muttering stubbornly, "No groveling, Death!" When he was out of danger he wrote seventy-some letters to friends from his hospital bed, each with a numbered series of thoughts directed to the recipient. The other man is that rare case where one can put one's finger exactly on the characteristics of which one is so fond. He married the same woman twice. Although it didn't work out either time, she was well worth marrying twice, and

---

[1] Latin for "in form only."

[2] Carving or statue expressing grief or suffering, from the Latin for "pain."

to my way of thinking this showed that he was at once a man of fervent, rash, abiding love, and yet a man of flexibility, ready to admit an error and to act to correct it.

Both my mother and country mentor were now on the mend, and my own doctor reported good news. Prospects began looking up. What I'd gained from the period, besides a flood of relief, was the memory of how certain I'd been that the intricacy and brilliance of life cannot simply fold up with one's death—that, as in the metaphor of a fountain, or the great paradigm of rain and the ocean, it sinks down but comes up, blooms up and sinks down again. ✍

What I Think, What I Am[1]

Our loneliness makes us avoid column readers these days. The personalities in the San Francisco *Chronicle*, Chicago *Daily News*, New York *Post* constitute our neighbors now, some of them local characters but also the opinionated national stars. And movie reviewers thrive on our yearning for somebody emotional who is willing to pay attention to us and return week after week, year after year, through all the to-and-fro of other friends, to flatter us by pouring out his/her heart. They are essayists of a type, as Elizabeth Hardwick° is, James Baldwin was.

We sometimes hear that essays are an old-fashioned form, that so-and-so is the "last essayist," but the facts of the marketplace argue quite otherwise. Essays of nearly any kind are so much easier than short stories for a writer to sell, so many more see print, it's strange that though two fine anthologies remain that publish the year's best stories, no comparable collection exists for essays.[2] Such changes in the reading public's taste aren't always to the good, needless to say. The art of telling stories predated even cave painting, surely; and if we ever find ourselves living in caves again, it (with painting and drumming) will be the only art left, after movies, novels, photography, essays, biography, and all the rest have gone down the drain—the art to build from.

One has the sense with the short story as a form that while everything may have been done, nothing has been overdone; it has a permanence. Essays, if a comparison is to be made, although they go back four hundred years to Montaigne, seem a mercurial, newfangled, sometimes hokey affair that has lent itself to many of the excesses of the age, from spurious autobiography to spurious hallucination, as well as to the shabby careerism of traditional journalism. It's a greased pig. Essays are associated with the way young writers fashion a name—on

---

[1]First published in *The New York Times Book Review*, June 27, 1976.

[2]*The Best American Essays* series, published by Ticknor and Fields and edited by Robert Atwan as well as an annual guest editor, began with Hardwick° as guest editor in 1986.

plain, crowded newsprint in hybrid vehicles like the *Village Voice*, *Rolling Stone*, the *New York Review of Books*, instead of the thick paper stock and thin readership of *Partisan Review*.

Essays, however, hang somewhere on a line between two sturdy poles: this is what I think, and this is what I am. Autobiographies which aren't novels are generally extended essays, indeed. A personal essay is like the human voice talking, its order the mind's natural flow, instead of a systematized outline of ideas. Though more wayward or informal than an article or treatise, somewhere it contains a point which is its real center, even if the point couldn't be uttered in fewer words than the essayist has used. Essays don't usually boil down to a summary, as articles do, and the style of the writer has a "nap" to it, a combination of personality and originality and energetic loose ends that stand up like the nap on a piece of wool and can't be brushed flat. Essays belong to the animal kingdom, with a surface that generates sparks, like a coat of fur, compared with the flat, conventional cotton of the magazine article writer, who works in the vegetable kingdom, instead. But essays, on the other hand, may have fewer "levels" than fiction, because we are not supposed to argue much about their meaning. In the old distinction between teaching and storytelling, the essayist, however cleverly he camouflages his intentions, is a bit of a teacher or reformer, and an essay is intended to convey the same point to each of us.

This emphasis upon mind speaking to mind is what makes essays less universal in their appeal than stories. They are addressed to an educated, perhaps a middle-class, reader, with certain presuppositions, a frame of reference, even a commitment to civility that is shared—not the grand and golden empathy inherent in every man or woman that a storyteller has a chance to tap.

Nevertheless, the artful "I" of an essay can be as chameleon as any narrator in fiction; and essays do tell a story quite as often as a short story stakes a claim to a particular viewpoint. Mark Twain's piece called "Corn-pone Opinions," for example, which is about public opinion, begins with a vignette as vivid as any in *Huckleberry Finn*. Twain says that when he was a boy of fifteen, he used to hang out a back window and listen to the sermons preached by a neighbor's slave standing on top of a woodpile: "He imitated the pulpit style of the several clergymen of the village, and did it well and with fine passion and energy. To me he was a wonder. I believed he was the greatest orator in the United States and would some day be heard from. But it did not happen; in the distribution of rewards he was overlooked. . . . He interrupted his preaching now and then to saw a stick of wood, but the sawing was a pretense—he did it with his mouth, exactly imitating the sound the bucksaw makes in shrieking its way through the wood. But it served its purpose, it kept his master from coming out to see how the work was getting along."

A novel would go on and tell us what happened next in the life of the slave—and we miss that. But the extraordinary flexibility of essays is what has enabled them to ride out rough weather and hybridize into forms that suit the times. And just as one of the first things a fiction writer learns is that he needn't actually be writing fiction to write a short story—that he can tell his own history or anybody else's as exactly as he remembers it and it will be "fiction" if it remains primarily a story—an essayist soon discovers that he doesn't have to tell the whole truth and nothing but the truth; he can shape or shave his memories, as long as the purpose is served of elucidating a truthful point. A personal essay frequently is not autobiographical at all, but what it does keep in common with autobiography is that, through its tone and tumbling progression, it conveys the quality of the author's mind. Nothing gets in the way. Because essays are directly concerned with the mind and the mind's idiosyncrasy, the very freedom the mind possesses is bestowed on this branch of literature that does honor to it, and the fascination of the mind is the fascination of the essay. ✐

Joan Didion

(1934 –)

Joan Didion, daughter of Frank Reese and Eduene Jerrett Didion, was born and raised in Sacramento, California, on land that her great-great-grandfather had farmed. Her great-great-great-grandmother, Nancy Hardin Cornwall, had been one of the original eighty-seven members of the Donner-Reed party that had set out from Illinois for California in 1846. Luckily Nancy Cornwall had turned north in Nevada, before the rest of the group became trapped by a blizzard in the Sierras. Rather than starve, the forty survivors cannibalized their dead. This unique family history shaped Didion's sense of self from her earliest years. From her lessons in the Trinity Episcopal Church, Didion remembers the catechismal equation of Nancy Cornwall's destination, the Sacramento Valley, with the Holy Land "in the type and diversity of its products." The memory is not merely a wry comment on the dubious validity of an equation based only on agricultural products. For Didion the Sacramento Valley is indeed holy because of the virtue of the frontier mentality. But the valley's fifth- and sixth-generation inhabitants inherited an "implacable insularity" that renders both them and Didion herself "paralyzed by a past no longer relevant." All that Didion had been taught to revere—the understated courage of her forebears, the character developed from "good upbringing"—eventually came to be, in one of her recurring phrases, "beside the point." This telling comment expresses in casual, cryptic language a characteristic of Didion that apparently appeared at an early age: a haunting dread that there is no point to anything, that life, anyone's life, is without meaning.

In "On Keeping a Notebook" Didion says that she began writing at age five; her first story, of a woman who thinks she is freezing in the Arctic but is really about to die of the heat in the Sahara, records the frightening extremes that, for Didion, articulate her dread. When she was seven, the Japanese attacked Pearl Harbor, and her father, an Army Air Corps finance officer, was shifted, with his family, from California to Washington, to North

Carolina, and finally to Colorado before returning to Sacramento near the end of the war. For Didion the war meant a sudden loss of the regular flow of daily life, an abrupt disjuncture that confirmed her sense of the world as a frightening place. Thus, like Woolf, Hoagland, and White, Didion was a nervous, fearful child despite her family's wealth.

In an interview with Didion in the late seventies, Michiko Kakutani unearthed an incident that encapsulates Didion's admittedly "theatrical temperament" and her fascination with fear. One summer evening following eighth grade, Didion told her parents she was taking her brother to a square dance but instead left Jimmy at the bus terminal while she went off to the ocean, notebook in hand, to see what it would be like to drown. Soaked but satisfied, she went back for her brother and both crept unnoticed into the house.

In high school Didion typed out sentences from Hemingway,° Conrad,° and James,° joined a sorority called the Mañana Club that met in the governor's mansion, and drank vodka and orange juice by the river. She applied to Stanford but was rejected, and again she toyed with suicide, as described in "On Being Unchosen by the College of One's Choice." Instead she went, in 1953, to the University of California at Berkeley, joined Tri Delt, majored in English, and won first prize in *Vogue's* Prix de Paris contest for writers.

In "Goodbye to All That," an eponymous allusion to Robert Graves's° book about his experiences in World War I, Didion describes her experiences in New York City from 1956 to 1964. She had arrived young, already out of love with the boy back home she had promised to marry, sick with fever, intending to stay only six months, and eager for "new faces," new experiences; she left no longer young, newly married but in a state of acute despair, homesick for Sacramento, and hunted by the press of time. During those eight years she worked for *Vogue*, *National Review*, and *Mademoiselle*, for "so little money that some weeks [she] had to charge food at Bloomingdale's gourmet shop in order to eat." She lived in nearly empty apartments, furnished only with a bed and two borrowed "French garden chairs" or "fifty yards of yellow theatrical silk" billowing unweighted from her bedroom windows. For Didion New York was Xanadu, a never-ending party of late nights oozing into early mornings, famous people, chiffon scarves, Bloody Marys and cheap red wine, Henry Bendel jasmine soap, and women at Gristede's with Yorkshire terriers that finally provoked Didion's contempt. During this time she had written her first novel, *River Run*, set in the Sacramento Valley; it was published in 1963 and received only a few mixed reviews. Soon after, a major battle with depression made it impossible for her to go anywhere without crying: "One day I could not go into a Schrafft's; the next day it would be Bonwit Teller."

In January of 1964 Didion married John Gregory Dunne, a fellow writer and friend of seven years who had helped her edit the galleys for her novel; in June, when Didion was no longer able to "get dinner with any degree of certainty," the couple left their jobs and moved to Los Angeles, California. Despite a heartbreaking miscarriage, Didion was able to work in California, publishing essays for *National Review*, a regular film column for *Vogue*, and a variety of pieces for *Holiday*, *The New York Times Magazine*, the *Saturday Evening Post*, and the *American Scholar*. Nevertheless, in 1965, as Didion records from Hawaii in "Letter from Paradise, 21° 19′ N., 157° 52′ W.," she "had been tired too long and quarrelsome too much and too often frightened of migraine and failure." Her trip to Hawaii led, if not to happiness, at least to the publication of another essay that helped her come to terms with the major event of her generation, the bombing of Pearl Harbor.

The following year, 1966, the couple adopted a baby daughter, Quintana Roo. In "Los Angeles Notebook," written shortly after the baby's arrival, Didion describes the hot wind called the Santa Ana that epitomizes for her the unpredictable violence of modern life, especially as it was played out in the late sixties. The period before the onset of the Santa Ana is a time of uneasy dread: "The baby frets. The maid sulks. I rekindle a waning argument with the telephone company, then cut my losses and lie down, given over to whatever it is in the air. To live with the Santa Ana is to accept, consciously or unconsciously, a deeply mechanistic view of human behavior." Clearly, despite the pleasures Quintana brought to both her parents, Didion remained the victim of periodic bouts of misery.

Struggling in their marriage, Didion and Dunne nonetheless collaborated on a column called "Points West" for the *Saturday Evening Post*, taking turns each issue, a venture which lasted until the demise of the magazine in 1969. *Slouching Towards Bethlehem*, published in 1968, is a collection of some of these and other essays that Didion had written in New York and in California. That summer Dunne moved out of their rented house in Hollywood to work out problems with his writing and to escape their faltering relationship. That summer also, Didion confesses in the title essay of *The White Album*, she was tested and treated at St. John's Hospital, Santa Monica, for "an attack of vertigo and nausea" prompted, Didion implies, by social and political events as much as by private ones. By December of 1969 their personal lives had not significantly improved: Didion began her first essay for *Life* by acknowledging that she, her husband, and her three-year-old daughter were in Honolulu "in lieu of filing for divorce."

Didion's second novel, *Play It As It Lays* (1970), was not only a best seller but was also nominated for a National Book Award. She continued writing for *Life* until June of 1970, while also publishing essays in *The New York Times Book Review* and *The New York Review of Books*. In 1971 she and Dunne again collaborated, this time on a screenplay, *Panic in Needle Park*, for Twentieth Century-Fox. Their marriage improving, they moved to a beach house in Malibu forty miles up the coast from Los Angeles, with room enough to display a quilt made by Didion's great-great-grandmother and a rosewood piano that had belonged to the Didions since 1848. Here Didion and Dunne wrote film scripts of *Play It As It Lays* (1972) and *A Star Is Born*

(1976) and shared a column called "The Coast" for *Esquire* (1976–1977). Here too Didion wrote her third novel, *A Book of Common Prayer* (1977).

The community the couple found on the Pacific Coast Highway, described in "On the Morning After the Sixties," was "one of shared isolation and adversity," reinforcing Didion's vision of a world of dangerous extremes: snakes lurked in the driveway, and fires and floods periodically cut off access to the highway. They lived in this house from the time Quintana was five until she was twelve, when "it rained until the highway collapsed, and one of her [Quintana's] friends drowned at Zuma Beach, a casualty of Quaaludes." A few months after the family had moved to a two-story colonial in Brentwood Park, Los Angeles, a Santa Ana blew a fire up the coast that stopped just before it reached their former house.

The next year, 1979, Didion published *The White Album*, her second collection of essays. Since then both she and Dunne have continued to work successfully, moving with ease among celebrities from the film industry as well as fellow writers and artists. Michiko Kakutani's article on Didion, written shortly after the publication of *The White Album*, describes Didion's life in Los Angeles as possessing "the soothing order and elegance of a *Vogue* photo spread." In her Los Angeles house Didion exerted control over her small and recurrently painful body through pills, painkillers, and the pleasing rituals of housekeeping: sewing curtains, cooking gourmet meals, polishing silver. But even in this comfortable, secure world, she admitted to her interviewer that she felt afraid.

In 1981 Didion and Dunne produced another screenplay, *True Confessions*, based on a novel by Dunne. In 1983 Didion published a work of nonfiction, *Salvador*, and another novel, *Democracy*, the following year. She continues to publish essays, more outward-looking than her earlier works, primarily for *The New York Review of Books*. Some of these were revised and included in her most recent book of nonfiction, *Miami* (1987). Among her several works since then is an essay on New York City written for *The New York Review of Books*.

Like Hoagland's, Didion's essays astonish the reader with their vivid, telling details of the author's personal life. Yet neither author tells all, and each finds in private suffering an etching of the public woe. Didion's recognition in "The White Album" that severe depression was a natural response to the events of the sixties articulates her stance as a writer. Another example of this congruence of the private and the public is the opening sentence of that essay: "We tell ourselves stories in order to live." The stories form a shape in the void, help her to forget that outside them lies nothing. Without their control, their limits, their narrative continuity and focus, Didion cannot perceive meaning, cannot find the point. Her essays, as much as her novels, are rituals of avoidance, ways to keep going. That first sentence is typical of Didion in its stark assertion of this fact and in its direct assumption that she speaks for all of us, whether we like it or not, whether or not we always agree.

Didion's early titles ("On Self-Respect" and "On Morality," for example) deliberately evoke those of Bacon, recalling his terse voice and his sense of noblesse oblige, an obligation to serve his public by recording useful observations. Didion's modern versions also voice the experience of the privileged class. Unlike many of her rich but liberal counterparts of the sixties, Didion does not reject her wealthy upbringing. But in place of Bacon's calm assurance and advice is Didion's sense of immediacy and panic, her desperate need to make the reader understand what it feels like to be Joan Didion in the last half of the twentieth century. Didion translates Bacon's short, concise sentences into cinematic fast cuts from one scene to another to articulate the oblique connections and disjunctures of modern life. However, just as Bacon's world was infinitely remote from the uneducated masses who could not read his essays, so Didion's psychic pain may be incomprehensible to the poor who live outside the periphery of her vision.

In "The Women's Movement" (1972) Didion conflates feminism with Marxism, seeing the political proponents of consciousness-raising as theorists compelled to undermine the individual and the family in the name of a new revolutionary class. Studiously apolitical herself (according to Kakutani she voted, like her parents, for Goldwater in 1964 and exercised her right to vote only two more times during the next fifteen years), she rejects such anticapitalist notions outright and sees in what has remained of the women's movement nothing at all of interest. The desire of some writers for *Ms.* to rewrite fairy tales seems to Didion a misguided urge to change history, to recreate, somehow, the body of the female. Didion prefers an awareness of her sex, the "apprehension of what it is like to be a woman, the irreconcilable difference of it . . . that dark involvement with blood and birth and death." The word *apprehension* here is particularly apt, signifying at once knowledge and fear.

Ozick and Didion—one an avowed feminist, the other avowedly not—are both strong-minded writers who are heavily influenced by their sense of the past. Ozick's strength springs from commitment to art and to Judaism; Didion's comes from resistance and the need to control what is, after all, beyond the scope of human understanding. Both assert their strength through style, the careful attention to the sound of words on the page. Didion's exact details and unflagging sensitivity to the horrors and ironies and absurdities of modern life have made her one of the most anthologized modern essayists—proof that her oppression by "some nameless anxiety," her longing to "go home again," is not, as she speculates in "On Going Home," confined to her generation alone. ✍

On Self-Respect[1]

Once, in a dry season,[2] I wrote in large letters across two pages of a notebook that innocence ends when one is stripped of the delusion that one likes oneself. Although now, some years later, I marvel that a mind on the outs with itself should have nonetheless made painstaking record of its every tremor, I recall with embarrassing clarity the flavor of those particular ashes. It was a matter of misplaced self-respect.

I had not been elected to Phi Beta Kappa. This failure could scarcely have been more predictable or less ambiguous (I simply did not have the grades), but I was unnerved by it; I had somehow thought myself a kind of academic Raskolnikov,[3] curiously exempt from the cause-effect relationships which hampered others. Although even the humorless nineteen-year-old that I was must have recognized that the situation lacked real tragic stature, the day that I did not make Phi Beta Kappa nonetheless marked the end of something, and innocence may well be the word for it. I lost the conviction that lights would always turn green for me, the pleasant certainty that those rather passive virtues which had won me approval as a child automatically guaranteed me not only Phi Beta Kappa keys but happiness, honor, and the love of a good man; lost a certain touching faith in the totem power of good manners, clean hair, and proven competence on the Stanford-Binet scale.[4] To such doubtful amulets[5] had my self-respect been pinned, and I faced myself that day with the nonplused apprehension of someone who has come across a vampire and has no crucifix at hand.

Although to be driven back upon oneself is an uneasy affair at best, rather like trying to cross a border with borrowed credentials, it seems to me now the one condition necessary to the beginnings of real self-respect. Most of our platitudes notwithstanding, self-deception remains the most difficult deception. The tricks that work on others count for nothing in that very well-lit back alley where one keeps assignations with oneself: no winning smiles will do here, no prettily drawn lists of good intentions. One shuffles flashily but in vain through one's marked cards—the kindness done for the wrong reason, the apparent triumph which involved no real effort, the seemingly heroic act into which one had been shamed. The dismal fact is that self-respect has nothing to do with the approval of others—who are, after all, deceived easily enough; has nothing to do with

---

[1]First published in *Vogue* in 1961.
[2]Probably alludes to the aridity of the sinful soul as well as to the weather.
[3]Main character in Dostoyevsky's *Crime and Punishment* who, driven by poverty, commits two murders under the illusion that he is exempt from moral law.
[4]A measurement of mental development achieved through psychological testing of children, it was invented by Alfred Binet (1857–1911) to identify and help slow learners.
[5]Objects worn as charms against evil or ill luck.

reputation, which, as Rhett Butler told Scarlett O'Hara,[1] is something people with courage can do without.

To do without self-respect, on the other hand, is to be an unwilling audience of one to an interminable documentary that details one's failings, both real and imagined, with fresh footage spliced in for every screening. *There's the glass you broke in anger, there's the hurt on X's face; watch now, this next scene, the night Y came back from Houston, see how you muff this one.* To live without self-respect is to lie awake some night, beyond the reach of warm milk, phenobarbital, and the sleeping hand on the coverlet, counting up the sins of commission and omission, the trusts betrayed, the promises subtly broken, the gifts irrevocably wasted through sloth or cowardice or carelessness. However long we postpone it, we eventually lie down alone in that notoriously uncomfortable bed, the one we make ourselves. Whether or not we sleep in it depends, of course, on whether or not we respect ourselves.

To protest that some fairly improbable people, some people who *could not possibly respect themselves*, seem to sleep easily enough is to miss the point entirely, as surely as those people miss it who think that self-respect has necessarily to do with not having safety pins in one's underwear. There is a common superstition that "self-respect" is a kind of charm against snakes, something that keeps those who have it locked in some unblighted Eden, out of strange beds, ambivalent conversations, and trouble in general. It does not at all. It has nothing to do with the face of things, but concerns instead a separate peace, a private reconciliation. Although the careless, suicidal Julian English[2] in *Appointment in Samarra* and the careless, incurably dishonest Jordan Baker[3] in *The Great Gatsby* seem equally improbable candidates for self-respect, Jordan Baker had it, Julian English did not. With that genius for accommodation more often seen in women than in men, Jordan took her own measure, made her own peace, avoided threats to that peace: "I hate careless people," she told Nick Carraway. "It takes two to make an accident."

Like Jordan Baker, people with self-respect have the courage of their mistakes. They know the price of things. If they choose to commit adultery, they do not then go running, in an access of bad conscience, to receive absolution from the wronged parties; nor do they complain unduly of the unfairness, the undeserved embarrassment, of being named co-respondent. In brief, people with self-respect exhibit a certain toughness, a kind of moral nerve; they display what was once called *character*, a quality which, although approved in the abstract, sometimes loses ground to other, more instantly negotiable virtues. The measure of its slipping prestige is that one tends to think of it only in connection with

---

[1] Main characters in the Pulitzer Prize–winning novel *Gone with the Wind* (1936) by Margaret Mitchell (1900–1949).

[2] Unhappy Gibbsville Cadillac dealer in John O'Hara's novel *Appointment in Samarra* (1934); he also appears in *A Rage to Live* (1949).

[3] Friend of Daisy Buchanan, romantically involved with Nick Carraway (see Fitzgerald°).

homely children and United States senators who have been defeated, preferably in the primary, for reelection. Nonetheless, character—the willingness to accept responsibility for one's own life—is the source from which self-respect springs.

Self-respect is something that our grandparents, whether or not they had it, knew all about. They had instilled in them, young, a certain discipline, the sense that one lives by doing things one does not particularly want to do, by putting fears and doubts to one side, by weighing immediate comforts against the possibility of larger, even intangible, comforts. It seemed to the nineteenth century admirable, but not remarkable, that Chinese Gordon[1] put on a clean white suit and held Khartoum against the Mahdi; it did not seem unjust that the way to free land in California involved death and difficulty and dirt. In a diary kept during the winter of 1846, an emigrating twelve-year-old named Narcissa Cornwall[2] noted coolly: "Father was busy reading and did not notice that the house was being filled with strange Indians until Mother spoke about it." Even lacking any clue as to what Mother said, one can scarcely fail to be impressed by the entire incident: the father reading, the Indians filing in, the mother choosing the words that would not alarm, the child duly recording the event and noting further that those particular Indians were not, "fortunately for us," hostile. Indians were simply part of the *donnée*.[3]

In one guise or another, Indians always are. Again, it is a question of recognizing that anything worth having has its price. People who respect themselves are willing to accept the risk that the Indians will be hostile, that the venture will go bankrupt, that the liaison may not turn out to be one in which *every day is a holiday because you're married to me*. They are willing to invest something of themselves; they may not play at all, but when they do play, they know the odds.

That kind of self-respect is a discipline, a habit of mind that can never be faked but can be developed, trained, coaxed forth. It was once suggested to me that, as an antidote to crying, I put my head in a paper bag. As it happens, there is a sound physiological reason, something to do with oxygen, for doing exactly that, but the psychological effect alone is incalculable: it is difficult in the extreme to continue fancying oneself Cathy in *Wuthering Heights*[4] with one's head in a Food Fair bag. There is a similar case for all the small disciplines, unimportant in themselves; imagine maintaining any kind of swoon, commiserative or carnal, in a cold shower.

---

[1]Charles George Gordon (1833–1885), British soldier who led a Chinese army, the Ever-Victorious, against the Taiping Rebellion in 1863 and later tried to defeat the Mahdi, Muhammad Ahmed (1843–1885), a Sudanese religious leader who believed himself destined to reconquer Egypt. General Gordon was besieged in Khartoum for ten months before he and his men were killed.

[2]One of Didion's ancestors; see biography.

[3]French for "given" or "fact"; what is understood to be basic.

[4]See Emily Brontë.°

But those small disciplines are valuable only insofar as they represent larger ones. To say that Waterloo was won on the playing fields of Eton[1] is not to say that Napoleon might have been saved by a crash program in cricket; to give formal dinners in the rain forest[2] would be pointless did not the candlelight flickering on the liana[3] call forth deeper, stronger disciplines, values instilled long before. It is a kind of ritual, helping us to remember who and what we are. In order to remember it, one must have known it.

To have that sense of one's intrinsic worth which constitutes self-respect is potentially to have everything: the ability to discriminate, to love and to remain indifferent. To lack it is to be locked within oneself, paradoxically incapable of either love or indifference. If we do not respect ourselves, we are on the one hand forced to despise those who have so few resources as to consort with us, so little perception as to remain blind to our fatal weaknesses. On the other, we are peculiarly in thrall to everyone we see, curiously determined to live out—since our self-image is untenable—their false notions of us. We flatter ourselves by thinking this compulsion to please others an attractive trait: a gist for imaginative empathy, evidence of our willingness to give. *Of course* I will play Francesca to your Paolo,[4] Helen Keller to anyone's Annie Sullivan:[5] no expectation is too misplaced, no role too ludicrous. At the mercy of those we cannot but hold in contempt, we play roles doomed to failure before they are begun, each defeat generating fresh despair at the urgency of divining and meeting the next demand made upon us.

It is the phenomenon sometimes called "alienation from self." In its advanced stages, we no longer answer the telephone, because someone might want something; that we could say *no* without drowning in self-reproach is an idea alien to this game. Every encounter demands too much, tears the nerves, drains the will, and the specter of something as small as an unanswered letter arouses such disproportionate guilt that answering it becomes out of the question. To assign unanswered letters their proper weight, to free us from the expectations of others, to give us back to ourselves—there lies the great, the singular power of self-respect. Without it, one eventually discovers the final turn of the screw: one runs away to find oneself, and finds no one at home. ✍

---

[1]This statement is attributed to the Duke of Wellington; it is characteristic of the British upper-class belief that school games prepared men for war, a view that was shattered for many on the battlefields of World War I.

[2]Allusion to British upper-class colonial values; see, for example, *The Riddle of the Sands* (1903) by Erskine Chalders, about men in the jungle who "have made it a rule to dress regularly for dinner in order to maintain their self respect and prevent a relapse into barbarism."

[3]A woody vine found in the tropics.

[4]The lovers whose lust condemned them to the second circle of hell in Dante's *Inferno*.

[5]Keller (1880–1986), who was graduated from Radcliffe in 1904 and became a writer and lecturer, was blind and deaf at the age of two. When she was seven, she was put in the care of Sullivan (1886–1936), herself partially blind, who taught Keller the manual alphabet. Sullivan remained Keller's devoted companion for the rest of Sullivan's life.

On Morality[1]

As it happens I am in Death Valley, in a room at the Enterprise Motel and Trailer Park, and it is July, and it is hot. In fact it is 119°. I cannot seem to make the air conditioner work, but there is a small refrigerator, and I can wrap ice cubes in a towel and hold them against the small of my back. With the help of the ice cubes I have been trying to think, because *The American Scholar* asked me to, in some abstract way about "morality," a word I distrust more every day, but my mind veers inflexibly toward the particular.

Here are some particulars. At midnight last night, on the road from Las Vegas to Death Valley Junction, a car hit a shoulder and turned over. The driver, very young and apparently drunk, was killed instantly. His girl was found alive but bleeding internally, deep in shock. I talked this afternoon to the nurse who had driven the girl to the nearest doctor, 185 miles across the floor of the Valley and three ranges of lethal mountain road. The nurse explained that her husband, a talc miner, had stayed on the highway with the boy's body until the coroner could get over the mountains from Bishop, at dawn today. "You can't just leave a body on the highway," she said. "It's immoral."

It was one instance in which I did not distrust the word, because she meant something quite specific. She meant that if a body is left alone for even a few minutes on the desert, the coyotes close in and eat the flesh. Whether or not a corpse is torn apart by coyotes may seem only a sentimental consideration, but of course it is more: one of the promises we make to one another is that we will try to retrieve our casualties, try not to abandon our dead to the coyotes. If we have been taught to keep our promises—if, in the simplest terms, our upbringing is good enough—we stay with the body, or have bad dreams.

I am talking, of course, about the kind of social code that is sometimes called, usually pejoratively, "wagon-train morality." In fact that is precisely what it is. For better or worse, we are what we learned as children: my own childhood was illuminated by graphic litanies of the grief awaiting those who failed in their loyalties to each other. The Donner-Reed Party,[2] starving in the Sierra snows, all the ephemera of civilization gone save that one vestigial taboo, the provision that no one should eat his own blood kin. The Jayhawkers,[3] who quarreled and separated not far from where I am tonight. Some of them died in the Funerals and some of them died down near Badwater and most of the rest of them died in the Panamints. A woman who got through gave the Valley its name. Some might say that the Jayhawkers were killed by the desert summer, and the Donner Party by the mountain winter, by circumstances beyond control; we were taught instead

---

[1]First published in the *American Scholar* in 1965.
[2]See biography.
[3]Free staters before the Civil War who fought with the slave staters over Kansas; they were scorned for their reputation as marauders.

that they had somewhere abdicated their responsibilities, somehow breached their primary loyalties, or they would not have found themselves helpless in the mountain winter or the desert summer, would not have given way to acrimony, would not have deserted one another, would not have *failed*. In brief, we heard such stories as cautionary tales, and they still suggest the only kind of "morality" that seems to me to have any but the most potentially mendacious meaning.

You are quite possibly impatient with me by now; I am talking, you want to say, about a "morality" so primitive that it scarcely deserves the name, a code that has as its point only survival, not the attainment of the ideal good. Exactly. Particularly out here tonight, in this country so ominous and terrible that to live in it is to live with antimatter, it is difficult to believe that "the good" is a knowable quantity. Let me tell you what it is like out here tonight. Stories travel at night on the desert. Someone gets in his pickup and drives a couple hundred miles for a beer, and he carries news of what is happening, back wherever he came from. Then he drives another hundred miles for another beer, and passes along stories from the last place as well as from the one before; it is a network kept alive by people whose instincts tell them that if they do not keep moving at night on the desert they will lose all reason. Here is a story that is going around the desert tonight: over across the Nevada line, sheriff's deputies are diving in some underground pools, trying to retrieve a couple of bodies known to be in the hole. The widow of one of the drowned boys is over there; she is eighteen, and pregnant, and is said not to leave the hole. The divers go down and come up, and she just stands there and stares into the water. They have been diving for ten days but have found no bottom to the caves, no bodies and no trace of them, only the black 90° water going down and down and down, and a single translucent fish, not classified. The story tonight is that one of the divers has been hauled up incoherent, out of his head, shouting—until they got him out of there so that the widow could not hear—about water that got hotter instead of cooler as he went down, about light flickering through the water, about magma, about underground nuclear testing.

That is the tone stories take out here, and there are quite a few of them tonight. And it is more than the stories alone. Across the road at the Faith Community Church a couple dozen old people, come here to live in trailers and die in the sun, are holding a prayer sing. I cannot hear them and do not want to. What I can hear are occasional coyotes and a constant chorus of "Baby the Rain Must Fall" from the jukebox in the Snake Room next door, and if I were also to hear those dying voices, those Midwestern voices drawn to this lunar country for some unimaginable atavistic[1] rites, *rock of ages cleft for me*, I think I would lose my own reason. Every now and then I imagine I hear a rattlesnake, but my husband says that it is a faucet, a paper rustling, the wind. Then he stands by a window, and plays a flashlight over the dry wash[2] outside.

---

[1] From *atavism*, or reversion to the primitive.
[2] A gully.

What does it mean? It means nothing manageable. There is some sinister hysteria in the air out here tonight, some hint of the monstrous perversion to which any human idea can come. "I followed my own conscience." "I did what I thought was right." How many madmen have said it and meant it? How many murderers? Klaus Fuchs[1] said it, and the men who committed the Mountain Meadows Massacre[2] said it, and Alfred Rosenberg[3] said it. And, as we are rotely and rather presumptuously reminded by those who would say it now, Jesus said it. Maybe we have all said it, and maybe we have been wrong. Except on that most primitive level—our loyalties to those we love—what could be more arrogant than to claim the primacy of personal conscience? ("Tell me," a rabbi asked Daniel Bell[4] when he said, as a child, that he did not believe in God. "Do you think God cares?") At least some of the time, the world appears to me as a painting by Hieronymous Bosch;[5] were I to follow my conscience then, it would lead me out onto the desert with Marion Faye, out to where he stood in *The Deer Park*[6] looking east to Los Alamos and praying, as if for rain, that it would happen: "*. . . let it come and clear the rot and the stench and the stink, let it come for all of everywhere, just so it comes and the world stands clear in the white dead dawn.*"

Of course you will say that I do not have the right, even if I had the power, to inflict that unreasonable conscience upon you; nor do I want you to inflict your conscience, however reasonable, however enlightened, upon me. ("We must be aware of the dangers which lie in our most generous wishes," Lionel Trilling[7] once wrote. "Some paradox of our nature leads us, when once we have made our fellow men the objects of our enlightened interest, to go on to make them the objects of our pity, then of our wisdom, ultimately of our coercion.") That the ethic of conscience is intrinsically insidious seems scarcely a revelatory point, but it is one raised with increasing infrequency; even those who do raise it tend to

---

[1]German-born physicist (1911–) who became a British citizen and in 1943 worked on the atomic bomb in the United States. The FBI eventually discovered that he was sending secret information to the Communists in the Soviet Union. After serving a term in prison from 1950 to 1959, he went to East Germany to direct the Institute for Nuclear Physics.

[2]In 1857 a group of 140 non-Mormon emigrants headed for California was murdered in southwest Utah by John D. Lee, a Mormon, and a band of Paiute Indians. Lee had promised the settlers safe passage, but when they proceeded according to his instructions, he and the Indians killed all but a few children.

[3](1893–1946) German Nazi leader and author of an anti-Christian and anti-Semitic book that contributed to Hitler's racist philosophy. He was convicted at Nuremberg as a war criminal and executed.

[4]Harvard sociologist (1919–), co-founder of the journal *Public Interest* and author of such works as *The Coming of Post Industrial Society* (1973) and *The Winding Passage* (1981).

[5]Flemish painter (1450–1516) known for his brilliantly colored and detailed pictures of bizarre plants, animals, people, devils, and allegorical or mythological figures.

[6]See Mailer.°

[7]American critic (1905–1975), professor at Columbia and author of *The Liberal Imagination* (1950), *The Opposing Self* (1955), and *A Gathering of Fugitives* (1956) as well as a novel, some short stories, and books on Matthew Arnold,° E. M. Forster,° and Sigmund Freud.°

segue[1] with troubling readiness into the quite contradictory position that the ethic of conscience is dangerous when it is "wrong," and admirable when it is "right."

You see I want to be quite obstinate about insisting that we have no way of knowing—beyond that fundamental loyalty to the social code—what is "right" and what is "wrong," what is "good" and what "evil." I dwell so upon this because the most disturbing aspect of "morality" seems to me to be the frequency with which the word now appears; in the press, on television, in the most perfunctory kinds of conversation. Questions of straightforward power (or survival) politics, questions of quite indifferent public policy, questions of almost anything: they are all assigned these factitious moral burdens. There is something facile going on, some self-indulgence at work. Of course we would all like to "believe" in something, like to assuage our private guilts in public causes, like to lose our tiresome selves; like, perhaps, to transform the white flag of defeat at home into the brave white banner of battle away from home. And of course it is all right to do that; that is how, immemorially, things have gotten done. But I think it is all right only so long as we do not delude ourselves about what we are doing, and why. It is all right only so long as we remember that all the *ad hoc* committees, all the picket lines, all the brave signatures in *The New York Times*, all the tools of agitprop[2] straight across the spectrum, do not confer upon anyone any *ipso facto*[3] virtue. It is all right only so long as we recognize that the end may or may not be expedient, may or may not be a good idea, but in any case has nothing to do with "morality." Because when we start deceiving ourselves into thinking not that we want something or need something, not that it is a pragmatic necessity for us to have it, but that it is a *moral imperative* that we have it, then is when we join the fashionable madmen, and then is when the thin whine of hysteria is heard in the land, and then is when we are in bad trouble. And I suspect we are already there. ✎

On Going Home[4]

I am home for my daughter's first birthday. By "home" I do not mean the house in Los Angeles where my husband and I and the baby live, but the place where my family is, in the Central Valley of California. It is a vital although troublesome distinction. My husband likes my family but is uneasy in their house, because once there I fall into their ways, which are difficult, oblique, deliberately inarticulate, not my husband's ways. We live in dusty houses ("D-U-S-T," he once wrote

---

[1]Musical term meaning a smooth transition from one movement or piece of music to another.
[2]Political agitation and propaganda, particularly in aid of leftist causes, from the Russian for a department of communist propaganda.
[3]Latin for "by the fact itself."
[4]First published in 1967.

with his finger on surfaces all over the house, but no one noticed it) filled with mementos quite without value to him (what could the Canton dessert plates mean to him? how could he have known about the assay scales,[1] why should he care if he did know?), and we appear to talk exclusively about people we know who have been committed to mental hospitals, about people we know who have been booked on drunk-driving charges, and about property, particularly about property, land, price per acre and C-2 zoning[2] and assessments[3] and freeway access. My brother does not understand my husband's inability to perceive the advantage in the rather common real-estate transaction known as "sale-leaseback,"[4] and my husband in turn does not understand why so many of the people he hears about in my father's house have recently been committed to mental hospitals or booked on drunk-driving charges. Nor does he understand that when we talk about sale-leasebacks and right-of-way condemnations we are talking in code about things we like best, the yellow fields and the cottonwoods and the rivers rising and falling and the mountain roads closing when the heavy snow comes in. We miss each other's points, have another drink and regard the fire. My brother refers to my husband, in his presence, as "Joan's husband." Marriage is the classic betrayal.

Or perhaps it is not any more. Sometimes I think that those of us who are now in our thirties were born into the last generation to carry the burden of "home," to find in family life the source of all tension and drama. I had by all objective accounts a "normal" and a "happy" family situation, and yet I was almost thirty years old before I could talk to my family on the telephone without crying after I had hung up. We did not fight. Nothing was wrong. And yet some nameless anxiety colored the emotional charges between me and the place that I came from. The question of whether or not you could go home again[5] was a very real part of the sentimental and largely literary baggage with which we left home in the fifties; I suspect that it is irrelevant to the children born of the fragmentation after World War II. A few weeks ago in a San Francisco bar I saw a pretty young girl on crystal[6] take off her clothes and dance for the cash prize in an "amateur-topless" contest. There was no particular sense of moment about this, none of the effect of romantic degradation, of "dark journey," for which my generation strived so assiduously. What sense could that girl possibly make of, say, Long Day's Journey into Night?[7] Who is beside the point?

---

[1]Devices for determining the proportion of precious metals in an ore.
[2]Zoning for neighborhood businesses such as small markets and other shops.
[3]Estimates of the value of property for purposes of taxation.
[4]The leasing of property by the new owner back to the previous owner.
[5]Reference to a lyrical and intense novel by Thomas Wolfe (1900–1938) called You Can't Go Home Again (1940), about his memories of the past and his search for self-discovery and a meaningful faith.
[6]Methamphetamine, an amphetamine derivative in powder or crystal form, soluble for injection and illicitly made; also called "speed."
[7]Autobiographical play by Eugene O'Neill (1888–1953) about the conflicts and loves within his family.

That I am trapped in this particular irrelevancy is never more apparent to me than when I am home. Paralyzed by the neurotic lassitude engendered by meeting one's past at every turn, around every corner, inside every cupboard, I go aimlessly from room to room. I decide to meet it head-on and clean out a drawer, and I spread the contents on the bed. A bathing suit I wore the summer I was seventeen. A letter of rejection from *The Nation*, an aerial photograph of the site for a shopping center my father did not build in 1954. Three teacups hand-painted with cabbage roses and signed "E. M.," my grandmother's initials. There is no final solution for letters of rejection from *The Nation* and teacups hand-painted in 1900. Nor is there any answer to snapshots of one's grandfather as a young man on skis, surveying around Donner Pass in the year 1910. I smooth out the snapshot and look into his face, and do and do not see my own. I close the drawer, and have another cup of coffee with my mother. We get along very well, veterans of a guerrilla war we never understood.

Days pass. I see no one. I come to dread my husband's evening call, not only because he is full of news of what by now seems to me our remote life in Los Angeles, people he has seen, letters which require attention, but because he asks what I have been doing, suggest uneasily that I get out, drive to San Francisco or Berkeley. Instead I drive across the river to a family graveyard. It has been vandalized since my last visit and the monuments are broken, overturned in the dry grass. Because I once saw a rattlesnake in the grass I stay in the car and listen to a country-and-Western station. Later I drive with my father to a ranch he has in the foothills. The man who runs his cattle on it asks us to the round-up, a week from Sunday, and although I know that I will be in Los Angeles I say, in the oblique way my family talks, that I will come. Once home I mention the broken monuments in the graveyard. My mother shrugs.

I go to visit my great-aunts. A few of them think now that I am my cousin, or their daughter who died young. We recall an anecdote about a relative last seen in 1948, and they ask if I still like living in New York City. I have lived in Los Angeles for three years, but I say that I do. The baby is offered a horehound drop, and I am slipped a dollar bill "to buy a treat." Questions trail off, answers are abandoned, the baby plays with the dust motes in a shaft of afternoon sun.

It is time for the baby's birthday party: a white cake, strawberry-marshmallow ice cream, a bottle of champagne saved from another party. In the evening, after she has gone to sleep, I kneel beside the crib and touch her face, where it is pressed against the slats, with mine. She is an open and trusting child, unprepared for and unaccustomed to the ambushes of family life, and perhaps it is just as well that I can offer her little of that life. I would like to give her more. I would like to promise her that she will grow up with a sense of her cousins and of rivers and of her great-grandmother's teacups, would like to pledge her a picnic on a river with fried chicken and her hair uncombed, would like to give her *home* for her birthday, but we live differently now and I can promise her nothing like that. I give her a xylophone and a sundress from Madeira, and promise to tell her a funny story. ✍

In Bed[1]

Three, four, sometimes five times a month, I spend the day in bed with a migraine headache, insensible to the world around me. Almost every day of every month, between these attacks, I feel the sudden irrational irritation and flush of blood into the cerebral arteries which tell me that migraine is on its way, and I take certain drugs to avert its arrival. If I did not take the drugs, I would be able to function perhaps one day in four. The physiological error called migraine is, in brief, central to the given of my life. When I was 15, 16, even 25, I used to think that I could rid myself of this error by simply denying it, character over chemistry. "Do you have headaches *sometimes? frequently? never?*" the application forms would demand. "Check one." Wary of the trap, wanting whatever it was that the successful circumnavigation of that particular form could bring (a job, a scholarship, the respect of mankind and the grace of God), I would check one. "*Sometimes,*" I would lie. That in fact I spent one or two days a week almost unconscious with pain seemed a shameful secret, evidence not merely of some chemical inferiority but of all my bad attitudes, unpleasant tempers, wrongthink.

For I had no brain tumor, no eyestrain, no high blood pressure, nothing wrong with me at all: I simply had migraine headaches, and migraine headaches were, as everyone who did not have them knew, imaginary. I fought migraine then, ignored the warnings it sent, went to school and later to work in spite of it, sat through lectures in Middle English and presentations to advertisers with involuntary tears running down the right side of my face, threw up in washrooms, stumbled home by instinct, emptied ice trays onto my bed and tried to freeze the pain in my right temple, wished only for a neurosurgeon who would do a lobotomy on house call, and cursed my imagination.

It was a long time before I began thinking mechanistically enough to accept migraine for what it was: something with which I would be living, the way some people live with diabetes. Migraine is something more than the fancy of a neurotic imagination. It is an essentially hereditary complex of symptoms, the most frequently noted but by no means the most unpleasant of which is a vascular headache of blinding severity, suffered by a surprising number of women, a fair number of men (Thomas Jefferson had migraine, and so did Ulysses S. Grant, the day he accepted Lee's surrender), and by some unfortunate children as young as two years old. (I had my first when I was eight. It came on during a fire drill at the Columbia School in Colorado Springs, Colorado. I was taken first home and then to the infirmary at Peterson Field, where my father was stationed. The Air Corps doctor prescribed an enema.) Almost anything can trigger a specific attack of migraine: stress, allergy, fatigue, an abrupt change in barometric pressure, a contretemps over a parking ticket. A flashing light. A fire drill. One inherits, of course, only the predisposition. In other words I spent yesterday in bed with a

---

[1]First published in 1968.

headache not merely because of my bad attitudes, unpleasant tempers and wrongthink, but because both my grandmothers had migraine, my father has migraine and my mother has migraine.

No one knows precisely what it is that is inherited. The chemistry of migraine, however, seems to have some connection with the nerve hormone named serotonin,[1] which is naturally present in the brain. The amount of serotonin in the blood falls sharply at the onset of migraine, and one migraine drug, methysergide, or Sansert, seems to have some effect on serotonin. Methysergide is a derivative of lysergic acid (in fact Sandoz Pharmaceuticals first synthesized LSD-25 while looking for a migraine cure), and its use is hemmed about with so many contraindications and side effects that most doctors prescribe it only in the most incapacitating cases. Methysergide, when it is prescribed, is taken daily, as a preventive; another preventive which works for some people is old-fashioned ergotamine tartrate,[2] which helps to constrict the swelling blood vessels during the "aura," the period which in most cases precedes the actual headache.

Once an attack is under way, however, no drug touches it. Migraine gives some people mild hallucinations, temporarily blinds others, shows up not only as a headache but as a gastrointestinal disturbance, a painful sensitivity to all sensory stimuli, an abrupt overpowering fatigue, a strokelike aphasia,[3] and a crippling inability to make even the most routine connections. When I am in a migraine aura (for some people the aura lasts fifteen minutes, for others several hours), I will drive through red lights, lose the house keys, spill whatever I am holding, lose the ability to focus my eyes or frame coherent sentences, and generally give the appearance of being on drugs, or drunk. The actual headache, when it comes, brings with it chills, sweating, nausea, a debility that seems to stretch the very limits of endurance. That no one dies of migraine seems, to someone deep into an attack, an ambiguous blessing.

My husband also has migraine, which is unfortunate for him but fortunate for me: perhaps nothing so tends to prolong an attack as the accusing eye of someone who has never had a headache. "Why not take a couple of aspirin," the unafflicted will say from the doorway, or "I'd have a headache, too, spending a beautiful day like this inside with all the shades drawn." All of us who have migraine suffer not only from the attacks themselves but from this common conviction that we are perversely refusing to cure ourselves by taking a couple of aspirin, that we are making ourselves sick, that we "bring it on ourselves." And in the most immediate sense, the sense of why we have a headache this Tuesday and not last Thursday, of course we often do. There certainly is what doctors call a "migraine personality," and that personality tends to be ambitious, inward, intolerant of error, rather rigidly organized, perfectionist. "You don't look like a migraine personality," a doctor once said to me. "Your hair's messy. But I suppose you're

---

[1] A chemical that can raise body temperature and contract smooth muscles.

[2] From a fungus growing on rye; a basic source of lysergic acid.

[3] Partial or total loss of the ability to articulate words; see Addison, *Spectator* No. 247.

a compulsive housekeeper.'' Actually my house is kept even more negligently than my hair, but the doctor was right nonetheless: perfectionism can also take the form of spending most of a week writing and rewriting and not writing a single paragraph.

But not all perfectionists have migraine, and not all migrainous people have migraine personalities. We do not escape heredity. I have tried in most of the available ways to escape my own migrainous heredity (at one point I learned to give myself two daily injections of histamine[1] with a hypodermic needle, even though the needle so frightened me that I had to close my eyes when I did it), but I still have migraine. And I have learned now to live with it, learned when to expect it, how to outwit it, even how to regard it, when it does come, as more friend than lodger. We have reached a certain understanding, my migraine and I. It never comes when I am in real trouble. Tell me that my house is burned down, my husband has left me, that there is gunfighting in the streets and panic in the banks, and I will not respond by getting a headache. It comes instead when I am fighting not an open guerrilla war with my own life, during weeks of small household confusions, lost laundry, unhappy help, canceled appointments, on days when the telephone rings too much and I get no work done and the wind is coming up. On days like that my friend comes uninvited.

And once it comes, now that I am wise in its ways, I no longer fight it. I lie down and let it happen. At first every small apprehension is magnified, every anxiety a pounding terror. Then the pain comes, and I concentrate only on that. Right there is the usefulness of migraine, there in that imposed yoga, the concentration on the pain. For when the pain recedes, ten or twelve hours later, everything goes with it, all the hidden resentments, all the vain anxieties. The migraine has acted as a circuit breaker, and the fuses have emerged intact. There is a pleasant convalescent euphoria. I open the windows and feel the air, eat gratefully, sleep well. I notice the particular nature of a flower in a glass on the stair landing. I count my blessings. ✍

Why I Write[2]

Of course I stole the title for this talk from George Orwell. One reason I stole it was that I like the sound of the words: *Why I Write*. There you have three short unambiguous words that share a sound, and the sound they share is this:

I

I

I

---

[1]Stimulates gastric secretions, contracts smooth muscle, and is released in allergic attacks.
[2]First published in *The New York Times Book Review*, December 5, 1976.

In many ways writing is the act of saying *I*, of imposing oneself upon other people, of saying *listen to me, see it my way, change your mind*. It's an aggressive, even a hostile act. You can disguise its aggressiveness all you want with veils of subordinate clauses and qualifiers and tentative subjunctives, with ellipses and evasions—with the whole manner of intimating rather than claiming, of alluding rather than stating—but there's no getting around the fact that setting words on paper is the tactic of a secret bully, an invasion, an imposition of the writer's sensibility on the reader's most private space.

I stole the title not only because the words sounded right but because they seemed to sum up, in a no-nonsense way, all I have to tell you. Like many writers I have only this one "subject," this one "area": the act of writing. I can bring you no reports from any other front. I may have other interests: I am "interested," for example, in marine biology, but I don't flatter myself that you would come out to hear me talk about it. I am not a scholar. I am not in the least an intellectual, which is not to say that when I hear the word "intellectual" I reach for my gun, but only to say that I do not think in abstracts. During the years when I was an undergraduate at Berkeley I tried, with a kind of hopeless late-adolescent energy, to buy some temporary visa into the world of ideas, to forge for myself a mind that could deal with the abstract.

In short I tried to think. I failed. My attention veered inexorably back to the specific, to the tangible, to what was generally considered, by everyone I knew then and for that matter have known since, the peripheral. I would try to contemplate the Hegelian dialectic[1] and would find myself concentrating instead on a flowering pear tree outside my window and the particular way the petals fell on my floor. I would try to read linguistic theory and would find myself wondering instead if the lights were on in the bevatron[2] up the hill. When I say that I was wondering if the lights were on in the bevatron you might immediately suspect, if you deal in ideas at all, that I was registering the bevatron as a political symbol, thinking in shorthand about the military-industrial complex and its role in the university community, but you would be wrong. I was only wondering if the lights were on in the bevatron, and how they looked. A physical fact.

I had trouble graduating from Berkeley, not because of this inability to deal with ideas—I was majoring in English, and I could locate the house-and-garden imagery in "The Portrait of a Lady"[3] as well as the next person, "imagery" being by definition the kind of specific that got my attention—but simply because I had neglected to take a course in Milton.° For reasons which now sound baroque I needed a degree by the end of that summer, and the English department finally agreed, if I would come down from Sacramento every Friday and talk about the cosmology of "Paradise Lost," to certify me proficient in Milton.° I did this. Some

---

[1] See Hegel.°
[2] A particle accelerator; *bev* stands for billions of electron-volts. The Lawrence Radiation Laboratory at Berkeley housed the 6.2 BEV synchroton, which was used to discover the antiproton.
[3] See James.°

Fridays I took the Greyhound bus, other Fridays I caught the Southern Pacific's City of San Francisco on the last leg of its transcontinental trip. I can no longer tell you whether Milton° put the sun or the earth at the center of the universe in "Paradise Lost," the central question of at least one century and a topic about which I wrote 10,000 words that summer, but I can still recall the exact rancidity of the butter in the City of San Francisco's dining car, and the way the tinted windows on the Greyhound bus cast the oil refineries around Carquinez Straits into a grayed and obscurely sinister light. In short my attention was always on the periphery, on what I could see and taste and touch, on the butter, and the Greyhound bus. During those years I was traveling on what I knew to be a very shaky passport, forged papers: I knew that I was no legitimate resident in any world of ideas. I knew I couldn't think. All I knew then was what I couldn't do. All I knew then was what I wasn't, and it took me some years to discover what I was.

Which was a writer.

By which I mean not a "good" writer or a "bad" writer but simply a writer, a person whose most absorbed and passionate hours are spent arranging words on pieces of paper. Had my credentials been in order I would never have become a writer. Had I been blessed with even limited access to my own mind there would have been no reason to write. I write entirely to find out what I'm thinking, what I'm looking at, what I see and what it means. What I want and what I fear. Why did the oil refineries around Carquinez Straits seem sinister to me in the summer of 1956? Why have the night lights in the bevatron burned in my mind for twenty years? *What is going on in these pictures in my mind?*

When I talk about pictures in my mind I am talking, quite specifically, about images that shimmer around the edges. There used to be an illustration in every elementary psychology book showing a cat drawn by a patient in varying stages of schizophrenia. This cat had a shimmer around it. You could see the molecular structure breaking down at the very edges of the cat: the cat became the background and the background the cat, everything interacting, exchanging ions.[1] People on hallucinogens describe the same perception of objects. I'm not a schizophrenic, nor do I take hallucinogens, but certain images do shimmer for me. Look hard enough, and you can't miss the shimmer. It's there. You can't think too much about these pictures that shimmer. You just lie low and let them develop. You stay quiet. You don't talk to many people and you keep your nervous system from shorting out and you try to locate the cat in the shimmer, the grammar in the picture.

Just as I meant "shimmer" literally I mean "grammar" literally. Grammar is a piano I play by ear, since I seem to have been out of school the year the rules were mentioned. All I know about grammar is its infinite power. To shift the structure of a sentence alters the meaning of that sentence, as definitely and inflexibly as the position of a camera alters the meaning of the object photographed. Many people know about camera angles now, but not so many know about sentences. The

---

[1] Electrically charged group of atoms.

arrangement of the words matters, and the arrangement you want can be found in the picture in your mind. The picture dictates the arrangement. The picture dictates whether this will be a sentence with or without clauses, a sentence that ends hard or a dying-fall sentence, long or short, active or passive. The picture tells you how to arrange the words and the arrangement of the words tells you, or tells me, what's going on in the picture. *Nota bene:*[1]

It tells you.

You don't tell it.

Let me show you what I mean by pictures in the mind. I began "Play It As It Lays" just as I have begun each of my novels, with no notion of "character" or "plot" or even "incident." I had only two pictures in my mind, more about which later, and a technical intention, which was to write a novel so elliptical and fast that it would be over before you noticed it, a novel so fast that it would scarcely exist on the page at all. About the pictures: the first was of white space. Empty space. This was clearly the picture that dictated the narrative intention of the book—a book in which anything that happened would happen off the page, a "white" book to which the reader would have to bring his or her own bad dreams—and yet this picture told me no "story," suggested no situation. The second picture did. This second picture was of something actually witnessed. A young woman with long hair and a short white halter dress walks through the casino at the Riviera in Las Vegas at one in the morning. She crosses the casino alone and picks up a house telephone. I watch her because I have heard her paged, and recognize her name: she is a minor actress I see around Los Angeles from time to time, in places like Jax[2] and once in a gynecologist's office in the Beverly Hills Clinic, but have never met. I know nothing about her. Who is paging her? Why is she here to be paged? How exactly did she come to this? It was precisely this moment in Las Vegas that made "Play It As It Lays" begin to tell itself to me, but the moment appears in the novel only obliquely, in a chapter which begins:

"Maria made a list of things she would never do. She would never: walk through the Sands or Caesar's alone after midnight. She would never: ball at a party, do S-M unless she wanted to, borrow furs from Abe Lipsey, deal. She would never: carry a Yorkshire in Beverly Hills."

That is the beginning of the chapter and that is also the end of the chapter, which may suggest what I meant by "white space."

I recall having a number of pictures in my mind when I began the novel I just finished, "A Book of Common Prayer." As a matter of fact one of these pictures was of that bevatron I mentioned, although I would be hard put to tell you a story in which nuclear energy figured. Another was a newspaper photograph of a hijacked 707 burning on the desert in the Middle East. Another was the night view from a room in which I once spent a week with paratyphoid, a hotel room on the Colombian coast. My husband and I seemed to be on the Colombian coast

---

[1]Latin for "Note well."

[2]A chain of four grocery stores in the Los Angeles area, catering to the Hispanic trade.

representing the United States of America at a film festival (I recall invoking the name "Jack Valenti"[1] a lot, as if its reiteration could make me well), and it was a bad place to have fever, not only because my indisposition offended our hosts but because every night in this hotel the generator failed. The lights went out. The elevator stopped. My husband would go to the event of the evening and make excuses for me and I would stay alone in this hotel room, in the dark. I remember standing at the window trying to call Bogotá (the telephone seemed to work on the same principle as the generator) and watching the night wind come up and wondering what I was doing eleven degrees off the equator with a fever of 103. The view from that window definitely figures in "A Book of Common Prayer," as does the burning 707, and yet none of these pictures told me the story I needed.

The picture that did, the picture that shimmered and made these other images coalesce, was the Panama airport at 6 A.M. I was in this airport only once, on a plane to Bogotá that stopped for an hour to refuel, but the way it looked that morning remained superimposed on everything I saw until the day I finished "A Book of Common Prayer." I lived in that airport for several years. I can still feel the hot air when I step off the plane, can see the heat already rising off the tarmac at 6 A.M. I can feel my skirt damp and wrinkled on my legs. I can feel the asphalt stick to my sandals. I remember the big tail of a Pan American plane floating motionless down at the end of the tarmac. I remember the sound of a slot machine in the waiting room. I could tell you that I remember a particular woman in the airport, an American woman, a *norteamericana*, a thin *norteamericana* about 40 who wore a big square emerald in lieu of a wedding ring, but there was no such woman there.

I put this woman in the airport later. I made this woman up, just as I later made up a country to put the airport in, and a family to run the country. This woman in the airport is neither catching a plane nor meeting one. She is ordering tea in the airport coffee shop. In fact she is not simply "ordering" tea but insisting that the water be boiled, in front of her, for twenty minutes. Why is this woman in this airport? Why is she going nowhere, where has she been? Where did she get that big emerald? What derangement, or disassociation, makes her believe that her will to see the water boiled can possibly prevail?

"She had been going to one airport or another for four months, one could see it, looking at the visas on her passport. All those airports where Charlotte Douglas's passport had been stamped would have looked alike. Sometimes the sign on the tower would say 'Bienvenidos' and sometimes the sign on the tower would say 'Bienvenue,' some places were wet and hot and others dry and hot, but at each of these airports the pastel concrete walls would rust and stain and the swamp off the runway would be littered with the fuselages of cannibalized Fairchild F-227's and the water would need boiling.

"I knew why Charlotte went to the airport even if Victor did not.

---

[1](1921–) Film executive, assistant to President Johnson (1963–1966), and president of the Motion Picture Association (1966–1990).

"I knew about airports."

These lines appear about halfway through "A Book of Common Prayer," but I wrote them during the second week I worked on the book, long before I had any idea where Charlotte Douglas had been or why she went to airports. Until I wrote these lines I had no character called "Victor" in mind: the necessity for mentioning a name, and the name "Victor," occurred to me as I wrote the sentence. *I knew why Charlotte went to the airport* sounded incomplete. *I knew why Charlotte went to the airport even if Victor did not* carried a little more narrative drive. Most important of all, until I wrote these lines I did not know who "I" was, who was telling the story. I had intended until that moment that the "I" be no more than the voice of the author, a 19th-century omniscient narrator. But there it was:

"I knew why Charlotte went to the airport even if Victor did not.

"I knew about airports."

This "I" was the voice of no author in my house. This "I" was someone who not only knew why Charlotte went to the airport but also knew someone called "Victor." Who was Victor? Who was this narrator? Why was this narrator telling me this story? Let me tell you one thing about why writers write: had I known the answer to any of these questions I would never have needed to write a novel. ✒

Stephen Jay Gould

(1941–)

Stephen Jay Gould was born in 1941 in Manhattan, the elder son of Leonard Gould, a court stenographer, Marxist, and intellectual, and Eleanor Rosenberg Gould, an artist. In "The Telltale Wishbone" Gould says that at age four he hoped to become a garbage man, planning to condense all the garbage of New York into one great truck. But at age five he saw something even more magnificent than his imagined garbage truck: the *Tyrannosaurus* at the American Museum of Natural History. His first reaction as he stood with his father before the immense creature was fear: "A man sneezed; I gulped and prepared to utter my *Shema Yisrael*." Minutes later, he told his father he had decided to become a paleontologist.

Gould grew up in Forest Hills, Queens, where he attended PS 26 and was taught by three excellent teachers (to whom he later dedicated his second collection of essays). He was devoted to baseball, betting, and science. In "Streak of Streaks" he reports that he and his father frequented Yankee Stadium in the Bronx, where, in an early encounter with improbability ("You never get them," his father said at the time), his father caught a foul ball hit by Joe DiMaggio. When Gould posted the ball to his hero, DiMaggio returned it—signed. At about age nine, Gould tells in "The Dinosaur Rip-off," he first realized how little some adults know about science. He had made a bet with a buddy about whether or not dinosaurs lived at the same time as humans and was out one chocolate bar when he discovered that the adult the boys agreed on as arbiter (the first one who claimed to know) was completely misinformed on the subject. At eleven, Gould read *Meaning of Evolution* by G. G. Simpson. Although he did not understand every point, he realized that the bones that had so impressed him in the museum could tell a tale about the history of the planet and its evolving life. In Jamaica High School, however, as Gould records in "Moon, Mann, and Otto," his textbook, *Modern Biology*, managed to avoid the controversial concept of evolution because, says Gould, no publishers are "as cowardly and conservative as the publishers of public school texts."

Like science, music was a great influence in Gould's life in high school. As he describes in "Madame Jeanette," Gould sang second bass, one of 250 disciplined and devoted members of the New York All-City High School chorus. When Gould was fourteen, he bet his eleven-year-old brother Peter (now a prominent set designer in New York) that Beethoven would outlast Chuck Berry's "Roll Over Beethoven." According to the *Rolling Stone* interviewer John Tierney, Gould admits that the results aren't in yet, but he's sure his brother will lose.

After high school, Gould earned a B.A. from Antioch College, where he became interested in the snail fossils that one of his teachers had collected in Bermuda. Two years after enrolling in the Ph.D. program at Columbia, in 1965, he married Deborah Lee, an artist. In 1966 he was hired as assistant professor of geology at Antioch College; in 1967 he completed the Ph.D., having worked at the American Museum of Natural History and written his dissertation on fossil snails in Bermuda. That year also he accepted a position at Harvard University, where he has been full professor since 1973 and continues to teach biology, geology, and the history of science. He and his wife, who teaches art at Groton Academy, have two sons: Jesse, born in 1970, and Ethan, born in 1974. In 1975 Gould won the first of many awards, the Schuchert Award for excellence in research in the field of paleontology.

Gould's work on snails of the West Indies and his collaboration with Niles Eldredge of the American Museum of Natural History, reported in "Punctuated Equilibria: An Alternative to Phyletic Gradualism" (published in *Models in Paleobiology* in 1972), gained him stature in the academic world. At the same time, his monthly essays, begun in 1974 for *Natural History*, established him as a popular essayist. As he explains in the prologue to *The Panda's Thumb* (his second collection), the title and impetus of his column, "This View of Life," comes from the last sentence of Charles Darwin's *Origin of Species*: "There is a grandeur in this view of life, with its several powers, having been originally breathed into a few forms or into one; and that, whilst this planet has gone cycling on according to the fixed law of gravity, from so simple a beginning endless forms most beautiful and most wonderful have been, and are being, evolved." His goal in these essays has been, he explains in the prologue to his latest collection (*Bully for Brontosaurus*) to explore "instructive oddities of nature" as well as "the enduring themes of evolution." To this end he has composed essays on flies, bees, worms, oysters, fish, hyenas, zebras, pandas, elk, humans, Hershey bars, Mickey Mouse, baseball, fairy tales, and more—all without condescending to the layperson.

Gould's first essay collection, *Ever Since Darwin*, was published the same year as his first purely academic book, *Ontogeny and Phylogeny* (Harvard's Belknap Press), in 1977. That collection, dedicated to his father, sets up a number of subjects that recur in one form or another in subsequent collections: Darwiniana, human evolution, theories of the earth, cultural and political influences on science, IQ and racism, and sociobiology. Although he has recently disparaged his writing in this book, he nonetheless establishes his stylistic signature in the structure of many of its essays, which move from some nonscientific aspect of culture to a scientific curiosity and from there to some overriding principle. Thus the opening paragraphs of these essays yield references to Groucho Marx, Ebenezer Scrooge, the yellowed notes of Gould's first paleontology teacher, Yankees announcer Mel Allen, Voltaire,° Rube Goldberg, and Bruno Bettelheim.

In each succeeding collection Gould has sharpened both the ideas he pursues and his skills as an essayist. For his second collection, *The Panda's Thumb* (1980), Gould won a Notable Book citation from the American Library Association and an American Book Award for the science category. The collection includes many of the categories of interest established in his first book of essays and adds material on convergence, that is, the different and quirky evolutionary paths leading to analogous features, such as the panda's "thumb." Another group of essays in this book explores the relationship between the size of a creature, the length of its life, and our conceptions of time. One of his most popular essays, "Women's Brains," comes from this collection, in a group of essays under the rubric "Science and Politics of Human Differences." In this essay Gould explains the damage wrought by "biological labeling" on "those whose dreams are flouted" as well as on "those who never realize that they may dream."

The following year, 1981, Gould won a MacArthur Foundation Award and became involved in the debate against creationists, which culminated in his testimony in December 1981 in Little Rock, Arkansas, in a trial challenging the state law that required public schools to treat creationism and evolution equally. In 1982 the Arkansas Act was declared unconstitutional in a ruling recognizing that creationism is a religious belief, not a branch of science. That year also Gould published *The Mismeasure of Man*, a study of the influence of prejudice on scientific attempts to assess intelligence. Enlarging on ideas he had presented in *Ever Since Darwin* and *The Panda's Thumb*, Gould enumerates the horrors committed by those who believed not only in craniometry and the reification and heritability of intelligence but also in the innate superiority of white European males. For this work he won the National Book Critics Circle Award in 1982.

That July, after a routine physical undertaken before a trip to Europe, Gould was told that he had mesothelioma, "a rare and serious cancer usually associated with exposure to asbestos." In "The Median Isn't the Message" Gould describes his reaction: he went straight to the library to research everything he could find on his disease. His inclination since childhood to take on a bet as well as his training as a scientist in statistics and probability helped him interpret his odds of survival, which were (and continue to be) much better than the prognosis first indicated ("Mesothelioma is incurable, with a median mortality of only eight months after discovery"). Although he does believe that a positive attitude increases the chances for survival, Gould does not support those who blame the victims for their disease or those who "look back at something like that and try to find a good side to it."

By 1983 Gould had published, with Niles Eldredge, two more academic books as well as his third collection of essays, *Hen's Teeth and Horse's Toes*, containing sections on oddities, adaptation, and further effects of politics on science. In "Science and Jewish Immigration," for example, Gould incorporates material he had presented in *The Mismeasure of Man*, a book he had dedicated to the memory of his maternal grandparents, who had come to America from Hungary. The definition of grandparents had been for him, he said in an interview, "people who spoke accented English." In this essay he shows how the quotas established for the Immigration Restriction Act of 1924, stemming from the eugenics developed by H. H. Goddard, director of research for an institute for the feebleminded, prevented millions of people from central and eastern Europe from fleeing the Nazis before the war. One of Gould's major themes is that ideas carry power "as surely as guns and bombs."

In the last six years, Gould has published two more collections of essays, *The Flamingo's Smile* (1985) and *Bully for Brontosaurus* (1991), as well as *An Urchin in the Storm* (1987), a children's book entitled *Illuminations* (1987), *Time's Arrow, Time's Cycle* (1987), and *Wonderful Life* (1989), about the tremendous and bizarre variety of fossils in the Burgess shale. This book emphasizes two ideas Gould has pursued all along: the importance of contingency, chance, and luck in the pattern of evolution and the implications of probability theory—the recognition that random patterns lack intrinsic meaning, that any meaning attributed to them is created by man. Humans are not the epitome or the goal of evolution; some well-adapted species lost out only by accident, discarded by time and chance.

Although Gould is active in the fight to preserve the environment and the diversity of species and although he sees a belief in evolutionary progress as "human arrogance," he would prefer to lose a species of land snail than allow people in the Bahamas to starve, he told Tierney in *Rolling Stone*. (As it happens, the land snail lives in an area unfit for agriculture, so such a choice need not be made.) He also predicted in that interview that further human evolution would not be significant—"we've built all of civilization without changing bodily form." Because we interbreed, we are unlikely to develop the isolated populations needed to speciate.

Like Hoagland, Gould is admittedly an optimist. He finds it a good sign that although we have the power we have not yet waged a nuclear war. Moreover, although such a catastrophe would wipe out mankind, it would not destroy the earth. As he explains in the prologue to his latest collection of essays, "Our planet is not fragile on its own time scale, and we, pitiful latecomers in the last microsecond of our planetary year, are stewards of nothing in the long run." Nevertheless, through the great pleasure afforded by his far-ranging, eclectic knowledge, Gould does much to repair the split between science and the humanities first noted and lamented by George Orwell and C. P. Snow. In "Darwin's Middle Road" Gould offers his definition of the characteristics of genius: "breadth of interest and the ability to construct fruitful analogies between fields." In his references to Aristotle,° Larry Bird, Winston Churchill, George Eliot,° Katherine Hepburn, Thomas Jefferson, Immanuel Kant,° Maria Montessori, James Randi, Dylan Thomas, Mark Twain, Arturo Toscanini, Christopher Wren, and many, many more, Gould finds connections between science and philosophy, sports, politics, literature, cinema, education, magic, music, and architecture, thus creating the bridge between the isolated academic and the curious layperson that Samuel Johnson advocates in "The Necessity of Literary Courage," where he compares the "elevated genius" who comes down from "the pinnacles of art" to the setting sun that "remits his splendor but retains his magnitude." 🍂

Darwin's Middle Road[1]

"We began to sail up the narrow strait lamenting," narrates Odysseus. "For on the one hand lay Scylla, with twelve feet all dangling down; and six necks exceeding long, and on each a hideous head, and therein three rows of teeth set thick and close, full of black death. And on the other mighty Charybdis sucked down the salt sea water. As often as she belched it forth, like a cauldron on a great fire she would seethe up through all her troubled deeps." Odysseus managed to swerve around Charybdis, but Scylla grabbed six of his finest men and devoured them in his sight—"the most pitiful thing mine eyes have seen of all my travail in searching out the paths of the sea."

False lures and dangers often come in pairs in our legends and metaphors— consider the frying pan and the fire, or the devil and the deep blue sea. Prescriptions for avoidance either emphasize a dogged steadiness—the straight and narrow of Christian evangelists—or an averaging between unpleasant alternatives—the golden mean of Aristotle.° The idea of steering a course between undesirable extremes emerges as a central prescription for a sensible life.

The nature of scientific creativity is both a perennial topic of discussion and a prime candidate for seeking a golden mean. The two extreme positions have not been directly competing for allegiance of the unwary. They have, rather, replaced each other sequentially, with one now in the ascendency, the other eclipsed.

The first—inductivism[2]—held that great scientists are primarily great observers and patient accumulators of information. For new and significant theory,

---

[1]From *The Panda's Thumb*, 1980.

[2]Based on inductive thinking, that is, drawing conclusions after amassing evidence; as opposed to deductive thinking, drawing conclusions from general principles or premises in the form of a syllogism.

the inductivists claimed, can only arise from a firm foundation of facts. In this architectural view, each fact is a brick in a structure built without blueprints. Any talk or thought about theory (the completed building) is fatuous and premature before the bricks are set. Inductivism once commanded great prestige within science, and even represented an "official" position of sorts, for it touted, however falsely, the utter honesty, complete objectivity, and almost automatic nature of scientific progress towards final and incontrovertible truth.

Yet, as its critics so rightly claimed, inductivism also depicted science as a heartless, almost inhuman discipline offering no legitimate place to quirkiness, intuition, and all the other subjective attributes adhering to our vernacular notion of genius. Great scientists, the critics claimed, are distinguished more by their powers of hunch and synthesis, than their skill in experiment or observation. The criticisms of inductivism are certainly valid and I welcome its dethroning during the past thirty years as a necessary prelude to better understanding. Yet, in attacking it so strongly, some critics have tried to substitute an alternative equally extreme and unproductive in its emphasis on the essential subjectivity of creative thought. In this "eureka" view, creativity is an ineffable something, accessible only to persons of genius. It arises like a bolt of lightning, unanticipated, unpredictable and unanalyzable—but the bolts strike only a few special people. We ordinary mortals must stand in awe and thanks. (The name refers, of course, to the legendary story of Archimedes° running naked through the streets of Syracuse shouting eureka [I have discovered it] when water displaced by his bathing body washed the scales abruptly from his eyes and suggested a method for measuring volumes.)

I am equally disenchanted by both these opposing extremes. Inductivism reduces genius to dull, rote operations; eurekaism grants it an inaccessible status more in the domain of intrinsic mystery than in a realm where we might understand and learn from it. Might we not marry the good features of each view, and abandon both the elitism of eurekaism and the pedestrian qualities of inductivism? May we not acknowledge the personal and subjective character of creativity, but still comprehend it as a mode of thinking that emphasizes or exaggerates capacities sufficiently common to all of us that we may at least understand if not hope to imitate?

In the hagiography[1] of science, a few men hold such high positions that all arguments must apply to them if they are to have any validity. Charles Darwin, as the principal saint of evolutionary biology, has therefore been presented both as an inductivist and as a primary example of eurekaism. I will attempt to show that these interpretations are equally inadequate, and that recent scholarship on Darwin's own odyssey towards the theory of natural selection supports an intermediate position.

So great was the prestige of inductivism in his own day, that Darwin himself fell under its sway and, as an old man, falsely depicted his youthful accomplishments in its light. In an autobiography, written as a lesson in morality for his

---

[1]Biographies of saints.

children and not intended for publication, he penned some famous lines that misled historians for nearly a hundred years. Describing his path to the theory of natural selection, he claimed: "I worked on true Baconian principles, and without any theory collected facts on a wholesale scale."

The inductivist interpretation focuses on Darwin's five years aboard the *Beagle* and explains his transition from a student for the ministry to the nemesis of preachers as the result of his keen powers of observation applied to the whole world. Thus, the traditional story goes, Darwin's eyes opened wider and wider as he saw, in sequence, the bones of giant South American fossil mammals, the turtles and finches of the Galapagos, and the marsupial fauna of Australia. The truth of evolution and its mechanism of natural selection crept up gradually upon him as he sifted facts in a sieve of utter objectivity.

The inadequacies of this tale are best illustrated by the falsity of its conventional premier example—the so-called Darwin's finches of the Galapagos. We now know that although these birds share a recent and common ancestry on the South American mainland, they have radiated into an impressive array of species on the outlying Galapagos. Few terrestrial species manage to cross the wide oceanic barrier between South America and the Galapagos. But the fortunate migrants often find a sparsely inhabited world devoid of the competitors that limit their opportunities on the crowded mainland. Hence, the finches evolved into roles normally occupied by other birds and developed their famous set of adaptations for feeding—seed crushing, insect eating, even grasping and manipulating a cactus needle to dislodge insects from plants. Isolation—both of the islands from the mainland and among the islands themselves—provided an opportunity for separation, independent adaptation, and speciation.

According to the traditional view, Darwin discovered these finches, correctly inferred their history, and wrote the famous lines in his notebook: "If there is the slightest foundation for these remarks the zoology of Archipelagoes will be worth examining; for such facts would undermine the stability of Species." But, as with so many heroic tales from Washington's cherry tree to the piety of Crusaders, hope rather than truth motivates the common reading. Darwin found the finches to be sure. But he didn't recognize them as variants of a common stock. In fact, he didn't even record the island of discovery for many of them—some of his labels just read "Galapagos Islands." So much for his immediate recognition of the role of isolation in the formation of new species. He reconstructed the evolutionary tale only after his return to London, when a British Museum ornithologist correctly identifed all the birds as finches.

The famous quotation from his notebook refers to Galapagos tortoises and to the claim of native inhabitants that they can "at once pronounce from which Island any Tortoise may have been brought" from subtle differences in size and shape of body and scales. This is a statement of different, and much reduced, order from the traditional tale of finches. For the finches are true and separate species—a living example of evolution. The subtle differences among tortoises represent minor geographic variation within a species. It is a jump in reasoning, albeit a valid one as we now know, to argue that such small differences can be amplified to produce a new species. All creationists, after all, acknowledged geographic variation (consider human races), but argued that it could not proceed beyond the rigid limits of a created archetype.

I don't wish to downplay the pivotal influence of the *Beagle* voyage on Darwin's career. It gave him space, freedom and endless time to think in his favored mode of independent self-stimulation. (His ambivalence towards university life, and his middling performance there by conventional standards, reflected his unhappiness with a curriculum of received wisdom.) He writes from South America in 1834: "I have not one clear idea about cleavage, stratification, lines of upheaval. I have no books, which tell me much and what they do I cannot apply to what I see. In consequence I draw my own conclusions, and most gloriously ridiculous ones they are." The rocks and plants and animals that he saw did provoke him to the crucial attitude of doubt—midwife of all creativity. Sydney, Australia—1836. Darwin wonders why a rational God would create so many marsupials on Australia since nothing about its climate or geography suggests any superiority for pouches: "I had been lying on a sunny bank and was reflecting on the strange character of the animals of this country as compared to the rest of the World. An unbeliever in everything beyond his own reason might exclaim, 'Surely two distinct Creators must have been at work.' "

Nonetheless, Darwin returned to London without an evolutionary theory. He suspected the truth of evolution, but had no mechanism to explain it. Natural selection did not arise from any direct reading of the *Beagle*'s facts, but from two subsequent years of thought and struggle as reflected in a series of remarkable notebooks that have been unearthed and published during the past twenty years. In these notebooks, we see Darwin testing and abandoning a number of theories and pursuing a multitude of false leads—so much for his later claim about recording facts with an empty mind. He read philosophers, poets, and economists, always searching for meaning and insight—so much for the notion that natural selection arose inductively from the *Beagle*'s facts. Later, he labelled one notebook as "full of metaphysics on morals."

Yet if this tortuous path belies the Scylla of inductivism, it has engendered an equally simplistic myth—the Charybdis of eurekaism. In his maddeningly misleading autobiography, Darwin does record a eureka and suggests that natural selection struck him as a sudden, serendipitous flash after more than a year of groping frustration:

> In October 1838, that is, fifteen months after I had begun my systematic inquiry, I happened to read for amusement Malthus[1] on Population, and being well prepared to appreciate the struggle for existence which everywhere goes on from long-continued observation of the habits of animals and plants, it at once struck

---

[1]Thomas Robert (1766–1834), English economist and sociologist who wrote *An Essay on the Principle of Population* (1798) showing that while population increases by a geometric ratio, "the means of subsistence" increases only by an arithmetical ratio. He also wrote *Principles of Political Economy* (1820), among other works.

me that under these circumstances favorable variations would tend to be preserved, and unfavorable ones to be destroyed. The result of this would be the
formation of new species. Here, then, I had at last got a theory by which to work.

Yet, again, the notebooks belie Darwin's later recollections—in this case by
their utter failure to record, at the time it happened, any special exultation over his
Malthusian insight. He inscribes it as a fairly short and sober entry without a
single exclamation point, though he habitually used two or three in moments of
excitement. He did not drop everything and reinterpret a confusing world in its
light. On the very next day, he wrote an even longer passage on the sexual
curiosity of primates.

The theory of natural selection arose neither as a workmanlike induction
from nature's facts, nor as a mysterious bolt from Darwin's subconscious, triggered by an accidental reading of Malthus. It emerged instead as the result of a
conscious and productive search, proceeding in a ramifying but ordered manner,
and utilizing both the facts of natural history and an astonishingly broad range
of insights from disparate disciplines far from his own. Darwin trod the middle
path between inductivism and eurekaism. His genius is neither pedestrian nor
inaccessible.

Darwinian scholarship has exploded since the centennial of the *Origin* in
1959. The publication of Darwin's notebooks and the attention devoted by
several scholars to the two crucial years between the *Beagle*'s docking and the
demoted Malthusian insight has clinched the argument for a "middle path"
theory of Darwin's creativity. Two particularly important works focus on the
broadest and narrowest scales. Howard E. Gruber's masterful intellectual and
psychological biography of this phase in Darwin's life, *Darwin on Man*, traces all
the false leads and turning points in Darwin's search. Gruber shows that Darwin
was continually proposing, testing, and abandoning hypotheses, and that he
never simply collected facts in a blind way. He began with a fanciful theory
involving the idea that new species arise with a prefixed life span, and worked his
way gradually, if fitfully, towards an idea of extinction by competition in a world
of struggle. He recorded no exultation upon reading Malthus, because the jigsaw
puzzle was only missing a piece or two at the time.

Silvan S. Schweber has reconstructed, in detail as minute as the record will
allow, Darwin's activities during the few weeks before Malthus (The Origin of the
Origin Revisited, *Journal of the History of Biology*, 1977). He argues that the final
pieces arose not from new facts in natural history, but from Darwin's intellectual
wanderings in distant fields. In particular, he read a long review of social scientist
and philosopher Auguste Comte's[1] most famous work, the *Cours de philosophie
positive*. He was particularly struck by Comte's insistence that a proper theory be

---

[1]French philosopher (1798–1857) and founder of positivism, a view of the intellectual history of
man as developing in three stages: the theological, in which the world is explained by the
supernatural; the metaphysical, in which the world is explained in terms of forces or energies;
and the positive or scientific, in which the world is explained through observation, hypotheses,
and experiment.

predictive and at least potentially quantitative. He then turned to Dugald Stewart's[1] *On the Life and Writing of Adam Smith*,[2] and imbibed the basic belief of the Scottish economists that theories of overall social structure must begin by analyzing the unconstrained actions of individuals. (Natural selection is, above all, a theory about the struggle of individual organisms for success in reproduction.) Then, searching for quantification, he read a lengthy analysis of work by the most famous statistician of his time—the Belgian Adolphe Quetelet.[3] In the review of Quetelet, he found, among other things, a forceful statement of Malthus's quantitative claim—that population would grow geometrically and food supplies only arithmetically, thus guaranteeing an intense struggle for existence. In fact, Darwin had read the Malthusian statement several times before; but only now was he prepared to appreciate its significance. Thus, he did not turn to Malthus by accident, and he already knew what it contained. His "amusement," we must assume, consisted only in a desire to read in its original formulation the familiar statement that had so impressed him in Quetelet's secondary account.

In reading Schweber's detailed account of the moments preceding Darwin's formulation of natural selection, I was particularly struck by the absence of deciding influence from his own field of biology. The immediate precipitators were a social scientist, an economist, and a statistician. If genius has any common denominator, I would propose breadth of interest and the ability to construct fruitful analogies between fields.

In fact, I believe that the theory of natural selection should be viewed as an extended analogy—whether conscious or unconscious on Darwin's part I do not know—to the laissez faire economics of Adam Smith. The essence of Smith's argument is a paradox of sorts: if you want an ordered economy providing maximal benefits to all, then let individuals compete and struggle for their own advantages. The result, after appropriate sorting and elimination of the inefficient, will be a stable and harmonious polity. Apparent order arises naturally from the struggle among individuals, not from predestined principles or higher control. Dugald Stewart epitomized Smith's system in the book Darwin read:

> The most effective plan for advancing a people . . . is by allowing every man, as long as he observes the rules of justice, to pursue his own interest in his own way, and to bring both his industry and his capital into the freest competition with those of his fellow citizens. Every system of policy which endeavors . . . to draw towards a peculiar species of industry a greater share of the capital of the society than would naturally go to it . . . is, in reality, subversive of the great purpose which it means to promote.

---

[1] Scottish philosopher and mathematician (1753–1828) known for his lectures and clear writing. His best-known works are *Outlines of Moral Philosophy* (1793) and his three-volume *Elements of the Philosophy of the Human Mind* (1792–1827).

[2] Scottish economist (1723–1790) and author of *An Inquiry into the Nature and Causes of the Wealth of Nations* (1776).

[3] (1796–1874) Also an astronomer, he developed methods for modern census taking and created the concept of the "average man."

As Schweber states: "The Scottish analysis of society contends that the combined effect of individual actions results in the institutions upon which society is based, and that such a society is a stable and evolving one and functions without a designing and directing mind."

We know that Darwin's uniqueness does not reside in his support for the idea of evolution—scores of scientists had preceded him in this. His special contribution rests upon his documentation and upon the novel character of his theory about how evolution operates. Previous evolutionists had proposed unworkable schemes based on internal perfecting tendencies and inherent directions. Darwin advocated a natural and testable theory based on immediate interaction among individuals (his opponents considered it heartlessly mechanistic). The theory of natural selection is a creative transfer to biology of Adam Smith's basic argument for a rational economy: the balance and order of nature does not arise from a higher, external (divine) control, or from the existence of laws operating directly upon the whole, but from struggle among individuals for their own benefits (in modern terms, for the transmission of their genes to future generations through differential success in reproduction).

Many people are distressed to hear such an argument. Does it not compromise the integrity of science if some of its primary conclusions originate by analogy from contemporary politics and culture rather than from data of the discipline itself? In a famous letter to Engels,[1] Karl Marx° identified the similarities between natural selection and the English social scene:

> It is remarkable how Darwin recognizes among beasts and plants his English society with its division of labor, competition, opening up of new markets, 'invention,' and the Malthusian 'struggle for existence.' It is Hobbes'° *bellum omnium contra omnes* (the war of all against all).

Yet Marx° was a great admirer of Darwin—and in this apparent paradox lies resolution. For reasons involving all the themes I have emphasized here—that inductivism is inadequate, that creativity demands breadth, and that analogy is a profound source of insight—great thinkers cannot be divorced from their social background. But the source of an idea is one thing; its truth or fruitfulness is another. The psychology and utility of discovery are very different subjects indeed. Darwin may have cribbed the idea of natural selection from economics, but it may still be right. As the German socialist Karl Kautsky[2] wrote in 1902: "The fact that an idea emanates from a particular class, or accords with their interests, of course proves nothing as to its truth or falsity." In this case, it is ironic that Adam Smith's system of laissez faire does not work in his own domain of economics, for it leads to oligopoly and revolution, rather than to order and harmony. Struggle among individuals does, however, seem to be the law of nature.

---

[1] See Marx.°

[2] Marxist (1854–1938) who rejected the Bolshevik Revolution (1917) in Russia because it was not, he said, truly Marxist.

Many people use such arguments about social context to ascribe great insights primarily to the indefinable phenomenon of good luck. Thus, Darwin was lucky to be born rich, lucky to be on the *Beagle*, lucky to live amidst the ideas of his age, lucky to trip over Parson Malthus—essentially little more than a man in the right place at the right time. Yet, when we read of his personal struggle to understand, the breadth of his concerns and study, and the directedness of his search for a mechanism of evolution, we understand why Pasteur[1] made his famous quip that fortune favors the prepared mind. ✐

Moon, Mann, and Otto[2]

Little Rock, Arkansas
December 10, 1981

This morning's *Arkansas Gazette* features a cartoon with searchlights focused on a state map. The map displays neither topography nor political boundaries, but merely contains the words, etched in black from Oklahoma to the Mississippi: "Scopes Trial II. Notoriety." I spent most of yesterday—with varying degrees of pleasure, righteousness, discomfort, and disbelief—in the witness box, trying to convince Federal Judge William R. Overton that all the geological strata on earth did not form as the result of a single Noachian deluge. We are engaged in the first legal test upon the new wave of creationist bills that mandate equal time or "balanced treatment" for evolution and a thinly disguised version of the Book of Genesis read literally, but masquerading under the nonsense phrase "creation science." The judge, to say the least, seems receptive to my message and as bemused as I am by the fact that such a trial can be held just a few months before the hundredth anniversary of Darwin's death.[3]

The trial of John Scopes in 1925 has cast such a long shadow into our own times that the proceedings in Little Rock inevitably invite comparison (see last essay).[4] I appreciate the historical continuity but am more impressed by the differences. I sit in a massive alabaster building, a combined courthouse and post office, a no-nonsense, no-frills edifice, surrounded by the traffic noises of downtown Little Rock. The Rhea County Courthouse of Dayton, Tennessee—the building that hosted Scopes, Darrow,[5] and Bryan in 1925—is a gracious, shaded,

---

[1]Louis (1822–1895), great French chemist who pioneered the germ theory of infection, developed a vaccine against anthrax, showed that sterilization destroys germs in liquids (pasteurization), and established the Pasteur Institute in Paris.

[2]From *Hen's Teeth and Horse's Toes*, 1983.

[3]April 1882.

[4]"A Visit to Dayton," in *Hen's Teeth and Horse's Toes*.

[5]Clarence Seward (1857–1938), lawyer famous for his unsuccessful defense of Eugene V. Debs in the Pullman strike case and his successful plea of temporary insanity for Leopold and Loeb.

and decorated Renaissance Revival structure that dominates the crossroads of its two-street town. The Scopes trial was directly initiated by Dayton's boosters to put their little town on the map; many, probably most, citizens of Arkansas are embarrassed by the anachronism on their doorstep. John Scopes was convicted for even mentioning that humans had descended from "a lower order of animals"; we have made some progress in half a century, and modern creationists clamor for the official recognition of their pseudoscience, not (at least yet) for the exclusion of our well-documented conclusions.

I decided to be a paleontologist when I was five, after an awestruck encounter with *Tyrannosaurus* at the Museum of Natural History in New York. The phenomenology of big beasts might have been enough to sustain my interest, but I confirmed my career six years later when I read, far too early and with dim understanding, G. G. Simpson's *Meaning of Evolution* and discovered that a body of exciting ideas made sense of all those bodies of bone. Three years later, I therefore approached my first high school science course with keen anticipation. In a year of biology, I would surely learn all about evolution. Imagine my disappointment when the teacher granted Mr. Darwin and his entire legacy only an apologetic two days at the very end of a trying year. I always wondered why, but was too shy to ask. Then I just forgot my question and continued to study on my own.

Six months ago, in a secondhand bookstore, I found a copy of my old high school text, *Modern Biology*, by T. J. Moon, P. B. Mann, and J. H. Otto. We all appreciate how powerful an unexpected sight or odor can be in triggering a distant "remembrance of things past."[1] I knew what I had the minute I saw that familiar red binding with its embossed microscope in silver and its frontispiece in garish color, showing a busy beaver at work. The book, previously the property of a certain "Lefty," was soon mine for ninety-five cents.

Now, more than half a life later (I studied high school biology in 1956), I finally understand why Mrs. Blenderman had neglected the subject that so passionately interested me. I had been a victim of Scopes's ghost (or rather, of his adversary, Bryan's). Most people view the Scopes trial as a victory for evolution, if only because Paul Muni and Spencer Tracy served Clarence Darrow so well in theatrical and film versions of *Inherit the Wind*, and because the trial triggered an outpouring of popular literature by aggrieved and outraged evolutionists. Scopes's conviction (later quashed on a technicality) had been a mere formality; the battle for evolution had been won in the court of public opinion. Would it were so. As several historians have shown, the Scopes trial was a rousing defeat. It abetted a growing fundamentalist movement and led directly to the dilution or

---

Although Darrow lost his case against William Jennings Bryan (1860–1925), lawyer, Democratic presidential candidate, and orator famed for his 1896 "Cross of Gold" speech favoring unlimited minting of silver, Darrow's interrogation of Bryan on the witness stand revealed that even Bryan thought the biblical seven days of creation might be symbolic, thus angering his fundamentalist supporters. Bryan died the week following the Scopes trial.

[1]See Proust.°

elimination of evolution from all popular high school texts in the United States (see bibliography for works of Grabiner and Miller, and of Nelkin[1]). No arm of the industry is as cowardly and conservative as the publishers of public school texts—markets of millions are not easily ignored. The situation did not change until 1957, a year too late for me, when the Russian Sputnik provoked a searching inquiry into the shameful state of science education in America's high schools.

Moon, Mann, and Otto commanded the lion's share of the market in the mid-1950s; readers of my generation will probably experience that exhilarating sense of *déjà vu* with me. Like many popular books, it was the altered descendant of several earlier editions. The first, *Biology for Beginners*, by Truman J. Moon, was published in 1921, before the Scopes trial. Its frontispiece substituted Mr. Darwin for the industrious beaver, and its text reflected a thorough immersion in evolution as the focal subject of the life sciences. Its preface proclaimed: "The course emphasizes the fact that biology is a unit science, based on the fundamental idea of evolution rather than a forced combination of portions of botany, zoology and hygiene." Its text contains several chapters on evolution and continually emphasizes Darwin's central contention that the *fact* of evolution is established beyond reasonable doubt, although scientists have much to learn about the *mechanism* of evolutionary change (see essay 19).[2] Chapter 35, on "The Method of Evolution," begins: "Proof of the *fact* of similarity between the various forms of living things and of their evident relationship, still leaves a more difficult question to be answered. *How* did this descent and modification take place, by what means has nature developed one form from another? [Moon's italics]"

I then examined my new purchase with a growing sense of amusement mixed with disgust. The index contained such important entries as "fly specks, disease germs in," but nothing about evolution. Indeed, the word evolution does not occur anywhere in the book. The subject is not, however, entirely absent. It receives a scant eighteen pages in a 662-page book, as chapter 58 of 60 (pp. 618–36). In this bowdlerized jiffy, it is called "The hypothesis of racial development." Moon, Mann, and Otto had gone the post-Scopes way of all profitable texts: eliminate and risk no offense. (Those who recall the reality of high school courses will also remember that many teachers never got to those last few chapters at all.)

This one pussyfooting chapter is as disgraceful in content as in brevity. Its opening two paragraphs are a giveaway and an intellectual sham compared with Moon's forthright words of 1921. The first paragraph provides a fine statement of historical continuity and change in the *physical* features of our planet:

> This is a changing world. It changes from day to day, year to year, and from age to age. Rivers deepen their gorges as they carry more land to the sea. Mountains

---

[1]Grabiner, J. V., and P. D. Miller. 1974. Effects of the Scopes Trial. *Science* 185:832–37. Nelkin, D. 1977. *Science Textbook Controversies and the Politics of Equal Time.* Cambridge, MA: Massachusetts Institute of Technology Press. [From Gould's bibliography.]

[2]"Evolution as Fact and Theory" in *Hen's Teeth and Horse's Toes.*

rise, only to be leveled gradually by winds and rain. Continents rise and sink into the sea. Such are the gradual changes of the physical earth as days add into years and years combine to become ages.

Now what could be more natural and logical than to extend this same mode of reasoning and style of language to life? The paragraph seems to be set up for such a transition. But note how the tone of the second paragraph subtly shifts to avoid any commitment to historical continuity for organic change:

> During these ages, species of plants and animals have appeared, have flourished for a time, and then have perished as new species took their places. . . . When one race lost in the struggle for survival, another race appeared to take its place.

Four pages later, we finally get an inkling that genealogy may be behind organic transitions through time: "This geological story of the rocks, showing fossil gradations from simple to complex organisms, is what we should expect to find if there had been racial development throughout the past." Later on the page, Moon, Mann, and Otto ask the dreaded question and even venture the closest word they dare to "evolution": "Are these prehistoric creatures the ancestors of modern animals?" If you read carefully through all the qualifications, they answer their question with a guarded "yes"—but you have to read awfully hard.

Thus were millions of children deprived of their chance to study one of the most exciting and influential ideas in science, the central theme of all biology. A few hundred, myself included, possessed the internal motivation to transcend this mockery of education, but citing us seems as foolish and cruel as the old racist argument, "what about George Washington Carver[1] or Willie Mays,"[2] used to refute the claim that poor achievement might be linked to economic disadvantage and social prejudice.

Now I can mouth all the grandiloquent arguments against such a dilution of education: we will train a generation unable to think for themselves, we will weaken the economic and social fabric of the nation if we raise a generation illiterate in science, and so on. I even believe all these arguments. But this is not what troubled me most as I read chapter 58 in Moon, Mann, and Otto. I wasn't even much angered, but merely amused, by the tortured pussyfooting and glaring omissions. Small items with big implications are my bread and butter, as any reader of these essays will soon discover. I do not react strongly to generalities. I can ignore a displeasing general tenor, but I cannot bear falsification and debasement of something small and noble. I was not really shaken until I read the last paragraph of chapter 58, but then an interior voice rose up and began to compose

---

[1]American chemist (1864–1943), born a slave, who earned a college degree, directed research in the Department of Agriculture at Tuskegee Institute, Alabama, and improved the economy of the South through his discoveries of a variety of uses for peanuts, cotton waste products, sweet potatoes, and other produce.

[2](1931–) Baseball player for the New York Giants who helped them win the 1954 World Series. He retired in 1973 having batted a total of 660 home runs.

this essay. For to make a valid point in the context of their cowardice, Moon, Mann, and Otto had perverted (perhaps unknowingly) one of my favorite quotations. If cowardice can inspire such debasement, then it must be rooted out.

The last paragraph is titled: Science and Religion. I agree entirely with its first two sentences: "There is nothing in science which is opposed to a belief in God and religion. Those who think so are mistaken in their science or their theology or both." They then quote (with some minor errors, here corrected) a famous statement of T. H. Huxley, using it to argue that a man may be both a Darwinian and a devout Christian:

> Science seems to me to teach in the highest and strongest manner the great truth which is embodied in the Christian conception of entire surrender to the will of God. Sit down before fact as a little child, be prepared to give up every preconceived notion, follow humbly wherever and to whatever abysses nature leads, or you shall learn nothing. I have only begun to learn content and peace of mind since I have resolved at all risks to do this.

Now a man may be both an evolutionist and a devout Christian. Millions successfully juxtapose these two independent viewpoints, but Thomas Henry Huxley did not. This quote, in its proper context, actually speaks of Huxley's courageous agnosticism. It also occurs in what I regard as the most beautiful and moving letter ever written by a scientist.

The tragic setting of this long letter explains why Huxley cited, only in analogy as Moon, Mann, and Otto did not understand, "the Christian conception of entire surrender to the will of God." Huxley's young and favorite son had just died. His friend, the Reverend Charles Kingsley° (best remembered today as author of *The Water-Babies* and *Westward Ho!*) had written a long and kind letter of condolence with a good Anglican bottom line: see here Huxley, if you could only abandon your blasted agnosticism and accept the Christian concept of an immortal soul, you would be comforted.

Huxley responded in tones that recall the chief of police in Gilbert and Sullivan's[1] *Pirates of Penzance* who, when praised by General Stanley's daughters for expected bravery in a coming battle that would probably lead to his bloody death, remarked:

> Still, perhaps it would be wise
> Not to carp or criticise,
> For it's very evident
> These attentions are well meant.

Huxley thanks Kingsley° for his sincerely proffered comfort, but then explains in several pages of passionate prose why he cannot alter a set of principles, established after so much thought and deliberation, merely to assuage his current grief.

---

[1]Sir William Gilbert (1836–1911), librettist, and Sir Arthur Sullivan (1842–1900), composer, collaborated from 1871 to 1896 to produce numerous popular operettas, such as *H.M.S. Pinafore*, *Iolanthe*, and *The Mikado*.

He has, he maintains, committed himself to science as the only sure guide to truth about matters of fact. Since matters of God and soul do not lie in this realm, he cannot know the answers to specific claims and must remain agnostic. "I neither deny nor affirm the immortality of man," he writes. "I see no reason for believing in it, but, on the other hand, I have no means of disproving it." Thus, he continues, I cannot assert the certainty of immortality to placate my loss. Uncomfortable convictions, if well founded, are those that require the most assiduous affirmation, as he states just before the passage quoted by Moon, Mann, and Otto: "My business is to teach my aspirations to conform themselves to fact, not to try and make facts harmonize with my aspirations."

Later, in the most moving statement of the letter, he speaks of the larger comfort that a commitment to science has provided him—a comfort more profound and lasting than the grief that his uncertainty about immortality now inspires. Among three agencies that shaped his deepest beliefs, he notes, "Science and her methods gave me a resting-place independent of authority and tradition." (For his two other agencies, Huxley cites "love" that "opened up to me a view of the sanctity of human nature," and his recognition that "a deep sense of religion was compatible with the entire absence of theology.") He then writes:

> If at this moment I am not a worn-out, debauched, useless carcass of a man, if it has been or will be my fate to advance the cause of science, if I feel that I have a shadow of a claim on the love of those about me, if in the supreme moment when I looked down into my boy's grave my sorrow was full of submission and without bitterness, it is because these agencies have worked upon me, and not because I have ever cared whether my poor personality shall remain distinct forever from the All whence it came and whither it goes.
>
> And thus, my dear Kinglsey,° you will understand what my position is. I may be quite wrong, and in that case I know I shall have to pay the penalty for being wrong. But I can only say with Luther, "Gott helfe mir, ich kann nichts anders [God help me, I cannot do otherwise]."

Thus we understand what Huxley meant when he spoke of "the Christian conception of entire surrender to the will of God" in the passage cited by Moon, Mann, and Otto. It is obviously not, as they imply, his profession of Christian faith, but a burning analogy: as the Christian has made his commitment, so have I made mine to science. I cannot do otherwise, despite the immediate comfort that conventional Christianity would supply in my current distress.

Today I sat in the court of Little Rock, listening to the testimony of four splendid men and women who teach science in primary and secondary schools of Arkansas. Their testimony contained moments of humor, as when one teacher described an exercise he uses in the second grade. He stretches a string across the classroom to represent the age of the earth. He then asks students to stand in various positions marking such events as the origin of life, the extinction of dinosaurs, and the evolution of humans. What would you do, asked the assistant attorney general in cross-examination, to provide balanced treatment for the 10,000-year-old earth advocated by creation scientists? "I guess I'd have to get a short string," replied the teacher. The thought of twenty earnest second graders, all scrunched up along a millimeter of string, created a visual image that set the court rocking with laughter.

But the teachers' testimony also contained moments of inspiration. As I listened to their reasons for opposing "creation science," I thought of T. H. Huxley and the courage required by dedicated people who will not, to paraphrase Lillian Hellman,[1] tailor their convictions to fit current fashions. As Huxley would not simplify and debase in order to find immediate comfort, these teachers told the court that mechanical compliance with the "balanced treatment" act, although easy enough to perform, would destroy their integrity as teachers and violate their responsibility to students.

One witness pointed to a passage in his chemistry text that attributed great age to fossil fuels. Since the Arkansas act specifically includes "a relatively recent age of the earth" among the definitions of creation science requiring "balanced treatment," this passage would have to be changed. The witness claimed that he did not know how to make such an alteration. Why not? retorted the assistant attorney general in his cross-examination. You only need to insert a simple sentence: "Some scientists, however, believe that fossil fuels are relatively young." Then, in the most impressive statement of the entire trial, the teacher responded. I could, he argued, insert such a sentence in mechanical compliance with the act. But I cannot, as a conscientious teacher, do so. For "balanced treatment" must mean "equal dignity" and I would therefore have to justify the insertion. And this I cannot do, for I have heard no valid arguments that would support such a position.

Another teacher spoke of similar dilemmas in providing balanced treatment in a conscientious rather than a mechanical way. What then, he was asked, would he do if the law were upheld? He looked up and said, in his calm and dignified voice: It would be my tendency not to comply. I am not a revolutionary or a martyr, but I have responsibilities to my students, and I cannot forego them.

God bless the dedicated teachers of this world. We who work in unthreatened private colleges and universities often do not adequately appreciate the plight of our colleagues—or their courage in upholding what should be our common goals. What Moon, Mann, and Otto did to Huxley epitomizes the greatest danger of imposed antirationalism in classrooms—that one must simplify by distortion, and remove both depth and beauty, in order to comply.

In appreciation for the teachers of Arkansas, then, and for all of us, one more statement in conclusion from Huxley's letter to Kingsley:°

> Had I lived a couple of centuries earlier I could have fancied a devil scoffing at me . . . and asking me what profit it was to have stripped myself of the hopes and consolations of the mass of mankind? To which my only reply was and is—Oh

---

[1]American playwright (1905-1984), author of *The Children's Hour* (1934), about a charge of lesbianism against two teachers; *The Little Foxes* (1939), about the South; and *Watch on the Rhine* (1941) and *The Searching Wind* (1944), about fascism. In 1952 in a letter to the House Committee on Un-American Activities,° Hellman wrote: "I cannot and will not cut my conscience to fit this year's fashions."

devil! truth is better than much profit. I have searched over the grounds of my belief, and if wife and child and name and fame were all to be lost to me one after the other as the penalty, still I will not lie.

Postscript

On January 5, 1982, Federal District Judge William R. Overton declared the Arkansas act unconstitutional because it forces biology teachers to purvey religion in science classrooms. ✿

Human Equality Is a Contingent Fact of History[1]

Pretoria, August 5, 1984

History's most famous airplane, Lindbergh's[2] *Spirit of St. Louis*, hangs from the ceiling of Washington's Air and Space Museum, imperceptible in its majesty to certain visitors. Several years ago, a delegation of blind men and women met with the museum's director to discuss problems of limited access. Should we build, he asked, an accurate scale model of Lindbergh's plane, freely available for touch and examination? Would such a replica solve the problem? The delegation reflected together and gave an answer that moved me deeply for its striking recognition of universal needs. Yes, they said, such a model would be acceptable, but only on one condition—that it be placed directly beneath the invisible original.

Authenticity exerts a strange fascination over us; our world does contain sacred objects and places. Their impact cannot be simply aesthetic, for an ersatz absolutely indistinguishable from the real McCoy[3] evokes no comparable awe. The jolt is direct and emotional—as powerful a feeling as anything I know. Yet the impetus is purely intellectual—a visceral disproof of romantic nonsense that abstract knowledge cannot engender deep emotion.

Last night, I watched the sun set over the South African savanna—the original location and habitat of our australopithecine ancestors. The air became chill; sounds of the night began, the incessant repetition of toad and insect, laced with an occasional and startling mammalian growl; the Southern Cross appeared in the sky, with Jupiter, Mars, and Saturn ranged in a line above the arms of Scorpio. I sensed the awe, fear, and mystery of the night. I am tempted to say (describing emotions, not making any inferences about realities, higher or lower) that I felt close to the origin of religion as a historical phenomenon of the human psyche. I also felt kinship in that moment with our most distant human past—for an *Australopithecus*

---

[1]From *The Flamingo's Smile*, 1985.

[2]Charles Augustus (1902–1974), American aviator who was first to fly solo, nonstop across the Atlantic Ocean, landing in Paris on 21 May 1927. He married Anne Morrow in 1929. After the kidnapping and death of their son in 1932, the Lindberghs moved to England, returning in 1939 as isolationists who appeared to be pro-Nazi. During the war, Lindbergh fought in the Pacific.

[3]Slang for the "real thing," after an American boxer, Norman Selby, aka Kid McCoy, (1873–1940).

africanus may once have stood, nearly three million years ago, on the same spot in similar circumstances, juggling (for all I know) that same mixture of awe and fear.

I was then rudely extricated from that sublime, if fleeting, sentiment of unity with all humans past and present. I remembered my immediate location—South Africa, 1984 (during a respite in Kruger Park from a lecture tour on the history of racism). I also understood, in a more direct way than ever before, the particular tragedy of the history of biological views about human races. This history is largely a tale of division—an account of barriers and ranks erected to maintain the power and hegemony of those on top. The greatest irony of all presses upon me: I am a visitor in the nation most committed to myths of inequality—yet the savannas of this land staged an evolutionary story of opposite import.

My visceral perception of brotherhood harmonizes with our best modern biological knowledge. Such union of feeling and fact may be quite rare, for one offers no guide to the other (more romantic twaddle aside). Many people think (or fear) that equality of human races represents a hope of liberal sentimentality probably squashed by the hard realities of history. They are wrong.

This essay can be summarized in a single phrase, a motto if you will: *Human equality is a contingent fact of history*. Equality is not true by definition; it is neither an ethical principle (though equal treatment may be) nor a statement about norms of social action. It just worked out that way. A hundred different and plausible scenarios for human history would have yielded other results (and moral dilemmas of enormous magnitude). They didn't happen.

The history of Western views on race is a tale of denial—a long series of progressive retreats from initial claims for strict separation and ranking by intrinsic worth toward an admission of the trivial differences revealed by our contingent history. In this essay, I shall discuss just two main stages of retreat for each of two major themes: genealogy, or separation among races as a function of their geological age; and geography, or our place of origin. I shall then summarize the three major arguments from modern biology for the surprisingly small extent of human racial differences.

Genealogy, The First Argument

Before evolutionary theory redefined the issue irrevocably, early to mid-nineteenth-century anthropology conducted a fierce debate between schools of monogeny and polygeny. Monogenists advocated a common origin for all people in the primeval couple, Adam and Eve (lower races, they then argued, had degenerated further from original perfection). Polygenists held that Adam and Eve were ancestors of white folks only, and that other—and lower—races had been separately created. Either argument could fuel a social doctrine of inequality, but polygeny surely held the edge as a compelling justification for slavery and domination at home and colonialism abroad. "The benevolent mind," wrote Samuel George Morton (a leading American polygenist) in 1839, "may regret the inaptitude of the Indian for civilization. . . . The structure of his mind appears to be different from that of the white man. . . . They are not only averse to the restraints of education, but for the most part are incapable of a continued process of reasoning on abstract subjects.''

Genealogy, The Second Argument

Evolutionary theory required a common origin for human races, but many post-Darwinian anthropologists found a way to preserve the spirit of polygeny. They argued, in a minimal retreat from permanent separation, that the division of our lineage into modern races had occurred so long ago that differences, accumulating slowly through time, have now built unbridgeable chasms. Though once alike in an apish dawn, human races are now separate and unequal.

We cannot understand much of the history of late nineteenth- and early twentieth-century anthropology, with its plethora of taxonomic names proposed for nearly every scrap of fossil bone, unless we appreciate its obsession with the identification and ranking of races. For many schemes of classification sought to tag the various fossils as ancestors of modern races and to use their relative age and apishness as a criterion for racial superiority. Piltdown,[1] for example, continued to fool generations of professionals partly because it fit so comfortably with ideas of white superiority. After all, this ''ancient'' man with a brain as big as ours (the product, we now know, of a hoax constructed with a modern cranium) lived in England—an obvious ancestor for whites—while such apish (and genuine) fossils as *Homo erectus* inhabited Java and China as putative sources for Orientals and other peoples of color.

This theory of ancient separation received its last prominent defense in 1962, when Carleton Coon[2] published his *Origin of Races*. Coon divided humanity into five major races—caucasoids, mongoloids, australoids, and, among African blacks, congoids and capoids. He claimed that these five groups had already become distinct subspecies during the reign of our ancestor, *Homo erectus*. *H. erectus* then evolved toward *H. sapiens* in five parallel streams, each traversing the same path toward increased consciousness. But whites and yellows, who ''occupied the most favorable of the earth's zoological regions,'' crossed the threshold to *H. sapiens* first, while dark peoples lagged behind and have paid for their sluggishness ever since. Black inferiority, Coon argues, is nobody's fault, just an accident of evolution in less challenging environments:

> Caucasoids and Mongoloids . . . did not rise to their present population levels and positions of cultural dominance by accident. . . . Any other subspecies that had evolved in these regions would probably have been just as successful.

Leading evolutionists throughout the world reacted to Coon's thesis with incredulity. Could modern races really be identified at the level of *H. erectus*? I shall always be grateful to W. E. Le Gros Clark, England's greatest anatomist at the

---

[1]The human bones found in Piltdown, Sussex, England, in 1908 fooled some scientists until 1950, when fluoride tests proved they were from modern man.

[2](1904–1981) Taught at Harvard from 1934 to 1948 and then became professor of anthropology at the University of Pennsylvania.

time. I was spending an undergraduate year in England, an absolute nobody in a strange land. Yet he spent an afternoon with me, patiently answering my questions about race and evolution. Asked about Coon's thesis, this splendidly modest man simply replied that he, at least, could not identify a modern race in the bones of an ancient species.

More generally, parallel evolution of such precision in so many lineages seems almost impossible on grounds of mathematical probability alone. Could five separate subspecies undergo such substantial changes and yet remain so similar at the end that all can still interbreed freely, as modern races so plainly do? In the light of these empirical weaknesses and theoretical implausibilities, we must view Coon's thesis more as the last gasp of a dying tradition than a credible synthesis of available evidence.

Genealogy, The Modern View

Human races are not separate species (the first argument) or ancient divisions within an evolving plexus (the second argument). They are recent, poorly differentiated subpopulations of our modern species, *Homo sapiens*, separated at most by tens or hundreds of thousands of years, and marked by remarkably small genetic differences.

Geography, The First Argument

When Raymond Dart[1] found the first australopithecine in South Africa sixty years ago, scientists throughout the world rejected this oldest ancestor, this loveliest of intermediate forms, because it hailed from the wrong place. Darwin, without a shred of fossil evidence but with a good criterion for inference, had correctly surmised that humans evolved in Africa. Our closest living relatives, he argued, are chimps and gorillas—and both species live only in Africa, the probable home, therefore, of our common ancestor as well.

But few scientists accepted Darwin's cogent inference because hope, tradition, and racism conspired to locate our ancestral abode on the plains of central Asia. Notions of Aryan supremacy led anthropologists to assume that the vast "challenging" reaches of Asia, not the soporific tropics of Africa, had prompted our ancestors to abandon an apish past and rise toward the roots of Indo-European culture. The diversity of colored people in the world's tropics could only record the secondary migrations and subsequent degenerations of this original stock. The great Gobi Desert expedition, sponsored by the American Museum of Natural History just a few years before Dart's discovery, was dispatched primarily to find the ancestry of man in Asia. We remember this expedition for success in discovering dinosaurs and their eggs; we forget that its major quest ended in utter failure because Darwin's simple inference was correct.

---

[1](1893–1988) Born in Australia, professor of anthropology and anatomy and dean of the medical school at the University of Witwaterstrand, Johannesburg, South Africa.

Geography, The Second Argument

By the 1950s, further anatomical study and the sheer magnitude of continuing discovery forced the general admission that our roots lay with the australopithecines, and that Africa had been our original home. But the subtle hold of unacknowledged prejudice still conspired (with other, more reasonable bases of uncertainty) to deny Africa its continuing role as the cradle of what really matters to us—the origin of human consciousness. In a stance of intermediate retreat, most scientists now argued that Africa had kindled our origin but not our mental emergence. Human ancestors migrated out, again to mother Asia, and there crossed the threshold to consciousness as *Homo erectus* (or so-called Java and Peking man). We emerged from the apes in Africa; we evolved our intelligence in Asia. Carleton Coon wrote in his 1962 book: "If Africa was the cradle of mankind, it was only an indifferent kindergarten. Europe and Asia were our principal schools."

Geography, The Modern View

The tempo of African discovery has accelerated since Coon constructed his metaphor of the educational hierarchy. *Homo erectus* apparently evolved in Africa as well, where fossils dating to nearly two million years have been found, while the Asian sites may be younger than previously imagined. One might, of course, take yet another step in retreat and argue that *H. sapiens*, at least, evolved later from an Asian stock of *H. erectus*. But the migration of *H. erectus* into Europe and Asia does not guarantee (or even suggest) any further branching from these mobile lineages. For *H. erectus* continued to live in Africa as well. Evidence is not yet conclusive, but the latest hints may be pointing toward an African origin for *H. sapiens* as well. Ironically then (with respect to previous expectations), every human species may have evolved first in Africa and only then—for the two latest species of *Homo*—spread elsewhere.

I have, so far, only presented the negative evidence for my thesis that human equality is a contingent fact of history. I have argued that the old bases for inequality have evaporated. I must now summarize the positive arguments (primarily three in number) and, equally important, explain how easily history might have happened in other ways.

The Positive (and Formal, or Taxonomic) Argument from Racial Definition

We recognize only one formal category for divisions within species—the subspecies. Races, if formally defined, are therefore subspecies. Subspecies are populations inhabiting a definite geographic subsection of a species' range and sufficiently distinct in any set of traits for taxonomic recognition. Subspecies differ from all other levels of the taxonomic hierarchy in two crucial ways. First, they are categories of convenience only and need never be designated. Each organism must belong to a species, a genus, a family, and to all higher levels of the hierarchy; but a species need not be formally divided. Subspecies represent a taxonomist's personal decision about the best way to report geographic variation. Second, the subspecies of any species cannot be distinct and discrete. Since all belong to a single species, their numbers can, by definition, interbreed. Modern quantitative methods have permitted taxonomists to describe geographic variation more precisely in numerical terms; we need no longer construct names to describe differences that are, by definition, fleeting and changeable. Therefore, the practice of naming subspecies has largely fallen into disfavor, and few taxonomists use the category any more. Human variation exists; the formal designation of races is passé.

Some species are divided into tolerably distinct geographic races. Consider, for example, an immobile species separated on drifting continental blocks. Since these subpopulations never meet, they may evolve substantial differences. We might still choose to name subspecies for such discrete geographic variants. But humans move about and maintain the most notorious habits of extensive interbreeding. We are not well enough divided into distinct geographic groups, and the naming of human subspecies makes little sense.

Our variation displays all the difficulties that make taxonomists shudder (or delight in complexity) and avoid the naming of subspecies. Consider just three points. First, discordance of characters. We might make a reasonable division on skin color, only to discover that blood groups imply different alliances. When so many good characters exhibit such discordant patterns of variation, no valid criterion can be established for unambiguous definition of subspecies. Second, fluidity and gradations. We interbreed wherever we move, breaking down barriers and creating new groups. Shall the Cape Colored, a vigorous people more than two million strong and the offspring of unions between Africans and white settlers (the ancestors, ironically, of the authors of apartheid and its antimiscegenation laws), be designated a new subspecies or simply the living disproof that white and black are very distinct? Third, convergences. Similar characters evolve independently again and again; they confound any attempt to base subspecies on definite traits. Most indigenous tropical people, for example, have evolved dark skin.

The arguments against naming human races are strong, but our variation still exists and could, conceivably, still serve as a basis for invidious comparisons. Therefore, we must add the second and third arguments as well.

The Positive Argument from Recency of Division

As I argued in the first part of this essay (and need only state in repetition now), the division of humans into modern "racial" groups happened yesterday, in geological terms. This differentiation does not predate the origin of our own species, *Homo sapiens*, and probably occurred during the last few tens (or at most hundreds) of thousands of years.

The Positive Argument from Genetic Separation

Mendel's[1] work was rediscovered in 1900 and the science of genetics spans our entire century. Yet, until twenty years ago, a fundamental question in evolutionary

---

[1]Gregor Johann (1822–1884), Austrian monk whose work with hybridization of peas, published in 1866, was ignored until it was rediscovered independently by three scientists.

genetics could not be answered for a curious reason. We were not able to calculate the average amount of genetic difference between organisms because we had devised no method for taking a random sample of genes. In the classical Mendelian analysis of pedigrees, a gene cannot be identified until it varies among individuals. For example, if absolutely every *Drosophila*[1] in the world had red eyes, we would rightly suspect that some genetic information coded this universal feature, but we would not be able to identify a gene for red eyes by analyzing pedigrees, because all flies would look the same. But as soon as we find a few white-eyed flies, we can mate white with red, trace pedigrees through generations of offspring, and make proper inferences about the genetic basis of eye color.

To measure the average genetic differences among races, we must be able to sample genes at random—and this unbiased selection can't be done if we can only identify variable genes. Ninety percent of human genes might be held in common by all people, and an analysis confined to varying genes would grossly overestimate the total difference.

In the late 1960s, several geneticists harnessed the common laboratory technique of electrophoresis[2] to solve this old dilemma. Genes code for proteins, and varying proteins may behave differently when subjected in solution to an electric field. Any protein could be sampled, independent of prior knowledge about whether it varied or not. (Electrophoresis can only give us a minimal estimate because some varying proteins may exhibit the same electrical mobility but be different in other ways.) Thus, with electrophoresis we could finally ask the key question: How much genetic difference exists among human races?

The answer, surprising for many people, soon emerged without ambiguity: damned little. Intense studies for more than a decade have detected not a single "race gene"—that is, a gene present in all members of one group and none of another. Frequencies vary, often considerably, among groups, but all human races are much of a muchness. We can measure so much variation among individuals *within* any race that we encounter very little new variation by adding another race to the sample. In other words, the great preponderance of human variation occurs within groups, not in the differences between them. My colleague Richard Lewontin (see bibliography),[3] who did much of the original electrophoretic work on human variation, puts it dramatically: If, God forbid, the holocaust occurs "and only the Xhosa people of the southern tip of Africa survived, the human species would still retain 80 percent of its genetic variation."

As long as most scientists accepted the ancient division of races, they expected important genetic differences. But the recent origin of races (second positive argument) affirms the minor genetic differences now measured. Human groups do vary strikingly in a few highly visible characters (skin color, hair form)—and these external differences may fool us into thinking that overall

---

[1] Fruit fly.

[2] The motion of charged particles in a stationary liquid.

[3] *Human Diversity* (New York: Scientific American Library, 1982).

divergence must be great. But we now know that our usual metaphor of superficiality—skin deep—is literally accurate.

In thus completing my précis, I trust that one essential point will not be misconstrued: I am, emphatically, not talking about ethical precepts but about information in our best current assessment. It would be poor logic and worse strategy to hinge a moral or political argument for equal treatment or equal opportunity upon any factual statement about human biology. For if our empirical conclusions need revision—and all facts are tentative in science—then we might be forced to justify prejudice and apartheid (directed, perhaps, against ourselves, since who knows who would turn up on the bottom). I am no ethical philosopher, but I can only view equality of opportunity as inalienable, universal, and unrelated to the biological status of individuals. Our races may vary little in average characters, but our individuals differ greatly—and I cannot imagine a decent world that does not treat the most profoundly retarded person as a full human being in all respects, despite his evident and pervasive limitations.

I am, instead, making a smaller point, but one that tickles my fancy because most people find it surprising. The conclusion is evident, once articulated, but we rarely pose the issue in a manner that lets such a statement emerge. I have called equality among races a *contingent* fact. So far I have only argued for the fact; what about the contingency? In other words, how might history have been different? Most of us can grasp and accept the equality; few have considered the easy plausibility of alternatives that didn't happen.

My creationist incubi,[1] in one of their most deliciously ridiculous arguments, often imagine that they can sweep evolution away in the following unanswerable riposte: "Awright," they exclaim, "you say that humans evolved from apes, right?" "Right," I reply. "Awright, if humans evolved from apes, why are apes still around? Answer that one!" If evolution proceeded by this caricature—like a ladder of progress, each rung disappearing as it transforms bodily to the next stage—then I suppose this argument would merit attention. But evolution is a bush, and ancestral groups usually survive after their descendants branch off. Apes come in many shapes and sizes; only one line led to modern humans.

Most of us know about bushes, but we rarely consider the implications. We know that australopithecines were our ancestors and that their bush included several species. But we view them as forebears, and subtly assume that since we are here, they must be gone. It is so indeed, but it ain't *necessarily* so. One population of one line of australopithecines became *Homo habilis*; several others survived. One species, *Australopithecus robustus*, died less than a million years ago and lived in Africa as a contemporary of *H. erectus* for a million years. We do not know why *A. robustus* disappeared. It might well have survived and presented us today with all the ethical dilemmas of a human species truly and markedly inferior in intelligence (with its cranial capacity only one-third our own). Would we have built zoos, established reserves, promoted slavery, committed genocide, or perhaps even practiced kindness? Human equality is a contingent fact of history.

---

[1]Evil spirits believed to lie with sleeping women, giving them nightmares; demons.

Other plausible scenarios might also have produced marked inequality. *Homo sapiens* is a young species, its division into races even more recent. This historical context has not provided enough time for the evolution of substantial differences. But many species are millions of years old, and their geographic divisions may be marked and deep. *H. sapiens* might have evolved along such a scale of time and produced races of great age and large accumulated differences—but we didn't. Human equality is a contingent fact of history.

A few well-placed mottoes might serve as excellent antidotes against deeply ingrained habits of Western thought that so constrain us because we do not recognize their influence—so long as these mottoes become epitomes of real understanding, not the vulgar distortions that promote "all is relative" as a précis of Einstein.°

I have three favorite mottoes, short in statement but long in implication. The first, the epitome of punctuated equilibrium, reminds us that gradual change is not the only reality in evolution: other things count as well; "stasis is data." The second confutes the bias of progress and affirms that evolution is not an inevitable sequence of ascent: "mammals evolved at the same time as dinosaurs." The third is the theme of this essay, a fundamental statement about human variation. Say it five times before breakfast tomorrow; more important, understand it as the center of a network of implication: "Human equality is a contingent fact of history." ✐

The Chain of Reason Versus the Chain of Thumbs[1]

The *Weekly World News*, most lurid entry in the dubious genre of shopping mall tabloids, shattered all previous records for implausibility with a recent headline: "Siamese Twins Make Themselves Pregnant." The story recounted the sad tale of a conjoined brother-sister pair from a remote Indian village (such folks never hail from Peoria, where their non-existence might be confirmed). They knew that their act was immoral, but after years of hoping in vain for ordinary partners, and in the depths of loneliness and frustration, they finally succumbed to an ever-present temptation. The story is heart-rending, but faces one major obstacle to belief: All Siamese twins are monozygotic, formed from a single fertilized egg that failed to split completely in the act of twinning. Thus, Siamese twins are either both male or both female.

I will, however, praise the good people at *Weekly World News* for one slight scruple. They did realize that they had created a problem with this ludicrous tale, and they did not shrink from the difficulty. The story acknowledged that, indeed, Siamese twins generally share the same sex, but held that this Indian pair had been formed, uniquely and differently, from two eggs that had fused! Usually, however, *Weekly World News* doesn't even bother with minimal cover-ups.

---

[1]First published in *Natural History,* July 1989, and collected in *Bully for Brontosaurus,* 1991.

Recently, for example, they ran a screaming headline about a monster from Mars, just sighted in a telescope and now on its way to earth. The accompanying photo of the monster showed a perfectly ordinary chambered nautilus (an odd-looking and unfamiliar creature to be sure). I mean, they didn't even bother to retouch the photo or hide in any way their absurd transmogrification of a marine mollusk into an extraterrestrial marauder!

The sad moral of this tale lies not with the practices of *Weekly World News*, but with the nature of a readership that permits such a publication to prosper—for if *Weekly World News* could not rely, with complete confidence, on the ignorance of its consumers, the paper would be exposed and discredited. The Siamese twin story at least showed a modicum of respect for the credulity of readers; the tale of the Martian monster records utter contempt both for the consuming public and for truth in general.

We like to cite an old motto of our culture on the factual and ethical value of veracity: "And ye shall know the truth, and the truth shall make you free" (John 8:32). But ignorance has always prospered, serving the purposes of demagogues and profitmongers. An overly optimistic account might try to link our increasing factual knowledge with the suppression of cruelties and abuses ranging from execution for witchcraft to human sacrifice for propitiating deities. But this hope cannot be sustained, for no century has exceeded our own in quantity of imposed cruelty (as "improvements" in the technology of genocide and warfare more than balance any overall gains in sensibility). Moreover, despite a great spread in the availability of education, the favored irrationalisms of the ages show no signs of abatement. Presidential calendars are still set by astrologers,[1] while charlatans do a brisk business in necklaces made of colored glass masquerading as crystals that supposedly bathe believers in a salutary and intangible "energy." An astounding percentage of "educated" Americans think that the earth might be less than 10,000 years old, even while their own kids delight in dinosaurs at the local museum.

The champions of beleaguered rationalism—all heroes in my book—have been uncovering charlatans throughout the ages: from Elijah[2] denouncing the prophets of Baal to Houdini[3] exposing the tricks of mediums to James Randi[4] on

---

[1]Reference to Nancy Reagan's habit of consulting an astrologer before President Ronald Reagan (1981 to 1988) traveled.

[2]See 1 Kings 18, where Elijah pits the power of the Lord against the power of the gods of Baal, causing a wooden altar and an offering of sliced bull to burst into flames after being drenched three times with water.

[3]Harry (1874–1926), stage name of Erich Weiss, brilliant locksmith and magician famous for his escapes from locks, handcuffs, straightjackets, and sealed chests submerged in deep water.

[4]Randall James Hamilton Zwinge (1928–), internationally known magician and escape artist, was born in Toronto and became a U.S. citizen in 1987. The author of numerous books, including *The Magic of Uri Geller* (1975; with Bert Sugar), *Houdini, His Life and Art* (1978), and *The Magic World of the Amazing Randi* (1989), Randi has been on the editorial board of the journal *Skeptical Inquirer* since 1976 and spends most of his time investigating and debunking claims of the supernatural or paranormal. In 1964 Randi offered $10,000 for proof of such claims, but has not yet had to pay up.

the trail of modern hoaxers and hucksters. Obviously, we have not won the war, but we have developed effective battle strategies—and would have triumphed long ago were our foe not able, like the Lernean Hydra,[1] to grow several new heads every time we lop one off. Still, tales of past victories—including the story of this essay—are not only useful as spurs of encouragement; they also teach us effective methods of attack. For reason is timeless, and its application to unfamiliar contexts can be particularly instructive.

How many of us realize that we are invoking a verbal remnant of "the greatest vogue of the 1780s" (according to historian Robert Darnton) when we claim to be "mesmerized" by a wonderful concert or a beautiful sunset? Franz Anton Mesmer was a German physician who had acquired wealth through marriage to a well-endowed widow; connections by assiduous cultivation (Mozart,[2] a valued friend, had staged the first performance of his comic opera *Bastien und Bastienne* at Mesmer's private theater); and renown with a bizarre, if fascinating, theory of "animal magnetism" and its role in human health. In 1778, Mesmer transferred to Paris, then the most "open" and vibrant capital of Europe, a city embracing the odd mixture so often spawned by liberty—intellectual ferment of the highest order combined with quackery at its most abject: Voltaire° among the fortune tellers; Benjamin Franklin surrounded by astrologers; Antoine Lavoisier[3] amidst the spiritualists.

Mesmer, insofar as one can find coherence in his ideas at all, claimed that a single (and subtle) fluid pervaded the universe, uniting and connecting all bodies. We give different names to this fluid according to its various manifestations: gravity for planets in their courses; electricity in a thunderstorm; magnetism for navigation by compass. The same fluid flows through organisms and may be called animal magnetism. A blockage of this flow causes disease, and cure requires a reestablishment of the flux and a restoration of equilibrium. (Mesmer himself never went so far as to ascribe all bodily ills to blocked magnetism, but

---

[1]In Greek mythology, a many-headed monster who grew two new heads when one was cut off. Hercules' second labor was to kill the Hydra, which he did by cauterizing the necks after cutting off the heads. Lernean refers to the name of the marsh where the Hydra lived.

[2]I thank Gerald A. Le Boff and Ernest F. Marmorek for informing me, after reading this essay at its initial publication, of another explicit link between Mozart (and his great librettist, DaPonte) and Mesmer. In *Cosī Fan Tutte*, the maid Despina, disguised as a physician, "cures" Ferrando and Guglielmo of their feigned illness by touching their foreheads with a large magnet and then gently stroking the length of their bodies. An orchestral tremolo recalls the curing mesmeric crisis, while Despina describes her magnet as:

pietra Mesmerica
ch'ebbe l'origine
nell' Alemagna
che poi si celebre
lá in Francia fù.

—a mesmeric stone that had its origin in Germany and then was so famous in France (a fine epitome of Mesmer's tactic and its geographic history). [Gould's note.]

[3]Antoine Laurent (1743–1794), French chemist and founder of modern chemistry, who described combustion and showed how oxygen works in the respiration of plants and animals.

several disciples held this extreme view, and such a motto came to characterize the mesmeric movement: "There is only one illness and one healing.")

Cure of illness requires the intervention of an "adept," a person with unusually strong magnetism who can locate the "poles" of magnetic flow on the exterior of a human body and, by massaging these areas, break the blockage within to reestablish the normal flux. When working one on one, Mesmer would sit directly opposite his patient, establishing the proper contact and flow by holding the sufferer's knees within his own, touching fingers, and staring directly into her face (most patients were women, thus adding another dimension to charges of exploitation). Mesmer, by all accounts, was a most charismatic man—and we need no great psychological sophistication to suspect that he might have produced effects more by power of suggestion than by flow of any fluid.

In any case, the effects could be dramatic. Within a few minutes of mesmerizing, sensitive patients would fall into a characteristic "crisis" taken by Mesmer as proof of his method. Bodies would begin to shake, arms and legs move violently and involuntarily, teeth chatter loudly. Patients would grimace, groan, babble, scream, faint, and fall unconscious. Several repetitions of these treatments would reestablish magnetic equilibrium and produce cures. Mesmer carried sheaves of testimonials claiming recovery from a variety of complaints. Even his most determined critics did not deny all cures, but held that Mesmer had only relieved certain psychosomatic illnesses by the power of suggestion and had produced no physical effects with his putative universal fluid.

Mesmer's popularity required the development of methods for treating large numbers of patients simultaneously (such a procedure didn't hurt profits either), and Mesmer imposed high charges, in two senses, upon his mostly aristocratic crowd. Moreover, as a master of manipulation, Mesmer surely recognized the social value of treatment in groups—both the reinforcing effect of numerous crises and the simple value of conviviality in spreading any vogue as a joint social event and medical cure. Mesmer therefore began to magnetize inanimate objects and to use these charged bodies as instruments of unblocking and cure.

Many contemporary descriptions and drawings of Mesmer's sessions depict the same basic scene. Mesmer placed a large vat, called a *baquet*, in the center of a room. He then filled the *baquet* with "magnetized" water and, sometimes, a layer of iron filings as well. Some twenty thin metal rods protruded from the *baquet*. A patient would grab hold of a rod and apply it to the mesmeric poles of his body. To treat more than twenty, Mesmer would loop a rope from those who surrounded the *baquet* (and held the iron rods) to others in the room, taking care that the rope contained no knots, for such constrictions impeded the flux. Patients would then form a "mesmeric chain" by holding a neighbor's left thumb between their own right thumb and forefinger, while extending their own left thumb to the next patient down the line. By squeezing a neighbor's left thumb, magnetic impulses could be sent all the way down the chain.

Mesmer, whether consciously or not, surely exploited both the art and politics of psychosomatic healing. Everything in his curing room was carefully arranged to maximize results, efficiency, and profit. He installed mirrors to reflect the action and encourage mass response; he heightened the effect with music played on the ethereal tones of a glass harmonica, the instrument that Benjamin Franklin had developed; he employed assistants to carry convulsive patients into a "crisis room" lined with mattresses, lest they should hurt themselves in their frenzy. To avoid the charge of profitmongering among the rich alone, Mesmer provided a poor man's cure by magnetizing trees and inviting the indigent to take their relief gratis and alfresco.[1]

I don't want to commit the worst historical error of wrenching a person from his own time and judging him by modern standards and categories. Thus, Franz Mesmer was not Uri Geller[2] teleported to 1780. For one thing, historical records of Mesmer are scanty, and we do not even know whether he was a simple charlatan, purveying conscious fakery for fame and profit, or a sincere believer, deluded no less than his patients in mistaking the power of suggestion for the physical effects of an actual substance. For another, the lines between science and pseudoscience were not so clearly drawn in Mesmer's time. A strong group of rationalists was laboring to free science from speculation, system building, and untestable claims about universal harmonies. But their campaign also demonstrates that all-embracing and speculative systems were still viewed by many scholars as legitimate parts of science in the eighteenth century. Robert Darnton, who has written the best modern book on mesmerism, describes the French intellectual world of the 1780s (*Mesmerism and the End of the Enlightenment in France*, 1968):

> They looked out on a world so different from our own that we can hardly perceive it; for our view is blocked by our own cosmologies assimilated, knowingly or not, from the scientists and philosophers of the 19th and 20th centuries. In the 18th century, the view of literate Frenchmen opened upon a splendid, baroque universe, where their gaze rode on waves of invisible fluid into realms of infinite speculation.

Still, whatever the differing boundaries and cultural assumptions, the fact remains that Mesmer based his system on specific claims about fluids, their modes of flow, and their role in causing and curing human disease—claims subject to test by the ordinary procedures of experimental science. The logic of argument has a universality that transcends culture, and late eighteenth century debunking differs in no substantial way from the modern efforts. Indeed, I write this essay because the most celebrated analysis of mesmerism, the report of the Royal Commission of 1784, is a masterpiece of the genre, an enduring testimony to the power and beauty of reason.

Mesmerism became such a craze in the 1780s that many institutions began to worry and retaliate. Conventional medicine, which offered so little in the way

---

[1] Italian for "free" and "outdoors."

[2] Self-proclaimed psychic and entertainer (1946–). Born in Tel Aviv, he lived in Cyprus and Israel before moving to the United States in the 1970s. He is especially known for bending spoons and starting stopped watches.

of effective treatment, was running scared. Empirical and experimental scientists viewed Mesmer as a throwback to the worst excesses of speculation. People in power feared the irrationalism, the potential for sexual license, the possibility that Mesmer's mass sessions might rupture boundaries between social classes. Moreover, Mesmer had many powerful friends in high circles, and his disturbing ideas might spread by export. (Mesmer counted Lafayette[1] among his most ardent disciples. King Louis XVI asked Lafayette before he departed for America in 1784: "What will Washington think when he learns that you have become Mesmer's chief journeyman apothecary?" Lafayette did proselytize for Mesmer on our shores, although Thomas Jefferson actively opposed him. Lafayette even visited a group of Shakers, thinking that they had discovered a form of mesmerism in their religious dances.)

The mesmeric vogue became sufficiently serious that Louis XVI was persuaded to establish a Royal Commission in 1784 to evaluate the claims of animal magnetism. The commission was surely stacked against Mesmer, but it proceeded with scrupulous fairness and thoroughness. Never in history has such an extraordinary and luminous group been gathered together in the service of rational inquiry by the methods of experimental science. For this reason alone, the *Rapport des commissaires chargés par le roi de l'examen du magnétisme animal* (Report of the Commissioners Charged by the King to Examine Animal Magnetism) is a key document in the history of human reason. It should be rescued from its current obscurity, translated into all languages, and reprinted by organizations dedicated to the unmasking of quackery and the defense of rational thought.

The commissioners included several of France's leading physicians and scientists, but two names stand out: Benjamin Franklin and Antoine Lavoisier. (Franklin served as titular head of the commission, signed the report first, and designed and performed several of the experiments; Lavoisier was the commission's guiding spirit and probably wrote the final report.) The conjunction may strike some readers as odd, but no two men could have been more appropriate or more available. Franklin lived in Paris, as official representative of our newborn nation, from 1776 to 1785. American intellectuals sometimes underestimate Franklin's status, assuming perhaps that we revere him *faute de mieux*[2] and for parochial reasons—and that he was really a pipsqueak and amateur among the big boys of Europe. Not at all. Franklin was a universally respected scholar and a great, world-class scientist in an age when nearly all practitioners were technically amateurs. As the world's leading expert on electricity—a supposed manifestation of Mesmer's universal fluid—Franklin was an obvious choice for the commission. His interest also extended to smaller details, in particular to Mesmer's use of the

---

[1]Marie Joseph, marquis de (1757–1834), French general, friend of Washington, who was wounded at Brandywine, fought at Valley Forge, and won at Yorktown. Following the American Revolution he returned to France and was made commander of the National Guard after the fall of the Bastille. In 1789 he devised the modern French flag, but he lost power in 1791; he then led the campaign in Austria, left his army, and was captured in Austria in 1792. When Napoleon liberated France in 1797, Lafayette returned to live out his life in his country.

[2]French for "for lack of a better."

glass harmonica (Franklin's own invention) as an auxiliary in the precipitation of crises. As for Lavoisier, he ranks as one of the half-dozen greatest scientific geniuses of all time: He wrote with chilling clarity, and he thought with commanding rigor. If the membership contains any odd or ironic conjunction, I would point rather to the inclusion of Dr. Guillotin among the physicians—for Lavoisier would die, ten years later, under the knife that bore the good doctor's name (see Essay 24).[1]

The experimental method is often oversold or promulgated as the canonical, or even the only, mode of science. As a natural historian, I have often stressed and reported the different approaches used in explaining unique and complex historical events—aspects of the world that cannot be simulated in laboratories or predicted from laws of nature (see my book *Wonderful Life*, 1989). Moreover, the experimental method is fundamentally conservative, not innovative—a set of procedures for evaluating and testing ideas that originate in other ways. Yet, despite these caveats about nonexclusivity and limited range, the experimental method is a tool of unparalleled power in its appropriate (and large) domain.

Lavoisier, Franklin, and colleagues conclusively debunked Mesmer by applying the tools of their experimental craft, tried and true: standardization of complex situations to delineate possible causal factors, repetition of experiments with control and variation, and separation and independent testing of proposed causes. The mesmerists never recovered, and their leader and namesake soon hightailed it out of Paris for good, although he continued to live in adequate luxury, if with reduced fame and prestige, until 1815. Just a year after the commission's report, Thomas Jefferson, replacing Franklin as American representative in Paris, noted in his journal: "animal magnetism dead, ridiculed." (Jefferson was overly optimistic, for irrationalism born of hope never dies; still, the report of Franklin and Lavoisier was probably the key incident that turned the tide of opinion—a subtle fluid far more palpable and powerful than animal magnetism—against Mesmer.)

The commissioners began with a basic proposition to guide their testing: "Animal magnetism might well exist without being useful, but it cannot be useful if it doesn't exist." Yet, any attempt to affirm the existence of animal magnetism faced an intense and immediate frustration: The mesmerists insisted that their subtle fluid had no tangible or measurable attributes. Imagine the chagrin of a group of eminent physical scientists trying to test the existence of a fluid without physical properties! They wrote, with the barely concealed contempt that makes Lavoisier's report both a masterpiece of rhetoric and an exemplar of experimental method (the two are not inconsistent because fair and scrupulous procedures do not demand neutrality, but only strict adherence to the rules of the craft):

> It didn't take the Commissioners long to recognize that this fluid escapes all sensation. It is not at all luminous and visible like electricity [the reference, of course, is to lightning before the days of "invisible" flow through modern wires].

---

[1] "The Passion of Antoine Lavoisier" in *Bully for Brontosaurus*.

Its action is not clearly evident, as the attraction of a magnet. It has no taste, no odor. It works without sound, and surrounds or penetrates you without warning you of its presence. If it exists in us and around us, it does so in an absolutely insensible manner. [All quotations from the commissioners' report are my translations from an original copy in Harvard's Houghton Library.]

The commissioners therefore recognized that they would have to test for the existence of animal magnetism through its effects, not its physical properties. This procedure suggested a focus either on cures or on the immediate (and dramatic) crises supposedly provoked by the flow of magnetism during Mesmer's sessions. The commissioners rejected a test of cures for three obvious and excellent reasons: Cures take too long and time was awasting as the mesmeric craze spread; cures can be caused by many factors, and the supposed effects of magnetism could not be separated from other reasons for recovery; nature, left to her own devices, relieves many ills without any human intervention. (Franklin wryly suspected that an unintended boost to nature lay at the root of Mesmer's successes. His fluid didn't exist, and his sessions produced no physical effect. But patients in his care stayed away from conventional physicians and therefore didn't take the ordinary pills and potions that undoubtedly did more harm than good and impeded natural recovery.) Mesmer, on the other hand, wanted to focus upon cures, and he refused to cooperate with the commission when they would not take his advice. The commission therefore worked in close collaboration with Mesmer's chief disciple, Charles Deslon, who attended the tests and attempted to magnetize objects and people. (Deslon's cooperation indicates that the chief mesmerists were not frauds, but misguided believers in their own system. Mesmer tried to dissociate himself from the commission's findings, arguing that Deslon was a blunderer unable to control the magnetic flux—but all to no avail, and the entire movement suffered from the exposé.)

The commissioners began by trying to magnetize themselves. Once a week, and then for three days in a row (to test a claim that such concentrated time boosted the efficiency of magnetism), they sat for two and a half hours around Deslon's *baquet* in his Paris curing room, faithfully following all the mesmeric rituals. Nobody felt a thing beyond boredom and discomfort. (I am, somehow, greatly taken by the image of these enormously talented and intensely skeptical men sitting around a *baquet*, presumably under their perukes,[1] joined by a rope, each holding an iron rod, and "making from time to time," to quote Lavoisier, "the chain of thumbs." I can picture the scene, as Lavoisier says—Okay boys, ready? One, two, squeeze those thumbs now.)

The commissioners recognized that their own failure scarcely settled the issue, for none was seriously ill (despite Franklin's gout), and Mesmer's technique might only work on sick people with magnetic blockages. Moreover, they acknowledged that their own skepticism might be impeding a receptive state of

---

[1]Wigs.

mind. They therefore tested seven "common" people with assorted complaints and then, in a procedure tied to the social assumptions of the *ancien régime*, seven sufferers from the upper classes, reasoning that people of higher status would be less subject, by their refinement and general superiority, to the power of suggestion. The results supported power of suggestion as the cause of crises, rather than physical effects of a fluid. Only five of fourteen subjects noted any results, and only three—all from the lower classes—experienced anything severe enough to label as a crisis. "Those who belong to a more elevated class, endowed with more light, and more capable of recognizing their sensations, experienced nothing." Interestingly, two commoners who felt nothing—a child and a young retarded woman—might be judged less subject to the power of suggestion, but not less able to experience the flow of a fluid, if it existed.

These preliminaries brought the commissioners to the crux of their experiments. They had proceeded by progressive elimination and concentration on a key remaining issue. They had hoped to test for physical evidence of the fluid itself, but could not and chose instead to concentrate on its supposed effects. They had decided that immediate reactions rather than long-term cures must form the focus of experiments. They had tried the standard techniques on themselves, without result. They had given mesmerists the benefit of all doubt by using the same methods on people with illnesses and inclined to accept the mesmeric system—still without positive results. The investigation now came down to a single question, admirably suited for experimental resolution: The undoubted crises that mesmerists could induce might be caused by one of two factors (or perhaps both)—the psychological power of suggestion or the physical action of a fluid.

The experimental method demands that the two possible causes be separated in controlled situations. People must be subjected to the power of suggestion but not magnetized, and then magnetized but not subject to suggestion. These separations demanded a bit of honorable duplicity from the commissioners—for they needed to tell people that nonmagnetized objects were really full of mesmeric fluid (suggestion without physical cause), and then magnetize people without letting them know (physical cause without suggestion).

In a clever series of experiments, designed mainly by Lavoisier and carried out at Franklin's home in Passy, the commissioners made the necessary separations and achieved a result as clear as any in the history of debunking: Crises are caused by suggestion; not a shred of evidence exists for any fluid, and animal magnetism, as a physical force, must be firmly rejected.

For the separation of suggestion from magnetism, Franklin asked Deslon to magnetize one of five trees in his garden. A young man, certified by Deslon as particularly sensitive to magnetism, was led to embrace each tree in turn, but not told about the smoking gun. He reported increasing strength of magnetization in each successive tree and finally fell unconscious in a classic mesmeric crisis before the fourth tree. Only the fifth, however, had been magnetized by Deslon! Mesmerists rejected the result, arguing that all trees have some natural magnetization anyway, and that Deslon's presence in the garden might have enhanced the effect. But Lavoisier replied scornfully:

But then, a person sensitive to magnetization would not be able to chance a walk in a garden without the risk of suffering convulsions, and such an assertion is therefore denied by ordinary, everyday experience.

Nevertheless, the commissioners persisted with several other experiments, all leading to the same conclusion—that suggestion without magnetism could easily produce full-scale mesmeric crises. They blindfolded a woman and told her that Deslon was in the room, filling her with magnetism. He was nowhere near, but the woman had a classic crisis. They then tested the patient without a blindfold, telling her that Deslon was in the next room directing the fluid at her. He was not, but she had a crisis. In both cases, the woman was not magnetized or even touched, but her crises were intense.

Lavoisier conducted another experiment at his home in the Arsenal (where he worked as Commissioner of Gunpowder, having helped America's revolution with matériel, as much as Lafayette had aided with men). Several porcelain cups were filled with water, one supposedly strongly magnetized. A particularly sensitive woman who, in anticipation, had already experienced a crisis in Lavoisier's antechamber, received each cup in turn. She began to quiver after touching the second cup and fell into a full crisis upon receiving the fourth. When she recovered and asked for a cup of water, the foxy Lavoisier finally passed her the magnetized liquid. This time, she not only held, but actually imbibed, although "she drank tranquilly and said that she felt relieved."

The commissioners then proceeded to the reverse test of magnetizing without unleasing the power of suggestion. They removed the door between two rooms at Franklin's home and replaced it with a paper partition (offering no bar at all, according to Deslon, to the flow of mesmeric fluid). They induced a young seamstress, a woman with particularly acute sensitivity to magnetism, to sit next to the partition. From the other side, but unknown to the seamstress, an adept magnetizer tried for half an hour to fill her with fluid and induce a crisis, but "during all this time, Miss B . . . made gay conversation; asked about her health, she freely answered that she felt very well." Yet, when the magnetizer entered the room, and his presence became known (while acting from an equal or greater distance), the seamstress began to convulse after three minutes and fell into a full crisis in twelve minutes.

The evident finding, after so many conclusive experiments—that no evidence exists for Mesmer's fluid and that all noted effects may be attributed to the power of imagination—seems almost anticlimactic, and the commissioners offered their result with clarity and brevity: "The practice of magnetization is the art of increasing the imagination by degrees." Lavoisier then ended the report with a brilliant analysis of the reasons for such frequent vogues of irrationalism throughout human history. He cited two major causes, or predisposing factors of the human mind and heart. First, our brains just don't seem to be well equipped for reasoning by probability. Fads find their most fertile ground in subjects, like the curing of disease, that require a separation of many potential causes and an assessment of probability in judging the value of a result:

The art of concluding from experience and observation consists in evaluating probabilities, in estimating if they are high or numerous enough to constitute proof. This type of calculation is more complicated and more difficult than one might think. It demands a great sagacity generally above the power of common people. The success of charlatans, sorcerers, and alchemists—and all those who abuse public credulity—is founded on errors in this type of calculation.

I would alter only Lavoisier's patrician assumption that ordinary folks cannot master this mode of reasoning—and write instead that most people surely can but, thanks to poor education and lack of encouragement from general culture, do not. The end result is the same—riches for Las Vegas and disappointment for Pete Rose.[1] But at least the modern view does not condemn us to a permanent and inevitable status as saps, dupes, and dunces.

Second, whatever our powers of abstract reasoning, we are also prisoners of our hopes. So long as life remains disappointing and cruel for so many people, we shall be prey to irrationalisms that promise relief. Lavoisier regarded his countrymen as more sophisticated than previous suckers of centuries past, but still victims of increasingly sly manipulators (nothing has changed today, as the Gellers and von Danikens[2] remain one step ahead of their ever-gullible disciples):

> This theory [mesmerism] is presented today with the more imposing apparatus [I presume that Lavoisier means both ideas and contraptions] necessary in our more enlightened century—but it is no less false. Man seizes, abandons, but then commits again the errors that flatter him.

Since hope is an ever-present temptress in a world of woe, mesmerism "attracts people by the two hopes that touch them the most: that of knowing the future and that of prolonging their days."

Lavoisier then drew an apt parallel between the communal crises of mesmeric sessions and the mass emotionalism so often exploited by demagogues and conquerors throughout history—"*l'enthousiasme du courage*" (enthusiasm of courage) or "*l'unité d'ivresse*" (unity of intoxication). Generals elicit this behavior by sounding drums and playing bugles; promoters by hiring a claque to begin and direct the applause after performances; demagogues by manipulating the mob.

Lavoisier's social theory offered no solution to the destructive force of irrationalism beyond a firm and continuing hegemony[3] of the educated elite. (As my

---

[1]National League Rookie of the Year in 1963, Rose (1941–) is the only player to perform in more than five hundred games in five different positions and be named an NL All Star at each one. He was named Man of the Year in 1985 for his work as manager-player of the Cincinnati Reds. In 1989 he was banned from baseball for betting on games.

[2]Erich (1935–), Swiss author of *Memories of the Future* (1966), translated and published in the United States as *Chariots of the Gods* (1970), which claims that the earth was visited by extraterrestrials that created the first *Homo sapiens*. The sequel, *Gods from Outer Space: Return to the Stars* (1971), concentrates on "evidence" for this hypothesis, such as similarities between Egyptian and Mayan cultures. These books were followed by three more such books, *The Gold of the Gods* (1973), *In Search of Ancient Gods* (1974), and *Miracles of the Gods* (1976).

[3]Predominance.

one criticism of the commissioners' report, Lavoisier and colleagues could see absolutely nothing salutary, in any conceivable form, in the strong emotionalism of a mesmeric crisis. They did not doubt the power of the psyche to cure, but as sons of the Enlightenment, children of the Age of Reason, they proclaimed that only a state of calm and cheerfulness could convey any emotional benefit to the afflicted. In this restriction, they missed an important theme of human complexity and failed to grasp the potential healing effect of many phenomena that call upon the wilder emotions—from speaking in tongues to catharsis in theatrical performance to aspects of Freudian° psychoanalysis. In this sense, some Freudians view Mesmer as a worthy precursor with a key insight into human nature. I hesitate to confer such status upon a man who attained great wealth from something close to quackery—but I see the point.)

I envision no easy solution either, but I adopt a less pessimistic attitude than Lavoisier. Human nature is flexible enough to avert the baleful effects of intoxicated unity, and history shows that revolutionary enthusiasm need not devolve into hatred and mass murder. Consider Franklin and Lavoisier one last time. Our revolution remained in the rational hands of numerous Franklins, Jeffersons, and Washingtons; France descended from the Declaration of the Rights of Man into the Reign of Terror. (I do recognize the different situations, particularly the greater debt of hatred, based on longer and deeper oppression, necessarily discharged by the new rulers of France. Still, no inevitability attended the excesses fanned by mass emotionalism.) In other words:

> Antoine Lavoisier
>   Lost his head
> Benjamin Franklin
>   Died in bed.

From which, I think, we can only conclude that Mr. Franklin understood a thing or two when he remarked, speaking of his fellow patriots, but extended here to all devotees of reason, that we must either hang together or hang separately. ✂

Alice Walker

(1944–)

Alice Walker was born in February 1944, the last of eight children of Willie Lee and Minnie Lou Walker, black sharecroppers in Eatonton, Georgia. Because her family lived in a house of only a few rooms, Walker remembers her childhood as a struggle for privacy in crowded conditions. Moreover, as blacks, all her family, friends, and neighbors were cut off from and disparaged by the whites, whose crops they picked, whose clothes they ironed, and whose children they looked after. Nonetheless, Walker also remembers the great happiness she found reading, fishing, swimming, and walking "through fields of black-eyed Susans."

When she was seventeen Walker went to Spelman College in Atlanta on a scholarship. That summer she attended a World Youth Peace Festival in Helsinki and two years later transferred to Sarah Lawrence, a less structured but academically elite school where, under the tutelage of the poet Muriel Rukeyser, Walker wrote her first book of poems.

After college, Walker registered black voters in Georgia, attended a writers' conference, and worked for the Welfare Department in New York City until she was awarded an Ingram Merrill Foundation Writing Fellowship. By 1967, when she married lawyer Mel Leventhal, she had published several essays and short stories; by 1968 she had published her poems in a collection called *Once*. Meanwhile, the couple had moved to Mississippi, where Leventhal worked for civil rights and Walker worked in Head Start projects, taught black studies at Jackson State College, and continued to write.

In 1971 Walker's daughter, Rebecca Leventhal, was born. Soon after mother and daughter went to Boston, where, as a Fellow of the Radcliffe Institute, Walker continued to write, supplementing her income by teaching part-time at Wellesley College. The family reunited in Mississippi in 1973 and returned to New York a few years later so that Leventhal could pursue his career as a civil rights lawyer. Meanwhile Walker had written a novel, *The Third Life of George Copeland* (1970), a second collection of poems,

Revolutionary Petunias and Other Poems (1973), and a collection of short stories, *In Love and Trouble: Stories of Black Women* (1973). The next year Walker began writing essays on the black experience and women's issues for *Ms.* magazine. In 1976 she published a novel, *Meridian*, about the civil rights movement. Also that year Leventhal and Walker were divorced.

Since then, Walker has continued to write poetry, short stories, essays, and novels. She published another volume of poems, *Goodnight, Willie Lee, I'll See You in the Morning*, in 1979, a collection of short stories, *You Can't Keep a Good Woman Down*, in 1981, and, in 1983, her most popular novel, *The Color Purple*, as well as her first collection of essays, *In Search of Our Mothers' Gardens*. In 1987 she published a second collection of essays, *Living by the Word*, and in 1989 another novel, *The Temple of My Familiar*. Her most recent book is *Her Blue Body Everything We Know: Earthling Poems 1965–1990 Complete*. Among her many awards, Alice Walker received a National Book Critics Circle Award nomination in 1982 and won both the American Book Award and the Pulitzer Prize for Literature in 1983.

Like Didion, Walker uses a cinematic cutting technique, juxtaposing events separate in time but connected by an underlying theme. Her analysis of these events is at first unobtrusive but gradually builds to an epiphany enlightened, as Walker explains in "Brothers and Sisters," by an outside context, an ideology that provides distance and insight: "All partisan movements add to the fullness of our understanding of society as a whole. They never detract; or, in any case, one must not allow them to do so." At its best, Walker's voice, like Hurston's, combines an informal, colloquial tone with an intense, concentrated diction. The last line of "Zora Neale Hurston: A Cautionary Tale and a Partisan View," for example, captures the political and the poetic in Walker's insistence that people need an artistic and intellectual tradition, that it is the duty of all *"witnesses for the future* to collect them [the geniuses] again for the sake of our children, and, if necessary, bone by bone." ✐

Zora Neale Hurston: A Cautionary Tale and a Partisan View[1]

I became aware of my need of Zora Neale Hurston's work some time before I knew her work existed. In late 1970 I was writing a story that required accurate material on voodoo practices among rural Southern blacks of the thirties; there seemed none available I could trust. A number of white, racist anthropologists and

---

[1] First published as the Foreword to *Zora Neale Hurston: A Literary Biography* (1977) and collected in *In Search of Our Mothers' Gardens* (1983).

folklorists of the period had, not surprisingly, disappointed and insulted me. They thought blacks inferior, peculiar, and comic, and for me this undermined, no, *destroyed*, the relevance of their books. Fortunately, it was then that I discovered *Mules and Men*, Zora's book on folklore, collecting, herself, and her small, all-black community of Eatonville, Florida. Because she immersed herself in her own culture even as she recorded its "big old lies," i.e., folk tales, it was possible to see how she and it (even after she had attended Barnard College and become a respected writer and apprentice anthropologist) fit together. The authenticity of her material was verified by her familiarity with its context, and I was soothed by her assurance that she was exposing not simply an adequate culture but a superior one. That black people can be on occasion peculiar and comic was knowledge she enjoyed. That they could be racially or culturally inferior to whites never seems to have crossed her mind.

The first time I heard Zora's *name*, I was auditing a black-literature class taught by the great poet Margaret Walker,[1] at Jackson State College in Jackson, Mississippi. The reason this fact later slipped my mind was that Zora's name and accomplishments came and went so fast. The class was studying the usual "giants" of black literature: Chesnutt,[2] Toomer,° Hughes,° Wright,° Ellison,[3] and Baldwin, with the hope of reaching LeRoi Jones[4] very soon. Jessie Fauset,[5] Nella Larsen,[6] Ann Petry,[7] Paule Marshall[8] (unequaled in intelligence, vision, craft by anyone of her generation, to put her contributions to our literature modestly), and Zora Neale Hurston were names appended, like verbal footnotes, to the illustrious all-male list that paralleled them. As far as I recall, none of their work was studied

---

[1]Poet and novelist (1915–), author of *Jubilee* (1966), *For My People* (1942, republished 1969), and *Richard Wright: Daemonic Genius* (1988).

[2]Charles Waddell (1858–1932), lawyer and author, said to be the first to deal with race from the black point of view. His works include three novels, *The House Behind the Cedars* (1900), *The Marrow of Tradition* (1901), and *The Colonel's Dream* (1905); two books of short stories; and a biography, *Frederick Douglass* (1899).

[3]Ralph (1914–), American novelist, professor at New York University, and essayist who wrote *The Invisible Man* (1952) and two collections of essays, *Shadow and Act* (1964) and *Going to the Territory* (1987).

[4](1934–) Also called Imamu Amiri Baraka, he is an American activist and author who wrote poems and plays such as *Dutchman*, *The Toilet*, and *The Slave* (all 1964), founded the Black Community Development and Defense Organization in 1968, and was one of the leaders of the National Black Political Caucus in 1972.

[5](1881–1961) An important figure in the Harlem Renaissance,° she was a novelist, a poet, and the first black woman admitted to Cornell University. Her novels include *There Is Confusion* (1924) and *Comedy: American Style* (1933).

[6]Librarian, nurse, and novelist (1891–1964). Her works include *Quicksand* (1928), *Passing* (1929), and several short stories.

[7]Novelist and short story writer (1908–) whose works include *The Narrows* (1953) and *Miss Muriel and Other Stories* (1971).

[8]Novelist and short story writer (1929–) best known for *Brown Girl, Brownstones* (1959) and *The Chosen Place, The Timeless People* (1969). Her stories were collected in *Reena and Other Stories* (1984).

in the course. Much of it was out of print, in any case, and remains so. (Perhaps Gwendolyn Brooks[1] and Margaret Walker herself were exceptions to this list; both poets of such obvious necessity it would be impossible to overlook them. And their work—owing to the political and cultural nationalism of the sixties— was everywhere available.)

When I read *Mules and Men* I was delighted. Here was this perfect book! The "perfection" of which I immediately tested on my relatives, who are such typical black Americans they are useful for every sort of political, cultural, or economic survey. Very regular people from the South, rapidly forgetting their Southern cultural inheritance in the suburbs and ghettos of Boston and New York, they sat around reading the book themselves, listening to me read the book, listening to each other read the book, and a kind of paradise was regained. For what Zora's book did was this: it gave them back all the stories they had forgotten or of which they had grown ashamed (told to us years ago by our parents and grandparents— not one of whom could *not* tell a story to make you weep, or laugh) and showed how marvelous, and, indeed, priceless, they are. This is not exaggerated. No matter how they read the stories Zora had collected, no matter how much distance they tried to maintain between themselves, as new sophisticates, and the lives their parents and grandparents lived, no matter how they tried to remain cool toward all Zora revealed, in the end they could not hold back the smiles, the laughter, the joy over who she was showing them to be: descendants of an inventive, joyous, courageous, and outrageous people; loving drama, appreciat- ing wit, and, most of all, relishing the pleasure of each other's loquacious and *bodacious* company.

This was my first indication of the quality I feel is most characteristic of Zora's work: racial health; a sense of black people as complete, complex, *undiminished* human beings, a sense that is lacking in so much black writing and literature. (In my opinion, only Du Bois° showed an equally consistent delight in the beauty and spirit of black people, which is interesting when one considers that the angle of his vision was completely the opposite of Zora's.) Zora's pride in black people was so pronounced in the ersatz black twenties that it made other blacks suspicious and perhaps uncomfortable (after all, *they* were still infatuated with things Euro- pean). Zora was interested in Africa, Haiti, Jamaica, and—for a little racial diver- sity (Indians)—Honduras. She also had a confidence in herself as an individual that few people (anyone?), black or white, understood. This was because Zora grew up in a community of black people who had enormous respect for them- selves and for their ability to govern themselves. Her own father had written the Eatonville town laws. This community affirmed her right to exist, and loved her as an extension of its self. For how many other black Americans is this true? It certainly isn't true for any that I know. In her easy self-acceptance, Zora was more

---

[1]Teacher and poet (1917–), she was the first black to win the Pulitzer Prize (1950). Her works include *Annie Allen* (1949), *Selected Poems* (1963), *Beckonings* (1975), and a novel, *Maud Martha* (1953).

like an uncolonized African than she was like her contemporary American blacks, most of whom believed, at least during their formative years, that their blackness was something wrong with them.

On the contrary, Zora's early work shows she grew up pitying whites because the ones she saw lacked "light" and soul. It is impossible to imagine Zora envying anyone (except tongue in cheek), and least of all a white person for being white. Which is, after all, if one is black, a clear and present calamity of the mind.

Condemned to a desert island for life, with an allotment of ten books to see me through, I would choose, unhesitatingly, two of Zora's: *Mules and Men*, because I would need to be able to pass on to younger generations the life of American blacks as legend and myth; and *Their Eyes Were Watching God*, because I would want to enjoy myself while identifying with the black heroine, Janie Crawford, as she acted out many roles in a variety of settings, and functioned (with spectacular results!) in romantic and sensual love. *There is no book more important to me than this one* (including Toomer's° *Cane*, which comes close, but from what I recognize is a more perilous direction).

Having committed myself to Zora's work, loving it, in fact, I became curious to see what others had written about her. This was, for the young, impressionable, barely begun writer I was, a mistake. After reading the misleading, deliberately belittling, inaccurate, and generally irresponsible attacks on her work and her life by almost everyone, I became for a time paralyzed with confusion and fear. For if a woman who had given so much of obvious value to all of us (and at such risks: to health, reputation, sanity) could be so casually pilloried and consigned to a sneering oblivion, what chance would someone else—for example, myself— have? I was aware that I had much less gumption than Zora.

For a long time I sat looking at this fear, and at what caused it. Zora was a woman who wrote and spoke her mind—as far as one could tell, practically always. People who knew her and were unaccustomed to this characteristic in a woman, who was, moreover, a. sometimes in error, and b. successful, for the most part, in her work, attacked her as meanly as they could. Would I also be attacked if I wrote and spoke my mind? And if I dared open my mouth to speak, must I always be "correct"? And by whose standards? Only those who have read the critics' opinions of Zora and her work will comprehend the power of these questions to riddle a young writer with self-doubt.

Eventually, however, I discovered that I repudiate and despise the kind of criticism that intimidates rather than instructs the young; and I dislike fear, especially in myself. I did then what fear rarely fails to force me to do: I fought back. I began to fight for Zora and her work; for what I knew was good and must not be lost to us.

Robert Hemenway was the first critic I read who seemed indignant that Zora's life ended in poverty and obscurity; that her last days were spent in a welfare home and her burial paid for by "subscription." Though Zora herself, as he is careful to point out in his book *Zora Neale Hurston: A Literary Biography*, remained gallant and unbowed until the end. It was Hemenway's efforts to define Zora's legacy and his exploration of her life that led me, in 1973, to an overgrown Fort Pierce, Florida graveyard in an attempt to locate and mark Zora's grave. Although by that time I considered her a native American genius, there was nothing grand or historic in my mind. It was, rather, a duty I accepted as naturally mine—as a black person, a woman, and a writer—because Zora was dead and I, for the time being, was alive.

Zora was funny, irreverent (she was the first to call the Harlem Renaissance°[1] literati[2] the "niggerati"), good-looking, sexy, and once sold hot dogs in a Washington park just to record accurately how the black people who bought the hot dogs talked. (A letter I received a month ago from one of her old friends in D.C. brought this news.) She would go anywhere she had to go: Harlem, Jamaica, Haiti, Bermuda, to find out anything she simply had to know. She loved to give parties. Loved to dance. Would wrap her head in scarves as black women in Africa, Haiti, and everywhere else have done for centuries. On the other hand, she loved to wear hats, tilted over one eye, and pants and boots. (I have a photograph of her in pants, boots, and broadbrim that was given to me by her brother, Everette. She has her foot up on the running board of a car—presumably hers, and bright red—and looks racy.) She would light up a fag—which wasn't done by ladies then (and, thank our saints, as a young woman she was never a lady) on the street.

Her critics disliked even the "rags" on her head. (They seemed curiously incapable of telling the difference between an African-American queen and Aunt Jemima.[3]) They disliked her apparent sensuality: the way she tended to marry or not marry men, but enjoyed them anyway—while never missing a beat in her work. They hinted slyly that Zora was gay, or at least bisexual—how else could they account for her drive? Though there is not, perhaps unfortunately, a shred of evidence that this was true. The accusation becomes humorous—and of course at all times irrelevant—when one considers that what she *did* write was one of the sexiest, most "healthily" rendered heterosexual love stories in our literature. In addition, she talked too much, got things from white folks (Guggenheims, Rosenwalds,[4] and footstools) much too easily, was slovenly in her dress, and appeared maddeningly indifferent to other people's opinions of her. With her easy laughter and her Southern drawl, her belief in doing "cullud" dancing authentically, Zora seemed—among these genteel "New Negroes" of the Harlem Renaissance°—*black*. No wonder her presence was always a shock. Though almost everyone agreed she was a delight, not everyone agreed such audacious black delight was permissible, or, indeed, quite the proper image for the race.

Zora was before her time, in intellectual circles, in the life style she chose. By the sixties everyone understood that black women could wear beautiful cloths on

---

[1]See also biography for Hurston, pp. 367–371.
[2]Italian for the "literary intelligentsia."
[3]Trademark of Quaker Oats, pictured on containers of syrup and packages of pancake mix.
[4]Guggenheims and Rosenwalds are foundation grants.

their beautiful heads and care about the authenticity of things "cullud" *and* African. By the sixties it was no longer a crime to receive financial assistance—in the form of grants and fellowships—for one's work. (Interestingly, those writers who complained that Zora "got money from white folks" were often themselves totally supported, down to the food they ate—or, in Langston Hughes's° case, *tried* to eat, after his white "Godmother"[1] discarded him—by white patrons.) By the sixties, nobody cared that marriage didn't last forever. No one expected it to. And I do believe that now, in the seventies, we do not expect (though we may wish and pray) every black person who speaks *always* to speak *correctly* (since this is impossible): and if we *do* expect it, we deserve all the silent leadership we are likely to get.

During the early and middle years of her career Zora was a cultural revolutionary simply because she was always herself. Her work, so vigorous among the rather pallid productions of many of her contemporaries, comes from the essence of black folk life. During her later life she became frightened of the life she had always dared bravely before. Her work too became reactionary, static, shockingly misguided and timid. (This is especially true of her last novel, *Seraphs on the Sewannee*, which is not even about black people, which is no crime, but *is* about white people for whom it is impossible to care, which is.)

A series of misfortunes battered Zora's spirit and her health. And she was broke.

Being broke made all the difference.

Without money of one's own in a capitalist society, there is no such thing as independence. This is one of the clearest lessons of Zora's life, and why I consider the telling of her life "a cautionary tale." We must learn from it what we can.

Without money, an illness, even a simple one, can undermine the will. Without money, getting into a hospital is problematic and getting out without money to pay for the treatment is nearly impossible. Without money, one becomes dependent on other people, who are likely to be—even in their kindness— erratic in their support and despotic in their expectations of return. Zora was forced to rely, like Tennessee Williams's Blanche,[2] "on the kindness of strangers." Can anything be more dangerous, if the strangers are forever in control? Zora, who worked so hard, was never able to make a living from her work.

She did not complain about not having money. She was not the type. (Several months ago I received a long letter from one of Zora's nieces, a bright ten-year-old, who explained to me that her aunt was so proud that the only way the family could guess she was ill or without funds was by realizing they had no idea where she was. Therefore, none of the family attended either Zora's sickbed or her funeral.) Those of us who have had "grants and fellowships from 'white folks' " know this aid is extended in precisely the way welfare is extended in Mississippi. One is asked, *curtly*, more often than not: How much do you need *just to survive?*

---

[1] Refers to Mrs. Charlotte Osgood Mason; see biography for Hurston.
[2] Blanche DuBois, the young, neurotic woman in his play *Streetcar Named Desire* (1947).

Then one is—if fortunate—given a third of that. What is amazing is that Zora, who became an orphan at nine, a runaway at fourteen, a maid and manicurist (because of necessity and not from love of the work) before she was twenty—with one dress—managed to become Zora Neale Hurston, author and anthropologist, at all.

For me, the most unfortunate thing Zora ever wrote is her autobiography. After the first several chapters, it rings false. One begins to hear the voice of someone whose life required the assistance of too many transitory "friends." A Taoist[1] proverb states that *to act sincerely with the insincere is dangerous*. (A mistake blacks as a group have tended to make in America.) And so we have Zora sincerely offering gratitude and kind words to people one knows she could not have respected. But this unctuousness, so out of character for Zora, is also a result of dependency, a sign of her powerlessness, her inability to pay back her debts with anything but words. They must have been bitter ones for her. In her dependency, it should be remembered, Zora was not alone—because it is quite true that America does not support or honor us as human beings, let alone as blacks, women, and artists. We have taken help where it was offered because we are committed to what we do and to the survival of our work. Zora was committed to the survival of her people's cultural heritage as well.

In my mind, Zora Neale Hurston, Billie Holiday,[2] and Bessie Smith[3] form a sort of unholy trinity. Zora *belongs* in the tradition of black women singers, rather than among "the literati," at least to me. There were the extreme highs and lows of her life, her undaunted pursuit of adventure, passionate emotional and sexual experience, and her love of freedom. Like Billie and Bessie she followed her own road, believed in her own gods, pursued her own dreams, and refused to separate herself from "common" people. It would have been nice if the three of them had had one another to turn to, in times of need. I close my eyes and imagine them: Bessie would be in charge of all the money; Zora would keep Billie's masochistic tendencies in check and prevent her from singing embarrassing anything-for-a-man songs, thereby preventing Billie's heroin addiction. In return, Billie could be, along with Bessie, the family that Zora felt she never had.

We are a people. A people do not throw their geniuses away. And if they are thrown away, it is our duty *as artists and as witnesses for the future* to collect them again for the sake of our children, and, if necessary, bone by bone. ✍

---

[1] From a Chinese philosophy, Taoism, said to have been founded by Lao-tzu, a sixth-century B.C. teacher who sought practical and spiritual harmony through a universal force. The proverbs come from the book *Tao-te-ching* or *Tao*, from the Chinese for "path."

[2] Great jazz singer (1915–1959) of the thirties and forties.

[3] Singer (1894–1937), called the "Empress of the Blues" in the twenties.

Beauty: When the Other Dancer Is the Self[1]

It is a bright summer day in 1947. My father, a fat, funny man with beautiful eyes and a subversive wit, is trying to decide which of his eight children he will take with him to the county fair. My mother, of course, will not go. She is knocked out from getting most of us ready: I hold my neck stiff against the pressure of her knuckles as she hastily completes the braiding and then beribboning of my hair.

My father is the driver for the rich old white lady up the road. Her name is Miss Mey. She owns all the land for miles around, as well as the house in which we live. All I remember about her is that she once offered to pay my mother thirty-five cents for cleaning her house, raking up piles of her magnolia leaves, and washing her family's clothes, and that my mother—she of no money, eight children, and a chronic earache—refused it. But I do not think of this in 1947. I am two and a half years old. I want to go everywhere my daddy goes. I am excited at the prospect of riding in a car. Someone has told me fairs are fun. That there is room in the car for only three of us doesn't faze me at all. Whirling happily in my starchy frock, showing off my biscuit-polished[2] patent-leather shoes and lavender socks, tossing my head in a way that makes my ribbons bounce, I stand, hands on hips, before my father. "Take me, Daddy," I say with assurance; "I'm the prettiest!"

Later, it does not surprise me to find myself in Miss Mey's shiny black car, sharing the back seat with the other lucky ones. Does not surprise me that I thoroughly enjoy the fair. At home that night I tell the unlucky ones all I can remember about the merry-go-round, the man who eats live chickens, and the teddy bears, until they say: that's enough, baby Alice. Shut up now, and go to sleep.

It is Easter Sunday, 1950. I am dressed in a green, flocked,[3] scalloped-hem dress (handmade by my adoring sister, Ruth) that has its own smooth satin petticoat and tiny hot-pink roses tucked into each scallop. My shoes, new T-strap patent leather, again highly biscuit-polished. I am six years old and have learned one of the longest Easter speeches to be heard that day, totally unlike the speech I said when I was two: "Easter lilies/pure and white/blossom in/the morning light." When I rise to give my speech I do so on a great wave of love and pride and expectation. People in the church stop rustling their new crinolines. They seem to hold their breath. I can tell they admire my dress, but it is my spirit, bordering on sassiness (womanishness), they secretly applaud.

"That girl's a little *mess*," they whisper to each other, pleased.

Naturally I say my speech without stammer or pause, unlike those who stutter, stammer, or, worst of all, forget. This is before the word "beautiful" exists in people's vocabulary, but "Oh, isn't she the *cutest* thing!" frequently floats my

---

[1]Published in *In Search of Our Mothers' Gardens*, 1983.
[2]Polished to a sheen like that on bisque pottery.
[3]Tufted with cotton to produce a textured pattern, usually across the upper third or half of a garment.

way. "And got so much sense!" they gratefully add . . . for which thoughtful addition I thank them to this day.

It was great fun being cute. But then, one day, it ended.

I am eight years old and a tomboy. I have a cowboy hat, cowboy boots, checkered shirt and pants, all red. My playmates are my brothers, two and four years older than I. Their colors are black and green, the only difference in the way we are dressed. On Saturday nights we all go to the picture show, even my mother; Westerns are her favorite kind of movie. Back home, "on the ranch," we pretend we are Tom Mix,[1] Hopalong Cassidy,[2] and Lash LaRue[3] (we've even named one of our dogs Lash LaRue); we chase each other for hours rustling cattle, being outlaws, delivering damsels from distress. Then my parents decide to buy my brothers guns. These are not "real" guns. They shoot "BBs," copper pellets my brothers say will kill birds. Because I am a girl, I do not get a gun. Instantly I am relegated to the position of Indian. Now there appears a great distance between us. They shoot and shoot at everything with their new guns. I try to keep up with my bow and arrows.

One day while I am standing on top of our makeshift "garage"—pieces of tin nailed across some poles—holding my bow and arrow and looking out toward the fields, I feel an incredible blow in my right eye. I look down just in time to see my brother lower his gun.

Both brothers rush to my side. My eye stings, and I cover it with my hand. "If you tell," they say, "we will get a whipping. You don't want that to happen, do you?" I do not. "Here is a piece of wire," says the older brother, picking it up from the roof; "say you stepped on one end of it and the other flew up and hit you." The pain is beginning to start. "Yes," I say. "Yes, I will say that is what happened." If I do not say this is what happened, I know my brothers will find ways to make me wish I had. But now I will say anything that gets me to my mother.

Confronted by our parents we stick to the lie agreed upon. They place me on a bench on the porch and I close my left eye while they examine the right. There is a tree growing from underneath the porch that climbs past the railing to the roof. It is the last thing my right eye sees. I watch as its trunk, its branches, and then its leaves are blotted out by the rising blood.

I am in shock. First there is intense fever, which my father tries to break using lily leaves bound around my head. Then there are chills: my mother tries to get me to eat soup. Eventually, I do not know how, my parents learn what has happened. A week after the "accident" they take me to see a doctor. "Why did you wait so long to come?" he asks, looking into my eye and shaking his head. "Eyes are sympathetic," he says. "If one is blind, the other will likely become blind too."

---

[1] Silent movie star (1880–1940) who wore a white suit, black boots, and a ten-gallon hat; he retired in 1928 after making one hundred pictures.
[2] Western hero played by William Boyd (1898–1972) in a series of films beginning in 1935 and a TV series in the fifties.
[3] Nickname of Frank H. LaRue (1878–1960), actor who played the whip-wielding cowboy in a series of films in the thirties and forties.

This comment of the doctor's terrifies me. But it is really how I look that bothers me most. Where the BB pellet struck there is a glob of whitish scar tissue, a hideous cataract, on my eye. Now when I stare at people—a favorite pastime, up to now—they will stare back. Not at the "cute" little girl, but at her scar. For six years I do not stare at anyone, because I do not raise my head.

Years later, in the throes of a mid-life crisis, I ask my mother and sister whether I changed after the "accident." "No," they say, puzzled. "What do you mean?"
What do I mean?

I am eight, and, for the first time, doing poorly in school, where I have been something of a whiz since I was four. We have just moved to the place where the "accident" occurred. We do not know any of the people around us because this is a different county. The only time I see the friends I knew is when we go back to our old church. The new school is the former state penitentiary. It is a large stone building, cold and drafty, crammed to overflowing with boisterous, ill-disciplined children. On the third floor there is a huge circular imprint of some partition that has been torn out.

"What used to be here?" I ask a sullen girl next to me on our way past it to lunch.

"The electric chair," says she.

At night I have nightmares about the electric chair, and about all the people reputedly "fried" in it. I am afraid of the school, where all the students seem to be budding criminals.

"What's the matter with your eye?" they ask, critically.

When I don't answer (I cannot decide whether it was an "accident" or not), they shove me, insist on a fight.

My brother, the one who created the story about the wire, comes to my rescue. But then brags so much about "protecting" me, I become sick.

After months of torture at the school, my parents decide to send me back to our old community, to my old school. I live with my grandparents and the teacher they board. But there is no room for Phoebe, my cat. By the time my grandparents decide there *is* room, and I ask for my cat, she cannot be found. Miss Yarborough, the boarding teacher, takes me under her wing, and begins to teach me to play the piano. But soon she marries an African—a "prince" she says—and is whisked away to his continent.

At my old school there is at least one teacher who loves me. She is the teacher who "knew me before I was born" and bought my first baby clothes. It is she who makes life bearable. It is her presence that finally helps me turn on the one child at the school who continually calls me "one-eyed bitch." One day I simply grab him by his coat and beat him until I am satisfied. It is my teacher who tells me my mother is ill.

My mother is lying in bed in the middle of the day, something I have never seen. She is in too much pain to speak. She has an abscess in her ear. I stand looking down on her, knowing that if she dies, I cannot live. She is being treated with warm oils and hot bricks held against her cheek. Finally a doctor comes. But I must go back to my grandparents' house. The weeks pass but I am hardly aware of it. All I know is that my mother might die, my father is not so jolly, my brothers still have their guns, and I am the one sent away from home.

"You did not change," they say.

Did I imagine the anguish of never looking up?

I am twelve. When relatives come to visit I hide in my room. My cousin Brenda, just my age, whose father works in the post office and whose mother is a nurse, comes to find me. "Hello," she says. And then she asks, looking at my recent school picture, which I did not want taken, and on which the "glob," as I think of it, is clearly visible, "You still can't see out of that eye?"

"No," I say, and flop back on the bed over my book.

That night, as I do almost every night, I abuse my eye. I rant and rave at it, in front of the mirror. I plead with it to clear up before morning. I tell it I hate and despise it. I do not pray for sight. I pray for beauty.

"You did not change," they say.

I am fourteen and baby-sitting for my brother Bill, who lives in Boston. He is my favorite brother and there is a strong bond between us. Understanding my feelings of shame and ugliness he and his wife take me to a local hospital, where the "glob" is removed by a doctor named O. Henry.[1] There is still a small bluish crater where the scar tissue was, but the ugly white stuff is gone. Almost immediately I become a different person from the girl who does not raise her head. Or so I think. Now that I've raised my head I win the boyfriend of my dreams. Now that I've raised my head I have plenty of friends. Now that I've raised my head classwork comes from my lips as faultlessly as Easter speeches did, and I leave high school as valedictorian, most popular student, and *queen*, hardly believing my luck. Ironically, the girl who was voted most beautiful in our class (and was) was later shot twice through the chest by a male companion, using a "real" gun, while she was pregnant. But that's another story in itself. Or is it?

"You did not change," they say.

It is now thirty years since the "accident." A beautiful journalist comes to visit and to interview me. She is going to write a cover story for her magazine that focuses on my latest book. "Decide how you want to look on the cover," she says. "Glamorous, or whatever."

Never mind "glamorous," it is the "whatever" that I hear. Suddenly all I can think of is whether I will get enough sleep the night before the photography session: if I don't, my eye will be tired and wander, as blind eyes will.

At night in bed with my lover I think up reasons why I should not appear on the cover of a magazine. "My meanest critics will say I've sold out," I say. "My family will now realize I write scandalous books."

---

[1]Also the name of a famous American short story writer (William Sidney Porter, 1862–1910) whose works are known for their ironic coincidences and surprise endings.

"But what's the real reason you don't want to do this?" he asks.

"Because in all probability," I say in a rush, "my eye won't be straight."

"It will be straight enough," he says. Then, "Besides, I thought you'd made your peace with that."

And I suddenly remember that I have.

I remember:

I am talking to my brother Jimmy, asking if he remembers anything unusual about the day I was shot. He does not know I consider that day the last time my father, with his sweet home remedy of cool lily leaves, chose me, and that I suffered and raged inside because of this. "Well," he says, "all I remember is standing by the side of the highway with Daddy, trying to flag down a car. A white man stopped, but when Daddy said he needed somebody to take his little girl to the doctor, he drove off."

I remember:

I am in the desert for the first time. I fall totally in love with it. I am so overwhelmed by its beauty, I confront for the first time, consciously, the meaning of the doctor's words years ago: "Eyes are sympathetic. If one is blind, the other will likely become blind too." I realize I have dashed about the world madly, looking at this, looking at that, storing up images against the fading of the light. *But I might have missed seeing the desert!* The shock of that possibility—and gratitude for over twenty- five years of sight—sends me literally to my knees. Poem after poem comes—which is perhaps how poets pray.

On Sight

I am so thankful I have seen
The Desert
And the creatures in the desert
And the desert Itself.

The desert has its own moon
Which I have seen
With my own eye.
There is no flag on it.

Trees of the desert have arms
All of which are always up
That is because the moon is up
The sun is up
Also the sky
The stars
Clouds
None with flags.

If there *were* flags, I doubt
the trees would point.
Would you?

But mostly, I remember this:

I am twenty-seven, and my baby daughter is almost three. Since her birth I have worried about her discovery that her mother's eyes are different from other people's. Will she be embarrassed? I think. What will she say? Every day she watches a television program called "Big Blue Marble." It begins with a picture of the earth as it appears from the moon. It is bluish, a little battered-looking, but full of light, with whitish clouds swirling around it. Every time I see it I weep with love, as if it is a picture of Grandma's house. One day when I am putting Rebecca down for her nap, she suddenly focuses on my eye. Something inside me cringes, gets ready to try to protect myself. All children are cruel about physical differences, I know from experience, and that they don't always mean to be is another matter. I assume Rebecca will be the same.

But no-o-o-o. She studies my face intently as we stand, her inside and me outside her crib. She even holds my face maternally between her dimpled little hands. Then, looking every bit as serious and lawyerlike as her father, she says, as if it may just possibly have slipped my attention: "Mommy, there's a *world* in your eye." (As in, "Don't be alarmed, or do anything crazy.") And then, gently, but with great interest: "Mommy, where did you *get* that world in your eye?"

For the most part, the pain left then. (So what if my brothers grew up to buy even more powerful pellet guns for their sons and to carry real guns themselves. So what, if a young "Morehouse man"[1] once nearly fell off the steps of Trevor Arnett Library because he thought my eyes were blue.) Crying and laughing I ran to the bathroom, while Rebecca mumbled and sang herself off to sleep. Yes indeed, I realized, looking into the mirror. There *was* a world in my eye. And I saw that it was possible to love it: that in fact, for all it had taught me of shame and anger and inner vision, I *did* love it. Even to see it drifting out of orbit in boredom, or rolling up out of fatigue, not to mention floating back at attention in excitement (bearing witness, a friend has called it), deeply suitable to my personality, and even characteristic of me.

That night I dream I am dancing to Stevie Wonder's song "Always" (the name of the song is really "As," but I hear it as "Always"). As I dance, whirling and joyous, happier than I've ever been in my life, another bright-faced dancer joins me. We dance and kiss each other and hold each other through the night. The other dancer has obviously come through all right, as I have done. She is beautiful, whole and free. And she is also me. ✿

---

[1]A student at Morehouse College in Atlanta, part of Atlanta University Center, with which Spelman College is also affiliated.

Richard Rodriguez

(1944–)

Richard Rodriguez was born in July of 1944 in San Francisco, California, the third child of Leopoldo and Victoria Moran Rodriguez. His parents met in California, both having come from Mexico hoping to improve their families' economic condition. When Rodriguez's father first arrived in America, he'd hoped to borrow money from a priest for his high school education, planning eventually to become an engineer. He courted Victoria Moran while they were attending night school and took her to the opera, each dressed in fancy clothes. But, as Rodriguez records in his autobiography, *Hunger of Memory: The Education of Richard Rodriguez*, the loan never came; after a number of janitorial and factory jobs, Rodriguez's father gave up going to the opera. His mother finished night school but "had been awarded a high school diploma by teachers too careless or busy to notice that she hardly spoke English." Unlike her sisters, who found work as maids, his mother taught herself to type so that she could work at "clean office jobs." Eventually Rodriguez's father found work as a dental technician and moved his young family to the middle-class neighborhood in Sacramento where Rodriguez grew up. After her last child entered school, his mother became a clerk-typist for a government office, proud of the words she could spell but not pronounce. Although neither of his parents read for pleasure, both knew the power of an education and saw to it that their children received the best they could find.

The four Rodriguez children attended the local Catholic parochial school, where the nuns insisted that they learn English and speak it, even at home. This introduction to public life as opposed to private, intimate life at home—and to reading, analysis, and quiet as opposed to family talk, spontaneity, and noise—gave Rodriguez the education so highly prized by his family but at the expense of their self-enclosed private world. His autobiography records this gain and its concomitant loss. Books and public language allowed all the Rodriguez children entrance into the upper middle class but cut them off in painful ways from the intimacies of a separate family life, from the differences that had permitted them to remain a close-knit family group.

Rodriguez argues that this pain and alienation are experienced by all children who move from the working class into professions requiring an academic background. For this reason he has written extensively opposing both bilingual education and affirmative action, contending that once people have entered the mainstream, supported by a solid education that allows them to achieve in the public world, they are no longer members of a minority, no longer in need of special consideration. The people, Rodriguez believes, who need special attention are those whose education is so inferior that, like his mother, they are unable to join the mainstream because they cannot speak the language and have no access to middle-class jobs and economic success.

Rodriguez was a successful student, earning a B.A. from Stanford in 1967 and an M.A. from Columbia University in 1969. From 1969 to 1972 he did graduate work at the University of California at Berkeley, and from 1972 to 1973 he studied at the Warburg Institute, London, on a Fulbright to do research for a dissertation in English Renaissance literature. When he returned to Berkeley in 1974, he found himself inundated with offers for speaking engagements and full-time teaching appointments at colleges and universities, even though he had not finished his dissertation. Gradually he came to believe that these offers were not based on his actual accomplishments, which he felt were no better than those of his fellow graduate students, who had not even been granted interviews. Instead, he believed, he was being courted because of his supposed minority status. After considerable anguish, angered by both right- and left-wing political groups who failed to understand his position, he rejected all offers, left graduate school, and devoted himself to writing.

Rodriguez was awarded a one-year fellowship from the National Endowment of the Humanities in 1976 to work on his autobiography. After that, he took on odd jobs until the book was published in 1981. In 1982 he won a Gold Medal from the Commonwealth Club, a Christopher Award, and the Anisfield-Wolf Award for Race Relations. A second book, *Mexico's Children*, is forthcoming. Richard Rodriguez is now an associate editor at the Pacific News Service in San Francisco and lives in a Victorian house in San Francisco's gay community.

Rodriguez's model is George Orwell (who was also a "scholarship boy"), and like him Rodriguez writes with compelling honesty about political and social issues, combining literature with journalism so that the art and richness of the language, the distinctive voice of the writer, is always on the page. He finds poetry in the details of everyday life: "One among the four chambers of the beating hearts of Mexicans is a cave of Mary. . . . You will see her image everywhere in Mexico as you will see it in the Southwest—in bubblegum colors or in lovely shades of melon—a decal on the car window;

the blue tattoo on an arm; a street mural in Los Angeles." Like Didion, whose upbringing, also in Sacramento, was worlds away from that of Rodriguez, he confronts his readers with direct questions that convey the immediacy of his concern for the lives of the people he describes. Asking "Can you understand?" he believes, like Orwell, that we must. ✒

Labor[1]

I went to college at Stanford, attracted partly by its academic reputation, partly because it was the school rich people went to. I found myself on a campus with golden children of western America's upper middle class. Many were students both ambitious for academic success *and* accustomed to leisured life in the sun. In the afternoon, they lay spread out, sunbathing in front of the library, reading Swift° or Engels[2] or Beckett.[3] Others went by in convertibles, off to play tennis or ride horses or sail. Beach boys dressed in tank-tops and shorts were my classmates in undergraduate seminars. Tall tan girls wearing white strapless dresses sat directly in front of me in lecture rooms. I'd study them, their physical confidence. I was still recognizably kin to the boy I had been. Less tortured perhaps. But still kin. At Stanford, it's true, I began to have something like a conventional sexual life. I don't think, however, that I really believed that the women I knew found me physically appealing. I continued to stay out of the sun. I didn't linger in mirrors. And I was the student at Stanford who remembered to notice the Mexican-American janitors and gardeners working on campus.

It was at Stanford, one day near the end of my senior year, that a friend told me about a summer construction job he knew was available. I was quickly alert. Desire uncoiled within me. My friend said that he knew I had been looking for summer employment. He knew I needed some money. Almost apologetically he explained: It was something I probably wouldn't be interested in, but a friend of his, a contractor, needed someone for the summer to do menial jobs. There would be lots of shoveling and raking and sweeping. Nothing too hard. But nothing more interesting either. Still, the pay would be good. Did I want it? Or did I know someone who did?

I did. Yes, I said, surprised to hear myself say it.

In the weeks following, friends cautioned that I had no idea how hard physical labor really is. ('You only *think* you know what it is like to shovel for eight hours straight.') Their objections seemed to me challenges. They resolved the

---

[1]From *Hunger of Memory: The Education of Richard Rodriguez*, 1982.
[2]See Marx.°
[3]Samuel (1906–1989), major playwright and novelist born in Dublin who lived in Paris and wrote such plays as *Waiting for Godot* (1952), *Endgame* (1957), and *Krapp's Last Tape* (1959), as well as poetry, short stories, and such novels as *Malloy* (1951), *Malone Dies* (1951), and *More Pricks than Kicks* (1970).

issue. I became happy with my plan. I decided, however, not to tell my parents. I wouldn't tell my mother because I could guess her worried reaction. I would tell my father only after the summer was over, when I could announce that, after all, I did know what 'real work' is like.

The day I met the contractor (a Princeton graduate, it turned out), he asked me whether I had done any physical labor before. 'In high school, during the summer,' I lied. And although he seemed to regard me with skepticism, he decided to give me a try. Several days later, expectant, I arrived at my first construction site. I would take off my shirt to the sun. And at last grasp desired sensation. No longer afraid. At last become like a *bracero*.[1] 'We need those tree stumps out of here by tomorrow,' the contractor said. I started to work.

I labored with excitement that first morning—and all the days after. The work was harder than I could have expected. But it was never as tedious as my friends had warned me it would be. There was too much physical pleasure in the labor. Especially early in the day, I would be most alert to the sensations of movement and straining. Beginning around seven each morning (when the air was still damp but the scent of weeds and dry earth anticipated the heat of the sun), I would feel my body resist the first thrusts of the shovel. My arms, tightened by sleep, would gradually loosen; after only several minutes, sweat would gather in beads on my forehead and then—a short while later—I would feel my chest silky with sweat in the breeze. I would return to my work. A nervous spark of pain would fly up my arm and settle to burn like an ember in the thick of my shoulder. An hour, two passed. Three. My whole body would assume regular movements; my shoveling would be described by identical, even movements. Even later in the day, my enthusiasm for primitive sensation would survive the heat and the dust and the insects prickling my back. I would strain wildly for sensation as the day came to a close. At three-thirty, quitting time, I would stand upright and slowly let my head fall back, luxuriating in the feeling of tightness relieved.

Some of the men working nearby would watch me and laugh. Two or three of the older men took the trouble to teach me the right way to use a pick, the correct way to shovel. 'You're doing it wrong, too fucking hard,' one man scolded. Then proceeded to show me—what persons who work with their bodies all their lives quickly learn—the most economical way to use one's body in labor.

'Don't make your back do so much work,' he instructed. I stood impatiently listening, half listening, vaguely watching, then noticed his work-thickened fingers clutching the shovel. I was annoyed. I wanted to tell him that I enjoyed shoveling the wrong way. And I didn't want to learn the right way. I wasn't afraid of back pain. I liked the way my body felt sore at the end of the day.

I was about to, but, as it turned out, I didn't say a thing. Rather it was at that moment I realized that I was fooling myself if I expected a few weeks of labor to gain me admission to the world of the laborer. I would not learn in three months what my father had meant by 'real work.' I was not bound to this job; I could

---

[1]A man who works with his arms, from *brazos*, Spanish for "arms."

imagine its rapid conclusion. For me the sensations of exertion and fatigue could be savored. For my father or uncle, working at comparable jobs when they were my age, such sensations were to be feared. Fatigue took a different toll on their bodies—and minds.

It was, I know, a simple insight. But it was with this realization that I took my first step that summer toward realizing something even more important about the 'worker.' In the company of carpenters, electricians, plumbers, and painters at lunch, I would often sit quietly, observant. I was not shy in such company. I felt easy, pleased by the knowledge that I was casually accepted, my presence taken for granted by men (exotics) who worked with their hands. Some days the younger men would talk and talk about sex, and they would howl at women who drove by in cars. Other days the talk at lunchtime was subdued; men gathered in separate groups. It depended on who was around. There were rough, good-natured workers. Others were quiet. The more I remember that summer, the more I realize that there was no single *type* of worker. I am embarrassed to say I had not expected such diversity. I certainly had not expected to meet, for example, a plumber who was an abstract painter in his off hours and admired the work of Mark Rothko.[1] Nor did I expect so many workers with college diplomas. (They were the ones who were not surprised that I intended to enter graduate school in the fall.) I suppose what I really want to say here is painfully obvious, but I must say it nevertheless: The men of that summer were middle-class Americans. They certainly didn't constitute an oppressed society. Carefully completing their work sheets; talking about the fortunes of local football teams; planning Las Vegas vacations; comparing the gas mileage of various makes of campers—they were not *los pobres*[2] my mother had spoken about.

On two occasions, the contractor hired a group of Mexican aliens. They were employed to cut down some trees and haul off debris. In all, there were six men of varying age. The youngest in his late twenties; the oldest (his father?) perhaps sixty years old. They came and they left in a single old truck. Anonymous men. They were never introduced to the other men at the site. Immediately upon their arrival, they would follow the contractor's directions, start working—rarely resting—seemingly driven by a fatalistic sense that work which had to be done was best done as quickly as possible.

I watched them sometimes. Perhaps they watched me. The only time I saw them pay me much notice was one day at lunchtime when I was laughing with the other men. The Mexicans sat apart when they ate, just as they worked by themselves. Quiet. I rarely heard them say much to each other. All I could hear were their voices calling out sharply to one another, giving directions. Otherwise, when they stood briefly resting, they talked among themselves in voices too hard to overhear.

---

[1]American painter (1903–1970) born in Russia and known for abstract paintings of brightly colored, floating rectangles.
[2]Spanish for "the poor."

The contractor knew enough Spanish, and the Mexicans—or at least the oldest of them, their spokesman—seemed to know enough English to communicate. But because I was around, the contractor decided one day to make me his translator. (He assumed I could speak Spanish.) I did what I was told. Shyly I went over to tell the Mexicans that the *patrón* wanted them to do something else before they left for the day. As I started to speak, I was afraid with my old fear that I would be unable to pronounce the Spanish words. But it was a simple instruction I had to convey. I could say it in phrases.

The dark sweating faces turned toward me as I spoke. They stopped their work to hear me. Each nodded in response. I stood there. I wanted to say something more. But what could I say in Spanish, even if I could have pronounced the words right? Perhaps I just wanted to engage them in small talk, to be assured of their confidence, our familiarity. I thought for a moment to ask them where in Mexico they were from. Something like that. And maybe I wanted to tell them (a lie, if need be) that my parents were from the same part of Mexico.

I stood there.

Their faces watched me. The eyes of the man directly in front of me moved slowly over my shoulder, and I turned to follow his glance toward *el patrón* some distance away. For a moment I felt swept up by that glance into the Mexicans' company. But then I heard one of them returning to work. And then the others went back to work. I left them without saying anything more.

When they had finished, the contractor went over to pay them in cash. (He later told me that he paid them collectively—'for the job,' though he wouldn't tell me their wages. He said something quickly about the good rate of exchange 'in their own country.') I can still hear the loudly confident voice he used with the Mexicans. It was the sound of the *gringo*[1] I had heard as a very young boy. And I can still hear the quiet, indistinct sounds of the Mexican, the oldest, who replied. At hearing that voice I was sad for the Mexicans. Depressed by their vulnerability. Angry at myself. The adventure of the summer seemed suddenly ludicrous. I would not shorten the distance I felt from *los pobres* with a few weeks of physical labor. I would not become like them. They were different from me.

After that summer, a great deal—and not very much really—changed in my life. The curse of physical shame was broken by the sun; I was no longer ashamed of my body. No longer would I deny myself the pleasing sensations of my maleness. During those years when middle-class black Americans began to assert with pride, 'Black is beautiful,' I was able to regard my complexion without shame. I am today darker than I ever was as a boy. I have taken up the middle-class sport of long-distance running. Nearly every day now I run ten or fifteen miles, barely clothed, my skin exposed to the California winter rain and wind or the summer sun of late afternoon. The torso, the soccer player's calves and thighs, the arms of the twenty-year-old I never was, I possess now in my thirties. I study the youthful

---

[1]Non-Hispanic American.

parody shape in the mirror: the stomach lipped tight by muscle; the shoulders rounded by chin-ups; the arms veined strong. This man. A man. I meet him. He laughs to see me, what I have become.

The dandy. I wear double-breasted Italian suits and custom-made English shoes. I resemble no one so much as my father—the man pictured in those honeymoon photos. At that point in life when he abandoned the dandy's posture, I assume it. At the point when my parents would not consider going on vacation, I register at the Hotel Carlyle in New York and the Plaza Athenée in Paris. I am as taken by the symbols of leisure and wealth as they were. For my parents, however, those symbols became taunts, reminders of all they could not achieve in one lifetime. For me those same symbols are reassuring reminders of public success. I tempt vulgarity to be reassured. I am filled with the gaudy delight, the monstrous grace of the nouveau riche.

In recent years I have had occasion to lecture in ghetto high schools. There I see students of remarkable style and physical grace. (One can see more dandies in such schools than one ever will find in middle-class high schools.) There is not the look of casual assurance I saw students at Stanford display. Ghetto girls mimic high-fashion models. Their dresses are of bold, forceful color; their figures elegant, long; the stance theatrical. Boys wear shirts that grip at their overdeveloped muscular bodies. (Against a powerless future, they engage images of strength.) Bad nutrition does not yet tell. Great disappointment, fatal to youth, awaits them still. For the moment, movements in school hallways are dancelike, a procession of postures in a sexual masque. Watching them, I feel a kind of envy. I wonder how different my adolescence would have been had I been free. . . . But no, it is my parents I see—their optimism during those years when they were entertained by Italian grand opera.

The registration clerk in London wonders if I have just been to Switzerland. And the man who carries my luggage in New York guesses the Caribbean. My complexion becomes a mark of my leisure. Yet no one would regard my complexion the same way if I entered such hotels through the service entrance. That is only to say that my complexion assumes its significance from the context of my life. My skin, in itself, means nothing. I stress the point because I know there are people who would label me 'disadvantaged' because of my color. They make the same mistake I made as a boy, when I thought a disadvantaged life was circumscribed by particular occupations. That summer I worked in the sun may have made me physically indistinguishable from the Mexicans working nearby. (My skin was actually darker because, unlike them, I worked without wearing a shirt. By late August my hands were probably as tough as theirs.) But I was not one of *los pobres*. What made me different from them was an attitude of *mind*, my imagination of myself.

I do not blame my mother for warning me away from the sun when I was young. In a world where her brother had become an old man in his twenties because he was dark, my complexion was something to worry about. 'Don't run in the sun,' she warns me today. I run. In the end, my father was right—though perhaps he did not know how right or why—to say that I would never know what real work is. I will never know what he felt at his last factory job. If tomorrow I worked at some kind of factory, it would go differently for me. My long education would favor me. I could act as a public person—able to defend my interests, to unionize, to petition, to speak up—to challenge and demand. (I will never know what real work is.) I will never know what the Mexicans knew, gathering their shovels and ladders and saws.

Their silence stays with me now. The wages those Mexicans received for their labor were only a measure of their disadvantaged condition. Their silence is more telling. They lack a public identity. They remain profoundly alien. Persons apart. People lacking a union obviously, people without grounds. They depend upon the relative good will or fairness of their employers each day. For such people, lacking a better alternative, it is not such an unreasonable risk.

Their silence stays with me. I have taken these many words to describe its impact. Only: the quiet. Something uncanny about it. Its compliance. Vulnerability. Pathos. As I heard their truck rumbling away, I shuddered, my face mirrored with sweat. I had finally come face to face with *los pobres*. ✐

Mañana[1]

The sea is blue. A dusty road leads through eucalyptus, past the cemetery, to the village. The house is empty, shuttered, locked. The clay stove is cold enough for spiders, which spin and twirl like uninterrupted angels. The echo answers all questions.

The future? What will happen if Latin American civil war spreads? What will happen if the Mexican government explodes from bloated corruption? Where is the end to the line of illegal immigrants?

It is 1986 and the border does not hold.[2] Entire families are coming, grandmothers, uncles, cousins. America is no longer the male's solitary journey as it was in the 1940s, the 1950s, the 1960s. More of the family is now here than there. But the decision to leave for the American city was not virtuous; it was governed by pragmatism. In their warm American kitchen, Mexicans talk among beer bottles of an eventual return to the empyrean.[3]

America wants to tell the new immigrants that she is sorry—and she is sorry—but there is not enough space, air, welfare—not enough America for all who would come. But then Americans take the Mexicans up on their offer of

---

[1]From "Mexico's Children," published in the *American Scholar*, Spring 1986.
[2]Echo of a well-known line from "The Second Coming" by Yeats°: "Things fall apart; the centre cannot hold; / Mere anarchy is loosed upon the world."
[3]The heights of heaven, the realm of pure light.

cheap labor. Mexicans are all around the neighborhood on Saturdays, making those pleasant faraway sounds, buzzing, chopping, mowing. They have become the new Americans, busy at a time when we grow more leisured, more Latin.

For the time being, Mexicans continue to arrive with punctual innocence. No intention to be disrespectful of American laws, *señor*, but necessity is necessity. The past meets the future in an opposing glance. The American wonders about the future; the Mexican immigrant broods over the past.

I can imagine a drama, perhaps a tragedy, an outburst of xenophobia[1] played out in the American Southwest. And because the poor have the most to lose from uncontrolled immigration, I imagine Mexican Americans joining the resistance to more immigrants, just as I imagine black Americans resisting illegal immigration.

Mexican Americans become a people whose future gets told in numbers. In the 1970s our population nearly doubled. We are now eight million officially; unofficially (guessing at those illegally here) we are eleven million, maybe more. On a statistical plane, we are twenty-two years old. We are married. We have babies. Mexican-American women show the highest fertility rate of any ethnic group in America. We are 60 percent of the nation's entire Hispanic population.

A commonplace of recent articles about us is that, along with other Hispanics, Mexicans Americans are destined to "displace" blacks as America's largest minority group by the year 2020 or sooner. This prediction is nonsensical in that Hispanics are an ethnic group not a racial group—many Hispanics are black. The dangerous future I envision is one in which Hispanic numbers will be used as a way of evading the black in America. The danger commonly conjured is that the numbers portend an American Quebec. And while we talk, the numbers race, the odds change like digits on a bookie's marquee. America is the fifth-largest Spanish-speaking country in the world (behind Mexico, Spain, Argentina, and Colombia).

Most articles on Mexico end up in a jumble of numbers, unreadable, usually accompanied by photographs that will casually break your heart. In one such paragraph, I see the teenaged father walking down the street with three children, and only here can I read the writing on the wall. The Shavian[2] life force belongs to them. I am unmarried, barren, witty. My day is spent with you; we are neighbors. As much as you could be, I am awed by the generosity of the Mexican immigrant's embrace of his child. I have heard these new immigrants sing hymns on Sundays, heard hymns in Catholic churches sung with stunning faith. The future is theirs. Their ascendancy has nothing to do with borders. It is simply a matter of time. I, meanwhile, have cast my lot with you in the America of *Time* magazine, the *Time* that had a cover story on Mexico titled "The Population Curse"—as though life, and not illness and poverty and death, was the true enemy.

---

[1] Fear of foreigners.
[2] Characteristic of George Bernard Shaw.°

In his office, the Catholic bishop, a Mexican American, points over my shoulder to a mosaic image of Our Lady of Guadalupe[1] on the wall. "That is the way I think of American society," the bishop says. "America is not a melting pot. America is more like that—a mosaic made up of different colors, each beautiful, but united to produce a work of art."

America's bishops have made headlines with their opinions about the MX missile and the morality of capitalism. Less publicized has been their "Pastoral Letter on Hispanic Ministry" issued in 1984, wherein the bishops announced themselves to be against assimilation as a social goal for Hispanics. They wrote: "The Church shows its esteem for the dignity of Hispanic culture by working to ensure pluralism, not assimilation and uniformity." But while the bishops piously fret themselves with the thought that Hispanics may be changed too much by America, Hispanics are destined to change America, change the very tenor of institutions like the Roman Catholic church. By the end of the century, half of the world's Catholics will be Spanish-speaking. Already in the United States, one Catholic in four is Hispanic. Numbers make it inevitable that Hispanics will reshape the character of an American church that has been, for over a century, largely Irish in cast.

I am speaking of assimilation. I am not speaking of tacos or bilingual voting ballots. I am speaking of the soul, the real soul, which passes matter and surpasses matter. The residue of the past is told in a mood, a gesture of hands, a tone of voice. A man who knows my family well tells me today that when I write in English he can recognize the sound of my father speaking in Spanish. This is the way Mexico will influence America in the future: American English will be changed by the Mexican immigrant children who put it in their mouths. Optimism will be weighted, in time, by some thicker mood.

Meanwhile, I am about as much of Mexico as you are going to get on paper. Diluted: a second-generation American, a middle-class man, a man born to the city, someone who is interested in Mexico. The obvious truth about assimilation is that it is never even. The advantage goes to the more numerous, the longer settled, the wealthy. The child of immigrant parents goes off to school and comes home knowing more about British kings than about his grandfather's travail. (So it was that America happened to me. I turned into you.) But if assimilation is never equal, assimilation is always reciprocal.

Mexican Americans are destined to become your neighbors, your boyfriends, your wives, your uncles. We will change you. Mexico will change you. But Mexico's greatest influence will be carried by an Americanized middle class and not by the less assimilated working class. The paradox of assimilation is that

---

[1]As Rodriguez explains earlier in the essay, "Mexicans believe that in the sixteenth century the Christian Mary, in the spangled raiment of an Aztec princess, appeared to an Indian. . . . To this Virgin Mary the Mexican turns today, not so much in hope of miraculous change, as for consolation in sorrow (all that she promised was to share human suffering)."

ethnic influence occurs not when people live apart, in distinct and separate neighborhoods, but—where it seems least likely to happen—in the arena of the middle class, the great American mall.

My nephews and nieces today. They will grow up and we will call them Hispanic. Hispanic is the word for their future. Already "Mexican American" as a political category, an idea, is being transposed to "Hispanic." The same has happened to other immigrant groups in this country. Think of the Jewish immigrants or the Italians. Many came, carefully observing Old World distinctions and rivalries. German Jews distinguished themselves from Russian Jews. The Venetian was adamant about not being taken for a Neapolitan.[1] But to America, what did such claims matter? All Italians looked and sounded the same. A Jew was a Jew. And now America shrugs again. Palm trees or cactus, it's all the same; Hispanics are all the same.

Puerto Ricans, Central Americans, Cuban Americans—all are becoming Hispanic. A new group consciousness is being forged on this side of the border. A new accent is being heard, a uniform American Spanish. Politicians already have gotten the point. There is strength in Hispanic numbers and there is bound to be influence. The Mexican-American activist (né the Chicano) is now a Hispanic politician.

A century ago, *Spanish* was the acceptable term. To those Mexican Americans who claimed to be Spanish came admission to circles of civility. Spanish meant light skin, of course, though it was not always an exact racial designation. To be Spanish meant that one had money or the memory of money or pretense to money. Spanish meant land. Today's term is *Hispanic*. It signals a movement out of the barrio,[2] the wider view taken. The smart coinage. The adjective that fits an emerging middle class of business executives and lawyers and doctors and writers like me.

But you have to wonder how far the term will take us. For the middle-class Mexican American, intermarriage outside the group has long been possible; it is common today. At the very moment of our numerical celebrity, we may be about to disappear into the melting pot. *Hispanic*, as our middle-class label, may turn out to be an ironic badge of influence that signals, in but another generation, our political decline.

My youngest nephew stares at me with dark eyes. He has blond hair. I think it is Mexico I see in his eyes, the unfathomable regard of the past, while ahead of him stretches Sesame Street. What will he think of his past, except to know that he has several? What will he know of Mexico except to know that his ancestors lived on land he will never inherit? What Mexico bequeaths to him passes silently through his heart, something to take with him as he disappears, like my father, into America. ✎

---

[1] From Naples.
[2] A Spanish-speaking community.

• • •

Annie Dillard

(1945–)

Annie Dillard was born in April of 1945 in Pennsylvania, the eldest of the three daughters of Frank and Pam Lambert Doak, members of Pittsburg's upper middle class. Her father, a Presbyterian, a Republican, and the only child of a banker, worked as the personnel manager of a firm founded in the 1840s by his mother's grandfather. Her mother, a witty, inventive woman, stayed home to oversee the household chores, arrange gatherings with friends, and drive the children to and from private school, art lessons, dancing school, ball games, and the pool at the country club. In her autobiography, *An American Childhood*, Dillard says her mother was underutilized, a "Samson in chains."

In the book Dillard describes her awakening to the outside world and "a life of concentration." She focuses on the year her father decided to quit his job, withdraw his investments in the firm, and, prompted by Twain's *Life on the Mississippi*, take his boat down the river to New Orleans. He left his wife, ten-year-old Annie, seven-year-old Amy, six-month-old Molly, the maid, and a nanny to keep up appearances until, lonely and worried about what people might think, he returned to civility six weeks later. This event, tying together reading and adventure in a brief escape from the dutiful life, is the touchstone of Dillard's autobiography. Even at ten, Dillard was intense, reading *Kidnapped*, *The Field Book of Ponds and Streams*, and *The Natural Way to Draw*, pitching ball, drawing, doing detective work, examining rocks and fossils, playing piano and field hockey, and looking through her microscope at hydra and rotifers, often "in a rapture," always testing her limits.

As a teenager, however, Dillard "vanished into a blinded rage," railing at the hypocrisy she believed she saw in church, at the men and women who paraded their wealth and power in "sable stoles" and "tailcoats" Sunday mornings and spent Sunday nights at the country club. Like the downed lines she had seen during a tornado, she was a "live wire, shooting out sparks that were digging a pit around me." She drew obsessively all over her school notebooks, got suspended briefly for smoking, read the French symbolists, wrote poetry, pounded out "Shake, Rattle, and Roll" on the piano, loved her boyfriend "so tenderly" that she thought she'd "transmogrify into vapor," and went on a drag race with boys she hardly knew, ending up in the hospital and later on crutches, an embarrassment and wonder to her family. Finally, mercifully, in 1963 she packed herself off to Hollins College in Virginia, where the English department could "smooth off her rough edges."

At Hollins she studied theology as well as English and married her creative writing teacher, Richard Dillard, a poet and novelist, at the end of her sophomore year. Her rejection of religion, she said in 1978, had lasted only a month during her senior year in high school. She has remained in "the arms of Christianity" ever since. After earning her B.A. in 1967 and M.A. in 1968, Dillard remained in the Hollins area, painting and writing. In 1974 she published two books: a collection of her poems, *Tickets for a Prayer Wheel*; and her eclectic notes on nature and theology, *Pilgrim at Tinker Creek*, for which she was awarded the Pulitzer Prize for nonfiction in 1975. That year she and her husband were divorced, and Dillard moved to Washington to teach poetry and creative writing at Western Washington State University. While there, she wrote a column for the periodical of the Wilderness Society, worked as contributing editor of *Harper's*, and wrote her third book, *Holy the Firm* (1977), an aesthetic, ecstatic exploration of God and pain. From 1979 to 1981 she taught at Wesleyan University; in 1980 she married Gary Clevidence, a novelist, but the two have separated. Since then Dillard has written a series of personal narratives entitled *Teaching a Stone to Talk* (1982) and a critical appreciation of stories and novels, *Living by Fiction* (1982). Her most recent books are her autobiography, *An American Childhood* (1987), and *A Writing Life* (1989), eclectic thoughts about writing books.

Like William Hazlitt, who also dabbled in art, Annie Dillard is a master of a range of styles, moving from the plain style of her critical essays in *Living by Fiction* and much of her autobiography to the baroque prose of *Pilgrim at Tinker Creek*, *Holy the Firm*, and *A Writing Life*. Dillard draws details from nature, defining with equal vividness the "parallel rods" at the back of a boy's neck, the abdomen of an earwig, or the "translucent" skin of a deer. Like Sir Thomas Browne, she is fascinated with God and death and nature; like his prose, hers reflects a mind intent on seeing the truth of death and the image of transfiguration. ✐

The Death of a Moth[1]

Transfiguration in a Candle Flame

I live alone with two cats, who sleep on my legs. There is a yellow one, and a black one whose name is Small. In the morning I joke to the black one, Do you remember last night? Do you remember? I throw them both out before breakfast, so I can eat.

There is a spider, too, in the bathroom, of uncertain lineage, bulbous at the abdomen and drab, whose six-inch mess of web works, works somehow, works miraculously, to keep her alive and me amazed. The web is in a corner behind the toilet, connecting tile wall to tile wall. The house is new, the bathroom immaculate, save for the spider, her web, and the sixteen or so corpses she's tossed to the floor.

The corpses appear to be mostly sow bugs, those little armadillo creatures who live to travel flat out in houses, and die round. In addition to sow-bug husks, hollow and sipped empty of color, there are what seem to be two or three wingless moth bodies, one new flake of earwig, and three spider carcasses crinkled and clenched.

I wonder on what fool's errand an earwig, or a moth, or a sow bug, would visit that clean corner of the house behind the toilet; I have not noticed any blind parades of sow bugs blundering into corners. Yet they do hazard there, at a rate of more than one a week, and the spider thrives. Yesterday she was working on the earwig, mouth on gut; today he's on the floor. It must take a certain genius to throw things away from there, to find a straight line through that sticky tangle to the floor.

Today the earwig shines darkly, and gleams, what there is of him: a dorsal curve of thorax and abdomen, and a smooth pair of pincers by which I knew his name. Next week, if the other bodies are any indication, he'll be shrunk and gray, webbed to the floor with dust. The sow bugs beside him are curled and empty, fragile, a breath away from brittle fluff. The spiders lie on their sides, translucent and ragged, their legs drying in knots. The moths stagger against each other, headless, in a confusion of arcing strips of chitin[2] like peeling varnish, like a jumble of buttresses for cathedral vaults, like nothing resembling moths, so that I would hesitate to call them moths, except that I have had some experience with the figure Moth reduced to a nub.

Two summers ago I was camped alone in the Blue Ridge Mountains of Virginia. I had hauled myself and gear up there to read, among other things, *The Day on*

---

[1]First published in 1976.
[2]Substance composing the outer crust on insects and crustaceans.

Fire, by James Ullman, a novel about Rimbaud[1] that had made me want to be a writer when I was sixteen; I was hoping it would do it again. So I read every day sitting under a tree by my tent, while warblers sang in the leaves overhead and bristle worms trailed their inches over the twiggy dirt at my feet; and I read every night by candlelight, while barred owls called in the forest and pale moths seeking mates massed round my head in the clearing, where my light made a ring.

Moths kept flying into the candle. They would hiss and recoil, reeling upside down in the shadows among my cooking pans. Or they would singe their wings and fall, and their hot wings, as if melted, would stick to the first thing they touched—a pan, a lid, a spoon—so that the snagged moths could struggle only in tiny arcs, unable to flutter free. These I could release by a quick flip with a stick; in the morning I would find my cooking stuff decorated with torn flecks of moth wings, ghostly triangles of shiny dust here and there on the aluminum. So I read, and boiled water, and replenished candles, and read on.

One night a moth flew into the candle, was caught, burnt dry, and held. I must have been staring at the candle, or maybe I looked up where a shadow crossed my page; at any rate, I saw it all. A golden female moth, a biggish one with a two-inch wingspread, flapped into the fire, dropped abdomen into the wet wax, stuck, flamed, and frazzled in a second. Her moving wings ignited like tissue paper, like angels' wings, enlarging the circle of light in the clearing and creating out of the darkness the sudden blue sleeves of my sweater, the green leaves of jewelweed by my side, the ragged red trunk of a pine; at once the light contracted again and the moth's wings vanished in a fine, foul smoke. At the same time, her six legs clawed, curled, blackened, and ceased, disappearing utterly. And her head jerked in spasms, making a spattering noise; her antennae crisped and burnt away and her heaving mouthparts cracked like pistol fire. When it was all over, her head was, so far as I could determine, gone, gone the long way of her wings and legs. Her head was a hole lost to time. All that was left was the glowing horn shell of her abdomen and thorax—a fraying, partially collapsed gold tube jammed upright in the candle's round pool.

And then this moth-essence, this spectacular skeleton, began to act as a wick. She kept burning. The wax rose in the moth's body from her soaking abdomen to her thorax to the shattered hole where her head should have been, and widened into flame, a saffron-yellow flame that robed her to the ground like an immolating monk. That candle had two wicks, two winding flames of identical light, side by side. The moth's head was fire. She burned for two hours, until I blew her out.

She burned for two hours without changing, without swaying or kneeling—only glowing within, like a building fire glimpsed through silhouetted walls, like a hollow saint, like a flame-faced virgin gone to God, while I read by her light,

---

[1]Arthur (1854–1891), French symbolist poet who lived from 1872 to 1873 in Paris, London, and Brussels with another poet, Paul Verlaine (1844–1896), until Verlaine, while drunk, shot and wounded him with a pistol. After returning home, Rimbaud wrote his autobiography, *Une saison en enfer* (*A Season in Hell*, 1873) and a series of prose poems, *Illuminations*. Among his most famous poems are "Le Bateau ivre" ("The Drunken Boat") and "Le Dormeur du val" ("The Sleeper in the Vale"). Rimbaud died in Marseilles after the amputation of his leg.

kindled, while Rimbaud in Paris burnt out his brain in a thousand poems, while night pooled wetly at my feet.

So. That is why I think those hollow shreds on the bathroom floor are moths. I believe I know what moths look like, in any state.

I have three candles here on the table which I disentangle from the plants and light when visitors come. The cats avoid them, although Small's tail caught fire once; I rubbed it out before she noticed. I don't mind living alone. I like eating alone and reading. I don't mind sleeping alone. The only time I mind being alone is when something is funny; then, when I am laughing at something funny, I wish someone were around. Sometimes I think it is pretty funny that I sleep alone. 🌣

The Deer at Providencia[1]

There were four of us North Americans in the jungle, in the Ecuadorian jungle on the banks of the Napo River in the Amazon watershed. The other three North Americans were metropolitan men. We stayed in tents in one riverside village, and visited others. At the village called Providencia we saw a sight which moved us, and which shocked the men.

The first thing we saw when we climbed the riverbank to the village of Providencia was the deer. It was roped to a tree on the grass clearing near the thatch shelter where we would eat lunch.

The deer was small, about the size of a whitetail fawn, but apparently full-grown. It had a rope around its neck and three feet caught in the rope. Someone said that the dogs had caught it that morning and the villagers were going to cook and eat it that night.

This clearing lay at the edge of the little thatched-hut village. We could see the villagers going about their business, scattering feed corn for hens about their houses, and wandering down paths to the river to bathe. The village headman was our host; he stood beside us as we watched the deer struggle. Several village boys were interested in the deer; they formed part of the circle we made around it in the clearing. So also did four businessmen from Quito who were attempting to guide us around the jungle. Few of the very different people standing in this circle had a common language. We watched the deer, and no one said much.

The deer lay on its side at the rope's very end, so the rope lacked slack to let it rest its head in the dust. It was "pretty," delicate of bone like all deer, and thin-skinned for the tropics. Its skin looked virtually hairless, in fact, and almost translucent, like a membrane. Its neck was no thicker than my wrist; it was rubbed open on the rope, and gashed. Trying to paw itself free of the rope, the deer had scratched its own neck with its hooves. The raw underside of its neck showed

---

[1]From *Teaching a Stone to Talk*, 1982.

red stripes and some bruises bleeding inside the muscles. Now three of its feet were hooked in the rope under its jaw. It could not stand, of course, on one leg, so it could not move to slacken the rope and ease the pull on its throat and enable it to rest its head.

Repeatedly the deer paused, motionless, its eyes veiled, with only its rib cage in motion, and its breaths the only sound. Then, after I would think, "It has given up; now it will die," it would heave. The rope twanged; the tree leaves clattered; the deer's free foot beat the ground. We stepped back and held our breaths. It thrashed, kicking, but only one leg moved; the other three legs tightened inside the rope's loop. Its hip jerked; its spine shook. Its eyes rolled; its tongue, thick with spittle, pushed in and out. Then it would rest again. We watched this for fifteen minutes.

Once three young native boys charged in, released its trapped legs, and jumped back to the circle of people. But instantly the deer scratched up its neck with its hooves and snared its forelegs in the rope again. It was easy to imagine a third and then a fourth leg soon stuck, like Brer Rabbit and the Tar Baby.[1]

We watched the deer from the circle, and then we drifted on to lunch. Our palm-roofed shelter stood on a grassy promontory from which we could see the deer tied to the tree, pigs and hens walking under village houses, and black-and-white cattle standing in the river. There was even a breeze.

Lunch, which was the second and better lunch we had that day, was hot and fried. There was a big fish called *doncella*, a kind of catfish, dipped whole in corn flour and beaten egg, then deep fried. With our fingers we pulled soft fragments of it from its sides to our plates, and ate; it was delicate fish-flesh, fresh and mild. Someone found the roe, and I ate of that too—it was fat and stronger, like egg yolk, naturally enough, and warm.

There was also a stew of meat in shreds with rice and pale brown gravy. I had asked what kind of deer it was tied to the tree; Pepe had answered in Spanish, "*Gama*." Now they told us this was *gama* too, stewed. I suspect the word means merely game or venison. At any rate, I heard that the village dogs had cornered another deer just yesterday, and it was this deer which we were now eating in full sight of the whole article. It was good. I was surprised at its tenderness. But it is a fact that high levels of lactic acid, which builds up in muscle tissues during exertion, tenderizes.

After the fish and meat we ate bananas fried in chunks and served on a tray; they were sweet and full of flavor. I felt terrific. My shirt was wet and cool from swimming; I had had a night's sleep, two decent walks, three meals, and a swim—everything tasted good. From time to time each of us, separately, would look

---

[1]Drawing on the stories he had heard from the slaves in his hometown of Eatonton, Georgia, Joel Chandler Harris (1846–1908) published *Uncle Remus: His Songs and Sayings* (1881), *The Tar Baby* (1904), and *Uncle Remus and Br'er Rabbit* (1906), on which Walt Disney (1901–1966) based his popular movie *Song of the South* (1946).

beyond our shaded roof to the sunny spot where the deer was still convulsing in the dust. Our meal completed, we walked around the deer and back to the boats.

That night I learned that while we were watching the deer, the others were watching me.

We four North Americans grew close in the jungle in a way that was not the usual artificial intimacy of travelers. We liked each other. We stayed up all that night talking, murmuring, as though we rocked on hammocks slung above time. The others were from big cities: New York, Washington, Boston. They all said that I had no expression on my face when I was watching the deer—or at any rate, not the expression they expected.

They had looked to see how I, the only woman, and the youngest, was taking the sight of the deer's struggles. I looked detached, apparently, or hard, or calm, or focused, still. I don't know. I was thinking. I remember feeling very old and energetic. I could say like Thoreau that I have traveled widely in Roanoke, Virginia. I have thought a great deal about carnivorousness; I eat meat. These things are not issues; they are mysteries.

Gentlemen of the city, what surprises you? That there is suffering here, or that I know it?

We lay in the tent and talked. "If it had been my wife," one man said with special vigor, amazed, "she wouldn't have cared *what* was going on; she would have dropped *everything* right at that moment and gone in the village from here to there to there, she would not have *stopped* until that animal was out of its suffering one way or another. She couldn't *bear* to see a creature in agony like that."

I nodded.

Now I am home. When I wake I comb my hair before the mirror above my dresser. Every morning for the past two years I have seen in that mirror, beside my sleep-softened face, the blackened face of a burnt man. It is a wire-service photograph clipped from a newspaper and taped to my mirror. The caption reads: "Alan McDonald in Miami hospital bed." All you can see in the photograph is a smudged triangle or face from his eyelids to his lower lip; the rest is bandages. You cannot see the expression in his eyes; the bandages shade them.

The story, headed MAN BURNED FOR SECOND TIME, begins:

> "Why does God hate me?" Alan McDonald asked from his hospital bed.
>   "When the gunpowder went off, I couldn't believe it," he said. "I just couldn't believe it. I said, 'No, God couldn't do this to me again.' "

He was in a burn ward in Miami, in serious condition. I do not even know if he lived. I wrote him a letter at the time, cringing.

He had been burned before, thirteen years previously, by flaming gasoline. For years he had been having his body restored and his face remade in dozens of operations. He had been a boy, and then a burnt boy. He had already been stunned by what could happen, by how life could veer.

Once I read that people who survive bad burns tend to go crazy: they have a very high suicide rate. Medicine cannot ease their pain; drugs just leak away, soaking the sheets, because there is no skin to hold them in. The people just lie there and weep. Later they kill themselves. They had not known, before they were burned, that the world included such suffering, that life could permit them personally such pain.

This time a bowl of gunpowder had exploded on McDonald.

> "I didn't realize what had happened at first," he recounted. "And then I heard that sound from 13 years ago. I was burning. I rolled to put the fire out and I thought, 'Oh God, not again.'
>
> "If my friend hadn't been there, I would have jumped into a canal with a rock around my neck."

His wife concludes the piece, "Man, it just isn't fair."

I read the whole clipping again every morning. This is the Big Time here, every minute of it. Will someone please explain to Alan McDonald in his dignity, to the deer at Providencia in his dignity, what is going on? And mail me the carbon.

When we walked by the deer at Providencia for the last time, I said to Pepe, with a pitying glance at the deer, "*Pobrecito*" — "poor little thing." But I was trying out Spanish. I knew at the time it was a ridiculous thing to say. ✍

The Dancing-School Boys[1]

The interior life expands and fills; it approaches the edge of skin; it thickens with its own vivid story; it even begins to hear rumors, from beyond the horizon skin's rim, of nations and wars. You wake one day and discover your grandmother; you wake another day and notice, like any curious naturalist, the boys.

There were already boys then: not tough boys—much as I missed their inventiveness and easy democracy—but the polite boys of Richland Lane. The polite boys of Richland Lane aspired to the Presbyterian ministry. Their fathers were surgeons, lawyers, architects, and businessmen, who sat on the boards of churches and hospitals. Early on warm weekday evenings, we children played rough in the calm yards and cultivated woods, grabbing and bruising each other often enough in the course of our magnificently organized games. On Saturday afternoons, these same neighborhood boys appeared wet-combed and white-shirted at the front door, to take me gently to the movies on the bus. And there were the dancing-school boys, who materialized at the front door on Valentine's Day, holding heart-shaped boxes of chocolates.

---

[1]From *An American Childhood*, 1987.

I was ten when I met the dancing-school boys; it was that same autumn, 1955. Father was motoring down the river.[1] The new sandstone wall was up in the living room.

Outside the city, the mountainside maples were turning; the oaks were green. Everywhere in the spreading Mississippi watershed, from the Allegheny and the Ohio here in Pittsburgh to the Missouri and the Cheyenne and the Bighorn draining the Rocky Mountains, yellow and red leaves, silver-maple and black-oak leaves, or pale cottonwood leaves and aspen, slipped down to the tight surface of the moving water. A few leaves fell on the decks of Father's boat when he tied up at an Ohio island for lunch; he raked them off with his fingers, probably, and thought it damned strange to be raking leaves at all.

Molly, the new baby, had grown less mysterious; she smiled and crawled over the grass or the rug. The family had begun spending summers around a country-club pool. Amy and I had started at a girls' day school, the Ellis School; I belted on the green jumper I would wear, in one size or another, for the next eight years, until I left Pittsburgh altogether. I was taking piano lessons, art classes. And I started dancing school.

The dancing-school boys, it turned out, were our boys, the boys, who ascended through the boys' private school as we ascended through the girls'. I was surprised to see them that first Friday afternoon in dancing school. I was surprised, that is, to see that I already knew them, that I already knew almost everyone in the room; I was surprised that dancing school, as an institution, was eerily more significant than all my other lessons and classes, and that it was not peripheral at all, but central.

For here we all were. I'd seen the boys in, of all places, church—one of the requisite Presbyterian churches of Pittsburgh. I'd seen them at the country club, too. I knew the girls from church, the country club, and school. Here we all were at dancing school; here we all were, dressed to the teeth and sitting on rows of peculiar painted and gilded chairs. Here we all were, boys and girls, plunged by our conspiring elders into the bewildering social truth that we were meant to make each other's acquaintance. Dancing school.

There in that obscure part of town, there in that muffled enormous old stone building, among those bizarre and mismatched adults who seemed grimly to dance their lives away in that dry and claustrophobic ballroom—there, it proved, was the unlikely arena where we were foreordained to assemble, Friday after Friday, for many years until the distant and seemingly unrelated country clubs took over the great work of providing music for us later and later into the night until the time came when we should all have married each other up, at last.

"Isn't he cute?" Bebe would whisper to me as we sat in the girls' row on the edge of the ballroom floor. I had never before seen a painted chair; my mother favored

---

[1]See biography.

wood for its own sake. The lugubrious[1] instructors were demonstrating one of several fox-trots.

Which?

"Ronny," she whispered one week, and "Danny," the next. I would find that one in the boys' row. He'd fastened his fists to his seat and was rocking back and forth from his hips all unconsciously, open-mouthed.

Sure.

"Isn't he cute?" Mimsie would ask at school, and I would think of this Ricky or Dick, recall some stray bit of bubbling laughter in which he had been caught helpless, pawing at his bangs with his bent wrist, his saliva whitening his braces' rubber bands and occasionally forming a glassy pane at the corner of his mouth; I would remember the way his head bobbed, and imagine those two parallel rods at the back of his neck, which made a thin valley where a short tip of hair lay tapered and curled; the way he scratched his ear by wincing, raising a shoulder, and rubbing the side of his head on his jacket's sleeve seam. Cute?

You bet he was cute. They all were.

Onstage the lonely pianist played "Mountain Greenery." Sometimes he played "Night and Day." It was Friday afternoon; we could have been sled riding. On Fridays, our unrelated private schools, boys' and girls', released us early. On Fridays, dancing school met, an hour later each year, until at last we met in the dark, disrupting our families' dinners, and at last certain boys began to hold our hands, carefully looking away, after a given dance, to secure us for the next one.

We all wore white cotton gloves. Only with the greatest of effort could I sometimes feel, or fancy I felt, the warmth of a boy's hand—through his glove and my glove—on my right palm. My gloved left hand lay lightly, always lightly, on his jacket shoulder. His gloved right hand lay, forgotten by both of us, across the clumsy back of my dress, across its lumpy velvet bow or its long cold zipper concealed by brocade.

Between dances when we held hands, we commonly interleaved our fingers, as if for the sheer challenge of it, for our thick cotton gloves permitted almost no movement, and we quickly cut off the circulation in each other's fingers. If for some reason we had released each other's hands quickly, without thinking, our gloves would have come off and dropped to the ballroom floor together still entwined, while our numbed bare fingers slowly regained sensation and warmth.

We were all on some list. We were to be on that list for life, it turned out, unless we left. I had no inkling of this crucial fact, although the others, I believe, did. I was mystified to see that whoever devised the list misunderstood things so. The best-liked girl in our class, my friend Ellin Hahn, was conspicuously excluded. Because she was precisely fifty percent Jewish, she had to go to Jewish dancing school. The boys courted her anyway, one after the other, and only made

---

[1]Excessively gloomy.

do with the rest of us at dancing school. From other grades at our school, all sorts of plain, unintelligent, lifeless girls were included. These were quiet or silly girls, who seemed at school to recognize their rather low places, but who were unreasonably exuberant at dancing school, and who were gradually revealed to have known all along that in the larger arena they occupied very high places indeed. And these same lumpish, plain, very rich girls wound up marrying, to my unending stupefaction, the very liveliest and handsomest of the boys.

The boys. There were, essentially, a dozen or so of them and a dozen or so of us, so it was theoretically possible, as it were, to run through all of them by the time you finished school. We saw our dancing-school boys everywhere we went. Yet they were by no means less extraordinary for being familiar. They were familiar only visually: their eyebrows we could study in quick glimpses as we danced, eyebrows that met like spliced ropes over their noses; the winsome whorls of their hair we could stare at openly in church, hair that radiated spirally from the backs of their quite individual skulls; the smooth skin on their pliant torsos at the country-club pool, all so fascinating, each so different; and their weird little graceful bathing suits: the boys. Richard, Rich, Richie, Ricky, Ronny, Donny, Dan.

They called each other witty names, like Jag-Off. They could dribble. They walked clumsily but assuredly through the world, kicking things for the hell of it. By way of conversation, they slugged each other on their interesting shoulders.

They moved in violent jerks from which we hung back, impressed and appalled, as if from horses slamming the slats of their stalls. This and, as we would have put it, their messy eyelashes. In our heartless, condescending, ignorant way we loved their eyelashes, the fascinating and dreadful way the black hairs curled and tangled. That's the kind of vitality they had, the boys, that's the kind of novelty and attraction: their very eyelashes came out amok, and unthinkably original. That we loved, that and their cloddishness, their broad, vaudevillian reactions. They were always doing slow takes. Their breathtaking lack of subtlety in every particular, we thought—and then sometimes a gleam of consciousness in their eyes, as surprising as if you'd caught a complicit wink from a brick.

Ah, the boys. How little I understood them! How little I even glimpsed who they were. How little any of us did, if I may extrapolate. How completely I condescended to them when we were ten and they were in many ways my betters. And when we were fifteen, how little I understood them still, or again. I still thought they were all alike, for all practical purposes, no longer comical beasts now but walking gods who conferred divine power with their least glances. In fact, they were neither beasts nor gods, as I should have guessed. If they were alike it was in this, that all along the boys had been in the process of becoming responsible members of an actual and moral world we small-minded and fast-talking girls had never heard of.

They had been learning self-control. We had failed to develop any selves worth controlling. We were enforcers of a code we never questioned; we were vigilantes of the trivial. They had been accumulating information about the world outside our private schools and clubs. We had failed to notice that there was such a thing. The life of Pittsburgh, say, or the United States, or assorted foreign continents, concerned us no more than Jupiter did, or its moons.

The boys must have shared our view that we were, as girls, in the long run, negligible—not any sort of factor in anybody's day, or life, no sort of creatures to be reckoned with, or even reckoned in, at all. For they could perhaps see that we possessed neither self-control nor information, so the world could not be ours.

There was something ahead of the boys, we all felt, but we didn't know what it was. To a lesser extent and vicariously, it was ahead of us, too. From the quality of attention our elders gave to various aspects of our lives, we could have inferred that we were being prepared for a life of ballroom dancing. But we knew that wasn't it. Only children practiced ballroom dancing, for which they were patently unsuited. It was something, however, that ballroom dancing obliquely prepared us for, just as, we were told, the study of Latin would obliquely prepare us for something else, also unspecified.

Whatever we needed in order to meet the future, it was located at the unthinkable juncture of Latin class and dancing school. With the declension of Latin nouns and the conjugation of Latin verbs, it had to do with our minds' functioning; presumably this held true for the five steps of the fox-trot as well. Learning these things would permanently alter the structure of our brains, whether we wanted it to or not.

So the boys, with the actual world before them, had when they were small a bewildered air, and an endearing and bravura show of manliness. On the golden-oak ballroom floor, every darkening Friday afternoon while we girls rustled in our pastel dresses and felt at our hair ineffectually with our cotton gloves, the boys in their gloves, standing right in plain view between dances, exploded firecrackers. I would be waltzing with some arm-pumping tyke of a boy when he whispered excitedly in my ear, "Guess what I have in my pocket?" I knew. It was a cherry bomb. He slammed the thing onto the oak floor when no one was looking but a knot of his friends. The instructors flinched at the bang and stiffened; the knot of boys scattered as if shot; we could taste the sharp gunpowder in the air, and see a dab of gray ash on the floor. And when he laughed, his face reddened and gave off a vaporous heat. He seemed tickled inside his jiggling bones; he flapped his arms and slapped himself and tears fell on his tie.

They must have known, those little boys, that they would inherit corporate Pittsburgh, as indeed they have. They must have known that it was theirs by rights as boys, a real world, about which they had best start becoming informed. And they must have known, too, as Pittsburgh Presbyterian boys, that they could only just barely steal a few hours now, a few years now, to kid around, to dribble basketballs and explode firecrackers, before they were due to make a down payment on a suitable house.

Soon they would enter investment banking and take their places in the management of Fortune 500 corporations. Soon in their scant spare time they would be serving on the boards of schools, hospitals, country clubs, and churches. No wonder they laughed so hard. These were boys who wore ties from the moment their mothers could locate their necks.

I assumed that like me the boys dreamed of running away to sea, of curing cancer, of playing for the Pirates, of painting in Paris, of tramping through the Himalayas, for we were all children together. And they may well have dreamed these things, and more, then and later. I don't know.

Those boys who confided in me later, however, when we were all older, dreamed nothing of the kind. One wanted to be top man at Gulf Oil. One wanted to accumulate a million dollars before he turned thirty. And one wanted to be majority leader in the U.S. Senate.

But these, the boys who confided in me, were the ones I would love when we were in our teens, and they were, according to my predilection, not the dancing-school boys at all, but other, oddball boys. I would give my heart to one oddball boy after another — to older boys, to prep-school boys no one knew, to him who refused to go to college, to him who was a hood, and all of them wonderfully skinny. I loved two such boys deeply, one after the other and for years on end, and forsook everything else in life, and rightly so, to begin learning with them that unplumbed intimacy that is life's chief joy. I loved them deeply, one after the other, for years on end, I say, and hoped to change their worldly ambitions and save them from the noose. But they stood firm.

And it could be, I think, that only those oddball boys, none of whom has inherited Pittsburgh at all, longed to star in the world of money and urban power; and it could be that the central boys, our boys, who are now running Pittsburgh responsibly, longed to escape. I don't know. I never knew them well enough to tell. ✐

Michael Dorris

(1945–)

Michael Dorris was born in 1945 in Dayton, Washington, the only child of Jim and Mary Betsy Burkhardt Dorris. He studied English and classics at Georgetown University, where he earned a bachelor's in 1967. In 1970 he earned a master's in the history of theater from Yale.

As a twenty-six-year-old Yale graduate student in anthropology and an assistant professor at Franconia College, Dorris became one of the first single men in the United States to adopt a young child. Part Modoc Indian on his father's side, Dorris asked for an Indian child and was given a three-year-old boy, born in South Dakota and a member of the Sioux tribe. Although happy and well adjusted, his son was slow to toilet-train and subject to frightening, inexplicable seizures. One year later, Dorris was hired as an assistant professor at Dartmouth College: "Within weeks I had to find a house, negotiate a move, locate child care, start a high-pressure job, and try to establish a new academic subdiscipline, Native American Studies—a subject in which I had no formal degree. I had not finished my Ph.D. thesis, and I was faced with the prospect of caring for a chronically ill little boy."

By 1974 Dorris had not only solved most of those problems, but he had also adopted a second son, a one-year-old, also a South Dakota Sioux, whom he named Sava. By 1975 he had published two articles, "Native Americans Today" and "Grandmother's Watch," and a book, *Native Americans: Five Hundred Years After* (photographs by Joseph Farber). He had also adopted a ten-month-old baby girl, Madeline, hinting to his social worker that a wonderful, young Indian lawyer was waiting to become his wife. Actually, he points out, he had been too busy with his children and career to find such a person. In 1976 he published *Man in the Northeast* and a chapter, "Native American Curriculum," in *Racism in the Textbook*, and in 1977 he published *A Sourcebook for Native American Studies*. He also published two textbooks, *Pre-Contact North America* in 1979 and *Introduction to Native American*

Studies in 1980. He won a grant from the National Endowment for the Humanities in 1976 and was a Guggenheim Fellow in 1978.

In 1979 Dorris met Louise Erdrich, whom he had known casually years before when he had been a first-year professor at Dartmouth and she had been one of his students in the Native American Program. A creative writer and editor of the Boston Indian Council newspaper, she is part Turtle Mountain Chippewa and the eldest in a family of seven children. Dorris found her the most beautiful woman he had ever seen. The attraction was mutual, and, after Dorris and his family spent a nine-month sojourn in New Zealand (where Dorris was a research fellow), he married Louise Erdrich in October of 1981. The following year Erdrich legally adopted the children. Since then, she has given birth to three daughters, Persia in 1984, Pallas in 1985, and Asa in 1989.

In 1985, after publishing *A Guide to Research on North American Indians* (with Arlene Hirschfelder and Mary Lou Byler), Dorris was awarded a grant from the Rockefeller Foundation to research fetal alcohol syndrome; the result is *The Broken Cord* (1989), an account of his search for an explanation for the disabilities suffered by his first son, Adam (a pseudonym). While working on the story of Adam, Dorris also published a novel, *A Yellow Raft in Blue Water* (1987). A full professor at Dartmouth, Dorris has given up tenure to pursue his career as a writer. Together, Dorris and Erdrich wrote *Crown of Columbus* (1991), a novel about a woman who finds part of a lost journal of Columbus. In addition to lecturing and giving readings from his books, Dorris is working on a collection of short stories called *Working Men*.

Michael Dorris writes in the plain style, mixing colloquial, even trite, phrases with academic English to underline his point: "On some gut level I didn't give a hoot about the anthropologically explained or politically correct *right* of individual choice, about a self-serving cultural apology that each person was beyond reproach even for destructive behavior that extended to babies." In this sentence, prompted by his discovery that Adam's mother had been drunk during much of her pregnancy, the trite phrases carry the burden of the emotion conveyed. At other times, however, Dorris tailors a commonplace saying to fit metaphorically and literally into the sentence, as in these two lines from "Life Stories": "Summer jobs were therefore a relief, an opportunity to pull a share of the load." "I decided to put an ocean between me and my former trusting clientele." (He quits his job and escapes to France.) In the essay included in this text, Dorris reveals his discomfort with his academic persona, aligning, instead, with the individual, common man. He adopts the informal, conversational voice of Charles Lamb and E. B. White. Also like them, Dorris creates comedy out of his own misfortunes, such as the time described in *The Broken Cord* when his desire to change his clothes to affect a clean appearance so overrode his desire to get to a doctor that a deep cut required a transfusion. Like Addison and Johnson before him, Dorris writes for the reading middle class, whom he hopes to entertain and to educate. Unlike them, however, he is an uneven stylist, sometimes slapdash and solipsistic, at other times both comic and moving. ✍

Life Stories[1]

In most cultures, adulthood is equated with self-reliance and responsibility, yet often Americans do not achieve this status until we are in our late twenties or early thirties—virtually the entire average lifespan of a person in a traditional non-Western society. We tend to treat prolonged adolescence as a warm-up for real life, as a wobbly suspension bridge between childhood and legal maturity. Whereas a nineteenth-century Cheyenne or Lakota[2] teenager was expected to alter self-conception in a split-second vision, we often meander through an analogous rite of passage for more than a decade—through high school, college, graduate school.

Though he had never before traveled alone outside his village, the Plains Indian male was expected at puberty to venture solo into the wilderness. There he had to fend for and sustain himself while avoiding the menace of unknown dangers, and there he had absolutely to remain until something happened that would transform him. Every human being, these tribes believed, was entitled to at least one moment of personal, enabling insight.

Anthropology proposes feasible psychological explanations for why this flash was eventually triggered: fear, fatigue, reliance on strange foods, the anguish of loneliness, stress, and the expectation of ultimate success all contributed to a state of receptivity. Every sense was quickened, alerted to perceive deep meaning, until at last the interpretation of an unusual event—a dream, a chance encounter, or an unexpected vista—reverberated with metaphor. Through this unique prism, abstractly preserved in a vivid memory or song, a boy caught foresight of both his adult persona and of his vocation, the two inextricably entwined.

Today the best approximations that many of us get to such a heady sense of eventuality come in the performance of our school vacation jobs. Summers are intermissions, and once we hit our teens it is during these breaks in our structured regimen that we initially taste the satisfaction of remuneration that is earned, not merely doled. Tasks defined as *work* are not only graded, they are compensated; they have a worth that is unarguable because it translates into hard currency. Wage labor—and in the beginning, this generally means a confining,

---

[1]First published in *Antaeus*, Autumn 1989.
[2]"The people," also called Sioux.

repetitive chore for which we are quickly over-qualified—paradoxically brings a sense of blooming freedom. At the outset, the complaint to a peer that business supersedes fun is oddly liberating—no matter what drudgery requires your attention, it is by its very required nature serious and adult.

At least that's how it seemed to me. I come from a line of people hard hit by the Great Depression. My mother and her sisters went to work early in their teens—my mother operated a kind of calculator known as a comptometer while her sisters spent their days, respectively, at a peanut factory and at Western Union. My grandmother did piecework sewing. Their efforts, and the Democratic Party, saw them through, and to this day they never look back without appreciation for their later solvency. They take nothing for granted. Accomplishments are celebrated, possessions are valuable, in direct proportion to the labor entailed to acquire them; anything easily won or bought on credit is suspect. When I was growing up we were far from wealthy, but what money we had was correlated to the hours some one of us had logged. My eagerness to contribute to, or at least not diminish, the coffer was countered by the arguments of those whose salaries kept me in school: My higher education was a sound group investment. The whole family was adamant that I have the opportunities they had missed and, no matter how much I objected, they stinted themselves to provide for me.

Summer jobs were therefore a relief, an opportunity to pull a share of the load. As soon as the days turned warm I began to peruse the classifieds, and when the spring semester was done, I was ready to punch a clock. It even felt right. Work in June, July, and August had an almost Biblical aspect: In the hot, canicular weather[1] your brow sweated, just as God had ordained.[2] Moreover, summer jobs had the luxury of being temporary. No matter how bizarre, how onerous, how off my supposed track, employment terminated with the falling leaves and I was back on neutral ground. So, during each annual three-month leave from secondary school and later from the university, I compiled an eclectic résumé: lawn cutter, hair sweeper in a barber shop, lifeguard, delivery boy, temporary mail carrier, file clerk, youth program coordinator on my Montana reservation, ballroom dance instructor, theater party promoter, night-shift hospital records keeper, human adding machine in a Paris bank, encyclopedia salesman, newspaper stringer, recreation bus manager, salmon fisherman.

The reasonable titles disguise the madness of some of these occupations. For instance, I seemed inevitably to be hired to trim the yards of the unconventional. One woman followed beside me, step by step, as I traversed her yard in ever tighter squares, and called my attention to each missed blade of grass. Another client never had the "change" to pay me, and so reimbursed my weekly pruning with an offering culled from his library. I could have done without the *Guide to Artificial Respiration* (1942) or the many well-worn copies of Reader's

---

[1]Hot days around August 11 when the dog star rises.
[2]See Genesis 3:19.

Digest Condensed Books, but sometimes the selection merited the wait. Like a rat lured repeatedly back to the danger of mild electric shock by the mystique of intermittent reenforcement, I kept mowing by day in hopes of turning pages all night.

The summer I was eighteen a possibility arose for a rotation at the post office, and I grabbed it. There was something casually sophisticated about work that required a uniform, about having a federal ranking, even if it was GS-1 (Temp/Sub), and it was flattering to be entrusted with a leather bag containing who knew what important correspondence. Every day I was assigned a new beat, usually in a rough neighborhood avoided whenever possible by regular carriers, and I proved quite capable of complicating what would normally be fairly routine missions. The low point came on the first of August when I diligently delivered four blocks' worth of welfare checks to the right numbers on the wrong streets. It is no fun to snatch unexpected wealth from the hands of those who have but moments previously opened their mailboxes and received a bonus.

After my first year of college, I lived with relatives on an Indian reservation in eastern Montana and filled the only post available: Coordinator of Tribal Youth Programs. I was seduced by the language of the announcement into assuming that there existed Youth Programs to be coordinated. In fact, the Youth consisted of a dozen bored, disgruntled kids—most of them my cousins—who had nothing better to do each day than to show up at what was euphemistically called "the gym" and hate whatever Program I had planned for them. The Youth ranged in age from fifteen to five and seemed to have as their sole common ambition the determination to smoke cigarettes. This put them at immediate and on-going odds with the Coordinator, who on his first day naively encouraged them to sing the "Doe, a deer, a female deer" song from *The Sound of Music*. They looked at me, that bleak morning, and I looked at them, each boy and girl equipped with a Pall Mall behind an ear, and we all knew it would be a long, struggle-charged battle. It was to be a contest of wills, the hearty and wholesome vs. prohibited vice. I stood for dodge ball, for collecting bugs in glass jars, for arts and crafts; they had pledged a preternatural allegiance to sloth. The odds were not in my favor and each waking dawn I experienced the lightheadedness of anticipated exhaustion, that thrill of giddy dissociation in which nothing seems real or of great significance. I went with the flow and learned to inhale.

The next summer, I decided to find work in an urban setting for a change, and was hired as a general office assistant in the Elsa Hoppenfeld Theatre Party Agency, located above Sardi's restaurant in New York City. The Agency consisted of Elsa Hoppenfeld herself, Rita Frank, her regular deputy, and me. Elsa was a gregarious Viennese woman who established contacts through personal charm, and she spent much of the time courting trade away from the building. Rita was therefore both my immediate supervisor and constant companion; she had the most incredible fingernails I had ever seen—long, carefully shaped pegs lacquered in cruel primary colors and hard as stone—and an attitude about her that could only be described as zeal.

The goal of a theater party agent is to sell blocks of tickets to imminent Broadway productions, and the likely buyers are charities, B'nai Briths, Hadassahs,[1] and assorted other fund-raising organizations. We received commissions on volume, and so it was necessary to convince a prospect that a play— preferably an expensive musical—for which we had reserved the rights to seats would be a boffo smash hit.

The object of our greatest expectation that season was an extravaganza called *Chu Chem*, a saga that aspired to ride the coattails of *Fiddler on the Roof* into entertainment history. It starred the estimable Molly Picon and told the story of a family who had centuries ago gone from Israel to China during the diaspora,° yet had, despite isolation in an alien environment, retained orthodox culture and habits. The crux of the plot revolved around a man with several marriageable daughters and nary a kosher suitor within 5,000 miles. For three months Rita and I waxed eloquent in singing the show's praises. We sat in our little office, behind facing desks, and every noon while she redid her nails I ordered out from a deli that offered such exotic (to me) delicacies as fried egg sandwiches, lox and cream cheese, pastrami, *tongue*. I developed of necessity and habit a telephone voice laced with a distinctly Yiddish accent. It could have been a great career. However, come November, *Chu Chem* bombed. Its closing was such a financial catastrophe for all concerned that when the following January one Monsieur Dupont advertised on the Placement Board at my college, I decided to put an ocean between me and my former trusting clientele.

M. Dupont came to campus with the stated purpose of interviewing candidates for teller positions in a French bank. Successful applicants, required to be fluent in *français*, would be rewarded with three well-paid months and a rent-free apartment in Paris. I headed for the language lab and registered for an appointment.

The only French in the interview was *Bonjour, ça va?*,[2] after which M. Dupont switched into English and described the wonderful deal on charter air flights that would be available to those who got the nod. Round-trip to Amsterdam, via Reykjavik, leaving the day after exams and returning in mid-September, no changes or substitutions. I signed up on the spot. I was to be a *banquier*,[3] with *pied-à-terre*[4] in Montparnasse!

Unfortunately, when I arrived with only $50 in travelers checks in my pocket—the flight had cleaned me out, but who needed money since my paycheck started right away—no one in Paris had ever heard of M. Dupont.

Alors.[5]

---

[1]B'nai Briths: Hebrew for "Sons of the Covenant"; Hadassahs: Hebrew for "Esther," large Jewish service organizations.

[2]French for "Hello, how's it going?"

[3]French for "banker."

[4]French for "foothold," that is, a small apartment.

[5]French for "then," meaning "So now what?"

I stood in the Gare du Nord[1] and considered my options. There weren't any. I scanned a listing of Paris hotels and headed for the cheapest one: the Hotel Villedo, $10 a night. The place had an ambiance that I persuaded myself was antique, despite the red light above the sign. The only accommodation available was "the bridal suite," a steal at $20. The glass door to my room didn't lock and there was a rather continual floor show, but at some point I must have dozed off. When I awoke the church bells were ringing, the sky was pink, and I felt renewed. No little setback was going to spoil my adventure. I stood and stretched, then walked to a mirror that hung above the sink next to the bed. I leaned forward to punctuate my resolve with a confident look in the eye.

The sink disengaged and fell to the floor. Water gushed. In panic I rummaged through my open suitcase, stuffed two pair of underwear into the pipe to quell the flow, and before the dam broke, I was out the door. I barreled through the lobby of the first bank I passed, asked to see the director, and told the startled man my sad story. For some reason, whether from shock or pity, he hired me at $1.27 an hour to be a cross-checker of foreign currency transactions, and with two phone calls found me lodgings at a commercial school's dormitory.

From eight to five each weekday my duty was to sit in a windowless room with six impeccably dressed people, all of whom were totaling identical additions and subtractions. We were highly dignified with each other, very professional, no *tutoye*ring.[2] Monsieur Saint presided, but the formidable Mademoiselle was the true power; she oversaw each of our columns and shook her head sadly at my American-shaped numbers.

My legacy from that summer, however, was more than an enduring penchant for crossed 7s. After I had worked for six weeks, M. Saint asked me during a coffee break why I didn't follow the example of other foreign students he had known and depart the office at noon in order to spend the afternoon touring the sights of Paris with the *Alliance Française*.[3]

"Because," I replied in my halting French, "that costs money. I depend upon my full salary the same as any of you." M. Saint nodded gravely and said no more, but then on the next Friday he presented me with a white envelope along with my check.

"Do not open this until you have left the Société Générale," he said ominously. I thought I was fired for the time I had mixed up krøners and guilders, and, once on the sidewalk, I steeled myself to read the worst. I felt the quiet panic of blankness.

"Dear Sir," I translated the perfectly formed script. "You are a person of value. It is not correct that you should be in our beautiful city and not see it. Therefore we have amassed a modest sum to pay the tuition for a two-week afternoon program for you at the *Alliance Française*. Your wages will not suffer, for

---

[1]North Station, a train station in Paris.
[2]French for "addressing each other as *tu or toi*," that is, using the informal form of "you."
[3]French language school for tourists and foreigners.

it is your assignment to appear each morning in this bureau and reacquaint us with the places you have visited. We shall see them afresh through your eyes." The letter had thirty signatures, from the Director to the janitor, and stuffed inside the envelope was a sheaf of franc notes in various denominations.

I rushed back to the tiny office. M. Saint and Mademoiselle had waited, and accepted my gratitude with their usual controlled smiles and precise handshakes. But they had blown their Gallic[1] cover, and for the next ten days and then through all the days until I went home in September, our branch was awash with sight-seeing paraphernalia. Everyone had advice, favorite haunts, criticisms of the *Alliance's* choices or explanations. Paris passed through the bank's granite walls as sweetly as a June breeze through a window screen, and ever afterward the lilt of overheard French, a photograph of *Sacré Coeur*[2] or the Louvre,[3] even a monthly bank statement, recalls to me that best of all summers.

I didn't wind up in an occupation with any obvious connection to the careers I sampled during my school breaks, but I never altogether abandoned those brief professions either. They were jobs not so much to be held as to be weighed, absorbed, and incorporated, and, collectively, they carried me forward into adult life like overlapping stairs, unfolding a particular pattern at once haphazard and inevitable. ✐

---

[1]Characteristic of the French, from the Latin for "French."
[2]French for "Sacred Heart," a famous basilica (cathedral with a nave and two side aisles) in Paris on top of Montmartre.
[3]The major museum of art in Paris.

· · ·

Shelby Steele

(1946–)

Shelby Steele, born in 1946, was raised in Phoenix, Illinois, a small, all-black, working-class suburb south of Chicago. He was one of the four children of Shelby Steele, Sr., a truck driver, and his wife, a social worker. His southern-born father was self-educated, having completed only third grade when "the white man's fields took permanent priority over his education."

Steele's grammar school, "a dumping ground for teachers with too little competence or mental stability to teach in the white school," taught him the cruelty of racists, who reinforce what he calls the "anti-self," that part of the self in every child that refuses to believe in the value or success of the self and "entrenches itself as a lifelong voice of doubt." His sixth-grade teacher, an ex-Marine who bit the caps off bottles of Coke, decided that Steele was "stupid" and made him pay for this "sin" by collecting with his bare hands all the broken glass on a playground so strewn with shards that it "glared like a mirror in sunlight." On another occasion the teacher instructed an older boy on a bike to chase Steele around the school until he fainted. Instead, Steele managed to get away, but he never returned to the school.

When Steele was fourteen and a member of the swimming team at the YMCA, one of the mothers, a white woman, corrected his grammar every time she heard him use black English, insisting that his "verbs and pronouns agree, that I put the 'g' on my 'ings,' and that I say 'that' instead of 'dat.' " Although his reaction was at first anger, he later decided that he had felt threatened by shame and had "recomposed" that unpleasant feeling into "a tableau of racial victimization." When a teammate reported Steele's accusation of racism, the white woman pulled Steele aside to tell him about her life: as a poor high school dropout she was qualified to do nothing but secretarial work. Steele realized that she had meant to be kind: "She said she didn't give a 'good goddamn' about my race, but that if I wanted to do more than 'sweat my life away in a steel mill,' I better learn to speak correctly."

Unlike his sixth-grade treacher, that woman, Steele saw, was helping to develop the believing self, the self that aims for success.

In his integrated high school, with a 40 percent black population, Steele says that he and the other black students, propelled by "integration shock," "racial vulnerability," and the doubt produced by their anti-selves, eased their academic anxieties by proclaiming themselves, as blacks, to be superior dancers: "Dancing was a manifestation of soul and cool and, as such, it was, among many other things, an advertisement for the race, a visible superiority through which we could recompose at least some of the hidden anxieties of being in an integrated situation." Like all children, says Steele, he found himself struggling to discover his identity, to survive the conflicts between the believing self and the anti-self; unlike white children, however, his anti-self was given constant reinforcement in the racist behavior of his teachers and, he says, in the expectation of prejudice that past racist behavior stimulates in its victims. The result, he believes, is defensiveness and rigidity of the black identity: "We need a collective identity that encourages diversity within the race, that does not make black unity a form of repression, that does not imply that the least among us are the most black, and that makes the highest challenge of 'blackness' personal development."

When Steele entered Coe College in Iowa in 1965, where only eighteen of the one thousand students were black, his heroes were Martin Luther King, Jr.,° and Malcolm X;° Steele soon became a leader of the school's black student organization. After graduation, he taught Afro-American literature to poor blacks in Illinois before enrolling in the graduate program in English at the University of Utah. He earned a Ph.D. in 1974 and is now a professor of English at San Jose State University in California. He is married to Rita Steele, a white clinical psychologist, and the couple has two children, a son, Eli, and a daughter, Loni.

In 1990 Steele published a collection of essays entitled *The Content of Our Character: A New Vision of Race in America*. Like Rodriguez, he opposes affirmative action, believing that "the unkindest cut is to bestow on children like my own an undeserved advantage while neglecting the development of those disadvantaged children on the East Side of my city who will likely never be in a position to benefit from a preference. Give my children fairness; give disadvantaged children a better shot at development—better elementary and secondary schools, job training, safer neighborhoods, better financial assistance for college, and so on." Steele is acutely aware of the controversy his views engender; he told one interviewer, "I never shine a light on anything I haven't experienced or write about fears I don't see in myself first. I'm my own first target. I spill my own blood first."

In his essays Steele combines personal anecdotes with close reasoning to convince his readers. Like Walker, he analyzes his own experiences and applies what he learns to the world at large, finding contexts that help him and us to understand their significance. His style is informal but more academic than Walker's or White's, yet less allusive than Hazlitt's or Ozick's. If he sometimes sounds stiff, he is just as likely to startle with his metaphors, as in this reaction to racists who yell "nigger" as they go by in their cars: "I don't like to think that these solo artists might soon make up a chorus, or worse, that this chorus might one day soon sing to me from the paths of my own campus." Like Rodriguez, he recognizes the separation between the "private self" and the "public reality" but finds "joy" in the freedom to write as an individual, in his own voice, his own style. ✐

On Being Black and Middle Class[1]

Not long ago, a friend of mine, black like myself, said to me that the term *black middle class* was actually a contradiction in terms. Race, he insisted, blurred class distinctions among blacks. If you were black, you were just black and that was that. When I argued, he let his eyes roll at my naïveté. Then he went on. For us, as black professionals, it was an exercise in self-flattery, a pathetic pretension, to give meaning to such a distraction. Worse, the very idea of class threatened the unity that was vital to the black community as a whole. After all, since when had white America taken note of anything but color when it came to blacks? He then reminded me of an old Malcolm X° line that had been popular in the sixties. Question: What is a black man with a Ph.D.? Answer: A nigger.

For many years I had been on my friend's side of this argument. Much of my conscious thinking on the old conundrum of race and class was shaped during my high school and college years in the race-charged sixties, when the fact of my race took on an almost religious significance. Progressively, from the mid-sixties on, more and more aspects of my life found their explanation, their justification, and their motivation in my race. My youthful concerns about career, romance, money, values, and even styles of dress became subject to consultation with various oracular sources of racial wisdom. And these ranged from a figure as ennobling as Martin Luther King, Jr.,° to the underworld elegance of dress I found in jazz clubs on the South Side of Chicago. Everywhere there were signals, and in those days I considered myself so blessed with clarity and direction that I pitied my white classmates who found more embarrassment than guidance in the fact of *their* race. In 1968, inflated by new power, I took a mischievous delight in calling them culturally disadvantaged.

But now, hearing my friend's comment was like hearing a priest from a church I'd grown disenchanted with. I understood him, but my faith was weak. What had sustained me in the sixties sounded monotonous and off-the-mark in

---

[1]First published in *Commentary*, January 1988, and collected in *The Content of Our Character*, 1990.

the eighties. For me, race had lost much of its juju,[1] its singular capacity to conjure meaning. And today, when I honestly look at my life and the lives of many other middle-class blacks I know, I can see that race never fully explained our situation in American society. Black though I may be, it is impossible for me to sit in my single-family house with two cars in the driveway and a swing set in the backyard and *not* see the role class has played in my life. And how can my friend, similarly raised and similarly situated, not see it?

Yet despite my certainty I felt a sharp tug of guilt as I tried to explain myself over my friend's skepticism. He is a man of many comedic facial expressions and, as I spoke, his brow lifted in extreme moral alarm as if I were uttering the unspeakable. His clear implication was that I was being elitist and possibly (dare we suggest?) anti-black—crimes for which there might well be no redemption. He pretended to fear for me. I chuckled along with him, but inwardly I did wonder at myself. Though I never doubted the validity of what I was saying, I felt guilty saying it. Why?

After he left (to retrieve his daughter from a dance lesson) I realized that the trap I felt myself in had a tiresome familiarity and, in a sort of slow motion epiphany, I began to see its outline. It was like the suddenly sharp vision one has at the end of a burdensome marriage when all the long-repressed incompatibilities come undeniably to light.

What became clear to me is that people like myself, my friend, and middle-class blacks in general are caught in a very specific double bind that keeps two equally powerful elements of our identity at odds with each other. The middle-class values by which we were raised—the work ethic, the importance of education, the value of property ownership, of respectability, of "getting ahead," of stable family life, of initiative, of self-reliance, et cetera—are, in themselves, raceless and even assimilationist. They urge us toward participation in the American mainstream, toward integration, toward a strong identification with the society, and toward the entire constellation of qualities that are implied in the word individualism. These values are almost rules for how to prosper in a democratic, free enterprise society that admires and rewards individual effort. They tell us to work hard for ourselves and our families and to seek our opportunities whenever they appear, inside or outside the confines of whatever ethnic group we may belong to.

But the particular pattern of racial identification that emerged in the sixties and that still prevails today urges middle-class blacks (and all blacks) in the opposite direction. This pattern asks us to see ourselves as an embattled minority, and it urges an adversarial stance toward the mainstream and an emphasis on ethnic consciousness over individualism. It is organized around an implied separatism.

The opposing thrust of these two parts of our identity results in the double bind of middle-class blacks. There is no forward movement on either plane that

---

[1]Supernatural power attributed to the West African fetish or charm of the same name.

does not constitute backward movement on the other. This was the familiar trap I felt myself in while talking with my friend. As I spoke about class, his eyes reminded me that I was betraying race. Clearly, the two indispensable parts of my identity were a threat to one another.

Of course when you think about it, class and race are both similar in some ways and also naturally opposed. They are two forms of collective identity with boundaries that intersect. But whether they clash or peacefully coexist has much to do with how they are defined. Being both black and middle class becomes a double bind when class and race are defined in sharply antagonistic terms, so that one must be repressed to appease the other.

But what is the "substance" of these two identities, and how does each establish itself in an individual's overall identity?

It seems to me that when we identify with any collective we are basically identifying with images that tell us what it means to be a member of that collective. Identity is not the same thing as the fact of membership in a collective; it is, rather, a form of self-definition, facilitated by images of what we wish our membership in the collective to mean. In this sense, the images we identify with may reflect the aspirations of the collective more than they reflect reality, and their content can vary with shifts in those aspirations.

But the process of identification is usually dialectical. It is just as necessary to say what we are *not* as it is to say what we are—so that, finally, identification comes about by embracing a polarity of positive and negative images. To identify as middle-class, for example, I must have both positive and negative images of what being middle-class entails; then I will know what I should and should not be doing in order to be middle-class. The same goes for racial identity. In the racially turbulent sixties the polarity of images that came to define racial identification was very antagonistic to the polarity that defined middle-class identification. One might say that the positive images of one lined up with the negative images of the other, so that to identify with both required either a contortionist's flexibility or a dangerous splitting of the self. The double bind of the black middle class was in place.

The black middle class has always defined its class identity by means of positive images gleaned from middle- and upper-class white society and by means of negative images of lower-class blacks. This habit goes back to the institution of slavery itself, when "house" slaves both mimicked the whites they served and held themselves above the "field" slaves. But, in the sixties, the old bourgeois impulse to dissociate from the lower classes (the we/they distinction) backfired when racial identity suddenly called for the celebration of this same black lower class. One of the qualities of a double bind is that one feels it more than sees it, and I distinctly remember the tension and strange sense of dishonesty I felt in those days as I moved back and forth like a bigamist between the demands of class and race.

Though my father was born poor, he achieved middle-class standing through much hard work and sacrifice (one of his favorite words) and by identifying fully with solid middle-class values—mainly hard work, family life, property ownership, and education for his children (all four of whom have advanced degrees). In his mind these were not so much values as laws of nature. People who embodied them made up the positive images in his class polarity. The negative images came largely from the blacks he had left behind because they were "going nowhere."

No one in my family remembers how it happened, but as time went on, the negative images congealed into an imaginary character named Sam who, from the extensive service we put him to, quickly grew to mythic proportions. In our family lore he was sometimes a trickster, sometimes a boob, but always possessed of a catalogue of sly faults that gave up graphic images of everything we should not be. On sacrifice: "Sam never thinks about tomorrow. He wants it now or he doesn't care about it." On work: "Sam doesn't favor it too much." On children: "Sam likes to have them but not to raise them." On money: "Sam drinks it up and pisses it out." On fidelity: "Sam has to have two or three women." On clothes: "Sam features loud clothes. He likes to see and be seen." And so on. Sam's persona amounted to a negative instruction manual in class identity.

I don't think that any of us believed Sam's faults were accurate representations of lower-class black life. He was an instrument of self-definition, not of sociological accuracy. It never occurred to us that he looked very much like the white racist stereotype of blacks, or that he might have been a manifestation of our own racial self-hatred. He simply gave us a counterpoint against which to express our aspirations. If self-hatred was a factor, it was not, for us, a matter of hating lower-class blacks but of hating what we did not want to be.

Still, hate or love aside, it is fundamentally true that my middle-class identity involved a dissociation from images of lower-class black life and a corresponding identification with values and patterns of responsibility that are common to the middle class everywhere. These values sent me a clear message: Be both an individual and a responsible citizen, understand that the quality of your life will approximately reflect the quality of effort you put into it, know that individual responsibility is the basis of freedom, and that the limitations imposed by fate (whether fair or unfair) are no excuse for passivity.

Whether I live up to these values or not, I know that my acceptance of them is the result of lifelong conditioning. I know also that I share this conditioning with middle-class people of all races and that I can no more easily be free of it than I can be free of my race. Whether all this got started because the black middle class modeled itself on the white middle class is no longer relevant. For the middle-class black, conditioned by these values from birth, the sense of meaning they provide is as immutable as the color of his skin.

I started the sixties in high school feeling that my class-conditioning was the surest way to overcome racial barriers. My racial identity was pretty much taken for granted. After all, it was obvious to the world that I was black. Yet I ended the sixties in graduate school a little embarrassed by my class background and with an almost desperate need to be "black." The tables had turned. I knew very clearly (though I struggled to repress it) that my aspirations and my sense of how to operate in the world came from my class background, yet "being black" required certain attitudes and stances that made me feel, secretly, a little duplicitous. The inner compatibility of class and race I had known in 1960 was gone.

For blacks, the decade between 1960 and 1969 saw racial identification undergo the same sort of transformation that national identity undergoes in times of war. It became more self-conscious, more narrowly focused, more prescribed, less tolerant of opposition. It spawned an implicit party line that tended to disallow competing forms of identity. Race-as-identity was lifted from the relative slumber it knew in the fifties and pressed into service in a social and political war against oppression. It was redefined along sharp adversarial lines and directed toward the goal of mobilizing the great mass of black Americans in this warlike effort. It was imbued with strong moral authority, useful for denouncing those who opposed it and for celebrating those who honored it as a positive achievement rather than a mere birthright.

The form of racial identification that quickly evolved to meet this challenge presented blacks as a racial monolith, a singular people with a common experience of oppression. Differences within the race, no matter how ineradicable, had to be minimized. Class distinctions were one of the first such differences to be sacrificed, since they not only threatened racial unity but also seemed to stand in contradiction to the principle of equality, which was the announced goal of the movement for racial progress. The discomfort I felt in 1969, the vague but relentless sense of duplicity, was the result of a historical necessity that put my class and race at odds, that was asking me to cast aside the distinction of my class and identify with a monolithic view of my race.

If the form of this racial identity was the monolith, its substance was victimization. The civil rights movement and the more radical splinter groups of the late sixties were all dedicated to ending racial victimization, and the form of black identity that emerged to facilitate this goal made blackness and victimization virtually synonymous. Since it was our victimization more than any other variable that identified and unified us, it followed logically that the purest black was the poor black. It was images of him that clustered around the positive pole of the race polarity; all other blacks were, in effect, required to identify with him in order to confirm their own blackness.

Certainly, there were more dimensions to the black experience than victimization, but no other had the same capacity to fire the indignation needed for war. So, again out of historical necessity, victimization became the overriding focus of racial identity. But this only deepened the double bind for middle-class blacks like me. When it came to class we were accustomed to defining ourselves against lower-class blacks and identifying with at least the values of middle-class whites; when it came to race we were now being asked to identify with images of lower-class blacks and to see whites, middle-class or otherwise, as victimizers. Negative lining up with positive, we were called upon to reject what we had previously embraced and to embrace what we had previously rejected. To put it still more personally, the Sam figure I had been raised to define myself against had now become the "real" black I was expected to identify with.

The fact that the poor black's new status was only passively earned by the condition of his victimization, not by assertive, positive action, made little difference. Status was status apart from the means by which it was achieved, and along with it came a certain power—the power to define the terms of access to that status, to say who was black and who was not. If a lower-class black said you were not really "black"—a sellout, an Uncle Tom—the judgment was all the more devastating because it carried the authority of his status. And this judgment soon enough came to be accepted by many whites as well.

In graduate school I was once told by a white professor, "Well, but . . . you're not really black. I mean, you're not disadvantaged." In his mind my lack of victim status disqualified me from the race itself.

To overcome marginal status, the middle-class black had to identify with a degree of victimization that was beyond his actual experience. In college (and well beyond) we used to play a game called "nap matching." It was a game of one-upmanship, in which we sat around outdoing each other with stories of racial victimization, symbolically measured by the naps[1] of our hair. Most of us were middle-class, and so had few personal stories to relate, but if we could not match naps with our own biographies, we would move on to those legendary tales of victimization that came to us from the public domain.

The single story that sat atop the pinnacle of racial victimization for us was that of Emmett Till, the Northern black teenager who, on a visit to the South in 1955, was killed and grotesquely mutilated for supposedly looking at or whistling at (we were never sure which, though we argued the point endlessly) a white woman. Oh, how we probed his story, finding in his youth and Northern up-bringing the quintessential embodiment of black innocence brought down by a white evil so portentous and apocalyptic, so gnarled and hideous, that it left us with a feeling not far from awe. By telling his story and others like it, we came to *feel* the immutability of our victimization, its utter indigenousness, as a thing on this earth like dirt or sand or water.

Of course, these sessions were a ritual of group identification, a means by which we, as middle-class blacks, could be at one with our race. But why were we, who had only a moderate experience of victimization (and that offset by opportunities our parents never had), so intent on assimilating or appropriating an identity that in so many ways contradicted our own? Because, I think, the sense of innocence that is always entailed in feeling victimized filled us with a corresponding feeling of entitlement, or even license, that helped us endure our vulnerability on a largely white college campus.

In my junior year in college I rode to a debate tournament with three white students and our faculty coach, an elderly English professor. The experience of being the lone black in a group of whites was so familiar to me that I thought nothing of it as our trip began. But then, halfway through the trip, the professor casually turned to me and, in an isn't-the-world-funny sort of tone, said that he had just refused to rent an apartment in a house he owned to a "very nice" black

---

[1]Fuzzy surfaces.

couple because their color would "offend" the white couple who lived downstairs. His eyebrows lifted helplessly over his hawkish nose, suggesting that he
too, like me, was a victim of America's racial farce.[1] His look assumed a kind of
comradeship: he and I were above this grimy business of race, though for expe-
diency we had occasionally to concede the world its madness.

My vulnerability in this situation came not so much from the professor's
blindness to his own racism as from his assumption that I would participate in it,
that I would conspire with him against my own race so that he might remain
comfortably blind. Why did he think I would be amenable to this? I can only guess
that he assumed my middle-class identity was so complete and all-encompassing
that I would see his action as nothing more than a trifling concession to the
folkways of our land; that I would in fact applaud his decision not to disturb
propriety. Blind to both his own racism and to me—one blindness serving the
other—he could not recognize that he was asking me to betray my race in the
name of my class.

His blindness made me feel vulnerable because it threatened to expose my
own repressed ambivalence. His comment pressured me to choose between my
class identification, which had contributed to my being a college student and a
member of the debating team, and my desperate desire to be "black." I could have
one but not both; I was double-bound.

Because double binds are repressed, there is always an element of terror in
them: the terror of bringing to the conscious mind the buried duplicity, self-
deception, and pretense involved in serving two masters. This terror is the stuff of
vulnerability, and since vulnerability is one of the least tolerable of all human
feelings, we usually transform it into an emotion that seems to restore the control
of which it has robbed us; most often, that emotion is anger. And so, before the
professor had even finished his little story, I had become a furnace of rage. The
year was 1967, and I had been primed by endless hours of nap-matching to feel,
at least consciously, completely at one with the victim-focused black identity.
This identity gave me the license, and the impunity, to unleash upon this professor one of those volcanic eruptions of racial indignation familiar to us from the
novels of Richard Wright.° Like Cross Damon in *The Outsider*, who kills in
perfectly righteous anger, I tried to annihilate the man. I punished him, not
according to the measure of his crime, but according to the measure of my
vulnerability, a measure set by the cumulative tension of years of repressed terror.
Soon, I saw that terror in *his* face as he stared black-eyed at the road ahead. My
white friends in the backseat, knowing no conflict between their own class and
race, were astonished that someone they had taken to be so much like themselves
could harbor a rage that for all the world looked murderous.

Though my rage was triggered by the professor's comment, it was deepened
and sustained by a complex of need, conflict, and repression in myself of which
I had been wholly unaware. Out of my racial vulnerability I had developed the
strong need of an identity with which to defend myself. The only such identity

---

[1]Steele is alluding to the fact that the professor is Jewish.

available was that of me as victim, him as victimizer. Once in the grip of this paradigm, I began to do far more damage to myself than he had done.

Seeing myself as a victim meant that I clung all the harder to my racial identity, which, in turn, meant that I suppressed my class identity. This cut me off from all the resources my class values might have offered me. In those values, for instance, I might have found the means to a more dispassionate response, the response less of a victim attacked by a victimizer than of an individual offended by a foolish old man. As an individual, I might have reported this professor to the college dean. Or, I might have calmly tried to reveal his blindness to him, and possibly won a convert. (The flagrancy of his remark suggested a hidden guilt and even a self-recognition on which I might have capitalized. Doesn't confession usually signal a willingness to face oneself?) Or I might have simply chuckled and then let my silence serve as an answer to his provocation. Would not my composure, in any form it might take, deflect into his own heart the arrow he'd shot at me?

Instead, my anger, itself the hair-trigger expression of a long-repressed double bind, not only cut me off from the best of my own resources, it also distorted the nature of my true racial problem. The righteousness of this anger and the easy catharsis it brought buoyed the delusion of my victimization and left me as blind as the professor himself.

As a middle-class black I have often felt myself *contriving* to be "black." And I have noticed this same contrivance in others—a certain stretching away from the natural flow of one's life to align oneself with a victim-focused black identity. Our particular needs are out of sync with the form of identity available to meet those needs. Middle-class blacks need to identify racially; it is better to think of ourselves as black and victimized than not black at all; so we contrive (more unconsciously than consciously) to fit ourselves into an identity that denies our class and fails to address the true source of our vulnerability.

For me, this once meant spending inordinate amounts of time at black faculty meetings, though these meetings had little to do with my real racial anxieties or my professional life. I was new to the university, one of two blacks in an English department of over seventy, and I felt a little isolated and vulnerable, though I did not admit it to myself. But at these meetings we discussed the problems of black faculty and students within a framework of victimization. The real vulnerability we felt was covered over by all the adversarial drama the victim/victimizer polarity inspired, and hence went unseen and unassuaged. And this, I think, explains our rather chronic ineffectiveness as a group. Since victimization was not our primary problem—the university had long ago opened its doors to us—we had to contrive to make it so, and there is not much energy in contrivance. What I got at these meetings was ultimately an object lesson in how fruitless struggle can be when it is not grounded in actual need.

At our black faculty meetings, the old equation of blackness with victimization was ever present—to be black was to be a victim; therefore, not to be a victim was not to be black. As we contrived to meet the terms of this formula, there was an inevitable distortion of both ourselves and the larger university. Through the prism of victimization, the university seemed more impenetrable than it actually was, and we more limited in our powers. We fell prey to the victim's myopia, making the university an institution from which we could seek redress, but which we could never fully join. This mind-set often led us to look more for compensations for our supposed victimization than for opportunities we could pursue as individuals.

The discomfort and vulnerability felt by middle-class blacks in the sixties, it could be argued, was a worthwhile price to pay considering the progress achieved during that time of racial confrontation. But what might have been tolerable then is intolerable now. Though changes in American society have made it an anachronism, the monolithic form of racial identification that came out of the sixties is still very much with us. It may be more loosely held, and its power to punish heretics has probably diminished, but it continues to catch middle-class blacks in a double bind, thus impeding not only their own advancement but even, I would contend, that of blacks as a group.

The victim-focused black identity encourages the individual to feel that his advancement depends almost entirely on that of the group. Thus he loses sight not only of his own possibilities but of the inextricable connection between individual effort and individual advancement. This is a profound encumbrance today, when there is more opportunity for blacks than ever before, for it reimposes limitations that can have the same oppressive effect as those the society has only recently begun to remove.

It was the emphasis on mass action in the sixties that made the victim-focused black identity a necessity. But in the nineties and beyond, when racial advancement will come only through a multitude of individual advancements, this form of identity inadvertently adds itself to the forces that hold us back. Hard work, education, individual initiative, stable family life, property ownership— these have always been the means by which ethnic groups have moved ahead in America. Regardless of past or present victimization, these "laws" of advancement apply absolutely to black Americans also. There is no getting around this. What we need is a form of racial identity that energizes the individual by putting him in touch with both his possibilities and his responsibilities.

It has always annoyed me to hear from the mouths of certain arbiters of blackness that middle-class blacks should "reach back" and pull up those blacks less fortunate than they—as though middle-class status was an unearned and essentially passive condition in which one needed a large measure of noblesse oblige[1] to occupy one's time. My own image is of reaching back from a moving train to lift on board those who have no tickets. A noble enough sentiment—but might it not be wiser to show them the entire structure of principles, effort, and

---

[1]French for "nobility obliges," meaning the generous and honorable behavior considered the responsibility of persons of high birth.

sacrifice that puts one in a position to buy a ticket[1] anytime one likes? This, I think, is something members of the black middle class can realistically offer to other blacks. Their example is not only a testament to possibility but also a lesson in method. But they cannot lead by example until they are released from a black identity that regards that example as suspect, that sees them as "marginally" black; indeed that holds *them* back by catching them in a double bind.

To move beyond the victim-focused black identity, we must learn to make a difficult but crucial distinction: between actual victimization, which we must resist with every resource, and identification with the victim's status. Until we do this, we will continue to wrestle more with ourselves than with the new opportunities that so many paid so dearly to win. ✍

---

[1]Possibly an allusion to Baldwin's title for his collected essays, *The Price of the Ticket.*

· · ·

Amy Tan

(1952–)

When Amy Tan's parents came to the United States from China in 1949 to escape the Communist takeover of Beijing, her mother left behind three daughters, Tan's half-sisters, as well as her own siblings. Her mother's brother, a high official in the Communist Party, has visited Tan's mother in San Francisco. Tan herself went to China in 1987 to attend her niece's wedding and to discover for herself the world her parents had fled in their search for freedom. For, however suffused her life has been by things Chinese, Amy Tan is an American, concerned with the development of herself as an individual, "wary," according to one interviewer, "of 'being cast as a spokesperson' for all Asian Americans."

Despite her teachers' opinion that she was better in math than English, and despite her mother's hopes that she would become a neurosurgeon and concert pianist "on the side," Tan opted to become a writer, first for businesses and now as a full-time novelist. Her first book, *The Joy Luck Club* (1989), a series of sixteen stories told by four mothers and their American-born daughters, was such a huge success that Tan began to doubt her ability to write a second, especially since so many people she met plied her with stories of failed second books. In "Angst & the Second Novel" (1991) Tan describes the result of all the pressure: "I developed a pain in my neck, which later radiated to my jaw, resulting in constant gnashing, then two cracked teeth and, finally, a huge dental bill. The pain then migrated down my back. . . . And while I was struggling to sit in my chair, with hot packs wrapped around my waist, I did not actually write fiction: I wrote speeches—30, 40, 50 speeches [about the first book]."

When she did finally get down to writing the second book, Tan had to begin and discard five different ones, having written between 30 and 88 pages of each before she finally found the right character and the right story. Even then, however, she rewrote 150 pages and "felt sick for about a week" before the second book, *The Kitchen God's Wife* (1991), was well under way.

In addition to the two novels, numerous speeches, and "Angst & the Second Novel," Tan has published several essays, including "Fish Cheeks" (1987), "Watching China" (1989), "Mother Tongue" (1990; originally a speech delivered in 1989), and "The Language of Discretion" (1990). At work on her third novel, she lives in San Francisco with her husband, a tax lawyer. She and her friends have started their own club, where they exchange "investment tips" as well as gossip, and have named it "The Fool and His Money."

As she says in "Mother Tongue," Tan is "fascinated by language," pleased by the artfulness and beauty of the several "Englishes" she knows. In her essays Tan employs her novelist's eye and linguist's ear to surprise the reader into an awareness of what it feels like to be someone else, to imagine what a single event might seem like to a minister's son, her mother, or herself. In "Mother Tongue" the "limited" English her mother speaks reveals her listeners' limits as well. For Tan, only through the multiple perspectives offered by language can the various and sometimes conflicting truths emerge. ✎

Fish Cheeks[1]

I fell in love with the minister's son the winter I turned fourteen. He was not Chinese, but as white as Mary in the manger. For Christmas I prayed for this blond-haired boy, Robert, and a slim new American nose.

When I found out that my parents had invited the minister's family over for Christmas Eve dinner, I cried. What would Robert think of our shabby Chinese Christmas? What would he think of our noisy Chinese relatives who lacked proper American manners? What terrible disappointment would he feel upon seeing not a roasted turkey and sweet potatoes but Chinese food?

On Christmas Eve I saw that my mother had outdone herself in creating a strange menu. She was pulling black veins out of the backs of fleshy prawns. The kitchen was littered with appalling mounds of raw food: A slimy rock cod with bulging eyes that pleaded not to be thrown into a pan of hot oil. Tofu,[2] which looked like stacked wedges of rubbery white sponges. A bowl soaking dried fungus back to life. A plate of squid, their backs crisscrossed with knife markings so they resembled bicycle tires.

And then they arrived—the minister's family and all my relatives in a clamor of doorbells and rumpled Christmas packages. Robert grunted hello, and I pretended he was not worthy of existence.

Dinner threw me deeper into despair. My relatives licked the ends of their chopsticks and reached across the table, dipping them into the dozen or so plates

---

[1]First published in *Seventeen*, December 1987.
[2]Soybean curd.

of food. Robert and his family waited patiently for platters to be passed to them. My relatives murmured with pleasure when my mother brought out the whole steamed fish. Robert grimaced. Then my father poked his chopsticks just below the fish eye and plucked out the soft meat. "Amy, your favorite," he said, offering me the tender fish cheek. I wanted to disappear.

At the end of the meal my father leaned back and belched loudly, thanking my mother for her fine cooking. "It's a polite Chinese custom to show you are satisfied," explained my father to our astonished guests. Robert was looking down at his plate with a reddened face. The minister managed to muster up a quiet burp. I was stunned into silence for the rest of the night.

After everyone had gone, my mother said to me, "You want to be the same as American girls on the outside." She handed me an early gift. It was a miniskirt in beige tweed. "But inside you must always be Chinese. You must be proud you are different. Your only shame is to have shame."

And even though I didn't agree with her then, I knew that she understood how much I had suffered during the evening's dinner. It wasn't until many years later—long after I had gotten over my crush on Robert—that I was able to fully appreciate her lesson and the true purpose behind our particular menu. For Christmas Eve that year, she had chosen all my favorite foods. ◢

Glossary

Achilles Hero of the *Iliad*. When Achilles refuses to fight because of Agamemnon's theft of Briseis, his loyal friend Patroclus wears the armor of Achilles, fights in his stead, and succumbs to Hector. The death of his friend finally moves Achilles to reenter the battle.

Aeneas Hero of Virgil's epic poem the *Aeneid*. In classical legend the Trojan prince, son of Aphrodite, escaped the fall of Troy, carrying his father Anchises on his back. He stayed with Dido in Carthage and then founded Rome.

Aeschylus (525–456 B.C.) The first of the three famed poets of Greek tragedy, he wrote over ninety plays, seven of which still exist in entirety: *The Suppliants*, *The Persians*, *The Seven Against Thebes*, *Prometheus Bound*, and the trilogy entitled *The Oresteia*, consisting of *Agamemnon*, *The Libation Bearers*, and *The Eumenides*.

Aesop (Sixth century B.C.) Presumed author of the *Fables* who, according to Herodotus, the first Greek historian, was born a Greek slave and later freed.

Agamemnon In Greek mythology, king of Mycenae, son of Atreus and brother to Menelaus. He sacrificed his daughter Iphigenia to Artemis to get the winds needed to sail to Troy. After the war, Agamemnon was murdered by his wife, Clytemnestra, and her lover, Aegisthus. His children, Orestes and Electra, killed their mother to avenge his death.

Alcott, Louisa May (1832–1888) American novelist, friend of Emerson and Thoreau, who was a servant and a seamstress before earning money through her writing. She published poems in the *Atlantic Monthly*, wrote about her duties as a nurse in the Civil War in *Hospital Sketches*, edited a children's magazine, and wrote several novels, her most famous being *Little Women*, perhaps the most popular girls' book ever.

Alexander the III or the Great (356–323 B.C.) King of Macedon, great leader tutored by Aristotle° who united Greece, conquered Persia, founded Alexandria in northern Egypt, and went from what is now Afghanistan to northern India, spreading Hellenism wherever he went. Among his many wives was Roxana, a Persian who bore his only son. Alexander encouraged his troops to intermarry with the Persians and, despite his multiple invasions of territory belonging to others, asserted the equality of all people. Before he could begin a journey by sea around Arabia, he caught a fever and died at age thirty-three.

Apollo In Greek and Roman mythology, the god of the sun, music, medicine, prophecy, poetry, archery, pastures, and flocks; Artemis (Diana) is his twin sister.

Archimedes (287–212 B.C.) Greek mathematician and inventor known for running naked through the streets of Syracuse shouting "Eureka" ("I have found it") after he realized, while in his bath, that he could determine the amount of gold in the king's crown by comparing the amount of water it displaced to the amount displaced by an equal weight of gold. He is also known for his confidence in the lever: "Give me a place to stand, and I will move the world." Much of his writing on geometry remains extant.

Aristophanes (fl. 420 B.C.) Greek comic poet whose eleven plays are the oldest complete comedies. He satirizes Socrates° in *The Clouds*, Euripides° in *The Women at Demeter's Festival*, Aeschylus° and Euripides° in *The Frogs*, and both war and sexual love in his most famous play, *Lysistrata*.

Aristotle (384–322 B.C.) Greek philosopher and pupil of Plato.° In his *Physics*, *Metaphysics*, and the *Organum*, Aristotle disagrees with his teacher Plato° by positing both form and matter within physical reality, matter being the substance of a thing and form being its source of movement. In this view only the Prime Mover is pure form and is the cause and goal of all being. Aristotle based his philosophy on logic, the syllogism, and categories such as substance, quality, quantity, relation, location in time and space, and action. He also introduced causal distinctions such as the material cause, the formal cause, the efficient cause, and the final cause. Thus his logic is used to describe nature through direct observation and to develop theory on the basis of such factual observation. His works on biology include *The Parts of Animals*, *On the Motion of Animals*, *On the Origin of Animals*, and *On the Generation of Animals*. Aristotle also wrote *De anima*, *Discourse on Conduct*, *Politics*, *De poetica*, *Rhetoric*, and *The Constitution of Athens*. He believed that the highest good is found in rationality and that happiness is found in contemplation. His prescriptions for tragedy and rhetoric continue to influence our appreciation of literature.

Arnold, Matthew (1822–1888) English poet and critic, educated at Rugby and Oxford, who held the post of inspector of schools for most of his life. He is best known for poems such as "Thyrsis," his elegy for his friend Arthur Hugh Clough, and the lyric "Dover Beach" on the isolation felt with the loss of faith, as well as for works of criticism such as *Essays in Criticism* and *Culture and Anarchy*.

Augustine, Aurelius Augustinus (A.D. 354–430) Bishop of Hippo who was raised as a Christian, indulged in a wild youth while studying in Carthage, became a Manichean, taught rhetoric in Rome and Milan, studied Plato,° and was baptized as a Christian in 387. A founder of theology, he wrote *Confessions*, *City of God*, and *On the Trinity*, among other works.

Augustus Caesar (63 B.C.–A.D. 14) Born Caius Octavius and named Caius Julius Caesar Octavianus (Octavian) when he was adopted by the Julian family. He was the first Roman Emperor, the grandnephew and heir of Caesar,° who with Mark Antony and Lepidus formed the Second Triumvirate and defeated Brutus° and Cassius at Philippi. He was made general over Antony after Antony's affair with Cleopatra, and when Antony and Cleopatra were defeated at Actium in 31 B.C., Octavian led the empire. The senate declared him emperor in 29 and in 27 named him Augustus ("revered"). As ruler Augustus maintained the lands gained by Caesar,° improved roads, built a forum, took a census, reformed taxation, and established the *Pax Romana*, the Roman Peace. He is the emperor referred to in Luke who ordered that all the world should be enrolled. His stepson Tiberius succeeded him.

Austen, Jane   (1775–1817) English novelist, daughter of a clergyman, she lived in Hampshire and Bath and wrote comedies of manners such as *Pride and Prejudice*, *Northanger Abbey*, *Emma*, *Sense and Sensibility*, and *Mansfield Park*.

Bacchus   Greek god of wine, grapes, and sensuous pleasure, often identified with Dionysus.

Bach, Johann Sebastian   (1685–1750) Great German composer and organist known for his preludes and fugues, *The Well Tempered Clavier*, the *St. John Passion*, the *St. Matthew Passion*, the *Magnificat*, the *Christmas Oratorio*, and many other wonderful compositions.

Belloc, Hilaire   (1870–1953) Roman Catholic essayist, satirist, and poet who was born in France and became a British subject in 1902. He wrote *The Path to Rome*, *Marie Antoinette*, *The Jews*, and *Napoleon* and edited, with his friend G. K. Chesterton,° an anticapitalist newspaper called *New Witness*.

Bilbo, Theodore Gilmore   Conservative U.S. senator (1935 to 1947) from Mississippi who espoused white supremacy and intimidated blacks to keep them from voting.

Boccaccio, Giovanni   (1313–1375) Italian poet and author of the *Decameron*, one hundred clever tales told by a group of wealthy men and women in retreat from the Black Death. He also wrote numerous other works, including the prose romance *Filocolo*, the poem *Filostrato* about Troilus and Cressida,° the satire *Corbaccio* against women, and biographies of famous men and women.

Boileau-Despréaux, Nicolas   (1636–1711) French poet and literary critic who was the foremost proponent of classicism. He is famous for his satires on Parisian life and on women.

Brontë, Charlotte   (1816–1855) English novelist, author of *Jane Eyre*, *The Professor*, *Shirley*, and *Villette*. She was the third daughter of a poor clergyman whose wife died after producing six children, and she herself died of toxemia due to pregnancy a year after her marriage.

Brontë, Emily   (1818–1848) Fourth Brontë daughter, author of *Wuthering Heights*. She died of tuberculosis a year after the funeral of her only brother, Branwell.

Brutus, Marcus Junius   (85?–42 B.C.) Roman soldier and statesman who sided with Pompey against Caesar.° After the battle of Pharsalia, Caesar° pardoned him and gave him a role in government. But Brutus joined Cassius in the plot to murder Caesar° and went on to battle Octavian and Mark Antony. When he lost the Battle of Philippi, he committed suicide.

Bruyère, Jean de La   (1645–1696) French lawyer and writer who lived as tutor to the son of the Prince of Condé and, after the boy's death, as a gentleman of the house. From this position he could study carefully the characters and customs of the idle nobility. His great work, *Les Caractères de Théophraste, traduit du grec; avec Les Caractères ou les moeurs de ce siècle*, which reached its ninth edition in 1696, was written to instruct and thus improve mankind.

Burke, Edmund   (1729–1797) British statesman and writer. Born in Dublin of a Protestant father and Catholic mother, he was educated at Trinity College, Dublin, and studied law in London before devoting himself to politics and writing. A member of Samuel Johnson's circle, he is best known for *Philosophical Enquiry into the Origin of Our Ideas of the Sublime and Beautiful* (1757), which helped shape the aesthetics of eighteenth-century

England, and *Reflections on the Revolution in France* (1790), which presented the conservative and negative view of the French Revolution. He favored political parties but believed in stable institutions.

Burns, Robert   (1759–1796) Scottish poet, oldest of seven children of a hardworking farmer. He wrote *Poems, Chiefly in the Scottish Dialect*, including such well-known songs as "Flow Gently, Sweet Afton," "Auld Lang Syne," and "Comin' thro' the Rye."

Byron, Lord   (1788–1824) George Gordon Byron, sixth Baron Byron, English Romantic poet and satirist who died from fever while working for Greek independence from the Turks. He is known for such poems as *Childe Harold* (1812) and *Don Juan* (1819–1824) and for creating the "Byronic hero," a mysterious, solitary, and defiant figure.

Caesar, Caius Julius   (102?–44 B.C.) Roman general, statesman, and writer who invaded Gaul and Britain (55 B.C.), returned a hero, and rode to power, heading with Pompey the popular party (popular with the people but hated by the senate). He organized a coalition government, the First Triumvirate, made up of Pompey, commander of the army, Marcus Crassus, the richest man in Rome, and himself. Crassus's death (53 B.C.) ended the coalition and set up an opposition between Pompey, supported by the senate, and Caesar, military hero beloved by the people. When Pompey incited the senate to order Caesar to give up his army, two tribunes, Mark Antony and Cassius, supported Caesar. Saying "the die is cast" ("*lacta alea est*"), Caesar defied the senate by commanding his troops to cross the Rubicon, defeat Pompey at Pharsalia, enter Italy, and march to Rome. During his consulship he passed agrarian and housing laws to benefit the people, established the Julian calendar, and developed public libraries, but he also set himself up as a dictator, and, on the ides of March, 15 March 44 B.C., he was stabbed to death by his republican friends, chiefly Cassius and Brutus.° His will left all to his grandnephew Octavian, eighteen, who became Augustus.°

Carlyle, Thomas   (1795–1881) British author, born in Scotland and educated in Edinburgh, who studied theology, mathematics, and law before turning to German literature. He is the author of many works, including a *Life of Schiller*; a translation of Goethe's *Wilhelm Meister*; *On Heroes, Hero-Worship, and the Heroic in History*; and *Past and Present*. He is best known for *Sartor Resartus*, in which he sees the material world as clothing for the spiritual world.

Cather, Willa Sibert   (1873–1947) American short story writer and novelist. She moved from Virginia to Nebraska when she was nine. After graduating from the University of Nebraska, she taught in Pennsylvania and then moved to New York City, where she wrote many novels, including *O Pioneers!*, *My Antonia*, *One of Ours*, *The Professor's House*, and *Death Comes for the Archbishop*. Many of her stories are collected in *My Mortal Enemy* and *The Old Beauty and Others*.

Cato the Elder or Cato the Censor   (234–149 B.C.) Roman statesman and moralist who disapproved of the ways of Carthage, telling the senate that Carthage must be destroyed and thus encouraging the Third Punic War, in which Carthage was indeed destroyed. Hating luxury, he took up rustic ways and wrote many works, including *De agri cultura* and probably *De originibus*, though few survive.

Cato the Younger   (95–46 B.C.) Roman statesman of great honesty who was an extreme opponent of Caesar,° sided and fought with Pompey in the Adriatic, and went to Africa to continue the fight until Caesar° defeated Scipio (46 B.C.). Cato then committed suicide. Caesar° wrote his *Anticato* against him.

Cervantes Saavedra, Miguel de   (1547–1616) Spanish novelist, playwright, and poet who studied in Italy, fought in the army, was captured by pirates, sold as a slave, ransomed for a vast sum, and imprisoned more than once. His burlesque masterpiece is *Don Quixote de la Mancha*.

Chagall, Marc   (1889–1985) Russian Jewish painter who settled in Paris in 1922, where he painted subjects drawn from folklore. Among his works are *The Lovers*, *The Bride with a Double Face*, *Girl on a Horse*, *Solitude*, and *The Fiancés at the Eiffel Tower*.

Chesterton, Gilbert Keith (G.K.)   (1874–1936) English author, convert to Catholicism, who wrote a series of detective stories with Father Brown as the hero. He also wrote novels (*The Man Who Was Thursday*, *The Napoleon of Notting Hill*) and poetry and edited *G. K.'s Weekly* as well as the *New Witness*.

Cicero, Marcus Tullius   (106–43 B.C.) Also called Tully. Great Roman orator, politician, and philosopher who sided with Pompey against Caesar° but was forgiven and lived in Rome after the civil war. Among his many works are his defenses against the attacks by Marc Antony, the *First and Second Philippic*; his philosophical pieces, such as *De natura deorum*, *De amicitia*, and *De senectute*; and his pieces on oratory, *Brutus°* and *De oratore*. Much of Cicero's fame rests on his own oratorical skills, as evidenced in speeches such as *On Behalf of Archias* and *On Behalf of Balbus*. Following Caesar's° assassination, Octavian (Augustus)° took Rome and put Cicero and many others to death.

Claude, Lorrain   (1600–1682) Originally Claude Gellée. French landscape painter whose works include *The Expulsion of Hagar*, harbor scenes, Roman countryside, and vast panoramas.

Claudius the Emperor or Claudius I   (10 B.C.–A.D. 54) Tiberius Claudius Drusus Nero Germanicus, Roman emperor (A.D. 41 to 54), nephew of Tiberius, proclaimed Emperor when Caligula was murdered. His fourth wife, Agrippina II, is said to have murdered him after convincing him to bypass his own son in favor of her son Nero° by a previous marriage. Claudius's historical writings are lost; much popular information about him comes from a fictional recreation of his life in *I, Claudius* (1934) and *Claudius the God* (1935) by Robert Graves.°

Coleridge, Samuel Taylor   (1772–1834) English poet and critic who, in 1798 with his friend Wordsworth,° published a collection of poetry, *Lyrical Ballads*, that began the romantic movement in English literature. Coleridge's "The Rime of the Ancient Mariner" appeared in that volume and was followed by "Kubla Khan," "Christabel," and "Dejection: An Ode." He is also known for his critical works, *Biographia Literaria* and *Confessions of an Enquiring Spirit*.

Congreve, William   (1670–1729) English Restoration dramatist who wrote *The Double Dealer*, *Love for Love*, and his masterpiece, *The Way of the World*—all comedies revolving around intrigue, manners, morals, and wit.

Conrad, Joseph   (1857–1924) Novelist born in Poland (Josef Teodor Konrad Walecz Korseniowski) who joined an English merchant ship, learned English, and became a British citizen. He wrote *The Nigger of the Narcissus*, *Lord Jim*, *Heart of Darkness*, *Typhoon*, and other novels.

Corneille, Pierre   (1606–1684) French dramatist who wrote *Mélite*, a comedy, *Médée*, a tragedy, and *Le Cid*, his masterpiece based on a Spanish play. He also wrote such classical tragedies as *Horace*, *Cinna*, and *Polyeucte* and the comedy *Le Menteur*.

Correggio, Antonio Allegri da   (1494–1534) Italian painter born in Correggio whose graceful, gentle paintings include the *Marriage of St. Catherine*, the *Madonna of St. Francis*, the *Ascension of Christ*, and the *Assumption of the Virgin*.

Cressida   Legendary lover of Troilus, a Trojan prince, who promises to be faithful when she is sent to the Greek camp in exchange for a Trojan prisoner but betrays her love with the Greek Diomed. Troilus is killed by Achilles.°

Cuvier, Baron Georges   (1769–1832) Originally born Léopold Chrétien Frédéric Dagobert. French naturalist who made advances in comparative anatomy, zoological classification, and paleontology, but rejected uniformitarianism and evolution.

Defoe, Daniel   (1660–1731) English writer and journalist who wrote his most famous works, *The Adventures of Robinson Crusoe* (1719), *Moll Flanders* (1722), and *A Journal of the Plague Year* (1722), in his late fifties and early sixties. The son of a butcher, Defoe was educated by Dissenters and turned from the ministry to become a merchant. In 1692 he went bankrupt, and in 1702 he was imprisoned for an ironic essay about the high church's treatment of nonconformists. After his release, Defoe became a journalist and later a novelist.

Democritus   (c. 460–c. 370 B.C.) Greek philosopher who believed that all things are composed of atoms, tiny invisible indestructible particles of the same matter but of different sizes, shapes, and weight. He also believed that happiness is the chief goal of life and that it can be attained through inner peace.

Descartes, René   (1596–1650) French philosopher and mathematician best known for his work in analytical geometry and his famous phrase *Cogito, ergo sum* ("I think, therefore I am"). From this assertion he derived the existence of God and the external world.

Diaspora   Dispersion, from the Greek for "scatter apart"; usually used in reference to Jews living outside Jerusalem after the destruction of the Temple in 586 B.C. and to their forced exile into Babylonia.

Dickens, Charles   (1812–1870) English novelist, the son of a clerk in the navy whose imprisonment for debt when Charles was twelve forced the boy to work in a blacking warehouse where shoe polish was made. He later became a court stenographer and a reporter of the sessions at Parliament, before writing his famous novels, which first appeared in monthly installments: *Oliver Twist*, *Nicholas Nickleby*, *A Christmas Carol*, *David Copperfield*, *Bleak House*, *Hard Times*, *Great Expectations*, and many others.

Dickinson, Emily   (1830–1886) American poet, daughter of a successful lawyer. She lived all her life in Amherst, Massachusetts, and after age thirty began to withdraw from all social contact. Although she published only seven poems in her lifetime, after her death her sister discovered over a thousand others. Among the best known are "I Felt a Funeral in My Brain," "The Soul Selects Her Own Society," "I Heard a Fly Buzz," "The Heart Asks Pleasure First," "Because I Could Not Stop for Death," and "A Narrow Fellow in the Grass."

Diogenes the Cynic   (c. 412–323 B.C.) Greek philosopher who believed that virtue lies in simplicity. He so disdained comfort that he lived in a tub and threw away his last cup when he saw a peasant drink from his hands. When Alexander the Great° asked what he could do to help, Diogenes is said to have replied, "Step out of my sunlight." Diogenes is best known for searching with his lantern in the daylight for "an honest man."

Dioscorides (First century A.D.) Greek physician whose major work, *De materia medica*, remained a respected reference book for 1700 years.

Disraeli, Benjamin (1804–1881) First Earl of Beaconsfield, British statesman, author, and leader of the Conservative Party, member of Parliament, chancellor of the exchequer, and two times prime minister, he is also known for his novels *Vivian Grey*, *Coningsby*, and *Sybil* and for his views on the rights and responsibilities of the social classes of England. Like his major rival, Gladstone,° Disraeli supported parlimentary reform and reforms in housing and public health, but he was best known for his acquisitive foreign policy and the support of Queen Victoria.

Donne, John (1572–1631) English metaphysical poet and divine who was born into a Roman Catholic family but later converted to Anglicanism. He ruined a promising career at court by secretly marrying Anne Moore, niece of his employer's second wife, in 1601, for which he was briefly imprisoned. After years of struggle, he entered the ministry in 1650 and, as dean of St. Paul's, became one of the best preachers of the century. His lyric poems fall into three categories: poems of the courtly rake such as "The Flea," poems to his wife such as "The Canonization" and "A Valediction: Forbidding Mourning," and his *Holy Sonnets* such as "Death be not proud." He also wrote satires, long poems, sermons, and other religious prose.

Dostoyevsky, Feodor Mikhailovich (1821–1881) Great Russian novelist who was born in Moscow and raised in a religious family. His father, a surgeon in the army and an alcoholic, was killed by his serfs. Dostoyevsky studied to be an engineer but turned to writing instead, publishing two novels before he became caught up in a group of radical idealists who were arrested for an illegal printing press. Dostoyevsky then spent four years of hard labor in Siberia, where he suffered from epilepsy and returned to the religious beliefs of his upbringing, rejecting the liberal western ideas of his youth. He was married twice, to a widow he met in Siberia and, after her death, to his secretary. Among his best-known novels are *Notes from the Underground*, *Crime and Punishment*, *The Idiot*, *The Possessed*, and *The Brothers Karamazov*.

Dreyfus Affair Two years after French captain Alfred Dreyfus (1859–1935) was convicted of treason in a secret court-martial and sent to Devil's Island in 1894, the chief of French Intelligence discovered that the real traitor was Walsin Esterhazy, but when he was tried in 1898, Esterhazy was quickly acquitted. Numerous left-wing writers and politicians, such as Georges Clemenceau, Anatole France, and Emile Zola,° came to the defense of the Jewish Dreyfus, who remained incarcerated amid intense anti-Semitism. When it was discovered that Colonel Henry of Army Intelligence had forged the evidence against Dreyfus, Henry committed suicide, but the military court persisted in sentencing Dreyfus to ten years in prison. Finally, in 1906 the supreme court of appeals exonerated Dreyfus, who was made a major and decorated with the Legion of Honor.

Dryden, John (1631–1700) English poet, dramatist, and critic who was made poet laureate in 1668. His many works include *Astrea Redux*, on the restoration of Charles II; *Annus Mirabilis*, on the Dutch war; *Absalom and Achitophel*, on politics; and *MacFlecknoe*, on the poet Shadwell. He also wrote several plays, including *The Conquest of Grenada* and *All for Love*. In *The Hind and the Panther*, he announced his conversion to Catholicism. His *Essay of Dramatic Poesy* shows his excellence as a critic, and the satirical poems and odes ensure his lasting fame.

Du Bois, William E. Burkhardt (W.E.B.) (1868–1963) Civil rights leader who graduated from Harvard, earned his M.A. and his Ph.D. there, and co-founded the National Negro Committee, which became the National Association for the Advancement of Colored People (NAACP). Convinced that blacks should struggle for economic, political, and civil equality, he nonetheless opposed black separatists. A professor of economics and history at Atlanta University, Du Bois also edited *Crisis*, the NAACP journal, worked with many African leaders, wrote *John Brown, Black Reconstruction, The World and Africa*, and other books, joined the Communist Party, and moved to Ghana, where he edited an *African Encyclopedia for Africans*.

Einstein, Albert (1879–1955) American theoretical scientist born in Germany who studied in Zurich and became a Swiss citizen, developed his theory of relativity, and explained the photoelectric effect and Brownian movement. He held full professorships in Prague, Zurich, and Berlin, where he again took German citizenship. He received the Nobel Prize in physics in 1921. During the reign of the Nazis, his property was confiscated and his citizenship revoked. In 1933 he accepted a position at Princeton University and became a citizen of the United States in 1940. In his search for a unified field theory, Einstein held to the belief that quantum theory, which he himself helped develop, would be proved wrong. Among his works are *Relativity: The Special and the General Theory, The Meaning of Relativity, About Zionism, The World As I See It*, and *Ideas and Opinions*.

Eliot, George (1819–1880) Mary Ann Evans, English novelist, daughter of a clergyman. She was a prodigious reader who studied languages, translated Strauss's *Life of Jesus* from the German, and helped edit *Westminister Review*. She shocked her community by living with G. H. Lewes; although his estranged wife prevented their marriage, Lewes was Eliot's faithful companion who supported her through periods of depression and uncertainty while she wrote her novels. Among her best-known works are *Adam Bede, Silas Marner, Mill on the Floss, Romula, Felix Holt, Daniel Deronda*, and *Middlemarch*, her masterpiece.

Eliot, Thomas Sterns (T. S.) (1888–1965) English poet and critic who was born in St. Louis, Missouri, and educated at Harvard. In 1914 he moved to London, where he worked as bank clerk and assistant editor of *Egoist* (1917 to 1919). He published his first book of poems, *Prufrock and Other Observations*, in 1917, which was followed by *Ara Vos Prec* in 1919, *Poems* in 1920, and *The Wasteland* in 1922. His first collection of critical essays was published in 1920 as *The Sacred Wood*. From 1922 to 1939 he edited his own journal, *Criterion*, and in 1925 he published *The Hollow Men* and joined Faber and Faber. In 1927 Eliot became both a British subject and a member of the Anglican church. His religious conversion provides the impetus for his later poetry, *Ash Wednesday* (1930) and *The Four Quartets* (1935–1942), as well as for his play *Murder in the Cathedral* (1935). Among his other publications are his critical works, *After Strange Gods* (1931), *The Use of Poetry and the Use of Criticism* (1933), *Elizabethan Essays* (1934), *Essays Ancient and Modern* (1936), and *Notes Toward a Definition of Culture* (1948); and his plays, *The Family Reunion* (1939), *The Cocktail Party* (1950), *The Confidential Clerk* (1954), and *The Elder Statesman* (1959).

Epstein, Sir Jacob (1880–1959) American sculptor born in New York City who studied with Rodin in Paris and worked in England. Among his most famous works are the Oscar Wilde Memorial in Paris, a marble *Venus* at Yale University, a bronze *Christ* in England, and bronze portraits of Albert Einstein,° Jawaharlal Nehru, and many others.

Euripides   (c. 480–406 B.C.) Greek poet of as many as ninety tragedies, of which nineteen survive, including *Alcestis, Medea, Hippolytus, The Trojan Women, Orestes*, and the *Bacchae*.

Falstaff   Comic character in three of Shakespeare's plays, *The First Part of King Henry the Fourth, The Second Part of King Henry the Fourth*, and *The Merry Wives of Windsor*, who pleases audiences with his wit, roguery, and instinct for self-preservation.

Faulkner, William   (1897–1962) American writer born in Mississippi who trained as a Canadian pilot in the Royal Air Force, attended the University of Mississippi, and lived in Paris before he moved to a mansion in Oxford, Mississippi, where he wrote about the South. He won the Nobel Prize for literature in 1949. Among his works are a book of poems called *The Marble Faun* (1924); novels such as *The Sound and the Fury* (1929), *As I Lay Dying* (1930), *Sanctuary* (1931), *Light in August* (1932), and *Absalom, Absalom!* (1936); and collections of stories such as *Go Down, Moses* (1942) and *Big Woods* (1955).

Fielding, Henry   (1707–1754) English novelist who studied law before writing comedies that attacked Walpole° and helped lead to the censoring of the stage in 1737. While a lawyer and later a magistrate, he wrote *Joseph Andrews*, a burlesque of Richardson's° *Pamela, Jonathan Wild*, an ironic novel, and his most famous work, *Tom Jones*, a comic adventure that explores a moral vision of the world. After writing his last novel, *Amelia*, he left the law to travel to Portugal. There he wrote *Voyage to Lisbon*, a humorous journal of the trip.

Fitzgerald, Francis Scott Key (F. Scott)   (1896–1940) American short story writer and novelist, born in Minnesota and educated at Princeton, where he was on probation his junior year. He left in 1917 for the army and was stationed in Alabama, where he met Zelda Sayre and began his first novel, *This Side of Paradise* (1920). That year he married Zelda, moved to New York, and became part of the rich, decadent society he detailed in *The Beautiful and Damned* (1922), *The Great Gatsby* (1925), *Tender Is the Night* (1934), and four collections of short stories written between 1920 and 1935. He died of a heart attack at age forty-four.

Flaubert, Gustave   (1821–1880) French novelist, son of a surgeon, he studied law but returned to his home to write with scrupulous care, always looking for *le mot juste*, "the right word." In addition to his masterpiece, *Madame Bovary*, he wrote *Salammbô, Three Tales, L'Éducation sentimentale, The Temptation of St. Anthony*, and the unfinished satire *Bouvard et Pécuchet*.

Forster, Edward Morgan (E. M.)   (1879–1970) English novelist who lived in Greece and Italy, served with the International Red Cross in Egypt in World War I, and wrote, among other works, *Where Angels Fear to Tread, The Longest Journey, A Room with a View, Howard's End, A Passage to India*, a critical work called *Aspects of the Novel*, and *Maurice*, a novel about homosexuality that was published after his death.

Freud, Sigmund   (1856–1939) Austrian founder of psychoanalysis who lived in Vienna until 1938, when he moved to Hampstead, London, after the Nazi occupation of Austria. Freud worked first with hypnotism and then developed his talking therapy and free association to help patients release repressed emotions. He presented his theories of the unconscious in such works as *The Interpretation of Dreams* (1900), *The Psychopathology of Everyday Life* (1904), *Three Contributions to Sexual Theory* (1905), *Totem and Tabu* (1913), *The Ego and the Id* (1923), and *Moses and Monotheism* (1939).

Galen   (c. A.D. 130–200) Greek physician who lived in Rome and was court physician for Marcus Aurelius. In his writings he correlates past knowledge with his own views based in part on experiment and dissection. Over eighty of his supposed five hundred works on medicine are extant; until the Renaissance they were considered the final statement on all things medical.

Gladstone, William Ewart   (1809–1898) British statesman and orator of the Liberal Party, four times Prime Minister, who as a religious moralist supported the secret ballot and other elements of parlimentary reform as well as home rule for the Irish but withdrew his support for the Irish nationalist and politician Charles Stewart Parnell (1846–1891) when he divorced his wife. Gladstone's great political rival was Benjamin Disraeli.°

Goldsmith, Oliver   (1730–1774) British writer and dramatist. Educated at Trinity College, Dublin, he studied medicine in Edinburg and Leiden but abandoned that career to become a man of letters in London. He is best known for a series of essays, *The Citizen of the World*; a novel, *The Vicar of Wakefield*; a poem, *The Deserted Village*; and a play, *She Stoops to Conquer*.

Graves, Robert   (1895–1985) British poet, novelist, and critic, best known for his work of nonfiction about his life in World War I, *Goodbye to All That* (1929), his novels *I, Claudius* (1934) and *Claudius the God* (1935), and his book of criticism *The White Goddess* (1948).

Gray, Thomas   (1716–1771) English poet who lived in Cambridge and is best known for his sonnet "On a Distant Prospect of Eton College" and his melancholy poem "Elegy Written in a Country Churchyard."

Guido, Reni   (1575–1642) Italian painter and engraver who painted frescoes in Rome, such as his *God the Father Above a Concert of Angels*, the *Aurora*, and, in Ravenna, the *Israelites Gathering the Manna*; versions of his *Ecce Homo* hang in London and Paris.

Hadrian   (A.D.76–138) Publius Aelius Hadrianus, Roman emperor born in Spain. An orphan, he was ward of and successor to Trajan. He expelled the Jews from Jerusalem, destroyed the Temple, and replaced it with a temple of Jupiter Capitolinus, renaming Jerusalem Colonia Aelia Capitolina. He built walls in Germany, Hadrian's Wall in Britain, and the Arch of Hadrian in Athens. He also rebuilt the Pantheon and increased the size of the Roman Forum.

Hardwick, Elizabeth   (1916–) American novelist, essayist, and professor, born in Lexington, Kentucky. Her works include the novels *Ghostly Lover* (1945) and *Sleepless Nights* (1979) and the books of essays *A View of My Own* (1962) and *Seduction and Betrayal: Women and Literature* (1974). She married the poet Robert Lowell in 1949 and was divorced in 1972.

Hardy, Thomas   (1840–1928) English novelist and poet. The son of a stonemason, he was trained to be a church architect in Dorcet, where he also wrote his poems and novels depicting a bleak, indifferent universe. Among his novels are *Far from the Madding Crowd*, *The Return of the Native*, *The Mayor of Casterbridge*, *Tess of the D'Urbervilles*, and *Jude the Obscure*.

Harlem Renaissance   Begun in 1912 with the publication of James W. Johnson's *Autobiography of an Ex-Colored Man* and continuing through the 1920s, the Renaissance was a time when whites recognized and paid tribute to black culture, particularly black authors, poets, dramatists, artists, and sculptors.

Harte, Walter   (1709–1774) Minor writer of essays, friend of Pope,° one-time vicar, and traveling tutor to Chesterfield's son. His expertise was more in Greek and Latin than in the graces Chesterfield so wished his son to possess.

Harvey, William (1578–1657) English physician, first to demonstrate the function of the heart and the circulation of the blood.

Hawthorne, Nathaniel (1804–1864) American novelist and short story writer, author of *Twice-Told Tales*, *The House of the Seven Gables*, *The Scarlet Letter*, *Tanglewood Tales*, *The Blythdale Romance*, and others.

Hegel, George Wilhelm Friedrich (1770–1831) German philosopher, theologian, and professor who presented his ideas in works such as *Phenomenology of Mind* (1807), *Science of Logic* (1812–1816), *Encyclopedia of the Philosophical Sciences* (1817), and *Philosophy of Right* (1821). He is known for the Hegelian dialectic, in which one idea, the thesis, generates its opposite, the antithesis, and their interaction leads to a new idea, the synthesis, which can in turn promote another antithesis. His most famous such triad is being, nonbeing, and becoming.

Hemingway, Ernest (1899–1961) American novelist and short story writer, born in Illinois, who worked as a reporter for the *Kansas City Star* and as an ambulance driver and a soldier in the Italian infantry in World War I. After the war he was a foreign correspondent in Paris and he also served as a correspondent during the Spanish Civil War. After fighting in World War II, he moved to Cuba; when expelled by Castro, he settled in Idaho. He is best known for his stories, particularly those in *In Our Time*, *Men Without Women*, *Winner Take Nothing*, *First Forty-nine Stories*, and for his novels, especially *The Sun Also Rises*, *A Farewell to Arms*, and *For Whom the Bell Tolls*.

Heraclitus (c. 535–c. 475 B.C.) Greek philosopher who believed that change is the only reality and that all things carry with them their opposites so that reality is always in a state of flux, of becoming, never of permanent being. He also believed that the universe is made of fire and that all elements are transformations of this universal fire, of which every man shares a part.

Hesiod (Eighth century B.C.?) Second great Greek epic poet (the first is Homer°) and a farmer in Boetia, he is best known for *Works and Days*, a book of advice for farmers, and *Theogony*, a genealogy of the gods.

Heywood, Thomas (c. 1570–1641) Prolific Jacobean dramatist best known for *A Woman Killed with Kindness*, about the English middle class. He also wrote classical plays, Roman plays, English history plays, romantic plays, and a variety of miscellaneous works, such as *Hierarchy of the Blessed Angels* (1635), a poem in nine books, the *History of Women* (1640), and *The Exemplary Lives and Memorable Acts of Nine of the Most Worthy Women of All the World: Three Jews, Three Gentiles, Three Christians*.

Hobbes, Thomas (1588–1679) English philosopher and tutor to the Cavendish family and, in France, to the exiled Prince Charles. He is best known for his mechanistic political philosophy as described in *De Cive* (1642), *Leviathan* (1651), *De Homine* (1658), and *Behemoth* (1680). He believed that man is naturally selfish and that fear causes man to make contracts with powerful authorities. The lives of the earliest men, he believed, were "nasty, brutish, and short."

Homer Ancient Greek poet who wrote two epics, the *Iliad* and the *Odyssey*, in literary Greek for an aristocratic society. According to legend, Homer was blind.

Horace (65–8 B.C.) Quintus Horatius Flaccus, Roman poet who fought alongside Brutus° at Philippi and later retired to a farming estate in the Sabine hills outside of Rome to write, publishing his *Epodes* in 30 B.C. and later his *Satires*, *Epistles*, and *Odes*, which won him admiration as the great humane lyricist of his time.

Hughes, Langston   (1902–1967) American poet active in the Harlem Renaissance° who used the rhythms of colloquial speech and jazz to depict the experiences of urban life. His poetic collections include *The Weary Blues* (1926), *Shakespeare in Harlem* (1942), and *One-Way Ticket* (1949). He also wrote plays, children's books, novels, and two autobiographies, *The Big Sea* (1940) and *I Wonder As I Wander* (1956).

Hume, David   (1711–1776) Scottish philosopher who attacked rationalism and developed a theoretical skepticism in such works as *A Treatise of Human Nature*, *An Enquiry Concerning Human Understanding*, and *Dialogues Concerning Natural Religion*. He also wrote the *History of England*, which, though popular at the time, is not always factually accurate.

Hutton, James   (1726–1797) Scottish geologist who asserted in *Theory of the Earth* that the history of the earth can be deduced because the forces at work on earth today are the same as those at work in the past (uniformitarianism).

Huxley, Aldous   (1894–1963) English novelist, grandson of T. H. Huxley, who moved in the 1930s to California. Among his novels are *Crome Yellow*, *Antic Hay*, *Point Counterpoint*, *Brave New World*, *After Many a Summer Dies the Swan*, and *Ape and Essence*.

Icarus   In Greek mythology, the son of the inventor Daedalus, who had been confined by King Minos to Crete for killing his apprentice. After building the Minotaur's labyrinth, Daedalus asked to be allowed to leave. When the King refused permission, Daedalus made wings of wax for himself and his son, but Icarus flew too close to the sun, his wings melted, and he fell to his death.

Italian-Ethiopian War   Under Mussolini, Italy attacked Ethiopia in 1935, causing Emperor Haile Selassie to flee for his life. In 1941 the British and South Africans defeated the Italians in Ethiopia, and Selassie was reinstated as ruler until his downfall in 1974.

James, Henry   (1843–1916) American novelist and critic known for his convoluted prose style. He was born in New York City and studied law at Harvard before settling in London, where he became a British subject in 1915. His works include *Roderick Hudson*, *The American*, *Daisy Miller*, *The Portrait of a Lady*, *The Bostonians*, *The Princess Casamassima*, *The Tragic Muse*, *The Aspern Papers*, *What Maisie Knew*, *The Spoils of Poynton*, *The Turn of the Screw*, *The Sacred Font*, *The Wings of the Dove*, *The Ambassadors*, and *The Golden Bowl*.

Jim Crow   Refers to the segregation and disparagement of blacks and specifically to laws passed in the 1880s in the South to enforce segregation and destroy gains made during the Reconstruction; from a nineteenth-century song of that name used by Thomas D. Rice (1808–1860) in his minstrels. The Jim Crow laws were finally destroyed by the Civil Rights Act of 1964, the Voting Rights Act of 1965, and the Fair Housing Act of 1968.

John   (1167–1216) King of England, son of Henry II and Eleanor of Aquitaine who led a rebellion against his brother Richard's° rule while Richard° was on the Third Crusade. Richard° forgave him, and John became king after Richard's° death. It is believed that John murdered his nephew Arthur, who had tried to overthrow him in 1203. Because of the extortion of money from his barons for his unsuccessful wars, the nobles rose against the king, and at Runnymede in June 1215 he signed the Magna Carta, ensuring feudal rights and preventing the king from usurping the rights of the barons.

Josephus, Flavius   (A.D. 37–95) Jewish historian and soldier who wrote *The Jewish War*, *Antiquities of the Jews*, *Against Apion*, and his autobiography. Although he defended Galilee against the Romans, when he was defeated he won the favor of Titus Flavius Vespasianus (see Vespasian°), whose name he took.

Joyce, James (1882–1941) Irish novelist, probably the greatest writer of the twentieth century. Educated by Jesuits, he left Ireland for Paris in 1902, returned shortly thereafter, and left again in 1904 with Nora Barnacle, living in Paris, Trieste, and finally in Zurich. The couple had two children but did not marry until 1931. The family, nearly always broke, was supported by Joyce's classes in English as a second language as well as by friends and patrons, particularly Harriet Shaw Weaver, who believed in Joyce's genius. Joyce suffered from glaucoma and became nearly blind in his later years, but he worked steadily to produce his short stories (*Dubliners*), his poems (*Chamber Music*), and his novels (*Portrait of the Artist as a Young Man*, *Ulysses*, and *Finnegans Wake*).

Jung, Carl Gustav (1875–1961) Swiss psychiatrist, founder of analytical psychology, who broke with Freud° in 1912 with the publication of *Psychology of the Unconscious* (later called *Symbols of Transformation*), in which he presented his theory of the archetypes held in the collective unconscious. His major works include *Two Essays on Analytical Psychology*, *Modern Man in Search of a Soul*, and *The Structure and Dynamics of the Psyche*.

Juvenal (c. A.D. 60–140) Decimus Junius Juvenalis, Roman satirical poet best known for his sixteen biting satires on the excessive luxury, the immorality, and the crime he saw in Rome between A.D. 100 and 128. His work is often contrasted with the mild satires of Horace,° which intend to ridicule rather than attack.

Kant, Immanuel (1724–1804) German philosopher who said that because the structure of the mind determines our perception of reality, we can never confirm or deny propositions such as God, immortality, or freedom since they lie outside of the mind's categorical reason. He is also known for his ethical test, the categorical imperative or moral law, which states that one should act as if one's behavior were a maxim for universal law. Among his works are *Critique of Pure Reason*, *Critique of Practical Reason*, and *Critique of Judgment*.

Keats, John (1795–1821) Major English romantic poet. The son of a stable keeper, he was apprenticed to a surgeon but, influenced by Leigh Hunt, became a poet. He fell in love with Fanny Brawne, caught tuberculosis from his brother Tom (who died in 1818), and died in Rome at the age of twenty-five. Among his works are *Endymion*, "On First Looking into Chapman's Homer," "Lamia," "The Eve of St. Agnes," "Ode to a Nightingale," "Ode on a Grecian Urn," and sonnets such as "When I have fears that I may cease to be" and "Bright star! Would I were steadfast as thou art."

King, Martin Luther, Jr. (1929–1968) American clergyman and civil rights leader who was born in Atlanta, Georgia, earned a Ph.D. from Boston University, and was ordained a Baptist minister in 1954 in Montgomery, Alabama. In 1955 he led a boycott against segregated bus lines and won national prominence when the lines were integrated the following year. Based on his belief in nonviolent resistance, King's civil rights activism led him to organize the Southern Christian Leadership Conference, to suffer imprisonment at the hands of segregationists, and to organize an enormous march on Washington in 1963. He won the Nobel Peace Prize the next year. On April 4, 1968, in Memphis, Tennessee, where he was supporting striking sanitation workers, King was assassinated by James Earl Ray.

Kingsley, Charles (1819–1875) English clergyman and novelist. An advocate of Christian socialism, he is best known for his childen's book *The Water Babies* (1863). In 1859 he was made chaplain to Queen Victoria; the next year he was appointed professor of modern history at Cambridge, and in 1873 he was made canon of Westminster.

Kipling, Rudyard (1865–1936) English writer born in India who wrote poems such as *Barrack-Room Ballads*, "The White Man's Burden," and "Gunga Din," children's stories such as *The Jungle Book* and *Just-So Stories*, and novels such as *Kim*, all depicting a romanticized version of imperialism.

La Bruyère See Bruyère.°

Lear Legendary English king about whom Shakespeare wrote his great tragedy *King Lear*, in which the King foolishly retires and divides his kingdom among his three daughters.

Leonardo da Vinci (1452–1519) Italian painter, sculptor, architect, musician, engineer, and scientist who was born near Vinci and worked in Florence, Milan, Rome, and Amboise, France. His notebooks reveal him as one of the greatest creative geniuses of all time; he is especially known for his *Last Supper, Mona Lisa*, and *St. John the Baptist*.

Linnaeus, Carolus (1707–1778) Swedish botanist and taxonomist, founder of the binomial system of nomenclature. He explained his system in *Systema Naturae* in 1735 and presented the genus and species of plants in *Species Plantarum* in 1753. In the tenth edition of *Systema Naturae* he classified both plants and animals (1758). In 1761 he was made a noble and took the name Karl von Linne.

Locke, John (1632–1704) English philosopher who founded empiricism. In *Essay Concerning Human Understanding* (1690), Locke asserted that the human mind is at first blank, a tabula rasa on which experience leaves its marks. What we learn from our senses allows us to reflect upon ideas. Locke is also known for his political ideas, such as the equality and independence of all men, the importance of property, the right to the fruits of one's own labor, the concept of checks and balances in government, and the right to revolt against an oppressive, unresponsive government. The United States Constitution owes much to the ideas of John Locke.

Longinus, Cassius (A.D.213–273) Greek philosopher and rhetorician who was executed by the Romans for treason. *On the Sublime*, thought to have been his work, is now attributed to an earlier writer of the same name who lived in the first century A.D.

Lucan (A.D. 39–65) Marcus Annaeus Lucanus, Roman poet, nephew to Seneca,° who was compelled to commit suicide when he was discovered to have conspired against Nero,° probably in retribution for Nero's° banning of the public recitation of Lucan's epic *Bellum civile*. Also called *Pharsalia*, the poem describes the civil war between Caesar° and Pompey.

Lyell, Sir Charles (1797–1875) British geologist who in his book *Principles of Geology* gained popular acceptance for Hutton's° theory of uniformitarianism, the slow development over time of the present geological formations, as opposed to catastrophism, which allowed for events like the Flood and a relatively short history of the earth attuned to the biblical projection of time.

Mailer, Norman (1923–) American author known for his politics and machismo as well as for his novels, particularly *The Naked and the Dead* (1948), *The Deer Park* (1955), *The White Negro* (1958), *The Armies of the Night* (1968), *The Executioner's Song* (1979), and *Harlot's Ghost* (1991).

Maimonides (1135–1204) Moses ben Maimon, Jewish rabbi, physician, philosopher, and scholar who was born in Spain and died in Cairo. He organized Jewish oral law, the

Mishna, in a work entitled *Mishneh Torah*. He also wrote commentary on the Mishna and works on logic, medicine, philosophy, and religion. His *Moreh Nevukhim*, or *Guide for the Perplexed*, has influenced thinkers of many faiths.

Malcolm X (1925–1965) Militant black leader who became a Muslim minister when he had finished a prison term in 1952. In 1963 he broke with Elijah Muhammad, the Muslim leader, and formed his own group. In 1964, after converting to orthodox Islam, he founded the Organization of Afro-American Unity, a militant but nonseparatist group. In 1965 he was assassinated, probably by a member of the Black Muslims.

Mann, Thomas (1875–1955) German novelist concerned with culture and psychology who wrote such novels as *Buddenbrooks*, *Tonio Kröger*, *Death in Venice*, *The Magic Mountain*, *Joseph and His Brothers*, *Doctor Faustus*, and *Confessions of Felix Krull, Confidence Man*, as well as many short stories (collected in *Stories of Three Decades*).

Martial (c. A.D. 40–104) Marcus Valerius Martialis, Roman epigrammatic poet who was born in Spain but lived in Rome after A.D. 64 and won fame there through his witty commentary on Roman life.

Marx, Karl (1818–1883) German philosopher and founder of communism who rejected Hegel° and turned to materialism. In Paris he met Friedrich Engels, a German socialist, and together they wrote *The German Ideology* describing dialectical materialism, in which the conflict of opposites leads to growth and change. In 1848 they wrote the *Communist Manifesto*, explaining Marx's view of the class struggle and the ultimate triumph of the working class. In London, poor, ill, and suffering from the deaths of more than one of his children, Marx studied in the British Museum, helped found the International Working Men's Association, and wrote the three volumes of *Das Kapital* explaining his views.

Melville, Herman (1819–1891) American author who spent four years aboard ship before writing *Typee: A Peep at Polynesian Life* and *White-Jacket; or The World in a Man-of-War*, as well as shorter fiction such as "Bartleby the Scrivener" and "Billy Budd, Foretopman." His masterpiece is *Moby Dick; or The White Whale*.

Meredith, George (1828–1909) English novelist and poet who was a lawyer and journalist before he wrote his best works, *The Ordeal of Richard Feverel* and *The Egoist*, among others.

Michelangelo, Buonarroti (1475–1564) Italian sculptor, painter, and architect known for his marble *Bacchus* and the huge *David*, as well as for his frescoes in the Pauline Chapel in the Vatican and his painting of the ceiling of the Sistine Chapel.

Milton, John (1608–1674) English poet who wrote many important poems, including "Ode on the Morning of Christ's Nativity," "L'Allegro," "Il Penseroso," numerous sonnets, the masque "Comus," the elegy "Lycidas," and the great epic *Paradise Lost*, as well as *Paradise Regained* and the classical tragedy *Samson Agonistes*. He also wrote pamphlets and essays supporting divorce, freedom of the press (*Areopagitica*), and the deposition of unworthy kings. After the restoration of Charles II, Milton went into hiding for a while, but he was later included in the general amnesty. He spent his last years blind, working on his writing with the aid of his daughters and his secretaries.

Minerva Roman goddess of wisdom and the arts, derived from Etruscans and from the Greek goddess Athena. Her temple was a gathering place for craftsmen, actors, and authors.

Modigliani, Amedeo (1884–1920) Franco-Italian Jewish sculptor and painter who worked in Paris, developing an elongated form for his nudes and portraits.

Molière, Jean Baptiste Poquelin (1622–1673) French actor and playwright best known for his comedies of character such as *Le Tartuffe*, *Le Misanthrope*, and *L'Avare*. He also wrote farces, masques, and ballets.

Morrison, Toni (1931–) Born Chloe Anthony Wofford. Teacher, editor, and novelist, author of *The Bluest Eye* (1969), *Sula* (1973), *Song of Solomon* (1977), *Tar Baby* (1981), and *Beloved* (1986), for which she won the Pulitzer Prize.

Nero, (Nero) Claudius Caesar (A.D. 37–68) Born Lucius Domitius Ahenobarbus, he was Roman emperor from 54 to 68, the last ruler from the line of Julius Caesar.° His mother was the great granddaughter of Augustus° and he himself was adopted by Claudius I° and given Claudius's° daughter Octavia as his wife to ensure his succession. While Seneca° was his advisor, Nero ruled well, but when his mother (Claudius's° wife Agrippina) began to favor Claudius's° son Britannicus over Nero, Nero poisoned him and later murdered his mother and his wife. That same year Seneca° retired, and two years later half of Rome went up in flames while, rumor had it, Nero recited the fall of Troy. Blaming Christians for the fire, he began the first Roman persecutions of adherents to the new religion. Despite his lavish rebuilding of Rome, Nero was by now hated and committed suicide during a revolt against him.

N.S. New Style: dating according to the Gregorian calendar. Continental Europe had shifted from the Julian calendar, established by Julius Caesar,° to the Gregorian calendar, established by Pope Gregory in 1582. Because the length of the Julian calendar year was 365 days and 6 hours, extra time accumulated year after year. The Gregorian calendar was instituted to correct for this excess. By the time the English aligned themselves with the rest of Europe, eleven days (3–13 September 1752) had to be omitted. The shift also changed the date of the new year from 25 March to 1 January.

Newton, Sir Isaac (1642–1727) English scientist, mathematician, and philosopher who discovered the law of universal gravitation, developed calculus, and discovered that white light is composed of all the colors of the spectrum. His *Philosophia naturalis principia mathematica* (1687) describes his three laws of motion and shows how gravity affects falling objects as well as heavenly bodies. In *Opticks* (1704) Newton presented his view that light is composed of corpuscles, a theory that prevailed until the early nineteenth century, when wave theory was developed. Newton was a professor at Cambridge (1669–1701), served in Parliament (1689–1690, 1701–1702), presided over the Royal Society (1703–1727), was made warden of the mint (1696), and was knighted in 1705.

O'Connor, Flannery (1925–1964) American author born in Georgia who was strongly influenced by her Roman Catholicism. She suffered from lupus and spent much of her life as an invalid. Her stories are collected in *A Good Man Is Hard to Find* and *Everything That Rises Must Converge*. Her novels are *Wise Blood* and *The Violent Bear It Away*.

O.S. Old Style: dating by the Julian calendar. See N.S.°

Ovid (43 B.C.–A.D. 18) Publius Ovidius Naso, Roman poet who originally studied law but soon became involved in the society of fellow poets and wrote love lyrics (*Amores*), fictional love letters from heroines (*Heroides*), instructions on making and keeping lovers (*Ars amatoria*), and his most famous work, a collection of lively, witty myths, the *Metamorphoses*. Perhaps because of his preference for pleasure over didactics, Ovid was suddenly banished from Rome by Augustus° in A.D. 8. Although he later wrote *Tristia* and *Fastia*, his poetic powers diminished in exile.

Paris   In the *Iliad*, son of Priam and Hecuba, brother of Hector. For choosing Aphrodite as most beautiful of the three goddesses (the others were Hera and Athena) quarreling over the apple of discord, Paris was awarded Helen, whom he abducted from the Greek Menelaus, thereby staring the Trojan War.

Patmore, Coventry Kersey Dighton   (1823–1896) English poet and librarian at the British Museum who wrote *The Angel in the House*, a poem in four books praising the joys of married life, and a series of poems on his conversion to Roman Catholicism.

Patrick, Saint   (c. 385–461) Missionary born to a Christian family of Roman citizens in Britain. After his capture and enslavement at sixteen by an Irish horde, he escaped to the Continent, where he took vows in a monastery and prepared himself to become a missionary to Ireland. He defied the pagan gods and won his first converts at Tara by lighting the Easter fire on a nearby hill. By the time of his death, he had converted almost all of Ireland. Much legend surrounds his life, including the story that he chased the snakes from Ireland.

Picasso, Pablo   (1881–1973) Spanish painter and sculptor who worked in France and was among the greatest painters of the twentieth century. Among his works are *The Old Guitarist* (Chicago), *Les Demoiselles d'Avignon* (New York City), *Female Nude* (Philadelphia), and his most famous painting, *Guernica* (Spain), condemning war.

Plato   (427?–347 B.C.) Greek philosopher and pupil of Socrates.° In his Socratic dialogues—the *Apology*, the *Meno*, and the *Gorgias*—he presents the defense of his master and questions the teaching of virtue and the nature of right and wrong. In his later works— the *Republic*, *Phaedo*, *Symposium*, *Phaedrus*, and others—Plato asserts the harmony of the universe, outlines the ideal state, and proposes his theory of forms or ideas, which are more real than physical reality and which impose order on the cosmos. His dialectical method of inquiry, in which man questions all assumptions, allows man to pursue ever higher forms to reach an understanding of the highest Good.

Pliny the Elder   (A.D. 23–79) Caius Plinius Secundus, Roman naturalist remembered for writing the encyclopedic *Natural History*, which consists of thirty-seven books of often amusingly erroneous information about the physical universe.

Pliny the Younger   (A.D. 62?–c. 113) Caius Plinius Caecilius Secundus, Roman orator and statesman, nephew and ward of Pliny the Elder,° whose letters reveal fascinating details of Roman life.

Plutarch   (A.D. 46?–c.120) Greek biographer whose great work is *Parallel Lives*, a collection of biographies of Greek and Roman heroes set in parallel form to reveal the moral character of each pair. Thus the Greek Alexander° is compared to the Roman Caesar,° the Greek Demosthenes to the Roman Cicero,° and the Greek Theseus to the Roman Romulus. Shakespeare used Sir Thomas North's translation of Plutarch for his Roman plays.

Pope, Alexander   (1688–1744) English satiric poet famed for his heroic couplets. He wrote *Essay on Criticism*, a poem setting out critical tastes; *Rape of the Lock*, a delightful mock heroic poem; *The Dunciad*, a satire attacking fools and hacks; *Imitations of Horace,*° a political satire; and *Essay on Man*, presenting his philosophical views. He also wrote translations of Homer° and an edition of Shakespeare, among other works.

Proust, Marcel   (1871–1922) French novelist born in Paris who, suffering from asthma and the death of his parents, withdrew from society to live in a room lined with cork, where he wrote his masterpiece of sixteen volumes, *Remembrance of Things Past*.

Pythagoras (582–507 B.C.) Greek philosopher who founded a school that believed in the transmigration of souls and in numbers as constituting reality. His followers believed in equality between the sexes, humane treatment of slaves, and kindness to animals. Astute mathematicians, they also made contributions to medicine and science.

Rabelais, François (1490–1533) French writer who was first a monk and humanist student, later a doctor and editor, and finally a writer of two great comic masterpieces: *Gargantua*, a collection of stories about the giant, and *Pantagruel*, about the son of Gargantua. At the time of his death, Rabelais had written a total of four books detailing the adventures of the giant and his son and covering a variety of topics, including education, politics, and philosophy, in a wildly comic and ribald style.

Racine, Jean (1639–1699) French classical dramatist who wrote *Andromaque*, *Les Plaideurs*, *Bérénice*, *Iphigénie en Aulide*, *Phèdre*, *Esther*, and *Athalie*. At first an imitator of Corneille,° Racine later replaced Corneille° as the foremost playwright in France, causing the older dramatist's friends, such as Moliere,° to turn against the younger playwright. Nevertheless, supported by the king and later by Boileau,° Racine maintained his popularity.

Raphael, Santi (1483–1520) Italian Renaissance painter who worked in Urbino, where he was born, and later in Florence and Rome. His works include *The Crucifixion*, *Pieta*, his *Self-Portrait* (at the Uffizi), *Madonna with the Fish*, *The Temptation of Eve*, and many others. His pictures are known for their balance and classical harmony.

Reade, Charles (1814–1884) English novelist, playwright, and reformer who wrote *The Cloister and the Hearth*, *It's Never Too Late to Mend* (advocating prison reform), *Hard Cash*, and *Put Yourself in His Place*, among other works. Thomas Mallon, in his book *Stolen Words* (Ticknor and Fields, 1989), reminds his readers of the status of Reade as a skilled plagiarist as well.

Reich, Wilhelm (1897–1957) Austrian psychiatrist, chief associate in Freud's° Psychoanalytic Polyclinic in Vienna, who broke with Freud,° left for New York City in 1939, and founded in 1942 the Orgone Institute, where he presented his belief that "orgone" energy must be repeatedly released through sexual means to avoid not only neuroses of the individual but social disorders as well. To that end he invented the orgone box, which was declared a fraud by the Food and Drug Administration. Reich died in prison, where he had been sentenced to two years for defying the Food and Drug Act.

Rembrandt, Harmenszoon van Rijn (1606–1669) Greatest master of the Dutch school of painters, he was born in Leiden and worked for some time there teaching and doing numerous self-portraits as well as paintings of the old and the poor. In 1632 he moved to Amsterdam, where he worked as an established portrait painter. Among his many works are *The Night Watch*, *Aristotle Contemplating the Bust of Homer*, and *The Polish Rider*.

Richard I, Richard or Richard the Lion-Heart (1157–1199) King of England from 1188 to 1199, third son of Henry II and Eleanor of Aquitaine. He fought in the Third Crusade and suppressed a revolt raised against him by his brother John,° but spent only six months of his reign in his own country.

Richardson, Samuel (1689–1761) English novelist who wrote three epistolary novels: *Pamela*, about a servant who, virtue intact, marries her employer's son; *Clarissa Harlowe*, about a virtuous girl who runs away with her seducer; and *The History of Sir Charles Grandison*, seven volumes about a gentleman deciding whom to marry.

Richelieu, Armand Jean du Plessis, duc de   (1585–1642) French cardinal of the Roman Catholic church and chief minister of King Louis XIII. Richelieu consolidated and greatly influenced the power of the monarchy and decreased the power of the nobility and the Huguenots.

Rodin, Auguste   (1840–1917) French sculptor born in Paris who first gained fame with his male nude *The Age of Bronze*, which was bought by the Luxembourg Gardens. His other works include *The Thinker*, *The Burghers of Calais* in bronze, his monuments to Balzac and Hugo, and *The Kiss* and *The Bather*, in marble.

Rousseau, Jean Jacques   (1712–1778) Swiss-French philosopher and author. He was born in Geneva, the son of a watchmaker, and spent his early years wandering with Louise de Warens, his patroness and lover, who took him to Turin, where he converted to Catholicism. In Turin, he was a footman for twelve years before he left for Paris and became part of a group of intellectuals that included Diderot. Here he took a new lover, a servant girl, and won first prize in 1749 in a contest to determine whether culture corrupted or improved human nature. Rousseau said man was by nature good and that society corrupted him. After returning to Geneva and converting back to Protestantism, he felt betrayed by his friends in Paris and lived for a while in England with David Hume° before settling in Paris. He is best known for *Du Contrat social*, his work of political theory; *Émile*, his philosophy of education; *Julie, ou La Nouvelle Héloïse*, his novel; and *Confessions*, his autobiography.

Sanger, Margaret   (1883–1966) American nurse who set up a clinic as well as national and international conferences to establish legal, medically supervised, birth control.

Sappho   Early sixth century B.C. Greek lyric poet who lived on the island of Lesbos and wrote at least six books of poetry, of which only a few fragments survive. She was of an aristocratic family, possibly married with a daughter, but her poems were about her love for young girls. Her classic, controlled lines influenced such later poets as Catullus and Ovid.°

Saracens   Name given in the Middle Ages to Arabs and other Muslims.

Scithian   Scythian: a member of the ancient nomadic group who from the eighth to the fourth century B.C. inhabited land from the Danube River to Asia. Scythians were considered barbarians by the Greeks. They withstood an onslaught from Alexander's° troops in c. 325 B.C.

Scott, Sir Walter   (1771–1832) Scottish novelist and poet, famous for his Waverly novels (about Scottish life), particularly *The Heart of Midlothian* and *The Bride of Lammermoor*, and for his historical novels, particularly *Ivanhoe*.

Seneca   (c. 4 B.C.–A.D. 65) Lucius Annaeus Seneca, Roman philosopher, playwright, and politician, born in Spain and sent to Rome to study. He was Nero's° tutor and advisor in the early years of Nero's° rule before he asked to retire from the intrigues of court life. Accused of conspiracy, he was required to commit suicide and did so by slashing his veins. His stoical and highly moral writings include *Epistolae morales ad Lucilium* and *Quaestiones naturales* (both philosophical inquiries) and *Diologi*. His eight extant tragedies, full of high rhetoric and passion, influenced Thomas Kyd and other early English dramatists.

Seven Sages   Greek men living from 620 to 550 B.C. who were known for their wisdom and wise maxims: Cleobulus, tyrant of Lindus ("Moderation is the chief good"); Periander, tyrant of Corinth ("Forethought in all things"); Pittacus of Mitylene ("Know thine opportunity"); Bias of Priene ("Too many workers spoil the work"); Thales of Miletus ("To feel confident brings ruin"); Chilon of Sparta ("Know thyself"); and Solon of Athens ("Nothing in excess").

Shaw, George Bernard   (1856–1950) Great Irish dramatist, socialist, and critic who wrote plays expressing his ideas on a number of issues and won the Nobel Prize in 1925. Among his many plays are *Mrs. Warren's Profession*, about prostitution; *Man and Superman*, about the roles of men and women; *Major Barbara*, about poverty as the source of evil; and *Pygmalion*, about the English class system.

Sidney, Sir Philip   (1554–1586) Model English courtier and poet in Queen Elizabeth's court who wrote *Arcadia*, pastoral poems connected by a prose narrative; *The Defense of Poesie*, a critical work on the nature of poetry; and *Astrophel and Stella*, a sonnet sequence describing the pattern of his unsuccessful courtship of Penelope Devereux. He died in battle at age thirty-two.

Smollett, Tobias   (1721–1771) Scottish surgeon turned novelist who worked as a surgeon's mate aboard ship and later married and set up a practice in England. His most famous works are *Roderick Random*, *The Adventures of Peregrine Pickle*, and *Ferdinand Count Fathom*, all three tough, picaresque, adventure stories, and *Humphrey Clinker*, a comic novel about traveling through England and Scotland.

Socrates   (469–399 B.C.) Greek philosopher of Athens whose belief in the identity of virtue and knowledge compelled him to seek out virtue through discussions with fellow citizens on the streets. Charged with corrupting youth, he was condemned to death by drinking hemlock. His questioning of statements by examining their implications through dialogue is called the Socratic method of teaching. Most of our information about Socrates comes from Plato,° his most famous pupil, who described the trial and death of Socrates in the *Apology*, the *Crito*, and the *Phaedo*.

Solomon   (c. 972–932 B.C.) King of Israel after the rule of his father, David. Solomon built the temple in Jerusalem. He is also known for his wisdom and is said to have written Proverbs, Ecclesiastes, and the Song of Solomon.

Sophocles   (c. 495–406 B.C.) Second of the three famed Greek tragic poets, he wrote over a hundred plays, of which seven survive intact: *Ajax*, *Antigone*, *Oedipus Rex*, *Electra*, the *Trachiniae*, *Philoctetes*, and *Oedipus at Colonus*.

Statius, Publius Papinius   (A.D. 40–96) Latin poet born in Naples who wrote two epics, the *Thebaid* and the *Achilleid*, as well as a collection of poems called the *Silvae*.

Sterne, Laurence   (1713–1768) Anglican vicar who wrote *Journal to Eliza*, *A Sentimental Journey*, and his comic masterpiece, *Tristram Shandy*, which plays with the possibilities inherent in the form of the novel.

Stoics   Greek school of philosophers founded by Zeno of Citium (c. 300 B.C.), who believed that all knowledge stems from the senses and that a universal force, God, shapes the material world and pervades all matter. Virtue, the law of nature, should determine human conduct.

Stowe, Harriet Beecher   (1811–1896) American novelist and humanitarian, author of *Uncle Tom's Cabin* (1852), a popular antislavery novel, and mother of six. She lived near Mark Twain in Nook Farm, Connecticut.

Stuyvesant Town   Stuyvesant Square District, from Fourteenth Street on the south to Eighteenth Street on the north and from First Avenue west to Third Avenue, was once part of the farm owned by Peter Stuyvesant. It was occupied by the Dutch until 1700 and then by Germans, Irish, Italians, Jews, and Slavs.

Suetonius   (c. A.D. 69–140) Caius Suetonius Tranquillus, Roman biographer, author of *De vita Caesarum* and *De viris illustribus*. He was also Hadrian's° secretary.

Swift, Jonathan   (1667–1745) Anglo-Irish author and dean of St. Patrick's Cathedral in Dublin, he wrote *The Battle of the Books*, defending the ancients over the moderns; *A Tale of a Tub*, a satire against religious excess; the ironic *Argument Against Abolishing Christianity*; and many political pamphlets, including the famous and bitter "A Modest Proposal" suggesting that the poor improve their condition by selling their children as food. His most famous work is his satire exposing human folly, *Gulliver's Travels*.

Tacitus   (c. A.D. 55–c.118) Publius Cornelius, Roman historian who wrote *De origine et situ Germanorum*, describing the early Germanic tribes, and the *Histories* and *Annals*, describing Roman life from about A.D. 68 to the first years of Nero's° rule.

Tennyson, Lord Alfred   (1809–1892) English Victorian poet, poet laureate, and author of such works as "The Lotus-Eaters," "The Lady of Shalott," "Ulysses," "The Charge of the Light Brigade," and "Crossing the Bar." His major works include *In Memoriam* (his response to the death of his friend Arthur Henry Hallam) and *Idylls of the King*.

Thackeray, William Makepeace   (1811–1863) English novelist born in India who studied law and art and wrote for various magazines before he published his best novels: *Vanity Fair*, *Pendennis*, *Henry Esmond*, *The Newcomes*, and *The Virginians*. He also delivered lectures, toured the United States, and edited *Cornhill Magazine*, a literary journal.

Tolstoy, Count Leo   (1828–1910) Russian philosopher and novelist. Born of a noble family, he was orphaned at nine and raised by his aunts. He studied languages and law but left the University of Kazan without a degree and entered the army. When he returned to his estate, he set up a school for his peasants, visited Europe, and married a well-educated girl who bore him thirteen children and remained faithful to him despite his infidelities until, after converting to a pacifist Christian love, Tolstoy insisted on rejecting all material goods. His extreme position led to a separation between him and his family, including his wife and all but one of his children. At eighty-three Tolstoy left home with his youngest daughter, caught a chill, and died in the home of a railroad stationmaster. Among his works are *War and Peace*, *Anna Karenina*, "The Death of Ivan Ilyich," and *What Is Art?* in which he rejects his own great works.

Toomer, Jean   (1894–1967) Teacher, writer, and leader of the Harlem Renaissance,° known for *Cane* (1923), a novel written in prose and poetry and composed of three parts chronicling the black experience in the rural South and urban North. His later work was rejected by publishers; he lived his last years as a Quaker recluse.

Un-American Activities, Committee on   This House committee was part of the communist witch hunt of the early 1950s, when all sorts of people, particularly writers, artists, and members of the film industry, were harassed and careers were ruined with little or no evidence. The fear of communist infiltration was stirred up in large part by Republican Senator Joseph McCarthy and ended in the Senate's censure of him in December 1954.

Vandyke, Sir Anthony   (1599–1641) Flemish artist who painted religious works and portraits, such as those of Italian nobility and of Charles I of England. He was knighted in England and made court painter.

Van Vechten, Carl (1880–1964) Music critic and novelist who encouraged positive interactions between blacks and whites; Huston's letters to Van Vechten provided a good source for her biographer.

Vespasian (A.D. 9–79) Titus Flavius Vespasianus, Roman emperor (69–79) who worked his way up through the army and was leader of the siege against the Jews in Judaea when the revolt against Nero° took place. He supported both Otho and Vitellius but was proclaimed emperor by his soldiers and took off for Rome to establish his claim. As emperor he built the temple of Pax and the Coliseum. His son Titus, who had destroyed Jerusalem in the war in Judaea, succeeded him.

Virgil (70–19 B.C.) Publius Vergilius Maro, Roman poet who studied in Rome and returned to his father's farm to work the land and write. When the farm was confiscated, he settled in Rome, wrote the *Eclogues*, idealized visions of rural life; the *Georgics*, realistic views of life on a farm; and the epic poem the *Aeneid*, establishing himself then and since as one of the greatest of poets.

Voltaire, François Marie Arouet de (1694–1778) French author and philosopher of the Enlightenment who completed his first work, a tragedy, while in the Bastille, wrongly accused of insulting the Regent. Later he became quite wealthy through clever financial transactions. In 1726 he was again imprisoned in the Bastille for witty remarks against a powerful family; he was set free only when he promised to go at once to England. There he was impressed by Newton,° Locke,° and the English views on freedom. His work in English, *Letters Concerning the English Nation*, was banned in France. After his return to France, he lived with the Marquise du Chatelet, a mathematician and physicist. When she died in 1749, he lived for a time in Berlin and later in Geneva, and died across the border on his estate in France. He knew and corresponded with most of the great men and women of his time, wrote voluminously, and championed the causes of religious freedom and justice. *Candide*, a rollicking satire, is his best-known work.

Walpole, Robert (1676–1745) First Earl of Oxford, English statesman and Whig who was a trusted advisor of both George I and George II and who served as lord of the treasury and as chancellor of the exchequer, controlling Parliament, especially the House of Commons, through patronage and through management of the electorate. Military setbacks during the War of Austrian Succession caused his resignation in 1742, but Walpole remained a major political force until his death. Although called the first prime minister, Walpole was in fact dependent on royal favor.

Waugh, Evelyn (1903–1966) English satirist, Roman Catholic, and author of novels such as *Decline and Fall*, *Vile Bodies*, *A Handful of Dust*, *Black Mischief*, *Put Out More Flags*, *Brideshead Revisited*, *The Loved One*, *Officers and Gentlemen*, and other works.

Wells, Herbert George (H. G.) (1866–1946) English author, pupil of T. H. Huxley, biology teacher, and writer of science fiction such as *The Time Machine*, *The Invisible Man*, *The War of the Worlds*, and *The Shape of Things to Come*.

Whitman, Walt (1819–1892) A major American poet, he was a journalist and carpenter before he published with his own money a volume of eleven poems, *Leaves of Grass*, in 1855. Like Wordsworth's° *Lyrical Ballads*, Whitman's book contained a preface stating his theory of poetry, but the volume did not sell well. He nonetheless expanded and reissued the book in 1856 and 1860; the last revision appeared in 1892. During the Civil War he worked as a volunteer hospital nurse and published another volume of poetry, *Drum-Taps*, in 1865 and *Sequel to Drum-Taps* in 1866. Among his most famous poems are "Song of Myself," in which he sees himself as the embodiment of all men, and "When Lilacs Last in the Dooryard Bloom'd," on the death of Lincoln. Whitman celebrates in his free verse freedom, democracy, and the dignity of the physical body.

Wilde, Oscar Fingal O'Flahertie Wills   (1854–1900) Irish writer and wit, educated at Trinity College, Dublin, and Magdalen College, Oxford, who wrote stories and fairy tales for children as well as the novel *The Picture of Dorian Gray*, plays such as *Lady Windermere's Fan*, *An Ideal Husband*, and *The Importance of Being Earnest*, and the poem *The Ballad of Reading Gaol*, which describes his experiences while imprisoned for homosexuality.

William the Conqueror   (1027–1087) Duke of Normandy who in 1066 defeated Harold of Wessex, the crowned king of England. William was crowned on Christmas Day, and, while putting down a number of rebellions, he succeeded in overpowering the native English nobility, establishing a feudal system, importing a new Norman elite, and introducing French as the language of nobility, thus significantly influencing the development of the English language and its literature. Although many English laws, customs, and institutions remained in place, his successful invasion is called the Norman Conquest.

Wordsworth, William   (1770–1850) English poet and leader of the romantic movement in England, who, with Coleridge,° published *Lyrical Ballads* in 1798, including the famous preface explaining his views on diction and meter, and such poems as "I wandered lonely as a cloud" and the Lucy poems. He also wrote longer poems, such as *The Prelude* and *The Excursion*. Among his most famous are "Tintern Abbey," "The world is too much with us," "Composed upon Westminster Bridge," and "Ode. Intimations of Immortality from Recollections of Early Childhood."

Wright, Richard   (1908–1960) American novelist born on a plantation in Mississippi who worked in Chicago for the Federal Writers' Project during the Depression, briefly joined the Communist Party in 1932, and moved to Paris in 1946. Among his works are a collection of four long stories called *Uncle Tom's Children* (1938), his most famous novel, *Native Son* (1940), his autobiography, *Black Boy* (1945), a novel, *The Outsider* (1953), and a description of his trip to Africa, *Black Power* (1954).

Yeats, William Butler   (1865–1939) Irish poet and dramatist. One of the greatest lyrical poets of the twentieth century, he was born in Dublin, the son of John Butler Yeats, a painter. Influenced by Irish mythology, mysticism, and nationalism, he founded with others the Irish Literary Theatre in Dublin. Among his plays are *The Countess Cathleen* and *Cathleen Ni Houlihan*. Among his works of prose are *The Celtic Twilight* and *Secret Rose*. But he is best known for poems such as "The Lake Isle of Innisfree," "The Second Coming," "Sailing to Byzantium," "The Wild Swans at Coole," "Easter 1916," "Among School Children," "Byzantium," and the Crazy Jane poems.

Zola, Émile   (1840–1902) French journalist and novelist known for his naturalism, that is, his minute observation of the sordid aspects of life, in such novels as *L'Assommoir* on the low life in Paris and *Germinal* on coal mining. He is also known for his article "J'accuse" supporting Dreyfus° in 1898

Author and Title Index

Copyright Acknowledgments